DATE DUE

ꜟDEC 03 1991	
ꜟMAR 06 1992 MAR 20 1992ꜟ	
APR 23 1992	
APR 20 1993	
NOV 02 1995	
MAR 14 1996	
MAR 27 1997	
APR 10 OCT 03 1997	

BRODART, INC.   Cat. No. 23-221

THE DIARY
OF VIRGINIA
WOOLF

Volume Three:

1925-1930

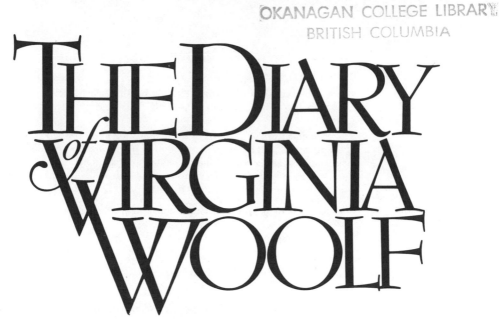

THE DIARY of VIRGINIA WOOLF

Edited by
Anne Olivier Bell
Assisted by Andrew McNeillie

VOLUME THREE
1925-1930

Harcourt Brace Jovanovich

New York and London

Printed in the United States of America

Library of Congress Cataloging in Publication Data

Woolf, Virginia Stephen, 1882–1941.
The diary of Virginia Woolf.

Includes index.
CONTENTS: V. 1. 1915–1919.—v. 2. 1920–1924.—v. 3. 1925–1930.—
1. Woolf, Virginia Stephen, 1882–1941—Diaries.
2. Authors, English—20th century—Biography.
PR6045.072Z494   1977   823'.9'12   [B]   77-73111
ISBN 0-15-125599-7

First American edition

B C D E

CONTENTS

EDITOR'S PREFACE

The division of this edition of Virginia Woolf's diaries into five volumes arises, it must be confessed, largely from practical considerations; nevertheless the span covered by this third volume—that is to say the years 1925 to 1930—has a unity which, though largely undesigned, is real and which corresponds to a distinct period in her life. It is the period in which she attained full maturity as an artist and at the same time achieved a secure and respected position in the world of letters. As a corollary, she became financially more stable and socially more adventurous. These are perhaps the most fruitful and satisfying years of her life.

This volume opens with Virginia revising and preparing both *The Common Reader* and *Mrs Dalloway* for their publication in the late spring of 1925. Her last book, *Jacob's Room*, which had appeared towards the end of 1922, had achieved a certain *succès d'estime*, but as a novelist she was still very unsure of herself; Middleton Murry's opinion that in that novel she had reached a dead end was a perpetual source of disquiet, and she awaited the reception of her new books—*Mrs Dalloway* in particular—with marked apprehensiveness. Her fluctuations of feeling as the opinions of individuals and the press reached her are almost obsessively recorded; but as she also wrote at this time: 'The truth is that writing is the profound pleasure & being read the superficial.' That this was true for her one cannot doubt.

But 'being read' brought its rewards, superficial or otherwise, in the way of greatly enhanced reputation (what she dubiously referred to as her 'fame', a condition she both relished and mistrusted); it brought acknowledgment by the literate public on both sides of the Atlantic that Virginia Woolf was an artist of authentic quality and originality, and a creative and illuminating critic. And this certainly reassured her and gave her greater confidence in following her own path; she could scarcely contain her impatience to start the writing of *To The Lighthouse* which had been simmering in her brain for many months. Fame also brought a greater demand for her books, for her opinions, and for her company; maintaining a balance between the pleasures and rewards of society and those of solitude became an ever more difficult operation.

In the spring of 1927, in the torpid period between finishing *To The Lighthouse* and its publication in May, Virginia began to amuse herself with an idea to which she attached a provisional title: *The Jessamy*

Brides. This protean concept developed finally, by way of *The Moths,* into *The Waves,* which she had almost completed as this volume closes; but it also branched out in a slighter form as *Orlando,* a work written at breakneck speed between October 1927 and March 1928. Although sterner critics, and among them Virginia herself, regarded this as little more than a *jeu d'esprit,* it delighted a large number of people and sold far better than any of her previous books. It is perhaps the most accessible of all of them and comes nearest to the simpler human passions.

Orlando may be regarded as an offering of love to Vita Sackville-West who, during these years, was to hold sway in both Virginia's heart and her imagination. They had first met at the end of 1922, but it was not until late in 1925 that their somewhat guarded interest in each other (Virginia had been told that Vita was a pronounced Sapphist who might have her eye on her) developed into an intensely absorbing passion. Virginia is at first reticent in her diary about her feelings for Vita, which may rather be inferred from the frequency of her letters to her; but gradually the paramount importance of the attachment becomes apparent. This is a passage in Virginia's life which has attracted a good deal of attention, but with the publication of her letters and her diary there is little more that I would wish to say concerning that delicate sentimental transaction of which *Orlando* is the permanent monument; and yet these sources reveal a seeming paradox: Virginia's one serious infidelity is remarkable in that it exhibits clearly the secure strength of her marriage. Nothing in the letters or the diary during her love affair with Vita is more manifest than her constant affection for Leonard, and his for her. Vita represented romance, the champagne and gold-dust aspect of the world by which Virginia always was fascinated; but with Leonard she could depend completely upon that spirit of trusting affection and mutual respect, of intimacy and ease, upon the solid comfort of day-to-day happiness which she described as the core of her life. It is a characteristic anomaly of the situation that if Leonard was discomposed by any of Virginia's lovers, it was not by Vita but by that formidable old egotist and eccentric Dame Ethel Smyth. He really liked Vita; but Ethel both exasperated and bored him.

The proximate cause of this later friendship, which was to absorb— and demand—so much of Virginia's time after their first meeting in February 1930, was *A Room of One's Own.* This little book, Virginia's most persuasive essay in feminist propaganda, had branched and flowered from the root-stock of two papers read to student societies at the two women's colleges at Cambridge in October 1928, and was published a year later. Ethel Smyth, a veteran in the struggle for women's suffrage, convinced that her failure as a musician could be ascribed to male prejudice, discerned in the author of *A Room of One's Own* a natural ally, resolved to claim her as such, and bore down upon her with all flags flying. Already predisposed, Ethel fell in love with Virginia at once; and Virginia, fascinated and impressed by the old campaigner's vigour and spirit, found her impossible to withstand. However, in this volume of the diary we see only the beginning of this relationship.

Virginia's relations with individual women, and her interest in the whole subject of women—in their particular qualities, their hidden and unrecorded lives, their disadvantages and struggles and triumphs in a male-dominated society—has become the focus for a great deal of attention, and she is rightly seen to have been both a profound analyst of women and an eloquent advocate of their rights. Yet the attention devoted to the 'feminist' aspect of her life and work threatens at times to distort and obscure the whole, and it seems almost necessary to insist that Virginia was not essentially a feminist zealot. A measure of the very wide-ranging and catholic nature of her thought and interest is given by her diary—the most direct and unpremeditated record of her immediate concerns—which is relatively little occupied with these matters.

Although Virginia continued to feel most at ease with her old Bloomsbury intimates, she extended her social circle and, always curious about people, embraced the opportunities her growing fame afforded her to observe or meet the eminent, particularly in her own profession of letters (though she did not disdain an invitation to dine in company with the Prime Minister). Her impressions of, for example, Thomas Hardy or W. B. Yeats, of Max Beerbohm, George Moore, or H. G. Wells, provide some of the most vivid and interesting pages in this volume. And her literary success brought more material advantages: amenities and comforts could be added to 52 Tavistock Square and to Monks House; Virginia could afford to buy nice clothes (always an agitating matter) and works of art, to give presents and parties, to buy a second-hand motor-car, to travel abroad. Leonard and Virginia were both frugal by nature and by habit, and what to them appeared free-handed spending would seem modest enough today; but their years of stringency and scraping were over; they had earned the liberty to order their lives free from the harsher restraints of financial anxiety.

This was indeed a period of new achievements, new affluence, new pleasures. There are inevitable vexations and dejections, illnesses and anxieties; nevertheless, allowing for Virginia's tendency to use her diary as a vent for ill humour, this volume is on the whole the record of a fortunate time: the record of a woman happy in her marriage, happy in her friendships, but above all happy in her work, in the fertility of her imagination, in the growing assurance of her own powers of expression, in the continued expansion of her genius.

Editorial Note

In 1953 Leonard Woolf published *A Writer's Diary*, a selection of excerpts from his wife's manuscript diaries, before making the dispositions which brought the originals to America after his death. They are now preserved in the Henry W. and Albert A. Berg Collection of English and American Literature in the New York Public Library (Astor, Lenox, and Tilden Foundations). Through a concord between the copyright holders, Virginia Woolf's English and American publishers, and the Curator of the Berg Collection, the series of diaries she kept from 1915 until her death in 1941 are now being published in their entirety in five volumes. The text for the six years included in this third volume is transcribed from Diaries XIV to XIX inclusive, plus a few pages from the end of Diary XIII, and the first forty pages of Diary XX. (See Volume I, Appendix I, in which the whole series is listed.)

The transcription follows the manuscript as closely and completely as possible, though it has to be said that Virginia Woolf's rapid handwriting gets progressively more difficult to decipher; my uncertainties or total defeats are revealed by the use of square brackets (reserved throughout for editorial interpolations) and question marks. Where she has crossed out or altered words or passages I have followed her reconsidered version, although when they seem of sufficient interest, the cancelled words are given within angled brackets: ⟨   ⟩. Her spelling is so consistently good that her rare aberrations are preserved; so is her often phonetic spelling of proper names, when the correct form is supplied between square brackets or in a footnote. Virginia Woolf's almost invariable use of the ampersand has been retained to suggest the pace of her writing (although the symbol in its printed form unfortunately rather negates this intention), and to give point to the occasions where she chooses to spell out the conjunction.

I have made some concession to the convenience of reader and printer in respect of certain features of the manuscript:

I have standardised the dating of the entries, and they are set out: day, date, month, and italicised thus: *Tuesday 6 January*; the month is repeated in the running headline on each page, together with the year. Virginia Woolf's own dating is inconsistent, and sometimes wrong, and there seems no particular point in perpetuating it. Where, from internal and external evidence, I have found her to be mistaken, I have indicated the fact.

Inconsistencies of punctuation, in particular a heedless insufficiency of inverted commas, brackets, and of apostrophes in the possessive case, have been amended. It is not always easy to determine what intention is implied by a single or double mark made at speed, but I have tried to interpret these faithfully. I have allowed myself some latitude in distinguishing paragraphs where they may not always be clearly apparent on the written page.

Autographical idiosyncrasies—in particular the habit of forming abbreviations with superior letters as in M^{rs}, Sq^{re}, 19th, and the like—have been brought as it were down to earth, the stops and dashes omitted; and the variety of marks following the single letter to which names are frequently abbreviated have been standardised to a full point.

Such annotations as I have thought could be helpful or interesting to readers are given at the foot of the page to which they relate; they are numbered in sequence *within each month*. (All methods of presenting annotations seem to me to have disadvantages, and this is admittedly a compromise solution.) I am of course aware that it is virtually impossible to suit everyone in the provision of supplementary information, and that much of my rather *terre-à-terre* annotation will prove superfluous to one or another reader. Readers' wants differ, and I can only remind them of their own power to choose to read, or to ignore, footnotes.

As in the previous volumes I have attempted to identify every person referred to in the diary; those regular players who must already be familiar to most readers I have relegated to Appendix I on p 349; the others—and as Virginia moved more into the world they become more numerous—are introduced in footnotes on their first appearance; the index should discover them. The summary information provided does not in general extend beyond the period covered by this volume.

I have where possible identified Virginia's own published writings according to B. J. Kirkpatrick's indispensable *Bibliography of Virginia Woolf*, prefixing the numbers therein by *Kp*; I use the abbreviation *HP Checklist* and number to indicate the books issued by Leonard and Virginia Woolf in their capacity as publishers, particulars of which are given in J. Howard Woolmer's *Checklist of the Hogarth Press, 1917-1938*; and *M & M* represents the volume on Virginia Woolf, edited by Robin Majumdar and Allen McLaurin, in *The Critical Heritage* series. A complete list of abbreviations employed for books and names is to be found on p 347; other books are cited by their author, full title, and date of publication in England, except for Virginia Woolf's own works, when reference is made, unless otherwise stated, to the uniform edition published in London by the Hogarth Press and in New York by Harcourt Brace Jovanovich.

Acknowledgments

Once again the greater part of the research for this volume (outside my home) has been pursued in the London Library and in the Library and Documents Centre of the University of Sussex; to the ever helpful staff, and to the incomparable facilities, of those institutions, I wish to pay tribute. My work is greatly eased by the publication in advance of this diary of *The Letters of Virginia Woolf* edited by Nigel Nicolson and Joanne Trautmann, now approaching its sixth and final volume; besides bestowing this great natural advantage, Nigel Nicolson has been unfailingly generous in providing me with information that only he could supply. Harry (Sir Henry) Lintott has solved several puzzles for me, and has nobly read through my notes and saved me from innumerable errors of fact and form, for which I am deeply grateful. Trekkie Parsons has again permitted me to make use of Leonard Woolf's laconic diaries, an inestimable assistance. And the following friends and correspondents have generously responded to my need for help of various kinds:

Anastasia Anrep; Igor Anrep; Barbara Bagenal; Rachel Cecil; David and Elisabeth Elwyn; Alan Clark; David Garnett; Richard Garnett; John Gere; Anthony Harris; Michael Henley; Grace Higgens; Michael Jamieson; John Jones; Dr John Kelly; Milo Keynes; Paul Levy; Averil Lysaght; Norman and Jeanne McKenzie; G. H. G. Norman; Ian Parsons; Frances Partridge; Angela Richards; S. P. Rosenbaum; Daphne Sanger; Desmond Shawe-Taylor; Brenda Silver; George Spater; Olivier Todd; John le Forest Thompson; and Veronica Wedgwood.

I also wish to acknowledge the courtesy and assistance I have received from librarians, officials, or staff of the following: Cambridge University Library; Cheltenham Art Gallery and Museum Service; Christie's, London; *Country Life*; Dorset County Museum; The English Association; Girton College Library; Goethe Institute, London; King's College Library, Cambridge; The National Maritime Museum, Greenwich; Newnham College Library; Oxford University Press; The Royal Academy of Arts; The Victoria and Albert Museum (Departments of Metalwork, of Prints and Drawings, and Textiles and Dress, and the Theatre Museum); *Vogue*.

The portion of the letter from W. B. Yeats which appears on p 331 does so with the kind permission of Michael and Anne Yeats and A. P. Watt Ltd.

I have referred to concessions made for the sake of reader and printer. I would like however to observe that Messrs T. &. A. Constable of Edinburgh need no concessions from me; they could print anything they were asked to—and indeed have most faithfully done so.

The maps forming the endpapers for the English edition have been specially drawn by my son Julian Bell.

The indispensability of my assistant Andrew McNeillie is, I trust, evidenced by his name on the title-page of this work. Essential preparation and research have been carried out by Virginia Bell and Victoria Walton. Sandra Williams has again borne the onerous responsibility of typing the final copy. To have such excellent and dependable helpers is an immeasurable asset for which I am constantly grateful.

My greatest debt is to those who have entrusted me with this task: the copyright holders Angelica Garnett and Quentin Bell, Lola Szladits the Curator of the Berg Collection, John Ferrone of Harcourt Brace Jovanovich, and Norah Smallwood of the Hogarth Press. Although naturally I sometimes curse both them and the day I was so bold and foolhardy as to undertake it, they have severally been so helpful, so encouraging, and above all so patient, that I count myself fortunate in my taskmasters, salute them for their virtues, and thank them for their confidence.

ANNE OLIVIER BELL

Sussex, November 1979

1925

1925

The Woolfs returned to London from Monks House on 2 January. VW continued to use her 1924 book (Diary XIII).

Tuesday 6 January

The disgraceful truth is that I shall run year into year, for I cant waste so many blank pages.

What a flourish I began 1924 with! And today, for the 165th time, Nelly has given notice— Won't be dictated to: must do as other girls do. This is the fruit of Bloomsbury.[1] On the whole, I'm inclined to take her at her word. The nuisance of arranging life to suit her fads, & the pressure of 'other girls' is too much, good cook though she is, & honest, crusty old maid too, dependable, in the main, affectionate, kindly, but incurably fussy, nervy, unsubstantial. Anyhow, the servant question no longer much worries me.

Last night we dined at 3 Albert Road Mary's new villa.[2] I like the new year to begin with warm friendly feelings—& it was a superb dinner. There were the children too, a nice girl & boy; a girl with lovely *womans* eyes, sympathetic, startled; & wild like a girl. (I want to begin to describe my own sex.) What do I mean about the expression? Extreme youth, & yet, one felt, this feeling has been existing forever; very feminine. Here I conceive my story—but I'm always conceiving stories now. Short ones —scenes—for instance The Old Man (a character of L.S.) The Professor on Milton—(an attempt at literary criticism)[3] & now The Interruption, women talking alone. However, back to life. Where are we?

I spent this morning writing a note on an E[lizabe]than play—for

1. The Woolfs had employed Nelly Boxall and Lottie Hope as living-in servants since 1916; they took Nelly with them when they moved to Tavistock Square, Bloomsbury, in 1924, and Lottie went to work for the Adrian Stephens in neighbouring Gordon Square.
2. For Mary Hutchinson and her husband St John Hutchinson see Appendix I. The Hutchinsons had recently moved to 3 Albert (now Prince Albert) Road, Regent's Park, from their previous home at River House, Hammersmith. The children were Barbara (b. 1911) and Jeremy (b. 1915).
3. VW was already envisaging her father Leslie Stephen as the subject of a 'scene' the previous autumn (see *II VW Diary*, 17 October 1924); it was to develop into *To the Lighthouse*. The professor is incorporated in *Mrs Dalloway*, pp 193-4.

which I have been reading plays all this year.[4] Then I found the minute hand of my watch had come off (this was talking to Lytton about [Samuel] Richardson last night—I found it off then): so I went into the printing room to see the time—found Angus & Leonard doing Simkin's bill. Stayed & laughed. L. went off to the office, when we had dog-walked round the Square. I came in & set a page of Nancy. Then out to Ingersoll to get my watch mended.[5] Then dog walked. Then here. It being a black grained winter day; lengths of the pavement ink black where not lighted. Never shall I describe all the days I have noticed. I cannot hit it off, quite, & yet perhaps if I read this again I shall see what I meant then.

Rodmell was all gale & flood; these words are exact. The river overflowed. We had 7 days rain out of 10. Often I could not face a walk. L. pruned, which needed heroic courage. My heroism was purely literary. I revised Mrs D[alloway]: the dullest part of the whole business of writing; the most depressing & exacting. The worst part is at the beginning (as usual) where the aeroplane has it all to itself for some pages, & it wears thin. L. read it; thinks it my best—but then has he not *got* to think so? Still I agree. He thinks it has more continuity than J[acob]s R[oom]. but is difficult owing to the lack of connection, visible, between the two themes.

Anyhow it is sent off to Clarks, & proofs will come next week. This is for Harcourt Brace, who has accepted without seeing & raised me to 15 p.c.[6]

I did not see very much at Rodmell, having to keep my eyes on the typewriter.

Angus was with us for Christmas, a very quiet, very considerate, unselfish deliberate young man, with a charming sense of humour—colourless, Lytton says: passive. But I think well of him, all the same.

4. VW's 'Notes on an Elizabethan Play' was published in the *TLS* of 5 March 1925 (Kp C259).
5. For Lytton Strachey see Appendix I. Angus Henry Gordon Davidson (b. 1898), graduate of Magdalene College, Cambridge, came to work at the Hogarth Press in December 1924 as successor to G. H. W. Rylands and stayed until the end of 1927. Simpkin, Marshall, Hamilton, Kent & Co were book wholesalers and distributors. The *Nation* office was at 38 Great James Street, WC1. Nancy Cunard (1896-1965), the rebellious daughter of the immensely wealthy Sir Bache and Lady Cunard; her long poem *Parallax* was to be published by the Hogarth Press in April 1925 (*HP Checklist* 57). The Ingersoll Watch Company had two establishments in Kingsway.
6. R & R Clark Ltd, the Edinburgh firm of printers. Harcourt, Brace and Company, VW's publishers in America.

Wednesday 18 March

These last pages belong to the Common Reader, & were written in bed with influenza;[1] & now, at last, having sent off the last proofs today, I have got my new diary made, & shall close this, with a thousand apologies, & some ominous forebodings at the sight of all the blank pages.

VW here begins a new book, Diary XIV, on the title-page of which is written:

52 Tavistock Square WC

1925

Wednesday 18 March[2]

This disgrace has been already explained—I think: two books to see through the press, mainly between tea & dinner; influenza, & a distaste for the pen.[3]

At the moment (I have 7½ before dinner) I can only note that the past is beautiful because one never realises an emotion at the time. It expands later, & thus we don't have complete emotions about the present, only about the past. This struck me on Reading platform, watching Nessa & Quentin kiss, he coming up shyly, yet with some emotion. This I shall remember; & make more of, when separated from all the business of crossing the platform, finding our bus &c. That is why we dwell on the past, I think.

We went to see the children at school: the young men, I should say. Julian was shut up in a pound, pounding Mr Eliot's tennis court by way of punishment. (That suggests a story about a man whose ambition it was to buy a field; this kept him alive; when he bought it, he died.) Mr Goddard came up, & Julian shouted out, "I'm at it till 5" as though they were undergraduates.[4] Not much public school about this; but oh

1. This entry follows a one-page, extensively rewritten draft of the final paragraph (on Sir Thomas Browne) of 'The Elizabethan Lumber Room', published as part of the *Common Reader* on 23 April 1925.
2. VW has written *Saturday 18 March*; Saturday was either 14 or 21 March, but the date rather than the day here seems more likely to be right.
3. Nancy Cunard's *Parallax* and R. C. Trevelyan's *Poems and Fables* (*HP Checklist* 78) were both hand-printed at the Hogarth Press and published in April 1925. VW probably caught influenza from LW, who was ill from 11-13 March.
4. Quentin Bell had followed his elder brother Julian to Leighton Park School, near Reading, and was now in his second term there. T. C. Elliott (d. 1969) taught French at the school from 1915-30; Scott Goddard (1895-1965) was music master, 1921-26, and later became a well-known music critic. For *pounding* read *rolling*.

the horror of being Mr Goddard, & wandering out, this bitter day (it snowed) to welcome home the steeplechasers. When they ran in, they at once rolled on the ground, & were covered with rugs & coats. The last lap, their legs rose very weakly. J. & Q. were utterly cynical about this, & said no one enjoyed it, but it was thought the right thing to do. But this nib scratches.

The Woolfs travelled from Victoria, via Newhaven-Dieppe, to Paris on Thursday 26 March, then on by overnight train to Marseilles and to Cassis, where they stayed at the Hotel Cendrillon; they returned to London on 6/7 April.

Wednesday 8 April

Just back from Cassis. Often while I was there I thought how I would write here frequently & so get down some of the myriad impressions which I net every day. But directly we get back, what is it that happens? We strip & dive into the stream, & I am obsessed with a foolish idea that I have no time to stop & write, or that I ought to be doing something serious. Even now, I pelt along feverishly, thinking half the time, but I must stop & take Grizzle [*dog*] out; I must get my American books in order;[1] the truth is, I must try to set aside half an hour in some part of my day, & consecrate it to diary writing. Give it a name & a place, & then perhaps, such is the human mind, I shall come to think it a duty, & disregard other duties for it.

I am under the impression of the moment, which is the complex one of coming back home from the South of France to this wide dim peaceful privacy—London (so it seemed last night) which is shot with the accident I saw this morning & a woman crying Oh oh oh faintly, pinned against the railings with a motor car on top of her. All day I have heard that voice. I did not go to her help; but then every baker & flower seller did that. A great sense of the brutality & wildness of the world remains with me—there was this woman in brown walking along the pavement— suddenly a red film car turns a somersault, lands on top of her, & one hears this oh, oh, oh. I was on my way to see Nessa's new house, & met Duncan in the square, but as he had seen nothing, he could not in the

---

1. VW's article 'American Fiction' appeared in the *Saturday Review of Literature*, New York, on 1 August 1925 (Kp C265).

least feel what I felt, or Nessa either, though she made some effort to connect it with Angelica's accident last spring. But I assured her it was only a passing brown woman; & so we went over the house composedly enough.[2]

Since I wrote, which is these last months, Jacques Raverat has died; after longing to die; & he sent me a letter about Mrs Dalloway which gave me one of the happiest days of my life.[3] I wonder if this time I have achieved something? Well, nothing anyhow compared with Proust, in whom I am embedded now. The thing about Proust is his combination of the utmost sensibility with the utmost tenacity. He searches out these butterfly shades to the last grain. He is as tough as catgut & as evanescent as a butterfly's bloom. And he will I suppose both influence me & make me out of temper with every sentence of my own. Jacques died, as I say; & at once the siege of emotions began. I got the news with a party here— Clive, Bee How, Julia Strachey, Dadie.[4] Nevertheless, I do not any longer feel inclined to doff the cap to death. I like to go out of the room talking, with an unfinished casual sentence on my lips. That is the effect it had on me—no leavetakings, no submission—but someone stepping out into the darkness. For her though the nightmare was terrific. All I can do now

2. For Vanessa Bell and Duncan Grant see Appendix I. An account of their daughter Angelica's accident is given in *II VW Diary*, 5 April 1924. 'Nessa's new house' was part of no. 37 Gordon Square.

3. Jacques Pierre Raverat (1885-1925), a Frenchman who had studied mathematics at Cambridge and was one of the group of friends called by VW the 'neo-Pagans', another of whom, the wood-engraver Gwendolen Mary Darwin (1885-1957), he married in 1911. They lived at Vence in the Alpes-Maritimes, and he became a painter. He had suffered for some years from a form of disseminated sclerosis, a paralysing disease, and his letters were dictated to his wife. About a month before his death on 7 March 1925, VW had sent him advance proofs of *Mrs Dalloway*, and he responded: 'Almost it's enough to make me want to live a little longer, to continue to receive such letters and such books ... I am flattered & you know how important an element that is in one's sensations, and proud & pleased . . .' The correspondence between VW and Jacques and Gwen Raverat is preserved in MHP, Sussex.

4. For Clive Bell see Appendix I. Beatrice Isabel Howe, later Mrs Mark Lubbock, author of *A Fairy Leapt Upon My Knee* (1927); she was painted by Duncan Grant in 1926 (see *Shone*, p 228) Julia Frances Strachey (1901-79), daughter of Oliver Strachey and his first wife Ruby Mayer, was to become a writer of unusual character and quality if of scant quantity. George Humphrey Wolferston ('Dadie') Rylands (b. 1902), Scholar of Eton and King's College, Cambridge, and an Apostle; he worked in the Hogarth Press for the last six months of 1924 and then left to work for his Cambridge Fellowship. His poem *Russet and Taffeta*, dedicated to VW, was published in December 1925 (*HP Checklist* 75).

is to keep natural with her, which is I believe a matter of considerable importance. More & more do I repeat my own version of Montaigne "Its life that matters".[5]

I am waiting to see what form of itself Cassis will finally cast up in my mind. There are the rocks. We used to go out after breakfast & sit on the rocks, with the sun on us. L. used to sit without a hat, writing on his knee. One morning he found a sea urchin—they are red, with spikes which quiver slightly. Then we would go a walk in the afternoon, right up over the hill, into the woods, where one day we heard the motor cars & discovered the road to La Ciota[t] just beneath. It was stony, steep & very hot. We heard a great chattering birdlike noise once, & I bethought me of the frogs. The ragged red tulips were out in the fields; all the fields were little angular shelves cut out of the hill, & ruled & ribbed with vines; & all red, & rosy & purple here & there with the spray of some fruit tree in bud. Here & there was an angular white, or yellow or blue washed house, with all its shutters tightly closed; & flat paths round it, & once rows of stocks; an incomparable cleanness & definiteness everywhere. At La Ciota[t] great orange ships rose up out of the blue water of the little bay. All these bays are very circular, & fringed with the pale coloured plaster houses, very tall, shuttered, patched & peeled, now with a pot & tufts of green on them, now with clothes, drying; now an old old woman looking. On the hill, which is stony as a desert, the nets were drying; & then in the streets children & girls gossiped & meandered all in pale bright shawls & cotton frocks, while the men picked up the earth of the main square to make a paved court of it. The Hotel Cendrillon is a white house, with red tiled floors, capable of housing perhaps 8 people. There were Miss Toogood, the Howards, Miss Betsy Roberts, Mr Gurney, Mr Francis &, finally, Mr Hugh Anderson & Mr Garrow Tomlin.[6] All deserve pages of description. And then the whole hotel atmosphere provided me with many ideas: oh so cold, indifferent, superficially polite, & exhibiting such odd relationships: as if human nature were now reduced to a kind of code, which it has devised to meet these emergencies, where people who do not know each other meet, & claim their rights as members of the same tribe. As a matter of fact, we got into touch all round; but our depths were not invaded. But L. & I were too too happy,

5. See 'Montaigne' in *The Common Reader*, p 95: 'But enough of death; it is life that matters.' VW wrote this day to Gwen Raverat; see *III VW Letters*, no. 1547; also no. 1550 of 1 May 1925.
6. Hew Anderson, see below, 19 July 1925; the Hon George Garrow Tomlin (1898-1931), elder brother of Stephen Tomlin, the sculptor (see below, 27 March 1926); other hotel guests unidentified.

as they say; if it were now to die &c.[7] Nobody shall say of me that I have not known perfect happiness, but few could put their finger on the moment, or say what made it. Even I myself, stirring occasionally in the pool of content, could only say But this is all I want; could not think of anything better; & had only my half superstitious feeling as the Gods who must when they have created happiness, grudge it. Not if you get it in unexpected ways though.

Sunday 19 April

It is now after dinner, our first summer time night, & the mood for writing has left me, only just brushed me & left me. I have not achieved my sacred half hour yet. But think—in time to come I would rather read something here than reflect that I did polish off Mr Ring Lardner successfully.[8] I'm out to make £300 this summer by writing, & build a bath & hot water range at Rodmell. But, hush, hush—my books tremble on the verge of coming out, & my future is uncertain. As for forecasts—its *just* on the cards Mrs Dalloway is a success (Harcourt thinks it "wonderful"), & sells 2,000—I dont expect it: I expect a slow silent increase of fame, such has come about, rather miraculously, since Js R. was published; my value mounting steadily as a journalist, though scarcely a copy sold. And I am not very nervous—rather; & I want as usual to dig deep down into my new stories, without having a looking glass flashed in my eyes— Todd, to wit; Colefax to wit et cetera.[9]

7.
        '. . . . . . If it were now to die,
        'Twere now to be most happy; for, I fear,
        My soul hath her content so absolute,
        That not another comfort like to this
        Succeeds in unknown fate.'   *Othello*, II, i

8. Ringgold Wilmer (Ring) Lardner (1885-1933), American short-story writer whose work is discussed by VW in her article 'American Fiction' (Kp C265); see above, 8 April 1925, n 1.

9. VW wrote several 'stories' concerned with 'the party consciousness, the frock consciousness' (see below, 27 April 1925) at this period, seven of which are collected in *Mrs Dalloway's Party* (1973) edited by Stella McNichol (whose editorial procedures were severely criticised by J. F. Hulcoop in the *VW Miscellany*, no. 3, Spring 1975, and defended in *ibid*, no. 9, Winter 1977). Manuscript and typescript versions of these stories are both now in the Berg. Dorothy Todd, who edited British *Vogue* from 1922-26, sought to make it an authoritative and sophisticated guide to high fashion in clothes and culture, and commissioned contributions from *avant-garde* writers (including VW) and artists in both France and England. Lady Colefax (*née* Sibyl Halsey, d. 1950) was celebrated for her indefatigable pursuit of 'interesting' people, whom she and her husband Sir Arthur entertained at their home, Argyll House, Chelsea.

Lytton came in the other night. He seemed to me autumnal; with that charming rectitude of spirit which no one else attains so perfectly I think. His justice of mind is considerable. But Christ is dismissed, to his disappointment, for he grows more & more fussy about subjects: Christ, he says did not exist: was a figment; & so much is known that really he couldn't pull it all together in one book. Then perhaps Philip Ritchie is waning.[10] We talked of old buggers & their lack of attraction for young men. My anti-bugger revolution has run round the world, as I hoped it would. I am a little touched by what appears their contrition, & anxiety to condone their faults. Yet if I cant say what's in my mind, & have a fling with Clive's Colonel now & then, what's the use of me?[11] The pale star of the Bugger has been in the ascendant too long. Julian agrees emphatically. We had Good Friday at Rodmell—June weather, & again this downy billowy wave beneath us: ah, but how quickly I sink; what violet shadows there are between the high lights, & one, perhaps, as unreasonable as another. But this properly belongs to a story.[12]

Yesterday we went to Max's show with dear shabby old Angus, who seems to me an elder brother, 20 years younger than I am.[13] We came back to tea (over all this the bloom of the past descends as I write—it becomes sad, beautiful, memorable) & ate a great many buns, & then discussed Murphy.[14] Alas!—she has a temper. She is an ill-conditioned mongrel woman, of no charm, a Bohemian scallywag, something like Irish stew to look at, & not destined for a long life here, I suppose. But Angus, though plaintive is gentlemanly; does not insist, & sees the drawbacks;

10. The Hon. Philip Charles Thomson Ritchie (1899-1927), eldest son of Lord Ritchie of Dundee, had been called to the Bar in 1924, and since the previous summer had engaged Lytton Strachey's affections.

11. The meaning is here equivocal. In most contexts 'Clive's Colonel' would mean his elder brother Lt. Col. William Cory Bell (1875-1961), Unionist MP for Devizes from 1918-23, whose views on buggery were likely to be more emphatic than VW's own. However, Clive Bell had recently published an article entitled 'The Colonel's Theory' (N & A, 7 March 1925), discussing Tolstoy on Art by Aylmer Maude, and referring to Tolstoy as 'a retired colonel—or lieutenant was it?'; but it is not easy to see in what way this was relevant to the matter in hand.

12. The Woolfs had motored down to Sussex with Clive Bell and Duncan Grant, and were at Rodmell from Maundy Thursday to Easter Monday, 9-13 April.

13. The Woolfs went to the opening day on 18 April of an exhibition of new caricatures by Max Beerbohm at the Leicester Galleries; it included the series 'The Old and the Young Self' and an unusual number of cartoons of political interest.

14. Bernadette Murphy came to work as secretary in the Hogarth Press on 4 February 1925.

Leonard will have to pull out the tooth on Thursday. I suspect some hidden grievance: I suspect she harbours scores.

Marjory & her Tom looked in at the basement this evening, very happy, L. says, & indeed I think she must enjoy her situation to the last ounce—money, food, security, & a supply of young men, & her faithful Tom, & a little dress allowance, & breakfast late, & consideration. She is a nice trusty creature into the bargain, & if I wished to see anyone, I daresay it would be her.[15]

At this moment, all we wish is to escape seeing anyone. Tomorrow I shall buy a new dress. I observe here that I am becoming jerky & jumpy, & my con[s]cience is asserting that I ought to read Mr Ring Lardner & earn my 50 guineas.

Monday 20 April

Happiness is to have a little string onto which things will attach themselves. For example, going to my dressmaker in Judd Street, or rather thinking of a dress I could get her to make, & imagining it made— that is the string, which as if it dipped loosely into a wave of treasure brings up pearls sticking to it. Poor Murphy is in the glumps, owing to Leonard's fiery harshness—each of which epithets he would most certainly deny. She has no string dipping into the green wave: things don't connect for her; & add up into those entrancing bundles which are happiness. And my days are likely to be strung with them. I like this London life in early summer—the street sauntering & square haunting, & then if my books (I never speak of L.'s pamphlet) were to be a success; if we could begin building at Monks, & put up wireless for Nelly, & get the Skeats to live at Shanks' cottage—if—if—if[16]—What will happen is *some* intensities of pleasure, some profound plunges of gloom. Bad reviews, being ignored; & then some delicious clap of compliment. But really what I should like would be to have £3 to buy a pair of rubber soled boots, & go for country walks on Sundays.

15. Marjorie Thomson (*c.* 1900-1931), at that time ostensibly married to C. E. M. Joad, had worked in the Hogarth Press from January 1923 until February 1925; she was about to marry Thomas Humphrey Marshall (b. 1893), Fellow of Trinity College, Cambridge, economist and social scientist, who taught at the London School of Economics. He was an elder brother of Frances Marshall (see below, 30 April, n 6).

16. LW's pamphlet *Fear and Politics. A Debate at the Zoo*, no. 7 in the first series of Hogarth Essays, was published in July 1925 (*HP Checklist* 79). The 'surly poet' and journalist Edward Shanks (see *II VW Diary*) had lived at Charnes Cottage, next door to Monks House. 'Skeats' unidentified.

One thing in considering my state of mind now, seems to me beyond dispute, that I have at last, bored down into my oil well, & can't scribble fast enough to bring it all to the surface. I have now at least 6 stories welling up in me, & feel, at last, that I can coin all my thoughts into words. Not but what an infinite number of problems remain; but I have never felt this rush & urgency before. I believe I can write much more quickly: if writing it is—this dash at the paper of a phrase, & then the typing & retyping—trying it over, the actual writing being now like the sweep of a brush; I fill it up afterwards. Now suppose I might become one of the interesting—I will not say great—but interesting novelists? Oddly, for all my vanity, I have not until now had much faith in my novels, or thought them my own expression.

Monday 27 April

The Common Reader was out on Thursday:[17] this is Monday, & so far I have not heard a word about it, private or public: it is as if one tossed a stone into a pond, & the waters closed without a ripple. And I am perfectly content, & care less than I have ever cared, & make this note just to remind me next time of the sublime progress of my books. I have been sitting to Vogue, the Becks that is, in their mews, which Mr Woolner built as his studio, & perhaps it was there he thought of my mother, whom he wished to marry, I think.[18] But my present
second selves is
what I mean
reflection is that people have any number of states of consciousness: & I should like to investigate the party consciousness, the frock consciousness &c. The fashion world at the Becks—Mrs Garland was there superintending a display—is certainly one;[19] where people secrete an envelope which connects them & protects

17. *The Common Reader* was published by the Hogarth Press on 23 April in an edition of 1250 copies (*HP Checklist* 81).

18. Maurice Adams Beck (1886-1960) and his partner Helen Macgregor were *Vogue*'s chief photographers at this period. Their studios at 4 Marylebone Mews had been built in 1861 at the rear of his new house at 29 Welbeck Street by the pre-Raphaelite sculptor Thomas Woolner (1825-1892), who about that time had sought leave to make a bust of Julia Jackson, for whom he cherished 'a more than artistic admiration', and to whom he made an offer of marriage; both overtures were declined. (See Leslie Stephen, *The Mausoleum Book*, edited by Alan Bell, 1977, p 28.) Beck and MacGregor had photographed VW the previous year, and one was reproduced by *Vogue* in its feature 'We Nominate for the Hall of Fame' in late May, 1924 (see also *In Vogue*, edited by Georgina Howell, 1975, p 61). A portrait from the present sitting was to appear in *Vogue*'s early May issue, 1926. (See also *QB II*, pl. 6a; Cecil Beaton, *British Photographers*, 1944, p 61.)

19. Madge Garland was Fashion Editor of *Vogue* under Dorothy Todd's editorship.

them from others, like myself, who am outside the envelope, foreign bodies. These states are very difficult (obviously I grope for words) but I'm always coming back to it. The party consciousness, for example: Sybil's consciousness. You must not break it. It is something real. You must keep it up; conspire together. Still I cannot get at what I mean. Then I meant to dash off Graves before I forget him.[20]

Figure a bolt eyed blue shirted shockheaded hatless man in a blue overcoat standing goggling at the door at 4.30, on Friday. "Mrs Woolf?" I dreading & suspecting some Nation genius, some young man determined to unbosom himself, rushed him to the basement, where he said "I'm Graves". "I'm Graves". Everybody stared. He appeared to have been rushing through the air at 60 miles an hour & to have alighted temporarily. So he came up, &, wily as I am, I knew that to advance holding the kettle in a dishclout was precisely the right method, attitude, pose. The poor boy is all emphasis protestation & pose. He has a crude likeness to Shelley, save that his nose is a switchback & his lines blurred. But the consciousness of genius is bad for people. He stayed till 7.15 (we were going to Caesar & Cleopatra—a strange rhetorical romantic early Shaw play[21]) & had at last to say so, for he was so thick in the delight of explaining his way of life to us that no bee stuck faster to honey. He cooks, his wife cleans; 4 children are brought up in the elementary school; the villagers give them vegetables; they were married in Church; his wife calls herself Nancy Nicolson; won't go to Garsington, said to him I must have a house for nothing; on a river; in a village with a square church tower; near but not on a railway—all of which, as she knows her mind, he procured. Calling herself Nicolson has sorted her friends into sheep & goats. All this to us sounded like the usual self consciousness of young men, especially as he threw in, gratuitously, the information that he descends from dean rector, Bishop, Von Ranker &c &c &c: only in order to say that he despises them. Still, still, he is a nice ingenuous rattle headed young man; but why should our age put this burden of

20. Robert Ranke Graves (b. 1895), poet and novelist; in 1918 he had married eighteen-year-old Nancy, daughter of the painter William Nicholson. The information concerning Graves's heredity and way of life here summarised by VW is amplified in his autobiography *Goodbye To All That* (1929). The Hogarth Press had already published two, and were to publish a further four, books by him (see *HP Checklist*, nos. 33, 46, 59, 63, 92 and 93).

21. Bernard Shaw's play, with Cedric Hardwicke and Gwen Ffrangcon-Davies in the name parts, was given by the Birmingham Repertory Theatre Company at the Kingsway Theatre; the Woolfs went on the evening of 23 April—a Thursday, which implies that VW was mistaken in supposing Graves's visit to have been on a Friday.

proof on us? Surely once one could live simply without protestations. I tried, perhaps, to curry favour, as my weakness is. L. was adamant. Then we were offered a ticket for the Cup tie, to see wh. Graves has come to London after 6 years; cant travel in a train without being sick; is rather proud of his sensibility. No I don't think he'll write great poetry: but what will you? The sensitive are needed too; the halfbaked, stammering stuttering, who perhaps improve their own quarter of Oxfordshire.

And on Sunday we had our first walk, to Epping.[22]

Wednesday 29 April

Hastily (Moore waiting[23]) I must record the fact of Tom's long gaslit emotional rather tremulous & excited visit last night, which informed us of his release (But I have not yet sent in my demission) from the Bank; some heavensent appointment, providing "4/5th's of my present salary" & a guarantee, being "humanly speaking" certain, to take effect next October—whether Lady Rothermere (who has become 'very nice') or the 4ly review, he sayeth not. Then he has a house near Sloane Sqre in view, rent £58 only, & so hopes to start fresh, & has been thinking over his state these past weeks, being alone, with time on his hands.[24] He has seen his whole life afresh, seen his relations to the world, & to Vivien in particular, become humbler suppler more humane—good, sensitive honourable man as he is, accusing himself of being the American husband, & wishing to tell me privately (L. gone to fetch the letters) what store V. sets by me, has done nothing but write since last June, because I told her to! He then defended not writing which is her device he said, & went into her p[s]ychology. Then he said to L. (having told us that he must space his remarks very carefully to fit in all he had to say) Do you know

22. Of this outing LW noted in his diary: 'Went Loughton train, & walked Epping Forest, High Beech & Chingford, & back by bus.'
23. VW was presumably reading for her article on George Moore's *Hail and Farewell* which was to be published in *Vogue*, early June, 1925 (Kp C263.1).
24. For T. S. Eliot and his wife Vivienne, see Appendix I. Heaven was sending Eliot, through several benevolent intermediaries, an appointment to the editorial board of the publishers Faber & Gwyer (later Faber & Faber), which he was to occupy from November 1925 until his death. The literary quarterly *The Criterion*, created for and edited by Eliot since 1922, had been subsidised by Lady Rothermere (d. 1937), wife of the newspaper proprietor Alfred Harmsworth, 1st Viscount Rothermere; Faber & Gwyer now undertook to share, and later to shoulder, the financial responsibility and it continued as *The New Criterion*, subsequently *The Monthly Criterion*, and once again as *The Criterion*, until its dissolution in 1939. The Eliots were to move to 57 Chester Terrace (now Row), a short distance from Sloane Square.

anything about psycho-analysis? L. said yes, in his responsible way; & Tom then told us the queer story—how Martin the dr. set V. off thinking of her childhood terror of loneliness, & now she cant let him, Tom, out of her sight. There he has sat mewed in her room these 3 months, poor pale creature, or if he has to go out, comes in to find her in a half fainting state.[25]

"Tomorrow will be wretched" he said, for he was now away from 8 to 11. We advised another doctor. But whether its doctors or sense or holiday or travel or some drastic method unknown thats to cure that little nervous self conscious bundle—heaven knows. She has the abstract, he the historic mind he said. The upshot was a queer sense of his emotion in coming to tell us all this—something not merely touching to my vanity but to my sense of human worth, I think; his liking for us, affection, trust in Leonard, & being so much at his ease in some subconscious way he said, not in conversation, with me, all making me lay my arm on his shoulder; not a very passionate caress, but the best I can do.

And now I'm a little fidgety about the *Common Reader*; not a single word of it from a soul, & perhaps a Review in the Lit Sup tomorrow. But this is quite recognisably superficial; beneath my fidgets being considerable stability.

Friday 1 May

This is a note for future reference as they say. The Common Reader came out 8 days ago, & so far not a single review has appeared, & no body has written to me or spoken to me about it or in any way acknowledged the fact of its existence; save Maynard, Lydia, & Duncan. Clive is conspicuously dumb; Mortimer has flu & cant review it; Nancy saw him reading it, but reported no opinion: all signs which point to a dull chill depressing reception; & complete failure.[1] I have just come through the hoping fearing stage, & now see my disappointment floating like an old

---

25. Sketches by Vivienne Eliot, using the pseudonyms Feiron Morris or Fanny Marlow, appeared in each quarterly issue of *The Criterion* between October 1924 and July 1925. Dr Marten was a physician and lay-psychologist of Freiburg much favoured by Lady Ottoline Morrell; Eliot had written to VW on 22 May 1924 (MHP Sussex, copy) warmly recommending him as a remarkable doctor who had done Vivienne a great deal of good the previous year—'in fact, made the turning point in that serious illness'; by 10 July 1925 he was writing to LW that he should consider suing Dr Marten did it not entail the necessity of going to Germany to do so.

1. For Maynard Keynes, Lydia Lopokova, Raymond Mortimer and Duncan Grant see Appendix I.

bottle in my wake & am off on fresh adventures. Only if the same thing happens to Dalloway one need not be surprised. But I must write to Gwen.[2]

Monday 4 May

This is the temperature chart of a book. We went to Cambridge, & Goldie said he thought me the finest living critic: the paralysed man, Hayward, said, in his jerky angular way: "Who wrote that extraordinarily good article on the Elizabethans 2 or 3 months ago in the Lit. Sup.?" I pointed to my breast.[3] Now there's one sneering review in Country Life, almost inarticulate with feebleness, trying to say what a Common reader is, & another, says Angus, in the Star, laughing at Nessa's cover.[4] So from this I prognosticate a good deal of criticism on the ground that I'm obscure & odd; & some enthusiasm; a slow sale, & an increased reputation. Oh yes—my reputation increases. But I am headachy, & cannot go to a concert with Angus, & Leonard is giving Randall his farewell dinner,[5] & it [is] a relief to sit quiet (the joy of giving up an engagement is supreme) & I wish I could describe Pernel, Cambridge, Braithwaite & Hayward, with a postscript for Thompson. A lovely place full, like all places, now, of this wave of the past. Walking past the Darwins I noticed the willows; I thought with that growing maternal affection which now comes to me, of myself there; of Rupert; then I went to Newnham, & kindled Mrs Palmer with talk of Pernel marrying an Archbishop.[6]

2. She did: see *III VW Letters*, no. 1550.
3. The Woolfs went to Cambridge on Saturday afternoon so that LW might attend an Apostles' meeting that evening; they returned to London on Sunday evening. Goldsworthy ('Goldie') Lowes Dickinson (1862-1932), Fellow of King's College and an Apostle, had resigned his lectureship in Political Science in 1920. John Davy Hayward (1905-65), who was to become a notable bibliophile and editor, was in his final year at King's; he suffered from muscular dystrophy.
4. *Country Life*, 2 May 1925, contained an unsigned review, 'What Does the "Common Reader" Read?' The critic in the *Star*, 1 May 1925, was Horace Thorogood; of the jacket design he wrote that 'only a conscious artist could have done it so badly'.
5. On 3 May 1925 John Randall completed fifty years of service as proof-reader on the *Athenaeum* (now amalgamated with the *Nation*); he finally retired the following January, when LW, on behalf of his colleagues, presented him with a barometer.
6. As LW was dining with his brother Apostles, VW walked to Newnham College to dine with the Principal, (Joan) Pernel Strachey (1876-1951), the fourth of Lytton's five sisters, passing Newnham Grange, the Darwin's house by the river, on her way. (Cf *A Room of One's Own*, chapter I.) Helen Elizabeth Palmer (1887-1954), Tutor at Newnham, was a widowed sister of VW's old admirer Walter Lamb (see *VW Diary* Volumes I and II). VW presumably saw Thompson and

No, I can't fire it off [?]; Mrs Asquith sticks in my gizzard;[7] I shall read Moore till dinner, & ⟨a paper⟩ then again till Leonard comes in. No, I dont want to hear Bach, & by giving Angus the tickets, secured him a charming young man for company.

Pernel was easier than I've ever known her. We sat over her fire, gossiping—how Kate died, taking the dog for a walk till a week of the end; entirely reserved; like a skeleton, like a dead person walking with sarcoma; no doctor. No mention of herself & the 58 brown diaries burnt, I suppose.[8]

Saturday 9 May

Just back from the Greek play at Chiswick with Lydia & Berta Ruck; a fine spring day, all the trees out driving across the Park; that transient journey being founded on a walk with Nessa Clive & Thoby, & Thoby & I agreed in calling Hyde Park 'urbane'.[9]

As for the Common Reader, the Lit. Sup. had close on 2 columns sober & sensible praise—neither one thing nor the other—my fate in the Times. And Goldie writes that he thinks "this is the best criticism in English—humorous, witty & profound."[10]—My fate is to be treated to all extremes & all mediocrities. But I never get an enthusiastic review in the Lit. Sup. And it will be the same for Dalloway, which now approaches.

Braithwaite, both Apostles, next day, as LW breakfasted with the one and lunched with the other. George Derwent Thompson (b. 1903) was a Fellow of King's who in 1937 became Professor of Greek at Birmingham; Richard Bevan Braithwaite (b. 1900), also a Fellow of King's, was to become a University lecturer and then Knightbridge Professor of Moral Philosophy at Cambridge, 1953-67.

7. VW's review, entitled 'Gipsy or Governess?', of Margot Asquith's *Places and Persons* appeared in the *N & A* on 16 May 1925 (KpC262·4).

8. VW's cousin Katherine Stephen (1856-1924) had been Principal of Newnham from 1911-20. See *II VW Diary*, 19 February 1924: '... there in a row on a shelf were her diaries from Jan 1 1877. ... And on her last day she will say to the charwoman who attends her, Bring me the diaries which you will find in the cabinet; & now, put them on the fire.'

9. The Cambridge Amateur Dramatic Company performed Euripides' *Helen* and *Cyclops* at the Chiswick Empire on 9 May in versions by J. T. Sheppard, who gave an introductory talk on 'Euripides and Comedy'. VW had unconsciously killed off the popular novelist Berta Ruck (Mrs Oliver ('Sally') Onions, 1878-1978) in *Jacob's Room* (see *II QB*, pp 91-2, where in her letter to the author Mrs Onions misremembers the performance as being of *The Frogs*). Thoby was VW's elder brother, who had died in 1906.

10. 'Mrs Woolf as Critic' appeared in the *TLS* of 7 May 1925 (see *M & M*, p 148); G. L. Dickinson's letter of the same date (accurately quoted) is in MHP, Sussex.

I'm jangled & jaded, having sat next the sea horse Sally Onions, who oozes lust at the sight of young men dancing. Last night we made a meagre meal with the Sangers,[11] whose mediocrity of comfort & taste saddens me: oh for a little beauty in life, as Berta Ruck might say—a lewd woman that, deposited in a lewd South Kensington House, like an equestrienne, in pale Jacon with a carnation, & her front teeth with a red ridge on them where her lips had touched them.[12] Little Lydia I liked: how does her mind work? Like a lark soaring; a sort of glorified instinct inspires her: I suppose a very nice nature, & direction at Maynard's hands.

Last night we had Morgan & Brace;[13] Morgan pleading with Leonard to come & see him—operated on for a broken bone in the wrist, I should have added, but it is now

Thursday 14 May

The first day of summer, leaves visibly drawing out of the bud, & the Square almost green. Oh what a country day—& some of my friends are now reading Mrs D. in the country.[14]

I meant to register more of my books temperatures. C.R. does not sell; but is praised. I was really pleased to open the Manchester Guardian this morning & read Mr Fausset on The Art of V.W. Brilliance combined with integrity; profound as well as eccentric.[15] Now if only the Times would speak out thus, but the Times mumbles & murmurs like a man sucking pebbles—did I say that I had nearly 2 mumbling columns on me there? But the odd thing is this: honestly I am scarcely a shade nervous about Mrs D. Why is this? Really I am a little bored, for the first time, at thinking how much I shall have to talk about it this summer. The truth is that writing is the profound pleasure & being read the superficial. I'm now all on the strain with desire to stop journalism & get on to *To the Lighthouse*. This is going to be fairly short: to have father's character done complete in it; & mothers; & St Ives; & childhood; & all the usual things I try to put in—life, death &c. But the centre is father's character,

11. C. P. (Charlie) Sanger (1871-1930), Chancery Barrister and an Apostle, and his wife Anna Dorothea (Dora), *née* Pease (1865-1955), lived in Oakley Street, Chelsea. VW had known them since before her marriage, and was very fond of him, but less so of his wife.
12. Jacon = jaconet, a plain light-weight cotton fabric, like muslin.
13. For E. Morgan Forster, see Appendix I. Donald Clifford Brace (1881-1955) was a co-founder of VW's American publishers, Harcourt, Brace; he came to tea.
14. *Mrs Dalloway* was published by the Hogarth Press on 14 May 1925.
15. The *Manchester Guardian*'s review of *The Common Reader* was by the author and literary critic Hugh I'Anson Fausset (1895-1965). It is reprinted in *M & M*, p 151.

sitting in a boat, reciting We perished, each alone, while he crushes a dying mackerel—However, I must refrain.[16] I must write a few little stories first, & let the Lighthouse simmer, adding to it between tea & dinner till it is complete for writing out.

Yesterday was a terrific chatter day—Desmond on top of Dr Leyes, Lord Olivier on top of Desmond, James & Dadie to finish off with, while L. had I forget how many press interviews & committees into the bargain. The League of Nations is booming (Innes, I mean.)[17] But I meant to describe my dear old Desmond, whom it rejoiced me to see again, & he held out both his hands, & I set him in his chair & we talked till 7 o'clock. He is rather worn & aged; a little, I think, feeling that here's 45 on him & nothing achieved, except indeed the children, whom he dotes on— Micky to write, Dermod & Rachel trilling & warbling on flute & piano:[18] all his human relations very fertile & flourishing, but oh, he said, talking of Houseman, don't let him give up the Corn Exchange & take to literature![19] I saw him thinking of his 50 articles for 5 years, his welter of old articles lying dusty in boxes, & now Geoffrey Scott promoted to do Donne, which Desmond should have done in the year 1912. I

16. From the last verse of William Cowper's poem, 'The Castaway':
  'No voice divine the storm allay'd,
   No light propitious shone,
  When, snatch'd from all effectual aid,
   We perish'd, each alone:
  But I beneath a rougher sea,
   And whelm'd in deeper gulfs than he.'

17. For Desmond MacCarthy and James Strachey, see Appendix I. Dr Norman Maclean Leys (d. 1944), had spent sixteen years in the Public Health Service in East and Central Africa; his controversial book *Kenya* had been published by the Hogarth Press six months earlier (*HP Checklist* 48). Sydney Olivier (1859-1943), 1st Baron Olivier of Ramsden, Fabian socialist and colonial administrator, had been ennobled in order that he might serve as Secretary of State for India in the shortlived Labour administration of 1924; four books by him were to be published by the Hogarth Press (*HP Checklist* 138, 139, 204 and 327). Kathleen E. Innes's book *The Story of the League of Nations told for Young People* had been published in April 1925 (*HP Checklist* 65).

18. The MacCarthy children were Michael (1907-1973), Rachel (b. 1909), and Dermod (b. 1911); Michael became a farmer and Dermod a doctor; Rachel was to marry a writer (Lord David Cecil) and to publish a novel.

19. This may be interpreted as Desmond's way of expressing his hope that his son Michael—whose ambition was to become a farmer—should stick to so useful and rewarding a profession (i.e. growing or selling corn) rather than suffer the financial and ethical doubts and insecurities of the literary life. (A. E. Housman had spent ten years in the Patent Office before becoming an academic and publishing his poetry.)

remember him telling me the story at Brunswick Square. So I said I would take the thing in hand & see it through which touched him, for children are not enough, after all; one wants something to be made out of oneself alone—& 5 boxes of dusty articles are rather raggy & rotten for 45 years. And he praised the C.R. with enthusiasm; & will write on it,[20] & so we chattered along; Vernon Lee, with her cheap rings in exquisite taste; & her idiomatic Italian; & her spiteful way of seeing things, so that she dare not write her memoirs; Lily Langtry coming down the playhouse steps & her daughter looming behind her, loveliness that "struck me in the breast"; also Logan & Ottoline—how Alys is ill of the cancer again— "a most unhappy miserable life poor woman—" L. having the new Mrs B.R. on one side, would be chafed to death by Ott. next door; but like a fool, Logan made none of this clear, & only complained that the village peace of Chelsea would be destroyed by O. wh. naturally she resented.[21] In all this, Desmond acts as solvent & go between, everyone sponging on his good nature & sense. What else did we discuss? The E[lizabe]thans? The Phoenix; poor Ray Litvin's miserable big mouth, & little body;[22]

20. Geoffrey Scott (1883-1929), whose second book *The Portrait of Zélide* appeared this year, never 'did' Donne. Desmond's aspirations in this respect are referred to in *I VW Letters*, no. 617 of 21 May [1912]: '. . . we go over the story of Donne's life. As the greater part of the history of England is somehow coming in, the book will be apoplectic.' His essay on Donne was republished in his book *Criticism* (1932), 'a selection from a selection made for me from the accumulation of many years of literary journalism'. VW went through his articles at this time (see below, 15 May and 1 June 1925, and *III VW Letters*, no. 1553, probably of 20, not 17, May) to encourage him to make a book from them, but her efforts were ineffective. 'Affable Hawk' (Desmond MacCarthy) reviewed *The Common Reader*—'a most uncommon book'—in the *New Statesman* of 30 May 1925.

21. Vernon Lee was the pseudonym of Violet Paget (1856-1935), a prolific writer, notably on Italian cultural history; she lived in Florence but made frequent visits to London. Emilie (Lillie), *née* Le Breton, widow of Edward Langtry and now Lady de Bathe (1853-1929), actress and famous beauty, was known as 'The Jersey Lily'; her daughter Jeanne-Marie was the child of Prince Louis of Battenberg. Logan Pearsall Smith (1865-1946), American-born man of letters, lived in St Leonard's Terrace, Chelsea, with his sister Alys (1867-1951), divorced wife of the Ho n.Bertrand Russell, who with his second wife Dora now lived near by in Sydney Street. Lady Ottoline Morrell (see Appendix I), who was at this time thinking of moving from Garsington to Chelsea, was credited by Logan with the break-up of his sister's marriage to Russell, with whom she had had a long affair.

22. The Woolfs had been to see the Phoenix Society's production at the Adelphi Theatre (Sunday 10 May) of *The Orphan* by Thomas Otway. Rachel (Ray) Litvin (d. 1977) played Monimia, the orphan; VW who knew her slightly had called her 'a Bohemian'; and indeed the action of the play is set in Bohemia.

when L. came, & then the dinner party, I just having time for a race round the Square; both Dadie & James very easy & affable, indeed for Dadie I feel considerable affection—so sensitive & tender is he, & one of these days will get a pull on himself, & be less of a quicksilver. Indeed, staying on he talked very seriously & excitedly of his dissertation & poets use of words, how they fix on to a word & fill it out with meaning & make it symbolic. But what these scholars want is to get at books through writing books, not through reading them.[23]

But I must remember to write about my *clothes* next time I have an impulse to write. My love of clothes interests me profoundly: only it is not love; & what it is I must discover.

Friday 15 May

Two unfavourable reviews of Mrs D (Western Mail & Scotsman[24]): unintelligible, not art &c: & a letter from a young man in Earls Court "This time you have done it—you have caught life & put it in a book . . ." Please forgive this outburst, but further quotation is unnecessary; & I dont think I should bother to write this, if I weren't jangled what by? The sudden heat, I think, & the racket of life. It is bad for me to see my own photograph. And I have been lunching with Desmond, & reading that dear old Owl's journalism. The thing is, he cant thrust through an article. Now, Lytton or I, though we mayn't think better or write better, have a drive in us, which makes an article whole. And yet there are things worth keeping, & he becomes moved, & irrational when he thinks of it, & I want him to be pleased— So we lunched in the grill of the Connaught Rooms where other men were talking business, had a bottle of wine & delved into the filth packets as he calls them.[25] Home to find Vogue sending photographs—more photographs: T.P. wants one, the Morning Post another.[26] & the C.R. sells 2 or 3 copies a day.

23. Rylands' Fellowship dissertation was to be published by the Hogarth Press in May 1928 as the first part of his book *Words and Poetry* (*HP Checklist* 175).
24. *Mrs Dalloway* was reviewed in the *Western Mail* of 14 May 1925. The reviewer said the book did not interest him 'very much' but supposed that 'readers of preternaturally nimble intellect may discover a consecutive story', while in *The Scotsman* of the same date the critic warned that 'None but the mentally fit should aspire to read this novel' and concluded: 'It may be said such is life, but is it art?'
25. The Connaught Rooms were in Great Queen Street, as were the offices of the *New Statesman*, of which Desmond MacCarthy was literary editor.
26. *Vogue* sent prints of the Beck-MacGregor photographs (see above, 27 April). No picture of VW appeared in either *T.P.'s Weekly* or the *Morning Post*.

We are going to the play out into this tawny coloured London—but journalism is the devil. I cannot write after reading it. No time—& I must change, & write about clothes some day soon.

Sunday 17 May[27]

A wire from Raymond in Paris—just read Mrs D. it is quite beautiful— & a very good, outspoken wholly praising review of C. R. in the Observer —"no living critic" &c.[28] But this is not all vanity; I'm recording for curiosity: the fate of a book. The only judgment on Mrs D. I await with trepidation (but thats too strong) is Morgan's. He will say something enlightening.

Just back (all my days here begin with this) from Sutton.[29] Oh it is full summer weather—so hot one can't walk on the sunny side, & all London—even Lavender Hill Lambeth which peels visibly in the sun— transmogrified. We had a bad walk, all along the cinder track, with soft footpaths inviting wh. we could not take, owing to L.'s lecture, delivered in a semi-religious sanctuary, with hymns & prayers & a chapter from the Bible. The whole of Sutton was hymning something: soft intense strains of human [word omitted by VW] went warbling about, as I sat; & I was touched & moved by it: the world so beautiful, God's gift to us, said the Chairman, who looked poor man as if he had never had an ounce of pleasure in his life. Things become very familiar to me, so that I sometimes think humanity is a vast wave, undulating: the same, I mean: the same emotions here that there were at Richmond. Please have some tea—we shall be hurt if you don't accept our hospitality. Accordingly we do; & the same queer brew of human fellowship, is brewed; & people look the same; & joke in the same way, & come to these odd superficial agreements, wh. if you think of them persisting & wide spread—in jungles, storms, birth & death—are not superficial; but rather profound, I think. We came home on top of a bus all the way for a shilling, with the usual glimpses down lanes, into farmyards, at running streams, persisting in between villas, & behind sunbaked yellow or black motor roads. A little girl on the bus asked her mother how many inches are there in a mile. Her mother repeated this to me. I said you must go to school &

27. VW has misdated this entry *Sunday May 16th.*
28. The anonymous reviewer in *The Observer* of 17 May 1925 wrote: 'Few books ... can show a deeper enjoyment, a wider range, or a finer critical intelligence than the volume of Mrs Woolf's.'
29. LW's diary note for 17 May reads: 'Train to Epsom. Walked Banstead. Bus Sutton. Address Adult School. Bus home.'

they'll tell you. But she is at school said her mother. She's seven; & *he* (the baby on her knee) goes to school. He's three. So I gave them two biscuits left over, & the little girl (see my egotism) with her bright excitable eyes, & eagerness to grasp the whole universe reminded me of myself, asking questions of my mother. We saw Lambeth, & I imagined the frolics of clergymen in the boscage, which is very thick; crossed Westminster Bridge; admired the Houses of Parliament & their fretted lacy look; passed the Cenotaph, which L. compromised by sitting with his hat off all the way up Whitehall,[30] & so home, passing a nigger gentleman, perfectly fitted out in swallow tail & bowler & gold headed cane; & what were his thoughts? Of the degradation stamped on him, every time he raised his hand & saw it black as a monkeys outside, tinged with flesh colour within?

Yesterday we had tea with Margaret in her new house. There are three poplars, & behind them St Paul's. But I don't want to live in the suburbs again. There we sat, & I teased her, & she me, & she minded a little, & got red & then white, as if her centre were not very firm. She is severe to Lilian, who has the small rooms & is not allowed to plant flowers, she said bitterly, for it worries Margaret, & so nothing is done to the garden, which too worries Margaret. For these worries, she takes Ethel M. Dell & Dickens. Why, she said, should D.s characters be like people, when he can create people?—an interesting criticism, I think. We hit it off very well, chiefly owing to my wildness & harum scarumness, I think; & I am very fond of her, & sorry for her, since how awful it would be to 'retire' at 60: to sit down & look at poplar trees? Moreover, she once said she had 'compromised'; her father making entire work impossible; & she now regrets things, I imagine; has seen so little of the world, & carried nothing to the extreme. Lilian irritates too, compared with what she might have had. But, after all, thats enough.[31]

The time is now ripe for dinner. And I must answer some of my admirers. Never have I felt so much admired—so tomorrow, snubs will snub me back again into trim.

30. Lambeth Palace in its extensive park has been the seat of the Archbishops of Canterbury since about 1200. It used to be the custom for men to raise their hats on passing the Cenotaph in Whitehall as a mark of respect for the fallen.

31. Margaret Caroline Llewelyn Davies (1861-1944), General Secretary of the Women's Co-operative Guild from 1889-1921. She had recently moved the short distance to Well Walk, Hampstead, from the house she had shared with her father until his death, aged ninety, in 1916. She was an old and staunch friend of the Woolfs. Her colleague and constant companion Lilian Harris (c. 1866-1949) had been Assistant Secretary to the Guild and had retired at the same time as Margaret. Ethel M. Dell (1881-1939) was an enormously popular romantic novelist.

Wednesday 20 May[32]

Well, Morgan admires. This is a weight off my mind. Better than Jacob he says; was sparing of words; kissed my hand, & on going said he was awfully pleased, very happy (or words to that effect) about it. He thinks—but I wont go into detailed criticism: I shall hear more; & this is only about the style being simpler, more like other peoples this time.

I dined with the Sitwells last night.[33] Edith is an old maid. I had never conceived this. I thought she was severe, implacable & tremendous; rigid in her own conception. Not a bit of it. She is, I guess, a little fussy, very kind, beautifully mannered, & a little reminding me of Emphie Case![34] She is elderly too, almost my age, & timid, & admiring & easy & poor, & I liked her more than admired or was frightened of her. Nevertheless, I do admire her work, & thats what I say of hardly anyone: she has an ear, & not a carpet broom; a satiric vein; & some beauty in her. How one exaggerates public figures! How one makes up a person immune from one's own pleasures & failings! But Edith is humble: has lived in a park alone till 27, & so described nothing but sights & sounds; then came to London, & is trying to get a little emotion into her poetry—all of which I suspected, & think promising. Then how eager she was to write for the Press, which had always been her great ambition, she said. Nothing could be more conciliatory & less of an eagle than she; odd looking too, with her humorous old maids smile, her half shut eyes, her lank hair, her delicate hands, wearing a large ring, & fine feet, & her brocade dress, blue & silver. Nothing of the protester or pamph[l]eteer or pioneer seemed in her—rather the well born Victorian spinster. So I must read her afresh. There were Francis [Birrell], Raymond [Mortimer], [Arthur] Waley & a little American toad called Towne, who soaked himself in liquor & became almost loving to us all.[35] The three Sitwells have

32. This entry is mistakenly dated *May 18th*.
33. VW had been (without LW, who dined with his mother) to a dinner party at 2 Carlyle Square, Chelsea, given by Osbert Sitwell (1892-1969) with his brother Sacheverell (b. 1897) and sister Edith (1887-1964), the poet. Since their production of *Façade* (see *II VW Diary*, 13 June 1923), the Sitwells had enjoyed wide notoriety in the popular press as eccentrics and poseurs, and had been the inspiration of a revue sketch by Noel Coward. The Woolfs were to publish Edith Sitwell's essay *Poetry and Criticism* later this year (*HP Checklist* 76).
34. Euphemia Case kept house with her youngest sister Janet (1862-1938), VW's old Classics teacher and friend.
35. For Francis Birrell, see Appendix I. Arthur David Waley (1889-1966) had already published several books of translations from the Chinese and Japanese. He

considerable breeding about them; I like their long noses, & grotesque faces. As for the house, Osbert is at heart an English squire, a collector, but of Bristol glass, old fashion plates, Victorian cases of humming birds, & not of foxes brushes & deers horns. His rooms are all stuck about with these objects. And I liked him too. But why are they thought daring & clever? Why are they the laughing stocks of the music halls & the penny a liners?

Not much talk; all easy goodnatured generalities after dinner, Francis bawling, Waley sombre & demure, & I very indulgent with my compliments: & now tomorrows Supt [*TLS*] & then (here L. came in & told me about R. Macdonald at the Labour party meeting).

Monday 1 June

Bank holiday, & we are in London. To record my books fates slightly bores me; but now both are floated, & Mrs D. doing surprisingly well. 1070 already sold. I recorded Morgan's opinion: then Vita was a little doubtful;[1] then Desmond, whom I see frequently about his book, dashed all my praise by saying that Logan thought the C.R. well enough, but nothing more. Desmond has an abnormal power for depressing one. He takes the edge off life in some extraordinary way; I love him; but his balance & goodness & humour, all heavenly in themselves, somehow diminish lustre. I think I feel this not only about my work, but about life. However, now comes Mrs Hardy to say that Thomas reads, & hears the C.R. read, with "great pleasure". Indeed, save for Logan, & he's a salt veined American, I have had high praise. Also Tauchnitz asks about them.[2]

---

was still at this time on the staff of the British Museum. The American was Charles Hanson Towne (1877-1949), novelist and editor, who in 1925 visited England in the capacity of a literary agent, specifically to meet 'new writers who were coming along'. In his book *So Far So Good* (New York, 1945), Towne related that he was invited to dine by Somerset Maugham, who 'asked me whom I should most care to meet, of all the writers. I begged for Arnold Bennett and H. G. Wells; and they both came. And, as a generous extra attraction, that wonderful writer, Virginia Woolf.' There is no record that VW ever met Somerset Maugham, and Towne has evidently confused different occasions.

1. For Vita Sackville-West, see Appendix I.
2. A copy of Florence Hardy's letter, dated 31 May 1925, is in MHP Sussex; it enclosed a poem by Thomas Hardy, 'Coming up Oxford Street: Evening' which was published in the *N & A* on 13 June 1925. Bernhard Tauchnitz of Leipzig published paper-cover editions in English of a very large number of British and American authors, from whom they acquired the European rights. Both *Mrs Dalloway* and *Orlando* were to be published by Tauchnitz in 1929 (Kp E1, E2).

We are now considering a change to a widow called by courtesy Smith, Jones' sister; which will despatch poor Murphy, but one can't be very sentimental over her, & to settle in with a placid powerful professional woman is precisely what we want to pull us together. Angus is a little languid—not that we in any way, I hasten to say, complain of him; but Murphy is temperamental, untidy, sloppy, & turns crusty about accounts.[3]

A week ago we had a great invasion—Ottoline surprising us with Julian Philip & a Gathorne Hardy.[4] Ottoline was very affectionate, & perhaps affection being so much time & habit, I too have some real affection for her. But how can I analyse my feelings? I like everyone, I said at 46 the other night; & Duncan said I liked everyone, & thought everyone quite new each time. That was at dinner to meet Miss Warner, the new Chatto & Windus poetess, & indeed she has some merit— enough to make me spend 2/6 on her, I think.[5] It is a sunny fitful day, & standing in Hyde Park to listen to the socialists, that furtive Jew, Loeb, who dogs my life at intervals of 10 years, touched us on the shoulder, & took 2 photographs of us, measuring his distance with a black tape, provided by his wife. He usually tells people to hold one end next their hearts: but this is a joke. He had been hanging about Covent Garden to photograph singers & had lunched at 2.30. I asked if he were a professional, which hurt his pride: he owned to taking a great interest in it, & said he had a large collection.[6]

Tom came in yesterday, rather rockier than last time, not quite so flushed with emotion, & inclined to particularise the state of Vivien's bowels too closely for my taste. We both almost laughed; she has a queer rib, a large liver, & so on. What is more to the point is that Tom is to be

3. Alice Louisa Jones, called by courtesy 'Mrs' (see *II VW Diary*, 29 August 1923), was secretary to the editor of the *N & A*; her sister did not succeed Murphy in the Hogarth Press.
4. For Lady Ottoline and Philip Morrell and their daughter Julian, see Appendix I. The Hon. Robert Gathorne-Hardy (1902-1973), third son of the 3rd Earl of Cranbrook, had got to know them while he was at Christ Church, Oxford, and became a very close friend of Lady Ottoline, whose memoirs he was to edit and publish in two volumes in 1963 and 1974.
5. Sylvia Townsend Warner (1893-1978), whose first book of poems, *The Espalier*, had just been published. 46 Gordon Square was Maynard Keynes's house.
6. Sydney J. Loeb (1876-1964), stockbroker and ardent Wagnerian. VW referred to him and his 'collection of operatic photographs' in a letter to Lytton Strachey written in 1910 (*I VW Letters*, no. 492); in 1912 he married Matilde (1881-1978), a daughter of the great Wagnerian conductor Dr Hans Richter. His vast collection remains in the family.

the editor of a new ⟨mag⟩ quarterly, which some old firm is issuing in the autumn, & all his works must go to them—a blow for us.[7]

He said nothing of my books. With great dignity, I did not ask for his opinion. People often dont read books for weeks & weeks. And anyhow, for my part I hate giving an opinion.

[Friday 5 June][8]

To work off the intense depression left by Desmond. What does this come from? But I have just made this beautiful image—how he is like a wave that never breaks, but lollops one this way & that way & the sail hangs on ones mast & the sun beats down—& its all the result of dining & sitting talking till 3 in the morning with El[izabe]th Bibesco, with whom I had tea yesterday.[9] She is a fat housekeeper of a woman, excellent manager, bustling, economical, entirely without nerves, imagination, or sensibility, but what a good housekeeper, how she keeps the books down, & what a good woman of business, how well she would suit an innkeeper, & how she would see to his interests—entertain his customers with her; sprightly rather broad jokes, standing with her thumbs in her armpits on the other side of the bar, with all her false *arms akimbo* diamonds flashing, & her little pig eyes, & her broad fat hips & cheeks. This is the spiritual truth about Bibesco: the fact being that she lies in bed, in green crepe de chine, with real diamonds on her fingers, & a silk quilt, & thinks she talks brilliantly to the most intellectual set in London—so she does, to Desmond, & Mortimer, & poor Philip Ritchie, & I was half in a rage, having sacrificed my Mozart 5tet to her, from which I should have got gallons of pure pleasure instead of the break- fast cup of rather impure delight. For it had its fun. There was old Asquith in [*page ends*].

And then I was ruffled by Nelly, but got over it, by spending £50 of charm. And now I remember—how fatal this is to remember after a quarrel what one did not say—how I might have said, If you have Lottie every day, why should I not have my friends? But one can't—& she is *jealous*, that is the truth. And next time I will say it—& it was Miss Mayor

7. See above, 29 April 1925 n 24, and below, 14 September 1925 n 5.
8. This entry is undated, but the date may be deduced from the fact that the Mozart recital here referred to was given at the Æolian Hall on Thursday 4 June.
9. Elizabeth Charlotte Lucy Bibesco (1897-1945), the only daughter of the former Liberal leader H. H. Asquith, recently created Earl of Oxford and Asquith, and his second wife Margot, had married the Roumanian diplomat Prince Antoine Bibesco in 1919. She wrote stories, plays and poems and had already published four books.

coming that upset us; 'always people when we have dinner parties". And we had Vita, Edith Sitwell, Morgan, Dadie, Kitty Leaf[10]—old Vita presenting me with a whole tree of blue Lupins, & being very uncouth & clumsy, while Edith was like a Roman Empress, so definite clear cut, magisterial & yet with something of the humour of a fishwife—a little too commanding about her own poetry & ready to dictate—tremulously pleased by Morgan's compliments (& he never praised Vita, who sat hurt, modest, silent, like a snubbed schoolboy).[11]

Monday 8 June

This is the hottest June on record. Do not take this seriously—only it is very hot. & we were at Karin's yesterday. There was Irene & her Phil [Noel-Baker]. I am too sleepy having got up at $\frac{1}{4}$ to 6 this morning to describe her. She has spread a little, has a double chin, an emphatic nose, & the feet of gulls on sand round her eyes, which are of the old staring sea green blue. And she has her old ways—her straightforwardness, downrightness, ideals; love of adventure, but none of this is so becoming as of old. For in fact she's grown stereotyped, metallic, harsh; her voice brazen, & her cheeks crude. She suspected me, & suspected Bloomsbury, & adored Leonard, whom she thought so salutary for Phil, but we both suspect [a] scheme for making Phil the foreign sec. in the next Labour Government. I liked her best when she talked about the Greek peasants, & that side may retain some charm. But she talks, talks, talks; thrusts her way with a hard kind of energy into whatever may be going forward— would like, I imagine, to wire pull, & be hostess, & know the right people, but instead protests a horror of success, & wants to keep Phil unspoilt. She also wants to be the mistress of men, I imagine, & a little resents that age should have unseated her from that familiar post, as it very obviously has. She veered, as usual, towards Desmond, professed her horror of "hurting Molly—a very gallant creature", & almost drove L. distracted by asking him what he thought of the character of every politician.[12]

10. Katherine ('Kitty') Leaf was the only daughter of Walter and Charlotte Leaf (see below, 9 April 1926). Fiona MacDonald Mayor (1872-1932), was the author of *The Rector's Daughter*, which the Woolfs had published in 1924 (*HP Checklist* 49).
11. The words in parenthesis were added on the date of the subsequent entry.
12. The Woolfs spent Saturday and Sunday in Essex with Adrian and Karin Stephen (see Appendix I) in their cottage, once an inn, on the tidal waters equidistant from Thorpe-le-Soken and Walton-on-the-Naze (where they kept their yacht). Their fellow-guests were Philip and Irene Noel-Baker. Irene (1889-1956) was the only child and heiress of Frank Noel of Achmetaga where VW and her brothers had

No, she has not worn well; the plating has come off & she's rather steely & common underneath. Needless to say, I had some waves of ancient emotion, chiefly at the sound of her voice & sight of her hands— hands expressing motherhood, perhaps; but mostly felt very flat, unable to pump up anything, & thus uncomfortable. To this, the sordid East End country, the woman who whispers with a gashed throat, the terrific pound home along the hot road, added. And the taxi never came, & we had a second night of it, hearing good, pure hearted Phil, with his principles & his ability, & his athleticism, read aloud to Irene till late.

Sunday 14 June

A disgraceful confession—this is Sunday morning, & just after ten, & here I am sitting down to write diary & not fiction or reviews, without any excuse, except the state of my mind. After finishing those two books, though, one can't concentrate directly on a new one; & then the letters, the talk, the reviews, all serve to enlarge the pupil of my mind more & more. I cant settle in, contract, & shut myself off. I've written 6 little stories, scrambled them down untidily, & have thought out, perhaps too clearly, To the Lighthouse. And both books so far are successful. More of Dalloway has been sold this month than of Jacob in a year. I think it possible we may sell 2,000. The Common one is making money this week. And I get treated at great length & solemnity by old gentlemen.

A powerful, heavy, light blue eyed woman of 50, Mrs Cartwright wants to succeed Murphy; & Murphy wants to stay.[13] How people want work! How tremendous a pull a very little money has in the world! But what the solution is to be, & how we are to find it, I know not. Here I salute Leonard with unstinted, indeed childlike, adoration. Somehow he will gently & firmly decide the whole thing, while Angus & I wobble & prevaricate. But then I have a child's trust in Leonard. Waking this morning, rather depressed that Mrs D. did not sell yesterday, that we

---

stayed on their visit to Greece in 1906. There had been some attachment between Irene and Desmond MacCarthy (see I VW Diary, 27 January 1918; and for Molly MacCarthy see Appendix I), but in 1915 she had married Philip Noel-Baker (b. 1889), who had been a scholar and noted athlete at King's College, Cambridge; he had subsequently worked for the League of Nations, and since 1924 had been Professor of International Relations at London University. He was seeking election to Parliament in the Labour interest, and was elected in 1929, when he became Parliamentary Private Secretary to the Secretary of State for Foreign Affairs.

13. Mrs Cartwright did succeed Bernadette Murphy in July, and remained at the Hogarth Press until 31 March 1930.

had Peter [Lucas], Eileen Power & Noll & Ray [Strachey] last night[14] & found it hard work, & not a single compliment vouchsafed me, that I had bought a glass necklace for £1, that I had a sore throat & a streaming nose, rather under the weather, I say, I snuggled in to the core of my life, which is this complete comfort with L., & there found everything so satisfactory & calm that I revived myself, & got a fresh start; feeling entirely immune. The immense success of our life, is I think, that our treasure is hid away; or rather in such common things that nothing can touch it. That is, if one enjoys a bus ride to Richmond, sitting on the green smoking, taking the letters out of the box, airing the marmots, combing Grizzle, making an ice, opening a letter, sitting down after dinner, side by side, & saying "Are you in your stall, brother?"—well, what can trouble this happiness? And every day is necessarily full of it. If we depended upon making speeches, or money, or getting asked to parties—which reminds me of Ottoline's ghastly party the other night. What possessed me to talk all the time to Helen Anrep? Partly that the plethora of young men slightly annoys me. Really, I am not a good lioness. With all my vanity, I'm come now to be a little cynical, or why don't I so much relish the admiration of the Turners, Kitchins, & Gathorne Hardys? A woman is much more warmly sympathetic. She carries her atmosphere with her. And Ott.'s powers of hostesry are all worn threadbare. People sat about at great distances, & one had a sense of the clock ticking & Ott. saying This is a failure, a failure, & not knowing how to pick the pieces up.[15]

Now I must answer Gerald Brenan, & read the Genji; for tomorrow

14. Frank Laurence (Peter) Lucas (1894-1967), an Apostle, and since 1920 a Fellow of King's College, Cambridge, was in 1926 to be appointed University Lecturer in English Literature. He was a prolific writer. Eileen Power (1889-1940), mediaeval historian, had studied and taught at Girton and was now Reader in Economic History in the University of London. They dined with the Woolfs, and were joined afterwards by Lytton's brother Oliver Strachey (1874-1960) and his second wife Rachel ('Ray', 1887-1940), Karin Stephen's elder sister, who had edited the *Woman's Leader* and was Chairman of the Women's Service Bureau.

15. Ottoline's 'ghastly party' was given in Ethel Sands' house, 15 The Vale, Chelsea, which she had rented for the season in order to launch her daughter Julian in society. The entrance hall was decorated by the Russian mosaicist Boris von Anrep (1883-1969), whose second wife Helen, *née* Maitland (1885-1965), a beautiful and perspicacious half-American woman trained as an opera singer in Europe, had gravitated into Augustus John's Bohemian circle, had married Anrep in 1917, and was soon to leave him for Roger Fry. W. J. Turner (1889-1946), author, critic, and journalist. C. H. B. Kitchin (1895-1967), whose first book *Streamers Waving* had been published by the Woolfs in April (*HP Checklist* 68). VW reverts to her unsocial behaviour on this occasion in *III VW Letters*, nos. 1560 and 1561.

I make a second £20 from Vogue.[16] Did I say that I am rejected by Sybil? From being Sybil, she has become Lady Colefax. No invitations for a month.

Tuesday 16 June

This is the fag end of my morning's work on Genji, which runs a little too easily from my pen & must be compressed & compacted. Dalloway, I fear, has hit her head against some impassable barrier of the public, just as Jacob did, & scarcely sells these last 3 days. Yet my friends are enthusiastic—really so, I think; & ready to acclaim me successful, arrived, triumphant with this book: Clive, Mary, Molly, Roger, my latest allies. We have sold 1240, I think; so the wave spread further than Jacob, & has a ripple left perhaps.

Tonight is Leonard's festival night, the feast of the Brethren Apostles, & presumably some overflow of them here. "Why do human beings invent these ways of torturing themselves?" Them's his words; for he has to preside & speak.[17] Old Lytton, I am reminded, has fairly passed from our lives. No word about my books; no visits since Easter. I imagine that when he takes a new love, & he has Angus, he gets surly, like a stag; he feels a little ridiculous, uneasy, & does not relish the company of old cynical friends like ourselves. And in fact, when I hear the story from Angus, of his agony & entreaty & despair, I only feel slightly nauseated. He makes the young men pity him & laugh at him, & there is a touch of senility in this exposure of himself, while, practically speaking, his amours land him in society of the most tepid, milk & watery kind; nothing that taxes his mind or stimulates; poor feeble Philip for instance, who is precisely like an Eton boy in an Eton jacket: give him an ice & a sovereign.

"Them's his words"—this reminds me I must get back to D. Copper-

16. Gerald Brenan (b. 1894) who had been the Woolfs' host in Spain in April 1923 (see *II VW Diary*, p 240), was temporarily living in lodgings in Wiltshire pursuing his tormented love affair with Carrington and his literary researches. His letter to VW, about her novels, is in MHP Sussex; for her reply, see *III VW Letters*, no. 1560. VW's review of Arthur Waley's translation of the first volume of *The Tale of Genji* by Lady Murasaki appeared in *Vogue*, late July 1925 (Kp C264).

17. In his address to the Society, of which he was current President, LW referred to an occasion in Cambridge when 'all of us, except Goldie, agreed that we had suffered the most extraordinary agonies connected with the Society', and with this in mind had taken as his subject 'the connection between reality and happiness and misery'. See LWP, Sussex.

field.[18] There are moments when all the masterpieces do no more than strum upon broken strings. It is very rare—the right mood for reading—in its way as intense a delight as any; but for the most part pain.

Thursday 18 June

No, Lytton does not like Mrs Dalloway, &, what is odd, I like him all the better for saying so, & don't much mind. What he says is that there is a discordancy between the ornament (extremely beautiful) & what happens (rather ordinary—or unimportant). This is caused he thinks by some discrepancy in Clarissa herself; he thinks she is disagreeable & limited, but that I alternately laugh at her, & cover her, very remarkably, with myself. So that I think as a whole, the book does not ring solid; yet, he says, it is a whole; & he says sometimes the writing is of extreme beauty. What can one call it but genius? he said! Coming when, one never can tell. Fuller of genius, he said than anything I had done. Perhaps, he said, you have not yet mastered your method. You should take something wilder & more fantastic, a frame work that admits of anything, like Tristram Shandy. But then I should lose touch with emotions, I said. Yes, he agreed, there must be reality for you to start from. Heaven knows how you're to do it. But he thought me at the beginning, not at the end. And he said the C.R. was divine, a classic; Mrs D. being, I fear, a flawed stone. This is very personal, he said & old fashioned perhaps; yet I think there is some truth in it. For I remember the night at Rodmell when I decided to give it up, because I found Clarissa in some way tinselly. Then I invented her memories. But I think some distaste for her persisted. Yet, again, that was true to my feeling for Kitty,[19] & one must dislike people in art without its mattering, unless indeed it is true that certain characters detract from the importance of what happens to them. None of this hurts me, or depresses me. Its odd that when Clive & others (several of them) say it is a masterpiece, I am not much exalted; when Lytton picks holes, I get back into my working fighting mood, which is natural to me. I don't see myself a success. I like the sense of effort better. The sales collapsed completely for 3 days; now a little dribble begins again. I shall be more than pleased if we sell 1500. Its now 1250.

July 20th. Have sold about 1550

18. VW's article 'David Copperfield', a review of *The Uncommercial Traveller; Reprinted Pieces and Christmas Stories* by Charles Dickens, appeared in the *N & A* of 22 August 1925 (Kp C266).
19. Katherine (Kitty) Maxse, *née* Lushington (1867-1922), a figure of considerable social consequence in VW's Kensington youth, had served as a model for Clarissa Dalloway.

Saturday 27 June

A bitter cold day, succeeding a chilly windy night, in which were lit all the Chinese lanterns of Roger's garden party. And I do not love my kind. I detest them. I pass them by. I let them break on me like dirty rain drops. No longer can I summon up that energy which when it sees one of these dry little sponges floating past, or rather stuck on the rock, sweeps round them, steeps them, infuses them, nerves them, & so finally fills them & creates them. Once I had a gift for doing this, & a passion, & it made parties arduous & exciting. So when I wake early now I luxuriate most in a whole day alone; a day of easy natural poses, a little printing, slipping tranquilly off into the deep water of my own thoughts navigating the underworld; & then replenishing my cistern at night with Swift. I am going to write about Stella & Swift for Richmond, as a sign of grace, after sweeping guineas off the Vogue counter. The first fruit of the C.R. (a book too highly praised now) is a request to write for the Atlantic Monthly.[20] So I am getting pushed into criticism. It is a great stand by—this power to make large sums by formulating views on Stendhal & Swift.

Jack dined here last night; & we said how many years is it since we three were alone in a room together? he & Nessa & I, waiting for dinner, & a little nervous.[21] I'm more nervous of these encounters than she is. She has a sweet cordiality (odd term to use) which impressed me, recalling mother, as she led him on; & laughed; so sincere, so quiet, & then, when we went on to Roger's rather dismal gathering, gay & spirited, kissing Chrissie & flirting with Mrs Anrep, so careless & casual & white-haired—but enough of this.[22] The truth is I am too random headed to describe Jack, yet he is worth describing. He made us laugh of course. He said such Wallerish things. "There are two kinds of biography, my dear Ginia"—in his old opinionative sententious way with enormous emphasis. He is red-copper coloured, with a pouch under his chin which rests on his collar; trusty brown eyes, a little hazy now, & one ear deaf, he said,

20. VW's article 'Swift's Journal to Stella' appeared in the *TLS* (of which Bruce Richmond was editor) on 24 September 1925 (Kp C268). Her first contribution to the *Atlantic Monthly* did not appear until November 1927.
21. John (Jack) Waller Hills (1867-1938), Unionist MP from 1906-22, and re-elected in December 1925. He was the widower of VW's half-sister Stella Duckworth; after her early death, he and Vanessa had injudiciously fallen in love. He it was who had encouraged the bug-hunting Stephen children to become serious lepidopterists (see *I QB*, p 33); he was also a keen fisherman.
22. Roger Fry(see Appendix I)'s party was at his home, 7 Dalmeny Avenue, Holloway. Christabel, the Hon. Mrs Henry McLaren (1890-1974), became Lady Aberconway on the death of her father-in-law in 1934.

& proceeded to tell us how he is cured by a Swiss every year, & gives the Nuns who keep the clinic a box of chocolates, which they love, being underfed. He looks in at the window & sees them handing the box round, & picking in turn. Then he told us, driving back from Roger's—I insist upon paying this taxi my dear Leonard—how he sugared for moths last summer & caught perhaps 150—& the man he was with (on a fishing club) left his electric light on & the moths came & sat on the curtain. He exaggerates, illuminates, appreciates everyone very generously. L. thinks he "might become a bit of a bore". Then we discussed his writing an autobiography: upon which he became very intent, & almost emotional. "But could one tell the truth? About one's affairs with women? About one's parents? My mother now—she was a very able woman—we all owe her an awful lot—but hard." She said an odd thing to Nessa once— that she hated girls, especially motherless girls. "There you go very deep— It was the terror of her life—that she was losing her charm. She would never have a girl in the house. It was a tragedy. She was a very selfish woman."[23] (But while I try to write, I am making up "To the Lighthouse"—the sea is to be heard all through it. I have an idea that I will invent a new name for my books to supplant "novel". A new —— by Virginia Woolf. But what? Elegy?)

Sunday 19 July

By bringing this book down here to the Studio, I have rather stinted it I think, as my mornings have all been spent writing—Swift or letters. So a whole tribe of people & parties has gone down the sink to oblivion[1] —Ott's parties & complaints; Gwen Raverat set sturdy dusty grim black, yesterday; Tom hedging a little over the Bank; Sybil Colefax drinking tea & protesting her desire to give up parties; her party when Olga Lynn dropped her music in a rage & had to be pacified by Balfour;[2] & Ott lost

23. Such autobiographical truths as J. W. Hills found proper to reveal are to be found in his books *A Summer on the Test* (1924) and *My Sporting Life* (1936). The motherless girls Vanessa and Virginia Stephen had encountered his mother when, following Stella's death in 1897, they had stayed at the Hills' family home, Corby Castle, near Carlisle. For VW's reactions then, see *I QB*, p 61, and her *1897 Diary* (Berg).

1. The veil of oblivion is lifted in *II QB*, p 113.

2. This scene, at a Colefax party probably given on 1 July at Argyll House, is described by Olga Lynn (1882-1957), a diminutive *Lieder* singer much favoured by Society, in her memoirs *Oggie* (1955); her rage was occasioned by the entry of Margot Asquith (Lady Oxford), who created such a disturbance that the singer had to stop. A somewhat different version of what appears to have been the same occasion is given in *IV LW*, pp 104-5.

her shawl; & the garden was lit like a stage, & Clive & Mary could be seen to the least eyelash; & so home to bed; & Mrs Asquith, Lady Oxford, called me the most beautiful woman in the room, which compliment was repeated to me the next night (so thick have parties been) by Jack Hutch. at Dadie's, where there were many faces again, & drink, & again home to bed; & then little Eddie Sackville-West & Julian Morrell to dine (& I am to have his piano) & Philip in to fetch her; & then a party at Ott's with Ching playing the piano; & the news of Hew Anderson's death there broken to Angus;[3] & Murphy going; & Mrs Cartwright coming; & my books—oh yes, the Calendar has abused Mrs D. which hurt me a little; & then the tide of praise has flowed over me again, & they both sell well, & my fears were ungrounded; & Maynard has brought us a pamphlet, wh. is called The Economic Consequences of Mr Churchill, & we are having 10,000 printed for Monday week to sell at a shilling.[4]

On Friday I went on a river party & we dined at Formosa, & Eddie [Sackville-West] played in the round drawing room, & there was George Young in a punt.[5] Not a moments reflection has gone to any of these statements; but I take them together, never knowing what withered straw doesn't vivify the whole bunch of flowers. They have shone bright & gay this summer in the incessant heat. For the first time for weeks I sit by a fire, but then I am in the thinnest silk dress; & for once, it is watery & windy though I see blue sky through my skylight. A happy summer, very busy; rather overpowered by the need of seeing so many people. I never ask a soul here; but they accumulate. Tonight Ottoline; Tuesday Jack Hutch; Wednesday Edith Sitwell, Friday dine with Raymond. These are my fixed invitations; & all sorts of unforseen ones will occur. I run out after tea as if pursued. I mean to regulate this better

3. The Hon. Edward Charles Sackville-West (1901-1965), the son and heir of 4th Baron Sackville and Vita's cousin, was a writer and extremely musical. James Ching was a young aspiring classical pianist who was to give three public concerts in the Wigmore Hall in the autumn. Hew Skelton Anderson (1900-1925), who had graduated from New College, Oxford, in 1923, died of meningitis on 15 July 1925; he had been at the Hotel Cendrillon at Cassis, when VW was there in April (see III VW Letters, no. 1546).

4. J. F. Holms wrote in the Calendar of Modern Letters, July 1925, that 'despite its pure and brilliant impressionism' Mrs Dalloway is 'sentimental in conception and texture, and is accordingly aesthetically worthless'. (See M & M, pp 169-71.) John Maynard Keynes's pamphlet The Economic Consequences of Mr Churchill was published this month in an edition of 7000 copies (HP Checklist 66).

5. Formosa Fishery, on the Thames near Cookham, was the home of the Youngs, old family friends of the Stephens. The present (4th) Baronet was the diplomat George Peregrine Young (1872-1952).

in future. But I dont think of the future, or the past, I feast on the moment. This is the secret of happiness; but only reached now in middle age.

Monday 20 July

Here the door opened, & Morgan came in to ask us out to lunch with him at the Etoile, which we did, though we had a nice veal & ham pie at home (this is in the classic style of journalists).[6] It comes of Swift perhaps, the last words of which I have just written, & so fill up time here. I should consider my work list now. I think a little story, perhaps a review, this fortnight; having a superstitious wish to begin To the Lighthouse the first day at Monks House. I now think I shall finish it in the two months there. The word 'sentimental' sticks in my gizzard (I'll write it out of me in a story—Ann Watkins of New York is coming on Wednesday to enquire about my stories).[7] But this theme may be sentimental; father & mother & child in the garden: the death; the sail to the lighthouse. I think, though, that when I begin it I shall enrich it in all sorts of ways; thicken it; give it branches & roots which I do not perceive now. It might contain all characters boiled down; & childhood; & then this impersonal thing, which I'm dared to do by my friends, the flight of time, & the consequent break of unity in my design. That passage (I conceive the book in 3 parts: 1. at the drawing room window; 2. seven years passed; 3. the voyage:) interests me very much. A new problem like that breaks fresh ground in ones mind; prevents the regular ruts.

Last night Clive dined with us; & Nelly is rather waspish about it this morning; & tried to run away before Ottoline came; but it proved to be Adrian; & then we talked of cancer, & Clive got set, & Ottoline came, in tea kettle taffeta, all looped & scolloped & fringed with silver lace, & talked about Rupert & Jacques, & re-told, with emendations, the story of Ka & Henry Lamb & herself.[8] She has been working over these old stories so often, that they hold no likeness to the truth—they are stale, managed, pulled this way & that, as we used to knead & pull the

6. The Etoile Restaurant, then as now at 30 Charlotte Street.
7. The galling word 'sentimental' is the keynote of the criticism of VW in *The Calendar* (see above, 19 July 1925, n 4). Ann Watkins was a New York literary agent.
8. The painter Henry Lamb (1883-1960), one-time protégé of Ottoline and a noted philanderer, had in 1911/12 attracted Ka Cox's love; this had excited an obsessive passion for her in her hitherto merely affectionate friend Rupert Brooke, and precipitated his nervous breakdown. (See Christopher Hassall, *Rupert Brooke*, 1964, pp 296-8.) Ka—Katherine Laird Cox (1887-1938), a friend of VW's since 1911, had married Will Arnold-Forster in 1918.

crumb of bread, till it was a damp slab. Then the old motor was heard hooting & there was Philip & Julian [Morrell], at which, at Julian that is, Clive cheered up, & was very brisk & obliging as he knows how. We argued the case of the aristocracy v. the middle class. I rather liked it. But one seldom says anything very profound. I like the sense of other people liking it, as I suppose the Morrells do, for they settle on us like a cloud of crows, once a week now. My vanity as a hostess is flattered. Sometimes a buttery crumb of praise is thrown to me—"Lady Desborough admires your books enormously—wants to meet you"—& then Clive, looking at my photographs in Vogue says of the one last year—"That is charming—but must be taken very long ago, I suppose"[9]—so you see how I switch back from pleasure to pain, & time was when I should have ended the evening fast stuck in black despair, gone to bed like a diver with pursed lips shooting into oblivion. But enough, enough—I coin this little catchword to control my tendency to flower into phrase after phrase. Some are good though.

What shall I read at Rodmell? I have so many books at the back of my mind. I want to read voraciously & gather material for the Lives of the Obscure—which is to tell the whole history of England in one obscure life after another. Proust I should like to finish. Stendhal, & then to skirmish about hither & thither. These 8 weeks at Rodmell always seem capable of holding an infinite amount. Shall we buy the house at Southease? I suppose not.

Thursday 30 July

I am intolerably sleepy & annulled, & so write here. I do want indeed to consider my next book, but I am inclined to wait for a clearer head. The thing is I vacillate between a single & intense character of father; & a far wider slower book—Bob T. telling me that my speed is terrific, & destructive.[10] My summer's wanderings with the pen have I think shown me one or two new dodges for catching my flies. I have sat here, like an improviser with his hands rambling over the piano. The result is perfectly inconclusive, & almost illiterate. I want to learn greater quiet, & force. But if I set myself that task, don't I run the risk of falling into the flatness of N[ight]. & D[ay].? Have I got the power needed if quiet

9. Lady Desborough (1867-1952) held a pre-eminent position in the world of wit and fashion. For *Vogue*'s photographs of VW, see above, 27 April 1925, n 18.
10. Robert (Bob) Calverly Trevelyan (1872-1951), poet and classical scholar, an Apostle, and an old friend.

is not to become insipid. These questions I will leave, for the moment, unanswered.

I should here try to sum up the summer, since August ends a season, spiritual as well as temporal. Well; business has been brisk. I don't think I get many idle hours now, the idlest being, oddly enough, in the morning. I have not forced my brain at its fences; but shall, at Rodmell. When the dull sleep of afternoon is on me, I'm always in the shop, printing, dissing addressing; then it is tea, & Heaven knows we have had enough visitors. Sometimes I sit still & wonder how many people will tumble on me without my lifting a finger: already, this week, uninvited, on the verge of the holidays too, have come Mary, Gwen, Julian & Quentin, Geoffrey Keynes, & Roger. Meanwhile we are dealing with Maynard. All Monday Murphy & I worked like slaves till 6 when I was stiff as a coal heaver. We get telegrams & telephones; I daresay we shall sell our 10,000. On Tuesday at 12.30 Maynard retires to St Pancras Registry office with Lydia, & Duncan to witness (against his will.) So that episode is over.[11] But, dear me, I'm too dull to write, & must go & fetch Mr Dobrée's novel & read it, I think.[12] Yet I have a thousand things to say. I think I might do something in To the Lighthouse, to split up emotions more completely. I think I'm working in that direction.

The Woolfs went to Monks House on the afternoon of Wednesday, 5 August. On Sunday 16 August they lunched with the newly-married Keyneses at Iford where they had rented a house; and on Wednesday 19 August they bicycled to Charleston for tea and dinner, it being Quentin's fifteenth birthday. The Keyneses were there too. During dinner VW fainted and was taken home by car, and remained in a delicate state of health for some time to come.

Saturday 5 September

And why couldn't I see or feel that all this time I was getting a little used up & riding on a flat tire? So I was, as it happened; & fell down in a faint at Charleston, in the middle of Q.'s birthday party: & then have lain about here, in that odd amphibious life of headache, for a fortnight. This has rammed a big hole in my 8 weeks which were to be stuffed so

11. Maynard Keynes and Lydia Lopokova were married at St Pancras Central Registry Office on 4 August 1925. Geoffrey Langdon Keynes (b. 1887), surgeon and bibliographer, was Maynard's younger brother.
12. Presumably a manuscript submitted by the writer and academic Bonamy Dobrée (1891-1974), whom the Woolfs were publishing in their Hogarth Essays series; but they published no novel by him until 1932.

full. Never mind. Arrange whatever pieces come your way. Never be unseated by the shying of that undependable brute, life, hag ridden as she is by my own queer, difficult nervous system. Even at 43 I dont know its workings, for I was saying to myself, all the summer, "I'm quite adamant now. I can go through a tussle of emotions peaceably that two years ago even, would have raked me raw."

I have made a very quick & flourishing attack on To the Lighthouse, all the same—22 pages straight off in less than a fortnight. I am still crawling & easily enfeebled, but if I could once get up steam again, I believe I could spin it off with infinite relish. Think what a labour the first pages of Dalloway were! Each word distilled by a relentless clutch on my brain.

I took up the pen meaning to write on "Disillusionment". I have never had any illusion so completely burnt out of me as my illusion about the Richmonds.[1] This they effected between 4 & 6 yesterday. But Elena has no beauty, no charm, no very marked niceness even! Any country parsons wife is her match. Her nose is red, her cheeks blowsed: her eyes without character. Even her voice & movements which used to be adorable, her distinction, her kindly charm—all have vanished; she is a thick, dowdy, obliterated woman, who has no feelings, no sympathies, prominences & angles are all completely razed bare. Seriously, one has doubts for her complete mental equipment. The conversation was practically imbecile: for instance: (E). I think I could get very fond of a house. But we are so lucky. There are some delightful people near. People who like the same sort of things we do. (B). We are very lucky. There are two fellows within 4 miles who were at Winchester with me. One went to Ceylon as a tea planter. They both farm now. Are you lucky in your clergyman? So much depends in the country on one's clergyman. (E). I really forget anything more from the lips of E. I believe it was all the same: how she would like a house with a piano: & they mean to retire & buy a house with a piano. She sees flowers, dogs, houses, people with the same quiet, stolid, almost coarse, at any rate dull indifference. Her hands are thick. She has a double chin. She wears a long American looking blueish coat, with a nondescript dowdy scarf, a white blouse, fastened with a diamond lizard—oh the colourlessness, drabness, & coldness of her personality—she whom I used to think arch & womanly & comforting! She is white haired too. Bruce is completely

1. Bruce Lyttelton Richmond (1871-1964), editor since 1902 of the TLS and VW's most regular employer, and his wife Elena, née Rathbone (1878-1964), who were married in 1913. She had formed part of the young Stephens' social circle in Kensington, and had been admired by VW's elder brother Thoby.

circular: round head, eyes, nose, paunch, mind. You can't stop him rolling from thing to thing. He never stops, he glides smoothly. It would shock him to mention writing, money, or people. All has to be dissolved in slang & kindliness.

Now the curious thing was that these qualities infected us both to such an extent that we were acutely miserable. I have sometimes felt the same when walking in the suburbs. Castello Avenue made me angry like this once.[2] As for L. he was indignant. That human nature should sink so low, he said; & then that people should lead such aimless evil lives— the most despicable he could imagine. They took the colour, the sting, the individuality out of everything. And to think that I have ever wasted a thought upon what that goodtempered worldly little grocer thought of my writing! But E. is the great disillusionment. Partly on Thoby's account, partly through my own susceptibility to certain shades of female charm, I had still some glow at the thought of her. Now that glow is replaced by a solid tallow candle. And I feel, this morning, having pitched into bed exhausted, physically worn out, mentally bankrupt, scraped; whitewashed, cleaned. An illusion gone.

Monday 14 September[3]

A disgraceful fact—I am writing this at 10 in the morning in bed in the little room looking into the garden, the sun beaming steady, the vine leaves transparent green, & the leaves of the apple tree so brilliant that, as I had my breakfast, I invented a little story about a man who wrote a poem, I think, comparing them with diamonds, & the spiders webs (which glance & disappear astonishingly) with something or other else: which led me to think of Marvell on a country life, so to Herrick, & the reflection that much of it was dependent upon the town & gaiety—a reaction. However, I have forgotten the facts. I am writing this partly to test my poor bunch of nerves at the back of my neck—will they hold or give again, as they have done so often?—for I'm amphibious still, in bed & out of it; partly to glut my itch ('glut' and 'itch'!) for writing. It is the great solace, & scourge. Leonard is in London this solitary perfect day; this day of the peculiar September mintage; talking to Murphy in the basement, while the vans rumble by, & peoples skirts & trousers appear at the top of the area. This leads us to think of selling Monks, & spending our summers, quit of Press, quit of Nelly, quit of Nation, quit

2. See *II VW Diary*, 31 January 1920. LW's brother Edgar and his wife lived at 7 Castello Avenue, Putney.
3. VW has written 'Monday Sept 13th perhaps'.

of polar blasts, in the South of France. The news that Mr Wilkinson is longing to buy Monks shakes our resolution to sell it.[4] A walk, in pearly mottled weather, on the marshes, plunges me in love again. Leonard then finds his potato crop good, & his autumn crocuses rising. We have been in the throes of the usual servant crisis—varied this time it is true: Nelly says Lottie wants to come back; we offer to have her; she denies it—to Karin; to Nelly she prevaricates. I was flung into a passion with Karin, & so precipitated another headache. But we are on the laps of the Gods: we don't intend to raise a finger either way. Only it is a curious reflection that a little strain with servants more effectually screws the nerves at the back of the head than any other I am aware of. Now why? It is because it is subterranean, partly.

Tom has treated us scurvily, much in the manner that he has treated the Hutchinsons. On Monday I get a letter that fawns & flatters, implores me to write for his new 4ly; & proposes to discuss press matters as soon as we get back; on Thursday we read in the Lit. Supt. that his new firm is publishing Waste Land & his other poems—a fact which he dared not confess, but sought to palliate by flattering me. also (Sept 23rd) that Read is being asked to write for Tom's Press He treated Jack in the same way over Vivien's story in the *Criterion*.[5] The Underworld—the dodges & desires of the Underworld, its shifts & cabals are at the bottom of it. He intends to get on by the methods of that world; & my world is really not the underworld. However, there is a kind of fun in unravelling the twists & obliquities of this remarkable man. How far will they make his poetry squint? Anyhow, at my age, without illusions of that sort any more—I mean in the greatness of Tom, or the greatness of any of us, or our power to influence each other intellectually—I remain detached, & composed. Plenty of other illusions remain to me—emotional, personal; the pleasures of inventing Wednesday walks this winter is now uppermost. I'm going to Greenwich, to Caen Woods, to Gunnersbury, all in the dripping autumn weather, with tea at an

4. Clennell Anstruther Wilkinson (1883-1936), journalist and writer of popular biographies, and brother-in-law of J. C. Squire, editor of the *London Mercury*. Squire and his cronies made a considerable and, as VW felt, wholly regrettable contribution to the social life of Rodmell village.
5. VW's reply to Eliot's entreaty is *III VW Letters*, no. 1577, misdated *3rd* for *8th* September; in it she adverts to the need for a reprint of the Hogarth Press edition of *The Waste Land* (1923). On 10 September the *TLS* carried an announcement by Faber & Gwyer of their forthcoming publication of T. S. Eliot's *Collected Poems* 'containing *The Waste Land*, now out of print, together with many other pieces no longer available and some not previously collected'. The parallel with Jack Hutchinson and Mrs Eliot has defied explanation. Read, see below, p 45 n 13.

A.B.C. & home to a hot bath.[6] Really I am going to let myself slacken in social ways: instead of feeling that I shirk a hedge, in refusing Lord Berners or Lady Colefax, I am going to allow myself to do so approvingly;[7] saying that I strengthen a paragraph in The Lighthouse thereby, or add another hour to the shabby crony talk which I love best. Not but what I shall dip here & there; but without anxiety or preparation of clothes or any of that struggle. This gives me a delicious sense of ease. And I have earned it, too, for I spread my £35 dress allowance to its furthest, & braved many a party spartanly 'on principle' as the marmots would say. The 'principle' which I find intermittently guiding my life is—to take one's fences. Heaven knows how I've dreaded them! Now, with my Studio habitable, & another servant perhaps, I shall aim at haphazard, bohemian meetings, music (we have the algraphone, & thats a heavenly prospect—music after dinner while I stitch at my wool-work—I go to Lewes this afternoon to meet Nessa & buy wools[8]) people of our own standard dropping in; ease, slippers, smoke, buns, chocolate. For I'm naturally sociable; it cannot be denied.

Tuesday 22 September

How my handwriting goes down hill! Another sacrifice to the Hogarth Press. Yet what I owe the Hogarth Press is barely paid by the whole of my handwriting. Haven't I just written to Herbert Fisher refusing to do a book for the Home University Series on Post Victorian?[9]—knowing

6. For VW's visit to Greenwich, see below, 27 March 1926. Ken (formerly Caen) Wood in Highgate was opened to the public by King George V on 18 July 1925; these meadows and woods surrounding the Adam mansion had, after protracted negotiations, been bought from Lord Mansfield and vested in the London County Council. (The house and collections were be to bequeathed by the 1st Earl of Iveagh in 1927.) The purchase by the Boroughs of Acton and Ealing of Gunnersbury Park, some 200 acres and two mansions, the property of a branch of the Rothschild family since 1876, was imminent; but it was not opened to the public until May 1926. A.B.C.: one of the chain of tea-rooms operated by the Aerated Bread Company.

7. Gerald Hugh Tyrwhitt-Wilson, 14th Baron Berners (1883-1950), was a witty and accomplished composer, author, and painter, whom VW had met in 1924.

8. *The Algraphone*, 'Gramophone Superior', was manufactured by Alfred Graham & Co of South London; it was at about this time that LW began to review gramophone records for the *N & A*, and this may have been part of his apparatus for so doing. VW was embroidering a cross-stitch chaircover from a design by Vanessa Bell; see *III VW Letters*, no. 1576 et seq.

9. Herbert Albert Laurens Fisher (1865-1940), the historian and one of the editors of the 'Home University Library', was VW's first cousin. He had been President

that I can write a book, a better book, a book off my own bat, for the Press if I wish! To think of being battened down in the hold of those University dons fairly makes my blood run cold. Yet I'm the only woman in England free to write what I like. The others must be thinking of series' & editors. Yesterday I heard from Harcourt Brace that Mrs D. & C.R. are selling 148 & 73 weekly—Isn't that a surprising rate for the 4th month? Doesn't it portend a bathroom & a w.c. either here, or Southease? I am writing in the watery blue sunset, repentance of an ill tempered morose day, which vanished, the clouds, I have no doubt, showing gold over the downs, & leaving a soft gold fringe on the top there.

Today is
Thursday 24 September

—sad to think a week only left whole of this partially wrecked summer; however, I don't complain, seeing as how I have dipped my head in health again & feel stabilised once more about the spinal cord, which is always the centre of my being. Maynard & Lydia came here yesterday— M. in Tolstoi's blouse & Russian cap of black astrachan—A fair sight, both of them, to meet on the high road![10] An immense good will & vigour pervades him. She hums in his wake, the great mans wife. But though one could carp, one can also find them very good company, & my heart, in this the autumn of my age, slightly warms to him, whom I've known all these years, so truculently pugnaciously, & unintimately. We had very brisk talk of Russia: such a hotch-potch, such a mad jumble, M. says, of good & bad, & the most extreme things that he can make no composition of it—can't yet see how it goes. Briefly, spies everywhere, no liberty of speech, greed for money eradicated, people living in common, yet some, L[ydia]'s mother for instance with servants, peasants contented because they own land, no sign of revolution, artistocrats acting showmen to their possessions, ballet respected, best show of

---

of the Board of Education in Lloyd George's coalition government from 1916 to 1922, and was still a Liberal MP; he was appointed Warden of New College, Oxford, in 1925 and gave up his seat in 1926.

10. Early in September the Keyneses had gone to Russia, officially for Maynard to attend the bicentenary celebrations of the Academy of Sciences in Leningrad as the representative of the University of Cambridge, and unofficially, to visit Lydia's family. His reactions to the Soviet régime were recorded in three articles in the *N & A*, subsequently published as a Hogarth Press pamphlet *A Short View of Russia* in December 1925 (*HP Checklist* 67).

Cezanne & Matisse in existence. Endless processions of communists in top hats, prices exorbitant, yet champagne produced, & the finest cooking in Europe, banquets beginning at 8.30 & going on till 2.30; people getting slightly drunk, say about 11, & wandering round the table. Kalinin getting up, & perambulating followed by a little crowd who clapped him steadily as he walked; then the immense luxury of the old Imperial trains; feeding off the Tsars plate; interview with Zinoviev who (I think) was a suave cosmopolital Jew, but had two fanatical watch dogs with square faces, guarding him, & mumbling out their mysteries, fanatically. One prediction of theirs, to the effect that in 10 years time the standard of living will be higher in Russia than it was before the war, but in all other countries lower, M. thought might very well come true. Anyhow they are crammed & packed with sights & talks: Maynard has a medal set in diamonds, & L. a gold sovereign wh. she was allowed to take from the bags at the mint.[11]

But the Keynes', I need hardly say, renewed my headache, & when Lytton came, I was drooping over the fire, & could not do much battle with that old serpent. What was said I think was to the effect that he had had a fire at Hamspray, which blistered the wall, but did not touch his books—& what fire could have the heart to do that? Then he had read Bunny "Really its very extraordinary—so arty,—so composed—the competence terrific, but . . . well, its like a perfectly restored Inn—Ye Olde . . . everything tidied up & restored." No Bunny in it, as there were signs of being in The Man in the Zoo; no humour; a perfect restoration.[12]

But to tell the truth, I am exacerbated this morning. It is 10.25, on a fine grey still day; Lily is doing my bedroom; the starlings are in the apple tree; Leonard is in London, & Nelly I suppose is settling the greatest question of her whole life—what marriage is to a woman—with Lottie. Lily is a wide eyed sheep dog girl who comes from Iford to

---

11. Mikhail Ivanovich Kalinin (1875-1946) was made a member of the Politburo and the Communist Party's Central Committee in 1925. Grigori Evseevich Zinoviev (1883-1936), a Ukrainian of Jewish parentage—the alleged author of the 'Zinoviev Letter'—was at the time of Keynes's visit chairman of the Executive Committee of the Communist International; dismissed by Stalin in 1926, he was shot in August 1936, a victim of the Great Purge.

12. Lytton this year stayed first at Charleston and then with the Keyneses at Iford, from whence he visited the Woolfs. David (Bunny) Garnett's recently published third book was The Sailor's Return; his second, A Man in the Zoo, had been published in 1924. Born in 1892, Garnett was an old, if younger, friend of both Lytton and VW; in the summer of 1924 he had given up his partnership in the bookshop he had started in 1919 with Francis Birrell to devote himself to writing and country life.

'do'; but can't scramble an egg or bake a potato, & is thus ill armed for life, so far as I can see.

Beginning at 9.45 I wrote two pages of a story, as a test again; & passed it well, I think, anyhow my cistern is full of ideas. But to the point: why am I exacerbated? By Roger. I told him I had been ill all the summer. His reply is—silence as to that; but plentiful descriptions of his own front teeth. Egotism, egotism—it is the essential ingredient in a clever man's life I believe. It protects; it enhances; it preserves his own vital juices entire by keeping them banked in. Also I cannot help thinking that he suspects me of valetudinarianism & this enrages me: & L. is away & I cant have my thorn picked out by him, so must write it out. There! it is better now; & I think I hear the papers come; & will get them, my woolwork, & a glass of milk.

[*Wednesday 30 September*]

This was I suppose successfully accomplished; & it is now Wednesday morning, damp & close & over all the sense already of transmigration, of shedding one habit for another. My autumn coat is grown. I begin to sympathise with Nelly's longing for the ease & speed of civilisation. But I vow here not to be misled into thinking this is life—this perpetual frenzy & stretch; or I shall again be deposited in a heap, as I was in August.

Today we are on Tom's track, riddling & reviling him. He won't let Read off that book, has been after him 3 or 4 months.[13] Dignity is our line; & really, as far as the poaching of authors goes, he won't harm us. Then there is the fascination of a breach; I mean, after feeling all this time conscious of something queer about him, it is more satisfactory to have it on the surface. Not that I want a breach: what I want is a revelation. But L. thinks the queer shifty creature will slip away now.

I actually forgot to record the finish of the Lottie drama—she's in love with the cowman at Thorpe [-le-Soken]! This emerged after an hours violent argument with Nelly. This explains & excuses all: & we are, for private reasons, thoroughly content. What is worse, is poor unfortunate Karin—in operating, they cut a nerve in her face, which is

13. Herbert Read (1893-1968), poet and critic, at this time an Assistant-Keeper in the Victoria & Albert Museum. The Woolfs had published his first book *Mutations of the Phoenix* in 1923, and were publishing his *In Retreat* in October 1925; his first book for Faber & Gwyer was to be *Reason & Romanticism. Essays in Literary Criticism* (1926).

half paralysed. She can't speak, I gather, without being all screwed up.[14] She refuses to see the children for fear of frightening them. This final malignancy on the part of fate seems to me her knock out blow; save that somehow she will, I suppose, find a way round, as people mostly do. This softens the heart towards her. It makes one think of her courage. But how quickly the *intense* feeling of sympathy passes, & she resumes her place in ones mind as a person one is conscious of being permanently, dully, sorry for. But then propinquity will revive it: Tavistock Sqre, being next door, will make one more conscious of the horror of screwing up one's own face.

The Woolfs returned to Tavistock Square on Friday 2 October; by Monday VW felt so unwell that her doctor, Elinor Rendel, was sent for, and for the rest of this month and most of November she was more or less ill, in and out of bed, with occasional walks or drives with LW and seeing a very limited number of visitors. She managed to write On Being Ill, *for T. S. Eliot's* New Criterion, *and a few reviews for the* Nation & Athenaeum.

Friday 27 November

Oh what a blank! I tumbled into bed on coming back—or rather Ellie tumbled me; & keeps me still prostrate half the day.[1] Next week I shall go to the ballet, my first night out. One visitor a day. Till 2 days ago, bed at 5. So visitors have become as usual, pictures hung on the wall. On the whole, I have not been unhappy; but not very happy; too much discomfort; sickness, (cured by eating instantly); a good deal of rat-gnawing at the back of my head; one or two terrors; then the tiredness of the body—it lay like a workman's coat. Sometimes I felt old, & spent. Madge died. Rustling among my emotions, I found nothing better than dead leaves. Her letters had eaten away the reality—the brilliancy, the warmth. Oh detestable time, that thus eats out the heart & lets the body go on. They buried a faggot of twigs at Highgate, as far as I am concerned.

14. The operation was intended to alleviate Karin Stephen's deafness. Her servant Lottie's *amour* (see *III VW Letters*, no. 1590) was likewise ill-fated.

1. Frances Elinor Rendel (1885-1942), daughter of Lytton's eldest sister Elinor, studied history and economics at Newnham College, Cambridge, and worked until 1912 for the National Union of Women's Suffrage Societies; she then qualified as a doctor, and after war service in Roumania and the Balkans, set up as a General Practitioner in London. She became VW's doctor when the latter moved to Tavistock Square in 1924.

I drove to the gate, & saw Nessa & Leonard, like a pair of stuffed figures, go in.[2]

My walks are extended to Oxford Street; only once so far; & then what about talks. Vita has been twice. She is doomed to go to Persia; & I minded the thought so much (thinking to lose sight of her for 5 years) that I conclude I am genuinely fond of her.[3] There is the glamour of unfamiliarity to reckon with; of aristocracy (Raymond says, But she's half a peasant—) of flattery. All the same, after sifting & filing, much, I am sure, remains. Shall I stay with her? Shall we go to Charleston for Christmas? The best of these illnesses is that they loosen the earth about the roots. They make changes. People express their affection. Nessa wants to have us— Indeed, I have seen more of her & Duncan than for many a day. Gwen [Raverat] comes in: threatens to dissolve, her hearty direct stodgy manner in floods of tears, as if the rivets that hold her must give way—such tragedies have beaten her, together for the moment; but suddenly she will break down & tell me something that she has not told anyone. She finds me understanding. And I suppose she is in love—or Marchand in love—& I don't altogether want to hear it.[4]

Reading & writing go on. Not my novel though. And I can only think of all my faults as a novelist & wonder why I do it—a wonder which Lytton increases, & Morgan decreases. Morgan is writing an article on me.[5] This may be very helpful. It may shove me off again. Then I want to write 'a book' by which I mean a book of criticism for the H.P. But on what? Letters? Psychology? Lytton is off. The Loves of

2. Margaret (Madge) Vaughan, *née* Symonds (1869-1925), wife of VW's cousin W. W. Vaughan, headmaster since 1921 of Rugby School. She was buried at Highgate Cemetery on 7 November after a service in Rugby School Chapel the previous day. Madge Vaughan had once been very much alive in VW's emotions; indeed she had been the first woman 'to capture her heart', see *I QB*, pp 60-1.
3. Vita Sackville-West had in 1913 married Harold George Nicolson (1886-1968), third son of the 1st Baron Carnock and, like his father, a career diplomatist. From 1920 he was at the Foreign Office in London, but had now been posted as Counsellor to the British Legation in Teheran. Vita, who had a horror of the constraints and formalities of the diplomatic life, remained at Long Barn, their Kentish home, but joined him in Persia for two months in the Spring of 1926, and again in 1927.
4. Jean-Hippolyte Marchand (1883-1914), French painter, whose work was shown at the Second Post-Impressionist Exhibition in 1912, and subsequently at the Carfax Gallery, in London, where he was much admired. He was a friend of the Raverats in Vence, Alpes-Maritimes.
5. 'The Novels of Virginia Woolf' by E. M. Forster was published in *The New Criterion* of April 1926 (and subsequently reprinted as 'The Early Novels of Virginia Woolf' in *Abinger Harvest*, 1936). For VW's 'book' see below, 7 December 1925, n 5.

the Famous. Q. Elizabeth &c. I thought him at his most intimate last night; all plumy, incandescent, soft, luminous. Something slightly repels (too strong) Leonard. His character is not so good as Morgan's, he said, walking round the square in the snow today. "There is something about all Stracheys—" Then, when we talk, L. & I, we rather crab Lytton's writing I observe. But all this vanishes, with me, when he comes, as yesterday, to talk, & talk, & talk. That Nessa is still most beautiful— that comes over me. That Ka is thinner—& very self conscious: but nothing, in my sentimental heart, can stand against these old loyalties. I cannot keep my wits altogether about me in talk. I begin to glitter & englobe people with a champagne mist. And then it fades. I was talking of this to Raymond—whose blunt nose & flashy clothes are, I think, one's chief grudge against him—the other day. That there is no substance in

ones friendships, that they fade like—For instance,
* A shrewd guess— did he regret Harold [Nicolson] in Persia?* Nothing
he does regret like a coin is struck & left for ever in one's pos-
Harold in Persia session. People die; Madge dies, & one cannot beat

up a solitary tear. But then, if 6 people died, it is true that my life would cease: by wh. I mean, it would run so thin that though it might go on, would it have any relish? Imagine Leonard, Nessa Duncan Lytton, Clive Morgan all dead.

Monday 7 December

I want to lie down like a tired child & weep away this life of care— & my diary shall receive me on its downy pillow.[1] Most children do not know what they cry for; nor do I altogether. It is 12 o'clock on Monday morning, a very cold day, but sunny, healthy, cheerful. Bells ring down-stairs; doors are slammed. I should be in full feather, for after all these drowsy dependent weeks I am now almost quit of it again; & can read & write, & walk a little, & mildly entertain. Well, it is partly that devil

Vita. No letter. No visit. No invitation to Long
Poor woman! she Barn. She was up last week, & never came. So many
did try to come— good reasons for this neglect occur to me that I'm
prevented, fog &c. ashamed to call this a cause for weeping. Only if I

do not see her now, I shall not—ever: for the moment for intimacy will be gone, next summer. And I resent this, partly because I like her; partly

1. 'I could lie down like a tired child,
And weep away the life of care
Which I have borne and yet must bear,
Till death like sleep might steal on me.'
Shelley, *Stanzas Written in Dejection near Naples.*

because I hate the power of life to divide. Also, I am vain. Clive will know *why* Vita did not come to see me. That old rat chased to his hole, there is Tom's postcard about *On Being Ill*—an article which I, & Leonard too, thought one of my best: to him characteristic &c: I mean he is not enthusiastic; so, reading the proof just now, I saw wordiness, feebleness, & all the vices in it.[2] This increases my distaste for my own writing, & dejection at the thought of beginning another novel. What theme have I? Shan't I be held up for personal reasons? It will be too like father, or mother: &, oddly, I know so little of my own powers. Here is another rat run to earth. So now for news.

We shall spend Xmas at Charleston, which I'm afraid Leonard will not like much. We walked at Hampstead on Saturday. It was very cold—skating everywhere, save there, L. having brought his skates. It had a foggy winter beauty. We went in to Ken Wood (but dogs must be led) & there came to the duelling ground, where great trees stand about, & presumably sheltered the 18th Century swordsmen (how I begin to love the past—I think something to do with my book) & it was here that we discussed Lytton, gravely, like married people. But my God—how satisfactory after, I think 12 years, to have any human being to whom one can speak so directly as I to L.! Well, it was a question of L[ytton]'s change of feeling. He has the faults of a small nature said L. He is ungenerous. He asks, but never gives. But I have always known that—often I have seen the dull eyelid fall over him, if one asked a little too much: some sheath of selfishness that protects him from caring too much, or committing himself uncomfortably. He is cautious. He is a valetudinarian. But—there are, as usual, the other things; & as I say, I have known about Lytton's leathern eyelid since I was 20. Nothing has ever shocked me more, I think. But L. said when they were at Cambridge Lytton was not like that to him. First there was the I[nternationa]l Review: & Lytton refused to write; then Ralph; then never a word of praise for other people.[3] Morgan, said Leonard, as we trod back over the

2. In response to T. S. Eliot's letter imploring her to write for his new quarterly (see above, 14 September 1925), VW had sent him her article 'On Being Ill' on 14 November. His unenthusiastic postcard has not been located, but the article appeared in *The New Criterion* in January 1926 (Kp C270).

3. LW had been editor of the monthly *International Review* from its inception in 1919 until its amalgamation with the *Contemporary Review* at the end of the year. Ralph Partridge (1894-1960) had distinguished himself academically and in the 1914-18 war, from which he returned to Oxford disillusioned with militarism. He became an intimate of Lytton Strachey's household with his devoted companion (Dora) Carrington (whom Partridge prevailed upon to marry him in 1921), and from October 1920 to March 1923 had worked with the Woolfs in the Hogarth Press; but

slippery hillocks seeing so little as we talked (& yet all this part of Hampstead recalls Katherine to me—that faint ghost, with the steady eyes, the mocking lips, &, at the end, the wreath set on her hair:[4]) Morgan has improved. Morgan is I think naturally more congenial to L. than Lytton is. He likes "Sillies"; he likes the dependent simplicity of Morgan & myself. He likes settling our minds, & our immense relief at this. Well, well.[5]

I am reading The Passage to India; but will not expatiate here, as I must elsewhere. This book for the H.P.: I think I will find some theory about fiction.[6] I shall read six novels, & start some hares. The one I have in view, is about *perspective*. But I do not know. My brain may not last me out. I cannot think closely enough. But I can—if the C.R. is a test—beat up ideas, & express them now without too much confusion. (By the way, Robert Bridges likes Mrs Dalloway: says no one will read it; but it is beautifully written, & some more, which L. who was told by Morgan, cannot remember.[7])

I don't think it is a matter of 'development' but something to do with prose & poetry, in novels. For instance Defoe at one end: E. Brontë at the other. Reality something they put at different distances. One would have to go into conventions; real life; & so on. It might last me—

---

his character and behaviour together with Lytton's covert promotion of his interests had been a source of increasing irritation to them. See *II VW Diary*, *passim*.

4. On learning of Katherine Mansfield's death, VW had written (*II VW Diary*, 16 January 1923); 'Then, as usual with me, visual impressions kept coming and coming before me—always of Katherine putting on a white wreath, & leaving us, called away; made dignified, chosen.'

5. For LW's definition of the 'silly' see *II VW Diary*, 11 September 1923, n 5.

6. Forster's last novel had been published eighteen months earlier; VW did not publish any comment upon it until the end of 1927 (Kp C292, 'The Novels of E. M. Forster'). LW and Dadie Rylands had planned a series, to be called 'Hogarth Lectures on Literature' (see *HP Checklist*, Appendix I, p 139), to which VW was intended to contribute a book on fiction. She refers to this several times in her diary between now and September 1928, and in letters during 1927, and it was announced as 'in preparation' in the introductory booklet *A Lecture on Lectures* by Sir Arthur Quiller-Couch (published ostensibly in 1927 but actually in February 1928; *HP Checklist* 144). VW's book never appeared in the series, but was eventually published as three articles under the title 'Phases of Fiction' in the New York *Bookman* in 1929 (Kp C312, reprinted in *Granite and Rainbow*). See also MHP, Sussex, B6 & 7.

7. Robert Seymour Bridges (1844-1930) was a long-standing friend of Roger Fry; he was appointed Poet Laureate in 1913. VW was to meet him on her visit to Garsington in 1926 (see below, 1 July 1926).

this theory—but I should have to support it with other things. And death—as I always feel—hurrying near. 43: how many more books?

Katie came here;[8] a sort of framework of discarded beauty hung on a battered shape now. With the firmness of the flesh, & the blue of the eye, the formidable manner has gone. I can see her as she was at 22 H[yde] P[ark] G[ate] 25 years ago: in a little coat & skirt; very splendid; eyes half shut; lovely mocking voice; upright; tremendous; shy. Now she babbles along.

"But no duke ever asked me, my dear Virginia. They called me the Ice Queen.

And why did I marry Cromer? I loathed Egypt; I loathed invalids. I've had two very happy times in my life—childhood—not when I grew up—but later, with my boys club, my cottage, & my chow—& now. Now I have all I want. My garden—my dog."

I don't think her son enters in very largely. She is one of these cold eccentric great Englishwomen, enormously enjoying her rank, & the eminence it lends her in St John's Wood, & now free to poke into all the dusty holes & corners, dressed like a charwoman, with hands like one, & finger nails clotted with dirt. She never stops talking. She lacks much body to her. She has almost effused in mist. But I enjoyed it. Though I think she has few affections, & no very passionate interests. Now, having cried my cry, & the sun coming out, to write a list of Christmas presents. Ethel Sands comes to tea.[9] But no Vita.

Monday 21 December

But no Vita! But Vita for 3 days at Long Barn, from which L. & I returned yesterday.[10] These Sapphists *love* women; friendship is never untinged with amorosity. In short, my fears & refrainings, my 'impertinence' my usual self-consciousness in intercourse with people who mayn't want me & so on—were all, as L. said, sheer fudge; &, partly

8. Katie was the Countess of Cromer, *née* Lady Katherine Thynne (1865-1933), second wife and since 1917 widow of Evelyn Baring, 1st Earl of Cromer, the British administrator and Consul-General in Egypt.
9. Ethel Sands (1873-1962), American-born painter who divided her year between the Château d'Auppegard, near Dieppe, which she shared with her lifelong friend Nan Hudson, and her house at 15 The Vale, Chelsea. Wealthy and gregarious, she was an active and benign hostess and patron of the arts.
10. VW went to stay with V. Sackville-West at Long Barn on 17 December; it was, according to Nigel Nicolson (*III VW Letters*, p 223), 'the beginning of their love affair'. LW joined them on the afternoon of 19 December, and Vita motored them to London next day.

thanks to him (he made me write) I wound up this wounded & stricken year in great style. I like her & being with her, & the splendour—she shines in the grocers shop in Sevenoaks with a candle lit radiance, stalking on legs like beech trees, pink glowing, grape clustered, pearl hung. That is the secret of her glamour, I suppose. Anyhow she found me incredibly dowdy, no woman cared less for personal appearance—no one put on things in the way I did. Yet so beautiful, &c. What is the effect of all this on me? Very mixed. There is her maturity & full breastedness: her being so much in full sail on the high tides, where I am coasting down backwaters; her capacity I mean to take the floor in any company, to represent her country, to visit Chatsworth, to control silver, servants, chow dogs; her motherhood (but she is a little cold & offhand with her boys[11]) her being in short (what I have never been) a real woman. Then there is some voluptuousness about her; the grapes are ripe; & not reflective. No. In brain & insight she is not as highly organised as I am. But then she is aware of this, & so lavishes on me the maternal protection which, for some reason, is what I have always most wished from everyone. What L. gives me, & Nessa gives me, & Vita, in her more clumsy external way, tries to give me. For of course, mingled with all this glamour, grape clusters & pearl necklaces, there is something loose fitting. How much, for example, shall I really miss her when she is motoring across the desert? I will make a note on that next year. Anyhow, I am very glad that she is coming to tea today, & I shall ask her, whether she minds my dressing so badly? I think she does. I read her poem; which is more compact, better seen & felt than anything yet of hers.[12]

Mary's stories, I fear, are bad.[13] Dear me—then Roger is in love with H[elen Anrep]. Morgan's article has cheered me very much.[14] L. is doing up rubber seals & fur rabbits at the moment. The workmen are hammering, their engines throbbing outside on the hotel. We go down to Charleston tomorrow, not without some trepidation on my part, partly because I shall be hung about with trailing clouds of glory from Long

11. Vita's sons were (Lionel) Benedict (1914-1978) and Nigel (b. 1917) Nicolson.
12. V. Sackville-West's journey from Cairo to Persia in March 1926 is described in her *Passenger to Teheran*, published by the Hogarth Press in 1926 (*HP Checklist* 107); the final four days travel, over high mountain passes and desert plains, was by Trans-Desert Mail car. Her poem was probably 'On the Lake' which appeared in the *N & A* on 26 December 1925.
13. Nonetheless the Hogarth Press published Mary Hutchinson's *Fugitive Pieces* in June 1927 (*HP Checklist* 122); only one of them is referred to by the author as a 'story', the others being categorized as 'Shuttlecocks' and 'Weathercocks'.
14. Forster sent his as yet unpublished article (see above, 27 November 1925) to VW to read.

Barn wh. always disorientates me & makes me more than usually nervous: then I am—altogether so queer in some ways. One emotion succeeds another.[15]

On 22 December the Woolfs went to Charleston for Christmas, as builders were making alterations to Monks House. Clive and Vanessa Bell and the three children were there; also, until 24th, Roger Fry. Vanessa reported to Duncan Grant (who was with his mother at Twickenham) that they had spent a fascinating evening reading VW's diary recalling early days at 46 Gordon Square, with the four Stephens' very full and 'rather high society' life there. (Berg, 1905 Diary). VW and Quentin Bell had again collaborated in a squib, called The Messiah, purporting to depict scenes from Clive's life. On Boxing Day Vita Sackville-West came to lunch. LW returned to London on 27th, and VW followed him on 28th December.

15. The entry for 21 December is written on two pages; but on an intervening and a succeeding page VW has twice written out the following passage:

> Such a being must have stood out conspicuously among his fellows; the facts of his life would have been the ground of the faith in his genius; & when his early death endeared & sanctified his memory, loving grief would generously grant him the laurels which he had never worn.   (written for Bridges)

Roger Fry was collaborating with Robert Bridges, one of the founders of the Society for Pure English, in producing two tracts on English Handwriting, and to this end was collecting specimens of handwriting from his friends; VW's sample was not however, included in the total of 65 facsimiles reproduced (Tracts nos. XXIII and XXVIII). See II RF Letters, no. 575 of 18 December 1925 to Robert Bridges.

1926

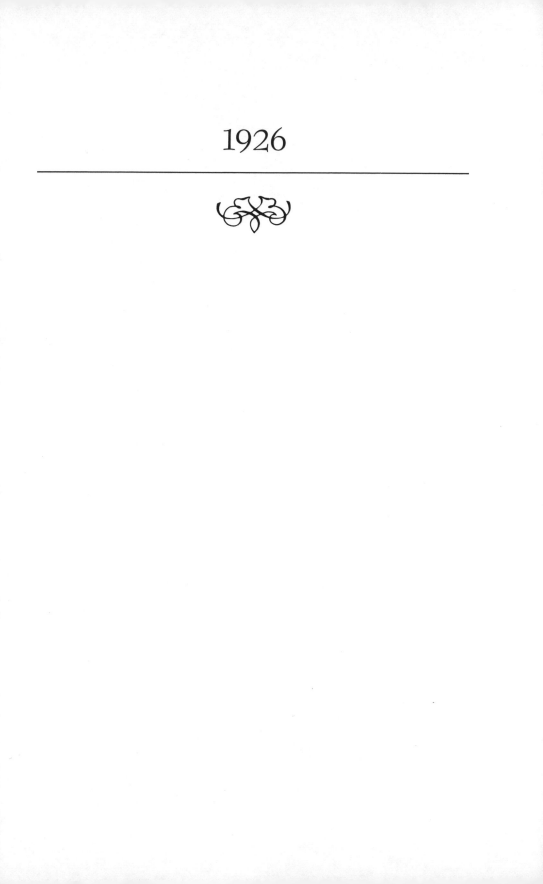

1926

VW wrote no diary between 21 December 1925 and 19 January 1926; her letters preserved from this interval are, with one exception, all to Vita Sackville-West, a significant indication of her preoccupation. After her return from Charleston to Tavistock Square on 28 December, she was again unwell, and on 8 January Dr Elinor Rendel diagnosed German Measles; but by 13th she was allowed out. Both the Woolfs and Vita were given dinner by Clive Bell at his favourite restaurant, the Ivy in West Street, WC2, on 18 January before his party, to which VW did not go.
The next entry was the last made in DIARY XIV; but there follow two pages of a preliminary version of the lecture she was to give at a private girls' school at Hayes Court in Kent on 30 January 1926 (later published as 'How Should one Read a Book?', Kp C277).

Tuesday 19 January

Vita having this moment (20 minutes ago—it is now 7) left me, what are my feelings? Of a dim November fog; the lights dulled & damped. I walked towards the sound of a barrel organ in Marchmont Street. But this will disperse; then I shall want her, clearly & distinctly. Then not— & so on. This is the normal human feeling, I think. One wants to finish sentences. One wants that atmosphere—to me so rosy & calm. She is not clever; but abundant & fruitful; truthful too. She taps so many sources of life: repose & variety, was her own expression, sitting on the floor this evening in the gaslight. We dined last night at the Ivy with Clive; & then they had a supper party, from which I refrained. Oh & mixed up with this is the invigoration of again beginning my novel, in the Studio, for the first time this morning. All these fountains play on my being & intermingle. I feel a lack of stimulus, of marked days, now Vita is gone; & some pathos, common to all these partings; & she has 4 days journey through the snow.

VW here begins DIARY XV, the title page of which is inscribed:

52 Tavistock Square

1926

Monday 8 February

Just back from Rodmell—to use again the stock opening. And I should explain why I've let a month slip perhaps. First, I think, the

German measles or influenza; next Vita; then, disinclination for any exertion, so that I never made a book till last week. But undoubtedly this diary is established, & I sometimes look at it & wonder what on earth will be the fate of it. It is to serve the purpose of my memoirs. At 60 I am to sit down & write my life. As rough material for that master-piece—& knowing the caprice of my own brain as record reader for I never know what will take my fancy, I here record that I come in to find the following letters waiting me. 1. Ottoline, on that wonderful essay On Being Ill. She is doing a cure. 2. A long letter of hysterical flattery from Miss Keiller [Kieffer] who is translating Jacob's Room. 3. a card, showing me her character in an unfavourable light from Miss Ethel Pye, who once met me in an omnibus & wishes to take a mask of my head; 4. a letter from Harcourt Brace enclosing cheque from the Forum for O[n]. B[eing]. Ill. 5. a letter asking me to become one of the Committee of the English Association; 6. a cutting on Hogarth Essays from the Dial; 7. a note from Clive asking me to dine to meet his brother.[1] I think this makes me out rather specially important. It is 3 days post. I am rather tired, a little tired, from having thought too much about To the Light-house. Never never have I written so easily, imagined so profusely. Murry says my works won't be read in 10 years time—Well, tonight I get a new edition of the V[oyage]. O[ut]. from Harcourt Brace—this was published 11 years ago.[2]

1. 1. VW's essay 'On Being Ill' had appeared in the January issue of Eliot's *New Criterion* (Kp C270). 2. Marie Kieffer and Claude Dravaine published their translation of two extracts from *Jacob's Room* in *La Revue nouvelle*, Paris, March 1927 (Kp D28) and *Revue politique et littéraire: Revue bleue*, Paris, 6 August 1927 (Kp D29). 3. Ethel Pye (*c.* 1882-1960) was an artist and sculptor peripherally connected with the 'neo-pagan' circle. 4. 'On Being Ill' was reprinted as 'Illness: An Unexplored Mine' in the New York *Forum* in April 1926 (Kp C270). 5. Mrs Leonard Woolf was co-opted on to the general committee of the English Association (founded in 1906 to promote the knowledge and appreciation of English language and literature) on 28 January 1926; though there is no record of her having ever attended a meeting, her name appeared each year until 1934. 6. *The Dial*, New York, commended the series in general and gave a fairly detailed comment upon each of the first six of the 'Hogarth Essays' (see *HP Checklist*), in its February number. 7. Clive's brother was Lt. Col. Cory Bell (see above, 19 April 1925, n 11).

2. John Middleton Murry (1889-1957), literary critic, author, widower of Katherine Mansfield (though now remarried), controlled and edited the *Adelphi*; in his article entitled 'The Classical Revival' in the issue of 9 February 1926, he wrote: 'Mrs Woolf's *Jacob's Room* and Mr Eliot's *The Waste Land* belong essentially to the same order. Both are failures; ... Fifty, ten years hence no one will take the trouble (no small one) to read either of these works, unless there should be some revolutionary happening to their authors—some liberation into a real spontaneity— which will cause these records of their former struggle ... to be studied.'

Tuesday 23 February

Here is the usual door bell/ & I think Gwen came in, & I was rather sodden & wretched, feeling that I had nothing to give her, & she everything to ask. As I foretold, she is enmeshed in a net of fire: that is the truth; loves net; the fiery net of—who was it?—that was scorched to death: & hers is more painful than his, & more enduring.[3] Yet how seldom one envisages what one knows! Her net lies on me; but it does not burn me. And I do little futile kindnesses to her, which are little good to anybody; & I don't do them, & I feel compunction. Of all this I have little appetite to write, being exacerbated 1. because Nelly won't make marmalade; 2. because a certain function impends; 3. because I can't go, in deference to L.'s wish, to Mortimer's farewell party, 4. because Dadie asked me to tea, & I did not go; 5. because—the last because I cannot now remember—a vague dissatisfaction: spring & funerals; yellow lights & white blossoms; beautiful black yellow pointed squares—& so on. Vita is a dumb letter writer, & I miss her. I miss the glow & the flattery & the festival. I miss her, I suppose, not very intimately. Nevertheless, I do miss her, & wish it were May 10th; & then I don't wish it; for I have such a razor edge to my palette that seeing people often disgusts me of seeing them.[4]

I am blown like an old flag by my novel. This one is To the Lighthouse. I think it is worth saying for my own interest that at last at last, after that battle Jacob's Room, that agony—all agony but the end, Mrs Dalloway, I am now writing as fast & freely as I have written in the whole of my life; more so—20 times more so—than any novel yet. I think this is the proof that I was on the right path; & that what fruit hangs in my soul is to be reached there.[5] Amusingly, I now invent theories that fertility & fluency are the things: I used to plead for a kind of close, terse, effort. Anyhow this goes on all the morning; & I have the devils own work not to be flogging my brain all the afternoon. I live entirely in it, & come to the surface rather obscurely & am often unable to think what to say when we walk round the Square, which is bad I know. Perhaps it may be a good sign for the book though. Of course

3. Semele was consumed by the fire of her lover Jupiter's full majesty; but it was Mars and Venus who were caught in a net by Vulcan.
4. Raymond Mortimer was shortly to set out for Teheran to join the Nicolsons; Vita was due to return to England on 10 May.
5.   'Hang there like fruit, my soul,
                       Till the tree die!'
                                   Cymbeline, V v 262.
See also *I QB*, p 69.

it is largely known to me: but all my books have been that. It is, I feel, that I can float everything off now; & "everything" is rather a crowd & weight & confusion in the mind.

Then I have seen Lytton: seen Eddy; Mary; I forget: I have been discreet in my society, & enjoyed it. Perhaps I am again brisking, after my lethargy. The publishing season is about to begin. Nessa says Why don't you give it up? I say, because I enjoy it. Then I wonder, but do I? What about Rome & Sicily? And Manning Sanders is not worth the grind.[6] Am I a fanatical enthusiast for work, like my father? I think I have a strain of that, but I don't relish it. Tonight Francis Birrell & Rose Macaulay dine with us.[7] To celebrate the occasion, I have bought a toast rack & a bedspread, which covers that atrocious chest of drawers wh. has worried me these 2 years. I am now so pleased with the colour that I go out & look at it.

Wednesday 24 February

To continue, the second day running which is a rarity, they came last night, Francis & Rose Macaulay—I daresay I shall be calling her Rose one of these days. Francis didn't much relish meeting her: my gnats of worries gave me little peace: Gwen ringing up; I not cordial; she shying off: I repentant; ringing up again. Then Rose—too chattery chittery at first go off; lean as a rake, wispy, & frittered. Some flimsy smartness & taint of the flimsy glittery literary about her: but this was partly nerves, I think; & she felt us alien & observant doubtless. Anyhow in the middle of dinner the lights went out: only a few candles in saucers to be had, & I left her & Francis alone in the dark to talk. After all, she has no humbug about her; is exactly on a par as far as conventions go, I imagine; only frosted & rather cheaply gilt superficially with all that being asked to speak at dinners, to give opinions to newspapers, & so on; lunching at the League of Nations; dining with Iolo Williams, meeting Jack Squire who has grown whiskers & looks like a verger.[8]

Let me see, there's some failure of sympathy between Chiswick & Bloomsbury, I think, she said. So we defined Bloomsbury. Her part is to

6. The second booklet of Ruth Manning-Sanders' verse to be printed by the Woolfs, *Martha Wish-You-Ill*, was published by the Hogarth Press in July 1926 (*HP Checklist* 102).
7. (Emilie) Rose Macaulay (1881-1958), the drily entertaining novelist and popular literary lady, whom VW met occasionally.
8. Iolo Aneurin Williams (1890-1962), author, journalist, and collector, was from 1920-39 the bibliographical correspondent of the *London Mercury*, founded and edited by the egregious man of letters, John Collings Squire (1884-1958).

stick up for common sense she said. I elaborated her being Cambridge. She is writing an article for an American paper on London after the War.[9] It is [this] sort of thing that one distrusts in her. Why should she take the field so unnecessarily? But I fancy our 'leading lady novelists' all do as they are asked about this, & I am not quite one of them. I saw my own position, a good deal lowered & diminished; & this is part of the value of seeing new people—still more of going to people's houses. One is, if anything, minimised: here in the eternal Bloomsbury, one is apt, without realising it, to expand. Then Gwen came. I like Francis. I like his laughter; & his random energy. He is a Victorian. Indeed we talked a lot, when L. was in the basement with the electrician, of father, who, said Francis, dominates the 20th Century. "He made it possible for me to have a decent life" he said. "He pulled down the whole edifice, & never knew what he was doing. He never realised that if God went, morality must follow. A remarkable man; for though he would not believe in God, he was stricter than those who did."

"He loved lamentation" said L. coming up. R.M. said her parents called him always "poor Leslie Stephen" because he had lost his faith. Also they said he was very gentle & charming. Gwen said her father & uncles had a great respect for him. They had a very romantic feeling for my mother.[10]

Because she was so beautiful, I said, proud that R.M. should know this; & felt rather queer, to think how much of this there is in To the Lighthouse, & how all these people will read it & recognise poor Leslie Stephen & beautiful Mrs Stephen in it. Then we talked of knowing people. R.M. said she always knew why she liked people. Gwen being perhaps tired, was a little mystical; or perhaps she has acquired views which are yet hardly articulate. Anyhow Leonard thought her 'almost imbecile'. They got talking about whether one knew more about pictures or books. R.M. showed up rather well in argument, & maintained that a book is a subjective thing; she attacks authority in literature. But people know about painting as it is a more technical art. Then she said (this makes me think she will wish to be called Rose) how she had dreamt she was staying with us in a cottage in Surrey, a 15th century house, full of old beams & candle lit. In some lights she has the beautiful eyes

9. Rose Macaulay had studied at Somerville College, Oxford; but her father, George Macaulay, was a Cambridge man, and for the last ten years of his life, when she still lived at home, was lecturer in English there. Her article, 'New London Since 1914', appeared in the *New York Times* in May 1926.
10. Gwen Raverat's father and four uncles were the sons of the great Charles Darwin; see her *Period Piece, A Cambridge Childhood*, 1952.

of all us distinguished women writers; the refinement; the clearness of cut; the patience; & humbleness. It is her voice & manner that make one edgy.

Saturday 27 February

I think I shall initiate a new convention for this book—beginning each day on a new page—my habit in writing serious literature. Certainly, I have room to waste a little paper in this year's book. As for the soul: why did I say I would leave it out? I forget. And the truth is, one can't write directly about the soul. Looked at, it vanishes: but look at the ceiling, at Grizzle, at the cheaper beasts in the Zoo which are exposed to walkers in Regents Park, & the soul slips in. It slipped in this afternoon. I will write that I said, staring at the bison: answering L. absentmindedly; but what was I going to write?[11]

Mrs Webb's book has made me think a little what I could say of my own life. I read some of 1923 this morning, being headachy again, & taking a delicious draught of silence.[12] But then there were causes in her life: prayer; principle. None in mine. Great excitability & search after something. Great content—almost always enjoying what I'm at, but with constant change of mood. I don't think I'm ever bored. Sometimes a little stale; but I have a power of recovery—which I have tested; & am now testing for the 50th time. I have to husband my head still very carefully: but then, as I said to Leonard today, I enjoy epicurean ways of society; sipping & then shutting my eyes to taste. I enjoy almost everything. Yet I have some restless searcher in me. Why is there not a discovery in life? Something one can lay hands on & say "This is it?" My depression is a harassed feeling—I'm looking; but that's not it— thats not it. What is it? And shall I die before I find it? Then (as I was walking through Russell Sqre last night) I see the mountains in the sky: the great clouds; & the moon which is risen over Persia; I have a great & astonishing sense of something there, which is 'it'— It is not exactly beauty that I mean. It is that the thing is in itself enough: satisfactory; achieved. A sense of my own strangeness, walking on the earth is there too: of the infinite oddity of the human position; trotting along Russell Sqre with the moon up there, & those mountain clouds. Who am I,

11. i.e.: those beasts which the public could see from the park through the railings without having to pay for admission to the Zoo.
12. Beatrice Webb's *My Apprenticeship*, consisting of extracts from her diary from 1868 up to the time of her marriage in 1892, with connecting and explanatory passages, had just been published. VW had been rereading her *own* diary for 1923.

what am I, & so on: these questions are always floating about in me; & then I bump against some exact fact—a letter, a person, & come to them again with a great sense of freshness. And so it goes on. But, on this showing which is true, I think, I do fairly frequently come upon this 'it'; & then feel quite at rest.

Is that what I meant to say? Not in the least. I was thinking about my own character; not about the universe. Oh & about society again; dining with Lord Berners at Clive's made me think that. How, at a certain moment, I see through what I'm saying; detest myself; & wish for the other side of the moon; reading alone, that is. How many phases one goes through between the soup & the sweet! I want, partly as a writer, to found my impressions on something firmer. I said to Lord B. All you must do in writing is to float off the contents of your mind. Clive & Raymond laughed & said Thats exactly what you do anyhow. And I don't want that to be all. Nor is it. Theres a good deal of shaping & composing in my books. However—the main idea of them is that, then; & I dont like it.

Lord B. was stockish, resolute, quick witted: analysed his own instability. His father was a sea captain; wished him not on any account to be a long haired artist; his mother used to say "My little boy plays so nicely—you should hear him play" but she minded his not hunting & riding. So, he said, he was inhibited as a musician. His talent clung (I think he said) like a creeper to the edge of a cliff. One day he wrote two marches for fun. Stravinsky saw them, thought them good, & they were published. So he was accepted as a serious musician, with only 4 lessons from Tovey in counterpoint. He had an astonishing facility. He could write things that sounded all right. Suddenly, last year, all his pleasure in it went. He met a painter, asked him how you paint; bought 'hogsheads' —(meant hog's bristles) & canvas & copied an Italian picture, brilliantly, consummately, says Clive. Has the same facility there: but it will come to nothing he said, like the other.[13]

What did we talk about? Tom & the Sitwells; Eddie Marsh & Lady Colefax,[14] & I felt one cd. go on saying these things for ever, & they

13. VW dined with Clive on 25 February. Lord Berners' autobiographical *First Childhood* (1934), amplifies this summary of his parents' characters. Donald Francis Tovey (1875-1940), pianist, composer and scholar, was one of the greatest personalities in the musical world of his day; he had been Reid Professor of Music at Edinburgh University since 1914.

14. Edward ('Eddie') Marsh (1872-1952), again private secretary to Winston Churchill (now Chancellor of the Exchequer), was like Lady Colefax inveterately sociable; his interests and patronage embraced writers, painters and actors.

mean nothing. Sure enough, he asked me to dine: & now I say I have a headache & can't.

Wednesday 3 March

And I did have a bit of a headache—yes; all this time is rather weathering headaches. Nailing a flag to a mast in a gale, I have just compared writing a novel in London to that, in a letter to Vita. The glow is off my visit to Herbert & Freda at Cookham: a very memorable day.[1] From their windows you look down on the top of old Mr Watkins' bald head skulling on the Thames. You look at two twisted stakes in the river which I took for cranes; & across Marlow to some hills. They motored us up into the hills, & it was oddly strangely still & bright & empty & full of unblown flowers. We saw a Queen Anne house called—I forget; so high & remote, with turf to its door; & broad alleys; capacious windows, a woman. Well; no one gets more pleasure from these sights than I do; only the wave of pleasure leaves some regret—all this beauty going—going—going: & I in Tavistock Sqre not seeing it. And spiritually it was very interesting. I thought I had found the real human being— something so simple & fitted to its surroundings as to be almost irreflective, in Freda. She is nearer humanity than I am: eats her way into the heart of it, as I cannot. Her thighs are thick with honey. But the impression is dying, as they do, under others—how I lost my little mother of pearl brooch, bought a 16/ hat which I do not like, & must go to tea at Ethel [Sands]'s tomorrow in what then? My own lack of beauty depresses me today. But how far does the old convention about 'beauty' bear looking into? I think of the people I have known. Are they beautiful? This problem I leave unsolved.

Raymond gave a fancy dress party on Sunday night. I was torpid with a sleeping draught; & was dozing off, as the carriages arrived at no. 6. Still I envied them; & thought, when Raymond telephoned about the copy of Old Kensington which I gave him & said how lovely Nancy [Cunard] had looked, that I had missed the greatest sight of the season.[2] Happily, Lucas comes to tea, & he says he hears it was a terrible sticky dull party, with not room to turn round in, which greatly pleases me. Lucas, Peter, I should call him, came, from friendship; which friendship,

1. See *III VW Letters*, no. 1622 for VW's letter to Vita; it also describes the Woolfs' visit to LW's stockbroker brother Herbert Sidney Woolf (1879-1949) and his wife Alfreda, *née* Major, at Cookham Dean on Sunday 28 February.
2. Raymond Mortimer lived at 6 Gordon (now Endsleigh) Place, which connected Gordon and Tavistock Squares. His present was the book published in 1873 by Miss Thackeray—subsequently Lady Ritchie, VW's 'Aunt Anny'.

as I suppose, was gently stimulated by my praise of his novel.[3] He is a
bony rosy little austere priest; so whole, & sane, & simple throughout
one can't help respecting him, though when it comes to books we disagree.
He says Tom &c: have thrown intellect to the winds; given up the ghost;
he says Houseman & de la Mare are the real poets.[4] I say poetry is defunct;
& Tom &c anyhow try to animate it. The Sitwells, he says, advertise.
They're aristocrats, I say, thinking criticism upstart impertinence on the
part of flunkeys. No merit in their works anyhow, he says. But what
about this drawing room singer, de la Mare, I ask. The most charming
of men. Granted. Granted, on Peter's side, that he has no coherency
whatever—is always darting after strange monsters—goldfish in bowls,
I say. Well, but we cant all be great philosophical poets, he says.
Anyhow Tom ain't a drawing room singer, I say. Tom has been down
lecturing, & not creating a good impression at Cambridge, I fancy.[5]
He tells the young men, in private, how they cook fish in Paris: his
damned selfconsciousness again, I suppose. But Peter is, to my mind,
too entire in his judgments; founded on book learning & prettiness into
the bargain. He has no ascendency of brain: he is not, & now never will
be, a personage: which is the one thing needful in criticism, or writing of
any sort, I think; for we're all as wrong as wrong can be. But character
is the thing.

Tuesday 9 March

Then I was at two parties: Ethel's tea; Mary's dinner.

Ethel's was a ghastly frizzly frying pan affair. I chattering in front
of the footlights.

Well, said Ott. how are you? You look wonderfully well; as if you
had never had an illness in your life.

3. F. L. Lucas's first novel, *The River Flows*, was published by the Hogarth Press in
October 1926 (*HP Checklist* 99); written in the form of a diary, it betrayed,
according to the *TLS* (14 October 1926): 'inexperience which was not so obvious
from his criticism' but shed 'a not uninteresting light on the Cambridge scene'.
4. A. E. Housman (1859-1936), Professor of Latin at Cambridge 1911-36, was
eminent in the fields of classical scholarship and of original poetry, although of the
latter he published nothing between *A Shropshire Lad* in 1896 and *Last Poems* in
1922. Walter de la Mare (1873-1956), poet, storyteller, and man of letters.
5. T. S. Eliot gave eight lectures (the Clark Lectures) on 'The Metaphysical Poetry
of the Seventeenth Century' at Trinity College between 26 January and 9 March
1926. (The unpublished texts are in the Hayward Bequest in King's College
Library, P6.) As described by Lucas, who did not admire him, the impression made
by Eliot upon Cambridge was inevitably poor.

(Now what does she say that for? To get pity for herself, sure enough.)
I can't say I'm any better.

But she is all dressed like a girl of 18; tomato coloured Georgette & fur.

Ethel says, tittering

What a nice hat.

I'm all windblown in my old felt, come through the snow, with Dadie.

Well, I say to myself, I'll see this through anyhow, take my seat as on a throne, & proceed, first to little smug Leigh Ashton: Read wrote that Times Leader this morning (quoting me & Joyce as examples of good prose versus death of Queen Victoria).[6]

I should so much like to know if you think its well written—such a charming man.

Then diversion: Ethel; Ottoline: Percy Lubbock.[7]

Are the Russians more passionate than we are?

No; I say; I have all the passions. Asked to define a dramatic scene; how Leonard says "I think the worse of you for ever" when I accept Ott's invitation. Suddenly I remember it was Ott's invitation. If Mr Lubbock had a daughter he would have scenes—this is sheer egotistical cruelty on Ott's part; so home, holding Dadie by the arm; talking about his fellowship, to be announced on Saturday, (But Peter thinks he won't get it[8]) & abusing Chelsea, & Ottoline; & saying how unpopular I made myself.

As for Mary's party, there, save for the usual shyness about powder & paint, shoes & stockings, I was happy, owing to the supremacy of literature. This keeps us sweet & sane, George Moore & me I mean.[9]

He has a pink foolish face; blue eyes like hard marbles; a crest of snowwhite hair; little unmuscular hands; sloping shoulders; a high stomach;

6. (Arthur) Leigh Bolland Ashton (b. 1897) had joined the staff of the Victoria & Albert Museum (of which he was later to become Director) in 1922. The leading article in the *TLS* of 4 March 1926, entitled 'English Prose', discussed *The Oxford Book of English Prose* (1925), chosen and edited by Sir Arthur Quiller-Couch. The examples VW refers to here were taken from her own *Mrs Dalloway*, from Joyce's *Ulysses*, and from *Queen Victoria* by Lytton Strachey, who was the only one of the three to be represented in Quiller-Couch's anthology.

7. Percy Lubbock (1875-1965), man of letters.

8. Peter Lucas was right; G. H. W. Rylands was not elected a Fellow of King's College, Cambridge, until March 1927.

9. George Augustus Moore (1852-1933), the admired Anglo-Irish novelist and writer, author of *Esther Waters* (1894), was a friend of the Hutchinsons; VW now apparently met him for the first time. His views on Thomas Hardy and Anne Brontë had been expressed at length in his *Conversations in Ebury Street* (1924).

neat, purplish well brushed clothes; & perfect manners, as I consider them. That is to say he speaks without fear or dominance; accepting me on my merits; every one on their merits. Still in spite of age uncowed, unbeaten, lively, shrewd. As for Hardy & Henry James though, what shall one say?

"I am a fairly modest man; but I admit I think Esther Waters a better book than Tess."

But what is there to be said for that man? He cannot write. He cannot tell a story. The whole art of fiction consists in telling a story. Now he makes a woman confess. How does he do it? In the third person—a scene that should be moving, impressive. Think how Tolstoi would have done it!

But, said Jack [Hutchinson] War & Peace is the greatest novel in the world. I remember the scene where Natasha puts on a moustache, & Rostov sees her for the first time as she is & falls in love with her.

No, my good friend, there is nothing very wonderful in that. That is an ordinary piece of observation. But my good friend (to me—half hesitating to call me this) what have you to say for Hardy? You cannot find anything to say. English fiction is the worst part of English literature. Compare it with the French—with the Russians. Henry James wrote some pretty little stories before he invented his jargon. But they were about rich people. You cannot write stories about rich people; because, I think he said, they have no instincts. But Henry James was enamoured of marble balustrades. There was no passion in any of his people. And Anne Brontë was the greatest of the Brontës & Conrad could not write, & so on. But this is out of date.

Saturday 20 March

But what is to become of all these diaries, I asked myself yesterday. If I died, what would Leo make of them? He would be disinclined to burn them; he could not publish them. Well, he should make up a book from them, I think; & then burn the body. I daresay there is a little book in them: if the scraps & scratches were straightened out a little. God knows.

This is dictated by a slight melancholia, which comes upon me sometimes now, & makes me think I am old: I am ugly. I am repeating things. Yet, as far as I know, as a writer I am only now writing out my mind.

Dining with Clive last night to meet Lord Ivor Spencer Churchill— an elegant attenuated gnat like youth; very smooth, very supple, with the semi-transparent face of a flower, & the legs of a gazelle, & the white waistcoat & diamond buttons of a dandy, & all an Americans desire to understand psycho-analysis—I thought of my own age.[10] I made a horrid gaffe early on: said I liked a picture, which I did not like, & found I was wrong. Now if I had followed my instinct, as one should do, I should have been right. For some extraordinary reason, this poisoned my evening, slightly. The Lord analysed everything very ingeniously: he is a clever boy. I was greatly impressed by masculine cleverness, & their ability to toss balls swiftly & surely to & fro: no butter fingers; all clean catches. Adrian Bishop came in; a ruddy bull frog;[11] & then I went, & Clive, with a discrimination which was affectionate, but not just, apologised, thinking I had not talked enough for my pleasure; whereas I had said the wrong thing, & been depressed over that. Otherwise the evening amused me, & I wanted, like a child, to stay & argue. True, the argument was passing my limits—how if Einstein is true, we shall be able to foretell our own lives. Fortune tellers can now read one's mind exactly according to Lord Ivor, who, by the bye, had read neither Henry James nor V.W., is about 23, & came to the Press this morning, obediently, to buy my complete works. No intellectual would have done that. They are excessively anxious to save their souls—these aristocrats; witness Lord Berners the other night, sending out for Peacock—on my recommendation.

Otherwise, we had Bea Howe to dinner; & went to Philip [Woolf]'s one hot still day of the usual loveliness, & saw the place, & the horses, & the pepper box towers of Waddesdon, & I liked the immense directness & uncloudedness of Babs;[12] but says Eddy [Sackville-West] who came to tea on Sunday, this is "I assure you" all my imagination. She would be very dull if you knew her. He knows dozens of her. Who is not dull? Only B[loomsbur]'y according to Eddy.

Then there was Sybil Colefax: she comes to heel promptly: no, I won't go there; she may have a little cheap tea here, which she does, gratefully.

10. Lord Ivor (Charles Spencer-) Churchill (1898-1956), younger son of the 9th Duke of Marlborough and his first wife, Consuelo Vanderbilt; uninterested in public affairs, he was devoting himself to connoisseurship and to forming his remarkable collection, in particular of French Impressionist and Post-Impressionist painting.
11. Herbert Frank ('Adrian') Bishop (1898-1942) was a Dubliner educated at Eton and at King's College, Cambridge (1919-23), where he was prominent as a scholar, a wit, and an actor. After leaving Cambridge, he lived mostly abroad—in Vienna, Persia, Germany and Italy, teaching and writing—until 1935.
12. Philip Sidney Woolf (1889-1962), LW's youngest brother, was estate manager to a distant cousin, James de Rothschild, owner of Waddesdon Manor, Buckinghamshire—a conspicuous mansion built in 1880 in the style of a French château (now National Trust property). Philip had married Marjorie ('Babs') Lowndes in 1922.

She has done America with the usual dashing, joyless efficiency; could not analyse, merely report. Charlie Chaplin such a mixture of subtlety & common[n]ess: but why? No instances available, so I infer that she picked this up second hand, perhaps from Esme Howard; perhaps from Coolidge, or from Douglas Fairbanks or from the Italian boy who drove the car. Like a good housewife, which she is, she is making Peter begin life hard, cooking his breakfast, down on Wall Street by 9. There is a strain of hard, serious, professionalism in her, quite unmitigated by all the splendours of Argyll House.[13]

Wednesday 24 March

"I'm going to hand in my resignation this morning" said L. making the coffee.

To what? I asked.

"The Nation".

And it is done; & we have six months only before us. I feel 10 years younger; the shafts off our shoulders again & the world before us. I can't pretend to make much of a to-do about this either way. It was a temporary makeshift job, amusing at first, then galling, & last night, after an argument of the usual kind about literary articles & space & so on with Maynard & Hubert L. came to the decision to resign now. There was no quarrel. Oddly enough, having tea with Nessa, she had set me thinking the same thing. Phil [Noel-]Baker had said to her he thought L. the best living writer, & what a pity it was he spent so much time on the Nation & the Press. So there was I beginning, don't you think we might give them up! —when L. came in with his contribution to the question. He was dining with Clive, so the discussion waited till this morning; was decided by 10; in the hands of the Chief by 11—& now thank God no more chiefs for either of us so long as we live I hope.[14]

The situation appears to be that L. shall make £300; I £200—& really I don't suppose we shall find it hard; & then the mercy of having no ties, no proofs, no articles to procure, & all that, is worth a little more exertion elsewhere, should it come to that. I'm amused at my own

13. Esme Howard (1863-1939), created 1st Baron Howard of Penrith in 1930, was from 1924-30 British Ambassador to the USA. Peter was one of Sibyl Colefax's two sons.

14. LW was dissuaded by Keynes ('the Chief') and Henderson from carrying out this intention to resign as literary editor of the *N & A*—a position he had held since the end of April 1923—and in fact continued to hold until the end of 1930. See correspondence in LWP, Sussex, section I. Hubert Douglas Henderson (1890-1952), economist, was editor of the paper from 1923-1930.

sense of liberation. To upset everything every 3 or 4 years is my notion of a happy life. Always to be tacking to get into the eye of the wind. Now a prudent life is, as L. pointed out in the Square the opposite of this. One ought to stick in the same place. But with £400 assured & no children, why imitate a limpet in order to enjoy a limpets safety? The next question will be, I see, the Press. Shall we give that up too, & so be quit of everything? Its not such an easy question, or so pressing. I sometimes wish it. For, speaking selfishly, it has served my turn: given me a chance of writing off my own bat, & now I doubt if Heinemann or Cape would much intimidate me. But then there's the fun—which is considerable. The time will come, at this rate, when we have nothing in the world to resign: then, to get the effect of change, one will have to accept. We say we will travel & see the world. Anyhow I make my usual prediction—we shall be richer this time next year without the Nation than with it.

I rather like feeling that I *have* to earn money. I intensely dislike being in office, in any post of authority. I dislike being in people's pay. This of course is part of the reason why I like writing for the Press. But I suppose freedom becomes a fetish like any other. These disjointed reflections I scribble on a divine, if gusty, day; being about, after reading Anna Karenina, to dine at a pot-house with Rose Macaulay—not a cheerful entertainment; but an experience perhaps.

Lydia came into the room when L. was talking to Maynard this morning to show him her Zebra shoes, which cost £5.8.6. & they were really lizard, L. says. Also it is curious how a change like this destroys formality[?]—dissipates the elements.

Saturday 27 March

To continue—I don't know why I should really tell the story of the Nation—it doesn't figure largely in our lives. But Leonard met Phil Baker, who says he will get £300 as lecturer at the School of Economics easily if he wants it. He came in that night & said this & then we went off on a blowing night to dine at Rose M.'s 'pothouse', as I so mistakenly called it. There were 10 second rate writers in second rate dress clothes, Lynds, Goulds, O'Donovan:[15] no, I won't in any spasm of hypocritical

15. Robert Wilson Lynd (1879-1949), journalist and essayist, regular contributor to the *New Statesman* and the Liberal *Daily News*; his wife, also a writer, was Sylvia, *née* Dryhurst (1888-1952). Gerald Gould (1885-1936), author and literary journalist; his wife Barbara Ayrton Gould (d. 1950), had worked on the *Daily Herald,* and was a Labour Party parliamentary candidate—finally elected in 1945. Jeremiah (Gerald) O'Donovan (1872-1942) had once been a Catholic priest in

humanity include Wolves. L. by the way was in his red brown tweed. Then the pitter patter began; the old yard was scratched over by these baldnecked chickens. The truth was that we had no interests private; literature was our common ground; & though I will talk literature with Desmond or Lytton by the hour, when it comes to pecking up grains with these active stringy fowls my gorge rises. What d'you think of the Hawthornden prize? Why isn't Masefield as good as Chaucer, or Gerhardi as good as Tchekov: how can I embark with Gerald Gould on such topics? He reads novels incessantly; got a holiday 3 years ago, & prided himself on reading nothing but Tchekhov; knows all about a novel in the first chapter. Sylvias & Geralds & Roberts & Roses chimed & tinkled round the table. A stout woman called Gould got steadily more & more mustard & tomato coloured. I said Holy Ghost? when Mr O'Donovan said the whole of the coast. Lodged on a low sofa in Rose's underground cheerful, sane, breezy room I talked to a young cultivated man, who turned out to be Hinks, Roger, British Museum, mild aesthete, variety of Leigh Ashton; but thank God, not a second rate journalist.[16] All the time I kept saying to myself Thank God to be out of that; out of the Nation; no longer brother in arms with Rose & Robert & Sylvia. It is a thinblooded set; so 'nice', 'kind', respectable, cleverish & in the swim.

Then our set at Nessa's last night, was hardly at its best. L. & Adrian silent & satirical; old Sickert rather toothless & set;[17] I driven to chatter, not well; but Nessa & Duncan don't consolidate & order these parties; so home in a spasm of outraged vanity, & not that altogether, for I had worked honestly if feebly, & L. had not; & then he was off early this morning to Rodmell where Philcox is in the thick of building & drains:[18]

Galway, had resigned, travelled, married, published novels and met Rose Macaulay while they were both working in the Ministry of Information towards the end of the war. Their ensuing clandestine love-affair lasted until his death.

16. Roger Packman Hinks (1903-1963), educated at Westminster School and Trinity College, Cambridge, had spent a year at the British School in Rome, and had just been appointed to an assistant-Keepership in the Department of Greek and Roman Antiquities in the British Museum.

17. Walter Richard Sickert (1860-1942), the painter, had suffered a long period of depression and misanthropy following the death of his second wife in 1920. He was living alone in a bed-sitting-room and studio at 15 Fitzroy Street. However in 1924 he had been elected ARA, much to his gratification, and later this year was to marry again.

18. Philcox Bros, builders, of 155 High Street, Lewes; they were carrying out alterations to Monks House.

so I had no time to uncrease my rose leaf; had to try & work, to finish the rather long drawn out dinner scene [in *To the Lighthouse*], & was just striking oil when in comes Angus to tell me Eddy was on the phone: would I go to Rimsky Korsakov with him on Tuesday.[19] I agreed— more, asked him to dinner. Then was all a whirl & flutter of doubts; detested the engagement; could not settle; suddenly shook my coat, like a retriever; faced facts; sent Eddy a wire, & a letter "Cant come—detest engagements", & pondered where shall I spend the day? decided on Greenwich, arrived there at 1; lunched; everything fell out pat; smoked a cigarette on the pier promenade, saw the ships swinging up, one two, three, out of the haze; adored it all; yes even the lavatory keepers little dog; saw the grey Wren buildings fronting the river; & then another great ship, grey & orange; with a woman walking on deck; & then to the hospital; first to the Museum where I saw Sir John Franklin's pen & spoons (a spoon asks a good deal of imagination to consecrate it)—I played with my mind watching what it would do,—& behold if I didn't almost burst into tears over the coat Nelson wore at Trafalgar with the medals which he hid with his hand when they carried him down, dying, lest the sailors might see it was him. There was too, his little fuzzy pigtail, of golden greyish hair tied in black; & his long white stockings, one much stained, & his white breeches with the gold buckles, & his stock—all of which I suppose they must have undone & taken off as he lay dying. Kiss me Hardy &c—Anchor, anchor,—I read it all when I came in, & could swear I was there on the Victory— So the charm worked in that case.[20] Then it was raining a little, but I went into the Park, which is all prominence & radiating paths; then back on top of a bus, & so to tea. Molly [McCarthy] came, a warm faithful bear, of whom I am really fond, judging from the steady accumulation of my desire to see her these last 3 or 4 weeks, culminating in my asking her to come, as I so rarely ask anyone to come. Saxon came, with his great grandfather's diary, which it pleases him I should like, & call like him;[21] & then reading & bed. I think my rose leaf is now uncrumpled. Certainly I shall remember

19. A concert performance of Rimsky Korsakov's opera *The Legend of the Invisible City of Kitezh* was to be given at the Royal Opera House, Covent Garden, on 30 March.
20. The relics of Sir John Franklin's ill-fated 1845 expedition to discover the North-West passage were displayed in the Naval Museum, at that time housed in King Charles' Block of the Royal Naval College (formerly hospital); the Nelson relics were exhibited in the Painted Hall. Since 1934 they have been assembled in the National Maritime Museum in the Queen's House, Greenwich.
21. Saxon had an idea that a book might be made of his great-grandfather Sharon Turner's diary, and be published by the Hogarth Press; but it never was.

the ships coming up (here Tomlin rings,[22] but I won't see him—solitude is my bride, & she is adulterated by Clive & Mary tonight) & Nelson's coat long after I have forgotten how silly & uncomfortable I was at Nessa's on Friday.

Friday 9 April

Life has been very good to the Leafs.[1] I should say it has been perfect. Why then all this pother about life? It can produce old Walter, bubbling & chubby; & old Lotta, stately & content; & little Kitty, as good & nice as can be; & handsome Charles, as loving & affectionate. Plunge deep into Walter's life & it is all sound & satisfactory. His son kisses him & says "Bless you father". He sinks back chuckling on his cushions. He chooses a maccaroon. He tells a story. Lotta purrs[?], in her black velvet dress. Only I am exiled from this profound natural happiness. That is what I always feel; or often feel now—natural happiness is what I lack, in profusion. I have intense happiness—not that. It is therefore what I most envy; geniality & family love & being on the rails of human life. Indeed, exaggeration apart, this is a very satisfactory form of existence. And it exists for thousands of people all the time. Why have we none of us got it, in that measure? Old & young agreeing to live together: & being normal; & clever enough of course; yet not stinted or self-conscious in emotion. Much of this may be the generalised & harmonious view which one gets of unknown people as a whole. I might not think it if I saw more of them. Writers do not live like that perhaps. But it is useless frittering away the impression which is so strong. Also I keep thinking "They pity me. They wonder what I find in life." Then I sink a little silent, & rouse myself to talk to Kitty. Also I know that nothing Leonard or I have done—not our books or the Press or anything means anything to Lotta & Walter & Charles & very little to Kitty. Charles has his

22. Stephen Tomlin (1901-1937), youngest son of a High Court judge, had abandoned study of the law to become a sculptor. He had become close friends with many of the younger adherents of 'Bloomsbury'. VW met him in 1924 when she recorded: 'Theres a little thrush like creature called Tomlin who wants to sculpt me.' (*II VW Diary*, 21 December 1924.)

1. The Woolfs had been to tea with the Leafs at Sussex Place, Regent's Park. Walter Leaf (1852-1927), Homeric scholar, Chairman since 1919 of the London & Westminster Bank, and President of the International Chamber of Commerce; he had married in 1894 Charlotte Mary (1867-1937), second daughter of John Addington Symonds and sister of Madge Vaughan (the wife of VW's cousin W. W. Vaughan) who had died the previous November. Their children were Charles (b. 1896), and Katherine (Kitty) (b. 1900), who was at Newnham College, Cambridge, from 1920-23.

motor at the door. They are perfectly happy, motoring off to Berk-hamstead, which will take an hour, so they are among the lanes even now. A spring night & so on.

Sunday 11 April

Cannot read Mrs Webb because at any moment S. Tomlin may ring the bell. Also I wanted to go on about the Leafs. I have almost forgotten the impression they made on me. I have wrapped myself round in my own personality again. How does it come about—these sudden intense changes of view? Perhaps my life, writing imagining, is unusually conscious: very vivid to me: & then, going to tea with the Leafs destroys it more completely than other people's lives because my life is saying to itself "This is life—the only life". But when I enter a complete world of its own; where Walter cracks a joke, I realise that this is existing whether I exist or not; & so get bowled over. Violent as they are, these impressions go quickly; leaving a sediment of ideas which I shall discuss with L. perhaps when we go to Iwerne Minster. About natural happiness: how it is destroyed by our way of life.

Mrs Webb's Life makes me compare it with mine. The difference is that she is trying to relate all her experiences to history. She is very rational & coherent. She has always thought about her life & the meaning of the world: indeed, she begins this at the age of 4. She has studied herself as a phenomenon. Thus her autobiography is part of the history of the 19th Century. She is the product of science, & the lack of faith in God; she was secreted by the Time Spirit. Anyhow she believes this to be so; & makes herself fit in very persuasively & to my mind very interestingly. She taps a great stream of thought. Unlike that self-conscious poseur Walter Raleigh she is much more interested in facts & truth than in what will shock people & what a professor ought not to say.[2] Tomlin does not seem to be coming, & L. is at Staines, so I will try a little reading.[3]

2. See in particular Chapter III of Beatrice Webb's *My Apprenticeship*: 'The Choice of a Craft: the Religion of Humanity.' VW was also reading *The Letters of Sir Walter Raleigh, 1879-1922*, edited by Lady Raleigh (2 vols., 1926); her withering review appeared under the title 'A Professor of Life' in the early May number of *Vogue*; it was reprinted in *A Captain's Deathbed* (Kp C273). Walter Raleigh (1861-1922), knighted in 1911, had been successively Professor of English Literature at Liverpool, Glasgow, and Oxford Universities.

3. LW, in one of his regular filial observances, launched with his mother at his brother Harold's home near Staines, and drove with her to his brother Herbert's at Cookham.

On Tuesday 13 April the Woolfs went by train to Blandford in Dorset, and motored out to the Talbot Inn at Iwerne Minster, where they stayed five nights; for the return journey on the 18th they went by bus to Bournemouth and took the train from there back to Waterloo.

Sunday 18 April

⟨This is written⟩

This is not written very seriously.—obviously not—to try a pen, I think. And it is now [*Friday*] *April 30th*, the last of a wet windy month, excepting the sudden opening of all the doors at Easter, & the summer displayed blazing, as it always is, I suppose; only cloud hidden. I have not said anything about Iwerne Minster. Now it would amuse me to see what I remember it by. Cranbourne Chase: the stunted aboriginal forest trees, scattered, not grouped in cultivations; anemones, bluebells, violets, all pale, sprinkled about, without colour, livid, for the sun hardly shone. Then Blackmore Vale; a vast air dome & the fields dropped to the bottom; the sun striking, there, there; a drench of rain falling, like a veil streaming from the sky, there & there; & the downs rising, very strongly scarped (if that is the word) so that they were ridged & ledged; then an inscription in a church "sought peace & ensured it", & the question, who wrote these sonorous stylistic epitaphs?—& all the cleanliness of Iwerne village, its happiness & well being, making me ask, as we tended to sneer. Still this is the right method, surely; & then tea & cream—these I remember: the hot baths; my new leather coat; Shaftesbury, so much lower & less commanding than my imagination, & the drive to Bournemouth, & the dog & the lady behind the rock, & the view of Swanage, & coming home.

And then it was horror: Nelly; faced her going; was firm yet desolate; on Tuesday she stopped me on the landing said "Please ma'am may I apologise?" & this time we had been so resolute & implicitly believed her that I had written 6 letters. No cooks however came; & I had enough look into the 'servant question' to be glad to be safe again with Nelly. Now I vow come what may, never never to believe her again. "I am too fond of you ever to be happy with anyone else" she said. Talking of compliments, this is perhaps the greatest I could have. But my mind is wandering. It is a question of clothes. This is what humiliates me— talking of compliments—to walk in Regent St, Bond Str &c: & be notably less well dressed than other people.

Yesterday I finished the first part of To the Lighthouse, & today began the second. I cannot make it out—here is the most difficult abstract piece of writing—I have to give an empty house, no people's characters, the passage of time, all eyeless & featureless with nothing to cling to: well, I rush at it, & at once scatter out two pages. Is it nonsense, is it brilliance? Why am I so flown with words, & apparently free to do exactly what I like? When I read a bit it seems spirited too; needs compressing, but not much else. Compare this dashing fluency with the excruciating hard wrung battles I had with Mrs Dalloway (save the end). This is not made up: it is the literal fact. Yes, & I am rather famous. For the rest, we dally about the Nation. Maynard, dressed in a light overcoat, is back; hums & haws about standing for the Provost of King's.[4] We tell him Lydia would like it. He says it means middle age & respectability. I feel some sympathy for him. This is because he is going grey, I tell Clive. Clive's back; Nessa departing,[5] & I worrying about my clothes, & how Roger last night upset me by saying that Nessa finds fault with my temper behind my back. Then (at Ralph's new left handed establishment[6]) Inez, rather like Vivien [Eliot] to look at, searches into my eyes with her greenish pink-rimmed ones, & says, I must tell you two things: then she tells me that she admires me. That swallowed (doubtfully) she says, Did you ever have an affair with Oliver?[7] The connection is this: she disliked me, from jealousy. I protest I never kissed him, & he never looked at me. She refuses to believe. So she has been refusing to believe for years— A queer little interview, stage managed by Oliver* & she: at last brought off. I called in Leonard, & I think convinced her.

* Oliver denied all knowledge of this; & said she invented it in order to have an excuse for an intimate conversation. "So many women are like that" said Rose Macaulay sitting spruce lean, like a mummified cat, in her chair (this is written Aug. 12th)

4. The Provostship of King's College was vacant because of the death on 7 April of Sir Walter Durnford; in the event the Rev. A. E. Brooke, Ely Professor of Divinity, was elected to succeed him.
5. Clive was back from Paris; Vanessa was about to go, with Duncan Grant and Angus Davidson, to Venice.
6. This was at 41 Gordon Square, where Ralph Partridge now lived during the week with Frances Marshall, returning each weekend to Ham Spray, his country home with his wife Carrington and Lytton Strachey. Frances Catherine Marshall (b. 1900), educated at Bedales and Newnham, worked in Birrell and Garnett's bookshop (David Garnett was her brother-in-law); she and Ralph Partridge were married after Carrington's death in 1932.
7. Inez Jenkins, née Ferguson (b. 1895), had had an affair with Oliver Strachey at the end of the war; she married in 1923. From 1919-29 she was General Secretary of the National Federation of Women's Institutes.

Wednesday 5 May

An exact diary of the Strike would be interesting.[1] For instance, it is now a ¼ to 2: there is a brown fog; nobody is building; it is drizzling. The first thing in the morning we stand at the window & watch the traffic in Southampton Row. This is incessant. Everyone is bicycling; motor cars are huddled up with extra people. There are no buses. No placards. no newspapers. The men are at work in the road; water, gas & electricity are allowed; but at 11 the light was turned off. I sat in the press in the brown fog, while L. wrote an article for the Herald. A very revolutionary looking young man on a cycle arrived with the British Gazette. L. is to answer an article in this.[2] All was military stern a little secret. Then Clive dropped in, the door being left open. He is offering himself to the Government. Maynard excited, wants the H[ogarth]. P[ress]. to bring out a skeleton number of the Nation.[3] It is all tedious & depressing, rather like waiting in a train outside a station. Rumours are passed round—that the gas wd. be cut off at 1—false of course. One does not know what to do. And nature has laid it on thick today—fog, rain, cold. A voice, rather commonplace & official, yet the only common voice left, wishes us good morning at 10. This is the voice of Britain, to wh. we can make no reply. The voice is very trivial, & only tells us that the Prince of Wales is coming back (*from Biarritz*), that the London streets present an unprecedented spectacle.

Thursday 6 May

(one of the curious effects of the Strike is that it is difficult to remember the day of the week). Everything is the same, but unreasonably, or

1. The General Strike was proclaimed by the Trades Union Congress on the evening of 2 May 1926 in support of the mineworkers who had struck on 1 May. Their dispute dated back to the summer of 1925. The coal strike that had seemed imminent then had been effectively postponed by a nine month government subsidy. This ran out on 30 April 1926. But any real hope of averting the coal strike had foundered with the rejection by both miners and coalowners of the Samuel Commission's recommendations published in March this year.
2. The *British Gazette* was the government-founded newspaper run for the duration of the strike under the management of Winston Churchill; no article by LW appeared at this period in the *Daily Herald*, which was published, in the same format and with identical contents, on eight occasions between 5 and 17 May.
3. The *N & A* was not published again until 15 May; but a special strike issue, consisting of a 'symposium of views' by Keynes, Gilbert Murray, Ramsay Muir, W. T. Layton and E. D. Simon, had been prepared for publication, but did not appear, the previous week. See *N & A* 15 May; also *III VW Letters*, no. 1635.

because of the weather, or habit, we are more cheerful, take less notice, & occasionally think of other things. The taxis are out today. There are various skeleton papers being sold. One believes nothing. Clive dines in Mayfair, & everyone is pro-men; I go to Harrison [*dentist*], & he shouts me down with "Its red rag versus Union Jack, Mrs Woolf" & how Thomas has 100,000.[4] Frankie dines out, & finds everyone pro-Government. Bob [Trevelyan] drops in & says Churchill is for peace, but Baldwin wont budge.[5] Clive says Churchill is for tear gas bombs, fight to the death, & is at the bottom of it all. So we go on, turning in our cage. I notice how frequently we break of[f] with "Well I don't know." According to L. this open state of mind is due to the lack of papers. It feels like a deadlock, on both sides; as if we could keep fixed like this for weeks. What one prays for is God: the King or God; some impartial person to say kiss & be friends—as apparently we all desire.

Just back from a walk to the Strand. Of course one notices lorries full of elderly men & girls standing like passengers in the old 3rd class carriages. Children swarm. They pick up bits of old wood paving. Everything seems to be going fast, away, in business[?]. The shops are open but empty. Over it all is some odd pale unnatural atmosphere— great activity but no normal life. I think we shall become more independent & stoical as the days go on. And I am involved in dress buying with Todd [*editor of* Vogue]; I tremble & shiver all over at the appalling magnitude of the task I have undertaken—to go to a dressmaker recommended by Todd, even, she suggested, but here my blood ran cold, with Todd. Perhaps this excites me more feverishly than the Strike. It is a little like the early hours of the morning (this state of things) when one has been up all night. Business improved today. We sold a few books. Bob cycled from Leith Hill, getting up at 5 a.m. to avoid the crowd. He punctured an hour later, met his tailor who mended him, set forth again, was almost crushed in the crowd near London, & has since been tramping London, from Chelsea to Bloomsbury to gather gossip, & talk, incoherently about Desmond's essays & his own poetry. He has secreted two more of these works which 'ought to be published'. He is ravenous greedy, & apelike, but has a kind of russet surly charm; like a dog one teases. He complained how Logan teased him. Clive calls in to discuss bulletins—indeed, more than anything it is like a house

4. James Henry Thomas (1874-1949), General Secretary of the National Union of Railwaymen 1918-24, 1925-31, had been Colonial Secretary in the Labour Government of 1924. He had directed and negotiated the settlement of a rail strike in 1919.
5. Stanley Baldwin (1867-1947) was Prime Minister in the current Conservative administration; Winston Churchill (1874-1965) his Chancellor of the Exchequer.

where someone is dangerously ill; & friends drop in to enquire, & one has to wait for doctor's news—Quennel, the poet, came; a lean boy, nervous, plaintive, rather pretty; on the look out for work, & come to tap the Wolves—who are said, I suppose to be an authority on that subject. We suggested Desmond's job.[6] After an hour of this, he left, —— here Clive came in & interrupted. He has been shopping in the West End with Mary. Nothing to report there. He & L. listened in at 7 & heard nothing. The look of the streets—how people "trek to work" that is the stock phrase: that it will be cold & windy tomorrow (it is shivering cold today) that there was a warm debate in the Commons—

Among the crowd of trampers in Kingsway were old Pritchard, toothless, old wispy, benevolent; who tapped L. on the shoulder & said he was "training to shoot him"; & old Miss Pritchard, equally frail, dusty, rosy, shabby. "How long will it last Mrs Woolf?" "Four weeks" "Ah dear!" Off they tramp, over the bridge to Kennington I think; next in Kingsway comes the old battered clerk, who has 5 miles to walk. Miss Talbot has an hours walk; Mrs Brown 2 hours walk.[7] But they all arrive, & clatter about as usual—Pritchard doing poor peoples work for nothing, as I imagine his way is, & calling himself a Tory.

Then we are fighting the Square on the question of leading dogs. Dogs must be led; but tennis can be played they say. L. is advancing to the fight, & has enlisted the Pekinese in the Square. We get no news from abroad; neither can send it. No parcels. Pence have been added to milk, vegetables &c. And Karin has bought 4 joints.

It is now a chilly lightish evening; very quiet; the only sound a distant barrel organ playing. The bricks stand piled on the building & there remain. And Viola was about to make our fortune. She dined here, Monday night, the night of the strike.[8]

6. Peter Quennell (b. 1905), who had had a precocious success as a schoolboy poet and became a protégé of Eddie Marsh and the Sitwells, had been rusticated from Balliol (to which he did not return) the previous October. LW had met him with the Sitwells; he did find reviewing work from Desmond MacCarthy on the *New Statesman*.

7. William Burchell Pritchard (d. 1940), admitted 1876, was the senior partner in the firm of solicitors, Dollman & Pritchard, which occupied the ground and first floors of 52 Tavistock Square; 'old Miss Pritchard' was his sister who acted as chief clerk. Rose Talbot (later Mrs Shrager) and Mrs Brown were clerks in the office.

8. Viola Tree (1884-1939), eldest daughter of the great actor-manager Sir Herbert Beerbohm Tree, was a performer in her own right. The expected success of her memoirs, *Castles in the Air. The Story of my Singing Days*, published by the Hogarth Press in April 1926 (*HP Checklist* 111), had miscarried owing to the general strike.

MAY 1926

Friday 7 May

No change. "London calling the British Isles. Good morning everyone". That is how it begins at 10. The only news that the archbishops are conferring, & ask our prayers that they may be guided right. Whether this means action, we know not. We know nothing. Mrs Cartwright walked from Hampstead. She & L. got heated arguing, she being anti-labour; because she does not see why they should be supported, & observes men in the street loafing instead of working. Very little work done by either of us today. A cold, wet day, with sunny moments. All arrangements unchanged. Girl came to make chair covers, having walked from Shoreditch, but enjoyed it. Times sent for 25 Violas.[9] Question whether to bring out a skeleton Roneo Nation. Leonard went to the office, I to the Brit[ish] Mus[eum]; where all was chill serenity, dignity & severity. Written up are the names of great men; & we all cower like mice nibbling crumbs in our most official discreet impersonal mood beneath. I like this dusty bookish atmosphere. Most of the readers seemed to have rubbed their noses off & written their eyes out. Yet they have a life they like—believe in the necessity of making books, I suppose: verify, collate, make up other books, for ever. It must be 15 years since I read here. I came home & found L. & Hubert [Henderson] arriving from the office—Hubert did what is now called "taking a cup of tea", which means an hour & a halfs talk about the Strike. Here is his prediction: if it is not settled, or in process, on Monday, it will last 5 weeks. Today no wages are paid. Leonard said he minded this more than the war & Hubert told us how he had travelled in Germany, & what brutes they were in 1912.[10] He thinks gas & electricity will go next; had been at a journalists meeting where all were against labour (against the general strike that is) & assumed Government victory. L. says if the state wins & smashes T[rades]. U[nion]s he will devote his life to labour: if the archbishop succeeds, he will be baptised. Now to dine at the Commercio to meet Clive.

Sunday 9 May

There is no news of the strike. The broadcaster has just said that we are praying today. And L. & I quarrelled last night. I dislike the tub

9. i.e. The Times Book Club, of 42 Wigmore Street, W1, a leading circulating library.
10. Troops had been used to maintain order during a brief but bitter coal strike in the Ruhr in March 1912. Over 1500 charges were preferred against individual strikers and a high proportion of these led to prison sentences. Reaction hardened and throughout the remainder of the year the German authorities set their face against the so-called 'red and gold international' of socialists and Jews and pursued policies hostile to organised labour and in particular to the right to picket.

thumper in him; he the irrational Xtian in me. I will write it all out later—my feelings about the Strike; but I am now writing to test my theory that there is consolation in expression. Unthinkingly, I refused just now to lunch with the Phil Bakers, who fetched L. in their car. Suddenly, 10 minutes ago, I began to regret this profoundly. How I should love the talk, & seeing the house, & battling my wits against theirs. Now the sensible thing to do is to provide some pleasure to balance this, which I cd. not have had, if I had gone. I can only think of writing this, & going round the Square. Obscurely, I have my clothes complex to deal with. When I am asked out my first thought is, but I have no clothes to go in. Todd has never sent me the address of the shop; & I may have annoyed her by refusing to lunch with her. But the Virginia who refuses is a very instinctive & therefore powerful person. The reflective & sociable only comes to the surface later. Then the conflict.

Baldwin broadcast last night: he rolls his rs; tries to put more than mortal strength into his words. "Have faith in me. You elected me 18 months ago. What have I done to forfeit your confidence? Can you not trust me to see justice done between man & man?" Impressive as it is to hear the very voice of the Prime Minister, descendant of Pitt & Chatham, still I can't heat up my reverence to the right pitch. I picture the stalwart oppressed man, bearing the world on his shoulders. And suddenly his self assertiveness becomes a little ridiculous. He becomes megalomaniac. No I dont trust him: I don't trust any human being, however loud they bellow & roll their rs.

Monday 10 May

Quarrel with L. settled in studio. Oh, but how incessant the arguments & interruptions are! As I write, L. is telephoning to Hubert. We are getting up a petition.[11] There was a distinct thaw (we thought) last night. The Arch B. & Grey both conciliatory.[12] So we went to bed happy. Today ostensibly the same dead lock; beneath the surface all sorts of

11. The petition called upon the government to 'restart negotiations immediately on the lines suggested by the Archbishop of Canterbury . . .' LW had undertaken to organise the collection of signatures of writers and artists, in which task he was helped by a company of active young people, with bicycles. See *IV LW*, 217-18.
12. The Most Rev. Randall Thomas Davidson (1848-1930), Archbishop of Canterbury 1903-28; his sermon on Sunday 9 May at St Martin in the Fields, preached on a text from *Ephesians* iv 1: 'Walk worthy of the vocation wherewith ye are called', was broadcast. Viscount Grey of Fallodon (1862-1933), now an Elder Statesman of the Liberal Party, also broadcast on Sunday evening, appealing to the public to help the Government so that wage negotiations might be conducted freely and not under duress.

currents, of which we get the most contradictory reports. Dear old Frankie has a story (over the fire in the bookshop) of an interview between Asquith & Reading which turned Reading hostile to the men. Later, through Clive, through Desmond, Asquith is proved to be at the Wharfe, 60 miles from Lord Reading.[13] Lady Wimbore gave a party—brought Thomas & Baldwin together.[14] Meeting mysteriously called off today. Otherwise strike wd. have been settled. I to H of Commons this morning with L.'s article to serve as stuffing for Hugh Dalton in the Commons this afternoon.[15] All this humbug of police & marble statues vaguely displeasing. But the Gvt. provided me with buses both ways, & no stones thrown. Silver & crimson guard at Whitehall; the cenotaph, & men bare heading themselves. Home to find Tom Marshall caballing with L.; after lunch to [Birrell & Garnett's] bookshop, where the gossip (too secret for the telephone) was imparted; to London Library where Gooch—a tall, pale mule, affable & long winded, was seen, & Molly dustily diligently reading the Dublin Review for 1840,[16] walk home; Clive, to refute gossip; James to get St Loe to sign;[17] then Maynard ringing up to command us to print the Nation as the N. Statesman is printed; to wh. I agreed, & L. disagreed; then dinner; a motor car collision—more telephones ringing at the moment 9.5.

13. Asquith (Lord Oxford), still leader of the Liberal Party, had a house, The Wharf, on the Thames at Sutton Courtney near Oxford. Rufus Isaacs (1860-1935), 1st Viscount (and newly created 1st Marquis) Reading, had only just returned from India, where he was Viceroy 1921-26.

14. Lady Wimborne, née the Hon. Alice Grosvenor (1880-1948), was the wife of the wealthy Ivor Churchill Guest, 1st Viscount Wimborne; for an extended account of her part in the behind-the-scenes negotiations, see Chapter 3 'The General Strike' of Osbert Sitwell's *Laughter in the Next Room*, 1949.

15. Hugh Dalton (1887-1962), educated at Eton and King's College, Cambridge, Reader in Economics at London University and Labour MP for Camberwell. Dalton may or may not have received his 'stuffing' in time but either way his only utterance before the House of Commons on 10 May was: 'A statement by the head of the Established Church.' This exclamation he directed at Winston Churchill who was attempting to explain why the views of the Archbishop of Canterbury and other leading churchmen on how to settle the Strike had not been reported in the government-run *British Gazette*.

16. George Peabody Gooch (1873-1968), the eminent historian, was from 1911-60 editor of the *Contemporary Review*, to which LW had been a regular contributor in 1920-22. Molly MacCarthy was researching for her collection of biographical sketches, *Fighting Fitzgerald and other Papers*, published in 1930, in the *Dublin Magazine*.

17. (John) St. Loe Strachey (1860-1927), a first cousin of James and Lytton from the senior branch of the Strachey family, had been the influential proprietor and editor of the Unionist weekly *The Spectator* from 1898 until December 1925.

Tuesday 11 May

I may as well continue to write—this book is used to scandalous mistreatment—while I wait—here interruptions began which lasted till the present moment/ when I write from 12.30 to 3 with Gerald Brenan in the study composing with infinite difficulty a letter to Mr Galsworthy.[18] Arguing about the Ar[chbisho]p of Canterbury with Jack Squire at 12 seems now normal, but not—how often do I repeat—nearly as exciting as writing To the Lighthouse or about de Q[uincey].[19] I believe it is false psychology to think that in after years these details willl be interesting. The war is now barren sand after all. But one never knows: & waiting about, writing serves to liberate the mind from the fret & itch of these innumerable details. Squire doesn't want to "knuckle under". To kneel is the duty of the Church. The Church has no connection with the nation. Events are that the Roneo workers refuse to set up L.'s article in the Nation, in which he says that the Strike is not illegal or unconstitutional. Presumably this is a little clutch of the Government throttle. Mr Baldwin has been visiting the Zoo.[20] In the middle of lunch admirable Miss Bulley arrives, having visited Conway unsuccessfully.[21] St Loe has joined. So Rose Macaulay & Lytton. Tonight the names are to be handed in; & then perhaps silence will descend upon us. Ralph & Gerald are our emissaries. But

18. According to *IV LW*, p. 218, John Galsworthy, the renowned author of *The Forsyte Saga*, was the only person approached who refused to sign the petition; however the editor of the *Observer*, J. L. Garvin, was certainly another (see LWP, Sussex).

19. VW's article on de Quincey, 'Impassioned Prose', was to appear in the *TLS* on 16 September 1926 (Kp C275).

20. It had been stated in the House of Commons on 6 May by Sir John Simon, Liberal MP and one-time Attorney-General, that the resolution of the General Council of the TUC to call a general strike was unlawful. The special Strike Issue of the *N & A* which had been prepared for publication this week was in any event scrapped since the strike ended; it appeared in a very truncated form dated 15 May.

    Although Regent's Park had been taken over by the authorities and closed, the Zoological Gardens were open, and were visited by the Prime Minister on Sunday afternoon.

21. Margaret H. Bulley, from a Northern Quaker family, rented the house at 19 Taviton Street, Bloomsbury, which had housed Birrell and Garnett's bookshop and several other congenial tenants. Much influenced by Roger Fry, she wrote several books on art, including *Art and Counterfeit* (1925). She was shortly to marry her cousin G. W. Armitage. Sir Martin Conway (1856-1937), raised to the Peerage by Ramsay MacDonald in 1931 as Lord Conway of Allington, mountaineer, art historian and collector, was Conservative MP for the Combined Universities, the seat which LW had unsuccessfully contested in 1922 (See *IV LW*, 46).

then everyone rings up—the most unlikely people—[Donald] Brace for instance, Kahan;[22] the woman comes with the new sofa cover. Yesterday Ralph & Frances Marshall were in a railway accident. She had her teeth jangled. One man was killed; another had his leg broken—the result of driving a train without signals, by the efforts of ardent optimistic undergraduates.[23] Billing has been in to say he will print anything, all his men being back & needing work. So, as poor MacDermott has been dead since January, perhaps the Nation will be done by them.[24] Come to think of it, almost all our type is standing, so our printing was in any case hardly feasible. Must I now ring up James? Day's Library boy was set upon by roughs, had his cycle overturned, but kept his books & was unhurt after calling here for 6 Tree. Tree dribbles along. There is an occasional order. Mrs C[artwright]. arrives on Faith's bicycle which is red with rust.[25]

Wednesday 12 May

Strike settled. (ring at bell)
The Strike was settled about 1.15—or it was then broadcast. I was in Tottenham Court Rd. at 1 & heard Bartholomew & Fletcher's megaphone declaim that the T.U.C. leaders were at Downing Street;[26] came home to find that neither L. or Nelly had heard this: 5 minutes later, the wireless. They told us to stand by & await important news. Then a piano played a tune. Then the solemn broadcaster assuming incredible pomp & gloom

22. Richard Ferdinand Kahn (b. 1905), Scholar, and in 1930 to be elected Fellow, of King's College, Cambridge, was at this period still an undergraduate; a member of the Political Economy Club which met weekly in Maynard Keynes's rooms in King's, he turned to the formal study of economics after graduating in Mathematics and Natural Sciences in 1927.
23. On the afternoon of 10 May a goods train had crashed into the rear of a stationary Cambridge-London passenger train at Bishop's Stortford, derailing two coaches; one man was killed, and another suffered a broken leg.
24. Billing & Sons Ltd were the printers of Philip Noel-Baker's *Disarmament* (*HP Checklist* 106), published in April 1926. F. J. McDermott, of the Prompt Press, Richmond, had advised and helped the Woolfs when they first embarked on their Hogarth Press venture, and had printed *Monday or Tuesday* for them in 1921—so badly that they had not employed him again.
25. Day's was the fashionable Mayfair circulating library to which VW had subscribed in 1915. Mrs Cartwright's vehicle was borrowed from Faith Henderson, *née* Bagenal (b. 1889), wife of the editor of the *N & A*, who like her lived in Hampstead.
26. Bartholomew & Fletcher was a firm of upholsterers, cabinet makers and decorators at 217-18 Tottenham Court Road. The General Council of the TUC decided on 12 May to terminate the general strike and resume negotiations with the Government; but directed affiliated unions to issue instructions to their own members.

& speaking one word to the minute read out: Message from 10 Downing Street. The T.U.C. leaders have agreed that Strike shall be withdrawn. Instantly L. dashed off to telephone to the office, Nelly to tell Pritchard's clerk, & I to Mrs C. (But N[elly]. was beforehand) then we finished lunch; then I rang up Clive—who proposes that we should have a drink tonight. I saw this morning 5 or 6 armoured cars slowly going along Oxford Street; on each two soldiers sat in tin helmets, & one stood with his hand at the gun which was pointed straight ahead ready to fire. But I also noticed on one a policeman smoking a cigarette. Such sights I dare say I shall never see again; & dont in the least wish to. Already (it is now 10 past 2) men have appeared at the hotel with drainpipes. Also Grizzle has won her case against the Square.

Thursday 13 May

I suppose all pages devoted to the Strike will be skipped, when I read over this book. Oh that dull old chapter, I shall say. Excitements about what are called real things are always unutterably transitory. Yet it is gloomy—& L. is gloomy, & so am I unintelligibly—today because the Strike continues—no railwaymen back: vindictiveness has now seized our masters. Government shillyshallies. Apparently, the T.U.C. agreed to terms wh. the miners now reject. Anyhow it will take a week to get the machinery of England to run again. Trains are dotted about all over England. Labour, it seems clear, will be effectively diddled again, & perhaps rid of its power to make strikes in future. Printers still out at the Nation. In short, the strain removed, we all fall out & bicker & backbite.[27] Such is human nature—& really I dont like human nature unless all candied over with art. We dined with a strike party last night & went back to Clive's. A good deal was said about art there. Good dull Janet Vaughan, reminding me of Emma, joined us.[28] I went to my

27. There had been no general resumption of work following the TUC General Council's decision to terminate the strike. The Cabinet declined to resume negotiations over miner's pay until all strikers had returned to work; the miners refused to be represented at discussions with the government; the TUC issued a memorandum saying that it no longer stood behind the miners; the miners repudiated the memorandum. The railway unions decided to continue to strike until satisfactory assurances as to re-instatement had been given by their employers; the railway companies considered that their employees had broken agreements and fresh ones must therefore be entered into. And so on.

28. Janet Maria Vaughan (b. 1899), daughter of VW's cousin W. W. Vaughan and his wife Madge (née Symonds); she was finishing her medical studies, and had been active in collecting signatures for the petition. Emma (1874-1960) was Janet's aunt, the youngest of VW's Vaughan cousins.

dressmaker, Miss Brooke, & found it the most quiet & friendly & even enjoyable of proceedings. I have a great lust for lovely stuffs, & shapes; wh. I have not gratified since Sally Young died.[29] A bold move this, but now I'm free of the fret of clothes, which is worth paying for, & need not parade Oxford Street.

Thursday 20 May

Waiting for L. to come back from chess with Roger: 11.25. I think nothing need be said of the Strike. As tends to happen, one's mind slips after the crisis, & what the settlement is, or will be, I know not.

We must now fan the books up again. Viola & Phil Baker were both struck on the wing. Viola comes, very tactfully, as a friend, she says, to consult after dinner. She is a flamboyant creature—much of an actress— much abused by the Waleys & Marjories; but rather taking to me. She has the great egotism, the magnification of self, which any bodily display, I think, produces. She values women by their hips & ankles, like horses. Easily reverts to the topic of her own charms: how she shd. have married the D. of Rutland. "Lord —— (his uncle) told me I was the woman John really loved. The duchess said to me 'Do make love to John & get him away from ——. At any rate you're tall & beautiful—' And I sometimes think if I'd married him—but he never asked me—Daddy wouldn't have died. I'd have prevented that operation: Then how he'd have loved a duke for a son in law! All his life was dressing up—that sort of thing you know."[30] So she runs on, in the best of clothes, easy & familiar, but reserved too; with the wiles & warinesses of a woman of the world, half sordid half splendid, not quite at her ease with us, yet glad of a room where she can tell her stories, of listeners to whom she is new & strange. She will run on by the hour—yet is very watchful not to bore; a good business woman, & floating over considerable acuteness on her charm. All this however, is not making her book move, as they say.

Eddy came in to tea. I like him—his flattery? his nobility? I dont know—I find him easy & eager. And Vita comes to lunch tomorrow, which will be a great amusement & pleasure. I am amused at my relations

---

29. Mrs Young made the rather grander dresses for VW and her sisters when they were Kensington young ladies.

30. John Henry Montagu Manners (1886-1940), who succeeded his father as 9th Duke of Rutland in 1925, married Kathleen Tennant in 1916; Viola Tree had married Alan Parsons, a civil servant, in 1912. Her daddy, Sir Herbert Beerbohm Tree, died unexpectedly after an operation on a ruptured tendon in his leg, on 2 July 1917, aged sixty-three.

with her: left so ardent in January—& now what? Also I like her presence
& her beauty. Am I in love with her? But what is love? Her being 'in
love' (it must be comma'd thus) with me, excites & flatters; & interests.
What is this 'love'? Oh & then she gratifies my eternal curiosity: who's
she seen, whats she done—for I have no enormous opinion of her poetry.
How could I—I who have such delight in mitigating the works even of
my greatest friends. I should have been reading her poem tonight:[31]
instead finished Sharon Turner—a prosy, simple, old man; the very spit
& image of Saxon. a boundless bore, I daresay, with the most intense zeal
for "improving myself", & the holiest affections, & 13 children, & no
character or impetus—a love of long walks, of music; modest, yet
conceited in an ant like way. I mean he has the industry & persistency in
recounting compliments of an ant, but so little character that one hardly
calls him vain!

Tuesday 25 May

The heat has come, bringing with it the inexplicably disagreeable
memories of parties, & George Duckworth; a fear haunts me even now,
as I drive past Park Lane on top of a bus, & think of Lady Arthur Russell
& so on.[32] I become out of love with everything; but fall into love as the
bus reaches Holborn. A curious transition that, from tyranny to freedom.
Mixed with it is the usual "I thought that when you died last May,
Charles, there had died along with you"—death being hidden among
the leaves: & Nessa's birthday among the little hard pink rosettes of the
may, which we used to stop & smell on the pavement at the top of
Hyde Pk. Gate & I asked why, if it was may, it did not come out on
the 1st; it comes out now, & Nessa's birthday, which must be her 47th,
is in a few days. She is in Italy: Duncan is said to have "committed a
nuisance" for which he has been fined 10 lira.

31. V. Sackville-West, who had returned from Persia on 16 May, had finished but had
    not yet published her long poem *The Land* on which she had been working since
    1923.
32. George Herbert Duckworth (1868-1934), the elder of VW's half-brothers, had
    entertained social ambitions for her and Vanessa. Lady Arthur Russell (d. 1910),
    a sister-in-law of their mother's cousin Adeline, Duchess of Bedford, was a
    hostess of considerable consequence in his eyes—and he was briefly engaged to
    her daughter Flora (see *I QB*, pp 81-2); she lived at 2 Audley Square, just behind
    Park Lane. VW described her as 'a rude, tyrannical old woman, with a blood-
    stained complexion and the manners of a turkey cock.' (*Moments of Being* (1976),
    p. 149)

L. has been having Nelly's poisonous cold, brought by Lottie—Do I hear him? Grizzle says Yes: stands tail wagging—She is right. Vita has it; or I should be dining—

Now we have been sitting in the Square. L. is better. I am happier. Tomorrow we go to Rodmell—to find the bath & the W.C. & the drawing room with the wall pulled down. This cherry has been dangled & withdrawn so often that I scarcely believe we shall now munch it. And I must notice that the Strike still makes it necessary for me to find out trains at Victoria.

I have finished—sketchily I admit—the 2nd part of To the Lighthouse —& may, then, have it all written over by the end of July. A record— 7 months, if it so turns out.

So Vita came: & I register the shock of meeting after absence; how shy one is; how disillusioned by the actual body; how sensitive to new shades of tone—something 'womanly' I detected, more mature; & she was shabbier, come straight off in her travelling clothes; & not so beautiful, as sometimes perhaps; & so we sat talking on the sofa by the window, she rather silent, I chattering, partly to divert her attention from me; & to prevent her thinking "Well, is this all?" as she was bound to think, having declared herself so openly in writing. So that we each registered some disillusionment; & perhaps also acquired some grains of additional solidity— This may well be more lasting than the first rhapsody. But I compared her state, justly, to a flock of birds flying hither thither, escaped, confused: returning, after a long journey, to the middle of things again. She was quieter, shyer, awkwarder than usual even. She has no ready talk—confronted by Nelly or Mrs Cartwright she stands like a schoolgirl. I think it quite likely she will get Harold out of his job. But then, as I always feel, with her 'grand life', Dotties & so on, whom I don't know at all, there may be many parts of her perfectly unillumined.[33] But I cannot write. For the most part I can write. Suddenly the word instinct leaves me. This is the permanent state of most people no doubt. Maynard met George & Lady M[argaret]. at the Darwins. He is a humbug & she a fiend, he writes. She now walks with a stick.[34] What a dreary world it is—these bubbles meeting once in 20 years or so.

33. Dottie was Dorothy (d. 1956), wife of Lord Gerald Wellesley, from whom she was soon to separate (he succeeded his nephew as 7th Duke of Wellington in 1943). She was a very wealthy woman in her own right, a poet, and an intimate friend of Vita, who dedicated The Land to her. VW had met her once in July 1922 when she visited Knole with Vita.

34. George Duckworth had married Lady Margaret Herbert (1870-1958) in 1904; she was a daughter of the 4th Earl of Carnarvon.

Wednesday 9 June

Then I got the flue, last Saturday; sat shivering at Lords, in the hot sunshine; so have seen no one, except basement dwellers, & put off Don Giovanni, Dadie & Hope tonight, & Osbert [Sitwell]'s dinner tomorrow.[1] All my bubbling up faculty at once leaves me. I grind out a little of that eternal How to read, lecture, as the Yale Review has bought it,[2] & cannot conceive what The Lighthouse is all about. I hope to whip my brains up either at Vita's or Rodmell this weekend.

Yes, Rodmell is a perfect triumph, I consider—but L. advises me not to say so. In particular, our large combined drawing eating room, with its 5 windows, its beams down the middle, & flowers & leaves nodding in all round us. The bath boils quickly; the water closets gush & surge (not quite sufficiently though). The weather again failed us, & we had a queer journey home, via Newhaven, Peacehaven & Brighton. Trains slow & scarce. The Strike, I should say, continues. We then went to a party at Edith Sitwell's (I in my new dress) 'to meet Miss Stein', a lady much like Joan Fry, but more massive; in blue-sprinkled brocade, rather formidable.[3] There was Morgan, Siegfried [Sassoon], Todd—to whom I proposed, wildly, fantastically, a book—which she accepts![4]—(& Viola so much criticised in the austere heights of Ham Spray) & Edith distraught; & cherries in handfulls, & barley water—as L. described it very brilliantly to Sybil the next day. She came: no one else; we sat & laughed—& wheres the harm in this stupidish, kindly, rather amusing woman, I asked? Then she expressed a wish to dine with us. L. is lunching with Wells today.

1. LW and VW had been to watch England v. The Rest at Lord's on 5 June. *Don Giovanni*, conducted by Bruno Walter, was given at Covent Garden on 7 June. Hope Mirrlees (1887-1978), whose poem *Paris* the Woolfs had printed in 1920, had since published two novels and was about to publish a third.
2. This was a revised version of the lecture she had given on 30 January at Hayes Court; it was published in the *Yale Review* in October 1926 (Kp C277).
3. The party, on 1 June at Edith Sitwell's Bayswater flat, was given for the American experimental writer Gertrude Stein (1874-1946), who had lived in Paris since 1903; she had been invited to lecture to literary societies at Cambridge and Oxford. Her address, entitled *Composition as Explanation*, was published as a Hogarth Essay in November 1926 (*HP Checklist* 110). Joan Mary Fry (1862-1955), the second of Roger's six unmarried sisters, had kept house for him at Guildford until 1919; she was an active Quaker.
4. Nothing came of this proposal, which was that Todd should write her own life (see *III VW Letters*, no. 1644). Siegfried Sassoon (1886-1967), poet.

JUNE 1926

Wednesday 9 June

Leonard back from Wells who chattered till $\frac{1}{4}$ to 4: likes to walk through the streets; has a house in France kept for him by a very intelligent Brazilian lady.[5] Called me "too intelligent—a bad thing": can't criticise; brings in social theories, because he says in an age when society is dissolving, the social state is part of the character. They lunched at Boulesteins. Leonard asked for him at the Automobile Club; "A very famous name" said the man.[6] And the warmth & clamour of Wells' fame seems to reach me, this chilly rainy evening; & I see how, if I stayed there, as he asks us, he would overwhelm me. (We are very hungry, by the way; Nelly is preparing a nice roast chicken & ices for dinner, which I shall enjoy. Then we shall play the Gramophone). I'm cheering up after my attack I'm glad to say, though a little undecided whether to stay with Vita or go to Monks House.

L. is going to make a book of his essays. I think of asking Lady Horner to write her memoirs.[7] Today we discussed the date of Nelly's holiday— & so we go on.

Following VW's influenza or 'nerve exhaustion headache' (III VW Letters, no. 1646), the Woolfs went to Rodmell on Saturday 11 June; LW returned to London on Sunday afternoon leaving Vita Sackville-West, who had come to lunch, to stay with VW until Tuesday. The next two weeks were very sociable, and included a dinner party at the Hutchinsons to meet Aldous Huxley who had just been round the world, and a visit to Garsington, when she met Robert Bridges, on 26-27 June.

Wednesday 30 June

This is the last day of June & finds me in black despair because Clive laughed at my new hat, Vita pitied me, & I sank to the depths of gloom.

5. For the past eighteen months H. G. Wells (1866-1946) had rented a provençal *mas* near Grasse, where he was about to build one of his own. The lady with whom he shared it he described as Levantine, not Brazilian; she was Odette Keun (1888-1978), a writer and journalist of Italo-Dutch parentage born in Constantinople.
6. Boulestin was (and is) a French restaurant in Southampton Street off the Strand; the Royal Automobile Club was (and is) in Pall Mall.
7. LW's *Essays on Literature, History, Politics, etc*, the majority of which were based upon material first published in the *N & A* and the *New Statesman*, were published by the Hogarth Press in May 1927 (*HP Checklist* 153). Frances Horner, *née* Graham (1860-1940), who had been a friend to many of the pre-Raphaelites, did write her memoirs, *Time Remembered*, but they were published by Heinemann in 1933.

This happened at Clive's last night after going to the Sitwells with Vita. Oh dear I was wearing the hat without thinking whether it was good or bad; & it was all very flashing & easy; & there I saw a man with braided hair, another with long red tongues in his button hole; & sat by Vita & laughed & clubbed. When we got out it was only 10.30—a soft starry night: I had refused to go to Colefax: it was still too early for her to go. So she said "Shall we go to Clive's & pick him up?" & I was then again so lighthearted, driving through the park, & seeing people scud before us. Also we saw all the Mayfair houses, & finally came to Gordon Sqre & there was Nessa tripping along in the dark, in her quiet black hat. So we had some lively talk. She said Duncan was having a sandwich at the public house: then he came, carrying an egg. Come on all of us to Clive's, I said; & they agreed. Well, it was after they had come & we were all sitting round talking that Clive suddenly said, or bawled rather, what an astonishing hat you're wearing! Then he asked where I got it. I pretended a mystery, tried to change the talk, was not allowed, & they pulled me down between them, like a hare; I never felt more humiliated. Clive said did Mary choose it? No. Todd said Vita. And the dress? Todd of course: after that I was forced to go on as if nothing terrible had happened; but it was very forced & queer & humiliating. So I talked & laughed too much. Duncan prim & acid as ever told me it was utterly impossible to do anything with a hat like that. And I joked about the Squires' party. & Leonard got silent, & I came away deeply chagrined, as unhappy as I have been these ten years; & revolved it in sleep & dreams all night; & today has been ruined.

Thursday 1 July

These reflections about the hat read rather amusingly I think. What a weathercock of sensibility I am! How I enjoy—or at least how (for I was acutely unhappy & humiliated) these gyrations interest me, conscious as I am of a strong lynch pin controlling them—Leonard in short. Coming out from lunching with Maynard today I ran (in the hat, in the dress) into Clive & Mary, & had to stand their fire: dress praised to the skies, hat passed. So thats over. Indeed the cloud began to lift at 7 last night.

But all this has obscured Garsington; Bridges; & Wells. These great men are so much like the rest of us. Wells remarkable only for a combination of stockishness with acuity: he has a sharp nose, & the cheeks & jowl of a butcher. He likes, I judge, rambling & romancing about the lives of other people; he romanced about the Webbs: said their books were splendid eggs, well & truly laid, but addled. Described Beatrice, as by a gipsy & a Jew: a flashing creature, become Quaker as we all do as we get on. That has nothing to do with ⟨God⟩ Christianity. Are you a Quaker, I asked. Of course I am. One believes that there is a reason for things (I think he said). But he did not rise steadily off the ground for long. Lunch is a hot stodgy hour too. I could see from the plaintive watery look on Mrs Wells' face (she has widely spaced teeth & in repose looks very worried, at the same time vacant) that he is arrogant lustful & bullying in private life.[1] The virtues he likes are courage & vitality. I said how ghastly! (That is the story of Dorothy Richardson's struggles.) No: nothing is ghastly where there is courage he said. He rambled over her life, amusingly. How she married Odel, a man who makes symbolical drawings—bubbles coming out of a human mouth & turning into womens legs & so on: which is so like life, Wells said: the heterogeneity— one thing leading to another, & the design so remarkable. But they dont sell. And now Duckworth won't publish any more of her books.[2]

As for Bridges: he sprang from a rhododendron bush, a very lean tall old man, with a curly grey hat, & a reddish ravaged face, smoky fierce eyes, with a hazy look in them; very active; rather hoarse, talking in-cessantly. We sat in his open room & looked past blue spikes of flowers to hills, which were invisible, but when they show, all this goes out he said—his one poetical saying, or saying that struck me as such. We talked about handwriting, & criticism; how Garrod had written on Keats; & they know a Petrarchan sonnet, but not why one alters it. Because they dont write sonnets, I suggested, & urged him to write criticism.[3] He is direct & spry, very quick in all his movements, racing

1. LW had seen a good deal of H. G. Wells during and after the war in connection with League of Nations matters and Wells's *Outline of History* (see *III LW*, pp 192-3); but it is not clear that VW had met him or his wife before this lunch party at the Keynes's on 1 July. Amy Catherine ('Jane') Wells, *née* Robbins (1872-1927) had for many years acquiesced in Wells's notorious infidelities, but always maintained her social position as his wife.
2. The novelist Dorothy Miller Richardson (1873-1957) had been at school in Putney with Mrs Wells, and through her met H. G., with whom she had an affair which ended with a miscarriage in 1907; in 1917 she had married Alan Odle, a tubercular artist fifteen years her junior (he died in 1948). Duckworth, who in the ten years up to 1925 had published eight successive volumes of her novel series *Pilgrimage*, were losing money on it, though they did in fact publish two further volumes.
3. Robert Bridges lived at Chilswell House on Boar's Hill near Oxford. On the subject of handwriting, see 21 December 1925, n 15, above. H. W. Garrod (1878-1960), at this time Professor of Poetry at Oxford, published his book on Keats in July 1926 (and his edition of the *Poetical Works* in 1939). Bridges himself had written on Keats in 1894, a critical essay published as the introduction to G. Thorn Drury's edition of the *Poems*, 1896.

me down the garden to look at pinks, then into his library, where he showed me the French critics, then said Michelet was his favourite historian; then I asked to see the Hopkins manuscripts; & sat looking at them with that gigantic grasshopper Aldous folded up in a chair close by. Ottoline undulated & vagulated.[4]

He asked me to come again: would read me his poems—not his early ones which want a beautiful voice, & aren't interesting he said: but his later ones, his hexameters. He skipped off & held the gate open. I said how much I liked his poems—true of the short ones: but was mainly pleased & gratified to find him so obliging & easy & interested. Ottoline flattered me on this point. But she had her points too; her dwindling charm reveals them, as we sat by the lake, discussing Mary Clive life, truth, literature. Then dressed, & Aldous & Eddie & Philip Nichols, & Miss Spender Clay, who can have £500 a year if she wants it Julian said.[5]

Sunday 4 July

Then Wells came again; & stayed till 4, when he had to meet an American.[6] He is getting to the drowsy stage: the 60s. Seems well wishing but not so spry as he used to be. He talked about his new book, the thoughts one has at 60. He brings in everything—a man called Lubin, for instance, who invented int[n] agriculture (I think) a man who died in poverty & was shuffled out of the way to his grave in Rome the day that Wilson made his entry—"that shallow, pretentious empty headed

4. The public recognition of Gerard Manley Hopkins (1844-89) as a poet was due to Robert Bridges, his contemporary and close friend at Oxford, who had first published his poems (in an edition of only 750 copies of which the Woolfs possessed one, sold at Sotheby's, 27 April 1970, lot 67) in 1918. Bridges collected Hopkins' poems and letters and assembled his posthumous papers (now mostly in the Bodleian). Aldous Huxley (1894-1963) was a fellow guest at Garsington.
5. Philip Bouverie Bowyer Nichols (1894-1962) had been at Balliol, served throughout the war, and was now in the Foreign Service; in 1932 he was to marry Phyllis Mary Spender-Clay (b. 1905), a granddaughter of the fabulously wealthy William Waldorf, 1st Viscount Astor.
  On the page opposite this last paragraph is a list, headed *Tavistock Cafe*!: '1 Nessa 2 Roger 3 Julia 4 Dadie 5 Eddie 6 V. 7 Clive 8 Raymond 9 Lytton.' This relates to one of VW's recurrent social projects, later this year to take shape as the 'Bloomsbury Bar'. (See *III VW Letters*, no. 1677.)
6. H. G. Wells and Desmond MacCarthy lunched with the Woolfs on Friday 2 July.

professor"— Lubin was the real thinker for peace.[7] What other ideas had he? Desmond asked. Well, to do away with Sunday. There should be [a] holiday once in 10 days. That was his own stint. 10 days work, then 4 or 5 days off. The present system is wasteful. The shadow of the week end begins on Friday, is not over till Monday afternoon. He said sometimes he wrote all day for days; sometimes not at all. He struck me again as an odd mixture of bubble & solidity—likes to blow a phrase now & then. We got him on to Hardy—a very simple, subtle old peasant man much impressed by clever people who write[;] very humble, delighted when Wells took Rebecca West to call on him, walked half way into Dorchester with them—"an impudent young journalist" Wells called her. Hardy had heard of her. Came to stay with Barrie to see an air raid— wrote his early books in chapters as the printers wanted them.[8] Then he got up to go: we asked him to stay & tell us about Henry James. So he sat down. Oh I should be delighted to stay & talk the whole afternoon, he said. Henry James was a formalist. He always thought of clothes. He was never intimate with anyone—not with his brother even: had never been in love. Once his brother wanted to see Chesterton, & climbed a ladder & looked over a wall. This angered Henry; who called in Wells & asked him for an opinion—as if I had one![9] Wells has learnt nothing from Proust—his book like the British Museum. One knows there are delightful interesting things in it, but one does not go there. One day it may be wet—I shall say God, what am I to do this afternoon? & I shall read Proust as I might go to the British Museum. Would not read Richardson—a man who knows all about feminine psychology (with some contempt) nobody ought to know that. I said on the contrary he

7. Book 5, § 6 of Wells's latest book, *The World of William Clissold* (to be published in the autumn of 1926), is a discourse upon 'that prophetic American Jew, David Lubin', a self-made man who by 1905 had set up the International Institute of Agriculture in Rome. He was buried in that city in January 1919, 'and his funeral passed disregarded through streets that were beflagged and decorated to welcome the visit of President Wilson'.
8. Rebecca West was the professional name of the writer Cicily Isabel Fairfield (b. 1892) who, as a young and ardent radical, wrote regularly for the militant feminist weekly *The Freewoman*; in 1912 her hostile review of one of H. G. Wells's novels led to their meeting and an extended love affair only terminated by her in 1923. In July 1917, Mr and Mrs Hardy had stayed with the novelist and playwright Sir J. M. Barrie, Bt, OM (1860-1937) and had watched the searchlights scanning the sky from his Adelphi flat overlooking the Thames.
9. Wells's story of Henry James's disapprobation of his brother William's unseemly behaviour is retold by Leon Edel in *Henry James. The Master. 1901-1916* (1972), pp 373-4. The elephantine figure of the writer G. K. Chesterton (1874-1936) perambulating the streets of Rye would indeed have been a sight to see.

knew very little: was conventional. Honour, chastity & so on. Wells said we had changed our ideas completely. That idea of chastity had vanished. Women were even more suggestible than men. Now they dont think about it—a chaste little couple (he talks of little couples) mixing with a promiscuous little couple. He said we are happier perhaps—children are certainly more at ease with their parents. But he thought they were beginning to miss restraints. They were wondering what things were for. They were very restless; discussing Henry James & Eliot, & how formal they are & overdone with manner—(he described H.J. pushing under a letter he was writing to talk to Wells "at the Reform"). I said it was American. They were alien to our civilisation. He said he had been that himself. His father was a gardener, his mother a ladies maid. He found it very strange to meet people who went to parties & wore dress clothes. Henry James could not describe love—there comes the ahh—laying on of hands. This Wells could do himself. I am a journalist. I pride myself upon being a journalist he said. Well I have a sort of feeling that all writing should be journalism—(done with an object)— One knows nothing of what posterity will want—may be a guide book. I tell Arnold [Bennett] they will read him for his topography.

In all this he showed himself, as Desmond said afterwards, perfectly content to be himself, aware of his powers,—aware that he need not take any trouble, since his powers were big enough.

Thursday 22 July

The summer hourglass is running out rapidly & rather sandily. Many nights I wake in a shudder thinking of some atrocity of mine. I bring home minute pinpricks which magnify in the middle of the night into gaping wounds. However, I drive my pen through de Quincey of a morning, having put The Lighthouse aside till Rodmell. There all virtue, all good, is in retreat. Here nothing but odds & ends—going to the dentist, buying combs; having Maynard & Bob to tea, & then Ralph & Frances to dinner, followed by Eddie & Kitchen [C. H. B. Kitchin]. But we are both jaded, & get no clear impression any more from the human face—must dine with Osbert Sitwell tonight though, & go to Hardy tomorrow. This is human life: this is the infinitely precious stuff issued in a narrow roll to us now, & then withdrawn for ever; & we spend it thus. Days without definite sensation are the worst of all. Days when one compels oneself to undergo this or that for some reason—but what reason?

There is nothing important at the moment to record: or if so, & one's

state of mind is overwhelmingly important, I leave that, too for Rodmell.
There I shall come to grips with the last part of that python, my book;
it is a tug & a struggle, & I wonder now & then, why I let myself in for
it. Rose Macaulay said "What else would one do with one's thoughts?"
I have not seen her again nor Gwen, nor written to Violet [Dickinson];
nor learnt French, nor finished Clarissa.

Desmond came in; talked about Shakespeare. Now to settle my mind
to Suspiria.[10]

Sunday 25 July

At first I thought it was Hardy, & it was the parlourmaid, a small
thin girl, wearing a proper cap. She came in with silver cake stands &
so on. Mrs Hardy talked to us about her dog.[11] How long ought we to
stay? Can Mr Hardy walk much &c I asked, making conversation, as I
knew one would have to. She has the large sad lack lustre eyes of a
childless woman; great docility & readiness, as if she had learnt her part;
not great alacrity, but resignation, in welcoming more visitors; wears a
sprigged voile dress, black shoes, & a necklace. We cant go far now, she
said, though we do walk every day, because our dog isn't able to walk
far. He bites, she told us. She became more natural & animated about the
dog, who is evidently the real centre of her thoughts—then the maid came
in. Then again the door opened, more sprucely, & in trotted a little puffy
cheeked cheerful old man, with an atmosphere cheerful & businesslike
in addressing us, rather like an old doctors or solicitors, saying "Well
now—" or words like that as he shook hands. He was dressed in rough
grey with a striped tie. His nose has a joint in it, & the end curves down.
A round whitish face, the eyes now faded & rather watery, but the whole
aspect cheerful & vigorous. He sat on a three cornered chair (I am too
jaded with all this coming & going to do more than gather facts) at a
round table, where there were the cake stands & so on; a chocolate roll;
what is called a good tea; but he only drank one cup, sitting on his

10. Violet Dickinson (1865-1948) was one of VW's oldest friends, a friendship now
maintained more through loyalty than interest. VW wrote to her on 26 July (see
III VW Letters, no. 1658). VW owned the 8-volume, 1792, edition of Samuel
Richardson's *Clarissa Harlowe*. "Suspiria de Profundis" was one of de Quincey's
'dream-visions', first published in *Blackwood's Magazine* in 1845.
11. The Woolfs went to Dorchester and back by train on the afternoon of Friday 23
July, in order to have tea with Mr and Mrs Hardy at Max Gate. Florence Emily,
née Dugdale (1878-1937), had married Thomas Hardy as his second wife in 1914;
he was then over twice her age. The two volumes of her *Life* of her husband,
written in effect by Hardy himself, were published in 1928 and 1930, after his death.

three cornered chair. He was extremely affable & aware of his duties. He did not let the talk stop or disdain making talk. He talked of father— said he had seen me, or it might have been my sister but he thought it was me, in my cradle. He had been to Hyde Park Place—oh Gate was it. A very quiet street. That was why my father liked it. Odd to think that in all these years he had never been down there again. He went there often. Your father took my novel—Far From the Madding Crowd. We stood shoulder to shoulder against the British public about certain matters dealt with in that novel—You may have heard. Then he said how some other novel had fallen through that was to appear—the parcel had been lost coming from France—not a very likely thing to happen, as your father said—a big parcel of manuscript; & he asked me to send my story. I think he broke all the Cornhill laws—not to see the whole book; so I sent it in chapter by chapter, & was never late.[12] Wonderful what youth is! I had it in my head doubtless, but I never thought twice about it— It came out every month. They were nervous, because of Miss Thackeray I think. She said she became paralysed & could not write a word directly she heard the press begin. I daresay it was bad for a novel to appear like that. One begins to think what is good for the magazine, not what is good for the novel.

You think what makes a strong curtain, put in Mrs Hardy jocularly. She was leaning upon the tea table, not eating gazing out.

Then we talked about manuscripts. Mrs Smith had found the MS of F. from the M.C. in a drawer during the war, & sold it for the Red Cross.[13] Now he has his MSS back, & the printer rubs out all the marks. But he wishes they would leave them, as they prove it genuine.

He puts his head down like some old pouter pigeon. He has a very long head; & quizzical bright eyes, for in talk they grow bright. He said when he was in the Strand 6 years ago he scarcely knew where he was, & he used to know it all intimately. He told us that he used to buy 2nd hand books—nothing valuable—in Wyck Street. Then he wondered why Great James Street should be so narrow & Bedford Row so broad.

12. Hardy contributed his own account of his relations with Leslie Stephen—who as editor of *The Cornhill Magazine* had commissioned and published his fourth novel in serial form in 1874—to F. W. Maitland's *The Life and Letters of Leslie Stephen*, 1906, pp 270-78.

13. Hardy's manuscript had been found by the widow of Reginald John Smith, son-in-law of the founder of *The Cornhill Magazine* and its editor from 1898, after his death in 1917; she persuaded Hardy to rewrite a missing page, had it bound in blue morocco, and sent it to the Red Cross Sale at Christie's on 22 April 1918. It is now the property of Mr Edwin Thorne in America.

He had often wondered about that. At this rate, London would soon be unrecognisable. But I shall never go there again. Mrs Hardy tried to persuade him that it was an easy drive—only 6 hours or so. I asked if she liked it, & she said Granville Barker had told her that when she was in the nursing home she had 'the time of her life'.[14] She knew everyone in Dorchester, but she thought there were more interesting people in London. Had I often been to Siegfried's flat? I said no. Then she asked about him & Morgan, said he was elusive, as if they enjoyed visits from him. I said I heard from Wells that Mr Hardy had been up to London to see an air raid. "What things they say!" he said. It was my wife. There was an air raid one night when we stayed with Barrie. We just heard a little pop in the distance— The searchlights were beautiful. I thought if a bomb now were to fall on this flat how many writers would be lost. And he smiled in his queer way, which is fresh & yet sarcastic a little: anyhow shrewd. Indeed, there was no trace to my thinking of the simple peasant. He seemed perfectly aware of everything; in no doubt or hesitation; having made up his mind; & being delivered of all his work; so that he was in no doubt about that either. He was not interested much in his novels, or in anybodies novels; took it all easily & naturally. "I never took long with them" he said. The longest was the *Din*nasts. (so pronounced). "But that was really 3 books" said Mrs Hardy. Yes: & that took me 6 years; but not working all the time. Can you write poetry regularly? I asked (being beset with the desire to hear him say something about his books); but the dog kept cropping up. How he bit; how the inspector came out; how he was ill; & they could do nothing for him. Would you mind if I let him in? asked Mrs Hardy, & in came We[s]sex, a very tousled, rough brown & white mongrel, got to guard the house, so naturally he bites people, said Mrs H.; Well, I dont know about that, said Hardy, perfectly natural, & not setting much stock by his poems either it seemed. Did you write poems at the same time as your novels? I asked. No. he said. I wrote a great many poems. I used to send them about, but they were always returned, he chuckled. And in those days I believed in editors. Many were lost—all the fair copies were lost. But I found the notes, & I wrote them from those. I was always finding them. I found one the other day; but I don't think I shall find any more.

Siegfried took rooms near here, & said he was going to work very hard, but he left soon.

14. Harley Granville Barker (1877-1946), actor, producer, dramatist and critic, was a friend of the Hardys. Mrs Hardy had spent ten days in a London nursing home in the autumn of 1924, when VW had visited her (see *II VW Diary*, 17 October 1924).

E. M. Forster takes a long time to produce anything—7 years, he chuckled. All this made a great impression of the ease with which he did things. "I daresay F. from the M. C. would have been a great deal better if I had written it differently", he said. But as if it could not be helped, & did not matter.

He used to go to the Lushingtons in Kensington Sqre & saw my mother there. She used to come in & out when I was talking to your father.[15]

I wanted him to say one word about his writing before we left & cd only ask wh. of his books he wd. have chosen, if like me, he had had to choose one to read in the train. I had taken the M[ayor] of C[asterbridge]. That's being dramatised, put in Mrs H. & then brought L[ove's]. L[ittle]. Ironies.[16]

And did it hold your interest? he asked.

I stammered that I could not stop reading it, which was true, but sounded wrong. Anyhow, he was not going to be drawn, & went off about giving a young lady a wedding present. None of my books are fitted to be wedding presents, he said. You must give Mrs Woolf one of your books, said Mrs Hardy, inevitably. Yes I will. But I'm afraid only in the little thin paper edition, he said. I protested that it would be enough if he wrote his name (then was vaguely uncomfortable).

Then there was de la Mare. His last book of stories seemed to them such a pity.[17] Hardy had liked some of his poems very much. People said he must be a sinister man to write such stories. But he is [a] very nice man—a very nice man indeed.

He said to a friend who begged him not to give up poetry, "I'm afraid poetry is giving up me." The truth is he is a very kind man, & sees anyone who wants to see him. He has 16 people for the day sometimes.

Do you think one can't write poetry if one sees people? I asked. "One might be able to—I dont see why not. Its a question of physical strength" said Hardy. But clearly he preferred solitude himself. Always however he said something sensible & sincere; & thus made the obvious business

15. Judge Vernon Lushington (1832-1912) and his wife had been close friends of Leslie and Julia Stephen in Kensington; and their daughters Katherine (Kitty Maxse), Margaret (Massingberd), and Susan played a not inconsiderable part in the social life of their children.

16. John Drinkwater's stage adaptation of *The Mayor of Casterbridge* opened for a limited run at the Barnes Theatre on 8 September 1926; a special matinée, attended by Mr and Mrs Hardy, was given in his honour at the Pavilion Theatre, Weymouth, on 20 September.

17. *The Connoisseur and other Stories*, published Spring 1926. LW had used it as the basis for his weekly article, 'The World of Books' in the *N & A* of 3 July 1926.

of compliment giving rather unpleasant. He seemed to be free of it all; very active minded; liking to describe people; not to talk in an abstract way: for example Col. Lawrence, bicycling with a broken arm "held like that" from Lincoln to Hardy listened at the door; to hear if there was anyone there.[18]

I hope he won't commit suicide, said Mrs Hardy pensively, still leaning over the tea cups, gazing despondently. He often says things like it, though he has never said quite that perhaps. But he has blue lines round his eyes. He calls himself Shaw in the army. No one is to know where he is. But it got into the papers.

He promised me ⟨to give up fly—⟩ not to go into the air, said Hardy.

My husband doesn't like anything to do with the air, said Mrs Hardy.

Now we began to look at the grandfather clock in the corner. We said we must go—tried to confess we were only down for the day. I forgot to say that he offered L. whisky & water, wh. struck me that he was competent as a host, & in every way.

So we got up & signed Mrs H's visitors books; & Hardy took my L. Little Ironies off, & trotted back with it signed, & Woolf spelt Wolff, wh. I daresay had given him some anxiety.[19] Then We[s]sex came in again. I asked if Hardy could stroke him. So he bent down & stroked him, like the master of the house. We[s]sex went on wheezing away.

There was not a trace anywhere of deference to editors, or respect for rank, an extreme simplicity: What impressed me was his freedom, ease, & vitality. He seemed very "Great Victorian" doing the whole thing with a sweep of his hand (they are ordinary smallish, curled up hands) & setting no great stock by literature; but immensely interested in facts; incidents; & somehow, one could imagine, naturally swept off into imagining & creating without a thought of its being difficult or remarkable; becoming obsessed; & living in imagination. Mrs Hardy thrust his old grey hat into his hand & he trotted us out on to the road. Where is that? I asked him, pointing to a clump of trees on the down opposite, for his house is outside the town, with open country (rolling, massive downs, crowned with little tree coronets before & behind) & he said, with interest, "That is Weymouth. We see the lights at night—not the

18. Thomas Edward Lawrence (1888-1935), 'Colonel Lawrence of Arabia', had become a close friend of the Hardys during the two and a half years he spent as Private Shaw, serving with the Royal Tank Corps at Bovington Camp, Dorset. In 1925 he had been allowed to rejoin the R.A.F. as an aircraftsman, and was posted to Cranwell, Lincolnshire; in March 1926 he had fractured his right arm but nonetheless came on his motorbicycle to visit the Hardys soon afterwards.

19. This copy was sold at Sotheby's on 27 April 1970, lot 65.

lights themselves, but the reflection of them." And so we left, & he trotted in again.

Also I asked him if I might see the picture of Tess which Morgan had described, an old picture: whereupon he led me to an awful engraving of Tess coming into a room from a picture by Herkomer.[20] "That was rather my idea of her" he said. But I said I had been told he had an old picture. "Thats fiction" he said. "I used to see people now & then with a look of her."

Also Mrs Hardy said to me, do you know Aldous Huxley? I said I did. They had been reading his book, which she thought 'very clever'. But Hardy could not remember it. Said his wife had to read to him— his eyes were now so bad. ⟨"Was that the book where the⟩ "Theyve changed everything now he said. We used to think there was a beginning & a middle & an end. We believed in the Aristotelian theory. Now one of those stories came to an end with a woman going out of the room."[21] He chuckled. But he no longer reads novels.

The whole thing—literature, novels &c—all seemed to him an amusement, far away, too, scarcely to be taken seriously. Yet he had sympathy & pity for those still engaged in it. But what his secret interests & activities are—to what occupation he trotted off when we left him—I do not know.

Small boys write to him from New Zealand, & have to be answered. They bring out a "Hardy number" of a Japanese paper, which he produced. Talked too about Blunden.[22] I think Mrs H. keeps him posted in the doings of the younger poets.

On the eve of her eleven-week summer retreat from London, VW spent the night of Monday 26 July at Long Barn with Vita Sackville-West, who motored her over to Rodmell the next afternoon. They arrived before LW,

20. Sir Hubert von Herkomer, R.A. (1849-1914) had illustrated the serialisation of *Tess of the D'Urbervilles* which appeared in the *Graphic* in 1891; he gave two of the original drawings to Hardy at Christmas 1891 (they are now in the Dorset County Museum). 'Tess's return from the Dance' shows Tess coming into a room, but it is a drawing in pen and wash, not an engraving.

21. Aldous Huxley's book was his collection *Two or Three Graces* published in May 1926; the story in question was 'Half-Holiday' which ends with a man, not a woman, going out of a room.

22. Edmund Charles Blunden (1896-1974), poet and critic; he had been awarded the Hawthornden Prize for his poetry in 1922, and had been on the staff of the *N & A* before going to Japan in 1924 as Professor of English at Tokyo University, a post he held until 1927.

who also came by car, with Clive and Julian Bell who were going to Charleston. Vita presented the Woolfs with a spaniel bitch puppy called Fanny, which they renamed Pinker (or Pinka).

The headed notes which follow were written at different times, only occasionally datable, between the end of July and the beginning of September. VW appears to have eschewed company to work at To the Lighthouse, *although Raymond Mortimer stayed one week-end. On 20 August the Woolfs dined with Maynard and Lydia Keynes at Tilton, the farmhouse half a mile from Charleston which, with its farm lands, Keynes had leased for 99 years from the local landowner, Viscount Gage. After dinner they all attended the now customary firework party at Charleston in celebration of Quentin's birthday.*

Rodmell. 1926

As I am not going to milk my brains for a week, I shall here write the first pages of the greatest book in the world. This is what the book would be that was made entirely solely & with integrity of one's thoughts. Suppose one could catch them before they became "works of art."? Catch them hot & sudden as they rise in the mind—walking up Asheham hill for instance. Of course one cannot; for the process of language is slow & deluding. One must stop to find a word; then, there is the form of the sentence, soliciting one to fill it.

Art & Thought

What I thought was this: if art is based on thought, what is the transmuting process? I was telling myself the story of our visit to the Hardys. & I began to compose it: that is to say to dwell on Mrs Hardy leaning on the table, looking out, apathetically, vaguely; & so would soon bring everything into harmony with that as the dominant theme. But the actual event was different.

Next,

Writing by living people

I scarcely ever read it. but, owing to his giving me the books, am now reading C by M. Baring.[23] I am surprised to find it as good as it is. But how good is it? Easy to say it is not a great book. But what qualities does it lack? That it adds nothing to one's vision of life, perhaps. Yet it is hard to find a serious flaw. My wonder is that entirely second rate work

23. *C* [Clarence], a novel by Maurice Baring (1874-1945), diplomat and man of letters; the two-volume American edition of 1924, with a long inscription by the author to VW, was sold at Sotheby's on 27 April 1970, lot 5.

like this, poured out in profusion by at least 20 people yearly, I suppose, has so much merit. Never reading it, I get into the way of thinking it non-existent. So it is, speaking with the utmost strictness. That is, it will not exist in 2026; but it has some existence now; which puzzles me a little. Now Clarence bores me; yet I feel this is important. And why?

[*Saturday 31 July*]

My own Brain

Here is a whole nervous breakdown in miniature. We came on Tuesday. Sank into a chair, could scarcely rise; everything insipid; tasteless, colourless. Enormous desire for rest. Wednesday—only wish to be alone in the open air. Air delicious—avoided speech; could not read. Thought of my own power of writing with veneration, as of something incredible, belonging to someone else; never again to be enjoyed by me. Mind a blank. Slept in my chair. Thursday. No pleasure in life whatsoever; but felt perhaps more attuned to existence. Character & idiosyncracy as Virginia Woolf completely sunk out. Humble & modest. Difficulty in thinking what to say. Read automatically, like a cow chewing cud. Slept in chair. Friday. Sense of physical tiredness; but slight activity of the brain. Beginning to take notice. Making one or two plans. No power of phrase making. Difficulty in writing to Lady Colefax. Saturday (today) much clearer & lighter. Thought I could write, but resisted, or found it impossible. A desire to read poetry set in on Friday. This brings back a sense of my own individuality. Read some Dante & Bridges, without troubling to understand, but got pleasure from them. Now I begin to wish to write notes, but not yet novel. But today senses quickening. No 'making up' power yet; no desire to cast scenes in my book. Curiosity about literature returning: want to read Dante, Havelock Ellis, & Berlioz autobiography; also to make a looking glass with shell frame. These processes have sometimes been spread over several weeks.

Proportions Changed

That in the evening, or on colourless days, the proportions of the landscape change suddenly. I saw people playing stoolball in the meadow: they appeared sunk far down on a flat board; & the downs raised high up, & mountainous round them. Detail was smoothed out. This was an extremely beautiful effect; the colours of the womens dresses also showing very bright & pure in the almost untinted surroundings. I knew, also, that the porportions were abnormal—as if I were looking between my legs.

Second Rate Art

i.e. C. by Maurice Baring. Within its limits, it is not second rate, or there is nothing markedly so, at first go off. The limits are the proof of its non-existence.. He can only do one thing: himself to wit; charming, clean, modest sensitive Englishman: outside that radius, & it does not carry far nor illumine much, all is—as it should be; light, sure, proportioned, affecting even; told in so well bred a manner that nothing is exaggerated, all related, proportioned. I could read this for ever, I said. L. said one would soon be sick to death of it.

Wandervögeln

of the sparrow tribe. Two resolute, sunburnt, dusty girls, in jerseys & short skirts, with packs on their backs, city clerks, or secretaries, tramping along the road in the hot sunshine at Ripe.[24] My instinct at once throws up a screen, which condemns them: I think them in every way angular, awkward & self assertive. But all this is a great mistake. These screens shut me out. Have no screens, for screens are made out of our own integument; & get at the thing itself, which has nothing whatever in common with a screen. The screen making habit, though, is so universal, that probably it preserves our sanity. If we had not this device for shutting people off from our sympathies, we might, perhaps, dissolve utterly. Separateness would be impossible. But the screens are in the excess; not the sympathy.

Returning Health

This is shown by the power to make images: the suggestive power of every sight & word is enormously increased. Shakespeare must have had this to an extent which makes my normal state the state of a person blind, deaf, dumb, stone-stockish & fish-blooded. And I have it compared with poor Mrs Bartholomew almost to the extent that Shre has it compared with me.[25]

[*Monday 2 August*]

Bank Holiday

Very fat woman, girl & man spend Bank Holiday—a day of complete sun & satisfaction—looking up family graves in the churchyard. 23

24. LW, who did not as a rule record his activities whilst at Rodmell, noted under 31 July: 'Bicycled Ripe'.
25. Mrs Rose Bartholomew of Style Cottages, Rodmell, cooked for the Woolfs at Monks House when Nelly was not there; 'she has been mad, squints, & is singularly pure of soul.' (*III VW Letters*, no. 1462.)

youngish men & women spend it tramping along with ugly black boxes on shoulders & arms, taking photographs. Man says to woman "Some of these quiet villages don't seem to know its bank holiday at all" in a tone of superiority & slight contempt.

The Married Relation

Arnold Bennett says that the horror of marriage lies in its 'dailiness'. All acuteness of relationship is rubbed away by this. The truth is more like this. Life—say 4 days out of 7—becomes automatic; but on the 5th day a bead of sensation (between husband & wife) forms, wh. is all the fuller & more sensitive because of the automatic customary unconscious days on either side. That is to say the year is marked by moments of great intensity. Hardy's 'moments of vision'.[1] How can a relationship endure for any length of time except under these conditions?

Friday 3 September

Women in tea garden at Bramber—a sweltering hot day: rose trellises; white washed tables; lower middle classes; motor omnibuses constantly passing; bits of grey stone scattered on a paper strewn green sward all thats left of the Castle.[1]

Woman leaning over the table, taking command of the treat, attended by two elder women, whom she pays for, to girl waitress (a marmalade coloured fat girl, with a body like the softest lard, destined soon to marry, but as yet only 16 or so)

Woman   "What can we have for tea?"

Girl   (very bored, arms akimbo) Cake, bread & butter, tea: Jam?

Woman   Have the wasps been troublesome? They get into the jam—
         as if she suspected the jam would not be worth having.

Girl   agrees.

Woman: Ah, wasps have been very prominent this year.

Girl   Thats right.

So she doesn't have jam.

This amused me, I suppose.

1. Hardy's *Moments of Vision, and Miscellaneous Verses* had been published in 1917.
1. Bramber, once a centre of Norman administration on the river Adur in West Sussex, with an imposing castle and chapel, had declined into romantic overgrown ruins overlooking a village along a busy main road.

For the rest, Charleston, Tilton, To the Lighthouse, Vita, expeditions: the summer dominated by a feeling of washing in boundless warm fresh air—such an August not come my way for years: bicycling; no settled work done, but advantage taken of air for going to the river, or over the downs. The novel is now easily within sight of the end, but this, mysteriously, comes no nearer. I am doing Lily on the lawn: but whether its her last lap, I don't know. Nor am I sure of the quality; the only certainty seems to be that after tapping my antennae in the air vaguely for an hour every morning I generally write with heat & ease till 12.30: & thus do my two pages.

[*Sunday 5 September*]

So it will be done, written over that is, in 3 weeks, I forecast, from today. What emerges? At this moment I'm casting about for an end. The problem is how to bring Lily & Mr R[amsay]. together & make a combination of interest at the end. I am feathering about with various ideas. The last chapter which I begin tomorrow is In the Boat: I had meant to end with R. climbing on to the rock. If so, what becomes [of] Lily & her picture? Should there be a final page about her & Carmichael looking at the picture & summing up R.'s character? In that case I lose the intensity of the moment. If this intervenes, between R. & the lighthouse, there's too much chop & change, I think. Could I do it in a parenthesis? so that one had the sense of reading the two things at the same time?

I shall solve it somehow, I suppose. Then I must go in to the question of quality. I think it may run too fast & free, & so be rather thin. On the other hand, I think it is subtler & more human than J[acob's] R[oom] & Mrs D[alloway]. And I am encouraged by my own abundance as I write. It is proved, I think, that what I have to say is to be said in this manner. As usual, side stories are sprouting in great variety as I wind this up: a book of characters; the whole string being pulled out from some simple sentence, like Clara Pater's, "Don't you find that Barker's pins have no points to them?"[2] I think I can spin out all their entrails this way; but it is hopelessly undramatic. It is all in oratio obliqua. Not quite all; for I have a few direct sentences. The lyric portions of To the L.

2. Clara Ann Pater (1841-1910), younger of Walter Pater's two sisters, became the first Classics Tutor and eventually Vice-President of Somerville College, Oxford. After their brother's death in 1894, the sisters moved to Canning Place, Kensington, and Clara gave VW lessons in Greek. Her question provided the starting point for ' "Slater's Pins have no Points" ' (Kp C295), first published in the *Forum*, New York, in January 1928.

are collected in the 10 year lapse, & dont interfere with the text so much as usual. I feel as if it fetched its circle pretty completely this time: & I dont feel sure what the stock criticism will be. Sentimental? Victorian?

Then I must begin to plan out my book on literature for the Press.[3] Six chapters. Why not groups of ideas, under some single heading—for example. Symbolism. God. Nature. Plot. Dialogue. Take a novel & see what the component parts are. Separate this, & bring under them instances of all the books which display them biggest. Probably this would pan out historically. One could spin a theory which wd bring the chapters together. I don't feel that I can read seriously[?] & exactly for it. Rather I want to sort out all the ideas that have accumulated in me.

Then I want to write a bunch of 'Outlines' to make money (for under a new arrangement, we're to share any money over £200 that I make): this I must leave rather to chance, according to what books come my way. I am frightfully contented these last few days, by the way. I dont quite understand it. Perhaps reason has something to do with it. Charleston & Tilton knocked me off my perch for a moment: Nessa & her children: Maynard & his carpets. My own gifts & shares seemed so moderate in comparison; my own fault too—a little more self control on my part, & we might have had a boy of 12, a girl of 10: This always rakes me wretched in the early hours. So I said, I am spoiling what I have. And thereupon settled [?] to exploit my own possessions to the full; I can make money & buy carpets; I can increase the pleasure of life enormously by living it carefully. No doubt, this is a rationalisation of a state which is not really of that nature. Probably I am very lucky. Mrs Allinson says she would like to look like me.[4] Mary says I'm the only woman she loves. Nelly cooks admirably. Then, I am extremely happy walking on the downs. I dont want to be talking to Eddy at Charleston. I like to have space to spread my mind out in. Whatever I think, I can rap out, suddenly to L. We are somehow very detached, free, harmonious. I don't in the least want to hurry up & finish the time here. I want to go to Seaford & walk back over the downs; to go & see the house at East Chiltington; to breathe in more light & air; to see more grey hollows & gold cornfields & the first ploughed land shining white, with the gulls flickering. No: I dont want anyone to come here & interrupt. I am immensely busy. Hence I come to my moral, which is simply to enjoy what one does enjoy, without teasing oneself oh but Nessa has

3. See above, 7 December 1925, n 6.
4. Elsie Allison was the wife of the Australian J. Murray Allison, of Hill Farm House, Rodmell, advertising director of Allied Newspapers Ltd, a prominent and gregarious local landowner.

children, Maynard carpets. I might go & stay with Ethel [Sands, *in Normandy*]. For my own wishes are always definite enough to give me a lead, one way or another; & the chief joy in life is to follow these lights; I am now almost entirely surrounded by sheep. God knows, I wish we could buy the terrace, & have a garden all round the lodge—but this is not a serious diminution of joy.[5]

Clive & Mary came over yesterday in brilliant sun. We sat on the millstones. (one sheep has a tail like a bell-rope—the others are all bit short.) Wells. Hardy. Maynard. Richardson. [*word illegible*]. Christabel—going to Greece for a month with Lesley Jowitt. Maupassant's metaphors —The Questionnaire. Lytton's harem—Their dulness—Carrington a cook who doesn't go out on Sundays. Whether Eddy is clever or not. Tonks & Steer & Moore—Tonks in love with Mary, Clive insists; she is modest. So we talked.[6] Then I drove with them to the Laye, walked up the down behind Asheham & let all that wind & sun blow through the crazy sails of my old windmill, which gives me so much pleasure still.[7] I forget what I thought about: did not think, I suppose; was all in a thrill of emotion at my being liked by Mary & being a success, &c. Home to music, my new 15/- table, talk with L.: a sense of great happiness & ease. Went & looked at the stars, but could not get quite the right sense of amazement (I can get this really well at times) because L. said "Now come in. Its too cold to be out"

5. The Woolfs had erected a wooden 'lodge' (often used by VW as a writing room) by the churchyard wall at the far end of their property; from it there was a view over the wide Ouse valley across a strip of land, adjoining theirs, which fell steeply away into a field. LW had for some time been trying to buy this 'terrace' and, if necessary, the rest of the field; and in 1928 he succeeded. (See below, 8 August 1928.)
6. Christabel McLaren (later Lady Aberconway) and Lesley Jowitt, wife of a future Lord Chancellor, were both ornaments of the smart artistic society in which Clive Bell and Mary Hutchinson were equally at home; the latter was also a great favourite with the elderly bachelor artists Henry Tonks and Philip Wilson Steer and their close friend the writer George Moore.

In successive issues in August and September 1926 the *N & A* had carried a supplement entitled 'Questionnaire on Religious Belief' which arose from an article by LW, 'Rationalism and Religion' published on 12 June; the results, finally reported in the *N & A* of 16 October 1926, gave as answer to the first question, "Do you believe in a personal God?" 743 affirmative and 1024 negative replies. (A wholly contrary result was obtained by the *Daily News* in a similar enquiry.) For Carrington (1893-1932), see above, 7 December 1925, n 3.
7. 'The Lay' was a farm cottage and buildings on the road half way between Asheham and Beddingham.

Monday 13 September

The blessed thing is coming to an [end] I say to myself with a groan. Its like some prolonged rather painful & yet exciting process of nature, which one desires inexpressibly to have over. Oh the relief of waking & thinking its done—the relief, & the disappointment, I suppose. I am talking of To the Lighthouse. I am exacerbated by the fact that I spent 4 days last week hammering out de Quincey, which has been lying about since June; so refused £30 to write on Willa Cather; & now shall be quit in a week I hope of this unprofitable fiction, & could have wedged in Willa before going back. So I should have had £70 of my years 200 ready made by October: (my greed is immense: I want to have £50 of my own in the Bank to buy Persian carpets, pots, chairs &c.) Curse Richmond, Curse The Times, Curse my own procrastinations & nerves. I shall do Cobden Sanderson & Mrs Hemans & make something by them however.[8] As for the book [*To the Lighthouse*]—Morgan said he felt 'This is a failure' as he finished The passage to India. I feel—what? A little stale this last week or two from steady writing. But also a little triumphant. If my feeling is correct, this is the greatest stretch I've put my method to, & I think it holds. By this I mean that I have been dredging up more feelings & character, I imagine. But Lord knows, until I look at my haul. This is only my own feeling in process. Odd how I'm haunted by that damned criticism of Janet Case's "its all dressing . . . technique. (Mrs Dalloway). The C.R. has substance". But then in ones strained state any fly has liberty to settle, & its always the gadflies. Muir praising me intelligently has comparatively little power to encourage —when I'm working that is—when the ideas halt.[9] And this last lap, in the boat, is hard, because the material is not so rich as it is with Lily on the lawn: I am forced to be more direct & more intense. I am making

8. VW's review of *The Journals of Thomas James Cobden-Sanderson, 1897-1922*, appeared in the *N & A* on 9 October 1926 under the title 'The Cosmos' (Kp C276). She wrote nothing on her contemporary Willa Cather (1876-1947), the American regionalist writer, nor on Felicia Hemans (1793-1835), chiefly remembered for 'The Boy Stood on the Burning Deck'; though there is an incomplete ms draft of an article on the latter in MHP, Sussex (B10a).

9. Edwin Muir (1887-1959), poet and critic, born and brought up in Orkney, came to London after his marriage in 1919 and worked on the Guild Socialist weekly *The New Age*. LW printed his poems at the Hogarth Press in 1925 and 1926, and employed him as a reviewer on the *N & A*, which first published his series of appraisals of contemporary writers which the Hogarth Press were about to issue in book form under the title *Transition* (*HP Checklist* 105). The long essay on VW had appeared in the *N & A* on 17 April 1926, and is also reprinted in *M & M*, p 178.

some use of symbolism, I observe; & I go in dread of 'sentimentality'. Is the whole theme open to that charge? But I doubt that any theme is in itself good or bad. It gives a chance to ones peculiar qualities—thats all. Then I'm concerned whether to stay with Ethel Sands or not: whether to buy a dress or not. Then I'm astonishingly happy in the country—a state of mind which, if I did not dislike hyphens, I should hyphen, to show that it is a state by itself.

We took Angus over the downs towards Falmer yesterday. After all these years, we have discovered some of the loveliest, loneliest, most surprising downland in these parts: lovelier I think than our rival the Seaford-Tilton down over which we walked in broiling sun last Thursday. How it beat on our heads, made poor puppy pant. Lydia & Maynard came to tea.

Wednesday 15 September

Sometimes I shall use the Note form: for instance this

A State of Mind

Woke up perhaps at 3. Oh its beginning its coming—the horror—physically like a painful wave swelling about the heart—tossing me up. I'm unhappy unhappy! Down—God, I wish I were dead. Pause. But why am I feeling this? Let me watch the wave rise. I watch. Vanessa. Children. Failure. Yes; I detect that. Failure failure. (The wave rises). Oh they laughed at my taste in green paint! Wave crashes. I wish I were dead! I've only a few years to live I hope. I cant face this horror any more—(this is the wave spreading out over me).

This goes on; several times, with varieties of horror. Then, at the crisis, instead of the pain remaining intense, it becomes rather vague. I doze. I wake with a start. The wave again! The irrational pain: the sense of failure; generally some specific incident, as for example my taste in green paint, or buying a new dress, or asking Dadie for the week end, tacked on.

At last I say, watching as dispassionately as I can, Now take a pull of yourself. No more of this. I reason. I take a census of happy people & unhappy. I brace myself to shove to throw to batter down. I begin to march blindly forward. I feel obstacles go down. I say it doesn't matter. Nothing matters. I become rigid & straight, & sleep again, & half wake & feel the wave beginning & watch the light whitening & wonder how, this time, breakfast & daylight will overcome it; & then hear L. in the passage & simulate, for myself as well as for him, great cheerfulness; &

generally am cheerful, by the time breakfast is over. Does everyone go through this state? Why have I so little control? It is not creditable, nor lovable. It is the cause of much waste & pain in my life.

Tuesday 28 September

Every day I have meant to record a state of mind. But it has always disappeared (characteristically) yet recurred often enough to make it one of some importance. It is raining hard this evening; we have entered the calm period of Nelly's departure. So I will try, before my fingers chill & my mind wanders to the fire, to write here what I can remember.

Intense depression: I have to confess that this has overcome me several times since September 6th (I think that, or thereabouts was the date.) It is so strange to me that I cannot get it right—the depression, I mean, which does not come from something definite, but from nothing. "Where there is nothing" the phrase came ⟨back⟩ to me, as I sat at the table in the drawing room. Of course I was interested; & discovered that, for the first time for many years, I had been idle without being ill. We had been walking, expeditioning, in the hot fine weather. I was writing the last pages of To the Lighthouse (finished, provisionally, Sept 16th). Somehow, my reading had lapsed. I was hunting no hares. One night I got hold of Geoffrey Scott's book on Architecture, & a little spark of motive power awoke in me.[10] This is a warning then; never to cease the use of the brain. So I used my brain. Then, owing to mismanagement, no one came to stay, & I got very few letters; & the high pure hot days went on & on; & this blankness persisted, & I began to suspect my book of the same thing; & there was Nessa humming & booming & flourishing over the hill; & one night we had a long long argument. Vita started it, by coming over with Plank,[11] & L. (I say) spoilt the visit by glooming because I said he had been angry. He shut up, & was caustic. He denied this, but admitted that my habits of describing him, & others, had this effect often. I saw myself, my brilliancy, genius, charm, beauty (&c. &c.— the attendants who float me through so many years) diminish & disappear. One is in truth rather an elderly dowdy fussy ugly incompetent woman vain, chattering & futile. I saw this vividly, impressively. Then he said our relations had not been so good lately. On analysing my state of mind

10. *The Architecture of Humanism. A Study in the History of Taste*, 1914.
11. George Plank (1883-1965), a Philadelphian Quaker who came to England in May 1914, stayed on and took British nationality in 1926. A modest but accomplished illustrator and wood-engraver, he regularly provided the covers for *Vogue*; and the wrapper of V. Sackville-West's poem *The Land*, published this month, was designed and cut on wood by him.

I admitted that I had been irritated, first by the prevalency of the dogs (Grizzle on heat too.[12]) Secondly by his assumption that we can afford to saddle ourselves with a whole time gardener, build or buy him a cottage, & take in the terrace to be garden. Then, I said, we shall be tying ourselves to come here; shall never travel; & it will be assumed that Monks House is the hub of the world. This it certainly is not, I said, to me; nor do I wish to spend such a measure of our money on gardens, when we cannot buy rugs, beds or good arm chairs. L. was, I think, hurt at this, & I was annoyed at saying it, yet did it, not angrily, but in the interests of freedom. Too many women give way on this point, & secretly grudge their unselfishness in silence—a bad atmosphere. Our atmosphere decidedly cleared, after this, Tommie [Tomlin] came for the week end, & I am once more full of work, at high pressure, interested, & quite unable, I see, to make plain even to my own eyes, my season of profound despondency.

If I wish to avoid this in future, I recommend, first, incessant brain activity; reading, & planning; second, a methodical system of inviting people here (which is possible, with Nelly obedient & gay); third, increased mobility. For next year, I shall arrange perhaps to go definitely to Ethel Sands. With my motor I shall be more mobile.

But it is always a question whether I wish to avoid these glooms. In part they are the result of getting away by oneself, & have a psychological interest which the usual state of working & enjoying lacks. These 9 weeks give one a plunge into deep waters; which is a little alarming, but full of interest. All the rest of the year one's (I daresay rightly) curbing & controlling this odd immeasurable soul. When it expands, though one is frightened & bored & gloomy, it is as I say to myself, awfully queer. There is an edge to it which I feel of great importance, once in a way. One goes down into the well & nothing protects one from the assault of truth. Down there I cant write or read; I exist however. I am. Then I ask myself what I am? & get a closer though less flattering answer than I should on the surface—where, to tell the truth, I get more praise than is right. But the praise will go; one will be left alone with this queer being in old age. I am glad to find it on the whole so interesting, though so acutely unpleasant. Also, I can, by taking pains, be much more considerate of L.'s feelings; & so keep more steadily at our ordinary level of intimacy & ease: a level, I think, no other couple so long married, reaches, & keeps so constantly.

12. Grizzle, the mongrel fox-terrier the Woolfs acquired in the summer of 1922, became infected with eczema, and was put down on 4 December 1926.

Thursday 30 September

I wished to add some remarks to this, on the mystical side of this solitude; how it is not oneself but something in the universe that one's left with. It is this that is frightening & exciting in the midst of my profound gloom, depression, boredom, whatever it is: One sees a fin passing far out. What image can I reach to convey what I mean? Really there is none I think. The interesting thing is that in all my feeling & thinking I have never come up against this before. Life is, soberly & accurately, the oddest affair; has in it the essence of reality. I used to feel this as a child—couldn't step across a puddle once I remember, for thinking, how strange—what am I? &c. But by writing I dont reach anything. All I mean to make is a note of a curious state of mind. I hazard the guess that it may be the impulse behind another book. At present my mind is totally blank & virgin of books.* I want to watch & see how the idea at first occurs. I want to trace my own process.

* Perhaps The Waves or moths (Oct. 1929)

I was depressed again today because Vita did not come (yet relieved at the same time); had to hold L.'s ladder in the garden, when I wanted to write or to try on Nessa's dress; & slightly afraid that this dress is not very successful.

But I am shelving the dress problem on these principles. I am having cheap day clothes; & a good dress from Brooke; & I am being less pernickety about keeping to limits, as I have only to write & stir myself, to make, I wager, quite £50 extra in the year for my own extravagances. No longer shall I let a coat for £3 floor me in the middle of the night, or be afraid to lunch out because "I've no clothes." A broader & bolder grasp is what is wanted. Here I am going into the question of order & so on, like a housekeeper, taking in supplies. Soon, this time next week, I shall have no time for glooming or introspection. It will be "When may I come & see you?" Already Betty Potter has begun.[13]

Now I must scheme a little at my book of criticism.

The Woolfs returned to London on 4 October; there are no entries in VW's diary until 30 October, nor does LW resume his laconic record until 21 October.

13. Betty Potter was the stage name of Elizabeth Meinertzhagen (1892-1948), an ambitious but not very successful actress whom VW had tried to help when she was suicidal a few years earlier. (See *II VW Letters*, 1235.)

OCTOBER 1926

Saturday 30 October

It will be when may I come & see you!—too true a prophecy, though made in the damp & solitude of Rodmell. Monday, Ozzie Dickinson, Wednesday, Lady Colefax, Thursday Morgan to meet Abel Chevalley, dine Wells to meet Arnold Bennett, Friday to Monday Long Barn.[1] So the week slips or sticks through my fingers; rage misery joy, dulness elation mix: I am the usual battlefield of emotions; alternately think of buying chairs & clothes; plod with some method revising To the Lighthouse; quarrel with Nelly (who was to catch the afternoon train today because I told a lie about a telephone) & so we go on. Maurice Baring & the Sitwells send me their books;[2] Leonard forges ahead, now doing what he calls "correspondence"; the Press creaks a little at its hinges; Mrs C[artwright]. has absconded with my spectacles: I find Buggers bores; like the normal male; & should now be developing my book for the Press. All these things shoulder each other out across the screen of my brain. At intervals, I begin to think (I note this, as I am going to watch for the advent of a book) of a solitary woman musing[?] a book of ideas about life. This has intruded only once or twice, & very vaguely: it is a dramatisation of my mood at Rodmell. It is to be an endeavour at something mystic, spiritual; the thing that exists when we aren't there.

Among external things, we were at Cambridge for the week end; kept warm at the Bull—& there's a good subject—The Hotel.[3] Many people from Macclesfield talking about motor cars. Mothers, to me pathetic, looking half shyly at their sons, as if deprecating their age. A whole life

1. Oswald Eden Dickinson (1869-1954), brother of VW's old friend Violet whose homes he shared, was secretary to the Home Office Board of Control in Lunacy from 1913-32. Abel Chevalley (1868-1933), French critic of English Literature, was to give a lecture, under the auspices of the P.E.N. Club, on 'Some Tendencies of the French Contemporary Novel' at King's College, Strand, on 4 November; E. M. Forster was presiding. The same day, LW noted that they 'Dined Wells Arnold Bennett & Bernard Shaw'.

2. In addition to *C* (see above, 31 July 1926, n 23), Maurice Baring gave VW his *Punch & Judy and other Essays*, 1924, *Daphne Adeane*, 1926, *Cat's Cradle*, 1926, and *The Glass Mender and other Stories*, 1926 (see *Holleyman*, MH II, pp 5, 6). On 2 October Osbert Sitwell inscribed his *Before the Bombardment*, 1926, 'For dear Virginia Tremblingly from the Author' (*Holleyman*, MH II, p 3); Sacheverell Sitwell presented her with his *All Summer in a Day*, 1926 (sold at Sotheby's on 27 April 1970, lot 93).

3. The Woolfs had stayed at the Bull Hotel, Trumpington Street (now a mere façade concealing new college buildings), on 23 and on 24 October when, after dining with Maynard Keynes, LW read a paper to the Heretics' Club.

opened to me: father, mother, son, daughter. Father alone has wine. An enormous man, like an advertisement of Power: sits in chair. Daddy you'll be miserable in it says girl, herself bovine. Mother a mere wisp; sits with eyes shut; had spent hours driving up writing characters of maids. Shall I remember any of this?

Then Gosse introducing Vita at Royal —— something. I never saw the whole hierarchy of lit. so plainly exposed. Gosse the ornament on the tea pot: beneath him file on file of old stout widows whose husbands had been professors, beetle specialists doubtless, meritorious dons; & these good people, ruminating tea, & reflecting all the depths of the suburbs tinctured with literature, dear Vita told them were "The Hollow Men."[4] Her address was read in sad sulky tones like those of a schoolboy; her pendulous rich society face, glowing out under a black hat at the end of the smoky dismal room, looked very ancestral & like a picture under glass in a gallery. She was fawned upon by the little dapper grocer Gosse, who kept spinning round on his heel to address her compliments & to scarify Bolshevists; in an ironical voice which seemed to ward off what might be said of him; & to be drawing round the lot of them thicker & thicker, the red plush curtains of respectability. There was Vita, who was too innocent to see it, Guedalla, & Drinkwater.[5] I dont regret my wildest, foolishest, utterance, if it gave the least crack to this respectability. But needless to say, no word of mine has had any effect whatever. Gosse will survive us all. Now how does he do it? Yet he seemed to me, with his irony & his scraping, somehow uneasy. A kind of black doormat got up & appeared to be Lady Gosse. So home, with Dotty in a rage, because she was palmed off with Plank. She did contrive to get here though in the end. One night I went in with Vita after the play. She was lying asleep at Mount Street, in a flat at the top of the house: large pale furniture about dimly seen—a dog on her bed. She woke up chattering & hysterical. Virginia Woolf Virginia Woolf My God! Virginia Woolf is in the room. For Gods Sake Vita dont turn the lights on. No light you fool! But I

---

4. V. Sackville-West gave a lecture at the Royal Society of Literature on the afternoon of 27 October on 'Some Tendencies of Modern English Poetry'. She ended her address with this fragment from T. S. Eliot's poem published in his *Poems 1909-1925*:

> 'Remember us—if at all—not as lost
> Violent souls, but only
> As the hollow men.'

The chair was taken by Sir Edmund Gosse (1849-1928), man of letters, high priest of the literary establishment, and dispenser of a weekly gospel in the *Sunday Times*.

5. Philip Guedalla (1889-1944), historian and biographer; John Drinkwater (1882-1937), playwright and poet.

cant see to get the allella, mumbled Vita.[6] She got it though. We sat & drank. Dusky shapes of glasses & things, a room I had never seen; a woman I scarcely knew; Vita there between us, intimate wi' both; flattery, extravagance, complete inner composure on my part, & so home.

The first three weeks of November, when no diary was written, appear to have been very fully taken up with work on To the Lighthouse, *with Vita (and a visit to her at Long Barn, 6-8 November), with social gatherings and innumerable people. The dinner party on 4 November at the H. G. Wellses', where the Woolfs met the Shaws and Arnold Bennett, was recorded by the latter in his journal; of the Woolfs he wrote: 'Both gloomy, these two . . . But I liked both of them in spite of their naughty treatment of me in the press.'*

Tuesday 23 November

Here I must resolve first of all to find some long solid book to read. What? Tristram Shandy? French memoirs? This is on top of a discussion, at tea about Angus. He dont do, L. says: will never make a manager. So then shall it be another attempt, or Cape, or Secker?[1] These difficulties recur. I should not much like writing for Cape; yet if the Press is sagging on our shoulders, there is little sense in waiting on. Next year L. thinks we could sell to advantage. It gives one a full life: but then life is so full already. Colefax complicates the scene—Colefax is the death of this book. Aren't I always reading her scrawls or answering them. This culminated last week in her dining alone with me, off cold chicken. I found us talking socially, not intimately, she in pearls (shams Vita says) popping up one light after another: like the switch board at the telephone exchange at the mention of names. Geoffrey Scott, Percy Lubbock[,] whoever it might be. Perfectly competent, &, for her purpose, efficient. She is, I maintain, a woman of the world: has all her senses tuned to that pitch. The machine doesn't work in private, though she was very anxious, poor aspiring, slightly suspicious & uneasy woman, that it should. She told me how she had lived till she married running after old ladies with their knitting. So, on marriage, but she was only 19, had kicked her

6. VW had been with Vita Sackville-West to the Barnes Theatre on 25 October to the first night of Komisarjevsky's production of *The Three Sisters*. Dorothy Wellesley had a London flat opposite Hyde Park. Alella is a white Catalonian wine.
1. LW noted his conclusion about Angus Davidson in the same words on the same day; see LWP, Sussex, Part II, Q.

heels up: determined to live, like Violet's mother, who leant out of the Palace window at Auckland & said, to an old man selling kippers, Is this life?[2] But now, aged 50, she asks, Is this life? again—rushing round, dining & giving dinners; never able to concentrate in a corner, & secretly, in my opinion, not desiring it but pretending it, as she has the habit of pretence. This is all right in her, but wrong in me. So we don't altogether amalgamate; but I have my reservations, she hers. In came Dadie, to our relief, somewhat; then Sir Arthur, breezy, cheery, competent, patting her, controlling her, petted by her (she reverted to her arch girlish days, when she could eat soup & potatoes without any thought of her figure) sitting on the edge of my shabby dirty down at heels arm chair.[3]

All this rushes on apace. Fame grows. Chances of meeting this person, doing that thing, accumulate. Life is as I've said since I was 10, awfully interesting—if anything, quicker, keener at 44 than 24—more desperate I suppose, as the river shoots to Niagara—my new vision of death; active, positive, like all the rest, exciting; & of great importance—as an experience.

'The one experience I shall never describe' I said to Vita yesterday. She was sitting on the floor in her velvet jacket & red striped silk shirt, I knotting her pearls into heaps of great lustrous eggs. She had come up to see me—so we go on—a spirited, creditable affair, I think, innocent (spiritually) & all gain, I think; rather a bore for Leonard, but not enought to worry him. The truth is one has room for a good many relationships. Then she goes back again to Persia, with Leigh Ashton— that putty faced low voiced rather beaten cur, who is always slinking off with his tail between his legs, but gives, they say, oyster suppers.

I am re-doing six pages of Lighthouse daily. This is not I think, so quick as Mrs D.: but then I find much of it very sketchy, & have to improvise on the typewriter. This I find much easier than re-writing in pen & ink. My present opinion is that it is easily the best of my books, fuller than J.'s R. & less spasmodic, occupied with more interesting things than Mrs D. & not complicated with all that desperate accompani- ment of madness. It is freer & subtler I think. Yet I have no idea yet of any other to follow it: which may mean that I have made my method perfect, & it will now stay like this, & serve whatever use I wish to put it to. Before, some development of the method brought fresh subjects in

2. Violet Dickinson's mother had been Emily Dulcibella Eden, third daughter of the 3rd Baron Auckland, Bishop of Bath and Wells from 1854-1869; his Palace was at Wells, not Auckland.

3. Sir Arthur Colefax (1866-1936), KC, was a specialist in patent and trade mark law. The Colefaxes had married in 1901.

view, because I saw the chance of being able to say them. Yet I am now
& then haunted by some semi mystic very profound life of a woman,
which shall all be told on one occasion; & time shall be utterly obliterated;
future shall somehow blossom out of the past. One incident—say the
fall of a flower—might contain it. My theory being that the actual event
practically does not exist—nor time either. But I dont want to force this.
I must make up my Series book.

*On 4 December VW went again to Long Barn to spend the week-end with
Vita Sackville-West; LW, having had Grizzle put down, spent the night
with his brother Herbert at Cookham.*

Saturday 11 December

I have never been able to afford 2/ for a good piece of washleather, yet
I buy a dozen boxes of matches for 1/6.

I am giving up the hope of being well dressed.

Violet Dickinson has just had a third serious operation & I went to
an old Curiosity shop instead of going to see her.[1]

Leonard is lunching with Maynard & a great registered parcel has just
been delivered containing Dadie's dissertation.[2]

It is now close on 3.30.

Some superstition prevents me from reading Yeats' autobiography as
I should like.[3]

I am very happy at the moment: having arranged my week on the
whole well.

But I have been rather unscupulous. I have put off the Stephens, at
Thorpe: & shall probably stay at Knole.

A few thoughts to fill up time waiting for dinner.

An article all about London:

How Vita's inkpot flowered on her table.

Logan's vanity: I write everything 8 times—

(So thats how its done I thought: he thought thats the only way to
produce writing like mine)

1. Violet Dickinson was convalescing in her own home in Manchester Street after a
   cancer operation.
2. A slightly revised version of G. H. W. Rylands' Fellowship dissertation was to be
   published by the Hogarth Press as *Words and Poetry* in 1928 (*HP Checklist* 175).
3. W. B. Yeats' *Autobiographies: Reveries over Childhood & The Trembling of the Veil*,
   first published in 1914 and 1922 respectively, were re-issued in November 1926 in
   Macmillan's 6-volume Collected Works of Yeats. The book was discussed by LW
   in his 'World of Books' article in the *N & A* on 1 January 1927.

But all my thoughts perish instantly. I make them up so vast. How to blunt the sting of an unpleasant remark: to say it over & over & over again. Walked to Violet's; took her a red carnation & a white one. My feelings quickened as I drew near. I visualised the operation as I stood on the doorstep.

I also have made up a passage for The Lighthouse: on people going away & the effect on one's feeling for them.

But reading Yeats turns my sentences one way: reading Sterne turns them another.

On 22 December the Woolfs went to Cornwall to spend Christmas with Ka and Will Arnold-Forster at Eagle's Nest, Zennor; they returned to London on 28 December.

1927

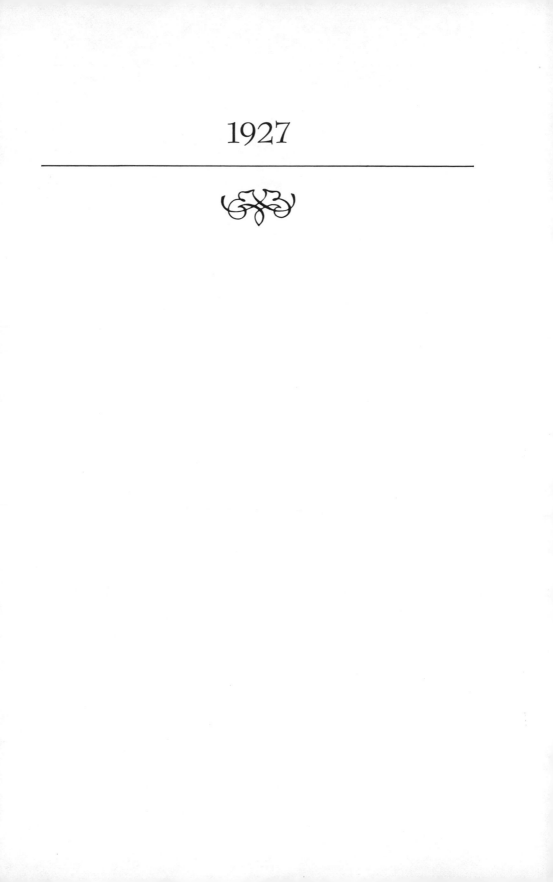

1927

The Woolfs returned to Tavistock Square from Cornwall on 28 December, a day earlier than intended, owing to the cold and the colds at Eagle's Nest; they went to Monks House from 4-8 January; and on 17 January VW was taken by Vita Sackville-West to stay with the latter's father at Knole for two nights. VW continued to write her diary in her 1926 book, DIARY XV.

Friday 14 January

This is out of order, but I have no new book, & so must record here (& it was here I recorded the beginning of The Lighthouse) must record here the end. This moment I have finished the final drudgery. It is now complete for Leonard to read on Monday. Thus I have done it some days under the year, & feel thankful to be out of it again. Since October 25th I have been revising & retyping (some parts 3 times over) & no doubt I should work at it again; but I cannot. What I feel is that it is a hard muscular book, which at this age proves that I have something in me. It has not run out & gone flabby, at least such is my feeling before reading it over.

Sunday 23 January

Well Leonard has read To the Lighthouse, & says it is much my best book, & it is a 'masterpiece'. He said this without my asking. I came back from Knole & sat without asking him. He calls it entirely new 'a psychological poem', is his name for it. An improvement upon Dalloway: more interesting. Having won this great relief, my mind dismisses the whole thing, as usual; & I forget it, & shall only wake up & be worried again over proofs & then when it appears.

We went to Cornwall (dare I characterise Will hearing him talk next door—it is Sunday—he is dining with us). He is a water-blooded waspish little man, all on edge, vain, peevish, nervous. Ka is matronly, but substantial. Some views I retain—one of the valley in the evening light—but others were only a dull impression of life suspended & frozen, & the chin sawing of Mervyn: all chapped, becolded.[1] We came home for these

1. William Edward Arnold-Forster (1885-1951) had married VW's old friend Ka Cox in 1918, when he was still in the RNVR. By training and inclination a painter, he now devoted much time to the work of the League of Nations, and in 1926 had

reasons a day early, & next morning I had a letter from the New York H[erald]. & T[ribune] asking me to go there, passage paid, 120 in my pocket &, perhaps, expenses, & write 4 articles. We accepted, on conditions; but have not heard yet. Meanwhile we hesitate, for if Leonard came, we should probably be £150 out of pocket. So it seems. The adventure is tempting. But the grind of moneymaking is scarcely to be endured unnecessarily. We could go to Greece, or Italy for less.

Then Nessa has gone, poor dear creature. I came in two days ago & found her white at the telephone; Elly at the other end saying that Duncan's illness was probably typhoid.[2] I think a left handed marriage makes these moments more devastating: a sense remains, I think of hiding one's anguish; of insecurity. Angus writes the most cautious alarming letters. Anyhow she went yesterday in a snowstorm, & we kissed on the pavement in the snow. We are very intimate—a great solace to me. Vita goes on Saturday.[3] Tomorrow I dine with her at Colefaxes: a brilliant party: no clothes: hair down my back as usual. Does it very much matter? I reached that point of philosophy at Knole the other night, with the bountiful womanly Mrs Rubens & his Lordship the figure of an English nobleman, decayed, dignified, smoothed, effete; respectable I think in his modest way.[4] But I never have enjoyed a party. Balls at Buckingham

---

been appointed a member of the Labour Party Advisory Committee on International Affairs, of which LW was Secretary. At a meeting on 19 January the two of them had been asked to draft a commentary, and presumably it was this they were discussing as VW wrote. Will's younger brother Mervyn Nevil Arnold-Forster (1888-1927), who had fought with the Grenadier Guards and was awarded a MC, was later this year to be considered as manager of the Hogarth Press, but died on 6 May 1927 from pneumonia and the delayed effects of his war service (see below, 16 May 1927).

2. Early in January Duncan Grant had gone to stay with his mother and aunt at Cassis, where they had rented a villa, 'Les Mimosas'; on arrival he collapsed with a fever. Angus Davidson who followed him to Provence for his winter holiday found him very ill and alarmed Vanessa, who had in any case planned to join Duncan and spend several months painting in the south. She left England, with Angelica and her servant Grace Germany, on 22 January; by the time they reached Cassis Duncan was on the mend, and Vanessa installed herself in a flat in the nearby Villa Corsica.

3. Vita in fact left London for Persia on Friday 28 January, after spending most of the morning with VW; Leigh Ashton and Dorothy Wellesley accompanied her.

4. Vita's father, Lionel Edward Sackville-West, 3rd Baron Sackville (1867-1928), was a conscientious JP and member of Kent County Council. In 1919 Lady Sackville had left Knole, to which she never returned, when he installed the singer Olive Rubens (d. 1973) and her husband Walter in the house; but she refused to set him free to marry Mrs Rubens.

Palace are worth looking at. He spends the day sitting on Com[mi]tees at Maidstone; interviews parsons about livings; likes chess & crime. Vita took me over the 4 acres of building, which she loves: too little conscious beauty for my taste: smallish rooms looking on to buildings: no views: yet one or two things remain: Vita stalking in her Turkish dress, attended by small boys, down the gallery, wafting them on like some tall sailing ship—a sort of covey of noble English life: dogs walloping, children crowding, all very free & stately: & [a] cart bringing wood in to be sawn by the great circular saw. How do you see that? I asked Vita. She said she saw it as something that had gone on for hundreds of years. They had brought wood in from the Park to replenish the great fires like this for centuries: & her ancestresses had walked so on the snow with their great dogs bounding by them. All the centuries seemed lit up, the past expressive, articulate; not dumb & forgotten; but a crowd of people stood behind, not dead at all; not remarkable; fair faced, long limbed; affable; & so we reach the days of Elizabeth quite easily. After tea, looking for letters of Dryden's to show me, she tumbled out a love letter of Ld Dorset's (17th century) with a lock of his soft gold tinted hair which I held in my hand a moment.[5] One had a sense of links fished up into the light which are usually submerged. Otherwise no particular awe or any great sense of difference or distinction. They are not a brilliant race. The space & comeliness of it all struck me. I came home to Marjorie Strachey,[6] Tom Eliot, Nessa & Roger. A little constricted our society: no talk of the clergy or of the country; but how lively & agile compared with the

[text ends]

DIARY XVI

Thursday 3 February

Fate always contrives that I begin the new year in February. I ask, why another volume? (but here's an innovation: this is not a book but a block —so lazy am I about making writing books nowadays). What is the purpose of them? L. taking up a volume the other day said Lord save him if I died first & he had to read through these. My handwriting deteriorates. And do I say anything interesting? I can always waste an idle hour reading them; & then, oh yes, I shall write my memoirs out of them, one of these days.

5. In her book *Knole and the Sackvilles* (1947) V. Sackville-West describes Dryden as a constant visitor at Knole, the guest of Charles Sackville, 6th Earl of Dorset (1638-1706); and refers (p 128) to a lock 'of reddish-brown hair of surprising length' enclosed in a love-letter to the Countess of Falmouth.
6. Marjorie ('Gumbo') Strachey (1882-1964), teacher, was Lytton's youngest sister.

That reminds me of the Webbs: those 36 strenuous hours at Liphook, in an emphatic lodging house, with blue books in the passages; & those entirely devoted—by which I mean those entirely integrated people.[1] Their secret is that they have by nature no divisions of soul to fritter them away: their impact is solid & entire. Without eyes & ears (but Mrs Webb listens in & prefers Mozart to Handel, if I may guess) one can come down with more of a weight upon bread & butter or whatever the substance is before one. On a steely watery morning we swiftly tramped over a heathy common talking, talking. In their efficiency & glibness one traces perfectly adjusted machinery; but talk by machinery does not charm, or suggest: it cuts the grass of the mind close at the roots. I'm too hurried to write. Mrs W. is far less ornamental than of old: wispy untidy drab, with a stain on her skirt & a key on her watch chain; as if she had cleared the decks & rolled her sleeves & was waiting for the end, but working.

Saturday 12 February

Exactly what has happened in the Clive Mary affair I cannot say. Did he not sheepishly admit in the kitchen the other night that he was putting it off till March? & then, casually & jauntily tell me as if by chance, the other afternoon, here, that he was going after all. But wont Mary mind? What if she does?—that was practically his answer.[2]

Vita's prose is too fluent. I've been reading it, & it makes my pen run. When I've read a classic, I am curbed &—not castrated: no, the opposite; I cant think of the word at the moment.

Had I been writing P[assenger] to T[eheran] I should have run off whole pools of this coloured water; & then (I think) found my own method of attack. It is my distinction as a writer I think to get this clear & my expression exact. Were I writing travels I should wait till some angle emerged: & go for that. The method of writing smooth narrative

1. The Woolfs stayed Saturday night, 29 January, with Sidney and Beatrice Webb at their Surrey home, Passfield Corner, which Beatrice described (*Diaries 1924-32*, edited by Margaret Cole, 1956, p 32) as a cottage with a comfortable study and delightful loggia; for her reflections on this renewal of relations with 'this exceptionally gifted pair' see *ibid.*, pp 130-31; and for LW's recollection of *her* fervour and appearance on this occasion, see *I LW*, pp 49-50.
2. Clive had announced his decision to break with Mary Hutchinson and to leave England for some months in order to write a book; he changed his mind several times, but eventually set out on 23 February to join Vanessa and Duncan at Cassis. VW's version of the matter at this time is given fully in her letters to Vanessa of 2 and 9 February (*III VW Letters*, nos. 1712, 1715); but the fluctuations of Clive's emotional life were apparent for some considerable time longer.

cant be right; things dont happen in one's mind like that. But she is very skilful & golden voiced.

This makes me think that I have to read To the L. tomorrow & Monday, straight through in print; straight through, owing to my curious methods, for the first time. I want to read largely & freely once: then to niggle over details.

But I am forgetting, after 3 days, the most important event in my life since marriage—so Clive described it: Bobo shingled me. Mr Cizec has bingled me.[3] I am short haired for life. Having no longer, I think, any claims to beauty, the convenience of this alone makes it desirable. Every morning I go to take up brush & twist that old coil round my finger & fix it with hairpins & then with a start of joy, no I needn't. In front there is no change; behind I'm like the rump of a partridge. This robs dining out of half its terrors; in token of which, I'm 'dining out' (the distinction is clear: Roger & Clive & Bloomsbury aint dining out) with Ethel [Sands] & with the [Hubert] Hendersons.

For the rest—its been a gay tropical kind of autumn, with so much Vita & Knole & staying away: we have launched ourselves a little more freely perhaps from work & the Press. But now with Nessa away, Clive away, Duncan away, Vita away, the strenuous time sets in: I'm reading & writing at a great pace; mean to 'do' Morgan;[4] have a fling at my book on fiction; & make all the money we want for Greece & a motor car. I may note that the first symptoms of Lighthouse are unfavourable. Roger, it is clear did not like Time Passes. Harpers & the Forum have refused serial rights; Brace writes, I think, a good deal less enthusiastically than of Mrs D. But these opinions refer to the rough copy, unrevised.[5] And

3. Beatrice ('Bobo') Mayor, née Meinertzhagen (1885-1971), wife of an Apostle and sister of the actress Betty Potter; she wrote plays. She and Clive, who were close friends at this time, dined with the Woolfs on 9 February. Charles Cizek was a hairdresser, of 116 Tottenham Court Road.

4. VW 'did' Morgan in her article 'The Novels of E. M. Forster' (Kp C292), not published until November in the *Atlantic Monthly*, though (as he had done with his article on her) she showed him a draft of it in June. Later in the year she also wrote on Forster's *Aspects of the Novel* (the published text of the Clark Lectures he was currently delivering at Cambridge) an article (Kp C288) which, though written considerably later, was published (in the *New York Herald Tribune*) before the one on his novels.

5. The centre section of *To the Lighthouse*, 'Time Passes', translated by Roger Fry's friend Charles Mauron, had been published in Paris in the Winter 1926 issue of *Commerce* (Kp D27). Fry wrote to his wife: 'To tell the truth I do not think this piece is quite of her best vintage' (see *II RF Letters*, no. 590). Both the English and American editions of *To the Lighthouse* were published on 5 May 1927 (Kp A10 a & b). From this diary entry it would appear that several proof copies

anyhow I feel callous: L.'s opinion keeps me steady; I'm neither one thing nor the other.

Yesterday Wells asked us to publish a pamphlet for him.[6] This is a great rise in the world for us; & comes on top of rather a flat talk with Angus. L. says he doesn't "manage". Angus refuses to budge an inch. He can't see the point of it. As he says, too, whats he to do if he leaves? He doesn't want to leave. Though sometimes 'fed up' he likes it better than most work. But I'm persuaded we need, the press needs, a fanatic at the moment; not this quiet easygoing gentlemanliness. I am annoyed at doing cards, & envelopes; & L. does twice the work I do.

Monday 21 February

Why not invent a new kind of play—as for instance
Woman thinks: . . .
He does.
Organ Plays.
She writes.
They say:
She sings:
Night speaks:
They miss

I think it must be something in this line—though I cant now see what. Away from facts: free; yet concentrated; prose yet poetry; a novel & a play.

But today is

Monday 28 February

& I have got into another stream of thought, if thought it can be called.

Let me collect a few logs, drifting in my mind, to represent the past few days.

Clive, standing at the door.

---

had been pulled (by R. & R. Clark, Edinburgh) and that three at least had been sent to America. There are discrepancies between the text of the English and of the American edition (printed for Harcourt Brace by Quinn & Boden Company, N.J.), notably in the section 'Time Passes'. It thus seems likely, particularly in view of Roger Fry's reported opinion, that VW made emendations on her proof which were effected by Clarks but not transmitted to America; and thus that the English edition embodies her final revision.

6. *Democracy Under Revision*, the text of a lecture to be given by H. G. Wells at the Sorbonne on 15 March 1927, was published by the Hogarth Press in March (*HP Checklist* 151).

She cries for the moon.

This was said of Mary. With it he went to Cassis for 3 months.

Again, If Mrs Woolf dont think me worth a penny stamp I said—this being Rose Bartholomew standing at her cottage door on Friday evening. Phrases suddenly seem to me very significant, & then I forget them. My brain is rather stale. Do I like The Lighthouse? I think I was disappointed. But God knows. I have to read it again.

A letter from Vita & Dottie just come. She is not an explicit letter writer. But I must be fond of her, genuinely, to start as I did at the sight of Dottie's hand, thinking she wrote to say V. was ill.

For the rest I think Cowper is a good poet. I'd like to write about him. Shall we go to Greece, Italy or France? I'm glad I didn't dedicate my book to Roger. This I verified in his presence, the other night [*23 February*]. He dined here with Raymond. Raymond is intellectually speaking underbred. Roger a pure aristocrat. Philip [Ritchie] came in, his little green eyes hazed bunged up with drink. So to Rodmell. And now the wind is making the tin screen over the gas fire rattle. How we protect ourselves from the elements! Coming back last night I thought, owing to civilisation, I, who am now cold, wet, & hungry, can be warm & satisfied & listening to a Mozart 4tet in 15 minutes. And so I was.

That ring may be Tom. No. Tom dont run upstairs—only the lower classes do that.

And I dont think I shall go out in the rain, though I am going to spend this week in long romantic London walks. I have successfully broken the neck of that screaming grey goose—society. There's nothing to be afraid of in dining with Ethel or Sibyl—& I'm shingled now. One spins round for a moment & then settles on one's feet. But about the Soul: the soul has sunk to the bottom. I am empty headed tonight, feeling the lack of Nessa rather, & all the prelude of Spring—the vague discomfort & melancholy & a feeling of having come to anchor. But I intend to work harder & harder. If they—the respectables, my friends, advise me against The Lighthouse, I shall write memoirs; have a plan already to get historical manuscripts & write Lives of the Obscure:[7] but why do I pretend I should take advice? After a holiday the old ideas will come to me as usual; seeming fresher, more important than ever; & I shall be off again, feeling that extraordinary exhilaration, that ardour & lust of creation—which is odd, if what I create is, as it well may be, wholly bad.

7. VW had already published two such 'Lives' (reprinted in *The Common Reader*); but her inclination to act as 'a deliverer advancing . . . to the rescue of some stranded ghost' was recurrent.

Today I bought a new watch. Last night I crept into L.'s bed to make up a sham quarrel about paying our fares to Rodmell. Now to finish Passage to India.

Saturday 5 March

Both rather headachy & fatigued. This is the last slope up of the year which is always worst. Finishing, correcting the last proofs that is to say, of a book is always a screw. Then I have written rather incessantly, one thing after another. A holiday, without dinner to order, or telephone to answer, or people to talk to, will be a divine miracle. We go to Cassis on the 30th; then to Sicily; so home by Rome. What could be more to my heart. Often I sit & think of looking at things. The greed of my eye is insatiable. To think of seeing a new place fills me with excitement. I now make up pictures of Sicily. Think of the Campagna grey in the evening.

I have been hard pressed about the Eliot fund, & behind the scenes of ladies diplomacy—Chrissie & Sibyl, that is:[1] so much suavity, so much distrust of each other, & so great a desire for compliments. Molly came to tea; could not get her mind off her troubles, first laughing at them— Desmond all right, & so on: then brushing laughter aside, & becoming more & more openly worried. Sibyl had cross examined her about her debts. To such indignities poverty exposes one. So I told her the truth, or what I hope will be the truth: that friends are subscribing enough to send them abroad, Oh how wonderful! she exclaimed, she never having seen Italy or Spain all these years. "I'm afraid Desmond has had rather an unhappy life," she said. "But then think of Lytton . . . Of course I was extravagant about doing the house up . . . but then we can let it." "Rachel goes for long walks at night & reads Coleridge—Oh Desmond's hopeless—he's like a dog who runs out if the door is open." So we laid our heads together over the fire; & felt very sisterly & sympathetic. I distrust though the pleasure one gets in helping one's friends.

Monday 14 March

Although annoyed that I have not heard from Vita by this post nor

1. The winding up of the abortive Eliot Fund (see *II VW Diary*, 19 July 1922, n 13; and *III VW Letters*, separately indexed) of which VW, Lady Ottoline Morrell and Richard Aldington were trustees, was protracted and not finally accomplished until January 1928. Now there was a scheme afoot, in which the prime movers were Christabel McLaren and Lady Colefax, to raise money for the perennially indigent MacCarthys, either to pay their debts, or to enable them to have a holiday abroad. To VW fell the task of transmitting a cheque for £300 to Molly MacCarthy; see *III VW Letters*, no. 1736 of 24 March 1927. See also LWP, Sussex, II D 17f, notebook labelled 'DM Fund March & April 1927'.

yet last week, annoyed sentimentally, & partly from vanity—still I must record the conception last night between 12 & one of a new book. I said I would be on the watch for symptoms of this extremely mysterious process. For some weeks, since finishing The Lighthouse I have thought myself virgin, passive, blank of ideas. I toyed vaguely with some thoughts of a flower whose petals fall; of time all telescoped into one lucid channel through wh. my heroine was to pass at will. The petals falling. But nothing came of it. I shirked the effort—seemed to have no impulse that way, supposed that I had worked out my vein. Faith Henderson came to tea, &, valiantly beating the waters of conversation, I sketched the possibilities which an unattractive woman, penniless, alone, might yet bring into being. I began imagining the position—how she would stop a motor on the Dover road, & so get to Dover: cross the channel: &c. It struck me, vaguely, that I might write a Defoe narrative for fun. Suddenly between twelve & one I conceived a whole fantasy to be called "The Jessamy Brides"—why, I wonder? I have rayed round it several scenes. Two women, poor, solitary at the top of a house. One can see anything (for this is all fantasy) the Tower Bridge, clouds, aeroplanes. Also old men listening in the room over the way. Everything is to be tumbled in pall mall. It is to be written as I write letters at the top of my speed: on the ladies of Llangollen; on Mrs Fladgate; on people passing.[2] No attempt is to be made to realise the character. Sapphism is to be suggested. Satire is to be the main note—satire & wildness. The Ladies are to have Constantinople in view. Dreams of golden domes. My own lyric vein is to be satirised. Everything mocked. And it is to end with three dots . . . so. For the truth is I feel the need of an escapade after these serious poetic experimental books whose form is always so closely considered. I want to kick up my heels & be off. I want to embody all those innum-erable little ideas & tiny stories which flash into my mind at all seasons. I think this will be great fun to write; & it will rest my head before starting the very serious, mystical poetical work which I want to come next. Meanwhile, before I can touch the Jessamy Brides, I have to write my book on fiction & that wont be done till January, I suppose. I might dash off a page or two now & then by way of experiment. And it is possible that the idea will evaporate. Anyhow this records the odd hurried unexpected way in which these things suddenly create themselves—one thing on top of another in about an

Orlando leading to The Waves. (July 8th 1933)

2. Lady Eleanor Butler (1739-1829) and the Hon. Sarah Ponsonby (1755-1831) foreswore matrimony and retreated to Plas Newydd overlooking Llangollen, where they became celebrated as eccentrics. Mrs Fladgate unidentified.

hour. So I made up Jacob's Room looking at the fire at Hogarth House; so I made up The Lighthouse one afternoon in the square here.

Monday 21 March

This is the kind of evening when one seems to be abroad: the window is open; the yellows & greys of the houses seem exposed to the summer; there is that rumour & clamour which reminds one of Italy. Almost in a week now we shall be starting. I dislike the days before going. I went to buy clothes today & was struck by my own ugliness. Like Edith Sitwell I can never look like other people—too broad, tall, flat, with hair hanging. And now my neck is so ugly . . . But I never think of this at home.

How disturbing the summer is! We shall sit reading with the windows open tonight, but my mind will only just touch the page & float off. Something unsettled & melancholy will be in the air. Also it seems the threshold of that vast burning London summer, which alarms me slightly, Vita & Harold will be back; my book will be out. We shall sit in the Square. But I shall not let things worry me much. (so I say—but it is still only March.) We shall have a week at Cassis—a strange resurrection of us all abroad. Many years have gone since Nessa, Clive & I met there. Never with Leonard of course.[3]

My brain is ferociously active. I want to have at my books as if I were conscious of the lapse of time, age & death. Dear me, how lovely some parts of The Lighthouse are! Soft & pliable, & I think deep, & never a word wrong for a page at a time. This I feel about the dinner party, & the children in the boat; but not of Lily on the lawn. That I do not much like. But I like the end.

I get too many letters to answer nowadays. Edith Sitwell came to tea: transparent like some white bone one picks up on a moor, with sea water stones on her long frail hands which slide into yours much narrower than one expects like a folded fan. She has pale gemlike eyes; & is dressed, on a windy March day, in three decker skirts of red spotted cotton. She half shuts her eyes; coos an odd little laugh, reminding me of the Fishers [*VW's cousins*]. All is very tapering & pointed, the nose running on like a mole. She said I was a great writer, which pleased me. So sensitive to everything in people & books she said. She got talking about her mother, blaspheming in the nursery, hysterical, terrible; setting Edith to kill bluebottles. 'But nobody can take a liberty with her' said Edith, who prides herself on Angevin blood. She is a curious product, likable to me:

3. VW had gone to Italy with Clive and Vanessa Bell both in 1908 and 1909.

sensitive, etiolated, affectionate, lonely, having to thread her way (there is something ghostlike & angular about her) home to Bayswater to help cook dinner. She said she would like to attach great bags & balloons of psychology, people having dinner, &c, to her poems, but has no knowledge of human nature, only these sudden intense poems—which by the way she has sent me.[4] In other ages she would have been a cloistered nun; or an eccentric secluded country old maid. It is the oddity of our time that has set her on the music hall stage. She trips out into the Limelight with all the timidity & hauteur of the aristocratic spinster.

On 30 March the Woolfs set out on a month's holiday, travelling via Paris to Cassis, where they again stayed at the Hotel Cendrillon but spent most of their days with the Bells and Duncan Grant at the Villa Corsica. On 6 April they left Toulon by train for Rome, going on next day to Palermo, where they stayed five days before moving on to Syracuse. On the return journey they spent three nights in Naples and a week in Rome, and came home to Tavistock Square late on 28 April. VW's letters give a spirited and detailed account of their travels; see III VW Letters, nos. 1741-7.

Sunday 1 May

We came back on Thursday night from Rome; from that other private life which I mean to have for ever now. There is a complete existence in Italy: apart from this. One is nobody in Italy: one has no name, no calling, no background. And, then, not only is there the beauty, but a different relationship. Altogether I dont think I've ever enjoyed one month so much. What a faculty of enjoyment one has! I liked everything. I wish I were not so ignorant of Italian, art, literature & so on. However, I cannot now write this out, or go into the great mass of feeling which it composed in me. Nelly was found, at 11.30, when we got back, in bed, with some mysterious affection of the kidney. This was a jar; the coffee was a jar; everything was a jar. And then I remember how my book is coming out. People will say I am irreverent—people will say a thousand things. But

4. Edith was the eldest and conspicuously unloved child of Sir George and his tempestuous wife Lady Ida, a daughter of the Earl of Londesborough, whom he had selected for her distinguished pedigree without regard to her character or feelings. After a miserable childhood and youth, Edith managed to leave home in 1914, since when she had lived in a 3-room flat in Pembridge Mansions, Moscow Road, with her ex-governess. (See *Façades: Edith, Osbert & Sacheverell Sitwell* by John Pearson, 1978.) The copy of her just published *Rustic Elegies*, inscribed to VW, was sold at Sotheby's on 27 April 1970, lot 88.

I think, honestly, I care very little this time—even for the opinion of my friends. I am not sure if it is good. I was disappointed when I read it through the first time. Later I liked it. Anyhow it is the best I can do. But would it be a good thing to read my things when they are printed, critically? It is encouraging that, in spite of obscurity, affectation & so on, my sales rise steadily. We have sold, already, 1220 before publication, & I think it will be about 1500, which for a writer like I am is not bad. Yet, to show I am genuine, I find myself thinking of other things with absorption & forgetting that it will be out on Thursday. Leonard never thinks of his book. Vita comes back on Friday. I am angry with Clive for gossiping about my letter to Nessa.[1] It is fine, cold, clear, we dine out, have a char.

Thursday 5 May

Book out. We have sold (I think) 1690 before publication—twice Dalloway. I write however in the shadow of the damp cloud of the Times Lit Sup. review, which is an exact copy of the JsR. Mrs Dalloway review, gentlemanly, kindly, timid & praising beauty, doubting character, & leaving me moderately depressed.[2] I am anxious about Time Passes. Think the whole thing may be pronounced soft, shallow, insipid, sentimental. Yet, honestly, don't much care; want to be let alone to ruminate. Odd how strong this feeling is in me. Now I think we are safe to get our motor car. The next fortnight we shall both be depressed about our books.

Dined with the Wests last night, all solid, shiny, spread & spacious; as if they were settling in; wedding presents; clean covers, carpets, &c. all too handsome for my taste.[3] I'm reverting to squalor as my milieu. And then why did she marry him? He is the type of any other cleverish young journalist, common, glib: uneasy last night, lest we should talk of Angus. But we talked of Madge.

I know why I am depressed: a bad habit of making up the review I should like before reading the review I get. I am excited about my article

1. VW's full and rapturous letters to Vanessa from Sicily and Italy had been read aloud to Clive and Duncan at Cassis, and Clive had retailed their contents to friends met in Paris on his return there. See *III VW Letters*, nos. 1748, 1750.
2. The *TLS* unsigned review of *To the Lighthouse* appeared on 5 May 1927, the day of its publication (*M & M*, p 193); for those of *Jacob's Room* and *Mrs Dalloway*, see also *M & M*, pp 95 and 160.
3. Katherine (Kitty) Leaf had married the journalist Douglas Hammill West on 22 January 1927; they were living at 23 Walpole Street, Chelsea.

on Poetry & Fiction. Writing for an audience always stirs me. I hope to avoid too many jokes.[4] Then Vita will come tomorrow. But I dont want people: I want solitude; Rome.

Nelly away; Pinker [*dog*] away; Clive coming back; Opera in swing; Francis to see me about writing; fine spring weather.

Wednesday 11 May

Vita back; unchanged, though I daresay one's relation changes from day to day. Clive & she together. I think Clive is pretty miserable: his stay at Cassis a failure, so far as writing goes. And then the question rises, has he not gone too far in eating, drinking, love making, to stop dead now? He seemed random & unsettled, much as when he left, only now with no absolute hard arm to cling to, as he fancied when he went to Cassis. He talked (always shifting away from himself yet returning, ambiguously to that centre) about going mad: sometimes thought he was going mad; then how one's life was over; one was spent, played out; this was clear when one saw Julian & Quentin. After all, its an ignominious position to have made the grand refusal, & gone back on it. Mary was at the opera, on a hot evening like this think of listening to Wagner, he said. There's Saxon upstairs, Mary & Sibyl Colefax below. This was all said half enviously, yet doubtfully; as if not knowing what line to take.

My book. What is the use of saying one is indifferent to reviews when positive praise, though mingled with blame, gives one such a start on, that instead of feeling dried up, one feels, on the contrary, flooded with ideas? I gather from vague hints, through Margery Joad, through Clive, that some people say it is my best book. So far Vita praises; Dotty enthuses; an unknown donkey writes. No one has yet read it to the end, I daresay; & I shall hover about, not anxious but worried for 2 more weeks, when it will be over.

Monday 16 May

The book. Now on its feet so far as praise is concerned. It has been out 10 days—Thursday a week ago. Nessa enthusiastic—a sublime, almost upsetting spectacle. She says it is an amazing portrait of mother; a supreme portrait painter; has lived in it; found the rising of the dead almost painful.

4. VW's article, 'Poetry, Fiction and the Future', first given as a lecture at Oxford (see below 6 June 1927, n 1), was published in the *New York Herald Tribune* on 14 and 21 August 1927 (Kp C284), and posthumously in *Granite and Rainbow* as 'The Narrow Bridge of Art'—a title perhaps given by LW.

Then Ottoline, then Vita, then Charlie [Sanger], then Lord Olivier, then Tommie, then Clive:[5] poor Clive—he came in, ostensibly to praise this 'amazing book—far the best you've ever written' but found Eddie who imposed himself resolutely, sharply; & so sat on, but how wandering & unhappy. I have scarcely seen him in this mood ever before—like a person awaked from a sweet dream. But what is it? A disillusionment? A shock? He sees Mary. Has he lost faith? Has the dancing mist of rhapsody failed him—he who was based so solidly on such beef & beer or champagne rather. Suppose one woke & found oneself a fraud? It was part of my madness—that horror. But then as Clive said, you go mad but you bound up again—the inference being that he was to stay mad.

Sold 1802 of The L.: if it makes 3,000 I
This it did on July 13th   shall be as they say more than content. Mervyn
[Arnold-Forster] dead—did I record; & I
haunted for a time by the sight of his prim pinched face, with the nice blue eyes, so suddenly stilled: so unseasonably. The eye plays a large part in these affairs.

Monday 6 June (Whit Monday)

I have been in bed a week with a sudden & very sharp headache, & this is written experimentally to test my brain. It is a horrid dull damp Bank holiday morning—(here L. comes in & we spend fifteen minutes discussing advertisements. The L. has sold 2,200 & we are reprinting). Nessa says its ugly weather when I ring up to offer her half a bottle of turpentine to paint her cupboard with.

But I would like to learn to write a steady plain narrative style. Then perhaps I could catch up with the last few weeks; describe my visit to Oxford;[1] & how I lunched with Clive & dined with Dadie & stood in the basement printing Gottstalk with a great sense of shade & shelter. I like the obscure anonymity of the Press better a good deal than I like Voltaire

5. Vanessa's letter to VW about *To the Lighthouse* is given in the Appendix to *III VW Letters*. Lady Ottoline's letter (14 May 1927) is in MHP, Sussex: 'The Beauty of it is overwhelming—especially to *me* the 2d Part—"Time Passes" . . . All these pages marked & marked, for they seem to me some of the loveliest pages in English prose.' Lord Olivier (see above, 14 May 1925, n 17) was a great admirer of VW's books, but his matter-of-fact comments upon *To the Lighthouse* riled her (see *III VW Letters*, no. 1760).

1. VW had been invited to speak to an audience of undergraduates of both sexes at Oxford on 18 May, and persuaded Vita Sackville-West to accompany her (see *III VW Letters*, no. 1760). Her subject was 'Poetry, Fiction and the Future'. See above, 5 May 1927, n 4.

by Riding.[2] And now, with Morgan's morganatic, evasive, elusive letter this morning, The Lighthouse is behind me:[3] my headache over; & after a week at Rodmell, my freedom from inspection, my deep dive into my own mind will begin.

How odd, it comes into my mind, is Nessa & my jealousy of each other's clothes! I feel her, when I put on my smart black fringed cape, anguished for a second: did I get it from Champco? in the same way I run my eye over her Paris dress, & compare it with my last year's Brooke.[4] Then she says she is going to wear earrings: I say at once that I will; this she resents. Yet, we are both fundamentally sensible, & soon recover from our umbrage.

I think, however, I am now almost an established figure—as a writer. They dont laugh at me any longer. Soon they will take me for granted. Possibly I shall be a celebrated writer. Anyhow, The Lighthouse is much more nearly a success, in the usual sense of the word, than any other book of mine.

A great knot of people came together suddenly last week, or the week before. Tom—so glad to gossip with me off handedly over a cup—no 6 cups—of tea; then he played the gramophone: & Logan, pink & spruce, doing his trick of culture & urbanity & good sense very efficiently.[5] He had been evoking the spirit of Henry James with Desmond in Paris. (Sibyl, by the way, takes to herself all credit for that fund, I observe. Sibyl, Clive & Raymond say, has sold her soul to the devil, & he's now come to fetch it—This phrase is common to them both, & gives the measure of

2. In October 1926 the Woolfs had published a collection of poems called *The Close Chaplet* (*HP Checklist* 91) by Laura Riding Gottschalk (b. 1901), an American poet who had come to England in December 1925, and was associated with Robert Graves. *Voltaire: A Biographical Fantasy*, a long poem written in 1921, was hand-printed at 52 Tavistock Square and published in November 1927 (*HP Checklist* 145). The author's name was printed on the title-page as Laura Riding Gottschalk; but Gottschalk was partially obliterated by overprinting with two 6 pt black rules and did not recur in her subsequent publications.
3. Forster's letter, in MHP, Sussex (copy) is dated from Cambridge on 5 June 1927. 'It is awfully sad, very beautiful . . .; it stirs me much more to questions of whether & why than anything else you have written. . . . I am inclined to think it your best work.'
4. Mme Elspeth Champcommunal (d. 1976), widow of a French painter and a friend of Roger Fry, had been editor of British *Vogue* from 1916 to 1922, when Dorothy Todd succeeded her. Miss Brooke was a dressmaker recommended to VW by the latter the previous year.
5. VW gave tea to T. S. Eliot on Monday 23 May, and the following day to Logan Pearsall Smith, Faith Henderson and Vita and Eddy Sackville-West, after lunching with Clive Bell, Dadie Rylands and Lady Violet Bonham Carter.

smart talk at lunch parties.) Lytton, too, I saw: an invalid after an attack of love, the most desperate since Duncan. We talked, with poor marble eyed Cynthia Noble attentive, as far as she can be, about the O'B. & his life.[6] I often glide into intimacy with Lytton about books. He is enthusiastic, his mind bare, his attention extremely alive, about books; whereas, about love, its more cryptic. Dadie & Douglas were both starched & powdered like pasteboard young men at the ballet;[7] legs quite straight; heads curled; shirts granulated; they were going on to Kitchin's party, to be bored, as they knew; but in perfect trim for it. This Lytton does not quite achieve. We dined ostentatiously rather, it being part of the game to order food from Fortnum & Mason's; part of the pathetic, rather attractive, yet also foolish, showing off, very youthful game of being precisely like other people.

Saturday 18 June

This is a terribly thin diary for some reason: half the year has been spent, & left only these few sheets. Perhaps I have been writing too hard in the morning to write here also. Three weeks wiped out by headache. We had a week at Rodmell, of which I remember various sights, suddenly unfolding before me spontaneously (for example, the village standing out to sea in the June night, houses seeming ships, the marsh a fiery foam) & the immense comfort of lying there lapped in peace. I lay out all day in the new garden, with the terrace. It is already being made. There were blue tits nested in the hollow neck of my Venus.[8] Vita came over one very hot afternoon, & we walked to the river with her. Pinker now swims after

6. For the fluctuations of Lytton Strachey's last great love affair, with Roger Senhouse, see *Holroyd*, ch. 16, 6. Cynthia was the younger daughter of the wealthy Saxton Noble and his cultivated and musical wife, a notable hostess in the world of diplomacy and the arts. Oscar Browning (1837-1923), an Apostle, always known as the 'O.B.', was a lifelong Fellow of King's, to which he returned after fifteen years as an Eton Housemaster; a provocative, stimulating and controversial teacher and educationalist, he was a very prominent Cambridge 'character'. A recently published life of him by H. E. Wortham provided VW's story about Browning and the stable boy in *A Room of One's Own* (p 81).
7. On 24 May, the day of Clive's lunch and VW's own tea-party, the Woolfs, Lytton Strachey and Cynthia Noble had dined at 37 Gordon Square (where they had rented rooms from Vanessa) with Dadie Rylands and Douglas Davidson, Angus's younger brother who, after taking a degree at Cambridge, was now a painter. Fortnum & Mason was and is the grand Piccadilly store specialising in high class provisions. Two days later VW had a headache and was ill for a week before going to Rodmell on 7 June.
8. A headless plaster cast from the antique which stood on a wall in the garden.

Leonard's stick. I read—any trash. Maurice Baring; sporting memoirs. Slowly ideas began trickling in; & then suddenly I rhapsodised (the night L. dined with the apostles) & told over the story of the Moths, which I think I will write very quickly, perhaps in between chapters of that long impending book on fiction.[9] Now the moths will I think fill out the skeleton which I dashed in here: the play-poem idea: the idea of some

The Waves

continuous stream, not solely of human thought, but of the ship, the night &c, all flowing together: intersected by the arrival of the bright moths. A man & a woman are to be sitting at table talking. Or shall they remain silent? It is to be a love story: she is finally to let the last great moth in. The contrasts might be something of this sort: she might talk, or think, about the age of the earth: the death of humanity: then moths keep on coming. Perhaps the man could be left absolutely dim. France: near the sea; at night; a garden under the window. But it needs ripening. I do a little work on it in the evening when the gramophone is playing late Beethoven sonatas. (The windows fidget at their fastenings as if we were at sea.)

We have been to Hyde Park, where the Church boys were marching; officers on horses in their cloaks like equestrian statues.[10] Always this kind of scene gives me the notion of human beings playing a game, greatly, I suppose, to their own satisfaction.

We saw Vita given the Hawthornden.[11] A horrid show up, I thought: not of the gentry on the platform—Squire, Drinkwater, Binyon only—of us all: all of us chattering writers. My word! how insignificant we all looked! How can we pretend that we are interesting, that our works matter? The whole business of writing became infinitely distasteful. There was no one I could care whether he read, liked, or disliked "my writing". And no one could care for my criticism either: the mildness, the conventionality of them all struck me. But there may be a stream of ink in them that matters more than the look of them—so tightly clothed, mild,

9. Vanessa had written on 3 May from the Villa Corsica at Cassis describing how they were beset by moths of a night-time (see *II QB*, p 126); VW was fascinated, and contemplated a story on the theme—the genesis of what was eventually to become *The Waves*. (VW had followed LW back to London on 14 June, the night of the Apostles' dinner.)

10. On the afternoon of Saturday, 18 June, over 6,000 members of the Church Lads' Brigade marched from Wellington and Chelsea Barracks to the parade ground near Marble Arch, where they were inspected by the Prince of Wales.

11. At a ceremony in the Æolian Hall, Bond Street, on 16 June, John Drinkwater presented the Hawthornden Prize for the best literary production of 1926 to V. Sackville-West for her long poem *The Land*; J. C. Squire and Laurence Binyon (1896-1943), poet and art-historian, were also on the selection committee.

& decorous—showed. I felt there was no one full grown mind among us. In truth, it was the thick dull middle class of letters that met; not the aristocracy. Vita cried at night.

Wednesday 22 June

Woman haters depress me, & both Tolstoi & Mrs Asquith hate women. I suppose my depression is a form of vanity. But then so are all strong opinions on both sides. I hate Mrs A.'s hard, dogmatic empty style. But enough: I shall write about her tomorrow:[12] I write every day about something, & have deliberately set apart a few weeks to money making, so that I may put £50 in each of our pockets by September. This will be the first money of my own since I married. I never felt the need of it till lately. And I can get it, if I want it, but shirk writing for money.

Clive's father died yesterday.[13] Harold Nicolson & Duncan dined with us, & Nessa came in afterwards, very silent, inscrutable &, perhaps critical. As a family we distrust anyone outside our set, I think. We too definitely decide that so & so has not the necessary virtues. I daresay Harold has not got them; at the same time, there is a good deal in him I like: he is quick & rash & impulsive; not in our sense, very clever; uneasy; seeming young; on the turn from diplomat to intellectual; not Vita's match; but honest & cordial. L. says he's too commonplace. I liked my little duet with him. He wears a green, or blue, shirt & tie; is sunburnt; chubby, pert[?]; vivacious. Talked of politics, but was flimsy compared with Leonard—I thought. Said it was with L. & me that he felt completely at his ease. Told stories wh. sound rather empty in the bare Bloomsbury rooms.

Thursday 23 June

This diary shall batten on the leanness of my social life. Never have I spent so quiet a London summer. It is perfectly easy to slip out of the crush unobserved. I have set up my standard as an invalid, & no one bothers me. No one asks me to do anything. Vainly, I have the feeling that this is of my choice, not theirs; & there is a luxury in being quiet in the heart of chaos. Directly I talk & exert my wits in talk I get a dull damp rather headachy day. Quiet brings me cool clear quick mornings, in which

12. VW's unsigned review of Margot Asquith (Lady Oxford)'s *Lay Sermons* appeared under the title 'The Governess of Downing Street' in the *N & A* of 30 July 1927 (Kp C283·1).
13. William Heward Bell, colliery owner and a director of the Great Western Railway, died at his Wiltshire home on 21 June, aged 78. Harold Nicolson had finally returned, with Vita, from Persia early in May; and Duncan and Vanessa from France early in June.

I dispose of a good deal of work, & toss my brain into the air when I take a walk. I shall feel some triumph if I skirt a headache this summer.

I sat with Nessa in the Square yesterday. Angelica sends Pinker after a ball. Nessa & I sit on the seat & gossip. She is to see Mary; she is to go to old Bell's funeral. She is learning to motor. She has sold a picture. The point of Clive's affair is that Mary is in love with another. This point was carefully hidden before Easter. His vanity was careful to hide it: her discretion. So I got my version out of proportion. The truth is odd enough though. Unless she will bed with him he is distracted. That she will not do; yet, for lack of him, is distracted herself. The love affair rather increases on her side. It is said to be for someone low in the world. This inclines us to think it Lord Ivor. But the point is one for curiosity only.

Vita's book [*The Land*] verberates & reverberates in the Press. A prize poem—that's my fling at it—for with some relics of jealousy, or it may be of critical sense, I can't quite take the talk of poetry & even great poetry seriously. But the subject & the manner, so smooth, so mild, may be what I dislike; & perhaps I am corrupt. I wonder what I should think if I could get a cool look at some writing of my own.

Oh & Sibyl has dropped me: & I don't feel the fall.

What is then the abiding truth in this phantasmagoria, I ask myself, seeking as I often do some little nugget of pure gold. I think, often, I have the happiest of lives, in having discovered stability. Now one stable moment vanquishes chaos. But this I said in The Lighthouse. We have now sold, I think, 2555 copies.

I am distressed by my failure to make cigarettes. I had a lesson from a man in Francis Street—cant do a thing with my fingers. Angelica is expert with hers already. Nessa says all painters are: this is a perquisite they get thrown in with their gift.

And Adrian came to tea on Sunday, & fairly sparkled. At last I think he has emerged. Even his analysis will be over this year. At the age of 43 he will be educated & ready to start life. I remember Harry Stephen saying that he had his fingers on the gear—the Indian judgeship that is to say—about then.[14] So we Stephens mature late. And our late flowers are rare & splendid. Think of my books, Nessa's pictures—it takes us an age to bring our faculties into play. And now I must write to Ethel Sands, & perhaps, go to the Ballet.[15]

14. Adrian Stephen, on the road to becoming a psychoanalyst, had completed his medical training in 1926; his cousin, Sir Harry Lushington Stephen (1860-1945), was made a judge of the High Court in Calcutta in 1901.
15. VW did write to Ethel Sands (*III VW Letters*, no. 1778), but did not go to the ballet (Diaghileff's season at the Princes Theatre).

Thursday 30 June

Now I must sketch out the Eclipse.[16]

About 10 on Tuesday night several very long trains, accurately filled (ours with civil servants) left King's Cross. In our carriage was Vita & Harold[,] Quentin, L. & I. This is Hatfield I daresay, I said. I was smoking a cigar. Then again, This is Peterborough, L. said. Before it got dark we kept looking at the sky: soft fleecy; but there was one star, over Alexandra Park. Look Vita, that's Alexandra Park, said Harold. The Nicolsons got sleepy: H. curled up with his head on V.'s knee. She looked like Sappho by Leighton, asleep; so we plunged through the midlands; made a very long stay at York. Then at 3 we got out our sandwiches, & I came in from the wc to find Harold being rubbed clean of cream. Then he broke the china sandwich box. Here L. laughed without restraint. Then we had another doze, or the N.'s did; then here was a level crossing, at which were drawn up a long line of motor omnibuses & motors, all burning pale yellow lights. It was getting grey—still a fleecy mottled sky. We got to Richmond about 3.30: it was cold, & the N.'s had a quarrel, Eddie said, about V.'s luggage. We went off in the omnibus, saw a vast castle (who does that belong to said Vita, who is interested in Castles). It had a front window added, & a light I think burning. All the fields were aburn with June grasses & red tasselled plants, none coloured as yet, all pale. Pale & grey too were the little uncompromising Yorkshire farms. As we passed one, the farmer, & his wife & sister came out, all tightly & tidily dressed in black, as if they were going to church. At another ugly square farm, two women were looking out of the upper windows. These had white blinds drawn down half across them. We were a train of 3 vast cars, one stopping to let the others go on; all very low & powerful; taking immensely steep hills. The driver once got out & put a small stone behind our wheel—inadequate. An accident would have been natural. There were also many motor cars. These suddenly increased as we crept up to the top of Bardon Fell. Here were people camping beside their cars. We got out, & found ourselves very high, on a moor, boggy, heathery, with butts for grouse shooting. There were grass tracks here & there, & people had already taken up positions. So we joined them, walking out to what seemed the highest point looking over Richmond. One light burnt down there. Vales & moors stretched, slope after slope, round us. It was like the Haworth country. But over Richmond, where the sun was rising, was a

16. Special trains were run from London to North Yorkshire, which was within the belt of totality for the total eclipse of the sun on 29 June 1927—the first to be visible in Britain for over 200 years. In London bad weather completely obscured the phenomenon.

soft grey cloud. We could see by a gold spot where the sun was. But it was early yet. We had to wait, stamping to keep warm. Ray [Strachey] had wrapped herself in the blue striped blanket off a double bed. She looked incredibly vast & bedroomish. Saxon looked very old. Leonard kept looking at his watch. Four great red setters came leaping over the moor. There were sheep feeding behind us. Vita had tried to buy a guinea pig— Quentin advised a savage[17]—so she observed the animals from time to time. There were thin places in the cloud, & some complete holes. The question was whether the sun would show through a cloud or through one of these hollow places when the time came. We began to get anxious. We saw rays coming through the bottom of the clouds. Then, for a moment we saw the sun, sweeping—it seemed to be sailing at a great pace & clear in a gap; we had out our smoked glasses; we saw it crescent, burning red; next moment it had sailed fast into the cloud again; only the red streamers came from it; then only a golden haze, such as one has often seen. The moments were passing. We thought we were cheated; we looked at the sheep; they showed no fear; the setters were racing round; everyone was standing in long lines, rather dignified, looking out. I thought how we were like very old people, in the birth of the world—druids on Stonehenge: (this idea came more vividly in the first pale light though;) At the back of us were great blue spaces in the cloud. These were still blue. But now the colour was going out. The clouds were turning pale; a reddish black colour. Down in the valley it was an extraordinary scrumble of red & black; there was the one light burning; all was cloud down there, & very beautiful, so delicately tinted. Nothing could be seen through the cloud. The 24 seconds were passing. Then one looked back again at the blue: & rapidly, very very quickly, all the colours faded; it became darker & darker as at the beginning of a violent storm; the light sank & sank: we kept saying this is the shadow; & we thought now it is over—this is the shadow when suddenly the light went out. We had fallen. It was extinct. There was no colour. The earth was dead. That was the astonishing moment: & the next when as if a ball had rebounded, the cloud took colour on itself again, only a sparky aetherial colour & so the light came back. I had very strongly the feeling as the light went out of some vast obeisance; something kneeling down, & low & suddenly raised up, when the colours came. They came back astonishingly lightly & quickly & beautifully in the valley & over the hills

The colour for some moments was of the most lovely kind—fresh, various —here blue, & there brown: all new colours, as if washed over & repainted.

17. QB can shed no light on this wild recommendation.

—at first with a miraculous glittering & aetheriality, later normally almost, but with a great sense of relief. It was like recovery. We had been much worse than we had expected. We had seen the world dead. This was within the power of nature. Our greatness had been apparent too. Now we became Ray in a blanket, Saxon in a cap &c. We were bitterly cold. I should say that the cold had increased as the light went down. One felt very livid. Then—it was over till 1999. What remained was a sense of the comfort which we get used to, of plenty of light & colour. This for some time seemed a definitely welcome thing. Yet when it became established all over the country, one rather missed the sense of its being a relief & a respite, which one had had when it came back after the darkness. How can I express the darkness? It was a sudden plunge, when one did not expect it: being at the mercy of the sky: our own nobility: the druids; Stonehenge; & the racing red dogs; all that was in ones mind. Also, to be picked out of ones London drawing room & set down on the wildest moors in England was impressive. For the rest, I remember trying to keep awake in the gardens at York while Eddy talked & falling asleep. Asleep again in the train. It was hot & we were merry. The carriage was full of things. Harold was very kind & attentive: Eddy was peevish. Roast beef & pineapple chunks, he said. We got home at 8.30 perhaps.

Monday 4 July

Back from Long Barn.[1] Thank heaven, I never had to change my dress. Such opulence & freedom, flowers all out, butler, silver, dogs, biscuits, wine, hot water, log fires, Italian cabinets, Persian rugs, books—this was the impression it made: as of stepping into a rolling gay sea, with nicely crested waves: as if the anxious worn life had suddenly been set on springs, & went bounding, springing for the week end. Yet I like this room better perhaps: more effort & life in it, to my mind, unless this is the prejudice one has naturally in favour of the display of one's own character. Vita very opulent, in her brown velvet coat with the baggy pockets, pearl necklace, & slightly furred cheeks. (They are like saviours flannel, of which she picked me a great bunch, in texture[2]) Of its kind this is the best, most representative human life I know: I mean, certain gifts & qualities & good fortunes are here miraculously combined—I liked Harold too.

1. The Woolfs went to stay with the Nicolsons at Long Barn on Saturday, 2 July; LW returned to Tavistock Square on Sunday evening, and VW on Monday.
2. Presumably *Stachys Lanate*, known variously as Saviour's Blanket, Jesus's Blanket, Lamb's, Donkey's or Rabbit's Ears.

He is a spontaneous childlike man, of no great boring power; has a mind that bounces when he drops it; he opens his eyes as he looks at one; has a little immature moustache; curled hair; an air of immaturity which is welcome. I should judge him very generous & kind hearted; an Englishman overlaid with culture; coming of a sunburnt country stock; & not much fined even by diplomacy. After dinner last night we discussed the Empire. "I prefer Sydney to Paris. Australia is more important than France. After all, its our younger sons out there. I feel proud of it. The point is, Raymond, our English genius is for government." "The governed don't seem to enjoy it" said Raymond. Silly ass, said Harold. "We do our job: disinterestedly; we dont think of ourselves, as the French do, as the Germans do. Take the British oil fields. There's a hospital there where they take any one, employee or not. The natives come from all over the place. Don't tell me thats not a good thing. And they trust us." So on to the system of bribery; to the great age of England being the age of colonial expansion. "I grant Shakespeare's a nasty snag." "But why not grow, change?" I said. Also, I said, recalling the aeroplanes that had flown over us, while the portable wireless played dance music on the terrace, "can't you see that nationality is over? All divisions are now rubbed out, or about to be." Raymond vehemently assented. Raymond is all for the triumph of mind. What action matters? Actions matter most of all, said Harold. I was sitting on a carved Italian stool over the log fire; he & Raymond bedded in the soft green sofa. Leonard's injustice to the aristocracy was discussed. Before this, Lord Sackville & Mrs Rubens had come over, partly to protect their respectability, partly to play tennis. (They won't stay at Knole alone if possible; & if they must, sanctify the proceeding by calling on Vita). He is a smooth worn man, inheriting noble nose & chin which he has not put much into himself; a straight, young looking man, save that his face has the lack lustre of a weak man whose life has proved too much for him. No longer does he struggle much for happiness, I imagine; accepts resignedly; & goes to Maidstone almost daily, as part of the routine of his nobility. He plays golf; he plays tennis. He thinks Bernard Darwin must be a man of surpassing brain power.[3] We sat together under a vast goat skin coat of Vita's, watching them play, & I found him smooth & ambling as a blood horse, but obliterated, obfusc, with his great Sackville eyes drooping, & his face all clouded with red & brown. One figured a screw or other tool whose worms & edges have been rubbed smooth, so that though they shine, plaid silver, they no longer grip.

3. Bernard Darwin (1876-1961), son of Sir Francis Darwin and step-son of VW's cousin Florence (Fisher), was golf correspondent of the *Times* and *Country Life* and a prolific writer on a variety of subjects.

Vita very free & easy, always giving me great pleasure to watch, & recalling some image of a ship breasting a sea, nobly, magnificently, with all sails spread, & the gold sunlight on them. As for her poetry, or intelligence, save when canalised in the traditional channels, I can say nothing very certain. She never breaks fresh ground. She picks up what the tide rolls to her feet. For example, she follows, with simple instinct, all the inherited tradition of furnishing, so that her house is gracious, glowing, stately, but without novelty or adventure. So with her poetry, I daresay. Raymond & I travelled up & discussed them. She the most noble character he said; both almost defiantly fortunate, so that Harold touches wood when he reflects on his own life, heaves a sigh & says how, if it were dashed down tomorrow, he would have had his day. But it wont be dashed down at all. It will grow freely & fully round them both; their fruit will ripen, & their leaves golden; & the night will be indigo blue, with a soft gold moon. They lack only what we have—some cutting edge; some invaluable idiosyncracy, intensity, for which I would not have all the sons & all the moons in the world.

Monday 11 July[4]

Waiting for what I do not exactly know. In a mood of random restlessness—Nelly having for 125th time 'given notice' this morning. Shall I go to Ashley Gardens [*Registry Office*] & engage Mrs Collins & her daughter? I am sick of the timid spiteful servant mind; yet perhaps Mrs Collins will be of the same feather. Never mind.

A great storm has torn off one wing of my double windows. But I have never mentioned the absorbing subject—the subject which has filled our thoughts to the exclusion of Clive & Mary & literature & death & life— motor cars. Every evening we go round with Pinker for a game in Gordon Sqre—I talk as if the evenings had been fine—no, we sit there in between the sulphur coloured storms; under the shelter of trees with the rain pattering between the leaves.[5] We talk of nothing but cars. Then, sometimes, word is brought that Mrs Bell is at the door in her car. I rush out, & find her, rather nervously in control of a roomy shabby Renault with Fred beside her. Three times I have been for a little tour with her. And yesterday we commissioned Fred to find us & bring instantly to our door,

4. VW has misdated this entry *10 July*; in it she refers to 'Clive's party' which in fact was a dinner party on 11 July (he was at his mother's in Wiltshire on the 10th).
5. The *Times* of 11 July 1927 reported great thunderstorms with consequent heavy flooding and damage in London.

a Singer. We have decided on a Singer.[6] And, the reason why I am distracted now is that Fred is going to ring me up & say if I am to have my first lesson this evening. The sun is shining; the trees dripping. Possibly I may go.

This is a great opening up in our lives. One may go to Bodiam, to Arundel, explore the Chichester downs, expand that curious thing, the map of the world in ones mind. It will I think demolish loneliness, & may of course imperil complete privacy. The Keynes' have one too—a cheap one. Nessa thinks it will break down at once. Nessa takes a very sinister view of the Keynes'. She anticipates ruin of every sort for them, with some pleasure too. Here's Leonard—So then I tell him about the storm, about the telephones, & about Pinker. Then Sibyl who has cut me these 3 months, suddenly writes to say she has been 'unwell', & will I come to tea. No I wont. And now I must quickly dress for Clive's party, where I am to meet Cory & Nessa & Duncan & Christabel: for there's a plethora of parties this week, & tomorrow I'm missing Lydia & Stravinsky;[7] but a kind of philosophy protects me: I shall make out a happy evening somehow; & find a curious pleasure in staying away, imagining. So I must stop & write to Sibyl. With any luck The Lighthouse will reach 3,000 this week.

Saturday 23 July

This is very near the end of the London season. I go to Ethel [Sand]'s at Dieppe (I'm rather proud of crossing the channel again) on Wednesday, then back to Newhaven, where I may be met by my own car. Since making the last entry I have learnt enough to drive a car in the country alone. On the backs of paper I write down instructions for starting cars. We have a nice light little shut up car in which we can travel thousands of miles. It is very dark blue, with a paler line round it. The world gave me this for writing The Lighthouse, I reflect, a book which has now sold 3,160 (perhaps) copies: will sell 3,500 before it dies, & thus far exceeds any other of mine.

The night I did not go to Stravinsky Desmond came, tender & garrulous & confidential. I remember leaning with him out of the window. He

6. The Woolfs acquired their second-hand Singer car for £275 on 15 July. Frederick Pape, husband of Angelica's nurse Louie, was a professional chauffeur who taught Vanessa to drive, and to some extent VW, though she fairly soon gave up. LW had six driving lessons and drove his car alone for the first time on 31 July.
7. *L'Histoire du Soldat*, a short entertainment with four characters by G. F. Ramuz and music by Igor Stravinsky, first performed in 1918, was being given in an English translation by the Arts Theatre Club; Lydia Lopokova took the part of the Princess. LW (but not VW) dined with the Keyneses before going to it.

was full of love for everyone. He said he loved the way Melinda [*unidenti-fied*] scratched her head or put on her gloves. He said he was now in love with his children. When Dermod asks him for a new perspective for his microscope he feels what he used to feel when he was in love with a woman. He resents his gift of money a little, since he was making £2,000 a year; but then he had 'arrears'; & has now, evidently—£200 to the Bank, £200 for income tax & so on. We talked of love owing to Clive. For that night after I dined with Clive & went through some rather artificial gambols with Christa[bel McLaren] (who has always thought of me as Virginia; & can't quite lose the sense of my being a perfect lady "Look at those hands") Clive walked me round, & standing under the lamp expressed his complete disillusion. "My dear Virginia, life is over. There's no good denying it. We're 45. I'm bored, I'm bored, I'm un-speakably bored. I know my own reactions. I know what I'm going to say. I'm not interested in a thing. Pictures bore me. I take up a book & put it down. No one's interested in what I think any more. I go about thinking about suicide. I admire you for having tried to kill yourself." To think that I should be listening to this in the moonlight from Clive! And he spoke with such dreary good sense too. I could scarcely whip up any ardour of denial. It was all true, it seemed to me. Not, indeed, true of me, but true of him. & so I feebly asked him to come & see me; & I would prove that I was interested in him. He agreed half heartedly, waved his hand, & went off, thinking about suicide. Then we met next night at Raymonds'.[8] Hardly had I come into the room but he started up boasting & professing, perfunctorily a little, but boldly enough. He had had an adventure. Life was changed; had met the loveliest of women, seemed the nicest too, was an aristocrat; she had been kind to him; would Raymond come on to supper on Monday? All this was blustered out, with many a cuff at me (for he always wishes he says to hurt me—even over a motor car) & it was about Valerie Taylor, an actress, whom he had met lunching at the Maclagans.[9] For my own part, I am once more at the stage of thinking Clive 'second rate'. It is all so silly, shallow, & selfish. Granted the charm of his vitality, still one would prefer a finer taste to it. How angry his 'secondrateness' used to make me, in connection with Nessa.

8. In fact, the night after, i.e. 13 July.
9. Valerie Taylor (b. 1902), daughter of an army officer, studied at the Royal Academy of Dramatic Art and first appeared on the London stage in 1924; she was currently appearing in Frederick Lonsdale's *On Approval* at the Fortune Theatre, which ran from April 1927 to June 1928. Eric Robert Dalrymple MacLagan (1879-1951), knighted in 1933, an authority on Italian sculpture, was Director of the Victoria & Albert Museum from 1924-45.

Now I think of it much less often, but I suppose the feeling is there. All this summer he has twanged so persistently on the one string that one gets bored. Love love love—Clive, Clive, Clive—that's the tune of it, thrummed with rather callous persistency; a thick finger & thumb. Now love I dare say nothing against; but it is a feeble passion, I mean a gross dull passion, when it has no part in it of imagination, intellect, poetry. Clive's love is three parts vanity. Now that he can say, or lie, I've been to bed with Valerie, his self love is assuaged. He remains Clive the undaunted lover, the Don Juan of Bloomsbury; & whether its true or not, so long as we think it true, scarcely matters. But I own that he pesters me with his jealousy, or whatever it is, does his best to annoy me, & so I'm not quite the impartial judge I might be. The interesting question remains—why does he always wish to hurt me?

So Desmond & I discussed all this. And The Lighthouse too; & I felt, susceptible as I am, he's doing this partly to thank me for having been generous to him. But I am enough mistress of myself now to let these feelings flow & not disturb my pleasure.

All images are now tinged with driving a motor. Here I think of letting my engine work, with my clutch out.

It has been, on the whole, a fresh well ordered summer. I am not so parched with talk as usual. I have dipped into society more easily. My illness in May was a good thing in some ways; for I got control of society at an early stage, & circumvented my headache, without a complete smash. Thus it has been a free quiet summer: I enjoyed the Eclipse; I enjoyed Long Barn; (where I went twice) I enjoyed sitting with Vita at Kew for 3 or 4 hours under a cloudy sky, & dining at the Petit Riche with her;[10] she refreshes me, & solaces me; I have worked very methodically & done my due of articles, so that with luck, I shall have made £120 *over* my proper sum by September. That is I shall have made £320 by journalism, & I suppose at least £300 by my novel this year. I have thought too much, though on purpose, with my eyes open, of making money; & once we have each a nest egg I should like to let that sink into my sub-consciousness, & earn easily what we need. Bruce Richmond is coming to tea on Monday to discuss an article on Morgan; & I am going to convey to him the fact that I can't always refuse £60 in America for the Times' £10. If I could make easily £350 a year, I would: if I could get some settled job.

At Rodmell I am going, seriously, to begin my book on fiction. With

10. On 21 July the Woolfs had driven in their car to Richmond Park; LW returned home, leaving VW and Vita Sackville-West to visit Kew Gardens and to dine together.

luck I might have this done by January. Then I shall have the Moths full in my brain to pour out. I am keeping it standing a long time, & rather fear that it may lose its freshness. Dadie has involved us (is the word wrong?) with Peter. Dadie dines with Topsy & she pumps him about the Wolves & Peter's book.[11] Dadie wants to crab it & puts it on to us. Leonard says it doesn't do; Virginia thinks it 'Academic'. The result is a long angry letter from Peter, half vanity, half righteous indignation; but we have explained, & all the burden now rests on Dadie. (& partly on me, for Topsy says I wrote her a rude letter about Jane Austen, but this has been explained).

The Press is going on. Novels are the great bloodsuckers. Mary's book will cost us £100; & we shall lose too on The Marionettes. So in the past two days I have rejected Butts & Daglish & Littell; I fancy that we don't do as well as we should with novels.[12] And I'm exposed to the hanging lips & clamorous vanity of Lucy Clifford today: she has an article on George Eliot which she wrote for a special fee (that is where I shall end if I dont take care—talking always of 'fees') for the Nineteenth Century.[13] Gottstalk is finished.

On 27 July LW saw VW off at Victoria on the boat train for Dieppe, when she went to stay with Ethel Sands and Nan Hudson at their Normandy home, the Château d'Auppegard; she returned via Newhaven on 30 July, rejoining LW at Monks House.

RODMELL

Monday 8 August

I was to have written here such a brilliant account of my 3 days at Dieppe. It was to have sprung, suddenly, in a beautiful fountain, out of the table in the window at (name forgotten) overlooking the Seine. The

11. 'Topsy' Lucas (1893-1966), the novelist E. B. C. Jones, was married to 'Peter' (F. L.) Lucas; the book in question was probably his *Tragedy in Relation to Aristotle's* POETICS, which was to be published in the series 'Hogarth Lectures in Literature' early in 1928 (*HP Checklist* 129).

12. Edwin Muir's *The Marionette* and Mary Hutchinson's *Fugitive Pieces* had been published in May and June 1927 respectively (*HP Checklist* 132, 122). The rejected authors were Mary Butts (1893-1937)—possibly her *Armed with Madness* subsequently published by Wishart in 1928; Doris Daglish of Wandsworth (see *III VW Letters*); and probably the American writer Philip Littell (1868-1943), who until 1924 had been editor of the *New Republic* in which a considerable number of VW's articles appeared.

13. Mrs W. K. Clifford (*c.* 1855-1929), a friend of VW's parents, who had supported herself by her pen after being widowed at twenty-four; the monthly review *Nineteenth Century and After* published no article by her on George Eliot.

Seine there is very broad, & round the bend come constantly steamers, Norwegian, with petrol, English French; & Nan kept looking to read their names, showing in all she did a sort of nervous tremulous pride in France (or do I imagine this?) which hints at the fact that she likes their life there, alone at Auppegard, better than Ethel.[1] "I'm gregarious" said Ethel a little waspishly, for she is brittle & acid, the spoilt pet of the more dour & upstanding Nan. We were, I think, looking over the cliff with the churchyard on it, the tombstones standing up against the blue sea. But I was to have written this, & now shall not, I suppose.— It is a very narrow house, all window, laid with pale bright Samarcand rugs, & painted greens & blues, with lovely 'pieces', & great pots of carefully designed flowers arranged by Loomas. A white bull terrier stalks from room to room, one ear bent over in his fights. Nan, stylishly dressed, sews dusters of an evening, & Ethel craves talk. Nessa & Duncan say that the talk skirts & flits & never settles very long; in fact that the house is built upon the finest silver wood ash: so soft so silver you don't at first notice how it gets into your throat & makes your skin dry & dusty.

We have motored most days. We opened one little window when we bought the gramophone; now another/ opens with the motor—I was going to say, but stopped.

Wednesday 10 August[2]

Yes, the motor is turning out the joy of our lives, an additional life, free & mobile & airy to live alongside our usual stationary industry. We spin off to Falmer, ride over the Downs, drop into Rottingdean, then sweep over to Seaford, call, in pouring rain at Charleston, pass the time of day with Clive—Nessa is at Bodiam—return for tea, all as light & easy as a hawk in the air. Soon we shall look back at our pre-motor days as we do now at our days in the caves. After a week here, Leonard has become perfectly efficient; I am held back by insufficient lessons, but shall be expert before September is half through. Various little improvements in the house keep me on the thrill with hope & despair. Shall I lavish £5 that will be mine on a new spare bed?—alas, I fear I must; then the great & distasteful operations of furnishing will be over, & next year I shall add ornament & comfort. Perhaps if I make an extra sum we might build a

1. Anna Hope (Nan) Hudson (1896-1957), an American painter, had met Ethel Sands in Paris in 1894, the beginning of their life-long loving companionship. Henry Lomas was their butler from 1925-34. Vanessa Bell and Duncan Grant were staying at Auppegard, having been commissioned to paint decorations in the loggia. See Wendy Baron, *Ethel Sands and her Circle*, 1977, pp 187-90.
2. VW has misdated this entry 'Wednesday Aug. 9th'.

bed sitting room for me in the attic, enlarge L.'s study, & so have a desirable, roomy, light house. For if we had £300 every year to spend, it is difficult to think of anything, except this, travel, & pocket money, to spend it on. Here at the age of 45 are Nessa & I growing little wings again after our lean years. She may rake in another £500; perhaps more.[3] Already she has bought a roll of linoleum & a cupboard. But my state is precarious. With The Lighthouse I may just have climbed to the top of my hill; or again we may wobble back; my journalism may pall on the Americans: no rich father in law will endow me; but Heaven knows, I have not much anxiety. We are flexible, adventurous still I hope.

An odd incident, psychologically as the vanished Kot used to say, has been Morgan's serious concern about my article on him. Did I care a straw what he said about me? Was it more laudatory? Yet here is this self-possessed, aloof man taking every word to heart, cast down to the depths, apparently, because I do not give him superlative rank, & writing again & again to ask about it, or suggest about it, anxious that it shall be published in England, & also that more space shall be given to the Passage to India. Had I been asked, I should have said that of all writers he would be the most indifferent & cool under criticism. And he minds a dozen times more than I do, who have the opposite reputation.[4]

This brings me back to those last days in London when I called on Ottoline, had a shabby easy intimate talk with her, & then, inadvertently as if by touching a button brought on me the whole shower bath of Philip's affection. He came the next day, inconveniently, & the day after when Sibyl was there. Once more I felt the uneasy excitement of 'love', that is of physical desire making someone restless, too restless & emotional to talk simply. But L. came in; Pinker came in, & the amorous Philip, who has lost most of his good looks & is coarse as an old ram, had to leave. But I found a letter at Rodmell, quoting J.'s Room—'Come back to me Darling'—with which I shall make Vita jealous tomorrow. But what course to take, especially now that he is our neighbour, I do not altogether know; nor whether to answer his letter or not.[5]

3. i.e. as a result of her father-in-law's death.
4. Forster's article on VW had 'cheered me very much' (see above, 21 December 1925); his direct response to the draft of her article on him, a letter and a postcard dated 28 June and 10 July respectively, are in MHP, Sussex, where there are also further letters to LW on the subject. 'The vanished Kot', S. S. Koteliansky (1881-1955), had collaborated with both LW and VW in translations from Russian authors published by the Hogarth Press; they had seen a good deal of him while they were still living at Richmond.
5. The Morrells had moved from Garsington to 10 Gower Street, WC1, in May 1927. Philip Morrell's letter of 27 July to VW is in MHP, Sussex. '. . . Yesterday I felt

This, however, is Nelly's first evening back, in the flush of good temper, with Gladys [*a niece?*], & I am beginning to think of my dinner. Since I dined at Auppegard I cannot be said to have dined at all: ham & eggs; cheese & raspberries; once a baked pudding—so we have fed at the hands of poor emaciated Mrs Bartholomew.

Sunday 21 August

Some little scenes I meant to write down.

One was on the flats towards Ripe one blazing hot day. We stopped in a bye road about 3 in the afternoon, & heard hymn singing. It was very lonely & desolate. Here were people singing to themselves, in the hot afternoon. I looked & saw a middle class 'lady' in skirt & coat & ribboned hat, by the cottage door. She was making the daughters of the agricultural labourers sing; it was about three o'clock on a Tuesday perhaps. Later we passed the ladies house; it had a wooden griffin nailed above the door—presumably her crest.

What I like, or one of the things I like, about motoring is the sense it gives one of lighting accidentally, like a voyager who touches another planet with the tip of his toe, upon scenes which would have gone on, have always gone on, will go on, unrecorded, save for this chance glimpse. Then it seems to me I am allowed to see the heart of the world uncovered for a moment. It strikes me that the hymn singing in the flats went on precisely so in Cromwell's time.

That was our only hot day, I think. One day the rain splashed down so fast that it rose again in a fountain, up off the road in our faces.

Sunday 4 September

Many scenes have come & gone unwritten, since it is today the 4th Sept, a cold grey blowy day, made memorable by the sight of a kingfisher, & by my sense, waking early, of being again visited by 'the spirit of delight'. "Rarely rarely comest thou, spirit of delight."[1] That was I singing this time last year; & sang so poignantly that I have never forgotten it, or my vision of a fin rising on a wide blank sea. No biographer could possibly guess this important fact about my life in the late summer of 1926: yet biographers pretend they know people.

A happy summer, this? Well, a striving working splashing social

that after all these years of silence I had really begun to talk to you, almost to be friends—yes; I think you are really very different from the writer of the books, but always adorable.'

1. See above, 30 September 1926. The song is Shelley's.

summer. Many meetings; & one or two gaieties.[2] I amuse myself by watching my mind shape scenes. We sat in a field strewn with cut grass at Michelham Priory the other day. It was roasting hot. There was Angus with his pink shirt open; Duncan strolling along with a sketchbook under his arm; the sound of rushing waters; Nessa driving her old blue bonnet with Angelica perched beside her. Nothing much is said on these occasions; but the memory remains: made of what? Of coloured shirts; the pink roof of the Gateway against a greyblue sky; & Pinker; & my being cross about my book on fiction; & Leonard silent; & a great quarrel that hot night; & I coming up here to sit alone in the dark, & L. following me; & sharp hard words; right & wrong on both sides; peace making; sleep; content.

A graveyard scene.

Mr Malthouse's son, a sailor, died of consumption & was buried in the churchyard under the big tree. I went into the churchyard with Angelica that fine afternoon. Avery was digging the grave, throwing up heavy showers of the yellow earth. Mrs Avery, immensely fat & florid, was sprawling on the edge of the grave, with her small children playing about. They were having tea, & dressed in their reds & blue looked more like a picture, by Millais, or some other Victorian, of life & death, youth & the grave, than any real sight. It was quite unconscious; yet the most deliberate picture making; hence, unreal, sentimental, overdone.[3]

The Flying Princess, I forget her name, has been drowned in her purple leather breeches.[4] I suppose so at least. Their petrol gave out about

2. Apart from their frequent meetings with the denizens of Charleston, the Woolfs had a visit from Roger Fry and three from Vita, including one on 27 August when she brought Harold Nicolson, Dorothy Wellesley, and Raymond Mortimer with her; the latter remained to spend two nights at Monks House. On 31 August they picnicked with the Charlestonians at Laughton Place, and drove on to the moated Michelham Priory with its 15th century gatehouse; (Vanessa's Renault was known as 'the Bonnet'). On 2 September the Woolfs and the Charleston party dined with the Keyneses at Tilton and witnessed an 'entertainment' in their new loggia (see *III VW Letters*, no. 1807).

3. Henry Malthouse was the landlord of the Rodmell pub, the Abergavenny Arms; his son Albert John Malthouse died on 28th August 1927. William Avery, the gravedigger, lived in the village. Cf. 'The Third Picture' of 'Three Pictures' in *The Death of the Moth* (Kp A27).

4. Attempting the first westbound transatlantic flight (it was achieved by a German crew in April 1928), Lt-Col. F. F. Minchin and Captain Leslie Hamilton, with Princess Löwenstein-Wertheim as passenger, took off from Upavon Aerodrome near Salisbury on Wednesday, 31 August, to fly the 3,600 miles to Ottawa in a Fokker monoplane named St Raphael; it was sighted the same evening some 800 miles out from the coast of Ireland, and was never seen again.

midnight on Thursday, when the aeroplane must have come gently down upon the long slow Atlantic waves. I suppose they burnt a light which showed streaky on the water for a time. There they rested a moment or two. The pilots, I think, looked back at the broad cheeked desperate eyed vulgar princess in her purple breeches & I suppose made some desperate dry statement—how the game was up: sorry; fortune against them; & she just glared; & then a wave broke over the wing; & the machine tipped. And she said something theatrical I daresay; nobody was sincere; all acted a part; nobody shrieked; Luck against us—something of that kind, they said, & then So long, & first one man was washed off & went under; & then a great wave came & the Princess threw up her arms & went down; & the third man sat saved for a second looking at the rolling waves, so patient so implacable & the moon gravely regarding; & then with a dry snorting sound he too was tumbled off & rolled over, & the aeroplane rocked & rolled—miles from anywhere, off Newfoundland, while I slept at Rodmell, & Leonard was dining with the Craniums in London.[5]

Monday 5 September

Having solidified the vision of the flying Princess into words, I have, strangely enough, laid a phantom which has been very prominent before my eyes. Why should this be so? Some dissatisfaction seems laid to rest. So, gradually, the urgency of the memory dies out too, as in one's own life; in about 48 or 96 hours all trace of the death of the Princess in her purple breeches is smoothed over.

As a matter of fact, we are just in from Brighton, & my mind is agitated by having bought a jersey, which I like, & by having let Leonard bump the back of the car on the gate post. So, to soothe these whirlpools, I write here. We went to Brighton today; & thus added a pounds worth of pleasure to life. Monotony is avoided. Oh, & I thought—but the thought is already escaping—about the enormous activity of the human kind; his feverish runnings about; Brighton & the roads being nothing but a swarm & agitation of human flesh; & yet it is not despicable.

And when I get back here, the same energy is bringing the men back from harvest across the fields; & old Mr Grey, & the poor plodding horse [?]. Now a really comprehensive magnificent statesmanlike mind would take stock of all this human activity & direct it & weld it together. I see this possibility by fits & starts: I see human beings as at the beginning of a vast enterprise, not merely with the usual writers care for the aesthetic

5. The Cranium was an elective dining club started by David Garnett, Francis Birrell, and Stephen Tomlin to enable dispersed friends to keep in touch with each other.

quality. This is a point of view which is more & more forced upon one by places like Peacehaven. All aesthetic quality is there destroyed. Only turning & tumbling energy is left. The mind is like a dog going round & round to make itself a bed. So, give me new & detestable ideas, I will somehow trample a bed out of them.

Tuesday 20 September[6]

A thousand things to be written had I time: had I power. A very little writing uses up my capacity for writing:

Laughton Place & Philip Ritchie's death

These as it happened, synchronised. When Vita was here 10 days ago we drove over to Laughton, & I broke in, & explored the house. It seemed, that sunny morning, so beautiful, so peaceful; & as if it had endless old rooms. So I came home boiling with the idea of buying it; & so fired L. that we wrote to the farmer, Mr Russell, & waited, all on wires, edgy, excited for an answer. He came himself, after some days; & we were to go & see it. This arranged, & our hopes very high, I opened the Morning Post & read the death of Philip Ritchie.[7] "He cant take houses, poor Philip" I thought. And then the usual procession of images went through my mind. Also, I think for the first time, I felt this death leaves me an elderly laggard; makes me feel I have no right to go on; as if my life were at the expense of his. And I had not been kind; not asked him to dinner & so on. So the two feelings—about buying the house & his death—fought each other: & sometimes the house won & sometimes death won; & we went to see the house & it turned out unspeakably dreary; all patched & spoilt; with grained oak & grey paper; a sodden garden & a glaring red cottage at the back. I note the strength & vividness of feelings which suddenly break & foam away. Now I forget to think about Philip Ritchie.

One of these days, though, I shall sketch here, like a grand historical

---

6. VW has misdated this entry 'Tuesday Sept. 18th'.
7. Vita and Harold Nicolson came to tea at Monks House on 8 September, and afterwards the two husbands went up to London together; the following day VW and Vita saw Laughton Place, the remains of an isolated sixteenth-century moated house in the flat country between Ringmer and Ripe; the only surviving portion, a tall and broad brick tower, had been converted in the eighteenth century into a farmhouse. Philip Ritchie died at Winchelsea on 13 September, aged 28, of septic pneumonia following a tonsillectomy. (Despite LW's scorn, VW used to take the arch-Conservative *Morning Post* during the summer months at Rodmell.)

picture, the outlines of all my friends. I was thinking of this in bed last night, & for some reason I thought I would begin with a sketch of Gerald Brenan. There may be something in this idea. It might be a way of writing the memoirs of one's own times during peoples lifetimes. It might be a most amusing book. The question is how to do it. Vita should be Orlando, a young nobleman. There should be Lytton. & it should be truthful; but fantastic. Roger. Duncan. Clive. Adrian. Their lives should be related. But I can think of more books than I shall ever be able to write. How many little stories come into my head! For instance: Ethel Sands not looking at her letters. What this implies. One might write a book of short significant separate scenes. She did not open her letters.

We motored to Long Barn & back yesterday, through suburbs for the most part. All Hampstead, red, sanitary, earnest, view gazing, breeze requiring is lodged in the heights of Ashdown Forest. Now & again one comes on something consciously preserved like the Wren house at Groombridge.[8] One stops the motor & looks. So do other motorists. We found Vita & Dotty sitting over a log fire. Dottie is going to spend £200 a year on poetry: to edit a series of books of unsaleable poetry. This £200 she was giving to the Poetry Bookshop, but deterred by his earnestness & his drunkenness she is crying off: & has laid it at our feet.[9] There will be much comment she says at this. People will say she is buying her way into Bloomsbury. The children were there; Nigel very shabby: Vita dressed him as a Russian boy "Dont. It makes me look like a little girl" he said. There was the French tutor who never spoke.[10] Dotty byronic in her dress, but much improved over the London Dotty. They do not yet know what is to become of Harold, who has refused to go to Buda Pesth.

And Quentin came, & the Keynes's came, & Morgan came. All of this I meant, perhaps, to describe: but then how hard I drive my pen through

8. Groombridge Place, a handsome moated H-plan house on the Kent-East Sussex border near Tunbridge Wells, was built in the third quarter of the seventeenth century in the manner of Inigo Jones rather than Wren.
9. Dorothy Wellesley, herself a poet and anxious to use some of her considerable wealth to encourage poets, became (by arrangement with LW who reserved some rights over choice) the sponsor and editor of the first series of the *Hogarth Living Poets*, in which 24 titles were published between 1928 and 1932. The Poetry Bookshop had been founded in 1913 by the poet and publisher Harold Edward Monro (1879-1932); it survived until his death as a centre for poetry readings and for those interested in poetry.
10. This was Maurice Couve de Murville (b. 1907), a future Prime Minister of France, who in the interval between leaving university and entering the French civil service, spent six summer weeks at the Nicolsons.

one article after another—Hemingway, Morgan, Shelley; & now Biography.[11]

Quentin wont let us play him Wagner: prefers Bach. Nessa's children are terrifyingly sophisticated: so Morgan said when Angelica, rigged up in a long black shawl, acted Lady Cornflax & Lady Ottoline at Charleston. They have grown up without any opposition: nothing to twist or stunt. Hence they have reached stages at 16 or 17 which I reached only at 26 or 27.

But the summer, has never burnt; & is now ashes. Already at half past five the light out here is greyish; the wind swirling; all children indoors; & I shall write a letter or two & go into the house: sit over a fire & read, I think, biography.

But we are very happy—seldom more so, I think. Perhaps things are doing rather well. Theres the motor; Dottie's £200;—& L. said about Laughton Place the other day, "The strange thing is that we always come to the same opinion about things"—which pleased me.

Sunday 25 September

On the opposite page I wrote notes for Shelley, I think by mistake for my writing book.[12]

Now let me become the annalist of Rodmell.

Thirty five years ago, there were 160 families living here where there are now no more than 80. It is a decaying village, which loses its boys to the towns. Not a boy of them, said the Rev. Mr Hawkesford, is being taught to plough. Rich people wanting week end cottages buy up the old peasants houses, for fabulous sums. Monks House was offered to Mr H. for £400: we gave £700. He refused it, saying he didn't wish to own country cottages. Now Mr Allinson will pay £1200 for a couple, & we he said might get £2,000 for this.[13]

11. E. M. Forster stayed the week-end of 10-12 September at Monks House. VW was writing four articles to be published in the *New York Herald Tribune*; they were on Hemingway's *Men Without Women* (see 'An Essay in Criticism', 9 October 1927, Kp C287); on E. M. Forster's *Aspects of the Novel* ('Is Fiction an Art?', 16 October 1927, Kp C288); on *Shelley: His Life and Work* by Walter Edwin Peck ('Not one of Us', 23 October 1927, Kp C289); and on *Some People* by Harold Nicolson ('The New Biography', 30 October 1927, Kp C290).

12. These notes relate to Professor Peck's 2-volume life of Shelley (see note 11 above) and read: '287 1../ Weavers. 2.45/ 2.120 prodigy of crime & pollution/ 2.166 S. shd have lived out of doors/ 167. knocked down for being a d—d atheist./ 172. appreciates the cloud because of an increased knowledge of physiography.'

13. The Rev. James Boen Hawkesford was Rector of Rodmell from 1896 until his death in January 1928. J. M. Allison, see above, 5 September 1926, note 4.

He is an old decaying man, run to seed. His cynicism, & the pleasant turn it gives his simple worn out sayings, amuses me. He is sinking into old age, very shabby, loose limbed, wearing black wool mittens. His life is receding like a tide, slowly; or one figures him as a dying candle, whose wick will soon sink into the warm grease & be extinct. To look at, he is like some aged bird; a little, small featured face, with heavily lidded smoky bright eyes; his complexion is still ruddy; but his beard is like an unweeded garden. Little hairs grow weakly all over his cheeks, & two strands are drawn, like pencil marks, across his bald head. He tumbles into an arm-chair; & tells over his stock of old village stories, which always have this slightly mocking flavour, as though, completely unambitious, & by no means successful himself, he recouped himself by laughing slyly at the humours of the more energetic. He has a hit at Allinson for building; drily tells us how Capt Stamper won't pay his tithes; how Miss Lucas signs the Captain's cheques for him.[14] The outlay these flashy newcomers make on their field & farms makes him sardonic. But he wont raise a finger either way; likes his cup of Indian tea, which he prefers to China, & doesn't much mind what anybody thinks. He smokes endless cigarettes, & his fingers are not very clean. Talking of his well, he said "It would be a different thing if one wanted baths"—which for some 70 years, presumably, he has done without. Then he likes a little practical talk about Aladdin lamps, for instance, & how the Rector at Iford has a device by which he makes the globe of the Veritas lamp wh. is cheaper serve. It appears that the Aladdin costs 10d & 2/-. But it blackens suddenly & is useless. Leaning over stiles, it is of lamp mantles that the two rectors talk.[15] Or he will advise about making a garage: how Percy shd. cut a trench, & then old Fears should line the walls with cement. That is what he advises; & I fancy many many hours of his life have passed hobnobbing with Percys & Fears, about cement & trenches. Of his clerical character there is little visible. He would not buy Bowen a riding school he said; her sister did that. He didn't believe in it. She has a school at Rottingdean, keeps 12 horses, employs grooms, & has to be at it all day, Sundays

14. Captain Edwin Poulden Fenton Byng-Stamper (1885-1939), late of the Royal Welch Fusiliers, of Northease House, near Rodmell, was one of the principal landowners in the district; he was to marry Miss Frances Byng Lucas, a great-granddaughter of Admiral George Byng, 6th Viscount Torrington.

15. 'Aladdin' and 'Veritas' lamps worked by burning vaporized paraffin oil in a mantle of asbestos filament, which gave a far brighter light than that obtained from a simple wick—though the sudden blackening of the mantle was a hazard of the system. There were Aladdin lamps at Monks House, but VW's summary of the rectors' talk suggests that she did not cope with them. The vicar (since 1909) of Kingston with Iford was the Rev. A. G. Green.

included.[16] But having expressed his opinion in the family conclave, he would leave it at that. Mrs H. would back Bowen. She would get her way. The Rector would slouch off to his study, where he does, heaven knows what. I asked him if he had work to do: a question which amused him a little. Not work he said; but a young woman to see. And then he settled into the armchair again, & so sat out a visit of over an hour & a half.

Wednesday 5 October

I write in the sordid doss house atmosphere of approaching departure. Pinker is asleep in one chair; Leonard is signing cheques at the little deal table under the glare of the lamp. The fire is covered with ashes, since we have been burning it all day, & Mrs B[artholomew]. never cleans. Envelopes lie in the grate. I am writing with a pen which is feeble & wispy; & it is a sharp fine evening with a sunset, I daresay.

We went to Amberley yesterday & think of buying a house there. For it is an astonishing forgotten lovely place, between water meadows & downs. So impulsive we both are, in spite of our years.

But we are not as old as Mrs Gray, who came to thank us for our apples. She won't send to buy, as it looks like begging, since we never take

1832
86
———
1918

money. Her face is cut into by wrinkles: they make wheals across her. She is 86, & can never remember such a summer. In her youth it was so hot in April often that they couldn't bear a sheet on them. Her youth must have been almost the same time as my fathers. She is 9 years younger, I make out: born in 1841. And what did she see of Victorian England I wonder?[1]

I can make up situations, but I cannot make up plots. That is: if I pass the lame girl, I can without knowing I do it, instantly make up a scene: (now I cant think of one). This is the germ of such fictitious gift as I have. And by the way I get letter after letter about my books, & they scarcely please me.

Further, we met Mary & Barbara [Hutchinson] in Brighton yesterday; grey, tailor made, elegant, with a touch of pink, & pink silk legs. Yet I fancied some wrinkles about Mary's eyes; & a sharp line or two, made by Clive. We were affable, as people are when they meet after a coolness; we gave them buns. We were extra affable, perhaps; & the shadow of Clive

16. Percy Bartholomew of Park Cottages, Rose's husband, was in 1928 to become LW's gardener and an important figure in his life at Rodmell. The Hawkesfords had two daughters, Olive and Boen; the latter ran the Rottingdean Riding School.

1. Cf. 'Old Mrs Grey' in *The Death of the Moth* (Kp A27). Leslie Stephen was born in 1832.

loomed above us. Going to fetch L.'s hat from Charleston I chanced on one of those evening autumn emotional hours when people want to be intimate, perhaps to boast. And he told me an absurd romantic story—of a girl, lovely, desired, half his age; & how she loved him, & he could not believe it; she must think me a cultivated elderly man, he said; & so "I try I try to control myself" but, wondrously, they went off the other day; had 4 days perfect bliss; & now "the drama begins". That is, it began two days ago, on Monday. Nobody has the least idea who she is. And is it lasting, or genuine, or only a set off against Mary? & will it survive Mary's attacks, & shall we be dragged in, & so on & so on? Those are the thoughts which agitate us this October, which is the birth of the year.

If my pen allowed, I should now try to make out a work table, having done my last article for the Tribune, & now being free again. And instantly the usual exciting devices enter my mind: a biography beginning in the year 1500 & continuing to the present day, called Orlando: Vita; only with a change about from one sex to another. I think, for a treat, I shall let myself dash this in for a week, while   [*text ends*]

The Woolfs returned to London on Thursday 6 October.

Saturday 22 October

This is a book, I think I have said before, which I write after tea. And my brain was full of ideas, but I have spent them on Mr Ashcroft & Miss Findlater, fervent admirers.[2]

"I shall let myself dash this in for a week"—I have done nothing, nothing, nothing else for a fortnight; & am launched somewhat furtively but with all the more passion upon Orlando: A Biography. It is to be a small book, & written by Christmas. I thought I could combine it with *Fiction*, but once the mind gets hot it cant stop; I walk making up phrases; sit, contriving scenes; am in short in the thick of the greatest rapture known to me; from which I have kept myself since last February, or earlier. Talk of planning a book, or waiting for an idea! This one came in a rush; I said to pacify myself, being bored & stale with criticism & faced with that intolerable dull Fiction, "You shall write a page of a story for a treat: you shall stop sharp at 11.30 & then go on with the Romantics". I had very little idea what the story was to be about. But the relief of

2. Mr Ashcroft, unidentified; Mary Findlater (1865-1963) and her sister Jane (1866-1946) who separately and jointly wrote a number of popular novels, had written appreciatively to VW; her reply, dated 22 October 1927, is published in Eileen MacKenzie, *The Findlater Sisters*, 1964, pp 116-17.

turning my mind that way about was such that I felt happier than for months; as if put in the sun, or laid on cushions; & after two days entirely gave up my time chart & abandoned myself to the pure delight of this farce: which I enjoy as much as I've ever enjoyed anything; & have written myself into half a headache & had to come to a halt, like a tired horse, & take a little sleeping draught last night: which made our breakfast fiery. I did not finish my egg. I am writing Orlando half in a mock style very clear & plain, so that people will understand every word. But the balance between truth & fantasy must be careful. It is based on Vita, Violet Trefusis, Lord Lascelles, Knole &c.[3]

A great many incidents to record. They come always in a rush together, these bright October days, with every one just back, fresh from solitude, cheerful, busy, sociable. Nessa has initiated, informally, Sunday evenings; & there Old Bloomsbury is to gather, after dinner—Helen Clive Roger & so on.

Then I asked the time in the Press a week ago.

"Leonard can tell you" said Angus very huffily.

"Ask Angus. I dont seem to know" said Leonard very grumpy. And I saw Mrs C. lower her head over her typing & laugh. This was the tail of a terrific quarrel about the time between them. Angus was dismissed; but tells Nessa he wants to stay, could tempers be made compatible. A bad year, this, financially, for the Press: yet prospects seem flourishing, if only Marys & Braithwaites didn't eat up all profits. Dottie (who comes to tea with great simplicity, but sits a little long afterwards) is investing her £200 a year in Stella Gibbons &c. & lends me her own poems, which I promptly throw down the W.C.[4] Vita stalks into the press, all red & black (so is Orlando) says Lizzie [a dog?] has been shot by a farmer, no, a publican (she respects farmers, not publicans): comes up here with me, & Harold drops in to say Good bye. We sit very cosy & intimate for all

3. Violet Trefusis, née Keppel (1894-1972), with whom Vita, often disguised as a man, had had a passionate and dramatic love affair between 1918-21 (see Nigel Nicolson, *Portrait of a Marriage*, 1973). Henry, Viscount Lascelles (1882-1974), who married the Princess Royal in 1922 and was to succeed his father as 6th Earl of Harewood in 1929, had courted Vita before she engaged herself to Harold Nicolson in 1913. Sasha the Russian Princess and the Archduchess Harriet in *Orlando* were based upon what VW learned of these two from Vita.

4. For the quarrel about the time, cf *II QB*, p 130. R. B. Braithwaite's *The State of Religious Belief* had been published by the Hogarth Press in February 1927 (*HP Checklist* 116); it was based upon the *N & A* Questionnaire (see above, 5 September 1926, n 6). Stella Gibbons (b. 1902), best known for her highly successful first novel *Cold Comfort Farm* (1932), was also a poet; but she was not included in Dorothy Wellesley's series of *Hogarth Living Poets*.

his man about the worldiness, over the gas: he has just been to the Foreign Office & they have been "ever so good. Really they spoil one" he said, being devoted to the Office, which now sends him to Berlin for 3 years.[5] Vita will only go for a short time she says. She likes him. She pets him: wants me to make him a fresh cup of tea.

Then there's Clive. He has laid his stairs with the vividest green, 5 inches thick: has every comfort & convenience. I dine there to meet Harold & Tom: Tom, of course, in white waistcoat, much the man of the world; which sets the key, & off they go telling stories about 'Jean' (Cocteau) about Ada Leverson, Gosse, Valery, &c. &c. & L. & I feel a little Bloomsburyish perhaps; no, I think this sort of talk is hardly up to the scratch. Harold does it best. He was in Petersburg when they blew up Stolypin, or his children; can describe the boom bum bum of a bomb falling from the life: & the Empress with her yellow eye whites; & King George throwing Mr Britling with a violence to the floor. & I 'may be lacking in distinction but I'm damned if I'm an alien' was his comment on some phrase of Wells'.[6]

And that reminds me how we saw the pale dove grey coffin of Mrs Wells slide through the gates at Golders Green. It had tassels like bell pulls on it. Wells sat in bottle blue overcoat by [George Bernard] Shaw, sobbing. One saw his white handkerchief going in & out of his pocket. Mr Page a shaggy shabby old scholar, read some typewritten sheets, by Wells, about "our friend Caroline."[7] "Poor things, poor silly things" she'd say,

5. Harold Nicolson left London for Germany on 25 October to take up his new appointment as First Secretary at the British Embassy.
6. Clive's dinner party was on 20 October. Harold Nicolson retold the story of the 1906 bomb attack by Socialist revolutionaries on the Russian Prime Minister P. A. Stolypin in his life (published 1920) of his father Lord Carnock who, as Sir Arthur Nicolson, was British Ambassador in St Petersburg from 1905-10; Harold himself had been sent by his father to see what had happened. Stolypin escaped unharmed (he was later murdered), but two of his children were among the many injured; the three assassins and twenty-five others were killed. Lord Carnock acted as assistant-secretary to the King in 1917 and was no doubt the source for Harold Nicolson's other story about his reaction to H. G. Wells's wartime novel *Mr Britling Sees It Through*, in which Wells wrote of the sad spectacle of England struggling under an 'alien and uninspiring court'. 'I may be uninspiring,' exclaimed the incensed King, 'but I'll be d---d if I'm an alien.' (See Harold Nicolson, *King George the Fifth. His Life and Reign*, 1952, pp 307-8.)
7. Mrs H. G. Wells, who died on the 6th and was cremated at Golders Green on 10 October, was generally known as 'Jane' although her name was Catherine (*not* Caroline). H. G., wishing to direct attention to a hidden side of her personality, published a memoir of her and several of her stories in *The Book of Catherine Wells* in 1928. Dr Thomas Ethelbert Page (1850-1936) was classical scholar, teacher, and a noted orator.

in their days of ill repute. This colloquialism merged in the burial service; & somehow the whole effect was a little nondescript. The aim was to emphasise life; & generosity & how generous lives continue; one thing touched me. "Some are set on a headland & their lives are a beacon to mankind. Others live retired & are hardly known; but their lives are the most precious" which reminds me of what my father wrote, & meant at the moment, of my mother.[8] Then the coffin slid away "into the furnace of material creation". She had become part of the roses she loved, & of the sun on snow. Poor Jane! It was desperate to see what a dowdy shabby imperfect lot we looked; how feeble; how ugly for the most part. And yet we were doing our best to say something sincere about our great adventure (as Wells almost called it). And he has been adventurous & plunged about in his bath & splashed the waters, to give him his due. Afterwards we stood about congratulating; Lydia sobbed; Shaw said "You mustnt cry. Jane is well—Jane is splendid" & we went off—I to Fortnum & Mason's to buy shoes.

Sunday 20 November

I will now snatch a moment from what Morgan calls 'life' to enter a hurried note. My notes have been few; life a cascade, a glissade, a torrent: all together. I think on the whole this *is* our happiest autumn. So much work; & success now; & life on easy terms: heaven knows what. My morning rushes, pell mell, from 10 to 1. I write so quick I can't get it typed before lunch. This I suppose is the main backbone of my autumn— Orlando. Never do I feel this, except for a morning or two, writing criticism. Today I began the third chapter. Do I learn anything? Too much of a joke perhaps for that; yet I like these plain sentences; & the externality of it for a change. It is too thin of course; splashed over the canvas; but I shall cover the ground by Jan. 7th (I say) & then re-write.

Vita comes; Dottie comes; Clive incessant; Tom; Roger; we have our Bloomsbury evenings; for the first time I have been spending money, on a bed, on a coat (the coat, at the moment, I regret) & had a delicious sense of affluence the other day when at Long Barn I tipped Loune [*the butler*] 5/- for a nights lodging. But the money psychology is odd; & that it doesn't give me enormous pleasure to spend. I doubt that I want anything

8. In October 1895, after the death of his wife, Leslie Stephen gave a lecture upon 'Forgotten Benefactors' at the Ethical Society, which was later published in volume II of his *Social Rights and Duties* (1896); his avowed intention was to 'speak of Julia without mentioning her name', and the text concludes: '. . . the good done by a noble life and character may last far beyond any horizon which can be realised by our imaginations'.

eno'; yet worry about spending wrongly; & must buy an evening dress which worries me too. I have refused Sibyl; accepted Ethel. Fame increases; I think. Young men write about me in their absurd random books. Domestic life, Nelly that is, good as gold.

This is a summary; for I have too many letters to write, & cant catch that cloud which was so heavy in my brain when I sat down.

I made Vita cry the other night; quietly, unself-consciously. "I hate being bored" I said, of her Campbells & Valery Taylors; & this she thought meant I should be tired of her.[1]

Wednesday 30 November

I have just been upstairs & tried on a hat (18/11) which I have just bought at B&H (so they call it) [*Bourne & Hollingsworth, Oxford Street*] to wear at Sibyl's lunch party tomorrow. With that money I could have bought a nightgown. Then I heard a man in a bus talk about quality & state of gentlemaness; & you would call me Sir; as I you Madam. This to a working woman, dowdy pasty plush with a baby. "Had more'n 8" she said to the conductor; whom she called young man; & he called her Ma. This is Dickens; or Shakespeare; or simple English cockney: whichever it is I adore it; & warm the cockles of my heart at it.

A very happy autumn this, I repeat. Nelly raised £5, & for that reason or another in constant spirits & kindness. Offered last night to clear away. She thinks it only fair, as we've raised her. No trouble about people coming. After Xmas discontent will set in no doubt; when I must write criticism; the light languishes; Nessa Vita Clive are all away. But I will steal a march on that depression. Moreover, aren't I proud at the moment. Ruth Draper admires me: I am to meet her on Friday at Elena Richmond's. What an incredible concatenation! So tonight I go to the Pit to see Ruth Draper.[2] Lunch with Sibyl; dine with Ethel; & a new dress, made from one 100 years old. These are the little waves that life makes; which keep us tossing & going up & down on top of them.

1. Vita, dining alone with VW at Tavistock Square on 10 November, had told her of the tribulations of her current affair with Mary Campbell, wife of the South African poet Roy Campbell; the Campbells had returned from his native Durban earlier in the year, and were now living in the gardener's cottage at Long Barn; he, on discovering his wife's liaison with Vita, had reacted violently and threateningly (see below, 7 July 1928). Ignatius Roy Dunnachie Campbell (1902-57) had married Mary Margaret Garman in London in 1922; in 1931 he published his highly disobliging satire on the Nicolsons (and Bloomsbury) *The Georgiad*.
2. Ruth Draper (1884-1956), the already celebrated American character actress, was appearing at the Criterion Theatre for a season of her solo performances.

DECEMBER 1927

[Thursday 1 December]

A rapid note about the lunch party, L. dining at the Cranium.[1]

An art of light talk; about people. Bogey Harris; Maurice Baring. B.H. 'knows' everyone: that is no one. Freddy Fossle? Oh yes I know him; knows Ly So & So; knows everyone: cant admit to not knowing. A polished, burnished diner out. Roman Catholic. In the middle M. Baring says—But Lady Beaverbrook died this morning.[2] Sibyl says Say that again. But BM. [?] was lunching with her yesterday, says Bogey. Well its in the papers: she's dead says M.B. Sibyl says But she was quite young. Lord Ivor asked me to meet the young man her daughter's to marry. I know Lord Ivor says, or wd say Bogey. Well its odd, says Sibyl, giving up the attempt to wrestle with the death of the young at a lunch party. So on to wigs: Lady Charlie used to have hers curled by a sailor on deck before she got up says Bogey. Oh I've known her all my life. Went yatchting with them. Lady . . . eyebrows fell into the soup. Sir John Cook was so fat they had to hike him up. Once he got out of bed in the middle of the night & fell on the floor where he lay 5 hours—couldn't move. BM. sent me a pear by the waiter with a long letter. Talk of houses & periods. All very smooth & surface talk: depends on knowing people: not on saying anything interesting. Bogey's cheeks are polished daily.

Tuesday 20 December

This is almost the shortest day & perhaps the coldest night of the year. We are in the black heart of a terrific frost. I notice that look of black atoms in a clear air, which for some reason I can never describe to my liking. The pavement was white with great powdery flakes the other night, walking back with Roger & Helen; this was from Nessa's last Sunday—last, I fear, for many a month. But I have as usual 'no time': let me count the things I should be doing this deep winters night with Leonard at his last lecture, & Pinker asleep in his chair. I should be reading Bagenal's story; Julian's play; Lord Chesterfield's letters; &

1. LW's Cranium dinner was on 1 December, which must therefore be the date of this entry and of Lady Colefax's lunch party.
2. Henry ('Bogey') Harris (c. 1871-1950), wealthy connoisseur and art collector of 9 Bedford Square, WC1, had been educated at Eton and Christ Church and was a prominent member of Edwardian society; from 1917-21 he was Secretary to the British Legation to the Vatican. Lady Beaverbrook, the somewhat overshadowed wife of the ebullient Press Lord, died of a heart attack at Stornoway House, St. James's, on 1 December.

writing to Hubert [Henderson] (about a cheque from the Nation).[3] There
is an irrational scale of values in my mind which puts these duties higher
than mere scribbling.

Angus is finally to go: we had another semi-painful interview in the
Studio; when he interrupted L.'s dismissal with his own resignation. Not
enough money. We think of Francis Birrell as partner; shall ask him
tomorrow; & broach the Hogarth Miscellany.[4]

This flashed to my mind at Nessa's children's party last night. The
little creatures acting moved my infinitely sentimental throat. Angelica so
mature, & composed; all grey & silver; such an epitome of all womanli-
ness; & such an unopened bud of sense & sensibility; wearing a grey wig
& a sea coloured dress. And yet oddly enough I scarcely want children of
my own now. This insatiable desire to write something before I die, this
ravaging sense of the shortness & feverishness of life, make me cling, like
a man on a rock, to my one anchor. I don't like the physicalness of having
children of one's own. This occurred to me at Rodmell; but I never
wrote it down. I can dramatise myself as parent, it is true. And perhaps I
have killed the feeling instinctively; as perhaps nature does.

I am still writing the 3rd Chap. of Orlando. I have had of course to
give up the fancy of finishing by February & printing this spring. It is
drawing out longer than I meant. I have just been thinking over the scene
when O. meets a girl (Nell) in the Park & goes with her to a neat room in
Gerrard Street. There she will disclose herself. They will talk. This will
lead to a diversion or two about women's love. This will bring in O.'s
night life; & her clients (thats the word). Then she will see Dr Johnson,
& perhaps write (I want somehow to quote it) To all you Ladies.[5] So I
shall get some effect of years passing; & then there will be a description of
the lights of the 18th Century burning; & the clouds of the 19th Century
rising. Then on to the 19th. But I have not considered this. I want to
write it all over hastily, & so keep unity of tone, which in this book is

3. Under the auspices of the Union of Democratic Control, LW had been giving a
   series, which began on 11 October, of six lectures on 'Imperialism and the Problem
   of Civilization' at Friends House, Euston Road. 'Bagenal's story' is untraced; as is
   Julian Bell's play: he appears to have sent more than one to VW for her criticism
   at this period (see *III VW Letters*, nos. 1836, 1865 to Julian Bell, and no. 1843 to
   Lady Cecil). VW was reading Chesterfield in connection with her review of *The
   Characters of Lord Chesterfield* edited by Charles Whibley, which was to appear in
   the *TLS* on 8 March 1928 (Kp C298).
4. Francis Birrell did not join the Press; and nothing ever came of the *Hogarth
   Miscellany*, or *Annual* as VW elsewhere refers to it.
5. 'To all you Ladies' was written in 1665 by Vita's ancestor Charles Sackville, Earl
   of Dorset. VW does not quote it in *Orlando*.

very important. It has to be half laughing, half serious: with great splashes of exaggeration.

Perhaps I shall pluck up courage to ask the Times for a rise. But could I write for my Annual I would never write for another paper. How extraordinarily unwilled by me but potent in its own right by the way Orlando was! as if it shoved everything aside to come into existence. Yet I see looking back just now to March that it is almost exactly in spirit, though not in actual facts, the book I planned then as an escapade; the spirit to be satiric, the structure wild. Precisely.

Yes, I repeat, a very happy, a singularly happy autumn.

Facts are: Clive is loved by a lady in Leicestershire: Mary loves (perhaps) Lord A. She wishes to have Clive back on terms. He forgets: has a twinge now & then, but is fancy free. Mary met them walking in Cavendish Square. Raymond will marry Valery. (so we think).

Thursday 22 December

I just open this for a moment, being dull of the head, to enter a severe reprimand of myself to myself. The value of society is that it snubs one. I am meretricious. mediocre; a humbug; am getting into the habit of flashy talk. Tinsel it seemed last night at the Keynes.[6] I was out of humour & so could see the transparency of my own sayings. Dadie said a true thing too: when V. lets her style get on top of her, one thinks only of that; when she uses clichés, one thinks what she means. But, he says, I have no logical power & live & write in an opium dream. And the dream is too often about myself.

Now with middle age drawing on, & age ahead it is important to be severe on such faults. So easily might I become a hare brained egotistic woman, exacting compliments, arrogant, narrow, withered. Nessa's children (I always measure myself against her, & find her much the largest, most humane of the two of us, think of her now with an admiration that has no envy in it: with some trace of the old childish feeling that we were in league together against the world; & how proud I am of her triumphant winning of all our battles: as she [battles?] her way so nonchalantly modestly, almost anonymously past the goal, with her children round her; & only a little added tenderness (a moving thing in her) which shows me that she too feels wonder surprise at having passed so many terrors & sorrows safe—

The dream is too often about myself. To correct this, & to forget one's

6. On 21 December Frankie Birrell and Dadie Rylands dined with the Woolfs before they all went on to the Keyneses' party.

own sharp absurd little personality, reputation & the rest of it, one should read; see outsiders; think more; write more logically; above all be full of work; & practise anonymity. Silence in company; or the quietest statement, not the showiest, is also 'indicated' as the doctors say. It was an empty party, rather, last night. Very nice here, though; & F.B. is I think willing.

On Christmas eve the Woolfs went by train to Lewes where they had left their car, and drove out to Charleston where they spent the next three nights before moving back to Monks House. The Bells were all away spending Christmas with Clive's widowed mother in Wiltshire.

1928

1928

The Woolfs returned from Monks House to Tavistock Square on Monday 2 January, and for the next two weeks VW saw few people besides her immediate Bloomsbury familiars and Vita Sackville-West, whose father was dying at Knole, and with whom she stayed the night of 14 January at Long Barn. She was absorbed in writing Orlando. DIARY XVII *which follows is written, like the last, on loose-leaf paper.*

Tuesday 17 January

In half an hour or so Nessa & Duncan will look in on their way to Roger's to say good bye. This is the true break in the year: Bloomsbury is dispersed today till May, I suppose. Clive was off to Germany this morning.[1]

Yesterday we went to Hardy's funeral. What did I think of? Of Max Beerbohm's letter, just read; or a lecture to the Newnhamites about women's writing.[2] At intervals some emotion broke in. But I doubt the capacity of the human animal for being dignified in ceremony. One catches a Bishops frown & twitch: sees his polished shiny nose; suspects the rapt spectacled young priest gazing at the cross he carries, of being a humbug; catches Robert Lynd's distracted haggard eye; then thinks of the mediocrity of Squire; next here is the coffin, an overgrown one; like a stage

1. This winter migration, henceforth to be a regular custom for the painters Duncan and Vanessa, was facilitated by their having acquired a secure base in Provence, 'La Bergère', a small house reconstructed from a ruin on his property at Fontcreuse, near Cassis, by Lt. Col. A. S. H. Teed (retd.), late of the Bengal Lancers; this year they were to remain there, with their daughter Angelica, until the end of May. Clive took Quentin to Munich, where he was to spend several months in a family, and then went on with Raymond Mortimer to Dresden, Berlin, and Paris, returning to London on 10 February.

2. Thomas Hardy died at his home on 11 January 1928; by a gruesome historic compromise between his own wishes and those of 'the nation', his heart was interred in his own parish churchyard at Stinsford and his ashes in Poet's Corner, Westminster Abbey; both funeral ceremonies took place at the same hour on 16 January. What appeared to VW an 'overgrown' coffin was in fact the pall-covered bier bearing the casket of ashes. Max Beerbohm had written (30 December 1927, copy MHP, Sussex) that he rated *The Common Reader* 'above any modern book of criticism', but that in her novels VW was 'so hard on us common readers'. VW had agreed to speak to the Newnham Arts Society in May; in the event her talk was postponed until October (see below, headnote before 27 October 1928).

coffin, covered with a white satin cloth: bearers elderly gentlemen rather red & stiff, holding to the corners: pigeons flying outside; insufficient artificial light; procession to poets corner; dramatic "In sure & certain hope of immortality" perhaps melodramatic. After dinner at Clive's Lytton protested that the great man's novels are the poorest of poor stuff; & can't read them. Lytton sitting or lying inert, with his eyes shut, or exasperated with them open. Lady Strachey slowly fading, but it may take years. Over all this broods for me, some uneasy sense, of change, & mortality, & how partings are deaths; & then a sense of my own fame—why should this come over me?—& then of its remoteness; & then the pressure of writing two articles on Meredith & furbishing up the Hardy.[3] And Leonard sitting at home reading. And Max's letter. & a sense of the futility of it all.

Saturday 11 February

I am so cold I can hardly hold the pen. The futility of it all—so I broke off; & have indeed been feeling that rather persistently, or perhaps I should have written here. Hardy & Meredith together sent me torpid to bed with headache. I know the feeling now, when I can't spin a sentence, & sit mumbling & turning; & nothing flits by my brain which is as a blank window. So I shut my studio door, & go to bed, stuffing my ears with rubber; & there I lie a day or two. And what leagues I travel in the time! Such 'sensations' spread over my spine & head directly I give them the chance; such an exaggerated tiredness; such anguishes & despairs; & heavenly relief & rest; & then misery again. Never was anyone so tossed up & down by the body as I am, I think. But it is over: & put away; & Lord Sackville is dead & lies at Withyam, & I passed Knole with Vita yesterday & had to look away from the vast masterless house, without a flag. This is what she minds most. When she left the house behind the old cart horses, she went for ever, she said, after complete rule for three days.[1]

3. Lady Strachey (1840-1928), *née* Jane Maria Grant, Duncan's aunt and mother of ten Stracheys, died in December (see below, 18 December 1928). VW's article on 'The Novels of George Meredith' appeared in the *TLS* of 9 February 1928 (Kp C297). Her tribute to Hardy had long been in preparation; it was begun in December 1921, having been effectively commissioned by Bruce Richmond as early as February 1919 (see *II VW Diary*, 9 August 1921, n 2). It was published, under the title 'Thomas Hardy's Novels', as the leading article in the *TLS*, 19 January 1928 (Kp C294).

1. Vita's father, the 3rd Baron Sackville, died at Knole on 28 January, aged sixty; he was buried, as the Sackvilles have been since the fourteenth century, in the family chapel at Withyham Church, his coffin drawn thither by carthorses. Since he had no son, his titles and estates passed to his brother Charles.

For some reason, I am hacking rather listlessly at the last chapter of Orlando, which was to have been the best. Always always the last chapter slips out of my hands. One gets bored. One whips oneself up. I still hope for a fresh wind, & dont very much bother, except that I miss the fun, which was so tremendously lively all October, November & December. I have my doubts if it is not empty; & too fantastic to write at such length.

For the rest, Bloomsbury today revives. Clive is back: whereupon Mary asks us to lunch: & so we return to some flicker of the snowdrop pallor of very early spring.

My pen protests. This writing is nonsense, it says. And L. is with M[argaret] Ll[ewelyn]. D[avies]. Pinker has the lice. [*Several ink blots.*]

Saturday 18 February

I am happy to say I have still a few pounds in the Bank, & my own cheque book too. This great advance in dignity was made in the autumn. Out of my £60 I have bought a Heal bed; a cupboard, a fur coat, & now a strip of carpet for the hall. This financial revision has been a great success. And I pan out articles so as to write one & earn £30 a month. And I should be revising Lord Chesterfield at this moment, but I'm not. My mind is woolgathering away about Women & Fiction, which I am to read at Newnham in May. The mind is the most capricious of insects—flitting fluttering. I had thought to write the quickest most brilliant pages in Orlando yesterday—not a drop came, all, forsooth, for the usual physical reasons, which declared themselves today. It is the oddest feeling: as if a finger stopped the flow of the ideas in the brain: it is unsealed, & the blood rushes all over the place. Again, instead of writing O. I've been racing up & down the whole field of my lecture. And tomorrow, alas, we motor; for I must get back into the book—which has brightened the last few days satisfactorily. Not that my sensations in writing are an infallible guide.

We dined with Ka.[2] She had unshaded all Nessa's lamps, & somehow commonplaced the house strangely. It was full too of those derelicts whom she collects—the earnest, the ugly, the unhappy. Never have I sat next such driftwood as Mrs Campbell. Garnett was as bad—an over-educated prig. So tired I cant talk—three large committees this afternoon —gave accurate information about cooking eggs.

Before that, there was Todd & Clive—Clive is ubiquitous. Todd like some primeval animal emerging from the swamp, muddy, hirsute. A

2. During her absence in France, Vanessa Bell had let her rooms at 37 Gordon Square to Ka and Will Arnold-Forster. Ka's other guests have not been identified.

woman who is commercial—rather an exception in my world. She spoke of "getting my money back" as Gerald Duckworth might have spoken with the same look of rather hostile & cautious greed, as though the world were banded to rob her. This money-grubbing way is not attractive; but it is lightened by a shimmer of dash & 'chic' even. She stands on her two feet as she expresses it. She is starting a paper—I'm so bored with people starting papers in May! There's Desmond for another.[3] But Todd has none of his bubble & gush. She finds work very dull. She likes life. [*Six words omitted*] flirting with Osbert I presume. She is tapir like, & the creatures nose snuffs pertinaciously after Bloomsbury.

Dadie came in for a moment, rather drawn & white, 'making money' too. We are a little out of that, Leonard & I: L. never makes a penny; I mean tries to: & I could almost wish we were more lavish in our ways. This is occasionally in my thoughts. And what else is? I doubt that I shall ever write another novel after O. I shall invent a new name for them.

Lunch with Mary; lunch with Clive; dinner with Clive; tea with Jane, raised in bed, with her old white head lifted up, on pillows, very aged & rather exalted, able only to talk or listen for 10 minutes or so.[4] Mary & Jack simmering with polished domestic affluence & prettiness: gay bunches everywhere; & paint, & carpets; but not much backing to it. Jack develops, before 3 strikes, the storytelling manner: by 3.30 all the stories are told. Home to shabbiness.

Sunday 18 March

I have lost my writing board; an excuse for the anaemic state of this book. Indeed I only write now, in between letters, to say that Orlando was finished yesterday as the clock struck one. Anyhow the canvas is covered. There will be three months of close work needed, imperatively, before it can be printed; for I have scrambled & splashed, & the canvas shows through in a thousand places. But it is a serene, accomplished

3. Dorothy Todd had been relieved of her editorship of British *Vogue* by its American owners in 1926 as she failed to make it profitable to them; she was now proposing to finance and produce a quarterly of similar quality herself, but did not succeed. Desmond MacCarthy's monthly, *Life and Letters*, subsidised by the Hon. Oliver Brett (later 3rd Viscount Esher), first appeared in June 1928, and he continued to edit it for five years.

4. Jane Ellen Harrison (1850-1928), one-time lecturer and Fellow of Newnham College, Cambridge, was a distinguished classical scholar, archaeologist, and anthropologist. The Hogarth Press had published her *Reminiscences of a Student's Life* in 1925 (*HP Checklist* 64). VW visited her at Mecklenburgh Street, WC1, where she now lived with Hope Mirrlees.

feeling, to write, even provisionally, The End, & we go off on Saturday, with my mind appeased.

I have written this book quicker than any: & it is all a joke; & yet gay & quick reading I think; a writers holiday. I feel more & more sure that I will never write a novel again. Little bits of rhyme come in. So we go motoring across France on Saturday, & shall be back on April 17th for the summer. Time flies—oh yes: that summer should be here again; & I still have the faculty of wonder at it. The world swinging round again & bringing its green & blue close to ones eyes.

Since February I have been a little clouded with headache, had a touch of influenza; & so, with the lights down, & all energy turned to forcing my book along, have not written here. I dislike these months. Shall we try Rome next year? Control of life is what one should learn now: its economic management. I feel cautious, like a poor person, now I am 46. But I may be dead then, I think, & so take my French lessons now, instead of waiting.

Thursday 22 March

There are the last pages at the end of Orlando, & it is twenty five minutes to one; & I have written everything I have to write, & on Saturday we go abroad.

Yes its done—Orlando—begun on 8th October, as a joke; & now rather too long for my liking. It may fall between stools, be too long for a joke, & too frivolous for a serious book. All this I dismiss from a mind avid only of green fields. The sun; wine; sitting doing nothing. I have been for the last 6 weeks rather a bucket than a fountain; sitting to be shot into by one person after another. A rabbit that passes across a shooting gallery, & one's friends go pop-pop. Heaven be praised, Sibyl today puts us off, which leaves Dadie only, & a whole days solitude, please Heaven, tomorrow. But I intend to control this rabbit shooting business when I come back. And money making. I hope to settle in & write one nice little discreet article for £25 each month; & so live; without stress; & so read— what I want to read. At 46 one must be a miser; only have time for essentials.

But I think I have made moral reflections enough, & should describe people, save that, when seen so colourlessly, by duty not wish, one's mind is a little slack in taking notes. Morgan & Desmond were here to tea. Morgan more of the blue butterfly than ever. Unless I talk, he says nothing. And any shadow sends him flitting. Desmond comes in, round as a billiard ball; & this is true of his dear bubbling lazy mind; which has such a glitter & lustre now from mere being at ease in the world that it puts me into a good temper to be with him. He describes, analyses, narrates; does not actually talk. All his blandishments are now active to get articles for "Life & Letters" which comes out in May. I am scarcely flattered now to be asked; yet of course dashed a little when I refuse Mrs van Doren's £120 & she takes no notice.[1] And a little dashed, too, not to get the Femina prize—partly because I've been exhibited as a competitor & people will think me dashed: which I'm not, innately.[2]

Roger & Helen, Ka & Will, the other night. Roger malicious a little, & vain. "I am the most read critic in England, & yet I have nowhere to write." Analysed, this amounts to the fact that The Nation only pays him £5, & Konody gets more, & the pages of the Burlington are more thumbed at his articles than at MacColl's.[3] There is an innocence in this vanity which is likeable; but I am touchy for the reputation of Bloomsbury. I thought I could see Ka & Will comparing us, & being glad we were not impeccable. They compare us with the political world: we them with our own. Will lay with his eyes shut, & I was rather sorry for him. He knows what Roger thinks of his pictures, & what I don't think—for I dont look at them; but he has the generosity to praise my books. We middleaged people now scarcely covet each others good opinion very seriously: are content to be different.

Watery blowy weather; & this time next week we shall be in the middle of France.

The Woolfs spent the week end of 24 March at Monks House, and made the Newhaven-Dieppe channel crossing on Monday 26 March. They drove via Beauvais, Troyes, Beaune, Vienne, Orange and Aix, and reached Cassis on

1. Irita Van Doren (1891-1966), wife of the writer Carl Van Doren, was currently editor of the weekly Book Supplement of the *New York Herald Tribune* and had, since 1925, commissioned a number of articles from VW, including a series of six reviews published in 1927 (Kp C284, 286-90) for which she paid her £120. Presumably she had now offered the same amount for a similar series and been refused; in 1929 she raised her price to £50 an article (see below, 13 April 1929).

2. VW's dejection was premature: on 23 March she read a *Times* report from Paris that she had been awarded the 1927-28 *Prix Femina* for *To the Lighthouse*; official intimation came in a letter from the Honorary Secretary of the British Femina-Vie Heureuse Committee dated 26 March 1928 (LWP, Sussex) by which time VW was in France. The two other final 'competitors' this year were Storm Jameson and Stella Benson.

3. Roger Fry and Ka Arnold-Forster dined with the Woolfs on 20 March; their spouses came in afterwards. Paul G. Konody (1872-1933) was art critic of the *Observer* and *Daily Mail* and author of numerous books on art and artists; D. S. MacColl (1859-1948) an influential administrator and writer upon art.

Sunday 1 April. There they stayed in rooms in the Château de Fontcreuse which belonged to Colonel Teed, taking most of their meals with Vanessa and her family at 'La Bergère'. The return journey, beginning on 9 April, took them, with overnight stops at Tarascon, Florac, Aurillac, Guéret, Blois and Dreux, to Dieppe; after a very rough crossing on 16 April, they left the car in Lewes and took the train to London.

Tuesday 17 April

Home again, as foretold, last night, & to settle the dust in my mind, write here. We have been across France & back—every inch of that fertile field traversed by the admirable Singer. And now towns & spires & scenes begin to rise in my mind as the rest sinks. I see Chartres in particular, the snail, with its head straight, marching across the flat country, the most distinguished of churches. The rose window is like a jewel on black velvet. The outside is very intricate yet simple; elongated; somehow preserved from the fantastic & ornate. Grey weather dashed all over this; & I remember coming in at night in the wet often, & hearing the rain in hotels. Often I was bobbing up & down on my two glasses of vin du pays.

It was rather a rush & a cram—as these jumbled notes testify. Once we were high up on a mountain in a snow storm; & rather afraid of a long tunnel. Twenty miles often cut us off from civilisation. One wet afternoon we punctured in a mountain village & I went in & sat with the family—a nice scrupulous polite woman, a girl who was pretty, shy, had a friend called Daisy at Earlsfield. They caught trout & wild boars. Then on we went to Florac, where I found a book Girardin's memoirs in the old bookcase that had been sold with the house. Always some good food & hot bottles at night. And there was Nessa & Duncan & Clive (who smacked me in public—curse him for an uneasy little upstart.) Oh & my prize—£40 from the French. And Julian. And one or two hot days & the Pont du Garde in the sun; & Les Beaux (this is where Dante got his idea of Hell Duncan said) & mounting all the time steadily was my desire for words, till I envisaged a sheet of paper & pen & ink as something of miraculous desirability—could even relish the scratch as if it were a divine kind of relief to me— And there was St Remy & the ruins in the sun. I forget now how it all went—how thing fitted to thing; but the eminences now emerge, & I noticed how, talking to Raymond at The Nation this afternoon we had already pitched on the high points. Before that, crossing the graveyard in the bitter windy rain, we saw Hope & a dark cultivated woman. But on they went past us, with the waver of an eye. Next moment

I heard Virginia, & turned & there was Hope coming back—"Jane died yesterday" she murmured, half asleep, talking distraught, 'out of herself.' We kissed by Cromwell's daughter's grave, where Shelley used to walk, for Jane's death.[1] She lay dead outside the graveyard in that back room where we saw her lately raised on her pillows, like a very old person, whom life has tossed up, & left; exalted, satisfied, exhausted. Hope the colour of dirty brown paper. Then to the office, then home to work here; & now to work & work, as hard as I can.

Saturday 21 April

A bitter windy rainy day. There is no blue, no red, no green in this detestable spring. Furs are in the shops. I have walked across the Park with Leonard; come home; find the char in the studio; must write here instead of making, as I had meant, some carefully polished sentences—for Orlando is to tell the truth, damned rough.

Life is either too empty or too full. Happily, I never cease to transmit these curious damaging shocks. At 46 I am not callous; suffer considerably; make good resolutions—still feel as experimental & on the verge of getting at the truth as ever. Oh & Vita—to change the subject & take up the burden of facts—has had a stupendous row with her mother—in the course of which she was made to take the pearl necklace from her neck, cut it in two with a pocket knife, deliver over the 12 central pearls, put the relics, all running loose, in an envelope the solicitor gave her. Thief, liar, I hope you'll be killed by an omnibus—so 'my honoured Lady Sackville' addressed her, trembling with rage in the presence of a secretary & a solicitor & a Chauffeur. The woman is said to be mad. Vita very gallant & wild & tossing her head & taking me to the Zoo & saying she was wild & free & wd. make her money now herself by writing.[2]

And I find myself again in the old driving whirlwind of writing against time. Have I ever written with it? But I vow I wont spend longer at Orlando, which is a freak; it shall come out in September, though the

1. Jane Harrison died on 15 April at 11 Mecklenburgh Street; the adjacent graveyard behind the Foundling Hospital, known as St George's Fields, was that of St George the Martyr Church, Queen Square, Bloomsbury. Oliver Cromwell's *grand-daughter* Mrs Gibson was buried there in 1727.
2. The dowager Lady Sackville, *née* Victoria Sackville-West (1862-1936), illegitimate daughter of Lionel Sackville-West (2nd Baron Sackville) and 'Pepita', a Spanish dancer, had married her cousin Lionel Edward Sackville-West (3rd Baron Sackville) in 1890. A woman of abounding vitality, charm, and wealth, she grew increasingly erratic and demanding with age; in 1919 she had left her husband and Knole, and now lived at Brighton. (See V. Sackville-West, *Pepita*, 1937, *HP Checklist* 419.)

perfect artist would revoke & rewrite & polish—infinitely. But hours remain over to be filled with reading something or other—I'm not sure what. What sort of summer do I desire? Now that I have 16 pounds to spend before July 1st (on our new system) I feel freer: can afford a dress or a hat, & so may go about, a little, if I want. And yet the only exciting life is the imaginary one. Once I get the wheels spinning in my head, I dont want money much, or dress, or even a cupboard, a bed at Rodmell or a sofa.

Dined with Lydia & Maynard: two couples, elderly, childless distinguished. He & she both urbane & admirable. Grey comes at Maynard's temples. He is finer looking now: not with us pompous or great: simple, with his mind working always, on Russian, Bolshevists, glands, genealogies; always the proof of a remarkable mind when it overflows thus vigorously into byepaths. There are two royal stocks in England he says from which all intellect descends. He will work this out as if his fortune depended on it. Lydia is composed, & controlled. She says very sensible things.

We went, also, to Jane's funeral, getting 'there' (somewhere out of the world where buses pass only one every 15 minutes), just as the service ended;[3] marching into the church clamorously; but it was only barely full of the dingiest people; cousins I fancy from the North, very drab: the only male relation afflicted, with a bubbly chin, a stubbly beard, & goggly eyes. Distinguished people drag up such queer chains of family when they die. They had hired Daimlers too, which succeeded the coffin at a foots pace. We walked to the grave; the clergyman, a friend, waited for the dismal company to collect; then read some of the lovelier, more rational parts of the Bible; & said, by heart, Abide with me. The gravedigger had given him, surreptitiously, a handful of clay, which he divided into three parts & dropped at the right moments. A bird sang most opportunely; with a gay indifference, & if one liked, hope, that Jane would have enjoyed. Then the incredibly drab female cousins advanced, each with a fat bunch of primroses & dropped them in; & we also advanced & looked down at the coffin at the bottom of a very steep brazen looking grave—But tho' L. almost cried, I felt very little—only the beauty of the Come unto me all ye that are weary; but as usual the obstacle of not believing dulled & bothered me. Who is 'God' & what the Grace of Christ? & what did they mean to Jane?

Raymond to tea—two hours animated admirable light & airy & well

3. Jane Harrison's funeral was at St Marylebone Cemetery, Finchley, on the afternoon of 19 April; it was that evening the Woolfs dined with the Keyneses.

seasoned talk, about facts mostly: ghosts; consciousness; novels: not people much. But he has his shirts made of figured tablecloths, shiny, hard.

And what am I to read? Pinker is back. And Leonard having tea with his mother. And perhaps the old woman has sighed herself through my room, & I can go down & do that typing, & write to the little man who smacks me in public & appeals for my pity—Clive I mean.[4]

Tuesday 24 April

Waiting for Gumbo [Marjorie Strachey]—how I hate waiting for anybody! Can't settle, read, think—so I write: an odd tribute to the uses I put this diary to. And I should be typing O. in the basement. Must now do 10 pages daily till June 1st. Well, I like being an ass on a mill round.

In from the triumph of buying a dress & a coat for about 5.10. What one must do is to face the girl with one's naked kindly searching eye: speak firmly; ask for a looking glass & study effects. Then they quail, under powder & paint. A lovely soaring summer day this: winter sent howling home to his arctic. I was reading Othello last night, & was impressed by the volley & volume & tumble of his words: too many I should say, were I reviewing for the Times. He put them in when tension was slack. In the great scenes, everything fits like a glove. The mind tumbles & splashes among words when it is not being urged on: I mean, the mind of a very great master of words who is writing with one hand. He abounds. The lesser writers stint. As usual, impressed by Shre. But my mind is very bare to words—English words—at the moment: they hit me, hard, I watch them bounce & spring. I've read only French for 4 weeks. An idea comes to me for an article on French; what we know of it.

Friday 4 May

And now theres the Femina prize to record before I go off this brilliant summer day to tea with Miss Jenkins in Doughty Street.[1] I am going dutifully, not to snub the female young. But I shall be overpowering I doubt not. But it is a wonderful day.

---

4. See *III VW Letters* no. 1885, dated 21 April; Clive was still at Cassis.
1. (Margaret) Elizabeth (Heald) Jenkins (b. 1905) a scholar and graduate of Newnham College, Cambridge, was at this time an unpublished novelist (she was to become a notable biographer). She had been invited to Tavistock Square with John Hayward one evening in March, when she had been the victim of Clive Bell's extravagant gallantries (see *III VW Letters*, no. 1867).

The prize was an affair of dull stupid horror: a function; not alarming; stupefying. Hugh Walpole saying how much he disliked my books; rather, how much he feared for his own. Little Miss Robins, like a red breast, creeping out.[2] I remember your mother—the most beautiful Madonna & at the same time the most complete woman of the world. Used to come & see me in my flat (I see this as a summer visit on a hot day). She never confided. She would suddenly say something so un-expected, from that Madonna face, one thought it *vicious*. This I enjoyed: nothing else made much impression. Afterwards there was the horror of having looked ugly in cheap black clothes. I cannot control this complex. I wake at dawn with a start. Also the 'fame' is becoming vulgar & a nuisance. It means nothing; & yet takes one's time. Americans perpetually. Croly; Gaige; offers:

We have seen an endless number of people—Eddie, Lytton, Miss Ritchie, Francis, Vita,—& now the minute Jenkins.[3]

Thursday 31 May

No I cannot read Proust at the moment—
Leonard is reading Orlando, which goes to the printer tomorrow. It is

2. The Femina-Vie Heureuse Prize ($£40$) was presented to VW at the Institut Français in South Kensington on 2 May by the popular novelist Hugh (Seymour) Walpole (1884-1941), whom she had once met at luncheon with Lady Colefax (see *II VW Diary*, 16 November 1923); their picture appeared on the back page of the *Times* on 3 May. Elizabeth Robins (1862-1952), actress, author, and feminist, born in Louisville, Kentucky. In 1888 she had settled in London where, in the 'nineties, she pioneered and acted in productions of Ibsen's plays, financed by a subscription fund of which Gerald Duckworth had been treasurer (her *Ibsen and the Actress* (*HP Checklist* 174) was published in the Hogarth Essays series in October 1928). She gave up acting in 1902, but wrote a play *Votes for Women!* (1907), and was a prolific novelist.
3. Herbert David Croly (1869-1930) had since 1914 been one of the editors of the *New Republic*, the New York journal which had published some twenty articles by VW; he and his wife had tea with the Woolfs on 26 April. Crosby Gaige (1882-1949), who came to tea on 5 May, was an American with wide-ranging interests in the theatre, in food and drink, bibliography, and book production; his privately printed $15 edition of *Orlando* was to appear in New York in October, a week before that of the Hogarth Press (see Kp A11; also LWP, Sussex, IID 16a). Alice MacGregor Ritchie (1897-1941), born in Natal, had studied at Newnham College, Cambridge, from 1917-20, and later worked in the League of Nations Secretariat at Geneva; she was now employed partly as traveller for Hogarth Press books, and partly in writing her own: her first novel *The Peacemakers* was published in May 1928 (*HP Checklist* 173).

very quiet at the moment. Whitsun is over. We were at Rodmell & saw the races, where the marsh used to be. And our field is sold to Allinson—who is going to build.[4] And what then? I have no brain left over to think with. And Leonard is arguing in the basement with Dadie. What can it be about? Pinker is asleep in the chair. Angelica comes back tomorrow. I feel a kind of drought caused by the lack of Nessa, & ask how shall I manage if we are apart 6 months, not only 4?[5] But my creed is to batter down opposition. I have seen—

I daresay a good many people, Rose Macaulay, Rebecca West, Maurois flash to mind in a bunch last week,[6] & Todd's room; rather to her credit, workmanlike; Garland pear[l]hung & silken; Todd as buxom as a badger. Rebecca a hardened old reprobate I daresay, but no fool; & the whole atmosphere professional; no charm, except the rather excessive charm of Garland.

Clive's book out—a very superficial one, L. says.[7]

The sun is out again; I have half forgotten Orlando already, since L. has read it & it has half passed out of my possession. I think it lacks the sort of hammering I should have given it if I had taken longer: is too freakish & unequal. Very brilliant now & then. As for the effect of the whole, that I cant judge. Not, I think 'important' among my works. L. says a satire.

Gosse is dead, & I am half reconciled to him by they're saying in the papers that he chose to risk a dangerous operation rather than be an invalid for life. This kind of vitality always gets me. But—lies otherwise

---

4. The races held on Whit Monday at Southease inaugurated what the local press referred to as 'a new Sussex sport' popularly termed 'galloping' or 'flapping'. 'Our field' of some $6\frac{1}{2}$ acres in all consisted of a strip adjoining and level with Monks House garden to the north, falling away down a steep bank to a larger area stretching in a wedge shape towards the Ouse Valley 'flats'. The recurrent threat of this field being built upon was removed when LW finally succeeded in buying it later this year (see below, 9 August 1928).

5. Angelica, with her friend Judith Bagenal, was brought home from Cassis by train by Grace Germany; Duncan and Vanessa, who came by car, spent some time in Paris on the way, and did not reach London until 16 June.

6. André Maurois (1885-1967), French biographer and man of letters. VW had read and enjoyed his biographies of Shelley (1923) and of Disraeli (1927); he was to write a preface to the French translation of Mrs Dalloway published in 1929 (Kp D11). She met him (and Arnold Bennett) at a tea party given by Lady Colefax before Whitsun.

7. Civilization: An Essay (1928); LW wrote of it in his weekly page 'The World of Books' in the N & A, 9 June 1928, that both 'Bell's method and his assumptions are wrong and are bound to lead to wrong conclusions'.

flourish round his grave, & poor dear Desmond with 3 children to keep has to be as profuse of them as anybody.[8]

We met him yesterday in Kingsway, just as I was thinking how I should describe him if I wrote a Memoir, as Molly insists. He loomed up as if my thought had made him visible. He gave me the first number of his paper.

Rose Macaulay says "Yes I won the prize"—rather peevishly.[9] I think at once that she is jealous, & test whatever else she says with a view to finding out whether she is or not. About Colefax: "I'm the only one of all my friends who isn't asked there." About work: 'I've got to work tomorrow' I say, excusing myself for not going to Raymond's party. "So have we all" rather sharply. & so on. This shows through a dozen little phrases, as we're talking of America, articles &c: she is jealous of me; anxious to compare us: but I may imagine it: & it shows my own jealousy no doubt, as suspicions always do. One cdn't know them if one hadn't got them. And now to Angelica with a packet of bulls eyes. I am again beginning to read.

L. takes Orlando more seriously than I had expected. Thinks it in some ways better than The Lighthouse; about more interesting things, & with more attachment to life, & larger. The truth is I expect I began it as a joke, & went on with it seriously. Hence it lacks some unity. He says it is very original. Anyhow I'm glad to be quit this time of writing 'a novel'; & hope never to be accused of it again. Now I want to write some very closely reasoned criticism; book on fiction; an essay of some sort (but not Tolstoy for the Times). Dr Burney's evening party I think for Desmond.[10] And then? I feel anxious to keep the hatch down: not to let too many projects come in. Something abstract poetic next time—I dont know. I rather like the idea of these Biographies of living people. Ottoline suggests herself—but no. And I must tear up all that manuscript, & write a great many notes & adventure out into the world—as I shall do tomorrow, when I go to have my ears pierced with Vita.

8. Sir Edmund Gosse died on 16 May, aged 76. Desmond MacCarthy's tribute to him appeared in the *Sunday Times* of 20 May 1928; its general tenor may be inferred from the opening sentence: ' "How beautifully *he* would do this" must be the first reflection of one who sits down to write a commemorative article in these columns.' MacCarthy was to succeed Gosse as the literary columnist of the *Sunday Times* on 12 August 1928.

9. Rose Macaulay dined alone with VW on 24 May. She had been awarded the *Prix Femina* in 1922 for her eleventh novel, *Dangerous Ages*.

10. For VW's 'book on fiction' see above, 7 December 1925, n 6. 'Dr Burney's Evening Party' was published first in the *New York Herald Tribune*, 21 and 28 July 1929, and reprinted in Desmond MacCarthy's *Life and Letters* in September 1929 (Kp C313).

JUNE 1928

June weather. Still, bright, fresh. Owing to the Lighthouse (car) I dont feel so shut in London as usual, & can imagine the evening on some moor now, or in France without the envy I used to have, in London on a fine evening. Also London itself perpetually attracts, stimulates, gives me a play & a story & a poem, without any trouble, save that of moving my legs through the streets. I walked Pinker to Grays Inn Gardens this afternoon, & saw—Red Lion Square: Morris'es house; thought of them on winters evenings in the 5oties; thought we are just as interesting;[11] saw the ⟨street⟩ Great Ormond St where a dead girl was found yesterday; saw & heard the Salvation Army making Xtianity gay for the people: a great deal of nudging & joking on the part of very unattractive young men & women; making it lively, I suppose; & yet, to be truthful, when I watch them I never laugh or criticise, but only feel how strange & interesting this is: wonder what they mean by 'Come to the Lord.' I daresay exhibitionism accounts for some of it: the applause of the gallery; this lures boys to sing hymns; & kindles shop boys to announce in a loud voice that they are saved. It is what writing for the Evening Standard is for Rose Macaulay & I was going to say myself: but so far I have not done it.[12]

Wednesday 20 June

So sick of Orlando I can write nothing. I have corrected the proofs in a week; & cannot spin another phrase. I detest my own volubility. Why be always spouting words? Also I have almost lost the power of reading. Correcting proofs 5, 6, or 7 hours a day, writing in this & that meticulously, I have bruised my reading faculty severely. Take up Proust after dinner & put him down. This is the worst time of all. It makes me suicidal. Nothing seems left to do. All seems insipid & worthless. Now I will watch & see how I resurrect. I think I shall read something—say a life of Goethe. Then I shall visit about. Mercifully, Nessa is back. My earth is watered again. I go back to words of one syllable: feel come over me the feathery change: rather true that: as if my physical body put on some soft comfortable, skin. She is a necessity to me—as I am not to her. I run to her as the wallaby runs to the old kangaroo. She is also very cheerful, solid, happy. The trifles that annoy other people, she passes off; as if her

11. After leaving Oxford, William Morris and Edward Burne Jones had in 1856-58 shared rooms and a studio at 17 Red Lion Square, which became a rendezvous for their lively circle.
12. In the 1920's Rose Macaulay contributed light articles to the popular press, including the *Evening Standard*, as a means of earning her living.

happiness were a million or two in the bank. And how masterfully she controls her dozen lives; never in a muddle, or desperate, or worried; never spending a pound or a thought needlessly; yet with it all free, careless, airy, indifferent: a very notable achievement.

Julian dines with us tonight to meet Miss Sylva Norman whom I fetched up from complete nonentity on the telephone last night.[1] Another marvel of science. There she was in 10 minutes after we thought of her saying she would LOVE to come. Julian is a vast fat powerful sweet tempered engaging young man, into whose arms I let myself fall, half sister, half mother, & half (but arithmetic denies this) the mocking stirring contemporary friend. Mercifully Julian has his instincts sane & normal: has a wide forehead, & considerable address & competence in the management of life. But my tooth is aching. They will dine with us; & that is what I am ripe for—to go adventuring on the streams of other peoples lives—speculating, adrift

Friday 22 June

So far I wrote & was interrupted—always interrupted; am now off to Ruislip with Pinker to wed her, & it is

Saturday 7 July

& a Saturday morning, very hot & fine.

All last night I dreamt of Katherine Mansfield & wonder what dreams are; often evoke so much more emotion, than thinking does— almost as if she came back in person & was outside one, actively making one feel; instead of a figment called up & recollected, as she is, now, if I think of her. Yet some emotion lingers on the day after a dream; even though I've now almost forgotten what happened in the dream, except that she was lying on a sofa in a room high up, & a great many sad faced women were round her. Yet somehow I got the feel of her, & of her as if alive again, more than by day.

At Long Barn yesterday, a good rather happy visit. I'm interested by the gnawing down of strata in friendship; how one passes unconsciously to different terms; takes things easier; dont mind at all hardly about dress or anything; scarcely feel it an exciting atmosphere, which, too, has its drawback from the "fizzing" point of view: yet is saner, perhaps deeper.

1. Sylva Norman (1901-1971), whose novel *Nature Has No Tune* the Woolfs were to publish in 1929 (*HP Checklist* 203), was a writer and journalist; she reviewed books for the *N & A*, was to become an authority on Shelley and, in 1933, the second wife of Edmund Blunden.

Lay by the black currant bushes lecturing Vita on her floundering habits with the Campbells for instance. Mrs C. beat by her husband, all because V. will come triumphing, with her silver & her coronets & her footmen into the life of a herring-cooker. She cooks herrings on a gas stove, I said, always remembering my own phrases.

But having thus scrambled in a page, I must go—& yet want to stay & write about Sterne.[1]

Monks House
Rodmell.

Wednesday 8 August[1]

Eddy has just gone, leaving me the usual feeling: why is not human intercourse more definite, tangible: why aren't I left holding a small round substance, say of the size of a pea, in my hand; something I can put in a box & look at? There is so little left. Yet these people one sees are fabric only made once in the world; these contacts we have are unique; & if E. were, say killed tonight, nothing definite would happen to me; yet his substance is never again to be repeated. Our meeting is—but the thread of this idea slips perpetually; constantly though it recurs, with sadness, to my mind: how little our relationships matter; & yet they are so important: in him, in me, something to him, to me, infinitely sentient, of the highest vividness, reality. But if I died tonight, he too would continue. Something illusory then enters into all that part of life. I am so important to myself: yet of no importance to other people: like the shadow passing over the downs. I deceive myself into thinking that I am important to other people: that makes part of my extreme vividness to myself: as a matter of fact, I dont matter; & so part of my vividness is unreal; gives me a sense of illusion. Eddy says he thinks "What impression am I making?" constantly & is agitated: as a matter of fact, he is probably making no impression: his agitation is about nothing: he is mistaken.

But, superficially speaking—for fundamentally I was thinking a thousand other thoughts; his presence was only I suppose a light on the surface of my mind—something green or iron-coloured or grey—while the water itself rushed on, in its old fierce way—thoughts about my writing; & about old age; & about buying the field (we bought it this morning) & about the children being noisy; & if I had bought Southease. All this went on sub-cutaneously. Yet his presence somehow checked the

1. VW's article on Sterne, 'A Sentimental Journey', was published in the *New York Herald Tribune*, 23 September 1928. Kp C303.
1. VW has written *Wednesday Aug. 9th.* She and LW had come to Rodmell for their summer stay on 24 July.

flow of sub-cutaneous life. I was always having to think what comes next? How am I to break into this other life which is 6 inches off mine in the deck chair in the orchard? So that my own thoughts could not flow deep or rapid, as they are doing now that Eddy is on his way to Tunbridge Wells. And what remains of Eddy is now in some ways more vivid, though more transparent, all of him composing itself in my mind, all I could get of him, & making itself a landscape appropriate to it; making a work of art for itself.

I am, as I write, wherever I come to a stop, looking out of the lodge window, at our field; & the little cottage boys with the cursed shrill voices, playing cricket half way down it; & as usual I am sentimental & worried. Children playing: yes, & interrupting me; yes & I have no children of my own; & Nessa has; & yet I dont want them any more, since my ideas so possess me; & I detest more & more interruption; & the slow heaviness of physical life, & almost dislike peoples bodies, I think, as I grow older; & want always to cut that short, & get my utmost fill of the marrow, of the essence.

I write thus partly in order to slip the burden of writing narrative, as for instance; we came here a fortnight ago. And we lunched at Charleston & Vita came & we were offered the field & we went to see the farm at Lime Kiln. Yet no doubt I shall be more interested, come 10 years, in facts; & shall want, as I do when I read, to be told details, details, so that I may look up from the page & arrange them too, into one of those makings up which seem so much truer done thus, from heaps of non-assorted facts, than now I can make them, when it is almost immediately being done ⟨by me⟩ under my eyes. It was a fine day, last Monday I rather think; & we drove through Ripe; & there was a girl & her feller at the gate in a narrow lane; & we had to interrupt them to turn the motor. I thought how the things they had been saying were dammed, like a river, by our interruption; & they stood there half amused, yet impatient, telling us to go to the left, but the road was up. They were glad when we went; yet gave us a flash of interest. Who are these people in their motor car: where are they going?—& then this sunk beneath the mind, & they forgot us completely. We went on. And then we reached the farm. The oasts had umbrella spokes poking out at the top: all was so ruined & faded. The Tudor farm house was almost blind; very small eyebrowed windows; old Stuart farmers must have peered out over the flat land, very dirty, ill-kempt, like people in slums. But they had dignity: at least thick walls; fireplaces; & solidity whereas now the house is lived in by one old, weedy pink faced man, who flung himself in his armchair. Go where you like— go anywhere, he said, loose jointed, somehow decayed, like the hop oasts;

& damp like the mildewed carpets, & sordid, like the beds with the pots sticking out under them. The walls were sticky; the furniture mid Victorian; little light came through. It was all dying, decaying; & he had been there 50 years, & it will drop to pieces, since there is not enough beauty or strength to make anyone repair it.[2]

Sunday 12 August

Shall I now continue this soliloquy, or shall I imagine an audience, which will make me describe?

This sentence is due to the book on fiction which I am now writing—once more, O once more.[3] It is a hand to mouth book. I scribble down whatever I can think of about Romance, Dickens &c. must hastily [?] gorge on Jane Austen tonight & dish up something tomorrow. All this criticism however may well be dislodged by the desire to write a story. The Moths hovers some where at the back of my brain. Janie & Julian have just gone. Julian a little in the style of Jem, only so much saner: broad browed, wavy haired, vast, fat, powerful, good-tempered.[4] He still laughs a great deal; but perhaps less than he did. Perhaps he is sticking his pitchfork in the ground. Janie is a little lapdog girl; like those pug faced prominent eyed wrinkled nosed little dogs that women carry about the streets; intelligent, vivacious, opening her mouth wide & snapping it shut; on one side a carpenters granddaughter—on the other a Strachey. Perhaps a little common do I mean? But Clive yesterday at Charleston said that there were no class distinctions. We had tea from bright blue cups under the pink light of the giant hollyhock. We were all a little drugged with the country: a little bucolic I thought. It was lovely enough—made me envious of its country peace: the trees all standing securely—why did my

2. Lime Kiln Farm is about 3½ miles north east of Selmeston; the farmer was appropriately named Deadman. The house was in fact restored, and still exists.
3. VW had been struggling with this 'book on fiction', originally intended for the Hogarth Press 'Lectures on Literature' series, for about two years (see above, 7 December 1925, n 6); it was finally to appear as an extended essay, 'Phases of Fiction', in three parts in *The Bookman*, New York, in April, May, and June 1929 (Kp C312). One of the eight items in MHP, Sussex, connected with this undertaking (95 pages of ms entitled *Phases of Fiction*) is dated 11 August 1928 (MHP/B 6c).
4. James Kenneth ('Jem') Stephen (1859-92), Leslie Stephen's favourite nephew, was both an heroic and alarming figure in VW's childhood; massive, handsome, ebullient, successful and popular, after an accidental blow on the head his behaviour became increasingly excitable and erratic, and he died insane. Jane-Simone ('Janie') Bussy (1906-60), only child of the French painter Simon Bussy and his wife Dorothy, *née* Strachey, was herself a painter.

eye catch the trees? The look of things has a great power over me. Even now, I have to watch the rooks beating up against the wind, which is high. & still I say to myself instinctively "Whats the phrase for that?" & try to make more & more vivid the roughness of the air current & the tremor of the rooks wing ⟨deep breasting it⟩ slicing—as if the air were full of ridges & ripples & roughnesses; they rise & sink, up & down, as if the exercise ⟨pleased them⟩ rubbed & braced them like swimmers in rough water. But what a little I can get down with my pen of what is so vivid to my eyes, & not only to my eyes: also to some nervous fibre or fan like membrane in my spine.

Janie Julian Leonard & I sat in the orchard till the wind got too strong, & I made them come out on the marsh & was sorry the river was low, or they might have praised it. And (irrelevantly) Miss Ritchie praises Orlando, & I was pleased till I thought, perhaps this is gratitude for our £20. Yet I dont think much either way about Orlando. Odd, how I feel myself under orders; always marching on a definite stage with each book, tho' it is one I set myself. And Duncan at Charleston was a little too aloof & supercilious seeming.

Tuesday 14 August

Just back from Long Barn & Dottie's new house, Penn in the Rocks.[5] Can one really be in love with a house? Is there not something sterile, so that one's mind becomes stringy in these passions? She is too anxious for other people to praise it. And I don't want possessions. I think this is true. I dont want to be Dottie collecting endless settees & arm chairs round myself. But then I have now a pressing sense of the flight of time; & if one is so soon to arrive, why pack all these things? More truthfully, if one is so soon to start, why prepare all these impedimenta. I feel on the verge of the world, about to take flight. Dottie on the other hand feels "I have at least, in spite of every other grudge on the part of fate, 10 or 15 thousand a year; & it is only fair that I should get from my money what I can." Somehow angrily then she sets to work to make her money slave for her. She has bought for ever & ever all these couchant rocks; rocks like kneeling elephants; agonised writhing rocks elongated rocks, rocks with grotesque roots grown into them, & Japanese trees on top. She runs about,

5. Penns-in-the-Rocks (or Penn's Rocks), near Withyham, was a mainly 18th century house of some architectural distinction, remarkable also for the multitude of great natural boulders or rocks of sandstone in the grounds. William Penn, the founder of Pennsylvania, had married the heiress to this property, but it had long since passed out of his family.

defiant strident a little discordant in her top boots with her dogs & says "I'm so tired—so worn out", gesticulates, exaggerates. I like the aristocratic tradition of space & a few good things. The house itself is now in sections. Half a ceiling ⟨overhangs⟩ intersects what were & will be dining room & bedroom above. This gives the house a provisional air; it is not a house that has been there 300 years, & housed Penn & other families; it is nothing—which in a house is distressing.

After that country, though, how I adore the emptiness, bareness, air & colour of this! Really. I would not give this view for Dottie's rocks. A relic I think of my fathers feeling for the Alps—this ecstasy of mine over the bare slope of Asheham hill. But then, as I remind myself, half the beauty of a country or a house comes from knowing it. One remembers old lovelinesses: knows that it is now looking ugly; waits to see it light up; knows where to find its beauty; how to ignore the bad things. This one can't do the first time of seeing. But they build with beautiful blocks of grey stone in Kent. D.'s farmhouse was the very house for me, solid, high, with the shape of the stone showing in the wall. This is all thrown in with her rocks. And she ecstasi[s]es over them, fancying them sympathetic to her genius, & makes them into part of her belief in her own genius.

Monks House looked very nice, unexpectedly so, & the great lily in the window has now four flowers. They opened in the night. So I was appeased aesthetically for my disappointment in having no letters—not one. I was going to remark however that Dottie's rocks are powdered pale greys & bright greens; they are grey as elephant backs. There are, too, bunches of scarlet berries hanging against them: only all too verdant, mossy, steamy, & enclosed for my taste. However, in the train it struck me that it is, even from one's own point of view, a great advantage that other people should like trees & so on; Why—I cant at the moment remember.

Friday 31 August

This is the last day of August, & like almost all of them of extraordinary beauty. Each day is fine enough & hot enough for sitting out; but also full of wandering clouds; & that fading & rising of the light which so enraptures me in the downs: which I am always comparing to the light beneath an alabaster bowl, &c. The corn is now stood about in rows of three for our [*four or*] five solid shaped yellow cakes—rich, it seems, with eggs & spice: good to eat. Sometimes I see the cattle galloping 'like mad' as Dostoevsky would say, in the brooks. The clouds—if I could describe them I would: one yesterday had flowing hair on it like the very fine white hair of an old man. At this moment they are white in a leaden sky; but the sun, behind the house, is making the grass green. I walked to the racecourse today & saw a weasel.

Morgan was here for the week end; timid, touchy, infinitely charming. One night we got drunk, & talked of sodomy, & sapphism, with emotion —so much so that next day he said he had been drunk. This was started by Radclyffe Hall & her meritorious dull book. They wrote articles for Hubert all day, & got up petitions; & then Morgan saw her & she screamed like a herring gull, mad with egotism & vanity. Unless they say her book is good, she wont let them complain of the laws. Morgan said that Dr Head can convert the sodomites.[6] "Would you like to be converted?" Leonard asked. "No" said Morgan, quite definitely. He said he thought Sapphism disgusting: partly from convention, partly because he disliked that women should be independent of men.

Probably the reason why I shall be so much bored this week end by Mrs Woolf is that we shall not be able to say a word we mean.[7] It is like talking to a child; a child, too, with 'feelings': a child with "rights" & a sense of propriety & respectability & what ought to be said & done. Having made up all these principles she is, & they all are, secretly dissatisfied; because they, naturally, get no pleasure from life; are cased in thick wool from any direct contact; & so these people—an immense class—are always uneasy unless they are eating, being flattered, or doing some natural task, like nursing a child. And then, if the child is Leonard, he grows up & is horribly bored by you.

I must now begin Peacock, without attempting to describe the extraordinary primeval appearance of the farm wagons; so laden with the hay in the brooks that they look like some vast shaggy animal moving on very short legs.

We have seen Mr James about the field; & will soon, I hope, sign the agreement, or cheque; & put up a fence, which is my first act as a

6. *The Well of Loneliness*, a novel of Lesbian love by Radclyffe Hall (1886-1943), had been published in July by Jonathan Cape, who had withdrawn it in the face of outraged objections in the popular press and from the Home Secretary. E. M. Forster and LW were united in their opposition, on principle, to such suppression, and organised protests, which included a joint letter from Forster and VW published in the *N & A*, 8 September 1928. (See also P. N. Furbank, *E. M. Forster: A Life*, vol. II (1978), pp 153-5.) Sir Henry Head (1861-1940; knighted 1927), FRS, neurologist. Roger Fry, who had a high opinion of him, had recommended that the Woolfs should consult him when VW was in a suicidal condition in 1913; and they did.

7. Marie Woolf, *née* de Jongh (1850-1939), LW's Dutch-born mother. Widowed in 1892, she had raised a family of six sons and three daughters.

landowner to keep the cottage children out.[8] Nessa, being a mother, & thus not sentimental about children, says "They can easily play somewhere else."[9]

Monday 3 September

The battle of Dunbar, the Battle of Worcester, & the death of Cromwell —how often it seems to me I said that to my father ("my" father, not 'father' any more) at St Ives; standing bolt upright in the dining room at Talland House. And it is a perfect 3rd of September day.[1] Leonard gave me the blue glass jug today, because he was cross when I slapped his nose with sweet peas, & because I was nice to his mother; & when I went into luncheon I saw it on the table. Indeed, I almost cried. He went to Brighton to get it for me. "I thought of it just as I was getting into the car" he said. Perhaps I have analysed his motives wrongly.

Seldom have I felt as tired as I did last night. This shaky ramshackle old lady of 76 wore us out. Her talk—I have written it for Nessa so cannot repeat[2]—never stops; never follows a line; is always about people; starts anywhere; at any moment; breaks into a Schubert trio: did you know Len that Mr Harris lives in Gordon Sqre? So on to his daughters; how she met one playing bridge &c. What makes it difficult is that she divines states of feeling to some extent, & would say pointedly "You must often think of your writing when you are not writing, Virginia", when through exhaustion I became silent. I had one moment of peculiar & acute discomfort this morning, when she became 'intimate', & said how much she had been touched when I sat beside her in the car yesterday. Why did I hate it so? I felt the horror of family life, & the terrible threat to one's liberty that I used to feel with father, Aunt Mary or George.[3] It is an

8. It would appear that Charles James, a local farmer, had enjoyed grazing rights on the field LW was now buying, and negotiations were proceeding for him to continue as tenant of the five acres of the lower part, leaving LW to incorporate the acre of the upper level (the 'terrace') into his garden.
9. This last sentence, written in a different ink, appears to have been added as an afterthought.
1. The historic battles, in 1650 and 1651, between the Parliamentary Army led by Oliver Cromwell, and the Scots supporting Charles II in his attempt to gain the throne, which were turning points in the Civil War. Cromwell died in 1658.
2. See *III VW Letters*, no. 1919 for this epistolary *tour de force*.
3. Mary Louisa Fisher, *née* Jackson (1841-1916), Julia Stephen's elder sister, had regarded it as her duty to supervise her nieces' conduct after their mother's death, as did George Duckworth. ('The meddling of aunts and the tyranny of brothers exasperated her.' Cf VW's review of Dorothy Osborne's letters which she was now reading, Kp C304.)

emotion one never gets from any other human relationship. She had the right to exact this on my part; & would feel pleasure & pain irrationally, & somehow put her claws in me. These feelings are as violent as any. And there was the sentimental, yet very vain & almost insanely selfish discourse about her love for her children; how they—these dull plain serviceable Jews & Jewesses—were all splendid men & women; at which my gorge rose. How strangely she made everything commonplace, ugly, suburban, notwithstanding a charm too: something fresh & vital such as old women have, & not, I think, old men. But to be attached to her as daughter would be so cruel a fate that I can think of nothing worse; & thousands of women might be dying of it in England today: this tyranny of mother over daughter, or father; their right to the due being as powerful as anything in the world. And then, they ask, why women dont write poetry. Short of killing Mrs W. nothing could be done. Day after day one's life would be crumpled up like a bill for 10 pen[ce] 3 farthings. Nothing has ever been said of this.

Monday 10 September

This is written, as 'this' is so often written, to fill up a little jagged piece of time, with Kennedy, the soft duckling boy, with a bill that opens wide & says 'Quack' in the drawing room, & Leonard talking to Mr James about the field.[4] Desmond, who lunched here with Julian has just gone. We spent the afternoon—hour after hour wasting away again, or why not say for once turning to gold & silver—for I should only have been reading Moby Dick otherwise—coining gold & silver talk then—talk very intimate now, more so than ever: a continuation of our talk in Tavistock Sqre the other day: there he said he had now 12 years to live; nine to be exact: & here we talked of his work, money, women, children, & writing; till I took him along the Roman road; & back to tea. I was amused to find that when Rebecca West says "men are snobs" she gets an instant rise out of Desmond; so I retorted on him with the condescending phrase used about women novelists 'limitations' in Life & Letters.[5] But there was no acrimony in this. We talked with fertility;

4. Richard Pitt Kennedy (b. 1910) had left Marlborough, a scholastic failure, at Easter and, thanks to his uncle the architect George Lawrence Kennedy (1882-1954), a fellow-member with LW of the Cranium Club, had started work as an apprentice at the Hogarth Press on 30 April. His illustrated account, *A Boy at the Hogarth Press* (1972), cast in the form of a diary, was written some forty years later and contains minor errors of fact.
5. The Woolfs had driven to London for the day on 5 September, and Desmond MacCarthy had lunched with them at Tavistock Square. In the August number of

never working a seam dry. Do you suppose then that we are now coming like the homing rooks back to the tops of our trees? & that all this cawing is the beginning of settling in for the night? I seem to notice in several of my friends some endearing & affecting cordiality: & a pleasure in intimacy; as if the sun were sinking. Often that image comes to me with some sense of my physical state being colder now, the sun just off one; the old disc of one's being growing cooler—but it is only just beginning: & one will turn cold & silver like the moon.

This has been a very animated summer: a summer lived almost too much in public. Often down here I have entered into a sanctuary; a nunnery; had a religious retreat; of great agony once; & always some terror: so afraid one is of loneliness: of seeing to the bottom of the vessel. That is one of the experiences I have had here in some Augusts; & got then to a consciousness of what I call 'reality': a thing I see before me; something abstract; but residing in the downs or sky; beside which nothing matters; in which I shall rest & continue to exist. Reality I call it. And I fancy sometimes this is the most necessary thing to me: that which I seek. But who knows—once one takes a pen & writes? How difficult not to go making 'reality' this & that, whereas it is one thing. Now perhaps this is my gift; this perhaps is what distinguishes me from other people; I think it may be rare to have so acute a sense of something like that—but again, who knows? I would like to express it too.

Pinker had 4 puppies the day (Friday) we went to the Bagenals & Dotty. Dotty was rust red, shabby, intense a little; she showed us the rocks. Leonard 'took against' her, as nurses say; violently.[6] We drove home very fast. I on the other hand took in favour of Barbara—& wished I had gone up alone with her on to the downs. I—perhaps Leonard interrupted here.

---

his monthly *Life and Letters*, in a review of *Another Country* by H. du Coudray, he had written: 'If, like the reporter, you believe that female novelists should only aspire to excellence by courageously acknowledging the limitations of their sex (Jane Austen and, in our own time, Mrs Virginia Woolf, have demonstrated how gracefully this gesture can be accomplished), Miss du Coudray's first novel may at the outset prove a little disappointing, since here is a writer definitely bent upon the attainment of masculine standards.'

6. The Bagenals, Nicholas Beauchamp (1891-1974) and Barbara, *née* Hiles (b. 1891), had married in 1918 when the former was still in the army and the latter working briefly as an assistant in the Hogarth Press in Richmond (see *I VW Diary*). He had become an expert on fruit trees and, since 1922, had been a lecturer at the East Malling Research Station near Maidstone. The Woolfs called on Dorothy Wellesley at Penn's Rocks on the way home. For LW's virulent reaction to her, see also *III VW Letters*, no. 1922.

Monday 17 September

I have precisely 5 minutes before dinner. Quentin has swallowed those precious two hours in which I was to have read Dorothy Osborne:[7] Quentin grown elegant & self conscious, liking to use French words; very sophisticated, showing in every movement now the shadow of our faults, as a set; uneasy, I doubt not; quick, sensitive; but wanting something of Julian's force & simplicity. So they change parts, growing, changing, turning from fat to thin. The drawing room smells with his paints—the gramophone like Moby Dick is white. Rachel came in with Angelica. She has quicksilver eyes, mended stockings, all the charm & dexterity of a poor clever man's child, whose wits are kept brushed, who mends her stockings, who lives on her adventures.

Desmond was here, talking the other day: intimate again, & yet too urbane, perhaps; or do I think this from the letter that so annoyed me— speaking of my paper's "butterfly lightness"—how angry I was, how depressed I became.[8] Leonard agrees that he has a complex, which leads him to belittle & fondle thus.

Saturday 22 September

This is written on the verge of my alarming holiday in Burgundy. I am alarmed of 7 days alone with Vita: interested; excited, but afraid—she may find me out, I her out. I may (& theres Mabel the Bride in her white dress at the pump. The bridegroom, a carter out of work, wears white socks. Are they pure? I doubt it. They are going to spend their honeymoon near Pevensey. He was 15 minutes late & we saw her come in wearing a wreath. And I felt this is the heart of England—this wedding in the country: history I felt; Cromwell; The Osbornes; Dorothy's shepherdesses singing: of all of whom Mr & Mrs Jarrad seem more the descendants than I am: as if they represented the unconscious breathing of England & L. & I, leaning over the wall, were detached, unconnected.[9] I suppose our

7. VW's review of *The Letters of Dorothy Osborne to William Temple*, edited by G. C. Moore Smith (1928), appeared in the *New Republic*, New York, on 24 October 1928, and in the *TLS*, 25 October 1928 (Kp C304). Quentin Bell was decorating the cabinet of the gramophone at Monks House.
8. Desmond's letter, presumably referring to VW's article 'The Niece of an Earl' (Kp C305) to be published in the October issue of his *Life and Letters*, does not survive.
9. Mabel Mockford, daughter of Mrs Mockford of Briar Cottage, Rodmell, and the late Mr Frank Mockford, married Percy William Jarrett of Northease at Rodmell Parish Church on Saturday, 22 September. The bride was 'prettily dressed in ivory crêpe-de-chine'.

thinking is the cause of this. We dont belong to any 'class'; we thinkers: might as well be French or German. Yet I am English in some way—)

But I was saying I should on the whole be confident about this French journey—that it will turn out well. I'm afraid of the morning most; & 3 o'clock in the afternoon; & wanting something Vita does not want. And I shall spend the money that might have bought a table or a glass. What one buys in foreign travel is a series of scenes; which gradually diminish to one or two, such as I still have of Greece & Venice as I saw them when I was 24 or 5. And I shall love the freedom from hours; & looking about; & the thought of coming back; & sitting talking, & some things I shall read; & one or two views, &—

This has been the finest, & not only finest, but loveliest, summer in the world. Still, though it blows, how clear & bright it is; & the clouds are opalescent; the long barns on my horizon mouse coloured; the stacks pale gold. Owning the field has given a different orient to my feelings about Rodmell. I begin to dig myself in & take part in it. And I shall build another storey to the house if I make money. But the news of Orlando is black. We may sell a third that we sold of The Lighthouse before publication—Not a shop will buy save in 6es & 12es. They say this is inevitable. No one wants biography. But it is a novel, says Miss Ritchie. But it is called a biography on the title page, they say. It will have to go to the Biography shelf. I doubt therefore that we shall do more than cover expenses—a high price to pay for the fun of calling it a biography. And I was so sure it was going to be the one popular book! Also it should be 10/6 or 12/6 not 9/- Lord, lord! Thus I must write some articles this winter, if we are to have nest eggs at the Bank. Down here I have flung myself tooth & nail on my fiction book, & should have finished the first draft but for Dorothy Osborne whom I'm dashing off. It will need entire re-writing but the grind is done—the rushing through book after book & now what shall I read? These novels have hung about me so long. Mercy it is to be quit of them; & shall I read English poetry, French memoirs— shall I read now for a book to be called "The Lives of the Obscure"? And when, I wonder, shall I begin the Moths? Not until I am pressed into it by those insects themselves. Nor have I any notion what it is to be like—a completely new attempt I think. So I always think.

A very gay active summer. Dined with the Keynes' to meet Lord Gage last Wednesday—found him with his flat face & Circassian blood, more of a character than I expected. Clive with inverse snobbery had run him down. We talked about the King, & he snubbed me by saying that he remarked an odd fact—everyone talks to him about the King. Every class, every kind of person, is interested to know what the King has for dinner.

And here was I, the intellectual, the labour woman, doing just the same thing. And there were the Russell Cookes; her I liked; him I hated.[10] A woman is in some ways so much better than a man—more natural, juicy, unfettered. But then he is a bounder, a climber, a shoving young man, who wants to be smart, cultivated, go-ahead & all the rest of it. I must use that cliché because I must do my Osborne article. & it is getting cold out here.

On 24 September VW and Vita Sackville-West sailed from Newhaven to spend a week together in Burgundy (their progress may be followed in III VW Letters, nos. 1926-32 to LW), coming back to England on 1 October. On 4 October the Woolfs returned to Tavistock Square, lunching with Vita at Long Barn on the way. Orlando was published on 11 October. On 20 October, taking Vanessa and Angelica, the Woolfs drove to Cambridge; they stayed the night with Pernel Strachey, the Principal of Newnham, where that evening VW read a paper to the Arts Society, and the next day lunched with George Rylands in his rooms at King's. The following week she again went to Cambridge, this time by train and with Vita, and spoke to the Girton ODTAA Society (26 October). These two papers, on 'Women and Fiction,' were to be expanded and published a year later as A Room of One's Own *(in which Mrs Rylands' lunch party is memorably if extravagantly described).*

Saturday 27 October

A scandal, a scandal, to let so much time slip, & I leaning on the Bridge watching it go. Only leaning has not been my pose: running up & down, irritably, excitedly restlessly. And the stream viciously eddying. Why do I write these metaphors? Because I have written nothing for an age.

Orlando has been published. I went to Burgundy with Vita. We did not find each other out. It flashed by. Yet I was glad to see Leonard again. How disconnected this is! My ambition is from this very moment, 8 minutes to six, on Saturday evening, to attain complete concentration again. When I have written here, I am going to open Fanny Burney's

10. Henry Rainald, 6th Viscount Gage (b. 1895) of Firle Place, Sussex landowner (and Keynes's and Vanessa's landlord); at this period, in addition to being PPS to the Secretary of State for India, he was a Lord-in-Waiting to King George V. The 'Circassian blood' is VW's fantasy. Sidney Russell Cooke (1892-1930), stockbroker, had been a student at King's College, Cambridge, from 1911-14; after war service and an unsuccessful Liberal candidature, he had made a successful career in the City, and the financial pages of the *N & A* had benefited from his advice. In 1930 he was found shot dead, his double-barrelled sporting gun beside him; the verdict was that it was accidental. His wife, *née* Helen Melville Smith, was the daughter of the captain of the ill-fated *Titanic*.

diaries, & work solidly at that article which poor Miss McKay cables about.[1] I am going to read; to think. I gave up reading & thinking on the 24th of Sept when I went to France. I came back, & we plunged into London & publishing. I am a little sick of Orlando. I think I am a little indifferent now what anyone thinks. Joy's life's in the doing—I murder, as usual, a quotation:[2] I mean its the writing, not the being read that excites me. And as I can't write while I'm being read, I am always a little hollow hearted; whipped up; but not so happy as in solitude. The reception, as they say, surpassed expectations. Sales beyond our record for the first week. I was floating rather lazily on praise, when Squire barked in the Observer, but even as I sat reading him on the backs last Sunday in the showering red leaves & their illumination, I felt the rock of self esteem untouched in me. "This doesn't really hurt" I said to myself; even now; & sure enough, before evening I was calm, untouched. And now theres Hugh [Walpole] in the Morning Post to spread the butter again, & Rebecca West—such a trumpet call of praise—thats her way—that I feel a little sheepish & silly. And now no more of that I hope.[3]

Thank God, my long toil at the women's lecture is this moment ended. I am back from speaking at Girton, in floods of rain. Starved but valiant young women—that's my impression. Intelligent eager, poor; & destined to become schoolmistresses in shoals. I blandly told them to drink wine & have a room of their own. Why should all the splendour, all the luxury of life be lavished on the Julians & the Francises, & none on the Phares & the Thomases?[4] There's Julian not much relishing it, perhaps. I fancy

1. Helen MacAfee, not McKay (1884-1956), managing editor and book critic of the *Yale Review* which had already published two articles by VW, had visited her at Tavistock Square at the end of May. VW failed to deliver her intended article on Dr. Burney's party (see *IV VW Letters*, no. 1985).
2.   '. . . Women are angels, wooing:
         Things won are done; joy's soul lies in the doing:
         That she belov'd knows naught that knows not this:
         Men prize the thing ungain'd more than it is:'
                          Cressida in *Troilus and Cressida*, I ii
3. J. C. Squire in his review entitled 'Prose-de-Société' in the *Observer*, 21 October 1928, wrote of his impression that 'the author had no gusto in the writing', and concluded that *Orlando* was 'a very pleasant trifle' that would 'entertain the drawing-rooms for an hour'. (See *M & M*, pp 227-9.) Hugh Walpole, 'On a Certain New Book' (*Morning Post*, 25 October 1928) lauded *Orlando* without naming it or its author; Rebecca West (*New York Herald Tribune*, 21 October 1928), called it 'a poetic masterpiece of the first rank'.
4. Elsie Elizabeth Phare (b. 1908), student at Newnham College 1926-29 and later an authority on Gerard Manley Hopkins and Andrew Marvell, was the current secretary of the Newnham Arts Society; Margaret Ellen Thomas (b. 1907) was one

sometimes the world changes. I think I see reason spreading. But I should have liked a closer & thicker knowledge of life. I should have liked to deal with real things sometimes. I get such a sense of tingling & vitality from an evenings talk like that; one's angularities & obscurities are smoothed & lit. How little one counts, I think: how little anyone counts; how fast & furious & masterly life is; & how all these thousands are swimming for dear life. I felt elderly & mature. And nobody respected me. They were very eager, egotistical, or rather not much impressed by age & repute. Very little reverence or that sort of thing about. The corridors of Girton are like vaults in some horrid high church cathedral—on & on they go, cold & shiny—with a light burning. High gothic rooms; acres of bright brown wood; here & there a photograph.

And we saw Trinity & King's this morning. Now to concentrate on English literature—forgetting Mary & Tom & how we went to be read aloud to, & Lady Cunard, & Clive back & Nessa back, & the Well of Loneliness. But Thank God to get back to writing again.[5]

Wednesday 7 November

And this shall be written for my own pleasure,—

But that phrase inhibits me: for if one writes only for one's own pleasure,—I dont know what it is that happens. I suppose the convention of writing is destroyed; therefore one does not write at all. I am rather headachy, & dimly obscured with sleeping draught. This is the aftermath (what does that mean?—Trench, whom I open idly apparently says nothing[1]) of Orlando. Yes, yes, since I wrote here I have become two inches & a half higher in the public view. I think I may say that I am now among the well known writers. I had tea with Lady Cunard—might have

---

of those responsible for inviting VW to speak at Girton, where she was a student from 1926-30. Before the Girton lecture on 26 October VW had seen her nephew Julian Bell, now in his second year at King's, and had then dined with Miss Thomas and another student at the Lion Hotel, Petty Cury (now demolished), where she and V. Sackville-West were staying.

5. The Woolfs had dined with Mary Hutchinson on 17 October and had afterwards gone to T. S. Eliot's house, where he read aloud his unpublished poem *Ash Wednesday*, a draft of which (now in King's College Library, Cambridge) he had previously sent them, inviting criticism. (See *IV LW*, pp 109-10.) Vanessa and Clive Bell had (independently) been in France; the former returned on 18th, the latter on 21st October.

1. *A Select Glossary of English Words used formerly in senses different from their present* (1859), compiled by Richard Chenevix Trench.

lunched or dined any day.[2] I found her in a little cap telephoning. It was not her atmosphere—this of solitary talk. She is too shrewd to expand, & needs society to make her rash & random which is her point. Ridiculous little parrokeet faced woman; but not quite sufficiently ridiculous. I kept wishing for superlatives: could not get the illusion to flap its wings. Flunkeys, yes; but a little drab & friendly. Marble floors, yes; but no glamour; no tune strumming, for me at least. And the two of us sitting there had almost to be conventional & flat—reminds me of Sir Thomas Browne—the greatest book of our times—said a little flatly by a woman of business, to me who don't believe in that kind of thing unless launched with champagne & garlands. Then in came Lord Donegall, a glib Irish youth, dark sallow slick, on the Press.[3] Dont they treat you like a dog? I said. "No, not at all" he replied, astonished that a marquis could be treated like a dog by anyone. And then we went up & up to see pictures on stairs in ballrooms & finally to Lady C.'s bedroom, hung entirely with flower pieces. The bed has its triangular canopy of rose red silk; the windows, looking on the square, are hung with green brocade. Her poudreuse—like mine only painted & gilt stood open with gold brushes looking glasses, & there on her gold slippers were neatly laid gold stockings. All this paraphernalia for one stringy old hop o' my thumb. She set the two great musical boxes playing & I said did she lie in bed & listen to them? But no. She has nothing fantastic in that way about her. Money is important. She told me rather sordid stories of Lady Sackville never visiting her without fobbing something off on her—now a bust, worth £5, for which she paid £100; now a brass knocker. "And then her talk—I didn't care for it . . ." Somehow I saw into these sordid commonplace talks, & could not sprinkle the air with gold dust easily. But no doubt she has her acuity, her sharp peck at life; only how adorable, I thought, as I tiptoed home in my tight shoes, in the fog, in the chill, could one open one of these doors that I still open so venturously, & find a live interesting real person, a Nessa, a Duncan, a Roger. Some one new, whose mind would begin vibrating. Coarse & usual & dull these Cunards & Colefaxes are—for all their astonishing competence in the commerce of life.

And I cannot think what to 'write next'. I mean the situation is, this

2. Maud ('Emerald') Cunard, *née* Burke (1872-1948), American-born widow of the wealthy Sir Bache Cunard of the steamship company, and mother of the rebellious Nancy, was a patroness of the arts and celebrated hostess whose invitations implied a recognition of social, intellectual, or artistic arrival. She lived in Grosvenor Square.
3. Edward Chichester (1903-1975) succeeded his father as 6th Marquess of Donegall the year after his birth. Educated at Eton and Christ Church, Oxford, he was beginning his successful career as a society journalist.

Orlando is of course a very quick brilliant book. Yes, but I did not try to explore. And must I always explore? Yes I think so still. Because my reaction is not the usual. Nor can I even after all these years run it off lightly. Orlando taught me how to write a direct sentence; taught me continuity & narrative, & how to keep the realities at bay. But I purposely avoided of course any other difficulty. I never got down to my depths & made shapes square up, as I did in The Lighthouse.

Well but Orlando was the outcome of a perfectly definite, indeed overmastering impulse. I want fun. I want fantasy. I want (& this was serious) to give things their caricature value. And still this mood hangs about me. I want to write a history, say of Newnham or the womans movement, in the same vein. The vein is deep in me—at least sparkling, urgent. But is it not stimulated by applause? over stimulated? My notion is that there are offices to be discharged by talent for the relief of genius: meaning that one has the play side; the gift when it is mere gift, unapplied gift; & the gift when it is serious, going to business. And one relieves the other.

Yes, but The Moths? That was to be an abstract mystical eyeless book: a playpoem. And there may be affectation in being too mystical, too abstract; saying Nessa & Roger & Duncan & Ethel Sands admire that: it is the uncompromising side of me; therefore I had better win their approval—

Again, one reviewer days that I have come to a crisis in the matter of style: it is now so fluent & fluid that it runs through the mind like water.

That disease began in The Lighthouse. The first part came fluid—how I wrote & wrote!

Shall I now check & consolidate, more in the Dalloway Jacob's Room style?

I rather think the upshot will be books that relieve other books: a variety of styles & subjects: for after all, that is my temperament, I think: to be very little persuaded of the truth of anything—what I say, what people say—always to follow, blindly instinctively with a sense of leaping over a precipice—the call of—the call of— now, if I write The Moths I must come to terms with these mystical feelings.

Desmond destroyed our Saturday walk; he is now mouldy & to me depressing. He is perfectly reasonable & charming. Nothing surprises, nothing shocks him. He has been through it all one feels. He has come out rolled, smoothed, rather sodden rather creased & jumbled, like a man who has sat up all night in a third class railway carriage. His fingers are stained yellow with cigarettes. One tooth in the lower jaw is missing. His hair is dank. His eye more than ever dubious. He has a hole in his blue sock. Yet he is resolute & determined—thats what I find so depressing. He seems to be sure that it is his view that is the right one; ours vagaries, deviations. And if his view is the right one, God knows there is nothing to live for: not a greasy biscuit. And the egotism of men surprises & shocks me even now. Is there a woman of my acquaintance who could sit in my arm chair from 3 to 6.30 without the semblance of a suspicion that I may be busy, or tired, or bored; & so sitting could talk, grumbling & grudging, of her difficulties, worries; then eat chocolates, then read a book, & go at last, apparently self-complacent & wrapped in a kind of blubber of misty self satisfaction? Not the girls at Newnham or Girton. They are far too spry; far too disciplined. None of that self-confidence is their lot.

We paid for our dinner at the Lion. Miss Thomas & Miss ——? were relieved, not to have to part with quite so many half crowns. And they showed us the chocolate coloured corridors of Girton, like convent cells; —

And there was the meeting in Mr Williams Ellises studio—a vast hall in Ebury street, with ostentatiously ragged chair covers.[4] Our raggedness, as a profession, was not ostentatious alas; it is part of our souls; a dowdiness that is not ragged, however; a meticulous respectability which is not my working state; for then I am, I think, almost picturesque. As a crowd together we achieve only dinginess & something egotistic & unreserved in our faces; as for old Garnett, I felt surely someone ought to put that surly shaggy unkempt old monstrosity (certainly his nails want cutting & his coat is matted with mud & burrs) in the lethal chamber. D[itt]o of his mistress: the top half Esquimaux, the bottom Maytime in Hampstead—sprigged muslin, sandals.[5] Vita as usual like a lamp or torch in all this petty bourgeoisdom; a tribute to the breeding of the Sackvilles, for without care of her clothes she appears among them ⟨in all the sanity & strength of a well made body⟩ like a lampost, straight, glowing. None of us have that; or know not how to carry it.

Poor Rose Macaulay—a mere chit; a wafer—& so on to the Hendersons in Hampstead, where my spleen & Frankie's were twin spleens: poor Frankie however kept his rattle & clapper going, hour after hour, sounding alone, while I sank in a tolerable arm chair & could say nothing;

4. Clough Williams-Ellis (1883-1978), already an influential architect, was married to the writer Amabel, daughter of St Loe Strachey; the meeting on 1 November at 22b Ebury Street was held to discuss support for the defence in the forthcoming *Well of Loneliness* case.
5. Edward Garnett (1868-1937), writer, influential publisher's reader, and father of David ('Bunny') Garnett; his mistress was the painter E. M. (Nellie) Heath, who had taken up prison welfare work.

though Mrs Enfield who has read the whole of Balzac made advances with Proust.[6] Faith, I think, saw in this languor, bad manners & conceit. She saw us despising her home & husband. She despised them herself. And she went to bed saying something bitter to Hubert, & looked back into the drawing room, wondering why all the colours were wrong. But then next morning there are the children at breakfast & she recovers somewhat but has to speak severely about Mrs Maypole, the hired help (10/- a night) who dropped the plates, & left Mr Birrell holding the ladle; & the ice was salt. Then she takes up Orlando & says, to Hubert, "This is a greatly over rated book— It is far far worse than The Lighthouse . . .' at the same time, 'What exciting lives these people lead! Bloomsbury . . ."

Thursday 8 November

Just to solace myself before correcting Hardy & Gissing,[7] I will note that we went to Karin's party last night. The truth is the stimulus is too brisk; one rattles; & only a shout can be heard, & one must stand; & one gets caught, like a bramble on a river by some branch; & hooked up out of the eddy. An emerald green Russian talked to me of seals & then gave me a card; I am to lecture 4 times a week for 8 weeks in America—oh yes—& she will arrange most advantageous terms. But won't mention money in a drawing room: so we lapse upon seals again, or Ann [Stephen]'s rabbit—a chinchilla animal lying languidly extended in the midst of the rumpus, exquisite, alien. Ethel Sands, fanning my vanity into a glow: yet she was downright the other night that Orlando isn't a patch on Lighthouse, with talk of luncheon parties where nothing is talked about but &c. &c.

Janet & Angus to dinner.[8] The young man who wants a job is not amiable; poor old Angus cuts up a little rough, & launches into anxious worried explanations about his play. He will never now break through that chrysalis core of gentlemanly reserve, caution, good manners which shells him in. I think he will meditate more & more upon the glories of

6. Doris Edith Enfield, *née* Hussey (d. 1951). For VW's views on her literary athletics see *II VW Diary*, 19 July 1922. The Hogarth Press had published her biography of 'L.E.L.' in March (*HP Checklist* 160).
7. VW's review of *The Early Life of Thomas Hardy* by Florence Emily Hardy appeared in the *N & A* of 24 November 1928 (Kp C306). She was also revising an earlier (1927) review of George Gissing's *Letters* to serve as an introduction to a selection from his writings to be published by Jonathan Cape in 1929 (see Kp C280).
8. Angus Davidson and Janet Vaughan dined at Tavistock Square before the Stephens' party on 7 November. Angus had not been successful in finding a congenial post since leaving the Hogarth Press almost a year earlier.

being a Davidson. Yet he has his scallywag side, the poor man, dancing & dining, which is to his credit. Janet in comparison seemed rapid, decided & lustrous, all in gold for Karin's party with Madge's gold necklace, & something very like Madge now & then; but tempered with the Vaughan decision. She is an attractive woman; competent; disinterested, taking blood tests all day to solve some abstract problem.

. . . think it

Saturday 10 November

This unexampled fluency here is due to the fact that I should be reading Miss Jewsbury,[9] answering letters (Lady Cunard to dine alone with George Moore) or correcting Hardy & Gissing. All these tasks are unworthy the sacred morning hours. Phrase tossing can only be done then; so I toss them privately here, feeling relieved not to be making money, once in a while. Shall I say that Bennett in the Ev[ening] Standard hurt me less than Squire in the Observer?[10] Not at all, I think;—an odd thing, though, how I am praised & abused: & what a sting I am in the flanks of Squires & Bennetts.

What is more interesting—& Lord knows this is true—I am speaking coolly & faithfully—is the trial yesterday at Bow Street.[11] We were all packed in by 10.30: the door at the top of the court opened; in stepped the debonair distinguished magistrate; we all rose; he bowed; took his seat under the lion & the unicorn, & then proceeded. Something like a Harley St. specialist investigating a case. All black & white, tie pin, clean shaven,

9. VW was reading the novels of Geraldine Jewsbury (1812-1880), the friend of Jane Welsh Carlyle, in preparation for her article 'Geraldine and Jane' to be published in the *TLS*, 28 February 1929 (Kp C309).

10. Arnold Bennett's review of *Orlando*, 'A Woman's High-Brow Lark', appeared in the *Evening Standard*, 8 November 1928. Bennett wrote that VW's 'best novel' *To the Lighthouse* had raised hopes which *Orlando* had now dashed to 'iridiscent fragments' at his feet. See *M & M*, pp 232-3. For Squire's article see above, 27 October 1928, n 3.

11. Jonathan Cape and a London bookseller had been summoned by the Public Prosecutor to show cause why Radclyffe Hall's novel *The Well of Loneliness* should not be destroyed as obscene. The case was heard on 9 November at Bow Street before the Chief Magistrate, Sir Chartres Biron (1863-1940), who ruled that the question of obscenity was one for him alone to determine, and that evidence as to literary merit was inadmissible. His judgement was delivered the following week, on 16 November, when he made an order for the book to be seized and destroyed. An appeal was entered and heard at London Sessions on 14 December when it was dismissed, the court concluding that the book was disgusting and obscene and prejudicial to the morals of the community.

wax coloured, & carved, in that light, like ivory. He was ironical at first: raised his eyebrows & shrugged. Later I was impressed by the reason of the law, its astuteness, its formality. Here have we evolved a very remarkable fence between us & barbarity; something commonly recognised; half humbug & ceremony therefore—when they pulled out calf bound books & read old phrases I thought this; & the bowing & scraping made me think it; but in these banks runs a live stream. What is obscenity? What is literature? What is the difference between the subject & the treatment? In what cases is evidence allowable? This last, to my relief, was decided against us: we could not be called as experts in obscenity, only in art. So Desmond who had got under the palanquin where he looked too indifferent, too calm, too completely at his ease to be natural, was only asked his qualifications & then, not allowed to answer the obscene question, was dismissed. In the hall I talked to Lady Troubridge (who used to sculpt & last time we met was a tea party, as children, in Montpelier Sqre) & John— John lemon yellow, tough, stringy, exacerbated.[12] Their costs run into 4 figures she said. And Leonard thinks this heralds a subscription. After lunch we heard an hour more, & then the magistrate, increasingly deliberate & courteous, said he would read the book again & give judgment next Friday at two, [on] the pale tepid vapid book which lay damp & slab all about the court. And I lost my little Roman brooch, & that is the end of this great day, so far. A curious brown top lighted scene; very stuffy; policemen at the doors; matrons passing through. An atmosphere quite decent & formal, of adult people.

Sunday 25 November

Leonard's 48th birthday. We were at Rodmell, where all has fallen into our hands, rapidly, unexpectedly: on top of the field we get a cottage, & Percy [Bartholomew] is 'our man'. Mrs Percy has inherited from that strange relationship of hers—I suspect her of being the illegitimate child of a circus manager—they travelled—she never speaks of her family— her father died alone—her Auntie left jewels & clothes—she has inherited £330 & some odd shillings. She has bought a set of big white teeth; & now thinks of a gramophone or a wireless set.

12. Una Elena Troubridge (d. 1963), *née* Taylor, was the widow of Admiral Sir Ernest Troubridge (d. 1926) who had obtained a legal separation in 1918 because of her decision to live with Radclyffe Hall—known as 'John'. She was a granddaughter of Sir Henry Taylor, a particular friend of VW's great-aunt Julia Margaret Cameron; her parents' home had been in Montpelier Square, Kensington, and she had studied sculpture at the Royal College of Art.

NOVEMBER 1928

I took Essex & E[th] (Lytton's) down to read, & Lord forgive me!—find it a poor book.[13] I have not finished it; & am keeping it to see if my [*text ends*]

Wednesday 28 November

1928

Father's birthday. He would have been $\frac{1832\ 96}{96}$ yes, today; & could

have been 96, like other people one has known; but mercifully was not. His life would have entirely ended mine. What would have happened? No writing, no books;—inconceivable. I used to think of him & mother daily; but writing The Lighthouse, laid them in my mind. And now he comes back sometimes, but differently. (I believe this to be true—that I was obsessed by them both, unhealthily; & writing of them was a necessary act.) He comes back now more as a contemporary. I must read him some day. I wonder if I can feel again, I hear his voice, I know this by heart?

Last night was one of our evenings—apparently successful; Adrian, Hope, Christa, Clive, Raymond, Bunny, Lytton, Vita & Valery towards the end: & Elizabeth Ponsonby.[14] People enjoyed it. Perhaps I didnt; perhaps I did. Half way through Lytton vanished (he lodges upstairs) brayed out of the room by Clive's vociferation, L. thinks. Clive makes it all very strident, gaslit, band played. I marked a queer change in my feeling when Lytton went. At other times I have felt his silence disapproving; have moderated my folly under it, & tried to keep him from going. But now that man writes Elizabeth & Essex; I kept thinking: well, if he can palm that off on us after years of effort—that lively superficial meretricious book—he can go or stay as he likes. I feel no bite in his disapproval. And though one of my vile vices is jealousy, of other writers' fame, though I am (& I think we all are) secretly pleased to find Lytton's

13. *Eli{z}abeth and Essex* was published in December 1928.
14. See Vanessa Bell to Roger Fry, 37 Gordon Square, 19 November 1928 (CH, Camb.): 'Virginia & I have started a most extraordinary series of entertainments on the line of the old Thursday evenings. We are at home here on Tuesday evenings to a most miscellaneous collection. Last week she provided Rose Macaulay . . . & Charlie Sanger, Clive brought Christabel, Raymond & Vita, I produced the Alan Clutton Brocks & a Davidson. It turned out quite amusing as everyone sate & listened while Virginia got wilder & wilder . . . tomorrow night . . . she is going to bring Hugh Walpole! It is an experiment which can be given up at any time . . .' This series of after-dinner At Homes continued until Christmas. The Hon. Elizabeth Ponsonby (1900-40) was a leader of the sophisticated post-war generation of 'bright young people'.

book a bad one, I also feel depressed. If I were to analyse, the truth is I think that the pleasure is mean, & therefore not deep or satisfying; one would, in the depths, have got real pleasure, though superficial pain, had E & E been a masterpiece. Oh yes, I should—for I have a mind that feeds perfectly dispassionately & apart from my vanities & jealousies upon literature; & that would have taken a masterpiece to itself. Mixed last night with my feeling was some curious personal dissatisfaction: that Lytton whom I loved & love should write like that. It is a reflection on my own taste. It is so feeble, so shallow; & yet Lytton in himself is neither. So one next accuses the public; & then the Carringtons & the young men. And one furbishes up a cloistered secluded invalidish Lytton whipping the flanks of the language & putting it to this foaming gallop, when the poor beast is all spavins & sores. And Dadie & Pernel & Janie Bussy & Dorothy [Bussy] all declared with emotion that this book was his best!

So the days pass, & I ask myself sometimes whether one is not hypnotised, as a child by a silver globe, by life; & whether this is living. Its very quick, bright, exciting. But superficial perhaps. I should like to take the globe in my hands & feel it quietly, round, smooth, heavy. & so hold it, day after day. I will read Proust I think. I will go backwards & forwards.

As for my next book, I am going to hold myself from writing till I have it impending in me: grown heavy in my mind like a ripe pear; pendant, gravid, asking to be cut or it will fall. The Moths still haunts me, coming, as they always do, unbidden, between tea & dinner, while L. plays the gramophone. I shape a page or two; & make myself stop. Indeed I am up against some difficulties. Fame to begin with. Orlando has done very well. Now I could go on writing like that—the tug & suck are at me to do it. People say this was so spontaneous, so natural. And I would like to keep those qualities if I could without losing the others. But those qualities were largely the result of ignoring the others. They came of writing exteriorly; & if I dig, must I not lose them? And what is my own position towards the inner & the outer? I think a kind of ease & dash are good;— yes: I think even externality is good; some combination of them ought to be possible. The idea has come to me that what I want now to do is to saturate every atom. I mean to eliminate all waste, deadness, superfluity: to give the moment whole; whatever it includes. Say that the moment is a combination of thought; sensation; the voice of the sea. Waste, deadness, come from the inclusion of things that dont belong to the moment; this appalling narrative business of the realist: getting on from lunch to dinner: it is false, unreal, merely conventional. Why admit any thing to literature that is not poetry—by which I mean saturated? Is that not my grudge against novel[ist]s—that they select nothing? The poets succeeding by simplifying: practically everything is left out. I want to put practically everything in; yet to saturate. That is what I want to do in The Moths. It must include nonsense, fact, sordidity: but made transparent. I think I must read Ibsen & Shakespeare & Racine. And I will write something about them; for that is the best spur, my mind being what it is; then I read with fury & exactness; otherwise I slip & skip: I am a lazy reader. But no: I am surprised & a little disquieted by the remorseless severity of my mind: that it never stops reading & writing; makes me write on Geraldine Jewsbury, on Hardy, on Women—is too professional, too little any longer a dreamy amateur.

Saturday 8 December

Here is a note barely dashed off (10 to one—just finished, very provisionally "Phases of Fiction") after Christabel MacClaren; & her 'winkle' party, as I call it, the other night. I mean she picked me out with a pin—about Lesbianism, & Dotty—(she is not one). My note was about her attitude to men; the adoring, flattering woman's attitude, which I so seldom see so purely. Like a flame leaping up. Clive "the most honourable of men"—yes but said with a devoutness, a radiancy, that made me laugh. Is this the 'natural' attitude between the sexes? What Clive has, the other way round for women? So cordial, so appreciative; I could hear it kindling her voice when she said "The men were bathing or writing letters or talking"—that was at Sherfield.[1] The men, good delightful creatures, were so engaged while that wretched furtive creature D. pursued me. And I can see man after man, Desmond, Clive &c, Wells, Shaw, warming his hands at this natural warmth, & expanding. It amused me. The other thought I had was about the limits of luxury: how far can the human soul stretch into rugs & rooms; at what point they suffocate its force. I have seen several rich people this autumn; & thought them, perhaps, dulled, coarsened by it: Lady Cunard; two days ago Mrs Bowen & Mrs Grenfell at Lydia's.[2]

1. Sherfield Court in Hampshire had been Lady Dorothy Wellesley's previous country house, the centre of her liberal hospitality.
2. Vera (Mrs Harold) Bowen (d. 1967), a friend of Lydia's from the world of music and ballet; her present husband was a wealthy business man. Florence Grenfell, née Henderson, was the wife of the banker E. C. Grenfell (later Lord St Just), Conservative MP for the City of London 1922-35.

Sunday 9 December

These reflections are written on a bitter cold evening to get the taste of a sentence into my mouth again. Angelica came this morning, & every time I lifted my pen she,—heavenly little creature that she is, demure, witty fantastic, neatly tipped the cup upside down; like a fool I went on trying to write, & only gave up when I was in a state of exasperation, not with her, but with my book: I was beginning a new beginning to Fiction. Now it is after tea; Angus will be coming to see Leonard about a character; & I am escaped, & can't be got at; & shall read Troilus & Cressida (Chaucer) till dinner. I have again seen too many people, without much intensity. Lydia's foolish tea party; & the Bagenals' lunch, & Christa; & then Long Barn, & being driven up by Dotty; "I cant say I understand Harold—I can't really say I do"—Then Vita, making a sacrifice of her quiet evening, drove up to London & heard her broadcast & went back with her, to save me the solitary drive. This worried me, rather: for whom would I give up this evening? & then Dotty with her pecking exacting ways "Please dear put the window up—put the window down" makes Vita seem to me pathetically gentle & kind. But none of this matters very much I agree, & Lord helping, I shall work all this week—save for the evenings. It is so cold my back is cold now, while the fire roasts my feet; fire is striking & many fire engines have rushed down Southampton Row. The King is dragging along, & the shop assistants are in fear lest they shall lose their Christmas bonus.[3] Christmas impends. And we shall spend it alone here, I think, & go to Rodmell afterwards & plan a new room, with Kennedy. And then to Berlin we say. Meanwhile Nessa & I give our Tuesday evenings, & too many people press to come.

But why I ask "see" people? Whats the point? These isolated occasions which come so often. May I come & see you? And what they get, or I get, save the sense of a slide passing on a screen, I cant say.

Tuesday 18 December

Here I should be pegging away at Fiction; rather an interesting little book I think; but I cannot get my mind down on to it, like a bird of prey firmly attached. I was switched off to write a eulogy of Lady Strachey, burnt yesterday with a bunch of our red & white carnations on top of her.[4]

3. George V was suffering from a general blood infection and toxaemia, and there were fears for his life. On 12 December he underwent an operation for the drainage of fluid from his right lung after which he made a slow recovery.
4. Lady Strachey died at 51 Gordon Square, aged 88, on 15 December 1928, and was cremated at Golders Green on 17th. VW's eulogy appeared in the *N & A* on 22 December 1928 (Kp C307; reprinted in VW, *Books and Portraits*, 1977).

It is odd how little her death means to me—for this reason. About a year ago she was said to be dying; & at once (Adrian told me) I made up my usual visualisation; felt the whole emotion of Lady Strachey's passing—her memories & so on—that night; & then she did not die; & now when she does die, not a vision, not an emotion comes my way. These little tricks of psychology amuse me.

L. has just been in to consult about a 3rd edition of Orlando. This has been ordered; we have sold over 6000 copies; & sales are still amazingly brisk—150 today for instance; most days between 50 & 60; always to my surprise. Will they stop or go on? Anyhow my room is secure. For the first time since I married 1912—1928—16 years—I have been spending money. The spending muscle does not work naturally yet. I feel guilty; put off buying, when I know that I should buy; & yet have an agreeable luxurious sense of coins in my pocket beyond my weekly 13/- which was always running out, or being encroached upon. Yesterday I spent 15/- on a steel brooch. I spent £3 on a mother of pearl necklace—& I haven't bought a jewel for 20 years perhaps! I have carpeted the dining room—& so on. I think one's soul is the better for this lubrication; & I am going to spend freely, & then write, & so keep my brain on the boil. All this money making originated in a spasm of black despair one night at Rodmell 2 years ago.[5] I was tossing up & down on those awful waves: when I said that I could find a way out. (For part of my misery was the perpetual limitation of everything; no chairs, or beds, no comfort, no beauty; & no freedom to move: all of which I determined there & then to win). And so came, with some argument, even tears one night (& how seldom I have ever cried!) to an agreement with Leonard about sharing money after a certain sum; & then opened a bank account; & now, at the lowest shall have £200 to put there on Jan. 1st. The important thing is to spend freely, without fuss or anxiety; & to trust to one's power of making more—Indeed, I cannot at this moment very seriously doubt that I shall earn more, this next 5 years, than ever before.

But to return to Max Beerbohm. I met him at Ethel's the other night.[6] As I came in a thick set old man (such was my impression) rose, & I was introduced. No freakishness, no fancy about him. His face is solidified; has a thick moustache; a red veined skin, heavy lines; but then his eyes are perfectly round, very large, & sky blue. His eyes become dreamy & merry when the rest of him is well groomed & decorous in the extreme.

5. See above, 15 September 1926.
6. VW (but not LW, who went to see his sick mother) dined with Ethel Sands on 13 December.

He is brushed, neat, urbane. Halfway through dinner he turned to me &
we began a 'nice', interesting, flattering, charming kind of talk; he told
me how he had read an article on Addison at Bognor during the war;
when literature seemed extinct; & there was his own name. I daresay V.W.
catches your eye as M.B. does mine. And nothing has encouraged me
more. So I said, as I think, that he is immortal. In a small way, he said;
but with complacency. Like a jewel which is hard & flawless, yet always
changing. A charming image he said, very kind, approving, & what half
flattered half saddened me, *equal*. Am I on that level? Virginia Woolf
says—V.W. thinks—how do you write? & so on: I was one of his
colleagues & fellows in the art of writing; but not I hoped quite so old.
Anyhow he asked me how I wrote. For he hacks every step with his
pen, & therefore never alters. He thought I wrote like this. I told him I
had to cut out great chunks. I wish you would send them to me, he said;
simply; Indeed, he was nothing if not kind; but looked long & steadily.
Looked at Lord David [Cecil]—that queer painters look, so matching, so
considering apart from human intent; yet with him not entirely. After
dinner, he leant on the mantelpiece & Maurice Baring & I flittered round
him like a pair of butterflies, praising, laughing, extravagant. And he said
he was so pleased by the praise of intelligent people like ourselves. But
always he had to be led off to talk politely to this person & that; finally
disappeared, very dignified, very discreet in his white waistcoat, pressing
my hand in his plump firm one long; & saying what a pleasure &c. I own
that I dont find much difference between the great & ourselves—indeed
they are like us: I mean they dont have the frills & furbelows of the small;
come to terms quickly & simply. But we got, of course, very little way.
He talked of Hardy, & said he couldnt bear Jude the Obscure: thought
it falsified life, for there is really more happiness than sorrow in life, &
Hardy tries to prove the opposite. And his writing is so bad. Then I ran
down—but he reads my essays & knows this—Belloc.[7] M.B. said that
Belloc, one must remember, poured out ten books a year on history
poetry &c. He was one of those full unequal people who were never
perfect, as he, M.B., might be called perfect in a small way. But he was
glad I didnt like him. Charles Lamb had the most beautiful things in him
& then he spoilt them. He had never read a book except Pendennis &
Tess of the d'Urbervilles till he left Oxford. And now at last, at Rapallo,
he reads. He is taking back Elizabeth & Orlando (pronounced in the
French way) to read; treats he looks forward to.

7. See VW's 'The Modern Essay' in *The Common Reader* where she praises Beerbohm,
   'the prince of his profession', and disparages Belloc.

Among others were present . . . Mrs Hammersley, Lord David, Hutchinsons, &c.[8]

And we dined last night with the Hutchinsons & met George Moor[e] —like an old silver coin now, so white so smooth; with his little flipper hands, like a walruses; & his chubby cheeks, & little knees—yet always saying the thing that comes into his head; fresh, juvenile almost for that reason; & very shrewd. Gave a description of Riceyman Steps[9]—the ferns covered in dust, the man with cancer marrying the woman with fits— Not what one calls a distinguished mind—& what a subject to choose! It seems as if he attaches much importance to subject. He was always praising or altering ways of treating stories. He is writing some Greek novel now, dictating to a charming lady, who has every virtue, save that she is not forthcoming & therefore will not marry. He dictates, & this gives him something to bite upon: then he re-dictates. He never writes. There are no mss of his in existence. Perhaps the dictated style is a true account of his style & H[enry]. J[ames]'s. & accounts for their fluidity, their verbosity.[10] And what it comes to is that the great are very simple; quick to come to terms with; reserved; & dont pay any attention to other peoples books (Moore throws scorn on them all—Shaw—a shriek of vulgarity—poisoned with vulgarity—never wrote a good sentence in his life—Wells—I spare myself Wells—& Galsworthy—) & live in an atmosphere very serene, bright, & fenced off: for all that they are more to the point than ordinary people; go to the heart of things directly. Moore toddled off & got quickly into a cab, Jack said, for all his look of an old silver coin.

8. Violet Mary Hammersley (1878-1964), hostess and patron of the arts, and an old friend of Ethel Sands. Lord David (Gascoyne-) Cecil (b. 1902), younger son of the 4th Marquess of Salisbury; VW had met him at Garsington in 1923 when he was still an undergraduate; he was now a Fellow of Wadham College, Oxford, and writing his life of Cowper. (He also was to write the life of Max Beerbohm, 1964.)

9. *Riceyman Steps* (1923), the novel by Arnold Bennett.

10. George Moore's 'Greek novel' was *Aphrodite in Aulis*, completed in November 1928 and published in 1930. Moore's later work was produced by a method of dictating and re-dictating from what he called 'rigmarole'. Henry James's later works were also dictated.

1929

1929

The Woolfs had spent Christmas in Bloomsbury, dining with Roger Fry on Christmas day; on 27 December they went to Rodmell, returning to London on 3 January 1929. This is Diary XVIII.

Friday 4 January

How odd to think that I have given the world something that the world enjoys—I refer to the Manchester Guardian—Orlando is recognised for the masterpiece that it is. The Times does not mention Nessa's pictures.[1] Yet, she said last night, I have spent a long time over one of them. Then I think to myself, So I have something, instead of children, & fall comparing our lives. I note my own withdrawal from those desires; my absorption in what I call, inaccurately, ideas: this vision.

We saw Koteliansky on Christmas day. Rather dryer & yellower in the cheeks, like an orange that is old. He was in his shirt sleeves. He had been washing up his Christmas dinner, which was "No, not a very good one . . . Come in Come in". This was Katherine's room he said. It is poverty stricken, tidy, clean—a bed, a table. It looks over back gardens to the trees of Regent's Park. We went straight into the old abuse of Murry; went back ten years, to Richmond; & those long visits; those difficult emphatic ways. He is, one says, the same. Very poor, as definite as ever. Still talking about Lawrence; a very very good writer but his last book DISGUSTING. You must read Counterpoint.[2] Why? Because

1. The third leader in the *Manchester Guardian* of 4 January 1929, headed 'The Year's Novels', developed the theme that 'the novel is the dominant art-form of this age' and said: '. . . a biography which proves on examination to be fiction is sure of a public, while a novel such as Virginia Woolf's "Orlando", which playfully masquerades as biography, is today recognised as the masterpiece it is'. Vanessa Bell and Duncan Grant were both showing with the 26th Exhibition of the London Group at the New Burlington Galleries; Vanessa's big picture was 'The Red Sofa'.

2. Koteliansky lived at 5 Acacia Road, St John's Wood, from 1915 until his death in 1955. The house had been Katherine Mansfield's for a brief happy period until the death of her brother in October 1915 made it unendurable to her. Kot lodged with her Russian successors and when after some years they left, took it over himself. D. H. Lawrence's *Lady Chatterley's Lover* had been published in Florence in the summer of 1928; and Aldous Huxley's *Point Counter Point* in October 1928.

he is a seerious man, a cultivated man. And it is typical of the age. It is a painful book a horrid book but it is that. Still the same seriousness, & concentration upon say 5 objects which he has been staring at these 40 years. Still he gnaws the bone of Katherine & Murry. And all the time some emotion was working in him. He was glad we had come. What could he give us? He gave me a red wooden box, a Russian toy, & stuffed it full of his Russian cigarettes. His voice quivered now & then. He looked at me with emotion. All the linoleum was shining, where he had cleaned it, & he had painted the woodwork with two sorts of Reckitt's blue: so that it shone very bright. He had painted it over & over. There he lives, how heaven knows. People will no longer buy his translations. His dog (a pure Jewish dog) is dead.

Now is life very solid, or very shifting? I am haunted by the two contradictions. This has gone on for ever: will last for ever; goes down to the bottom of the world—this moment I stand on. Also it is transitory, flying, diaphanous. I shall pass like a cloud on the waves. Perhaps it may be that though we change; one flying after another, so quick so quick, yet we are somehow successive, & continuous—we human beings; & show the light through. But what is the light? I am impressed by the transitoriness of human life to such an extent that I am often saying a farewell—after dining with Roger for instance; or reckoning how many more times I shall see Nessa.

Before Christmas Vita Sackville-West had gone to join her husband Harold Nicolson for a ten-week stay in Berlin, where he was Counsellor at the British Embassy. This provided the impulse for the Woolfs to visit Berlin; on 16 January they travelled overnight by Harwich and the Hook of Holland, and stayed at the Prinz Albrecht Hotel, where they were joined on 18 January by Vanessa and Quentin Bell and Duncan Grant who were making a tour of picture galleries in Germany and Austria. They all spent what Vanessa termed 'a very rackety' week in Berlin in the company of the Nicolsons, and the Woolfs returned the way they had come on 21 January; VW reach home in a state of collapse, and for the next six weeks led a virtually invalid life.

Thursday 28 March

It is a disgrace indeed; no diary has been left so late in the year. The truth was that we went to Berlin on the 16th of January, & then I was in bed for three weeks afterwards, & then could not write; perhaps for another three, & have spent my energy since in one of my excited outbursts of composition—writing what I made up in bed, a final version of Women & Fiction.[1]

And as usual, I am bored by narrative. I want only to say how I met Nessa in Tottenham Court Road this afternoon, both of us sunk fathoms deep in that wash of reflection in which we both swim about. She will be gone on Wednesday for 4 months. It is queer how instead of drawing apart, life draws us together. But I was thinking a thousand things as I carried my teapot, gramophone records & stockings under my arm. It is one of those days that I called 'potent' when we lived in Richmond.

Perhaps I ought not to go on repeating what I have always said about the spring. One ought perhaps to be forever finding new things to say, since life draws on. One ought to invent a fine narrative style. Certainly there are many new ideas always forming in my head. For one, that I am going to enter a nunnery these next months; & let myself down into my mind; Bloomsbury being done with. I am going to face certain things. It is going to be a time of adventure & attack, rather lonely & painful I think. But solitude will be good for a new book. Of course, I shall make friends. I shall be external outwardly. I shall buy some good clothes & go out into new houses. All the time I shall attack this angular shape in my mind. I think the Moths (if that is what I shall call it) will be very sharply cornered. I am not satisfied though with the frame. There is this sudden fertility which may be mere fluency. In old days books were so many sentences absolutely struck with an axe out of crystal: & now my mind is so impatient, so quick, in some ways so desperate.

Old age is withering us; Clive, Sibyl, Francis—all wrinkled & dusty; going over the hoops, along the track. Only in myself, I say, forever bubbles this impetuous torrent. So that even if I see ugliness in the glass, I think, very well, inwardly I am more full of shape & colour than ever. I think I am bolder as a writer. I am alarmed by my own cruelty with my friends. Clive, I say, is intolerably dull. Francis is a runaway milk lorry.

I feel on the verge of some strenuous adventure: yes; as if this spring day were the hatching; the portal; the opening through which I shall go upon this experience. So when I wake early, I brace myself out of my terrors by saying that I shall need great courage: after all, I say, I made £1000 all from willing it early one morning. No more poverty I said; & poverty has ceased. I am summoning Philcox next week to plan a room—

1. An interim version of 'Women and Fiction'—based on the lectures VW had given at Cambridge in October—had been sent to New York presumably before she went to Berlin, for it was published there in the *Forum* in March (Kp C310). The 'final version' was to become *A Room of One's Own*.

I have money to build it, money to furnish it. And we have the new car, & we can drive to Edinburgh in June if we like, & go to Cassis.[2]

The new year was threatened with a pumping machine, making this studio a trial; for it pumped every 25 minutes. Now for a fortnight it has not pumped. Am I saved? Now it is so quiet that I only hear sparrows; & a voice singing in the hotel. A perfect room for me. Nessa has taken a studio & will let 37, thus ending, for ever I suppose, her Gordon Square life.[3] How much I admire this handling of life as if it were a thing one could throw about; this handling of circumstance. Angelica will go to school. I have now many admiring letters to answer. Simpkins said today that many great publishers would be proud to have our list. In 10 years we shall be rather celebrated. At anyrate, without any trouble to write well, as there should have been, I have once more launched this diary.

Saturday 13 April

Habits gradually change the face of ones life as time changes one's physical face; & one does not know it. Here am I using this studio to sit in, & with my diary to write down here; almost always after tea I retire here. And then I never print now or address envelopes. So perhaps habit will snuff out this diary one day.

I am sordidly debating within myself the question of Nelly; the perennial question. It is an absurdity, how much time L. & I have wasted in talking about servants. And it can never be done with because the fault lies in the system. How can an uneducated woman let herself in, alone, into our lives? —what happens is that she becomes a mongrel; & has no roots any where. I could put my theory into practice by getting a daily of a civilised kind, who had her baby in Kentish town; & treated me as an employer, not friend. Here is a fine rubbish heap left by our parents to be swept.

It is very quiet & very cold. I walked Pinka through the Saturday streets this afternoon & was woken to the fact that it is April by a primrose on the pavement. I had been thinking I was on one of my January walks, with lights lit at 3.30 in peoples bedrooms. Rodmell was impracticable because of the cold; & until I have a room, I cannot go there meaning to work.

2. In February LW replaced his second-hand Singer car by another with a sunshine roof.

3. The area behind 52 Tavistock Square fronting Woburn Place had been cleared for the construction of an enormous hotel (the *Royal*, 789 rooms)—with the inevitable contamination of the neighbourhood by noise and dirt in the process. Vanessa had acquired a large studio at the back of 8 Fitzroy Street adjacent to Duncan's; now when in London, they lived and worked in these studios until 1940.

We always do mean to work.

I have just agreed to do another 4 articles for Mrs Van Doren, because she has raised her price to £50 an article—so that, whatever the cost, I can have my new room.[1] And all this money is changing my habits. I'm not sure it is not the memorable fact about this spring—for the first time since 1912—16 years that is—I am able to look say at blue lustre cups in a shop & decide, well why not buy them? But they cost £6 ... But then I am making over £1000 a year. I can make as much as I want. This little colloquy still takes place before I can unbend my old penurious muscles. But it is always better to buy than not to buy I think.

1928
1912
—
16

Hugh Walpole was here the other day, from 4.30 to 7.15 alone, over the fire. The same uneasy talk as usual; brisk & breezy, hating war; & then this morbid egotism & desire to scratch the same place over & over again—his own defects as a writer & how to remedy them, what they spring from; all mixed up with his normal, & usual sense of being prosperous & admired—from which, as he admits when I ask him, he gets great pleasure. He starts indeed to protest that he gives pleasure, does good, but can't bring that out in my presence; which is why he seeks my presence —a scratching stone to rid him of the world's mud. He protests too much. On the other hand, I like these bustling vigour[ous] characters: I like talk of Russia, & war & great doings & famous people— If I don't see them I romanticise them.

Leonard is upstairs finishing the Hogarth Press accounts. Yesterday he gave the three stall hands a bonus: Mrs C. £25; Belcher £20; Kennedy £20.[2] They sent up a bunch of roses later in the day. For the first time we have made over £400 profit. And 7 people now depend on us; & I think with pride that 7 people depend, largely, upon my hand writing on a sheet of paper. That is of course a great solace & pride to me. Its not scribbling; its keeping 7 people fed & housed: a great big man like Percy; a carrot faced woman like Cartwright; they live on my words. They will be feeding off Women & Fiction next year for which I predict some sale. It has considerable conviction. I think that the form, half talk half soliloquy allows me to get more onto the page than any how else. It made itself up & forced itself upon me (in this form—the thinking had been done & the

1. See above, 22 March 1928, n 1. These four commissioned articles, to be published in the autumn in the *New York Herald Tribune* and just previously in the *N & A*, were: 'Cowper and Lady Austen' (Kp C314); 'Beau Brummel' (Kp C315); 'Mary Wollstonecraft' (Kp C316); and 'Dorothy Wordsworth' (Kp C317).

2. Miss Belsher began work as a clerk at the Hogarth Press about two months before Richard Kennedy.

writing stiffly & unsatisfactorily 4 times before) as I lay in bed after Berlin.
I used to make it up at such a rate that when I got pen & paper I was like
a water bottle turned upside down. The writing was as quick as my hand
could write; too quick, for I am now toiling to revise; but this way gives
one freedom & lets one leap from back to back of one's thoughts.

Happily, for my health of soul, I am now very little noticed, & so can
forget the fictitious self, for it is half so, which fame makes up for one: I
can see my famous self tapering about the world. I am more comfortable
when shut up, self-contained as now.

The great pleasure of money is to spend a pound—as on a dinner at
Richmond—without accounting for it— I dined there with Vita. It was
cold. We drove round the Park. I saw a man leading a large cat on a chain.
I saw many odd parties in the hotel. How can they come here tonight,
I said? There was the old woman gorged like a vulture. The woman with
her foot cocked under the table at this ✔ angle, all through dinner:
the young spark in grey with the pink carnation; the two prominent-
eyed daughters in velvet; & all kinds of emotions, of ridicule & interest
crossing the vast room perpetually from one table to another. The waiters,
I thought, are only here this one night; everything is unreal & will vanish.
But it is going on precisely the same at this moment. Have you had a tiring
day Miss ——? says Mrs —— leaning out to speak to her. Oh dread-
fully tiring says Miss —— taking her seat at the table with the reserved
private bottle of soda water. And in complete desolation she waits for the
courses to be brought.

Monday 29 April

And it is pouring. Oh this cold spring! Dry as a bone, though until
today, but with never a blue sky. So that my red coat, which is like haws
in winter, suits it. I heard the nightingale at Vita's a week or two ago—
the one warm night. And we were cold at Rodmell last week, when we
went down to see Philcox, who will build two rooms for £320, & take
only two months. It was cold; but how silent, how safe from voices &
talk! How I resented our coming back; & quickly changed into the social
sphere of my soul; & went to lunch with Sibyl; & there had, for my pains,
precisely six minutes of tolerable talk with Max Beerbohm. But dear me,
how little talk with great men now disturbs me. Are we all chilling &
freezing, & do we look into each others old faces as into the craters of the
moon? (These I saw silver white & like the spots that are made by water
dropping into plaster of paris through Vita's telescope the other day.) I

begin to think that youth is the only tolerable thing to look at; & am taking Judy to the Coliseum on Wednesday.[3]

I forgot to say that the pump has begun again & is grinding away at this moment. But I say I shall get used to it—certainly I shall.

This morning I began to revise Phases of Fiction, & with that done, I can see my way clear to a complete imaginative book.

Meanwhile, I am eddying quicker & quicker into the stream, into London: tomorrow Christabel; then Mauron's lecture & Mary & the Keynes' & the Eliots.[4]

Poor Tom—a true poet, I think; what they will call in a hundred years a man of genius: & this is his life. I stand for half an hour listening while he says that Vivien cant walk. Her legs have gone. But whats the matter? No one knows. And so she lies in bed—cant put a shoe on. And they have difficulties, humiliations, with servants. And after endless quibbling about visiting—which he cant do these 8 weeks, owing to moving house & 15 first cousins come to England, suddenly he appears overcome, moved, tragic, unhappy, broken down, because I offer to come to tea on Thursday. Oh but we dont dare ask our friends, he said. We have been deserted. Nobody has been to see us for weeks. Would you really come—all this way? to see us? Yes I said.[5] But what a vision of misery, imagined, but real too. Vivien with her foot on a stool, in bed all day; Tom hurrying back lest she abuse him: this is our man of genius.— This is what I gathered yesterday morning on the telephone.

Sunday 12 May

Here, having just finished what I call the final revision of Women & Fiction so that L. can read it after tea, I stop: surfeited. And the pump, which I was so sanguine as to think ceased, begins again. About W. & F. I am not sure—a brilliant essay?—I daresay; it has much work in it, many opinions boiled down into a kind of jelly, which I have stained red as far as I can. But I am eager to be off—to write without any boundary coming

3. VW's niece Judith (1918-1972) was Adrian and Karin Stephen's younger daughter; the Coliseum was presenting a Variety programme.
4. Charles Mauron (1899-1966), a Provençal intellectual whom Roger Fry had 'discovered' about 1920 and introduced to Bloomsbury. A scientist by training, he was forced by progressive blindness to give up his University research post and, encouraged by Fry, turned to literature and criticism, in which field he produced much original writing, and to translation (he was to translate both *Orlando* and *Flush*). His present lecture (to which VW did not go; see *IV VW Letters*, no. 2025) was on Mallarmé and was given at 37 Gordon Square on 1 May.
5. Eliot wrote on 2 May to postpone VW's visit, saying circumstances were too much for them (copy, MHP, Sussex).

slick in ones eyes: here my public has been too close: facts; getting them malleable, easily yielding to each other.

A wet day, or we should be at Hampton Court with Roger & Mauron. And I am glad of the rain, because I have talked too much. We have seen too many people—Sydney Waterlow perhaps the most notable, as a resurrection. A desperate looking pompous sad respectable elderly man; worldly; but quivering as usual in his shell. Any pin pricks him in the unarmoured skin. I liked him. We met in the dark hall, glad of its darkness. We talked almost too easily, of Lucy Clifford buried with a service; & then his lancers & state at Bangkok—all to his liking. His importance very clear to him. At Oare he is nobody. And so he would like to go back to Bangkok & be important in the East for ever.[1] He can seek the truth no more—has indeed seen through the search for truth, which was in him the search for power. He believes in nothing any more, he said, & is convinced now that nothing will ever change him— So, talking of something else for a moment, he suddenly burst out into a terrific peroration about Spengler; who has changed the world for him—made infinitely more difference than anybody—so fixed & stable & independent is he.[2]

Also we had a party: Roger a little old—to my mind he needs Nessa to fertilise & sweeten him. Some queer rancour often seems to exacerbate him. When his stomach heals his leg aches. And Plomer came—a little rigid, I fear; & too much of a gentleman; & little Blunden, the very image of a London house sparrow, that pecks & cheeps & is starved & dirty.[3] And Julian, to me a very satisfactory young man at present; full of ardour, yet clear, precise; & genial too—with all his apostolic fervour & abstrac-

1. Sydney Waterlow (1878-1944), one-time suitor and old friend of VW (see *VW Diary*, vols. I & II) had rejoined the Diplomatic Service after the war, and had served as British Minister in Bangkok, 1926-28, and then in Addis Ababa, which post he had recently relinquished on grounds of health. His home in England was at Oare, Wiltshire. Mrs Clifford was a figure from VW's even more distant past; she had died on 21st, and was buried at Highgate Cemetery on 24th April. The Woolfs were at Rodmell on that day.

2. Oswald Spengler (1880-1936), German philosopher, whose influential study of the philosophy of history, *The Decline of the West*, had appeared in an English translation in 1926 and 1928.

3. William Plomer (1903-1973), English poet and novelist, was born in South Africa and returned there at the age of fifteen after war-time schooling in England. For the past two years he had been living by teaching in Japan, and had just reached England after a ten years' absence, and met the Woolfs for the first time; in 1925 he had sent them his novel *Turbott Wolfe* from Zululand, and they published it (*HP Checklist* 73) and his other books until 1932. Plomer had known Edmund Blunden in Tokyo where from 1924-27 the latter had been Professor of English Literature at the Imperial University.

tedness a good fellow, warm, kindly; much more apt to see the good than the bad. For example he thought poor little grey mouse Jenkins very nice & very intelligent & sat screwed up on the floor at her feet. He had been consoling Topsy all the afternoon. For Topsy & Peter have separated. Yes they have separated for ever, owing to her flirtatious ways.

Monday 13 May

How odd this is—here I am sitting at 3.10 with nothing much to do— nothing that I need do. I must take up printing again. But we have been to the Singers with the car—its clutch in trouble; & as we started, up came Saxon, on his holiday— Going to the Ring of course, & having a day off. For how many years has he done this—strange methodical character that he is. We dont meet for months, & take up the subject again. He took out his cheque book & said he thought the pattern was changed, with the same interest in that minute detail as he had 30 years ago. He has the same umbrella hanging by a hook on his arm; the same gold watch chain; & his pirouetting attitudes; & sprightly bird-like ways.

What then has life given you, I asked, (myself) looking at the Church at the top of Portland Street.[4] Well, he is free to go to the Opera, to read Plato to play chess. And he will continue doing these things, as if they were the chosen things till he dies. There is a certain dignity in this steady doing of things which seem chosen. Yet—thus one always ends a comparison of lives—I wouldn't for the whole world live yours.

And at 4 I must change & wash & go to the Mauron lecture at Argyll House; & then to Molly & then to dine with Sibyl—which will, I hope finish this lap of my race. Did I say that I still think of life as a series of laps—& still take my fences dutifully & then enjoy nothingness? So if I dine with Sibyl I need not dine with Christabel. I have never got in the frame of mind which makes these fences negligible. Then we go to Rodmell for 6 days; & then home; & then to Cassis; & then home. & then Rodmell; & then the autumn; & then the winter— Oh this pump! I wish I could say I never notice it. Moreover, the idea has come to me that I ought now to be re-reading my own books, for our 'Collected Edition'. L. & Kennedy are working at a dust cover this moment. Shall I run away from my duty & the pump & go & see?[5]

4. Presumably Trinity Church, opposite Great Portland Street Station.
5. The 'Uniform Edition of the Works of Virginia Woolf', printed by photo-litho-offset from the original editions, was initiated with four volumes—*The Voyage Out*, *Jacob's Room*, *The Common Reader*, and *Mrs Dalloway*—issued by the Hogarth Press on 26 September 1929. The typographical design of the dust jacket was improved by Vanessa Bell (see *IV VW Letters*, no. 2040).

MAY 1929

The election draws near, & the Derby.[6] I will go upstairs & read Proust
I think, since I am fabricating a few remarks on him for that cursed book
—that stone that plunges me deeper & deeper in the water. The reason
I dislike dining with Sibyl is that she exacts it: I am to give her a display
of intimacy, which she cannot acquire, poor woman, for herself.

Wednesday 15 May

This is written, as many pages in the past used to be written, to try a
new pen; for I am vacillating—cant be sure to stick to the old pen any

I make a note here
that I will one of
these days read the
whole of Matthew
Arnold.

more. And then every gold pen has some fatal drawback. Never have I met one without. And then one
cant be sure till one's written a long screed. And then
one's ashamed to go back—& then one does—&
then it all begins again, like Mathew Arnold's river,
or sea (brings in again &c &c).[7]

I went to Sibyl's dinner; but Heavens, how little real point there is to
these meetings—save indeed that the food is good; & there is wine, & a
certain atmosphere of luxury & hospitality. This, on the other hand, tends
to drug one; one has been given something, for which one has to pay.
And I don't like that feeling. The old white haired baby [George Moore]
sat propped up in his high chair; his hair now white like flax, like silk; his
cheeks tinted a childs pink; his eyes with their marble hardness; his boneless
ineffective hands. For some reason, he paid me compliments, indeed
referred to me as an authority on English; & even offered, which I daresay
was kindly meant, though nothing has happened, to send me one of his
books.[8]

What did we discuss? Mostly himself & his books, I think; & how he
had known various old dim figures, far away in the past. I told them
about Lord Alfred's threat, & this launched him on stories about Robbie

6. Having been in office since October 1924, the Conservatives had called the General
   Election for 30 May 1929. Derby Day was 5 June.
7.   'Listen! you hear the grating roar
    Of pebbles which the waves suck back, and fling,
    At their return, up the high strand,
    Begin, and cease, and then again begin,
    With tremulous cadence slow, and bring
    The eternal note of sadness in.'

    Dover Beach, published 1867.
8. An uncut presentation copy, inscribed by the author to VW, 1929, of George
   Moore's *The Making of an Immortal*, was lot 79 in Sotheby's sale on 27 April 1970.

Ross, & his own lawsuits.[9] But he is a detached shrewd old man; without many illusions & not very dependent on anyone, I should say. He wanted to walk back to Ebury Street, but it was raining & they made him take a cab. He talked about Henry James, & a proof sheet which nobody could read; & he said that a sentence ought to form like a cloud at the end of the pen—dont you think so? he said to me. These little compliments were due to my Geraldine & Jane which he said   & references, was an admirable story & should be published as such. It had nothing to do with fact. And I rather think he will die soon—he has to have another operation;[10] but in his detached way. I think these artists are slightly bored by all physical transactions. Let my body die, I can imagine him saying, so long as I can go on forming sentences at the end of my pen—& why not? Save that of course he says he enjoys the pleasures of the body. But that I rather doubt.

And I doubt too if Clive does. Clive is I fancy in bad odour everywhere at the moment, with his silly egotistic ways—writing to me to boast of a 'mystery', which it is clear that I am to impart; but I shant. He is like Lottie *au fond*; & Lottie by the way is dismissed; & is said to owe Karin £8 which she can't pay, & great scenes take place, poor Adrian, as I imagine, moping & glooming in discomfort alone; with Karin savage & violent & competent spasmodically, rushing out to pay bills & put her house in order in ten minutes when she has neglected it all these years: sordid & squalid it all is, & hardly gives me any pleasure, to tell the truth, these sufferings of my friends.

I am depressed. Brace has done it. The oval faced sallow man. They want to keep W. & F., which I like, till the spring, & make P. of F. come out this autumn—a book I hate; & was, as I think, wrongly pressed to undertake.[11] And then Roger wants to come to Rodmell, & I don't like

9. The litigious Lord Alfred Douglas (1870-1945) had threatened to sue the *N & A* and LW for libel unless they published an apology for LW's disparaging review (6 April 1929) of his *Autobiography*. A particular target of Lord Alfred's retributory litigation had been Robert Ross, Oscar Wilde's literary executor, whom LW appeared to him to be defending. In the event the *N & A* published a letter from Lord Alfred (27 April 1929) and no further action ensued. George Moore had won an action for libel brought against him in 1917 by a Louis N. Seymour in respect of his novel *Lewis Seymour and Some Women*.

10. George Moore had undergone preliminary surgery in April 1928, and was anticipating a second, major, operation; but the danger was considered too great, and it was not performed. He lived until 21 January 1933, a month before his eighty-first birthday.

11. In the event Harcourt Brace published *A Room of One's Own* (W[omen] & F[iction]) on the same day as the Hogarth Press, 24 October 1929 (Kp A12); for *Phases of Fiction* see above, 7 December 1925, n 6.

after my protests, to say no; & yet to have to talk & talk—& then Philcox can't get my rooms done, all because of Durrant's long waiting.[12] So my wheel is turning low. & do I like this pen or dont I? Such are my sorrows Mr Wesley, as the man said when the servant put on too many coals.

What Clive says is that he has a mystery; something he cant share; & this annoys me too; the sensation mongering, like Dotty; the desire to be talked of. Oh, I say, if only I could plunge my mind into the delights of pure imagination, & so get some pull on this horrid world of real life!

But I must some how wind up this account of flies in the eye & go up to dinner & try to think of some cause of pleasure with Leonard. Something cheerful. Oh but then I must grind on at Proust, I suppose; & then copy out passages. Never mind, I will try my new pen & see if that doesn't cheer me. Because clearly these miseries are very small trivial miseries, & fundamentally I am the happiest woman in all W.C.1. The happiest wife, the happiest writer, the most liked inhabitant, so I say, in Tavistock Square. When I count up my blessings, they must surely amount to more than my sorrows; even when I have all these flies in my eyes.

Well, what am I going to have for dinner? And I will hastily try my new pen on this last page, making it rapidly describe my complete renovation of domestic life—odd, I didn't do it before: that I order dinner no longer; but write it in a book & thus put glass between me & Nelly.

Oh & George [Duckworth] rang up this morning. A French couple who admire me: could I lunch: & my teeth he says, drop out, while I talk, while I eat; & they preferred Brighton to Penshurst.

Tuesday 28 May

It is an odd summer, this one, unexampled perhaps in our history. We are going off to Cassis on Tuesday for a week. This is a revolution. We have never been abroad so late in the year I think. The Election will be over. We shall be governed by a Tory or a Labour party—Tory, I suppose. For the benefit of posterity I may say that nobody pretends to know, with the exception of the candidates. They are all—even Hubert—confident.[13] And I feel, rather oddly, that this is an important election. Walking down the King's Road with Sidney Waterlow the other night—having been to dine at his club off a mahogany table surrounded by the portraits of statesmen—I had a cocktail, but no wine—& it was a thundery day—

12. G. L. Kennedy had been asked in December 1928 to advise on an extension to Monks House; Durrants were the builders asked to estimate the cost. Philcox's estimate was lower, and the building was entrusted to him in April.
13. Hubert Henderson was standing as Liberal candidate for Cambridge University; he was not elected.

Leonard had a headache—& we sat in the ladies reception room—a ducks egg coloured room with globes of light sending their light up, not down— very cool, smooth solid, something like sitting inside a shape of blanc mange—then said Sidney, feeling that something must be done, shall we go & see the Sangers? It was a thing that one ought to do. It would give them such pleasure. And he bought me 3 bunches of violets at the door from a woman who said it was her 40th wedding day: a tribute to my having once been asked in marriage by Sidney was it?— I held them in my hand all the evening, & we found the Sangers out; only a menial man came up from the basement. So we said we will call on the MacCarthys. And so it was that we walked along the King's Road, talking about the Election.[14] Sidney said that human nature has improved. We are all becoming gentler & wiser. Even the dogs are. One never sees a dog fight now he said, & sure enough the big mongrel trotted across the road very peacefully to sniff at the door of a public house. There the story stops. For I dont think much happened at the MacCarthys. One had to talk. I noticed nothing, I think. The memorable things happen when there is a great space of silence all round them perhaps. I dont know.

Now about this book, The Moths. How am I to begin it? And what is it to be? I feel no great impulse; no fever; only a great pressure of difficulty. Why write it then? Why write at all? Every morning I write a little sketch, to amuse myself.[15]

I am not saying, I might say, that these sketches have any relevance. I am not trying to tell a story. Yet perhaps it might be done in that way. A mind thinking. They might be islands of light—islands in the stream that I am trying to convey: life itself going on. The current of the moths flying strongly this way. A lamp & a flower pot in the centre. The flower can always be changing. But there must be more unity between each scene than I can find at present. Autobiography it might be called. How am I to make one lap, or act, between the coming of the moths, more intense than another; if there are only scenes? One must get the sense that this is the beginning: this the middle; that the climax—when she opens the window & the moth comes in. I shall have the two different currents—the moths flying along; the flower upright in the centre; a perpetual crumbling & renewing of the plant. In its leaves she might see things happen. But who is she? I am very anxious that she should have no name. I dont want a

14. The Woolfs dined with Sydney Waterlow at the United University Club, Suffolk Street, off Pall Mall East; the Sangers lived in Oakley Street, Chelsea, and the MacCarthys in Wellington Square, further east along the King's Road.
15. Professor John Graham, in his monumental edition of the holograph drafts of *The Waves* (University of Toronto Press, 1976), does not identify these sketches.

Lavinia or a Penelope: I want 'She'. But that becomes arty, Liberty, greenery yallery somehow: symbolic in loose robes. Of course I can make her think backwards & forwards; I can tell stories. But thats not it. Also I shall do away with exact place & time. Anything may be out of the window—a ship—a desert—London.

Friday 31 May

The oculist said to me this afternoon "Perhaps you're not as young as you were". This is the first time that has been said to me; & it seemed to me an astonishing statement. It means that one now seems to a stranger not a woman, but an elderly woman. Yet even so, though I felt wrinkled & aged for an hour, & put on a manner of great wisdom & toleration, buying a coat, even so, I forget it soon; & am 'a woman' again. Another light on my character or appearance— Coming up Southampton Row, a man snapped me & then said stop; & made me pay 6d for a silly little damp film, which I did not want; nor did I want to stay talking politics to a ferrety little rascal, having had little lunch. But my face marked me for his victim.

"We are winning" Nelly said at tea. I was shocked to think that we both desire the Labour party to win—why? partly that I dont want to be ruled by Nelly. I think to be ruled by Nelly & Lottie would be a disaster. It is dribbled out. Last night at Charleston we heard election results spoken very distinctly in the drawing room. Driving home through Lewes there was not a single light downstairs. No one was even listening in. The streets were perfectly empty. One man was pumpshipping against the station wall. I had imagined a crowd, flares, shouts, white sheets—only three black cats, out on business with the mice. So we shall be ruled by labour.[16]

We went down to Worthing to see Leonard's mother, laid like an old rose—rather lovely this time—in a narrow room; with the sea opposite. I watched the porpoises, & some reflections of people walking on the beach. And she cried; & was very dismal; & then rambled off about Caterham 50 years ago; & the Stannards, & how Herbert had rolled all the way down stairs, & drank so much milk that people were astonished. Nothing of life, as we see it, remains to her—only this curious lit up page

16. The Woolfs were registered as voters in the Lewes constituency, so, going *via* Worthing to visit LW's mother, they drove to Rodmell to vote on 30 May, and returned next day to London. Francis Birrell and Raymond Mortimer were living at Charleston in the Bells' absence, and the Woolfs had driven over after dinner on election day. The results of the General Election were: Labour 287; Conservatives 261; Liberals 59; others 8; in consequence, on 5 June Ramsay MacDonald formed his second Labour Government.

of the past, which she turns over & over lying in bed; & cant read or sleep, yet anxiously demands, does Leonard think she will get well? We had been saying driving down that one should take poison. She has every reason; & yet demands more life, more life, at 78. She quarrels; she cant walk; she is alone; she is looked after by nurses; lives in an hotel, but demands more life, more life. One odd thing she said was that she had slept with a governess as a child who had given her a terrible disease, & been expelled from Holland on that account. I fancy she had never told anyone this; it was her offering of intimacy to us; a thanksgiving perhaps for our having come. I was moved by her; could hardly speak. I suppose human nature, so emotional, so irrational, so instinctive, as it is in her, but not in me, has this beauty; this what they call 'elemental' quality. One may get it too, when one is 76. One may lie sobbing, & yet cry does doctor think I shall recover? One will not perhaps go to the writing table & write that simple & profound paper upon suicide which I see myself leaving for my friends. What a day it was—the sea flowing in & out of the bays, all the way, like the Adriatic, or Pacific; & the sand yellow; & the boats steaming along; & behind the downs like long waves, gently extending themselves, to break very quickly; smooth & sloping like the waves. Even bungalows are all burnt up & made part of this beauty; made of vapour not zinc. We voted at Rodmell. I saw a white gloved lady helping an old farm couple out of her Daimler. We have bought a motor lawn mower. I liked Francis last night. He is so abundant & fertile, so generous & warm hearted A most divine man—a man I adore—these phrases recur. And then he amused me with his imitation of Esther talking like Macaulay [*unexplained*]. When they read the results he was always talking so loud: & had to stop short. We called in on Long Barn & left Pinker, & here we are again after one of these little journeys which seem to have last[ed] 600 years. Everything looks a little strange & symbolical when one comes back. I was in a queer mood, thinking myself very old: but now I am a woman again—as I always am when I write. It is scattering & heatening, this motoring about.

The Woolfs went to Cassis by train via Folkestone-Boulogne-Paris-Marseilles on 4 June; they took rooms in Fontcreuse but meals with Vanessa and Duncan Grant, who drove them to Arles on their homeward journey. They reached home on 14 June.

Saturday 15 June

Home last night from Cassis; that is to say from Arles. The hottest holiday I have ever had. And in some ways different from others; partly

that it was so hot; then that we were alone with Nessa & Duncan; then
that I have become, almost, a landowner. A window owner, anyhow. Yes,
I almost bought La Boudard (& am not sure of the spelling) & have a
contract, to go there at the cost of £2.10 a month.[1] And this means an
infinite number of things—perhaps a complete change; as buying a house
so often does. Already this morning I feel an attachment—say a little
island—floating some way off, but in my possession. And this island means
heat, silence, complete aloofness from London; the sea; eating cakes in
the new hotel at La Ciotat; driving off to Aix; sitting on the harbour dining;
seeing the sardine boats come in; talk with people who have never heard
of me & think me older, uglier than Nessa, & in every way inferior to her;
that odd intimate, yet edgy, happy free yet somehow restrained intercourse
with her & Duncan. It means also buying French books at Toulon &
keeping them in my lovely cool room in the wood; Leonard in his shirt-
sleeves; an Eastern private life for us both; an Indian summer running in &
out of the light of common day; a great deal of cheap wine & cigars; new
alliances, with Currys, Cruthers, & other anomalous oddities[2]—all this
my engagement to make three windows at Boudard means to me.

I forget what the facts of our stay were. We were there for a week,
coming the day before they expected us, oddly enough as we did last year.
There was Duncan in his blue shirt; Angelica & Judith doing lessons on
the terrace. Nessa drove Miss Campbell into the town & brought up the
food every morning. I wrote a little article on Cowper, but lifting the
words with difficulty in the heat, surrounded by black & white butterflies.[3]
And L. & I were very extravagant, for the first time in our lives, buying
desks, tables, sideboards, crockery for Rodmell. This gave me pleasure; &
set my dander up against Nessa's almost overpowering supremacy. My
elder son is coming tomorrow; yes, & he is the most promising young man
in King's; & has been speaking at the Apostles dinner. All I can oppose
that with is, And I made £2,000 out of Orlando & can bring Leonard
here & buy a house if I want. To which she replies (in the same inaudible
way) I am a failure as a painter compared with you, & cant do more than

1. See *IV LW*, p 181: 'we began to buy a villa for ourselves near Fontcreuse; it was
   in fact a small, rather tumbled-down, whitewashed house. But we did not complete
   the purchase.' He saw the practical disadvantages of having three dwellings, and
   the dream evaporated during 1930.
2. English residents at Cassis.
3. Judith, the daughter of Barbara and Nick Bagenal, was born a few weeks before
   Angelica in 1918, and came more than once to Cassis as a companion for her.
   Jean Campbell (d. *c.* 1955?) lived at Fontcreuse with Colonel Teed; they met during
   the war when she had been a nurse. The article was one of those VW was writing
   for the *New York Herald Tribune* (see above, 13 April 1929, n 1).

pay for my models. And so we go on; over the depths of our childhood. Do you remember going down to the town to fetch — which ancient memories Duncan cannot share. He was divinely charming; & praised Nessa too. I put in shred after shred of feeling so that one may compose the salad, & am now running out to get my books from Riley if I can.[4]

VW here begins DIARY XIX.

Saturday 15 June

Against all laws, I am going to make this the first volume of a diary, though as ill luck has it, it is not even the first of the month. But it is the fault of practical life. I can't write any longer in books whose leaves perish. I don't know how to keep them. Here in a bound volume, the year has a chance of life. It can be stood on a shelf.

Pinker has just come home, very fat. And a sense of nothingness rolls about the house; what I call the sense of "Where there is nothing." This is due to the fact that we came back from France last night & are not going round in the mill yet. Time flaps on the mast—my own phrase I think. There are things I ought to do. I ought to correct A Room of one's own: I ought to read & correct the Common Reader. I ought to write several dull silly letters; to gentlemen in Maidstone & Kingston who tell me facts about dahlias; to Sir Philip Sassoon who most unexpectedly sends me, by motor car, his book of travels.[5] But I cant—not for five minutes or so. Time flaps on the mast. And then I see through everything. Perhaps the image ought to have been one that gives an idea of a stream becoming thin: of seeing to the bottom. Lytton once said,—I connect it with a visit to Kew Gardens—that we can only live if we see through illusion. & that reminds me (it is odd by the way, how small a thought is which one cannot express pictorially, as one has been accustomed to thinking it: this saying of Lytton's has always come pictorially, with heat, flowers, grass, summer, & myself walking at Kew) reminds me how the day before we went Lytton came, & we talked about Elizabeth & Essex. This was for the first time. And it was painful, because he minded what we had not said; & we had, to some extent to say it; but it was also a relief, on both sides, because we were glad to say it, & have this reserve over; & glad, I daresay, that Lytton minded; I daresay there was some discreditable element, at least in my

4. R. E. Riley, bookbinder, of 19 Woburn Buildings, Tavistock Square.
5. Sir Philip Sassoon (1888-1939), Under-Secretary of State for Air, 1924-29, in whose company VW had lunched on 25 April as a guest of Sibyl Colefax. His book was *The Third Route, A description of a Voyage to India by Air* (1929).

gladness; yet not much. I daresay, among my disagreeables, is this that I am jealous enough of other writers to be glad when they are made to own their failures; but this was trifling. More important much was the relief that one could say openly that one had disliked E & E for such reasons; & we began to go into them. His suppression of irony; his being tied by the story; the difficulty of using reality imaginatively; a wrong subject for him; could only be treated exactly. He said he had been very doubtful himself; & this is what I liked—that though his surrounders—Carrington Dadie & the rest—all praised, he himself felt, he was not pleased unless we Bloomsbury, praised too. What we said mattered. And I daresay, owing to success, he minds these reservations a great deal more than I should; for I kept thinking of all the criticism I had had. One is pleased when 'after long yea[r]s' such feelings have sway.[6] And I felt, among the discreditable feelings, how I had no longer anything to envy him for; & how, dashing off Orlando I had done better than he had done; & how for the first time I think, he thought of me, as a writer, with some envy. Yet he amused me by protesting that to write like that would be to write like Virginia—a fatal event, it seems.

Now time must not flap on the mast any more. Now I must somehow brew another decoction of illusion. Well, if the human interest flags—if its that that worries me, I must not sit thinking about it here. I must make human illusion—ask someone in tomorrow after dinner; & begin that astonishing adventure with the souls of others again—about which I know so little. Is it affection that prompts?

Sunday 16 June

As I finished those words, in came Leonard to say that Desmond was coming round in two minutes—which he did, so that the sail filled out again & the ship went on. (The reason why I write this is that I cannot go on correcting A Room of one's own. I have read till my own sentences jingle in my ear—& so I begin to make more). Desmond was shabby & baggy in grey. He was bubbling & simmering, off to dine with Crompton Davies at Kettner's, & determined to be punctual.[7] A vein of determination lies in him; & he is the most cooked & saturated of us all. Not an atom remains crude; basted richly over a slow fire—an adorable man, a divine

6. Cf Byron's *When we Two parted*.
7. Crompton Llewelyn Davies (1868-1935), one of Margaret Llewelyn Davies's six brothers, had been at Trinity College, Cambridge, and was an Apostle; he was now a partner in a firm of solicitors, and lived in Gledhow Gardens, South Kensington. Kettner's was (and is) a restaurant in Church (now Romilly) Street, Soho.

man, as Francis would say, for all his power of taking the spine out of me. Happily we did not get on to that—writing that is to say. Julian broke down in his Apostle speech; came dressed as for a ball, & got muddled in his notes & sat down; but with his admirable Stephen solidity did not mind. Also Desmond lost £5 to Lord Rothermere, & another man lost £2,000, over the Election. What circles you live in, said Leonard; & he said that this was only due to the Empire Review. Maynard he said looked as if he were conscious of discord at the Apostle dinner.[8] We talked of Lytton's books. But talk ran into talk; nothing could be spread out; he must not be late for Crompton. He (C.) lives in Gledhow Terrace, with two leather chairs in the dining room; behind it his bedroom; he has his Virgil & a Milton that Desmond gave him. My Milton, said Leonard; & I offered to give Desmond a new despatch box. Off he went talking all the way. And Pinker came back &—

Sunday 23 June

It was very hot that day, driving to Worthing to see Leonard's mother, my throat hurt me. Next morning I had a headache. So we stayed on at Rodmell till today. At Rodmell I read through the Common Reader; & this is very important—I must learn to write more succinctly. Especially in the general idea essays like the last, How it strikes a Contemporary, I am horrified by my own looseness. This is partly that I dont think things out first; partly that I stretch my style to take in crumbs of meaning. But the result is a wobble & diffusity & breathlessness which I detest. One must correct A room of one's own very carefully before printing. And so I pitched into my great lake of melancholy. Lord how deep it is! What a born melancholiac I am! The only way I keep afloat is by working. A note for the summer I must take more work than I can possibly get done. ⟨I am⟩—no, I dont   Aug. 31st This vow I kept know what it comes from. Directly I stop working I feel that I am sinking down, down. And as usual, I feel that if I sink further I shall reach the truth. That is the only mitigation; a kind of nobility. Solemnity. I shall make myself face the fact that there is nothing—nothing for any of us. Work, reading, writing are all disguises; & relations with people. Yes, even having children would be useless.

We went into the beechwood by the Race Course. I like these woods; & the waters of the greenery closing over one; so shallow, with the sun on

8. The Apostles' dinner had taken place while LW was in France. The April and May issues of the *Empire Review* had predicted a Conservative victory in the General Election of 30 May 1929.

them; then so deep in the shade. And I like the beech boughs, laced about, very intricate; like many arms; & the trunks, like the stone pillars in a church. But if I were Mrs Bartholomew I should certainly do something violent. This thought kept coming to me. What though could one do, at the bottom of that weight[?]; with that incubus of injustice on top of one? Annie Thompsett & her baby live on 15/ a week. I throw away 13/- on cigarettes, chocolates, & bus fares. She was eating rice pudding by the baby's cradle when I came in.[9]

However, I now begin to see the Moths rather too clearly, or at least strenuously, for my comfort. I think it will begin like this: dawn; the shells on a beach; I dont know—voices of cock & nightingale; & then all the children at a long table—lessons. The beginning. Well, all sorts of characters are to be there. Then the person who is at the table can call out any one of them at any moment; & build up by that person the mood, tell a story; for instance about dogs or nurses; or some adventure of a childs kind; all to be very Arabian nights; & so on: this shall be Childhood; but it must not be my childhood; & boats on the pond; the sense of children; unreality; things oddly proportioned. Then another person or figure must be selected. The unreal world must be round all this—the phantom waves. The Moth must come in: the beautiful single moth. There must be a flower growing.

Could one not get the waves to be heard all through? Or the farmyard noises? Some odd irrelevant noises. She might have a book—one book to read in—another to write in—old letters.

Early morning light—but this need not be insisted on; because there must be great freedom from 'reality'. Yet everything must have relevance.

Well all this is of course the 'real' life; & nothingness only comes in the absence of this. I have proved this quite certainly in the past half hour. Everything becomes green & vivified in me when I begin to think of the Moths. Also, I think, one is much better able to enter into other's—

Sunday 30 June

I broke off; somebody I imagine interrupted. My melancholy has been broken, like a lake by oars, since I wrote. I have been so active. We have seen so many people. Last night we dined with Roger, tonight with Clive; Lytton came; Vita came; we had a party. I brought a dress in Shaftesbury Avenue. It was very hot, I think; & is now cold, indeed, for the first time for weeks, it is, or has been raining. I am writing idly, to solace my eyes

9. Annie, who was to become the Woolfs' cook and domestic at Monks House, was a daughter of the Mrs Thomsett who had sometimes worked for them in earlier years.

after two hours of intense correction—that much corrected book, Women & Fiction. It shall go to the printer tomorrow I swear. And then I can bask entirely in the light of some fiction. But I have written myself out of that mood, & find it difficult to get back to it. This last half year I made over £1800; almost at the rate of £4000 a year; the salary almost of a Cabinet minister; & time was, two years ago, when I toiled to make £200. Now I am overpaid I think for my little articles— And I still think that the great pleasure of prosperity is to be able to go into a shop & buy a pocket knife. Well, after tomorrow I shall close down article writing, & give way to fiction for six or seven months—till next March perhaps. And I here record my intention to see to the writing of this new book much more carefully; to strike out redundancies. Now that I have, I think, gained the free use of my pen, I must begin to curb it. Hitherto my freedom has had to be fought for.

Helen Anrep last night was distracted & worried, like a wet overblown Rose. Baba got out of her bed & went on the roof & fell asleep there. So Miss Cox proposes to put her down into a lower class for a year. And Roger had news that her Hampstead House was falling down; would need £500 spent on it. And how could she live on the income of £3,000 if she sold it to the Hampstead Hospital?[10] The other day in Paris she thought she was going to have a child by Roger. "And I've failed utterly with the children I have—And I feel a hundred." So she plained & crooned, sitting beside Roger, with her hand on the arm of his chair. Sometimes he put his hand on hers. They were affectionate & private; this is Roger's private life. And it keeps him happy, while superficially he whirls from doctor to doctor; & springs & spins, & looks out places on the map—unable not to verify & track down any statement, however pointless. He told us how in some great French cave, there is a patch of green vegetation wherever the torchlight has fallen. And Mauron ran his hand along a ledge & thought it was moss. But it was bats dung. The bats fly up into the air.

Desmond is being very brilliant about the Byron letters & the Boswell papers. Think! There are 18 volumes of Boswell's diaries now to be published. With any luck I shall live to read them. I feel as if some dead

10. Anastasia (Baba) Anrep was the elder of Boris and Helen Anrep's two children; she was a boarder at Hayes Court School, near Bromley, of which Miss Catherine Cox was headmistress. (It was at this school that VW had given a lecture on 30 January 1926 (see Headnote, 1926), when she was driven there by Mary Hutchinson whose daughter was also a pupil.) Baba's punishment was commuted from a year to a term. Helen had left her husband and her house in Pond Street (adjacent to the then Hampstead General Hospital) to live with Roger Fry at 42 Bernard Street, WC1.

person were said to be living after all—an odd effect, this disinterment of a mass more of Boswell when one had thought all was known, all settled. And father never knew; & Sir Edmund Gosse is dead. These papers were in a cabinet in Ireland.[11]

And now it is almost time for lunch; & after lunch I must again read my book; with a view, if possible, to shortening & condensing the last pages.

The Woolfs spent each week-end in July at Rodmell, and on 27th moved there for ten weeks' respite from the metropolitan 'helter skelter'. VW had been suffering intermittently from headaches and depression. Ka Arnold-Foster came to Monks House for the night of 4 August.

Monday 5 August

Yes that is the date, & the last was June 30th—a tribute to the helter skelter random rackety summer I spent. Far the pleasantest memories, standing out like green weed on some civet grey pond, were the week ends here: the divine fresh week ends, with the hay cutting & the lights lambent; Leonard's new room, Hedgehog Hall a-building, & my lodge being made into the palace of comfort which it now is. For I am now sitting here, oppressed by the Bank holiday atmosphere which gets into the wild country air, the lonely marshes, & makes the village seem smug & suburban. The girls & men are playing stool ball; Leonard & Percy are making a pipe conduct water into the Pond. It is a chocolate brown, & lived in by small fish. Yes it was a scattered summer; I felt as if the telephone were strung to my arm & anybody could jerk me who liked. A sense of interruption bothered me. And then these people one 'sees'—how blurred the image becomes! What damp blotting paper my mind was, as I left Ottoline's on Thursday afternoon, & determined not to speak to another soul. There is a sort of irreverence in treating thus the venerable soul of man: one curses it, & bites it & gets embittered by it. More pleasure is to be had from one nights talk with old dunderheaded Ka than from these flittering &

11. Desmond MacCarthy, in reviewing a new edition of James Boswell's *The Hypo-chondriac* in his 'World of Books' column in the *Sunday Times* of 30 June, wrote: 'I used to think that when the Great Book was opened in the Valley of Jehoshaphat, it would be the entries under the head "Byron" which would contain fewest surprises for us, but apparently it is Boswell who after all has succeeded most triumphantly in anticipating the Day of Judgment.' Boswell's private papers discovered at Malahide Castle, near Dublin, in 1925-26, were issued in a privately printed and costly limited edition in eighteen volumes between 1928-34—the first six edited by Geoffrey Scott.

glitterings. In London I should only have girded at her. Here, spreading herself out in her slow heavy footed way one took in an easy half critical, half appreciative impression—the chief element being amusement at her protestations. When the story was not to her credit as a social centre, it was to his as a speaker, politician, gardener, artist, husband, thinker—everything. Indeed I cut her short this morning, as she exalted his brain, by saying we all live on illusion; Will's brain is one of them. Thus pulled up she jibbed a moment, & then recovered, & saw the sense; not quite, perhaps; but in her slow way, larded over with these shams & gentilities & politics & appearances, she is honest too. And we talked about Rupert. But my reflection—every visit leaves one with a reflection—was this, about talking in protest, to impress, its futility, its universality: only she is more open & insistent, for some reason, than we are—or so I hope. Take away that motive from one's talk, & how much would be left? How often don't I vaguely feel blessing my sentence, the face of my own vanity, which demands that I shall pay it this tribute.

And then I'm cross with Vita: she never told me she was going abroad for a fortnight—didnt dare; till the last moment, when she said it was a sudden plan.[1] Lord Lord! I am half amused though; why do I mind? what do I mind? how much do I mind? I shall fire up & accuse her, & see to the bottom of her vessel. One of the facts is that these Hildas are a chronic case; & as this one won't disappear & is unattached, she may be permanent. And, like the damned intellectual snob I am, I hate to be linked, even by an arm, with Hilda. Her earnest aspiring competent wooden face appears before me, seeking guidance in the grave question of who's to broadcast. A queer trait in Vita—her passion for the earnest middle-class intellectual, however drab & dreary. And why do I write this down? I have not even told Leonard; & whom do I tell when I tell a blank page? The truth is, I get nearer feelings in writing than in walking [sic]—I think: graze the bone; enjoy the expression; have them out of me; make them a little creditable to myself; I daresay suppress something, so that after all I'm doing what amounts to confiding. Why did Pepys write his diary after all?

I should be tackling Mary Wollstonecraft. I am in the thick of my four Herald articles,[2] thus cutting into my Moths (but I had proofs of A Room to correct) & hope to be quit of it all by August 14th & then go down step by step into that queer region. I must make a great try for it—for this

1. On 16 July Vita had gone for a walking holiday in the Val d'Isère with Hilda Matheson (1888-1940), first Director of Talks for the BBC, who had become one of her intimate friends.

2. The articles commissioned by the *New York Herald Tribune*; see above, 13 April 1929, n 1.

difficult book—& after that? Always adventure: with that sense to guide me, I shant stagnate anyhow.

You can choose between us, I say, stopping writing; & get some satisfaction from making up caustic phrases. Yet I'm not very caustic, only by starts.

Thursday 8 August

This is written to while away one of those stupendous moments—one of those painful, ridiculous, agitating moments which make one half sick & yet I dont know—I'm excited too; & feel free

Another scene, Aug. 30th; but these reflections stood me in good stead—& I laughed. But what a confounded bore it is

& then sordid; & unsettled; & so on—I've told Nelly to go; after a series of scenes which I wont bore myself to describe. And in the midst of the usual anger, I looked into her little shifting greedy eyes, & saw nothing but malice & spite there, & felt that that had come to be the reality now: she doesn't care for me, or for anything: has been eaten up by her poor timid servants fears & cares & respectabilities. And so at lunch L. & I settled it; & I spoke two words, which she almost pulled out of my mouth in her eagerness to show herself delighted & eager & hard & untouched—a sordid painful scene after 15 years; but then how many I have had, & how degrading they are. & if we dont break now we drift on endlessly—oh but all these old arguments I know by heart. Whats new & strange is to have made an end of it, for though we only speak of her staying away till October, I dont think we shall ever begin again. This is an occasion for some of the small virtues of life—cheerfulness, & decision, & the determination to start fresh & better. In truth we never should have gone on, I daresay, if it hadn't been for the war; I dont know: I'm confirmed in my wish to have no resident servants ever again. That is the evil which rots the relationship. But now I must go to Annie Thomsett again.

Saturday 10 August[3]

Well, Heaven be praised; it is all over & calm & settled. Nelly—how long ago that seems!—is staying—Yes, we found we cdnt get Mrs Thomsett; & I had two minutes of energetic courage; & so, Nelly saying, she thought—but I'm too bored. And I'm too deliciously relieved to have seen Vita this moment & find that her story to me was precisely true—& she brought documents to prove it—& was very upset—& had gone

3. VW has mis-dated this entry *Saturday Aug 9th.*

like a donkey & telephoned to Hilda—who is also very upset, & was altogether so simple & sincere & saw that my position was reasonable—oh yes, she could not have stood it a moment—but why, I ask myself, does it bore me so insufferably to write down what is so acutely exciting at the moment? My own lack of narrative power. Indeed I was more worried & angry & hurt & caustic about this affair than I let on, even to the blank page; yet afraid too of exaggeration. Of course, one is right about Nelly—right that she is, in bad moods almost insufferably mean, selfish & spiteful; but—& this is an interesting psychological remark, she is in a state of nature; untrained; uneducated, to me almost incredibly without the power of analysis or logic; so that one sees a human mind wriggling undressed—which is interesting; & then, in the midst of one's horror at the loathesome spectacle, one is surprised by the goodness of human nature, undressed; & it is more impressive because of its undress. For example, she thought I had given her notice permanently; but instead of giving way, —& yet she had nowhere to go to—to rage or spite, she bicycled into Lewes to get us cream for dinner: the motive being genuine I think; we must not suffer; & how could she leave us without a cook? It is this mixture that one can't understand; & that makes one always plunge so heavily in dealing with her. She said too that she would find it very difficult to get a place; since it is all the fashion now to engage cooks only who will live out (& this sentence is another example of my inability to write narrative). And it will happen again, her spite & meanness; but we shan't part now, I think. And I'm half pleased to find that it is harder to part after 15 years than I thought. And I'm pleased—oh very pleased—about Vita.

Thursday 15 August

These tumults over, then I had a headache. And two ideas come to me—to break my rule & write about the soul for once; & to write some exact dialogue: I just note this, it being dinner time.

We are back from Brighton where I brought a corner cupboard. And if I had time, I would here dissect a curious little spotted fruit: this melancholy. It comes with headache, of course. And I had come to the blind alley —the cul de-sac. Writing this compressed article, where every word is like a step cut in the rock—hard work, if ever writing was; & done largely for money; & whats money, compared with Nessa's children; & then the—

Monday 19 August

I suppose dinner interrupted. And I opened this book in another train of mind—to record the blessed fact that for good or bad I have just set the last correction to Women & Fiction, or a Room of One's Own. I shall never read it again I suppose. Good or bad? Has an uneasy life in it I think: you feel the creature arching its back & galloping on, though as usual much is watery & flimsy & pitched in too high a voice.

William Plomer has been for the week end & gone. A compressed inarticulate young man, thickly coated with a universal manner fit for all weather & people: tells a nice dry prim story; but has the wild eyes which I once noted in Tom, & take to be the true index of what goes on within. Once or twice he almost cracked his crust—sitting on the stones this morning for instance.

I dont suppose you know how separate I feel myself from all my contemporaries. I am afraid I was very inadequate last night (at Charleston). I apologised for the family party. No that was delightful; except that Clive Bell seemed inharmonious. What d'you think of Wyndham Lewis, of Joyce ?[4] (V.) I dont like scolds. It spoils the voice. I like old men of 80 like Moore & Yeats who have kept their minds working. "Exactly. That's the precise point" (these are William's words). And fathers are difficult. Mine has no interest in anything. But I dont live at Pinner for choice. I dislike Roy Campbell's pose.[5] He used to fly a kite at the end of a fishing rod. William (he said the Mr was awkward) is notably trying to be like other people: to justify his life among natives & colonels, which has given him this composure. Beside him Julian seemed a mere child, & Duncan a contemporary. May he bring Butts to see us?[6] He is a very self-contained independent young man, determined not to be rushed in any way, & having no money at all, he gave Nelly 5/ for a tip. I think he shows up well against the Raymonds & the Frankies—is somehow solid; to their pinchbeck lustre.

I have now written myself out of a writing mood; & cannot attack melancholy, save only to note that it was much diminished by hearing Nessa say she was often melancholy & often envied me—a statement I

4. The Woolfs took Plomer to dine at Charleston on Sunday. The family party felt inclined to apologise to Plomer on VW's behalf: by declaring that this shy and modest poet claimed descent from both Shakespeare and William Blake she made everyone feel ill at ease. (See *II QB*, p 149.) Percy Wyndham Lewis (1882-1957) the aggressive, contentious writer and artist; and James Joyce (1882-1941) were both VW's exact coevals.

5. William Plomer had known the poet Roy Campbell and his wife Mary in South Africa; he and Campbell had collaborated in the production of *Voorslag*, a magazine intended to serve as a lash or goad to the 'mental hindquarters' of South Africa's 'bovine citizenry'; see Chapter 17, *The Autobiography of William Plomer* (1975).

6. Anthony Butts (1900-1941), an old-Etonian painter with whom Plomer formed a deep and close friendship.

thought incredible. I have spilt myself among too many stools she said (we were sitting in her bedroom before dinner). Other peoples melancholy certainly cheers one. And now, having written my four little brief hard articles, I must think of that book again, & go down step by step into the well. These are the great events & revolutions in one's life—& then people talk of war & politics. I shall grind very hard; all my brakes will be stiff; my springs rusty. But I have now earned the right to some months of fiction. & my melancholy is brushed away, so soon as I can get my mind forging ahead, not circling round.

Wednesday 21 August

Geoffrey Scott died last week of pneumonia in New York. Let me think what I can remember of him. I met him first in 1909 at Florence at Mrs Berenson's. We went out for lunch, & he was there; & they discussed Francis Thompson. Afterwards we went to a party at Mrs Ross's: Mary came in with a brother, both disguised as Barnes, & had to reveal themselves as Stracheys before Mrs Ross would take any interest. Then she emphasised the fact that she was Meredith's mistress, leading us all down a lawn; —a terrace I suppose, overlooking Fiesole. I was unhappy that summer, & bitter in all my judgments; & cannot remember anything of Geoffrey Scott save that he was part of that unnatural Florentine society; & therefore in my mood, rather contemptible— long & familiar & aesthetic & at his ease, where I was rustic, provincial & badly dressed.[7] This impression then waits without a second till that summer evening, in 1925, I think, at Long Barn.[8] I had motored down with Dotty & Vita for my first visit & had sat shyly in the motor observing their endearments rather awkwardly, & how they stopped the Rolls Royce to buy great baskets of strawberries; & again I felt, not provincial, but ill-dressed, under-equipped; & so stepped on to the terrace at Long Barn; & forth came Geoffrey, smiling a little superciliously, as of old; & shook hands. Harold [Nicolson] was behind him, much more downright & burly & to my taste. That night we sat in

7. Geoffrey Scott, who died on 16 August, aged 46, had once been assistant to Bernard Berenson, the authority on Italian painting, at his villa *i Tatti* outside Florence; Berenson's neighbour, and a close friend of his wife Mary (*née* Pearsall Smith, the mother of Rachel and Karin Costelloe), was the formidable Janet Ross, *née* Duff-Gordon (1842-1927), who had lived in Italy since 1867; she was the model for more than one of Meredith's heroines, and wrote many books herself. (See Appendix II for VW's description of her.) Mary Hutchinson's mother, a cousin of Lytton Strachey's, married Sir Hugh Barnes; the brother was James Strachey Barnes. Francis Thompson (1859-1907), poet.
8. The year was in fact 1924. See *II VW Diary*, 5 July 1924.

the long room, & after Harold had grown sleepy sitting on the fender knocking his head against the fringe of the Italian cover on the mantelpice, Geoffrey sat with us, & was drawn by Dotty into telling stories for my amusement. He did this very well; I remember, though I dont remember what the stories were about. He was a very clever man, I thought; & I tried to place him, & concluded that he had some grudge against me as member of a circle he somehow respected but was not of; told me, I remember, that he could not distinguish an article by me in the Nation from one by Morgan or Lytton—we all wrote the same ironic style—& that I felt was said by way of showing me—& we were the two scallywags at that particular party—that he was up to our little ways & had no respect for them. Then next day we went over Knole, where again, as at Florence, he was very much at his ease, & knew every piece of furniture or silver & called Lord Sackville Lionel as if he had known him & Vita familiarly many years, just as he had known the Rosses & the Berensons. And he was tall, & dark & had the distinguished face of a failure; reminded me a little of Bernard Holland & other 'brilliant' young men,[9] who remain 'brilliant' & young well into the 40ties & never do anything to prove it. Harold walked back through the Park to think out some speech about Byron, simply & straightforwardly, rather to my & I think Geoffrey's amusement. The others—Dotty Vita & Geoffrey—took me to the station; & I said goodbye to him there, & never spoke to him again. I had the feeling that he & Dotty & Vita & Harold were all a set; very intimate & familiar, & indeed said so, when they challenged me, as usual, with Blooms-bury & its closed walls. "But you are the same—you make me feel that you are all very intimate" I said, & they half denied it; but only half. For, as I learnt later, I had broken in upon the height of his affair with Vita. It was flaming very strongly that particular month, or week; it was the time when she returned his passion, for a moment; when he was swearing that she must leave Harold & live with him. After that, my intercourse with him was only by hearsay—through messages—Karin said her mother wished her to arrange a meeting between Geoffrey & me —& then through Vita's explanations, later, when she told me how he was waiting for her, had left his Villa Medici & Lady Sybil on her account;[10] & was now fuming in a mews off Regent's Park expecting her while she sat at Tavistock Square talking to me. One night, she said, he almost strangled her—seized her by the throat; & she turned black & he was

9. See below, note 12.
10. Geoffrey Scott had in 1918 married the widowed Lady Sibyl Cutting who owned the Villa Medici, Fiesole; his love affair with Vita Sackville-West began in the autumn of 1923 and lasted with considerable intensity for a little less than a year.

frightened. And I heard how furious he was on the downs above Rodmell that summer, late at night, when they were driving home, from Lady Sackville I suppose. Vita saw lights in the valley & said that I was down there asleep. Whereupon he flew into another rage—they were calling the dogs who had gone hunting, & the wind blew his hat off. He called me 'that woman'. And I saw him, in full evening dress, at the ballet with Sybil [Colefax]. And then never again.

He is dead in New York, & all those papers about Boswell—what will become of them; & the life that was to have made him immortal will never be written; & he remains the brilliant young man for ever.[11]

> I was offered
> £2000 to write it

And I have turned over two pages by mistake. Perhaps I can think of some other figure to write in there, going backwards, before I need go in: & it is a lovely evening; & I want to stay out here writing, & trying my new pen.

Nobody has died, to my knowledge, of much interest. And if it comes to putting down talk, the truth is that, except in novels, people don't talk.

Well, Bernard Holland, as I have mentioned him.[12] But I cannot put my hand on any first meeting or even second. I believe I first heard him mentioned when I was say ten years old; & he had just become engaged to Helen Duckworth. Stella said to mother, "But can they know what he thinks then?"—or words which made me surmise that there was something dark & queer about this young man; something that to Stella seemed incongruous with the rusticity & conventionality of her Duckworth aunt & uncle. Then that little light, revealing as it was, goes out; & there is only hearsay about Bernard till, in 1902 or 3 perhaps, Dorothea took me uninvited to stay at Canterbury with Canon Holland;[13] & there was Bernard; & he was saturnine, with his great eyebrows almost meeting; & his sunk cheeks; & his gloom; & his height; & about him there hung, now more authentically, that reputation for brilliance & strangeness that was his, years ago, at Cambridge. Poor old Bernard—he's a genius, I once

11. At the time of his death Geoffrey Scott had been engaged in editing the Boswell papers, see above 30 June 1929, n 11. For the offer in the marginal postscript, see below, 1 March 1930.
12. Bernard Henry Holland (1856-1926), son of Rev. F. J. Holland, Canon of Canterbury, and his wife Mary Sibylla, née Lyall; educated at Eton and Trinity College, Cambridge, called to the Bar in 1882. He was private secretary to the Duke of Devonshire 1892-94 and to the Secretary of State for the Colonies 1903-8 and served as secretary to various Royal Commissions 1891-1908. In 1895 he married Florence Helen Duckworth, a cousin of VW's half-sister Stella Duckworth.
13. Dorothea Jane Stephen (1871-1965), youngest child of Sir James Fitzjames Stephen, and VW's cousin.

heard Harry Stephen say. He interested me because I imputed to him 'imagination'—the quality I most admired & missed most in my father & his agnostic friends. Bernard had edited his mother's letters, & I liked them in a sentimental way, seeing in them something imaginative, too; something that was coloured & pensive & intimate, unlike anything the Stephen family produced.[14] So that I looked at Bernard in the low room under the Cathedral with interest, & even hoped he might think me clever or imaginative or something. But I doubt that he detached me from the shadow of Dorothea. He was occupied & mysterious, in touch with politics & Cabinet ministers; highly thought of by the Lytteltons, & vaguely credited with being himself much more able & capable than they were; but he was too much of a genius, too queer & individual, so people said, to do anything for himself. And Helen played up to this version of Bernard very femininely; wandering about vague eyed, cherry cheeked, ecstatic, religious; like some woman I thought in a novel by Charlotte Yonge.[15] We were taken to see a sister of Mary Sibylla's, & she said, clasping her tea cup, that whenever she heard thunder she imagined that someone had been killed by it. There was all that kind of imagination afloat. Bernard stalked about in it, aloof, intellectual, silent; appreciative perhaps, but never said so. Helen played little melancholy scraps of Beethoven; which moved me; but Bernard snapped "Whats that? Gilbert & Sullivan?" to snub her sentimentality I suppose. And then, when there was talk of going back in the train together, he stopped it. He said that he must be alone & work. So I suppose I made no impression; & received one that was not altogether favourable. A sort of false gloom was his I thought; unless indeed he were tremendously imaginative. I read a book he wrote anonymously about becoming a Roman Catholic & got a faint seductive whiff of a world where people were very brilliant & thought about their souls; a semi-worldly world it seemed; rather fluent; rather too clear & plausible & pensive, but still attractive & unfamiliar. And then again I met him at Ottoline's; & then I was older, & he was more pronounced. That is he was still sardonic; cavernous; but no longer so lean, or so silent. He flirted, even I could see, with Ottoline; & had become one of those distinguished young men who are very brilliant when they dine out—like Herbert Paul perhaps;[16] they appear without

---

14. *Letters of Mary Sibylla.* Selected and edited by her son, Bernard Holland (1898).
15. The Lytteltons were a large aristocratic family with influence and connections in Church and State—part in fact of the Ruling Class. Charlotte M. Yonge (1823-1901), the prolific writer whose popular romances purvey a highly religious view of life.
16. Herbert Woodfield Paul (1853-1935) had been President of the Oxford Union, a Liberal MP, and then settled down as a Civil Service Commissioner and a writer

their wives, who are deaf or mad; influence politics; write unsigned articles; & flirt with ladies of title. Ottoline told me that Bernard had written her a sonnet, after another dinner party. And then he turned Roman Catholic. He wrote a vast life of the Duke of Devonshire; he wrote a vast history of the Holland family;[17] but that was all that came of his gloom & his imagination & his genius, & when he died, a year or two ago, even his friends never wrote to the Times about him.

Thursday 22 August

And so I might fill up the half hour before dinner writing.

I thought, on my walk that I would begin at the beginning: I get up at half past eight & walk across the garden. Today it was misty & I had been dreaming of Edith Sitwell. I wash & go into breakfast which is laid on the check table cloth. With luck I may have an interesting letter; today there was none. And then bath & dress; & come out here & write or correct for three hours, broken at 11 by Leonard with Milk, & perhaps newspapers. At one luncheon—rissoles today & chocolate custard. A brief reading & smoking after lunch; & at about two I change into thick shoes, take Pinker's lead & go out—up to Asheham hill this afternoon, where I sat a minute or two, & then home again, along the river. Tea at four, about; & then I come out here & write several letters, interrupted by the Post, with another invitation to lecture; & then I read one book of the Prelude. And soon the bell will ring, & we shall dine & then we shall have some music, & I shall smoke a cigar; & then we shall read—La Fontaine I think tonight & the papers—& so to bed. Here I will copy some lines I want to remember,

> The matter that detains us now may seem,
> To many, neither dignified enough
> Nor arduous, yet will not be scorned by them,
> Who, looking inward, have observed the ties
> That bind the perishable hours of life
> Each to the other, & the curious props
> By which the world of memory & thought
> Exists & is sustained.

---

of biography and history. He was married to a sister-in-law of Lady Ritchie, VW's 'Aunt Anny'.
17. *The Life of Spencer Compton, 8th Duke of Devonshire* (2 vols. 1911), and *The Lancashire Hollands ... With illustrations and pedigrees* (1917). In 1923 he published *Belief and Freedom*, a popular argument on behalf of Roman Catholicism.

They are from the 7th book of the Prelude.[18] A very good quotation I think.

But my skeleton day needs reviving with all sorts of different colours. Today it was grey & windy on the walk; yesterday generous & open; a yellow sun on the corn; & heat in the valley. Both days differ greatly; both are among the happiest of my life—I mean among the happy undistinguished days, ripe & sweet & sound; the daily bread; for nothing strange or exalted has happened; only the day has gone rightly & harmoniously; a pattern of the best part of life which is in the country like this; & makes me wish to command more of them—months of them.

Now my little tugging & distressing book & articles are off my mind my brain seems to fill & expand & grow physically light & peaceful. I begin to feel it filling quietly after all the wringing & squeezing it has had since we came here. And so the unconscious part now expands; & walking I notice the red corn, & the blue of the plain & an infinite number of things without naming them; because I am not thinking of any special thing. Now & again I feel my mind take shape, like a cloud with the sun on it, as some idea, plan, or image wells up, but they travel on, over the horizon, like clouds, & I wait peacefully for another to form, or nothing—it matters not which.

One picture I saw—Phil Burne Jones sitting in the square of St Mark's, in evening dress, alone one August night in 1912—for we were on our honeymoon. He looked dissipated & lonely, like a pierrot who had grown old & rather peevish. He wore a light overcoat & sat, his foolish nervous white face looking aged & set unhappy & eager & disillusioned, alone at a little marble table, while everyone else paraded or chattered & the band played—he had no companion—none of his smart ladies—nobody to chatter to, in his affected exaggerated voice; paying astonishing compliments, using dears & darlings & going into that once fashionable whinny of laughter which must I think have come down from Burne Jones himself —& Phil was a kind of dissipated degenerate, spending all the thousands that were paid for those wan women on staircases, on love affairs, on luxuries, on being a fashionable bachelor & fairy God father to the Trees & Taylors & other fashionable young ladies—a very timid conventional man at bottom, with a horrid taste in pictures, presumably, but a way with children. Lowell noticed that at St Ives. And I am still grateful for pictures that he drew for us. He belongs to the gallery of brilliant young men of 50, for he died a year or two ago.[19]

18. Wordsworth's *Prelude* (1850 version) Book VII, 458-466.
19. Philip Burne-Jones (1861-1926) succeeded his father Edward, the pre-Raphaelite artist, as 2nd Baronet in 1898; an un-serious painter with a gift for caricature, he

The best part of my walk this afternoon was certainly on the top of the down leading to Juggs Corner.

Yes, yes, but that is days ago. I saw a woman in white sitting against soft snow banks of blue & white sky; & a child in blue: I saw all the downs glooming & brightening. But it is now

Monday 2 September

& I am writing these words because Lyn (yes, she is Lyn) is reading in the garden, & I am talk-dried, & cant begin the Moths as I should, or patch up finally those old articles.[1] A long day it was yesterday—rather exhausting —hard work talking to someone one hardly knows in the orchard. A very nice young woman, with that essential bareness—I cant think of the word—that young women so often have—without illusions, about herself; an honesty bred of poverty. Keeping going on £200 a year in London which she earns. Pays her way week by week on articles; & her father has £600 as a presbyterian minister in Aberdeen, & will have £400 to retire on, & has 5 children. So that she will never have a penny of her own. All this breeds a kind of veracity & clear sightedness & austerity which I prefer, perhaps, to the lush undergrowth which surrounds Dotty. One gardener more or less, one persian pot more or less, what does it matter— her life is crowded & otiose; but Lyn knows every object in her room, & has saved up & bought them by saving so that they are exact & polished. Well, but of her? Oh I'm so sick of talk, & analysis.

This book would form in me could I let my mind lie asleep, calm like a tideless sea; but all this time I'm breaking my mind up; destroying the growth underneath. Never mind, after tomorrow when I go to Vita, solitude begins.* I shall ruminate for a month. Lyn has this austerity. She is direct & sensible, goes to the W.C. frankly; but is not sexually

* This was a sanguine guess—not fulfilled

---

led a frivolous social life as a man about town. The 'wan women on staircases' is an allusion to his father's painting of 1872-80 in the Tate Gallery, 'The Golden Stairs'. The Trees were the three vivacious daughters of Sir Herbert Beerbohm Tree; and the Taylors, Viola and Una, the granddaughters of Sir Henry Taylor (see above, 10 November 1928, n 12). James Russell Lowell (1819-1891), poet and man of letters, was American Ambassador in London, 1880-85, and in effect, VW's godfather.

1. Lyn Lloyd Irvine (1901-1973) had got to know the Woolfs as a result of her submitting poetry to the N & A and a novel to the Hogarth Press; though he did not publish it, LW thought well enough of her writing to invite her to contribute reviews to the N & A. Enid Welsford (below), a lecturer in English at Newnham, was a friend of hers.

advanced I should say; has had no indulgences with young men or wine; has something cool headed & sensible about her, derived from her theological father, her Scots farmer birth no doubt. She has been trained in English literature & is, what young women so seldom are, or were, a trained critic. She gives her opinion precisely & methodically, rather as Janet Vaughan would do on a case. (Janet was here last week end, by the way.) This trained mind is new & rather strange. It seems to eliminate enthusiasm, perhaps too drastically. Its odd to find everything weighed & criticised. & words of sobriety & insight issuing from this innocent round pink face; these candid blue eyes. She will spend money on face powder—went to buy a special brand & bought a cactus instead. Oh & she told a story about the dead man on the sands. She & Enid Welsford were motoring. One night they came to a bay & Enid wanted to walk to a long stretch of sand. So they went; & Lyn saw a coat & a pair of boots in the sand; & found it was a dead man. She stopped & went back, giving Enid the slip, not thinking that children might find it; absolutely horrified; her first sight of a dead person. This was made vivid to me. Enid came back. Did you see something? Yes I saw it. So they told the villagers. The man had been unhappily married & had seemed depressed & so killed himself, to be found that sad grey night—his boots sticking out of the sand, the face I suppose very ghastly.

I have just read a page or two of Samuel Butler's notebooks to take the taste of Alice Meynell's life out of my mouth.[2] One rather craves brilliance & cantankerousness. Yet I am interested; a little teased by the tight airless Meynell style; & then I think what they had that we had not—some suavity & grace, certainly. They believed in things & we didn't; & she had 7 children & wrote about 5 paragraphs a day for society papers & so on—all the time looking like a crucified saint; & was also very merry & witty perhaps—anyhow absolutely steeped in various sorts of adventure & life—went to America lecturing & made £15 a lecture, which she sent back to help Wilfrid. But it is not exactly this that I mean. When one reads a life one often compares one's own life with it. And doing this I was aware of some sweetness & dignity in those lives compared with ours—even with ours at this moment. Yet in fact their lives would be intolerable—so insincere, so elaborate; so I think—all this word paring &

2. *The Notebooks of Samuel Butler*, a selection edited by Henry Festing Jones, was first published in 1912. *Alice Meynell. A Memoir*, by her daughter, Viola Meynell, 1929. Alice Meynell, *née* Thompson (1847-1922), poet and essayist, had married the journalist and editor Wilfred Meynell in 1877; they had three sons and four daughters, many of whom, as they grew up, were accommodated in cottages in the grounds of the large farmhouse the Meynells owned at Greatham in Sussex.

sweetness & charity. Viola cant help dropping in lump after lump of sugar
—only two sharp & therefore memorable things survive—her mother
failed as a friend. She never gave enough. Old Coventry Patmore, whom
she thought the equal of Sh[akespea]re, complained that he had lost the
primacy among her friends & dropped out; whereupon she went alone
into the drawing room, for she hated to express her feelings, & also hated
long accounts of illness & death in biographies, turning her face away
from her son in her last illness, & letting him only kiss her hand. Secondly
there was the oddity of her admiration for Chesterton. Had I been a man &
very big I could have been Chesterton. That is, her views were all peculiar
& angular, & stuck to pedantically. She had a line of her own. But it would
be a wonderful relief if Viola would give up being pointed & precise &
tell us something casual & familiar—only she cant: her mind in stays.
Katherine Mansfield described a visit to the house in Sussex—All the Ms.
in barns & cottages; & the daughters singing long monotonous ballads, &
then, by way of contrast & to surprise a scallywag I daresay with their
liveliness breaking into music hall songs taught them by their brothers in
law. Katherine described them like so many B[urne]. J[ones]. mermaids
with long lush hair, plucking at mediaeval instruments & intoning those
verses. Mrs M. sat by. And I saw her in 1910 (?) at Mrs Ross's, & heard
her say that saying about the climate & then there she was ecstatic in an
omnibus.—I recorded my regret that one ever saw poetesses in the flesh.[3]
For she was a poetess too—it strikes me that one or two little poems will
survive all that my father ever wrote. But its odd—this comparing that
goes on as one reads a life—I kept thinking how little good could be said
of me.

Wednesday I think the 4 .September

I am just back from Long Barn, that is from Ashdown forest, where L.
fetched me; & I have just eaten a pear warm from the sun with the juice
running out of it, & I have thought of this device: to put

The Lonely Mind

separately in The Moths, as if it were a person. I don't know—it seems
possible. And these notes show that I am very happy.

I daresay it is the hottest day this year—the hottest September day

3. VW described having tea with Mrs Ross at Poggio Gherardi during her visit to
   Florence in 1909, and her impression of Alice Meynell, in her *Greece/Italy Notebook,
   1906-09* (Copy, MHP Sussex, A7): see Appendix II.

these twenty years. So the papers may say tomorrow. Really it was too hot in the garden at Long Barn. The children were querulous—Nigel riding round in between the flower beds on his bicycle, & Ben stretched on the seat saying in a reasonable sad voice, Nigel you aren't well—you dont look well. Boski says you dont. Mummy he ought to wash his feet. Vita (from the window) but he has washed his feet. Ben. Well they're dirty again. Boski came in with the time table. The buses dont fit. They cant get back from Fairlawn before 8. Vita. Then ring up Mrs Cazalet & say they cant come. I must tell them they must put it off. She went to Harold's room where they sat working with Mr O'Connor, & told them. Nigel began arguing. She was firm, & strode away. All this happened in blazing heat.[4] The car was very hot. George brought a bottle of soda water. We lunched among some pine trees in Ashdown Forest, & lay full length afterwards, I with my straw hat over my face. Then L. met us, punctually at 4, at Duddimans (no—not that name) & we sat on some prickly holly leaves on the heath & talked to Vita about Harold's letter. He says her poems aren't worth publishing. She is very calm & modest, & seems not to mind much—a less touchy poet never was. But then can a real poet be an un-touchy poet?[5]

She was very much as usual [?]; striding; silk stockings; shirt & skirt; opulent; easy; absent; talking spaciously & serenely to the Eton tutor, an admirable young man, with straight nose & white teeth who went to bed, or to his room, early, leaving us alone. I remarked the boys calling him Sir & bending with salaams over his hand & then kissing Vita—how English—how summery & how upper class—how pleasant—how without accent. This has been going on a thousand years I felt; at least, I can remember summers like this—white flannels & tennis, mothers, & tutors & English houses & dinner with moths getting in the candles & talk of tennis tournaments & ladies asking one to tea all my life—so pleasant, so without accent. And the tutor was the eternal tutor of young men— joking, affectionate, stern: watching Nigel with a sort of amusement & tenderness "There spoke the real Nigel" when N. said he hoped he had

4. For the past year Boski—Audrey le Bosquet—had been Vita's secretary. Fairlawne, the Cazalet's home, was at Tonbridge. Vincent Mansfield O'Connor (1904-1930), a junior classical master at Eton, was acting as the Nicolson boys' tutor during the summer holidays.

5. George Thomsett was the Nicolson's butler. The meeting place was probably Duddleswell, roughly half way between Monks House and Long Barn. Harold Nicolson had written to advise Vita against the publication of *King's Daughter*, a collection of her poems which included some of a lesbian character; it was due to appear in the 'Hogarth Living Poets' series, and was in fact published in October 1929 (*HP Checklist* 207).

spilt the gravy on his trousers:—like a stream flowing deep & correct & unruffled through narrow banks. This kind of thing we now do to perfection. It is not interesting, but from its admirable completeness & sameness makes one tender towards it.

Nelly has been out this afternoon & picked, I think, 7 lbs of blackberries to make into jam. Please remember this as her way of thanking me for having Lottie—after all, she has no other. And one tends to forget it.

Monday 16 September

Leonard is having a picnic at Charleston & I am here—'tired'. But why am I tired? Well I am never alone. This is the beginning of my complaint. I am not physically tired so much as psychologically. I have strained & wrung at journalism & proof correction; & underneath has been forming my Moths book. Yes, but it forms very slowly; & what I want is not to write it, but to think it for two or three weeks say—to get into the same current of thought & let that submerge everything, writing perhaps a few phrases here at my window in the morning. (And they've gone to some lovely place—Hurstmonceux perhaps, in this strange misty evening;—& yet when the time came to go, all I wanted was to walk off into the hills by myself. I am now feeling a little lonely & deserted & defrauded, inevitably). And every time I get into my current of thought I am jerked out of it. We have the Keynes's: then Vita came; then Angelica & Eve; then we went to Worthing, then my head begins throbbing—so here I am, not writing—that does not matter, but not thinking, feeling or seeing—& seizing an afternoon alone as a treasure—Leonard appeared at the glass door at this moment; & they didn't go to H[urstmonceu]x or anywhere; & Sprott was there & a miner, so I missed nothing—one's first egotistical pleasure.[6]

Really these premonitions of a book—states of soul in creating—are very queer & little apprehended.

Another reflection—nothing is so tiring as a change of atmosphere. I am more shattered & dissipated by an hour with Leonard's mother than by 6 hours—no, 6 days, of Vita. (Nessa doesn't count). The tremendous gear changing that has to take place grinds one's machinery to bits. And

6. Walter John Herbert ('Sebastian') Sprott (1897-1971), a Cambridge Apostle, had been appointed Lecturer in Psychology at Nottingham University College in 1925. On 13 September, on one of LW's regular filial visits to his mother, ensconced in a Worthing hotel for the summer, the Woolfs took Nelly Boxall and Angelica and her friend Eve Younger with them; the little girls then stayed the night at Monks House.

I have done this constantly—& what is more than doing it, I've foreboded doing it—I've counted up the days & felt Worthing brooding over me. & then, psychologically again, having Nelly in the car is to me a strain—imposes another forced atmosphere. None of these things would matter much if one's engine were going at full speed—how I tossed off every interruption when I was writing Orlando!—but it is as if they got in to the spokes—clogged the wheels—always just prevented me from getting the machine swinging round. And then I am 47: yes: & my infirmities will of course increase. To begin with my eyes. Last year, I think, I could read without spectacles; wd. pick up a paper & read it in a tube; gradually I found I needed spectacles in bed; & now I can't read a line (unless held at a very odd angle) without them. My new spectacles are much stronger than the old, & when I take them off, I am blinded for a moment. What other infirmities? I can hear, I think, perfectly: I think I could walk as well as ever. But then will there not be the change of life? And may that not be a difficult & even dangerous time? Obviously one can get over it by facing it with common sense—that it is a natural process; that one can lie out here & read; that one's faculties will be the same afterwards; that one has nothing to worry about in one sense— I've written some interesting books, can make money, can afford a holiday—Oh no; one has nothing to bother about; & these curious intervals in life—I've had many—are the most fruitful artistically—one becomes fertilised—think of my madness at Hogarth—& all the little illnesses—that before I wrote To The Light-house for instance. Six weeks in bed now would make a masterpiece of Moths. But that wont be the name. Moths, I suddenly remember, dont fly by day. And there cant be a lighted candle. Altogether, the shape of the book wants considering—& with time I could do it.

Here I broke off.

Saturday 21 September

Angelica goes to school for the first time today I think;[7] & I daresay Nessa is crying to herself—one of the emotions I shall never know—a child, one's last child—going to school, & so ending the 21 years of Nessa's children—a great stretch of life; how much fuller than I can guess —imagine all the private scenes, the quarrels, the happinesses, the moments of excitement & change, as they grew up. And now, rather sublimely she

7. Hitherto, when Vanessa had been in London, Angelica had had lessons from Miss Rose Paul in Mecklenburgh Square; now she was sent as a boarder to a small private girls' school, Langford Grove, near Chelmsford, of which the headmistress was Mrs Curtis.

ends her childhood years in a studio alone, going back, perhaps rather sadly to the life she would have liked best of all once, to be a painter on her own. So we have made out our lives, she & I, propelled into them by some queer force; for me, I always think of those curious long autumn walks with which we ended a summer holiday, talking of what we were going to do—'autumn plans' we called them. They always had reference to painting & writing & how to arrange social life & domestic life better. Often we thought about changing a room, so as to have somewhere to see our own friends. They were always connected with autumn, leaves falling, the country getting pale & wintry, our minds excited at the prospect of lights & streets & a new season of activity beginning—October the dawn of the year. But I am rambling off like an old woman into the past, when as I sat down, waiting for tea, I said to myself I have so many things to write in my diary.

Another of those curious plums, things falling unexpectedly in our way, has just happened. Annie the large eyed sad young woman has been to ask us to buy her a cottage, & let her do for us always, in fact be our servant here. She & her baby, aged two, have been turned out at a fortnights notice to make room for two spinster dog breeders. Humanity says we ought to buy her her cottage, & take no rent—let her work it off. Another £350, & repairs—more articles. She would make an ideal servant, I believe; she would be a great standby; one could come here as long as one liked—& poor dear Nelly could be left in London,—for she gave notice again this morning, to Leonard this time, about his coal scuttle. It seems we are settling & rooting almost daily. I should have to dismiss poor spindly Bartholomew. It needs some thinking—meanwhile Annie is up against this terrific high black prison wall of poverty—has to manage with a child on 15/- a week.

These reflections, which branch off down so many paths make me linger, over the two other records—Peter, & my future, which I thought I was going to write; but it is tea time, & then I want to wander off up the downs or along the river, straightening my ideas.

Please God nobody comes to tea. Yet Lytton & Antony Blunt & Peter are all at Charleston.[8] Please God I say these delightful & divine people dont come & make me concentrate again all in my face & brain. I want to swim about in the dark green depths. By the way last night in the Evening Standard James Laver called me a great writer "nobody need seek to

8. Peter Lucas had stayed at Monks House on 18 and 19 September, before going on to Charleston. Anthony Frederick Blunt (b. 1907), later to become an eminent art historian, was at Trinity College, Cambridge, an Apostle, and a friend of Julian Bell.

qualify the greatness of Miss Virginia Woolf"—hah! I hope Arnold Bennett sees that.[9]

Sunday 22 September

And it is ten minutes past ten in the morning, & I am not going to write a word. I have resolved to shut down my fiction for the present. My head aches too easily at the moment; I feel The Moths a prodigious weight which I can't lift yet. And yet, so odd a thing is the mind, I am never easy, at this early hour, merely reading or writing letters. Those occupations seem too light & diffused. Hence, though write letters I will & must— to Dotty, to Gerald Brenan, to peevish Eddy, I will canter here a moment. It is a fine September morning; the rooks cawing, the shadows very long & shallow on the terrace. The body has gone out of the air. It is thinning itself for winter. It is becoming pale & pure like the eyes of an old man. An exacting & rather exhausting summer this has been. What with going to London, going to Worthing & having people here, I have never settled in; I feel I should like to stay on & avoid London for a time. The car makes us almost too movable. On the other hand, this is the best appointed summer we have ever had. Never has the garden been so lovely—all ablaze even now; dazzling one's eyes with reds & pinks & purples & mauves: the carnations in great bunches, the roses lit like lamps. Often we go out after dinner to see these sights. And at last I like looking about the drawing room. I like my rug; my carpet; my painted beams. And for some odd reason I have found lovelier walks this year than ever—up into the downs behind Telscombe. Partly it is the weather, perhaps; we have had day after day of cloudless warm sun; the sky has been blue day after day; the sun has gone down clean, clear, leaving no feathers or battlements in the west. And lying out here I have seen the sun rise, & the moon shining one night like a slice of looking glass, with all the stars rippling & shining; & one night I had that curious feeling of being very young, travelling abroad, & seeing the leaves from a train window, in Italy—I cant get the feeling right now. All was adventure & excitement.

As for Peter, how right how charming how good he is!—but damn it

9. LW went to London for the day on 20 September and presumably brought back the *Evening Standard* which contained James Laver's article headed 'Supreme Gift Denied to Women'. Though expressing the view that in general women had failed to reach the front rank in the creative arts, he conceded that the novel was today almost a feminine preserve: 'Who would wish to deny the quality of greatness to Miss Virginia Woolf, for example, . . .' James Laver (1899-1975), an assistant-keeper in the Victoria and Albert Museum since 1922, was also a fertile writer and journalist. Arnold Bennett contributed an article each week to the *Evening Standard*.

all, what an uninteresting mind, intellectually. I cant put my finger on it, but nothing remains in one's mind after seeing him, nothing interesting, no suggestion. Incessant similes, perpetual quotation; he sees life with great ardour through books. And then he is now all agog to copulate, which makes his stories centre round that fascinating subject too inevitably —copulation & King's College Cambridge. He went through the war, & has had 4 years of battle & blood & wounds, & yet his mind keeps the virginal simplicity of a girls; he has the rigidity, at 36, of a crusted college character. I suppose the mixture is not very rich in him—thats all: father a schoolmaster, mother a housekeeper, life in the suburbs, scholarships &c: that was his upbringing; & then coming out of his shell, he deliberately vowed to be pagan, to be individual, to enjoy life, to explore his own sensations when there wasn't much matter to go on. Hence the repetition, the egotism, the absence of depth or character; but I feel all this far more when he writes than in talk. In talk his charm & niceness, his integrity, his brightness, all make him a very nice, dear, delightful, memorable (yes, but not interesting) human being. He will marry; he will become Prof. of Engl. Lit. at Camb.

Wednesday 25 September

But what interests me is of course my oil stove.[10] We found it here last night on coming back from Worthing. At this moment it is cooking my dinner in the glass dishes perfectly I hope, without smell, waste, or confusion: one turns handles, there is a thermometer. And so I see myself freer, more independent—& all one's life is a struggle for freedom— able to come down here with a chop in a bag & live on my own. I go over the dishes I shall cook—the rich stews, the sauces. The adventurous strange dishes with dashes of wine in them. Of course Leonard puts a drag on, & I must be very cautious, like a child, not to make too much noise playing. Nelly goes on Friday & so I shall [have] a whole week to experiment in—to become free in.

Yesterday morning I made another start on The Moths, but that wont be its title. & several problems cry out at once to be solved. Who thinks it? And am I outside the thinker? One wants some device which is not a trick.

The greenhouse began to be built yesterday. We are watering the earth with money. Next week my room will begin to rise. It strikes me that one is absurd to expect good temper or magnanimity from servants, considering what crowded small rooms they live in, with their work all about them.

10. Cooking at Monks House had hitherto been done on a solid fuel range.

Then, old Mrs. Woolf—(I mean I am making a few notes, heaven knows why, but one always thinks there is a reason.) She has come to wear a charm & dignity to me, unknown before, now her old age is crumbling down all the cheerful sentimental small talk—she becomes curiously more humane & wise, as old women are; so pliable, so steeped in life that they seem to become philosophic, & more mistress of the art of living than much cleverer people. So many many things have happened before her; illnesses, births, quarrels, troubles—nothing much surprises her, or long upsets her. True she is peevish & bored as a child; but has attained some carelessness of show & pomp & respectability, as if she had washed her hands of most things & were playing on a beach, rather an enviable old age in many ways, though intolerable too. Always take opportunities I heard her murmuring to Pinka who had eaten all our soup. And then the long stories about her cooks, & how she had taught them cooking when she was rich. 'Now you are poor & plain' one of them wrote 'after my great sorrow' here she sighs, & would cry, but is easily diverted & presses a tin of toffee on me.

I must go into the kitchen to see my stove cooking ham now

Wednesday 2 October

We have just been over Annie's cottage—so I suppose it is. & we therefore own another fair sized house; but the arrangement with Annie seems another of those plums which since this time, or August, last year, have dropped into our hands here. She will cook; my oil stove makes hot meals practicable at all hours; but I am dazed with the Brighton conference; hearing Henderson orate & seeing him get red slowly like a lobster; we went on Monday too (how my days of reflection have dwindled! one must give it all up now) & heard a good, interesting, debate.[1] The audience makes an extraordinary baaing noise; not talk, not footsteps—& I thought how politics was no longer an affair of great nobles & mystery & diplomacy, but of commonsense, issuing from ordinary men & women of business—not very exalted, but straight forward, like any other business affair.

The light is dying; I hear the village boys kicking footballs; & all those reflections, comments, that occur to me walking are died out—the atmosphere, winter, change, London's imminence, scatter, finally, my poor efforts at solid concentration. Yet I have, these last days, set my book

1. The Labour Party annual conference opened in the Dome, Brighton, on Monday, 30 September, when the main debate was on Family Allowances. On Wednesday, 2 October, the Foreign Secretary Arthur Henderson gave a survey of Government policy in foreign affairs.

alight I think—got it going; but at a rate like that of Jacob's Room Mrs Dalloway days—a page at most, & long sitting sucking my pen. And all the Americans write & cable for articles. And I shall go in & read Phedre, having picked some apples. Leonard in the cold windy road is cleaning the car.

LW packed up and drove to London on Thursday 3 October, leaving VW at Monks House; he returned on Saturday, when Maynard and Lydia Keynes came to tea, and they both drove back to Tavistock Square on Sunday afternoon, 6 October.

Friday 11 October

And I snatch at the idea of writing here in order not to write Waves or Moths or whatever it is to be called. One thinks one has learnt to write quickly; & one hasn't. And what is odd, I'm not writing with gusto or pleasure: because of the concentration. I am not reeling it off; but sticking it down. Also, never, in my life, did I attack such a vague yet elaborate design; whenever I make a mark I have to think of its relation to a dozen others. And though I could go on ahead easily enough, I am always stopping to consider the whole effect. In particular is there some radical fault in my scheme? I am not quite satisfied with this method of picking out things in the room & being reminded by them of other things. Yet I cant at the moment devise anything which keeps so close to the original design & admits of movement.

Hence, perhaps, these October days are to me a little strained & surrounded with silence. What I mean by this last word I dont quite know, since I have never stopped 'seeing' people—Nessa & Roger, the Jeffers', Charles Buxton, & should have seen Lord David & am to see the Eliots— oh & there was Vita too.[2] No; its not physical silence; its some inner loneliness—interesting to analyse if one could. To give an example—I was walking up Bedford Place is it—the straight street with all the boarding houses this afternoon, & I said to myself spontaneously, something like this. How I suffer, & no one knows how I suffer, walking up this street,

2. Charles Roden Buxton (1875-1942), whom LW described as a 'nineteenth-century non-conformist Liberal of the best type' (*IV LW*, p 245); disillusioned with the Liberal Party he joined the Labour Party and was at this time an MP. He and LW were respectively Chairman and Secretary of the Labour Party Advisory Committees on International and Imperial Affairs. Robinson Jeffers (1888-1962), the American poet, and his wife Una had tea with the Woolfs on 7 October; the Hogarth Press published three books of his poems in their 'Hogarth Living Poets' series (*HP Checklist* 167, 196, 226).

engaged with my anguish, as I was after Thoby died—alone; fighting something alone. But then I had the devil to fight, & now nothing. And when I come indoors, it is all so silent—I am not carrying a great rush of wheels in my head— Yet I am writing—oh & we are very successful—& there is—what I most love—change ahead. Yes, that last evening at Rodmell when Leonard came down against his will to fetch me, the Keynes's came over. And Maynard is giving up the Nation, & so is Hubert, & so no doubt shall we.[3] And it is autumn; & the lights are going up; & Nessa is in Fitzroy Street—in a great misty room, with flaring gas & unsorted plates & glasses on the floor,—& the Press is booming—& this celebrity business is quite chronic—& I am richer than I have ever been—& bought a pair of earrings today—& for all this, there is vacancy & silence somewhere in the machine. On the whole, I do not much mind; because, what I like is to flash & dash from side to side, goaded on by what I call reality. If I never felt these extraordinarily pervasive strains—of unrest, or rest, or happiness, or discomfort—I should float down into acquiescence. Here is something to fight: & when I wake early I say to myself, Fight, fight. If I could catch the feeling, I would: the feeling of the singing of the real world, as one is driven by loneliness & silence from the habitable world; the sense that comes to me of being bound on an adventure; of being strangely free now, with money & so on, to do anything. I go to take theatre tickets (The Matriarch) & see a list of cheap excursions hanging there, & at once think that I will go to Stratford on Avon Mob fair tomorrow—why not?—or to Ireland, or to Edinburgh for a week end.[4] I daresay I shant. But anything is possible. And this curious steed, life; is genuine— Does any of this convey what I want to say?—But I have not really laid hands on the emptiness after all.

Its odd, now I come to think of it—I miss Clive.

It occurs to me that Arthur Studd was another of the brilliant young men.[5] But there was something innocent about him, compared with

3. Since April 1923, when Maynard Keynes and his associates had acquired control of it, Hubert Henderson had edited the *N & A*; he was now leaving at the end of the year to take up an appointment as joint secretary to the newly-formed Economic Advisory Council. Keynes, as chairman of the *N & A* board, was seeking an amalgamation with the *New Statesman*—which was eventually effected in 1931.

4. Stratford-on-Avon's ancient 'mop' or fair was held each year on 12 October; on this date the Woolfs went to the Royalty Theatre to see Mrs Patrick Campbell in *The Matriarch* by G. B. Stern.

5. Arthur Haythorne Studd (1863-1919), educated at Eton and King's College, Cambridge; then studied painting at the Slade School and in Paris. He became obsessed by Whistler, three of whose paintings he bequeathed to the National Gallery.

Bernard & Geoffrey: he spoke through his nose, & had a soft guttural voice; & a bald forehead, & rather handsome brown eyes, like a dogs: he was canine, in some ways; travelled, distinguished, rich; with a stout mother he disliked, & thus won my mother's sympathy. He had thick red hands, but painted in the manner of Whistler—gesticulating over the canvas, & then producing some little pleasing melodious still life, with which, rather mystically, he was very pleased. It was 'being an artist' that took his fancy. He had lovely rooms in Cheyne Walk; & the white girls & pink clouds & rivers & fireworks of Whistler hung in them. He went to Samoa, to paint Whistlers perhaps, & came back when Stella was dead & grieved for her I think. He had loved her, in his fumbling ineffective way. Then he wrote little poems, about Eton, which he loved, & hoped to be buried there— But why should he think of being buried, with all his advantages? There was something ineffective about him—he could not do anything; but had, to us as children, a kind of romance; was supposed to do extravagant impossible things—like hiring a cab & taking us all off suddenly to play cricket at Lords—that I remember. I suppose he was the flower of Eton & the 90ties, getting itself varnished with art & Paris & studio life, & Chelsea. He sent me a post card from St Ives once, & a poem about Eton—& then—clap came the war; & being endlessly kind & generous & inefficient, no doubt he did great things for refugees, & died, without any notice being taken, that I am aware of—a rich bachelor; not much over 50 I suppose. Another 'young man'—not brilliant exactly, but congenial in my memory, modest, fresh, unexpected, & always so nasal.

Sunday 13 October

It comes to me to ask, how far could I live at this moment in Nessa being with Angelica at school? Can one supplement one's life? I think a little. Julian has driven her over from Cambridge, this still soft grey morning. It is sunny & misty in the country. She got into the car in the King's Parade, where the paper sellers are & the young men are hurrying I suppose along to breakfast. Then they drive, with a map on their knees; Julian rather tense, staring through his spectacles. Some very intimate things are hinted at—of wh. I know nothing—or rather he grunts & half says things, which she understands. She is very excited, at the same time practical. Julian is excited too. They are both very anxious to see Angelica. How will they see her first? She will come running down the stairs into the private room, on the left; with the Adams fireplace. And then? She will 'fly into Nessa's arms'. Nessa will hold her very tight to get the sensation of her child's body again. Julian will call her "dear". They will go out together into the park. Angelica will like to show off her knowledge of rules & ways & the best places to sit in; other girls will smile, & she will say 'Thats Claudia' or Annie. Thats Miss Colly—Thats Mrs Curtis. And all the time they will be feeling the comfort & excitement of being together—of having only just broached their time together. Nessa will get at ever so many things: questions of happiness, teaching, liking, loneliness—change. They will be very proud of each other & aloof. & Julian will peer about, through his glasses, liking Nessa & Angelica better than anybody I daresay; the simple crude boy—whom I shall now never know, I daresay. For—as I am going to say to Nessa on Wednesday— you are a jealous woman, & dont want me to know your sons, dont want to take, but always to give; are afraid of the givers. What will she answer?

But Leonard will go on moving the apples, & so I cannot write anything except my—what I am pleased to call—my diary. I wish I could write more succinctly, by the way, & with less use of the present participle. My carelessness shocks me. Nature is having her revenge, & is now making me write one word an hour.

Wednesday 23 October

As it is true—I write only for an hour—then sink back feeling I cannot keep my brain on that spin any more—then typewrite, & am done by 12— I will here sum up my impressions before publishing a Room of One's Own.[6] It is a little ominous that Morgan wont review it.* It makes me suspect that there is a shrill feminine tone in it which my intimate friends will dislike. I forecast, then, that I shall get no criticism, except of the evasive jocular kind, from Lytton, Roger & Morgan; that the press will be kind & talk of its charm, & sprightiness; also I shall be attacked for a feminist & hinted at for a sapphist; Sibyl will ask me to luncheon; I shall get a good many letters from young women. I am afraid it will not be taken seriously. Mrs Woolf is so accomplished a writer that all she says makes easy reading . . . this very feminine logic . . . a book to be put in the hands of girls. I doubt that I mind very much. The Moths; but I think it is to be waves, is trudging along; & I have that to refer to, if I am damped by the other. It is a trifle, I shall say; so it is, but I wrote it with ardour & conviction.

We dined last night with the Webbs, & I had Eddy & Dottie to tea.

* He wrote yesterday 3rd Dec. & said he very much liked it

6. It was published on 24 October 1929 in both England and America, though a small limited edition was issued three days previously in the United States (see Kp A12).

As for these mature dinner parties one has some friendly easy talk with one man—Hugh Macmillan—about the Buchans & his own career;—the Webbs are friendly but can't be influenced about Kenya:[7] we sit in two lodging house rooms (the dining room had a brass bedstead behind a screen) eat hunks of red beef; & are offered whisky. It is the same enlightened, impersonal, perfectly aware of itself atmosphere. "My little boy shall have his toy"—but dont let that go any further "—that's what my wife says about my being in the Cabinet". No they have no illusions. And I compared them with L. & myself, & felt (I daresay for this reason) the pathos, the symbolical quality of the childless couple; standing for something, united.

As for 'seeing' Eddy & Dottie, there is not much to it; an occasional phrase one remembers—Eddy's being in love with two people: Dotty's rational account of a bore whom she helps: Eddy wishes me to read his diary, but some, nameless, friend objects; but he agreed, before long: it is a gratification to him. And so $1\frac{1}{2}$ hours passed. Dotty deplored Vita's too early fame. Yet I suppose she loves her; is devoted; queer things lodge in people's souls;

I am very carefully & cautiously becoming a reader & a thinker again. Since I have been back I have read Virginia Water (a sweet white grape); God; —all founded, & teased & spun out upon one quite simple & usual psychological experience; but the man's no poet & cant make one see; all his sentences are like steel lines on an engraving;[8] I am reading Racine, have bought La Fontaine, & so intend to make my sidelong approach to French literature, circling & brooding—

Saturday 2 November

It takes precisely 10 days for anything to happen to a book—It is now Saturday 2nd. Nov: & the R. of ones O. has sold, I think 100 copies

7. Hugh Pattison Macmillan (1873-1952), created Lord Macmillan of Aberfeldy in 1930, was a Scottish lawyer who became Lord Advocate in the Labour administration of 1924, and served as chairman on innumerable committees and commissions. John Buchan, the author (later, as Lord Tweedsmuir, governor-general of Canada), was married to Susan Grosvenor, one of the aristocratic circle VW had known through Violet Dickinson in her youth. LW, who as secretary of the Labour Party Advisory Committee on Imperial Affairs had played a significant part in formulating the party's policy, was urging Sidney Webb, now Secretary of State for Colonial Affairs, to implement Labour's promises to finance the provision of education and roads for the native population of Kenya.

8. *Virginia Water* (1929), a first novel by Elizabeth Jenkins. *God: an Introduction to the Science of Metabiology* (1929), by John Middleton Murry.

this morning; none before, or scarcely any, this largely due to Vita's flamboyant broadcast. And I cant remember all the things I was intending to say,— like Renard—the man who kept a diary of the things that occur to one.[1]

I dreamt last night that I had a disease of the heart that would kill me in 6 months. Leonard, after some persuasion, told me. My instincts were all such as I should have, in order, & some very strong: quite unexpected, I mean voluntary, as they are in dreams, & have thus an authenticity which makes an immense, & pervading impression. First, relief—well I've done with life anyhow (I was lying in bed) then horror; then desire to live; then fear of insanity; then (no this came earlier) regret about my writing, & leaving this book unfinished; then a luxurious dwelling upon my friends sorrow; then a sense of death & being done with at my age; then telling Leonard that he must marry again; seeing our life together; & facing the conviction of going, when other people went on living. Then I woke, coming to the top with all this hanging about me; & found I had sold a great many copies of my book; & was asked to lunch by Madame Kallas[2] —the odd feeling of these two states of life & death mingling as I ate my breakfast feeling drowsy & heavy.

[*Tuesday 5 November*]

Oh but I have done quite well so far with R. of one's Own: & it sells, I think; & I get unexpected letters. But I am more concerned with my Waves. I've just typed out my mornings work; & can't feel altogether sure. There is *something* there (as I felt about Mrs Dalloway) but I can't get at it, squarely; nothing like the speed & certainty of The Lighthouse: Orlando mere childs play. Is there some falsity, of method, somewhere? Something tricky?—so that the interesting things aren't firmly based? I am in an odd state; feel a cleavage; here's my interesting thing; & there's no quite solid table on which to put it. It might come in a flash, on re-reading —some solvent. I am convinced that I am right to seek for a station whence I can set my people against time & the sea—but Lord, the difficulty of digging oneself in there, with conviction. Yesterday I had conviction; it has gone today. Yet I have written 66 pages in the past month.

1. Vita Sackville-West spoke of *A Room of One's Own* on 31 October in her bimonthly talk on books for the BBC; it was printed in *The Listener* on 6 November 1929 (see *M & M*, p 257). Jules Renard (1864-1910), author of *Poil de carotte* (1894); his *Journal* was published in 17 volumes in 1925-27.
2. Mme Kallas was the wife of Dr Oskar Kallas, the Estonian Minister in London.

Yesterday Sibyl came; & I told her that she was like a bird holding a
stinking mouse in its claws—& the mouse was life. She admitted it. She
said she had to go through an unpleasant busi-
ness; was going to Paris this morning; would
tell me of it afterwards. Then she bemoaned
her lot, guardedly; how she had grown up so
late, & only now began to see what it was she
wanted. I gather that it is intimacy, simplicity,
& friendship that she wants; & it is a little late in life to demand them; &
how can she get them now, needing £20,000 a year too? So Arthur cant
retire; they must sit there & see the season through; she cant, at the
moment, master life; it is not a dead mouse after all; but wriggles. She
looked ringeyed, puckered—I saw her in a flash, quite old. Her eyes were
very tragic.

The unpleasant business
was that she lost her nest
egg—said to be £50,000,
in America. Now gives
tea parties only

And today Stephen Tennant comes to tea.[3] & Arthur Waley. On
Sunday we were at Rodmell; & my room is now about three feet of brick,
with the window frames in; rather an eyesore, for it cuts off the garage
roof & the downs—both pleasanter sights than I had thought. They have
driven a small hole through the little room, for the passage; so that by
this time, no doubt, that is in being. & things fall & rise & disappear &
re-appear. And most of my joy was turned to rage because I let Southease
sale of furniture slip, & could have furnished my room perfectly for £20
I daresay. Such is one's life—yes, such: (a convenient phrase;) And I
am asked daily to lecture; & L.'s freedom draws near. Wright will inherit,
& is making his dispositions.[4] I keep saying "We shall be able to do that
when you have left the Nation". Still, you see what with oil stoves &
Annie, battling my way to freedom. Jan. 1st is the day. We have had the
Nation for nearly seven years, without making it blood & bone of ours,
as once I thought possible. A tepid paper; neither this nor that, with the
perpetual drag of Hubert & Harold, Hubert kindly incompetent, Harold
competent but to me, all wood, red apple, sawdust, plausibility, respectability, hesitation & compromise.

3. The Hon. Stephen James Napier Tennant (b. 1906), the fourth son of 1st Baron
Glenconner, was a painter and an aesthete.
4. LW's previous attempts to throw off the shackles of the literary editorship of the
N & A had been subverted by Maynard Keynes; now with the impending change
of editor (see above, 11 October 1929, n 3), he re-asserted his resolve to resign on
31 December (see also letters to Keynes and Henderson, LWP Sussex, 14 December
1929). Henderson was to be succeeded by his assistant-editor Harold Wright
(1883-1934), and LW by Edmund Blunden; but as the latter was not free until
mid-February, in the event LW continued his work until then.

Sunday 17 November

A horrid date. Yes, I am feeling a little sick, a little shivery; I cant settle to anything; I am in a twitter; I try to read Mauron—to write—& my lips begin forming words; I begin muttering long conversations between myself & Vita about Dotty on the telephone; about Miss Matheson: I act parts: I find myself talking aloud; I say things over & over again like this "I want to know if after what happened the other morning you want to give me notice? . . . Well, then, as you wont answer, I am afraid I must now give you notice . . . But I want to explain exactly why it is. After you told me to leave your room I went to Mr Woolf & said that I could not keep you as my maid any longer. But I haven't made up my mind in a hurry. I have been thinking about it since June. I tried to arrange not to order dinner so that we might avoid scenes. But the scenes at Rodmell were worse than ever. And now this is the last. I am afraid I can't go on with it. This is the 17th of Nov. I shall expect you to go on the 17th Dec." Yes, this is what I have to say to Nelly at 9.30 tomorrow, & then I go to Mrs Hunt's [*Domestic Agency*]. And I am almost trembling with this nervous anticipation as I write. But it must be done.

Monday 18 November

Well it is over, & much better than I expected—at least for the present. To my question Do you want to give me notice? she replied "I have given you notice— . ." Further argument was attempted & cut short by me. "Then you wish to go at the end of your month—12th December." "As we refused her an hours extra help when she was ill, yes." But this was said without conviction. I clinched it by looking at the calendar (which I could not see, blind as I am) & then left her, in the calmest flattest way possible—which means I'm afraid that she has no more intention of going on Dec. 12th than I have of taking ship to Siberia. So be it. My mind is like a gum when an aching tooth has been drawn. I am having a holiday—reading old Birrell[5], & shall hope that the dust will be settled now for a week or two. The Horsham tiles are being put on my roof, so Percy writes this morning; which means that my rooms must be almost done. And now I have an extra room there—Nelly's—yes; & no servant in the house

5. Augustine Birrell (1850-1933), the author and Liberal statesman, and Frankie's father, had been at Charleston when the Woolfs had tea there with Frankie and Raymond Mortimer on 7 July; on 13 July, old Birrell sent VW the three volumes of his *Collected Essays, 1880-1920* (1922), with an inscription and a note. See *Holleyman*, VS II 1.

here—thank God—two friends to come in one early t'other late; no more Bloomsbury gossip—no more Lottie barging in & out; no more fear of having people to lunch & tea & dinner; no more pains in the back, swollen ankles, & ups & downs of passion & effusion. And so, what with the oil stove, Annie, giving up the Nation, new rooms new servants, the new year will be one of the most interesting—a great advance towards freedom which is the ideal state of the soul. Yet it must not be thought that I have suffered acutely from servitude. My one claim on my own gratitude is that, directly I feel a chain, I throw it off: think of leaving Fitzroy; leaving Hogarth—leaving Hyde Park Gate I was going to say to round the sentence & indeed I think I have been an old struggler after my fashion—not so valiant I daresay as Nessa, but tenacious too & bold.

Monday 25 November

I merely add idly (ought I not to be correcting To the Lighthouse[6]) that the difficulties with Nelly are to avoid an apology. She has weakened, & is now all out to catch us weakening. She wished L. many happy returns this morning. She came to me on Friday & asked me why I did not speak. I had some difficulty in being stiff & angry & saying that after her behaviour & accusations it was impossible. Mrs Hunt promises an abundance of permanent dailies, & so I think the die is cast. I have no doubt difficulties will begin, again; but not the old intolerable difficulties, no, no, never again.

I broadcast; & poured my rage hot as lava over Vita. She appeared innocent—I mean of telling H[ilda] M[atheson]. that I could easily cut my Brummell to bits.[7] And then I discussed her friends, Vita's friends, & said that here, in their secondrateness, was the beginning of my alienation. I cant have it said "Vita's great friends—Dottie, Hilda & Virginia". I detest the 2ndrate schoolgirl atmosphere. She sat silent for the most part, & only said I was right. Harold had said the same. The thing to do is to check it. She cant stop what she's begun. And then in a hurry to Rodmell, where the roof is on, & the floor stretched with planks. The bedroom will be a lovely wonderful room what I've always hoped for.

6. *To the Lighthouse* was the fifth volume in 'The Uniform Edition of the Works of Virginia Woolf' (see above, 13 May 1929, n 5); it was published by the Hogarth Press on 19 February 1930 (Kp A1oc).
7. VW broadcast her piece about Beau Brummell on the BBC on 20 November; Hilda Matheson, the Talks Director, insisted on alterations to VW's script—'made me castrate Brummell'. (See *IV VW Letters*, no. 2100 to T. S. Eliot; also no. 2099).

Saturday 30 November

I fill in this page, nefariously; at the end of a morning's work. I have begun the second part of Waves—I dont know, I dont know. I feel that I am only accumulating notes for a book—whether I shall ever face the labour of writing it, God Knows. From some higher station I may be able to pull it together—at Rodmell, in my new room. Reading The Lighthouse does not make it easier to write; nor these impending final interviews with Nelly & new servants. We had a party—dining out at the Red Lion—last night; Julian & Rachel; Lyn, Hope, Plomer, Brian Howard, Nessa afterwards. Too many people, Leonard said. I dont know. I dislike B. Howard; I dislike his decadence, & protruding eyes, & unbuttoned waistcoat & floating tie.[8] On the make, Leonard says. Plomer, on the other hand, was very plump & vigorous, fresh from the Bayswater murder; the details of which he said—how he had cleaned scraps of brain from the carpet apparently—could not be told.[9] The young Jewess was attacked in bed at 4 last Sunday morning by a mad husband with a razor. First he locked the door, so that she banged & kicked, with the razor slashing her all the time in vain: at last burst out, with her head hanging by the skin to die on the landing. If William had not been away that week end the Chinese man would have come to him; & he thinks, killed him too. But this is not his line, he says as a novelist; & the psychic ladies who invest the house, like the coarser kind of bug & beetle, disgust him with their sea-ants. They table turn, & hear the voice of Mrs Frip—(not her name) from the other side; one, very fat with curled hair, said, "And it all happened a million years ago." Disgusting, William said. His eyes—the representative part of him—flashed & goggled.

It is said that Hope has become a Roman Catholic on the sly. Certainly she has grown very fat—too fat for a woman in middle age who uses her brains, & so I suspect the rumour is true. She has sat herself down under the shade. It is strange to see beauty—she had something elegant & individual—go out, like a candle flame. Julian, for instance, could not see,

8. Brian Howard (1905-1958), of American parentage, had been educated at Eton and Oxford, where he achieved notoriety as an extravagant dandy and aesthete. He was presumably brought to the after-dinner gathering at Tavistock Square by William Plomer.
9. Plomer's landlady, Sybil Sarah de Costa, known as Mrs Sybil Starr, was brutally murdered by her putative husband James Achew, alias James Starr, on Sunday 24 November, at Pembridge Villas, Bayswater. Achew, an American citizen said to have Red Indian blood, was sentenced to death at the Old Bailey on 17 January, but reprieved on grounds of insanity and committed to Broadmoor. Plomer's novel *The Case is Altered* (1932, *HP Checklist* 302) is based on this drama.

I think, that Hope had ever been a young & attractive woman. She has some vigour of mind though. Lyn has less than I could wish. When she has written her review, there is not much left. And her 'niceness'—housekeeping & nursing her sister who is ill—take the edge off. Had she £100, she would insure against illness, she said; because illness means that one cant work; this week, neither she nor her sister has made a penny. On that foundation it is hard to rear any very robust character; she is fretted & anxious.

Certainly it is true that if one writes a thing down one has done with it.

Saturday 30 November

It is still Saturday the 30th November, & we have been to Greenwich, leaving Nessa & Duncan to paint Dottie's tables in Mr James' shed.[10] Mr James is one of the Morris craftsmen; & has a tile making works near the river. He wears striped trousers & spats & will sit up all night, indulging himself with cups of tea, when the tiles are firing. Now & then you take out a tile to test it. He has three Kilns, the most expensive costing £300: & the Rotherhithe tunnel is near at hand. Leonard & I walked under the river (I thinking of the pressure of grey water round it; & of the absurd sublimity of errand boys & nursemaids walking on dry land under the river) & we came up in Greenwich & walked there on the parade where I walked a year or two ago in a temper. A man in a jersey was sitting in a glass shelter. How odd—to sit there, with nothing to do! And we saw the hospital, yellow & pink; & then it rained, & we went back & talked to Mr James about his tiles & then drove through the East End to the garage. I bought two crumpets for a penny; & we came home. Duncan began telling me the story of the London artists; & how Roger is so much hated by the critics that they wont notice the London artists. This is said to mean that Keith Baynes doesn't sell. And so Nessa is having a tea party tomorrow to discuss the matter with Porter & Keith Baynes. For this she bought some cakes. And they are having Angus to dinner. So am I not thank God.[11]

10. Mr L. J. James had his works at Wharf (now Saunders Ness) Road on the Isle of Dogs; Vanessa and Duncan were decorating tiles destined for the dining room at Penns-in-the-Rocks. It was not the Rotherhithe but the Millwall-Greenwich foot tunnel which was near at hand.

11. With the backing of Maynard Keynes, the London Artists Association had been founded in 1925 on co-operative principles to enable a small group of artists to work in relative freedom from financial anxiety. There were seven original members, including Vanessa, Duncan, Roger Fry, Keith Baynes (1887-1977), and the New Zealander Frederick J. Porter (1883-1944). Angus Davidson had become the LAA's secretary in the summer.

DECEMBER 1929

Sunday 8 December

Dear me; last Monday, as L. advised, I asked Nelly if she wished to go: & so (as I foreboded) she said reasonably no; & proposed solutions; we were landed; not emotionally, rather weariedly, & disillusionedly on my part, in a compromise: to try Mansfield for a month,—(here is L. to ask about alterations—that is a 2nd E.C. & new lavatory basin which being settled—& its a roaring wind) we ⟨then⟩ if the trial is unsatisfactory then to part without further discussion for ever.[1]

Just back from Rodmell. The roof is on; the floors are made; the windows in; giving, it seemed vast sweeping views of flooded meadows; but there was only a blink of light even at midday; we were engulfed in whirling wet; working up to such a storm on Friday night as I have, I think, never been in. It went round & round; & there was thunder in the crash of the wind; & great zigzags of lightning; & hail drumming on the iron roof outside my room; & such a fury of noise one could not sleep. So at one I went up to L. & looked at the lighted windows in the village; & thought, really with some fear, of being out alone that moment. Suppose the tree crashed, or the slates came off? We were not very securely sheltered, there under our slate roof; still better than being at sea. Dreams were all blown about, elongated, distorted, that night. A tree down in the churchyard. Trees down all the way up today. A curious sense of community brought by the storm. A man killed at Chailey sleeping in a shed; a woman at Eastbourne; a boy at Worthing. However, the mind was very still & happy. I read & read & finished I daresay 3 foot thick of MS read carefully too; much of it on the border, & so needing thought. Now, with this load despatched, I am free to begin reading Elizabethans—the little unknown writers, whom I, so ignorant am I, have never heard of, Puttenham, Webb, Harvey.[2] This thought fills me with joy—no overstatement. To begin reading with a pen in my hand, discovering, pouncing, thinking of theories, when the ground is new, remains one of my great excitements. Oh but L.

1. The plan was to employ Mrs Mansfield, who lived in the basement of 37 Gordon Square, to relieve the discontented Nelly of some of the burden of housework at 52 Tavistock Square.
2. VW made notes (see Holograph Reading Notes, vols XI and XII in the Berg Collection) on George Puttenham's *The Arte of English Poesie* (1589); on William Webbe's *A Discourse of English Poetrie* (1586)—both in Constable's English Reprint editions of 1895; and on Gabriel Harvey's *Works*, ed. A. B. Grosart, 1884; his Commonplace Book, ed. G. C. Moore Smith, 1913; and his *Letter Book, 1573-1580*, ed. E. J. L. Scott, 1884. Cf 'The Strange Elizabethans' in *The Common Reader, Second Series*, 1932 (Kp A18).

will sort apples, & the little noise upsets me; I cant think what I was going to say.

So I stopped writing, by which no great harm was done; & made out a list of Elizabethan poets.

And I have, with great happiness, refused to write Rhoda Broughton & Ouida for de la Mare. That vein, popular as it is, witness Jane & Geraldine, is soon worked out in me. I want to write criticism. Yes, & one might make out an obscure figure or two. It was the Elizabethan prose writers I loved first & most wildly, stirred by Hakluyt, which father lugged home for me—I think of it with some sentiment—father tramping over the Library with his little girl sitting at HPG in mind. He must have been 65; I 15 or 16, then; & why I dont know, but I became enraptured, though not exactly interested, but the sight of the large yellow page entranced me. I used to read it & dream of those obscure adventurers, & no doubt practised their style in my copy books. I was then writing a long picturesque essay upon the Christian religion, I think; called Religio Laici, I believe, proving that man has need of a God; but the God was described in process of change; & I also wrote a history of Women; & a history of my own family—all very longwinded & El[izabe]than in style.[3]

Tuesday 10 December

A bad day yesterday, because I had Vita to lunch, which I hate, & lost one of my green leather gloves. We had tea with Leonard's mother, who, sitting in a new room, fairly flabbergasted us by her accident. The hotel was struck by lightning on Friday; a chimney stack fell; her room was filled with soot & sparks—& there she was, dramatising it, shivering, shocked, yet buoyant & secretly pleased to be the centre of catastrophe again As usual she had behaved with perfect calm—"but I feel these things so much afterwards" & was anxious to give pounds of tobacco to the workmen engaged in mending the roof. "What right, I said to myself, have we to sit here & see those poor fellows carrying bricks? Oh their lives—carrying bricks to the roof in this gale—& I sitting here" (in a pink hotel bedroom). This is her fluid imagination—pounds of tobacco, as Harold [Woolf] said, wdn't do much to cure the social system.[4]

It is I think a proof of the pressure at which we live that I have said

3. Nothing remains of these juvenile works.
4. LW's mother lived in hotels, moving from London to Worthing for the summer months. Her present abode was in Earls Court. Harold (1882-1967) was her third son.

nothing of our lawsuit—or have I? against the hotel, against the jazz band.[5] Rachel, William Plomer & ourselves go to court on Friday. Why are the facts so intolerably dull? I shrink from writing them. I rather liked Scadding & Bodkin's office; & swearing by almighty God; but Rachel & Wm. enjoy it more than I do. It is more unexpected. Rachel will tell her friends about it—as I should have done. But whole days knocked out of the week bore me. I feel that my greatest triumph is to achieve a quiet evening—in which to read El[izabe]thans. And Charlie Sanger is very ill—I figure him lying worn out, worn out & without much solid happiness to show for it; like some old gold link—so good, so genuine; affectionate; honourable; but a worn disappointed man I think: no natural happiness: a conscience; & then Dora.

Thursday 12 December

Here, just back from Rodmell, & some rather forced conversation with Mr Philcox (the wife & I went to America—I dont like America—you pay separate for breakfast—room, double 24 dollars). I will rapidly note my evidence for tomorrow though Pritchard now says we shall be postponed—for the hotel cant get a witness. What I shall say—(I have the pump all right,) is this about the autumn.

We came back early in October & the music was very bad. My husband wrote to the Secretary who wrote & assured him that everything wd. be done. Next night the music was so bad that my husband rang up the hotel; but they said they could do nothing. The music slightly improved, & we waited till the end of Nov. when it became so bad we were unable to sit in the room. The party was on 29th: on the 30th it was intolerable.

Case settled; expenses paid: 15th Jan. (about)

How easily facts escape me!

Saturday 14 December

No I am too tired to write; have been rushed, what with the lawsuit &c; have had toothache: & so sit passive, hoping that some drops will form in my mind. By the way, the sales of A Room are unprecedented—have beaten Orlando; feels like a line running through ones fingers; orders

5. Since the opening of the Royal Hotel (see above, 28 March 1929, n 3), the Woolfs had been disturbed in the evenings by the noise of dance music from its ballroom. LW's complaints proving ineffective, he took legal action against the hotel company, and eventually won his case (see *IV LW*, pp 124-7). Scadding and Bodkin were solicitors of 2 Endsleigh Street, Tavistock Square.

for 100 taken as coolly as 12's used to be. We have sold, I think 5500; & our next years income is made.

Had I married Lytton I should never have written anything. So I thought at dinner the other night. He checks & inhibits in the most curious way. L. may be severe; but he stimulates. Anything is possible with him. Lytton was mild & damp, like a wet autumnal leaf. Lonely, & growing elderly; so he compares notes with Clive apparently. Our case stands over till next Thursday, & will probably be settled in the interval—some compromise made. Yesterday they screwed down some windows—the law had that instant effect. The law was sad-coloured, impressive. We saw Mr Preston at 10; he was in a black court coat, with dirty white bands; a self confident sandy, polite man. What a pugnacious chap you are! I heard another K.C. say to him in court. An admirable manly atmosphere— schoolboys come to responsibility they seemed; all so aquiline & definite under their frizzled grey wigs. Then the Judge (Farwell) came in. We rose. He bowed. He looked superhumanly sage, dignified, sad; the wig again cutting his forehead off & accentuating the deep reflective eyes—a sallow, sodden wearied face; so intent that he was monosyllabic—could not afford to open his mouth unnecessarily; merely nodded. All was over in 10 minutes I suppose. I felt the stress of it all; that man sitting there intent under his canopy in the small crowded court, never dropping a word, till 4 in the afternoon.[6]

Sunday 15 December

Tooth better, but not what I call a vigorous head; an idling, unconcentrated head—too much doing in Tavistock Sqre these last days. Last night we went to The Calendar (by Edgar Wallace) with Ann; & there was a cheer, & behold a great golden Queen bowing in a very small bow windowed box.[7] Also, when the lights went up, the King, red, grumpy, fidgeting with his hands; well groomed, bluff; heavy looking, with one white flower in his buttonhole, resenting the need, perhaps, of sitting to be looked at between one of the acts—his duty to be done; & then not

6. LW's case against the Imperial Hotel Company was heard before Mr Justice Farwell (Sir Christopher Farwell, 1877-1943) in the Chancery Division of the High Court on Friday 13 December; Herbert Sansome Preston, KC (d. 1935), appeared for the Woolfs. The case was several times adjourned, and finally settled out of court in LW's favour on 31st, not 15th, January 1930 (according to LW's diary).

7. Ann (b. 1916) was the elder of Adrian and Karin Stephen's two daughters; the play was at Wyndham's Theatre. The Duchess of York, daughter-in-law of King George V and Queen Mary, is now better known as Queen Elizabeth the Queen Mother.

much liking the little remarks cast at him, to minimise his labour, by the Queen. Once the D[uche]ss of York sat with the Queen; a simple, chattering, sweethearted little roundfaced young woman in pink: but her wrist twinkling with diamonds, her dress held on the shoulder with diamonds. The Queen also like a lit up street with diamonds. An odd feeling came to me of the shop window decorated for the public: these our exhibits, our show pieces. Not very impressive—no romance or mystery—the very best goods. Yet he descends, I daresay, from Hengist; goes straight back, this heavy bluff grumpy looking man, to Elizabeth & the rest;[8] will have his face forever in our history. He took spectacles out of a bright red case.

I thought (as I so often think things) of many comments to be written. One remains. If I were reading this diary, if it were a book that came my way, I think I should seize with greed upon the portrait of Nelly, & make a story—perhaps make the whole story revolve round that—it would amuse me. Her character—our efforts to be rid of her—our reconciliations.

The Woolfs drove to Rodmell for two weeks' Christmas break on Saturday 21 December. It rained heavily; the Bells were at Seend; LW pruned the fruit trees.

[*Thursday 26 December*]

Rodmell. Boxing day

And I am sitting in my new room—bedroom, not sitting room; with curtains fire table; & two great views; sometimes sun over the brooks & storm over the church. A violent Christmas; a brilliant serene Boxing day; & both very happy—completely, were it not for the damnable Byng-Stamper & his power to sell the down to a syndicate to exploit. That this is his intention comes through Percy; & I am wrought up to protest; indeed I must write to Ottoline & ask her the name of the little man who protects downs. This place is always being risked & saved; & so perhaps will be again. Cutting down trees & spoiling downs are my two great iniquities—what the Armenians were to Mrs Cole.[9] I find it almost

8. This suggests a rather inattentive reading of *Elizabeth and Essex* by VW.

9. Percy's story was that the landowner Captain Byng-Stamper was to sell a forty-acre field on Rodmell Hill for building. LW made various moves to avert this, including writing to the Prime Minister (see LWP, Sussex, II Ia), but failed to prevent the erection of several houses and bungalows in the following years. VW wrote to Ottoline, but not until February 1930 (*IV VW Letters* no. 2141). Mrs Cole was headmistress of the girls' school in Kensington where LW had attended the Kindergarten; she had been 'obsessed with the horrors and barbarism of the Armenian massacres' (*V LW*, pp 22-3; see also *I LW*, p 52).

incredibly soothing—a fortnight alone—almost impossible to let oneself have it. Relentlessly we have crushed visitors—Morgan, Roger, Adrian. We will be alone this once, we say; & really, it seems possible. Then Annie is to me very sympathetic; my bread bakes well. All is rather rapt, simple, quick effective—except for my blundering on at The Waves. I write two pages of arrant nonsense, after straining; I write variations of every sentence; compromises; bad shots; possibilities; till my writing book is like a lunatic's dream. Then I trust to some inspiration on re-reading; & pencil them into some sense. Still I am not satisfied. I think there is something lacking. I sacrifice nothing to seemliness. I press to my centre. I dont care if it all is scratched out. And there is something there. I incline now to try violent shots—at London—at talk—shouldering my way ruthlessly—& then, if nothing comes of it—anyhow I have examined the possibilities. But I wish I enjoyed it more. I dont have it in my head all day like The Lighthouse & Orlando.

Before I went Clive came to tea; sat alone for an hour or two. He asked me if I had been told that he had criticised A Room? I said no. He was a little rasped; said the jokes were lecture jokes. "Girls come round me"—too much of that—little ideas—nothing to compare with Orlando. And then, inconsistently, he praised O. above L[ighthouse]. against what he said at the time. But his criticism is founded upon the theory that I cant feel sex: have the purple light cut off; & *therefore* must write Orlando's not Lighthouses. I daresay there's some truth—especially in his saying that my soliloquies, trains of thought, are better than my silhouettes. But, as always, his own axe wants grinding: that Love is enough—or if love fails, down one goes for ever. For we got on Mary of course; & again he protested that no one could have acted other than he did—& then he vaguely threatened an alliance, in France, with his loved—or the lady who loves. But does she love? Does she take him to Egypt? All trembles now on some unreality. Everything has been shifted by Mary; no fundament left. And I always feel, how jolly, how much hunting, & talking & carousing there is in you! How long we have known each other—& then Thoby's form looms behind—that queer ghost. I think of death sometimes as the end of an excursion which I went on when he died. As if I should come in & say well, here you are. And yet I am not familiar with him now, perhaps. Those letters Clive read made him strange & external.[10]

But a dog barks, & my lamp flickers—even in my perfect room. So down to Leonard, to read Elizabethans & put our glass dish on the fire.

10. There was a proposal in the air at this time that the Hogarth Press should publish a collection of Thoby Stephen's letters, but nothing came of it. See *IV VW Letters*, no. 2118, to Vanessa.

DECEMBER 1929

Saturday 28 December

Bernard Shaw said the other night at the Keynes'[11]—& the Keynes's have just wrecked my perfect fortnight of silence, have been over in their Rolls Royce—& L. made them stay, & is a little inclined to think me absurd for not wishing it—but then Clive is his bugbear at present— Bernard Shaw said to me, I have never written anything except poetry. A man has written a book showing how by altering a word or two a whole act of the D[octo]rs Dilemma is in rhythm. In fact my rhythm is so strong that when I had to copy a page of Wells the other day in the midst of my own writing my pen couldnt do it. I was wanting to write my own rhythm —yet I hadn't known till then that I had so strong a rhythm. Heartbreak House is the best of my plays. I wrote it after staying with you at the Webbs in Sussex—perhaps you inspired it.[12] And Lydia is making the Lady into Queen Victoria. No I never saw Stevenson—Mrs Stevenson thought I had a cold.

You write Irish Mr Shaw. So does Mr Moore. Moore's an odd man— a very small talent cultivated with the utmost patience. We used to laugh at him in the old days. He was our butt. He was always telling us stories about himself & a lady—a grand lady—& she was always throwing something at his head & just missing it—& he used to say "Wait wait, there's a good passage coming". Nobody was better tempered. But he was our laughing stock. And one day Zola said to me I've discovered your great English novelist! Who's that said I. His name is George Moore. And I burst out laughing not our little George Moore, with his stories about himself? But it was. A lesson, you see, not to be too quick in judging ones friends.

But all his stories are autobiographic, I said.

Yes, they are all about George Moore & the lady who throws something at his head. —is writing a life of Moore & has asked me to tell the story of his early days. I am collecting my works. I find that I wrote a million words about the theatre. I dont know what to do with it. My wife wants me to leave out. But I think it gives a curious picture of the time. I am ashamed to think that I could ever have written so badly. The collection is limited

---

11. VW had talked to Shaw at an evening party given by the Keyneses on 19 December at 46 Gordon Square.
12. The Woolfs had spent the weekend of 17-19 June 1916 with the Sidney Webbs at Turner's Hill in Sussex; the Bernard Shaws were fellow-guests. Shaw was to repeat his compliment associating VW with *Heartbreak House* in a letter to her of 10 May 1940 (see *III LW*, p 126); he had in fact been occupied with the play some years before meeting her.

to 21 volumes. Theyre going to be sold in different bindings in America—some in leather very expensive—others quite cheap—hawked about all over America by peddlars. Im not a modest man but even I blushed at the stuff I've had to write for my publishers. Essential to every home & so on. I say out of twelve people, there will always be 3 women as clever as the men. What I've always told them is go for the governing bodies—dont mind about the vote. Insist upon representation. Now women are far more enthusiastic about business than men. They get things done. Men gossip in clubs. Oh but youve done more for us than anyone, Mr Shaw. My generation, & Francis Birrell's (he was sitting behind) we might be nice people, but we're different owing to you.

Happier said Francis.

Then Lydia came & broke in, with Mrs Shaw.

1930

1930

Saturday 4 January

This is the new year, & I shall continue this book—from economy. I am having a holiday; it is fine; & so inveterate an habitual am I, I find it easier to walk after lunch than before. Far from doing nothing, I intend to write some letters, & have been pondering the early works of Miss Easedale.[1]

The idea has come to us that we will live here from April onwards. And merely because of that idea, the view from my window looks different. It becomes usual[?], something for a long unstressed time; hitherto I have always seen it as an interlude; a breathing space. I note, for that Portrait of Nelly that I should write, if I were editing these pages, that her letter to me began Dear Madam—which I hold to be as Carlyle used to say "Significant of much". But these are notes merely; for some reason it bores me to enlarge.

Vita came yesterday with a green glass tank in which Japanese flowers expand in water. Here my mind would expand like that—the advent of the Keynes' made it shrivel.[2] And we wasted our fine day, that should have been spent at Rye, talking in their very ugly room. But I am not saying that *they* are ugly: that would be blasphemous. This perpetual denigration of human nature & adoration of solitude is suspect. Only, here I'm bound to the board, like an insect, for another three months; & my one fine day I grudge to society. Tonight we dine at Charleston & so home tomorrow to the pump, to the dance music; to Braithewaite, Goldie, Ottoline, Sprott & so on—to be 'seen' to 'see'. A little music though—the opera—that I shall like. And now I must answer letters & so start London free from that anyhow.

The Woolfs returned to Tavistock Square on 5 January.

1. Joan Adeney Easdale, a sixteen-year-old girl from Kent, had sent her 'piles of dirty copy books written in a scrawl without any spelling', in which VW discerned real merit. Her *A Collection of Poems (written between the ages of 14 and 17)* was published as no. 19 in the Hogarth Living Poets series (*HP Checklist* 253) in February 1931, and a further volume *Clemence and Clare* as no. 23 in 1932 (*HP Checklist* 287).
2. The Keyneses had turned up at Monks House in a chauffeur-driven car on the 28th, and persuaded the Woolfs to lunch with them at Tilton on 31 December.

JANUARY 1930

Thursday 9 January

I merely note that I am going to try to keep next week entirely free from 'seeing' people, bating my dinner at Bogy Harrises to meet the Prime Minister, & Angelica's party. I am going to see if I can keep 7 days out of the clutch of the seers. I have arranged to do my seeing all this week, & have plodded along faithfully, & industriously: Braithewait & Miss Matthews, Dottie, Ottoline, Goldie, Sprot, Quentin, Miss Matheson & Plomer last night & Eddy to tea today, Vita tomorrow, Quentin on Saturday; & then nobody I swear on Sunday.[3]

Sunday 12 January

Sunday it is. And I have just exclaimed, And now I can think of nothing else. Thanks to my pertinacity & industry, I can now hardly stop making up The Waves. The sense of this came acutely about a week ago on beginning to write the Phantom party: now I feel that I can rush on, . after 6 months hacking, & finish: but without the least certainty how its to achieve any form. Much will have to be discarded: what is essential is to write fast & not break the mood—no holiday, no interval if possible, till it is done. Then rest. Then re-write.

As for keeping a week free—I am now going to visit L.'s mother: then to the Frys after dinner. Marjorie Strachey to tea tomorrow: Duncan, I think, on Tuesday; Vita on Friday; Angelica on Saturday; Bogey Harris Wednesday: one day remains entire—Thursday—& thats the end of my week.

Thursday 16 January

A page of real life. Last night at Bogey Harrises. I came in, flung into the room in my red coat. A very painted raddled tall, pink woman (Mrs Graham Murray [*unidentified*]); & the rest, in an oval room, with painted ceiling, & books—"given me by Horne with Ben Johnson's autograph—

---

3. For Bogey Harris's dinner, see below, 16 January; Angelica's party was to be a fancy-dress one in Vanessa's studio on 18 January (see *II QB*, p 150); the Woolfs gave dinner to Richard Braithwaite and his friend Marjorie Matthews (1903-1972, Newnham 1922-25) at Boulestin on 6 January; on 8th, G. L. Dickinson, Sebastian Sprott and Hilda Matheson dined with them at Tavistock Square, and Lady Ottoline, William Plomer, and Quentin Bell came in afterwards; on the evening of the 9th, the Woolfs went to a performance of Mozart's early opera, *La Finta Giardiniera*, at the Scala Theatre.

the first edition of Dante— Lady Londonderry will be late; but we wont wait".[4] I have forgotten the prime minister—an unimpressive man; eyes disappointing; rather heavy; middle class; no son of the people; sunk; grumpy; self-important; wore a black waistcoat; had some mediocrity of personality. In came Lady L. very late; in ruby velvet, cut to the middle of the back, small, running, quick, current, energised. All went in to dinner, & I was too blind to read Sir Robert Vansittart on the man's card, so had to jumble for my neighbours pursuit.[5] Never mind. They all called each other Van, Bogey, Ramsay, Eadie, across the table; engaged in governing England: A mazer bowl fingered by Roger, drew Ramsay for two minutes, rather heavily into the open; took it; looked at it, laying his shabby drab spectacle case on the table; said he had never signed any authority for the sale of the mazer to America;[6] then lapsed into tete à tête with the ladies—murmuring, unresonant. And so upstairs, Ly L. running ahead, opening doors, taking us into little rooms to look at Majolica, at altarpieces. Then round the fire she started off, fluent, agreeable, hard hitting, like a rider, or Captain, without an ounce of spare flesh, telling stories—old men who had operations & were then mad—left their money in a muddle—her own father mad for two years—Farquhar muddling up the Fife Settlements & the Liberal Party fund[7]—all indiscreet, open, apparently; the chat of a perfectly equipped, un nonsensical, well fed, athletic woman, riding her horse at every fence. We discussed Birth

4. 'Bogey' Harris had been greatly influenced by the scholar and collector Herbert Horne (1864-1916) who spent his later years in Florence, to which city he bequeathed his palazzo and his collection (that of Harris was sold at auction after his death). Lady Londonderry, née Edith (Edie) Helen Chaplin (1878-1959), wife of the 7th Marquess of Londonderry and daughter of the 1st Viscount Chaplin (1840-1923) whose life (*Henry Chaplin. A Memoir*, 1926) she wrote, was a Conservative political hostess who had charmed the Labour Prime Minister, Ramsay MacDonald.
5. Sir Robert Gilbert Vansittart (1881-1957), civil servant and diplomatist, and like his host an old Etonian. He had risen steadily in the Foreign Office until in 1928 he was appointed Principal Private Secretary to the Prime Minister—a post he retained temporarily under Ramsay MacDonald. On 1 January 1930 he had returned to the Foreign Office as Permanent Under-Secretary.
6. The 'Pepys' or Saffron Walden mazer, hallmarked 1507, was sold at Christie's in July 1929 and, through Harris, was acquired by J. Pierpont Morgan. At that time the export of works of art was unrestricted.
7. The first Earl Farquhar (1844-1923), Master of the Household to Edward VII, had been Treasurer of the Unionist (Tory) Party; after the war he refused to relinquish to them funds collected while the party had been in coalition with the Liberals. At his death he made lavish bequests, in particular to King Edward's niece Princess Arthur of Connaught, Duchess of Fife, who was both his executor and principal beneficiary.

Control. 'Dear Edie, you wont let me convert you. But when you see your miners, with those terrible illegitimate children—

Eight in a room. One bed. What can you expect? They speak straight out to me, the old fashioned ones. Cant do anything else. What would you do? What should we do, if we lived like that? But we're not beasts. We can control ourselves. I detest Prohibition for that reason.'

Swept on, energetically, confidently, to the Webbs (woman sprung up beside me like a cobra) "Our class & yours can never meet. What difference is there? But these clever people! Yeats & Lady Gregory on a committee are hopeless—but both very clever people. Cant do anything."[8]

Ly L. can do whatever she wishes. She looked like an early Victorian picture—a Lawrence, I thought; a small pinched well cut face; healthy; without paint; very pink, pearls knotted about her wrists. The other woman garish, like a ruined almond tree. The rooms all set out with cases, chests, pictures objects. "I never give more than £10: I hunt about in rag & bone shops." Bogy has the glazed stuffed look of the well fed bachelor. Is evidently one of those elderly comfortable men of taste & leisure who make a profession of society; a perfectly instinctive snob. Knows everyone; lunches with Lord Lascelles; has taken the measure of it all exactly; nothing to say; proficient; surly; adept; an unattractive type, with all his talk of Lords & ladies, his belief in great houses; something of a gorged look, which connoisseurs have; as if he had always just swallowed a bargain. Something airless & too tidy in the house; a plethora of altar pieces. He pads about, gorged, without anything to seek for, save in old rag & bone shops; at the crest (I suppose) of his world. I suppose that this centre to one's mind—an altarpiece—is a bad one; too still & capable of acquisition. He never wants anything unattainable, I daresay: & so has feathered his nest. Roger says he has 'flair'; Roger who looks like a ravaged scavenger & lives with sardine tins & linoleum; yes, but Roger's house seems alive, with a living hand in it, manipulated, stretched. Why do interesting people never fix them down among objects (beautiful) & Duchesses (desirable). I tried, sitting on a priceless settee, picked up in Whitechapel for £10 (I never give more) to analyse my sensations. The ladies showed a perfect commercial grasp of the situation. Ramsay was tossed between them like a fish among cormorants. I had the impression that they did not rate this acquisition high; but took it as part of the days work. Ly L. had him to herself in a shaded room for an hour. Failing this, she had her claims written down to hand him.

Angelica said at the pantomime, as we watched the spangled lady dance,

8. Lady Gregory (1852-1932) was co-founder in 1902 with the poet W. B. Yeats of the Irish National Theatre.

"I shall never be able to dance like that but I may be able to paint like she dances."[9]

Sunday 26 January

I am 48: we have been at Rodmell—a wet, windy day again; but on my birthday we walked among the downs, like the folded wings of grey birds; & saw first one fox, very long with his brush stretched; then a second; which had been barking, for the sun was hot over us; it leapt lightly over a fence & entered the furze—a very rare sight. How many foxes are there in England? At night I read Lord Chaplin's life. I cannot yet write naturally in my new room, because the table is not the right height, & I must stoop to warm my hands. Everything must be absolutely what I am used to.

I forgot to say that when we made up our 6 months accounts, we found I had made about £3,020 last year—the salary of a civil servant: a surprise to me, who was content with £200 for so many years. But I shall drop very heavily I think. The Waves wont sell more than 2,000 copies. I am stuck fast in that book—I mean, glued to it, like a fly on gummed paper. Sometimes I am out of touch; but go on; then again feel that I have at last, by violent measures—like breaking through gorse—set my hands on something central. Perhaps I can now say something quite straight out; & at length; & need not be always casting a line to make my book the right shape. But how to pull it together, how to compost it—press it into one—I do not know; nor can I guess the end—it might be a gigantic conversation. The interludes are very difficult, yet I think essential; so as to bridge & also give a background—the sea; insensitive nature—I dont know. But I think, when I feel this sudden directness, that it must be right: anyhow no other form of fiction suggests itself except as a repetition at the moment.

It has sold about 6,500 today, Oct. 30th 1931—after 3 weeks. But will stop now I suppose.

Lord Buckmaster sat next me. I was talking to Desmond about Irene. Suddenly Ethel said leaning across,

But did you ever know Lord Tennyson? & my evening was ruined. Typical of these parties.[10]

9. As the Woolfs took Angelica to the Pantomime (*Puss in Boots* at the *Lyceum*) on 20 January, the above entry cannot all have been written on 16 January.
10. VW dined with Ethel Sands on 21 January (LW went to his mother). Stanley Owen Buckmaster, 1st Viscount Buckmaster (1861-1934), Law Lord, appellate judge and member of the Judicial Committee of the Privy Council, had been a Liberal MP and became Lord Chancellor in Asquith's government, 1915-16. Ethel's ill-judged enquiry is later ascribed by VW to Lord Buckmaster (see *IV VW Letters*, nos. 2128, 2133).

FEBRUARY 1930

Monday 10 February

Charlie Sanger died yesterday,[1] the very fine cold day, when we were driving up. I feel sorry in gusts. I wish we had dined there. I shall miss some peculiar thing—loyal, worn, romantic; flowing with affection. He knew us when Thoby died; had always clasped my hand warmly, sat sparking, glittering, elfish; very sympathetic, very serious, in the right way. He had a stern view, I think; had found life hard; & envisaged its hardness for others. Yes; I have a peculiar feeling for him—can one say more? And this is the sorrow for him—feeling one will never again have that. (I cant analyse—have indeed a slight temperature, & am in two minds if it is influenza, & whether to tell Leonard, who has had it—to put off Ethel Smyth, & Nessa—to go to bed—what is the sensible thing to do?[2]

Sunday 16 February

To lie on the sofa for a week. I am sitting up today, in the usual state of unequal animation. Below normal, with spasmodic desire to write, then to doze. It is a fine cold day & if my energy & sense of duty persist, I shall drive up to Hampstead.[3] But I doubt that I can write to any purpose. A cloud swims in my head. One is too conscious of the body & jolted out of the rut of life to get back to fiction. Once or twice I have felt that odd whirr of wings in the head which comes when I am ill so often—last year for example, at this time I lay in bed constructing A Room of One's Own (which sold 10,000 two days ago). If I could stay in bed another fortnight (but there is no chance of that) I believe I should see the whole of The Waves. Or of course I might go off on something different. As it is I half

1. C. P. Sanger died on the 8th not the 9th of February.
2. Dame Ethel Smyth (1858-1944), composer, author and feminist; daughter of an army general, she had to fight for a musical career and became an inveterate campaigner. She studied music in the circle of Brahms in Leipzig, wrote many operas (VW saw the first production of *The Wreckers* at His Majesty's Theatre in 1909), was a militant (and imprisoned) suffragist, and published a sequence of books of recollections; VW recorded her views of *Impressions that Remained* in the year of its publication (see *I VW Diary*, 28 November 1919), and reviewed her *Streaks of Life* in 1921 (Kp C218). Dame Ethel had now written in praise of *A Room of One's Own* and proposed a meeting; owing to VW's health this was several times postponed (see *IV VW Letters*, nos. 2136, 2138, 2140, 2143), but took place on 20 February.
3. The Woolfs *did* drive to Hampstead, and LW took a walk; he too had been ill and in bed with a temperature the previous week, but as usual recovered more quickly than VW.

incline to insist upon a dash to Cassis; but perhaps this needs more determination than I possess; & we shall dwindle on here. Pinker is walking about the room looking for the bright patch—a sign of spring. I believe these illnesses are in my case—how shall I express it?—partly mystical. Something happens in my mind. It refuses to go on registering impressions. It shuts itself up. It becomes chrysalis. I lie quite torpid, often with acute physical pain—as last year; only discomfort this. Then suddenly something springs. Two nights ago, Vita was here; & when she went, I began to feel the quality of the evening—how it was spring coming: a silver light; mixing with the early lamps; the cabs all rushing through the streets; I had a tremendous sense of life beginning; mixed with that emotion, which is the essence of my feeling, but escapes description—(I keep on making up the Hampton Court scene in The Waves —Lord how I wonder if I shall pull this book off! It is a litter of fragments so far). Well, as I was saying, between these long pauses (for I am swimmy in the head, & write rather to stabilise myself than to make a correct statement), I felt the spring beginning, & Vita's life so full & flush; & all the doors opening; & this is I believe the moth shaking its wings in me. I then begin to make up my story whatever it is; ideas rush in me; often though this is before I can control my mind or pen. It is no use trying to write at this stage. And I doubt if I can fill this white monster. I would like to lie down & sleep, but feel ashamed. Leonard brushed off his influenza in one day & went about his business feeling ill. Here am I still loafing, undressed, with Elly coming tomorrow. But as I was saying my mind works in idleness. To do nothing is often my most profitable way.

I am reading Byron: Maurois: which sends me to Childe Harold; makes me speculate.[4] How odd a mixture: the weakest sentimental Mrs Hemans combined with trenchant bare vigour. How did they combine? And sometimes the descriptions in C.H. are "beautiful"; like a great poet.

There are the three elements in Byron:

1 The romantic dark haired lady singing drawing room melodies to the guitar.

> "Tambourgi! Tambourgi! thy 'larum afar
> Gives hope to the valiant, & promise of war;

. . . . .

4. André Maurois' *Byron*, 1930. VW had the French edition in 2 volumes. The quotations which follow are from *Childe Harold's Pilgrimage*: 1: Canto II, lxxii, from verses i and ii of the Albanians' song; 2: Canto II, lxxvi; 3: Canto II, xxxvii; 4: i.e. Canto I, lxix, lxx, 'two Stanzas of a buffooning cast (on London's Sunday)' (Byron to Dallas, 21 August 1811); 5: Canto II, xcvi.

> Oh! who is more brave than a dark Suliote,
> In his snowy camese & his shaggy Capote"
> —something manufactured: a pose; silliness.

2 Then there is the vigorous rhetorical, like his prose, & good as prose.

> Hereditary Bondsmen! Know ye not
> *Who* would be free *themselves* must strike the blow?
> By their right arms the conquest must be wrought?
> Will Gaul or Muscovite redress ye? No! . . .

3 Then what rings to me truer, & is almost poetry.

> Dear Nature is the kindest mother still!
> Though always changing, in her aspect mild;

(all in Canto From her bare bosom let me take my fill,
11 of C H.) Her never-weaned, though not her favoured child.

* * *

> To me by day or night she ever smiled,
> Though I have marked her when none other hath,
> And sought her more & more, & loved her best in wrath.

4 And then there is of course the pure satiric, as in the description of
5 a London Sunday; & finally (but this makes more than three) the
inevitable half assumed half genuine tragic note, which comes as a
refrain, about death & the loss of friends.

> All thou could have of mine, stern Death! thou hast;
> The parent, Friend, & now the more than Friend:
> Ne'er yet for one thine arrows flew so fast,
> And grief with grief continuing still to blend,
> Hath snatched the little joy that life had yet to lend.

These I think make him up; & make much that is spurious, vapid, yet very
changeable, & then rich & with greater range than the other poets, could
he have got the whole into order. A novelist, he might have been. It is odd
however to read in his letters his prose an apparently genuine feeling
about Athens: & to compare it with the convention he adopted in verse.
(There is some sneer about the Acropolis). But then the sneer may have
been a pose too. The truth may be that if you are charged at such high
voltage you cant fit any of the ordinary human feelings; must pose; must
rhapsodise; don't fit in. He wrote in the Inn Album that his age was 100.
And this is true, measuring life by feeling.

Monday 17 February

And this temperature is up;
but it has now gone down; & now

[*Thursday 20 February*]

Feb. 20th, I must canter my wits if I can. Perhaps some character sketches.

Snow:[5]

She came in wrapped in a dark fur coat; which being taken off, she appeared in nondescript grey stockinette & jay blue stripes. Her eyes too are jay blue, but have an anguished starved look, as of a cat that has climbed on to a chimney piece & looks down at a dog. Her face is pale, & very small; indeed, has a curious preserved innocency which makes it hard to think that she is 50. However, her neck is very loose skinned; & there are the dewlaps of middle age. The preserved look seems to indicate lack of experience; as if life had put her in a refrigerator. And we talked— She brought me a parcel, & this was a book from Ethel Smyth, with a letter, which to veil the embarrassment which I supposed her to feel, I read aloud. Her comment was "What miles away all this is from Cheltenham!" Then we talked—but it was her starved & anguished look that remains & the attitude of mind. She seemed to be saying inwardly "I have missed everything. There are Vanessa & Virginia, They have lives full of novels & husbands & exhibitions. I am fifty & it has all slipped by." I gathered this from the jocose pertinacity with which she kept referring to herself. She said the climate of Cheltenham is so sleepy that she often cant paint; & after lunch they put on the gramophone; & then she goes most days to her mother at Bockhampton, where she likes meeting the village people. Farmers wives shake hands. After her mothers death—but she is only 80 & as firm as a rock—she & Lily who is political, but of course that doesn't take up all her time exactly, are going to live at Harrogate, where the climate is not so sleepy, & they know more people. Nothing long distracted her from her central concern—I have had no life & life is over. Even clothes suggested the same old theme. A dressmaker had told her that one enjoyed life more if one was well dressed. So she was

5. Margaret (Margery) Kemplay Snowden (1878-1966?), daughter of a Yorkshire vicar, had been a fellow-student of Vanessa's at the Royal Academy Schools at the beginning of the century; she remained her faithful friend and correspondent, living in Cheltenham, with her sister and near her mother. She came to tea with VW on 18 February.

trying this specific, to the tune of £8.8 at Pomeroy's in Old Burlington Street. But this worried & fretted her too. In fact I have seldom got a more dismal impression of suffering—too ignoble & petty to be called suffering: call it rather frustration, non-entity; being lifted on a shelf, & seeing things pass; "but then I am very lazy—thats what it is—I lapse into comfort." I should call it lapsing into despair. "What can three women do alone in the country?" Lord, how I praise God that I had a bent strong enough to coerce every minute of my life since I was born! This fiddling & drifting & not impressing oneself upon anything—this always refraining & fingering & cutting things up into little jokes & facetiousness—thats whats so annihilating. Yet given little money, little looks, no special gift, but only enough to make her devastatingly aware that other people have more gift, so that she sees her still lives against the superior still lives of Margaret Gere & the Cotswold school,—what can one do?[6] How could one battle? How could one leap on the back of life & wring its scruff? One would joke, bitterly; & become egotistical & anxious to explain & excuse; & plaintive. What I thought most pathetic was the fact that about 5.30 she began to fidget (she never does anything boldly & directly) with her gloves, & say she must be going. But where? I asked. To the Polytechnic to hear a lecture upon French literature. But why? "Oh one never hears French talked in Cheltenham." Dear dear, but I could tell you all about French literature, I said. However, she shillied shallied; & whether she wanted to go or to stay, I don't know. And when I asked her what she was going to do that night, Well that depends how long the lecture lasts, she said, feebly laughing. Wont you go to a play? No I think I shall have what is called a snack at the Temperance hotel;—Lord Lord, I repeat again. And it isn't as if she were unconscious & oblivious: no, she knows that the dog is there, & arches her back & puts out her paw, but ever so feebly & fussily.

Friday 21 February

No two women could be more extravagantly contraposed than Marjorie Snowden & Ethel Smyth. I was lying here at four yesterday when I heard the bell ring then a brisk tramp up the stairs; & then behold a bluff, military old woman (older than I expected), bounced into the room, a little glazed flyaway & abrupt; in a three cornered hat & tailor made suit.

"Let me look at you".

6. Margaret Gere (1878-1965) studied painting at Birmingham and at the Slade; she lived at Painswick in Gloucestershire and was, like Margery Snowden, a member of the Cheltenham Group of Artists. She was primarily a figure painter.

That over, Now I have brought a book & pencil. I want to ask.

Here there was a ring at the bell. I went to look over. Then we went to tea.

First I want to make out the genealogy of your mothers family. Old Pattle—have you a picture? No. Well now—the names of his daughters.

This lasted out tea. Afterwards, on the sofa, with Ethel stretching her legs out on Pinker's basket, we talked ceaselessly till 7—when L. came in. We talked—she talked considerably more than I. (On the stairs going up to tea I had asked to be Virginia; about ten minutes after tea she asked to be Ethel: all was settled; the basis of an undying friendship made in 15 minutes:—how sensible; how rapid;) & she got off; oh about music—"I am said to be an egoist. I am a fighter. I feel for the underdog. I rang up Hugh Allen & suggested lunch.[7] My dear Sir Hugh—my dear Ethel—there are facts you dont know about your sex. Believe me I have to go on coming to London, bullying, badgering—at last, they promise me 14 women in the orchestra. I go & find 2. So I begin ringing up." She has a vein, like a large worm, in her temple which swells. Her cheeks redden. Her faded eyes flash. She has a broad rounded forehead. She recurred to dress. I have to go to Bath to hear dear Maurice Baring's little plays; & then we go to (here Elly interrupted) Rottingdean.[8] And I must take an evening suit. Thats what worries me. I'm only happy in this—I have one gown I wear for conducting. And then I have to pack (here is a pineapple from Leonard's mother who waits outside). "My maid? But she's only a general—an Irish woman. "Dr (she calls me Dr) Mrs Woolf doesn't mean to see you. Heres another letter from her—to put you off." But I've come. And dont it show that my appetite for life is still great? I've thought of nothing but seeing you for 10 days. And this friendship has come to me now." So sincere & abrupt is she, & discri

minating withal—judging Vita & her secondrate women   Enid Bagnold
friends shrewdly—that perhaps something gritty & not
the usual expansive fluff, may come of it. I like to hear her talk of music. She has written a piece—on Brewster's Prisoner; & will have the gorgeous fun of orchestrating it this summer.[9] She says writing music is like

---

7. Sir Hugh Percy Allen (1869-1946), Professor of Music in the University of Oxford from 1918 until his death and Director of the Royal College of Music, 1918-37.

8. Maurice Baring, since 1893 one of Ethel Smyth's closest friends, had a house at Rottingdean, near Brighton. He had published two volumes of *Diminutive Dramas*, 1910 and 1919.

9. Henry Bennet Brewster (1859-1908), a cosmopolitan Anglo-American philosopher and writer whom Ethel Smyth had met in Florence when she was twenty-five. He was the only man with whom she was ever to be in love; he was married, a fact

writing novels. One thinks of the sea—naturally one gets a phrase for it. Orchestration is colouring. And one has to be very careful with one's 'technique'. Rhapsodises about A Room; about Miss Williamson;[10] about the end of some book of Maurice Baring's. "I'm in the street. I belong to the crowd. I say the crowd is right." Perhaps she is right to belong to the crowd. There is something fine & tried & experienced about her besides the rant & the riot & the egotism—& I'm not sure that she is the egotist that people make out. She said she never had anybody to admire her, & therefore might write good music to the end. Has to live in the country because of her passion for games. Plays golf, rides a bicycle; was thrown hunting two years ago. Then fell on her arm & was in despair, because life wd. be over if she could not play games. 'I am very strong' which she proved by talking till 7.30; then eating a biscuit & drinking a glass of vermouth & going off to eat a supper of maccaroni when she got to Woking at 9.

"I'll tell you all about it" she grinned at her maid, who asked if I was a nice woman. A fine old creature, certainly, Ethel. She talks French 'méringues' with a highly French accent.

Saturday 22 February

I had meant to write a sketch of George—Sir George Duck-worth[11]— as he announced himself to Nelly—& of Lytton; both unexpected visitors yesterday—for I'm not to go down to the studio till Monday; & so must canter my pen amateurishly here; but ten minutes ago the idea came to me of a possible broadsheet; which I wd. like to adumbrate, before discussing with L. My notion is a single sheet, containing say 2,000 or if printed back & front 4,000 words. Art, politics, Lit., music: an essay by a single writer to be printed at irregular intervals; sent to subscribers; costing 6d. Sometimes only a reproduction. It should be a statement about life: something somebody wants to say; not a regular comment. Very little

---

which complicated an already intense relationship. Brewster had written the libretto, based on his own drama, for her opera *The Wreckers*, and her last large-scale work, the oratorio *The Prison*, took its inspiration from his metaphysical work *The Prison: A Dialogue* (1891), republished with a memoir by Ethel Smyth in 1930.

10. Elizabeth Williamson (b. 1903), a great-niece of Ethel Smyth, was an astronomer and a mathematician who taught at University College, London.

11. George Duckworth had been knighted in 1927; in 1924-7 he had served as English Trustee and chairman of the Irish Land Trust for the provision of houses and land for ex-servicemen in Ireland under the Act of Settlement.

expense wd. be involved. It would have a spring & an urgency about it wh. the regular sheets lack. Sometimes only a picture. To be closely under L. & my thumbs, so as to give character & uniformity. To lapse for a month if necessary. No incubus of regular appearance. A circular signed by L. & me to be sent round. Young writers enlisted. Signed articles. Everything of the humblest, least ostentatious. The Hogarth News. The

And in June, I was offered the Editorship of a 4ly; by ⟨the Graphic⟩ Mr Bott & Mr Turner of the Book Club: L. is refusing it at this moment (30th June)[12]

Broadsheet.—name to be decided. You see I wd. like to write on Scott this week, & cant, because Richmond has sent the book already.[13] L. wd. do politics. Roger art. The young would have their fling. Possibly, if expenses were kept down, they could get £5 or so, & have their names. But they must not be essays—always—must be topical to some extent.

That being enough to go upon in talk after lunch—& it is a fine still day & perhaps we may drive to Richmond & try my legs walking—I will obediently, like a student in the art school—sketch Sir George. First his jowl: it is of the finest semi-transparent flesh; so that one longs to slice it, as it rests, infinitely tender, upon his collar. Otherwise he is as tight as a drum. One expects his trousers to split as he sits down. This he does slowly & rises with difficulty. Still some sentiment begins to form misty between us. He speaks of 'Mother'. I daresay finds in me some shadowy likeness—well—& then he is not now in a position to do me harm. His conventions amuse me. I suppose these family affections are somehow self-protection. He preserves a grain or two of what is me—my unknown past; my self; so that if George died, I

should feel something of myself buried. He is endlessly self-complacent. His stories, once started, roll comfortably—he is immensely comfortable—into the pocket of his solid self esteem. I ask, What about the hogs (the Chesterfield hogs) & he replies

See Sir George Duckworth on 'Pigs' in todays Times. Pigs are the most intelligent of animals. I own a small herd of white pedigree hogs."[14]

that the cowman's wife has had a very long labour. Margaret has been very worried. Dalingridge was lit up all night. They had to use the

12. No further details of this offer have been found.
13. The book VW hoped for must have been Stephen Gwynne's recently published *The Life of Sir Walter Scott*; a review of it appeared in the *TLS* on 27 February. But see below, 1 May 1930, when Bruce Richmond *did* send her a book on Scott.
14. This marginal note was added on 30 June 1930; that day's *Times* had published a letter from Sir George Duckworth of Dalingridge Place, Sussex, 'Owner of a small herd of pedigree Middle White pigs'; it was a response to a speech by Lloyd

telephone—to send for the dr. The womans mother slept in the house—
& so it goes on, singing cosily & contentedly the praises of the good
master & mistress—which I have no doubt they are. And he trots out his
little compliments—asked to be Sheriff. And he wishes to know if I am
making fabulous sums—& he chuckles & dimples & respects me for
being asked to a party by the Lord Mayor. And he twits Eddy Marsh for
being fond of the society of the great. And he deplores the nudity of
Nessa's pictures—& so prattles & chortles & gives me turtle soup &
advises about the preparation & so takes himself off, to meet Henry &
return to Dalingridge & the cowman & the hogs—a very incestuous
race—& his cook Janet & his Bronnie, home on leave from the Navy—
well, it does appear as if human life were perfectly tolerable; his voltage
is absolutely normal. The world has been made for him.[15]

Lytton came in after dinner. Very twinkly, lustrous, easy & even warm.
Leonard made cigarettes. I lay on the sofa in the twilight of cushions.
Lytton had been sent a book about Columbus & told us the story making
it into a fantastic amusing Lytton book[16]—Columbus a mad religious
fanatic who sailed west & west because he had read in Isaiah a prophesy;
his crew being convicts let out from prison; & they came to Cuba & he
made them sign a statement that this was India, because it was too large
to be an island; & they picked up gold & gems & went back to Spain &
the King & Queen rose as he came in. Here are all the elements of a Lytton
concoction, told with great gusto; irony; a sense of the incongruous &
dramatic. Then we warbled melodiously about Dadie, & Cambridge; &
Charlie; & so on. He has a new gramophone. He is editing Greville.[17]
He is very content too—not for George's reasons; & very well equipped,
& buys books; & likes us; & is going to Cambridge this week end. Its

George who was reported as saying he was 'not surprised that Mr Baldwin has
always expressed a preference for the society of pigs'. Sir George wrote that
whereas townsmen were apt to speak of both farm labourers and pigs as the last
word in stupidity, his considerable experience led him to conclude that the skill
of the former ranked well above all other labourers', 'while the "pig" is markedly
superior to all other farm animals in general intelligence'.

15. George Duckworth had three sons; Auberon and Henry were the two eldest.
16. Lives of Columbus by André de Hevesy and Jacob Wasserman had recently been
    issued in translation. Lytton published nothing on this subject.
17. An expurgated edition of the memoirs of Charles Greville had been published in
    1888 and Lytton, who had been engaged in a long campaign for the publication
    of the complete text, had for the past six months been working on the manuscripts
    in the British Museum, helped by Ralph Partridge and Frances Marshall. His
    edition of *The Greville Memoirs from 1814-1860* eventually appeared in 8 volumes
    in 1938, the editorial work completed by Roger Fulford.

odd how little one remembers what is actually said. I am thinking of the new paper.

Saturday 1 March

And then I went for a walk & brought on a headache, & so lay down again till today, Saturday—a fine day—when we propose to drive off—oh Thank God a thousand times—to Rodmell & there be at rest. This *To Hampstead Garden suburb [on 22 February]* little affair has taken 3 weeks, & will land me in 4, of non-writing inexpressiveness. Yet I'm not sure that this is not the very thing for The Waves. It was dragging too much out of my head— If ever a book drained me, this one does. If I had wisdom, no doubt I should potter at Rodmell for a fortnight, not writing. I shall take a look at it one of these mornings in my sunny room.

One evening here I had the odd experience of perfect rest & satisfaction. All the bayonets that prod me sank. There I lay (I daresay for an hour) happy. And the quality was odd. Not an anxiety, not a stir, anywhere. No one coming. Nothing to do. All strain ceased. A supreme sailing with ... through the dominion (I am *[word illegible]* quoting—I think Shelley—& it makes nonsense.) This is the rarest of all my moods. I cant recall another. Perhaps at Rodmell sometimes. Everything is shut off. It depends upon having been in the stir of London for some time. Not to have to get up & see Sibyl or Ethel or anybody— what a supreme relief! And now I have a chance to brew a little quiet thought. Yesterday I was offered £2,000 to write a life of Boswell by Doran Heinemann. L. is writing my polite refusal this moment.[1] I have bought my freedom. A queer thought that I have actually paid for the power to go to Rodmell & only think of The Waves by refusing this offer. If I accepted I would buy houses, tables & go to Italy, not worth it. Yesterday we went over 57 Russell Sqre wh. we may take. But I rather dread the noise & the size—I dont know. A lovely view.

Monday 3 March

Rodmell again. My new bedroom again. Children playing in the school. A thick pearl grey blue day; water drops on the window. Suppose health were shown on a thermometer I have gone up 10 degrees since yesterday,

1. LW's diary, 28 February 1930: 'Reeves came fr Doubleday Doran ask V write Boswell'. A. S. Frere Reeves was a director of William Heinemann Ltd, which at this time was owned by Doubleday Doran of New York.

when I lay, mumbling the bones of Dodo: if it had bones;[2] now I sit up, but cannot face going down & bringing an MS to read. Curiosity begins to stir all the same. Such is the effect of 24 hours here, & one ramble for 30 minutes on the flats. The sun wells up, like a pulse, behind the clouds. Tremendous shoals of birds are flying,—& the flop eared trains meeting as usual under Caburn.[3]

Molly Hamilton writes a d—d bad novel.[4] She has the wits to construct a method of telling a story; & then heaps it with the dreariest, most confused litter of old clothes. When I stop to read a page attentively I am shocked by the dishabille of her English. It is like hearing cooks & scullions chattering; she scarcely articulates, dashes it off, I imagine, on blocks of paper, on her knee, at the House of Commons perhaps; or in the Tube. And the quality of the emotion is so thick & squab, the emotions of secondrate women painters, of spotted & pimpled young men: I dont know how she conveys such a sense of the secondrate without gift: the soft pedal too, & the highminded pedal; & no wit; & not precision; & no word standing alone, but each flopping on to the shoulder of another—Lord what a style! What a mind. It has energy & some ability—chiefly shown in the method; but that breaks down; & that too is laboriously lifted. Now being still flabby in the march of the mind, I must read Sea Air—a good manuscript.[5]

Tuesday 11 March

all because I have to buy myself a dress this afternoon, & cant think what I want, I cannot read. I have written, fairly well—but it is a difficult book—at Waves; but cant keep on after 12; & now shall write here, for 20 minutes.

My impressions of Margaret [Llewelyn Davies] & Lilian [Harris] at Monks House were of great lumps of grey coat; straggling wisps of hair; hats floppy & home made; thick woollen stockings; black shoes, many

2. *Dodo* (1893) was a once celebrated novel by E. F. Benson in which the eponymous heroine is based on Margot Tennant (Mrs Asquith), and her candid friend Edith Staines on Ethel Smyth.

3. This train image occurs in *II VW Diary*, 7 January 1920, and in *The Waves*, p 204; but the word used is *lop* not *flop*.

4. Mary Agnes (Molly) Hamilton (1882-1966), a vigorous and able writer and journalist, of whom VW had seen a good deal in the years after the war. She had been elected Labour MP for Blackburn in 1929. Her latest novel was *Special Providence* (1930).

5. Author unidentified; *Sea Air* was the title of a book by the popular romantic novelist Isobel C. Clarke published in 1932—but it seems unlikely that it was submitted to the Hogarth Press.

wraps, shabby handbags, & shapelessness, & shabbiness & dreariness & drabness unspeakable. A tragedy in its way. Margaret at any rate deserved better of life than this dishevelled & undistinguished end. They are in lodgings—as usual. Have, as usual, a wonderful Xtian Scientist landlady; are somehow rejected by active life; sit knitting perhaps & smoking cigarettes, in the parlour where they have their meals, where there is always left a dish of oranges & bananas. I doubt if they have enough to eat. They seemed to me flabby & bloodless, spread into rather toneless chunks of flesh; having lost any commerce with looking glasses. So we showed them the garden, gave them tea (& I dont think an iced cake had come Lilian's way this 6 weeks) & then—oh the dismal sense of people stranded, wanting to be energised; drifting—all woollen & hairy. (It is odd how the visual impression dominates.) There is a jay blue spark in Margaret's eye, now & then, But she had not been out of the lodging for 5 weeks because of the East wind. Her mind has softened & wrinkled, sitting indoors with the oranges & cigarettes. Lilian is almost stone deaf, & mumbles & crumbles, emerging clearly only once, to discuss politics. Something has blunted Margaret's edge, rusted it, worn it, long before its time. Must old age be so shapeless? The only escape is to work the mind. I shall write a history of English literature, I think, in those days. And I shall walk. And I shall buy clothes, & keep my hair tidy, & make myself dine out. But perhaps life becomes repetitious, & one takes no trouble; is glad to be shovelled about in motor cars. M. has her tragic past. She is pathetic to me now—conciliatory & nervous where she used to be trenchant & severe. Janet she says writes endless notes; has sisters for ever staying with her to convalesce; & Emphie caught up their little white dog the other day from a wild herd of racing greyhounds, & had it bitten to death in her arms.[6] This is the sort of adventure that only befalls elderly unmarried women, on whom it makes a tremendous & very painful impression—so defence-less are they, so unable to throw off the damp blanket that surrounds them. What I miss is colour, energy, any clear reflection of the moment. I see those thick stockings & grey hairy wraps everywhere.

Monday 17 March

The test of a book (to a writer) [*is*] if it makes a space in which, quite naturally, you can say what you want to say. As this morning I could say

6. Janet Case lived with her sister Emphie at Minstead in the New Forest; she was the youngest of six sisters. From 1925-37 she contributed a weekly 'Country Diary' to the *Manchester Guardian*.

what Rhoda said. This proves that the book itself is alive: because it has not crushed the thing I wanted to say, but allowed me to slip it in, without any compression or alteration.

Friday 28 March

Yes, but this book is a very queer business. I had a day of intoxication when I said Children are nothing to this: when I sat surveying the whole book complete, & quarrelled with L. (about Ethel Smyth) & walked it off, felt the pressure of the form—the splendour & the greatness—as—perhaps, I have never felt them. But I shan't race it off in intoxication. I keep pegging away; & find it the most complex, & difficult of all my books. How to end, save by a tremendous discussion, in which every life shall have its voice—a mosaic—a——. I do not know. The difficulty is that it is all at high pressure. I have not yet mastered the speaking voice. Yet I think something is there; & I propose to go on pegging it down, arduously, & then re-write, reading much of it aloud, like poetry. It will bear expansion. It is compressed I think. It is—whatever I make of it—a large & potential theme—wh. Orlando was not perhaps. At any rate, I have taken my fence.

Home from tea with Nessa & Angelica. A fine spring day. I walked along Oxford St. The buses are strung on a chain. People fight & struggle. Knocking each other off the pavement. Old bareheaded men; a motor car accident; &c. To walk alone in London is the greatest rest.

Tuesday 1 April

And we have got to go & dine with Raymond now, this very potent, astonishingly exciting warm evening. I sit with my window open & hear the humming see a yellow window open in the hotel: I walked back from Leicester Square. What queer memories have got themselves mixed into this evening I asked. Something from a very soft, rather mystic evening; not feverish & fretful; no; by the sea; blue; gentle. And I dropped in at the dressmaker. She has no teeth. She was stitching. She said like a friend Mrs Woolf we are going to move. And I thought you wdnt mind if I left out the stitching as my eyes ached. All that is said tonight is gentle & happy & seems to thrust into some soft tide. I cant get it right, naturally.

Nessa is at Charleston. They will have the windows open; perhaps even sit by the pond. She will think This is what I have made by years of unknown work—my sons, my daughter. She will be perfectly content (as I suppose) Quentin fetching bottles; Clive immensely good tempered.

They will think of London with dislike. Yet it is very exciting; I shall sip my wine at Raymond's, & try & elicit something from Lytton. And so must change.

Friday 4 April

I am trying to sketch my last chapter—unsuccessfully; so will use 10 minutes to note my observations at Raymond's. Chiefly upon the atmosphere of buggery. Lytton's face lit up with love & rapture when I deserted the delightful women, with all their gifts, for Mr Williamson, brilliant & beautiful, but unknown, of Oxford. Raymond sat on the arm of Lytton's chair. Morgan came in from Meleager. And I went to see Ronnie behind the scenes. He was looking very nice in shorts. Eddy came in from Cochran's latest.[1] He had had to stand & was (I am making up The Waves) peevish. (humour is what it lacks). Anyhow, he said, Ensor (I forget) looked very pretty in a white suit—the rest oh so hideous. At this the other buggers pricked their ears & became somehow silly. I mean rather giggly & coy. An atmosphere entirely secluded, intimate, & set on one object; all agreed upon the things they liked. Raymond barked once or twice rudely (he is underbred, in voice anyhow) his feeling that I was noting, scoffing. Told me how Gerbault loathed women; then protested that I was not to believe all the stories of D'Annunzio & Duse: there was another side, *she* had maltreated him.[2] A protest; raucous, & obtrusive. A photograph of Stephen Tennant (Siegfried Sassoon goes to the same dressmaker) in a tunic, in an attitude was shown about; also little boys at a private school. Morgan became unfamiliar, discussing the beauties of Hilton Young's stepson.[3] "His skating is magnificent" (then in an undertone deploring some woman's behaviour). This all made on me a tinkling, private, giggling, impression. As if I had gone in to a men's urinal.

1. Mr Williamson, still unknown. R. C. Trevelyan's verse tragedy *Meleager* was being performed by the Players Company at the Rudolf Steiner Hall. *Cochran's 1930 Revue* at the London Pavilion was the latest in the succession of spectacular entertainments put on by the showman C. B. Cochran (1872-1951).
2. Alain Gerbault (1893-1941), French navigator and former international tennis player, had sailed round the world single-handed in 1925-9. Gabriele D'Annunzio (1863-1938), Italian poet, novelist and playwright whose liaison with the celebrated Italian actress Eleonora Duse (1859-1924) was in every sense a theatrical one.
3. (Edward) Hilton Young (1879-1960), whom VW had once thought of as a possible husband (see *I QB*, p 131), was now a Conservative MP: he had married in 1922 the widow of Captain R. F. Scott ('Scott of the Antarctic') and his stepson was Peter Scott (b. 1909) the artist and naturalist.

Wednesday 9 April

What I now think (about the Waves) is that I can give in a very few strokes the essentials of a person's character. It should be done boldly, almost as caricature. I have yesterday entered what may be the last lap. Like every piece of the book it goes by fits & starts. I never get away with it; but am tugged back. I hope this makes for solidity; & must look to my sentences. The abandonment of Orlando & Lighthouse is much checked by the extreme difficulty of the form—as it was in Jacob's Room. I think this is the furthest development so far; but of course it may miss fire somewhere. I think I have kept stoically to the original conception. What I fear is that the re-writing will have to be so drastic that I may entirely muddle it somehow. It is bound to be very imperfect. But I think it possible that I have got my statues against the sky.

Friday 11 April

Yesterday walked through the Waddesdon Greenhouses with Mr Johnson.[4] There were single red lines taking root in sand. Cyclamen by the hundred gross. Azaleas massed like military bands. Carnations at different stages. Vines being picked thin by sedulous men. Nothing older than 40 years, but now ready made in perfection. A fig tree that had a thousand lean regular branches. The statues tied up, like dead horses, in sheets. The whole thing dead. Made, planted, put into position in the year 1880 or thereabouts. One flower wd. have given more pleasure than those dozens of grosses. And the heat, & the tidiness & the accuracy & the organisation. Mr Johnson like a nectarine, hard, red, ripe. He was taught all he knew by Miss Alice, & accepted admiration as his income. Sir he called us.

Sunday 13 April

I read Shakespeare *directly* I have finished writing, when my mind is agape & red & hot. Then it is astonishing. I never yet knew how amazing his stretch & speed & word coining power is, until I felt it utterly outpace & outrace my own, seeming to start equal & then I see him draw ahead & do things I could not in my wildest tumult & utmost press of mind

4. The Woolfs lunched with LW's brother Philip at his home at Upper Winchendon, and in the afternoon were shown over the Waddesdon greenhouses by Mr Johnson, the head gardener. Miss Alice de Rothschild (d. 1922) had inherited the Waddesdon estate from her brother Baron Ferdinand in 1898; at her death her heir, James de Rothschild, had appointed Philip Woolf, a relation by marriage, estate manager.

imagine. Even the less known & worser plays are written at a speed that is quicker than anybody else's quickest; & the words drop so fast one can't pick them up. Look at this, Upon a gather'd lily almost wither'd (that is a pure accident: I happen to light on it.)[5] Evidently the pliancy of his mind was so complete that he could furbish out any train of thought; &, relaxing lets fall a shower of such unregarded flowers. Why then should anyone else attempt to write. This is not 'writing' at all. Indeed, I could say that Shre surpasses literature altogether, if I knew what I meant.

I meant to make this note of Waddesdon greenhouses. There were rows of hydrangeas, mostly a deep blue. Yes, said Mr Johnson, Lord Kitchener came here & asked how we blued them . . .[6] I said you put things in the earth. He said he did too. But sometimes with all one's care, they shot a bit pink. Miss Alice wouldn't have that. If there was a trace of pink there, it wouldnt do. And he showed us a metallic petalled hydrangea. No that wouldnt do for Miss Alice. It struck me, what madness, & how easy to pin ones mind down to the blueness of hydrangeas, & to hypnotise Mr Johnson into thinking only of the blueness of hydrangeas. He used to go to her every evening, for she scarcely saw anyone, & they would talk for two hours about the plants & politics. How easy to go mad over the blueness of hydrangeas & think of nothing else.

The Woolfs drove to Rodmell on 16 April for Easter and did not return to London until 27th.

Wednesday 23 April

This is a very important morning in the history of The Waves, because I think I have turned the corner & see the last lap straight ahead. I think I have got Bernard into the final stride. He will go straight on now, & then stand at the door; & then there will be a last picture of the waves. We are at Rodmell, & I daresay I shall stay on a day or two (if I dare) so as not to break the current & finish it. O Lord & then a rest; & then an article; & then back again to this hideous shaping & moulding. There may be some joys in it all the same.

5.   'When I did name her brothers, then fresh tears
        Stood on her cheeks, as doth the honey-dew
        Upon a gather'd lily almost wither'd.'

Titus Andronicus, III, i.

6. Horatio Herbert Kitchener, 1st Earl of Khartoum and Broome (1850-1916), Field-Marshal and popular military hero.

Saturday 26 April

Having had no letters for 3 days I feel my balloon shrink. All that semi-transparent globe wh. my fame attaches to me is pricked; & I am a mere stick. This is very wholesome; & grey; & not altogether displeasing though flat.

Sunday 27 April

A queer adventure, to come back & find Lottie in the house (her great box under the kitchen table) having been dismissed by Karin for stealing. She was sent with a policeman to the station. She is to sleep here tonight. And I am to see Karin.

Tuesday 29 April

And I have just finished, with this very nib-full of ink, the last sentence of The Waves. I think I should record this for my own information. Yes, it was the greatest stretch of mind I ever knew; certainly the last pages; I dont think they flop as much as usual. And I think I have kept starkly & ascetically to the plan. So much I will say in self-congratulation. But I have never written a book so full of holes & patches; that will need re-building, yes, not only re-modelling. I suspect the structure is wrong. Never mind. I might have done something easy & fluent; & this is a reach after that vision I had, the unhappy summer—or three weeks—at Rodmell, after finishing The Lighthouse. (And that reminds me—I must hastily provide my mind with something else, or it will again become pecking & wretched, —something imaginative, if possible, & light; for I shall tire of Hazlitt & criticism after the first divine relief—. & I feel pleasantly aware of various adumbrations in the back of my head; a life of Duncan: no, something about canvases glowing in a studio: but that can wait.)

I must run upstairs & peep in & tell Leonard & ask about Lottie, who has been after a place; & by the way injured yesterdays lap I am afraid with her vicissitudes.

Pm. And, I think to myself as I walk down Southampton Row "And I have given you a new book."

Thursday 1 May

And I have completely ruined my morning. Yes that is literally true. They sent a book from The Times, as if advised by Heaven of my liberty; & feeling my liberty wild upon me, I rushed to the cable & told Van

Doren I would write on Scott. And now having read Scott, or the perky & impertinent editor whom Hugh provides to dish up tasty fragments, I wont & cant:[1] & have got into a fret trying to read it, & writing to Richmond to say I cant; & have wasted the brilliant first of May which makes my skylight blue & gold; have only a rubbish heap in my head; cant read, & cant write, & cant think. The truth is, of course, I want to be back at The Waves. Yes that is the truth. Unlike all my other books in every way, it is unlike them in this, that I begin to re-write it, & conceive it again with ardour, directly I have done. I begin to see what I had in my mind; & want to begin cutting out masses of irrelevance, & clearing, sharpening & making the good phrases shine. One wave after another. No room. & so on. But then we are going touring Devon & Cornwall on Sunday which means a week off; & then I shall perhaps make my critical brain do a months work, for exercise. What could it be set to? Or a story?—no, not another story now. Perhaps Miss Burney's half sister's story,[2]

On Sunday 4 May the Woolfs set out on a week's tour by car of South-Western England, travelling Hogarth Press books in Bath, Bristol, Exeter, Truro and Penzance, and staying in hotels; they lunched at St Ives on 7 May, and then turned homewards, driving via Exeter, Shaftesbury, Salisbury and Winchester to Lewes, spending two nights at Monks House before returning to London on 11 May.

Sunday 18 May

The thing is now to live with energy & mastery, desperately. To despatch each day high handedly. To make much shorter work of the day than one used. To feel each like a wave slapping up against one. So not to dawdle & dwindle, contemplating this & that. To do what ever comes along with decision; going to the Hawthornden prize giving rapidly & lightheartedly; to buy a coat; to Long Barn; to Angelica's School;

1. Irita van Doren was anxious to publish further articles by VW in the Book Supplement of the *New York Herald Tribune*. *The Private Letter-Books of Sir Walter Scott*, edited by Wilfred Partington, was reviewed in the *TLS* on 15 May 1930; but not by VW. The book has an introductory letter by Hugh Walpole.
2. Probably written for Mrs van Doren (who paid well), 'Fanny Burney's Half-Sister' was first published in the *TLS* of 28 August 1930; it appeared in two parts under the more legitimate title of ' "Evelina's" Step Sister' in the *New York Herald Tribune* on 14 and 21 September 1930 (Kp C324).

thrusting through the mornings work (Hazlitt now) then adventuring.[3]
And when one has cleared a way, then to go directly to a shop & buy a
desk, a book case. No more regrets & indecisions. That is the right way
to deal with life now that I am 48: & to make it more & more important
& vivid as one grows old.

This is all very well; but what if Nelly then gets taken ill with her
kidneys, must have an operation. Soberly & seriously a whole fortnight
has been blown from my life; because I have had to hang about to see
Elly, to buy food, to arrange with Taupin, to arrange with the hospital;
to go there in an ambulance. My mind in order to work needs to be
stretched tight & flat. It has been broken into shivers. With great plodding
I have managed to write about the Women's Guild. And I consider
setting to work on The Waves. I have had over 6 weeks holiday from it.
Only again, this morning is ruined because I sit waiting a char, who does
not come. And we have Lyn & Sir R. Storrs to tea.[4]

*VW stayed the night of 23 May at Long Barn, after being taken by V.
Sackville-West to see her prospective home, the ruined Sissinghurst Castle;
the following day LW drove her, Vanessa and Duncan to visit Angelica at
her school near Colchester. Nelly Boxall went into hospital on 28 May, and
was operated on 3 June. On 29 May the Hogarth Press installed a new
printing machine; the old one was given to Vita Sackville-West, and is still
at Sissinghurst Castle. From 5-10 June the Woolfs were at Rodmell for
Whitsun; on 11th they went to see Paul Robeson, Sibyl Thorndike and Peggy
Ashcroft in Othello at the Savoy Theatre.*

Sunday 15 June

How many skips there are here! Nothing said of our tour through the
West; nothing said of N.'s operation; of Taupin, who lost my key broke

3. The 1930 Hawthornden Prize was presented by Stanley Baldwin to Lord David
   Cecil for his biography of Cowper, *The Stricken Deer* (1929), at the Æolian Hall
   on 22 May. VW's article on William Hazlitt was being written for the *New York
   Herald Tribune*, in which it appeared on 7 September 1930 (Kp C325).
4. This paragraph, undated, appears to have been added late in May. Mrs Tauplin
   was an elderly and incompetent Frenchwoman recommended by Vanessa and
   Helen Anrep as a temporary domestic in Nelly Boxall's absence. Margaret Llewelyn
   Davies had persuaded VW to write an introductory letter to a collection of letters
   by Co-operative working women which she was editing; *Life as We have Known It*
   was published by the Hogarth Press in March 1931 (*HP Checklist* 250; see also
   Kp B11). Sir Ronald Henry Amherst Storrs (1881-1955), diplomat, linguist,
   connoisseur of the arts and writer, was a friend of Ethel Smyth's; at this period he
   was Governor of Cyprus.

tumblers & cooked with the faded inspiration of one who had been a good cook; & nothing said of the divine relief of my quiet evenings, without servants; & how we dine out at the Cock; & how we say, can't this last? & then how I rang up Mrs Walters; & that experiment, an arduous one, begins tomorrow.[1] Leonard is not apt at a crisis. I mean his caution sticks his back up. He foresees obstacles. He has a philanthropic side too, which I distrust. Must be good to dependants. I am too hurried to spread these notes wider. At anyrate, Mrs W. an American who wishes to work, has been a journalist, is an intellectual, comes into our service tomorrow; being, as it were, Miss Ritchie, or Lyn Eirven. I have to give her orders; & she has to empty the slops. Will it work? will it last? Anyhow—every sentence begins anyhow—an interesting experience.

Monday 16 June

Mrs Walters is now here. And she says "What do you want with a Char?" But then new brooms &c. She is not new in one sense; rather old & lined; no, younger than I am; but a hard face, I think; but I forbear to crack her kernel. The interest will be to get a new light on housekeeping. My books are now my idol. Can I manage on less? How many pints? How many pounds of butter? Oh to be rid of servants—for all the emotions they breed—trust, suspicion, benevolence, gratitude, philanthropy, are necessarily bad.

And Nellie is now deposited on us for a day; turned out of hospital at a moments notice. I am amused to witness the conflict between L. & me. I hold a brief (hiddenly) for Walters; he (hiddenly) for Nelly. If the books are high, he secretly rejoices. If the food is good, I secretly denigrate Nelly's cooking. It is odd how those old scenes rankle in my mind—how unwilling I am to have her back. Partly the silence is so grateful; & partly the absence of lower classes. I think with real shrinking of having her in control again. Yet she is obliging friendly affectionate; & I cannot bring myself to talk to her as I should. I am always seeing myself told to "leave my room".

But enough—a useful phrase.

I dont know why, but I have stinted this book. The summer is in full swing. Its elements this year are Nessa & Duncan, Ethel Smyth, Vita & re-writing The Waves. We are very prosperous. On making up half yearly accounts, we find that we each get £425: & next year is sure, owing

---

1. Mrs Karl Walter, *née* Margaret Hardy, acted as cook-housekeeper to the Woolfs for six weeks—until they went to Rodmell for the summer.

to the gigantic sale of The Edwardians—it verges on the 20,000. And it is not a very good book. Ethel Smyth drops in; dropped in yesterday for instance, when I was so methodically devoting my morning to finishing the last page of type setting: On Being Ill;[2] I heard a ring, went up, & saw an old char in her white alpaca coat; sat her down; disburdened her of cardboard boxes; full of white pinks; & looked at her rather monumental old colonel's face (girt round with an inappropriate necklace, for she was going to lunch with Beecham.[3]) I get, generally, two letters daily. I daresay the old fires of Sapphism are blazing for the last time. In her heyday she must have been formidable—ruthless, tenacious, exacting, lightning quick, confident; with something of the directness & [single-?] ness of genius, though they say she writes music like an old dryasdust German music master. Her style in writing memoirs though is to her credit—indeed she has ridden post haste through life; & accumulated an astonishing number of observations, with which she qualifies her conversation so as to drive L. almost frantic. One speech of hers lasted 20 minutes unbroken, he says, the other night. We were starting for a picnic at Ken Wood with Nessa & Duncan. Their sublime ineptitude made me laugh & made Ethel laugh & made Eddy peevish. There we sat in the garage, heaving, rotating, stinking. Then we stuck in Gower Street. The night drew on & the wind rose. A spot of rain descended. We heaved our way up to Hampstead. The house was cadaverous; the rhododendrons blanched. Where should we dine? Better go back to Fitzroy St—which we did, & dined off sandwiches & strawberries about 10 o'clock in the highest glee. She is a game old bird—an old age entirely superior in vitality to Margaret's.

[*Sunday 6 July*]

And to tell the truth in the 15 minutes that remain before I go up to Mrs Walter's cold & exquisite but rather expensive lunch—to tell the truth I am slightly annoyed, both with Margaret & with Mr Birrell. Those were two kind acts of mine: the Women's Guild article & the article on

2. The sales of *The Edwardians* by Vita Sackville-West published on 29 May 1930 (*HP Checklist* 235) quite outstripped all expectations; the initial printing had been 3,030; by 19 June it had sold 18,000 copies. A special limited edition of 250 numbered and signed copies of VW's *On Being Ill* was published in November 1930 (*HP Checklist* 245).

3. Sir Thomas Beecham, Bt (1879-1961), conductor and impresario, was a staunch champion of Ethel Smyth's music and did much—though never as much as she would have liked—to bring her work before the public.

B.[1] Neither has thanked me. M. sent a postcard. Yet I spent two or even 3 weeks on that Letter; & worked & worked. Never—this is the moral—do a kindness in writing. Never agree to use one's art as an act of friendship. And therefore refuse to write about Maurice Baring, as he wishes.

We came into Ethel's drawing room last Thursday & found a row standing against the window—the D[uche]ss of Sermoneta, M. Baring, & Joyce Wethered.[2] Can I tell the story? I said to Maurice as we plodded after Joyce—Ethel running helter skelter after her great fuzzy dog—I said "This is like a party in literature—like Jane Austen's box hill party." There was a space & a formality & a definiteness about it that made it a real entertainment—with longueurs, with crises, with lapses, with culminations. We all had to wash. We all had to do this, to do that. Ethel's home is better than I expected. She has more beauty & even comfort about than I expected from her alpaca coat. The red & pink roses were thick on the walls. The flowers were lush in the beds. All was glowing & bright. She has white rough cast walls; & no furniture that has cost more than a pound or two—much is old schoolroom furniture endeared to her by her intense egotistic imagination. "It was there I sat, when Mary played the piano . . . And I said Mary couldn't you play G. sharp instead of G. natural . . . Thats the bed—Virginia you will have this room when you come to stay—where Sargent used to sleep, lying across: (because it is an old iron bed). And thats my father & mother—*she* was the artist . . ."[3]

1. In response to the persistence of Miss MacAfee, VW had offered her (*IV VW Letters*, no. 2166) an article based on Augustine Birrell's *Collected Essays* (see above, 18 November 1929, n 5) which was duly published in the June 1930 number of the *Yale Review* (Kp C323). For the Women's Guild article, see above 18 May 1930, n 4.
2. The Woolfs drove to Woking on the afternoon of 3 July for a party at Ethel Smyth's house, Coign (and did not get home until 11.30 p.m.). The Roman Duchess of Sermoneta, *née* Vittoria Colonna (1880-1954), wife of the 15th Duke (who lived in Canada), a lady-in-waiting to the Queen of Italy and an energetic member of international high society, contributed frequent articles to the *Daily Mail*; she was initially an admirer of Mussolini. Joyce Wethered (b. 1901) was British Ladies Open Golf champion in 1922, 1924, 1925 and 1929; she encouraged Ethel's passion for the game.
3. Mary (1857-1933) was the second (Ethel was the third) of the six daughters of Major-General J. H. Smyth, Royal Artillery, and his wife Nina, *née* Struth. Her preference for G natural is recalled in Ethel Smyth's memoirs, *Impressions that Remained* (1919), vol. I, p 83. Mary married Charles E. Hunter (d. 1916), and dissipated his immense fortune on lavish entertainment, on writers, musicians, and painters; she had been a particular friend of the American painter John Singer Sargent (1856-1925), who had achieved a unique position in English society with his portraits of the rich and fashionable.

But I got the impression of a very genuine, breeze blown mind; a free, entirely energised character—no impediments no inhibitions—the freest talk with Maurice. "I met a nephew of yours Ethel, with two names". "Well you might have—with two names". No, I cant give the sense of her largeness, & space & ease & good breeding & character. She is, oddly, much more expert as a hostess than as a guest; doesn't talk too much; is penetrating & quick, & has this delicious ease in summoning, conjuring up, people, like Lady Balfour & Mrs Lyttelton from the neighbourhood.[4] They sat on the sofa while I, sipping champagne, talked fast & furious to Maurice B. who turned lobster colour & trembled, & chattered about his books. There were 5 people who used to help me: all are now dead. He has had his sorrows: I dont know what: loved ladies, I daresay.

[*Monday 21 July*]

And I went down again to Woking on Tuesday (this is written waiting for Vita, on a very wet cold afternoon. She is going to drive us round to look at a wardrobe. I am going to buy a gilt wardrobe I think. Well, it is very wet, & I am rather discomposed, with making 2 articles into one & so on.[5] And I am not dining (here)

Wednesday 23 July

Edith Sitwell has grown very fat, powders herself thickly, gilds her nails with silver paint, wears a turban & looks like an ivory elephant, like the Emperor Heliogabalus.[6] I have never seen such a change. She is mature, majestical. She is monumental. Her fingers are crusted with white coral. She is altogether composed. A great many people were there—& she presided. But though thus composed, her eyes are sidelong & humorous. The old Empress remembers her Scallywag days. We all sat at her feet—cased in slender black slippers, the only remnants of her slipperiness & slenderness. Who was she like? Pope in a nightcap? No; the imperial majesty must be included. We hardly talked together, & I

---

4. Lady Betty Balfour (1867-1942), whose husband had just succeeded his brother as 2nd Earl of Balfour, lived at Fishers Hill, Woking; Dame Edith Lyttelton, *née* Balfour (d. 1948), was the widow of the Rt. Hon Alfred Lyttelton, PC, MP.

5. VW was converting the two parts of ' "Evelina's" Step Sister' (Kp C324) for publication as a single article in the *TLS* (see above 1 May 1930, n 2).

6. VW went to one of Edith Sitwell's tea-parties at Pembridge Mansions on 22 July. Heliogabalus, real name Varius Avitus, Roman Emperor (AD 218-222); his profligacy was so great as to shock even the Romans.

felt myself gone there rather mistakenly, had she not asked me very affectionately if she might come & see me alone. Her room was crowded with odds & ends of foreigners: the uncrowned King of Barcelona; Gerald's partner; Osbert; Lady Lavery &c.[7] Lady L. discussed the air crash. She said le Bon Dieu had taken them all at the right time. They had all done with life. Once too she would have been glad to die . . . This refers to the deaths of Lord Dufferin Lady Ednam &c.[8] I was driving down to the Temple with Vita, & we bought a Standard in the gateway. 'Titled victims' she said. Well it cant be Harold I said. Then I read out Lady Ednam, Marquis Dusserre (for so they reported him) & then in the stop press Lord Dufferin— What Lady Ednam? Dufferin? she cried. There was Harold on the pavement before their house.[9] "Yes, he said, Its Lady Ednam" "But its Freddy too" cried Vita (no she spoke composedly). God said Harold & read the stop press. Now what are we to do? I cant broadcast said Vita. I must tell my mother said Harold. First I'll get the paper though. Good Lord—Yes its Dufferin & Lady Ednam. "Is that Lady Carnock. Darling I have some bad news for you. Have you seen the paper? Freddy's been in a smash. He's killed, they think. Could you tell Aunt Lal?" What did your mother say Harold? Just 'Oh'. Now we cant dine with Lady Cunard. Oh yes dear we must. Perhaps I shall have to go down & see them— It was, as one says, like a scene in a play. The newspaper: the telephoning. The extreme simplicity & composure of it all: Boski typing; the man cleaning shoes; Harold telephoning, like a man in a play. So they drove off that wet grey evening to Lady Cunard's: dinner at 9. 30 people; & I did not go. (& I hear the whole party waited for me for half an hour)[10]

7. Thomas Balston (1883-1967) was a partner in Duckworth & Co, publishers, from 1921-34. Hazel Lavery (d. 1935), the beautiful Irish-American second wife of the painter Sir John Lavery, was a prominent figure in London society. The 'uncrowned king of Barcelona' was possibly Antonio de Ganderillas (1886-1970), wealthy international man of the world and friend of artists, who was attached to the Chilean Embassy in London.

8. On 21 July a private Junker monoplane flying from Le Touquet to Croydon crashed at Meopham, Kent; the crew of two and the four passengers—the Marquess of Dufferin and Ava, Viscountess Ednam, Sir Edward Ward, and Mrs Hennik Loeffler, wife of a company director of Grosvenor Square—were all killed.

9. Since leaving the Diplomatic Service at the end of 1929 to join the *Evening Standard*, Harold Nicolson had rented a flat at 4 King's Bench Walk, Inner Temple. Lady Carnock was his mother.

10. '. . . to dinner at Lady Cunard's. A very large party. Some of the young women did not see fit to turn up so that I found myself with an empty chair on one side . . .' (see *The Diaries of Evelyn Waugh*, edited by Michael Davie, 1976, p 323, 21 July 1930).

Saturday 26 July

Just back from a night at Long Barn, where I retrieved that fact about Emerald's party, waiting half an hour, all in the sulks too for the smash of their best friends. And Lady E. & Mrs S. strewed Kent with £62,000 worth of jewels.[11] Jewels in their hats, round their necks: somehow this makes me less sorry for them; undemocratic though I am. I rather like thinking of pearls pendant from oak trees.

I have 15—no 12—minutes before lunch; & am all of a quiver with home coming to L., to 2 newts in the bathroom, Letters (from Ethel, & flowers) books &c. A very nice homecoming; & I daresay a sample of my life, picked out of the mass (as it is, when one comes back) makes me a little amazed at my own happiness. I daresay few women are happier— not that I am consistently anything; but feel that I have had a good draught of human life, & find much champagne in it. It has not been dull—my marriage; not at all.

I liked rambling over Vita's new fields,[12] & talking to Mrs Page about the haycrop; & then champagne for dinner—an extravagance of Harold's; sleep in the sitting room; a log fire; dogs; aeroplanes at night; dogs again; & breakfast in bed—mushroom & peach & hot bath, & so home, as I say, to the newts & Leonard. Clive will come to tea. Perhaps we may go to the play.[13] And perhaps I might decide to have a new educated woman as servant. This comes on top of a day of Nelly Lottie & Mrs Mansfield. Their jokes their presence their familiarity, wh. rouse the usual reflections.

Passing the public House this Sunday afternoon, the buzz of voices through the door was exactly the same as at an evening party. My first thought was censorious: people in public houses. But this was soon corrected. I dont see much difference between the Marchmont Arms & Argyle [Argyll] House; or 3 Albert Road if it comes to that; except that we drink champagne & wear satin, & I sit between Lord Gage & Bernstorf.[14]

11. VW has definitely, if mistakenly, written *Mrs S* in place of *Mrs L*.
12. In March, before she had seen Sissinghurst, Vita had bought four fields at Long Barn.
13. The Woolfs went with Vanessa and Quentin Bell to a production of *The Importance of Being Earnest* at the Lyric Theatre, Hammersmith, on 28 July. John Gielgud took the part of John Worthing.
14. Albrecht Bernstorff (1890-1945), diplomatist, was on the staff of the German Embassy in London from 1922 to 1933, when he was recalled, and later murdered, by the Nazis.

Monday 28 July

A queer inconclusive but possibly fruitful conversation with Mrs Walter this morning. I think she would like to stay, if we could offer more wages. The truth is her husband has mistresses; or flirts. And she wishes to devote herself to us entirely—to do everything—that I should never have to order coffee. But she is going to think it out in August in Italy with Karl. I rather suspect (in my private mind) that we shall make a break here with Nelly, & take her—a great risk; rather fun: I feel 10 years younger instantly at the thought of a change. Anyhow, my constant relief at the absence of Nelly seems to prove that the system is as wrong as I've always said. Rooms empty of servants; to sit quietly; to have no jag [?], no unreal condescending talk. Other drawbacks suggest themselves —still anything for experiment—anything.

The Woolfs went to Rodmell for their summer break on 21 July.

Wednesday 6 August

This is written at Rodmell; oh yes, & it is the best, the freest, the comfortablest summer we have ever had. Figure to yourself feet swollen in boots. One takes them off—that is my state without poor dear Nelly; with nice bright Annie. The rain pelts—look at it (as the people in The Waves are always saying) now. My dinner is cooking. I have so many rooms to sit in, I scarcely know which to choose. And new chairs. And comfort everywhere, & some beginnings of beauty. But it is the freedom from servants that is the groundwork & bedrock of all this expansion. After lunch we are alone till Breakfast. I say, as I walk the downs, never again never again. Cost what it may, I will never put my head into that noose again.

I walk; I read; I write, without terrors & constrictions. I make bread. I cook mushrooms. I wander in & out of the kitchen. I have a resource besides reading. Why we ever suffered that discomfort so long, that presence always grumbling, always anyhow (for thats unfair) at a different angle from ours, needing gramo [*text ends*]

Wednesday 20 August

Last night was Quentin's birthday. "Another Quentin birthday over" said Maynard, at the gate after the fireworks, counting perhaps the remaining years. The rockets went roaring up & scattered their gold grain. That is an old phrase; but I always think of grain when I see them.

I can never find another. The willows were lit grey over the pond. The bonfire was forked, like branches in a wind. Nessa, in red, threw on a screen. Angelica, whirring & twirling like an old screaming witch, danced round it. "Childhood—true childhood" said Lydia. For some minutes everything that was said had the quality of sayings in a Tchekhov play.

I am writing while my potatoes boil. It has been a hot heavy ugly crusty[?] day; still, sulphurous; & the dogs have barked all round the village, one starting another. And the men have hammered on the spire. And I have been driven out & in. I have slept here, over an article by Vernon Lee, sent me in Ethel's daily letter. Ethel's letters are daily: for we have so much to make up. Time is short. "I would like to see Italy before I die" she says in todays letter. Should I curtail her & curb them? I think not. If one adventures, adventure wholly. And she is so courageous, remarkable shrewd, that it would be mere poltroonery for me to hold off for fear of ridicule (still they hammer, at 6.45.) So I let that old bonfire rage red & perhaps throw a screen on it. It is a very happy free, & indeed to me occasionally sublime summer. Yes, I think I have decided against Nelly: but dont let me rub that sore. I think I am on the back of The Waves now. Then my walks. How lovely it was exploring yesterday to the Hump! How strange that in almost 20 years I have never been that way—out along the marsh road beyond Sutton house. I see a line I might make to Lewes. I fell in & twisted my ankle. I saw an astonishing assortment of cones & angles of grey & gold down, back against back. I was very happy. I like the still, the profound slow happiness best. One day I walked to Firle, in a shower & found a 4 bladed pocket knife.

The Waves is I think resolving itself (I am at page 100) into a series of dramatic soliloquies. The thing is to keep them running homogeneously in & out, in the rhythm of the waves. Can they be read consecutively? I know nothing about that. I think this is the greatest opportunity I have yet been able to give myself: therefore I suppose the most complete failure. Yet I respect myself for writing this book. Yes—even though it exhibits my congenital faults.

Janet Vaughan is engaged, & Gerald Brenan married.[1]

Barbara [Bagenal] last night was aged, out of her element, peevish, & very red & beaky.

Julian silent. Clive undoubtedly on a fresh tack which does not allow of intimacy with me. I make these notes waiting in vain for that very

1. Janet Vaughan's engagement to David Gourlay was announced in *The Times* on 13 August 1930. Gerald Brenan and Gamel (Elizabeth Gammell) Woolsey (1899-1968), an American poetess, were ostensibly but not legally married from August 1930. See Gerald Brenan, *Personal Record, 1920-72* (1974), pp 220-29.

interesting remark to occur wh. was on the tip of my tongue; & will not now emerge, though I bait & wait. If one writes little notes, suddenly one thinks of something profound. I am reading Dante, & I say, yes, this makes all writing unnecessary. This surpasses 'writing' as I say about Shre. I read the Inferno for half an hour at the end of my own page: & that is the place of honour; that is to put the page into the furnace—if I have a furnace. Now to mash the potatoes. & L. has laid my carpet.

Monday 25 August

Ethel came for a night on Friday, & in order to drown Percy's mowing I will write here; for the friction of writing is a protection; & the dogs & the spire have been bad today. But they are bad because I am re-writing Hazlitt; having stopped The Waves at the break; & I am happy; & it is a very hot day; & we have been into Lewes, & I walked home part of the way. This is the only really hot day we have had. But I wish if I can to describe Ethel. At least let me pelt in a few notes of this curious unnatural friendship. I say unnatural because she is so old, & everything is incongruous. Her head is an enormous size over the temples. Music is there, she said, tapping her temples. That way lies insanity. What Walter said; what Wach (or someone) said—she cannot refrain from repeating what I guess to be very worn compliments, often repeated to herself at dead of night.[2] For she cannot get over unfortunately her own ill-treatment. A refrain occurs; & it is all the more marked for being in contrast with the generosity, sense, balance, & shrewdness of all else. Off her own music, & the conspiracy against her—for the Press are determined to burke her, though she fills every hall—thats the line of it—she is an admirable guest. Oh yes & more. I went through some odd vicissitudes, in the way of emotion. Lying in my chair in the firelight she looked 18; she looked a young vigorous handsome woman. Suddenly this vanishes; then there is the old crag that has been beaten on by the waves: the humane battered face that makes one respect human nature: or rather feel that it is indomitable & persistent. Then, she is worldly; by which I mean something I like; unembarrassed, aired, sunned, acquainted with this way of life & that; lived in many societies; taken her own way in shirt & tie vigorously unimpeded; then I am conscious, I suppose, of the compliment she pays me. But then she is over 70. And (oh the dogs—oh Percy!—& I had

2. The conductor Bruno Walter (1878-1962) was a loyal admirer of Ethel Smyth's music; the Prussian Adolf Wach (d. 1926), Professor of Jurisprudence at Leipzig University, and his wife Lili, who was Mendelssohn's daughter, were close friends from her student days in Germany.

marked off such a lovely evening—what am I to do?) She is sometimes startlingly quick. She has a lightning speed of perception which I liken to my own. But she is more robust; better grounded on fact than I am. She takes in a situation in one word. I told her about Margaret & my difficulties with the paper. No woman of 30 could have seen so swiftly or put the matter more succinctly in a nutshell. (her fault as a talker is diffusity). I had some interesting moments. About jealousy for instance. "D'you know Virginia, I dont like other women being fond of you." "Then you must be in love with me Ethel". "I have never loved anyone so much" (Is there something senile in this? I dont know). "Ever since I saw you I have thought of nothing else &c. I had not meant to tell you." But I want affection. "You may take advantage of this". No. Well, this, so far as I can boil it down, is Ethel's state. But what I like in her is not I think her love for how difficult it is to make that intelligible—it is compact of so many things—she exaggerates—I am sensitive to exaggeration—what I like is the indomitable old crag; & a certain smile, very wide & benignant. But dear me I am not in love with Ethel. And oh yes—her experience.

Thursday 28 August

It is the hottest day of the year: & so it was last year, almost on this day; & I was at Long Barn, & there was the Eton tutor, a nice young man with blue eyes white teeth & straight nose—& he now lies at the bottom of a crevasse in Switzerland—this very hot evening—lies crushed beside his Mary Irving: there are the two bodies for ever. I suppose some ice drips, or shifts: the light is blue, green; or wholly black; nothing stirs round them. Frozen, near together, in their tweeds & hobnail boots there they lie.[3] And I am here; writing in my lodge, looking over the harvest fields.

I suppose they felt whirled, like hoops; battered; senseless, after the first horror of feeling out of control.

A very violent summer.

So I said to Janie Bussy Julian & Quentin on the terrace last Sunday.

The church was finished today & the scaffolding taken down. I am reading R. Lehmann, with some interest & admiration[4]—she has a clear hard mind, beating up now & again to poetry; but I am as usual appalled by the machinery of fiction: its much work for little result. Yet I see no other outlet for her gifts. And these books dont matter—they flash a clear

3. Vincent O'Connor, the junior classical master at Eton who had tutored the Nicolson boys the previous summer, and his fiancée Mary Irving died in a climbing accident in the Swiss Alps on 21 August.
4. *A Note in Music* (1930), Rosamund Lehmann's second novel.

light here & there; but I suppose no more. But she has all the gifts (I suppose) that I lack; can give story & development & character & so on.

Annie offered me a paper weight of Strahn [? *Strachan*] in Scotland today in return for our paying her oculists bill.

Tuesday 2 September

I was walking down the path with Lydia. If this dont stop, I said, referring to the bitter taste in my mouth & the pressure like a wire cage of sound over my head, then I am ill: yes, very likely I am destroyed, diseased, dead. Damn it! Here I fell down—saying "How strange—flowers". In scraps I felt & knew myself carried into the sitting room by Maynard, saw L. look very frightened; said I will go upstairs; the drumming of my heart, the pain, the effort got violent at the doorstep; overcame me; like gas; I was unconscious; then the wall & the picture returned to my eyes; I saw life again. Strange I said, & so lay, gradually recovering till 11 when I crept up to bed. Today, Tuesday, I am in the lodge & Ethel comes—valiant old woman!

But this brush with death was instructive & odd. Had I woken in the divine presence it wd. have been with fists clenched & fury on my lips. "I dont want to come here at all!" So I should have exclaimed. I wonder if this is the general state of people who die violently. If so figure the condition of Heaven after a battle.

I think one might write a fantasia called Reflections on the sight of a daddy long legs. There was one just now (I have moved in from the lodge, thus disturbing both L. & Annie) crawling over the handmade paper on wh. I have to sign my name 600 times.[1] This bright sunny patch was his only pleasure. Yes, & then one dislikes daddies because they eat one's plants. One has some kindness for their very few pleasures. What is one's relation to insects?

It suddenly comes over me how I used to hook a piece of paper to me out of the nurse's eye in other illnesses—what a tremendous desire to write I had.

I will use these last pages to sum up our circumstances. A map of the world.

Leaving out the subject of Nelly, which bores me, we are now much freer & richer than we have ever been. For years I never had a pound

---

1. An exaggeration: the edition of *On Being Ill*, typeset by VW herself, was limited to 250 copies (Kp A14). See above, 16 June 1930.

extra; a comfortable bed, or a chair that did not want stuffing. This morning Hammond [*Lewes furnishers*] delivered 4 perfectly comfortable arm chairs—& we think very little of it.

I seldom see Lytton; that is true. The reason is that we dont fit in, I imagine, to his parties nor he to ours; but that if we can meet in solitude, all goes as usual. Yet what do one's friends mean to one, if one only sees them 8 times a year? Morgan I keep up with in our chronically spasmodic way. We are all very much aware of life, & seldom do anything we do not want to. My Bell family relations are young, fertile & intimate. Julian & Quentin change so much. This year Q. is shabby easy natural & gifted; last year he was foppish, finicky & affected. Julian is publishing with Chatto & Windus.[2] As for Nessa & Duncan I am persuaded that nothing can be now destructive of that easy relationship, because it is based on Bohemianism. My bent that way increases—in spite of the prodigious fame (it has faded out since July 15th: I am going through a phase of obscurity; I am not a writer: I am nothing: but I am quite content) I am more & more attracted by looseness, freedom, & eating one's dinner off a table anywhere, having cooked it previously. This rhythm (I say I am writing The Waves to a rhythm not to a plot[3]) is in harmony with the painters'. Ease & shabbiness & content therefore are all ensured. Adrian I never see. I keep constant with Maynard. I never see Saxon. I am slightly repelled by his lack of generosity; yet would like to write to him. Perhaps I will. George Duckworth, feeling the grave gape, wishes to lunch with Nessa; wishes to feel again the old sentimental emotions. After all, Nessa & I are his only women relations. A queer cawing of homing rooks this is. I daresay the delights of snobbishness somewhat fail in later life—& we have done—'made good'—that is his expression.

My map of the world lacks rotundity. There is Vita. Yes—She was here the other day, after her Italian tour, with 2 boys; a dusty car, sand-shoes & Florentine candlepieces, novels & so on tumbling about on the seats. I use my friends rather as giglamps: Theres another field I see: by your light. Over there's a hill. I widen my landscape.

Diary XX. The first page is inscribed:

September 8th 1930

Monks House

Rodmell

2. *Winter Movement* was published in October 1930.
3. Cf *IV VW Letters*, no. 2224 of 28 August to Ethel Smyth.

Monday 8 September

I will signalise my return to life—that is writing—by beginning a new book, & it happens to be Thoby's birthday, I remark. He would have been, I think, 50 today.

After coming out here I had the usual—oh how usual—headache; & lay, like a fibre of tired muscle on my bed in the sitting room, till yesterday. Now up again & on again; with one new picture in my mind; my defiance of death in the garden.

But the sentence with which this book was to open ran "Nobody has ever worked so hard as I do"—exclaimed in driving a paper fastener through the 14 pages of my Hazlitt just now. Time was when I dashed off these things all in the days work. Now, partly because I must do them for America & make arrangements far ahead, I spend I daresay a ridiculous amount of time, more of trouble on them. I began reading Hazlitt in January I think. And I am not sure that I have speared that little eel in the middle—that marrow—which is one's object in criticism. A very difficult business no doubt to find it, in all these essays; so many; so short; & on all subjects. Never mind; it shall go today; & my appetite for criticism is, oddly, whettened. I have some gift that way, were it not for the grind & the screw & the torture—

Vita comes tomorrow; we go to Sissinghurst on Wednesday; I shall attack The Waves on Thursday. So this illness has meant two weeks break—but as I often think, seasons of silence, & brooding, & making up much more than one can use, are fertilising. I was raking my brain too hard.

Anyhow, this is the happiest summer since we had Monks House; the most satisfactory. We hope on Percy's evidence—P. was tidying old Hawkesworth's grave—that the Byng Stamper farm has been bought by a horsebreeder, & all the land is to be under grass—not bungalows. And Annie surprises one daily with her amenity, dexterity & sympathy—the most convincing argument in favour of living out that I know. Yesterday I sent an advertisement to Time & Tide—but hush! Profound secrecy is essential.[4] The weather is September weather, bright, sunny, cool. We have a project of making my bedroom the sitting room—for the view. To let it waste, day after day, seems a crime: elderly eyes cannot waste. No, I would like to have another life, & live it in action. So I thought.

---

4. *Time and Tide*, 13 September 1930: 'Woman of intelligence and initiative wanted to do entire work of flat, WC1, for two writers. Live out. Good cooking essential. Might suit two friends half-day each. Wages by arrangement. Long summer holidays, also at Easter and Christmas. Box 8415.'

looking at Caburn, & imagining the feelings of a strong young man, who was walking up it, with wife & children, & a career in the City . . . I think. No he was a politician; & I think he was also an Indian civil servant. He was not a writer: These are the stories one invents. And this: "At the age of 50 Priestley will be saying "Why don't the highbrows admire me? It isn't true that I only write for money." He will be enormously rich; but there will be that thorn in his shoe—or so I hope. Yet I have not read, & I daresay shall never read, a book by Priestley. And I (to solace myself) get a letter from a Mr Spender saying he cares for my praise more than for that of any critic—& he sends me his poems.[5] And I invent this phrase for Bennett & Priestley "the tradesmen of letters".

Wednesday 24 September[6]

I have taken up my staff again; I wish I could say that my book was my staff; but oh dear, how many people I have seen—dashing that support from my hand! It must have been the afternoon I wrote this—yes, because L. & Percy were in the middle of moving the furniture into the sitting room—that Mary & Barbara [Hutchinson]'s little medicine bottle heads appeared at the window. How I scowled! And then there was Alice Ritchie, then the Wolves, then Morgan, then a party at Charleston then London, & then those curious women, Miss Ibbotson & Mrs Starr.[7]

"I am a cousin of Florence Nightingale" said Mrs Starr. When I said I was also related, her rather shifty eyes became shiftier. "I cant make

5. J. B. Priestley (b. 1894), whose best-selling books *The Good Companions* and *Angel Pavement* were published in 1929 and 1930 respectively. Stephen Spender (b. 1909) had recently left Oxford, where his passion for poetry and his ambition to be a poet had intensified. (See his autobiography, *World Within World*, 1951.)

6. The following calculation appears on the opposite page:

$$
\begin{array}{r}
280 \\
120 \\
\hline
116 \\
280 \\
\hline
29{,}160
\end{array}
$$

(the length of the Waves at this moment—a 3rd done, I suppose)

7. LW's mother, his sister Bella and her husband Thomas Southorn, on leave from Hong Kong, came to tea at Monks House on 12th (and again, with Harold Woolf, on 26th) September; Alice Ritchie came for the night on 17 September; E. M. Forster for the weekend of 20-22 September. On 23rd the Woolfs drove to London for the day to interview applicants who had responded to VW's advertisement in *Time and Tide* (see above, 8 September, n 4)—Miss Ibbotson, Mrs Starr, and Miss Rivett-Carnac. On 25th Ka Arnold-Forster came to lunch at Monks House, and Dorothy Bussy with her niece and nephew, Ellie and Dick Rendel, to tea.

omelettes" said Miss Ibbotson, addressing herself plaintively & at the same time peevishly to Mrs Starr. "It would be a great disaster of course if you sent in your dishes all burnt" said Mrs Starr. "You would give me notice, I suppose" said Miss Ibbotson. Miss Ibbotson was bankrupt; "Beggars can't be choosers" she said, "& so thats why I'm back again at *this*". Miss Ibbotson had once owned two motor cars & driven them for hire in London, but competition with the men had been too much. She had also been ill. She was skinny, raddled; wore a small corduroy jacket, & a rather dirty white shirt; had a red pocket-handkerchief; thick mended stockings & thick shoes. Mrs Starr was dressed in blue Liberty silk & a straw hat. She reproved Miss I. for being too diffident. "If I could have a trial" Miss I. repeated. But you will soon pick it up" said Mrs S. "I cant do fancy cooking" said Miss I. "And I would like to do some of the cleaning." "I shall do the cleaning" said Mrs S. "& you will do the kitchen." These remarks were shot at each other, & plainly represented much previous argument, though why Mrs S., so compact, if sly, had come into touch with Miss I., so wild, with her staring blue eyes & her wideawake, I could not say. An indefinable aroma of sordidity, instability, shadiness, shiftiness pervaded them. They were sure, I think almost at once, that we had seen through them, & that the place was not for them. "We live on Salads" said Mrs S. "though I am not a vegetarian." Sure enough the brown holland bag which they left behind them contained a number of lettuces wrapped in paper.

Miss Rivett-Carnac is the scion of a great Indian family who let her live in Wimbledon with her mother on a pound a week.[8] She has been through a good deal: social work; hostels; running clubs. She is about 35; a perfect lady, enough to be careless of being one; only anxious for shelter, & wages, & a little time to herself. She might do—she might be a superior Walter. She has, oh dear, suffered much. And is perhaps, vengeful, acid, worn, trusty, starved of happiness.

Could anything be done to make us less popular? we ask. For instance if I pied Leonard's hair—would that make his mother, Bella, Tom [Southorn], Harold [Woolf], Dorothy Bussy, Ellie Rendel & Ka Cox refuse to invite themselves to see us?

When I offered Miss Rivett-Carnac £50 yesterday it seemed to me nothing, because I was thinking that I can make that by writing 2,000 words. But 5 years ago, £50 was a substantial sum. How money has

8. The Rivett-Carnacs were an old Derbyshire family, a great number of whose sons served in the army or civil administration in India. VW engaged Miss Rivett-Carnac as a temporary replacement for the still convalescent Nelly; she came to Tavistock Square on 13 October and stayed until Christmas.

shrunk in my mind! This is one of the most curious things in my existence
—the shrinkage of money.

A perfect September day, after some very imperfect November days;
the swallows skimming the terrace; Percy asking if it will be fine tomorrow;
if so, he will mow the lawn. The bees are suspected to have been busy. In
that case we shall take honey tonight. L. & P. spent the afternoon—
Trim & Uncle Toby—mending the fence;[9] I spent it walking the downs.
I still have in spite of building a perfect stretch, & by juggling a little,
can convert distant houses into haystacks.

I am reading Dante; & my present view of reading is to elongate
immensely. I take a week over one canto. No hurry.

Our friends work us very hard. Heres Tom Eliot: when are you back?
Here's Miss Bartlett [*unidentified*], may we come to tea. Heres— & my
two months' respite nibbled at by all who choose. I think I will spend
August next year in Northumberland.

Monday 29 September

So all those days were completely ruined by the assiduity of our friends.
When one has to tidy the table, pick fresh flowers, collect chairs & be
ready, at 4, or at one, to welcome, & all the rest of it the circumjacent
parts of the day are ruined. On the whole L.'s family do the trick most
thoroughly. Everything is such an effort; so unreal; what I say is so
remote from what I feel; their standards are so different from mine; I
strain myself perpetually with trying to provide the right cakes, the right
jokes, the right affection & inquiries. Naturally it often goes wrong, as on
Friday. Harold, who is to me the most sympathetic of them, told a story
of the Woolf temper; how Philip had broken down the servants bedroom
door in a rage, because they had put a bottle, unfastened, into Bab's bed,
& refused to come & make it. Mrs W. who is the vainest of women (poor
old lady—yes, ones feeling of poor old woman churns[?] & muddles all
one's feelings of her egotism, her vanity) took this as a slur upon herself;
& began querulously & peevishly to defend her methods of education, &
to pay herself the usual compliments upon her wonderful management of
so many fatherless & penniless children. And then of course she requires
to have these praises corroborated, & will not be satisfied until I have also
wondered & exclaimed at her amazing unselfishness & courage & agreed
that the Woolf temper is merely a proof of their intelligence. Here of
course, I begin to see very plainly how ugly, how nosey, how irreparably
middle class they all are. Indeed, my aesthetic sense is the one that protests

9. See Sterne's *Tristram Shandy*.

most obstinately—how they cheapen the house & garden— How they bring in an atmosphere of Earls Court & hotels, how impossibly out of place, & stuffy & towny & dressy & dowdy they look on the terrace, among apple trees & vegetables & flowers! But there I am pinned down, as firmly as Prometheus on his rock, to have my day, Friday 26th of September 1930, picked to pieces, & made cheap & ugly & commonplace; for the sting of it is that there is no possible escape—no escape that wont make old Mrs Woolf begin to dab her eyes & feel that she is not being welcomed—she who is so "painfully sensitive"—so fond of cakes, so incapable of amusing herself, so entirely without any interest in my feelings or friends; so vampire like & vast in her demand for my entire attention & sympathy, while she sits over the fire, in her dreary furs & ugly bonnet & large boots, with her pendulous cheeks & red nose & cheap earrings, talking about Worthing & the charms of Dr Watson & the niceness of everybody, & how she will come to Worthing every year, & will expect to come to tea with us. Lord Lord! how many daughters have been murdered by women like this! What a net of falsity they spread over life. How it rots beneath their sweetness—goes brown & soft like a bad pear!

At the same time I cannot make out a case for myself as a maltreated person. No, because I have an interest beyond my own nose. But let me note that old age can only be made tolerable by having a firm anchor outside gossip, cakes, & sympathy. Think of imposing even one afternoon of such a burden upon Quentin Julian & Angelica! I shall spend my day at the British Museum. (This is one of those visual images, without meaning when written down, that conveys a whole state of mind to me)

Rodmell is full of incident, drama, &, sometimes I think, coming home over the flats, of beauty & solemnity. Mr Fears the epileptic died on Thursday. He had been locked in his room for weeks; but escaped, made off to Southease, & called on the Thomases to present his grievance to the Rector.[10] One of his grievances was that Mrs Dedman had stolen part of his garden—& it is said—& I can believe it—that this was no figment. There she stands in the street, ominous, glum, predatory, grasping, complaining. Then a doctor taps at the window: someone has been taken ill in the street & carried into a cottage. It was the mother of Miss Emery the dog breeder.[11] She now lies dying perhaps, & her husband must be taken for a motor drive while they are burying Mr Fears to distract him

10. The Rev. Walter Webb Thomas, Rector of Southease since 1904. For a description of this eccentric clergyman see *III LW*, pp 66-7.
11. Miss Emery was now the Woolfs immediate neighbour at Charnes Cottage.

from the thought of death. It is the most miserable of days, cold & drizzling, the leaves falling; the apples fallen; the flowers sodden; mist hiding Caburn. Yet I have written well, & cannot make out a case for myself as a maltreated person.

The great game of diplomacy is begun with Nelly. I have told Dr McGlashan that we will pay her wages, but not have her back till she is well.[12]

The Woolfs went to Charleston on 1st October whither, at his suggestion, George Duckworth brought his wife and one son to a family luncheon party. On 4th October the Woolfs returned to Tavistock Square.

Saturday 11 October

The fifty coffins have just trundled by, in lorries, spread rather skimpily with Union Jacks—an unbecoming pall—& stuck about with red & yellow wreaths. The only impressive sight was the rhythmical bending backward slow march of the Guards: for the rest, the human face is often pock marked & ignoble; poor gunners[?] look bored & twitch their noses; the crowd smells; the sun makes it all too like birthday cakes & crackers; & the coffins conceal too much. One bone, one charred hand, wd. have done what no ceremony can do: & the heap of a ceremony on ones little coal of feeling presses uneasily. I refer to the burial this morning of the 48 'heroes' of the R101.[1] But why 'heroes'? A shifty & unpleasant man, Lord Thomson by all accounts, goes for a joy ride with other notables, & has the misfortune to be burnt at Beauvais. That being so, we have every reason to say Good God how very painful—how very unlucky—but why all the shops in Oxford St & Southampton Row shd. display black dresses only & run up black bars; why the Nation should be requested to think of nothing else; why the people should line the streets & parade through Westminster Hall, why every paper should be filled

12. Nelly was staying with her relations at Peaslake, Shamley Green, Surrey, while recuperating from her operation; Dr Alan McGlashan was her doctor there.

1. The experimental flight of the R101 from Britain to India ended in disaster when the airship crashed near Beauvais in the early hours of Sunday 5 October. Of the 54 passengers 48 were killed, among them the Secretary of State for Air, Lord Thomson of Cardington. On the day of burial at Cardington churchyard crowds lined the route taken by the funeral procession from Westminster Hall, where the coffins had lain, to Euston. In addition to this show of public mourning there had been a memorial service at St Paul's on 10 October attended by heads of state, ministers and ambassadors.

with nobility & lamentation & praise, why the Germans should muffle their wireless & the French ordain a day of mourning & the footballers stop for two minutes' silence—beats me & Leonard & Miss Strachan.[2]

Wednesday 15 October

I say to myself "But I cannot write another word". I say "I will cut adrift—I will go to Roger in France—I will sit on pavements & drink coffee—I will see the Southern hills; I will dream; I will take my mind out of its iron cage & let it swim—this fine October". I say all this; with energy: but shall I do it? Shant I peter out here, till the fountain fills again? Oh dear oh dear—for the lassitude of the spirit! Rarely rarely comest thou now, spirit of delight. You hide yourself up there behind the hotel windows & the grey clouds. (I am writing this with a steel pen which I dip in the ink, so as to forestall the day when my German pens are extinct). It is dismal to broach October so languidly. I rather think the same thing happened last year. I need solitude. I need space. I need air. I need the empty fields round me; & my legs pounding along roads; & sleep; & animal existence. My brain is too energetic; it works; it throws off an article on Christina Rossetti; & girds itself up to deal with this & that.

Rivett is installed. And she cooks like a freehanded lady. Light sketchy dishes arrive. This is only our second day, & Annie, infinitely happy garrulous & anxious to stay—how can I put up with Rodmell now, she says. I shall feel shut up inside something—Annie goes today. A curious little interlude this. Alas, one day last week Nelly appeared—of course on her best behaviour—very much the old & trusted servant, with, I think, a dash of suspicion. Why did I not have her back & give her help, seeing that she had been with us 15 years?—that I think was in her mind. But we kept it down; & she is off to Colchester for 10 days & then—oh dear, I say again, oh dear. Nessa & Duncan are at Cassis, which brings the delicious vision of France too near me—Oh to walk among vineyards I cry again. And lots of people are on the buzz: dined last night with Raymond, a shabby & diminished Raymond, whom I like better than the dashing. Not much wine & so on. He has given up parties & takes Wyndham Lewis much to heart "A middle aged man-milliner" said Lewis in that pamphlet which is like the gossip & spite & bickering of a

---

2. Miss Strachan was one of the clerks at the Hogarth Press. The following page—that between the entries for 11 and 15 October—is given up to part of a draft of 'I am Christina Rossetti' (Kp C328) which VW has crossed through, noting in the margin: 'Written here by mistake'.

suburban housemaid who has been given notice & is getting a bit of her own back.[3]

Saturday 18 October

But behold, I think the spirit of delight is hovering over me, after 2 days at Rodmell, in spite of Ethel Smyth, in spite of Emmie Fisher.[4] Two teasing & tormenting letters from them were, of course, forwarded. But we walked to Lewes over the fields—yes, reached our goal, came out under that tunnel; now I have planned this walk for almost 20 years & never taken it. Home now, & find another letter, shaken & remorseful from Ethel, & Tom's new edition of Johnson,[5] & ever so many flowers.

Wednesday 22 October

Just back from headache cheating—there should be a name for these peregrinations—at Hampton Court. My misery at the sere & yellow leaves,[6] & the ships coming in & I not there & I not there—drove me to take a day off; indeed to plan 2 days off; but no: it rains now; & I'm for the fire.

My misery is Leonard's. Rivett cant cook. Poor woman! Bowed down with a sense of the failure of her life, creeping broken winged, arid, deprecatory, diffident, she sends in meagre savourless dishes & attempts nervous combinations of tapioca & orange. No, no: go she must. And then I think Annie—for ever. But the misery of these trifles can be devastating. Brown sole, brown sauce, & nothing else. And when I make a joke she laughs, as she laughed once in some tennis court to some subaltern I imagine, vainly. She is inve[r]tebrate; crushed; & what, I ask, is to become of her? And how am I to detach her seaweed clinging from my kitchen? For naturally this was a chance, a new start for her; something

3. Wyndham Lewis's satire *The Apes of God* had been published by him in a limited edition in June 1930; Mortimer reviewed it under the heading 'Mr Gossip' in the *N & A* of 12 July. A favourable review by Roy Campbell had been rejected by the incoming editor of the *New Statesman*, upon which, in September, Lewis brought out a pamphlet entitled *Satire & Fiction* incorporating Campbell's review, laudatory letters of support, and fighting comments by Lewis himself.

4. Emmeline (1868-1941) was the fourth of VW's eleven Fisher cousins; in 1915 she had married the musician R. O. Morris. VW did not preserve her letter, and the nature of the tease and torment is unknown.

5. T. S. Eliot had written an introductory essay to a reprint of *London: A Poem/ and/ The Vanity of Human Wishes/ by Samuel Johnson Ll.D*, produced in a limited edition, Autumn 1930 (see Gallup, *T. S. Eliot: A Bibliography*, 1969, B15).

6. 'my way of life/ is fall'n into the sear, the yellow leaf;' *Macbeth* V iii.

untried. And when I say No you can't cook, she will see her hope go bang like a rabbit in a shooting gallery. And I detest these dislodgments. Nelly again yesterday: apprehensive & suspicious; though I think not shaken seriously in her belief that she will come back to her [*sic*]. Thank the Lord, it rains, & I can bring myself to heel easily now. Winter has set in; draw the curtains; light the fire; & so to work.

Thursday 23 October

Behold, the rather familiar experiment—a new pen, new ink. "I'm afraid ma'am", said the youth at Partridge & Cooper's, "that the Penkala's are extinct." A voice on the telephone had spoken their doom. I went along Faringdon market this afternoon looking for the man with the barrow. I saw the grey towers of, I suppose, Smithfield. I almost went into St Paul's & saw Dr Donne, now uncovered again;[7] but being as I say to myself, pressed for time, I walked on, down the Strand.

Ethel came in yesterday evening; rather battered in an old moleskin coat; in the triangular hat which the hotel proprietor at Bath has made into its shape with a few pins. Well, I begin to make note of her, because, among other things—how many others—she said would I like her to leave me some of her letters—the Maggie Benson & Mrs Benson & Lady Ponsonby letters in her will?[8] Would you like me to write something about you? I said. Oh yes; what fun! But I should try some experiments. Oh what fun! How I should enjoy it! But I should get it all wrong. Yes, of course; or tear them up. Do just as you like. H. B.'s letters I'm leaving to Maurice Baring; but he'll do nothing. He'll tear them up.

So I am to some extent Ethel's literary executor, a post I have always vaguely desired; & so I now make a few notes as she talks, for a portrait. One would have to bring out her enormous eagerness. She was telling me how she reads Travel books; & her eyes—her blue, rather prominent eyes, positively glitter. And this is not talk about herself, or her music— simply about how people climb—their adventures. Her cheeks burn too. But she looks now & then aged: she said that she was a very brave woman.

7. Extensive restoration work had just been completed at St Paul's; the monument representing Donne in his shroud by Nicolas Stone, 1631, stands in the south choir aisle.

8. Mary Benson, *née* Sidgwick (1842-1918), wife of an Archbishop of Canterbury; her elder daughter Margaret (1865-1916); and Lady Ponsonby, wife of the private secretary to Queen Victoria and herself a sometime Maid of Honour—three ladies who had been deeply involved in Ethel's tempestuous emotional life and correspondence.

It is a quality I adore. And I have it. One of the bravest things I ever did

This she copied from Mrs Pankhurst was to tell people my age. My vivacity &c— Everyone thinks I'm 20 or 30 years younger. *Well* —(a characteristic word, indicating what really becomes necessary—a break—a new paragraph—a wedge inserted in the flood) Well—when I wanted people to realise how long I'd waited for recognition—& have never really had it—I did that—though I hated it: I told them my age, so that they couldn't go on saying Oh but she came into her own—she was recognised. This referred I think, but it is difficult to insert one's own wedges, to the Jubilee Concert at Berlin, on which occasion Lady Jones behaved so badly.[9] She was on her way—is now I suppose in the train or on the ship, this cold grey day—to Belfast, to conduct her Sea Songs[10] (one of my best things) & then, directly thats done, back she comes, across the Irish channel, & returns to Woking & goes on writing about H.B.: that looming imponderable figure: who has so queer an existence; for if I ask about him Logan, Ottoline &c. say Oh a petit maitre; a drawing room philosopher; to which Logan adds the son of a dentist, & Ottoline adds, he made love to me, & I found him intolerable. This was the man who dominated Ethel's life, this wraith who wanders about in Logan's & Ethel's lives. What a strange job then to write, as I may one day, the life of a woman whose past is thus nebulous. And I have only come in time to hear about the past. Everything is past. She hopes not to live another seven years; gives me to understand that now that her last barren years have been fructified by knowing me, she can sing her nunc dimittis. Since all the fiery years of desire are over. Yet I doubt if they are quite over. Yet it is a fine spectacle, & a curious one, this old woman summing up her experience & hymning her love for H.B. as a swan song (& people say an ugly song, for they say, her musical genius is another delusion—all her life then has been based on illusions; & that as I perceive when I talk to her is manifestly untrue). I must now write to the living Ethel—so one's perspective shifts.

Monday 27 October

How comfortless & uneasy my room is,—a table all choked with papers. &c. I'm now grinding out Waves again, & have perhaps an hour & a half to spend: a short time on Dante; a short time on MSS: a short time here—

9. Occasion unidentified; Ethel Smyth wrote several autobiographical books: *Impressions that Remained*, 2 vols. 1919; *Streaks of Life*, 1921; *A Final Burning of Boats*, 1928; *As Time Went On*, 1936; *What Happened Next*, 1940.
10. Presumably her 'Three Moods of the Sea', 1913.

with another pen. Yesterday we went to Warlingham & sat in a gravel pit, like a Cezanne. I made this comparison, to appease myself for not being in France. And we walked along a bridle path; & saw old quiet farms, & rabbits, & downs, all preserved as by a magic ring from Croydon. Never was the division between London & country so sharp. Home, & made dinner; & read MSS: But rather casually & unanimously we have decided within the last week to stop the Press. Yes; it is to come to an end. That is we are to go on only with my books & Ls. & Dotty perhaps; & what we print ourselves. In short, we shall revert next October to what we were in the Hogarth House days—an odd reversal, seeing that we are now financially successful. But what's money if you sell freedom? we say. And what's the point of publishing these innocuous novels & pamphlets that are neither good nor bad? So we make this decision, casually, walking round the Square after lunch & thus slip another shackle from our shoulders. This is what I call living with a pilot in the ship—not mere drifting ahead.

Sunday 2 November

And tonight the final letter to Nelly is to be sent; there it rests in my red bag, but I have great reluctance to read it over, as I had to write it. Yet I don't suppose she will mind acutely. For one thing, she has been prepared, I think, by our readiness to do without her; & then since the famous scene last November I think she has been aware of a change. These 5 months at any rate have proved that we are freer, easier & no less comfortable, indeed more comfortable, without her, for all her good humour, sense & niceness; which now that I have written the letter, I see once more in their true proportions. And I am vague & in the air, because I doubt that Annie will come—doubt if she should—wish indeed to have livers out in future. Oh never again to have scenes with servants—that is my ambition. How we used to walk round the Sqre considering Nelly's ultimatums; what hours we have spent & should still spend. No: this is a wholesome break, & takes 10 years off my shoulders. Oh, but I shall have to see her—

[? *Wednesday 5 November*]

These are further notes about Nelly, since it is a queer little bit of life broken off; servant psychology & so on. To my long, explicit & affectionate letter she has returned one word: Dear Mr & Mrs Woolf. Thank you for your cheque: Yrs truly.

But yesterday evening, an embittered, frightened angry voice, this is

Rivett's description, & by the sound she identified Nelly, was heard on the telephone. She asked for me; but I was, happily, out or down here. We conjecture that after launching her snub, she came up to consult Lottie, perhaps see Mrs Hunt, & for some reason they decided upon an interview. I imagine she has now gone back. And the sense of freedom spreads wider & wider. The letter is sent; the shock over. And I come in & find the house empty & silent.

A slight inaccuracy, if applied to the past few days. Ethel Lyn & Hugh Walpole to tea on Monday; Vita Clive & Hilda Matheson to dine; Hugh again later, & his piteous, writhing & wincing & ridiculous & flaying alive story of Willie Maugham's portrait.[1] Indeed it was a clever piece of torture; Hugh palpably exposed as the hypocritical booming thick skinned popular novelist, who lectures on young novelists & makes his own books sell: who is thick fingered & insensitive in every department. But said Hugh, turning round on his bed of thorns again & yet again, & pressing them further & further in, Thats not what I mind so much. What I mind are a few little things—little things Willie & I had together—only he & I knew—those he has put into print. Thats what I cant get over. For instance I cant tell you all the meanings there are to me in his saying I was like a man in love with a duchess—(the meaning is that Hugh is in love with a male opera singer[2]). Would you mind Virginia? (this said past midnight, Vita & I alone) And I said I should. "And he wrote to me & said he could not believe that I could be hurt. He said he had written without a thought of me. But that letter is almost worse than the book."

Clive is home blind of one eye & much in need of society. I thought him, why heaven knows, rather admirable & touching; determined not to be a burden on his friends, yet very grateful for our kindness (& I must ask him to come in tonight). So much instructed somehow in the little graces & also the inevitable lonelinesses, without his Mary, but then I think he has his Joan. And he cant read or write, & has hired a reader. Its the evenings that will be bad he said. Nessa characteristically writes from Cassis that she doesn't think much of it, & supposes that spectacles, 'which we all wear' will put it right.

And Julian's poems are out, & I am relieved—but why, vanity of my own critical powers? jealousy of his fame?—to hear that Vita agrees with me that for all his admirable good sense & observation & love of country life, he is no poet. People who treat words as he does rather afflict me—

1. The character of Alroy Kear in W. Somerset Maugham's novel *Cakes and Ale* was closely based upon that of his old friend Hugh Walpole.
2. This was Lauritz Melchoir (1890-1973), the Danish *Heldentenor*, whom for some years Walpole regarded as his 'perfect friend'.

I say this to discharge me partially of vanity & jealousy. Common sense & Cambridge are not enough, whatever Bunny may say.

Saturday 8 November

I pressed his hand when we said goodbye with some emotion: thinking This is to press a famous hand: It was Yeats, at Ottoline's last night. He was born in 1865 so that he is now a man of 65—& I am 48: & thus he has a right to be so much more vital, supple, high charged & altogether seasoned & generous. I was very much impressed by all this in action. He has grown very thick (Last time I met him—& I may note that he had never heard of me & I was slightly embarrassed by O.'s painstaking efforts to bring me to his notice, was in 1907—or 8 I suppose, at dinner at 46).[3] He is very broad; very thick; like a solid wedge of oak. His face is too fat; but it has its hatchet forehead in profile, under a tangle of grey & brown hair; the eyes are luminous, direct, but obscured under glasses; they have however seen close, the vigilant & yet wondering look of his early portraits. I interrupted a long dream story of de la Mares when I came in: about seeing Napoleon with ruby eyes & so on. Yeats was off, with vehemence even, kindling & stumbling a little, on dreams; those which have colour are rare & mean—I forget what. De la Mare told another very cryptic dream about a book with circles in it; the outermost ring black, the inner blue & so on. Yeats identified this dream at once as the dream of the soul in some particular state—I forget what. Tagore had told him he said that he had dreamed once as a young man; & if he could find the dream again it would become permanent.[4] And so on to dreaming states, & soul states; as others talk of Beaverbrook & free trade—as if matters of common knowledge. So familiar was he, that I perceived that he had worked out a complete psychology, which I could only catch on to momentarily in my alarming ignorance. De la M. had just been to the National Gallery, & had got no pleasure from the pictures. I said this flow & ebb of consciousness made all criticism unstable. He said one must go by the plus's always. Yeats said he could get nothing from Rembrandt, nothing from El Greco. He then explained our pleasure in pictures, or other works of art, by an elaborate metaphor, taken from his psychology; about the sharp edges of things being brought into contact; & the same

3. William Butler Yeats lived to be seventy-three; he died early in 1939. From 1895-1919 he had a London foothold at 18 Woburn Buildings (now Woburn Walk), Bloomsbury. He knew Clive slightly, and must have accepted an invitation to dine with the Bells at 46 Gordon Square early in their married life there.
4. Rabindranath Tagore (1861-1941), the Bengali poet and mystic.

order then coming in our consciousness: & thus our closest contact results from some sudden clicking to of edges, which—I have lost the metaphor now completely. Then, discussing what poems we could come back to unsated, I said Lycidas; De la M. said no. Not Milton for him: he could never recognise his own emotions there. Milton's woodbine was not his woodbine, nor M.'s Eve his Eve. Yeats said he could not get satisfaction from Milton; it was Latinised poetry (as somebody said, Milton had (in some way irreparably) damaged the English language). This attached itself to a cosmology evidently, in which Latins & Romans play their part. And so to modern poetry, & the question of the spade. Yeats said that "we", de la M. & himself, wrote 'thumbnail' poems only because we are at the end of an era. Here was another system of thought, of which I could only snatch fragments. He said that the spade has been embalmed by 30 centuries of association; not so the steam roller. The great age of poetry, Shakespeare's age, was subjective; ours is objective; civilisations end when they become objectified. Poets can only write when they have symbols. And steam rollers are not covered in symbolism —perhaps they may be after 30 generations. He & de la M. can only write small fireside poems. Most of emotion is outside their scope. All left to the novelists I said—but how crude & jaunty my own theories were beside his: indeed I got a tremendous sense of the intricacy of the art; also of its meanings, its seriousness, its importance, which wholly engrosses this large active minded immensely vitalised man. Wherever one cut him, with a little question, he poured, spurted fountains of ideas. And I was impressed by his directness, his terseness. No fluff & dreaminess. Letters he said must be answered. He seemed to live in the centre of an immensely intricate briar bush; from wh. he could issue at any moment; & then withdraw again. And every twig was real to him. He also spoke about the necessity of tragedy. It is necessary to attempt the impossible; but it must be possible. All creation is the result of conflict. James Stephens, some of whose poems he much admires, & I have never read, was so poor as a boy that he used to pick up the bread thrown to the ducks & eat it.[5] There must be tragedy in order to bring out the reverse of the soul. (This belongs to another theory about the soul & its antitype, which I vaguely remember in his poems). He said that Tom very cleverly made use of mythologies, for instance the Fisher King in the Waste Land; & mythologies are necessary. Ezra Pound writes beautifully when he uses them. Then suddenly must speak of—some common object—& at once his

5. James Stephens (1880?-1950), Irish writer, author of *The Crock of Gold* (1912), had been brought up in an orphanage and at times had gone so hungry as to have 'fought with swans for a piece of bread' (*DNB*).

rhythm breaks. I said we did not talk enough, not easily & equally. He told us of men he had met in trains. I liked his transitions to dialect & humour. With men perhaps he might be coarse. He had been staying with Masefield who, to celebrate the 30th year of their friendship, had got young women to recite Yeatses lyrics at Boars Hill. Their voices had been too small for the theatre; but Yeats had been greatly touched.[6] Judith M. is nice & good but not pretty. Hence she will have to marry a man she knows; not at first sight. And Mrs M. seemed simple & he liked her better than usual. Indeed, he seemed very cordial, very generous; having been warmed up by his 65 years; & being in command of all his systems, philosophies, poetics & humanities; not tentative any more. Hence no doubt his urbanity & generosity. Compare him with Tom for instance, who came to tea the day before, & may be, for anything I know, as good a poet. Poor Tom is all suspicion, hesitation & reserve. His face has grown heavier fatter & whiter. There is a leaden sinister look about him. But oh—Vivienne! Was there ever such a torture since life began!—to bear her on ones shoulders, biting, wriggling, raving, scratching, unwholesome, powdered, insane, yet sane to the point of insanity, reading his letters, thrusting herself on us, coming in wavering trembling—Does your dog do that to frighten me? Have you visitors? Yes we have moved again. Tell me, Mrs Woolf, why do we move so often? Is it accident? Thats what I want to know (all this suspiciously, cryptically, taking hidden meanings). Have some honey, made by our bees, I say. Have you any bees? (& as I say it, I know I am awaking suspicion). Not bees. Hornets. But where? Under the bed. And so on, until worn out with half an hour of it, we gladly see them go. Vivienne remarked that I had made a signal that they should go. This bag of ferrets is what Tom wears round his neck.

6. John Masefield (1878-1967), who in May 1930 had been appointed Poet Laureate, had built a small theatre, the Music Room, beside Hill Crest, his home at Boar's Hill, and it was there that the recital attended by Yeats had been given on 5 November. In a letter to his wife, dated 8 November, Yeats wrote of this occasion and of his visit to Lady Ottoline's: 'I had a rather moving experience at Masefield's. At his little theatre he made a long eulogy on my work & myself—very embarrassing—& then five girls with beautiful voices recited my lyrics for three quarters of an hour. I do not think the whole audience could hear but to me it was strangely overwhelming . . . Yesterday I met De la Mare & Virginia Wolf [*sic*] at Lady Ottoline's and here is the upshot of my talks and a metaphor of Lady Ottoline's

We that had such thought;
That such deeds have done,
Must ramble on—thinned out,
Like milk on a flat stone.'

On second thoughts, Yeats & de la Mare talk too much about dreams to be quite satisfactory. This is what makes de la Mare's stories (lent me by Ottoline) wobbly.[7]

[? *Tuesday 11 November*]

Now what will happen next, when The Waves is done? I think some book of criticism; (Mrs Stiles to take away wastepaper) But I am dissatisfied with my own smart endings. I must get on to a peak & survey the question. These are our stages.

I thought, to give this book continuity, I would copy every day the headlines in the paper. But I cant remember them.

Mr Scullin & Labour. Armistice day celebrations. The Blazing Car murder. Prince of Wales's next Expedition.—at a shot.[8]

William Plomer is back.[9] Nessa returns, wifely ready to read or sit with Clive, on Thursday. Roger too. And I cry O Solitude—& look towards Rodmell. And the weather goes on blue & balmy. And I go to the dentist, & so does Leonard. And Rivett is a nervous but clean cook. And Nelly has appealed to Dr McGlashan. And we await development.

The other night, sitting on the floor by my side, Vita suffered considerably from jealousy of Ethel. She praised her, stoutly, but bitterly. She has all the abandonment that I, living in this age of subtlety & reserve, have lost. She claims you; rushes in where I force myself to hold back. When Hugh was here he said casually that he had met Ethel at tea. Such agony went through her she could not speak. And I noticed nothing; & in my usual blind way, made my usual mocking joke. This V. took seriously & brought out my letter for me to read.

[*Wednesday 12 November*]

Alas, too numb brained to go on with Bernard's soliloquy this morning. A very little weight on me brings me low. And Clive has been a little

7. De la Mare's most recently published collection of stories was On the Edge (1930).
8. James Scullin, prime minister of Australia, was currently visiting Britain and Europe; during his absence a schism had broken out in the Australian Labour Party as to how to deal with the country's financial crisis. Alfred A. Rouse was to be executed on 10 March 1931 for the murder of an unknown man whose remains had been found in a burnt-out car in a village near Northampton on 6 November. The Prince of Wales was due to sail on 15 January to South America where he would open the British Empire Trade Exhibition in Buenos Aires on 14 March 1931.
9. Since the beginning of the year Plomer had been wandering in Europe with his friend Anthony Butts.

weight, added to the usual round; the dentist, shops & callers &c. So I
cant write. And last night we sat through a sticky valiant evening at
Hope's. Hope liberated from all restraint by [*illegible*] was it? Hope school
girlish, voluble, excited, the first time I have seen it since Jane's death.
Mrs Plunket Greene there (20 years added since we met at Savage's dinner
party) now she is grey, pendulous; with the oddest bird technique of the
head & eyes I have ever seen—for ever craning, peering, advancing,
exactly like a lively arch bird of some kind. A Roman Catholic—not,
unless you remembered her 20 years ago, a very nice or clever woman—
something too insinuating.[10]

Wednesday 12 November

And I had my talk with Nelly last night. Going up to sit still for an
hour, & read perhaps Dotty's poem I heard a shop bell, I thought, looked
down the stairs & saw Nelly. So we sat for two hours. An odd meandering
contradictory, mainly affectionate & even intimate talk. One of her pre-
occupations to establish her own hard lot & innocence of all offence
among the servants of the click.[11] We had treated her badly, turning her
off because of ill-health. Confronted by me, she advanced this more as an
excuse, almost a joke than anything. "Still I can't understand why you
won't have me back . . ." But Nelly, you gave me notice 10 times in the
past 6 years—& more . . . But I always took it back. Yes, but that sort of
thing gets on the nerves. Oh ma'am I never meant to tire you—dont go on
talking now if it tires you—but you wouldnt give me any help. Now
Grace had all the help she wants—Well, I says, this is long service. But
then Nelly you forgot that when you were with us. But then for 3 years
I've been ill. And I shall never like any mistress as much as I like you . . .
& so on & so on—all the old tunes, some so moving; so pathetic, some
(I'm glad to say) so irrational hysterical & with that curious senseless
reiteration of grievances which used to drive me frantic. The truth—but
I could never tell her this—is that that kind of dependence & intimacy,
with its exactness, & jealousy & its infinite minuteness wears one down;
is a psychological strain. And then the gossip. Oh I wont say how I've

10. Mrs Plunkett Greene was one of the two daughters of Sir Hubert Parry, the
composer and director of the Royal College of Music, 1894-1918; they had been
Kensington neighbours of the Stephen family. Gwen had married the baritone
Harry Plunkett Greene (d. 1936) in 1899. Sir George Savage (1842-1921),
consulting physician and a specialist in mental illness who had been both friend
and medical adviser to the Stephens, particularly on VW's problems.
11. The Bloomsbury servants referred to themselves as a clique.

heard, but I've heard—. You say——& so at last, after every variety of feeling, I was left with the one feeling No I could not have you sleeping here again. To be free of this inspection this frying in greasy pans, at all costs. None of this can be said, & the situation, if far less stormy than I feared, has its sharp edges. Poor old Nelly one thinks, finding a place— packing up—going to Registrys—after 15 years.

[*Added later*] And then I let her come back, for 3 months, from Jan. 1st. How am I ever to apologise to myself sufficiently?

Sunday 23 November

Ethel yesterday in a state of wonderment at her own genius. "Cant think how I happened" she says, putting on my hat, & bidding me observe what a nutshell it is on top of her gigantic brow.

Another observation, based on parties at Rhondda's & lunch with Harold:[12] given clothes I could soon dine & lunch every day & get so easily the hang of it that it mattered nothing. And so would have no point.

Sunday 30 November

"Oh I have had so much unhappiness in my life" said Mary, sobbing "It has been so dangerous, so difficult. How I envy you!"

Tuesday 2 December

No I cannot write that very difficult passage in The Waves this morning (how their lives hang lit up against the Palace) all because of Arnold Bennett & Ethel [Sands]'s party.[1] I can hardly set one word after another. There I was for 2 hours, so it seemed, alone with B. in Ethel's little back room. And this meeting I am convinced was engineered by B. to 'get on good terms with Mrs Woolf'—when heaven knows I don't care a rap if I'm on terms with B. or not. B. I say;

Soon after this A B. went to France, drank a glass of water, & died of typhoid. (March 30th, his funeral today)

12. Margaret Haig Thomas, Viscountess Rhondda (1883-1958), feminist, founder and editor (from 1926) of the weekly *Time and Tide*. The Woolfs had dined with her on 20 November and the following day went to a luncheon at the Garrick Club in celebration of Harold Nicolson's 44th birthday before going to Long Barn for the night.

1. Ethel Sands' dinner party, for fourteen guests, was on 1 December. Arnold Bennett died in London on 27 March 1931.

because he can't say B. He ceases—shuts his eyes—leans back. One waits. "*b*egin" he at last articulates quietly, without any fluster. But the method lengthens out intolerably a rather uninspired discourse. Its true, I like the old creature: I do my best, as a writer, to detect signs of genius in his smoky brown eye: I see certain sensuality, power, I suppose: but O as he cackled out "what a blundering fool I am—what a baby—compared with Desmond McCarthy—how clumsy—how could I attack professors?" This innocence is engaging; but wd. be more so if I felt him, as he infers, a "creative artist". He said that George Moore in The Mummer's Wife had shown him the Five Towns: taught him what to see there: has a profound admiration for G.M.: but despises him for boasting of his sexual triumphs. "He told me that a young girl had come to see him. And he asked her, as she sat on the sofa, to undress. And he said, she took of[f] all her clothes & let him look at her— Now that I dont believe . . . But he is a prodigious writer—he lives for words. Now he's ill. Now he's an awful bore—he tells the same stories over & over. And soon people will say of me "He's dead"." I rashly said "Of your books?" No, of me—he replied, attaching, I suppose, a longer life than I do to his books.

"Its the only life" he said (this incessant scribbling, one novel after another, one thousand words daily) I dont want anything else. I think of nothing but writing. Some people are bored. "You have all the clothes you want, I suppose" I said. "And baths—And beds. And a yacht." "Oh yes, my clothes cd.nt be better cut."

And at last I drew Lord David in. And we taunted the old creature with thinking us refined. He said the gates of Hatfield were shut "shut away from life". 'But open on Thursdays' said Lord D. "I dont want to go on Thursdays" said B. "And you drop your aitches on purpose" I said "thinking that you possess more 'life' than we do." "I sometimes tease" said B. "But I dont think I possess more life than you do. Now I must go home. I have to write one thousand words tomorrow morning".

And this left only the scrag end of the evening: & this left me in a state where I can hardly drive my pen across the page.

Question: Why does Desmond like talking to Lord Esher?[2]

Reflection: it is presumably a bad thing to look through articles, reviews &c. to find one's own name. Yet I often do.

Resolution: To say to Ethel one day—How can you attach this importance to everything you do when you call yourself a Christian (inspired by this mornings letter & its emphasis about the score of the Prison)

2. Oliver Brett (1881-1963), who provided both financial and editorial support for Desmond's monthly *Life and Letters*, had succeeded as 3rd Viscount Esher on the death of his father in January 1930.

DECEMBER 1930

Thursday 4 December

One word of slight snub in the Lit. Sup. today makes me determine, first, to alter the whole of The Waves; second, to put my back up against the public—one word of slight snub.[3]

Friday 12 December

This, I think, is the last days breathing space I allow myself before I tackle the last lap of The Waves. I have had a week off—that is to say I have written three little sketches; & dawdled, & spent a morning shopping, & a morning, this morning arranging my new table & doing odds & ends —but I think I have got my breath again & must be off for 3 or perhaps 4 weeks more. Then, as I think, I shall make one consecutive writing of the waves &c—the interludes—so as to work it into one—& then—oh dear, some must be written again; & then, corrections; & then send to Mabel; & then correct the type; & then give to Leonard. Leonard perhaps shall get it some time late in March. Then put away; then print, perhaps in June.[4]

Meanwhile we dine with Mary on Sunday to meet Mr Hart Davis who may come to the press—but in what capacity?[5] And two days ago we saw over 25 T[avistock]. S[quare]. to which we may move, if we decide to leave this, & can let it. But there too are obstacles; an hotel building alongside, & fewer rooms, & more expense.

Paper headlines.	Spanish Revolution. Russian timber yard scandal. Burst water main in Cambridge Circus.[6]

---

3. A half-column review of the limited edition of *On Being Ill* appeared in the *TLS*, 4 December 1930. The reviewer approved of the theme but thought that he reader was led away from it: 'The subject has shown a new, precipitous face for an instant, and once more vanished into the mist. The essay with its vellum and green covers, beautiful end-papers and fine type, remains placidly on the table.'
4. *The Waves* was to be published on 8 October 1931.
5. Rupert Hart Davis (b. 1907), educated at Eton and Oxford and who was later to found his own publishing firm, was at this time what he calls an office boy at William Heinemann Ltd.
6. It had been reported from Madrid on 12 December that the garrison at Jaca in the Spanish province of Huesca had revolted under the rumoured leadership of Major Franco. Evidence from three 'escaped Russian prisoners' as to the conditions under which the timber industry was currently being conducted at Archangel and in other Soviet prison camps had recently been published in the newspapers; Sir Edward Hilton Young MP had called on the Government to take action to put a stop to 'a trade stamped with the worst features of servile labour'.

Tuesday 16 December

I will never dine out again. I will burn my evening dress. I have gone through this door. Nothing exists beyond. I have taken my fence: & now need never whip myself to dine with Colefax, Ethel, Mary again.

These reflections were hammered in indelibly last night at Argyll House. The same party: same dresses; same food. To talk to Sir Arthur about Q. V.'s letters, & the dyestuff bill, & I forget[7]—I sacrificed an evening alone with Vita, an evening alone by myself—an evening of pleasure. And so it goes on perpetually. Lord & Lady Esher, Arnold Bennett—old Birrell. Forced, dry, sterile, infantile conversation. And I am not even excited at going. So the fence is not only leapt, but fallen. Why jump?

Thursday 18 December

Spain strikes. Illness of M. Poincaré. Suicide of Peter Warlock. Dyestuff Bill.[8]

Lord David, Lytton & Clive last night. Told them how I had burnt my evening dress in the gas fire—general agreement that parties are a folly. Clive specially emphatic. Talk about the riddle of the universe (Jeans' book) whether it will be known; not by us; found out suddenly: about rhythm in prose; Lytton is bringing out a new book of essays; what shall it be called; on living abroad; Clive says we (L. & I) are provincial. I say no mud abroad & fireflies in one's hair; Blenheim discussed; Lytton against it; Clive in favour; I say no sense of human personality; Lord David's aunt perpetually tears up her life of Ld Salisbury; feels the cause of the lunatics; no Cecils like dogs; Q.V. discussed; Bitter tea; A Lion

7. *The Letters of Queen Victoria (Third Series)*, Vol. I, 1886-1890, edited by G. E. Buckle, had recently been published. The Dyestuffs Act was due to lapse in January 1931 but under the Expiring Laws Continuance Bill the Conservative majority in the House of Lords secured a prolongation of the Act for a further twelve months. In 'Am I a Snob?' (*Moments of Being*, p 190) VW asserts that she was once 'the second leading authority in England on the Dyestuffs question'.

8. Martial law had been proclaimed in Spain on 15 December and labour unrest was widespread. Raymond Poincaré, the French statesman, was reported from Paris on 15 December as being seriously ill with congestion of the lungs and uraemia. Philip Heseltine (1894-1930), musicologist and under the pseudonym Peter Warlock a composer, had died of gas poisoning at his home in Chelsea on 17 December. The inquest concluded that there was insufficient evidence to decide whether his death was the result of suicide or an accident.

rages; Clive's eyes; Ld D. sneezed across the table; my bag came; fog all day.[9]

[*Friday 19 December*]

Spanish Rising. Prince of Wales' Chill. Carnera beats M.[10]

"Violet so delighted me", said Ethel, "by saying precisely what I wished her to say. I was so struck by the terrific strength & gentleness of V. & by her nose". Now I dont like this: I dont like that Ethel should know that I like compliments; I dont like liking them; I dont like Mrs Woodhouse fabricating them on the telephone.[11]

Saturday 20 December

W. H. D. Douglas drowned: six English lost: New motor regulation. Lord Willingdon appointed Viceroy of India.[12]

And Kingsley Martin lunched with us (sweeping up turkey as a char sweeps feathers) & said that the Nation & the N.S. are to amalgamate; & he is to be editor (highly secret, like all nonsense) & would L. be literary editor? No; L. wd. not.[13]

9. James Jeans' Rede Lecture, *The Mysterious Universe*, had been published in November. Strachey's *Portraits in Miniature and other Essays* appeared in May 1931. *Blenheim* (1930) was by G. M. Trevelyan. Lady Gwendolen Cecil published three volumes (1922, 1924, 1932) of her *Life* of her father the third Marquess of Salisbury, but never completed it. *Bitter Tea* by the American novelist Grace Zaring Stone had recently been published by Cobden Sanderson; 'A Lion rages', unidentified.

10. The rising in Spain had been declared a 'Republican failure' in the newspapers. The Prince of Wales had a 'slight' chill which prevented him visiting Windsor Great Park and caused him to miss a dinner at the Savoy. The Italian heavyweight Primo Carnera beat Reggie Meen of Britain in Round 2 at the Albert Hall on Thursday 18 December.

11. Violet Kate Eglinton Gordon-Woodhouse, *née* Gwynne (1872-1948), an amateur but outstanding harpsichordist and clavecinist, a pioneer of the revival of early music, whom Ethel regarded as the most musical of all her musical friends.

12. The English cricketer J. W. H. T. Douglas was among the 42 passengers who died aboard the steamer *Oberon* when it sank after colliding with the *Arcturus* in the Kattegat on the night of 19 December. The Ministry of Transport had banned motor coaches from certain Central London streets to relieve congestion. It had been announced on 19 December that Lord Willingdon, Governor-General of Canada, was to succeed Lord Irwin as Viceroy of India.

13. Basil Kingsley Martin (1897-1969) took up his post as the first editor of the newly merged *New Statesman and Nation* early in 1931 and retained it until his retire-

Monday 22 December[14]

Horror death of Douglas: Indian Conference. Fog. Intermittent. Weather to be colder.[15]

It occurred to me last night while listening to a Beethoven quartet that I would merge all the interjected passages into Bernard's final speech, & end with the words O solitude: thus making him absorb all those scenes, & having no further break. This is also to show that the theme effort, effort, dominates: not the waves: & personality: & defiance: but I am not sure of the effect artistically; because the proportions may need the intervention of the waves finally so as to make a conclusion.

Tuesday 23 December

I will make this hasty note about being robbed. I put my bag under my coat at Marshall & Snelgrove's. I turned; & felt, before I looked "It is gone". So it was. Then began questions & futile messages. Then the detective came. He stopped a respectable elderly woman apparently shopping. They exchanged remarks about 'the usual one—no she's not here today. Its a young woman in brown fur." Meanwhile I was ravaged, of course, with my own futile wishes—how I had thought, as I put down my bag, this is foolish. I was admitted to the underwor[l]d. I imagined the brown young woman peeping, pouncing. And it was gone my 6 pounds—my two brooches—all because of that moment. They throw the bags away, said the detective. These dreadful women come here—but

---

ment in December 1960; his first literary editor was R. Ellis Roberts whom he inherited from the *New Statesman*. For an account of the amalgamation of the *N & A* and the *New Statesman* see *The New Statesman. The History of the First Fifty Years* (1963) by Edward Hyams, pp 118-23.

14. On the opposite page VW has copied these lines from Dante, *Inferno*, 26, 94-102:

> Nè dolcezza di figlio, nè la piéta
> del vecchio padre, nè il debito amore
> Lo qual dovea Penelope far lieta
> Vincer poter dentro da me l'ardore
> Ch'i' ebbi a divenir del mondo esperto,
> E degli vizii umani e del valore;
> Ma misi me per l'alto mare aperto
> Sol con un legno e e con quella compagna
> Picciola, dalla qual non fui deserto

15. The Round Table Conference on India was held in London from 12 November 1930-19 January 1931.

not so much as to some of the Oxford St. shops. Fluster, regret, humiliation, curiosity, something frustrated, foolish, something jarred, by this underwor[l]d—a foggy evening—going home, penniless—thinking of my green bag—imagining the woman rifling it—her home—her husband —Now to Rodmell in the fog.[16]

Rodmell.

Saturday 27 December

But whats the use of talking about Bernard's final speech? We came down on Tuesday, & next day my cold was the usual influenza, & I am in bed with the usual temperature, & cant use my wits or, as is visible, form my letters. I daresay 2 days will see me normal; but then the sponge behind my forehead will be dry & pale—& so my precious fortnight of exaltation & concentration is snatched; & I shall go back to the racket & Nelly without a thing done. I cheer myself by thinking that I may evolve some thoughts[?]. Meanwhile it rains; Annie's child is ill; the dogs next door yap & yap; all the colours are rather dim & the pulse of life dulled. I moon torpidly through book after book: Defoe's Tour; Rowan's auto[bio-graph]y; Benson's Memoirs; Jeans; in the familiar way.[17] The parson—Skinner—who shot *Diary of a Somerset Rector*

himself emerges like a bloody sun in a fog. a book worth perhaps looking at again in a clearer mood. He shot himself in the beech woods above his house; spent a life digging up stones & reducing all places to Camelodunum; quarrelled; bickered; yet loved his sons; yet turned them out of doors—a clear hard picture of one type of human life—the exasperated, unhappy, struggling, intolerably afflicted. Oh & I've read Q.V.'s letters; & wonder what wd. happen had Ellen Terry been born Queen. Complete disaster to the Empire? Q.V. entirely unaesthetic; a kind of Prussian competence, & belief in herself her only prominences; material; brutal[?] to Gladstone; like a mistress with a dishonest footman.

16. LW's diary, 23 December 1930: 'Packed. Drove Marylebone Police Station get V's bag then to Monks.' See also *IV VW Letters* no. 2291 to Vanessa Bell.

17. VW's sickroom reading appears to have been Defoe's *Tour Through the Whole Island of Great Britain* (1724-27); *The Autobiography of Archibald Hamilton Rowan* published in Dublin by the Rev. W. Hamilton Drummond, 1840; *As We Were: A Victorian Peep-Show* by E. F. Benson, 1930; James Jeans' popular *The Mysterious Universe*, or his earlier *The Universe Around Us*; and *The Journal of a Somerset Rector*, edited by Howard Coombs and the Rev. Arthur N. Bax, 1930 (upon which VW based her essay 'The Rev. John Skinner' in *The Common Reader. Second Series*, 1935).

Knew her own mind. But the mind radically commonplace. only its inherited force, & cumulative sense of power, making it remarkable.

Monday 29 December

One of my trial runs to exercise my hands. (Still in bed). Skinner was bred to the Bar, but became, unfortunately, a clergyman. Unfortunately too his wife died, of consumption, leaving him with 3 children. Of these the only satisfactory one was Laura, who inherited her father's love of collecting & tabulating, but also her mother's consumption, so that before she had collected, in a very orderly way, many cabinets of shells, she died; & the other children were unsatisfactory.

Skinner was rector of Camerton in Somerset, & there he remained, year after year, without any aptitude whatsoever for the souls of the living. A clever, upright conscientious man, he did his duty by his flock, by perpetually admonishing them. That they were always bad, seems strange, but was to him true. A colliery was being formed at the village. The morals of colliers are perhaps loose. At any rate, no village in England seems to have contained so many insolent, wicked, ungrateful villagers. And Skinner was forever comparing them with the Romans. His only comfort was to dream himself back into Camelodunum, & to forget 1828. But being a disciplinarian, he was tormented by the need for reproving the living. His conscience refused to let him shut his eyes upon the sufferings of the halfwitted Mrs Goold, or the iniquities practised upon imbecile paupers at the workhouse, & he must perpetually go his rounds among the sick & dying, for accidents among the miners were frequent. He was always on the side of the afflicted; never on the side of the happy. He considered himself one of the worst treated of men, & imagined malignancies & insolences on all sides. Mrs Jarrett, the Squiress, was an arch-hypocrite. All her kindness had deceit behind it. Then he was sometimes asked to a ball—to a dinner party with French dishes. He much preferred solitude to the most brilliant society. Perpetually censorious, he found fault with French dishes, with dressing up, with all enjoyment— save only that of writing & writing, long accounts of places, catalogues of antiquity, & in special, his great work upon Etymology. He met with only ridicule here too. At a parsons dinner, he was asked to explain, on his system, the name of Bumstead, which he did—& then suspected that it was all a joke against him. Suspicion always came after a moments pleasure. Perhaps the only unalloyed pleasure was found in his visits to Stourhead, the seat of [*blank in ms*], where a party of antiquaries stayed for a day or two, giving themselves up to questions of Romans & Britons, of camps & buried cities. There, sitting alone in the luxurious library, he enjoyed the exquisite pleasure of copying extracts from—shall we say?—Ptolemy Theophrastus; & the good Bishop of Bath & Wells made him happy too in spite of a few suspicions—by asking him to spend the week end at Wells. These however were his only alleviations. Home life at Camerton became more & more sordid, humiliating, comfortless & by degrees violent. Jeered at & insulted by the rude peasants & farmers, who told him to his face that he was mad, his treatment was no better in his own vicarage, & from his own flesh & blood. There were terrible scenes with his sons. Once Joseph told him that he was making himself ridiculous by his writings, & was insane. Attempts to keep his son from drinking cider ended—so irritating was his manner—in violent curses. The sons were always being sent to stay with their grandmother at Bath. It was his temper that was at fault, he said; but they were at fault to irritate his temper. The servants left, because he wd. not let them walk out after dinner. The farmers cursed him because he suspected them of stealing his tythes; he nervously, irritatingly & imcompetently tried to exact his due of lambs & haycocks, He knew nothing of farming, nothing of country life. All he knew was that Camerton had been Camelodunum, & his obsession on this point made even the good natured Baronet protest that he carried Camelodunum too far. So at last—all he could do was to write & write & write. The blank pages of his diary alone neither sneered, nor hawked in his face, nor mocked him behind his back, nor plotted his downfall, nor called him mad. Eighty four volumes of antiquarian lumber & daily complaint & journalising were scribbled & put away in certain great iron chests which were bequeathed to the British Museum. At last his confidant was the future—in 50 years after his death, he said, these 84 volumes were to be given to the world—which world would understand his great contribution to etymology, & take his side against the Church-warden, Mrs Jarrett, Owen, the servant girl & all the rest of his ungrateful perpetually afflicting tribe. Fame & comfort would then be his. No doubt this secret confidence kept him going, through the gathering miseries of life. For the unhappy man was not blind to his faults. His chief misery must have come from the struggle of love & irritation. He loved his sons—yet drove them away. They fell ill, & he became all kindness & consideration—& yet how could the unfortunate Owen endure to have his father with him?—his egotistic, exacting, morose, but devoted father? He gave pain even by his affection. And suddenly the diary, written in a crabbed & illegible hand, ceases to be copied out any longer. The brother whose task it was died.

Skinner went on writing, but nobody could read his script. Perhaps the knowledge that even this confidant had failed him finally decided him. At any rate, 7 years later, he went out one December morning in the beechwoods, & fired. They found his dead body & buried it—exacerbated, scarred, covered with infernal irritation—in the grave of his wife & Laura.

Now this little narrative being run off,—& Lord, how difficult to write in bed—I report that the machine is not seriously damaged; & if I can get out, & move about, & yet not get a headache, I daresay in 3 days I shall be beginning to play gently with the waves. I dont have the temptations here of London. Not normal, but being normal is I daresay rather a fetish. All Mrs Dalloway was written with a temp. of 99 I think. How difficult though to get back into the right mental state: what a queer balance is needed. This little Skinner sketch is in the wrong order; but I dont fumble for words. Could let my mind fly, am not as I prove now, used up by an hour's exercise.

It rains. Nessa is driving from Seend today. Vita broadcasting. That bedroom voice, singing Bach, talking of the weather, has come in handy.

Tuesday 30 December

What it wants is presumably unity; but it is I think rather good (I am talking to myself over the fire about The Waves). Suppose I could run all the scenes together more?—by rhythm, chiefly. So as to avoid those cuts; so as to make the blood run like a torrent from end to end—I dont want the waste that the breaks give; I want to avoid chapters; that indeed is my achievement, if any here: a saturated, unchopped, completeness; changes of scene, of mood, of person, done without spilling a drop. Now if it cd. be worked over with heat & currency thats all it wants. And I am getting my blood up. (temp. 99)

But all the same I went to Lewes, & the Keynes's came to tea; & having got astride my saddle the whole world falls into shape; it is this writing that gives me my proportions.

ABBREVIATIONS
AND
APPENDIXES

ABBREVIATIONS

CH, Camb.	Charleston Papers deposited in the Library of King's College, Cambridge
Holleyman	Holleyman & Treacher Ltd: *Catalogue of Books from the Library of Leonard and Virginia Woolf, taken from Monks House, Rodmell, and 24 Victoria Square, London, and now in the possession of Washington State University.* Privately printed, Brighton, 1975
Holroyd	Michael Holroyd: *Lytton Strachey. A Biography.* Revised edition, Penguin Books, 1971
HP Checklist	*A Checklist of the Hogarth Press 1917-1938.* Compiled by J. Howard Woolmer. With a short history of the Press by Mary E. Gaither, Hogarth Press, London, 1976
Kp	B. J. Kirkpatrick: *A Bibliography of Virginia Woolf.* Revised edition, Hart-Davis, London, 1967
LW	Leonard Woolf. Five volumes of his *Autobiography*, Hogarth Press, London.
I LW	*Sowing: . . . 1880-1904.* 1960
II LW	*Growing: . . . 1904-1911.* 1961
III LW	*Beginning Again: . . . 1911-1918.* 1964
IV LW	*Downhill all the Way: . . . 1919-1939.* 1967
V LW	*The Journey not the Arrival Matters: . . . 1939-1969.* 1969
LWP, Sussex	*Leonard Woolf Papers.* University of Sussex Library Catalogue, 1977
M & M	Robin Majumdar and Allen McLaurin: *Virginia Woolf. The Critical Heritage,* Routledge & Kegan Paul, London, 1975
MHP, Sussex	*Monks House Papers.* University of Sussex Library Catalogue, July 1972
N & A	*Nation and Athenaeum*
RF Letters	*Letters of Roger Fry.* Edited by Denys Sutton. Chatto & Windus, London, 1972
I RF Letters	Volume I, 1878-1913
II RF Letters	Volume II, 1913-1934
QB	Quentin Bell: *Virginia Woolf. A Biography.* Hogarth Press, London, 1972
I QB	Volume I: *Virginia Stephen,* 1882-1912
II QB	Volume II: *Mrs Woolf,* 1912-1941
Shone	Richard Shone: *Bloomsbury Portraits,* 1976
TLS	*Times Literary Supplement*

VW   Virginia Woolf
  VW Diary   *The Diary of Virginia Woolf.* Edited by Anne Olivier
                 Bell. Hogarth Press, London.
  I VW Diary   Volume I: *1915-1919.* 1977
  II VW Diary Volume II: *1920-1924.* 1978
  VW Letters   *The Letters of Virginia Woolf.* Edited by Nigel Nicolson.
                 Hogarth Press, London
  I VW Letters   Volume I: *The Flight of the Mind* (1888-1912), 1975
  II VW Letters Volume II: *The Question of Things Happening* (1912-
                 1922), 1976
  III VW Letters Volume III: *A Change of Perspective* (1923-1928), 1977
  IV VW Letters Volume IV: *A Reflection of the Other Person* (1929-
                 1931), 1978

NOTE

The Uniform Edition of the Works of Virginia Woolf, published by the
Hogarth Press, is used for reference purposes.

APPENDIX I

*Biographical Outlines of Persons
Most Frequently Mentioned*

BELL, Clive (Arthur Clive Heward Bell, 1881-1964), art critic, married Vanessa Stephen in 1907, and thereafter played an important part in VW's life. His marriage had become a matter of convenience and friendship, for since about 1915 Mary Hutchinson held pride of place in his affections. In the period immediately preceding that covered by the present volume Bell published *Poems* (1921), *Since Cézanne* (1922), *The Legend of Monte della Sibilla* (1923) and *On British Freedom* (1923).

BELL, Vanessa ('Nessa'), *née* Stephen (1879-1961), painter, VW's elder sister and, after LW, the most important person in her life. She married Clive Bell in 1907, and though they always remained on amicable terms, from about 1914 and until her death she lived and worked with the painter Duncan Grant. Her children were Julian Heward (1908-1937); Quentin Claudian Stephen (b. 1910); and Angelica Vanessa (b. 1918)—the last-named being the daughter of Duncan Grant.

BIRRELL, Francis ('Frankie') Frederick Locker (1889-1935), critic, elder son of Augustine Birrell, educated at Eton and King's College, Cambridge. He and his friend David Garnett had together served with a Quaker Relief Unit in France during the war. In 1919 he and Garnett entered into partnership to establish a bookshop *Birrell & Garnett* in Taviton Street, near Gordon Square, and subsequently in Gerrard Street. He wrote regularly for the *Nation & Athenaeum* of which LW was the literary editor.

ELIOT, Thomas Stearns (1888-1965), American-born poet, educated at Harvard and Oxford; married in 1915 Vivienne Haigh-Wood. Eliot had known VW since 1918; despite her efforts and those of others to free him, he was until 1925 on the London staff of Lloyds Bank, which he had joined in 1917; he nonetheless edited a literary review, *The Criterion*, founded in 1922. The Hogarth Press had published his *Poems* (1919), *The Waste Land* (1923), and his essays *Homage to John Dryden* (1924).

FORSTER, Edward Morgan (1879-1970), novelist, educated at King's College, Cambridge, 1897-1902, an Apostle. Towards the end of 1921 he had returned from his second visit to India, after which he resumed writing *A Passage to India*, published in 1924. In 1925 he moved with his mother from Weybridge to Abinger in Surrey, and also found a *pied-à-terre* in Brunswick Square,

Bloomsbury. His *Pharos and Pharillon* had been published by the Hogarth Press in 1923.

FRY, Roger Eliot (1866-1934), art critic and painter, descended from generations of Quakers, gained first class honours in Natural Sciences at King's College, Cambridge, where he became an Apostle. He abandoned science for the study and practice of art; he had created a scandal by introducing the British public to Post-Impressionist art, but remained an established and respected figure in the museum and art world in England, France and America. His *Vision and Design* was published in 1920, and *Twelve Original Woodcuts* by the Hogarth Press, in 1921.

GRANT, Duncan James Corrowr (1885-1978), painter, only child of Major Bartle Grant whose sister was Lady Strachey; he spent much of his youth with the Strachey family. From about 1914 until her death in 1961, he lived and worked with Vanessa Bell; their daughter Angelica Bell was born on Christmas Day, 1918.

HUTCHINSON, Mary, *née* Barnes (1889-1977), a first cousin once removed of Lytton Strachey, married in 1910 the barrister and friend to the arts St John ('Jack') Hutchinson (1884-1942). She had for many years been paramount in Clive Bell's affections.

KEYNES, John Maynard (1883-1946), economist, scholar of Eton and King's College, Cambridge, an Apostle, a Fellow and from 1924 First Bursar of the College, and University lecturer in economics; he married in August 1925 the Russian ballerina Lydia Lopokova. In 1923 Keynes had become chairman of the new Board of the *Nation & Athenaeum* and had appointed LW literary editor. His publications up to the present period include *The Economic Consequences of the Peace* (1919), *A Revision of the Treaty* (1922), and his first major work in economics *A Tract on Monetary Reform* (1923).

LOPOKOVA, Lydia (b. 1892), Russian ballerina, studied at the Imperial School of Ballet, St Petersburg: she married Maynard Keynes in August 1925. She had visited London with the Diaghilev Company in 1918, 1919 and again in 1921 when Keynes had fallen in love with her and persuaded her to live in Gordon Square among his friends.

MacCARTHY, (Charles Otto) Desmond (1877-1952), literary journalist and editor, graduate of Trinity College, Cambridge, and an Apostle; married Mary ('Molly') Josefa Warre-Cornish in 1906. In 1920 he became literary editor of the *New Statesman*, for which he wrote a weekly column "Books in General", under the pseudonym "Affable Hawk".

MacCARTHY, Mary ('Molly') Josefa, *née* Warre-Cornish (1882-1953), married Desmond MacCarthy in 1906. Like VW she was a niece by marriage of 'Aunt Anny'—Lady Anne Thackeray Ritchie. In 1924 she published *A Nineteenth-Century Childhood*, a book made from a series of articles contributed to the *Nation & Athenaeum* in 1923-24.

MORRELL, Lady Ottoline, *née* Cavendish-Bentinck (1873-1938), hostess and patroness of the arts, married in 1902 Philip Morrell (1870-1943), barrister and Liberal MP, 1906-18. From 1915-1927 they lived at Garsington Manor in Oxfordshire, where they gave generous hospitality to pacifists, writers, and artists, and thenceforward in Gower Street, Bloomsbury. Their daughter Julian was born in 1906.

MORTIMER, Raymond (b. 1895) critic, a graduate of Balliol College, Oxford. VW first met him in 1923. In the 1920s he was active as a journalist in Paris and in London. He was a close friend of Clive Bell and of the Harold Nicolsons, whom he visited in Persia in 1926.

NICOLSON, Harold (1886-1968), diplomat and author, son of 1st Baron Carnock, married Vita Sackville-West in 1913. In 1925 he was posted to the British Embassy in Teheran, and in 1927 transferred to Berlin. His publications up to the present period include *Paul Verlaine* (1921), *Tennyson* (1923), and *Byron, The Last Journey* (1924).

SACKVILLE-WEST, Victoria ('Vita') Mary (1892-1962), novelist and poet, only child of 3rd Baron Sackville, married Harold Nicolson in 1913. VW first met her at a dinner given by Clive Bell in December 1922. From 1924, the Hogarth Press published thirteen of her books altogether, including her best selling novel *The Edwardians* in 1930.

STEPHEN, Adrian Leslie (1883-1948), VW's younger brother. Trinity College, Cambridge, 1902-05. A conscientious objector during the war, he married in 1914 Karin Elizabeth Conn Costelloe (1889-1953), a philosophy graduate of Newnham; they had two daughters, Ann (b. 1916) and Judith (1918-72). From 1919-26 they both studied medicine and psychology, and thereafter practised as analysts.

STRACHEY, (Giles) Lytton (1880-1932), critic and biographer, a contemporary and friend of both VW's brother Thoby Stephen and LW at Trinity College, Cambridge, and like the latter an Apostle. Since 1924 he had lived at Ham Spray House in Wiltshire with Carrington and her husband Ralph Partridge. After *Eminent Victorians* (1918), he had published *Queen Victoria* (1921), and *Books and Characters* (1922).

STRACHEY, James Beaumont (1887-1967), psychoanalyst, Lytton's youngest brother; he too went to Trinity College, Cambridge, and became an Apostle. He had married Alix Sargant-Florence in 1920 and with her went in the same year to Vienna to study under Freud; he was to become the English translator and general editor of Freud's works, which the Hogarth Press published.

APPENDIX II

Virginia Woolf and 'That Unnatural Florentine Society'

VW went with Vanessa and Clive Bell to Florence in April 1909. The notebook recording her impressions of this and other foreign journeys—to Greece in 1906, to Siena and Perugia in 1908, and to Florence in 1909—is lost, but a typed copy (MH/A7) made for Leonard Woolf is among the Monks House Papers in the University of Sussex Library, by whose permission the following passage is printed. It illuminates VW's reflections upon learning of the death of Geoffrey Scott (see Diary, 21 August 1929), and upon reading the life of Alice Meynell (see Diary, 2 September 1929).

Today we had another experience of society. We had lunch with the art critic [Bernard Berenson] and his wife; and tea with Mrs Ross. In case space should fail me (the candle gutters intolerably, and the ink oozes) I will describe the tea party. The worst of distinguished old ladies, who have known everyone and lived an independent life, is that they become brusque and imperious without sufficient wits to alleviate the manner. Mrs Ross lives in a great villa, is the daughter of distinguished parents; the friend of writers, and the character of the country side. She sells things off her walls. She is emphatic, forcible, fixes you with her straight grey eye as though it were an honour to occupy, even for a moment, its attention. The head is massive, it is held high; the mouth is coarse and the upper lip haired. Such old women like men, and have a number of unreasonable traditions. Pride of birth, I thought I detected; certainly she has that other pride, the pride which comes to those who have lived among the chosen spirits of the time. A word of family, and her wits were at work at once.

I know not why, but this type . . . does not much attract me. Only one position is possible if you are a young woman: you must let them adopt queenly airs, with a touch of the maternal. She summons you to sit beside her, lays her hand for a moment on yours, dismisses you the next, to make room for some weakly young man. She has them to stay with her for months —likes them best when they are big and strong but will tolerate weakness for the sake of the sex. She has led a bold life, managing for herself, and an English-woman who dictates to peasants is apt to become domineering. However, there can be no question of her spirit—many portraits showed the intent indomitable face, in youth and middle age, it is still the same, beneath white hair. It proved her power that her drawing room filled with guests. She seemed to enjoy sweeping them about, without much ceremony. Parties were bidden to admire the garden; young men were commanded to hand cake. Among the guests was a lean, attenuated woman, who had a face like that of a transfixed hare—the lower part was drawn out in anguish, while the eyes appealed piteously. This was Mrs Meynell, the writer, who somehow made one dislike the notion of women who write. She clasped the arm of a chair, and seemed uncomfortably out of place.

This was no atmosphere for chaste expression—there was nothing to lay hold of. She walked with a curious forward spring which, seeing that the body was spare and bony, encased too in black velvet, had an incongruous air. Once, no doubt, she was a poetess, and trod the fields of Parnassus. It is melancholy to trace even such words as Mrs Meynell's to a lank, slightly absurd and altogether insignificant little body, dressed with some attempt at the fashion. Did Mrs Browning look like that too? And yet, poor woman, had the fire of Sappho burnt in her what else could she have done? These gatherings are brutal things. Or is my theory proved—a writer should be the furnace from which his words come—and tepid people, timid and decorous, never coin true words. The poor thing looked furtive, as though found out—run to earth. She had a plain aesthetic daughter. The wine further watered.

INDEX

Addison, Joseph: 213

Albert Road, No. 3, home of Mr and Mrs St John Hutchinson: 3 & n, 310

Allen, Sir Hugh: 291 & n

Allison, Elsie, resident of Rodmell: 107 & n

Allison, James Murray, resident of Rodmell: 107 & n, 158, 159, 184

Amberley, Sussex: 160

America: 69, 185, 205, 250, 272, 277

Anderson, Hew Skelton: 8 & n, 35 & n

Annie see Thompsett, Annie

Anrep, Anastasia ('Baba'): 237 & n

Anrep, Boris: 30n, 33

Anrep, Helen: VW talks with, 30 & n; loved by Roger, 52; and Old Bloomsbury, 162; distracted & worried, affectionate & private, 237 & n; ref: 166, 178

Apostles, The, Cambridge Conversazione Society or The Society: LW's festival night, 31 & n; Julian's speech before, 232; discord at dinner, 235 & n

Argyll House, Chelsea: 69, 225, 310, 337

Arnold, Matthew: 226 & n; Dover Beach, 226n

Arnold-Forster, Katherine ('Ka'), née Cox: Ottoline on, 36 & n; thinner & self conscious, 48; matronly but substantial, 123; unshades Nessa's lamps, 175 & n; old dunderhead, 238; ref: 119, 123n, 178 & n, 319

Arnold-Forster, Mervyn: 123 & n, 136

Arnold-Forster, William (Will): in Bloomsbury, 178 & n; illusion about his brain, 239; ref: 119, 123 & n, 175n

Ashcroft, Mr, unidentified: 161

Ashcroft, Peggy, in Othello: 304

Ashdown Forest: 157, 251, 252

Asheham Hill: 102, 108, 192, 247

Ashton, Leigh: 66 & n, 117

Asquith, H. H.: and general strike, 82 & n

Asquith, Margot, née Tennant (Lady Oxford): sticks in gizzard, 17 & n; on VW's beauty, 35; hates women, 140 & n; ref: 296n; Lay Sermons, 140n; Places and Persons, 17 & n

Atlantic Monthly, periodical: 33 & n

Auppegard, home of Ethel Sands and Nan Hudson: 150, 151 & n, 153

Austen, Jane: 190, 307

Avery, William, Rodmell gravedigger, and family: 154 & n

Babs see Woolf, Marjorie

Bach, J. S.: 17, 158, 343

Bagenal, Barbara: VW favours, 196 & n; ref: 166, 167n, 211, 312

Bagenal, Judith: 232 & n

Bagenal, Nicholas: 196 & n, 211

Bagnold, Enid: 291, 326

Baldwin, Stanley: and General Strike, 78 & n; broadcasts to nation, 81; meets J. H. Thomas, 82; visits zoo, 83 & n

Balfour, Arthur James, 1st Earl of: pacifies Lieder singer, 34 & n

Balfour, Lady Betty: 308 & n

Balston, Thomas, partner in Duckworth & Co: 309 & n

Balzac: 205

Barbara see Bagenal

Barcelona, 'uncrowned' king of: 309 & n

Baring, Evelyn, see Cromer, 1st Earl of

Baring, Maurice: his novel, 102 & n, 103, 104; sends his books to VW, 114 & n; and E. Smyth, 291 & n; VW won't write on, 307; at E. Smyth's, 307, 308; ref: 139, 166, 213, 292, 325; C, a novel, 102 & n, 104, 114n; Diminutive Dramas, 291n

Barnes, James Strachey: 243n

Barrie, J. M.: 94 & n, 98

Bartholomew, Percy, of Rodmell: 'our man', 207, 221; and local story, 274 & n, 317; Trim & Uncle Toby, 320; ref: 159, 160n, 238, 266, 313, 318

Bartholomew, Rose: compared with VW, 104 & n; worth a penny stamp?, 129; poor emaciated, 153; never cleans grate, 160; inherits fortune, 207; were VW her, 236; her prospects, 255; ref: 160n

Bartholomew & Fletcher, upholsterers: 84 & n

Bartlett, Miss (unidentified): 320

Bath: 291, 303, 325, 342

Bath and Wells, Bishop of: 342

Baynes, Keith: 269 & n

Bayswater: murder in, 268 & n; ref: 133

Beaverbrook, Lady: 166 & n

Beaverbrook, Lord: 329

Beck, Maurice Adams, photographer: 12 & n

view of the Keyneses, 147; Clive's secondrateness and, 148; on Ethel and Nan, 151 & n; growing little wings, 152; driving car, 154; initiates Old Bloomsbury evenings, 162; about to migrate, 173 & n; her lamps unshaded, 175 & n; at La Bergère, 179; lack of causes drought, 184; is a necessity, 186; unsentimental mother, 194; a real person, 202; gives Tuesday evenings, 211; exhibits pictures, 217 & n; visits Germany and Austria, 218; sunk fathoms deep, 219; takes a studio, 220 & n; fertilizes Roger, 224; her supremacy, 232; praised by Duncan, 233; often melancholy, often envious, 242; in Fitzroy St., 260; imagined at Angelica's school, 261, 262; VW not so valiant as, but ..., 267; paint and politics, 269 & n; at Seend, 274; Thoby's letters to, 275n; and Margery Snowden, 289 & n; her nudes deplored, 294; content at Charleston, 298; her sublime ineptitude, 306; stokes bonfire, 312; easy Bohemian, 316; recommends spectacles, 328; reads for Clive, 332; *ref*: 6, 7n, 17, 42 & n, 53, 73, 113, 125, 127, 133, 134, 136, 165, 166, 169, 199, 201, 203, 231, 259, 268, 286, 304, 305, 323, 343, 352; 'The Red Sofa', 217n
Bell, (Lt Col William) Cory: the anti-bugger, 10 & n; *ref*: 58, 147
Bell, William Heward: 140n, 141
Belloc, Hilaire: 213 & n
Belcher, Miss, Hogarth Press clerk: 221 & n
Bennett, Arnold: Wells on—his topography, 95; on horror of marriage, 105, dining with, 114 & n; on Woolfs, 116; on *Orlando*, 206 & n; George Moore on, 214; tradesman of letters, 318; VW meets and portrays, 334-5; *ref*: 256, 334n, 337; *Riceyman Steps*, 214 & n
Benson, E. F.: *As We Were: A Victorian Peep-Show*, 340 & n; *Dodo*, 296 & n
Benson, Margaret: 325 & n
Benson, Mary: 325 & n
Berenson, Bernard: 244, 352
Berenson, Mrs Bernard: 243 & n
Berlin: Woolfs visit, 218; *ref*: 163, 211, 222, 326

Berlioz, Hector: 103
Bernard (fict): 301, 332, 339, 340
Berners, Lord: on himself, 63 & n; anxious for salvation, 68; *ref*: 42 & n; *First Childhood*, 63n
Bernstorff, Albrecht: 310 & n
Bibesco, Elizabeth: the truth about, 27 & n
Billing & Sons Ltd, printers: 84 & n
Binyon, Laurence: 139 & n
Birrell, Augustine: VW annoyed with, 306; *ref*: 266 & n, 307 & n, 337; *Collected Essays*, 266n
Birrell, Francis: for Biographical Note *see* Appendix I; bawling, 25; on Leslie Stephen, 61; and General Strike, 78, 82; to join Press?, 167 & n, 169; benefits lavished on, 200; his rattle & clapper, 204; a runaway milk lorry, 219; 'a man I adore', 231; made happier by Shaw, 277; *ref*: 24, 60, 135, 168n, 183, 205, 235, 242
Birrell & Garnett, bookshop: 82
Bishop, Adrian: 68 & n
Bloomsbury, a group of friends: influence on Nelly Boxall, 3; suspected by Irene Noel-Baker, 28; and Chiswick, 60; eternal, 61; and E. Sackville-West, 68; H. Nicolson on trial in, 140; Clive the Don Juan of, 149; Dottie buying her way in, 157 & n; Old Bloomsbury evenings, 162, 164; dispersed, 173 & n; reviving, 175; VW touchy for its reputation, 178; 'done with', 219; its praise and Lytton, 234; its closed walls, 244; and gossip, 267; *ref*: ix, 176, 205
Bloomsbury, a part of London: 78, 127, 217
Blunden, Edmund: 101 & n, 224
Blunt, Anthony: 255 & n
Boar's Hill, near Oxford: 331 & n
Boski *see* Le Bosquet, Audrey
Boswell, James: the Malahide papers, 237, 238 & n; VW asked to write life of, 295 & n; *ref*: 245; *The Hypochondriak*, 238n
Bott, Mr, of *The Graphic*: 293
Boulestin, restaurant: 90
Bourne & Hollingsworth: 165
Bowen, Vera: 210 & n
Bow Street Magistrates' Court: 206 & n

Boxall, Nelly: has given notice, 3; a wireless for?, 11; is *jealous*, 27; rather waspish, 36; to be quit of, 40; usual crisis, 41; discussing marriage, 44; longs for civilization, 45; won't make marmalade, 59; finally loses credibility, 75; holidays discussed, 90; cooks admirably, 107; calm follows departure, 111; obedient & gay, 112; lie causes quarrel, 114; mysterious kidney affection, 133; gives notice for 125th time, 146; first evening back, 153; good as gold, is given rise, 165; a victim of the system?, 220; at a distance, 228; fellow socialist, 230; to go . . . to stay, 240; 'in a state of nature', 241; her way of thanking, 253; strain of her company, 254; gives notice over coal scuttle, 255; goes on Friday, 257; another showdown, 266; out to catch Woolfs weakening, 267; final interview impending, 268; a compromise, 270 & n; VW's 'book' on, 274, 281; undergoes operation, 304; turned out of hospital, 305; relief at her absence, 311; decided against her, 312; boring subject of, 315; more diplomacy, 322 & n; on best behaviour, 323; apprehensive & suspicious, 325; final letters, 327, 328; appeals to doctor, 332; all the old tunes, 333, 334; *ref:* 3n, 85, 88, 242, 292, 310, 340

Brace, Donald: and *To the Lighthouse*, 127; depresses VW, 227 & n; *ref:* 18 & n, 84

Braithwaite, Richard Bevan: 16 & n, 162, 281, 282; *The State of Religious Belief*, 162n

Bramber, Sussex: 105 & n

Brenan, Gerald: emissary to PM, 83; a sketch of?, 157; 'married', 312; *ref:* 30, 31n, 83, 256

Brett, Hon. Oliver *see* Esher, Lord

Brewster, Henry Bennett: 291 & n, 325, 326; *The Prison: A Dialogue*, 291 & n

Bridges, Robert: praises *Mrs Dalloway*, 50; springs from rhododendron bush, on sonnets, criticism & Hopkins, 92-3; *ref:* 50n, 53n, 90, 91, 103

Brighton: Labour Party conference at, 258 & n; *ref:* 89, 155, 160, 194, 228, 241

Briscoe, Lily (fict): on the lawn, 106, 109, 132

British Gazette: LW to answer, 77; *ref:* 77n

British Museum: 80, 94, 321, 342

Broadsheet, The, projected periodical: 293

Brontë, Anne: George Moore on, 66n, 67

Brontë, Charlotte: 67

Brontë, Emily: 50, 67

Brooke, Miss, dressmaker: 86, 113, 137

Brooke, Rupert: Ottoline on, 36 & n; *ref:* 16, 239

Broughton, Rhoda: 271

Brown, Mrs, of Dollman & Pritchard: 79 & n

Browne, Sir Thomas: 5n, 202

Browning, Elizabeth Barrett: 353

Browning, Oscar (O.B.): 138 & n

Brunswick Square, No. 38: 20

Buchan, John: 263 & n

Buchan, Susan: 263 & n

Buckmaster, Lord: 285

Bulley, Margaret H.: 83 & n

Bull Hotel, Cambridge: 114 & n

Bunny *see* Garnett, David

Burlington Magazine: 178

Burne-Jones, Edward: 251

Burne-Jones, Philip: brilliant young man of 50, 248 & n

Burney, Dr: 185 & n

Burney, Fanny: 199-200, 303 & n

Bussy, Dorothy, *née* Strachey: 190n, 209, 319

Bussy, Jane-Simone (Janie): 190 & n, 191, 209, 314

Butler, Samuel: 250 & n; *The Notebooks of Samuel Butler*, 250n

Butts, Anthony (Tony): 242 & n

Butts, Mary: 150 & n; *Armed With Madness*, 150n

Buxton, Charles Roden: 259 & n

Byng Lucas, Miss Frances: 159 & n

Byng-Stamper, Captain E. P. F.: 159 & n, 274 & n, 317

Byron, Lord: 237, 238n, 244, 287-8; *Childe Harold's Pilgrimage*, 287 & n, 288

Caburn, Mount: 296, 318, 322

Caen Wood *see* Ken Wood

Calendar of Modern Letters: abuses *Mrs Dalloway*, 35 & n

165; lunch party, 166 & n, 222; dinner at a price, 226; loses nest-egg, 265; *ref*: 9 & n, 42, 63, 103, 114, 124, 135, 152, 177, 185, 202, 219, 225, 245, 262, 295, 337
Coleridge, S. T.: 130
Coliseum, The London: 223 & n
Collins, Mrs, and daughter: to replace Nelly?, 146
Columbus, Christopher: Lytton on, 294 & n
Commercio, restaurant: 80
Connaught Rooms: lunch with Desmond at, 21
Conrad, Joseph: George Moore on, 67
Constantinople: 131
Conway, Sir Martin: and strike petition, 83 & n
Cook, Sir John: 166
Cooke, Sidney Russell and Helen *née* Smith: 199 & n
Cookham: 64, 118
Coolidge, Calvin: 69
Cornhill Magazine, The: and Thomas Hardy, 97 & n
Cornwall: 119, 123, 303
Country Life: 16 & n
Couve de Murville, Maurice: 157n
Cowper, William: a good poet, 129; article on, 232 & n; 'The Castaway', 19n
Cox, Miss Catherine: 237 & n
Cox, Ka, *see* Arnold-Forster, Katherine
Cranbourne Chase: 75
Cranium Club: 155 & n, 166
Criterion, The, literary quarterly, later *The New Criterion*: 14n, 41, 46
Croly, Herbert David, editor: 183 & n
Cromer, Evelyn Baring, 1st Earl of: 51 & n
Cromer, Katherine, Countess of: framework of discarded beauty, 51 & n
Cromwell, Oliver: 153, 180 & n, 194 & n, 197
Cruthers, residents of Cassis: 232
Cunard, Lady: stringy old hop-o'-my-thumb, 201-2; *ref*: 202n, 206, 210, 309 & n, 310
Cunard, Nancy: 4 & n, 15, 64; *Parallax*, 4 & n, 5n
Currys, residents of Cassis: 232
Curtis, Mrs, headmistress: 254n, 262

Daglish, Doris, of Wandsworth: 150 & n
Daily Herald: 77
Dalingridge Place, Sussex: 293 & n, 294
Dalloway, Clarissa (fict): disagreeable & limited, 32
Dalton, Hugh: stuffed by LW, 82 & n
D'Annunzio, Gabriele: and Duse, 299 & n
Dante: makes writing unnecessary, 313; *ref*: 103, 179, 283, 320, 326, 339n; *Inferno*, 313, 339n
Darwin (family): 16 & n, 88
Darwin, Bernard: 145 & n
Davidson, Angus: unselfish and charming, 4; like an elder brother, 10; a little languid, 26; wobbles & prevaricates, 29; on Lytton in love, 31; 'He don't do', 116 & n; his cautious alarm, 124 & n; doesn't 'manage', and won't budge, 128; in pink shirt, 154; quarrels about time—and is dismissed, 162; finally to go, 167; his anxieties and gentlemanly reserve, 205 & n; comes for 'character', 211; secretary of London Artists, 269 & n; *ref*: 4 & n, 16, 17, 35 & n, 72, 110, 134
Davidson, Douglas: in perfect trim, 138
Davies, Crompton Llewelyn: 234 & n, 235
Davies, Margaret Llewelyn: in retirement, 23 · & n; dishevelled and undistinguished, 296, 297; VW annoyed with, 306, 307; *ref*: 175, 314
Day's Library, Mayfair: 84 & n
Dedman, Mrs, of Rodmell: 321
Defoe, Daniel: 50, 131, 340; *Tour Through the Whole Island of Great Britain*, 340n
De La Mare, Walter: Hardy on, 99 & n; dream talk with Yeats, 329, 330, 332 & n; *ref*: 65 & n, 271; *The Connoisseur and Other Stories*, 99n; *On the Edge*, 332
Dell, Ethel M.: 23 & n
De Quincey, Thomas: VW writing on, 83 & n, 95, 109; 'Suspiria de Profundis', 96 & n
Derby, The: 226
Desborough, Lady: 37 & n
Devonshire, Woolfs tour in: 303
Devonshire, 8th Duke of: Bernard Holland's Life of, 247 & n

Emery, Miss, dog breeder, of Rodmell: 321

Empire Review: 235 & n

Enfield, Dorothy, *née* Hussey: 205 & n

English Association: VW on committee of, 58 & n

Esher, Lady: 337

Esher, Lord (Hon. Oliver Brett): 176n, 335 & n, 337

Esther, unidentified: talking like Macaulay, 231

Etoile Restaurant, Charlotte Street: 36 & n

Eton College: 252 & n, 261, 314

Eve *see* Younger, Eve

Evening Standard: on writing for, 186; VW praised in, 255-6, 256n; *ref:* 309 & n

Faber & Gwyer, publishers: 14n, 41n

Fairbanks, Douglas: 69

Fairlawne, Tonbridge, home of Cazalet family: 252 & n

Faringdon Market: 325

Farquhar, Earl: 283 & n

Farwell, Mr Justice: 273 & n

Fausset, Hugh I'Anson: praises *Common Reader*, 18 & n

Fears, Mr, of Rodmell: 159, 321

Femina-Vie Heureuse, literary prize: awarded to VW, 178 & n, 179, 182, 183 & n; to Rose Macaulay, 185 & n

Fife Settlements: 283 & n

Findlater, Mary: 161 & n

Fisher, Emmeline: 324 & n

Fisher, Herbert Albert Laurens: 42 & n

Fisher, Mary, *née* Jackson: a threat to liberty, 194 & n

Fitzroy Square, No. 29: 267

Fitzroy Street, No. 8 (Vanessa's studio): 220n, 260, 306

Fladgate, Mrs (unidentified): 131

Florence: 243 & n, 244, 352

Fontcreuse, near Cassis: 173n, 179, 231, 232n

Formosa Fishery, near Cookham, home of the Youngs: 35 & n

Forster, E. M. (Morgan): for Biographical Note *see* Appendix I; operation on wrist, 18; his judgment on Mrs D., 22, 24; compliments E. Sitwell, snubs Vita, 28; asks Woolfs out to lunch, 36; his article on VW, 47 & n; his death imagined, 48; his character compared with Lytton's, 48, 49-50; cheers VW, 52 & n; Hardy on, 98, 99; and Tess's picture, 101; on finishing novel, 109; and Abel Chevalley, 114 & n; VW to do, 127 & n; morganatic letter on *Lighthouse*, 137 & n; VW's article on, 149; reacts to criticism, 152 & n; VW reviews, 158 & n; on the Bell children, 158; what he calls 'life', 164; the blue butterfly, 177; on sodomy, and Radclyffe Hall, 193 & n; his articles indistinguishable, 244; and *A Room of One's Own*, 262; in atmosphere of buggery, 299; kept up with, 316; *ref:* 25, 89, 157, 275, 318; *Abinger Harvest*, 47n; *A Passage to India*, 50 & n, 109, 130, 152; *Aspects of the Novel*, 158n

Fortnum & Mason, Piccadilly: 138, 164

Forum, periodical: 58 & n, 127

France: 6, 41, 90, 129, 139, 145, 151, 177, 178, 179, 186, 200, 233, 275, 323, 327

Francis, Mr, at Cassis: 8

Franklin, Sir John: 72 & n

Fred *see* Pape, Frederick

Fry, Joan Mary: 89 & n

Fry, Roger: for Biographical Note *see* Appendix I; an ally, 31; his garden party, 33 & n; his exacerbating egotism, 45; loves Helen Anrep, 52; reports Nessa's criticism of VW, 76; chess with LW, 86; dislikes 'Time Passes', 127 & n; a pure aristocrat, 129; in grand historical picture, 157; and Old Bloomsbury, 162; malicious & vain, 178 & n; a real person, 202; needs Nessa, 224; his life with Helen, 237; hated by critics, 269; ravaged scavenger, 284; *ref:* 34, 38, 53 & n, 125, 164, 166, 173, 203, 217, 218, 227, 236, 259, 262, 275, 282, 283, 293, 323, 332

Gage, 6th Viscount: 102, 198, 199n, 310

Gaige, Crosby: 183 & n

Galsworthy, John: and General Strike, 83 & n; George Moore scorns, 214

Garland, Madge: 12 & n, 184

Garnett, David ('Bunny'): Lytton on, 44; wrong about Julian, 329; *ref:* 208; *A Man in the Zoo*, 44 & n

Garnett, Edward: 204 & n

Garrod, H. W., 92 & n
Garsington Manor, home of Philip and
    Ottoline Morrell: 13, 90, 91
Garvin, J. L., editor of *The Observer*:
    83n
Gathorne-Hardy, Robert: 26 & n, 30
General Election, 1929: draws near, 226
    & n; Labour confident, 228; Labour
    winning, 230 & n; a gamble on, 235
General Strike: exact diary of, 77-85;
    petition, 81 & n, 82; LW asserts
    legality of, 83 & n; settlement
    announced, 84 & n, 85 & n; con-
    tinuing, 85, 86, 88, 89; ref: 77n, 80n
Genji *see* Murasaki, Lady
George V: dispatches Wells, 163 & n;
    dragging along, 211 & n; at the play,
    273, 274
Gerbault, Alain, circumnavigator: mis-
    ogynist, 299 & n
Gere, Margaret: 290 & n
Gerhardi, William: 71
Germany: and labour relations, 80 & n;
    ref: 173
Germany, Grace: 124n, 333 & n
Gibbons, Stella: 162 & n
Gilbert and Sullivan: 246
Girardin: memoirs, 179
Girton College, Cambridge: its young
    women, 200 & n, 204; its buildings,
    201; ref: 199
Gissing, George: 205 & n; 206
Gladstone, William: 340
Gladys, niece? of Nelly Boxall: 153
Goddard, Scott, master at Leighton Park
    School: 5 & n, 6
Goethe: 186
Goldie *see* Dickinson, Goldsworthy
    Lowes
Gooch, George Peabody: 82 & n
Goold, Mrs, of Camerton: 341
Gordon Square, No. 37: Nessa's new
    house, 6, 7n; let, 175n; to let, 220 & n
Gordon Square, No. 46: early days at,
    53; ref: 26
Gordon-Woodhouse, Violet: 338 & n
Gosse, Sir Edmund: introduces Vita's lec-
    ture, 115 & n; mortuary humbug on,
    184-5; deprived of Boswell, 238; ref:
    163, 185n
Gosse, Lady: 115
Gottschalk *see* Riding, Laura
Gould, Barbara Ayrton :70 & n ,71

Gould, Gerald: 70 & n, 71
Grant, Duncan: for Biographical Note
    see Appendix I; on VW, 26; reluctant
    witness at Keynes's wedding, 38; his
    death imagined, 48; doesn't consoli-
    date parties, 71; 'commits nuisance',
    87; egg in hand, prim and acid, 91;
    typhoid suspect, 124 & n; and Lytton,
    138; on Ethel and Nan, 151 & n;
    sketchbook under arm, 154; in grand
    historical picture, 157; about to
    migrate, 173 & n; and Dante's hell,
    179; aloof & supercilious, 191; a real
    person, 202; exhibits pictures, 217n;
    visits Germany and Austria, 218; at
    Cassis, 232; divinely charming, 233;
    paint and politics, 269 & n; a life of?,
    302; sublime ineptitude, 306; easy
    Bohemian, 316; ref: 6, 7n, 15, 47, 53,
    127, 133, 147, 203, 231, 242, 282, 304,
    305, 323
Granville Barker, Harley: 98 & n
Graphic, The, periodical: 293
Graves, Robert: described, 13-14; ref: 13n
Greece: 108, 124, 127, 129, 198, 352
Green, Rev. A. S., vicar of Kingston with
    Iford, Sussex: 159n
Greenwich: visit to described, 72-3, 269
    & n; ref: 41, 72n
Gregory, Lady: 284 & n
Grenfell, Florence, *née* Henderson: 210
    & n
Greville, Charles: memoirs edited by
    Lytton Strachey, 294 & n
Grey, Mr, of Rodmell: 155
Grey, old Mrs, of Rodmell: 169 & n
Grey, Viscount: and General Strike, 81
    & n
Grizzle, a mongrel dog: 6, 62, 85, 112, 118
Groombridge Place, Kent: 157 & n
Guedalla, Philip: 115 & n
Gumbo *see* Strachey, Marjorie
Gurney, Mr, at Cassis: 8

Hakluyt, Richard: 271
Hall, Radclyffe: petition got up for, 193
    & n; the trial, 206 & n, 207; *The Well
    of Loneliness*, 193n, 201
Hamilton, Mary Agnes ('Molly'): 296
    & n
Hammersley, Violet Mary: 214 & n
Hammond, furnishers, of Lewes: 316
Hampstead: recalls Katherine Mansfield,

50 & n; red, sanitary, earnest, 157;
ref: 49, 80, 204, 286, 306
Hampstead General Hospital: 237 & n
Hampton Court: scene in *The Waves*,
287; *ref:* 224, 324
Ham Spray House, near Hungerford:
fire at, 44; *ref:* 89
Handel: 126
Harcourt Brace & Co, publishers, New
York: on *Mrs Dalloway*, 9; new
edition of *The Voyage Out*, 58; *ref:*
4 & n, 43
Hardy, Florence: conveys husband's
pleasure, 25 & n; docile & ready, 96;
on serialisation, 97; and London, 98
& n; on T. E. Lawrence and suicide,
100; reads Huxley to Hardy, 101 & n;
ref: 96n, 99, 102
Hardy, Thomas: takes pleasure in *Common Reader*, 25 & n; George Moore
on, 66n, 67; Wells on, 94 & n; VW
to visit, 95; portrayed at home, 96-
101; 'moments of vision', 105 & n;
his funeral, 173-4; VW's article on,
174 & n; a further article, 205 & n;
Beerbohm on, 213; *ref:* ix, 96n, 97n,
98n, 99n, 101n, 102, 108, 173n, 206,
210; *The Dynasts*, 98; *Far from the
Madding Crowd*, 97 & n, 99; *Jude the
Obscure*, 213; *Life's Little Ironies*, 99,
100; *The Mayor of Casterbridge*, 99
& n; *Moments of Vision*, 105n; *Tess
of the D'Urbervilles*, 67, 213
Hardy, Thomas, flag captain to Nelson:
72
Harper's Magazine, New York: 127
Harris, Henry ('Bogey'): entertains VW
and prime minister, 282, 283 & n;
well fed bachelor, 284; *ref:* 166 & n
Harris, Lilian: life with Margaret, 23 & n;
mumbling & crumbling, 296, 297
Harrison, Edward, dentist: 78
Harrison, Jane: aged and exalted, 176 &
n; her death, 178 & n; and funeral,
181 & n; *ref:* 333; *Reminiscences of a
Student's Life*, 176n
Hart-Davis, Rupert: 336 & n
Harvey, Gabriel: 270 & n
Hawkesford, Boen: 159, 160 & n
Hawkesford, Rev. James Boen, rector of
Rodmell: described, 159-60; *ref:* 158
& n, 317
Hawkesford, Mrs: 160 & n

Hawthornden Prize: awarded to Vita,
139 & n; and to David Cecil, 304n;
ref: 71, 303
Hayward, John: praises VW's article, 16
& n
Hazlitt, William: 302, 304 & n, 313, 317
Head, Sir Henry, neurologist: 193 & n
Heal & Son, Tottenham Court Road:
175
Heinemann, publishers: 70, 295 & n
Heliogabalus, Emperor: 308 & n
Hemans, Felicia: 109 & n, 287
Hemingway, Ernest: VW article on, 158
& n; *Men Without Women*, 158n
Henderson, Arthur: at party conference,
258 & n
Henderson, Faith, *née* Bagenal: her
reactions imagined, 205; *ref:* 84 & n,
127, 131, 204
Henderson, Hubert: *N & A* arguments,
69 & n; and strike prediction, 80;
confident of Labour victory, 228 & n;
to give up *N & A*, 260 & n; his
perpetual drag, 265 & n; *ref:* 81, 127,
167, 204, 205
Hengist: 274
Herkomer, Sir Hubert von: and Hardy's
Tess, 101 & n
Heseltine, Philip *see* Warlock, Peter
Herrick, Robert: 40
Highgate Cemetery: 46
Hilda *see* Matheson, Hilda
Hills, John Waller ('Jack'): described,
33-4; *ref:* 33n; *A Summer on the Test*,
34n; *My Sporting Life*, 34n
Hills, Stella, *née* Duckworth: 245 & n,
261
Hogarth Essays: 58 & n
Hogarth House: madness at remembered,
254; *ref:* 132, 267, 327
Hogarth Miscellany: 167 & n
Hogarth News: 293
Hogarth Press: E. Sitwell eager to write
for, 24 & n; to be quit of, 40; Eliot
and, 42; its compensations, 43; VW
to write for, 47; book on fiction for,
50 & n, 107; give it up?, 69; the next
question, 70; to strike break?, 77;
creaking at hinges, 114; sagging on
shoulders, 116; Wells gives boost to,
128 & n; obscure anonymity of, 136;
failure with novels, 150; bad year
financially, 162; bonuses all round,

366

221; booming, 260; travelling for, 303; to be stopped, 327; *ref:* 68, 127, 304

Holland, family: history of, 247 & n

Holland, Bernard: 'brilliant young man' portrayed, 244-7; *ref:* 245n, 246n, 247n, 261; *Belief and Freedom,* 247n; *The Lancashire Hollands,* 247n; *The Life of Spencer Compton, 8th Duke of Devonshire,* 247n

Holland, Helen, *née* Duckworth: 245 & n, 246

Holland, the Rev. Canon F. J.: 245 & n

Holland, Mary Sibylla: her letters, 246 & n

Home University Library: 42 & n

Hope, Lottie: wants to return?, 41; discussing marriage, 44; loves cowman, 45; brings poisonous cold, 88; dismissed amid scenes, 227; to be ruled by?, 230; no more barging in by, 267; dismissed for stealing, 302; *ref:* 3n, 27, 253, 310; 328

Hopkins, Gerard Manley: and Bridges, 93 & n

Horne, Herbert: 282, 283n

Horner, Lady: 90 & n; *Time Remembered,* 90n

Hotel Cendrillon, Cassis: 6, 8, 133

House of Commons: warm debate in, 79; LW's stuffing for, 82 & n; *ref:* 296

Housman, A. E.: 19 & n, 65 & n

Howard, Brian: 268 & n

Howard, Esme: 69 & n

Howards, the, at Cassis: 8

Howe, Beatrice Isabel ('Bea'): 7 & n, 68, *A Fairy Leapt Upon My Knee,* 7n

Hudson, Nan: described, 151 & n; *ref:* 150

Hunt, Mrs, domestic agency: 266, 267, 328

Hunter, Mary, *née* Smyth: 307 & n

Hutchinson, Barbara: her lovely *woman's* eyes, 3; *ref:* 3n, 160, 318

Hutchinson, Jeremy: 3 & n

Hutchinson, Mary: for Biographical Note *see* Appendix I; entertains Woolfs, 3; VW's ally, 31; illumined, 35; her stories 'bad', 52 & n; gives literary party, 66; adulterates solitude, 73; loves VW, 107; VW a success with, 108; Clive to break with, 126 & n; cries for moon, 129; at the opera,

135; and Clive, 136; and Vanessa, 141; no match for motor cars, 146; her book's cost, 150; shadowed by Clive, 160, 161; eats Press profits, 162; loves Lord A, 168; simmers with Jack, 176; and Janet Ross, 243 & n; Clive on, 275; so much unhappiness, 334; *ref:* 3n, 38, 41, 60, 65, 79, 90, 91, 93, 175, 201, 214, 223, 318, 328, 336, 337; *Fugitive Pieces,* 52n, 150n, 162

Hutchinson, St John: for Biographical Note *see* Appendix I; entertains Woolfs, 3; compliment to VW repeated, 35; Eliot's scurvy treatment of, 41 & n; on Tolstoy, 67; simmering with Mary, 176; and George Moore, 214; *ref:* 3n, 90

Huxley, Aldous: gigantic grasshopper, 93 & n; read by the Hardys, 101 & n; approved by Kot, 217-18; *ref:* 90; *Point Counter Point,* 217n; *Two or Three Graces,* 101 & n

Huxley, Maria: 90

Hyde Park: 17, 26, 139

Hyde Park Gate: recollections of, 87; remembered by Hardy, 97; *ref:* 267, 271

Ibbotson, Miss, prospective housekeeper: 318 & n, 319

Ibsen, Henrik: 183n, 210

India, Round Table Conference on: 339 & n

Ingersoll, watch company: 4 & n

Innes, Kathleen E.: *The Story of the League of Nations told for Young People,* 19 & n

International Review: 49 & n

Irvine, Lyn Lloyd: honesty bred of poverty, 249 & n, 250; 'niceness' takes edge off, 269; *ref:* 268, 304, 305, 328

Irving, Mary: killed in Alps, 314 & n

Isaiah, Book of: 294

Italy: 87, 124, 129, 130, 132, 133, 295, 311

Ivy, The, restaurant: 57

Iwerne Minster: 74, 75

James, Charles, Rodmell farmer: 193, 194n, 195

James, Henry: George Moore on, 67; Wells on, 94 & n, 95; his spirit evoked, 137; his style, 214 & n; *ref*: 68, 227

James, L. J., Morris craftsman: 269 & n
James, William: and Chesterton, 94 & n
Janet, cook to the Duckworths: 294
Jarrett, Mrs, Squiress of Camerton: 341, 342
Jarrett, Mr and Mrs: their Rodmell wedding, 197 & n
Jeans, James: 337, 340 & n; *The Mysterious Universe*, 338n
Jeffers, Robinson and Una: 259 & n
Jenkins, Elizabeth: 182 & n, 183, 225; *Virginia Water*, 263 & n
Jenkins, Inez, *née* Fergusson: jealous of VW and Oliver Strachey, 76 & n
Jewsbury, Geraldine: 206 & n, 210
Joad, Marjorie *see* Thomson, Marjorie
John, Augustus: 207
Johnson, Dr: in *Orlando*, 167; Eliot's edition of, 324 & n
Johnson, Mr, gardener at Waddesdon: 300 & n, 301
Jones, Alice Louisa: 26 & n
Jones, Lady Roderick *see* Bagnold, Enid
Jonson, Ben: 282
Jowitt, Lesley: 108 & n
Joyce, James: 66 & n, 242; *Ulysses*, 66n
Judy *see* Stephen, Judith

Kahn, Richard Ferdinand: 84 & n
Kalinin, Mikhail Ivanovich: 44 & n
Kallas, Madame: 264 & n
Keats, John: 92 & n
Kennedy, George Lawrence, architect: 195n, 211
Kennedy, Richard: soft duckling boy, 195 & n; a bonus for, 221; making dust jacket, 225 & n
Ken (Caen) Wood: 41, 42n, 49, 306
Keun, Odette: 90n
Kew Gardens: with Vita, 149 & n; and Lytton, 233
Keynes, Geoffrey: 38 & n
Keynes, John Maynard: for Biographical Note *see* Appendix I; directs Lydia, 18; pamphlet for Press, 35 & n; marriage impending and effected, 38 & n; view of Russia, 43-4; *N & A* arguments, 69 & n; hums & haws over provostship, 76 & n; excited about strike, 77; and his carpets, 107, 108; has cheap car, 147; and a remark-

able mind, 181; senses Apostolic discord, 235; giving up *N & A*, 260 & n; entertains Woolfs and Shaw, 276 & n; celebrates Quentin's birthday, 311; carries VW indoors, 315; keeping constant with, 316; *ref*: 15, 43n, 70, 88, 91, 95, 102, 110, 118, 157, 168 & n, 198, 223, 253, 259, 281, 343; *A Short View of Russia*, 43n; *The Economic Consequences of Mr Churchill*, 35 & n, 38
Keynes, Lydia *see* Lopokova, Lydia
Kieffer, Marie: translator of *Jacob's Room*, 58 & n
King's College, Cambridge: Maynard and provostship, 76 & n; and Julian's promise, 232; *ref*: 201, 257
Kitchener, Lord: 301 & n
Kitchin, C. H. B.: 30 & n, 95, 138; *Streamers Waving*, 30n
Knole: VW entertained at, 124-5; and *Orlando*, 162; vast masterless house, 174 & n; Geoffrey Scott at, 244; *ref*: 118, 123, 127, 145, 173
Konody, Paul G., art critic: 178 & n
Koteliansky, S. S. ('Kot'): the vanished, 152 & n; definite as ever, 217 & n, 218

La Bergère, near Fontcreuse: 173n, 179
La Boudarde, near Cassis: 232 & n
Labour Party: wins general election, 230 & n; annual conference, 258 & n; *ref*: 25, 28, 123n, 228
La Fontaine: 247, 263
Lamb, Charles: Max Beerbohm on, 213
Lamb, Henry: Ottoline on, 36 & n
Lambeth Palace: 23
Langtry, Lily: 20 & n
Lardner, Ring (Ringgold Wilmer): 9 & n, 11
Lascelles, Lord: and *Orlando*, 162 & n; *ref*: 284
Laughton Place, in Sussex: 156 & n, 158
Laver, James: on VW, 255-6, 256n
Lavery, Lady: 309 & n
Lawrence, D. H.: disgusts Kot, 217; *Lady Chatterley's Lover*, 217n
Lawrence, Sir Thomas: 284
Lawrence, Col. T. E.: Hardy on, 100 & n
Leaf, Charles: 73 & n, 74
Leaf, Charlotte, *née* Symonds: 73 & n, 74
Leaf, 'Kitty' *see* West, Katherine
Leaf, Walter, 73 & n, 74

League of Nations: 19 & n, 60, 123n
Le Bosquet, Audrey: 252 & n, 309
Lee, Vernon: 20 & n, 312
Lehmann, Rosamund: 314 & n; *A Note in Music*, 314n
Leighton, Lord: 142
Leighton Park School: 5 & n, 6
Leverson, Ada: 163
Lewes, Sussex: 42, 169, 179, 230, 241, 303, 313, 324, 343
Lewis, Percy Wyndham: 242, 323; *The Apes of God*, 324n; *Satire & Fiction*, 324n
Leys, Dr Norman: 19 & n; *Kenya*, 19n
Liberal Party: muddle over funds, 283 & n
Life and Letters, periodical: 176n, 178, 185 & n, 195 & n, 335n
Lily, Rodmell housemaid: 44
Lime Kiln Farm, Sussex: 189, 190n
Lion, The, Cambridge hostelry: 204
Littell, Philip: 150 & n
Litvin, Rachel ('Ray'): a Bohemian, 20 & n
Llangollen, Ladies of: 131 & n
Loeb, Sydney J., amateur photographer: 26 & n
Loeffler, Mrs Hennik: 309 & n, 310n
Lomas, Henry, butler: 151 & n
London: street sauntering in, 11; novel writing in, 64; during General Strike, 77, 78, 79, 80; Hardy's view of, 98; article all about, 118; summer in, 132, 140; near end of season, 147; perpetual attraction of, 186; plunged into, 223; out of the window, 230; complete aloofness from, 232; £200 a year in, 249; its imminence, 258; violent shots at, 275; in the stir of, 295; walking alone in, 298; very exciting, 299; *ref*: 3, 6, 14, 22, 24, 25, 40, 44, 53, 61, 90, 101, 113, 144, 152, 155, 157, 161, 179, 217, 224, 239, 255, 256, 281, 301, 303, 318, 319, 327, 343
London Artists Association: 269 & n
Londonderry, Lady: 283 & n, 284
London Library: 82
London School of Economics (LSE): 70
Long Barn, V. Sackville-West's house: no invitation to, 48; 3 days at, 51 & n; clouds of glory from, 52-3; such opulence & freedom at, 144; happy to visit, 187; another visit, 211; Geoffrey

Scott at, 243; in the garden, 252; *ref*: 101, 114, 116, 118, 149, 157, 164, 173, 191, 199, 231, 251, 303, 304, 310, 314
Lopokova, Lydia (wife of Maynard Keynes): for Biographical Note *see* Appendix I; a lark soaring, 18; marriage impending and effected, 38 & n; home from Russia, 43-4; her 'zebra' shoes, 70; would like provostship, 76; performs Stravinsky, 147 & n; sobs at funeral, 164; very sensible, 181; and the Shaws, 276, 277; and true childhood, 312; *ref*: 15, 17, 43n, 102, 110, 157, 168 & n, 198, 210, 211, 223, 253, 259, 281, 315, 343
Lords, cricket ground: 89 & n, 261
Lottie *see* Hope, Lottie
Loune, butler at Long Barn: 164
Lowell, James Russell: 248 & n
Löwenstein-Wertheim, Princess: 'the Flying Princess', 154 & n, 155
Lubbock, Percy: 66 & n, 116
Lubin, David: Wells on, 93, 94 & n
Lucas, Emily Beatrice Coursolles ('Topsy'), *née* Jones: pumps Dadie, 150 & n; leaves husband, 225
Lucas, Frank Laurence ('Peter'): no ascendancy of brain, 64-5; doubts Dadie's fellowship, 66 & n; Dadie doubts his book, 150 & n; leaves wife, 225; an uninteresting mind, 256-7; *ref*: 30 & n, 65n, 255 & n; *The River Flows*, 65n; *Tragedy in Relation to Aristotle's Poetics*, 150n
Lushington, Judge Vernon, and family: 99 & n
Lynd, Robert: 70 & n, 71, 173
Lynd, Sylvia: 70 & n, 71
Lyn *see* Irvine, Lyn
Lynn, Olga, *Lieder* singer: 34 & n
Lyttleton (family): 246 & n
Lyttleton, Dame Edith (Mrs Lyttleton): 308 & n

Mabel, a typist: 336
MacAfee, Helen, of the *Yale Review*: 200 & n
Macaulay, Lord: 231
Macaulay, Rose: described, 60-2; her 'pothouse' dinner-party, 70-1; on women, 76; signs strike petition, 83; on writing, 96; and *Prix Femina*, 185 & n; and the *Evening Standard*, 186

& n; a mere chit, 204; *ref*: 60n, 61n, 70n, 184; *Dangerous Ages*, 185n
MacCarthy, Dermod: 19 & n, 148
MacCarthy, Desmond: for Biographical Note *see* Appendix I; worn & aged, 19-20; gives VW lunch and his 'filth packets', 21; lovable but depressing, 25; a wave that never breaks, 27; and the 'Ireniad', 28 & n, 285; lunching with Woolfs and Wells, 93n, 94; on Wells, 95; talks about Shakespeare, 96; Molly on, and the DM fund, 130 & n; and Henry James, 137; tender and garrulous and confidential, 147-148; his gratitude, 149; and *Life and Letters*, 176 & n, 185 & n; his bubbling lazy mind, 177-8; his homage to Gosse, 185 & n; gold & silver talk, 195-6; his letter annoys VW, 197 & n; his armchair egotism, 203-4; at Bow Street, 207; an adorable man, 234; loses £5 bet, 235; brilliant about Byron and Boswell, 237, 238n; *ref*: 19n, 20n, 71, 78, 79, 82, 195n, 210, 229, 335 & n; *Criticism*, 20n
MacCarthy, Mary ('Molly'): for Biographical Note *see* Appendix I; and Irene Noel-Baker, 28 & n; an ally, 31; warm faithful bear, 72; dusty, diligent, at London Library, 82 & n; her worries and debts, 130 & n; insists on VW memoir, 185; *ref*: 225, 229; *Fighting Fitzgerald and other Papers*, 82n
MacCarthy, Michael: 19 & n
MacCarthy, Rachel: 19 & n, 130, 197, 268, 272
MacColl, D. S.: 178 & n
MacDermott, F. T., printer: 84 & n
MacDonald, Ramsay: at Bogey Harris's dinner party, 283 & n, 284; *ref*: 25, 282
McGlashan, Dr Alan: 322 & n, 332
MacLagan, Mr and Mrs Eric: 148 & n
McLaren, Christabel ('Chrissie'): and the Desmond fund, 130 & n; artificial gambols with, 148; her 'winkle' party, 210; *ref*: 33 & n, 108 & n, 147, 208, 211, 223, 225
Macmillan, Hugh: 263 & n
Malthouse, Henry, Rodmell publican: 154 & n
Manchester Guardian: praises *Common*

Reader, 18 & n; *Orlando* 'a masterpiece', 217 & n
Manning-Sanders, Ruth: 60 & n; *Martha Wish-You-Ill*, 60n
Mansfield, Katherine: recalled, 50 & n; a dream of, 187; Kot's obsession with, 217, 218; on the Meynells, 251
Mansfield, Mrs, Bloomsbury char: 270 & n, 310
Marchand, Jean-Hippolyte: 47 & n
Marsh, Edward ('Eddie'), 63 & n, 294
Marshall, Frances: 76n, 84 & n, 95
Marshall, Thomas Humphrey (Tom): 11 & n, 82
Marshall & Snelgrove: VW robbed at, 339
Marten, Dr, of Freiburg: treats Vivienne Eliot, 15 & n
Martin, (Basil) Kingsley: 338 & n
Marvell, Andrew: 40
Mary, Aunt *see* Fisher, Mary
Mary, Queen: 273, 274
Masefield, John: and Yeats' anniversary, 331 & n; *ref*: 71
Masefield, Judith: 331
Masefield, Mrs: 331
Matheson, Hilda: abroad with Vita, 239 & n; very upset, 241; alters VW's broadcast, secondrate, 267 & n; *ref*: 266, 282, 328
Matisse: exhibited in Russia, 44
Matriarch, The, play, 260 & n
Matthews, Marjorie: 282 & n
Maugham, William Somerset: and Hugh Walpole, 328 & n; *Cakes and Ale*, 328n
Maupassant, Guy de: 108
Maurois, André: 184 & n, 287 & n; *Byron*, 287n
Mauron, Charles: 223 & n, 224, 225, 237, 266
Maxse, Kitty, *née* Lushington: and Clarissa Dalloway, 32 & n
Mayor, Beatrice ('Bobo'), *née* Meinertzhagen: shingles VW, 127 & n
Mayor, F. M.: 27, 28n; *The Rector's Daughter*, 28n
Meen, Reggie, boxer: 338 & n
Meinertzhagen, Elizabeth (Betty Potter): 113 & n
Meleager, see Trevelyan, R. C.
Melinda, unidentified: 148
Melville, Herman: *Moby Dick*, 195, 197

Meredith, George: VW's article on, 174 & n; claimed by Mrs Ross, 243 & n

Meynell, Alice: her life, 250-1; in Florentine Society, 352-3; ref: 250n, 251n

Meynell, Viola: memoir of mother, 250 & n, 352; sugar lumps, 251

Meynell, Wilfred: 250 & n

Michelet, Jules, historian: 93

Michelham Priory, Sussex: 154

Millais, Sir John Everett: 154

Milton, John: Yeats on, 330; ref: 3 & n, 235; Lycidas, 330

Mirrlees, Hope; crossing graveyard, 179; and Jane Harrison's death, 180 & n; sly convert, 268; liberated, 333; ref: 89 & n, 208, 269

Monks House, Rodmell: think of selling, 40; resolve shaken, 41; not hub of world, 112; rise in value, 158; unexpectedly nice, 192; gastronomy at, 257 & n; ref: ix, 3, 11, 36, 38, 53, 90, 123, 169, 173, 178, 188, 238, 259, 296, 303, 316, 317

Monro, Harold, poet and publisher: 157n

Montaigne: 8 & n

Moore, George: holds forth on writers, 66-7; on Bennett and others, 214 & n; on himself & his books, 226; compliments VW, 227; is liked, 242; Shaw and Zola on, 276; Bennett on, 335; ref: ix, 14 & n, 17, 66n, 206, 227n; Aphrodite in Aulis, 214n; Esther Waters, 67; The Mummer's Wife, 335

Morning Post: 21, 156 & n, 188 & n

Morrell, Julian: for Biographical Note see Appendix I; part of invasion, 26; cheers up Clive, 37; ref: 35, 93

Morrell, Lady Ottoline: for Biographical Note see Appendix I; a threat to Chelsea, 20; VW's affection for, 26; gives ghastly party, 30 & n; re-tells old stories, 36 & n; doing a cure, 58; seeking pity, 65-6; dressed like a girl of 18, 66; her dwindling charm, 93; on To the Lighthouse, 136 & n; shabby, easy, intimate, 152 & n; acted by Angelica, 158; & Bernard Holland, 246, 247; and conservation, 274 & n; on Henry Brewster, 326; hostess to Yeats, 329; ref: 20n, 34, 35, 37, 185, 238, 281, 282, 332

Morrell, Philip: for Biographical Note see Appendix I; part of invasion, 26; amorous, 152 & n; ref: 35, 37

Morris, William: and his circle, 186 & n; ref: 269 & n

Mortimer, Raymond: for Biographical Note see Appendix I; wires praise of Mrs Dalloway, 22; on Vita, 47; regrets Harold Nicolson's absence, 48; on VW's method, 63; his smart talk, 137-8; on Empire and nationality, 145; on Vita and Harold, 146; to marry?, 168; animated admirable talk with, 181-2; compared to Plomer, 242; his company, 299; shabby and likeable, 323, 324n; ref: 15, 24, 27, 35, 59 & n, 64 & n, 102, 129, 148, 179, 185, 208, 298

Mozart: 27, 126, 129, 282n; Don Giovanni, 89 & n; La Finta Giardiniera, 282n

Muir, Edwin: 109 & n; The Marionette, 150 & n; Transition, 109n

Murasaki, Lady: The Tale of Genji, 30, 31n

Murphy, Bernadette, assistant at Hogarth Press: described, 10; in the glumps, 11; turns crusty, 26; wants to stay, 299 & n; 'going', 35; works like slave, 38; in the basement, 40; ref: 10n, 26n

Murray, Mrs Graham, unidentified: 282

Murry, John Middleton: perpetual source of disquiet, vii; on VW's failure, 58 & n; Kot's abuse of, 217; ref: 218; God: an Introduction to the Science of, Metabiology, 263 & n

Napoleon: 329

Natasha (fict), in War and Peace: 67

National Gallery: 329

National Maritime Museum, Greenwich: 72 & n

Nation & Athenaeum: to be quit of, 40; LW to resign, 69 & n; richer without it, 70; Thank God to be out of, 71; dallying about, 76; skeleton Strike number, 77 & n, 80; Keynes commands Hogarth Press to print, 82; LW's article for blacked, 83 & n; printers still out, 85; 'The Questionnaire', 108 & n; and Lord Alfred Douglas, 227n; homogeneity of articles in, 244; Keynes and Henderson to leave, 260 & n; Wright to inherit, 265 & n; to amalgamate, 338 & n; *ref:* 13, 46, 84, 167, 178, 267

Nation & Athenaeum, offices: 85, 179

Nelly *see* Boxall, Nelly

Nelson, Admiral Lord: 72 & n, 73

Newnham College, Cambridge: VW to lecture at, 173n, 175, 199; projected history of, 203; its spry and disciplined students, 204; *ref:* 16 & n

New Statesman: in General Strike, 82; to amalgamate with *N & A*, 338 & n

New York Herald and Tribune: 124, 158n, 161, 221n, 239

Nichols, Philip: 93 & n

Nicholson, Nancy, wife of Robert Graves: 13 & n

Nicolson, Benedict: 52n, 252

Nicolson, Harold: for Biographical Note *see* Appendix I; to Persia, 47 & n; regretted by Mortimer, 48; and his job, 88; not Vita's match, 140; kind & attentive, 144; views on Empire, 145; almost defiantly fortunate, 146; refuses Buda Pesth, 157; reviewed by VW, 158 & n; bound for Berlin, 162, 163n; able story-teller, 163 & n; posted to Berlin, 218; against publishing Vita's poems, 252 & n; affected by air disaster, 309; *ref:* 132, 142, 156n, 211, 244, 309n, 310, 334 & n; *Some People*, 158n

Nicolson, Nigel: shabby . . . and bolshie, 157; with dirty feet?, 252; *ref:* 52n

Nightingale, Florence: 318

Nineteenth Century and After, periodical: 150 & n

Noble, Cynthia: 138 & n

Noel-Baker, Irene: described, 28-9; *ref:* 28n, 81, 285

Noel-Baker, Philip: fellow-guest, 28 & n; his character, 29; thinks LW 'best living writer', 69; advises LW on LSE, 70; *ref:* 28n, 81

Norman, Sylva: 187 & n; *Nature Has No Tune*, 187n

Observer, The: praises *Common Reader*, 22 & n; Squire barks in, 200 & n

O'Connor, Vincent: killed in the Alps, 314 & n; *ref:* 252 & n

Odel, Alan: and Dorothy Richardson, 92 & n

O'Donovan, Gerald: 70 & n, 71

ODTAA (One Damn Thing After Another), a Girton society: 199

Olivier, Lord: and *To the Lighthouse*, 136 & n; *ref:* 19 & n

Onions, Sally *see* Ruck, Berta

Orlando (fict): 157, 167

Osborne, Dorothy: 197 & n, 198, 199

Otway, Thomas: 20n

Ouida, pseudonym of Marie Louise de la Ramée, novelist: 271

Oxford: 136 & n

Oxford, Lady *see* Asquith, Margot

Oxford Street: armoured cars in, 85; *ref:* 47, 86, 298, 322, 340

Page, Dr Thomas Ethelbert: 163 & n

Page, Mrs, at Long Barn: 310

Palmer, Helen Elizabeth, *née* Lamb, of Newnham: 16 & n

Pankhurst, Mrs: 326

Pape, Frederick, chauffeur and driving instructor: 146, 147 & n

Paris: 6, 22, 65, 133, 137, 145, 231, 237, 261, 265

Partridge, Ralph: new left-handed establishment, 76 & n; emissary to PM, 83; derailed, 84 & n; *ref:* 49 & n, 95

Partridge & Cooper, stationers: 325

Pater, Clara: 106 & n

Patmore, Coventry: Shakespeare's 'equal', 251

Pattle, James, VW's great-grandfather: 291

Paul, Herbert: brilliant young man, 246 & n

Peacehaven, Sussex: 156

Peacock, Thomas Love: 68, 193

Penn, William: 191n, 192

Penns-in-the-Rocks, Withyham: 191 & n, 192, 269n

Pepys, Samuel: why did he write?, 239

Percy *see* Bartholomew, Percy

Persia: 47 & n, 48, 62, 117

Peter *see* Lucas, F. L.

Petit Riche, restaurant: 149

Phare, Elsie Elizabeth, Newnham student: 200 & n

Philcox Bros, Lewes builders: 71 & n, 219, 222, 228, 272

Phoenix Society: production of Otway, 20 & n

Pinka (Pinker), a cocker spaniel: 135, 146, 147, 154, 160, 166, 175, 182, 184, 186, 187, 196, 220, 231, 233, 235, 247, 258, 287, 291

Pitt, William: 81

Plank, George, artist: 111 & n, 115

Plato: 225

Plomer, William: first impression of, 224 & n; stays week-end with Woolfs, 242 & n; fresh from murder, 268 & n; *ref*: 272, 282, 332 & n; *The Case is Altered*, 268n; *Turbott Wolfe*, 224n

Plunket Greene, Mrs: 333 & n

Poetry Bookshop: 157 & n

Ponsonby, the Hon. Elizabeth: 208 & n

Ponsonby, Lady: 325 & n

Pope, Alexander: 308

Porter, Frederick J., artist: 269 & n

Potter, Betty *see* Meinertzhagen, Elizabeth

Pound, Ezra: Yeats on, 330-1

Power, Eileen, historian: 30 & n

Preston, Herbert Sansome, KC: 273 & n

Priestley, J. B.: tradesman of letters, 318 & n

Prinz Albrecht Hotel, Berlin: 218

Pritchard, Miss: 79 & n

Pritchard, William Burchell, solicitor: 79 & n, 272

Proust, Marcel: VW embedded in, 7; would like to finish, 37; Wells on, 94; *ref*: 183, 186, 205, 209, 226, 228

Puttenham, George: 270 & n

Pye, Ethel, sculptor: 58 & n

Quennell, Peter: 79 & n

R101, airship: 322 & n

Racine: 210, 263; *Phèdre*, 259

Raleigh, Professor Sir Walter: 74 & n

Ramsay, Mr (fict): 106

Randall, John, proof-reader: 16 & n

Raverat, Gwen, *née* Darwin: and Jacques' death, 7 & n; sturdy & grim, 34; threatens to dissolve—and Marchand, 47 & n; enmeshed in love, 59; a little mystical, 61 & n; *ref*: 8n, 16 & n, 38, 96

Raverat, Jacques: his death, and letter on *Mrs Dalloway*, 7 & n; *ref*: 36

Read, Herbert: Eliot after him, 45 & n; his *TLS* leader, 66 & n; *ref*: 41 & n; *In Retreat*, 45n; *Mutations of the Phoenix*, 45n; *Reason & Romanticism. Essays in Literary Criticism*, 45n

Reading, Lord: and General Strike, 82 & n

Red Cross: and Hardy ms, 97 & n

Red Lion Square, WC1: 186

Reform Club: 95

Regent's Park: 62, 217

Rembrandt: 329

Renard, Jules: 264 & n

Rendel, Dr Elinor (Elly, Ellie): tumbles VW into bed, 46 & n; and Duncan's typhoid, 124 & n; *ref*: 57, 287, 291, 304, 319

Rhoda (fict): 298

Rhondda, Lady: 334 & n

Richardson, Dorothy: Wells on, 92 & n

Richardson, Samuel: Wells on, 94; *ref*: 4, 108; *Clarissa Harlowe*, 96 & n

Richmond: 22, 30, 217, 219, 222, 293

Richmond, Bruce: VW to write on Swift for, 33 & n; a burnt-out illusion, 39-40; curse him, 109; to discuss article, 149; *ref*: 39n, 293, 303

Richmond, Elena: 'an illusion gone', 39-40; *ref*: 39n, 165

Riding, Laura: 136, 137 & n, 150; *The Close Chaplet*, 137n; *Voltaire*, 136, 137n

Riley, R. E., bookbinder: 233 & n

Rimsky Korsakov: 72; *The Legend of the Invisible City of Kitezh*, 72n

Ripe, Sussex: 104 & n, 153, 189

Ritchie, Alice: praises *Orlando*, 191; *ref*: 183 & n, 198, 305, 318 & n; *The Peacemakers*, 183n

Ritchie, Lady (Aunt Anny), *née* Anne Isabella Thackeray: 97; *Old Kensington*, 64 & n

Ritchie, Philip: and Lytton, 10 & n; his death, 156 & n; *ref*: 27, 31, 129

Rivett-Carnac, Miss, temporary domestic: 319 & n, 323, 324, 328, 332

Roberts, Betsy, at Cassis: 8

Robeson, Paul, in *Othello*: 304

Robins, Elizabeth: on Julia Stephen, 183 & n; *Ibsen and the Actress*, 183n; *Votes for Women!*, 183n

kind, 211; Woolfs visit in Berlin, 218; dining in Richmond, 222; VW cross with, 239 & n; and very pleased about, 241; her passion for Geoffrey Scott, 244, 245; untouchy poet, 252 & n; Dottie deplores her fame, 263; broadcasts on 'A Room', 264 & n; and 2nd rate schoolgirl atmosphere, 267; so full & flush, 287; shrewdly judged by E. Smyth, 291; affected by air disaster, 309; agrees Julian Bell is 'no poet', 328; jealous of Ethel, 332; *ref*: viii, 49, 51n, 53, 58, 59n, 64, 87n, 89, 101, 102, 106, 118, 123, 124, 127, 132, 134, 136 & n, 138, 142, 143, 145, 152, 156, 164, 183, 189, 208, 236, 253, 259, 266, 282, 304, 305, 308, 310, 316, 337, 343; *The Edwardians*, 306 & n; *King's Daughter*, 252 & n; *Knole ana the Sackvilles*, 125n; *The Land*, 87n, 88n, 111n, 139n, 141; *Passenger to Teheran*, 52n, 126

St Ives, Cornwall: 194, 261, 303
St Paul's Cathedral: 325 & n
Salisbury, Lord: 337, 338n
Sands, Ethel: her tea, a frying pan affair, 65; VW to stay with?, 108, 110, 112, 147; VW visits, 150-1; and grand historical picture, 157; downright about *Orlando*, 205; Tennyson blunder, 285; *ref*: 51 & n, 64, 66, 127, 129, 141, 151n, 165, 203, 212, 285n, 295, 334, 337
Sanger, Charles: very ill, 272; his death, 286 & n; *ref*: 18 & n, 136, 229, 294
Sanger, Dora: 18 & n, 229, 272
Sargent, John Singer: 307 & n
Sassoon, Sir Philip: 233 & n; *The Third Route. A description of a voyage to India by air*, 233n
Sassoon, Siegfried: 89 & n, 98, 299
Savage, Sir George: 333 & n
Savoy Theatre: *Othello* at, 304
Scadding and Bodkin, solicitors: 272 & n
Schubert: 194
Scotsman, The: reviews *Mrs Dalloway*, 21 & n
Scott, Geoffrey: his death—a portrait, 243-5; *ref*: 19, 20n, 111, 116, 238n, 243n, 244n, 245n, 261, 352; *The Architecture of Humanism*, 111 & n; *The Portrait of Zélide*, 20n

Scott, Lady Sibyl: abandoned by Geoffrey Scott, 244 & n
Scott, Sir Walter: 293 & n, 303 & n
Scullin, James, Prime Minister of Australia: 332 & n
Sea Air, unidentified novel: 296 & n
Secker, Martin, publisher: 116
Sermoneta, Duchess of, *née* Vittoria Colonna: 307 & n
Shakespeare: VW compared with, 104; uses too many words, 182; Patmore compared with, 251; his amazing speed and pliancy of mind, 300-01 & n, *ref*: 96, 165, 210, 313; *Othello*, 9n, 182, 304; *Titus Andronicus*, 301n
Shanks, Edward: 11 & n
Shaw, George Bernard: at Mrs Wells's funeral, 163, 164; George Moore on, 214; on George Moore, and himself, 276-7; *ref*: 116, 210, 276n; *Caesar and Cleopatra*, 13 & n; *Doctor's Dilemma*, 276; *Heartbreak House*, 276 & n
Shaw, Mrs Bernard: 116, 276n, 277
Shelley: biography reviewed, 158 & n; *ref*: 13, 48n, 153, 180, 295
Sheppard, John Tresidder: 17n
Sickert, Walter Richard: 71 & n
Simpkin & Marshall, book wholesalers and distributors: 4 & n, 220
Sissinghurst Castle, Kent: 304, 317
Sitwell, Edith: 'an old maid', described, 24 & n, 25; a Roman Empress, 28; meritless aristocrat?, 65; gives party for Gertrude Stein, 89 & n; described, 132-3 & n; VW dreaming of, 247; like Emperor Heliogabalus, 308; *ref*: 35, 63, 91
Sitwell, Osbert: an English squire, 25; meritless aristocrat?, 65; presents book to VW, 114 & n; *ref*: 24 & n, 63, 89, 91, 95, 176, 309; *Before the Bombardment*, 114n
Sitwell, Sacheverell: meritless aristocrat?, 65; presents book to VW, 114 & n; *ref*: 24 & n, 63, 91; *All Summer in a Day*, 114n
Skeats, fancied as neighbours: 11 & n
Skinner, Rev. John, Rector of Camerton, and family: 340-3; *The Journal of a Somerset Rector*, 340 & n
Smith, Mrs, considered for Press: 26 & n
Smith, Logan Pearsall: threatened by Ottoline, 20 & n; *Common Reader*

Literary Supplement]: praises *Common Reader*, 17 & n; Read's leader in, 66 & n; curse it, 109; and *To the Lighthouse*, 134 & n; its low remuneration, 149; ask for a rise?, 168; a book from, 302; slight snub from, 336; *ref*: 15, 25, 33n, 182, 185

Toby, Uncle (fict): 320

Todd, Dorothy, editor of *Vogue*: dress buying with, 78; and book proposal, 89 & n; hirsute and commercial, 175-176; buxom as a badger, 184; *ref*: 9 & n, 91, 176n

Tolstoy: George Moore on, 67; hates women, 140; *ref*: 43, 185; *Anna Karenina*, 70; *War and Peace*, 67

Tomlin, George Garrow: 8 & n

Tomlin, Stephen ('Tommie'), sculptor: 73 & n, 74, 112, 136

Tonks, Henry: 108 & n

Toogood, Miss, at Cassis: 8

Topsy *see* Lucas, E. B. C.

Tovey, Donald, musician: 63 & n

Towne, Charles Hanson: little American toad, 24 & n

T.P.'s Weekly: 21

Trades Union Congress (TUC): and strike settlement, 84 & n, 85 & n

Trafalgar, Battle of: 72

Tree, family: 248 & n

Tree, Sir Herbert Beerbohm: 86 & n

Tree, Viola: to make our fortune, 79 & n; dribbles along, 84; flamboyant creature, 86; criticised, 89; *ref*: 80; *Castles in the Air*, 79n

Trefusis, Violet: and *Orlando*, 162 & n

Trench, Richard Chenevix: 201 & n; *A Select Glossary of English Words*, 201n

Trevelyan, R. C. ('Bob'): 37 & n, 78, 95; *Meleager*, 299 & n; *Poems and Fables*, 5n

Trim, Corporal (fict): 320

Trinity College, Cambridge: 201

Troubridge, Una Elena, Lady: 207 & n

Turner, Mr, of the Book Club: 293

Turner, Sharon, Saxon's great-grandfather: 72 & n, 87

Turner, W. J.: 30 & n

Valery Paul: 163

Van Doren, Irita, New York editor:

commission from refused, 178 & n; 4 articles for, 221 & n; *ref*: 302, 303n,

Vansittart, Sir Robert: 283 & n

Vaughan, Emma: 85 & n

Vaughan, Janet: 'good dull', 85 & n; dines with Angus, 205 & n; competent disinterested woman, 206; and the trained mind, 250; engaged, 312 & n

Vaughan, Madge: reflections on her death, 46, 48; *ref*: 47n, 134, 206

Victoria, Queen: her only prominences, 340-1; *ref*: 276, 337 & n; *The Letters of Queen Victoria*, 337 & n, 340

Virgil: 235

Vogue, magazine: 12 & n, 21 & n, 31 & n, 33, 37

Wach, Professor Adolf, of Leipzig: 313 & n

Waddesdon Manor, Buckinghamshire: 68 & n, 300 & n, 301

Wagner: 135, 158

Wales, Prince of: 77, 332 & n, 338

Waley, Arthur, 24 & n, 25, 86, 265

Wallace, Edgar: *The Calendar*, 273 & n

Walpole, Hugh: presents Femina prize to VW, 183 & n; spreads butter over *Orlando*, 200 & n; protests too much, 221; provides impertinent editor for Scott, 303 & n; and *Cakes and Ale*, 328 & n; *ref*: 332

Walter, Bruno, conductor: 313 & n

Walter, Mrs, temporary cook-housekeeper: 305 & n, 306, 311, 319

Warlock, Peter, pseudonym of Philip Heseltine: 337 & n

Warner, Sylvia Townsend, poet: 26 & n; *The Espalier*, 26n

Waterlow, Sydney: notable resurrection, 224 & n; buys violets, 229; *ref*: 228

Watkins, Ann, New York literary agent: 36 & n

Webb, Beatrice: causes in her life—none in VW's, 62; the difference explained, 74; described by Wells, 91-2; 36 strenuous hours with, 126 & n; the Kenya question, and her little boy, 263 & n; and Shaw's inspiration, 276 & n; and class difference, 284; *ref*: 262; *My Apprenticeship*, 62n, 74n

Webb, Sidney: strenuous hours with, 126 & n; Beatrice's little boy, and Kenya,

315; with pied hair?, 319; Trim &
Uncle Toby, 320

(2) *The Hogarth Press and literary
work*: harsh to Murphy, his pamphlet,
11; gives farewell dinner, 16; doing
up parcels, 52; *N & A* resignation, 69
& n; and dallying about it, 76; to
collect Essays, 90 & n; forging ahead,
114; and Angus Davidson, 116, 128,
162, 167, 211; discusses advertisements, 136; consults about *Orlando*,
212; gives bonuses, 221; works on
dust cover, 225; and Lord Alfred's
libel, 227n; giving up *N & A*?, 260
& n; freedom draws near, 265 & n;
on Press tour, 303; no to *N S & N*,
338

(3) *Political activities*: countless
committees, 19, 123n; and lectures,
22 & n, 166, 167n; and R.MacDonald,
25; adored by Irene Noel-Baker, 28;
to answer *British Gazette*, 77; labour
... or baptism, 80; tub thumper, 80-1;
not a scab, 82; asserts strike's legality,
83; urges Webb over Kenya, 263 & n;
Works mentioned: *Fear and Politics*,
11 & n; *Essays on Literature, History,
Politics, etc*, 90n
Woolf, Marie (VW's mother-in-law): a
child with feelings, 193 & n; non-stop
talk, 194 & n, 195; like an old rose,
230-1; grinds one to bits, 253; her
charm & dignity, 258; soot, sparks,
and tobacco, 271; vainest of women,
320; painfully sensitive, 321; *ref*: 182,
235, 282, 318 & n
Woolf, Marjorie ('Babs') (wife of Philip):
68 & n, 320
Woolf, Philip: 68 & n, 300n, 320
Woolf, Virginia. Entries are divided thus:
(1) Early life and relationships. (2)
Personality and health. (3) Relationship with LW. (4) Diversions. (5)
Domestic matters. (6) Literary activities. (7) Her own published books.
(1) *Early life and relationships*:
St Ives and childhood, 18-19; Jack
Hills, 33-4; George Young, 35 & n;
Katie Cromer, 51 & n; disagreeable
memories, 87; history at St Ives, and
threats to liberty, 194; scenes of
travel, 198; Geoffrey Scott and
Florentine society, 243, 352-3; Bernard Holland and Canterbury society,
245-6; Phil Jones in Venice, 248;
'autumn plans', 255; Thoby Stephen,
260, 275, 317; Arthur Studd recalled,
260-1; throwing off chains, 267; early
literary loves and endeavours, 271;
tremendous desire to write, 315

(2) *Personality and health*: attitude
to fame, vii; her own sex, 3; and
influenza, 5; past, present, and future,
5, 36; impressions from Cassis, 6, 8,
from an accident, 6; on Jacques
Raverat's death, 7-8, 34, 47; her
version of Montaigne, 8; and her
own image, 9, 12, 21, 37, 132; her
anti-bugger revolution, 10; Marjorie
Thomson and happiness, 11; on
clothes, 11, 12, 21, 42, 90-1, 113, 296,
334; party consciousness, 12, 13;
fidgety, 15; her reputation, 16, 21, 22;
on Kate Stephen's death, 17 & n;
jangled, 18, 21; on human fellowship,
22; £50 worth of charm, 27; no
lioness, 30; 'I do not love my kind',
33; most beautiful, 35; aristocracy *v.*
middle class, 37; faints at Charleston,
38-9; still amphibious, 40-1; to take
fences, 42; headache renewed, 44;
tumbled into bed, 46; on Madge
Vaughan's death, 46, 48; imagines
death, 48; K. Mansfield recalled, 50,
187; Sapphist love, 51; wish for
maternal protection, 52; measles ...
and Murry, 58; spring and funerals,
59; fanatical like father?, 60; life
and discovery, 62-3; headaches and
beauty, 64; a horrid gaffe, 68; ten
years younger, 69-70; in underworld,
70-1; untrustworthy humanity, 81;
transitory reality, 85; 'flu and shivers,
89; integrity and art, 102, 104;
miniature nervous breakdown, 103,
110-11; marriage, 105; on parenthood,
107-8; haunting criticism, 109; symbolism and sentimentality, 110; intense depression, 111-12; mystical
solitude, 113; emotional battlefield,
114; complete inner composure, 116;
vision of death, 117; 'something in
me', 123; shingled and bingled, 127;
and fearless, 129; headachy, 130;
summer disturbances, 132; on opinions, 133, 134, 135-6; in bed, 136;

celebrated?, 137; and women haters, 140; abiding truth, 141; restlessness and the road, 164; the amorous Philip, 152; 'the spirit of delight', 153; scene making, 153-5, 160; the flying princess, a phantom laid, 154-5; a vision of humanity, 155-6; on Philip Ritchie's death, 156; 'grand historical picture', 156-7; at Mrs Wells' funeral, 163-4; money psychology, 164-5, 176, 212, 219, 241, 285, 319-320; incredible concatenation!, 165; 'an art of light talk', 166; children scarcely wanted, 167; middle-age prescription, 168-9; on Hardy's funeral, 173-4; anguishes and despairs, 174; dignity advanced, 175; miserly at 46, 177, and experimental, 180; at Jane Harrison's funeral, 181; 'suicidal' 186; human intercourse and subcutaneous life, 188-9, 209; possessed by ideas, 189; phrase-making, 191; on Dottie and her house, 191-2; pleasure in intimacy, and 'reality', 196; heart of England, 197; Lord Gage's snub, 198; speaking at Cambridge, 199-201; 'the rock of self-esteem', 200; well-known writer, 201; on talent and genius, 203; and male egotism, 204; thoughts on father's 96th birthday, 208; the 'moment' defined, 209; on men and women, 210; black despair, 212; on Koteliansky, 217-18; life, solid or shifting?, 218; three weeks in bed, 218-19; to enter nunnery, 219; effects of habit, 220; 'an elderly woman', 230; at the poll, 231; painful talk with Lytton, 233-4; work ethic, 235; 'if I were Mrs Bartholomew', 236; random rackety summer, 238; sordid and unsettled, 240; tumults and headache, 241; happy days, 248; life on £200 p.a., 240-50; psychologically tired, 253-4; change of life?, 254; 'greatness', 255-6; contrary summer, 256; suffering and emptiness, 259-60; dream of disease and death, 264; in a twitter, 266; sense of community, 270; the conservationist, 274, 317; crushes visitors, 275; suspects solitude, 281; aged 48, 285; on Charlie Sanger's death, 286; partly mystical illness, 287; family affections and George

Duckworth, 293-4; drained by book, 295; perils of retirement, 296-7; rather mystic evening, 298-9; as if in men's urinal, 299; how to live, 303; pub and private parties, 310; comfortablest summer, 311; on death in the alps, 314; fainting fit, 315; homing rooks, 316; on Woolf family, 320-1; questionable heroes, 322-3; lassitude, 323; O solitude, 332, 339; provincial Woolfs, 337; on being robbed, 339-340; torpid mooning, 340

(3) *Relationship with LW*: his constant affection, viii; their frugality, ix; perfect happiness with, 8, 9, 30; her child's trust in, 29; satisfaction of talking with, 49; her 'sheer fudge', 51; his maternal affection, 52; and protection, 59; and her diaries, 67; and the *N & A*, 69-70; tub-thumper *v.* Christian, 80-1; sitting in Square, 88; detached . . . harmonious, 107; relations not so good, 111-12; holds LW's ladder, 113; Vita a bore for LW, 117; his steadying opinions, 128; quarrel over fares, 130; sharp hard words, 154; in collision, 155; harmony of opinions, 158; fiery breakfast, 162; a little Bloomsburyish?, 163; out of 'making money', 176; his peace-offering, 194; in agreement over Desmond, 197; and money, 212; fundamentally happiest wife, 228; the childless couple, 263; dream of dying, and life together, 264; LW severe but stimulating, 273; his caution and philanthropy, 305; home coming to, 310; to stop the Press, 327

(4) *Diversions*: to Cassis, 6, 178-9, 231-2; Max Beerbohm's show, 10 & n; *Caesar and Cleopatra*, 13 & n; weekends at Cambridge, 16, 114, 199, 200-201; Euripides at Chiswick, 17 & n; outing to Sutton, 22-3; dinner-party at Sitwells, 24; listening to socialists, 26; week-end with Stephens, 28; Ottoline's ghastly party, 30; Roger's garden party, 33; people and parties, 34-5; Quentin's birthday parties, 38, 311-12; music after dinner, 42; to ballet, 46; visit to Cookham, 63; Ethel Sands' tea-, and Hutchinsons' dinner-party, 65-7; to Waddesdon, 68, 300,

THE AIRPLANE

A History of Its Technology

THE AIRPLANE

A History of Its Technology

John D. Anderson Jr.

National Air and Space Museum
Smithsonian Institution
and
Department of Aerospace Engineering
University of Maryland

American Institute of Aeronautics and Astronautics
1801 Alexander Bell Drive
Reston, VA 20191–4344

Publishers since 1930

American Institute of Aeronautics and Astronautics, Inc., Reston, Virginia

Library of Congress Cataloging-in-Publication Data

Anderson, John David.
  The airplane, a history of its technology / John D. Anderson Jr.
    p.   cm.
  Includes bibliographical references and index.
    ISBN 1-56347-525-1 (alk. paper)
  1. Airplanes—Design and construction—History.   2. Aerospace
engineering—History.   I. Title.
  TL670.3 .A49   2002
  629.133′34′09—dc21   2002153182

Cover design by Sara Bluestone.

Table of Contents

Preface

If you are a general reader without a background in engineering and science, but are interested in airplanes and the history of flight, this book is for you. If you are an engineer, scientist, or technician who wants to learn more about the technical evolution of the airplane, this book is also for you. It tells a story—a story of the technical development of the airplane. In reality, the story is so exciting that it essentially tells itself. All I have done is gather its essence, and put it on a plate for you to enjoy.

A history of the technology of the airplane can be treated as a scholarly subject within the broader field of the history of technology. By my choice, however, this is not intended to be a scholarly book. There are no footnotes, endnotes, or numbered references within the text because I want this book to be a smooth, conversational, and enjoyable read for you. There is, however, a brief bibliography at the end of the book that lists many of the sources I used to obtain material for this book and suggestions for further, more in-depth reading. Also, I have fallen back on the scholar's techniques of numbering many of the illustrations in this book and referring to them in the text by figure number; this is simply a convenience to focus your attention on a particular illustration. In addition, however, the book is peppered with numerous photographs of airplanes that augment the general discussion. These have self-contained captions and are not numbered.

The history of the technology of the airplane is a vast subject, impossible to cover completely in a book this size. What you read here is my personal choice of subjects and examples, sewn together in an overall tapestry, giving a broad and somewhat philosophical overview. Another author would most likely choose a different set of subjects and examples. That is why the title of this book states that it is *a* history of the technology, not *the* history. I hope that you will find my choices to be interesting and exciting to you and that this book will put you on course to probe more deeply and expansively into the subject.

I wish to acknowledge all my colleagues in the Aeronautics Division at the National Air and Space Museum (NASM), who provide a wonderful intellectual environment in which to study and discuss the history of aeronautics. In particular, I wish to thank Dr. Howard Wolko, an aerospace engineer now retired from NASM, for his enlightening discussions on the history of aircraft structures; Hal Andrews, NASM research associate, for use of many photographs from his vast collection and for sharing his unlimited knowledge about airplanes; Jeremy Kinney, propulsion curator at NASM for his insight into the development of the propeller; Dr. Tom Crouch and Dr. Peter Jakab, curators at NASM, for sharing their vast knowledge of early flight; Dr. Dom Pisano, chairman of the NASM Aeronautics Division, for his thoughts on the social history of the airplane; the American Aviation Historical Society for use of photographs from its archives; and Brian Riddle, Librarian of the Royal Aeronautical Society, London, for his invaluable help during my research at the Library. Special thanks go to Rodger Williams, head of business development for book publications for AIAA, who encouraged me to write this book and whose constant interest and encouragement have been a beacon for me throughout my writing. Special thanks also go to my wife, Sarah Allen, for giving up countless hours of family time for my writing, and to Susan Cunningham, long-time friend of the family and scientific typist, who typed the manuscript.

These are opening lines of Pilot Officer John Magee's famous poem, *High Flight*, written in September 1941:

> "Oh, I have slipped the surly bonds of Earth
> and danced the skies on laughter-silvered wings"

In your mind, I hope you do the same while reading this book. More than that, when you finish I hope you have a better appreciation of how inventors and aeronautical engineers have toiled over the past two centuries to design and build flying machines to slip "the surly bonds of Earth," and to build "laughter-silvered wings" that worked.

John D. Anderson Jr.
November 2002

1

CHAPTER

Introduction

Not within a thousand years will man ever fly.
Wilbur Wright, 1901
In a fit of despair

SUCCESS FOUR FLIGHTS THURSDAY MORNING ALL
AGAINST TWENTY ONE MILE WIND STARTED FROM LEVEL
WITH ENGINE POWER ALONE AVERAGE SPEED THROUGH
AIR THIRTY ONE MILES LONGEST 57 SECONDS INFORM
PRESS HOME CHRISTMAS.
OREVELLE WRIGHT

A telegram, with the original misprints.
(From Orville Wright to his father)
December 17, 1903

 The scene: Wind-swept sand dunes on Kill Devil Hill, 4 miles south of Kitty Hawk, North Carolina. The time: About 10:35 a.m. on Thursday, December 17, 1903. The characters: Orville and Wilbur Wright and five local witnesses. The action: Poised, ready to make history, is a flimsy, odd-looking machine, made from spruce and cloth in the form of two wings, one placed above the other, a horizontal elevator mounted on struts in front of the wings, and a double vertical rudder behind the wings. A 12-horsepower engine is mounted on the top surface of the bottom wing, slightly right of center. To the left of this engine lies a man, Orville Wright, prone on the bottom wing, facing into the brisk and cold December wind. Behind him rotate two ungainly looking airscrews (propellers), driven by two chain and pulley arrangements connected to the same engine. The machine begins to move along a 60-foot launching rail on level ground. Wilbur Wright runs along the right side of the machine, supporting the wingtip so that it will not drag the sand. Near the end of the starting rail, the machine lifts into the air; at this moment, John Daniels of the Kill Devil Life Saving Station takes a photograph, which preserves for all time the most historic moment in aviation history. This photograph is shown in Figure 1.1 and is perhaps the most important photograph in the annals of

FIGURE 1.1

The Wright Flyer taking off on its historic first flight, December 17, 1903, at 10:35 a.m. at Kill Devil Hill, North Carolina.

aviation. The machine flies unevenly, rising suddenly to about 10 feet, then ducking quickly toward the ground. This type of erratic flight continues for 12 seconds, when the machine darts to the sand, 120 feet from the point where it lifted from the starting rail. Thus ends a flight which, in Orville Wright's own words, was "the first in the history of the world in which a machine carrying a man had raised itself by its own power into the air in full flight, had sailed forward without reduction of speed, and had finally landed at a point as high as that from which it started."

The machine was the Wright Flyer I, now preserved for posterity in the National Air and Space Museum of the Smithsonian Institution in Washington, D.C. The flight on that cold December 17 was momentous; it brought to a realization the dreams of centuries, and it gave birth to a new way of life. With it, and with the further successes to come over the next five years, came the Wright brothers' clear right to be considered the first true aeronautical engineers.

Contrary to popular belief, however, the Wright brothers did not invent the airplane; rather, they invented the first *successful* airplane. The concept of the airplane was invented a hundred years earlier, and the Wrights inherited a century's worth of prior aeronautical research and development. The time was ripe for the attainment of powered flight at the beginning of the 20th century. Indeed, let us go back seven years before the Wright's first successful flight. The scene: A houseboat moored off Chopawamsic Island near the western bank of the Potomac River at Quantico, Virginia. The time: About 3:05 p.m. on May 6, 1896. The characters: Samuel Pierpont Langley (third secretary of the Smithsonian Institution), his close friend Alexander Graham Bell, and four assistants. The action: Slung underneath a catapult mounted on the roof of the houseboat is a flying machine in the form of two equal-sized rectangular wings placed one behind the other (a tandem wing arrangement) made from spruce and covered with China silk, measuring 13.1 feet from wingtip to wingtip. A horizontal and vertical tail is located at the rear of the machine. Between the two wings are dual propellers powered by a single lightweight steam engine producing about 1 horsepower. The machine is too small to carry a pilot but is much too large to be considered a model. This is a serious

FIGURE 1.2

Samuel Langley's Aerodrome Number 5 moments after its successful launch, May 6, 1896, over the Potomac River near Quantico, Virginia.

flying machine, designed by Langley on the basis of seven prior years of painstaking research. The flying machine, called an "aerodrome" by Langley, is launched into a gentle breeze from a height of 20 feet above the river's surface. Immediately after launch, the aerodrome slowly descends about 3 or 4 feet, then begins to climb steadily. Bell, who is in charge of photographing the flight, takes the picture shown in Figure 1.2 moments after the launch. Now wealthy from his invention of the telephone, Bell is present because of his intense interest in powered flight and his close friendship with Langley. The aerodrome begins to circle toward the right, constantly ascending during the first two turns. After reaching a height of 100 feet, the engine begins to run out of steam, and the aerodrome slowly descends, finally touching the surface of the water after being in the air for $1\frac{1}{2}$ minutes and covering a total distance of 3300 feet through the air.

This flight was momentous. It was the first successful sustained flight of a heavier-than-air, powered flying machine in history. It demonstrated to the world without a shadow of a doubt the technical feasibility of such powered flight. This demonstration was not lost on the Wright brothers, who subsequently took the technical feasibility essentially for granted. The machine, Langley's Aerodrome Number 5, is now preserved along with the Wright Flyer in the National Air and Space Museum. By 1896, it was clear to some people that the invention of a successful human-piloted airplane was nearly at hand. But this honor was not to be Langley's, although he ultimately designed a much larger human-carrying aerodrome, which failed to fly on two separate attempts in 1903 (for reasons to be discussed in Chapter 2).

Instead, it was the Wrights, through ingenuity, dedication, and persistence who invented the first *successful* airplane. Virtually every conventional airplane flying today incorporates the same basic elements of the Wright Flyer—wings to create lift, horizontal and vertical tail planes, a form of propulsion to create forward thrust, and, especially, a means of control to allow rolling, pitching, and yawing motion of the aircraft at the will of the pilot. Although the first flight on that epochal December 17th at Kill Devil Hill lasted only 12 seconds, and the longest of the three subsequent flights by the Wright brothers that morning covered 852 feet in 59 seconds, by 1905 in an improved machine the Wrights were staying

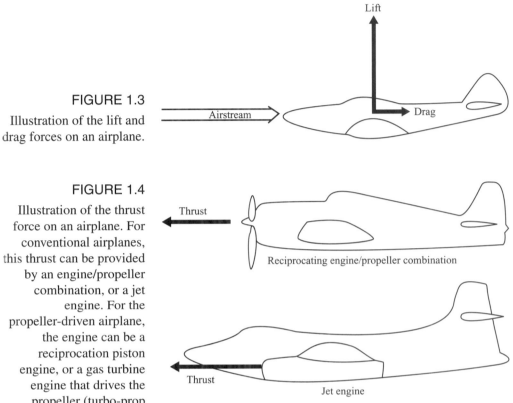

FIGURE 1.3

Illustration of the lift and drag forces on an airplane.

FIGURE 1.4

Illustration of the thrust force on an airplane. For conventional airplanes, this thrust can be provided by an engine/propeller combination, or a jet engine. For the propeller-driven airplane, the engine can be a reciprocation piston engine, or a gas turbine engine that drives the propeller (turbo-prop engine).

in the air for periods of up to 38 minutes covering 24 miles, ending only when they literally ran out of gasoline.

Look again at the Wright Flyer in Figure 1.1. What you see is a machine that was "high tech" for its day. Indeed, it was a symphony of high technology working in unison. The Wrights conceived of their machine as a *system*, embodying the mutually supportive elements of aerodynamics, propulsion, structures, and flight dynamics. Just as the quality of a modern stereophonic sound system today is no better than that of its weakest component, the same is true of a flying machine. You can design an airplane with great aerodynamics, propulsion, and flight control, but if the structure is weak, the machine will fail. (Samuel Langley found this out the hard way, as we will see in Chapter 2.) One reason for the success of the Wright brothers was that each component of their system was sufficient for the job—they made certain of this by intensive experiments and calculations.

This book is a history of the technology of the airplane, written with the nontechnical reader in mind, but telling a story that the technical reader can also enjoy. This history begins centuries before the Wright brothers and takes us to the present day.

The history of the technology of the airplane is the history of advancements in aerodynamics, propulsion, structures and materials, and flight control: the four essential technical features of powered flight. Imagine an airplane in flight, moving rapidly through the air. There is a rush of air over the airplane, which creates an aerodynamic force on the vehicle. This aerodynamic force can be resolved for convenience into *lift* perpendicular to the airstream and *drag* parallel to the

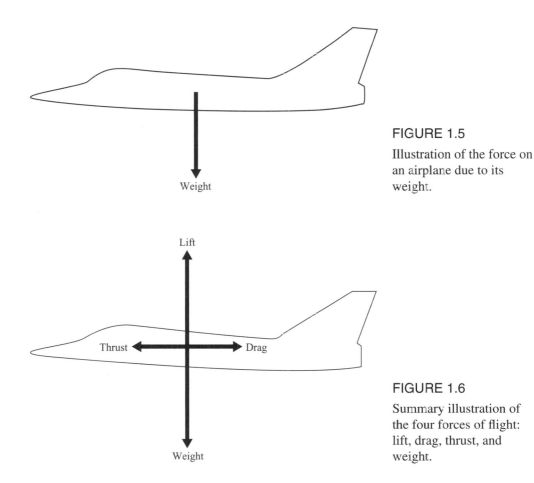

FIGURE 1.5

Illustration of the force on an airplane due to its weight.

FIGURE 1.6

Summary illustration of the four forces of flight: lift, drag, thrust, and weight.

airstream. The lift and drag forces are illustrated in Figure 1.3. The airplane must be pushed or pulled through the air by some type of propulsion device that creates *thrust*, as illustrated in Figure 1.4. The thrust overcomes the drag. The airplane must be structurally sound; you do not want the tail to crumple or the wings to collapse in flight. In the same vein, the materials used for the structure should be strong, but also lightweight. The *weight* of the airplane, illustrated in Figure 1.5, is the sum of the weight of the structure, as well as the weight of everything else being carried by the airplane. In steady level flight, the lift exactly balances the weight. Lift, drag, thrust, and weight—these are the four forces of flight that critically influence the performance of an airplane. The four forces of flight are shown together in Figure 1.6. Finally, the pilot of the airplane must have some means of controlling the motion of the airplane in flight—means to turn, bank, climb, and dive at will. This is the function of various control surfaces on the wings and tail, identified in Figure 1.7. Common control surfaces are the rudder on the vertical tail, the elevators on the horizontal tail, and the ailerons on the wings.

Our history of the technology of the airplane will be chronological, and we will treat aerodynamics, propulsion, structures and materials, and flight controls in parallel, as appropriate to each evolutionary era of the airplane. Recall that the Wright brothers appreciated that all four of these aspects must work together as a system and that the success of the Wright Flyer on December 17, 1903, was due in part to this appreciation.

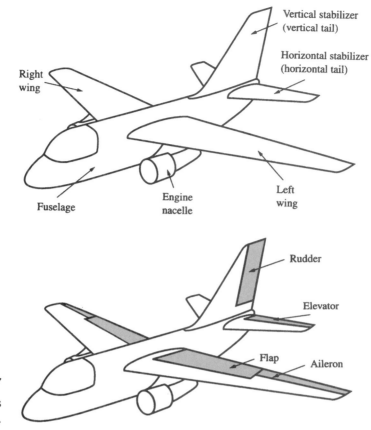

FIGURE 1.7

Illustration of the various parts of an airplane.

The Wrights did not work in a vacuum; they admitted that they "worked on the shoulders of giants." Efforts to solve the technical problems of powered, heavier-than-air flight began as early as the 15th century with Leonardo da Vinci and particularly gained momentum during the 19th century. The advent of the industrial revolution, first in England and then throughout western Europe, provided advancements in technology as well as an intellectual awareness of the machine age that were used to advantage by those individuals struggling to build flying machines in the 19th century. At the beginning of the 19th century, there was virtually no understanding of the physical principles of powered flight; at the end of the 19th century, enough was understood so that primitive flying machines were beginning to hop momentarily off the ground in England, France, and Russia. With those few individuals dedicated to the idea of powered flight, the end of the 19th century was a period of guarded (and sometimes unbridled) optimism that the invention of a successful flying machine was just around the corner. And they were right. Indeed, if Orville and Wilbur had never entered the field of aeronautics, and their momentous flights on December 17, 1903, had never taken place, the first successful airplane would have been invented by someone else within the decade. The time was right. The Wrights were the right people at the right time.

Just what aeronautical technology did the Wrights inherit from their predecessors? How much was right? How much was wrong? Who were the major players in the development of this technology and why? We will address these and other questions in the first part of this book. The course of aeronautical technology in the 19th century was a checkerboard pattern of false starts, replete with many blind alleys, with a few important forward advances. Octave Chanute, a famous American civil engineer near the end of the 19th century and one of the first Americans to become interested in powered flight, in his definitive survey of flying machines published in 1894 had this to say about the situation existing at that time: "Failures, it is said, are more instructive than successes; and thus far in flying machines there have been nothing but failures." Chanute was correct about learning from failures. Against the dark background of failure and technological ignorance in aeronautics, there were a few bright lights in the 19th century in the form of George Cayley in England, Alphonse Penaud and Clement Ader in France, Otto Lilienthal in Germany, and Samuel Langley in the United States. Who were these people? What did they accomplish? We will examine the work of these aeronautical investigators, as well as that of other self-styled inventors, in Chapter 3. In Chapter 4 we will put ourselves in the shoes of the Wright brothers in 1899 as they started their quest to solve the problem of powered flight. We will see what they used of the existing aeronautical technology at that time, what they rejected, and how they developed their own technology that within four years led to success. Finally, in the remaining chapters we will highlight the exponential growth of the technology of the airplane in the 20th century, growth which is still taking place today.

The history of science, from the ancient Greeks to the 20th century, has a common thread; there was generally a cultural and formal educational gap between the "academicians," who were trying to advance the intellectual understanding of science, and the "craftsmen," who were struggling to design things and make them work. With a few exceptions, these two cultures did not interact with each other, creating a chronic technology transfer gap that only in the 20th century seems to have been bridged (somewhat). This dichotomy was alive and well during the 19th century in terms of the advancement of aeronautics. For example, the fundamental understanding of the science of fluid mechanics was advanced considerably in the 19th century by such people as Louis Navier at the Ecole Polytechnic in Paris; George Stokes at Cambridge; Herman von Helmholtz at the Universities of Konigsberg, Bonn, Heidelberg, and Berlin; and Osborne Reynolds at the University of Manchester. These gentlemen were all university-educated academicians, none of whom had the slightest interest in flying machines. Indeed, the disdain for any work in aeronautics is reflected in Lord Kelvin's statement: "I have not the smallest molecule of faith in aerial navigation other than ballooning." Kelvin was expressing the prevailing opinion on the matter.

On the other hand, there was a group of craftsmen struggling to understand the fundamental laws of flight so that they could build successful flying machines. They were George Cayley, Francis Wenham, Horatio Phillips, and Hiram Maxim in England, all of whom were not university educated, but who were well read and self-educated. Among others, these technically oriented people were trying to apply their own intuitive understanding of the physical laws of flight to the design of flying machines. The Aeronautical Society of Great Britain was formed in 1866 to encourage discussion and exchange of ideas among these investigators. Ultimately, from this group of aeronautical engineering craftsmen, the profession of aeronautical engineering began to take on an embryonic form. But with little help from the academicians. For example, there remained throughout the 19th century a great divide between the rapid development of the science of fluid dynamics by academicians and the desperate need to understand the applied laws of aerodynamics by the craftsmen. This lack of technology transfer had an impact on the technological state of the art inherited by the Wright brothers. We will paint a more detailed picture of this great divide later in this book.

Let us get on with our discussion of the technology of early flight. After you finish this book, I hope that the next time you get on an airplane, you will *feel* the history of its technology. If you do, then I will have accomplished my goal.

CHAPTER

Flailing in the Dark: Aeronautics Before the 19th Century

> To me it seems that all sciences are vain and full of errors that are not born of experience, mother of all certainty, and that are not tested by experience...
>
> **Leonardo da Vinci**
> ***"Trattato della Pittura,"***
> ***Codex Urbina***
> **15th century**

> The genius of man may make various inventions, encompassing with various instruments one and the same end; but it will never discover a more beautiful, a more economical, or a more direct one than nature's, since in her inventions nothing is wanting and nothing is superfluous.
>
> **Leonardo da Vinci**
> **15th century**
> **(From manuscript now in the Royal Library**
> **at Windsor, England, U.K.)**

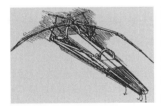

Imagine that you are relaxing on a beach. The sky is a light blue, which makes a sharp contrast at the horizon with the dark blue of the water. Profiled against this hue are white seagulls, flying seemingly effortlessly, alternately flapping their wings for speed and altitude and soaring majestically with outstretched wings. Without consciously knowing it, these seagulls are a perfect example of one of nature's inventions in which, as da Vinci wrote, "nothing is wanting and nothing is superfluous." Moreover, these seagulls have something you do not—the ability to move at will in the third dimension of the sky. Nature invented you differently, giving you the ability to walk and run in only the seemingly two-dimensional space of the Earth's surface. But you nevertheless might have the urge, indeed the dream, of being able to break the bounds of your two-dimensional world and fly effortlessly through the air along with those seagulls.

You would not be alone. Since the dawn of the human race, these thoughts and feelings about flight were shared by many. The importance given to flight in ancient times can be seen in the depictions of flying beings in mythology and religion. Flight had status. For example, angels were given wings. But you as an earthbound human being, how can you get into the air and fly? Since the ancient Greeks, people grappled with this question and made efforts to get off the ground. It became an intellectual quest, a mechanical challenge, and an exercise in shear boldness and courage. How did we do it? What intellectual understanding and constructs, and what mechanical advancements, finally led to successful human flight? The answers are contained in the story told in this book.

TOWER JUMPERS

Consider the following thought experiment. Assume that you were born on a desolate island, completely isolated from the 21st century, devoid of any newspapers, radio, television, etc. You have never seen an automobile, airplane, or any modern machine for that matter. However, moved by your observations of seagulls in flight, or by the flight of birds in general, you decide that you want to fly. What would you do? Would you immediately conceive of a machine made up of fixed wings, a fuselage, and a tail, such as shown in Figure 1.7? Would you imagine a flimsy biplane made of cloth and wood, such as the Wright Flyer shown in Figure 1.1? I think not. Rather, you mostly likely would try to emulate the birds. You would fashion some wings out of wood or feathers, strap them to your arms, climb to the roof of your hut, and jump off, flapping madly. If you were stubborn, you might even try it a second time.

In so doing, you would join a large group of would-be flyers labeled "tower jumpers." Beginning about 400 B.C., there are numerous tales of humans who attempted flight in this manner. For example, there was the Benedictine monk, Eilmer (sometimes called Oliver) of Malmesbury, who in 1020 constructed some wings and jumped from the roof of Malmesbury Abbey. For his effort, he received two broken legs and blamed his problem on the fact that he had no tail surfaces attached to his feet. In the same century, Saracen of Constantinople fitted a cloak with stiffeners, climbed to the top of a tower, and jumped off, attempting to flap and glide. He was killed. Tower jumping recognized no social strata or economic divide. For example, in 1742 the Marquis de Bacqueville attempted to fly across the Seine River in Paris with wings fixed to his arms and legs. Jumping from a house by the riverside, all he managed was to flutter down on a washerwoman's barge, breaking both his legs.

Tower jumpers contributed nothing to the technology of early flight. Indeed, Giovanni Borelli, a mathematics professor at the University of Messina and later at Pisa, in a book entitled *De Motu Animalium* published in 1680 one year after his death, proved that humans did not have the muscular strength to lift themselves and their apparatus and fly though the air. He noted that the ratio of muscle power to body weight is much larger for a bird than a human. Later tower jumpers should have paid more attention to Borelli. (Finally on August 23, 1977, cyclist Bryan Allen became the first human to fly successfully under his own muscle power. Flying the Gossamer Condor, a huge ultra-lightweight airplane that was a wonderful synthesis of modern aerodynamics, propulsion, and structures designed by Dr. Paul B. MacCready, Allen won the $50,000 Kremer Prize for the first

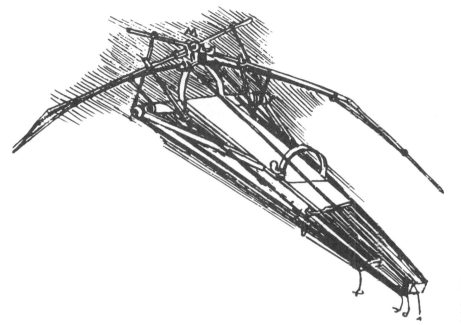

FIGURE 2.1
An ornithopter design by
Leonardo da Vinci, 1490.

man-powered flight on a figure-eight course around two points at least a half mile apart. The Gossamer Condor now hangs in the National Air and Space Museum of the Smithsonian Institution, looking very much like the world's first "cellophane" aircraft.)

However, in the history of aeronautics, and particularly in the development of the technology of the airplane, tower jumping contributed nothing.

ORNITHOPTERS AND LEONARDO DA VINCI

After jumping from the roof of your hut one or two times, you might get discouraged and give up on your quest for flight. Most tower jumpers did. Or you might try to think of a better way. You might conceive of a machine in which you could push or pull levers with your hands and arms, or pump with your legs, and this machine would have wings that would flap up and down and lift you into the air. Such flapping-wing machines are called ornithopters. This idea fascinated Leonardo da Vinci (1452–1519). More than 500 sketches concerning flight survive from da Vinci's notebooks. One of these sketches, shown in Figure 2.1, is da Vinci's idea for an ornithopter, wherein the pilot lies prone and operates the wings by pushing and pulling a variety of levers. Take a close look at the machine in Figure 2.1. You do not have to be an expert aeronautical engineer to recognize that it has no redeeming aerodynamic value whatsoever. At the time of writing, no ornithopter has successfully flown under human power. In the development of the technology of the airplane, ornithopters contributed nothing.

However, da Vinci introduced a new dimension in the quest for flight—intellectual inquiry into the physical fundamentals that governed flight. Da Vinci was an artist, sculptor, mathematician, physicist, engineer, and physician—the epitome of the Renaissance man. In his notes, there are numerous flashes of insight about how aerodynamic lift and drag are generated on a flight vehicle moving through the air; some of this insight was misguided and some was remarkably prescient.

For example, we know today that the lift on an airplane wing is generated by lower air pressure on the top surface of the wing and higher air pressure on the bottom surface, with this pressure difference creating a force perpendicular to the direction of motion of the airplane—lift. In his earlier thinking, da Vinci's concept of the generation of lift was flawed. He argued that when a surface struck the air (such as the downward movement of a bird's wing), the air would be compressed below the surface, and this higher density compressed air would tend to support the surface. In his *Codex Trivultianus*, we find the following statement:

> When the force generates more velocity than the escape of the resisting air, the same air is compressed in the same way as bed feathers when compressed and crushed by a sleeper. And that object by which air was compressed, meeting resistance on it, rebounds in the same way as a ball striking against a wall.

This mental image is flawed. Today, we know that usually about 70 percent of the pressure difference creating lift is due to the *lower* pressure exerted on the top surface compared with the higher pressure acting on the bottom surface of the wing. That is, the difference between the lower pressure on the top surface of the wing and the surrounding ambient atmospheric pressure is larger than the difference between the higher pressure on the bottom surface of the wing and the surrounding ambient atmospheric pressure. It is the lower pressure on the top of the wing that is the major player in the generation of lift.

Toward the end of his life, however, da Vinci recorded an observation that qualitatively was closer to identifying the actual source of lift. In *Codex E*, written around the year 1513, we find the following statement:

> What quality of air surrounds birds in flying? The air surrounding birds is above thinner than the usual thinness of the other air, as below it is thicker than the same, and it is thinner behind than above in proportion to the velocity of the bird in its motion forwards, in comparison with the motion of its wings towards the ground; and in the same way the thickness of the air is thicker in front of the bird than below, in proportion to the said thinness of the two said airs.

Interpreting da Vinci's "thinner" and "thicker" with "lower" and "higher" pressure respectively, we see for the first time the intellectual thought that the pressure exerted on the top of the wing is lower than ambient, hence contributing to lift. Moreover, he is stating that the air pressure exerted on the front of the object is higher than that exerted on the back. Today, we know this to be a major source of drag on a flight vehicle, called pressure drag.

Da Vinci believed that the aerodynamic force on an object, both lift and drag, varied directly as the velocity of the object through the air. That is, if the object's velocity is doubled, the force is doubled. Actually, this sounds intuitively reasonable, but it is wrong. How the aerodynamic force varied with velocity was a question addressed by many investigators in the Middle Ages, and they all agreed with da Vinci that it seemed reasonable that the force varied directly with velocity. The discovery of the true variation of aerodynamic force with velocity was a major intellectual and practical breakthrough in the early technology of flight, and we will tell this story later in the chapter.

Another major intellectual contribution by da Vinci was an appreciation of the "wind-tunnel principle." Today, we plunk a stationary flight vehicle in a wind tunnel and blow air over it at a given velocity, and we say that the aerodynamic force and other aerodynamic effects are identical to those associated with the same flight vehicle *moving* at the same velocity through still air. This principle, almost self-evident today, is the basis of all modern testing in wind tunnels. But it has not always been so self-evident. As late as the beginning of the 20th century, many aeronautical investigators were not so sure about this, and this uncertainty tended to discourage the use of wind tunnels by some at that time. Da Vinci, however, was certain about the equivalence. He emphatically stated the following in the *Codex Atlanticus*: "As it is to move the object against the motionless air so it is to move the air against the motionless object." In the same set of notes, he says the same thing slightly differently: "The same force as is made by the thing against air, is made by air against the thing." Da Vinci was the first person to clearly and unequivocally state the wind-tunnel principle.

Did da Vinci's work represent a contribution to the state of the art of flight technology? On the surface of it, you might be inclined to say yes. After all, some of the intellectual advances made by da Vinci as just described certainly represented advanced thinking at that time. However, his work on aeronautics was essentially bottled up in his notes, which were unavailable to others during his lifetime and for long afterward. Also, his work was further masked by his unique reverse "mirrorlike" handwriting. He did nothing to promulgate his thoughts on flight to other potential investigators during his time. Da Vinci's work on aerodynamics really came to light only in the 19th and 20th centuries, by which time the state of the art had advanced well beyond his thinking, and therefore, his thinking is of only historical interest. Because of this, da Vinci's work unfortunately did not contribute to the technology of the airplane.

SCIENTIFIC REVOLUTION

At the time that Leonardo da Vinci died, Europe was experiencing an explosive intellectual growth of inquiry about the laws that govern the physical world around us. The scientific revolution spanned the 16th and 17th centuries. During this period, Copernicus postulated his heliocentric model of the solar system, which had the planets revolving around the sun (in contrast to the prevailing geocentric theory that the Earth was the center of the universe). The experimental method of inquiry took hold in the early 1600s, exemplified by William Gilbert's experiments on magnetism and Francis Bacon's philosophy of learning that emphasized the marriage of rational thought with empirical observation—the scientific method. Galileo struggled to piece together a rational theory of mechanics, and Decartes championed the use of mathematics in the study of physical science. And the zenith of this scientific revolution was Issac Newton's system of rational mechanics, preserved for ages in his famous book *Philosophiae Naturalis Principia Mathematica*, first published in 1687.

During the scientific revolution, some progress was made toward the understanding of the physical laws that would eventually lead to the principles of flight. Before the 19th century, none of this progress was aimed specifically at solving the problem of heavier-than-air powered flight. Also, there was no progress toward the actual design of a viable machine. During the 17th and 18th centuries, however, there was intellectual progress that would eventually help the cause. This intellectual progress is the subject of the rest of the chapter.

THE VELOCITY-SQUARED LAW: A CONTROVERSY

For the design of a flying machine, one of the most basic and important pieces of information needed is how the aerodynamic force on the machine varies with the flight velocity of the machine. Without this knowledge, it is impossible to design a viable aircraft. And through the middle of the 17th century, this knowledge was not in hand. We know today that the aerodynamic force varies as the square of the velocity. How did we find out? The answer is an interesting story in human dynamics as well as scientific inquiry.

First, put yourself in the shoes of a self-styled natural philosopher in the Middle Ages. In thinking about the question as to how the forces on an object moving through a fluid varies with the velocity of the object, intuition is most likely to tell you that when the velocity doubles the force doubles. That is, you are inclined to feel that force is directly proportional to velocity. This seems logical, although up to the 17th century there was no proper experimental evidence or theoretical analysis to say one way or another. Like so much of ancient science, this feeling was based simply on the image of geometric perfection in nature, and what could be more "perfect" than the force doubling when the velocity doubles. Indeed, both da Vinci and Galileo, two of the greatest minds in history, held this belief. Had da Vinci ever progressed further with his thoughts on flying machines, reaching the point of an actual design on the basis of just the principles known to him, the machine would have had a much larger wing than necessary. The reasoning is this: 1) Assuming that aerodynamic lift is proportional to velocity results in a prediction of the lift that is too small. 2) The wing must create a lift at least equal to the weight of the machine. 3) If the prediction of the lift is too small, and the wing is designed to create a lift equal to the weight, then the resulting wing design will be too large, hence adding a lot of unnecessary weight and drag to the flying machine. Clearly, in the design of a flying machine, one of the most fundamental aerodynamic quantities that must be known is how the force varies with velocity. And up to the middle of the 17th century, the prevailing thought was the incorrect notion that force was directly proportional to the flow velocity.

Within the space of 17 years at the end of the 17th century, this situation changed dramatically. Between 1673 and 1690, two independent sets of experiments due to Edme Mariotte (1620–1684) in France and Christiaan Huygens (1629–1695) in The Netherlands, along with the theoretical fundamentals published by Issac Newton (1642–1727) in England, clearly established that the force on an object varies as the square of the flow velocity. That is, if the velocity doubles, the force goes up by a factor of four. In comparison with the previous centuries of halting, minimal progress in aerodynamics, the rather sudden realization of the velocity-squared law for aerodynamic force represents the first major scientific breakthrough in the historical evolution of aerodynamics. This result is so important to the history of the technology of the airplane that we need to look at its evolution in more detail.

Credit for the velocity-squared law rests with Edme Mariotte, who first published it in 1673. Mariotte lived in absolute obscurity for about the first 40 years of his life. There is a claim that he was born in Dijon, France, in 1620, but there are no documents to verify this, let alone to pinpoint an exact birthdate. We have no evidence concerning his personal life, his education, or his vocation until 1666, when very suddenly he was made a charter member of the newly formed Paris Academy of Sciences. Most likely, Mariotte was self-taught in the sciences. He came to the attention of the academy through his pioneering theory that sap circulated through plants in a manner analogous to blood circulating through animals. Controversial at that time, his theory was confirmed within four years by numerous experimental investigators. Mariotte quickly proved to be an active member and contributor to the academy. His areas of work were diverse; he was interested in experimental physics, hydraulics, optics, plant physiology, meteorology, surveying, and general scientific and mathematical methodology. Mariotte is credited as the first in France to develop experimental science, transferring to that country the same interest in experiments that grew during the Italian Renaissance with the work of da Vinci and Galileo. Indeed, Mariotte was a gifted experimenter who took pains to try to link existing theory to experiment—a novel thought in that day. The academy was essentially Mariotte's later life; he remained in Paris until his death on May 12, 1684.

In the period before 1673, Mariotte was particularly interested in the force produced by various bodies impacting on other bodies or surfaces. One of these "bodies" was a fluid; Mariotte examined and measured the force created by a moving fluid impacting on a flat surface. The device he used for these experiments was a beam dynamometer wherein a stream of water impinged on one end of the beam, and the force exerted by this stream was balanced and measured by a weight on the other end of the beam (Figure 2.2). The water jet emanated from the bottom of a filled vertical tube, and Mariotte could calculate its velocity from Torricelli's Law. (Evangelista Torricelli was an Italian physicist and mathematician, who in 1644 proved that the velocity of a fluid streaming from a hole in the bottom of a tank was proportional to the square root of the height of the fluid in the tank.) From the results obtained with this experimental apparatus, Mariotte was able to prove that the force of impact of the water on the beam varied as the square of the flow velocity. He presented these results in a paper read to the Paris Academy of Sciences in 1673—the first time in history that the velocity-squared law was published. For this work, Edme Mariotte deserves the credit for the first major advancement toward the understanding of velocity effects on aerodynamic force.

The esteem in which Mariotte was held by some of his colleagues is reflected by the words of J. B. du Hamel, who said the following after Mariotte's death in 1684:

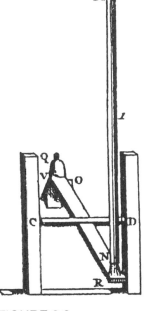

FIGURE 2.2
Mariotte's mechanism for measuring the force exerted on an object in a fluid flow.

> The mind of this man was highly capable of all learning, and the works published by him attest to the highest erudition. In 1667, on the strength of a singular doctrine, he was elected to the Academy. In him, sharp inventiveness always shone forth combined with the industry to carry through, as the works referred to in the course of this treatise will testify. His cleverness in the design of experiments was almost incredible, and he carried them out with minimal expense.

There was at least one colleague, however, who was not so happy with Mariotte, and who represents another side of the historical claim of the first to uncover the velocity-squared law. This man was Christiaan Huygens. Huygens's background is better known than that of Mariotte. He was born on April 15, 1629, in The Hague,

The Netherlands, to a family prominent in Dutch society. Huygens was well-educated; he was tutored by his father until the age of 16, after which he studied law and mathematics at the University of Leiden. Devoting himself to physics and mathematics, Huygens made substantial contributions, including improving existing methodology, developing new techniques in optics, and inventing the pendulum clock. Even today, all textbooks on basic physics discuss Huygens's law of optics. For his accomplishments, Huygens was made a charter member of the Paris Academy of Sciences in 1666, the same year as Mariotte. Huygens moved to Paris to participate more closely in the activities of the academy; he lived in Paris until 1681. During this period, both Mariotte and Huygens worked, conversed, and argued together as colleagues in the academy. In 1681, Huygens moved back to The Hague, where he died on July 8, 1695. During his life, Huygens was recognized as Europe's greatest mathematician. However, he was a somewhat solitary person who did not attract a following of young students. Moreover, he was reluctant to publish, mainly because of his inordinately high personal standards. For these two reasons, Huygens's work did not greatly influence the scientists of the next century; indeed, he became relatively unknown during the 18th century.

In 1668, Huygens began to study the fall of projectiles in resisting media. Following da Vinci and Galileo, he started out with the belief that "resistance" (drag) was proportional to velocity. However, within one year his analysis of the experimental data convinced him that resistance was proportional to the square of the velocity. This was four years before Mariotte published the same result in 1673; however, Huygens delayed until 1690 in publishing his data and conclusions. This somewhat complicates the question as to whom the velocity-squared law should be attributed. The picture is further blurred by Huygens himself, who accused Mariotte of plagiarism; however, Huygens levied this charge after Mariotte's death in 1684. Huygens stated that "Mariotte took everything from me." In regard to Mariotte's paper in 1673, Huygens complained, "He should have mentioned me. I told him that one day, and he could not respond." Here is a classic situation that frequently occurs in scientific and engineering circles even in modern times. We have a learned society, the Paris Academy of Sciences, the members of which frequently gathered to discuss their experiments, theories, and general feelings about the natural world. Ideas and preliminary results were shared and critiqued in a collegial atmosphere. Mariotte and Huygens were colleagues, and from Huygens's own words, they clearly discussed and shared thoughts. In such an atmosphere, the exact origin of new ideas is sometimes not clear; ideas frequently evolve as a result of discussion among groups. What is clear is this: Mariotte published the velocity-squared law in a paper given to the Academy in 1673; Huygens published the same conclusion 17 years later. Moreover, in 1673 Huygens critiqued Mariotte's paper and said *nothing* about plagiarism or not being referenced. Why did he wait until after Mariotte's death 11 years later to make such charges? We have no answer to this question. Using the written scientific literature as a measure, however, Mariotte is clearly the first person to publish the velocity-squared law. Taken in conjunction with Huygens's silence at the time of this publication, we have to conclude that Mariotte deserves first credit for this law. Of course, of great importance to the development of aerodynamics is simply the fact that, by the end of the 17th century, we have direct experimental proof from two independent investigations that aerodynamic force varies as the square of the velocity. This important experimental finding was supported later by the theoretical work of Isaac Newton (1642–1727). The entire Book II of Newton's *Principia*, published in 1687, was devoted to the science of fluid dynamics and hydrostatics. Entitled *The Motions of Bodies (in Resisting Mediums)*, this book was evidence of the importance Newton ascribed to the subject of bodies moving through fluids. He calculated that the resistance acting on a body moving through a fluid with a velocity V is proportional to the square of that velocity V^2. When it is considered that Newton was the father of rational mechanics, to have such a famous scientist prove theoretically the velocity-squared law should have resolved the question completely. It did not; even at the end of the 19th century, some investigators still felt compelled to verify the law.

Was Newton's interest in fluid dynamics driven in part by an interest in flying machines? Absolutely not! During the last part of the 17th century, practical interest in fluid dynamics was driven by naval architecture, in particular the desire to predict and understand the hull drag on ships. (By this time in history, the English had clearly demonstrated that a country with a powerful navy could rule large portions of the world. A powerful navy was dependent on the performance of its ships, which in turn was partly dependent on the ability to understand and predict the drag of ship's hulls.) Newton's interest in fluid mechanics may have been due in a small part to such a practical problem; however, there was a much more compelling reason in Newton's mind for calculating the resistance of a body moving through a fluid. There was a prevailing theory at that time, advanced by René Descartes, that interplanetary space was filled with matter that moved in vortex-like motion around the planets. However, astronomical observations showed that the motion of the heavenly bodies through space was not dissipated, but rather executed regular and repeatable patterns. The only way for this to be the case, if the bodies were moving through a space filled with a continuous medium as Descartes had theorized, would be for the aerodynamic drag on each body to be zero. The central purpose of Newton's fluid mechanics was to prove that a finite drag existed on a body, including the heavenly bodies, while moving through a continuous medium. If this were true, then Descartes's theory would be disproved. Indeed, in Proposition 23 of the *Principia*, Newton calculated a finite resistance on bodies moving through a fluid and showed that this resistance is "in a ratio compounded of the squared ratio of their velocities, and the squared ratio of their diameters, and the simple ratio of the density of the parts of the system." That is, Newton derived the velocity-squared law, while at the same time showing that the resistance varied with the cross-sectional area of the body (the "squared ratio of their diameters") and the first power of the density (the "simple ratio of the density"). In so doing, Newton, for the first time in history, presented a theoretical derivation of the essence of an aerodynamic force, namely,

$$R \propto \rho S V^2$$

where R is the force, ρ is the fluid density, and S is a reference cross-sectional area.

In Newton's mind, however, his contribution was simply to dispel Descartes theory. This is specifically stated by Newton in the scholium accompanying Proposition 40 dealing with the experimental measurements of the resistance of spheres moving through a continuous medium. Because such spheres were shown both theoretically and experimentally to exhibit a finite resistance while moving through a fluid, then, in Newton's words, "the celestial spaces, through which the globes of the planets and comets are continually passing towards all parts, with the utmost freedom, and without the least sensible diminution of their motion, must be utterly void of any corporeal fluid, excepting, perhaps, some extremely rare vapors and the rays of light." For Newton, this was the crowning accomplishment of his study of fluid dynamics. For modern aerodynamicists, the meaningful accomplishment was the theoretical proof that aerodynamic force varied 1) with the first power of the fluid density, 2) with the first power of the body reference area, and 3) with the second power of the velocity. Of course, this was simply the theoretical justification of such variations that were, by Newton's time, already established by experimental evidence.

NEWTONIAN SINE-SQUARED LAW—A RETROGRADE

At the time of Newton, the aerodynamic force that was of interest was simply the aerodynamic drag on an object. The objects investigated were usually flat plates oriented with their flat surface perpendicular to the flow, or spheres, or symmetric bodies at zero incidence angle to the flow (such as the hull of a ship oriented in line with its forward motion). For these cases, the net aerodynamic force is indeed all drag; such configurations do not generate lift. However, the wings of flying machines are designed to generate lift, and this usually entails some incidence angle (angle of attack) of the wings to the flow. How the aerodynamic lift varies with regard to the angular orientation of a body in the flow is a question that was not seriously addressed over the centuries ranging from the ancient Greeks through the time of Newton. This author has not found any mention of this concern in, for example, the works of da Vinci, Galileo, Mariotte, or Huygens. This is somewhat surprising because windmill blades strike the air at an angle of attack, and windmills were in use in Europe since the 12th century; hence, one might think that angle-of-attack effects would have been considered for this application. Also, such matters must have crossed da Vinci's mind in the course of his work on winged flying machines. In any event, no recorded study, either qualitative or quantitative, seems to exist on this question as late as the end of the 17th century.

In an indirect sense, Issac Newton provided the first technical contribution toward the analysis of angle of incidence effects on aerodynamic force. In Book II of the *Principia*, the fluid is postulated as a collection of individual particles that impact directly on the surface of the body, much like a stream of BBs impacting directly on the surface. This fluid model is simply an hypothesis on the part of Newton; it does not accurately model the action of a real fluid—a fact that Newton himself readily acknowledged. Consistent with this mathematical model, we find buried deep in the proof of Proposition 34 the result that the impact force exerted by the fluid on a segment of a curved surface is proportional to $\sin^2\theta$, where θ is the angle between a tangent to the surface segment and the freestream direction. This result, when applied to a flat surface (such as a flat plate) oriented at an angle of attack α to the freestream (Figure 2.3), gives for the resultant aerodynamic force on the plate

$$R = \rho V^2 S \sin^2 \alpha$$

where ρ is the fluid density, V is the flow velocity, and S is the area of the face of

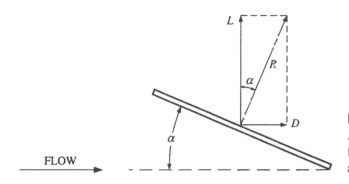

FIGURE 2.3
Aerodynamic force on a flat plate at an angle of attack α.

the flat plate. This equation is called "Newton's sine-squared law"; it does not appear explicitly in the *Principia*, although it follows directly from the derivation given by Newton in Proposition 34. The first application of Newton's sine-squared law to a flat plate at angle of attack is historically obscure. It is such a simple extrapolation of the work in Proposition 34 that we have to assume that it followed shortly after the publication of the *Principia*. As we will see shortly, it was part of the technical bag of tools used by 18th-century hydrodynamicists.

As innocent as it may seem, the sine-squared law later became the source of much discussion and controversy in the 19th century, and calculations based on it were used to show that heavier-than-air flight was not feasible. To see how these arguments went, return to Figure 2.3. From the relationship between L, R, and D, where L is the lift, R is the resultant aerodynamic force, and D is the drag, we use trigonometry to write

$$L = R \cos \alpha = \rho V^2 S \sin^2 \alpha \cos \alpha$$

and

$$D = R \sin \alpha = \rho V^2 S \sin^3 \alpha$$

Consider the flat lifting surface shown in Figure 2.3. Assume that the flat surface is at a small angle of attack, say 3 degrees. The sine of 3 degrees is a number much less than one and the cosine of 3 degrees is very close to one. In turn, the square of the sine is particularly small. Examining the preceding equation for lift, we note that, for a flying machine at a given velocity and with a given wing area, the sine-squared variation predicts a very small lift at small angles of attack. For a flying machine in level flight, the lift must equal the weight. Hence, if we are to accept the Newtonian sine-squared law as correct (which, as we will see shortly, it is not), then we are led to only two options to counter the small value of $\sin^2 \alpha$ and to increase the lift so that it will equal the weight of the flying machine:

1) Increase the wing area S. This can lead to enormous wing areas that make the flying machine totally impractical.
2) Increase the angle of attack α. Unfortunately, this leads to higher drag along with higher lift; indeed, according to the Newtonian sine-squared law, the drag increases faster than the lift when α is increased. In turn, to overcome this

drag, a more powerful (hence, heavier) engine would be needed. This would require the flying machine to produce even more lift, which results in even more drag.

For these reasons, the use of the Newtonian sine-squared law leads to very pessimistic calculations for the aerodynamic characteristics of flying machines—so pessimistic that these results were used by some people during the 19th century to argue against the practical feasibility of heavier-than-air flight. For example, let us see what would have happened if the Wright brothers had relied on the sine-squared law. The weight of the 1903 Wright Flyer with pilot was 750 pounds. To produce a lift of 750 pounds at, say, six degrees angle of attack at their design flight speed of 24 miles per hour, the sine-squared law predicts that the necessary wing area would have to be a whopping 23,448 square feet—*an impossibly large area for a flying machine*. In comparison, the wing area of the Wright Flyer was only 510 square feet, and that was sufficient to do the job. If the Wrights had based their design on the sine-squared law, they would have quit their efforts immediately.

So the Newtonian sine-squared law was a retrograde in the technology of early flight. It became so entrenched, however, that other investigators and inventors in the 19th century trying to prove the technical feasibility of heavier-than-air powered flight had to go to extra efforts to disprove the sine-squared law. They finally did, as we will discuss later. Of course, Newton himself can not be directly blamed for this situation. He never explicitly discussed the force on a flat plate at angle of attack as shown in Figure 2.3. He never explicitly derived the sine-squared law for such a configuration. So it is a bad rap to blame Newton for the pessimistic calculations used in the 19th century to torpedo the idea of heavier-than-air flying machines. In this, Newton was just an innocent bystander.

INVENTION OF THE WHIRLING ARM—BENJAMIN ROBINS

Imagine that you are living in the 18th century, and you want to go head-to-head with the question as to what is the aerodynamic force acting on a body moving through the air. Moreover, you want to get some hard data; you are more of an inventor or an engineer than a scientist and want to have some numbers to help build a flight vehicle. How do you get these numbers? You could always build a machine based on your intuition without the benefit of hard data and try to fly it. Again, you would not be alone—this is what many inventors did through the end of the 19th century. But this is certainly not a rational engineering approach. Instead, you would want to carry out controlled experiments on the ground to study the aerodynamic force on models of various shapes at various angles of attack. But how do you do this? How do you get air to move over your model in such a fashion to make controlled measurements of the aerodynamic force?

One person's answer to this question was the invention of the whirling arm by the noted British military engineer Benjamin Robins (1707–1751). The whirling arm influenced aeronautical testing for the next 150 years. Let us take a closer look at Robins and his whirling arm.

In 1746, the understanding of aerodynamic forces in flight was summarized succinctly by Robins, who in a paper published in the *Philosophical Transactions of the Royal Society of London* wrote, "All the theories of resistance hitherto established are extremely defective, and that it is only by experiments analogous to those here recited, that this important subject can even be completed." Robins simply was reacting to the situation that the contemporary theory did not contribute to the accurate calculation of aerodynamic forces. The Newtonian sine-squared law was essentially the only available practical tool, and the accuracy of that law was already in serious question. The time was ripe for some serious experimental advances to fill the void, and Benjamin Robins took the lead in this respect.

Robins was born in Bath, England, in 1707 to Quaker parents. He never espoused the Quaker pacifist philosophy; he studied to be a teacher, but quickly gave this up to pursue a scientific career as a military engineer. Intensely interested in mathematics, in 1727 he published a paper in the *Philosophical Transactions* on a demonstration of the 11th proposition of Newton's "Treatise on Quadratures." This paper was published in the year of Newton's death, at a time when Newton was embroiled in serious controversy with Leibniz over the development of calculus and, in turn, with a substantial part of the European scientific community. Robins became a strong supporter of Newton, almost to an extreme; in particular he attacked in writing both Leibniz and several of the Bernoullis, who were perceived to be enemies of Newton. In addition to his interest in mathematics, Robins was also an experimentalist, and it is in this respect that he made his lasting contributions. Toward the end of his relatively short life, Robins became interested in the investigation of rockets for the purpose of military signaling. Having never married, Robins traveled to India to work for the British East India Company to renovate some fortifications. He never returned to England and died in St. David, India, on July 29, 1751.

Robins's contributions to experimental aerodynamics were centered around two testing devices that he invented and used for the first time, namely, the whirling arm for measuring aerodynamic forces at low speeds and the ballistic pendulum for examining the aerodynamic characteristics of bodies at high speeds. Robins's whirling arm is illustrated in Figure 2.4; here we see a device where an

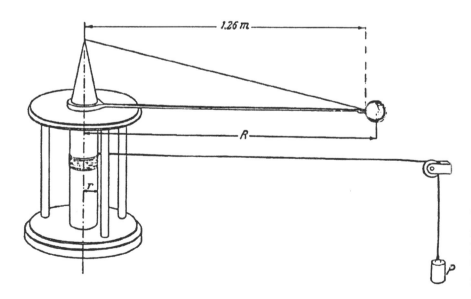

FIGURE 2.4
Whirling-arm mechanism designed by Benjamin Robins, 1746. This was the first significant device for aerodynamic testing.

aerodynamic shape (in this figure, a sphere) is mounted at the end of a long arm. The other end of the arm is attached to a shaft, which in turn is rotated by a falling weight attached to the shaft via a cable and pulley system. As the arm rotates, the aerodynamic body moves through the air at some relative velocity and experiences an aerodynamic resistance that can be measured. Whirling arms, however, have a distinct, built-in problem; after a period of time of operation, the air in the vicinity of the whirling arm starts to rotate in the same direction as the arm, and it becomes difficult to know what the relative velocity is between the moving body and the moving air. This tends to diminish the accuracy of any force measurements as a function of relative velocity. This is why whirling arms are passé in the world of modern aerodynamics, their role being completely taken over by modern wind tunnels. In lieu of wind tunnels (which are a late-19th century development), however, Robins's whirling arm provided the only aerodynamic testing device for the direct measurement of aerodynamic force in the 18th century and throughout most of the 19th century. His invention of the ballistic pendulum was equally as novel. Here a projectile is fired into a massive pendulum, the deflection of which is a measure of the momentum (hence, velocity) of the projectile.

Using these two devices, Robins made extensive measurements of aerodynamic drag on various bodies. Of these, three particular sets of measurements were relevant to the later technology of the airplane. First, Robins verified that the aerodynamic force varied with the square of the relative velocity between the body and the airstream (at speeds less than the speed of sound), reinforcing the earlier results of Mariotte, Huygens, and Newton. Second, he was the first to show that two aerodynamic bodies with different shapes but the same projected frontal area have different values of drag. The prevailing intuition at that time was that drag was mainly due to the projected frontal area of a body, and that the shape was secondary. Robins tested pyramid shapes first with the apex forward toward the incoming flow and then with the flat base forward. The latter case produced more drag. He also tested oblong flat plates at 45-degree angle of attack, first with the long side as the leading edge and then with the short side as the leading edge. He found that the drag was quite different, with the latter case producing more drag. In this respect, Robins was the first to observe the influence of wing aspect ratio on the aerodynamic force. [The aspect ratio for a rectangular-shaped wing is the ratio of the wing span (distance from one wing tip to the other) divided by the chord (distance from the front to the back of the wing).] Third, Robins was the first person to observe the large increase in drag associated with speeds near the speed of sound—today, this is called the transonic drag rise. Indeed, when the projectiles were moving at near the speed of sound, from his ballistic pendulum measurements Robins observed that the aerodynamic force began to vary as the velocity cubed, not squared as in the lower-speed cases. Today, we know that the transonic drag rise is due to shock waves that occur in local pockets of supersonic flow in the flowfield around a body flying at a velocity slightly less than the speed of sound. This phenomenon has been one of the most serious problems in modern aerodynamics; it has a major impact on the design of modern commercial jet transports, which cruise at high subsonic Mach numbers, and for all vehicles designed for supersonic and hypersonic flight because they have to fly through the transonic flight regime in the process of going supersonic. It is indeed amazing to this author that the transonic drag rise was first observed in the 18th century. For this discovery alone, Robins observes a high place in the history of aerodynamics.

Robins published his results in two publications; the first, entitled *New Principles of Gunnery Containing the Determination of the Force of Gunpowder and Investigation of the Difference in the Resisting Power of the Air to Swift and Slow Motions*, was published as a book in London in 1742, and the second, entitled "Resistance of the Air and Experiments Relating to Air Resistance," was published as a paper in the *Philosophical Transactions of the Royal Society of London* in 1746.

In Chapter 1, we mentioned the great divide that frequently separated the academic scientists and the craftsmen practitioners. Benjamin Robins's work transcended this divide. His work was read by many researchers, including one of the greatest 18th century mathematicians and scientists, Leonhard Euler. Indeed, Euler was so excited about Robins's book that he personally translated it into German in 1745, adding some commentary of his own. In 1751, the year of Robins's death, it was translated into French. Robins's discovery of the transonic drag rise was particularly extolled by Euler, who agreed completely with the result. Indeed, both Euler and Robins suggested the use of bodies with reduced frontal area at the nose of the body to reduce this drag rise—a precursor to our modern understanding that sharp, slender bodies tend to delay and reduce this drag in the transonic regime.

As a final remark on Robins, his work was appreciated by his contemporaries in England as well as on the continent; in 1747, he was awarded the Copely Medal by the Royal Society, Britain's most prestigious, venerable, and entrenched scientific society, whose membership included the crème de la crème of England's scientists. On the other hand, perhaps because he was viewed as a ballistician working on projectiles, his work was lost on future developers of the airplane in the 19th century. In 1894, Octave Chanute in the United States published his book *Progress in Flying Machines*, the most definitive survey of work on the technical development of the airplane to that date. Chanute did not even mention Robins.

JOHN SMEATON AND SMEATON'S COEFFICIENT

Eight years after Robins's death, another Englishman made a contribution that was to have an important but controversial impact on flying machine design—an impact that lasted to the beginning of the 20th century. This person was John Smeaton (1724–1792), a professional civil engineer who is recognized as the first person to make engineering a respected endeavor in the eyes of British society. Although Smeaton made only one, almost singular, contribution to experimental aerodynamics, its influence was so strong that it deserves major attention here. First, let us examine Smeaton, the man.

John Smeaton was born in Austhrope, Yorkshire, England, on June 8, 1724, descending from a long lineage of Scots. His father was a lawyer, which led Smeaton to begin his education in law. However, he quickly found that his talents were more along the lines of mechanical matters, and with the approval of his family, he became a successful maker of scientific instruments. Smeaton's life coincided with the beginning of the industrial revolution in England, which created the demand for massive civil engineering projects. Smeaton took advantage of these opportunities; he designed and constructed several harbors in England and established a reputation as a structural engineer. By far his most outstanding accomplishment in this area was the rebuilding of the Eddystone lighthouse after the failure of two previous contractors—an accomplishment that earned him general fame in England. He became a Fellow of the Royal Society and a charter member of the first professional engineering society, the Society of Civil Engineers, which after his death became known as the Smeatonian Society.

In 1759, Smeaton was awarded the Copley Medal by the Royal Society, the same prize given to Robins 12 years earlier. The work for which he earned this medal is the reason why Smeaton has a place in the history of aeronautics. With more than 10,000 windmills in England at that time, as well as a number of mills driven by water power, Smeaton carried out experiments on the force of both air and water on the vanes of such devices. For these experiments, Smeaton used Robins's invention of the whirling arm and adapted it such that the windmill blades not only translated in space via movement of the arm, but also such that the blades themselves rotated, thus simulating the actual operation of a windmill in the face of wind. The windmill blades at the end of the whirling arm were spun by a cable and pulley mechanism activated by a falling weight.

Smeaton published his experimental results in a paper entitled "An Experimental Enquiry Concerning the Natural Powers of Water and Wind to Turn Mills, and Other Machines Depending on a Circular Motion" in the *Philosophical Transactions of the Royal Society of London*, Volume 51, in 1759. In this paper Smeaton included a table of aerodynamic force measurements on a flat surface perpendicular to the flow. These force measurements were tabulated versus the wind velocity. A correlation of these tabulated results were given by Smeaton as

$$F = kSV^2$$

where F is the force in pounds exerted on the perpendicular surface, S is the surface area in square feet, and V is the wind velocity in miles per hour. The numerical value of k found by Smeaton was 0.005. The constant k became known as *Smeaton's coefficient*, and the value of 0.005 was used by many aerodynamic experimenters through the end of the 19th century. However the accuracy of this value was soon questioned, starting as early as 1809 by George Cayley (to be discussed in Chapter 3). Indeed, inaccuracies in Smeaton's coefficient had a major adverse impact on the early work of the Wright brothers in 1900 and 1901 (to be discussed in Chapter 4).

John Smeaton died at Austhorpe on October 28, 1792. He left behind a major contribution—information and an empirical relation on the aerodynamic force on a surface oriented perpendicular to an airstream. Later, Smeaton's coefficient was used and modified by subsequent investigators for the estimation of lift and drag on wings and airfoil surfaces. But by no means was it a final or definitive contribution, due to the subsequent uncertainties found in the value of Smeaton's coefficient; indeed, much controversy was generated by these uncertainties. Perhaps the final judgment of Smeaton's contribution is that the concept of Smeaton's coefficient is no longer a viable part of the modern, 21st-century state of the art in aerodynamics. However, for the 19th century, it was a critical segment of the state of the art at that time.

FIGURE 2.5
The first aerial voyage.
The Montgolfier hot-air
balloon lifts from the
ground near Paris on
November 21, 1783.

BALLOONING

Human efforts to fly literally got off the ground on November 21, 1783, when a
balloon carrying Pilatre de Rozier and the Marquis d'Arlandes ascended into the
air and drifted five miles across Paris (Figure 2.5). The balloon was inflated and
buoyed up by hot air from an open fire burning in a large wicker basket underneath.
The design and construction of the balloon was the work of the Montgolfier
brothers, Joseph and Etienne. In 1782, Joseph Montgolfier, gazing into his
fireplace, conceived the idea of using the "lifting power" of the hot air rising from a
flame to lift a person from the surface of the Earth. The brothers instantly set to
work, experimenting with bags made of paper and linen, in which hot air from a
fire was trapped. Joseph and Etienne had been carrying on their father's paper
manufacturing business in Annonay, and so they were familiar with the material
and had the skills for construction of the balloon. After several public
demonstrations of flight without human passengers, including the 8-minute voyage
of a balloon carrying a cage containing a sheep, a rooster, and a duck, the

Montgolfiers were ready for the big step. At 1:54 p.m., on November 21, 1783, the first flight with human passengers rose majestically into the air and lasted for 25 minutes. It was the first time in history that a human being had been lifted off the ground for a sustained period of time. Very quickly after this, the noted French physicist, J.A.C. Charles (of the Charles gas law in physics) built and flew a hydrogen-filled balloon from the Tuileries Gardens in Paris on December 1, 1783.

So people were finally off the ground! Balloons, or "aerostatic machines" as they were called by the Montgolfiers, made no real technical contributions to the technology of airplanes. On the other hand, they served a major purpose in triggering the public's interest in flight through the air. They were living proof that people could really leave the ground for an extended period of time and sample the environs heretofore exclusively reserved for birds. They were the only means of flight for more than another 100 years.

CHAPTER

Starts and Stops: Aeronautical Progress in the 19th Century

> The whole problem is confined within these limits, viz, to make a surface support a given weight by the application of power to the resistance of air.
>
> **Sir George Cayley**
> **"On Aerial Navigation,"**
> *Nicholson's Journal*
> **November 1809**

Put yourself in the shoes of a reasonably educated person at the end of the 18th century, a person who is also interested in developing a flying machine. You have not gone to Oxford University or Cambridge University, or any university for that matter, but you are well read and self-educated. You are familiar with the new scientific thought coming out of the scientific revolution, especially the rational mechanics of Issac Newton. Unfortunately, you still have very little to go on in terms of the *design* of a flying machine. Indeed, some progress had been made on basic intellectual fundamentals that would eventually contribute to the understanding of the scientific principles of powered flight, but a void existed in practical engineering approaches to the proper design of a flying machine. The popular image of a flying machine still involved flapping wings for both lift and thrust—the ornithopter concept exemplified by da Vinci's thinking. Certainly, humans had broken the bond of gravity and lifted into the air in a balloon built by the Montgolfier brothers. This was quickly followed by a host of other balloon flights and led to a ballooning craze at the end of the 18th century. But balloons contributed nothing to the technical advancement of heavier-than-air flight. They provided, however, some inspiration for would-be flying machine designers to dream of designs that would allow humans to have control of their destiny in the air; to be able to accelerate, climb, and turn, at will; and to *navigate* through the air—degrees of freedom not available to balloonists who had to go where the wind took them. So, as a person interested in building a flying machine at the end of the

18th century, the field was absolutely virgin, and you were on your own with precious little to guide you. In particular, the concept of the modern airplane as we know it today—a machine with fixed wings for lift, a fuselage and tail, and a separate mechanism for thrust—had not occurred to anybody. However, this situation was about to change dramatically.

THE CONCEPT OF THE MODERN CONFIGURATION AIRPLANE—GEORGE CAYLEY

The concept of the modern configuration airplane came about because of a stroke of genius on the part of one man, George Cayley, in England. Figure 3.1 shows a sketch made in 1804 by Cayley of a hand-launched glider of his own design. The glider was approximately 1 meter in length; a full-scale model is on view at the British Science Museum in South Kensington, London. Today, such a glider is trivial and is almost in the sphere of child's play. However, in 1804, this glider represented a technological breakthrough of immense proportion; indeed, it was the first modern configuration airplane in history. In Figure 3.1, we see a heavier-than-air machine with a *fixed-wing*, *fuselage*, and *horizontal and vertical tail*. This was totally at variance with contemporary thought, which focused on ornithopter concepts. In terms of the practical advancement of aeronautics, George Cayley was responsible for the concept of the modern configuration aircraft. He proposed a *fixed* wing to generate lift, a separate mode of propulsion to overcome the "resistance" (drag) of the machine's motion through the air, and both vertical and horizontal tail surfaces for directional and longitudinal static stability. Cayley first illustrated the concept in a very unconventional manner; in 1799 he engraved on a silver disk an outline of a fixed-wing aircraft. Both sides of this disk are shown in Figure 3.2. At the left of Figure 3.2 is a sketch of the aircraft; here we see a machine with a fixed wing, fuselage (occupied by a person), horizontal and vertical tails at the rear end of the fuselage, and a pair of "flappers" for propulsion. Clearly, the means of lift (the fixed wing) and propulsion (the flappers) are totally separate, in contrast to the action of ornithopter wings, which were intended to provide lift and propulsion all in the same motion. The flappers shown on Cayley's sketch leave much to be desired as a practical mode of propulsion; in this category, Cayley was far off the mark. However, this does not detract from the basic contribution shown on the disk, namely, the separation of lift and propulsion, wherein a fixed wing is employed solely for lift. This is further emphasized by the sketch on the flip side of the disk, shown at the right of Figure 3.2. Here we see, for the first time in history, a lift and drag diagram for a lifting surface. The arrow shows flow from right to left, and the large diagonal line represents a wing cross section at an angle of attack to the flow. The resultant aerodynamic force, drawn perpendicular to the wing, is resolved into two components, lift perpendicular to

FIGURE 3.1
Cayley's sketch of his model glider, 1804, the first modern-configuration airplane in history.

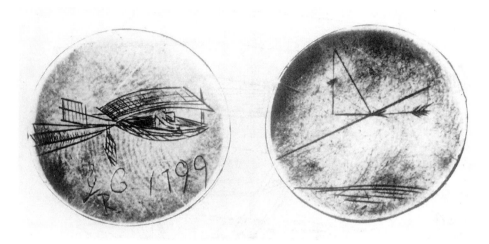

FIGURE 3.2
The silver disk on which George Cayley engraved his concept for a fixed-wing aircraft, the first in history, 1799. The reverse side of the disk shows the resultant aerodynamic force on a flat wing at angle of attack. This is the first lift-drag diagram in the history of aeronautical engineering. The disk is in the collection of the Science Museum in London.

the flow and drag parallel to the flow. Today, the silver disk is in the collection of the British Science Museum; it is no larger than the size of a U.S. quarter.

Sir George Cayley was born on December 27, 1773, in Scarborough, England. His mother, Isabella Seton Cayley, was a member of a well-known Scottish family descended from Robert Bruce. His father, Sir Thomas Cayley, was descended from the Norman invaders of England in 1066. Because of the chronic ill health of his father, Cayley's parents spent much time abroad, and Cayley's early days were spent at the family's house at Helmsley, where he enjoyed much freedom. There he acquired an early interest in mechanical devices, and he frequently visited the village watchmaker. After the death of his grandfather (also Sir George Cayley), the extensive family estate at Brompton passed quickly to his father, who lived for only another 18 months, and then to George Cayley. By the year 1792, Sir George Cayley had become the sixth baronet at Brompton Hall—at the early age of 19. He was to spend the rest of his life as a moderately well-to-do Yorkshire country squire.

As was not unusual in the 18th century, Cayley had virtually no formal education. There is some evidence that he went to school briefly in York, but his main education stemmed from two powerful and influential tutors: George Walker, a mathematician of high reputation, a Fellow of the Royal Society, and a man of extensive intellect, and George Morgan, a Unitarian minister, scientist, and lecturer on electricity. Both tutors were free thinkers, and they had a major impact on the wide breadth of education and open mindedness acquired by Cayley during the first 25 years of his life. Cayley never lost his enthusiasm for knowledge and invention; by the early 1800s he was recognized and sought after as one of England's leading scholars in matters of science, technology, and social ethics.

Struck by the beauty and intelligence of his first tutor's daughter, Sarah Walker, Cayley fell deeply in love in 1792, the same year in which he acquired the family estate at Brompton. Three years later they were married; their marriage lasted for 62 years and ended only with Cayley's death in 1857.

Return to Cayley's drawing of his 1804 glider shown in Figure 3.1. The wing was essentially a kite fixed to the wooden rodlike fuselage and was inclined 6 degrees to the rod by a small peg at the leading edge of the wing. The tail could

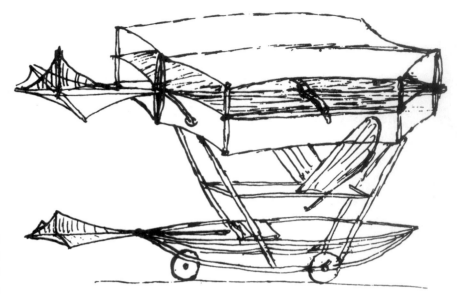

FIGURE 3.3
Cayley's sketch of his
triplane from 1849—the
boy carrier.

be set to any angle with the rod. A small weight dangled from the nose to adjust the location of the center of gravity. When Cayley successfully flew this hand-launched glider in 1804, it became the first modern configuration airplane in history to fly.

In concert with his aeronautical interests, Cayley carried out extensive work on the design of internal combustion engines. He recognized that existing steam engines, with their huge external boilers, were much too heavy in relation to their power output to be of any practical application to airplanes. To improve on this situation, Cayley invented the hot-air engine in 1799 and spent the next 58 years of his life trying to perfect the idea, along with a host of other mechanical designers of that day. The invention of the successful gas-fueled engine in France in the mid-1800s finally superseded Cayley's hot-air engine.

For reasons not totally understood, Cayley directed his aeronautical interest to lighter-than-air balloons and airships during the period from 1810 to 1843, making contributions to the understanding of such devices and inventing several designs for steerable airships. Then, from 1843 until his death in 1857, he returned his interest to the airplane, designing and testing several full-scale aircraft. One was a machine with triple wings (a triplane) and human-actuated flappers for propulsion, shown in Figure 3.3. In 1849, this machine made a floating flight off the ground, carrying a 10-year-old boy for several yards down a hill at Brompton. Another was a single-wing (monoplane) glider, which in 1853 flew across a small valley (no longer than 500 yards) with Cayley's coachman aboard as an unwilling pilot. (At the end of this flight, the coachman was quoted as saying, "Please, Sir George, I wish to give notice . . . I was hired to drive and not to fly.")

Although Cayley's standing in history is based on his aeronautical contributions, this broadly educated and liberal-thinking man (Figure 3.4) accomplished much more during his long life of 84 years. Of particular note is his invention in 1825 of the caterpillar treaded land vehicle, the forerunner of the Caterpillar tractor and the military tanks of the 20th century. In 1847, he invented an artificial hand. This artificial limb was a breakthrough in such devices, replacing

FIGURE 3.4
A portrait of Sir George
Cayley, painted by Henry
Perronet Briggs in 1841.

the simple hook that had been in use for centuries. Cayley's interests were purely
humane; he expected and received virtually no financial compensation for this
invention.

In addition to designing flight vehicles, Cayley also performed extensive
aerodynamic research using a whirling arm. Because his seminal concept for a
flying machine involved a fixed wing that generates lift at a small angle of attack to
the airflow, Cayley needed data on the variation of lift with angle of attack—data
that did not exist. Beginning in 1804, this lack of data drove him to build and
operate the whirling arm device shown in Figure 3.5. Cayley was the first person to
use a whirling arm for aeronautical purposes. At the end of the arm, he mounted a
flat surface made of paper stretched tightly over a frame. He tested this "flat plate"
lifting surface at angles of attack ranging from −3 degrees (3 degrees below the
horizontal) to 18 degrees. The area of the surface, for convenience of reducing the
data, was exactly 1 square foot. For example, he measured a lift of 1 ounce on the
flat surface at an angle of attack of 3 degrees at a velocity through the air of 21.8
feet per second, a measurement I found to be accurate to within 10 percent based
on modern aerodynamic calculations [see J. D. Anderson, *A History of
Aerodynamics, and Its Impact on Flying Machines*, Cambridge University Press,
1997 (hardback), 1998 (paperback)].

The importance of Smeaton's coefficient was not lost on Cayley. Indeed, with
his whirling arm he carried out measurements of the aerodynamic drag on a flat

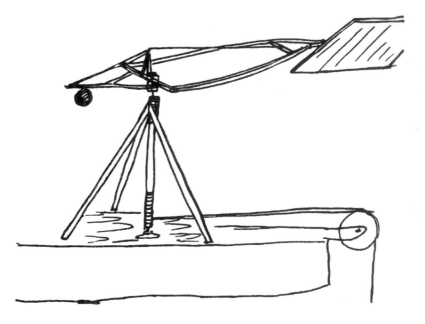

FIGURE 3.5
George Cayley's whirling arm apparatus for testing airfoils.

plate oriented perpendicular to the airstream. His results gave a value of 0.0037 for Smeaton's coefficient, in contrast to the value of 0.005 published by Smeaton. Today we know that a proper value of Smeaton's coefficient is 0.003; Cayley's measurements were getting closer to the truth.

A portrait of Sir George Cayley (Figure 3.4) was painted when he was 68 years old. It shows a still-handsome man with a soft, kindly, and scholarly countenance. It is no surprise that Cayley was well liked and respected by his family as a father and husband; by his friends as a kind, thoughtful, and humorous country squire; and by his scientific and technical colleagues as one of the most innovative, knowledgeable, and well-read people in England at the time. When Cayley died peacefully at Brompton Hall on December 15, 1857, many members of social and scientific England strongly felt his loss, as evidenced by numerous obituaries and statements at that time.

Cayley was also conscious of the inherent stability of a flying machine, that is, the ability of the airplane to right itself if disturbed by a gust during its flight. Returning to Figure 3.1, Cayley's 1804 glider, we note that he could adjust the center of gravity of the glider by changing the position of the weight hung from the fuselage. He found that the glider flew best when the center of gravity was about 7.5 inches behind the root leading-edge juncture of the wing. For this case, the lift on the wing acted at a point (the center of pressure of the wing) located *ahead* of the center of gravity. By itself, this would rotate the airplane upward around the center of gravity, flipping it over and on its back. However, Cayley trimmed the glider by having a horizontal tail inclined at a positive angle of 11.5 degrees relative to the fuselage (as seen in Figure 3.1), thus producing a lift on the tail that counteracted the pitching motion due to the lift on the wing and keeping the glider on a rather straight flight path. The concern over inherent stability became almost an obsession with flying machine inventors during the 19th century; George Cayley was the first person to set this idea in motion.

In total, the contributions made by Cayley to the design of the flying machine were momentous—by comparison, all previous investigators pale in Cayley's light. As a final tribute to George Cayley, the French aviation historian Charles Dollfus wrote the following in 1923:

> The aeroplane is a British invention: it was conceived in all essentials by George Cayley, the great English engineer who worked in the first half of the last century. The name of Cayley is little known, even in his own country, and there are very few who know the work of this admirable man, the greatest genius of aviation. A study of his publications fills one with absolute admiration both for his inventiveness, and for his logic and common sense. This great engineer, during the Second Empire, did in fact not only invent the aeroplane entire, as it now exists, but he realized that the problem of aviation had to be divided between theoretical research—Cayley made the first aerodynamic experiments for aeronautical purposes—and practical tests, equally in the case of the glider as of the powered aeroplane.

THE AERIAL STEAM CARRIAGE—WILLIAM SAMUEL HENSON

In 1835, a 30-year old mechanic and lace-machinery operator in Somerset, England, began to dream of making a flying machine. William Samuel Henson had a talent for the ingenious design of mechanical devices, with several patents already in his name. He experimented with model gliders and in 1842 obtained a patent for the large passenger-carrying flying machine shown in Figure 3.6. Henson was a contemporary of George Cayley and was aware of Cayley's work. The flying machine in Figure 3.6 is a beautiful rendering of Cayley's concept of the modern configuration airplane. Here we see a flying machine with a fixed wing, fuselage, and tail, powered by a steam engine driving two propellers mounted behind the wing. Here is Cayley's idea exemplified—a wing to produce lift and a separate propulsive mechanism to produce thrust. Henson embodied this idea in a flying machine that was much larger and indeed much more aesthetically pleasing than Cayley's designs. (Compare Henson's design in Figure 3.6 with Cayley's triplane in Figure 3.3.) The flying machine in Figure 3.6 is called Henson's Aerial Steam Carriage, and because the beautiful print shown in Figure 3.6 as well as

FIGURE 3.6
Henson's Aerial Steam Carriage, 1842–1843.

others like it were widely published and distributed worldwide, the Aerial Steam Carriage branded on the minds of the general public just what a heavier-than-air flying machine should look like—fixed wings, fuselage, tail, and an engine–propeller combination for thrust. Henson's design served to carve in stone George Cayley's seminal concept. However, ironically Henson's Aerial Steam Carriage was never built and, hence, never flown. Let us explore why.

Henson brought his friend and fellow lace-making engineer, John Stringfellow, into the picture, and they formed the Aerial Transit Company with the financial backing of such men as D. E. Colombine, the Regent Street attorney who had negotiated Henson's patent; John Marriott, a journalist whose value was the he "knew a Member of Parliament;" and a Mr. Roebuck, who was expected to promote a bill in Parliament for a shareholders company to operate an Aerial Steam Carriage. Henson and Stringfellow busied themselves with developing the technology that might enable the Aerial Steam Carriage to fly. They turned to model testing. In 1843, they obtained the help of John Chapman, a mathematician, who also had a whirling arm device. Chapman made more than 2000 recorded aerodynamic experiments on the whirling arm for Henson and Stringfellow. This led to a model with a 20-foot wing span and a wing area of 62.9 square feet powered by a nicely working small steam engine designed primarily by Henson but improved by Stringfellow. From 1845 to 1847, they tested this model at Balsa Down, near Chard, England. Try as they did, they could not get the machine to sustain itself after launching down a ramp. The financial supporters got cold feet. Henson became very discouraged and gave up. He married and migrated to the United States in 1848.

Had the Aerial Steam Carriage shown in Figure 3.6 ever been built, could it have flown? It was a large machine, with a wing span of 150 feet and a wing area of 4500 square feet. (By comparison, the wing span and area of the popular Boeing 737 twin jet transport are only 95 feet and 1135 square feet, respectively. Clearly, Henson's machine was big!) Henson reasoned that a square foot of wing area would generate about a half-pound of lift. Including the tail area of 1500 square feet with the wing area of 4500 square feet, Henson must have designed for a total weight of 3000 pounds. He was laboring under the lack of lightweight but strong materials for construction of the structure of the machine, and of course, the steam engine was heavy. There was no precedent for the construction of lightweight structures to fall back on. He also felt that a powerplant would have to produce 25–30 horsepower to propel this heavy flying machine into the air. Defining the power loading as the ratio of the weight of the airplane to the horsepower of the engine, Henson's design had a power loading of 100 pounds per horsepower. By comparison, the power loading of the Wright Flyer in 1903 was 62.5 pounds per horsepower, which was barely small enough to get them into the air. Later, a typical power loading for a World War I biplane such as the Sopwith Camel was about 11 pounds per horsepower. So Henson's Aerial Steam Carriage was grossly underpowered for its heavy weight, and on this characteristic alone it is extremely unlikely that it would have flown.

A prescient favorable design feature of the Aerial Steam Carriage was the relatively high aspect ratio of its wing. The aspect ratio of a wing is defined as b^2/S, where b is the wingspan (distance from one wingtip to the other) and S is the planform area (the projected area you see when looking directly down on the wing from above). If the wing is rectangular in shape, the aspect ratio is simply b/c,

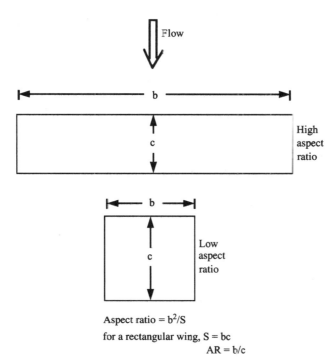

Aspect ratio = b^2/S

for a rectangular wing, $S = bc$

$$AR = b/c$$

FIGURE 3.7
Illustration of high and
low aspect ratio wings.

where c is the chord length (distance from the leading edge to the trailing edge of the wing), as shown in Figure 3.7. High and low aspect ratio rectangular wings are contrasted in Figure 3.7. The aspect ratio is a very important design feature of an airplane because, at speeds less than the speed of sound, an airplane with a high aspect ratio wing will have more lift and less drag than an airplane with a low aspect ratio wing, everything else being equal. Hence, it is good modern design practice to have a wing with as high an aspect ratio as possible. As the aspect ratio increases, however, the location of the center of pressure on the wing (the point through which the total wing lift effectively acts) moves along the span of the wing to a point father away from the fuselage. This causes the lift to create a larger bending moment at the fuselage that, if large enough, could cause the wings to tear off the airplane. To prevent this from happening, the structure of the wing must be made very strong at the root. In turn, this adds a considerable amount of extra structural weight to the wing, which is a limiting design factor on the aspect ratio for an airplane. Aerodynamicists would love to design wings that look like slats out of a venetian blind—very high aspect ratios. Structural designers would love to have wings that are short and stubby—very low aspect ratios. The compromise usually results in wing aspect ratios in the range from 5 to 10. For example, the aspect ratio of the 1903 Wright Flyer is 6.4, that of the famous Douglas DC-3 transport of the 1930s is 9.14, and that of the Boeing 747 jumbo jet is 7.0. The beneficial effect of high aspect ratio was not understood in the early part of the 19th century. The aspect ratio of the kitelike wing of Cayley's 1804 glider in Figure 3.1 is about 1; the aspect ratio of the machine etched on Cayley's silver disk shown in Figure 3.2 is 1.27. Obviously, George Cayley was dealing with almost square-shaped wings. However, in Figure 3.6 we see a flying machine with an aspect ratio of 5, much higher than any machine seen before. Was this because William Samuel Henson had a technical understanding of the beneficial aerodynamic performance of high aspect ratio wings? Most likely not. The Aerial Steam Carriage was patented in 1842, a year before John Chapman carried out his aerodynamic experiments for Henson and Stringfellow. And there is no evidence that these whirling arm experiments examined the effect of aspect ratio. Also, there was nothing in the aerodynamic state of the art inherited by Henson that would allow him to design for a high aspect ratio. Therefore, the high aspect ratio of the Aerial Steam Carriage was most likely an aesthetic feature—part of the overall beauty of this design compared with previous concepts for flying machines. Henson had no idea that he was using good aerodynamics. Neither did anybody else.

It is interesting to read George Cayley's comments on Henson's Aerial Steam Carriage, as published in the April 1843 issue of *Mechanics Magazine*:

> The magnitude of the proposed vehicle will, I fear, militate against its success. The extent of the leverage [of the great wingspan], however well guarded by diagonal braces, is in this necessarily light structure, terrific. For, although the wings are not meant to be wafted [encountering air gusts], the atmosphere, even in moderately calm weather, near the earth is subject to eddies; and the weight of the engine and cargo in the central part of this vast extensive surface would, in the case of any sudden check, operate with enormous power to break the slender fabric. This consideration shows that in order to obtain a sufficient quantity of surface to sustain great weights in the air, the extension ought not to be made in one plane but in parallel planes one above the other at a convenient distance, so as to form a more compact fabric of a three-decker, each deck being 8 to 10 feet from the other, to give free-room for the passage of air between. This vast surface [of Henson's] is all extended in one nearly horizontal plane, which is not the form experimentally proved to give lateral stability. The surface should be made in the form (elevation) of the letter V, though of much more obtuse angle.

In terms of the technology of early flight, Cayley's comments are important on four fronts:

1) He is criticizing the high aspect ratio wing of the Aerial Steam Carriage, saying that it would fail structurally under the forces of flight. Given the lack of understanding of aircraft structural design at that time, Cayley's intuition is most likely correct.

2) Instead, Cayley is suggesting that the total wing area be distributed over two or three smaller wings, mounted above each other. That is, he is recommending the biplane or triplane configuration. Recall that, in 1849, Cayley designed a triplane, called Cayley's boy carrier because it made several halting test glides with a young boy onboard. In this respect, the design concept of biplanes and triplanes originated with George Cayley. Later, the Wright brothers adopted the biplane configuration for all their machines, and biplanes and triplanes were the mainstay of World War I airplane designs. Indeed, biplanes were the dominant airplane configuration until the 1930s. It is interesting to note that Cayley's written comments refer to a triplane as a *three-decker*. This nomenclature using the word "decker" carried through to the Wright brothers who referred to their biplane designs as "double-deckers." The term "biplane" was coined by the Englishman D. S. Brown, who exhibited a biplane model in 1874 at a meeting of the Aeronautical Society of Great Britain under the label "aero-bi-plane."

3) Cayley is very conscious of the need for stability in roll for an airplane, for which he recommends a V form for the wings when seen from the front. Today we call this *dihedral*, and it is an essential design feature for stability in roll for many airplanes. Cayley uses the term "lateral stability," a term still used today in

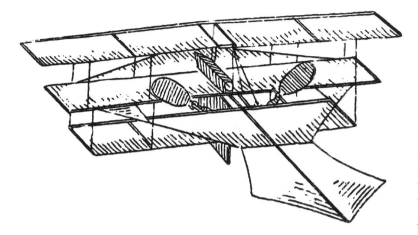

FIGURE 3.8
Stringfellow's triplane model of 1868, as sketched by Octave Chanute in his book *Progress in Flying Machines*, 1894.

association with the rolling motion of an airplane (rotation about the longitudinal axis that extends from the front to the back of the fuselage).

4) In his criticism of the Aerial Steam Carriage, Cayley uses no specific technical data or calculations, but rather refers to his own general experience and intuition. Indeed, he could do little else. Here is an excellent example of the still technically undeveloped state of the art of airplane design in the first part of the 19th century. *Intuition ruled supreme!*

Stringfellow continued with his experiments on models after Henson left England in 1848, but he was unable to get any machine to sustain itself in the air. His efforts concluded when he exhibited a model steam-powered triplane at the first aeronautical exhibition in history, an exhibition sponsored by the newly formed Aeronautical Society of Great Britain at the Crystal Palace in London in June 1868. Stringfellow's triplane is shown in Figure 3.8. During the exhibition, the model hung underneath a small trolley attached by pully-type wheels to a long cable stretched above the heads of the visitors. The best the model could do was to run along the cable. Even though Stringfellow's triplane was unsuccessful, like Henson's Aerial Steam Carriage it was extremely influential because of worldwide publicity. Illustrations of this triplane appeared throughout the end of the 19th century. These illustrations were later a strong influence on Octave Chanute, and through him on the Wright Brothers, strengthening the concept of superimposed wings. Stringfellow's triplane was the main bridge between George Cayley's aeronautics and the 20th century biplane.

THE FIRST PILOTED HOP—FELIX DU TEMPLE

The 19th century witnessed a long string of failures in the efforts to achieve a successful, sustained flight of a heavier-than-air flying machine. Among these were the efforts of Felix du Temple, a French naval officer who received a patent in 1857 for a large flying machine with swept-forward wings covered by silk fabric stretched by several curved spars in the span direction. Du Temple understood the need for lateral stability because his wings had a small degree of dihedral. The wings were fixed to a short, stubby fuselage containing a motor. The patent did not specify the type of motor; later, Octave Chanute theorized, "it might be steam, electricity, or some other type of prime mover." Within a year after his patent, du

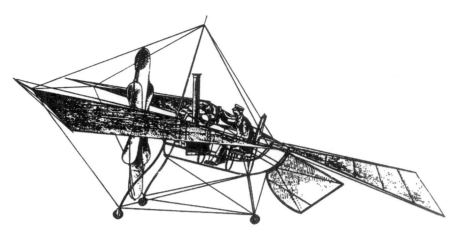

FIGURE 3.9
Du Temple's airplane, the
first piloted flying machine
to achieve a powered
hop off the ground.

Temple was experimenting with small models powered by some type of clockwork mechanism.

With the aid of his brother, Louis du Temple, Felix eventually constructed a full-size flying machine based on his patent and model tests. Shown in Figure 3.9, this machine had sweptforward wings and weighed approximately 1 ton. Du Temple estimated that a powerplant producing 6 horsepower would be sufficient to propel the machine, giving a very high power loading of 333 pounds per horsepower—his machine was woefully underpowered for its weight. Nevertheless, in 1874 this machine, piloted by a young sailor and powered by some type of hot-air engine (the precise type is unknown), was launched down an inclined ramp at Brest, France. It left the ground for a moment, but did not come close to resembling a sustained flight. However, du Temple's flying machine earned the credit for the first powered hop in history. Felix du Temple and his brother continued to work on a lightweight engine, but without success. Du Temple died in 1890 without contributing anything more to aeronautics.

THE SECOND PILOTED HOP—ALEXANDER MOZHAISKI

In the 19th century, Russia spawned some aeronautical enthusiasts, one of whom, Alexander F. Mozhaiski, a captain of the Imperial Russian Navy, designed and built a noteworthy flying machine. Beginning with a study of the flight of birds, Mozhaiski graduated to experiments with kites, some of which were large enough to carry him into the air when pulled at high speed by a horse-drawn carriage. In 1877, he tested a small model propelled by three clockwork-driven propellers; these short flights on the grounds of the St. Petersburg Riding School were observed by a host of spectators, including members of the Russian Academy of Sciences. The model flights were successful enough that a committee of scientists from the Academy approved Mozhaiski's design and encouraged the construction of a full-size machine for piloted flight. This flying machine was patented in 1881 and completed in 1883. It was partially based on Henson's design for the Aerial Steam Carriage—a large steam-powered monoplane with a cruciform tail, with one larger tractor propeller in front of the wing and two smaller pusher propellers at the trailing edge of the wing. The general arrangement of Mozhaiski's design is shown in Figure 3.10.

FIGURE 3.10
The second flying machine
to make a powered hop,
Mozhaiski's aircraft,
Russia, 1884.

In 1884, with I. N. Golubev as the pilot, Mozhaiski's flying machine was launched down an inclined ramp at Krasnoye Selo, near St. Petersburg, Russia. Building momentum, it became airborne for a distance of about 80 feet. In the 20th century Communist Soviet Union, this flight was heralded as the first successful airplane flight. In the Russian book *Meet Aerospace Vehicles* (by N. Zhemechughin et al., Mir Publishers, Moscow, 1974) we find the following statement: "A. Mozharsky (sic) is rightly claimed to have created the world's first aeroplane. . . . This was the world's first successful flight of an aeroplane." This claim is not accepted by most historians of technology. In his book *The World's First Aeroplane Flights* (1965), the dean of historians of aeronautics, C. H. Gibbs-Smith, states the following criteria used by aviation historians to judge a successful powered flight:

> In order to qualify for having made a simple powered and sustained flight, a conventional aeroplane should have sustained itself freely in a horizontal or rising flight path—without loss of airspeed—beyond a point where it could be influenced by any momentum built up before it left the ground: otherwise its performance can only be rated as a powered leap, i.e., it will not have made a fully self-propelled flight, but will only have followed a ballistic trajectory modified by the thrust of its propeller and by the aerodynamic forces acting upon its aerofoils. Furthermore, it must be shown that the machine can be kept in satisfactory equilibrium. Simple sustained flight obviously need not include full controllability, but the maintenance of adequate equilibrium in flight is part and parcel of sustentation.

On this basis, Mozhaiski's flying machine accomplished the second powered hop in history; neither his machine nor that of du Temple before him satisfied the described criteria for a successful piloted flight. After his attempt in 1884, Mozhaiski bowed out of the flying machine arena.

INHERENT STABILITY—ALPHONSE PENAUD

Alphonse Penaud was a particularly tragic figure in 19th century aeronautics—an engineer with a very promising future in the design of flying machines, which

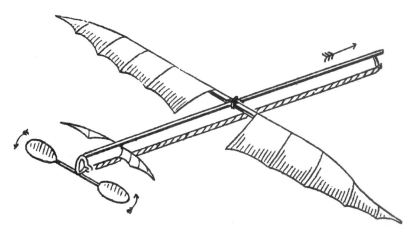

FIGURE 3.11
Penaud's planophore,
1871, as sketched by
Octave Chanute in 1894.

abruptly came to a premature end. Born in Paris in 1850 as the son of a French admiral, Penaud had a serious hip disease that prevented him from following his father into the Navy. Instead, he obtained an excellent engineering education and at an early age devoted himself to aeronautics. Penaud studied the design features that would ensure the inherent stability of a flying machine—features that would tend to restore the machine to equilibrium flight after being disturbed by an eddy or gust in the atmosphere. George Cayley was also concerned with this matter, but Penaud was not aware of Cayley's work until much later in his short career.

In 1871 Penaud built a small rubber-powered aircraft, which he called a "planophore," shown in Figure 3.11. Weighing only 0.56 ounces with a wing surface of 0.53 square feet and a wing span of 18 inches, the planophore was exhibited in August 1871 to members of the French Society of Aerial Navigation in the Jardin des Tuileries in Paris. The planophore had a main wing forward, a horizontal tail at the rear, and a pusher propeller driven by twisted strands of rubber that stretched almost the entire length of the sticklike fuselage. The wings had dihedral for lateral stability. The model flew for 131 feet, staying in the air for 11 seconds with 240 turns of the rubber. This may not seem particularly spectacular, but of most importance was that Penaud had set the horizontal tail at a negative incidence angle of −8 degrees relative to the chord line of the wing. This is in contrast to Cayley's 1804 glider, which had a positive incidence angle relative to the chord of the wing, as seen in Figure 3.1. We know today that a *negative* tail setting angle for a rear-mounted tail is necessary for the longitudinal balance of an airplane, and most airplane designs throughout the 20th century have such a negative tail incidence angle. Penaud is responsible for this design breakthrough. He located the wing such that its center of pressure (the point in the wing through which the lift force on the wing effectively acts) is behind the center of gravity of the whole machine. Penaud knew that the wing lift must act behind the center of gravity to have longitudinal stability, again a design feature that is present on all modern statically stable airplanes. By itself, this would cause the nose of the airplane to pitch down. But the negative tail setting angle results in a downward lift on the tail, which tends to pitch the nose up. These two effects—the pitching down of the nose due to the wing lift being behind the center of gravity and the pitching up of the nose due to the download on the tail—compensate each other, and the equilibrium is maintained.

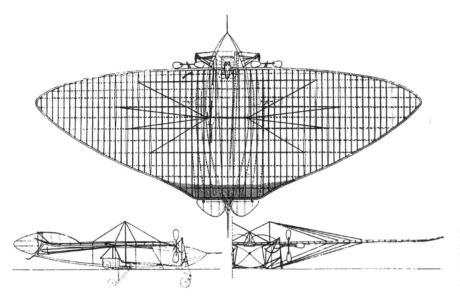

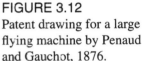

FIGURE 3.12
Patent drawing for a large flying machine by Penaud and Gauchot, 1876.

This fundamental understanding of the design criteria for longitudinal stability and balance was Penaud's major contribution to aeronautics. Referring back to Cayley's 1804 glider shown in Figure 3.1, with its rather large positive tail setting angle necessitated by the extreme forward location of the wing with the center of gravity behind the center of pressure of the wing, we see that Cayley had really gotten it wrong in this case. His glider flew to his satisfaction, but it was basically a longitudinally unbalanced airplane. Penaud set the standard and provided the fundamental understanding of what was necessary for stability and balance that we use today. Moreover, Penaud worked out both the theory and the practice of stability. Because of this, Penaud is credited as one of the aeronautical giants—ranking with Cayley and the Wrights.

With the assistance of his mechanic Paul Sauehot, Penaud went on to design a large, full-size flying machine, which was patented in 1876; the patent drawing is shown in Figure 3.12. This machine embodied all of Penaud's ideas for the airplane of the future. It was a two-seat monoplane with two tractor propellers, which rotated in opposite directions to cancel the torque effect of each. (When the engine of an airplane applies torque to rotate a propeller in one direction, there is an equal and opposite reaction that acts to rotate the airplane in the opposite direction. This is the torque effect.) The wings had an elliptical planform. (Penaud had no way of knowing, but modern 20th-century wing theory shows that an elliptic planform results in optimum aerodynamic efficiency, more lift and less drag, than other planform shapes.) The airfoil sections of the wing were cambered. The wings had a small dihedral angle of 2 degrees for lateral stability. Two elevators and a fixed vertical fin with an attached vertical rudder were placed at the rear. The cockpit had a glass dome, a single control column to operate the elevators and rudder, and instruments such as a compass, a level, and a barometer (for measuring altitude). Penaud included retractable landing gear with shock absorbers and a tail skid. This could almost be a description of a modern airplane. Moreover, the machine was designed as an amphibian, because Penaud felt that any full-scale flight experiments should be conducted over water. Finally, the estimated weight of the

Penaud–Gauchot machine including two aviators was 2640 pounds (which looks like a figure reflecting more preciseness than actually was attainable at that time). Penaud had calculated that it would require 20–30 horsepower to fly the machine at 60 miles per hour, and that the angle of attack of the wings to the airflow would be about 2 degrees at that flight condition. This results in a power loading of 88 pounds per horsepower, from which we conclude that the flying machine would have been much underpowered, similar to the situation of Henson's Aerial Steam Carriage.

Penaud never had the chance to try to fly his machine. He was unsuccessful in finding the funds to construct it. Moreover, he was criticized and decried for his efforts. This is an important point. The general public in the 19th century felt that efforts to build a heavier-than-air piloted flying machine were shear lunacy. Only madmen would try such a thing. Serious investigators and inventors had to deal with this public attitude in addition to facing the tremendous technical challenges of flight. This extreme negative public attitude is a recurring theme that haunted all of the major contributors to powered flight through the 19th century, coming to an abrupt end only with the proven success of the Wright brothers.

Discouraged, depressed, and in ill health, Alphonse Penaud lost all hope and committed suicide in October 1880 at the relatively young age of 30. He had, however, made his mark in aeronautics. His work did not die with him; on the contrary, it became widely known and continued to influence other inventors into the 20th century. Unlike Cayley's work, which for unexplainable reasons had became obscure by the 1870s, Penaud's work was well known by all investigators after him. There is some irony in the fact that, until late in his life, Penaud was not aware of Cayley's work and, hence, repeated some of it, but later was responsible for a revival of interest in Cayley and his work. Ultimately, Penaud held Cayley in great admiration and reestablished Cayley's reputation in the minds of future investigators.

The tragic, premature end of Penaud's life was an interruption to the road to success in 19th century aeronautics. He was in many respects an aeronautical genius, who may have catalyzed, or even himself achieved, successful powered flight before the Wright brothers. We will, of course, never know.

THE GREAT DIVIDE—ACADEMIC RESEARCHERS AND WOULD-BE INVENTORS OF THE FLYING MACHINE

Today, aeronautics researchers in the academic community, researchers in government laboratories, and designers in the aerospace industry are literally wired together for the instant exchange of technical information. Each feeds on the others. New technical developments can be flashed on the internet and through e-mail, technical papers describing recent progress are given at meetings of the American Institute of Aeronautics and Astronautics (AIAA) and the Royal Aeronautical Society, among others, and archival journals recording peer-reviewed research abound in libraries around the world. Moreover, there is a dialogue between researchers and designers. We take the modern environment almost for granted. It was not always this way, however. The environment in the 19th century in regard to the technology transfer between academic researchers in aerodynamics and would-be designers of flying machines was diametrically opposite to that which prevails today.

The scientific revolution in the 17th and 18th centuries provided stunning advances in the mathematical analysis and experimental understanding of classical physics. In particular, the understanding of force and its effect on the movement of objects finally came into focus with the work of Newton. In the 19th century, Newtonian physics became so well developed that there was a feeling within the academic science community that almost everything was understood. This perceived well-developed state also pertained to the science of fluid dynamics—the study of the motion of liquids and gases. Along with these developments, a basic understanding of aerodynamics evolved which, had there been an interest among academicians in applying this knowledge to flying machines, might have expedited the development of the successful airplane. That did not happen, however, for reasons now discussed.

First, let us survey the state of the art of the science of fluid dynamics and aerodynamics in the 19th century. Four pivotal advances had been achieved in the intellectual understanding of fluid dynamics, as follows:

1) Daniel Bernoulli (1700–1782) at the St. Petersburg Academy in Russia had experimented with the relation between velocity and pressure in a fluid and pointed out that, in a given flowfield, as the fluid velocity increases its pressure decreases and vice versa. Although he gallantly tried, Bernoulli was never able to precisely quantify this effect, today called the "Bernoulli principle." This was left to his friend and colleague, Leonhard Euler (1707–1783), also in St. Petersburg, who used the principles of the newly developed calculus to derive *Bernoulli's equation*,

$$p + \tfrac{1}{2}\rho V^2 = \text{constant}$$

where p denotes pressure, ρ the density of the fluid, and V the velocity. Clearly from this equation, as V increases, p must decrease for the sum of the two terms to remain constant. Bernoulli's equation is perhaps the most famous equation from classical fluid dynamics. Today, we use the Bernoulli principle to explain the source of lift on a wing.

2) When a fluid (liquid or gas) moves over a body or through a duct of some shape, a field of flow is established, where the pressure, velocity, and density take on different values at different spatial locations throughout the flow. The quantitative values of these flowfield variables must obey the basic laws of physics, namely, mass conservation (mass can be neither created nor destroyed), Newton's second law (force equals mass times acceleration), and energy conservation. Mathematically, these laws are expressed for a flow in the form of some elegant and complex partial differential equations called the Navier–Stokes equations. In principle, the solution of these equations yields the variation of the flowfield variables as a function of spatial location and time. These equations have terms in them that account for internal friction within the flow. They were first derived by Claude Louis Marie Henri Navier (1785–1836) in 1822 at the Ecole des Ponts et Chaussees in France. Quite independently, and without the knowledge of Navier's work, in 1845 Sir George Stokes (1819–1903) at Cambridge University in England obtained the same equations. Because of the dual ownership of these equations, they are called the *Navier–Stokes* equations. Formulating these equations is one thing; however, solving them is quite another. The Navier–Stokes equations are a

system of nonlinear, coupled partial differential equations that are exceptionally difficult to solve. Nevertheless, before the mid-19th century, the complete governing equations for a fluid flow were known and available to those people who understood them.

3) Because of the difficulty in finding solutions to the Navier–Stokes equations, efforts were made by mathematicians and scientists to find other, more simplified means of predicting the motion of fluids. Such an "end run" was introduced by the famous German physicist Hermann von Helmholtz (1821–1894). Helmholtz introduced the concept of vorticity and studied the shedding and propagation of vortices in a fluid flow. This rather esoteric-sounding concept provided a new approach for fluid dynamicists to calculate the flow of a fluid. Although not applicable in all cases, this vortex theory expanded the repertoire of fluid dynamicists and formed the basis for the stunning breakthrough in the calculation of lift—the circulation theory of lift, which appeared in 1906.

4) If you were to take this book and give it a shove over a table top, the book would slide a certain distance and then come to a stop. Why does it come to a stop? The answer is friction between the surface of the book and the surface of the table. The same type of frictional force acts between a fluid moving over a solid surface and the surface itself. The surface friction tends to retard the motion of the fluid, and in turn, the fluid exerts a frictional tugging force on the surface in the direction of the fluid motion. The importance of this friction force as a contributor to the aerodynamic drag on a body moving through the air was totally lost on most investigators in the 19th century. And even if they had realized the significance of this friction drag, they had no way of theoretically predicting its magnitude. However, an intellectual breakthrough in the eventual understanding of such matters occurred in the late 19th century. Osborne Reynolds (1842–1912), a professor at Owens College (later to become the University of Manchester) in England, performed some dramatic experiments in 1883 that identified two types of flow under the influence of friction: laminar flow, where the streamlines were smooth and regular, and turbulent flow, where the streamlines were tortuous and irregular. Reynolds studied the conditions under which an initially laminar flow would become turbulent. Because the frictional force due to a turbulent flow is much greater than that for a laminar flow, the transition from laminar to turbulent flow is of vital interest to aerodynamicists. Moreover, Reynolds established a theoretical basis for the analysis of turbulent flow that is still in use today.

Hence, we see that the academic community was busy in the 19th century developing the science of fluid dynamics to a rather mature state. However, these same academicians had no interest in helping to transfer this technology to the development of flying machines. Indeed, these scientists, and most of the general public as well, considered those individuals attempting to invent flying machines as madmen wasting their time. Working on flying machines was not a popular endeavor in the 19th century. Such an attitude is reflected by a comment from the famous English scientist, Lord Kelvin, who stated, "I have not the smallest molecule of faith in aerial navigation other than ballooning." Kelvin was simply expressing the prevailing opinion on the matter.

Moreover, there was a cultural difference between the two communities. The science of fluid dynamics was being developed by university-educated scholars who carried out their work predominately in the academic world. Efforts to design flying machines were being made by people who were not university educated, but who were self-educated and, frequently, like George Cayley, well read and knowledgeable. Therefore, a great divide existed between these two communities. The technology of early flight owes practically nothing to the relatively mature state of the science of fluid dynamics in the 19th century. Rather, flying machine technology advanced along different paths, as we will see.

THE AERONAUTICAL SOCIETY OF GREAT BRITAIN

The group of would-be inventors of flying machines felt disfranchised from the established scientific community. By the middle of the 19th century, this became a more serious problem to these inventors, who were becoming larger in number. It was time to band together in a more formal and professional sense. This group of self-educated men, whether they knew it or not, were beginning to establish a new profession—that of aeronautical engineering. And they needed some professional identity. That came with the formation of the Aeronautical Society of Great Britain in 1866.

In the development of any aspect of science and technology, *technical credibility* is essential. Today, such credibility in any discipline is established by an intricate mechanism of peer evaluation, widespread publishing in technical journals and books, and dynamic interaction among various scientists and engineers via the many technical conferences around the world, the telephone, video, etc. This type of mechanism was first formalized in 1662, when the Royal Society of London was incorporated under a royal charter, becoming the first formal learned society in science. The Royal Society was formed for the reading and publishing of scientific papers, for the interchange of ideas among scientists, and for the recognition of excellence.

Therefore, it is no surprise that the growing number of enthusiasts in powered flight would eventually lead to the founding of a technical society for the purpose of formally exchanging ideas and publishing papers on aeronautics. The first of these was the Societe Aerostatique et Meteorologique de France, founded in Paris in 1852. The second, and by far the most important, was the Aeronautical Society of Great Britain, founded in London in 1866. The first meeting of the council of the society was held at the residence of the Duke of Argyll on January 12, 1866. The purpose of the society, in the first official words of the society published by its first Honorary Secretary, Fred W. Brearey, is as follows:

> Before proceeding to the reading of papers, which it is the object of this meeting to encourage and discuss, it is necessary to claim on behalf of the Council perfect immunity in respect of any complicity with the views of their respective authors. It cannot be too often repeated that the Council, as a body, *has no theories of its own....* The Aeronautical Society of Great Britain has been formed to encourage, to observe, to record, and to aid, in proportion as its ability is strengthened by the support of its members.

With the formation of the Aeronautical Society of Great Britain, a formal mechanism for the establishment of technical credibility in aeronautics was finally in place. Here was living proof that the technical aspects of aeronautics were becoming a more accepted field of endeavor. The technical prestige associated with investigations in aeronautics, however, was at first slow in coming. Witness the following quote from the society's fifth annual report in 1870:

> Now let us consider the nature of the mud in which I have said we are stuck. The cause of our standstill, briefly stated, seems to be this: men do not consider the subject of "aerostation" or "aviation" to be a real science, but bring forward wild, impracticable, unmechanical, and unmathematical schemes, wasting the time of the Society, and causing us to be looked upon as a laughing stock by an incredulous and skeptical public.

One of the most interesting of the early papers to be published by the society came in the first year of its existence. The paper was entitled "On Aerial Locomotion and the Laws by Which Heavy Bodies Impelled through Air are Sustained" by Francis H. Wenham. Delivered on June 27, 1866, and published in the first annual report, this was indeed the first technical paper to be given under the aegis of the Society. Wenham's paper contained a statement. From extensive studies of the flight of birds, he noted, "It may be remarked that the swiftest—flying birds possess extremely long and <u>narrow</u> wings and the slow, heavy flyers short and wide ones." The underline in the preceding quote is Wenham's. From this, he went on to suppose that the wings of flying machines should be long and narrow. This was the first time in history where the advantage of a high aspect ratio wing for a flying machine was recognized, although, as we noted earlier, Henson's Aerial Steam Carriage was designed with a rather large aspect ratio for its time and Benjamin Robins had measured lower drag for higher aspect ratio flat plates. Today, we understand the scientific reasons for the aerodynamic advantages of high aspect ratio wings for subsonic flight. In 1866, Wenham and everybody else did not even have a clue. The advantage is related to induced drag, a concept that was not understood until 1918. In any event, Wenham theorized (correctly) that most of the lift on a wing at moderate angle of attack comes from the front portion of the wing. It follows, he said, that the most efficient wing configuration would be that of a number of long, narrow wings superimposed above each other—a multiwing concept. (This design feature, a large number of venetian-blind shaped wings stacked above each other, in four tandem decks, was actually used by Horatio Phillips in an actual airplane in 1908. The flight was successful; Phillips was airborne for approximately 500 feet. Of course, by that time the Wright brothers had triumphed, and Phillips's airplane was nothing but a curious footnote in history.)

So this is how the technical tradition of the Aeronautical Society of Great Britain started—with a pioneering paper by Francis H. Wenham wherein the advantage of high aspect ratio wings was set forth. An interesting indication of the level of technical sophistication (or, really the lack of it) that existed in aerodynamics at that time is dramatically evident in Wenham's 1866 paper—there are absolutely *no* equations of any sort in the paper. Applied aerodynamics, as a *quantitative* engineering science, had a long way to go.

The society did more than present and discuss papers. In 1868, just two years after its founding, the Aeronautical Society of Great Britain organized the first aeronautical exhibition in history—a display of flying machines and balloons at the famous Crystal Palace in London. Outside of the steam-powered model by John Stringfellow discussed earlier, the exhibition was an odd collection of unsuccessful artifacts. However, the importance of the exhibition was its very existence—the fact that the development of flying machines was taking on an enhanced status, spearheaded by the society itself.

An interesting comment on the role of advanced engineering research can be found in the third annual report of the society in 1868. The Duke of Argyll is discussing some aspects of aeronautical propulsion, as follows:

> The steam engine at the present day represents the greatest force to be obtained as yet. It is, however, not only a very heavy cumbrous, metallic body in itself, but it requires a large supply of water and fuel to enable it to do its work; these are additional heavy bodies, and the combined weight of the machine altogether precludes the hope that an engine can be so made as to raise or move itself in the air. <u>Still, the absence of the lighter motive power required ought not to stop us from investigating the principle upon which it is to be applied.</u>

The underlined sentence is a call for investigations of the principles of flight, even though a tacit recognition is made that an engine does not exist that could successfully power a flying machine. This is an early recognition of the value of engineering research, which is to provide fundamental information on physical principles, even though an application of these principles is not yet at hand.

Another interesting statement, quite prophetic, is found in the third annual report, namely, that "a large machine is more likely to succeed than a model." This statement was based on data that showed the "effect produced on one area will not be produced on another." This is a precursor to what today is called *scale effects* in aerodynamics. An example of the scale effects is that the friction drag on a small model is a much larger percentage of total drag than it is for the full-size airplane. Because airplane designers want to reduce the effect of friction drag on their airplanes, then the larger the airplane, the better. This is consistent with the preceding statement from the third annual report. It is, to the author's knowledge, the first statement in history of scale effects in aerodynamics.

Also found in the third annual report are statements by both Wenham and Stringfellow that the airscrew is the "best method of propelling through the air." This is in spite of the fact that no real experience had proven this. The writings of the society at this time are peppered with debates as to which is the best mechanism, a propeller or a beating wing, for propulsion. In regard to an engine to power the airscrew (propeller), the statement was made that "steam was, undoubtedly, the most economical, but in their present state, *gas* would answer better." Here, "gas" did not mean gasoline but rather literally an engine run by some type of hot gas such as might be formed from carbonic acid. Cayley had pursued a similar line of thinking.

The technical frustration felt by members of the society is summed in the following excerpt from the third annual report, which certainly reflects the state of the art in 1868:

> With respect to the abstruse question of mechanical flight, it may be stated that we are still ignorant of the rudimentary principles which should form the basis and rules for construction. No one has yet ventured to give a correct experimental definition of the primary laws and amount of power consumed in the flight of birds; neither, on the other hand, has any tangible evidence been brought forward to show that mechanical flight is an impossibility for man. . . . We are equally ignorant of the force of the wind exerted on surfaces of various sizes, forms, and degrees of inclinations: these are

generally <u>assumed</u> on the mathematical laws of the resolutions of forces, considered as the rigid impulse of inelastic weight and matter, and demonstrated by the aid of diagrams combined with a systems of weights, cords, and pulleys, which convey but a very distant idea, relative to the conditions of the present inquiry, where the elastic and yielding nature of the air is the cause of such unforeseen results, differing in according to the width, form, angle, and speed of the surface of impact.

Here, the mysteries associated with aerodynamics are riding high, and frustration is rampant.

This is not to say that optimism did not exist. In a paper delivered in Paris by De Lucy, translated and printed by the society, we find the following quote: "Science is ripe, industry is ready, everybody is in expectation; the hour of aerial locomotion will soon arrive." Little did De Lucy know that it would take another 34 years until the "arrival." In the meantime, the collective group of nascent aeronautical engineers, as typified by the members of the Aeronautical Society of Great Britain, would continue to press on toward their goal.

THE INVENTION OF THE WIND TUNNEL

Francis Wenham's 1866 paper to the Aeronautical Society of Great Britain, in which he theorized that long, narrow (high aspect ratio) wings were preferable for aerodynamic efficiency, was just the beginning of his contributions to the technology of early flight. Wenham followed his 1866 paper with other lectures, as well as frequent comments on, and criticisms of, the work of others presented to the society. On April 17, 1867, Wenham made a statement that serves as a rather definitive assessment of the state of the art at that time:

> Our knowledge of Aeronautics, as far as regards the navigation of the air by mechanical means, amounts to but very little, and the information recorded is of a contradictory character . . . without a definite law of the acting and counteracting forces of the elastic air, we have not even entered the threshold of aeronautical discovery, and attempts at obtaining mechanical flight cannot be foreseen in their results.

Wenham is clearly venting a sense of frustration on this state of affairs. However, this statement is followed by an intended course of action, as follows:

> In the present state of inquiry, a series of experiments is much needed, in order to furnish the data for construction. Should these establish the law of the capability of an atmospheric stratum for supporting heavy weights by means of very slightly inclined surfaces traveling at high speeds, we shall then have a certain fact to start from, and let it be borne in mind that the air as a means of transit has in one respect an unequaled advantage, that of a ready made highway, without hills, turnings, or irregularities to damage or break machinery; consequently, the only limit on speed is not in safety, but the amount of propelling force that can be applied.

Here we have Wenham appealing to his natural tendency to resolve technical questions by experiment. In fact, his next statement is "I propose shortly to try a series of experiments by the aid of an artificial current of air of known strength, and to place the Society in possession of the results."

This statement was a harbinger of the development, by Wenham, of the first wind tunnel in the history of aeronautical engineering. Its development was further encouraged at the May 1870 meeting of the council, where the absence of data on "reactions and lifting forces" was duly noted, as well as that experiments to obtain such data might not be very difficult. By June, the aeronautical society formed a committee for acquiring experimental data consisting of four reputable engineers, including Wenham, and funds were raised to carry out this objective. Wenham designed the experimental device—a long, rectangular 10-foot duct, with a square cross section 18 inches on a side. The air was driven through this duct by a fan powered by a steam engine. The fan was mounted at the front of the straight duct, and the air was simply pushed through the duct by means of the momentum from the fan. The actual device was fabricated by John Browning, an optician and a member of the society. The wind tunnel was located at Penn's Marine Engineering Works at Greenwich, England. The first wind-tunnel experiments in the world took place in a shadow of the famous Greenwich Observatory—somehow a fitting venue for an experimental aerodynamic device which, in more modern versions, would later become the very lifeblood of aeronautical progress in the 20th century.

By modern standards, the performance of Wenham's wind tunnel left much to be desired. The maximum velocity was only 40 miles per hour, and the airstream was considerably unsteady, making accurate and repeatable measurements virtually impossible. Even the mean direction of the airstream was in question because no vanes for guiding the air were used. The device was a straight, constant-area, rectangular duct; no convergent section resembling a nozzle was employed. Unfortunately, no contemporary sketch or picture of this first tunnel exists. The test model (a planar lifting surface at some angle of attack to the airstream) was mounted on a crude balance, and lift and drag were measured by vertical and horizontal springs. The "test section" of the tunnel was a region in the open air 2 feet downstream of the duct exit; today we call this type of wind tunnel an "open jet" facility. The largest of the flat plate lifting surfaces spanned 18 inches—the full width of the wind tunnel. The angle of attack ranged from 15 to 60 degrees. Wenham strongly (and properly) wanted to obtain data at lower angles of attack than 15 degrees, but the aerodynamic force at low angle of attack was too small to be measured accurately by the rather crude balance.

Despite these difficulties, the wind-tunnel results, being the first of their kind, were welcomed by the members of the society. The experimental data showed that meaningful lift was created at low angle of attack and that the lift was considerably larger than the accompanying drag. In this sense, Wenham confirmed the earlier whirling arm results of George Cayley, which seem to have retreated into obscurity by the time of Wenham's work. Wenham proved that lift-to-drag ratios considerably greater than one can be achieved. This was great and profound news for the aeronautical community.

CAMBERED AIRFOILS—HORATIO PHILLIPS

In the audience listening to Francis Wenham's report to the society on his wind-tunnel experiments was a young man from Streatham, a suburb of London; Horatio F. Phillips, at the impressionable age of 27, was not impressed. He was dissatisfied with the quality of the flow in Wenham's wind tunnel and with the total use by Wenham of *flat* lifting surfaces. Phillips, in the early 1880s, took the initiative to do better and designed and operated the second wind tunnel in history. A drawing of Phillips's wind tunnel is given in Figure 3.13, which from left to right

FIGURE 3.13
Phillips's sketch of his
wind tunnel showing, from
left to right, cross-
sectional views from the
front and side, 1884.

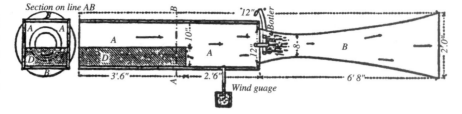

shows cross-sectional views from the front and side, respectively. Phillips was much concerned with the flow imperfections in Wenham's tunnel. In an effort to avoid flow fluctuations, Phillips choose a steam injector as a means to suck in air through the entrance of the wind tunnel. He may have been inspired by railway engines, where a jet of steam was sometimes used to drive air up the funnel to create a draft for the firebox. As shown in Figure 3.13, the injector was located in the exact center of the wind tunnel. In Figure 3.13, the flow direction is from left to right. To the left of the injector was a rectangular box with a 6-foot length and a square cross section 17 inches on each side. Mounted inside the rectangular section was a large block of wood (D in Figure 3.13), which reduced the flow area; hence, the region above block D represented a type of "throat region," where the flow velocity was a maximum value—up to 60 feet per second (about 41 miles per hour). It was in this region where the aerodynamic test model was mounted. The steam injector itself was a ring of iron pipe perforated with a number of holes facing in the downstream direction (toward the right in Figure 3.13). Steam from a large Lanchashire boiler (32 feet long and 7 feet in diameter) at a pressure of 70 pounds per square inch expanded at high speed through the holes in the injector ring, entraining the surrounding airflow and creating a local region of low pressure in the center of the tunnel, which in turn sucked air into the entrance of the tunnel at the left. Both the air and expanded steam then exhausted at the right through a circular duct labeled B in Figure 3.13. Although not perfect, the steam injector produced an airflow through the test section of better quality than in Wenham's tunnel. [It is interesting to note that Phillips's use of a steam injector to drive his wind tunnel was certainly an innovative idea for that time. Although the number and use of wind tunnels proliferated in the 20th century, none of those facilities were driven by an injector until the National Advisory Committee for Aeronautics (NACA) at the Langley Memorial Aeronautical Laboratory in 1928 jury-rigged an 11-inch high-speed wind tunnel driven by an annular injector downstream of the test section. Air (not steam) blasted through this annular injector, where the source of air through the injector was the high-pressure exhaust from another wind tunnel, the NACA variable density wind tunnel. The air velocity in the 11-inch high-speed tunnel was near Mach one, providing NACA with its first wind tunnel for transonic testing. The use of an injector in this case was a means to an end, namely, the piggybacking of a new facility on the hardware of an older facility. For the most part, injectors are not used as the *main* drive for modern wind tunnels, although some supersonic and hypersonic tunnels use air injectors at the diffuser entrance to enhance diffuser performance.]

Although the development of the second wind tunnel in history, especially a much improved facility over the first, would have established Phillips's name in the annals of aeronautical history, his main contribution to the advancement of aeronautics was the results he obtained by using the tunnel. Unhappy with

Wenham's use of flat plate lifting surfaces, Phillips experimented with cambered (curved) airfoils. Inspired by the shape of bird wings, Phillips designed a series of cambered airfoils with greater curvature over the top than on the bottom—so-called "double-surface" airfoils. Several of these airfoils shapes are shown in Figure 3.14. Phillips measured the aerodynamic performance of these airfoils in his wind tunnel and compared it with that of a flat plate also tested in the same tunnel. The results were dramatic—*the cambered airfoils were considerably more efficient lifting shapes than a flat plate*. Phillips clearly recognized the significance of his work because he obtained a patent for the six airfoil shapes shown in Figure 3.14. The patent was granted in 1884—one year *before* Phillips published his results for all to see in the journal *Engineering*. (Phillips was obviously covering his bases.) These cambered airfoils were the first modern airfoils in the history of aerodynamics. Moreover, the rationale used by Phillips for the basic design principle was sound. He properly recognized that when the flow moved over the curved upper surface of the airfoil the pressure decreased; hence, the lifting action of the airfoil is due to a *combination* of the lower pressure exerted on the upper surface and the higher pressure exerted on the lower surface. Although George Cayley had also alluded to this fact, the prevailing intuition throughout most of the 19th century was that the lifting action of an inclined plane moving through the air was due to the "impact" of air on the lower surface—a mental picture wrongly reinforced by the Newtonian flow model. Phillips, by designing double-surface airfoils, with more curvature over the top than the bottom, was qualitatively trying to encourage the formation of low pressure on the top surface, hence taking advantage of this fact to obtain a more efficient airfoil. Phillips's results were widely disseminated, and all serious flying machine developers after him used cambered airfoils.

Phillips is best known for the development of the second wind tunnel in history and for his design and testing of cambered airfoils. However, he later became a developer of flying machines himself. In 1893, he constructed a large device consisting of 50 wings, each with a span of 19 feet and a chord of 1.5 inches—an ungodly high aspect ratio of 152! (Phillips had clearly adopted Wenham's philosophy of wing design.) The wings were arrayed vertically above a long, cigar-shaped fuselage; the machine, shown in Figure 3.15, resembled a huge

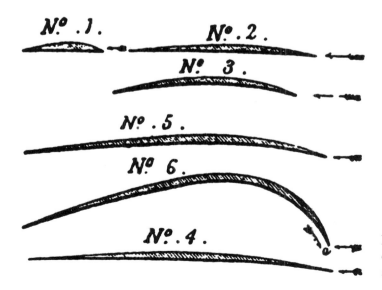

FIGURE 3.14
Phillips's patent sketches of his cambered-airfoil shapes, 1884.

FIGURE 3.15
Phillips's 1893 flying machine.

venetian blind. Powered by a 6-horsepower steam engine connected to a single pusher propeller, this unmanned flying machine lifted a total weight of 385 pounds at a speed of 40 miles per hour, tethered to move in a circular track with a 628-foot circumference. On the basis of this tethered flight experiment, Phillips felt that the viability of cambered airfoils had been established, and he halted his testing until the turn of the 20th century. His last sojourn into flight was in 1907, when he actually became airborne for about 500 feet in a larger derivative of his 1893 "venetian blind." This machine had four venetian blinds in tandem, powered by a 22-horsepower engine with a tractor propeller. This final culmination of his work, however, was somewhat anticlimatic in light of the success of the Wright brothers four years earlier. After this, Phillips dropped completely from the aeronautical scene. He died in Streatham in 1924, having witnessed the explosive growth of aviation during World War I.

GIGANTIC FLYING MACHINE—HIRAM MAXIM

The 19th century witnessed some success in advancing the technology of flight—the first wind tunnel, the cambered airfoil, and a mechanism of dissemination of information through the Aeronautical Society of Great Britain. During this same time, however, would-be inventors of the flying machine continued the tradition of failure in getting off the ground. Although the intellectual understanding of aeronautics was beginning to take off, real flying machines were not.

But people were getting closer to success. In England, on July 31, 1894, a new flight record was set by a huge 8000-pound flying machine designed and built by Hiram Maxim, which had a sustained flight covering a distance of about 400 feet in the air, *at an altitude of 2 feet*. What was this all about?

Hiram Maxim was born in 1840, in Sangerville, Maine. His father, Isaac Maxim, was a pioneer farmer. As Maxim later wrote, he grew up as "a poor little bare-headed, bare-footed boy with a pair of drill trousers, frayed out at the bottom, open at the knees, with a patch on the bottom, running wild but very expert on catching fish." Maxim had limited schooling and at the age of 14 went to work for a carriage maker, where he acquired mechanical skills. At the age of 20, he entered the engineering works at Fitchburg, Massachusetts, run by his uncle. Maxim's competence soon led him to make design changes on gas machines made by the company, improving their efficiency. Five years later, he became a draftsman in the gas machine factory of Oliver P. Drake in Boston. Maxim's star rapidly ascended. By 1873, he was senior partner in the firm of Maxim and Welch, builders of gas and steam engines in New York City. In 1878, he helped establish the United States Electric Lighting Company and was appointed chief engineer. In that same year, he obtained the first of his patents dealing with electricity, on "Improvements in Electric Lamps." Clearly, Maxim had joined the ranks of those self-educated inventors who were beginning to constitute the core of the profession of engineering.

On the 14th of August, 1881, Maxim departed on the S.S. Germanic for England to set up the office of the Maxim–Webster Company, which represented the interests of the U.S. Lighting Company in London. He was to live the rest of his life in England. Within two years, Maxim had invented and patented the first automatic repeating gun—the first machine gun in history. The Maxim gun became famous and was used until the beginning of World War I. The machine gun brought Maxim fame and fortune. He formed the Maxim Gun Company in 1884, with the financial backing of "the best men in London," in Maxim's words, including Albert, Thomas, and Edward Vickers. This was the first time that the Vickers brothers had been involved in armaments manufacture; they were later to become a powerhouse in arms, including the design and manufacture of airplanes. Outgrowing his London premises, Maxim moved his gun works in 1888 to Crayford in Kent, England.

At this time Maxim began to work on a flying machine. Approached by several wealthy gentlemen who asked him if it was possible to make such a machine, Maxim took his usual "I can do anything" attitude and presented a very positive outlook. His response was, "Certainly; the domestic goose is able to fly and why not man be able to do as well as the goose." He estimated that it would take him five years at an estimated cost of 100,000 English pounds to accomplish this feat. Rising to the challenge, Maxim rented a large open space, Baldwyns Park at Kent, and hired two skilled American mechanics, built a large hanger, and started to work on building a flying machine.

Maxim was not happy with the prevailing theoretical approaches to flying machine design, and he certainly was no supporter of the academicians who were developing the sometimes rather esoteric science of fluid mechanics. In 1908, in his book *Natural and Artificial Flight*, he reflected his desire for engineering simplicity and wrote, "What is required by experimenters in flying machines—and there will soon be a great number of them—is a treatise which they can understand, and which required no more delicate instruments than a carpenter's two foot rule and a grocer's scales." In the same book, he sarcastically stated his opinion of theoreticians: "I think we might put down all of their results, add them together, and divide by the number of mathematicians, and then find the average coefficient of error." Clearly, Maxim's attitude did nothing to shrink the "great divide" between academic science and the engineering of flying machines.

On the other hand, Maxim did not set out blindly to design his flying machine. He began with a series of aerodynamic tests on different airfoil and wing shapes, using both a wind tunnel and a whirling arm. Both of these facilities were large; the wind tunnel had a 3-foot square test section, and the whirling arm had a

64-foot diameter, with a wire extension that yielded a 318-foot diameter. With his whirling arm device, Maxim achieved a relative velocity through the air of 80 miles per hour using models as large as 25 square feet in planform area. From his wind-tunnel experiments, conducted in a test airstream of 40 miles per hour, he concluded that in the angle of attack range of 3–7 degrees—the range at which he expected to fly—the lift was directly proportional to the angle of attack. Today, the linear variation of lift with angle of attack, up to the stalling angle of attack at which the lift drops precipitously, is well known. Maxim was the first to explicitly point out this linear variation, although two of his contemporaries, Otto Lilienthal in Germany and Samuel Langley in the United States, were making the same observation. Maxim's single purpose for carrying out these experiments was to provide data for his flying machine. He later wrote in 1908, "When I made my experiments, I only had in mind the obtaining of current data, to enable me to build a flying machine that would lift itself from the ground." In this sense, Maxim was the first to conduct wind-tunnel tests for the explicit purpose of obtaining design data for a flying machine. (Later, the Wright brothers would conduct an extensive series of wind-tunnel experiments for the same purpose—to provide airfoil and wing data for their 1902 glider and ultimately the 1903 Wright Flyer. In comparison to Maxim's experiments, the Wrights' wind-tunnel data were much better organized, more extensive, and more focused on their design, and from this point of view, the Wrights were the first to conduct wind-tunnel tests that were actually responsible in a major way for the success of the flying machine.)

Maxim also noted the variation of aerodynamic force with velocity. Again in 1908, he wrote the following:

> I think it is quite safe to state that the lifting effect of well-made airplanes [i.e., wings], if we do not take into consideration the resistance due to the framework holding them in position increases as the square of their velocity. Double their higher speed and they give four times the lifting effect. The higher the speed, the smaller the angle of the plane, the greater the lifting effect in proportion to the power employed.

Here, Maxim is simply reiterating the velocity-squared law, first confirmed about two and one-half centuries before. He was, however, just one out of several investigators at the end of the 19th century who felt compelled to justify the velocity-squared law. The last sentence in Maxim's statement applies to an airplane in steady, level flight, where the lift must always equal the weight. As the velocity increases, to keep the lift from exceeding the weight, the airplane must fly at a smaller angle of attack, which is precisely what Maxim is saying.

Maxim conducted propeller tests, experimenting with the influence of blade pitch, shape, and size. His comment on the *location* of the propeller on the airplane is interesting: "What is true of ships is true of flying machines. Good results can never be obtained by placing the screw in front instead of in the rear of the machine. If the screw is in front the backwash strikes the machine and certainly has a decidedly retarding action." Maxim's logic was flawed; most propeller-driven airplanes designed in the 20th century have the propellers in front (the tractor configuration) rather than in the back (the pusher configuration). Maxim used the pusher configuration for his flying machine. So did the Wright brothers a decade later.

FIGURE 3.16
Hirman Maxim and his
large flying machine,
1894.

Maxim's wind-tunnel and whirling arm tests were conducted during the
period of 1889–1891. Then the design process took over. Maxim designed a huge
machine, as shown in Figure 3.16. The upper wing had a 40-foot hexagonal
section, with attached extensions that increased the wing span to 104 feet. The total
planform area of all of the horizontal surfaces was 4000 square feet. Maxim had
originally intended to use an internal combustion, gasoline-powered Otto cycle
engine, which certainly would have been an advanced feature. However, he soon
changed to steam power because steam engines were much more mature at that
time. In the final design, the boiler alone weighed 1000 pounds, and steam was fed
upward to two engines, each driving a large pusher propeller with a diameter of
17 feet, 10 inches. The propellers were made of laminated American white pine
covered with Irish linen and painted zinc white. The total power of the steam
powerplant was 362 horsepower. The weight of the flying machine was 8000
pounds, giving a power loading of 22 pounds per horsepower—a very respectable
value at that time and considerably better than the value of 62.5 pounds per
horsepower of the Wright Flyer. Maxim's machine had plenty of power to do the
job. For directional control, instead of having a rudder, Maxim used unequal thrust
between the two engines. The outer wing panels had dihedral for lateral stability.

On the field at Baldwyns Park, Maxim laid out 1800 feet of dual railway
tracks, along which the four-wheel undercarriage would run during takeoff.
Maxim's goal, however, was to demonstrate that the machine would generate
enough lift to leave the ground—and only that. He was not interested in attempting
a full-fledged, controlled, flight. Hence, he attached four extra raised wheels on
outriggers, which, if the flying machine climbed any higher than 2 feet, would
engage a wooden guard rail directly above them, keeping the machine from
climbing any higher.

Test trials began on July 31, 1894. On the third test run that day, Maxim
applied full power, and the machine took a rolling distance of only 600 feet before
it lifted off the track. The outrigger wheels engaged the upper guard rail, and the

machine and its three-man crew could not attain any higher altitude than 2 feet. At a speed of 42 miles per hour, after covering a total distance of 1000 feet along the track, one of the upper guide rails broke, and the machine lifted free for a moment "giving those on board the sensation of being in a boat." Maxim instantly shut off the steam. In settling back to the ground, the machine was damaged. Nevertheless, Maxim had demonstrated that a heavier-than-air flying machine could generate enough lift to leave the ground under its own power. The machine was repaired, and according to reports in the *Times* of London, Maxim held a public demonstration on November 3, 1894. Another flying demonstration was held in July 1895 with a visit by members of the Aeronautical Society of Great Britain. That was the last such demonstration of the Maxim flying machine. Maxim received a notice from his landlords that Baldwyns Park had been sold to the London County Council for a mental home. Also, his financial backers got cold feet, even though by this point Maxim had spent only 20,000 English pounds of the 100,000 he had originally estimated to be the cost. This was the end of Maxim's flying machine.

Maxim described himself as a "chronic inventor." He was knighted in 1901; in the same year he became involved with the development of a lightweight gasoline engine. Maxim, along with A. P. Thurston, designed a new flying machine during 1909–1910 powered by a gasoline engine. It was a pusher biplane with steel tubing and Duralumin—a new aluminum alloy—for the fuselage framework. This was perhaps the first use of Duralumin in aircraft structures. However, the airplane was of no consequence in light of the rapid developments after the Wright brothers success.

Sir Hiram Maxim worked almost to the end; he was granted two patents in 1916. On November 24, 1916, he died from bronchopneumonia at his home at Sandhurst Lodge in Streatham High Road, England. He left an estate valued at 33,000 English pounds.

There is some controversy about the extent of Maxim's contributions to the technology of early flight. On one hand, the respected aviation historian Charles H. Gibbs-Smith categorically dismisses his countryman as simply wasting time and money. He states, "Maxim's contribution to aviation was virtually nil, and he influenced nobody." On the other hand, Harald Penrose, also a respected aviation historian, in his book entitled *British Aviation: The Pioneer Years 1903–1914*, considers that Maxim should get the credit for the first successful sustained flight in England. Maxim himself, by his own admission, wanted only to build a flying machine that could generate enough lift to leave the ground. He accomplished that. In his book *Natural and Artificial Flight*, published late in 1908 after Wilbur Wright had so dramatically demonstrated the art of flying in the Wright Type A machine in France in August 1908, Sir Hiram Maxim rather arrogantly wrote this:

> It is very gratifying to me to know that all the successful flying machines of today are built on the lines which I had thought out at that time [i.e., 1893–1894], and found to be the best. All have superimposed aeroplanes [wings] of great length from port to starboard, all have fore and aft horizontal rudders, and all are driven with screw propellers . . . the fact that practically no essential departure has been made from my original lines, indicates to my mind that I had reasoned out the best type of machine even before I commenced a stroke of the work.

Maxim is really stepping out of bounds with this statement. His flying machine incorporated no new idea that had not already been put forth by Cayley,

Stringfellow, and the other early inventors discussed in this chapter, except that Maxim built a bigger and more powerful machine than ever before, and he did get off the ground. There is no evidence that the Wright brothers were influenced by any of Maxim's work.

Maxim's efforts did nothing to change the prevailing public attitude toward flying machines and their inventors. In 1894, even after taking a ride in Maxim's machine, the famous English scientist Lord Kelvin, in comments during a meeting of the British Association at Oxford, derided Maxim's machine as "a kind of child's perambulator with a sunshade magnified eight times." Lord Kelvin did not believe in the airplane. In 1896 in a letter to Aeronautical Society of Great Britain, he wrote, "I have not the smallest molecule of faith in aerial navigation other than ballooning."

Sir Hiram Maxim can best be described as a man with a powerful frame and untiring energy, bearded, square-shouldered, dynamic, highly inventive, and often grossly overbearing. In total, he had over 100 patents. Among his close friends were Rudyard Kipling and H. G. Wells. Also, Maxim and Samuel Langley, the third secretary of the Smithsonian Institution, knew each other well. As for Maxim's contributions to flight, we have to step a line between the completely negative opinion of Gibbs-Smith and the rather positive feeling of Penrose, who claimed, "with Maxim, the real prologue of England's aeroplanes commences." In this author's opinion, perhaps the best we can say about Maxim is that, without him, the flying machine community in the late 19th century would have been poorer—and we will leave it at that.

In the sense that England had Hiram Maxim, who built a flying machine that lifted off the ground under its own power, so, too, France had Clement Ader, who also built a flying machine that lifted off the ground under it own power. Ader (1841–1925) was a distinguished French electrical engineer, who, like Maxim, became interested in powered flight near the end of the 19th century. Ader's approach to the problem of flight, however, was quite different than that of Maxim. Hiram Maxim followed the more traditional design characteristics established by Cayley, Stringfellow, and Penaud and carried out an extensive series of wind-tunnel and whirling arm tests to collect design data for his machine. In contrast, although he was familiar with the existing aeronautical literature at that time, Ader carried out no organized experiments to collect design data; he patterned the design of his flying machine after the shape and flight of birds and bats.

Ader's interest in flight dates back to at least 1872, when he built a rather large ornithopter with a wing span of 26 feet and weighing 53 pounds. Octave Chanute called Ader's machine an "artificial bird." Needless to say, it was not successful. Ader's obsession with emulating birds, however, grew stronger. He obtained eagles and large bats from the zoological gardens in Paris and studied their flight in his workshop. He went to Algeria to study large vultures; disguising himself as an Arab, he traveled into the interior with two Arab guides. There he observed a number of vultures in flight, some of them with wingspans of about 10 feet.

Using these birds as his "design" base, Ader built a large flying machine that resembled a bat (Figure 3.17). Finished in 1890, this machine, called the Eole, had a wing span of about 50 feet. The Eole was a monoplane powered by a tractor propeller connected to a steam engine. Indeed, Ader had designed a very nice, lightweight, powerful steam engine producing 20 horsepower, which was by far

FIGURE 3.17
Clement Ader's flying
machine, the Eole, 1890.

the only real technical contribution made by his machine. On October 9, 1890, on
the grounds of a chateau at Armainvilliers, the Eole with Ader as the pilot rolled
along the level ground for about 90 feet, and then took off under its own power. It
sustained itself in the air for another 165 feet before touching down. This was the
first piloted, powered airplane to take off under its own power, and, therefore, Ader
deserves some credit. However, the Eole had no meaningful flight controls. There
was no elevator; instead Ader tried to reproduce mechanically as many of the
motions of a bat's wing as possible, except for propulsion. Because of this, and in
spite of the fact that the Eole got into the air under its own power, Ader and his
machine made no meaningful contribution to the technology of the airplane.

Amazingly, Ader obtained funding from the French War Ministry to build a
new and bigger airplane. He patterned the new machine, called the Avion III, after
the Eole. It had a wing span of 56 feet, weighed about 900 pounds, and was
powered by two of his excellent steam engines, each producing 20 horsepower and
each driving its own tractor propeller. The power loading of Ader's machine was
22.5 pounds per horsepower—on par with Maxim's machine and with plenty of
power to do the job. The earlier Eole had a similar power loading, and this is most
likely the only reason why it got into the air—by brute force. The Avion III was
tested only twice, on October 12th and 14th of 1897; neither test was successful.
Ader's efforts simply added to the list of failures in the 19th century.

THINGS ARE LOOKING UP—THE AERODYNAMICS AND GLIDERS OF OTTO LILIENTHAL

Otto Lilienthal's neighbors in the fashionable Berlin suburb of Gross-Lichterfield
were treated to some unusual goings-on during the year of 1888. In his garden,
Lilienthal had set up a large whirling arm with a 23-foot diameter, towering 15 feet
above the ground. In the calm, early morning hours, Otto, with the assistance of his
brother, Gustav, would crank up the whirling arm and send multitudinous model
wings with different airfoil shapes swishing through the air. During this year, the
Lilienthals carried out thousands of tests in Otto's garden. The neighbors certainly
had a new and interesting topic for conversation. But these aerodynamic
experiments were only the tip of the iceberg, coming at the end of more than
22 years of aerodynamic testing by Lilienthal in various locations in Germany.

Commencing in 1866, Otto Lilienthal carried out a protracted series of
aerodynamic measurements of the lift and drag on a variety of different-shaped
lifting surfaces, in Lilienthal's words continuing "with some long interruptions
until 1889." He used a whirling arm and, later, a device mounted outside in the
natural wind. Lilienthal published his results in a book entitled *Der Vogelflug als*

Grundlage der Fliegekunst, or *Birdflight as the Basis of Aviation*, published in 1889. This book contains by far the most coherent and useful presentation of aerodynamic data to appear in the 19th century. It was a blockbuster in advancing the technology of early flight, and everybody who was anybody in the world of flying machines read it.

The most important contribution of Lilienthal's aerodynamic experiments is that they proved beyond the shadow of a doubt the superiority of *cambered airfoils* over flat plates. Although Horatio Phillips in England had tested and patented cambered airfoils, he had not amassed a great deal of data to demonstrate their viability. Lilienthal did, and we have to give Lilienthal the credit for making cambered airfoils the norm for the successful flying machines that were to follow after the turn of the century. (Lilienthal did not find out about the Philliips airfoils until he went to file a German patent on cambered airfoils in 1889; he withdrew his patent application.)

Another seminal contribution by Lilienthal was his use of aerodynamic *coefficients* to report the aerodynamic force data measured on his test models. Rather than reporting just the raw data, the actual values of the aerodynamic force, Lilienthal divided his measured forces at various angles of attack by the force measured when the wing was at a 90-degree angle of attack—when the wing was perpendicular to the flow. These *ratios* were dimensionless values, called force *coefficients*, which vary with angle of attack. In so doing, Lilienthal's coefficients are not compromised by any uncertainty in Smeaton's coefficient and are not a function of velocity. When the aerodynamic force is reported in coefficient form, the influence of Smeaton's coefficient and velocity are simply divided out. In modern aerodynamics today, we generally deal with aerodynamic lift and drag in terms of lift and drag *coefficients* exclusively. The origin of this modern use can be traced to Lilienthal. Some of Lilienthal's data were published and disseminated widely in the form of a table of coefficients, called "the Lilienthal tables" by the Wright brothers and others. The Lilienthal tables became famous.

Lilienthal's contributions to aerodynamics were seminal, but in the bigger picture of the history of the technology of the airplane he lived a second life—as the inventor, builder, and flyer of the first practical gliders. He developed a passion for flight as early as 1861 at the age of 13, when he and his brother constructed wings, strapped them to their arms, and attempted to fly. Otto earned a degree in mechanical engineering at the Berlin Trade Academy (now the respected Technical University of Berlin) in 1870, becoming the only 19th-century flight experimenter with a college degree. He designed a compact, efficient, low-cost boiler and in 1881 opened a factory for manufacturing the boiler. This factory was his source of a rather modest income; it maintained operation until the end of World War I, well after Otto's death. During this period, he completed his aerodynamic experiments and dreamed of building flying machines. In the summer of 1889, Lilienthal built a large wing, 11 meters long with a 1.4-meter maximum chord; the planform was patterned after that of a bird's wing (including pointed wing tips). The wing sections were cambered, reflecting the basic finding of his aerodynamic experiments. An opening in the middle of the wing was large enough for a human body. Lilienthal never left the ground with this wing; he simply used it to experiment with the strength of the lifting force (noted by Lilienthal to be considerable) and on how the wing might be balanced in the natural wind. A year later, he was still conducting such tests with a slightly modified wing. Finally, in a

FIGURE 3.18
Otto Lilienthal flying one
of his gliders, 1894.

lecture to the German Society for Advancement of Airship Travel in March 1891, Lilienthal outlined a plan for flying; the title of his lecture was "On the Theory and Practice of Free Flight." In this outline, he suggested trying only short, downhill hops. By the late spring, he put his words into practice. Using a glider designed with both a wing and a tail, Lilienthal was jumping into the air for short hops in a field in Derwitz, a small farm town beyond Potsdam, Germany. By the end of the summer, he had jumped into the air more than a thousand times. (A photograph of Lilienthal flying one of his gliders is shown in Figure 3.18.) In his annual report to the Society in 1891 about these tests, Lilienthal said, "In this way I acquired the ability to glide down the gentle slopes of the hill in moderate winds and land at the foot of the hill with no accident of any kind." In this fashion, in the year 1891, Lilienthal became the first person to achieve sustained success with manned-glider flights. Later, in 1898, the French aviation pioneer Ferdinand Ferber wrote, "I conceive of the day in 1891 when Lilienthal first sliced fifteen meters through the air as the moment in which humanity learned to fly."

For the years 1892 and 1893, Lilienthal moved his glider experiments to a new practice field on Rauh Hill in Steglitz, Germany, only 20-minutes walking time from his house in Berlin. By this time his gliders had progressed through five design evolutions, each with differences in wing span, area, and planform and with some structural changes. He was limited in the design of the size of his gliders. Because Lilienthal's gliders were hang gliders, where the only mode of control was by shifting the position of his body and, hence, shifting the center of gravity, the gliders could not be made too large or else his body shifting would not be effective. By 1893, his current glider had a wingspan of 7 meters with a wing area of 14 square meters, yielding an aspect ratio of 3.5. It weighed only 20 kilograms (44 pounds). The design was sufficiently advanced that it formed the basis of Lilienthal's first aircraft patent in 1893. A schematic of this glider as it appears in the patent is shown in Figure 3.19. An English patent was granted in 1894 and a U.S. patent in 1895.

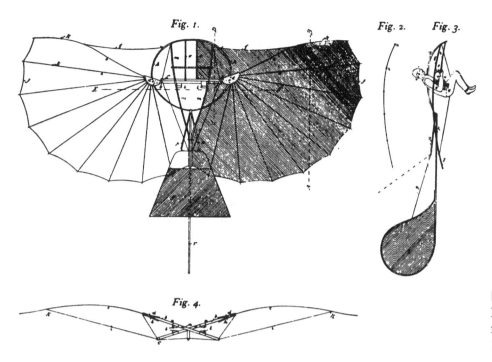

Fig. 1.

Fig. 2.   *Fig. 3.*

Fig. 4.

FIGURE 3.19
Lilienthal's patent drawing
for one of his gliders,
1893.

In the summer of 1893, Lilienthal also began to fly from some open hills in
the Rhinow Mountains, about 100 kilometers northwest of Berlin. Lilienthal had
long felt that this terrain was ideally suited for gliding flights, and his machines and
flying expertise had matured to the extent that it was worth the hour-long train ride
and subsequent wagon trip to the flying field. In addition, in 1894 he built with his
own money a conical-shaped hill in Lichterfelde, a suburb of Berlin; he could fly
from the top of this hill irrespective of the wind direction. Lilienthal's Flying Hill
was 15 meters high (about 50 feet) and was built from an existing rubble heap. The
cost has been estimated around 3000 German marks. He constructed a windowless
shed at the apex of the hill, where his gliders were stored. This Flying Hill became
the main location for his flying experiments after 1894; it exists to the present day.
In 1932, it became an official monument to Lilienthal. Today it is in the middle of a
garden-like park, adjacent to a large pond. The top of the Flying Hill is reached by
75 steps and provides a panoramic view of the Berlin suburbs. At the top of the hill
is a small pavilion with a ring-shaped roof, under which sits a stone globe on a
square basalt base. At the foot of the hill are stone plaques commemorating some
of Lilienthal's supporters and helpers. Originally dedicated on August 10, 1932, by
the Lord Mayor of Berlin, this memorial stands as a lasting posthumous symbol of
Germany's tribute to their first aeronautical pioneer.

At both locations, the Flying Hill at Lichterfelde and the chain of hills in the
Rhinow Mountains, Lilienthal continued to perfect his flying abilities and his
glider designs for the remaining two years before his death. His gliders were
predominantly single-wing monoplane designs, such as shown in his patent sketch
in Figure 3.19 and in the photograph in Figure 3.18. However, in 1895 he designed
and built several biplane gliders, testing them with success for the first time in
August 1895. Thereafter, he continued to fly both types of gliders. During the
course of his experimentation with gliders, from 1891 to 1896, Lilienthal

accumulated a great deal of flight time, successfully completing more than 2000 flights in both his monoplane and biplane machines.

Lilienthal's ultimate objective with this work was the design of an engine-powered, manned flying machine. However, his approach toward this objective was technically unsound, which stands in stark contrast to his innovative and well-conceived programs of aerodynamic experiments and glider development. Lilienthal was convinced that the route to successful powered flight was to directly emulate bird flight. Hence, all his work on a powered machine was focused on ornithopters. In fact, an ornithopter design was included as part of his 1893 patent. The idea was to have an engine (a 1-cylinder engine in his patent) drive the up-and-down wing-beating motion of the outer portion of the wings. The beating sections of the wings were a slatlike design, which were closed during the downstroke (to maximize the "lifting" action) and were open like a fan during the upstroke (to minimize resistance). Lilienthal built such a machine in the autumn of 1893 and began to test it as a glider at his Flying Hill in the spring of 1894. With the engine, the machine weighed more than 90 pounds, twice the weight of his unpowered gliders. This machine, with its heavier weight, resulted in faster landing speeds, making it more difficult for Lilienthal to fly it as a glider. When he attempted to operate the engine, which was powered by compressed carbon dioxide, it froze after a few strokes. These efforts were totally unsuccessful. In spite of this failure, Lilienthal began to build a second ornithopter during the summer of 1896, using a new engine, to be mounted on a larger airframe, with a wing area of more than 20 square meters. Lilienthal was killed before he had a chance to bring this second ornithopter to fruition.

This author finds it totally out of character that Lilienthal, a sensible, accomplished, practical mechanical engineer, would pursue so blindly the concept of a powered ornithopter. This is in spite of his knowledge of other work carried out in the 19th century on propeller-driven fixed-wing designs, emanating from George Cayley's seminal concept of separating the mechanisms of the production of lift and propulsion. Indeed, there were many reports in the German *Journal of Aviation* about work on propeller-driven, fixed-wing machines. Lilienthal, however, preached his advocacy of ornithopters to his colleagues; he was concerned about the slip stream from the propeller affecting the flying qualities of the machine. Because no propeller-driven aircraft had successfully flown by that time, Lilienthal felt that his concerns were confirmed. Indeed, he thought that the only practical use of the propeller was in the role of a helicopter rotor. In a letter to a colleague, Eugen Kreiss, on March 16, 1894, Lilienthal wrote the following:

> The sole method that in my estimation would be capable of offering a certain measure of the advantage of wing-flapping is the propeller which provides both lift and thrust. With such devices, if they are thoughtfully executed, quite advantageous results might perhaps be achieved. Practice alone will decide: we must see what the air and wind will say about them, and for that reason it would be desirable to see some of the ideas that have now surfaced transformed into reality, to put an end to this fruitless debate at last.

Lilienthal's premature death made certain that he would contribute no more to the technical resolution of this debate.

Otto held out the hope that he could make money in the flying machine business. In a letter to his sister in September 1893, he wrote, "Recently I have pushed the matter of flying more because I have been making such good progress with it. I even think that inventions which have stemmed from it could be used to make money. If the business becomes a hit, we would all be helped by it."

At the time, his boiler factory was not doing well financially. He hoped to make flying a sport in which other people would participate, hence providing revenue for himself. Indeed, he began to receive orders for his gliders, which he priced at 300 German marks per machine. By 1895, the price was increased to 500 marks for an improved design; namely, his "normal glider," a monoplane design with which he accomplished the majority of his flights. He sold only eight copies of his normal glider; the purchasers were from countries throughout Europe and the United States. One machine was sold to Nikolai Joukowski in Moscow; Joukowski was to become the most famous of Russian aerodynamicists, primarily through his contributions to the circulation theory of lift at the beginning of the 20th century. The one Lilienthal glider to come to the United States was purchased in the spring of 1896 by the newspaper publisher William Randolph Hearst. After passing through several hands, this glider (after being restored in 1967) hangs in the Early Flight Gallery at the National Air and Space Museum of the Smithsonian Institution in Washington, D.C.

On Sunday morning, August 9, 1896, Otto Lilienthal left Berlin for the Rhinow hills. The weather was perfect for flying. The air temperature was 20 °C (68 °F) and a steady breeze prevailed from the east at about 7 miles per hour. At noon, Lilienthal took his first flight of the day, a long glide from a takeoff point high on Gollenberg Hill. It took about 30 minutes to lug the machine back to the takeoff point, and then Otto took off for a second time. He would never fly again. A thermal eddy caught Lilienthal by surprise. The glider virtually stopped, motionless, in the air. In spite of violent body motion to control the machine, Lilienthal was unable to pick up speed. The glider completely stalled, and then nosed down, crashing into the ground from a height of 50 feet. Lilienthal, with a broken spine, was lifted from the glider. Conscious, Otto called out several times, "I'm still alive, I am Otto Lilienthal from Lichterfelde." A physician from Rhinow, Dr. Niendorf, attended him at a nearby inn. Much later, Dr. Niendorf described the situation:

> I can still see him today, lying on his back with his beautiful, full, blond beard, not remarking about any pain. I basically did not take his injury very seriously, as he could still move both arms well, though he was completely paralyzed from the waist down, a sure sign that his spine must have been broken.

Gustav Lilienthal was notified by telegram, and was by his brother's side in Stolln by early Monday morning. Otto recognized his brother, but soon lost consciousness. He was driven to the Neustadt-on-the-Dosse train station and placed on board the 2:00 p.m. train to Berlin, where he was immediately transferred to the Bergmann Clinic. He died at 5:30 that afternoon, Monday, August 10, 1896, without regaining consciousness.

If Lilienthal had not crashed, would he have been the first to successfully develop manned, powered flight? He certainly had a head start on the Wright brothers. Octave Chanute felt the answer is yes. In an article in the *Aeronautical Annual* in 1897, Chanute stated about Lilienthal, "Had he lived, success would probably not have been denied him." In flying gliders as well as in basic aerodynamic knowledge, Lilienthal had a considerable head start. But his design of a powered machine focused on the ornithopter principle; he was going down the wrong track with a full head of steam. Had he lived, he most likely would have spent much effort and time in perfecting his flapping wing machine. Otto was a strongly optimistic person; he would not have given up easily. However, he would have eventually been forced to redirect his efforts toward a fixed-wing design with a propeller, and by that time he most likely would have lost his head start on the Wright brothers.

There is no doubt that Otto Lilienthal was a giant in 19th century aeronautics and that he did more to advance manned, heavier-than-air flight than anybody else in that century after George Cayley. Perhaps some of the most reverent words written about Lilienthal came from Wilbur Wright, ironically in the last article that Wilbur was ever to write before his untimely death from typhoid fever on May 30, 1912. In the *Bulletin of the Aero Club of America* in September 1912 (published posthumously), Wilbur said this:

> Of all the men who attacked the flying problem in the 19th century, Otto Lilienthal was easily the most important. His greatness appeared in every phase of the problem. No one equaled him in power to draw new recruits to the cause; no one equaled him in fullness and clearness of understanding of the principle of flight; no one did so much to convince the world of the advantages of curved wing surfaces; and no one did so much to transfer the problem of human flight to the open air where it belonged. As a scientific investigator none of his contemporaries was his equal.

DEMONSTRATING THE TECHNICAL FEASIBILITY OF THE AIRPLANE—SAMUEL LANGLEY

The last decade of the 19th century was a heady and invigorating period for advancing the technology of the airplane. Maxim in England and Ader in France had powered themselves off the ground, although in a very halting manner. Lilienthal was almost routinely gliding smoothly through the skies near Berlin. Octave Chanute was cautiously optimistic in 1894, suggesting that the technology for powered flight was almost at hand: "It will be seen that the mechanical difficulties are very great; but it will be discerned also that none of them can now be said to be insuperable, and that material progress has recently been achieved toward their solution." Indeed, enough technical progress in flying machines had been made that Chanute was able to write and publish a book in 1894 that surveyed and analyzed this progress. Aptly titled *Progress in Flying Machines*, this book was widely read by the aeronautical community, including the Wright brothers. Into this vortex of activity stepped Samuel Pierpont Langley.

Samuel Langley became interested in flying machines after hearing a lecture on soaring effigies of birds, models launched in the air, at a meeting of the American Association for the Advancement of Science in Buffalo, New York, in 1886. At that time, Langley was a distinguished physicist and observational astronomer and director of the Allegheny Observatory in Pittsburgh. After his return from Buffalo, Langley successfully obtained the observatory's board of trustees' permission to construct a whirling arm device for aerodynamic experiments. Although the observatory's mission was astrophysical observation, and Langley's reputation was built on his contributions in astronomy, especially his studies of the sun and sun spots, Langley was allowed to construct and operate a major facility for the sole use of obtaining aerodynamic data. Funding for the whirling arm and the initial experiments came from a wealthy friend, William Thaw. At its completion in September 1887, Langley's whirling arm was the largest built to date; the arms swept out a circle of 60-foot diameter, revolving eight feet above the ground. By comparison, Lilienthal's largest whirling arm had a diameter of 7 meters (23 feet). In 1887, Langley began a series of carefully designed and executed aerodynamic experiments with his whirling arm—experiments that continued for more than four years, resulting in the publication of a book that elevated Langley to world-class status in the circle of late 19th century aerodynamic researchers. This book, entitled *Experiments in Aerodynamics* and published in 1891, constituted the first substantive American contribution to aerodynamics. With it, and with Langley's subsequent work on actual flying machines after he became secretary of the Smithsonian Institution in Washington, D.C., in 1887, the virtual monopoly in aerodynamic experimentation held by western Europe was broken.

To begin with, there is absolutely no doubt about the ultimate goal of Langley's experiments. He intended to explore and uncover the basic physical laws of aerodynamics that would scientifically prove the practicability of powered, heavier-than-air flight. Specifically, he wrote the following in the introduction to *Experiments in Aerodynamics*:

> To prevent misapprehension, let me state at the outset that I do not undertake to explain any art of mechanical flight, but to demonstrate experimentally certain propositions in aerodynamics which prove that such flight under proper direction is practicable. This being understood, I may state that these researchers have led to the result that mechanical sustentation of heavier bodies in the air, combined with very great speeds, is not only possible, but within the reach of mechanical means we actually possess, and that while these researchers are, as I have said, not meant to demonstrate the art of guiding such heavy bodies in flight, they do show that we now have the power to sustain and propel them.

These comments reflect Langley the scientist. Later, Langley was driven to design a series of actual flying machines to confirm without a shadow of doubt his conclusion from his whirling arm data, as just stated. In this regard, we see Langley the engineer.

When Langley began his whirling arm experiments in 1887, he had read the works of Wenham and Phillips, but was not aware of the yet-unpublished experiments of Lilienthal. In any event, Langley felt as if he was breaking new ground and was entering into a subject that was essentially a technological void. Much later, in 1897, he wrote of the prevailing situation and attitudes that existed when he began his earlier experiments:

> The whole subject of mechanical flight was so far from having attracted the general attention of physicists or engineers, that it was generally considered to be a field fitted rather for the pursuits of the charlatan than for those of the man of science. Consequently, he who was bold enough to enter it, found almost none of those experimental data which are ready to hand in every recognized and reputable field of scientific labor.

Langley's published aerodynamic data obtained with the whirling arm were all for *flat plates*, although he later examined cambered surfaces. The measurements on cambered surfaces were never published; they can only be found in Langley's wastebooks (his laboratory records), which are presently kept in the

Ramsey Room (the rare book room) of the National Air and Space Museum. Some of his flat plate data were obtained at a 90-degree angle of attack, that is, with the plate oriented perpendicular to the flow. From these 90-degree results, he readily calculated values for Smeaton's coefficient—the plural "values" is intentionally used here because the numbers obtained by Langley varied moderately from one test to another. Taking an average value of his measurements, Langley declared that the "final value" of Smeaton's coefficient k is 0.003 when the force is expressed in pounds, the plate area in square feet, and the velocity in miles per hour. This value is very close to the modern, 20th century value of $k = 0.0029$ established by the Royal Aeronautical Society. It is also a far cry from the earlier accepted value of 0.005 obtained from Smeaton's tables. Langley's measurement is *quite accurate*—a testimonial to the accuracy of his experiments for these conditions.

Langley was a master instrument designer. In contrast to the simple weight, pulley, and spring mechanisms developed by Lilienthal for his aerodynamic force measurements, Langley designed rather sophisticated electromechanical instruments for measuring various types of forces. He reported his results in terms of aerodynamic force coefficients. Although Lilienthal was the first to use aerodynamic force coefficients, Langley was not far behind. Lilienthal published his data in 1889, and Langley's *Experiments in Aerodynamics* was published in 1891. Their work established the use of aerodynamic force coefficients as part of the way of doing business in airplane aerodynamics. The usefulness of these coefficients is that *any* investigator at that time could take the coefficient value for a given angle of attack, multiply it by Smeaton's coefficient (hopefully using the correct value), the area of the plate in question, and the square of the velocity (whatever it may be), and obtain the aerodynamic force on the plate at the given angle of attack and velocity. Today, the use of Smeaton's coefficient is passé. Instead, the aerodynamic coefficient, say, a lift coefficient C_L, is simply multiplied by one-half the air density $\rho/2$, the planform area of the wing S, and the square of the velocity V^2, to give the lift force L:

$$L = \tfrac{1}{2}\rho V^2 S C_L.$$

[When this formula is used, consistent units must be used. For the lift in pounds, ρ must be in units of slugs per cubic feet (a slug is the consistent unit of mass in the engineering system of units, equal to 32.2 pounds mass), V in feet per second, and S in square feet. For the lift in newtons, ρ must be in kilograms per cubic meter, V in meters per second, and S in square meters. The value of the lift coefficient C_L, being dimensionless, is the same for *any* consistent system of units. See J. D. Anderson, *Introduction to Flight*, 4th edition, McGraw–Hill, 2000, for a basic discussion of such matters.]

We have already emphasized the importance of the aspect ratio of the wing in airplane design (Figure 3.7). Langley was the first person to obtain *definitive data* showing the aerodynamic superiority of high aspect ratio wings—his most important aerodynamic contribution. These data were obtained from his "plane-dropper apparatus." This was an iron frame mounted vertically at the end of his whirling arm, on which was mounted an aluminum falling piece that ran up and down on rollers. He attached his flat plate lifting surfaces to this falling piece. With the lifting surface locked into its highest position, the whirling arm was started, and when the desired airspeed over the plate was reached, the plate was released. It

WEIGHT OF MODELS : 0.465 kg

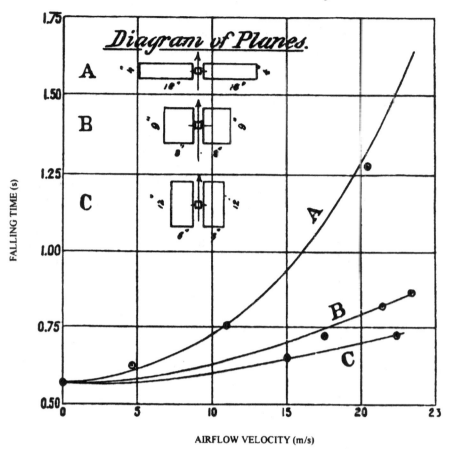

FIGURE 3.20
The first concrete data
showing the effect of
aspect ratio on lift.
Langley's data for flat
plates of different aspect
ratios, obtained from his
"plane-dropping" tests,
1891.

would then proceed to fall a maximum distance of 4 feet (as allowed by the height
of the iron frame). The *time* it took the plate to fall this distance was recorded by
Langley. The higher the lift, the longer the time it took for the plate to fall the
distance of 4 feet. Hence, a measurement of the time required to fall the distance of
4 feet is an index of the lifting capacity of the plate. Using this apparatus, Langley
tested flat plate wings of different aspect ratios. His plane-dropper tests clearly
showed that the higher aspect ratio wings took longer to drop than those with lower
aspect ratios and proved conclusively that wings with high aspect ratio produce
more lift than wings with low aspect ratio.

Langley's graph showing these data is reproduced in Figure 3.20. Here, the
time required to fall 4 feet is plotted versus the horizontal velocity for three plates
of equal weight and surface area but different aspect ratio. The highest aspect ratio
wing is labeled A, the lowest is labeled C, and an intermediate wing is labeled B.
Clearly, at any given velocity, the higher the aspect ratio, the longer the falling
time. Although Langley was not the first to appreciate the aerodynamic efficiency
of high aspect ratio wings (recall that Francis Wenham was the first to point out
this effect), he was the first to produce an organized set of definitive experimental
data that clearly proved the superiority of such wings. Moreover, Langley later put
these data to use in the design of his aerodromes. Note that the highest aspect ratio
model shown in Figure 3.20 is that consisting of two 18 × 4 inch planes; here, the

aspect ratio of each plane is 4.5—a fairly high value for the state of the art at that time. Influenced by these results, Langley later designed his successful Aerodrome Number 5 with a relatively high aspect ratio of 5.

Parenthetically, we note that Langley introduced the word "aspect" (the quotation marks are his) to describe the orientation of a plate in regard to what edge of the plate is perpendicular to the flow. For example, consider a 12 × 6 inch plate. If the plate is oriented in the flow such that the 12-inch side is the advancing (leading) edge, that is, the 12-inch side is perpendicular to the flow, in Langley's nomenclature this is a different aspect than if the plate is oriented such that the 6-inch side is the advancing edge. Although Langley did not define the concept of aspect *ratio* as we know it today, could Langley's introduction of the word aspect in this context be the root source of the term "aspect ratio"? It appears that the word aspect had not been used in the aeronautical literature before Langley's book.

The most *controversial* conclusion made by Langley on the basis of his experimental data is the "Langley Law," which simply states that the power required for a vehicle to fly through the air *decreases* as the velocity increases. Langley considered this to be one of his most important contributions. It is immediately stated in *Experiments in Aerodynamics*, right up front on page 1:

> These new experiments [and theory also when reviewed in their light] show that if in such aerial motion, there be given a plane of fixed size and weight, inclined at such an angle, and moved forward at such a speed, that it shall be sustained in horizontal flight, then the more rapid the motion is, the *less* will be the power required to support and advance it. This statement may, I am aware, present an appearance so paradoxical that the reader may ask himself if he has rightly understood it.

This conclusion is repeated no less than three other times in his book, twice in italics. For example, in summarizing his soaring experiments with the component pressure recorder, he stated, "The most important conclusion may be said to be the confirmation of the statement that *to maintain such planes in horizontal flight at high speeds, less power is needed than for low ones.*"

This conclusion flies in the face of intuition, which is why Langley labeled it as "paradoxical." It was considered to be misleading at best by some contemporaries and outright wrong by others. Lilienthal and the Wright brothers rejected this conclusion outright. In a meeting of the British Association for the Advancement of Science at Oxford in August 1894, Langley presented a short paper summarizing his work and conclusions; he was criticized and taken to task by both Lord Kelvin and Lord Rayleigh—formidable opposition to say the least. Indeed, Langley has been derided for this power law to the present day.

Langley's conclusion, however, was based on his experimental data, and these data *consistently* supported it. To make an assessment of the validity of Langley's conclusion, this author made a calculation of the *power required curve* for Langley's flat plate in soaring flight. (A power required curve is today a standard feature in the prediction of the performance of a given airplane. It is a graph of the power required for a given airplane at a given altitude to fly in steady, level flight, as a function of the flight velocity. The power required curve is shaped somewhat like a parabola, as shown in Figure 3.21. At the lowest possible velocity at which an airplane can sustain itself in the air, the angle of attack is very high, and the airplane is requiring a lot of power; it is simply clawing at the air to stay up. At a slightly higher velocity, the angle of attack is decreased because more of

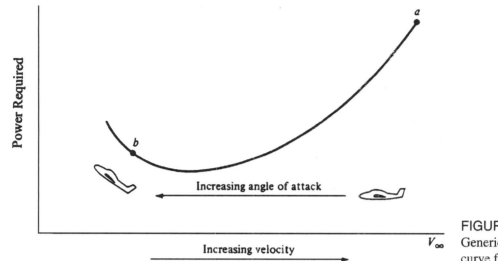

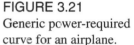

FIGURE 3.21
Generic power-required
curve for an airplane.

the lift is obtained from the higher dynamic pressure due to the higher velocity.
This decrease in angle of attack actually reduces the drag, and hence, the power
required to fly faster is actually less, as shown by point b in Figure 3.21. As the
flight velocity increases further, the decreases in angle of attack become smaller
and the power required will reach some minimum value, and then it will start to
increase at higher velocities, as shown by point a in Figure 3.21. Hence, the power
required to fly in steady level flight follows the variation shown in Figure 3.21.
That part of the curve to the left of the minimum in Figure 3.21, the low-speed part,
is called the *back side of the power curve*. It is an unstable region of flight, and
pilots generally try to avoid flight on the back side of the power curve.) This
author's calculations *clearly show that all of Langley's experimental data were
obtained on the back side of the power curve—the region where the power required
for steady, level flight indeed decreases with an increase in velocity.* The calculated
powered required curve for Langley's flat plate is shown in Figure 3.22; it pertains
to a flat plate of aspect ratio 6.25, planform area of 1 square foot, and a weight of
500-grams-force. The shape of this curve is like that for all conventional flight
vehicles. It has a local minimum point, for *minimum* power required. In Figure
3.22, this local minimum occurs at a velocity equal to about 22 meters per second
(about 50 mph). Examining *all* of Langley's data, we note that they were all taken
at velocities of 20 meters per second or less. This range of velocity is identified in
Figure 3.22. *Clearly, all of Langley's data were obtained on the back side of the
power curve.* Hence, his conclusions that led to the Langley power law were
correct for his range of test velocity. It is interesting to note that had his whirling
arm allowed testing at velocities greater than 22 meters per second, Langley would
have noted a reversal in his data trend, and most likely the Langley power law
would never have existed. [For more details on this calculation, see Appendix E of
J. D. Anderson, *A History of Aerodynamics and Its Impact on Flying Machines*,
Cambridge University Press, New York, 1997 (hardback) or 1998 (paperback).]

Samuel Langley was a self-educated scientist. Born in 1934 in Roxbury,
Massachusetts, he graduated from Boston High School. He chose not to go to
college, but rather worked as a civil engineer and architect for a dozen years in the

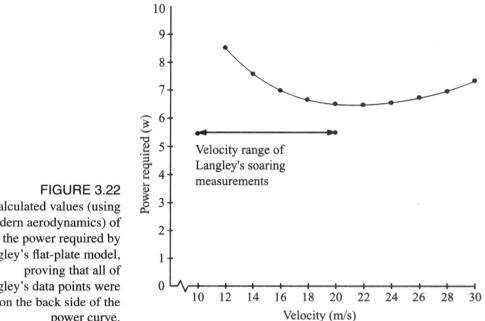

FIGURE 3.22
Calculated values (using
modern aerodynamics) of
the power required by
Langley's flat-plate model,
proving that all of
Langley's data points were
on the back side of the
power curve.

midwest. During the height of the American Civil War, he returned to Boston and
directed his attention to astronomy. In 1867, he became the director of the
Allegheny Observatory at the Western University of Pennsylvania (now the
University of Pittsburgh), and over the next 20 years he carved out a distinguished
reputation in observational astronomy, becoming an expert in characteristics of the
sun. In 1887, Langley became the third secretary of the Smithsonian Institution in
Washington, D.C., a position viewed by many as that of the most prestigious
scientist in the United States. It was with this viewpoint as a scientist that Langley
carried out his aerodynamic experiments. Langley's original goal was simply to
demonstrate the physical laws that would prove the practicality of mechanical
flight. This was the objective of his whirling arm experiments. At the end of
Experiments in Aerodynamics, Langley summarizes the impact of his data: "The
most important general influence from these experiments, as a whole, is that, so far
as the mere power to sustain heavy bodies in the air by mechanical flight goes,
such mechanical flight is possible with engines we now possess." The italics are
Langley's.

It had already become clear to Langley, however, that to convince the rest of
the world that his conclusion was correct, he had to do more than conduct
laboratory experiments. Indeed, during Langley's participation in the August 1894
meeting of the British Association for the Advancement of Science at Oxford,
Lord Rayleigh commented that the ultimate proof of the validity of Langley's
aerodynamic data would be "if he . . . succeeded in doing it [flying] he would be
[proven] right." Little did Rayleigh realize that Langley already had undertaken
activities aimed at the design, construction, and flying of a heavier-than-air
machine. Part I of the *Langley Memoir on Mechanical Flight*, published in 1911,
five years after Langley's death, was written by Langley in 1897. In the
introduction to Part I, Langley wrote:

> I beg the reader, therefore to recall as he reads, that everything here has been done with a view to putting a trial aerodrome successfully in flight within a few years, and thus giving an early demonstration of the only kind which is conclusive in the eyes of the scientific man, as well as of the general public—a demonstration that mechanical flight is possible —by actually flying.

Langley's goal was clear—he had to build a successful flying machine.

Toward this end, Langley could already draw on experience obtained with small, rubber-powered aircraft models. This work had commenced in April 1887, at the Allegheny Observatory, and continued for four years, mostly in Washington, D.C. The earlier models were made of pine; later Langley replaced those wooden frames with light metal tubes, which proved too heavy, and still later with shellacked paper tubes, which proved to have the best strength-to-weight ratio. The wings were made of paper, stretched over a supporting frame. Over the course of these flying model tests, Langley experimented with nearly 100 different configurations. Langley described these configurations as follows:

> some with two propellers, some with one, some with one propeller in front and one behind; some with plane, some with curved wings; some with single, some with superimposed wings (biplanes); some with two pairs of wings, one preceding and one following (tandem wings); some with the Penaud tail; and some with other forms.

Some of these rubber-powered models are shown in Figure 3.23. It must have been quite a sight observing these rubber-powered model airplanes being tossed out the north window of the dome of the Allegheny Observatory and later flying inside the upper hall of the original Smithsonian Building. In Langley's words, "The objects of these experiments . . . were to find the practical conditions of equilibrium and of horizontal flight . . . ." However, Langley's efforts with these model aircraft were not very productive. The results were mixed and not definitive. In *Memoirs* Langley describes the problem:

> The difficulties of these long-contained early experiments were enhanced by the ever-present difficulty which continued through later ones, that it was almost impossible to build the model light enough to enable it to fly, and at the same time strong enough to withstand the strains which flight imposed upon it. The models were broke up by their falls after a few flights, and had to be continuously renewed, while owing to the slightness of their construction, the conditions of observation could not be exactly repeated; and these flights themselves, as has already been stated, were so brief in time (usually less than six seconds), so limited in extent (usually less than twenty metres), and so wholly capricious and erratic, owing to the nature of the rubbermotor and other causes, that very many experiments were insufficient to eliminate these causes of mal-observation.

Finally, Langley gave up with the rubber-powered models, stating, "The final results . . . were not such as to give information proportioned to their trouble and cost, and it was decided to commence experiments with a steam-driven aerodrome on a large scale."

With this, Langley embarked on the next stage of his aeronautical work, namely, the development of steam-powered, flying machines. Ultimately, this was to prove much more successful. Langley had labeled his rubber-powered models as "aerodromes," and he carried this nomenclature over to all his subsequent flying

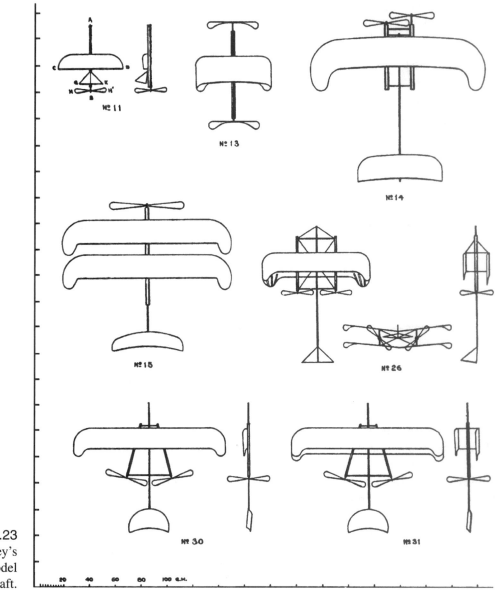

FIGURE 3.23
A selection of Langley's
rubber-powered model
aircraft.

machines. The source of the term aerodrome stems from December 1890, when at
the suggestion of a classical scholar who had been asked by Langley for a
reasonable choice of appellations from the classical languages, Langley chose the
Greek word "aerodromo," which meant air runner. Henceforth, he would call all
his flying machines aerodromes. Unfortunately, strictly translated, the word
aerodrome in Greek means a *place* from which a machine would fly, rather than
the machine itself. Probably because of this, the term aerodrome for a flying
machine did not stick; it was never used by anyone except Langley. It was,
however, used in the early 20th century as a British variant for the word airdrome,
a landing field.

At the time, Langley felt that steam was the power mode of choice. Writing
in *Memoirs*, he stated his purpose: "In November 1891 . . . I commenced the

construction of the engines and the design of the hull of a steam-driven aerodrome, which was intended to supplement the experiments given in *Aerodynamics* by others made under the construction of actual flight." Over the next four years, Langley built seven such aerodromes, numbering them consecutively from 0 to 6. Numbers 0–3 were quickly abandoned because they were too heavy and underpowered. However, the lessons learned with numbers 0–3 led to more successful designs for numbers 4–6. Of these, Aerodrome Number 5 achieved the highest degree of flying success.

Aerodrome Number 5 was representative of all of Langley's aerodromes. It was a tandem wing design—one feature that stemmed from the rubber-powered model tests. Both the tandem wings were the same shape and size. The planform was rectangular with a relatively high aspect ratio of 5; here Langley was using to advantage the important conclusions from his whirling arm experiments. Both wings had a wing span of 4 meters (13.1 feet), and the total sustaining wing area including both wings was 6.4 square meters (68.9 square feet). The total flying weight of the aerodrome was 26 pounds, yielding a wing loading (weight divided by wing area) of 0.38 pounds per square foot. The airfoil shape was highly cambered, in the ratio of 1–12 (the same as the airfoil in the Lilienthal tables), with the maximum camber at the 23.8 percent chord location—quite close to the quarter-chord point. This cambered shape, along with front and side views of Langley's Aerodrome Number 5, is shown in Figure 3.24. Although all of the aerodynamic data published by Langley in 1891 were for flat plates, a few years later his assistants were experimenting with cambered airfoils. These data were never published, but Langley chose to use a cambered airfoil on his aerodromes, following in the footsteps of Otto Lilienthal.

To launch the aerodromes, Langley chose the unique arrangement of a catapult mounted on top of a houseboat in the middle of the Potomac River. Langley explained:

> As the end of the year 1892 approached and with it the completion of an aerodrome of large size which had to be started upon its flight in some way, the method and place of launching it pressed for decision. One thing at least seemed clear. In the present stage of experiment, it was desirable that the aerodrome should—if it must fall—fall into water where it would suffer little injury and be readily recovered, rather than anywhere on land, where it would almost certainly be badly damaged.

In regard to the aerodrome itself, the four big problems with which Langley felt challenged were weight, structural strength, power, and vehicle stability. The matters of strength and weight combine into the strength-to-weight ratio—an important consideration in aircraft structures to the present day. Langley ultimately solved this problem for the aerodromes, but not without effort and continued problems. For example, Langley commented on observations of some abortive tests of Aerodromes Numbers 4 and 5 in 1894:

> Observations of the movement of the two aerodromes through the air, as seen by the writer from the shore, seemed to show, however, that the wings did not remain in their original form, but that at the moment of launching there was a sudden flexure and distortion due to the upward pressure of the air.

That is, the wing bent upward along the span and twisted so that airfoil sections at different locations along the wing were not at the angle of attack that they were

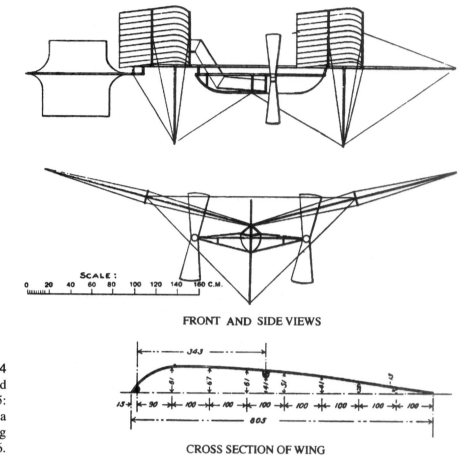

FRONT AND SIDE VIEWS

FIGURE 3.24
Langley's steam-powered
Aerodrome Number 5:
front and side views, and a
cross section of the wing
(airfoil section), 1896.

CROSS SECTION OF WING

supposed to be. Langley successfully fixed this problem for the small aerodromes, but this observation was a foreboding precursor to the disasters to come with Langley's full-scale aerodrome in 1903. In terms of power, Langley was able to design and build a small steam engine producing a maximum of 1 horsepower (he had calculated the power required to attain the theoretical soaring velocity of 24 feet per second to be 0.35 horsepower). But most of all, Langley was almost obsessed with the need for inherent stability of the aerodrome in flight. Langley understood the basic principles of static stability. To obtain lateral stability, he designed his wings with a substantial dihedral angle of 15 degrees, as seen in Figure 3.24. It was much more difficult to obtain longitudinal stability because Langley could not predict with any certainty the location of the center of pressure for the wings let alone that for the complete aerodrome. His flat plate data obtained with the whirling arm were of no real use in this regard; Langley was well aware that the center-of-pressure variation for a cambered airfoil was quite different. Moreover, he was concerned about the mutual interaction of the tandem-wing arrangement and the effect of the propeller slip stream on center-of-pressure location. Langley, however, was faced with the engineering problem of actually having to design and build a vehicle in spite of the incomplete information. To this end, he finally made a decision:

The curved wings used on the aerodromes in late years have a rise of one in twelve, or in some cases one in eighteen, and for these latter the following empirical local rule has been adopted: The center-of-pressure on each wing with a horizontal motion of 2000 feet per minute, is two-fifths of the distance from front to rear.

This was just for design purposes. When Langley was finally prepared to fly his aerodromes, he adjusted the location of the center of gravity by moving various components (the tail, the hull, etc.), and he adjusted the center-of-pressure location by changing the tail inclination angle as well as the angle made by the wing to the fuselage. Indeed, through his system of structural guy wires, he would set the inclination angle of the wing tip to a different inclination angle than that at the wing root. One typical combination of root and tip angle was 8 and 20 degrees, respectively. After a trial-and-error process with these adjustments, Langley would find the proper arrangement that provided longitudinal stability as well as balance for horizontal flight.

On May 6, 1896, after three years of frustrating failures in attempting to fly his aerodromes, Langley finally met with success, as described in the first pages of this book.

Samuel Langley had achieved the first successful flight of an engine-powered, heavier-than-air flying machine in history. Langley did not loose any time in spreading the news. By May 26, he was at the French Academy of Sciences in Paris, giving a short communication about his success and emphasizing that it was proof positive of the ultimate conclusion he had drawn five years earlier in *Experiments in Aerodynamics*, namely, that heavier-than-air powered flight was technically feasible and that it could be accomplished with existing technology. For reinforcement, Langley also attached to his report to the Academy a letter from Alexander Graham Bell describing in detail the flights that Bell himself had observed. Bell ended his letter with the statement, "It seemed to me that no one could have witnessed these experiments without being convinced that the possibility of mechanical flight had been demonstrated." This had been Langley's goal all along, and who more prestigious than Bell himself could have confirmed the realization of this goal.

Little did either of them know that this success would turn to disastrous failure seven years later.

THINGS ARE LOOKING DOWN—THE FAILED LANGLEY AERODROME

After his stunning success with the steam-powered aerodromes in 1896, there was a hiatus in Langley's aeronautical research. After all, he had proven without a shadow of a doubt the technical feasibility of heavier-than-air powered flight—the fundamental goal of his earlier work. Langley, however, was not content to sit on this accomplishment. In a letter to Octave Chanute in June 1897, Langley stated, "If anyone were to put at my disposal the considerable amount—fifty thousand dollars or more—for . . . an aerodrome carrying a man or men, with a capacity for some hours of flight, I feel that I could build it and should enjoy the task." He went on to predict that he could accomplish this feat within two or three years from the time he would start. Indeed, behind the scenes in Washington, D.C., Langley became proactive in searching for a sponsor for such a large aerodrome, thinking that his best chances for support were from the U.S. government. Circumstances for such a windfall became more likely with the approach of the Spanish–American War, and finally in 1898 Langley received an award of $50,000 from the War Department for the construction of a large, piloted flying machine.

The design of such a machine started in earnest in May 1898, when Langley hired as an assistant, Charles Manly, a young, new graduate from the Sibley School of Mechanical Engineering of Cornell University. The two men got along very well; Manly soon became an instrumental force behind the design and construction of the new aerodrome. The design philosophy behind the new aerodrome was to scale it up from the previous successful Aerodrome Number 5 from 1896. This was also to become the Achilles heel of the machine; you cannot simply take a previously successful flying machine, make it four times larger, and expect it to be equally as successful. Langley ignored certain "scaling laws" for both structures and aerodynamics, laws which are certainly better understood today than in Langley's time.

Departing from his earlier use of steam, Langley correctly decided that a gasoline-fueled engine was the proper prime mover for an aircraft. By that time, the internal combustion engine had reached a state of rapid development in Europe. August Otto in Germany designed a four-stroke, gasoline-fueled engine in 1876, and by 1895 more than 50,000 of these engines had been sold. These engines, per horsepower, were much lighter than steam engines with their accompanying boiler. Techniques for cracking crude oil had been developed, with gasoline as one of the products. So Langley made a good engineering decision to power his full-scale aerodrome with a gasoline-fueled, internal combustion engine. He first commissioned Stephan Balzer of New York to produce an engine, but dissatisfied with the results, Langley eventually had Manly redesign the power plant. Langley encountered the same problem to be faced later by the Wright brothers in early 1903—the horsepower-to-weight ratio required for the engine was beyond the standard state of the art of engine manufacture for that day. However, Charles Manly pulled off a technological miracle. The result of his redesign was a 5-cylinder radial engine that produced 52.4 horsepower and yet weighed only 208 pounds, a spectacular achievement for that time. Using a smaller, 1.5-horsepower gasoline-fueled engine, Langley accomplished a successful flight with a quarter-scale model aircraft in June 1901 and then an even more successful flight of the model powered by a 3.2 horsepower engine in August of 1903.

Encouraged by this success, Langley stepped directly to the full-size airplane, top and side views of which are shown in Figure 3.25. Following the technique used for launching his steam-powered aerodrome in 1896, Langley mounted this tandem-winged aircraft on a catapult to provide an assisted takeoff. In turn, the airplane and catapult were placed on top of a houseboat on the Potomac River. On October 7, 1903, with Manly at the controls, the airplane was ready for its first attempt. The launching had wide advance publicity, and the press was present to watch what might be the first successful powered flight in history. Here is the resulting report from the *Washington Post* the next day:

> A few yards from the houseboat were the boats of the reporters, who for three months had been stationed at Widewater. The newspapermen waved their hands. Manly looked down and smiled. Then his face hardened as he braced himself for the flight, which

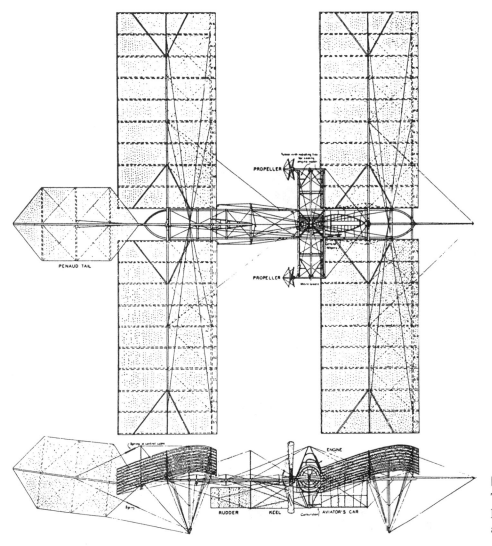

FIGURE 3.25
Top- and side-view of
Langley's full-scale
aerodrome, 1903.

might have in store for him fame or death. The propeller wheels, a foot from his head,
whirred around him one thousand times to the minute. A man forward fired two
skyrockets. There came an answering "toot, toot" from the tugs. A mechanic stopped,
cut the cable holding the catapult; there was a roaring, grinding noise—and the
Langley airship tumbled over the edge of the houseboat and disappeared in the river,
sixteen feel below. It simply slid into the water like a handful of mortar....

Manly was unhurt. Langley believed the airplane was fouled by the launching
mechanism, and he tried again on December 8, 1903. Figure 3.26, a photograph
taken moments after launch, shows the rear wings in total collapse and the
aerodrome going through a 90-degree angle of attack. Again the aerodrome fell
into the river, and again Manly was fished out, unhurt. It was not entirely certain
what happened this time; again the fouling of the catapult was blamed, but some
experts at the time maintained that the tail boom cracked due to structural
weakness. At any rate, that was the end of Langley's attempts. The War
Department gave up, stating that "we are still far from the ultimate goal [of human

FIGURE 3.26
Langley's aerodrome an
instant after launch on
December 8, 1903. This
was his second failure,
which ended his
aeronautical work.

flight]." Members of Congress and the press leveled vicious and unjustified attacks on Langley. (Human flight was still looked upon with much derision by most people.) In the face of this ridicule, Langley retired from the aeronautical scene. He died on February 27, 1906, a man in despair.

Most modern experts feel that Langley's aerodrome would not have been capable of sustained, equilibrium flight had it been successfully launched. (In 1914, after making 93 technical modifications to the Langley aerodrome, not the least of which included the addition of pontoons, Glenn Curtiss flew the aerodrome from Lake Keuka in upstate New York. But with the modifications, the aerodrome was a different machine.) Langley made no experiments with piloted gliders to get the feel of the air. He ignored completely the important aspects of flight control. He attempted to launch Manly into the air on a powered machine without Manly's having one second of flight experience. Nevertheless, Langley's aeronautical work was of some importance because he lent the power of his respected technical reputation to the cause of mechanical flight and his aerodromes were to provide encouragement to others.

In terms of contributions to the technology of the airplane, Langley's full-size aerodrome made none, except for its powerful, lightweight engine. Recent studies have shown that the Langley aerodrome was structurally unsound and that was the primary reason for its failure. The aerodrome failed as a system; it had marginal aerodynamics, excellent propulsion, and marginal longitudinal and directional control (movable horizontal tail and vertical rudder controlled by the pilot). It had no lateral control, and, of course, the structures aspect of the system was a total failure. So the system as a whole failed. Even the excellent propulsion was a potential source of failure; had the aerodrome been able to stay together long enough for a flight, it would have been greatly *overpowered* and may not have been able to withstand the heavier airloads that would have resulted from flying too fast.

TECHNOLOGY OF THE AIRPLANE IN THE 19TH CENTURY— IN RETROSPECT

The technology of the airplane advanced in fits and starts during the 19th century—some successes, some failures, some permanent contributions, and some designs best forgotten. The century began in glory—the invention of the concept of the modern configuration airplane by George Cayley. Every airplane flying today inherited its genes from Cayley's work. The century also ended in glory—major contributions by Lilienthal with his successful hang gliders and aerodynamic experiments and Langley's successful steam-powered aerodromes that proved beyond a shadow of a doubt the technical feasibility of heavier-than-air powered flight. In between, the evolution of airplane technology was that of two steps forward and one step backward. By the end of the 19th century, however, one thing was certain—the invention of the first successful airplane was just around the corner. It simply remained for the right person (or persons) to put the elements of aerodynamics, propulsion, structures, and flight controls together in a viable system.

CHAPTER

The Real Beginning: The Wright Flyer

I am an enthusiast, but not a crank in the sense that I
have some pet theories as to the construction of a flying
machine. I wish to avail myself of all that is already known and
then if possible add my mite to help on the future worker who
will attain final success.

Wilbur Wright, 1899

Wilbur Wright wrote the above words in a letter to the
Smithsonian on May 30, 1899, requesting information
about publications on flight. Wilbur and Orville
Wright had shown interest in mechanical flight as early
as childhood when their father, Milton Wright, brought
home a small toy helicopter. The year was 1878;
Wilbur was 11 and Orville, 7. By then, Alexander Graham Bell had filed for a
patent for the telephone in 1876, and Thomas Edison had invented the phonograph
in 1877. The Wrights' interest in flight appeared again when they read about Otto
Lilienthal's successful gliding experiences in 1896, and in Orville's words from his
recollections much later: "His death [Lilienthal's] a few months later while making
a glide off the hill increased our interest in the subject, and we began looking for
books pertaining to flight." Wilbur's May 30th letter to the Smithsonian in 1899,
however, is the first official record of the Wright brothers' serious intent to take up
the challenge of mechanical flight. Little did Wilbur Wright know that it was they
who were destined to "attain final success."

ORVILLE AND WILBUR—WHO WERE THEY?

Much has been written about the Wright brothers, the most recent being the
definitive biography by the noted aviation historian Tom Crouch. In *The Bishop's
Boys*, aptly titled by Crouch because Wilbur and Orville were the sons of a bishop
of the Church of the United Brethren in Christ, Crouch weaves a most interesting
story of the father and mother, the family and household atmosphere they created,
the environment in which Wilbur and Orville grew up, and the compelling work

ethic that drove them to success. A trusted confidant of the Wright's heirs, Crouch has had access to family correspondence and diaries overlooked by, or simply not available to, previous writers. His book is at present *the* definitive biography of the Wright brothers. Because of Crouch's work, and the many other good sources that exist for biographical material on the Wright brothers, here we will give only a brief sketch of their lives, appropriate only for understanding the way they worked and thought. We need to walk at least a short distance in their shoes.

Wilbur and Orville were products of the post–Civil War age; Wilbur was born near Millville, Indiana, on April 16, 1867, and Orville in Dayton, Ohio, on August 19, 1871. There was a total of seven children in the family: two older brothers, Reuchlin and Lorin; a set of twins, who died in infancy; a younger sister, Katharine; and, of course, Wilbur and Orville themselves. Their father, Milton Wright, was an active minister, administrator, and (later) bishop in the United Brethren church and was frequently away from home on business. About Milton, Crouch says the following:

> Milton was not adept at the skills required to win friends and influence people. As an administrator he had "personally offended" a number of presiding elders. His limitations as a politician were apparent. Reconciliation, negotiation, and compromise, the tools of the effective vote-getter, were foreign to him. Moreover, he would never trust men who possessed those skills. His written descriptions of various Dayton political contests over the years are studded with words like "scheming," "malicious," and "treacherous." There were no moral gray areas in his world. Right was right. Wrong was wrong. No amount of under the table negotiating would ever change that.

Much of the staunchly ethical and unbending nature of Wilbur's and Orville's personalities can be attributed to that of their father.

Their mother, Susan Koerner Wright, was born in Virginia. Susan married Milton on Thanksgiving day, 1859, at the age of 28. She was shy, quiet, and scholarly. Before her marriage, she had attended Hartsville College, coming within three months of graduation. She excelled at school, and was gifted with considerable mechanical ability. According to Crouch, "She designed and built simple household appliances for herself and made toys, including a much-treasured sled, for her children. When the boys wanted mechanical advice or assistance, they came to their mother. Milton was one of those men who had difficulty driving a nail straight." Clearly, the joy of mechanical devices shared by the Wright brothers was mainly due to their mother. It was a tragic loss to them when Susan died of tuberculosis in 1889. Katharine, who had been looking after the family during her mother's illness, inherited the formal responsibility of caring for the family after Susan's death. There were four people left in the Wright's home at 7 Hawthorn Street in Dayton—Milton, Wilbur, Orville, and Katharine. They fused into a self-support group of extreme tightness, sharing all problems and collectively working out solutions; whenever one of them was away, they corresponded on almost a daily basis. In spite of her family responsibilities, Katharine was able to graduate from Oberlin College, near Cleveland, Ohio, in 1898, after which she took a job teaching the classics at Steele High School in Dayton. (The closeness of the Wright family reached an unpleasant extreme in 1926 when Katharine married Henry Haskell, editor and part owner of the Kansas City *Star*. Orville considered this a rejection of him. Wilbur had been dead for 14 years, and he completely cut off all contact with Katharine. In his mind, Katharine had broken the sacred pact forged after their mother's death. Even when Katharine was dying of pneumonia in 1929, Orville steadfastly refused to visit her, until the very end when he was at her bedside—but this only at the insistence of his older brother, Lorin. The unusually close family ties of the Wrights was a double-edged sword.)

Wilbur and Orville never officially graduated from high school, let alone went to college. Wilbur attended high school in Richmond, Indiana, where the family was living at the time. He was an accomplished scholar, taking courses in Greek, Latin, geometry, natural philosophy, geology, and composition and earning grades well above 90 percent in them all. In addition, he was an athlete, excelling in gymnastics. Wilbur was doing so well that Milton and Susan were considering sending him to Yale. Unfortunately, just before Wilbur was to graduate in June 1884, Milton abruptly moved the family to Dayton; there were compelling political reasons dealing with church business for this quick move. Wilbur was not able to officially complete the courses required for graduation, nor able to attend the commencement exercises. Consequently, Wilbur never officially received a high school diploma, and he never attended Yale. However, Wilbur continued to be a scholar, ultimately becoming better read than most college graduates.

Orville attended Central High School in Dayton. In contrast to Wilbur, Orville was not an outstanding student, but he managed. His grades were in the 70–90 percent range. He was not the scholar that Wilbur was; Orville had little interest in higher education. Just before he was to return for his senior year, Orville's mother died. However, Orville had already decided not to return mainly because he had taken several special advanced courses in his junior year and, as a result, was going to be several credits shy of the necessary number for graduation. Because he would not be able to graduate with his classmates, Orville decided not to return. Instead, he was interested in being a printer, and he began to pursue this activity, including building his own printing press. His commercial ventures in the printing business, however, were not successful. In short, the inventors of the first practical flying machine never received high school diplomas.

By 1892, both Wilbur and Orville were bicycle enthusiasts, competing in local races. In December of 1892, they opened a bicycle shop on West Third Street in Dayton. At first, they only sold and repaired bicycles. However, by 1895 they were manufacturing and selling their own line of bicycles. It was a profitable business. The bicycle had become a major mode of transportation by 1890; at the height of its popularity in the 1890s, there were more than 300 companies in the United States manufacturing over a million bicycles a year. The Wrights' talent in designing and building bicycles had a nontrivial impact on their later flying machine work. Peter Jakab, in his definitive book *Visions of a Flying Machine*, nicely summarizes the situation, as follows:

> While the major bicycle manufacturers were employing mass-production techniques adopted from the firearm and sewing-machine industries, the Wrights remained small scale and continued to produce handmade originals. At a time when manufacturing was becoming increasingly mechanized and rapidly rushing toward the twentieth century, the Wrights stayed firmly within the classic artisan tradition of handcrafted, carefully finished individual pieces. This kind of attention to detail and craftsmanship would be a hallmark of their flying machines. Every component of their aircraft was designed and built with great care and served a specific and essential function. It is a bit ironic that an invention that has been so influential in the twentieth century was a product of men whose approach was so firmly anchored in the nineteenth century.

FIGURE 4.1
The Wrights' bicycle shop
in Dayton (circa 1900).

FIGURE 4.2
The Wrights' house at
7 Hawthorn Street in
Dayton (circa 1900).

The Wrights were also anchored to another 19th century phenomenon, namely, they were among the group of self-educated engineers who, without the benefit of a university education, proceeded to make significant engineering advances. The Aeronautical Society of Great Britain was originally composed of such men. The label "aeronautical engineer" was beginning to appear; both Lilienthal and Chanute used this term in their writings. However, the Wright brothers were the first to deserve, in the fullest sense, to be called aeronautical engineers.

Hence, in the year 1899, we find the brothers Wright firmly entrenched in the bicycle business in modest surroundings at 1127 West Third Street in Dayton; Figure 4.1 is a photograph of the Wrights' shop taken about that time. We also find them living rather comfortably in the Wrights' house at 7 Hawthorn Street in Dayton, shown in Figure 4.2. (Both the bicycle shop and the house are now located in Greenfield Village, Dearborn, Michigan, having been purchased and moved by Henry Ford in 1936 and 1937, respectively. These structures are part of the museum that Ford created to honor American ingenuity and industrial achievement; they are continuously maintained at Dearfield Village and are open to the public.) In Figure 4.3, we see them as a team, embodying well-read intellectuality, innate mechanical talents, a penchant for quality craftsmanship, a staunchly moral attitude, and an extremely dedicated work ethic. What fertile soil for the sowing of the seeds of the engineering challenge of powered flight.

In 1899, before Wilbur drafted his letter to the Smithsonian, how familiar was he with the existing technology of the airplane? Although the records are sketchy on this matter, the answer is this: very little. The Wrights had read some of the popular literature, such as articles about Lilienthal's glider flights in *McClure's Magazine*, which was in wide circulation at the time. In fact, the Wrights were aware of Lilienthal as early as 1890 because they published two short articles about him in a newspaper they printed and sold for a brief time in that year. In Wilbur's letter to the Smithsonian, he states, "The works on the subject to which I have had access are Marey's and Jamieson's published by Appleton's and various magazines and cyclopaedic articles." These were articles of not much consequence. If we take Wilbur literally, then the Wrights were pretty much in the dark about the *technical* state of the art of flying machines. It is curious, however, that Wilbur began his letter with the statement, "I have been interested in the problem of mechanical and human flight ever since as a boy I constructed a number of bats of various sizes after the style of Cayley's and Penaud's machines." Clearly he was aware at an early time of some of the basic configurations developed by George Cayley and Alphonse Penaud, but it is not clear where he got his information. A question comes immediately to mind: Why had the Wrights not read Chanute's *Progress in Flying Machines*? It was published five years before Wilbur wrote to the Smithsonian and was written by a well-known civil engineer who lived in Chicago, less than 250 miles from the Wrights' home in Dayton. The answer most likely resides in the limited public interest in the subject at that time, plus the limited funding most likely available to Dayton's Montgomery County Library. Chanute's book was by no means a best seller; most likely a copy was not available within the sphere of the Wrights' every day activities.

In any event, the Smithsonian replied quickly to the request in Wilbur's letter for "such papers as the Smithsonian Institution has published on this subject

FIGURE 4.3
Wilbur (left) and Orville
Wright on the back steps
of their home in Dayton.

[mechanical flight], and if possible a list of other works in print in the English language." Assistant Secretary of the Smithsonian Richard Rathburn replied on June 2, 1899, enclosing a list of publications on aeronautics. On this list were several of the most important sources available, sources we have discussed earlier in this book, namely, Chanute's *Progress in Flying Machines*, Langley's *Experiments in Aerodynamics*, and Means's *The Aeronautical Annual* for 1895, 1896, and 1897. Included in the reply were copies of four Smithsonian pamphlets, including one written by Langley and another by Lilienthal. Wilbur wrote back on June 14, thanking the Smithsonian and enclosing a dollar for the purchase of *Experiments in Aerodynamics*. Clearly, this interaction with the Smithsonian, initiated by Wilbur's letter, was a watershed in their lives; it jump-started their study of the important and substantive aeronautical literature. With that, they quickly immersed themselves in the existing state of the art. Among other sources, they obtained a copy of *Progress in Flying Machines* in 1899 and studied it carefully. We have no precise record of the full extent of what they read and when and of their detailed reactions at that time. In 1920, however, when reflecting on this period of their work, Orville stated this:

> On reading the different works on the subject we were much impressed with the great number of people who had given thought to it (mechanical flight), among some of the greatest minds the world has produced. . . . After reading the pamphlets sent to us by the Smithsonian we became highly enthusiastic with the idea of gliding as a sport.

During the summer of 1899, the Wrights took a quantum leap in their familiarity with the existing aeronautical literature.

From our earlier discussions, we see that the Wrights were not working in a vacuum when they began their activities in aeronautics. Indeed, they inherited a technical legacy, which was in many respects rich in content and ideas, and it focused the Wrights in a general direction, which was to lead them to success. Jakab, in *Visions of a Flying Machine*, states it this way:

> The phase of aeronautical development just prior to the Wrights' entry into the field had yielded much productive research and had laid a foundation of critical inquiry that would be invaluable to the next generation of experimenters. The status of the invention of the airplane was still much like searching for a needle in a haystack, but now at least it was known in which haystack to look.

Jakab goes on to give his view of the impact that previous work had on the Wrights:

> The experience of their predecessors did more to reveal fundamental questions than to provide answers, but wading through the failures and the misunderstandings of others aided the brothers in focusing quickly on the basic problems that needed to be addressed. Much of what the Wrights accomplished was highly original, but the findings of the late nineteenth century definitely gave them several useful pieces to the puzzle, as well as saving them from many unfruitful avenues of research. If the brothers had been a generation older, it is not at all certain that they would have avoided the stumbling blocks of those who were working in the second half of the nineteenth century. The Wrights were especially talented to be sure, but there is no reason to believe their genius operated in a vacuum, and that they would have invented the airplane no matter when they took up the problem.

In the discipline of aeronautics, the field was poised for almost immediate enlightenment and success. The Wright brothers were the right people at the right time; they used their innate inventive ability and took advantage of the opportunity. Had the Wright brothers never embarked on their aeronautical work, most likely the successful airplane would have been invented in Europe about 10 years later. As it turned out, the first credible airplane flights in Europe took place in 1907 in an ungainly machine called the "14-bis," developed and flown in Paris by the dashing Brazilian engineer, Alberto Santos-Dumont. The first flight, on September 13, covered only 7 meters, but a second flight, on October 23, remained airborne over a distance of close to 60 meters and won the Archdeacon prize for the first flight of 25 meters. After this, Santos-Dumont fitted octagonal-shaped ailerons to the machine and on November 12 executed a flight that covered 220 meters, staying in the air for 21.2 seconds. These were officially the first powered airplane flights in Europe, and because at that time most people were oblivious to the Wrights, Santos-Dumont was heralded by many as the first person to successfully fly a heavier-than-air, powered machine. For almost a year, the French felt that the airplane had been invented in France. The 14-bis, however, was not a practical aircraft. Nevertheless, had the Wrights never existed, the airplane would have been invented by others sometime very early in the 20th century.

But the Wright brothers *were* the first ones to do it, and they did it with dispatch, achieving their historic flight on December 17, 1903—just a little over four years after Wilbur wrote his fateful letter to the Smithsonian. This was due to much more than just extending the technical legacy they inherited. The Wright brothers had an engineering methodology unlike any of their predecessors. Jakab has written what is perhaps the clearest and most precise statement about this, as follows:

> If close attention is paid to their methodology, it becomes quite apparent that there were a number of specific personality traits, innate skills, and particular research techniques present in the Wrights' approach that came together in a unique way and largely explain why these two men invented the airplane. In short, the Wrights had a definable method that in very direct terms led them to the secrets of flight.

THE WRIGHTS' EARLIEST TECHNOLOGY—THE 1899 KITE

The Wrights' most important and most original contribution to the technology of the airplane occurred very early in their aeronautical development program—the appreciation of the need for lateral control and a mechanical mechanism for achieving it. Although the Wrights were to go on and pioneer many aspects of aeronautical engineering and applied aerodynamic research, their early recognition of the importance of lateral control, and the invention of a mechanical means of achieving it, is perhaps the crowning single element of their technology.

Lateral motion of an aircraft is, by definition, the rolling motion about an axis through the fuselage and parallel to the flight direction. Consider the front view of an airplane, as shown in Figure 4.4. The rolling motion is indicated by the curved arrow. In a modern airplane, the common mechanical device for inducing rolling motion is control surfaces called ailerons. Ailerons are flaplike elements at the trailing edge of the wings; like a wing flap, if an aileron is defected downward, the lift on that wing is increased, and, conversely, if the aileron is deflected upward, the

FIGURE 4.4
Front view of an airplane, illustrating rolling motion induced by aileron deflection.

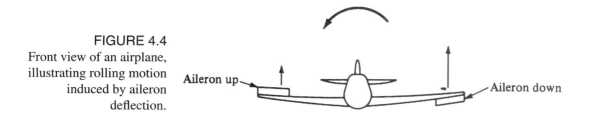

Aileron up — Aileron down

wing lift is decreased. In Figure 4.4, the aileron at the right is deflected downward, increasing the lift on the wing at the right, and the aileron on the left is deflected upward, decreasing the lift on the wing at the left. The net imbalance of lift on the two wings results in a rolling motion about the fuselage, shown by the counterclockwise arrow in Figure 4.4.

The Wrights were well aware that Lilienthal achieved both lateral and longitudinal control by shifting and swinging his body as it hung beneath his glider; in this way Lilienthal was able to keep the aircraft's center of gravity (including his body weight) and the aerodynamically generated center of pressure (that point on the aircraft through which the net aerodynamic force acts) on top of each other—the necessary condition for equilibrium flight in pitch, roll, and yaw. This was not easy to do. Wilbur's own description of this problem can be found in in a paper he delivered to the Western Society of Engineers in Chicago on September 18, 1901, where he commented on the overall problem of stability and control:

> The balancing of a gliding or flying machine is very simple in theory. It merely consists of causing the center of pressure to coincide with the center of gravity. But in actual practice there seems to be an almost boundless incompatibility of temper which prevents their remaining peaceably together for a single instant, so that the operator, who in this case acts as peacemaker, often suffers injury to himself while attempting to bring them together.

This was a clear and accurate statement of the phenomenon, one example out of many that reflected the Wrights' basic understanding of the problems of flight by that time. (*Note*: Wilbur Wright was an excellent technical writer—clear, knowledgeable, and to the point. A hundred years later, his papers still stand as an excellent example of the art of good technical writing, some interspersed with his subtle humor.)

The Wrights rejected the hang glider technique immediately. The adjusting of the center of gravity by swinging one's body seemed too ad hoc. Also, it was inherently dangerous due to physical fatigue. Besides, there was an inherent limitation on this technique for larger and heavier gliders: The heavier the machine, the smaller the effect of a person's body weight (which is a fixed value) on the movement of the overall center of gravity. In Orville's words, "We at once set to work to devise a more efficient means of maintaining the equilibrium . . . ."

Obtaining longitudinal (pitching) and directional (yawing) control by means of the deflection of the horizontal and vertical tail, respectively, had been examined during the 19th century. This was part of the technical legacy inherited by the Wrights. However, no attention had been paid to lateral control. The Wrights solution to this problem was both intellectual and mechanical. First came the intellectual understanding that a rolling moment, hence, lateral control, could be obtained by simultaneously setting the right wing at one angle of attack to the flow and the left wing at another angle of attack, such that the different lift forces on the two wings would induce a rolling motion. There is some uncertainty as to how this intellectual concept came to the Wrights. Early in 1900, in a letter to Octave Chaute, Wilbur stated, "My observation of the flight of buzzards leads me to believe that they regain their lateral balance, when partly overturned by a gust of wind, by a torsion of the tips of the wings."

This statement has led some people to think that the intellectual concept of differentially changing the angle of attack of the two wings came to Wilbur as a result of observing bird flight. But much later, Orville dispelled this idea in a letter to J. Horace Lytle on December 27, 1941, where he wrote the following:

> I cannot think of any part bird flight had in the development of human flight excepting as an inspiration. Although we intently watched birds fly in a hope of learning something from them I cannot think of anything that was first learned in that way. After we had thought out certain principles, we then watched the bird to see whether it used the same principles. In a few cases we did detect the same thing in the bird's flight.
>
> Learning the secret of flight from a bird was a good deal like learning the secret of magic from a magician. After you once know the trick and know what to look for you see things that you did not notice when you did not know exactly what to look for.

So the precise time and manner at which the intellectual solution to lateral control occurred to the Wrights is not known. The fact is, however, that it did, and it came sometime before July 1899. Because in that month they proof tested the concept using a kite, as will be discussed shortly.

The next question was this: by what mechanical means can this differential angle of attack of the two wings be achieved? Their first concept involved pivoting both wings via a gear and shaft arrangement; one wing would be pivoted so as to increase the angle of attack and, hence, increase the lift on that wing, and the other wing would be simultaneously pivoted in the reverse direction so as to decrease the angle of attack and, hence, decrease the lift on it. The difference in lift on the two wings would set up a rolling motion, similar to that shown in Figure 4.4. They rejected this approach, however, because, as Orville stated much later, "... we did not see any method of building this device sufficiently strong and at the same time light enough to enable us to use it."

Their mechanical solution to obtaining lateral control was conceived by Wilbur, almost by chance. A customer dropped into the Wrights' bicycle shop to buy an inner tube for a tire. Wilbur, who was alone in the shop at the time, removed the inner tube from its cardboard box and began casually to twist the box between his fingers while talking with his customer. He became aware that, when pressing the corners of the long box together in a certain manner, one end of the box flexed downward and the other upward. If the box were an airplane wing, this would be much like the orientation of the wing necessary to obtain an imbalance of the lift over the span of the wing, hence, inducing a rolling moment. The history of technology is peppered with instances where breakthroughs were a result of serendipity. This is one such case. Wilbur, who had been looking for a mechanical solution for lateral control, found it quite by accident while he was playing with the innertube box.

This invention by the Wrights of twisting the wingtips, which they achieved by removing the fore-and-aft diagonal wire bracing of the trussed biplane configuration used by Chanute, but retaining the spanwise trussing, and twisting the wings across the chord by wires controlled by the pilot, came to be known as *wing warping*. It was used in all of their flying machines until 1911.

The viability of wing warping for lateral control was proven simply, rapidly, and to their satisfaction by the Wrights less than two months after Wilbur had written to the Smithsonian. They designed a kite made of two superimposed

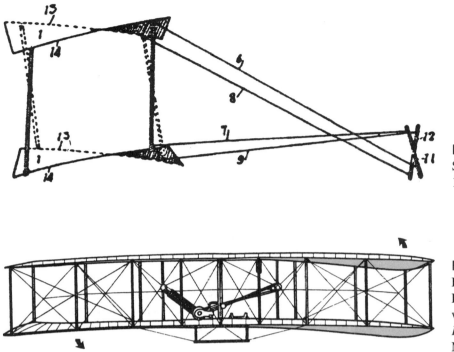

FIGURE 4.5
Side-view of the Wrights'
1899 kite.

FIGURE 4.6
Front-view of the Wright
Flyer, illustrating wing
warping. (From Combs,
Kill Devil Hill, Houghton
Mifflin, Boston, 1979.)

planes, each with a span of 5 feet and a constant chord of 13 inches (giving a wing aspect ratio of 4.62). Orville's drawing of this kite, from his deposition in 1921, is shown in Figure 4.5. The kite was controlled by string from two sticks, one held in each hand; the wing warping, clearly illustrated in Figure 4.5, was achieved by simultaneously moving the top of one stick forward and the top of the other backward. Note that there are no fore-and-aft diagonal struts, as seen in the side view of Figure 4.5, only vertical struts. The Wrights called these vertical struts "uprights." This strut arrangement allowed the wingtips (labeled 13 and 14 in Figure 4.5) to be warped in opposite directions by moving the two sticks (11 and 12) connected to the wings by strings (6–9). The basic design of this wing warping concept was carried over to their subsequent gliders and powered machines. Figure 4.6 shows the front view of the 1903 Wright Flyer with wing warping in action, rolling the machine in the counterclockwise direction.

The kite was flown by Wilbur sometime during the last week in July—the precise date was not recorded by Wilbur, and Orville was not present. (Crouch theorizes that, because the Wrights had no assistant in the bicycle shop at that time, one or the other brothers had to be at the shop, and that person was Orville when the kite was flown.) The only witnesses were a group of schoolboys. Wilbur was pleased with the results; the kite responded to the warping of the wings, always lifting the wing that was twisted upward. In Orville's words, "We felt that the model (the kite) had demonstrated the efficiency of our system of control." Here we see the first demonstration of the Wrights' engineering methodology; in this case, it was the direct use of a flight test to prove a vital concept. This was a necessary first step; without it the Wrights could not have logically progressed. As it turned out, with the success of their kite tests, the Wrights were encouraged to take the next step. They instantly made the decision to construct a machine large enough to carry a person, but embodying the basic design features of their kite. This was to lead a year later to their 1900 glider.

THE 1900 GLIDER

The bicycle business regularly peaked in the summer, and so the block of time that the brothers had for aeronautical work was approximately between September and January. During 1900, however, before September, they found time to design a glider large enough, they felt, to carry a person into the air. With the exception of the incorporation of wing warping for lateral control, which was uniquely their development, they used existing technology for this glider design. A photograph of the Wrights' 1900 glider is shown in Figure 4.7. Here we see the biplane configuration that evolved throughout the 19th century, strengthened by a strut and wire truss system between the wings, a modification of that championed by Octave Chanute in the 1890s. The Wrights chose to place a horizontal surface, much smaller than the wing surface, several feet ahead of the wings. Its purpose was to help in the longitudinal balance of the machine. Its location in front of the wings instead of the more conventional horizontal tail position behind the wings was an intentional effort to ensure more safety. The Wrights were always conscious of the gliding accident that killed Lilienthal in 1896, and they reasoned that a horizontal surface placed ahead of the pilot would help to compensate for a rearward shift in the center pressure on the wing caused by unexpected pitch-up due to wind gusts. As it turned out in their future designs, the forward tail location, which is called a *canard configuration*, helped them when the machine would stall by cushioning

FIGURE 4.7
The Wrights' 1900 glider.

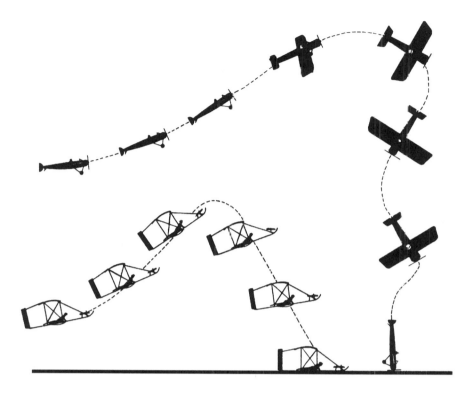

FIGURE 4.8
The design of the 1902 glider, with its forward canard surface, cushioned a stall, allowing the machine and pilot to "parachute" to the ground (bottom). This is in contrast to the design of a conventional airplane that normally would fall off on one wing and go into a spin (top and right). (From Combs, *Kill Devil Hill*, Houghton Mifflin, Boston, 1979.)

this stall and allowing the machine in the stall to descend rather gently in an almost "parachute" style. (This is in contrast to the nose dive encountered by Lilienthal when his glider stalled and he was fatally injured in the crash.) This behavior is shown at the bottom of Figure 4.8, where the 1902 glider with its canard surface is shown pitching up, stalling, and then parachuting gently to the ground. In contrast, a more conventional airplane, shown at the top of Figure 4.8, goes into a stall, falls off on one wing, and spins toward the ground. At the time they were designing the 1900 glider, the Wrights had no understanding of the nature of stall. With their later flight experience, however, the Wrights were convinced that the canard configuration was right for them, and they stuck with it for all of their flying machine designs until 1910, when in their Wright Model B of that year, they placed the horizontal tail in the rear.

The aerodynamic performance of the 1900 glider was calculated by the Wrights using Lilienthal's table of normal and axial force coefficients, from which they easily obtained the lift and drag coefficients. Their access to this table was via a paper by Octave Chanute entitled "Sailing Flight" published in 1897 in the *Aeronautical Annual*, in which he republished the Lilienthal table. (The original table had appeared in 1895 in Moedebeck's handbook in German.) The Wrights had gained a great deal of respect for Lilienthal during their study of the literature, and it was natural that they would feel comfortable in using his aerodynamic data for the design of their flying machine. This general respect for Lilienthal remained with them over the years.

The design point for their 1900 glider was the production of enough lift to sustain the machine plus pilot in the air when the airflow velocity relative to the machine was 18 miles per hour. At this flight velocity (airspeed), and for the estimated weight of the machine, their calculations based on the Lilienthal table indicated that the total wing planform area (the area of both wings combined) should be 200 square feet to generate enough lift when the angle of attack was 3 degrees—a value chosen by the Wrights as being reasonable. They knew that at higher angles of attack, the drag would be much larger—an undesirable feature. Hence, right from the beginning, the Wrights functioned as reasoned aeronautical engineers; they carried out analysis and made calculations to design their glider intelligently. For these calculations they took "off-the-shelf" technology—they used selectively the pertinent results from the existing literature. Lilienthal's table is one such example.

On September 6, 1900, Wilbur Wright left Dayton's Union Station on a Big Four train: destination—Kitty Hawk, North Carolina. Packed in his baggage were the prefabricated parts of the glider that the Wrights had designed. He was about to commence a series of flight tests with the glider, and the choice of Kitty Hawk as the venue was based on U.S. Weather Bureau data on locations in the United States where the prevailing winds average over 18 miles per hour. If it were possible for Orville to break away from the bicycle shop, it was planned for him to join Wilbur as soon as Wilbur was able to get the glider ready for flying. The train took Wilbur as far as Old Point, Virginia, from which he took a steamboat to Norfolk, Virginia. There he tried to find some spruce to make the long wing spars, but was unsuccessful; he ended up with white pine. Moreover, their wing design called for 18 foot lengths of spar material, and the white pine had only a maximum length of 16 feet. Consequently, Wilbur was forced to reduce the design wing area from 200 to 165 square feet. Based on the Lilienthal table, Wilbur calculated that the wind velocity necessary for sustaining the redesigned glider at a 3-degree angle of attack would be 21 miles per hour. From Norfolk he took the train to Elizabeth City, North Carolina, carrying his glider materials with him. The final leg of the trip was by boat across Albemarle Sound to Kitty Hawk. This part of the trip was extremely harrowing for Wilbur; the boat was essentially not seaworthy, and they encountered gale force winds and high waves during the crossing that almost sank the boat. What should have been an overnight trip was in fact almost two days from the time Wilbur left Elizabeth City to the moment he knocked on the door of the home William J. Tate at Kitty Hawk, where he was to stay during part of that season. Bill Tate was considered to be the most educated person in the small town; he was also the unofficial leader of Kitty Hawk. He was a fisherman, postmaster, notary public, and local county commissioner, as well as serving on the local lifesaving crew. The date was September 13, 1900. Wilbur had survived what was perhaps the most dangerous and life-threatening experience in his life.

He immediately set about the construction of the glider from the pieces that he had brought with him. His progress as well as his technical objectives were nicely described by him in a letter on September 23 to his father, in which he noted,

> I have my machine nearly finished. It is not to have a motor and is not expected to fly in any true sense of the word. My idea is merely to experiment and practice with a view to solving the problem of equilibrium. I have plans which I hope to find much in advance of the methods tried by previous experimenters . . . . I am constructing my machine to sustain about five times my weight and am testing every piece. I think there is no possible chance of its breaking while in the air . . . My machine will be trussed

like a bridge and will be much stronger than that of Lilienthal, which, by the way was upset through the failure of a movable tail and not by breakage of the machine ... My trip would be no great disappointment if I accomplish practically nothing. I look upon it as a pleasure trip pure and simple, and I know of no trip from which I could expect greater pleasure at the same cost ...

Here is a wonderful indication of Wilbur's innate engineering philosophy. He was not going for the whole prize; rather, he was constructing a glider that, for the most part, reflected the existing 19th century technology, but that was structurally more sound and that contained one major engineering advancement—wing warping for the purpose of lateral control and balance. Wilbur wanted to obtain *experience* and *data*, and that was all. He was looking to make a logical and incremental contribution to the state of the art of aeronautical technology.

On September 28, Orville arrived at Kitty Hawk. By October 4, they had set up their own camp in a tent about a half mile away from the Tate house. There they set about finishing the construction of their glider. Because Wilbur had not been able to find the length of wood long enough to make a wing spar according to their original design, they had to be satisfied with wings of smaller area—165 square feet instead of the originally designed 200 square feet of total area. (The total wing area of 165 square feet accounted for an 18-inch-wide cutout in the middle of the lower wing where the pilot would lie.) For each rectangular wing, the span was 17 feet and the chord was 5 feet, giving an aspect ratio of 3.4. The wings were covered with French sateen fabric, put on bias so that no wires were needed to brace the wing surface diagonally. The Wrights were already sensitive to the importance of aerodynamic drag reduction, and they buried the wing ribs and the rear spar, which had a square cross section, in pockets of fabric sewn over the top and bottom of the wood sections to create locally a faired-in shape to reduce the drag. For the truss mechanism, 15-gauge steel wire was used, in addition to wooden vertical supports, the uprights, between the wing.

The Wrights fully understood the consequence of the smaller wing area. Their original design point was to have the glider generate sufficient lift to fly at a 3-degree angle of attack in an 18-mile per hour wind. Now, with the smaller wing area, the amount of lift necessary to overcome the weight could only be obtained at a higher angle of attack (hence, more drag) and/or at a higher wind speed. However, they were not too worried about this because their primary purpose was to obtain technical data and, hopefully, to achieve some successful piloted glides in the process.

The initial flight of the glider was made during the first week of October; the precise date is not known. It was performed as a tethered flight with Wilbur onboard. This apparently was not satisfactory because they quickly moved to flying the glider as an unmanned kite from the ground. These kite flights were carried out systematically, loading the glider to different weights with various lengths of chain and measuring the drag. (The term used by the Wrights and others at the time was "drift.") On October 10 they tried flying the glider suspended from a derrick that they had constructed for the purpose. During these tests, the glider was carried away by a gust of wind and severely damaged. In Orville's words in a letter to Katharine Wright on October 14, "We dragged the pieces back to camp and began to consider getting home. They next morning we had cheered up some and began to think there was some hope of repairing it."

The Wrights did just that and continued with their flight tests. They abandoned the derrick idea, and most of the remaining flights were in the mode of a kite flown from the ground. A few of these were man carrying. Beginning on October 18, however, they started some free flights, the first simply being a free flight of the unmanned glider down a hill. Finally, on October 20, Wilbur climbed aboard the glider. With Orville and Bill Tate holding the wing tips and running down the slope of the Kill Devil Hill (where they had moved for the manned flights), the glider generated enough lift to carry Wilbur into the air on his own. Other flights followed; beginning with a few halting flights of about 5–10 seconds duration about 1 foot above the ground, Wilbur gradually managed to stay in the air for 15–20 seconds, covering 300–400 feet over the ground. On October 20, they ceased operations, and on October 23 they started their journey home.

Wilbur had done all the manned flying. He had managed a dozen flights into the air and amassed a total of two minutes of flight time. The Wrights were disappointed about this short length of flying experience; they had expected to do much more. But on the whole, they seemed to be somewhat satisfied with their first efforts to learn first-hand about the nature of a flying machine. Later, in 1901 in a paper given to the Western Society of Engineers, Wilbur noted the following about their experience at Kitty Hawk in 1900:

> Although the hours and hours of practice we had hoped to obtain finally dwindled down to about two minutes, we were very much pleased with the general results of the trip, for setting out as we did, with almost revolutionary theories on many points, and an entirely untried form of machine, we considered it quite a point to be able to return without having our pet theories completely knocked in the head by the hard logic of experience, and our own brains dashed out in the bargain.

Of the few advances in aeronautical technology achieved by the Wrights during their experiments at Kitty Hawk in 1900, the most important contribution was the absolute validation of wing warping as an effective mechanical means of achieving lateral control. Although the total amount of flying time that Wilbur achieved was only two minutes, this was enough to prove beyond a shadow of a doubt that lateral control was essential for successful flight and that the creation of differential lift by presenting the left and right wingtips at different angles of attack to the flow provided a viable mechanical mechanism to achieve this lateral control. This was a fundamental contribution to the development of the airplane.

In regard to wing dihedral, which earlier experimenters such as Penaud, Lilienthal, and Langley had felt to be very important for lateral stability, the Wrights were not convinced. Indeed, in their earliest tests in 1900, they found that dihedral made their glider very sensitive to sidewise gusts; they felt this was unsatisfactory and went to straight wings for the remainder of their flights that year. Throughout their subsequent development of the flying machine, the Wrights eschewed dihedral. They felt that they could control their machines much easier without it. Indeed, looking at the front view of the Wright Flyer in Figure 4.6, we note a certain amount of droop (anhedral) of the wings. This, however, was not a meaningful contribution to the early technology of the airplane; indeed, it might be viewed as somewhat retrograde. It was a precursor to their slowly developing philosophy that inherent stability was not all that important to successful airplane flight; they could readily dispense with the inherently stabilizing effect of dihedral and not think twice about it. Their 1903 Wright Flyer was intentionally designed to be statically *unstable*. This philosophy was not accepted by the rest of the aeronautical community, and most airplanes developed in the 20th century were statically *stable*, many of them employing dihedral for lateral stability, as needed.

Of all of the technical observations made by the Wrights in 1900, the one that was to eventually have the strongest impact on their future work was that their measurements of lift on the glider did not agree at all with their calculations of lift. Wilbur wrote about the 1900 glider, ". . . it appeared sadly deficient in lifting power as compared with the calculated lift of curved surfaces of its size." Indeed, their calculations indicated that, with a pilot onboard, a 21-mile-per-hour wind would lift the glider at an angle of attack of 3 degrees. The actual case was much worse; it took a 25-mile-per-hour wind to lift the glider plus pilot, and the angle of attack was 20 degrees. Because they used the Lilienthal table for their calculations, they began to have their first misgivings about the accuracy of Lilienthal's aerodynamic coefficients.

In the final assessment, with the exception of the concrete validation of their wing warping for lateral control, the Wrights' 1900 glider experiments contributed only incrementally to the aeronautical state of the art. But the Wrights were satisfied. When they left Kitty Hawk for home on October 23, they left the 1900 glider behind—they simply discarded it. They were already planning to return the following summer with a new, bigger, and better glider. (With the Wrights' permission, Bill Tate salvaged the 1900 glider for its materials. Mrs. Tate used the French sateen fabric to make dresses for her two young daughters.)

THE 1901 GLIDER

The year 1901 was busy for the Wrights. They set about designing a new glider. The characteristics of the new design were driven by the insufficient lift produced by their 1900 glider in comparison to their calculations based on Lilienthal's table of aerodynamic coefficients. What would you do if your glider was producing about one-third the lift you calculated and you desperately needed more lift at lower airspeeds? The most likely answer would be to make the glider bigger. That is exactly what the Wrights did. The new glider had almost twice the wing area, 290 square feet compared with the 165 square feet of the 1900 glider. The 1901 glider (with pilot) weighed 240 pounds compared with 190 pounds for the 1900 glider. The new glider had a wing loading of 0.83 pounds per square foot compared with 1.15 pounds per square foot for the 1900 glider. The Wrights were rapidly maturing as aeronautical engineers. They knew that an aircraft with a smaller wing loading could lift itself off the ground at a lower velocity, and so they intentionally designed their new glider with a smaller wing loading. They incorporated a second feature that they hoped would improve the lift; they increased the airfoil camber to 1/12 compared with the value of 1/23 for the 1900 glider. Lilienthal's table was for an airfoil with a camber of 1/12, and the Wrights thought that by matching Lilienthal's value they would remove some of the earlier discrepancy between their calculations and what was actually measured. But at the same time they hedged their bets; they designed a mechanism in the wings that would allow them to readily change the camber in the field from one flight to the next, simply by retrussing the wings. The wingspan of the 1901 glider was 22 feet, which gave a wing aspect ratio of 3.3; this was actually smaller than the 3.5 aspect ratio of their

1900 glider. The Wrights still did not appreciate the aerodynamic value of high aspect ratio wings, and their new design was actually going in the wrong direction in this respect. With the exception of the design features just mentioned, in virtually every other respect, the new glider was essentially the same as the 1900 glider.

The Wrights were anxious to test their new glider. Orville and Wilbur left Dayton together for Kitty Hawk on July 7, 1901, more than two months earlier than they had originally planned and two months earlier than the previous year. They set up camp at Kill Devil Hill, about four miles south of Kitty Hawk. Camp consisted of a tent and a shed; the shed (Wilbur called it "a cheap frame building") was large enough to hold the new glider and to serve as a workshop. By July 27, they had finished the construction of the flying machine, and on that day they went for broke. Wilbur made 17 glides that day, in the face of prevailing winds of about 13 miles per hour. Although from the point of view of an observer these glides appeared to be successful, one of them covering a distance of 300 feet, Wilbur knew differently. The new glider was almost uncontrollable in pitch. On the first few glides, it nosed almost immediately into the ground. Wilbur, lying prone, shifted his position (hence, the center of gravity) farther back on the wing for several subsequent flights, until finally he found a position that placed the center of gravity at the center of pressure; the center of pressure was clearly a foot back of where they had expected it to be. With the center of gravity in a more favorable position, the next flight covered more than 300 feet, remaining airborne for 19 seconds, and appeared successful. But Wilbur had to deflect the horizontal canard surface ahead of the wings the full amount, back and forth, to correct for an undulating motion. He was not happy about this, later writing the following:

> To the onlookers this flight seemed very successful, but to the operator it was known that the full power of the rudder (the Wrights' label for the forward-placed, movable horizontal canard surface) had been required to keep the machine from either running into the ground or rising so high as to lose all headway. In the 1900 machine one fourth as much rudder action had been sufficient to give much better control. It was apparent that something was radically wrong, though we were for some time unable to locate the trouble.

The Wrights soon correctly diagnosed the problem. They knew that the center of pressure of any airfoil shape changes its location on the airfoil as the angle of attack is changed. The movement of the center of pressure as the angle of attack of the airfoil is decreased is illustrated in Figure 4.9. For a cambered airfoil, starting at a very high angle of attack, say, 90 degrees, the center of pressure is near the middle of the airfoil. As the angle of attack decreases, the center of pressure moves forward, toward the leading edge. However, at some relatively small angle of attack, the movement of the center of pressure reverses itself, and at yet smaller angles of attack, the center of pressure moves rapidly toward the trailing edge as the angle of attack is further decreased. The larger the camber of the airfoil, the larger the angle of attack at which this reversal occurs, and the faster the travel of the center of pressure. With the increased camber of the 1901 glider wings compared with that of the previous year, the Wrights were experiencing more radical movement of the center of pressure, hence making their machine more

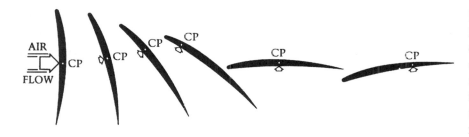

FIGURE 4.9
Movement of the center-of-pressure (CP) on an airfoil as the airfoil angle of attack is reduced from 90 degrees to a negative value (left to right). (From Combs, *Kill Devil Hill*, Houghton Mifflin, Boston, 1979.)

difficult to control. They made some measurements of the movement of the center of pressure and found it to be unacceptably large. Recall that with much prescience they had designed their 1901 glider such that the airfoil camber could be easily changed in the field. They immediately decreased the camber to 1/17. This fixed the longitudinal stability problem, and in the next glides, the machine handled much more like their 1900 glider, much to the relief of the Wrights.

Much to their consternation, the Wrights found that the lift of their new glider was as woefully deficient as their 1900 glider. Although the 1901 glider was larger, and indeed did produce more lift than their smaller 1900 glider, the measured lift was still far below their predictions based on Lilienthal's table. Wilbur wrote in his diary on July 29, 1901, "Afternoon spent in kite tests. Found lift of machine much less than Lilienthal tables would indicate, reaching only about 1/3 as much." The next day, he wrote again:

> The most discouraging features of our experiments so far are these:
>
> 1. The lift is not much over 1/3 that indicated by the Lilienthal tables. As we had expected to devote a major portion of our time to experimenting in an 18-mile wind without much motion of the machine, we find that our hopes of obtaining actual practice in the air are decreased to about one fifth of what we hoped, as now it is necessary to glide in order to get a sustaining speed. Five minutes' practice in free flight is a good day's record. We have not yet reached so good an average as this even.

Wilbur went on to list other discouraging features such as the poorer control compared with their 1900 glider, a higher measured drag (almost double) than expected, and more sluggishness in free flight.

The lift being much smaller than they expected ruined any hope of long hours of flight testing with the glider tethered as a kite and a pilot aboard. They had counted on this mode of operation to give them long hours of practice controlling the machine in the air. It was not to be. Although Wilbur achieved far more free-flight gliding time with the 1901 machine than he had in 1900, he was by no means satisfied with the state of affairs.

An interesting sidelight to their stay at Kill Devil Hill in 1901 was that they had visitors. Octave Chanute arrived on August 5 and remained with the Wrights for six days, taking close notes of the experiments, snapping photographs of the 1901 machine in flight, and generally providing good fatherly company for Wilbur and Orville. In addition, two other visitors, Edward Huffaker and George Spratt, joined them at Chanute's suggestion. Huffaker had experience with flying machines, having worked as an assistant to Samuel Langley at the Smithsonian between 1894 and 1898. Spratt was a Pennsylvania farmer with an informed interest in flying machines. The Wrights soon found Huffaker to be a disagreeable visitor, but they liked Spratt; the Wrights and Spratt were to remain close friends, and Wilbur and George were frequent letter correspondents over the ensuing years.

Their spirits dampened by rain and with growing confusion and despair about their test results, the Wrights left for home on August 20. Wilbur later recalled that on the trip back to Dayton he dejectedly said to Orville "that men would not fly for fifty years." Much later, in 1940 Orville recalled this statement as "not within a thousand years would man ever fly." The Wrights' spirits were at low ebb.

WHAT WAS WRONG?

Back in Dayton, the Wrights struggled to make sense of their flying experience. Fortunately, Octave Chanute provided an almost therapeutic mechanism for the Wrights. Chanute was impressed by what he saw during his visit to Kill Devil Hill. On August 29, 1901, he wrote to Wilbur, stating the following:

> I have been talking with some members of the Western Society of Engineers. The conclusion is that the members would be very glad to have an address, or a lecture from you, on your gliding experiments. We have a meeting on the 18th of September, and can set that for your talk. If you conclude to come I hope you will do me the favor of stopping at my house.

(Note that Chanute's invitation was to Wilbur, not Orville. Chanute obviously realized that Wilbur was the intellectual leader of the Wrights' team effort. Virtually all of Chanute's correspondence was with Wilbur. Also, it was Wilbur who had piloted the 1900 and 1901 gliders; Orville was not to get into the air until the following year.)

Wilbur was at first hesitant about Chanute's invitation. Their flight experiments to date introduced so many unanswered questions to their minds. Besides, Wilbur had never given a technical paper to a professional audience. On the other hand, receiving such a kind invitation from a man of the technical stature of Octave Chanute had to be uplifting to both brothers at a time when they were quite discouraged about their perceived lack of progress in flying. On September 2 Wilbur replied with a mild "yes" to Chanute's invitation. In reality, their sister Katherine, always a staunch supporter and close companion to Wilbur and Orville, played a strong role in Wilbur's decision. In a letter to her father on September 3, Katharine wrote:

> Through Mr. Chanute, Will has an invitation to make a speech before the Western Society of Civil Engineers, which has a meeting in Chicago in a couple of weeks. Will is to perform on the eighteenth. His subject is his gliding experiments. Will was about to refuse but I nagged him into going. He will get acquainted with some scientific men and it may do him a lot of good.

Although he had only a few weeks to prepare his paper, this was an excellent opportunity for Wilbur to collect his thoughts and reflect on the results of their flight experiments. At 8 p.m. on September 18, 1901, Wilbur stood before a friendly and willing audience of the Western Society of Engineers in Chicago and delivered a profound technical paper. It was simply entitled "Some Aeronautical Experiments," but it represented a comprehensive survey and commentary on their progress to date. Wilbur ended his paper by itemizing what seemed to him their most important technical findings, quoted as follows (with my added parenthetical comments):

> In looking over our experiments of the past two years, with models and full-sized machines, the following points stand out with clearness:
>
> 1. That the lifting power of a large machine, held stationary in a wind at a small distance from the earth, is much less than the Lilienthal table and our own laboratory experiments would lead us to expect. When the machine is moved through the air, as in gliding, the discrepancy seems much less marked. [Some of the author's recent research has shown that the Lilienthal table is basically sound and that the discrepancy between the Wrights' calculations and their measurements was due to their misinterpretation of Lilienthal's table in three distinct aspects. More on this later.]
>
> 2. That the ratio of drift to lift in well-shaped surfaces is less at angles of incidence of 5 degrees to 12 degrees than at an angle of 3 degrees. [The ratio of drift to lift is the reciprocal of what today we call the lift-to-drag ratio, L/D. Wilbur is noting that the lift-to-drag ratio is higher at angles of attack between 5 and 12 degrees than it is at lower angles of attack. Using Wilbur's estimate that the maximum L/D for the 1901 glider with pilot aboard was about 7, and employing standard modern analytical techniques (see, for example, J. D., Anderson, *Introduction to Flight*, 4th edition, McGraw-Hill, 2000), I estimate that the angle of attack at which the maximum L/D would be achieved is about 8 degrees. This data point is consistent with Wilbur's observation. As was usually the case, Wilbur knew what he was talking about.]
>
> 3. That in arched surfaces the center of pressure at 90 degrees is near the center of the surface, but moves slowly forward as the angle becomes less, till a critical angle varying with the shape and depth of the curve is reached, after which it moves rapidly toward the rear till the angle of no lift is found. [Here, Wilbur is spelling out for the first time in the literature what is today a well-known characteristic of cambered airfoils. See again Figure 4.9.]
>
> 4. That with similar conditions, large surfaces may be controlled with not much greater difficulty than small ones, if the control is effected by manipulation of the surfaces themselves, rather than by a movement of the body of the operator. [With the few successful glide flights of their 1901 glider, Wilbur had flown under control the largest and heaviest flying machine in history. He is pointing out that such flight of a large machine can be safely achieved, but with mechanical controls, not by shifting body weight as Lilienthal had done.]
>
> 5. That the head resistances of the framing can be brought to a point much below that usually estimated as necessary. [Head resistance, a term of the Wrights adopted from the aeronautical literature at that time, is today essentially what we term as parasite drag—drag due to friction acting on the surface of the airplane, plus drag due to pressure imbalance caused by separation of the flow over various parts of the airplane. It can be reduced by proper streamlining of the airplane shape. Wilbur's statement reflects two points: 1) They went to some efforts to reduce the drag of their 1901 glider, for example by locating the leading-edge wing spar underneath the nose of the cambered airfoil to present a more streamlined shape to the flow. The author suspects that their glider was aerodynamically more efficient than the data on which existing calculations for head resistance in the literature were based. 2) The existing calculational techniques for head resistance were themselves somewhat ad hoc and subject to considerable error. Wilbur's statement is simply saying two things—that their attention to drag reduction paid some dividends and that the existing techniques for calculating head resistance probably resulted in predicted values that were too large.]
>
> 6. That tails, both vertical and horizontal, may with safety be eliminated in gliding and other flying experiments. [Here, Wilbur is simply touting their design with the forward-placed horizontal canard surface. They had no rearward-placed tail in the more conventional sense as used by Cayley, Penaud, Lilienthal, Chanute, and Langley, and, of course, as used today on conventional airplane designs. Wilbur is simply saying that their configuration worked. The Wrights clung to their canard design until their Model B in 1910, when they moved the horizontal tail to the rear of the airplane.

However, as early as 1902 they found it necessary to mount a vertical tail surface in the rear for all of their subsequent machines. So this statement by Wilbur was a statement of fact for them in 1901, but it soon lost its significance.]

7. That a horizontal position of the operator's body may be assumed without excessive danger, and thus the head resistance reduced to about one fifth that of the upright position. [The Wrights' choice of a prone position for the pilot was not adopted by others; indeed by 1908 the Wright Type A machine had the pilot and passenger sitting upright. So the prone position for the pilot was not a lasting contribution to the technology of the airplane.]

8. That a pair of superposed, or tandem surfaces, has less lift in proportion to drift than either surface separately, even after making allowance for weight and head resistance of the connections. [This is the first statement in the aeronautical literature of the adverse interference effect due to the biplane configuration. The Wrights already recognized that by placing one wing above the other, or one directly behind the other, the lift of the combined wings is less and the drag is more in comparison to a single wing with the same total area and the same aspect ratio. The biplane effect became a subject for intensive theoretical study in the period around 1918–1920. It is amazing that the Wrights had discovered this effect as early as 1901.]

The single most perplexing problem to the Wrights at this time was the lack of agreement between their measurements of lift and their calculations based on the Lilienthal tables. What was wrong? It was fairly clear what the Wrights were thinking. They began to suspect the validity of Lilienthal's tables. In spite of their obvious respect for the contributions made by Lilienthal, their suspicion of his tables was so strong that Wilbur was bold enough to put in writing in his 1901 paper to the Western Society the statement that "the Lilienthal tables might themselves be somewhat in error." As time went on that fall, the Wrights became even more convinced of this. The question as to the validity of Lilienthal's table, and its adverse effect on the early glider design of the Wrights, has continued to recent times. However, some research has been carried out by the author that explains and reconciles the discrepancy. Simply stated, the Wrights misinterpreted the Lilienthal tables in three respects, and when these misinterpretations are accounted for, the Lilienthal tables predict a lift about one-third that calculated by the Wrights—exactly what the Wrights measured.

The first misinterpretation has to do with Smeaton's coefficient (see Chapter 2). By the fall of 1901, the Wrights suspected that the classic value of 0.005 for Smeaton's coefficient was in error. In his paper to the Western Society, Wilbur states, "The well-known Smeaton coefficient of $0.005 \, V^2$ for the wind pressure at 90 degrees is probably too great by at least 20 percent." Of course, Samuel Langley had published his measurements for Smeaton's coefficient in his *Experiments in Aerodynamics*, giving an average value for his measurements of 0.003. We know that Wilbur and Orville had bought a copy of Langley's book in 1899 and presumably they were aware of Langley's measurements. However, in both 1900 and 1901, while making the lift and drag calculations from the Lilienthal tables, they used the classic value of 0.005. This may have been because they were under the impression that Lilienthal had used the value of 0.005 to obtain his force coefficients from his measured values of the actual force. Therefore, to convert the tabulated coefficients back to force, the Wrights logically would have used the same value of 0.005, no matter what they might have thought the correct value of Smeaton's coefficient to be. In reality, Lilienthal did not use Smeaton's coefficient to reduce his data. Instead, he formed his aerodynamic coefficients at different angles of attack by dividing the respective force measurements by his measured force on the wing at a 90-degree angle of attack. In so doing, the Smeaton coefficient, and any uncertainty thereof, was simply divided out. Hence, the numbers in Lilienthal's table are independent of any value of Smeaton's coefficient. The Wrights should have used 0.003 to obtain more accurate force data from the Lilienthal tables. Instead, they used the higher value of 0.005.

Their second misinterpretation has to do with aspect ratio. Lilienthal's aerodynamic force measurements were made on a model wing with an aspect ratio of 6.48. Therefore, his table should have been used to predict forces only on wings with the same aspect ratio. (In 1918, Ludwig Prandtl in Germany published a theoretical method for modifying aerodynamic data measured for wings of a given aspect ratio to apply to wings of another aspect ratio. At the time of the Wrights' experiments, no such method existed.) The Wright brothers, however, readily used Lilienthal's table for their gliders, which had aspect ratios far smaller than 6.48. The Wrights acted as if they had no appreciation for the effect of aspect ratio on lift. This is in spite of the fact that Langley had published the first definitive experimental data on the effect of aspect ratio in his book *Experiments in Aerodynamics* and had conclusively shown that, at a given angle of attack, the lift coefficient decreases as the aspect ratio decreases. In 1900 and 1901, the Wrights appeared oblivious to this effect. Moreover, the effect is not trivial by any means. For example, take the case of the Wrights' 1900 glider, which had an aspect ratio of 3.5. Using Prandtl's theory, the lift coefficient for an aspect ratio 3.5 wing will be smaller than an aspect ratio 6.48 wing by the factor 0.814. The Wrights used an angle of attack of 3 degrees as their design point. They obtained a lift coefficient of 0.545 from Lilienthal's tables for a 3-degree angle of attack. They should have immediately multiplied this value by 0.814 to account for the aspect ratio effect. That is, for their aspect ratio of 3.5, the Wrights should have modified the value in Lilienthal's table to be $(0.814)(0.545) = 0.44$.

This number for the lift coefficient needs to be modified once more, this time to account for the location along the airfoil of the maximum camber. Lilienthal's test wing had a thin airfoil in the shape of a circular arc, with maximum camber at the midchord location. The Wrights, on the other hand, placed their location of maximum camber near the leading edge. This was done intentionally because they felt that this shape would reduce the movement of the center of pressure as the angle of attack changed. Because of the radically different maximum-camber locations, the Wrights' airfoils and Lilienthal's airfoil were aerodynamically different. This is yet another reason why the data from the Lilienthal table were not directly applicable to the Wrights' gliders. At the time, the Wrights did not realize that. In fact, during their designs of the 1900 and 1901 gliders, the Wrights tended to view the numbers in the Lilienthal table as almost universal values for cambered airfoils, independent of wing shape and location of maximum camber. For reference, the shape of the Wrights airfoil for their 1900 glider, the initial shape for their 1901 glider, and the circular arc shape of Lilienthal's airfoil are compared in Figure 4.10. The Wright airfoil shapes shown in Figure 4.10 are Wilbur's own freehand sketches; the apparent notch at the leading edge of the 1901 airfoil is the wing spar.

We know today that a more forward location of the maximum camber gives a smaller lift coefficient at a given angle of attack. At the design angle of attack of 3 degrees used by the Wrights, their forward camber location results in a smaller lift coefficient than was the case of Lilienthal's circular arc at the same 3 degrees of

FIGURE 4.10
Sketches of airfoil shapes:
a) Wilbur's sketch of their
1900 glider airfoil;
b) Wilbur's sketch of their
1901 glider airfoil;
c) circular-arc airfoil.

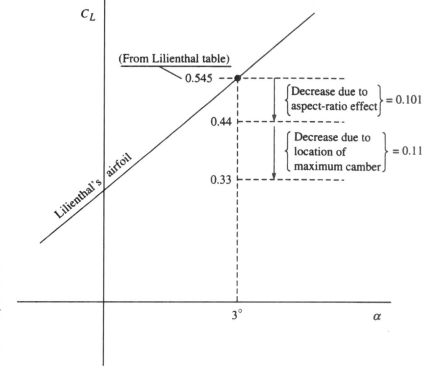

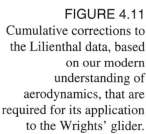

FIGURE 4.11
Cumulative corrections to
the Lilienthal data, based
on our modern
understanding of
aerodynamics, that are
required for its application
to the Wrights' glider.

attack. Moreover, today we can calculate the change in the lift coefficient due to these different locations of maximum camber. The details of the calculation are spelled out in the author's *A History of Aerodynamics*; the result is that the already reduced lift coefficient of 0.44 discussed earlier should be further reduced by the amount of 0.11. Hence, at 3-degrees angle of attack, the Wrights should have used $0.44 - 0.11 = 0.33$ as their lift coefficient.

The combined effect of aspect ratio and location of maximum camber for the Wrights' airfoil is illustrated in Figure 4.11, which is a schematic of the linear variation of lift coefficient C_L with angle of attack α. For an angle of attack of 3 degrees, the Lilienthal table gives the lift coefficient as 0.545. The aspect ratio effect reduces that value to 0.44. The effect of location of the maximum camber further reduces the value to 0.33. The Wrights used 0.545 to calculate the lift for their 1900 and 1901 gliders; they should have used 0.33. On that basis alone, their calculations of lift were in error by a factor of $0.33/0.545 = 0.60$. When the error in Smeaton's coefficient is factored into this calculation (the Wrights used 0.005, but should have used 0.003), the Wrights' lift calculations were in error by a factor $(0.003/0.005)(0.60) = 0.36$. That is, the actual lift as predicted from the Lilienthal table, *with Lilienthal's value modified as just discussed*, gives a value about 0.36, or about one-third of what the Wrights calculated. This was precisely what the Wrights' observed experimentally, as recorded in Wilbur's diary July 29, 1901: "Afternoon spent in kite tests. Found lift of machine much less than Lilienthal tables would indicate, reaching only about 1/3 as much."

This argument finally explains the apparent discrepancy between the Lilienthal table and the Wrights' measurements of lift on their glider; the numbers in the Lilienthal table and the Wrights measurements were both reasonably valid.

The Wrights' calculations, however, were not correct because they misinterpreted the numbers in the Lilienthal table and used these numbers incorrectly. In their defense, even if they had recognized the *qualitative* effects of different aspect ratios and different locations of maximum camber on lift coefficient, at that time there were no theoretical methods by which they could have *quantitatively* modified the Lilienthal data to apply to their gliders. We have done that now, because almost 100 years later, we have the theoretical methods to make the modifications.

The discrepancies between their calculations and measurements were a major cause of Wilbur and Orville's depressed state as they returned home from Kitty Hawk in August 1901. But their discontent would soon fade. Sometime after returning home, but before Wilbur gave his paper to the Western Society, they made an intellectually courageous decision. Problem: They had been using the best aerodynamic data available at that time (at least to the extent that they understood the data), and yet their gliders had been performing considerably below par (in comparison with their calculations). Conclusion: Something must be wrong with the existing data. Solution: Start over and compile their own aerodynamic data. That decision—essentially to do everything themselves, starting with the very basics—was a primary reason for the success of the Wright Flyer in 1903.

WIND-TUNNEL EXPERIMENTS

Whether or not the Lilienthal table was accurate, the important point at that time was that the Wrights *thought* that it might not be accurate. This served as a catalyst for the Wright brothers' own experiments in aerodynamics. During early October 1901, the Wrights designed and built a wind tunnel out of wood. With experiments carried out in this wind tunnel, the Wrights found what constitutes "the right aerodynamics." Their wind-tunnel testing program in the fall of 1901 was a pivotal aspect that eventually led to a new, spectacularly successful glider in 1902 and in the next year to the powered Wright Flyer and ultimate success. Without these wind-tunnel tests, the achievement of successful, powered human flight might not have happened as early as December 17, 1903, and it might not have happened to the Wright brothers. In this light, it is a good thing that the Wrights did not use the Lilienthal table correctly and that they used the wrong value of Smeaton's coefficient; that is, it is a good thing that their calculations disagreed with their measurements on their 1900 and 1901 gliders. Without this, the Wrights may not have been driven to discover the right aerodynamics.

The wind tunnel was operating by mid-October. A photograph of a replica of the wind tunnel is shown in Figure 4.12. (No photograph of the actual wind tunnel exists, and the Wrights junked the tunnel at some unknown later date.) The flow duct was 6 feet long with a square cross section 16 inches on each side. There was a glass window on top for observing the tests. The airflow was driven by a fan powered by the central power plant of the Wrights' bicycle shop—a 1-horsepower gasoline engine connected to the fan via shafts and belt drives. The maximum velocity attainable in the wind tunnel was about 30 miles per hour. The tunnel was housed on the second floor of the bicycle shop, where all of the testing took place. With this tunnel, the Wrights were following in the tradition of Francis Wenham, Horitio Phillips, and about a dozen other developers who had built and operated wind tunnels before the Wrights.

FIGURE 4.12
The Wrights' wind tunnel,
1901–1902.

The Wrights' wind-tunnel testing was unique, however, in that more wing and airfoil shapes were tested than in any previous wind tunnel. Moreover, the Wrights were the next people after Hiram Maxim to generate wind-tunnel data for the specific purpose of designing a flying machine, and they were unique in that these data led to the first *successful* airplane.

The instruments designed by the Wrights for measuring lift and drag coefficients on models in the wind tunnel were also unique—they were ingenious devices. A photograph of their lift balance is shown in Figure 4.13. What looks like a rather crude and lashed-up device is in reality a very precise instrument for the direct measurement of lift coefficient (rather than just the lift force). The wing model on which the lift coefficient is to be measured is mounted vertically, as seen at the top of Figure 4.13. The device is mounted in the tunnel such that the flow direction is parallel to the left and right sides of the wood base (or perpendicular to the ruler shown resting on the base). The four "fingers" that hang below the wing are flat surfaces oriented perpendicular to the flow. The mechanical details of the balance are nicely described by Jakab in *Visions of a Flying Machine*. Suffice it to say here that the lift force on the wing and the drag on the flat surface create torques about the vertical pivot rods on the instrument. With the airflow turned on, there will be one angular position of the pivot rods where these torques are balanced. An indicator on the bottom of the device registers this angle. A mathematical calculation based on this torque balance shows that the lift coefficient is equal to the sine of this indicated angle. See Jakab for the details. Note that the device registers the lift coefficient directly, not the lift force itself. When the drag of the flat surfaces perpendicular to the flow is properly combined with the lift generated on the wing, the influence of velocity, surface area, and (most important of all) Smeaton's coefficient is completely divided out of the measurement. *The Wrights had designed a force balance that measured directly the lift coefficient in such a manner that the result was independent of Smeaton's coefficient and the airflow velocity.* They did mechanically what Lilienthal did mathematically in the presentation of his data. (See the discussion of Lilienthal's data in Chapter 3.)

The Wrights built a second balance, this one to measure directly the drag-to-lift ratio D/L. This balance is shown in Figure 4.14. The wing model is mounted vertically on one of the arms of the balance. As before, an angular measurement of the orientation of the balance is the basic measurement. From this, the drag-to-lift ratio can be directly obtained. Again, this measurement is independent of velocity and Smeaton's coefficient. Of course, knowing the lift coefficient (from the first balance) and the ratio of drag-to-lift (from the second balance), the drag coefficient C_D falls out directly from the relation

$$C_D = (D/L)C_L.$$

From mid-October to December 7, 1901, the Wrights tested in their wind tunnel more than 200 different wing models, with different planform and airfoil shapes. Just a few of these models are shown in the photograph in Figure 4.15. They tested camber ratios from 1/6 to 1/20; the location of maximum camber ranged from near the leading edge to the midchord position. The planform shapes included squares, rectangles, ellipses, surfaces with raked tips, and circular arc segments for leading and trailing edges meeting at sharp points at the tip. They also examined tandem wing configurations (after Langley's aerodromes), biplanes, and triplanes. Finally, Wilbur and Orville had to end these experiments because of the

FIGURE 4.13
The Wrights' clever design of a wind tunnel balance for measuring the lift coefficient directly.

FIGURE 4.14
The Wrights' wind tunnel balance for direct measurement of the drag-to-lift ratio.

press of business. In a letter from Katharine Wright to Bishop Wright dated December 7, 1901, she wrote, "The boys have finished their tables of the action of the wind on various surfaces, or rather they have finished their experiments. As soon as the results are put in tables, they will begin work for next season's bicycles." These experiments, conducted over less than an two-month period, produced the most definitive and practical aerodynamic data on wings and airfoils obtained to that date. They gave the Wrights proper aerodynamic information on which to design a proper flying machine.

The Wrights chose to tabulate data from 48 of their wing models. One table gives lift coefficient tabulated versus angle of attack α. Another table gives the drag-to-lift ratio as a function of α. These tables supplanted the Lilienthal table in all respects. At the time, they represented the most valuable technical data in the history of applied aerodynamics.

But as it turned out, during the seminal period of the birth of the airplane, when these tables could have found widespread use, they remained for the Wrights' and Chanute's eyes only. This does not appear to be the original intention of Wilbur and Orville. They had been feeding Chanute bits and pieces of their lift and drag measurements during the course of their wind-tunnel experiments. Indeed, in a letter to Wilbur dated November 27, 1901, Chanute mentions that he has been invited by Major Moedebeck from Germany to write a new chapter for an updated version of the Moedebeck *Handbook for Aeronauts and Aviators*, the source of the original publication of the Lilienthal table in Berlin in 1895. Chanute

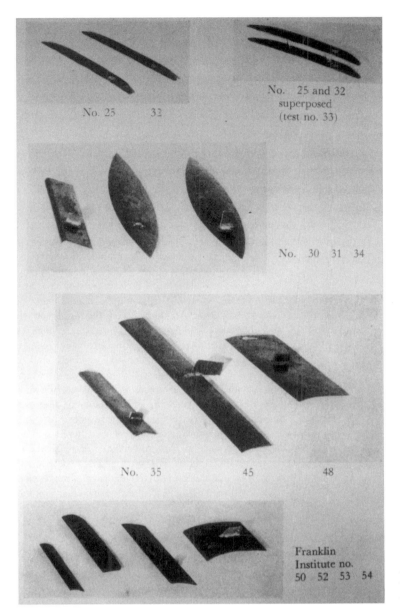

No. 25   32

No.   25 and 32
superposed
(test no. 33)

No.   30   31   34

No.   35   45   48

Franklin
Institute no.
50   52   53   54

FIGURE 4.15
A few of the Wrights'
wing models tested in their
wind tunnel.

gently hints that some of the Wrights' data might be included in his contribution to
the handbook. Chanute goes on to make Wilbur an offer: "Now, I will either
prepare the whole of the notes, including your experiments, or prepare the notes up
to the latter point, and let you describe your own work, as you may prefer. Please
let me know." Wilbur's rather modest reply was penned on December 1:

> I think very well of your plan to republish the Lilienthal section of Moedebeck's
> handbook substantially in its present form and add your own notes as a supplementary
> article. . . . You will be better able than we to preserve a proper perspective in
> describing our experiments, so you had better keep the matter in your own hands. It is a
> question whether any table additional to his should be inserted, but if deemed advisable
> it should preferably be of a surface of a markedly different character so that instead of
> contradicting Lilienthal it should emphasize the necessity of considering shape,
> relative dimensions, and profile in calculating the expected performance of a machine.

Chanute agreed with Wilbur, responding on December 11:

> I quite agree with you that it will be preferable to give in Moedebeck's handbook the coefficients for a surface of differing markedly from Lilienthal's, and to emphasize the necessity of considering shape. Please furnish me the necessary data and comments when you consider that you have arrived at such definite results as to warrant publication.

Wilbur did not address this matter until January 5, 1902, when he included in a letter to Chanute tables of aerodynamic data for 17 different models. In regard to these data, and the publication thereof, Wilbur had the following to say:

> In a recent letter you inquired what of our tables I thought ought to be given to Moedebeck. My failure to answer sooner was for the simple reason that I did not know what to say. On the one hand, the value of our tables lies chiefly in the opportunity they afford of comparisons of the effect of aspect, curvature, thickening, and chord, upon the lift, the tangential, and the angle at which the maximum occurs. But on the other, there is the objection that to include all would make more than would be advisable in so brief a work as a handbook. And then there is the further and greater objection that to insert in an authoritative work like a handbook a set of tables which are not claimed to be perfect, in advance of their general public acceptance, would entail a personal responsibility on your part which ought not to be assumed lightly. Although I have great confidence myself in their substantial accuracy, yet there comes the haunting thought that all previous experimenters in this line have made mistakes and that though we have avoided or corrected ninety-nine sources of error there may be one that has escaped attention. We could assume the responsibility of issuing them with a clear conscience, but the case would be somewhat different with you even though you should disclaim personal responsibility. However, when you have figures and studied all our measurements, you will be better able to determine the best course, whether to make a general statement of the tendency of the results, or whether to say nothing at all. We will send on the data of the measurements of the other surfaces shortly.

Here, Wilbur is showing various degrees of modesty, coyness, conservativeness, and deference to Chanute. However, in a roundabout way, Wilbur is still leaving up to Chanute the decision to publish the Wrights' data. There is the definite impression left by Wilbur, however, that he is dragging his feet on the matter. Chanute appeared to pick up on this veiled reluctance in his letter to Wilbur on February 6. Chanute complained that Moedebeck was rushing him for the contribution to the new handbook. He went on to say, "I had come to quite the same conclusion as yourself, i.e., that it would be unwise to give the public full information as to the properties of curved surfaces at present, and I wrote him [Moedebeck] that the article would not contain your data."

After this, Wilbur obviously considered the publishing of the Wrights' tables in the Moedebeck handbook to be a dead matter. Instead, he made a short comment in his letter to Chanute on February 7: "In considering the matter of publishing our tables of pressures and tangentials, . . . I think I shall prepare to make them public sometime during this summer."

Wilbur never did. After all of the preceding correspondence and discussion, the complete aerodynamic tables compiled by the Wrights were never published in their lifetime. Finally, from the Wrights' notebooks McFarland compiled the tables for 48 different wing models and published them as an Appendix to his collection of *The Papers of Wilbur and Orville Wright*, in 1953. Fifty-one years after the data were taken, the Wrights' aerodynamic tables were published.

By December 1901, the Wrights had uncovered what was for them the right aerodynamics. In particular, they had demonstrated to themselves the aerodynamic advantage of high aspect ratio. Their wind-tunnel models ranged in aspect ratio from 1 to 10. Although Langley's results published in *Experiments in Aerodynamics* clearly showed that higher aspect ratio wings produced more lift, the Wrights appeared not to have noted Langley's data, or they simply ignored it. There is no mention whatsoever of Langley's aspect ratio data in the correspondence between Wilbur and Chanute. In any event, the advantage of higher aspect ratio was clearly demonstrated to the Wrights by their own wind-tunnel tests. Of all of the models tested, Wilbur noted that the model with a 5 percent camber (1/20) and an aspect ratio of 6 had "the highest dynamic efficiency of all the surfaces shown." As we will discuss later, the data from this model had a strong effect on the wing design of their 1902 glider.

There is no doubt that by the beginning of 1902 the Wrights possessed far more aerodynamic data and understanding than anyone else before them. In the field of applied aerodynamics, the Wrights were unquestioned leaders. Orville was justified in making the following statement years later, in a deposition dated February 2, 1921:

> Cambered surfaces were used prior to our experiments. However, the earlier experimenters had so little accurate knowledge concerning the properties of cambered surfaces that they used cambered surfaces of great inefficiency, and the tables of air pressures which they possessed concerning cambered surfaces were so erroneous as to entirely mislead them. They did not even know that the center of pressure traveled backward on cambered surfaces at small angles of incidence, but assumed that it traveled forward. I believe we possessed in 1902 more data on cambered surfaces, a hundred times over, than all of our predecessors put together.

In this statement, Orville is unintentionally short-changing Langley; the reversal in center-of-pressure movement had been observed and measured by Langley and Huffaker before the Wrights, but the data were never published. Therefore, the Wrights never knew about it. Also, Orville is not paying enough respect to the reasonable accuracy of the Lilienthal table for air pressures. However, in the main, Orville is justified in emphasizing that he and Wilbur were the sole owners of the most advanced, most precise, and most viable database in applied aerodynamics at that time. This is just another reason why the Wright brothers were the first true aeronautical engineers.

THE 1902 GLIDER

By late November 1901, the Wrights' wind-tunnel results had made them aware of the importance of wing aspect ratio on aerodynamic performance. Also, because Chanute had provided them in October with a partially translated version of Lilienthal's *Birdflight as the Basis of Aviation*, they were finally aware of the shape and aspect ratio of Lilienthal's test model wings. With this, the Wrights no longer mistakenly considered the Lilienthal table as a set of universal values, but properly as a tabulation of aerodynamic coefficients pertaining only to a certain wing and airfoil shape. Indeed, the Wrights felt they had been a little misled by Octave Chanute, who had republished Lilienthal's table in his paper "Sailing Flight," which appeared in *The Aeronautical Annual* in 1897; it was from this source that the Wrights obtained the table. Chanute never qualified the limitations on the table, giving the impression that it was universal in nature. The author believes that Chanute was as much in the dark about Lilienthal's table as were the Wrights. Indeed, in a letter written to Chanute on November 22, 1901, Wilbur gently takes Chanute to task, stating the following:

> In the Lilienthal table I would suggest that it be stated in connection with the table that it is for a surface 0.4 meters × 1.8 meters, of the shape [here Wilbur draws the planform shape of Lilienthal's wing model] and a curvature of 1 in twelve, and measured in the natural wind. Any table is liable to great misconstruction if the surface to which it is applicable is not clearly specified. No table is of universal application.

As far as the Wrights were concerned the Lilienthal table was now moot. From their wind-tunnel tests, they had their own tables of aerodynamic coefficients, which were much more extensive and detailed than any from the past. Besides, the Wrights had a reasonable degree of confidence in the accuracy of their own measurements. They never again used the Lilienthal table for their design calculations.

(*Note*: The Wrights never referred to their testing device as a "wind tunnel" as we do today. In a letter to George Spratt on December 15, 1901, Wilbur referred to a "lift measuring machine," which could be the lift coefficient balance or the whole tunnel. Indeed, the inventor of the wind tunnel, Francis Wenham, called it an "artificial current." Horatio Phillips referred to a "delivery tube," and sometimes the Wrights simply called it "the apparatus." The term "wind tunnel" was not coined until 1910, when Gustave Eiffel used it in his descriptions of his aerodynamic experiments in Paris.)

During their work on "next season's bicycles" in early 1902, the Wrights found time to design "next season's" glider. The new design was based on knowledge gained from their wind-tunnel tests; its most striking difference from the previous gliders was a wing aspect ratio of 6.7—more than twice that for their 1901 glider. The Wrights had learned their lesson well. The total wing area was not much greater—305 square feet compared with the 1901 glider wing area of 290 square feet. Each wing was simply longer and more narrow. The airfoil camber was quite small—1/25 compared with the value of 1/12 they had started with in their 1901 flight trials. Even the aspect ratio of their forward canard surface was increased over that of the previous year.

There was another striking difference in the new design—it had a vertical tail at the rear of the machine, consisting of two vertical surfaces side-by-side, giving a total vertical tail area of 11.7 square feet. The reason for the vertical tail was to counteract a disturbing yawing motion that Wilbur had sensed in a few of his glides in 1901, but had not mentioned in his later paper to the Western Society, presumably because he had no plausible explanation for its occurrence. However, he briefly mentioned the problem in a letter to Chanute on August 22, 1901: "The last week (of flights in 1901) was without very great results though we proved that our machine does not turn (i.e., circle) toward the lowest wing under all circumstances, a very unlooked for result and one which completely upsets our theories as to the causes which produce the turning to the right or left."

What happened to Wilbur is this. If you are piloting an airplane, and you wish to turn, say, to the right, you induce a roll to the right. (You deflect the ailerons so that the right wing drops and the left wing raises up.) This rotates the aerodynamic lift vector toward the right, and hence, the airplane begins to make a circle to the right. That is, you execute a turn by "pointing" the lift vector in the direction toward which you want to turn. Wilbur understood this—this was his "theory as to the causes which produce the turning to the right or left." However, there is a side effect to this rolling motion of the wing. To get the right wing to drop and the left wing to raise up, you decrease the lift on the right wing and increase it on the left wing—this the Wrights accomplished by wing warping. There is an increase in wing drag due to the production of lift—today called "induced drag," or "drag due to lift." (It is associated with the generation of aerodynamic vortices at the wingtips, and for this reason it is sometimes identified as "vortex drag," particularly in England.) Thus, when the lift is increased on the left wing to raise it up, the drag on the left wing increases. Similarly, when the lift is decreased on the right wing, the drag on the right wing decreases. The net result is for the airplane to yaw (pivot) toward the left. That is, the nose of the airplane wants to swing toward the left, in the opposite direction of the desired turning direction to the right. This yawing motion is precisely what Wilbur had experienced but had not expected. They did not understand what was making it happen, but they correctly theorized that this undesirable yawing action could be supressed by adding a vertical tail at the rear of the machine. Such a vertical tail provides a "weather vane" effect, which would swing the glider back to its proper zero-yaw position if any unexpected yaw motion occurred during a turn. Hence, their new design had a vertical tail (indeed, a double vertical tail, to begin with).

Wilbur and Orville left Dayton on Monday, August 25, bound for Kitty Hawk and Kill Devil Hills. During the week before that, the Wrights worked on the prefabricated parts of their new 1902 glider. On August 20, Katharine wrote to her father:

> The flying machine is in process of making now. Will spins the sewing machine around by the hour while Orv squats around marking the places to sew. There is no place in the house to live but I'll be lonesome enough by this time next week and wish that I could have some of their racket around.

After arriving at their camp at Kill Devil Hills on August 28, the brothers first set about improving their living conditions. Their shed from the previous year was in disrepair; they remodeled and enlarged the building, as well as improved the interior. They dug a 16-foot well nearby the shed; Wilbur claimed that "it is the best (water) in Kitty Hawk." The brothers were in much better spirits than the previous year. Wilbur wrote to George Spratt on September 16 that "we are having a splendid time."

On September 8 they finally started to assemble their 1902 glider. It was finished 11 days later. After a midday dinner, they flew the glider as a kite and were

FIGURE 4.16
The 1902 glider in flight.

very encouraged by its behavior. Orville noted in his diary for September 19, "We made no entirely free flights, but from several glides made are convinced that the machine will glide on an angle of seven degrees, or maybe less." Over the next two days, this proved to be the case. Wilbur made nearly 50 glides, most of them at glide angles between 7 and 7.5 degrees. This is to be compared with glide angles of around 10 degrees or higher for their earlier 1901 glider.

The angle of glide (the angle between the descending flight path of the glider and the horizontal) is strictly a function of the lift-to-drag ratio of the glider: The higher the value of L/D, the smaller is the glide angle. Wilbur knew this. In his 1901 paper to the Western Society, he succinctly stated, "In gliding experiments, however, the amount of lift is of less relative importance than the *ratio* of lift to drift (drag), as this alone decides the angle of gliding descent." Their new machine in 1902, gliding at the smaller glide angle of about 7 degrees, clearly had a much improved L/D ratio. The improvement in L/D was primarily due to the much larger wing aspect ratio for the 1902 glider.

On September 23, Orville made his first free-flight glide. Before that, Wilbur had made all of the free gliding flights for all of their machines, beginning in 1900. After that, the Wrights shared the piloting of the machine. The Wrights' primary goal with the 1902 glider was to fly as long and as frequently as possible to gain experience in the air. A photograph of the 1902 glider soaring almost effortlessly through the air is shown in Figure 4.16. The high aspect ratio of the wings is clearly seen in this photograph; the machine is an object of aesthetic beauty in flight. In 20th century aeronautical engineering, there is a well-worn saying that "an airplane that looks beautiful will fly beautifully." Although not always a true statement, the author suggests that the Wrights' 1902 glider was the first flying machine to fit this description. During the almost two months that the Wrights spent at Kill Devil Hills that year, they finally accomplished their goals for gliding, successfully executing somewhere between 700 and 1000 flights, the longest being 26 seconds in the air covering 623 feet over the ground.

In terms of advancing the technology of the airplane, the Wrights' 1902 glider made three important contributions. The first is the clear demonstration in flight of the aerodynamic efficiency of high aspect ratio wings. We have discussed the nature of such wings and how the Wrights were finally led to appreciate this design feature; no further elaboration will be made here.

The second is in regard to the vertical tail that the Wrights used for the first time on their 1902 glider. Fixed vertical tails were not new—the concept goes back as far as 1799 with George Cayley. However, during the course of their flying in 1902, the Wrights made a modification to the vertical tail that was pivotal (no pun intended); they modified the tail so that it could be rotated about its vertical axis, thus acting as a movable rudder. The circumstances that led to this change, and the Wrights' intelligent dealing with them, is yet another example of their logical, reasoned, engineering talent. The 1902 glider started with a fixed double vertical tail, which the Wrights correctly reasoned would solve the adverse yaw problem that Wilbur encountered the year before when he banked the glider for a turn. As they began their flights in 1902, they found that, indeed, this particular problem had been solved. In fact, the Wrights shortly removed one of the vertical surfaces because a single vertical tail proved just as effective. But now a new problem surfaced. Whenever an airplane rolls (banks), it also experiences a slideslip (sidewise motion) in the direction of the lower wing. Because of this sidewise slipping, the entire side of the airplane that faces into the slideslip feels a component of the relative air velocity at right angles to the side. This includes the fixed vertical tail, which feels a component of force perpendicular to its surface due to the slideslip. In turn, this swings the tail away from, and hence the nose into, the direction of the slideslip. If left uncontrolled, this can set up a spiraling motion of the airplane into the turn, that is, a corkscrewing motion around the tip of the lower wing. Today, this is called a spin. Such spins happened a few times during the early flights in 1902, with the result of the glider falling out of the sky and the wing tip slamming into the sand. The Wrights called such an event "well digging."

The manner in which the Wrights came to a solution to this problem reveals an intellectual molding together of their two minds. Until this point in time, Wilbur had been the intellectual drive behind most of their developments and advancements, whereas Orville provided organizational skill as well as serving as a sounding board in their many spirited discussions about flying machines over the years. The two of them made a great team. It was Orville's turn, however, to have a great idea. Not able to sleep the night of October 3, and mulling over the well-digging problem in his mind, he came to an inspired and straightforward solution to the problem. The next morning at breakfast he shared his idea with Wilbur, namely, that the vertical tail should be made to pivot as a rudder. In this way, when the tail started to swing in an undesirable direction in a slideslip, rudder deflection controlled by the pilot would counteract and stop the undesirable yawing motion. Orville fully expected Wilbur to say something like, "Oh yes, I was already considering that," because, as the older brother, Wilbur sometimes unconsciously took priority for himself in the conception of new ideas. But after listening carefully, and pausing for a minute or two, Wilbur immediately accepted Orville's idea and then instantly improved the concept. Wilbur felt that the pilot already had a lot to do handling the other controls, so he suggested that the movable rudder be connected with the wing warping mechanism so that the rudder would automatically deflect in the correct direction when the wings were warped. Within a few hours that morning, meshing their ideas, the Wrights developed an effective control mechanism for yaw on their flying machine. With this, their flight control system was complete, and the 1902 glider became the first flying machine with full control around all three axes—pitch, yaw, and roll. After the movable rudder was installed, their tailspins and well digging disappeared. The problem was solved.

The third technical contribution was the overall structural design of the glider—its lightness and durability. They used lightweight, flexible, and resilient wood that yielded but did not usually break whenever the glider would have a hard encounter with the ground. The fabric of the wings, canard, and vertical tail played a structural role, being applied on the bias so as to add strength to the machine. Also, amazingly enough, the wooden ribs and spars were not rigidly attached to each other; the cloth covering and pockets around the joints held the structure together. This is one reason why their machines were readily repaired whenever any damage occurred.

These three contributions added up to produce an excellent *system*. In the 1902 glider, the Wrights had good aerodynamics, good flight control, and good structures, and these elements all worked together to make that glider a tremendous success. The Wrights' 1902 glider was the first truly successful *aeronautical system*, and that is perhaps its most important contribution to the technology of the airplane.

With their very successful flying experiences in 1902, Wilbur and Orville Wright pulled themselves far ahead of any other would-be inventor of the flying machine, although hardly anybody else knew it. But the Wrights knew it. Their technical maturity was growing by leaps and bounds and along with it their self-confidence and steadfastness to press ahead.

The position of the Wrights' technology was almost unintentionally contrasted with that of Octave Chanute during the 10-day period following October 5. For the second year in a row, Chanute visited the Wrights' camp, this time bringing with him Augustus Herring and two flying machines. Herring, like Huffaker, who had visited the Wrights' camp the year before, had worked for Samuel Langley at the Smithsonian, but only briefly. Since 1896 Herring was employed off and on by Chanute to help build and fly gliders. Herring made a few marginally successful flights from sand dunes on the Indiana shore of Lake Michigan during the summers of 1896 and 1897. Now, in the summer of 1902, Chanute had again hired Herring to rebuild a multiple-wing glider of Chanute's design and to fly it at Kill Devil Hills, possibly with the help of the Wrights. Chanute also shipped to Kill Devil Hills a second flying machine, an oscillating wing machine for which he contracted with Charles Lamson to construct. Both Chanute and Herring arrived at Kill Devil Hills on October 5. The multiple-wing machine had arrived two weeks earlier, and the oscillating wing machine showed up a few days after Chanute's arrival. The multiple-wing glider was an ungainly looking machine, with 12 wings, summing to a total area of 150 square feet. The Lamson machine was a triplane with wings that could oscillate in the forward and backward directions, a feature that Chanute believed might enhance longitudinal stability. On October 6 and 10, Herring attempted a few glides with the multiwing machine—all unsuccessful. From Orville's diary on October 11, we have the following results:

> Mr. Herring had decided that it is useless to make further experiments with the multi-wing. I think that a great deal of the trouble with it came from its structural weakness, as I noticed that in winds which were not even enough for support (winds with not enough velocity to lift the machine), the surfaces were badly distorted, twisting so that, while the wind at one end was on the underside, often at the other extreme it was on top.

Orville then goes on to make a rather sad but important observation: "Mr. Chanute seems much disappointed in the way it works." Basically, Octave Chanute, the fine and gracious old man of American aeronautics, the dean and assimilator of the state of the art, and an accomplished engineer, was finding his machines to be completely upstaged by the excellent performance of the Wrights' 1902 glider. This was compounded by events on October 14. From Orville's diary, we have this: "After breakfast we took the Lamson machine out in front of the building ready for gliding, but Herring soon decided to take it inside again to take its weight and ascertain its center of lift." The machine was never flown. That same day both Chanute and Herring left the camp rather abruptly to return home, leaving both machines behind. Most likely Chanute was embarrassed by the lack of performance of his machines in the face of the Wrights' obviously successful glider. Later, Chanute gave both his machines to the Wrights, a gift they graciously accepted but never intended to do anything with. When the Wrights left camp that year, Chanute's two machines remained behind, stored in the shed along with their 1902 glider. There they remained until they were destroyed in a violent storm late in 1907.

The Wrights left Kill Devil Hills for home on October 28. What a change from the year before! They now had the most successful flying machine ever developed, and they each had more than an hour of total flight time in the air. Moreover, their aeronautical technology had advanced far beyond that of any other—more than Langley, more than Chanute, even more than Lilienthal. Their 1902 glider was a functioning system with good aerodynamics, good flight control, and good structures. Only one element was missing—propulsion. To date, gravity had been their mode of propulsion—gliding downhill. The Wrights were now ready to take the next step.

THE 1903 WRIGHT FLYER

The time between the end of 1902 and the date when Wilbur wrote his letter to the Smithsonian on May 30, 1899, was less than $3\frac{1}{2}$ years, but there was an almost infinite amount of progress over that period. In his 1899 letter, Wilbur had stated his original goal to "add my mite to help on the future worker who will attain final success." Now, he and his brother were about to become "the future worker," and moreover, they knew it. By the end of 1902, the Wrights had for all intents and purposes invented the practical airplane. All they needed for final success was an adequate propulsion device.

To begin, the Wrights planned to construct a machine much larger than their 1902 glider, with a wing area of 500 square feet and a wing span of 40 feet (compared with 305 square feet and 32 feet, respectively, for the 1902 glider). They had already calculated this wing size to account for the increased weight due to an engine. They estimated the engine weight to be about 180 pounds, thus giving them a total design weight of 625 pounds. Using their tables of lift coefficients obtained from their wind-tunnel tests, they felt that a coefficient of about 0.8 could be achieved at a reasonable angle of attack. Using the equation

$$L = W = kV^2SC_L$$

where the lift L is equal to the weight W and k is Smeaton's coefficient, V is the flight velocity, S is the wing area, and C_L is the lift coefficient, the Wrights were able to estimate the velocity they would have to achieve to lift off the ground. They used the much more appropriate value of 0.003 for Smeaton's coefficient, which is for the case when V is in miles per hour. The result was

$$V = \sqrt{\frac{W}{kSC_L}} = \sqrt{\frac{625}{(0.003)(500)(0.8)}} = 23 \text{ miles per hour}$$

This would be the minimum velocity to which the thrust from the engine–propeller combination would have to accelerate the machine to get off the ground. In turn, the Wrights calculated this required thrust to be 90 pounds, based on their wing drag coefficient measurements from their wind tunnel plus an estimate of the "framing resistance," that is, the drag of everything else—struts, wires, frame, pilot, etc. Once again, we see an example of the careful and systematic methodology used by the Wrights—they calculated virtually everything needed to design the new machine before building it. They were functioning as mature aeronautical engineers.

When Bishop Wright met Wilbur and Orville at the Dayton train station on their return home on October 31, 1902, there was an air of success and optimism, in contrast to the return trip in the previous year. The brothers had already made the decision to build a new machine for 1903 and had decided that this machine would be powered. On December 3, 1902, a number of letters went out under the Wright Cycle Company letterhead to engine manufacturers, inquiring about the availability of a gasoline-fueled engine that could develop 8–9 horsepower, and weigh no more than 180 pounds. All of the replies were negative. Such a high horsepower-to-weight ratio was deemed beyond the state of the art of engine manufacture at that time. Once again, the Wrights were faced with doing it all by themselves, in the same spirit of their wind-tunnel tests.

The brothers divided their responsibilities; Orville took charge of designing and building the engine, and Wilbur assumed the responsibility for the propeller design and construction. These self-imposed assignments were a matter of expedient and efficient engineering management—they felt it was the best way to get the job done. However, even with these focused assignments, the brothers continued to work as a team, sharing their thoughts and progress and each providing technical advice to the other.

Orville, along with Charlie Taylor, a mechanic they had hired in 1901 to relieve them of some of the bicycle shop work so that they could devote more time to their flying machine activities, began to design and build the engine in December. Taylor was the right man at the right time. He played a role in the design of the engine and did virtually all of the machining. There were no engineering drawings made during its design—just hand sketches and Taylor's personal handcrafting. The first tests of the engine were run on February 12, 1903. A day later, Bishop Wright noted in his diary, "The boys broke their little gas motor in the afternoon." The failure was caused by dripping gasoline, which froze the bearings, breaking the engine body and frame. A new aluminum casting for the engine block was received on April 20, and the rebuilt engine was running successfully in May. Even the short testing period before the engine broke on February 13 gave the Wrights optimism that their engine was going to be sufficient. Wilbur wrote to George Spratt on February 28 the following details:

> We recently built a four-cylinder gasoline engine with 4″ piston and 4″ stroke, to see how powerful it would be, and what it would weigh. At 670 revolutions per min. it developed 8 1/4 horsepower brake test. By speeding it up to 1,000 rev. we will easily get eleven horsepower and possibly a little more at still higher speed, though the increase is not in exact proportion to the increase in number of revolutions. The weight including the 30-pound flywheel is 140 pounds.

According to their calculations of the power required for their new flying machine, the performance of their handmade engine was marginal, but sufficient.

An assembly cutaway drawing of the engine is shown in Figure 4.17, and a photograph is given in Figure 4.18. The Wrights chose an inline, four-cylinder arrangement to minimize vibration. The problem of engine roughness was a major concern for them because severe vibrations from the engine would compromise the structural integrity of the lightweight airframe as well as that of the engine itself. By distributing the power generation over four cylinders and incorporating a 26-pound cast iron flywheel, they hoped to reduce vibration to an acceptable level. The lightweight crankcase was designed as one solid casting, made from an aluminum alloy containing 8 percent copper. This design feature was different than the standard engine practice of building the crankcase from multiple parts. Also, the crankcase was designed to contain the major portion of the engine, adding to strength and lightness. The cylinders were cast iron, machined as thin as possible to save weight. The engine was cooled by water, which circulated by convection—no waterpump was used. Gasoline was gravity fed from a 0.4-gallon tank into the top of a sheet metal can, mixed with air, and then sucked into an induction chamber, where it circulated over the hot surface of the crankcase and was vaporized. The fuel–air mixture then entered the manifold and then the cylinders, where the mixture was ignited by a spark made by opening and closing two contact points connected to a direct current magneto friction driven by the flywheel. Exterior dry batteries and a coil were used for starting the engine, but were not carried as part of the airplane. Although the Wrights' engine did not represent a breakthrough in engineering design (Charles Manly at the Smithsonian had earlier designed an engine with a higher power-to-weight ratio), it was unique to them. With the aid of Charlie Taylor, they did everything themselves, from

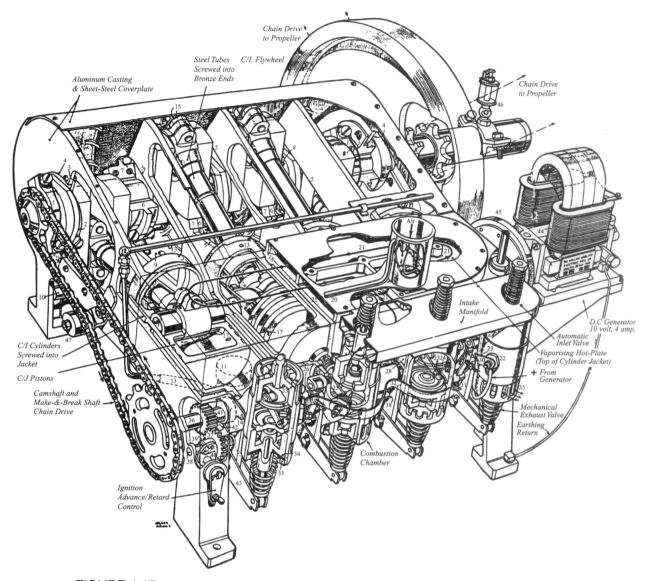

Chain Drive
to Propeller

Steel Tubes
Screwed into
Bronze Ends

C/I. Flywheel

Chain Drive
to Propeller

Aluminum Casting
& Sheet-Steel Coverplate

Air

Intake
Manifold

D.C Generator
10 volt, 4 amp.

Automatic
Inlet Valve

Vaporising Hot-Plate
(Top of Cylinder Jacket)

From
Generator

C/I Cylinders
Screwed into
Jacket

C/J Pistons

Camshaft and
Make-&-Break Shaft
Chain Drive

Mechanical
Exhaust Valve

Earthing
Return

Combustion
Chamber

Ignition
Advance/Retard
Control

FIGURE 4.17
Cutaway drawing of the
engine for the 1903
Wright Flyer.

design to manufacture and testing the engine. When it was all finished, the engine produced about 12 horsepower and, complete with all accessories, weighed about 200 pounds. It was sufficient to do the job.

The reciprocating engine itself does not produce forward *thrust*, which is what is needed to propel the airplane forward. Rather, the engine provides power in the form of a rotating shaft driven by the engine. Thrust must be provided by a propeller connected to the engine shaft. Wilbur assumed the responsibility for the propeller design, although in the process he had many stimulating, and sometimes heated, intellectual discussions with Orville about the aerodynamic complexities of propeller design and performance. Between them, they produced the first viable propeller theory in the history of aeronautical engineering. It was essentially a version of what is called "blade-element theory" today, and it used aerodynamic information about airfoils from their previous wind-tunnel tests. Of most importance, Wilbur was the first person to recognize the fundamental aspect of propellers in air, namely, that a propeller is nothing more than a twisted wing

FIGURE 4.18
The engine for the 1903 Wright Flyer. (National Air and Space Museum, Smithsonian Institution.)

oriented in such a fashion that the "lift force" produced on this twisted wing is oriented in the general flight direction, that is, in the thrust direction. The technical development of their propeller theory and subsequent testing of their propeller design was masterful. Orville summed up the results in a succinct statement in his rather long letter of June 7, 1903, to George Spratt:

> During the time the engine was building we were engaged in some very heated discussions on the principles of screw propellers. We had been unable to find anything of value in any of the works to which we had access, so that we worked out a theory of our own on the subject, and soon discovered, as we usually do, that all the propellers built heretofore are *all wrong*, and then built a pair of propellers 8 1/8 feet in diameter, based on our theory, which are *all right*! (till we have a chance to test them down at Kitty Hawk and find out differently). Isn't it astonishing that all these secrets have been preserved for so many years just so that we could discover them!! Well, our propellers are so different from any that have been used before that they will have to either be a good deal better, or a good deal worse.

For comparison, the crude propellers employed by would-be European flying machine inventors in the 19th century had efficiencies on the order of 40–50 percent. (Propeller efficiency is defined as the power output of the propeller divided by the shaft power input from the engine, expressed in terms of percentage.) Samuel Langley ran tests with his whirling arm on a propeller of his own design and measured a propeller efficiency of 52 percent; in *Experiments in Aerodynamics* Langley admitted that the "form of the propeller blades" was "not a very good one." In contrast, from their propeller theory the Wrights predicted an efficiency of 66 percent for their propeller. In reality it was most likely even better. For example, much later, in an anonymous article published in the November 1909 issue of the magazine *Aeronautics* in New York entitled "Wrights' Propeller Efficiency," it was reported that a certain Captain Eberhardt in Berlin had taken detailed measurements of the propeller used by Wilbur in his European flights during 1908 and 1909. From this, Eberhardt was able to ascertain a value of 76 percent for propeller efficiency.

There is no doubt that the Wrights made a quantum jump in the art of propeller design. And it was no fluke. Their blade-element propeller theory was a spectacular advancement over any existing means of designing propellers. The underlying basis of this theory was the Wrights' fundamental understanding of the true aerodynamic function of a propeller—*a major contribution to the technology of the airplane.* Their propeller theory exhibited a degree of technical maturity in applied aerodynamics never seen before in history. And their application of this theory to the design of a real propeller was masterful. The importance of the Wrights' propeller theory in the history of early flight technology and the degree to which their highly efficient propeller design contributed to the success of the 1903 Wright Flyer are not always well recognized by the public. However, it is the opinion of the author that this work was so significant that, had such an award existed in 1903, the Wrights deserved the Collier Trophy just for their advancements in the aerodynamics of propellers.

Following their now-entrenched policy of doing everything themselves, the brothers carved out of laminated spruce two propellers, each 8.5 feet in diameter. They covered the tips with a thin layer of light duck canvas, which was glued to the wood to keep it from splitting. Finally, they coated the propellers with aluminum paint. A photograph of one of their propellers is shown in Figure 4.19. When mounted on their new flying machine, the two propellers were connected to the engine shaft via two chain drives much like a bicycle chain (Figure 4.20), arranged so that the two propellers rotated in opposite directions to negate the torque effect.

FIGURE 4.19
The propeller for the 1903 Wright Flyer. (National Air and Space Museum, Smithsonian Institution.)

FIGURE 4.20
The chain drive mechanism connecting the propellers to the engine for the 1903 Wright Flyer. (National Air and Space Museum, Smithsonian Institution.)

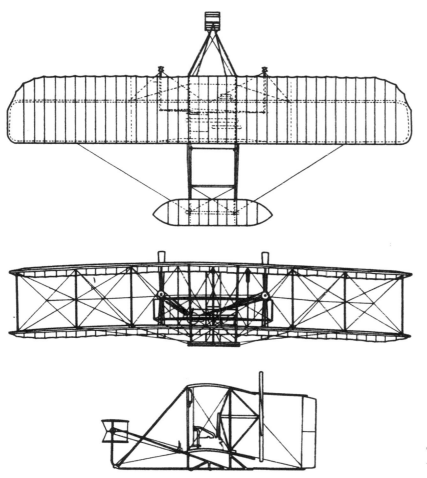

FIGURE 4.21
Three-view of the 1903
Wright Flyer.

SUCCESS

With everything done, Wilbur and Orville left Dayton on September 23, 1903, arriving at Kill Devil Hills two days later. They began work on a new building, to add to their earlier shed, and also took the 1902 glider out of storage. On September 28, they executed between 60 and 100 flights with their old glider, just to brush up on their piloting skills. On October 8, the parts for the new flying machine, which they had shipped from Dayton, arrived at the camp. Delayed and hampered by bad weather, including some strong storms, it took them almost a month to assemble the Wright Flyer. During this time they continued to gain experience flying the 1902 glider. When the Flyer was finished on November 5, the weight of the machine had crept upward to a total of 750 pounds including the pilot. (Most airplanes designed after 1903 have ended up with final weights larger than the initial estimates—a fact of life for airplane designers due to the natural tendency to add extra features as the design progresses. This phenomenon goes all of the way back to the Wright Flyer.) The total wing area was 510 square feet, and the wing span was 40.33 feet, yielding a very reasonable wing aspect ratio of 6.4. A three-view of the Wright Flyer is shown in Figure 4.21. Note that the forward canard is now a biplane configuration—two surfaces instead of the single surface used on their earlier machines. Also, the vertical rudder at the rear of the machine is a double surface, reminiscent of the first configuration of their 1902 glider. These control surfaces for both pitch and yaw were made with double surfaces to increase the control authority commensurate with a larger and heavier machine.

Unfortunately, more delays set in. While testing the engine on the same day that the assembly of the Flyer was completed, the jerking of the unsteady rotation of the propellers damaged the propeller shafts. They had to be returned to Dayton for repairs. Charlie Taylor tried to minimize the turnaround time, and on November 20 the engine was ready for another test. The engine still ran roughly, loosening the sprockets that held the shafts in place. Nothing seemed to keep the sprockets tight for any length of time. Finally, the Wrights, in frustration, glued the sprocket nuts in place, using bicycle tire cement. In a letter written to Charlie Taylor on November 23, Orville notes, "Thanks to Arnstein's hard cement, which will fix anything from a stop watch to a thrashing machine, we stuck those sprockets so tight I doubt whether they will ever come loose again." This "low-tech" solution worked fine.

The Wrights had calculated that the drag on their machine at the design speed of 23 miles per hour would be 90 pounds. Now, with the increase in weight, their calculations showed that a thrust of 100 pounds would be required. The Wrights were worried that their engine–propeller system might not be able to produce this higher thrust. You can imagine their elation when static tests of the propulsion mechanism yielded 132 pounds of thrust, far higher than what they had calculated as necessary. With this, by November 23, the Wrights knew that success was imminent. However, Murphy's law prevailed; on November 28 one of the propeller shafts cracked during further testing of the engine. They decided not to waste any more time with the old shafts. Orville promptly left for Dayton to make new, more durable shafts. The new shafts were made larger and from spring steel.

He arrived back at the camp on December 11, the new shafts in hand. By December 12, everything was in readiness. The Wrights had not had the chance to fly their new machine first as a glider, as they had originally planned. Such glider tests would have been in keeping with their cautious, engineering approach, to check the flying qualities of this much larger and heavier machine and to get some practice at the controls before attempting a powered flight. But the inclement weather and the bad fortune with the propeller shafts had delayed them throughout the fall, and now they were running out of time. They decided to fly the powered machine at the earliest possible moment, without the benefit of any glider trials. That moment came on December 14. On that day, the Wrights called witnesses from Kitty Hawk to the camp and then flipped a coin to see who would be the first pilot. Wilbur won. The Wright Flyer had no wheels. For takeoff, the Wrights had designed a detachable small wheel dolly on which the Flyer was mounted. The dolly rode on a 60-foot launching rail laid on the sand; the rail was made from four 15-foot, 2 × 4 inch boards laid end to end, covered with a thin metal strip. As soon as the Flyer would lift off the ground, the dolly would fall away. Wilbur started the engine. In Orville's words, "I grabbed the upright the best I could and off we went. By the time we had reached the last quarter of the third rail [about 35 to 40 feet] the speed was so great I could stay with it no longer." Wilbur took off, but the Flyer suddenly went into a steep climb, lost speed, stalled, and thumped back to the sand. Wilbur admitted to "an error in judgment." He had deflected the elevator too much and brought the nose too high. This is perfectly understandable considering neither of the brothers had been able to obtain any flight time with the Flyer as a glider and, hence, were not used to the controls of the bigger machine. In thumping back to the ground, the front canard surfaces were slightly damaged.

With minor repairs, and with the weather again favorable, the Wright Flyer was again ready for flight on December 17. This time it was Orville's turn at the controls. The launching rail was again laid on level sand. A camera was adjusted to take a picture of the machine as it reached the end of the rail. The engine was put on full throttle, the holding rope was released, and the machine began to move. The rest is history, as portrayed in the opening paragraphs of this book.

One cannot read or write of this epoch-making event without experiencing some of the excitement of the time. Wilbur Wright was 36 years old; Orville was 32. Between them, they had done what no one before them had accomplished. By their persistent efforts, their detailed research, and their superb engineering, the Wrights had made the world's first successful piloted heavier-than-air flight, satisfying all of the necessary criteria laid down by reasonable aviation historians. After Orville's first flight on that December 17, three more flights were made during the morning, the last covering 852 feet and remaining in the air for 59 seconds. The world of flight, and along with it the world of successful aeronautical engineering, had been born!

The Wrights continued to fly in 1904 and 1905, each year with a better flying machine. They were now flying out of a cow pasture named Huffman Praire, just outside of Dayton. They had a powered machine now, and no longer had to rely on the winds of Kitty Hawk. (Huffman Praire is now swallowed by Patterson Field, part of the massive Wright–Patterson Air Force Base.) Their 1905 machine was so successful that it could remain in the air until it ran out of fuel—a duration of approximately half an hour. Many aeronautical historians credit the 1905 machine as being the first *truly* practical airplane. A three-view of their 1905 machine is shown in Figure 4.22. It was not to be for another three years, however, that the world would appreciate what happened on that cold morning on December 17, 1903, at Kill Devil Hills. In August of 1908, Wilbur made the first public demonstration of their invention (by now, an improved design labeled the Wright Type A); it took place at the Hunaudieres race track just outside of Le Mans, France. A month later Orville was demonstrating the same type of airplane to the U.S. Army at Fort Myer in Virginia, just outside of Washington, D.C. Finally, the Wrights were fully recognized for what they had done—they had invented the world's first practical airplane.

THE TECHNOLOGY OF THE AIRPLANE— WHAT DID THE WRIGHTS CONTRIBUTE?

What did the Wrights contribute to the technology of the airplane? This may seem a rhetorical question after devoting this chapter completely to their design evolution that led to the first successful airplane. In retrospect, most aspects of the 1903 Wright Flyer represented a mature application of existing technology. The overall biplane configuration traces all of the way back to George Cayley. The use of a cambered airfoil stems from Horatio Phillips and later Otto Lilienthal. The aerodynamic advantage of their high aspect ratio wing was understood by Francis

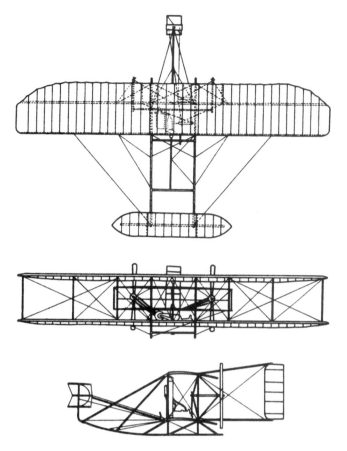

FIGURE 4.22
Three-view of the 1905
Wright airplane.

Wenham and experimentally confirmed by Samuel Langley, although the Wrights seemed to have to rediscovered this advantage in their wind-tunnel tests. The structural design borrowed considerably from Octave Chanute. Their use of a gasoline-fueled internal combustion engine was predated by Samuel Langley, and the generation of thrust by propellers goes back to Samuel Henson and George Stringfellow. The need for horizontal and vertical tail surfaces for longitudinal and directional stability and control also goes back to Cayley, with a major contribution from Alphonse Penaud, although the Wrights were the first to place the horizontal surfaces in front of the wing (canard configuration), and they bucked the prevailing practice of inherent static stability by designing their airplanes to be intentionally statically unstable. Their use of canard surfaces and intentional instability were eschewed by virtually all airplane designers in the 20th century until the recent use of both design features in modern fighter airplanes that are flown by wire with computer-driven controls and the recent design of some small kit-built canard airplanes. So none of the noted features of the 1903 Wright Flyer were *new* contributions to the technology of the airplane.

The Wrights, however, made it all work successfully—they designed the first successful aeronautical *system* wherein aerodynamics, propulsion, structures, and flight control worked synergistically together. This is the first of the three unique contributions to the technology of the airplane made by the Wright brothers—the recognition of the airplane as a system wherein all of the components must work successfully together.

Second, the Wrights' use of a propeller for generating thrust was not unique, but their fundamental understanding of the aerodynamic nature of the propeller as a twisted wing and their development of the first practical theory for the design of the propeller were unique. Every successful propeller-driven airplane carries the genes of the Wrights' innovative propeller design.

The third unique contribution was by far the most important—the design of successful flight control around all three axes of the airplane, with particular emphasis on lateral (roll) control. They were absolutely the first to appreciate the need for rolling the airplane to point the lift vector in the direction they wished to turn. The mechanism they used for lateral control, wing warping, was soon superceded by the use of ailerons by other airplane designers. But every successful airplane since the 1903 Wright Flyer had some form of lateral control—a contribution to the technology of the airplane made uniquely by the Wright brothers. The beautifully orchestrated control around the pitch, yaw, and roll axes of the Wright Flyer is shown in Figure 4.23. This figure embodies the Wrights' lasting contribution to the technology of the airplane.

AERONAUTICAL ENGINEERING TAKES OFF

The Wright brothers' innovative engineering methodology and their invention of the first successful airplane jump-started the profession of aeronautical engineering. Although such men as Cayley, Langley, and Lilienthal in the 19th century attempted to engineer flying machines, these efforts were given little formal recognition by professional engineers during the period, and worse, were derided as the activities of madmen by the general public. In the writings of Lilienthal and Chanute, the term "aeronautical engineering" can actually be found. But it was not until August 8, 1908, near Le Mans France, when Wilbur Wright gave the first public demonstration of their flying machine (a greatly improved version of the 1903 Flyer called the Wright Type A), that the general public suddenly recognized that the airplane had indeed been successfully invented. With this, almost overnight, the engineering profession suddenly recognized a new discipline—aeronautical engineering. Because there was so much to learn about the engineering principles of flying machines, and because the future of designing faster, higher-flying, and safer airplanes was wide open, aeronautical engineering became an important activity in both Europe and the United States. As a result of the inspired work of aeronautical engineers, the technology of the airplane experienced an exponential growth in the 20th century—a growth that continues to the present day.

In the remaining chapters we highlight the essential features of this rapid growth in the technology of the airplane after the Wright brothers. We can identify three major eras of growth: 1) the strut-and-wire biplane, 2) the mature propeller-driven monoplane, and 3) the jet-propelled airplane. These eras are set apart by major configuration changes reflecting quantum improvements in the aerodynamics of the airplane. For example, let us use the zero-lift drag coefficient and the maximum lift-to-drag ratio as two figures of merit for a given airplane. To explain these two figures of merit, first consider the aerodynamic drag on an

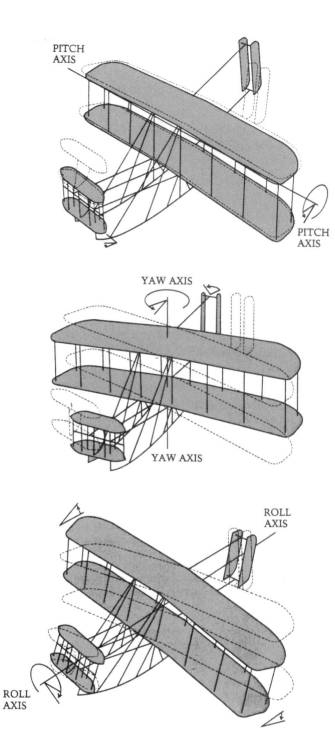

FIGURE 4.23
Illustration of (from top to bottom) pitch, yaw, and roll of the Wright Flyer. (From Combs, *Kill Devil Hill*, Houghton Mifflin, Boston, 1979.)

airplane flying at an airspeed V_∞ and at an altitude where the air density is ρ. The aerodynamic drag exerted on the airplane, D, is given by

$$D = \tfrac{1}{2}\rho V_\infty^2 S C_D$$

where S is the planform area of the wing and C_D is the drag coefficient. If the airplane is pitched to the angle of attack where the lift is zero (usually a small

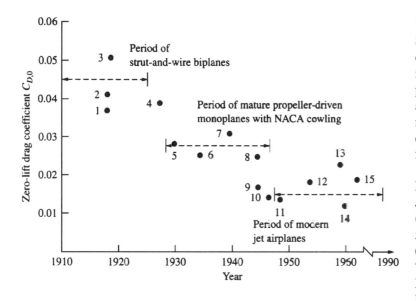

FIGURE 4.24

Step decreases in the drag coefficient over time, illustrating three general periods of 20th century airplane design. The numbered data points correspond to the following aircraft: 1) SPAD XIII, 2) Fokker D-VII, 3) Curtiss JN-4H Jenny, 4) Ryan NYP (Spirit of St. Louis), 5) Lockheed Vega, 6) Douglas DC-3, 7) Boeing B-17, 8) Boeing B-29, 9) North American P-51, 10) Lockheed P-80, 11) North American F-86, 12) Lockheed F-104, 13) McDonnell F-4E, 14) Boeing B-52, 15) General Dynamics F-111D.

negative angle of attack) called the zero-lift angle of attack, then the corresponding drag is called the *zero-lift drag* D_0 and the corresponding zero-lift drag coefficient $C_{D,0}$ is defined from

$$D_0 = \tfrac{1}{2}\rho V_\infty^2 S C_{D,0} \qquad \text{(zero-lift drag)}$$

The zero-lift drag coefficient $C_{D,0}$ is very close to the minimum drag coefficient for the airplane; hence, the value of $C_{D,0}$ is a good measure of the aerodynamic "streamlining" of the airplane. When comparing the values of $C_{D,0}$ for different airplanes, those with smaller values of $C_{D,0}$ usually reflect a greater degree of drag reduction. Everything else being equal, the lower the $C_{D,0}$ is the higher the maximum velocity of the airplane. In Figure 4.24 the values of $C_{D,0}$ for different aircraft are plotted versus the year the aircraft entered service. Figure 4.24 suggests that airplane design has gone through three major periods, distinguished from one another by a dramatic change. For example, the period of the strut-and-wire biplane, where values of $C_{D,0}$ are typically on the order of 0.04, extends from the turn of the century to the end of the 1920s. Breakthroughs in drag reduction in the early 1930s created a design revolution that ushered in the period of the mature propeller-driven monoplane, with values of $C_{D,0}$ on the order of 0.027. In the mid-1940s, the jet-propelled airplane created another design revolution, with values of $C_{D,0}$ on the order of 0.015. The data in Figure 4.24 clearly show three levels of $C_{D,0}$, each reflecting a different era in the technology of the airplane. Not shown in Figure 4.24 is the 1903 Wright Flyer, which had a very high value of $C_{D,0}$, about 0.074. By present standards, the Wright Flyer was not an aerodynamic masterpiece, but in 1903 it was the only successful airplane in existence.

The second figure of merit is the maximum lift-to-drag ratio $(L/D)_{max}$. An airplane wing is like an aerodynamic lever; if the L/D for an airplane is 20, that means that it can lift 20 pounds of weight at the cost of only 1 pound of drag—a dramatic mechanical advantage. As an airplane pitches through different angles of attack, its value of L/D changes. At some specific angle of attack, the L/D will

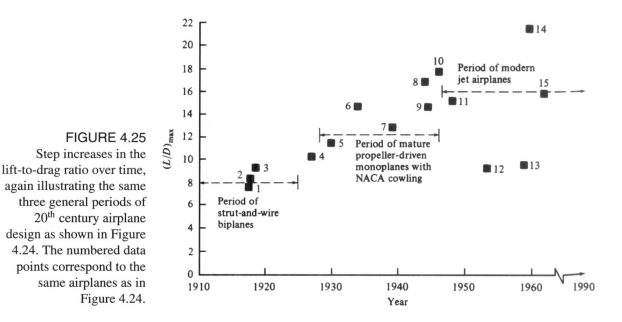

FIGURE 4.25
Step increases in the lift-to-drag ratio over time, again illustrating the same three general periods of 20th century airplane design as shown in Figure 4.24. The numbered data points correspond to the same airplanes as in Figure 4.24.

achieve a maximum value, $(L/D)_{\max}$. This maximum value is a direct measure of the aerodynamic efficiency of the aircraft. Everything else being equal, an airplane with a higher $(L/D)_{\max}$ can fly farther and climb faster. Figure 4.25, a companion to Figure 4.24, shows values for $(L/D)_{\max}$ for the same airplanes in Figure 4.24, plotted versus the year the airplane entered service. Once again we can identify the three eras of the growth of the airplane. The era of the strut and wire biplane is characterized by values of $(L/D)_{\max}$ on the order of 8—not a great improvement over the value of 5.7 for the 1903 Wright Flyer (not shown in Figure 4.25). The era of the mature propeller-driven monoplane reflects a much higher value of around 12, and the era of modern jet airplanes is characterized by values ranging from 12 or 13 for high-performance military jet fighters to 20 and above for large jet bombers and civilian transports.

The advances made in the technology of the airplane since the Wright Flyer are nothing short of phenomenal. The remaining chapters tell this story.

Seat-of-the-Pants Design: The Era of the Strut-and-Wire Biplane

No definitive aircraft configuration types had emerged by 1914, the beginning of World War I, and flying was regarded by most intelligent people—if at all—as a sort of curiosity not unlike tightrope walking at the circus. These viewpoints were utterly changed by the tactical and strategic uses of aircraft in the First World War. The demands of combat aviation, together with the opposing powers constantly vying for air superiority, resulted in the development of the airplane from a curiosity in 1914 to a highly useful and versatile vehicle, designed to fulfill specific roles, by the end of the war in November 1918.

Laurence K. Loftin Jr.
NASA Aeronautical Engineer, 1985

The scene: The balmy June sky over France in 1917. The action: A stubby, yet powerful biplane fighter, painted in a brown and green camouflage pattern with red, white, and blue French roundels prominently displayed on each wing, is maneuvering violently, locked in combat with an almost equally agile German biplane. At the controls of his Societe pour les Appareils Deperdussin (SPAD) built biplane, the legendary French air ace Georges Guynemer rolls, loops, and weaves for 20 minutes, attempting without success to find an advantageous position to shoot down his adversary. Flying an Albatros DVa, the German ace Ernst Udet also tries in vain to best his opponent. Suddenly Guynemer realized that Udet's guns have jammed. Waving goodbye, Guynemer breaks off the combat and returns home, leaving Udet to become Germany's second-highest-scoring ace, later to play a strong role in the buildup of the Luftwaffe in Nazi Germany.

Besides being a display of gallantry, this vignette illustrates the technological advance of the airplane by 1917. The SPAD XIII (Figure 5.1) and the Albatros DVa (Figure 5.2) are examples of the best of airplane design in 1917. Compared with the 1903 Wright Flyer with its 12-horsepower engine and airspeed of 30 miles per

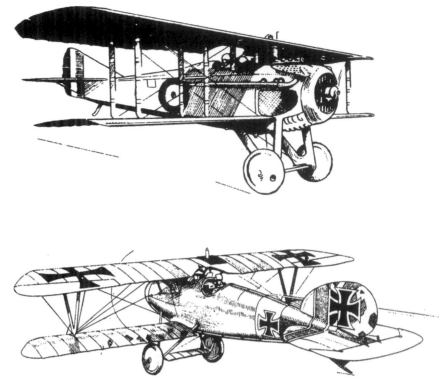

FIGURE 5.1
The French SPAD XIII (circa 1917). (From Rolfe and Dawydoff, *Airplanes of the World*, Simon and Schuster, New York, 1954.)

FIGURE 5.2
The German Albatross D-Va (circa 1917). (From Rolfe and Dawydoff, *Airplanes of the World*, Simon and Schuster, New York, 1954.)

hour, the SPAD XIII had a 200-horsepower Hispano–Suiza engine and a top speed of 130 miles per hour, and the Albatros DVa was about on par with a 180-horsepower Mercedes engine and a top speed of 116 miles per hour. By 1917, the airplane had evolved into an effective flying machine that achieved its increasing speed and performance mainly due to the brute force of ever-increasingly more powerful engines. However, the airplanes illustrated in Figures 5.1 and 5.2 did not represent any revolutionary technical breakthrough or change in airplane design—they simply were evolutionary improvements over the Wrights' original design. Airplanes in the era of the strut-and-wire biplane were, for the most part, simply "souped-up" Wright Flyers.

CONFIGURATION EVOLUTION—FIRST PHASE

Some sense of technical evolution can be seen by looking at a parade of airplane configurations from 1905 to the end of World War I, as shown in Figure 5.3. To begin with, just look at this parade from a broad perspective; we will examine the technical details later in this chapter. Beginning with the 1905 Flyer II, with its totally open fuselage, we see the 1909 Bleriot XI with the forward part of the fuselage enclosed. (The rear part was left open to have access for adjustments and tightening of the rod structure of the fuselage.) By 1915, most aircraft had totally enclosed fuselages. We see, for the most part, biplane configurations in Figure 5.3, with a few monoplanes interspersed. The choice of the biplane configuration was driven mainly by structural considerations—the wing area distributed over two (or more) smaller wings trussed together by struts and wires made a sturdy boxlike structure that had a better chance of surviving the stresses and strains of flight, especially violently maneuvering flight, than a larger and longer single wing. On the other hand, monoplane configurations have certain aerodynamic advantages, as well as providing a broader field of view for the pilot, both of which were somewhat appreciated at that time. The monoplane structure, however, was a problem. Given the thin airfoils in use at the time, there was little room inside the wing for massive spars and other internal structure, and like their biplane counterparts, monoplanes had to have their wings externally braced by wires. The Bleriot XI became famous on July 25, 1909, when Louis Bleriot became the first to fly across the English channel, piloting his little monoplane from a field near Calais, France, to a landing in a meadow near Dover Castle, England. After this, over a hundred Bleriot XI aircraft were sold, and the monoplane momentarily became a favorite configuration. In 1912, however, after several crashes of Bleriot XIs due to wing structural failure, and a report by Bleriot on structural problems associated with several monoplane types, this configuration fell out of favor, aided by the temporary ban of the use of such airplanes by the armies of both England and France. In spite of all this, Fokker in Germany designed a successful monoplane fighter, the Fokker EI–EIII series, in 1915 that for a few months in World War I became the "Fokker scourge" that dominated the sky. (This was mainly due to its use of the first forward-firing machine gun with an interrupter gear, allowing firing through the propeller disk, rather than due to the monoplane configuration.) The Fokker monoplanes experienced a higher-than-normal rate of wing failures. Because of such structural problems, the strut-and-wire biplanes remained the most dominant configuration during this period.

Examining Figure 5.3, one configuration stands out as an aberration—the beautifully streamlined Deperdussin racer in 1912. Designed by the French engineer Louis Bechereau, who later was also the designer of the SPAD XIII, this aircraft pioneered a new type of fuselage construction—the monocoque technique, which formed the fuselage from a single wooden shell, allowing the smooth, aerodynamically clean shape. Also a monoplane, this aircraft was point-designed for high speed as a racer. With Marcel Prevost at the controls, a Deperdussin won the Gordon Bennett Trophy race in 1913 with a record-breaking speed of 124.5 miles per hour. Although most airplane designers took a more conservative approach for operational airplanes—Bechereau himself later used the standard boxlike biplane configuration for his SPAD airplanes—the Albatross D series of airplanes beginning in 1916 also had a smooth, aerodynamically shaped fuselage using semimonocoque construction (to be discussed later).

Multiengine airplanes came on the scene in the big way in 1913 with the exceptionally large Le Grand, designed by the young Russian engineer Igor Sikorsky. A biplane configuration, it was the first airplane with four engines, as well as the first with an enclosed cabin for the pilots and crew. Its first flight took place in May of 1913, and it achieved 52 subsequent flights before it was destroyed later in the year during army maneuvers when another airplane accidentally dropped an engine on it. Sikorsky went on to build an even larger four-engine biplane, the Il'ya Moromets, in 1915—it was 14 times heavier than the Wright Flyer, with a wing area and wing span about three times that of the Flyer. The four Argus engines produced a total of 400 horsepower, in comparison with the 12 horsepower of the Flyer. The Sikorsky designs were the precursors to the large multiengine biplane bombers of World War I, such as the British Handly–Page 0/400 and the German Gotha G-VIII. The small, somewhat flimsy-looking Flyer had evolved into gigantic, flimsy-looking, two- and four-engined giants.

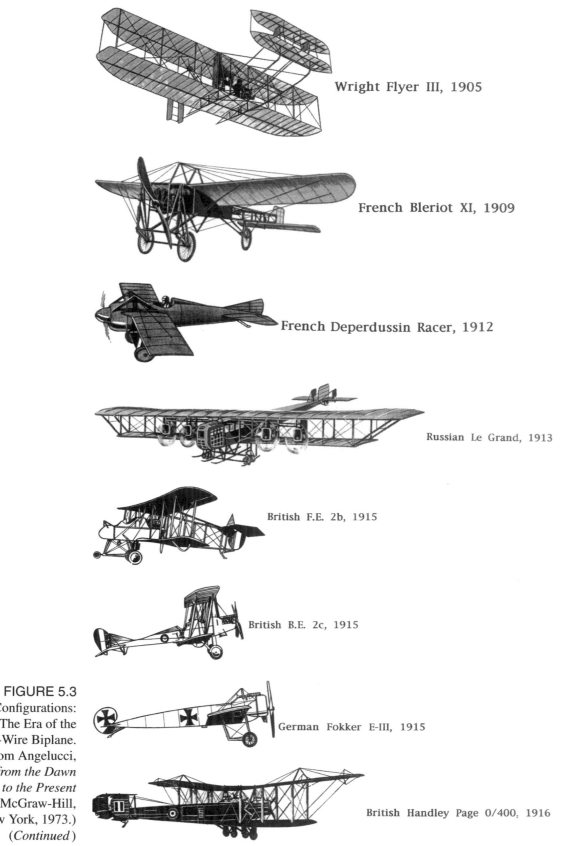

Wright Flyer III, 1905

French Bleriot XI, 1909

French Deperdussin Racer, 1912

Russian Le Grand, 1913

British F.E. 2b, 1915

British B.E. 2c, 1915

German Fokker E-III, 1915

British Handley Page 0/400, 1916

FIGURE 5.3
Parade of Configurations:
The Era of the
Strut-and-Wire Biplane.
(From Angelucci,
*Airplanes from the Dawn
of Flight to the Present
Day*, McGraw-Hill,
New York, 1973.)
(*Continued*)

British Sopwith Camel, 1917

German Albatros D III, 1917

British S.E. 5, 1917

German Fokker D-VII, 1918

German Gotha G-VIII, 1918

British Vickers-Vimy IV, 1919

American Curtiss NC, 1919

FIGURE 5.3
(*Continued from page 134.*)

AN EXAMPLE OF AERONAUTICAL ENGINEERING IN 1917—SPAD XIII

On September 2, 1916, deliveries began of a new fighter, the SPAD VII, which in its later variant, the SPAD XIII, was to become France's best combat aircraft of World War I. Both SPADs were designed by Louis Bechereau, who first gained fame as the designer of the earlier, streamlined Deperdussin racer (Figure 5.3). Bechereau was hired in 1910 by Armand Deperdussin, a wealthy, debonair silk broker, to design and build airplanes in a small factory near Reims. At that time, airplane manufacture had not progressed much beyond the handcrafting tradition set by the Wright brothers. Deperdussin's company was called the Societe pour les Appareils Deperdussin, hence, the acronym SPAD. In 1913 Deperdussin was jailed for the embezzlement of 28 million francs, and the company was reorganized as the Societe pour Aviation et Derives, keeping both the acronym and Bechereau. Bechereau's experience in designing monoplanes such as the Deperdussin racer had to be set aside in 1912 when both the British and French banned the use of monoplanes, and although the ban was later lifted, Bechereau was now deep in the design of biplanes.

The SPAD VII and SPAD XIII were designed around new, powerful engines, provided by the Hispano–Suiza company. Designed by the talented Swiss engineer, Marc Birkigt, these V-8 engines provided 180 hp for the SPAD VII in 1916 and an upgraded 220 horsepower for the SPAD XIII. The Hispano–Suiza 8BA engine used in the SPAD XIII was one of the best and most advanced engines produced during World War I, serving as the leading edge of the Curtiss and Rolls–Royce liquid-cooled engines to follow during the next 25 years. A photograph of the SPAD XIII, an airplane that is literally wrapped around its powerful engine, is shown in Figure 5.4. In this photograph, the young Captain Eddie Rickenbacker stands in front of his SPAD that he flew in 1918 as a member of the "hat in the ring"

FIGURE 5.4
The French SPAD XIII.
Captain Eddie
Rickenbacker is shown at
the front of the airplane.

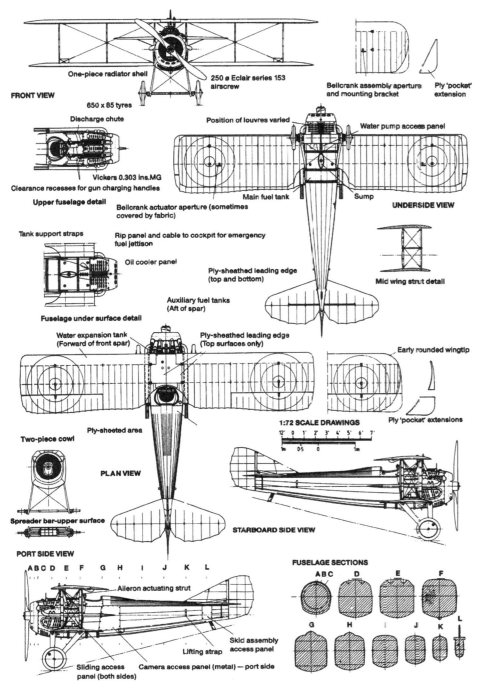

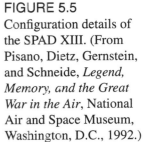

FIGURE 5.5
Configuration details of
the SPAD XIII. (From
Pisano, Dietz, Gernstein,
and Schneide, *Legend,
Memory, and the Great
War in the Air*, National
Air and Space Museum,
Washington, D.C., 1992.)

94th Aero Squadron. The airplane in Figure 5.4 is a picture of *brute force*—the 130
mile-per-hour high speed of the SPAD XIII was mainly due to the power from the
engine rather than any dramatic decrease in aerodynamic drag. The acceleration of
an airplane is a function of the thrust minus the drag, $T - D$; everything else being
equal, the higher is $T - D$, the faster is the airplane. The SPAD XIII had a lot of
$T - D$ just on the brute power provided by the Hispano–Suiza engine.

Some technical details of the SPAD XIII are shown in the multiview diagram
in Figure 5.5. The overall picture is that of a standard biplane configuration, with

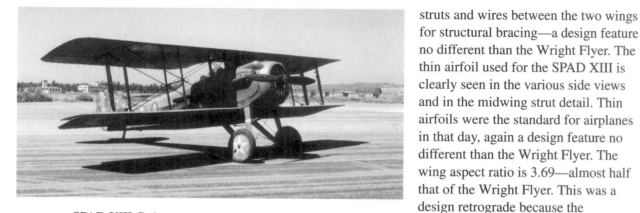

SPAD XIII C. 1.
Photograph of the SPAD
in Paul Mantz's collection,
Tustin, California.
(American Aviation
Historical Society, from
Warren Bodie.)

struts and wires between the two wings for structural bracing—a design feature no different than the Wright Flyer. The thin airfoil used for the SPAD XIII is clearly seen in the various side views and in the midwing strut detail. Thin airfoils were the standard for airplanes in that day, again a design feature no different than the Wright Flyer. The wing aspect ratio is 3.69—almost half that of the Wright Flyer. This was a design retrograde because the aerodynamic advantages of high aspect ratio wings were appreciated, although not theoretically understood, at the time Bechereau designed the SPAD. The SPAD was designed around the most powerful engine available, and the brute force aspect of thrust tended to make the increase in drag due to the lower aspect ratio wing less of a concern. Moreover, the lower aspect ratio allowed a smaller rolling moment of inertia and, hence, more rapid acceleration in roll—an important feature for a combat fighter. Furthermore, the rather streamlined configuration of the SPAD gave it a slightly lower (for its time) zero-lift drag coefficient of 0.037, which tended to compensate for the increased drag-due-to-lift due to the low aspect ratio wing. Aerodynamically, the SPAD exhibited no revolutionary features.

Ailerons on the top wings, as clearly seen in Figure 5.5, exercised lateral control. The Wrights' pioneered lateral control for airplanes—a feature quickly adopted by all subsequent successful airplane designers. Most of these designers, however, just as quickly eschewed the Wrights' use of wing warping as the mechanism for lateral control and used ailerons instead. The initial reason was legal, as an effort to avoid conflict with the Wrights' 1906 patent on their lateral control system. However, experience quickly proved ailerons to be a more effective design feature for lateral control, although Wright-designed airplanes clung to the old wing warping feature and did not incorporate ailerons until 1915. The origin of ailerons (a French word for the extremity of a bird's wing) can be traced to the Englishman M. P. W. Boulton, who patented the idea for an otherwise impractical ornithopter in 1868. In 1870, Richard Harte, a member of the Aeronautical Society of Great Britain, suggested a more modern flaplike aileron for use on a fixed-wing aircraft; his concept is shown in Figure 5.6. He envisioned that aileron deflection

FIGURE 5.6
Harte's design for an
aileron, 1870.

on one wing would increase drag on that wing and swing the nose of the aircraft in the direction of the higher-drag wing. He was not thinking of controlling roll, except for counteracting the effect of the torque of the propeller. Of course, at that time no practical aircraft existed, so that the concept could not be demonstrated and verified, and Boulton's and Harte's inventions quickly retreated to the background and were forgotten. The concept of ailerons again surfaced with the "June Bug" biplane designed by Glenn Curtiss in 1908, which used triangular flaplike surfaces extending outward from all four wing tips. Some other designs used separate movable winglets mounted either above, below, or between the wings. But in 1909, Henri Farman designed a biplane called the "Henri Farman III," which included a flaplike aileron at the trailing edge of all four wingtips for roll control; this was the true ancestor of the conventional modern-day aileron. Farman's design was soon adopted by most designers, and wing warping quickly became passé.

The heart of the SPAD, the 220-horsepower Hispano–Suiza engine, is neatly enclosed in the nose, with a rounded cowl at the front providing some semblance of streamlining. Inside the cowl, the radiator faces squarely into the airstream; vertical shutters (not visible in Figure 5.5) cross in front of the radiator, and variable louvers are placed around the engine housing, all to control engine cooling. Engine power is converted into forward thrust via the wooden two-blade propeller. Compared with the 12-horsepower nonthrottable engine of the 1903 Wright Flyer, the 220-horsepower Hispano–Suiza engine with throttle controls in the SPAD represented a considerable, but still evolutionary, improvement. The total enclosure of the engine within the fuselage of the SPAD was another improvement over the totally exposed engine of the Wright Flyer, again representing evolutionary progress in the efforts to reduce aerodynamic drag. (Recall that the zero-lift drag coefficient for the SPAD was 0.037 compared with 0.074 for the Wright Flyer—a reduction by a factor of two.) The Éclair series propeller on the SPAD was an improved shape over the Wrights' 1903 propeller, representing gradual evolution of the Wrights' stunningly effective propeller design. (Compare the SPAD propeller shown in Figure 5.5 with the Wrights' propeller in Figure 4.19.)

The engine and propeller of the SPAD exuded brute force, which meant higher flight speeds. However, flight speed is not directly proportional to engine power. That is, if engine power is doubled, the flight speed is *not* doubled—it increases by a much smaller amount. To see why, consider the drag, given by

$$D = \tfrac{1}{2}\rho_\infty V_\infty^2 S C_D$$

For an airplane in steady level flight, the drag is exactly counteracted by the thrust,

$$T = D = \tfrac{1}{2}\rho_\infty V_\infty^2 S C_D$$

The *power* available from the engine-propeller combination in flight, P, is

$$P = T V_\infty = \tfrac{1}{2}\rho_\infty V_\infty^3 S C_D$$

Hence, power varies as the *cube* of the airspeed. Turning this equation inside out, and solving for velocity, we see that flight velocity varies as the *cube root* of power. Hence, if the engine power is doubled, the speed of the airplane will increase by only 26 percent. You can easily see why the design of the higher speed

TABLE 5.1   Fundamental design parameters

Design	W/P, lb/hp	W/S, psf	$C_{D,0}$	$(L/D)_{max}$
Wright Flyer	62.5	1.47	0.074	5.7
SPAD XIII	8.25	8.0	0.037	7.4

propeller-driven airplanes in the first half of the 20th century required the design of reciprocating engines with phenomenal increases in horsepower.

The SPAD, like the Wright Flyer before it, was essentially a "vegetable" airplane, made primarily from wood and cloth. With the exception of the plywood sheeting along the top of the fuselage and along the top of the leading edge of the wings, the airplane was fabric covered. The basic structural components of the SPAD represented a graduate evolution from those of the Wright Flyer.

One of the most obvious differences between the SPAD and the Wright Flyer is that the SPAD had wheels, whereas the Wright Flyer had a simple landing skid. Other airplane designers did not follow the Wrights' landing gear arrangement. Wheels were used almost exclusively from 1907 onward. Santos-Dumont in his 14-bis in 1907 used wheels. Glenn Curtiss and his June Bug in 1908 used wheels. A Wright-designed airplane did not have wheels until the Model B in 1910. The early wheels had exposed radial spokes, like those of bicycles. By the beginning of World War I, designers covered these spokes with wheel covers to reduce drag; the wheel disk of the SPAD was fabric covered.

The strut-and-wire biplane of 1917 (the SPAD XIII is a good example) had evolved from the Wright Flyer into a faster, higher-flying airplane. What is it about an airplane that generates higher speeds, higher rates of climb, higher altitudes, etc.? Intuition says more thrust and less drag. But that is not the whole story. You could have an airplane that produces 100 pounds of thrust, with relatively low drag, but that is not going to do anything for you if the airplane weighs a half-million pounds. Clearly, the weight and size of the airplane must come into the picture. Interestingly enough, the important quantities that drive airplane performance are not power P by itself, or weight W by itself, or size as indicated by the wing planform area, S, by itself. Rather, certain *ratios* of these quantities dictate the performance of the airplane, namely, the *power loading*, W/P, *wing loading* W/S, *drag coefficient*, and the *maximum lift-to-drag ratio* $(L/D)_{max}$. Detailed analysis of airplane performance (such as described by J. D. Anderson in *Aircraft Performance and Design*, McGraw–Hill, New York, 1999) clearly shows the following:

1) Maximum velocity of the airplane at any given altitude depends *only* on power loading, wing loading, and drag coefficient (not drag itself, but rather drag *coefficient*). When designing a new airplane, maximum velocity can be *increased* by *decreasing* W/P, *increasing* W/S, and *lowering* drag coefficient.

2) Maximum rate-of-climb of the airplane at any given altitude depends *only* on power loading, wing loading, drag coefficient, and maximum lift-to-drag ratio. When designing a new airplane, maximum rate-of-climb can be *increased* by *decreasing* W/P, *increasing* W/S, *decreasing* the drag coefficient, and *increasing* $(L/D)_{max}$.

3) Maximum altitude occurs when the airplane runs out of rate-of-climb capability, that is, when the maximum rate-of-climb becomes zero. Hence, when designing a new airplane, maximum altitude can be increased by increasing the same quantities that increase maximum rate-of-climb.

The importance of these fundamental parameters, W/P, W/S, drag coefficient, and $(L/D)_{max}$, were recognized in some intuitive sense by designers such as Louis Bechereau during World War I. Table 5.1 compares these parameters for the Wright Flyer and the SPAD XIII. You can easily see why the SPAD XIII flew faster and higher.

ADVANCES IN AERODYNAMICS

The most important advance in the aerodynamics of the airplane during the strut-and-wire biplane era was the rather sudden use of thick rather than thin airfoil shapes. This is not immediately obvious, say, to the average visitor walking through the World War I Gallery of the National Air and Space Museum. Near the entrance, you see the SPAD XIII (Figure 5.7), and as you leave the Gallery, you pass by the Fokker D-VII (Figure 5.8), Germany's best fighter of the war. Both are biplanes of rather classic design, and at first glance you might not observe a subtle but important difference. The Fokker D-VII has struts between the two wings, *but no wires*. This is because the Fokker's wings are supported internally by a strong cantilever design using thick spars. In turn, the thick spars are allowed because the airfoil shape of the D-VII is thick in comparison with the thin airfoil used on the SPAD XIII. This is easily seen by comparing the SPAD XIII in Figure 5.5 with the Fokker D-VII in Figure 5.9. Note the airfoil shape for the SPAD XIII in Figure 5.5—a thin cambered shape with a rather sharp leading edge. Compare this with

FIGURE 5.7
The SPAD XIII in the National Air and Space Museum, Smithsonian Institution, Washington, D.C.

FIGURE 5.8
The Fokker D-VIII in the National Air and Space Museum, Smithsonian Institution.

the airfoil shape for the Fokker D-VII in Figure 5.9—a thick cambered shape with a large rounded leading edge.

In 1917, the thick airfoil flew in the face of conventional wisdom. Thin wing sections had started with da Vinci and were carried through the 19th century by such pioneers as George Cayley and Otto Lilienthal, perhaps following nature's design in birds' wings. At the turn of the 20th century, embryonic wind-tunnel tests, including those of the Wright brothers, indicated that thinner airfoils had much less drag than thick airfoils. Today we know this result to be an artifact of the small wind-tunnel models tested at the low wind speeds created in the early wind tunnels. Define the important aerodynamic parameter Reynolds number Re as

$$Re = \rho V c / \mu$$

where ρ is the air density, V is the airspeed, c is the chord length of the airfoil (an index of the size of the airfoil), and μ is the viscosity coefficient (an index of the effect of friction on the flow over the airfoil). All of the early airfoil experiments in wind tunnels were conducted at *low* Reynolds number because of the low values of V and c. [To obtain a physical understanding of Reynolds number, visualize a small parcel of air flowing over an object such as a wing. The Reynolds number is proportional to the ratio of the inertia of the parcel (due to its mass and velocity) to the friction force exerted on the surface of the parcel by the surrounding air. With the lower Reynolds number, the flow feels a stronger friction force compared with the inertia force.] It was not appreciated at that time, but, at low Reynolds number, a small bubble of flow separation can occur near the leading edge of the airfoil, called the laminar-separation bubble, and if this bubble burst, it would cause flow separation over the entire top surface of the airfoil, decreasing the lift and increasing the drag. Low Reynolds number laminar-separation bubbles are much more likely to occur on thick airfoils than thin shapes. Hence, the early wind-tunnel tests at low Reynolds numbers favored the performance of thin airfoils. When used

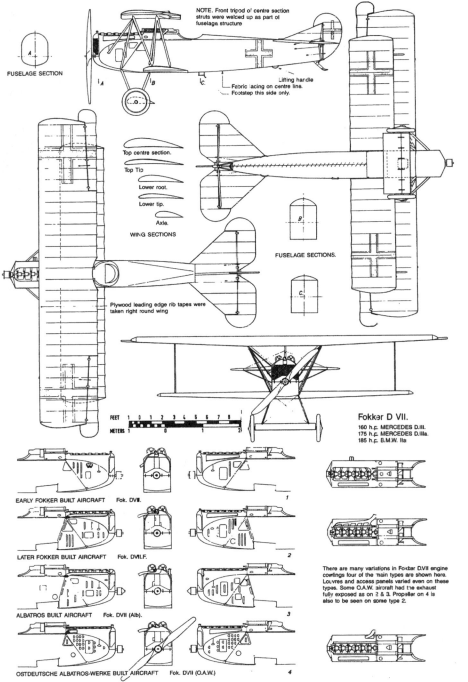

FIGURE 5.9
Configuration details of
the Fokker D-VII. (From
Pisano, Dietz, Gernstein,
and Schneide, *Legend,
Memory, and the Great
War in the Air*, National
Air and Space Museum,
Washington, D.C., 1992.)

on real airplanes, however, which were much larger and flew at higher speeds, the
Reynolds number was much larger, and the actual airfoil performance was much
different than measured in the early wind tunnels. Of course, nobody knew that at
the time. It was not recognized that thicker airfoils would actually perform better at
higher Reynolds numbers, producing higher maximum lift coefficients. Indeed, the
thin airfoils used on most airplanes until 1918, when inclined to larger angle of
attack, experienced premature flow separation, hence, stalling earlier with
consequently smaller maximum lift coefficients.

The 1903 Wright Flyer in the National Air and Space Museum, Smithsonian Institution.

The SPAD XIII at the National Air and Space Museum, Smithsonian Institution. This view highlights the thin airfoil section of the wing, characteristic of most World War I aircraft.

Let us compare some actual airfoil data. Figures 5.10 and 5.11 are historic graphs reproduced from NACA Technical Report TR-124, published in 1921; for historic purposes they are shown as exact facsimiles. Figure 5.10 gives data for the "Bleriot" airfoil, essentially like that used on the SPAD XIII; the data were obtained in 1916 by Gustave Eiffel in his large aerodynamic laboratory in Paris. Figure 5.11 gives data for the Göttingen 298 airfoil, used on the Fokker Dr.1 triplane and very similar to the airfoil used on the Fokker D-VII; the data were obtained in the large wind tunnel built by Ludwig Prandtl at Göttingen University in Germany. The respective airfoil shapes are shown at the top of Figures 5.10 and 5.11; you can easily compare the very thin shape of the Bleriot with the thick profile of the Göttingen 298. These graphs show the variation of lift and drag coefficients, L_c and D_c, respectively, and lift-to-drag ratio, as functions of angle of attack. In 1917, lift and drag coefficients were defined slightly differently than they are today, resulting in the numbers being half of what we use today. That is, a value of $L_c = 0.5$ in Figures 5.10 and 5.11 corresponds to a value of $C_L = 1.0$ in modern usage. The Reynolds numbers at which the data were taken were still low. For example, for the Göttingen 298 airfoil results in Figure 5.11, the Reynolds number is 73,000; the Reynolds number for the actual Fokker D-VII flying at 124 miles per hour at sea level is 4,361,000—a much larger value. When these two sets of data are compared, especially note the following:

1) The minimum drag coefficient for the thick Göttingen 298 is $D_c = 0.018$, about twice the value of $D_c = 0.01$ for the thin Bleriot. This is the typical low Reynolds number result and the major factor why thin airfoils were the shape of choice before 1917.

2) On the other hand, even in the face of low Reynolds numbers, the thick Göttingen 298 produces a maximum lift coefficient of $L_c = 0.14$, quite large compared with the much smaller value of 0.095 for the Bleriot.

The higher maximum lift coefficient is the important hallmark of the thick airfoil. In air combat, for example, the turn radius of an airplane is an important factor. Where two airplanes are compared, the one with a smaller turn radius can turn inside the other, gaining a considerable maneuver advantage. Turn radius is inversely proportional to the maximum lift coefficient. Everything else being equal, an airplane with a 30 percent higher maximum lift coefficient will have a 30 percent smaller turn radius. This is one of the reasons why the Fokker D-VII with its thick airfoil could outmaneuver any of the opposition.

The Fokker Dr.1 triplane, shown in Figure 5.12, was the first mass-production combat airplane to use a thick airfoil. It was not, however, the first airplane in general to use a thick airfoil. Professor Hugo Junkers at the Technical College in Aachen, Germany, in the process of pioneering the design of all-metal airplanes during World War I, was the first to recognize and prove the aero-

The Fokker D-VII at the National Air and Space Museum, Smithsonian Institution. This view highlights the thick section of the wing, a German breakthrough in airfoil design at the end of World War I.

dynamic advantages of thick airfoils. We will highlight Junkers's contributions to airplane design later in this chapter. Junkers felt that an all-metal airplane should have a cantilevered wing—no external supports. To achieve this, the airfoil section had to be thick. Junkers knew that such airfoils would be a complete departure from conventional practice. Much later, in a paper to the Royal Aeronautical Society in 1923, Junkers stated the following:

> Up to this time [1914] only aeroplanes with the very thinnest wing sections had been constructed and the aerodynamical investigations in this province of science—as, for example, those of Eiffel or of the "Gottingen Aerodynamics Institute"—had likewise been conducted exclusively in this direction. There prevailed the general opinion that good results, both in lift and drag, could only be obtained with a thin wing.

Then Junkers stated the design challenge:

> We have to view at present the question of the practical realization of the thick cantilever metal wing. We had to investigate whether it was feasible to produce a wing which would combine with a thick section a low drag and a sufficient lift, and whether such wings could be constructed in metal in such a way that the aerodynamical attributes would not be suppressed by the drawback of too high a weight.

Because no data existed on thick airfoils, to realize his design goal Junkers knew "they had to be freshly created." To this end he built a wind tunnel at Aachen and later another tunnel at his firm Hugo Junkers and Company in Dessau, Germany. In these tunnels he studied the properties of lift, drag, and center of pressure on both thin and thick airfoils. Some of the airfoil shapes he examined are shown in Figure 5.13. Junkers was elated with the test results. "My most extravagant expectations were surpassed," he wrote. "The thick airfoils proved not only equivalent to the thin ones of some series, but even superior, within certain limits." With a feeling of relief, Junkers went on to design his all-metal airplanes with thick airfoil sections. Not only were they thick, but the shapes were convex on *both* the top and bottom surfaces, as seen in the thicker profiles shown near the end of Figure 5.13. This was yet another departure from conventional practice.

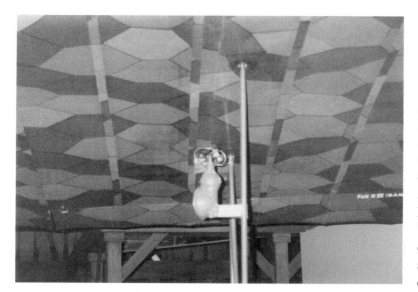

Method of airspeed measurement. This photo shows a rotating cup anemometer mounted between the two wings of the Fokker D-VII. This is a type of early airspeed measuring instrument.

Junkers's use of thick airfoils, originally driven by structural reasons, internally supported cantilevered wings, was not immediately followed by other designers. This author suspects that Junkers kept the airfoil data to himself for proprietary reasons, although the thick airfoil was there for everybody to see when his all-metal Junkers J1 came out in 1915 (Figure 5.14). The thick airfoil did not surface again until the Fokker Dr.1 triplane was designed in 1917 (Figures 5.12 and 5.15). An otherwise conventional fabric-covered airplane, the Dr.1 had wooden cantilevered wings that required thick airfoils for structural reasons. The Fokker Dr.1 was designed by Anthony Fokker's chief airplane designer, Reinhold Platz. Platz was a welder who rose through the ranks of the Fokker company to become Chief Designer in 1916. He did not have a university education; his engineering knowledge was intuitive and self-learned. A. R. Weyl, in his book *Fokker: The Creative Years* (Putnam, 1965) stated that Platz was not aware of any airfoil data from Junkers, or from Prandtl's laboratory at Göttingen; indeed, Weyl claims that Fokker himself kept any real technical data from reaching Platz for selfish personal reasons not fully understood. According to Weyl, Platz drew the airfoil shape by eye, knowing only that it had to be thick but streamlined. Weyl states this: "For Platz, a cantilever wing was simply a compromise between the weight of the structure that was required to resist given bending loads, and acceptable wing thickness. Aerodynamic considerations did not come into his design philosophy." This story is somewhat at odds with other technical sources that identify the Göttingen 298 airfoil (Figure 5.11) as the airfoil used on the Dr.1 triplane and the D.VII. We note, however, that the Dr.1 went into service during the later summer of 1917, and the technical report containing the data for the Göttingen 298 airfoil was not published until February of 1918. Also, the aerodynamic properties of airfoils depend critically on the details of the airfoil shape; small changes in shape, almost imperceptible to the eye, can sometimes cause major changes in the airfoil performance. To design the Dr.1 airfoil by eye, without any benefit of testing and subsequent fine tuning, and to have that airfoil shape perform as well as it did on the Dr.1 and the D.VII, seems fortuitous beyond belief.

In any event, the aerodynamic merits of thick airfoils were conclusively demonstrated by the German wind-tunnel experiments and the superiority of the Fokker airplanes at the end of World War I, especially the Fokker D.VII. In aerodynamics, this represented a dramatic and rapid evolutionary development, bordering on revolutionary. In spite of all this, the virtues of thick airfoils were slow to dawn on English and American aeronautical engineers. The first recognition in the United States came from the fledgling National Advisory Committee for Aeronautics (NACA). In 1919, F. H. Norton, then Chief Physicist at the brand new NACA Memorial Aerodynamical Laboratory at Langley Field, Virginia, published a report describing wind-tunnel measurements of lift, drag, and center of pressure on thick airfoils shaped like that shown in Figure 5.16.

Discussing thick airfoil sections, Norton stated the following:

> This type of wing is of interest—first, because it eliminates the resistance of the interplane bracing, a portion of the airplane that sometimes absorbs one-quarter of the total power required to fly; second, because it simplifies the construction and assembly of the wing structure, and third, because these wings may be made to give a very high maximum lift. At the present time, thick internally braced sections are used with considerable success on several German machines, notably the Fokker and Junker Biplanes.

Clearly, in 1919, NACA was aware of the advantages of thick airfoils. However, the British seemed to be dragging their feet. In the April 22, 1920, issue of the British magazine *Flight*, Norton's NACA technical report was reprinted in full, with the following editor's statement:

> Up to the time of writing our own authorities have not thought it of sufficient interest to have carried out experiments on thick wing sections in any of the Government wind tunnels. The subject is, however, one of the very greatest interest, and it is therefore with considerable satisfaction that we have received this proof of American farsightedness in a matter upon which our own experimenters have shown a singular lack of interest.

The widespread use of thick airfoils was slow in coming. Most biplanes designed in the 1920s were the standard strut-and-wire configuration using uncantilevered wings with thin airfoils—a testimonial to the prevailing conservative design philosophy of building a new airplane with only small departures from the previous airplane.

And talking about wires, the support wires for most airplanes through World War I had ordinary, circular cross sections, which, believe it or not, have an inordinately high drag coefficient. The SPAD XIII, for example, had round wires. Aeronautical engineers at the time knew that the interplane struts and wires caused high drag, and efforts were made to reduce this drag by streamlining the cross sections of both the struts and the wires. Figure 5.17 illustrates the front view and cross section of a relatively streamlined "standard" strut discussed by Captain F. S. Barnwell, a well-known airplane designer serving in the Royal Air Force (RAF), in a paper in *Flight* in early 1919. And Figure 5.18 shows a streamlined cross section for bracing wires, called "Rafwire" because it was developed by the Royal Aeronautical Factory in 1914. The drag coefficient of Rafwire was about 1/10 that of round wire. Rafwire was used on several British airplanes, including the Sopwith Pup, triplane, and Camel. It was, however, not used by manufacturers in other nations, perhaps out of ignorance, or more likely due to reluctance to incur the extra manufacturing cost. In any event, the streamlining of the interplane struts and wires represented an evolutionary aerodynamic advance over the boxlike struts and round wires used on the Wright Flyer.

The aerodynamics of the airplane is greatly influenced by aspect ratio. The benefits of high aspect ratio wings were first advanced (intuitively) by Francis

Method of airspeed measurement. This photo shows a Pitot-static tube for measuring airspeed, mounted on the 1918 Sopwith Snipe at the National Air and Space Museum, Smithsonian Institution. This type of airspeed instrument was used by many British World War I airplanes, and it became the normal device for measuring airspeed, continuing to the present day.

Method of airspeed measurement. A Pitot-static tube mounted on the vertical tail of the XP-80 at the National Air and Space Museum, Smithsonian Institution. Virtually all airplanes since the 1930s have used some type of Pitot tube for airspeed measurement.

Wenham in 1866, definitely proven by the experiments of Samuel Langley as published in 1891, and rediscovered by the Wright brothers in their wind-tunnel experiments of 1901–1902. After that, the design aspect ratio of an airplane wing became a compromise between aerodynamics, which said high aspect ratio, and structural design and weight, which said low aspect ratio. Table 5.2 lists the aspect ratios for several aircraft representative of the strut-and-wire biplane era.

Fighter airplanes of World War I had lower aspect ratios than the Wright Flyer, driven by structural concern for the high stresses and strains of air combat. The Handley Page 0/400 and Gotha G.V (Figure 5.3) were twin engine bombers, where the design for longer range demanded the improved aerodynamic efficiency provided by higher aspect ratio wings.

However, the author does not think that the value of high aspect ratios was fully appreciated by most aeronautical engineers at that time. The full theoretical understanding and calculation of the aerodynamic effect of aspect ratio was set forth by Ludwig Prandtl at Göttingen University in Germany, based on ideas proposed earlier by the Englishman Frederick Lanchester; however, Prandtl's theory did not appear until 1918 and was not made available in English language reports until the early 1920s. At the time that Bechereau designed the SPAD XIII, for example, the effect of high aspect ratio was still not fully understood; indeed, the picture was somewhat muddled. For example, by 1918 the U.S. Army had established an aeronautical research and development center at McCook Field in Dayton, Ohio, and in their bulletin of the Airplane Engineering Department of August 1918, the question of aspect ratio was addressed. In that bulletin, an article entitled "Effects of Varying Aspect Ratios" started with the following first

TABLE 5.2   Strut-and-wire biplane era aspect ratios

Airplane	Aspect ratio
Wright Flyer	6
Ablatross D-III (1917)	4.65
Fokker Triplane Dr.1 (1917)	4.04
Sopwith Camel (1917)	4.11
SPAD XIII (1917)	3.69
Fokker D-VII (1918)	4.70
Handley Page 0/400 (1916)	7.31
Gotha G.V (1917)	7.61
Curtiss JN-4 (Jenny) (1918)	7.76

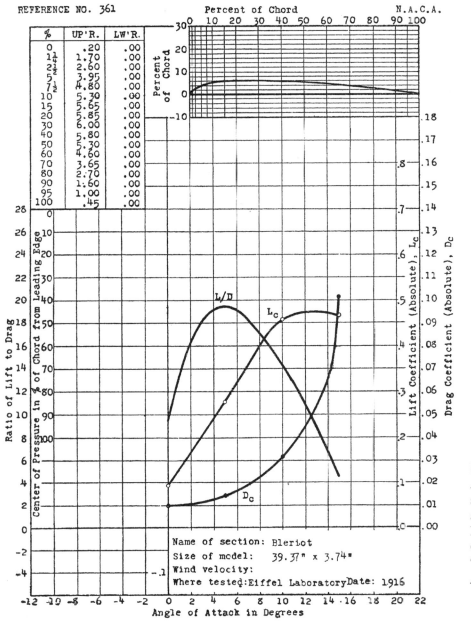

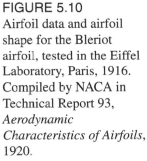

FIGURE 5.10
Airfoil data and airfoil shape for the Bleriot airfoil, tested in the Eiffel Laboratory, Paris, 1916. Compiled by NACA in Technical Report 93, *Aerodynamic Characteristics of Airfoils*, 1920.

sentence: "Considerable controversy exists as to the precise effects of varying aspect ratio." The report quoted results from Eiffel's laboratory showing that, with increasing aspect ratio, maximum lift coefficient actually diminished while the maximum lift-to-drag ratio was not improved. (We know today that both of these results are wrong.) Conflicting results from the National Physical Laboratory in England were also noted in the U.S. Army report, where measurements indicated that with increasing aspect ratio, lift coefficient slightly increased and the maximum lift-to-drag ratio was "very much improved." New test results "in an effort to clear the matter" were conducted "with great experimental care" at the Massachusetts Institute of Technology. As reported in the Army bulletin, these

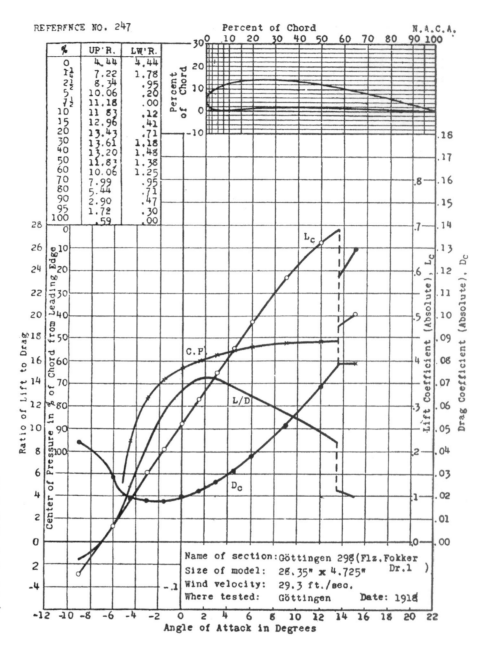

FIGURE 5.11
Airfoil data and airfoil shape for the Göttingen 298 airfoil, tested in the Göttingen University wind tunnel, Germany, 1918. Compiled by NACA in Technical Report 124, *Aerodynamic Characteristics of Airfoils II*, 1921.

results definitely showed that, with increasing aspect ratio, the maximum lift coefficient increases and lift-to-drag ratio "improves steadily." The Army report ends with the terse but definite statement that "we may conclude that increased aspect ratio means increased efficiency." All of these trends are correct. So, in regard to the Wrights' knowledge in 1903 about the advantages of high aspect ratio wings, the ensuing 15 years did not provide any real improvement, and in some cases the thinking was retrograde.

Finally, we note that in the three-views of the SPAD XIII (Figure 5.5), the Fokker D-VII (Figure 5.9), the Junkers J1 (Figure 5.14), and the Fokker Dr.1

(Figure 5.15) we see ailerons on the wings, but no flaps. The basic plain flaps evolved directly from the trailing-edge ailerons first used by Henri Farman in 1908. However, designers of the relatively slow World War I biplanes were not inclined to bother with flaps. Plain flaps were first used on the S.E.4 biplane built by the Royal Aircraft Factory in 1914; they became standard on airplanes built by Fairey in England from 1916 onward. The pilots of these aircraft, however, rarely bothered to use flaps; the landing and takeoff speeds of these airplanes were already low enough that the use of flaps was unnecessary.

Fokker D-VII. (American Aviation Historical Society, from K. M. Moulton.)

ADVANCES IN PROPULSION

The evolution of the airplane included an insatiable hunger for power—but power from engines as light weight as possible. At the turn of the 20th century, the conventional reciprocating engine was water cooled, necessitating a heavy radiator and associated plumbing—it remains so today. The heavy weight of water-cooled engines discouraged their use in the early airplanes. The Wrights' engine in 1903 (Figure 4.18) was water cooled, but only in a crude sense; water was fed to a water jacket around the cylinders by gravity from a narrow reservoir mounted on one of the forward center-section struts. There was no water pump, and the water did not circulate; it simply evaporated around the cylinders. The design was simple and

FIGURE 5.12
The Fokker DR.1 triplane.

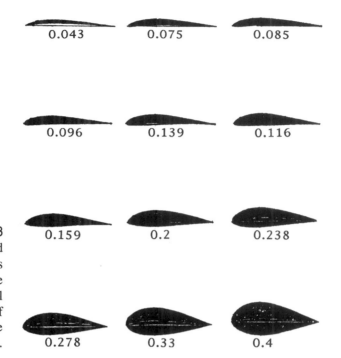

FIGURE 5.13
Some airfoil shapes tested by Hugo Junkers in his wind tunnel, 1915. The numbers under each airfoil shape give the ratio of maximum thickness to the chord length.

light weight, just what the Wrights wanted. The engine could only run for a few minutes, however, before overheating.

The ratio of the weight of an engine to its power output is an important figure of merit for propulsion. Because minimizing weight is a cardinal principle of airplane design, a fact well understood by Lilienthal, Langley, the Wright brothers, and every airplane designer after them, the lower the ratio of engine weight per horsepower, the better suited is the engine for aircraft use. (Note that this ratio is strictly an index for *engines*; it is not the same as the airplane power loading, which is the ratio of the gross weight of the *whole airplane* to the engine power. The power loading is one of the parameters that affect the performance of the airplane, whereas the engine weight-to-power ratio is a one of the figures of merit used for choosing an engine for a given airplane design.) The weight-to-power ratio for the Wrights' engine in 1903 was about 16 pounds per horsepower.

In 1905 the Frenchman Leon Levavasseur designed a much more advanced water-cooled engine, which produced 50 horsepower and weighed only 110 pounds, giving a weight-to-power ratio of 2.2 pounds per horsepower—much improved over the Wrights' engine. Named after a friend's daughter, the Antoinette engine had features ahead of its time but, unfortunately, was unreliable. It was designed originally for use on speedboats. Another 10 years would pass before water-cooled engines would become a standard for aircraft. The use of direct air cooling for the conventional engine was also not very effective because airplanes at that time flew too slowly.

A unique, but temporary solution to the cooling problem was found in 1908 by Laurent Sequin whose family firm, Gnome, was founded in 1905 in France to build reciprocating engines. Because the airflow over a conventional engine was too slow for adequate cooling, Sequin's idea was to rotate the engine itself, thus

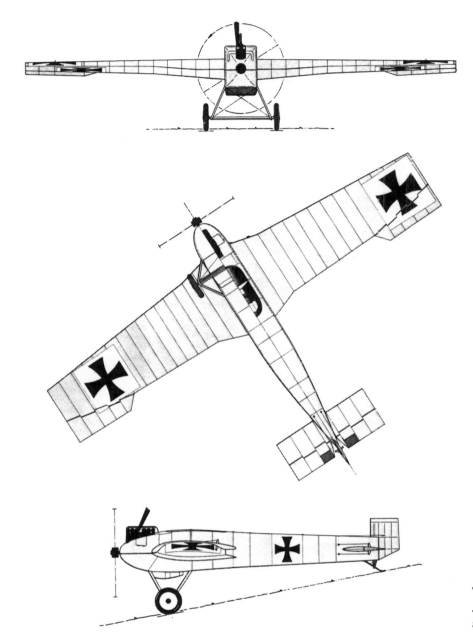

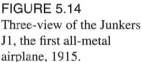

FIGURE 5.14
Three-view of the Junkers
J1, the first all-metal
airplane, 1915.

obtaining a sufficient movement of cooling air relative to the rotating cylinders. The conventional reciprocating engine, the type we have in our automobiles, is stationary, and the crankshaft rotates. In an airplane, the propeller is connected to the rotating crankshaft. For the rotary engine, the crankshaft is fixed, and the rest of the engine rotates around it. The propeller is fixed to the engine and rotates with it. In 1908, the Gnome rotary was a five-cylinder engine, but evolved quickly into a seven-cylinder 50-horsepower, 165-pound engine in 1909, and later achieved more than 100 horsepower. A longitudinal section of the Gnome seven-cylinder Monosoupape (single-valve) rotary engine is shown in Figure 5.19. By 1911, other companies were building their slightly different versions of rotary engines, Le Rhone and Clerget in France and Oberusel in Germany, for example. The

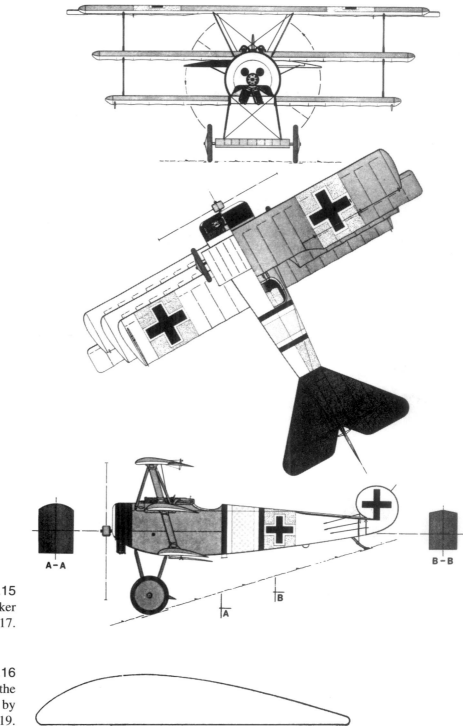

FIGURE 5.15
Three-view of the Fokker
Dr.1, 1917.

FIGURE 5.16
The Durand 13 airfoil, the
first thick airfoil tested by
NACA, 1919.

weight-to-power ratios of these rotary engines were on the order of 3 pounds per horsepower. Rotary engines powered more than 80 percent of the airplanes built in World War I before 1917. Figure 5.20 shows the Le Rhone 9-cylinder rotary engine, which produced 110 horsepower.

The heyday of the rotary engine was temporary. Because of the tremendous centrifugal force associated with the rotating heavy mass of the engine, its size, and hence, its horsepower, was limited. There were other disadvantages of rotary engines. In lieu of a standard oil pump and lubricating system, castor oil was added to the fuel mixture passing through the crankcase and bearing surfaces, lubricating the engine. The unused fuel and oil, sometimes flaming, would shoot out of the revolving cylinders, impinging harmlessly on the inside of a rounded cowling designed to keep the airplane from catching fire. The rounded cowling at the nose of the Fokker Dr.1 can be seen in Figure 5.15; the Fokker triplane was powered by an Oberusel rotary engine. Not so harmless was the effect of the castor oil fumes on the pilot; these fumes proved to be an effective intestinal lubricant. Another disadvantage of the rotary was the inability to throttle the engine because it had no carburetor; pilots had to cut the ignition intermittently to obtain reduced power for landing, relying on the flywheel action of the engine and the uninterrupted fuel flow to restart. Finally, the rotating engine created a strong gyroscopic action that caused new pilots some problems during maneuvering and turning. In spite of these disadvantages, the lightweight rotary engine was widely used until the horsepower requirements for new airplanes in 1918 began to exceed that available from practical-sized rotary engines.

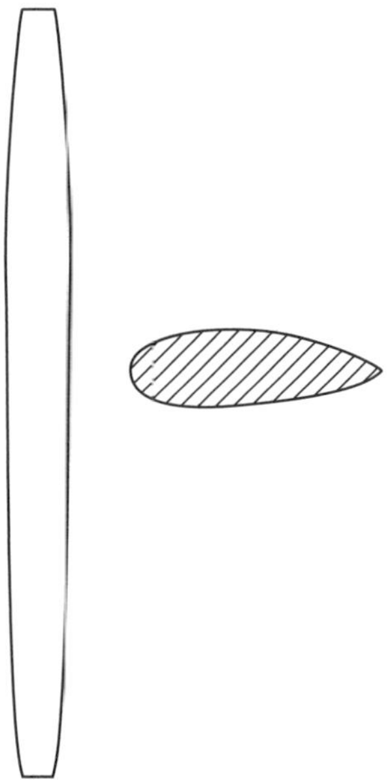

By 1918, the rotary engine was obsolete. The water-cooled engine came back into the picture because new designs effectively reduced the weight-to-power ratio. For example, the Wright Company made a six-cylinder in-line engine in 1913 that produced 70 horsepower and weighed 5 pounds per horsepower, a factor of three improvement over the original 1903 Wright engine with a lot more horsepower. In 1915, Mercedes in Germany made a six-cylinder, in-line, water-cooled engine (Figure 5.21) that provided 180 horsepower with a weight-to-horsepower ratio of 3.43 pounds per horsepower—on par with the best rotary engines. Mercedes engines powered the Albatros series of fighters (Figure 5.2) and the large German Gotha bombers (Figure 5.3). In an effort to better fit the noses of aircraft with a reduced frontal area, engine designers went to the V-type engine with the cylinders distributed in two rows inclined to the engine block through an angle that ranged from 60 to 90 degrees. During the same period in the United States, Curtiss built the OX-5 engine, a water-cooled V-8 that yielded 90 horsepower at 3.55 pounds per horsepower.

The leading water-cooled engine, however, was the series of Hispano–Suiza engines, which powered, for example, the SPAD VII and SPAD XIII fighters. This engine was the brainchild of the young Swiss engineer Marc Birkigt, who in 1905 had become linked with Spanish capital to enable Spain to compete in the field of automobiles. The trade name Hispano–Suiza quickly became known and respected in the automotive world. When World War I began, Birkigt derived an airplane engine from his successful automobile engines, and by 1915 his aircraft engine was successfully passing through test results and was ready for large-scale production. Birkigt made several innovations compared with the standard engine design. He constructed the cylinders from an aluminum single-block casting to which a very light crankcase was attached. Contrary to standard practice, which usually involved a heavy crankcase on which steel cylinders were individually bolted, Birkigt's engine had the crankcase hung on the cylinders rather than having the cylinders attached to the crankcase. The cylinder valve mechanism and overhead crankshaft were entirely encased in an oil-tight cover that fitted neatly over the cylinder block. As a result, the Hispano–Suiza was a compact unit ideally suited to aeronautical use. A cross section of the 200-horsepower Hispano–Suiza is shown in Figure 5.22, and a photograph is shown in Figure 5.23. Birkigt's

FIGURE 5.17
Front view and streamlined cross-section (not to constant scale) of a standard interwing vertical strut, used in the design of British airplanes during World War I.

FIGURE 5.18
Streamlined elliptic cross-section of "RAF" wire, developed by the Royal Aircraft Factory in 1914.

The Bentley BR-2 rotary engine, 1918, at the National Air and Space Museum, Smithsonian Institution. The Bentley powered the Sopwith Snipe, the airplane selected in 1918 to replace the famous Sopwith Camel.

outstanding talents in precision engineering also resulted in exceptional reliability for the Hispano–Suiza, with a weight-to-power ratio of 3.1 pounds per horsepower.

The Hispano–Suiza influenced engine design for the next two decades. Indeed, as the engine was being tested in 1915, two representatives of the Wright–Martin Company arrived in France from the United States. Wright–Martin, successor to the original Wright Company established by Wilbur and Orville, felt that a great future lay in engine manufacturing and that the easiest and quickest way of entering mass production in this market was to copy the best engine being built in Europe. This lead them to Birkigt and to an agreement between Wright–Martin and the French and Spanish parties for the granting of a license for manufacture in the United States. In a domino effect, the Curtiss Company, which had previously cornered the market for aircraft engines in the United States, was motivated to enlarge and improve their existing V-8 engine, the Curtiss OX-5. This ultimately evolved into the famous Curtiss D-12 engine that, with its 325 horsepower at 2.16 pounds per horsepower, powered a series of Curtiss racing airplanes to victory in the early 1920s. In Europe, the Hispano–Suiza inspired a series of designs that ultimately evolved into the famous Rolls–Royce Merlin engine of the 1930s; the Merlon engine went on to distinction in World War II.

The genes of the Hispano–Suiza can also be found in the most famous American engine of the strut-and-wire biplane era—the ubiquitous Liberty engine. Edward A. Deeds, an engineer and industrialist, who, on May 17, 1917, was appointed to the Aircraft Production Board, catalyzed the U.S. government into deciding that a standardized engine must be designed and put into production as quickly as possible. It was to be one of America's contributions to the war effort. Deeds believed that such an engine had to be designed for maximum power and efficiency, with minimum weight, and that it had to be capable of maximum power and speed during most of its operational time. Moreover, it had to be economical in the consumption of fuel and oil. The two engineering minds that were to design such an engine were serendipitously in Washington, D.C., during May 1917. Elbert John Hall, a partner in the Hall–Scott Motor Car Company that was producing four- and six-cylinder aircraft engines, and who had just designed a new 12-cylinder engine intended to produce 450 horsepower, had been summoned to the Navy Department on official business. Jesse G. Vincent, vice president for engineering for the Packard Motor Car Company, was in Washington, D.C., at the same time to campaign for the standardization of aircraft engine production, afraid that the United States may fall into the same pit as Europeans with their multiplicity of engines being produced. Deeds seized the moment. Giving Hall and Vincent (who had not met before) the use of his suite at the famous Willard Hotel

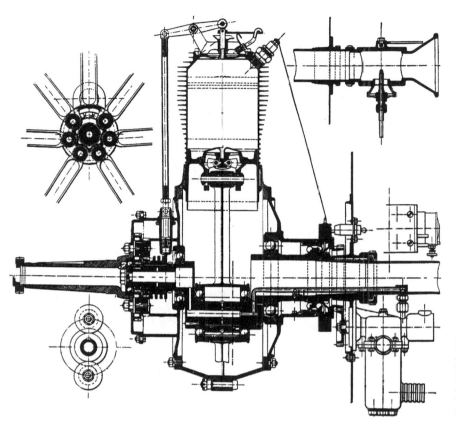

FIGURE 5.19
Longitudinal section of the
Gnome 7-cylinder
Monosoupape rotary
air-cooled engine, 1910.

in Washington, D.C., Deeds sequestered the two engineers on May 29. Within
hours they were laying down two views of a proposal eight-cylinder aircraft
engine. Deeds needed a design quickly, and he asked the two men to favor
simplicity for mass production, cautioning them not to use untried technology or
designs in the new engine. Drafting tools, a table, and paper were brought in. At
midnight, Vincent called Dr. Samuel Stratton, Director of the Bureau of Standards,
to obtain the latest data on French and British engines. On May 30, 1917, the
Washington, D.C., branch of the Society of Automotive Engineers provided a
volunteer draftsman, J. N. Schoonmaker, to help. On June 1, two layout men came
in from Detroit to work on construction features being thought out by Vincent,
Hall, and Schoonmaker. At midnight on June 4, Hall and Vincent presented their
finished drawings to the U.S. Army–Navy Aircraft Production Board, which
approved the production of five 8-cylinder and five 12-cylinder engines for testing.
What was to be the Liberty engine had been born in six days at the Willard Hotel.
But it reflected years of experience on the part of Hall and Vincent, experience that
ensured a quality product. Ultimately, the Liberty engine was mass produced as a
12-cylinder engine, with a total of 20,478 units produced. The V-12 engine
produced 400 horsepower at a remarkable 2.04 pounds per horsepower.
Figure 5.24 shows a cross section of the Liberty V-12 engine. The engine was
produced much faster than the airframes to use it; at the end of the war, many
thousands of Liberty engines were sitting around, waiting for some application. It
was used on airplanes well into the 1930s and found use as a lightweight and
powerful marine engine. (During prohibition, many Liberty engines were sold at

FIGURE 5.20
A nine-cylinder Le Rhone
rotary air-cooled engine,
rated at 110 horsepower.

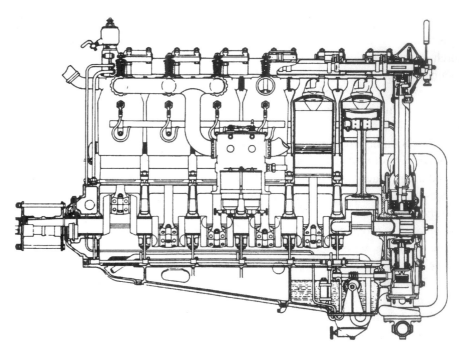

FIGURE 5.21
Longitudinal section of the
Mercedes 6-cylinder
liquid-cooled engine,
1915, 180 horsepower.

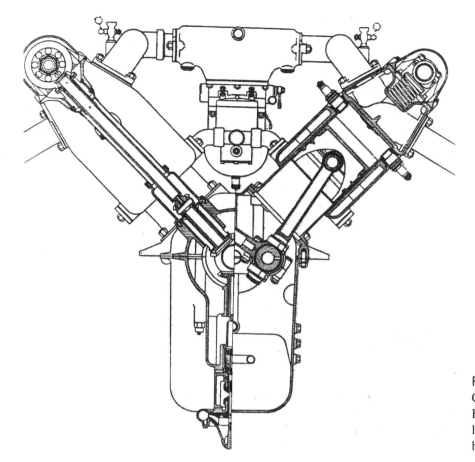

FIGURE 5.22
Cross-section of the
Hispano–Suiza
liquid-cooled engine, 200
horsepower.

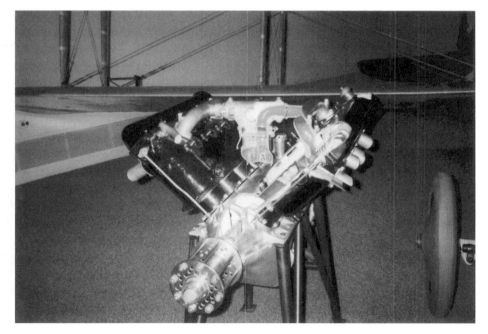

FIGURE 5.23
Photograph of the
8-cylinder Hispano–Suiza
in the National Air and
Space Museum,
Smithsonian Institution.

The first Liberty L-8 aircraft engine, number one, in the National Air and Space Museum, Smithsonian Institution.

low prices to bootleggers, whose Liberty-powered boats far outclassed those of the Coast Guard.)

So, propulsion during the era of the strut-and-wire biplane was dominated by the evolution of larger and more powerful reciprocating engines. These engines contained features refined well beyond the original Wright brothers' engine in 1903, but there was no dramatic revolutionary feature. Perhaps the greatest departure from the normal was the rotary engine, but it had only a limited place in the sun; it did not influence subsequent designs in the 1920s and beyond.

And, of course, we are reminded that reciprocating engines produce power in the form of rotating motion —they must be connected to a propeller to produce thrust to propel the airplane forward. During the era of the strut-and-wire biplane, at least through 1920, the propeller experienced only small incremental improvements in design; it basically remained the same type of wooden, fixed-pitch propeller used by the Wrights. By 1920, propellers routinely were designed by means of the blade element theory, which divides the propeller into a number of different sections located at different distances along the propeller blade from the hub. Each section is studied individually, using experimental wind-tunnel data for the lift and drag coefficients of each airfoil section. The pitch (twist) of each section relative to the plane of rotation is designed so that each airfoil section sees a local angle of attack to the local relative air velocity (where the relative air velocity, magnitude, and direction are the combination of the forward motion of the airplane and the rotational motion of the propeller) that corresponds to the maximum lift-to-drag ratio for each airfoil section. The force generated by the whole propeller is then treated as a summation of the forces on each airfoil section. The resulting layout of the propeller is shown in Figure 5.25, taken from *The Theory and Practice of Aeroplane Design*, 1920, by Andrews and Benson. This blade element design approach is essentially the same used by Wilbur and Orville Wright for their propeller in 1903; the propeller shown in Figure 5.25 simply reflects improved data for the airfoil sections. Compared with the Wrights' propeller, did propeller efficiency improve markedly by 1920? Absolutely not! A. W. Judge in his respected book *The Design of Airplanes* first published in 1916 wrote, "The efficiency of an air propeller varies from 60 percent to 80 percent. The average value for a well-designed propeller may be taken at from 70 percent to 75 percent." By comparison, the efficiency of the Wrights' 1903 propeller was about 76 percent, on par with the best of 1916—not much improvement there. Once again, the large improvement in power available in aircraft during this era was due completely to the brute force of the engines and not to any remarkable improvement in propeller efficiency.

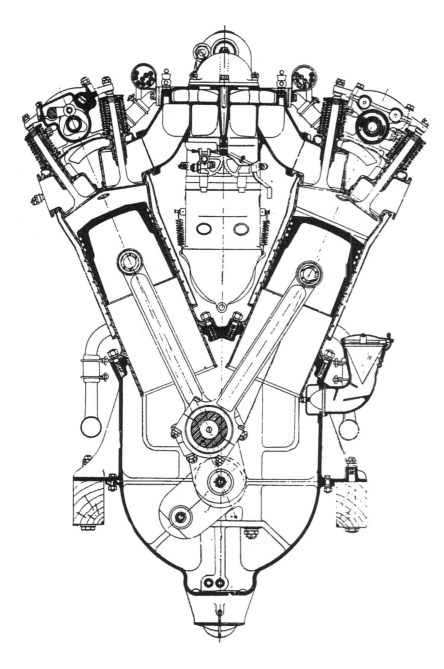

FIGURE 5.24
Cross-section of the
Liberty V-12 liquid-cooled
engine, 1918. Rated at 420
horsepower.

ADVANCES IN STRUCTURES

Take another look at the 1903 Wright Flyer shown in Figure 4.21. What you see, structurally, is a flying machine with wings braced by struts and wires and made up of thin airfoil-shaped ribs. Although not apparent from Figure 4.21, the ribs are fitted into cloth pockets attached to the fabric that covers the lower surface. Unlike the Wrights' earlier gliders, which had fabric covering only over the upper surface, the wings of the 1903 Flyer are covered over both the top and bottom. There is no fuselage per se; the horizontal canard surfaces at the front and the vertical tail surfaces at the rear are supported on longitudinal wooden bars attached to the

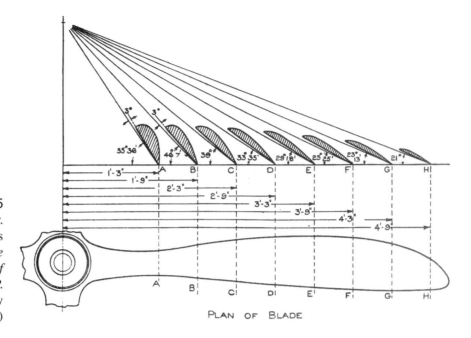

FIGURE 5.25
Layout of a propeller.
(From S. T. G. Andrews
and S. F. Benson, *The
Theory and Practice of
Aeroplane Design*, E. P.
Dutton and Co., New
York, 1920.)

upper and lower wings. The structural design of the Wright Flyer was bare bones, but it worked.

After 1908, when Wilbur Wright carried out his first public demonstration flights in France, interest in the airplane exploded all over Europe. With this began a rapid evolution of aircraft structural design in Europe. The wing structure is the most critical of any component of the airplane because it carried by far most of the aerodynamic load on the airplane. The Wrights appreciated this, but when they designed the structure of their wings, they had no detailed knowledge of how the aerodynamic force was distributed over the wings. What parts of the wing experienced more aerodynamic force than others? Without this knowledge, wing structural design was purely intuitive. This situation began to change in 1910 when Gustave Eiffel started to measure detailed pressure distributions over wings in his large wind tunnel in Paris. An example of Eiffel's measurements is shown in Figure 5.26 for the wing of a Nieuport, obtained from an early book on aeronautical engineering published by the American engineer Alexander Kleimin in 1918. At the right of Figure 5.26, the pressure distributions are shown over the upper and lower surfaces of four airfoil sections located at different stations along the span of the wing. (The pressures are couched in pounds per square foot per mile per hour of airspeed, with negative and positive values denoting pressures below and above the surrounding freestream pressure, respectively). At the left top and bottom of Figure 5.26, contours of constant values of pressure are shown over the top and bottom surfaces of the wing, respectively. This type of detailed pressure distribution data led to the understanding that the lifting force on the wing is distributed along the span, from wingtip to wingtip, in the manner shown in Figure 5.27. Figure 5.27 is from the early and highly respected airplane design book published by the British engineer Arthur W. Judge in 1916. In Figure 5.27, the lift coefficient is plotted versus spanwise location, and it shows that the lift force is greatest at the middle of the wing and tapers off progressively toward the wingtips. Also shown in Figure 5.27 is the variation of the local lift-to-drag ratio

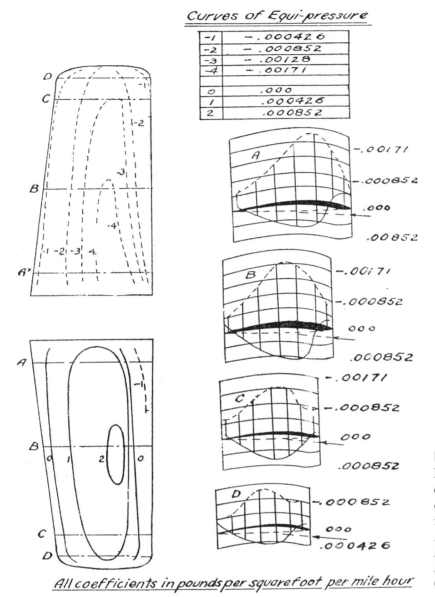

FIGURE 5.26
Measured pressure
distributions over the wing
of a Nieuport. (An exact
facsimile of Figure 8 from
A. Klemin, *Aeronautical
Engineering and Airplane
Design*, Gardner-Moffat
Co., New York, 1918.)

along the span. (Note that Judge is still using the term "drift" for drag of the wing. At that time, drift was a term for the drag of the wing alone, and "total head resistance" denoted the drag of the complete airplane. By 1920, these terms were generally supplanted by the term "drag" in both cases.) The type of aerodynamic information illustrated in Figures 5.26 and 5.27 made wing structural design during World War I a little less intuitive.

A typical wing structure of the 1918 time period is shown in Figure 5.28, taken from the early book by the American Grover Loening, who was to become a leading and respected airplane designer in the early 20th century. The basic construction was a series of ribs attached to front and rear spars, which ran along the span of the wing. Holes were cut in most of the ribs to reduce weight; these ribs were mainly to maintain the airfoil shape of the wing; hence, they were called former ribs. Some of the ribs were solid; these were strut ribs (compression ribs)

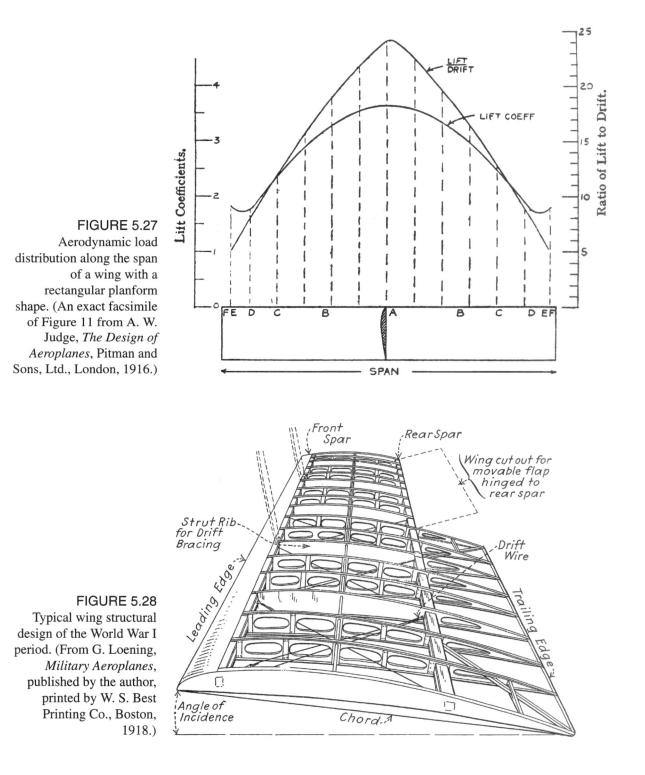

FIGURE 5.27
Aerodynamic load distribution along the span of a wing with a rectangular planform shape. (An exact facsimile of Figure 11 from A. W. Judge, *The Design of Aeroplanes*, Pitman and Sons, Ltd., London, 1916.)

FIGURE 5.28
Typical wing structural design of the World War I period. (From G. Loening, *Military Aeroplanes*, published by the author, printed by W. S. Best Printing Co., Boston, 1918.)

designed to brace the wing against the drag (drift) force. The drag force was also resisted by drift wires connected to the front and rear spars, as shown in Figure 5.28. The drag force, however, is much smaller than the lift force (which is resisted by the spars). Note from Figure 5.27 that the lift-to-drag ratio for such wings ranges from 10 to 25 over the span of the wing. The leading edge was either wood or metal, and the rest of the structure was covered with fabric.

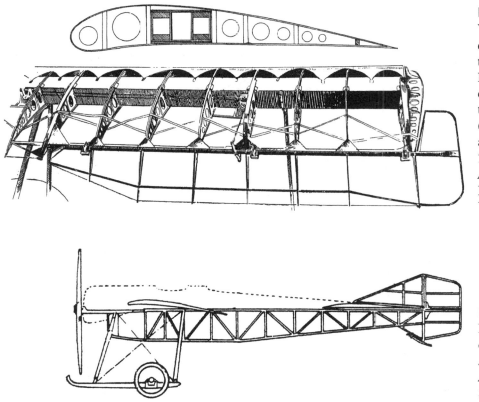

FIGURE 5.29
Wing and rib structural design for the Fokker Dr.1 triplane and the Fokker D-VII. Both had cantilevered wings with thick airfoil sections. (From S. T. G. Andrews and S. F. Benson, *The Theory and Practice of Aeroplane Design*, E. P. Dutton and Co., New York, 1920.)

FIGURE 5.30
Rigid girder fuselage construction. (From A. W. Judge, *The Design of Aeroplanes*, Pitman and Sons, Ltd., London, 1916.)

The advent in Germany toward the end of World War I of the cantilevered wing with thick airfoils not only changed the aerodynamic characteristics of such airplanes, but changed the wing structural design as well. A drawing of the basic wing design used for the Fokker triplane and the D-VII is shown in Figure 5.29. Here, in place of the conventional isolated front and rear spars, we see a massive central support system, which is essentially two thick spars placed very close to each other, united by sheets of plywood. This type of cantilevered, box–spar wing construction was used by Fokker well into the 1930s.

After 1908, airplanes started to have identifiable fuselages. Three types of fuselage structure were used. The girder type was the most common and is illustrated in Figures 5.30–5.33. Here we see a boxlike structure made up of several longitudinal rods, called longerons, running the entire length of the fuselage. These are supported by struts and wires, and the whole system forms a box lattice girder, which can withstand vertical and side loads and torsion (twisting) about the longitudinal axis. The girder structure was usually constructed of wood and wire. The chief designer for Fokker, Reinhold Platz, however, came from a welding background, and the later Fokker aircraft such as the Dr.1 triplane and D-VII had welded steel tube girder fuselages.

The second type of fuselage structure, developed as early as 1912 for the Deperdussin racer (Figure 5.3), was the monocoque, a French word meaning single shell. First developed by the Swiss engineer Ruchonnet, the monocoque structure was adopted by Louis Bechereau for the design of the highly streamlined (for its day) Deperdussin airplane. A Deperdussin racer was the winning airplane in the 1913 Gordon Bennett Cup at Reims, with a phenomenal speed of 124.5 miles per hour. A Duperdussin equipped with pontoons also won the Schneider Cup race in

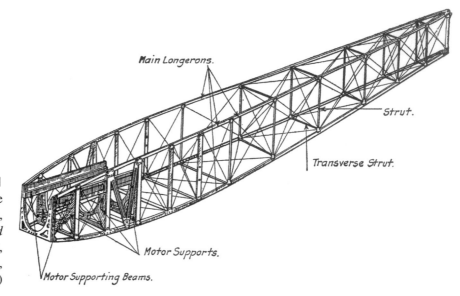

FIGURE 5.31
Generic girder fuselage design. (From O. Pomilio, *Airplane Design and Construction*, McGraw-Hill Book, Inc., New York, 1919.)

FIGURE 5.32
Girder fuselage of the Sopwith Camel. (From S. T. G. Andrews and S. F. Benson, *The Theory and Practice of Aeroplane Design*, E. P. Dutton and Co., New York, 1920.)

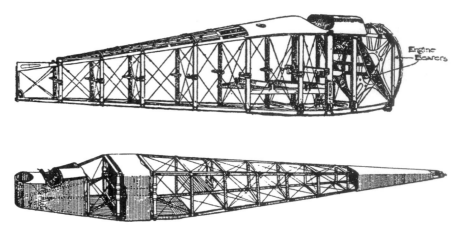

FIGURE 5.33
Girder fuselage with partial plywood covering for the Handley-Page 0/400 bomber. (From S. T. G. Andrews and S. F. Benson, *The Theory and Practice of Aeroplane Design*, E. P. Dutton and Co., New York, 1920.)

the same year. A monocoque fuselage, such as that shown in Figure 5.34, was made by laying thin strips of wood over a mold contoured to the desired fuselage shape. (Tulip wood was used for the Duperdussins.) Usually three layers of wood were used in this fashion, with the strips of wood running at right angles to the layer underneath. Each layer was glued to the other. Then two layers of fabric were glued to the outside of the shell and one layer of fabric on the inside. The fuselage was molded in two half-shells, which were subsequently glued together to form one single shell. The monocoque shells were amazingly thin, from 3 to 4 millimeters, and were both lightweight and strong. A clear advantage of the monocoque design was that fuselages could be made aerodynamically clean (streamlined). Disadvantages were that battle damage was more difficult to repair and the cost of manufacture was considerably more than for the conventional girder type. For these reasons, only a few airplane designs during World War I used monocoque fuselages.

The third type of fuselage construction, which became popular toward the end of World War I, was a combination of the first two. Called the monocoque–girder type, or more commonly the veneer type, it consisted of a

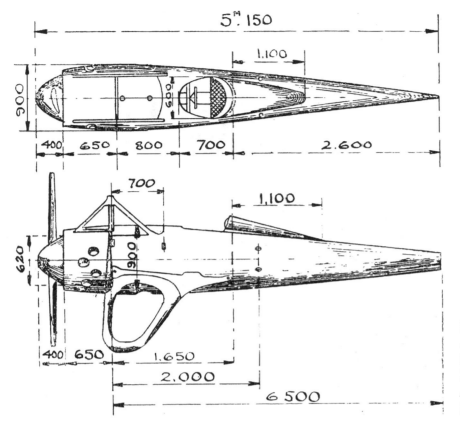

FIGURE 5.34
A generic monocoque
fuselage. (From A. W.
Judge, *The Design of
Aeroplanes*, Pitman and
Sons, Ltd., London, 1916.)

boxlike structure made up of four longitudinal longerons and internal bulkheads to
which wood panels were glued, as shown in Figure 5.35. Compare the
then-conventional girder construction shown in Figure 5.31 with the veneer
construction in Figure 5.35. Missing in Figure 5.35 are all of the internal struts and
bracing seen in Figure 5.31; the wood panels, glued or attached by nails or screws,
provided the required stiffening.

Not all fuselages made with longerons were boxlike, nor did they fall in any
of the described categories. Shown in Figure 5.36 is the structure used by Pfalz in
Germany, where a number of longerons were attached to rounded formers. The
structure was then covered with fabric, forming a rounded, aerodynamically
streamlined fuselage.

Instead of covering the structure shown in Figure 5.36 with fabric, the
German designers of the Albatros family of fighters covered it with wood. This
gave the outward appearance of a monocoque fuselage, but because the fuselage
was also internally strengthened with bulkheads and longerons, this style of
construction was called semimonocoque. The Albatros D-Va, with its
semimonocoque fuselage, is shown in Figure 5.37. Here we see another example of
the aerodynamic streamlining afforded by such a construction technique. (The
semimonocoque structure would become the gold standard of fuselage design by
the 1930s, so much so that the term semimonocoque became redundant. The term
stressed-skin construction has basically replaced it.)

We end this section with Figure 5.38, which is a structural side view of a
conventional airplane of the strut-and-wire biplane era. This side view shows the
typical distribution of the component parts. The airplane is a two-seat biplane, with

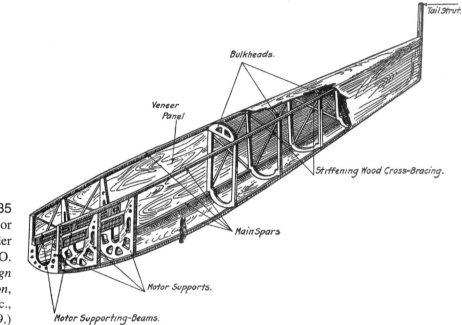

FIGURE 5.35
A generic "veneer," or monocoque-girder fuselage. (From O. Pomilio, *Airplane Design and Construction*, McGraw-Hill Book, Inc., New York, 1919.)

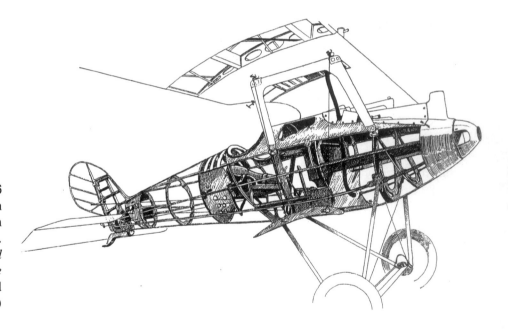

FIGURE 5.36
Fuselage of the German Pfalz D-III fighter. (From S. T. G. Andrews and S. F. Benson, *The Theory and Practice of Aeroplane Design*, E. P. Dutton and Co., New York, 1920.)

the engine, radiator, and tractor propeller in the nose. The gasoline tanks are directly behind the engine, located approximately around the center of gravity of the airplane. This location is important; as fuel is consumed, the location of the center of gravity stays essentially the same. Directly behind the fuel tanks are the pilot's and observer's seats. The wings are attached to the fuselage at a location so that the point through which the wing lift effectively acts is very near the center of gravity. And of course, the horizontal and vertical stabilizers (the tail) are at the back end of the fuselage.

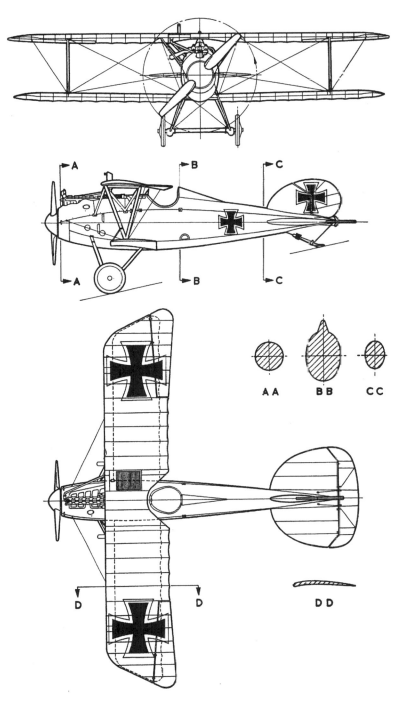

FIGURE 5.37
Three-view of the German
Albatros D-Va, 1917.

Look closely at the airplane shown in Figure 5.38, and then compare it with the Wright Flyer shown in Figure 4.21. Clearly, over the space of 16 years, aircraft structural design had gone through a remarkable evolution.

ADVANCES IN THE PROCESS OF AIRPLANE DESIGN

The Wright brothers obviously had no handbook of airplane design to work with. The intellectual process they intuitively followed for the design of the 1903 Flyer

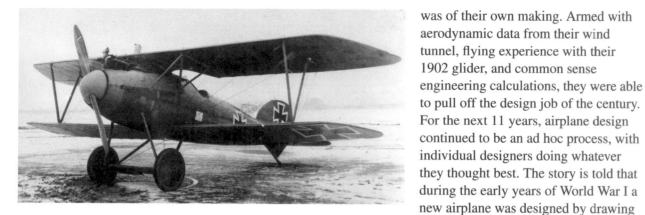

Albatros D-Va, 1917.
(American Aviation
Historical Society,
AAHS, from Peter
M. Bowers.)

was of their own making. Armed with aerodynamic data from their wind tunnel, flying experience with their 1902 glider, and common sense engineering calculations, they were able to pull off the design job of the century. For the next 11 years, airplane design continued to be an ad hoc process, with individual designers doing whatever they thought best. The story is told that during the early years of World War I a new airplane was designed by drawing chalk outlines on the factory floor, and the completed airplane was rolled out two weeks later. This may be anecdotal, but the real status of airplane design was clearly stated by C. G. Grey, editor of the periodical *The Airplane*, who wrote the following in 1915 in a preface to the first book on airplane design:

> It seems well to make clear why these two writers should be taken seriously by trained and experienced engineers, especially in these days when aeronautical science is in its infancy, and when much harm has been done both to the development of aeroplanes and to the good repute of genuine aeroplane designers by people who pose as "aeronautical experts" on the strength of being able to turn out strings of incomprehensible calculations resulting from empirical formulae based on debatable figures acquired from inconclusive experiments carried out by persons of doubtful reliability on instruments of problematic accuracy.

The two writers referred to by Grey were F. S. Barnwell and W. H. Sayers, and their combined book entitled *Aeroplane Design* (written by Barnwell) and *A Simple Explanation of Inherent Stability* (written by Sayers), based on articles by both authors published in *The Aeroplane* in 1915, was the first meaningful book on airplane design. Although it was a short book (100 pages), it was read and referenced by aeronautical engineers for the next decade. Barnwell became a captain in the RAF by the end of World War I and through his book and a number of published articles was responsible for putting airplane design on a more rational engineering basis. The first thoroughly engineering text book on airplane design, earmarked for the university classroom as well as the engineering staffs of the

FIGURE 5.38
Structural side-view of a conventional airplane from the period around 1919. (From O. Pomilio, *Airplane Design and Construction*, McGraw-Hill Book, Inc., New York, 1919.)

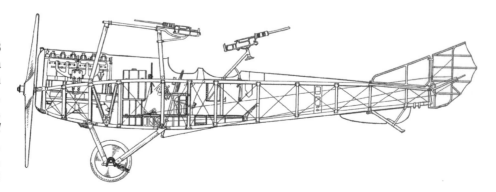

airplane industry, was written by Arthur W. Judge, and published by Putnam and Sons, London, in 1917. Judge was a Whitworth Scholar and obtained his engineering degree at the prestigious Imperial College of Science and Technology in London. At that time a member of the Institute of Automobile Engineers and an Associate Fellow of the Aeronautical Society of Great Britain, Judge put down a rational engineering methodology for airplane design—some aspects of which are still followed today. This methodology included the establishment of the design requirements for a given type of airplane; the estimation of weights early in the design process, including a detailed weight breakdown of all of the elements of the aircraft; a preliminary performance analysis of the design; and the determination of stresses. Wrapped around the methodology was a considerable amount of engineering data and formulas for making design calculations, as well as such details as undercarriage design and propeller slip-stream effects. This is the stuff on which rational airplane design is based. Over the next three years, approximately a half-dozen other airplane design textbooks were published, including two in the United States—one by Grover Loening, who went on to become a noted designer of a series of Loening airplanes in the 1920s, and one by Alexander Klemin, who later was to become one of America's most respected academicians in aeronautical engineering, founding the Department of Aeronautical Engineering at New York University in the early 1930s. By 1920, airplane design had moved from the intuitive, ad hoc process of the Wright brothers to a textbook subject—an important evolution during the era of the strut-and-wire biplane.

THE ALL-METAL AIRPLANE—HUGO JUNKERS

On January 4, 1923, members of the Royal Aeronautical Society in London gathered in anticipation of a lecture by the controversial Professor Hugo Junkers from the University of Aachen in Germany. Junkers, however, had been unable to make the trip due to illness, so he sent Herr Ingenieur Mierginsky, a consulting engineer at Junker's aircraft factory in Dessau, with his manuscript and lantern slides for the lecture. The manuscript was received only the day before the lecture, and W. J. Stern of the Air Ministry Laboratory in South Kensington stayed up late that night translating the paper so that he could read it to the Society that next day. What the members heard from Stern, using Junkers's slides, was the story, replete with technical details on aerodynamics and structures, of the first successful all-metal airplane, the Junkers J.1, shown in Figure 5.14, as well as some of its successors. The first flight of the J.1 was on December 11, 1915, which puts it squarely in the era of the strut-and-wire biplane, although the J.1 had no external struts and wires and, as you see from Figure 5.14, was a monoplane, not a biplane. The J.1 in many respects was ahead of its time because the all-metal airplane did not come into its own until the 1930s. Nevertheless, the J.1 was designed, built, and flown in an era when virtually every other airplane was a vegetable airplane—made from wood, fabric, and glue. Even though it does not fit the category of this chapter, Hugo Junkers development of the all-metal airplane during World War I was *revolutionary*, especially when compared in light of the 1903 Wright Flyer. It is an important part of the history of the technology of the airplane, and its place is right here, right in the middle of the strut-and-wire biplane era.

Hugo Junkers was educated in the engineering sciences and machine construction at the Technische Hochschules (technical colleges) in Berlin,

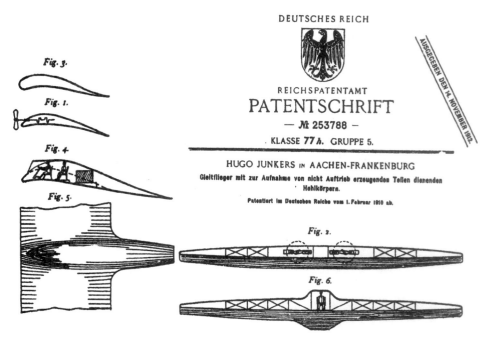

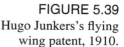

FIGURE 5.39
Hugo Junkers's flying
wing patent, 1910.

Karlsruhe, and Aachen, Germany. In 1879, he was given a professorship at
Aachen, where he held a chair in thermodynamics and engines in the Department
of Mechanical Engineering. Motivated by the work of Nikolaus Otto and Gottlieb
Daimler on internal combustion engines, Junkers made a number of improvements
on such engines and was granted patents for his inventions. At the University of
Aachen, he worked to bring together the engineering science of thermodynamics
and engineering practice. After the Wright brothers' public flights in 1908, Junkers
shifted his attention to the airplane. He quickly came to the conclusion that proper
airplane design should involve thick cantilevered wings that internally could carry
fuel, and even people if made large enough. He considered drag reduction to be the
primary driver of airplane design. Nothing should be hanging out of the main wing
structure—all parasite drag-producing elements of the conventional airplane
should be neatly contained inside the large, smooth wing contour. This led to his
patent for a large flying wing with everything stored inside the wing. Figure 5.39 is
from that patent, granted in 1910. Junkers bought an old chateau in Frankenburg,
part of Aachen, which he converted to a private laboratory called the Workshop for
Innovations. There, in 1912, he built a wind tunnel, which he used to test thick
wing models. As we have already discussed, thick wing sections were considered
to be aerodynamically inferior at that time, and Junkers's wind-tunnel tests broke
new ground, demonstrating that thick airfoils actually gave improved performance
over thin airfoil shapes. Virtually nobody paid attention, except Junkers himself.
To prove his point, Junkers compared the performance of his thick airfoil shape
with that of three thinner airfoils, each airfoil being the best of its class. The results
are shown in Figure 5.40, which is precisely the graph he later used for his 1923
paper to the Royal Aeronautical Society. The thick airfoil (a) yielded higher lift
and lower drag than either of the thinner airfoils (b), (c), or (d).

Junkers had built a factory in Dessau to build experimental internal
combustion engines and portable gas water heaters, the latter eagerly snapped up
by German hotels. At this factory in 1914, he began the first studies for a

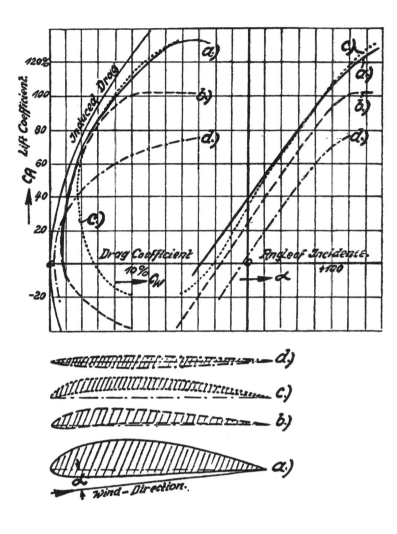

FIGURE 5.40
Junkers's airfoil data,
demonstrating the
effectiveness of a thick
airfoil.

monocoque midwing monoplane made completely of iron. This led to the J.1 in
1915. Many people felt that his "iron bird" was so heavy (more than 2200 pounds)
that it would never get off the ground. A series of successful flight tests beginning
on December 11, 1915, and lasting into early 1916 quickly dispelled such
pessimism. Indeed, the J.1 demonstrated a top speed of 107 miles per hour, a full
31 miles per hour faster than an Albatros LDD biplane flown over the same course
for comparison. The J.1 also faired well in a comparison with the ' best biplane" of
1915, the Rumpler R.C.1, as reported by Junkers in his 1923 paper to the Royal
Aeronautical Society. Figure 5.41, taken directly from this paper, compares the
lift-to-drag ratio and the drag polars (lift coefficient plotted versus drag coefficient)
for both airplanes. Both sets of curves show that the J.1 was aerodynamically
superior. The design parameters of both airplanes were roughly comparable. The
wing loadings for the J.1 and the Rumpler were 8.9 and 6.6 pounds per square foot,
respectively; the power loadings were 18 and 15.6 pounds per horsepower,
respectively. The big differences were that the J.1 had an all-iron skin, had thick
airfoils, and was a cantilevered monoplane.

Why iron? We know iron is heavy, and because minimizing weight is a
cardinal principle of airplane design, why did Junkers build an airplane out of iron?
The answer lies in part with the iron sheets themselves, which were very thin,
varying from 0.1 to 0.5 millimeters. The sheets were smooth on the outside (the J.1

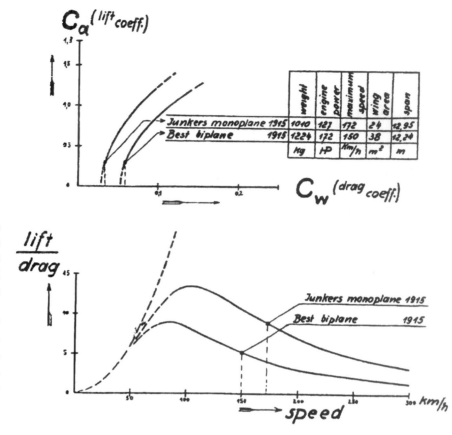

FIGURE 5.41
Comparison of the aerodynamic characteristics of the Junkers J.1. all-metal monoplane of 1915 with the Rumpler R.C.1 biplane, one of the better standard German airplanes in the same year. This comparison was presented in Junkers's paper to the Royal Aeronautical Society in 1923.

had a perfectly smooth external surface) and were reinforced by welded corrugations on the inside. As a result, the weight of the J.1 was perfectly respectable, a total of 2288 pounds, which resulted in a very reasonable wing loading and power loading.

The J.1, however, was Junkers only iron airplane. He shifted to the use of a special form of aluminum called *Duralumin*, an exceptionally strong and hard alloy of aluminum containing copper, manganese, magnesium, iron, and silicon. The development in Germany of Duralumin in the autumn of 1906 would change the course of aircraft structural development in the 20th century and beyond. The discovery of Duralumin was through two related events, one resulting from years of careful research and the other a purely chance discovery of a new and unexpected field of metallurgical endeavor that would remain unexplained for a decade. The story of Duralumin is interesting and revealing, as told to the author by Dr. Howard Wolko, an aeronautical structures expert recently retired from the National Air and Space Museum. Because Duralumin is an essential part of the history of the technology of the airplane, we pause for a moment in our discussion of the all-metal airplane and Hugo Junkers to examine how Duralumin came about. Here is the story, as passed on by Dr. Wolko.

Duralumin was developed by the German metallurgist, Alfred Wilm (1869–1938). Wilm was born on a farm in Silesia, southeastern Germany. While a student in an agricultural school, he became interested in chemistry and attended lectures given by the chemistry department of the Technische Hochschule Berlin–Charlottenburg. He was subsequently employed at the University of

Göttingen as an assistant in chemistry. In 1897, he was named head of the Chemical Laboratories at the Goldschmidt Chemical factories. In the spring of 1901, he became metallurgist for the Zentralstelle fur Wissenschaftlic–Technische Untersuchungen, a well-equipped laboratory for scientific research in Neubabelsberg near Berlin. Wilm, who had become interested in aluminum while with the Goldschmidt Chemical Factories, concentrated on improving the characteristics of aluminum alloys. For two years he studied the process by which the strength of aluminum–copper alloys is increased by heating to elevated temperatures and rapidly cooling to room temperatures (solution heat treatment). On October 10, 1903, Wilm filed for a patent covering his process.

In 1903, as his study was nearing completion, the task was given to the Institute by one of its founders, the German War Munitions Factory of Berlin and Karlsruhe, to find an aluminum alloy with the characteristics of brass. By refinement of an aluminum–copper–manganese alloy, Wilm almost attained the strength, but strength alone was not sufficient. The main thing to change was hardness. To accomplish this Wilm added $\frac{1}{2}$ percent magnesium to the alloy he had been working with and rolled it into a sheet about 3 mm thick. To further improve the alloy, he annealed it in a salt bath maintained at 520 °C and gave his assistant, engineer Jablonski, a small piece of the metal directly after annealing for determination of its mechanical properties.

As Wilm would later recall, "It was on a Saturday in September 1906, about an hour before noon and Jablonski had to leave about that time to keep an appointment." Wilm, of course, was anxious to determine whether the addition of magnesium had produced the improvement he wanted and persuaded Jablonski to run a quick hardness test before leaving. The full set of tests was delayed until Monday. An increase in hardness was recognizable but disappointingly small.

The following Monday, as Jablonski carried out the complete sequence of tests in Wilm's presence, both men were astounded to find the hardness was much higher than previously recorded. Wilm immediately called the laboratory assistant responsible for calibration of the material testing machines only to find that the equipment was just as they left it.

When Wilm could not account for the difference in hardness he proceeded to make another sample of the alloy following the same procedures as before. He then made hourly tests of hardness beginning immediately after annealing to determine how the change took place. At first, there was no obvious change but after 2 hours he observed a gradual increase in hardness. He continued to monitor the change from morning until evening. Resuming his watch the next morning, he again continued to record the increase in hardness until the material became stable after about four days. He would later write the following:

> The hardening process in aluminum alloys takes place in quite a different way than in steel containing carbon. If the latter, in order to harden them, are brought to a suitable temperature and then quenched, they have their characteristic hardness immediately after quenching. Aluminum alloys containing magnesium, in contrast, are soft immediately after quenching, however, after a few hours an increase in hardness begins, which is very considerable in the first few hours and gradually becomes slower in subsequent hours.

When investigation of the remaining properties such as stability, strength, and elongation showed all were improved, Wilm began the laborious task of determining by experiment how variations from laboratory conditions would affect

FIGURE 5.42
Junkers J-13, 1919. The first all-metal transport. (From D. Rolfe and A. Dawydoff, *Airplanes of the World*, Simon and Schuster, New York, 1954.)

production practice. By the autumn of 1908, his experimental work had advanced to the point where he considered his alloy ready to be released for commercial production. The earliest publication describing the still-unexplained aging effect of aluminum–copper–magnesium alloys appeared in 1911.

In 1909, with the retirement of the director of the institute, a major shift in research emphasis occurred with the institute. The new director was less appreciative of metallurgical research, and so Wilm filed for a patent before resigning. There followed a period of negotiation during which Wilm succeeded in acquiring patent rights to the alloys he had developed. Rasmus Beck, Technical Director of Durener Metalwerke, had previously expressed an interest in the Wilm alloys. As successor to the German War Munitions Factory, Durener Metalwerke negotiated for production rights. In the final arrangement, Wilm was allowed to acquire all patent rights on agreeing to license Durener Metalwerke for the exclusive right to manufacture in Germany. "Duralumin," a contraction of "Durener" and "aluminum," was copyrighted on October 8, 1909.

As soon as word of Wilm's alloy reached the United States, work began to develop an alloy of this type at Alcoa. Laboratory samples were made and tested in 1911, and Alcoa commercialized its version, an alloy known as 17S, in 1916. But an explanation for the peculiar room-temperature aging of Duralumin would remain a mystery until it was proven, in 1919, that the hardening mechanism was due to precipitation of a copper–aluminum compound in which magnesium played a secondary, but vital, part.

When Junkers was looking for an improved material for his all-metal airplanes, Duralumin was there, waiting for him. Using corrugated Duralumin, the Dessau works of Professor Junkers continued to produce a long line of all-metal airplanes well beyond the end of World War I. Among them was the J.13 (Figure 5.42), which found widespread use as a small single-engine commercial airplane. First flown in 1919, this six-passenger airplane was economical to fly, and in Junkers own words "has been used from tropical Columbia in South America up to the snow fields of Northern Canada and Finland."

The advantages of all-metal construction for airplanes were clearly set forth by Junkers in his 1923 paper. He wrote,

> Among the advantages the first is the greater durability. Wood is subject to the dangers of fire and decay, and splinters when breaking; it bursts and warps from the effect of humidity and change of temperature and the glued joints split; finally it is attacked by insects. No wooden aeroplane, serviceable for any length of time in the Tropics, has been produced as yet. Metal is free from all such drawbacks.

(Junkers did not know it at the time, but this statement was prescient. Eight years later one of the most highly publicized airplane crashes in the United States took the life of the famous Notre Dame football coach Knute Rockne. He was a passenger in a Fokker trimotor transport, a popular airplane at the time. The airplane was of wood construction. The cause of the crash was wing failure. Subsequent investigation showed that the main wooden spar had rotted. This hastened the end of the wooden airplane.)

Junkers went on to state,

> Structural parts made in wood also change shape and size; they swell or warp under the influence of heat and humidity, making necessary a continuous re-setting and truing-up of the aeroplane. All this does not apply to metal, and a constancy of form is necessarily important in aeroplane wings, slight changes frequently producing a distinct deterioration of the aerodynamic qualities.

With this last statement, Junkers shows that he is well aware that the airflow over a wing, hence, the lift and drag, is very sensitive to small changes in the shape of the airfoil. Aeronautical engineers have constantly rediscovered this fact throughout the century.

With all of this in mind, Junkers concluded that "metal aeroplanes have the advantage of greater durability, smaller expenditure for repairs and maintenance and preservation of form." Then he went on to list several other, less obvious advantages of metal construction:

> Besides these we have the superiority of metal from the standpoint of the designer and constructor. The designer is less handicapped in the choice of dimensions and structural contours. Wood is obtainable only in fixed sizes and shapes of trunk and branch, furnished by nature, whereas metal may be obtained in a nearly unlimited variety of qualities and dimensions. We have sheet metal down to a thickness of 0.004 inch, plates of more than 100 yards length, tubes, rolled section girders, etc.
>
> Shaping of wood is limited, while metal might be given nearly any form by pressing, forging, casting, rolling, drawing, overlapping, etc.
>
> And it is just as workable as wood for turning, planing, milling, boring, filing, and punching.
>
> Connections and joints, confined in the case of wood to gluing, bolting, mortising and wrapping with fabric, all of limited reliability, are much more varied and dependable with metal; as, for example, welding—autogeneous or electric—riveting, screwing, folding and soldering.
>
> Furthermore, the strength of metal is constant and can be stated any time in a reliable manner by tests, whereas the properties of wood are liable to change, wood being altogether highly inhomogeneous. Thus, the safety margin to be kept with wooden constructions must be much higher without giving a sufficient guarantee against undesirable surprises.

Finally, Junkers does allow two advantages of wood construction—it requires less expensive tools, and the wood is of smaller density. These appear insignificant compared with the advantages of metal construction so clearly laid out by Junkers.

Before the all-metal airplane became a design standard, 15 years would go by. Until the beginning of the 1930s, the wood and fabric airplane reigned supreme. Why? Junkers had clearly shown the advantages of all-metal construction, and his airplanes were flying successfully. Airplane designers, however, tended to be conservative in their thinking. Typically, a new airplane design was usually a small evolutionary step beyond existing designs. Airplane designers, for the most part, stuck with what worked in the past, and for many of them, wood and fabric construction was just fine. Indeed, there was explicit resistance to the all-metal airplane by government agencies in the United Kingdom and the United States. At

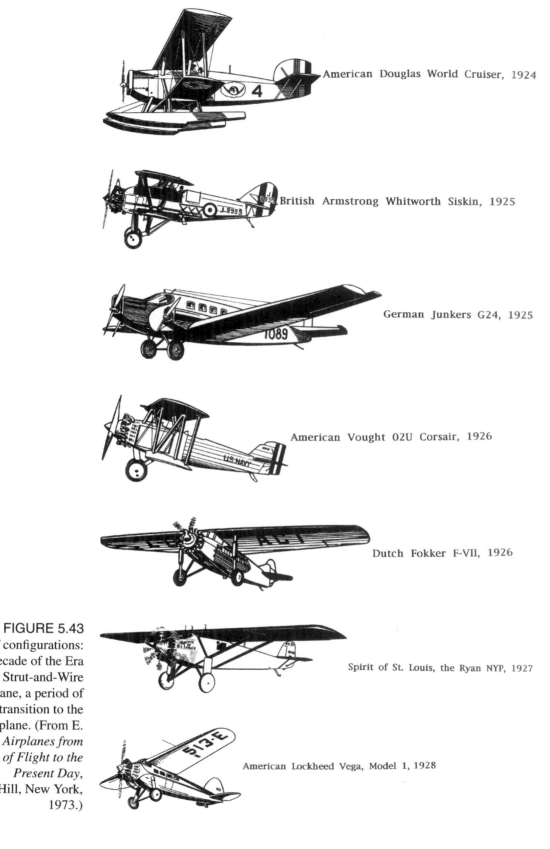

American Douglas World Cruiser, 1924

British Armstrong Whitworth Siskin, 1925

German Junkers G24, 1925

American Vought 02U Corsair, 1926

Dutch Fokker F-VII, 1926

Spirit of St. Louis, the Ryan NYP, 1927

American Lockheed Vega, Model 1, 1928

FIGURE 5.43
Parade of configurations:
The last decade of the Era
of the Strut-and-Wire
Biplane, a period of
transition to the
monoplane. (From E.
Angelucci, *Airplanes from
the Dawn of Flight to the
Present Day*,
McGraw-Hill, New York,
1973.)

the time Junkers's paper was presented to the Royal Aeronautical Society, the Air Ministry in Britain forbade the British aircraft industry to use Duralumin, especially for parts of the airplane likely to be highly stressed. Because that included almost all of the airplane, the industry in the United Kingdom did not use Duralumin. About the same time, NACA in the United States recommended against the use of Duralumin. In both countries, the case was made that Duralumin was subject to corrosion and, therefore, was unsafe for airplane use.

A line-up of Sopwith Camel F.1s, 1917. The Camel was one of the most famous Allied fighter planes of World War I, and in recent times it has been immortalized in the comic strip "Peanuts." (Harold Andrews Collection.)

The disdain of the all-metal airplane can clearly be seen in the sarcastic comment made by Handley Page after he had heard Junkers's paper read to the Royal Aeronautical Society. He shared with the audience that the first Junkers machine that he saw was one that had crashed in landing, the fuselage having broken in a rather unfortunate place. The name Junkers had been painted on its sides, and the break had occurred just behind the k, so that when he walked around the machine to attempt to find out what it was he read the letters "Junk." The *Aeronautical Journal* reported that this story caused "considerable amusement" among the audience.

The era of the strut-and-wire biplane continued with vegetable airplanes. The development of the first all-metal airplanes was a relatively isolated phenomenon in this era, a revolution ahead of its time. The evolution of the configuration of the airplane in the 1920s is reflected in Figure 5.43. For the most part, these airplanes represented only small evolutionary steps beyond their predecessors. This even applies to the famous Ryan NYP, the "Spirit of St. Louis" flown nonstop by Charles Lindbergh from New York to Paris in May 1927. The Spirit of St. Louis represented conventional airplane technology; it was simply optimized and point designed for one performance characteristic—maximum range. The Ryan NYP was also optimized for something else—reliability. Near the end of the 1920s, the end of the strut-and-wire biplane era, the airplane was evolving into a reliable flying machine—a precursor to the design revolution that dominated the next decade. This is our next subject—the era of the mature propeller-driven airplane.

Zeppelin R.XV, 1917. The "R" stands for Riesenflugzeug or "gigantic airplane," one of a series built in Germany for bombing London. It is an example of some of the exceptionally large strut-and-wire biplanes built during World War I. (Harold Andrews Collection.)

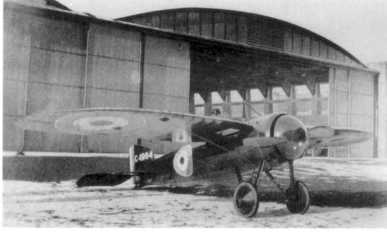

Bristol M.1C monoplane fighter, 1917. Designed by the noted designer Frank Barnwell. In spite of the prevailing bias against monoplanes at the time, the M.1C reflected some aspects of streamlining. (Harold Andrews Collection.)

Breguet Br-14B2, 1917. This French biplane bomber has a predominantly aluminum structure, and enjoyed success at the end of World War I as well as into the post-war period. The Br-14B2 shown here has the markings of the 96th Squadron of the American Expeditionary Force. (Harold Andrews Collection.)

Bristol F.2b two-seat fighter, 1917. Another airplane designed by Frank Barnwell, the F.2b went into combat in March 1917, and was so well liked and successful that it remained in service with the Royal Air Force until 1932. (Harold Andrews Collection.)

Curtiss JN-4D Jenny, 1915. The famous Jenny was America's main airplane contribution to World War I. Even at that, Glenn Curtiss commissioned the Englishman B. Douglas Thomas, previously of Sopwith, to design the Jenny. (Harold Andrews Collection.)

Boeing 80A transport biplane, 1928. With its fixed landing gear and biplane configuration, the 80A continued the tradition of the strut-and-wire biplane era, bumping up against the design revolution of the 1930s. (Harold Andrews Collection.)

Curtiss F9C-2 Sparrow Hawks flying in formation. Designed in 1931, the Sparrow Hawk was carried by Navy dirigibles; the airplanes shown here are from the dirigible Macon. Part of the "skyhook" mechanism that engaged the retractable trapeze carried by the Macon can be seen mounted above the top wing of the Sparrow Hawks. The F9C-2 was Curtiss's first semi-monocoque, all-metal fighter. (Harold Andrews Collection.)

Boeing P-12E fighter, 1931. The P-12E had a Townend ring wrapped around the cylinders of the radial engine, a design feature favored by Boeing in the early 1930s. With its biplane configuration, open cockpit, and fixed landing gear, the P-12E was a bit anachronistic at the beginning of the design revolution of the 1930s. (Harold Andrews Collection.)

Curtiss P-6E fighter, 1931. An aesthetically beautiful design, the P-6E was another example of a biplane that overlapped the beginning of the era of the mature propeller-driven airplane. (Harold Andrews Collection.)

6
CHAPTER

The First Design Revolution: The Era of the Mature Propeller-Driven Airplane

A beautiful aircraft is the expression of the genius of a great engineer who is also a great artist.

Nevil Shute
No Highway, **1947**

Instead of a palette of colors, the aeronautical engineer has his own artist's palette of options. How he mixes these engineering options on his technological palette and applies them to his canvas [design] determines the performance of the airplane. When the synthesis is best it yields synergism, a result that is dramatically greater than the sum of its parts. This is hailed as "innovation." Failing this, there will result a mediocre airplane that may be good enough, or perhaps an airplane of lovely appearance, but otherwise an iron peacock that everyone wants to forget.

Richard K. Smith
Milestones of Aviation, **1989**

The scene: Clover Field, Santa Monica, California, bathed in a gentle breeze blowing in from the ocean, with a comfortable air temperature of 76 °F. The time: Exactly 12:36 p.m. on July 1, 1933. The characters: Carl Cover, vice president of sales and chief test pilot for the Douglas Aircraft Corporation; Fred Herman, a senior designer for Douglas; a crowd of the Douglas employees, including Donald Douglas and his assistant chief designer, Arthur Raymond; and a sleek, aesthetically beautiful new airplane, the first commercial airplane ever designed at Douglas, aptly labeled the DC-1. The action: With Cover at the controls and Herman as copilot, the twin-engine DC-1, powered by two Wright Cyclone engines of 710 horsepower each, throttles wide open, roars down the runway, and lifts off for its maiden flight. Douglas and his small company have a great deal riding on the success of this airplane. Designed to meet stringent specifications set down by the Transcontinental and Western Air, Inc. (TWA), the DC-1 embodies the absolute synergistic best of modern aeronautical engineering technology in 1933. If successful, the DC-1 would be, by far, the most economic, most comfortable, highest speed, highest flying, and safest airplane to exist at that time. Jack Frye, vice president of TWA, who had drafted the specifications, is looking forward to this airplane revolutionizing commercial air travel. Little does anybody know that potential disaster looms on the horizon. As Cover puts the DC-1 in a climb about 30 seconds after takeoff, the left engine quits; a moment later the right engine sputters to a stop. As the airplane noses over, however, the engines start again. Cover starts to climb again, but once again the engines stop. They start again when the nose dips down. For the next 10 minutes, Cover puts on a display of expert piloting, coaxing the DC-1 up to 1500 feet, following a sawtooth flight path alternating between a climb, the engines cutting off, a noseover, the engines starting again, and another climb until the engines quit again. At 1500 feet, Cover judges that the DC-1 is at a safe enough altitude to allow him to bank and return safely to the runway. A few minutes later, the airplane and its occupants are on the ground, unscathed.

But what is wrong? The airplane and its engines appear to be mechanically sound. Five days go by as the engines are taken apart and reassembled more than a dozen times. On the test block, the engines run perfectly. During the process, Carl Cover suggests to the technicians from the Wright Aeronautical Corporation that they look at the carburetors, but they object, thinking the problem is elsewhere. On the fifth day, Cover's suggestion is finally carried out. To the amazement of the technicians, the carburetors, which meter fuel to the engine, are found to be installed backward. In this position, the carburetor floats would cut off the fuel flow when the airplane is in a nose-up altitude. The carburetors are quickly rotated 180 degrees. The problem is fixed. On July 7, the DC-1 takes off again, and the engines perform perfectly.

Such is the saga of the beginning of the most successful series of commercial airliners for the next 30 years. Only one DC-1 was built; a photograph of it is shown in Figure 6.1. The DC-1 was essentially an experimental airplane. It was

FIGURE 6.1
The Douglas DC-1, 1933.
(Photo courtesy of David
W. Ostrowski and Hal
Andrews.)

quickly followed by the look-alike but slightly larger DC-2, of which Douglas was to manufacture 156 in 20 different models that were used by airlines around the world. The DC-2, in turn, quickly evolved into the look-alike but still larger DC-3, which was to become one of the most successful airplanes in the history of flight and aeronautical engineering. When the DC-3 production line was finally shut down at the end of World War II, 10,926 had been built. The Douglas DC-3 is the epitome of the mature, propeller-driven airplane. Let us take a closer look.

SETTING THE STANDARD FOR THE MATURE PROPELLER-DRIVEN AIRPLANE—FROM THE DC-1 TO THE DC-3

We introduce our discussion of the history of the technology of the airplane during the era of the mature propeller-driven airplane by examining one of the most important case histories from that period. We will draw extensively from the case history given in the author's book *Airplane Performance and Design* (McGraw Hill, 1999).

The genesis of any airplane designs is competition. So it was in 1932, when Boeing was putting the final touches to the prototype of its 247 airplane—a pioneering, low-wing monoplane, all metal, with twin engines wrapped in the new NACA low-drag cowling and with retractable landing gear. A three-view of the 247 is shown in Figure 6.2. The Boeing 247 carried 10 passengers in a soundproof cabin at speeds near 200 miles per hour. This airplane was expected to revolutionize commercial air travel. Because of this, the airlines were standing in line for orders. However, Boeing at that time was a member of the United Aircraft Group, which included Pratt and Whitney Engines and United Airlines. Hence, United Airlines was first in line and was programmed to receive the first 70 new 247s to come off the production line. This put the other airlines in an untenable competitive position.

Because of this, on August 5, 1932, Donald W. Douglas, president of Douglas Aircraft Corporation, received a letter from TWA. Dated August 2, the same letter had been sent to the Glenn Martin Company in Baltimore, Maryland, and the Curtiss–Wright Corporation in St. Louis, Missouri, as well as to Douglas in Santa Monica. Jack Frye, a vice president of TWA, signed the letter. Frye was inquiring about Douglas's interest in designing a new commercial transport airplane; because TWA could not readily obtain the new Boeing 247, in an aggressive fashion they went after their own state-of-the-art airplane. Attached to Frye's letter was a one-page list of general performance specifications for the new airplane. (We note that the U.S. Army's list of specifications that led to the purchase of the Wright Military Flyer in 1908 was also one-page long; clearly, 25 years later airplane specifications could still be given in a short, concise, clear-cut manner.) A facsimile of Frye's letter and his one page of specifications is given in Figure 6.3.

The specifications called for an all-metal trimotor airplane that would have a cruising range of 1080 miles at a cruise velocity of 150 miles per hour. Of greatest importance, however, was the requirement listed at the bottom of the page, that is,

The Douglas DC-1, 1933. With its beautiful streamlining, NACA engine cowlings, retractable landing gear, variable-pitch propeller, and split flaps, this airplane is perhaps the best example of the beginning of the era of the mature propeller-driven airplane. (American Aviation Historical Society, AAHS, from Peter M. Bowers.)

The Boeing 247, 1932. This transport airplane helped to lead the way to the mature propeller-driven airplane. (Harold Andrews Collection.)

that the new airplane at a full takeoff gross weight of 14,200 pounds be able to takeoff safely from any TWA airport with one engine out. At that time, the highest airport in the TWA system was in Winslow, Arizona, at an elevation of 4500 feet. Other aspects of the specifications called for a maximum velocity of at least 185 miles per hour, landing speed of not more than 65 miles per hour, a minimum rate of climb at sea level of 1200 feet per minute, and a minimum service ceiling of 21,000 feet, compromised downward to 10,000 feet with one engine out.

Donald Douglas and Jack Frye had met several times before, at various aviation functions in the Los Angeles, California, area. They held a strong mutual respect for each other. Since the formation of his company in 1921, most of Douglas's business dealt with designing and constructing military airplanes, especially a successful line of torpedo airplanes for the Navy. However, he had been recently thinking about venturing into the commercial airplane market as well. (Airline passenger service had skyrocketed since Charles Lindbergh's historic solo flight across the Atlantic Ocean in 1927.) So Douglas paid serious attention to Frye's letter. He took it home with him that night, staying awake until 2 a.m. pondering the ramifications. The next day he met with his core engineering design group and went over the TWA specifications one by one. The discussion lasted well into the evening. The group had already made the decision to submit a proposal to TWA; Friday's discussion was to be about the basic nature of the airplane design itself.

A view of the Boeing 247 in flight. (American Aviation Historical Society, AAHS, from Peter M. Bowers.)

The TWA specifications (Figure 6.3) called for a "trimotored monoplane" as being preferred, but held out the possibility of the design's being a biplane. Trimotor monoplanes were not new; the Fokker F-10 and the Ford trimotor had been flying in airplane service for almost five years. However, this airplane configuration suffered a public setback on March 31, 1931, when a TWA Fokker trimotor crashed in a Kansas wheat field, killing among the passengers the famous Notre Dame University football coach Knute Rockne. As for the biplane configuration, the early 1930s was a period of drag reduction via streamlining, and biplanes with their higher drag were on the way out.

So when the Friday meeting started out, it was no surprise that the chief engineer, James H. "Dutch" Kindelberger, stated emphatically,

I think that we're damn fools if we don't shoot for a twin-engined job instead of a trimotor. People are skeptical about the trimotors after the Rockne thing. Why build

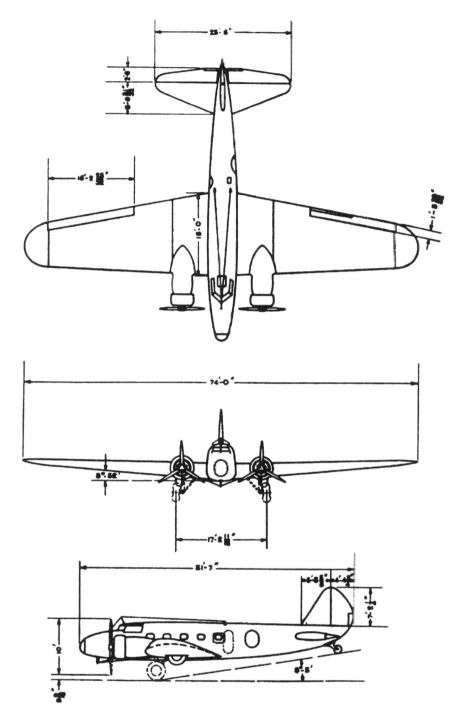

FIGURE 6.2
Three-view of the Boeing
247D airliner, 1933.

anything that even looks like a Fokker or Ford? Both Pratt & Whitney and
Wright-Aeronautical have some new engines on the test blocks that will be available
by the time we're ready for them. Lots of horses . . . any two of them will pull more
power than any trimotor flying right now.

Douglas agreed. An essential design decision was made without making a single
calculation.

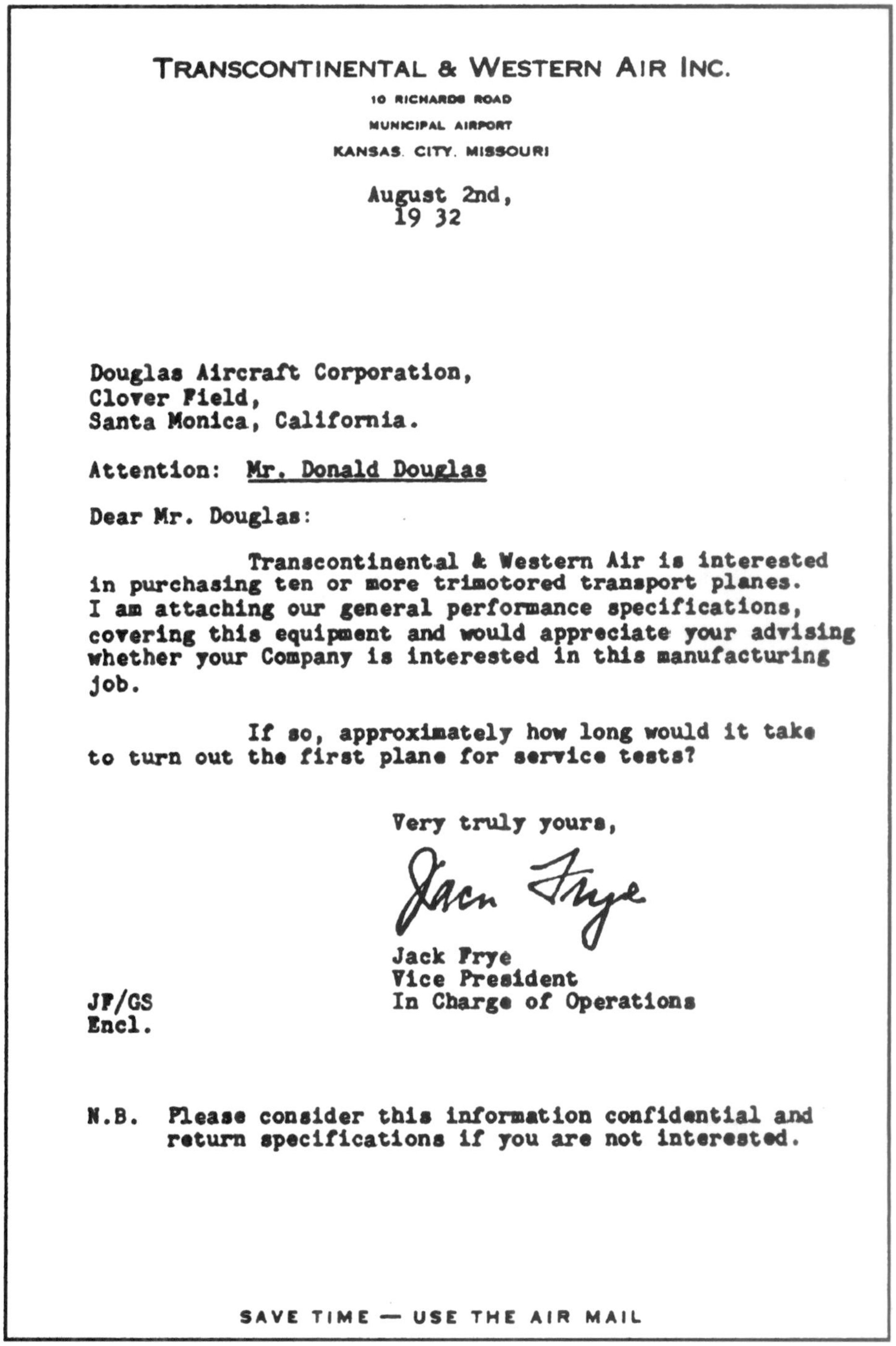

TRANSCONTINENTAL & WESTERN AIR INC.

10 RICHARDS ROAD
MUNICIPAL AIRPORT
KANSAS. CITY. MISSOURI

August 2nd,
19 32

Douglas Aircraft Corporation,
Clover Field,
Santa Monica, California.

Attention: Mr. Donald Douglas

Dear Mr. Douglas:

Transcontinental & Western Air is interested
in purchasing ten or more trimotored transport planes.
I am attaching our general performance specifications,
covering this equipment and would appreciate your advising
whether your Company is interested in this manufacturing
job.

If so, approximately how long would it take
to turn out the first plane for service tests?

Very truly yours,

Jack Frye

Jack Frye
Vice President
In Charge of Operations

JF/GS
Encl.

N.B. Please consider this information confidential and
return specifications if you are not interested.

SAVE TIME — USE THE AIR MAIL

FIGURE 6.3a
Facsimile of the letter
from TWA to Donald
Douglas. Douglas is later
quoted as saying this letter
was "the birth certificate of
the modern airliner."

Arthur Raymond, Kindelberger's assistant, who had earned a master's degree
in aeronautical engineering at Massachusetts Institute of Technology in 1921 (one
of the few people with graduate degrees in aeronautical engineering at that time),
was immediately thinking about the wing design. He suggested, "Why not use a
modified version of Jack Northrop's taper wing? Its airfoil characteristics are good.
The taper and slight sweepback will give us some latitude with the center of

```
            TRANSCONTINENTAL & WESTERN AIR., INC.

            General Performance Specifications
                     Transport Plane

                  C

1.     Type:  All metal trimotored monoplane preferred but
       combination structure or biplane would be considered.
       Main internal structure must be metal.

2.     Power:  Three engines of 500 to 550 h.p. (Wasps with 10-1
       supercharger; 6-1 compression O.K.).

3.     Weight:  Gross (maximum)                    14,200 lbs.

4.     Weight allowance for radio and wing mail bins    350 lbs.

5.     Weight allowance must also be made for complete instruments,
       night flying equipment, fuel capacity for cruising range
       of 1080 miles at 150 m.p.h., crew of two, at least 12 pas-
       sengers with comfortable seats and ample room, and the usual
       miscellaneous equipment carried on a passenger plane of this
       type.  Payload should be at least 2,300 lbs. with full equip-
       ment and fuel for maximum range.

6.     Performance

       Top speed sea level (minimum)            185 m.p.h.
       Cruising speed sea level - 79 % top speed    146 m.p.h. plus
       Landing speed not more than               65 m.p.h.
       Rate of climb sea level (minimum)        1200 ft. p.m.
       Service ceiling (minimum)                21000 ft.
       Service ceiling any two engines          10000 ft.



       This plane, fully loaded, must make satisfactory take-offs
       under good control at any TWA airport on any combination of
       two engines.



Kansas City, Missouri.
August 2nd, 1932
```

FIGURE 6.3b
Facsimile of the specifications from TWA, attached to the letter.

gravity." Raymond was referring to the innovative wing design by Jack Northrop, who had worked for Douglas between 1923 and 1927 and then left for Lockheed, finally forming his own company in 1931. (This is the same company that today builds the B-2 stealth bomber.) Northrop had developed a special cantilever wing that derived exceptional strength from a series of individual aluminum sections fastened together to form a multicellular structure. The wing is the heart of an airplane, and Raymond's thinking was immediately focused on it. He also wanted to place the wing low enough on the fuselage that the wing spars would not cut through the passenger cabin (as was the case with the Boeing 247). Such a structurally strong wing offered some other advantages. The engine mounts could be projected ahead of the wing leading edge, placing the engines and propellers far enough forward to obtain some aerodynamic advantage from the propeller slip stream blowing over the wing, without causing the wing to twist. Also, the decision was to design the airplane with a retractable landing gear. In that regard Douglas said, "The Boeing's got one. We'd better plan on it too. It should cut down on the drag by 20 percent." Kindelberger then suggested, "Just make the nacelles bigger. Then we can hide the wheels in the nacelles." The strong wing design could handle the weight of both the engines and the landing gear.

The early 1930s was a period when airplane designers were becoming appreciative of the advantages of streamlining to reduce aerodynamic drag. Retracting the landing gear was part of streamlining. Another aspect was the radial engines. Fred Stineman, another of Douglas's talented designers, added to the discussion: "If we wrap the engines themselves in the new NACA cowlings, taking advantage of the streamlining, it should give us a big gain in top speed." This referred to the research at the NACA Langley Memorial Aeronautical Laboratory, beginning in 1928, that rapidly led to the NACA cowling, a shroud wrapped around the cylinders of air-cooled radial engines engineered to reduce drag greatly and to increase the cooling of the engine. At this stage of the conversation, Ed Burton, another senior design engineer, voiced a concern: "The way we're talking, it sounds like we are designing a racing plane. What about this 65 miles per hour landing speed Frye wants?" This problem was immediately addressed by yet another senior design engineer, Fred Herman, who expressed this opinion: "The way I see it, we're going to have to come up with some kind of an air brake, maybe a flap deal that will increase the wing area during the critical landing moment and slow the plane down.... Conversely, it will give us more lift on takeoff, help tote that big payload."

The deliberation extended into days. However, after a week of give-and-take discussions, they all agreed that the airplane design would have the following features.

1) Be a low-wing monoplane.
2) Use a modified version of the Northrop wing.
3) Be a twin-engine airplane, not a trimotor.
4) Have retractable landing gear, retracted into the engine nacelles.
5) Have some type of flaps.
6) Use the NACA cowling.
7) Locate the engine nacelles relative to the wing leading edge at the optimum position as established by some recent NACA research.

The design methodology and philosophy exemplified by these early discussions between Douglas and his senior design engineers followed a familiar pattern. *No new, untried technology was being suggested.* All of the design features itemized were not new. However, the *combination* of all seven items in the *same* airplane was new. The Douglas engineers were looking at past airplanes and past developments and were building on these to scope out a new design. To a certain extent, they were building on the Northrop Alpha (Figure 6.4). Although the Alpha was quite a different airplane (single-engine transport carrying six passengers inside the fuselage with an open cockpit for the pilot), it also embodied the

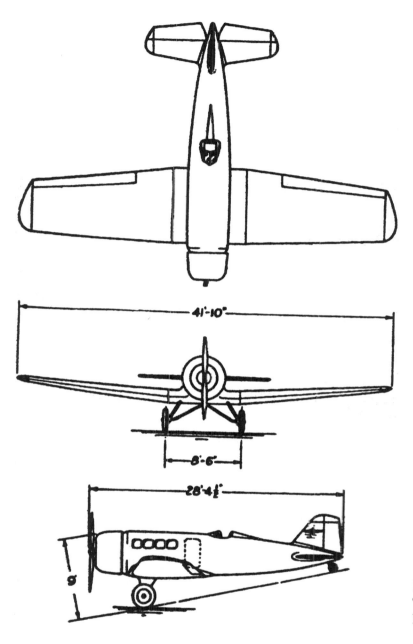

FIGURE 6.4
Three-view of the
Northrop Alpha, 1930.

Northrop multicellular cantilevered wing and an NACA cowling. Also, it was not lost on Douglas that TWA had been operating Northrop airplanes with great success and with low maintenance.

During this first critical work of their deliberations, the small team of Douglas designers had progressed through an intellectual process that reflected the maturing discipline of airplane design. In addition, they used more than a slide rule for calculations; they drew also on the collective intuitive feelings of the group, honed by experience. They practiced the *art* of airplane design to the extreme. At the end of that week, a proposal to TWA was prepared, and Arthur Raymond and Harry Wetzel (Douglas's vice president and general manager) took a long train ride across the country to deliver their proposal to the TWA executive office in New York. There, a three-week series of intense discussions took place; among the

TWA representatives present at many of these meetings were Richard Robbins (president of TWA), Jack Frye, and Charles Lindbergh (the same Charles Lindbergh who had gained fame for his transatlantic solo flight in 1927 and who served as a technical consultant to TWA).

Although there were other competitors for the TWA contract, Raymond and Wetzel were successful in convincing TWA of the merits of a twin-engine ("bimotor") airplane over a trimotor. A major aspect of this consideration was the ability of the airplane to fly successfully on one engine, especially to takeoff at full gross weight from any airport along the TWA route and to be able to climb and maintain level flight over the highest mountains along the route. This was not a trivial consideration, and Raymond's calculations had a certain degree of uncertainty—the uncertainty that naturally is associated with the early aspects of the conceptual design process period. Raymond called from New York to tell Douglas about the critical nature of the one-engine-out performance's being a pivotal aspect of the discussions with TWA. When Douglas asked Raymond about his latest feelings as to whether the airplane design could meet this performance requirement, Raymond's reply was, "I did some slide-rule estimates. It comes out 90 percent yes and 10 percent no. The 10 percent is keeping me awake at nights. One thing is sure, it's never been done before with an aircraft in the weight class we're talking about." Douglas conferred with Kindelberger, who took the stand: "There's only one way to find out. Build the thing and try it." Douglas made the decision—Raymond should tell TWA that the Douglas Company would be able to construct such an airplane.

On September 20, 1932, in Robbin's office, the contract was signed between TWA and Douglas to build the airplane. Douglas christened the project as the DC-1, the Douglas Commercial One. The contract called for the purchase by TWA of one service test airplane at the cost of $125,000, with the option (indeed, clear intent) of purchasing up to 60 additional airplanes, in lots of 10, 15, or 20 at $58,000 each. The contract was 42 typewritten pages long, 29 of which dealt specifically with the technical specifications. There was a detailed breakdown of the empty weight and an expanded five-page list of performance specifications. The contract even went to the detailed extent of specifying such items as this: "Air sickness container holders shall be located adjacent to each seat in such a position as to be easily reached with seat in any adjustment." (Actually, this was not as trivial as it may seem today; the airplane was unpressurized, and hence, it would be flying, as did all aircraft at that time, at low altitudes where there was plenty of air turbulence, especially in bad weather.)

The concern that the Douglas designers put into the aspect of one-engine-out flight is reflected in a detailed technical paper written by Donald Douglas and presented by Douglas at the Twenty-Third Wilbur Wright Memorial Lecture of the Royal Aeronautical Society in London on May 30, 1935. The annual Wilbur Wright Lectures were (and still are) the most prestigious lectures of the society. It was a testimonial to Douglas's high reputation that he had received the society's invitation. The paper was entitled "The Development and Reliability of the Modern Multi-Engine Air Liner with Special Reference to Multi-Engine Airplanes after Engine Failure." Douglas began his paper with a statement that is as apropos today as it was then: "Four essential features are generally required of any form of transportation: speed, safety, comfort, and economy." However, today we would add *environmentally clean* to the list. Douglas went on:

> The airplane must compete with other forms of transportation and with other airplanes. The greater speed of aircraft travel justifies a certain increase in cost. The newer transport planes are comparable with, if not superior to, other means of transportation. Safety is of special importance and improvement in this direction demands the airplane designer's best efforts.

Douglas then concentrated on engine failure as it related to airplane safety. He wrote:

> Statistics show that the foremost case of accident is still the forced landing. The multi-engine, capable of flying with one or more engines not operating, is the direct answer to the dangers of an engine failure. It is quite apparent, however, that for an airplane that is not capable of flying with one engine dead the risk increases with the number of engines installed. Hence, from the standpoint of forced landings, it is not desirable that an airplane be multi-engine unless it can maintain altitude over any portion of the air line with at least one engine dead. Furthermore, the risk increases with the number of remaining engines needed to maintain the required altitude. In general, therefore, the greatest safety is obtained from
>
> 1. The largest number of engines that can be cut out without the ceiling of the airplane falling below a required value;
> 2. The smallest number of engines on which the airplane can maintain this given altitude.
>
> For airplanes equipped with from one to four engines, it follows that the order of safety is according to the list following.

Douglas followed with a list of 10 options, starting with the category "four-engine airplane requiring one engine to maintain given altitude" as the most safe and "four-engine airplane requiring four engines to maintain given altitude" as obviously the least safe. Fourth down on the list was the two-engine airplane requiring one engine to maintain given altitude—this was the category of the DC-1 (and the DC-2 and DC-3 to follow). It is statistically safer than a three-engine airplane requiring two engines to maintain given altitude, which was fifth on Douglas's list.

Another hallmark governed the early design of the DC-1, namely, creature comfort. This was particularly emphasized by Art Raymond who, after the TWA contract negotiations were over in New York, chose to fly back to Santa Monica. Flying from coast to coast at that time was an endurance test, especially in the Ford trimotor that Raymond was on. Raymond suffered from the noise, vibration, cold temperature at altitude, small and primitive lavatory facilities, uncomfortable seats, and even mud splashed on his feet. Indeed, he complained later, "When the airplane landed on the puddle-splotched runway, a spray of mud, sucked in by the cabin air vents, splattered everybody." After returning to the Douglas plant, Raymond stated, "We've got to build comfort, and put wings on it. Our big problem is far more than just building a satisfactory performing transport airplane." The team set about immediately to design an airplane that included soundproofing, cabin temperature control, improved plumbing, and no mud baths

In 1932, the Guggenheim Aeronautical Laboratory at the California Institute of Technology (GALCIT) had a new, large subsonic wind tunnel. It was the right facility in the right place at the right time. Situated at the heart of the southern California aeronautical industry at the time when that industry was set for rapid

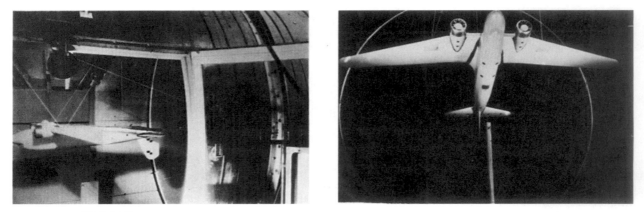

FIGURE 6.5
A model of the Douglas DC-1 mounted upside-down in the Cal Tech wind tunnel, late 1932.

growth in the 1930s, the California Institute of Technology (Cal Tech) wind tunnel performed tests on airplane models for a variety of companies that had no such testing facilities. Douglas was no exception. As conceptual design of the DC-1 progressed into the detailed design stage, wind-tunnel tests on a scale model of the DC-1 were carried out in the Cal Tech wind tunnel. Over the course of 200 wind-tunnel tests, the following important characteristics of the airplane were found:

1) The use of a split flap increased the maximum lift coefficient by 35 percent and increased the drag by 300 percent. Both effects are favorable for landing; the increase in $(C_L)_{max}$ allowed a higher wing loading, and the corresponding decrease in L/D allowed a steeper landing approach.

2) The addition of a fillet between the wing and fuselage increased the maximum velocity by 17 miles per hour.

3) During the design process, the weight of the airplane increased, and the center of gravity shifted rearward. For that case, the wind-tunnel tests showed the airplane to be longitudinally unstable. The design solution was to add sweepback to the outer wing panels, hence, shifting the aerodynamic center sufficiently rearward to achieve stability. The mildly swept-back wings of the DC-1 (also used on the DC-2 and DC-3 airplanes) gave these airplanes enhanced aesthetic beauty as well as a distinguishing configuration.

A photograph of the DC-2 model mounted upside down in the Cal Tech wind tunnel is shown in Figure 6.5. The upside-down orientation was necessary because the model was connected by wires to the wind-tunnel balance above it, and in this position the downward-directed lift kept the wires taunt. Dr. W. Bailey Oswald, at that time a professor at Cal Tech who was hired by Douglas as a consultant on the DC-1 aerodynamics, later said, "If the wind tunnel tests had not been made, it is very possible that the airplane would have been unstable, because all the previous engineering estimates and normal investigations had indicated that the original arrangement was satisfactory." (We note that this is the same Bailey Oswald who introduced the Oswald efficiency e to be discussed in a later section). Beginning in 1928, Arthur Raymond taught a class on the practical aspects of airplane design at Cal Tech, and Oswald attended the class in the first year. The two became trusted colleagues. Finally, reflecting on his first action on returning to Santa Monica after his trip to the TWA offices in New York, Raymond later wrote,

> The first thing I did when I got back was to contact Ozzie (Oswald) and ask him to come to Santa Monica to help us, for that one-engine-out case still bothered me. I told him we only needed him for a little while, but he stayed until retirement in 1959, and ultimately had a large section working for him.

On July 1, 1933, the prototype DC-1 was ready for its first flight. It took less than one year from the day the original TWA letter arrived in Douglas's office to the day that the DC-1 was ready to fly. The story of that first flight is told at the beginning of this chapter. At the end of its test-flight program, the airplane had met all its flight specifications, including the one-engine-out performance at the highest altitudes encountered along the TWA routes. It was a wonderful example of successful, enlightened airplane design.

An interesting contrast can be made in regard to the time from design conception to the first flight. During World War I, some airplanes were designed by laying out chalk markings on the floor and rolling out the finished airplane two weeks later. Fifteen years later, the process was still relatively quick, that for the DC-1 being about 11 months. Compare this to the design time for today's modern civil and military airplanes, which sometimes takes close to a decade between design conception and first flight.

Only one DC-1 was built. The production version, which involved lengthening the fuselage by 2 feet and adding two more seats to make it a 14-passenger airplane, was labeled the DC-2. The first DC-2 was delivered to TWA on May 14, 1934. Altogether, Douglas manufactured 156 DC-2s in 20 different models, and the airplane was used by airlines around the world. It set new standards for comfort and speed in commercial air travel. But the airplane that really made such travel an *economic success* for the airlines was the next outgrowth of the DC-2, namely, the DC-3.

As in the case of the DC-2, the DC-3 was a result of an airline initiative, not a company initiative. Once again, the requirements for a new airplane were being set by the customer. This time the airline was American Airlines, and the principal force behind the idea was a tall, soft-spoken, but determined Texan, Cyrus R. Smith. C. R. Smith had become president of American Airlines on May 13, 1934. American Airlines was operating sleeper service, using older Curtiss Condor biplanes outfitted with Pullman-sized bunks. On one flight of this airplane during the summer of 1934, Smith, accompanied by his chief engineer, Bill Littlewood, almost subconsciously remarked, "Bill, what we need is a DC-2 sleeper plane." Littlewood said that he thought it could be done. Smith lost no time. He called Douglas to ask if the DC-2 could be made into a sleeper airplane. Douglas was not very receptive to the idea. Indeed, the company was barely able to keep up with its orders for the DC-2. Smith, however, would not take no for an answer. The long-distance call went on for two hours, costing Smith more than $300. Finally, after Smith virtually promised that American Airlines would buy 20 of the sleeper airplanes, Douglas reluctantly agreed to embark on a design study. Smith's problem was that he had just committed American Airlines to a multimillion-dollar order for a new airplane that was just in the imagination of a few men at that time, and the airline did not have that kind of money. However, Smith then traveled to

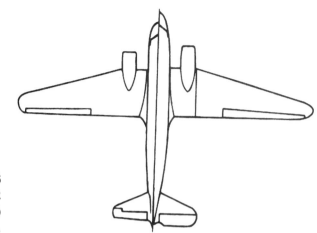

FIGURE 6.6
Comparison of the DC-2
(left) and DC-3 (right)
planforms.

Washington, D.C., to visit his friend and fellow Texan Jesse Jones, who was the head of Reconstruction Finance Corporation, a New Deal agency set up by President Franklin Roosevelt to help U.S. business. Smith got his money—a $4,500,000 loan from the government. The new project, the Douglas Sleeper Transport (DST), was on its way.

Design work on the DST, which was quickly to evolve into the DC-3, started in earnest in the fall of 1934. Once again, model tests from the Cal Tech wind tunnel were indispensable. The new design outwardly looked like a DC-2. But the fuselage had been widened and lengthened, the wingspan increased, and the shape of the rudder and vertical stabilizer were different. In the words of Arthur Raymond, "From the DC-1 to the DC-2, the changes were minor; from the DC-2 to the DC-3, they amounted to a new airplane." The different plan view shapes of the DC-2 and DC-3 are shown in Figure 6.6. The wind-tunnel tests at Cal Tech were overseen by Professor A. L. Klein and Bailey Oswald. During the tests, a major stability problem was encountered. Klein stated, "The bigger plane with its change in the center of gravity had produced the stability of a drunk trying to walk a straight line." However, by slightly modifying the wing and changing the airfoil section, the airplane was made stable; indeed, the DST finally proved to be one of the most stable airplanes in existence at that time. The first flight of the DST was on December 17, 1935. After the efforts of more than 400 engineers and drafters, the creation of 3500 drawings, and some 300 wind-tunnel tests, the airplane flew beautifully. American Airlines began service of the DST on June 25, 1936.

The distinguishing aspects of the DST compared with the DC-2 were that its payload was one-third greater and its gross weight was about 50 percent larger. These aspects did not go unappreciated by Douglas. If the bunks were taken out and replaced by seats, the airplane could carry 21 passengers in a relative state of luxury. This was yet another new airplane—the DC-3. In fact, by the time Douglas gave his 1935 annual report to his board of directors, the DC-3 was already moving down the production line in parallel with the DST.

Less than 100 airplanes in the sleeper configuration, DST, were produced. But when the DC-3 production line was finally shut down at the end of World War II, 10,926 had been built. The vast majority of these were for the military, 10,123 compared with 803 for the commercial airlines. The DC-3 was an amazing

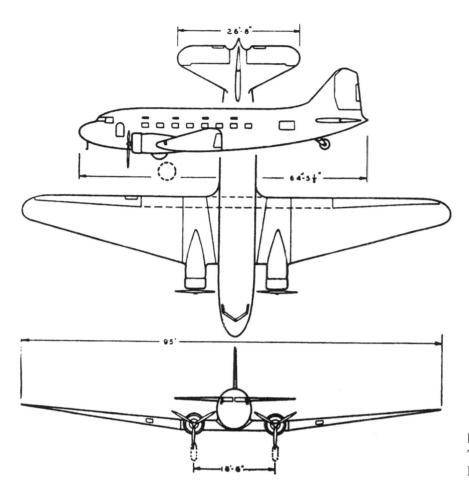

FIGURE 6.7
Three-view of the Douglas
DC-3, 1936.

success, and today it is heralded by many aviation enthusiasts as the most famous airplane of its era.

A three-view of the DC-3 is given in Figure 6.7. Compare this with the three-view of the SPAD XIII in Figure 5.5. What a difference! This comparison dramatically illustrates the design revolution that ushered in the era of the mature propeller-driven airplane. Only 19 years separate these two airplanes, but they are eons apart technically. Concentrating on Figure 6.7, let us examine the advances in aeronautical engineering technology that were synergistically embodied in the DC-3 and that thereafter characterized all airplanes of the period.

The most obvious difference is the streamlined appearance of the DC-3, one of the most aesthetically beautiful of all aircraft. In fact, the configuration of the DC-3 screams *drag reduction*. This is more than just appearance. The zero-lift drag coefficient of the DC-3 is 0.0249, much smaller than the value of 0.367 for the SPAD XIII (which itself is lower than many other World War I aircraft). The drag-reduction features of the DC-3 are as follows:

1) *Streamlining of the basic airframe.* There is a smooth, somewhat round in cross section, elongated fuselage and a wing with a relatively new airfoil shape generated by the National Advisory Committee for Aeronautics (NACA), designed to produce reasonable lift with little drag. Aerodynamicists had made progress in

the theoretical understanding of the physical mechanisms that cause drag, and this understanding was beginning to feed into the design of airplanes. These advances in theoretical aerodynamics will be highlighted in a later section.

2) *High aspect ratio wing.* The wing of the DC-3 had an aspect ratio of 9.14, considerably larger than its closest competitor, the Boeing 247, with an aspect ratio of 6.55, and certainly much larger than the SPAD XIII, as can be seen from a comparison of Figures 5.5 and 6.7. By the time the DC-3 was designed, the aerodynamic theory of wings had advanced to the point that the mysteries of aspect ratio were fully revealed, and accurate mathematical equations were available to predict the effect of aspect ratio on both lift and drag. We will examine this breakthrough in theoretical aerodynamics in a later section.

3) *NACA cowlings on the engines.* The DC-3 is powered by two Wright Cyclone engines—air-cooled radial engines. Looking at Figure 6.7, however, the cylinders of the engines are nowhere to be seen; they are covered over by streamlined shrouds, cowlings, specially designed by NACA based on a concerted wind-tunnel test program that began in 1928. The story of the development of the NACA cowling is an exacting chapter in the history of aerodynamics; this story is told in a later section. In some cases, the addition of the NACA cowling to a fuselage with engine cylinders previously exposed to the airstream resulted in a dramatic 60 percent reduction in drag.

4) *Retractable landing gear.* The fixed landing gear constantly protruding into the airstream and causing high drag, such as seen in Figure 5.5 for the SPAD XIII and characteristic of virtually all airplanes from the era of the strut-and-wire biplane (see, for example, the parade of configurations in Figures 5.3 and 5.43), is missing in Figures 6.1, 6.2, and 6.4–6.7. Indeed, one of the hallmarks of the era of the mature propeller-driven airplane is that the landing gear is retracted after takeoff and is neatly buried in the fuselage, wing, or nacelle. It is simply no longer hanging out in the airstream, thus reducing the parasite drag of the airplane. Aeronautical engineers as early as World War I appreciated the aerodynamic advantages of retractable landing gear, but the extra weight and mechanical complexity of the retracting mechanism worked against its implementation. Finally, in the early 1930s, the attention to drag reduction had brought about such dividends that the fixed landing gear was the next thing to go. For the DC-3, as well as several of the pioneering aircraft of the new era, the wheels were not completely retracted out of the airstream. Note in Figure 6.7 that the landing gear is retracted into the engine nacelle, and because of competition for space in the nacelle between the engine and the wheels, the landing gear does not fit flush inside the nacelle. A small portion of the wheel is still exposed to the flow, but this is a small sacrifice to pay for the overall drag reduction obtained by getting most of the bulky landing gear out of the airstream. By the end of this era, most airplane designs had fully retracted landing gear, with a totally flush external airframe.

All of these features contributed to the streamlined airplane. Streamlining became a cardinal design principle in the era of the mature propeller-driven airplane; drag reduction was paramount.

Although you can not easily tell from looking at the three-view in Figure 6.7, the DC-3 was equipped with *variable-pitch propellers* manufactured by the Hamilton Standard Company. In contrast, the SPAD XIII, along with all airplanes of that era, had a fixed-pitch propeller. Before the 1930s, this was a weak link in all propeller-driven aircraft. As discussed in Chapter 4, Wilbur Wright was the first to recognize that a propeller is essentially a twisted wing oriented in such a fashion that the principle part of the aerodynamic force is in the thrust direction. For a propeller of fixed orientation, the twist of the propeller is designed so that each airfoil section of the propeller is at its optimum angle of attack to the local relative airfoil direction, usually that angle of attack that corresponds to the maximum lift-to-drag ratio of the airfoil. The relative airflow seen by each airfoil section is the sum of the forward motion of the airplane and the rotational motion of the propeller. Clearly, when the forward velocity of the airplane is changed, the local flow direction is changed, and hence, the angle of attack of each airfoil is changed. As a result, a fixed-pitch propeller is operating at maximum efficiency only at its design airspeed; for all other airspeeds of the airplane, the propeller efficiency decreases. This is a tremendous disadvantage of a fixed-pitch propeller. The solution to this problem is to vary the pitch of the propeller during flight to operate at near-optimum efficiency over the whole flight range of the airplane, that is, to rotate the propeller blade about its longitudinal axis so that the local angle of attack seen by each airfoil section of the propeller is close to its optimum value. As the direction of the local flow velocity at each airfoil section changes with airspeed, then the optimum local angle of attack can be maintained by rotating the blade itself accordingly. This is the principle of the variable-pitch propeller. The aerodynamic advantage of varying the pitch of the propeller during flight was appreciated as early as World War I, but the mechanical solution was easier said than done. The first practical variable-pitch propeller was not available until 1933, just in time for its use on a later model of the Boeing 247 and on the DC-1, followed by the DC-2 and DC-3. The story of the technical development of the variable pitch propeller will be told in a later section.

Return to Figure 6.7; the only evidence that the DC-1 has a variable-pitch propeller is the small hub that projects slightly forward of the center of the propeller blades. This hub houses part of the hydromechanical control mechanism for varying the pitch of the propeller. The improved efficiency, and hence increased thrust, provided by the variable-pitch propeller allowed the DC-1 to meet the single-engine, high-altitude performance requirements set down by TWA. The variable-pitch propeller is one of the most essential ingredients of the mature propeller-driven airplane. It allows the airplane to, so to speak, shift gears in flight.

The DC-3 had a maximum speed of 212 miles per hour, which made it the fastest commercial transport of its day. One design feature of the DC-3 that allowed this higher speed was its high wing loading of 25.3 pounds per square foot; by comparison, the wing loading of the slower Boeing 247 was much smaller, 16.3 pounds per square foot. Everything else being equal between two airplanes, the one with the higher wing loading will have a higher maximum velocity. A higher wing loading, however, comes with a price—a higher landing speed, unless something special is done about it. The Douglas engineers knew what they had to do to keep the stalling speed and hence the landing speed, a safe, low value. Because stalling speed varies inversely with the square root of the maximum lift coefficient $C_{L,max}$, the wings of the DC-3 were designed with split flaps, which, when deflected downward, artificially increased the value of $C_{L,max}$ and, hence, reduced the landing speed. The stalling speed of the DC-3 with its flaps deployed was a respectable 67 miles per hour, only slightly faster than the 61-mile per hour stalling speed for the Boeing 247, which was not equipped with flaps. A split flap is shown schematically in Figure 6.8; it forms part of the bottom surface of the wing, and this bottom surface is the only part that deflects downward, whereas the

TABLE 6.1   Comparison of performance parameters

Configuration	W/P, pounds per horsepower	W/S, pounds per square foot	$C_{D,0}$	$(L/D)_{max}$
Handley Page 0/400	20.5	8.7	0.0427	9.7
DC-3	10.9	25.3	0.0249	14.7

FIGURE 6.8
A split flap.

top surface remains straight. This is in contrast to a plain flap, where the entire trailing edge is deflected. Examining the top view of the DC-3 shown in Figure 6.7, the flaplike surfaces shown at the trailing edges of the wings are long ailerons, not flaps. The hidden-view dashed lines connecting the two ailerons, traversing the rest of the span of the wings, represent the split flaps that are hidden from view from the top. Although plain flaps had been used on a few airplanes as early as World War I (see discussion in Chapter 5), the DC-3 was the first major airplane where flaps were an essential design feature. Moreover, the Douglas engineers chose to use split flaps, invented by Orville Wright in 1920, because the split flap produces a slightly higher $C_{L,max}$ and less of a change in pitching moment compared with a plain flap. Many of the fighter airplanes used during World War II were equipped with split flaps. The use of flaps of some type is a feature of the mature propeller-driven airplane.

Another feature that made the DC-3 a fast airplane for its time was the two powerful Wright Cyclone engines, each producing 1100 horsepower, giving the DC-3 a power loading of 10.9 pounds per horsepower. The Wright Cyclone was a powerful, 14-cylinder, air-cooled radial engine, with the cylinders arranged in two rows. After the demise of the rotary engines near the end of World War I, the basic radial engine experienced a hiatus until the late 1920s, when both Pratt and Whitney and Wright Aeronautical designed successful, reliable radials. The Pratt and Whitney Wasp engines and the Wright Cyclone engines, when combined with the low-drag NACA cowling, became the engines of choice for many airplane designers at the beginning of the era of the mature, propeller-driven airplane.

The Douglas DC-3 hanging in the Air Transportation Gallery at the National Air and Space Museum, Smithsonian Institution, Washington, D.C.

Again return to Figure 6.7. We mention an obvious feature of the DC-3—it is a *monoplane*. Moreover, it is an *all-metal airplane*. The design features embraced by Hugo Junkers in 1915 (see Chapter 5) had finally become the dominant airplane configuration by the early 1930s. For the most part, gone is the biplane configuration, gone is the vegetable airplane of wood and fabric, and gone is the thin airfoil. With the DC-3, we have an aluminum airplane with a cantilevered wing, made up of a 15 percent thick NACA 2215 airfoil shape at the root, tapering to a 6 percent thick NACA 2206 airfoil shape at the tip.

The Douglas DC-3, the most technically and commercially successful transport of the 1930s. (American Aviation Historical Society, AAHS, from Peter M. Bowers.)

Once again, compare the DC-3 in Figure 6.7, which is the epitome of the era of the mature propeller-driven airplane, with the SPAD XIII in Figure 5.5, which is representative of the era of the strut-and-wire biplane. From the point of view of the technology of the airplane, there is no comparison. Perhaps a more revealing comparison is to examine the twin-engine DC-3 in light of a twin-engine airplane from the strut-and-wire biplane era, such as the Handley Page 0/400. You will find the 0/400 included in the parade of configurations in Figure 5.3. The Handley Page was one of the most successful bombers of World War I, and after the war it served as a civil transport and airmail carrier until the mid-1920s. A comparison of the performance parameters for the Handley Page 0/400 and the Douglas DC-3 is given in Table 6.1.

Clearly, between the SPAD XIII and the Handley Page 0/400 from World War I and the DC-3 in the mid-1930s, there has been a revolution in aeronautical engineering, particularly in the design of the airplane. In the remainder of this chapter, we will look more closely at various aspects of this revolution.

In regard to the Douglas DC-3, we note in closing this section that the airplane itself embodied no new revolutionary design features per se. No new untried technology was used on the DC-3. Each aspect of the design revolution, such as the NACA cowling, wing flaps, retractable landing gear, etc., had been tested and demonstrated separately. But what was revolutionary about the DC-3 was that it contained in its design, for the first time, *all* of the features of the mature propeller-driven airplane and that the designers of the DC-3 combined all of these features in a synergistic fashion, resulting in one of the most technologically successful airplanes in history.

PARADE OF CONFIGURATIONS—1930–1953

The fruits of the design revolution are clearly seen in the parade of configurations typical of the era of the mature propeller-driven airplane, as shown in Figure 6.9. Here (with a few exceptions), we see a parade of all-metal monoplanes with enclosed cockpits, retractable landing gear, and a streamlined airframe. Just cast your eyes over the airplanes. Now flip back to Figures 5.3 and 5.43 for a reminder of what airplanes looked like in the previous era. Clearly the period of the 1930s saw a transformation of the airplane. Some historians have called this period the "golden age" of aviation; indeed, that is the title of a whole gallery at the National

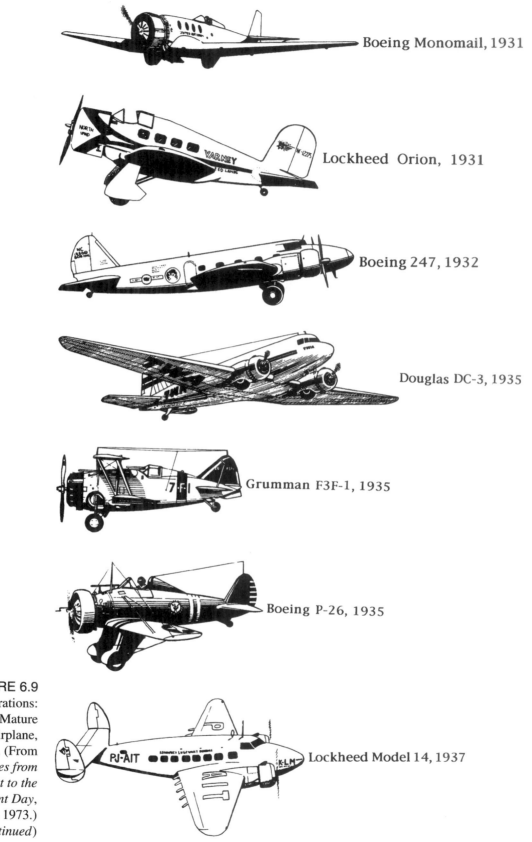

Boeing Monomail, 1931

Lockheed Orion, 1931

Boeing 247, 1932

Douglas DC-3, 1935

Grumman F3F-1, 1935

Boeing P-26, 1935

Lockheed Model 14, 1937

FIGURE 6.9
Parade of Configurations:
The Era of the Mature
Propeller-Driven Airplane,
1930–1953. (From
Angelucci, *Airplanes from
the Dawn of Flight to the
Present Day,*
McGraw-Hill, 1973.)
(*Continued*)

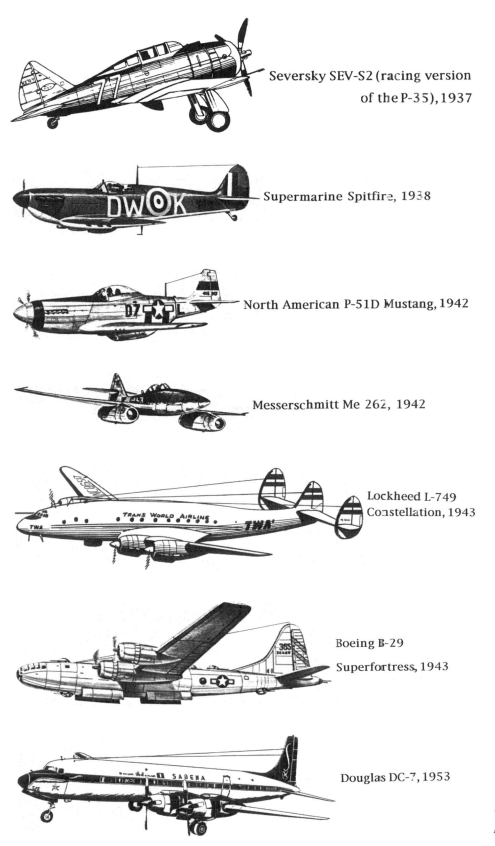

Seversky SEV-S2 (racing version of the P-35), 1937

Supermarine Spitfire, 1938

North American P-51D Mustang, 1942

Messerschmitt Me 262, 1942

Lockheed L-749 Constellation, 1943

Boeing B-29 Superfortress, 1943

Douglas DC-7, 1953

FIGURE 6.9
(*Continued from page 202.*)

Air and Space Museum. There is no doubt in the author's mind that it was the first of two *golden ages in aeronautical engineering.* (We will discuss the second in the next chapter.) Imagine being a young aeronautical engineer during the design revolution, when there was an explosion of new aeronautical technology that paved the way toward the design of faster and higher flying airplanes—the sky was indeed the limit to these aeronautical engineers. Imagine the excitement to participate in the inception of new, sleek airplanes that looked like they were doing 400 miles per hour even sitting on the ground. Added to this was the excitement of discovery; research in aeronautical technology was beginning to lay bare the secrets of aerodynamics, propulsion, and structural mechanics and materials. During the first 30 years of flight, airplanes had been designed on the basis of purely empirical knowledge and past experience. Now, through the research programs of government laboratories such as the NACA in the United States and the Royal Aeronautical Establishment in England and in select universities in the United States and Europe, people were finally beginning to understand why airplanes flew as they did and how to tailor nature's processes to improve the flight of airplanes. There is a whole lot of truth to the statement by the noted aeronautical historian Richard Smith that "the airplane did more for science than science ever did for the airplane."

Figure 6.9 begins with the Boeing Monomail in 1931, the first commercial transport with retractable landing gear (actually, semiretractable). It was Boeing's first all-metal airplane, and it laid the path to Boeing's 247 transport and the B-17 and B-29 bombers of World War II. The Monomail's open cockpit was a bit anachronistic, however. The Lockheed Orion was a development of the earlier Vega; like the Vega, the Orion was made from wood. The beautiful streamlining, enclosed cockpit, and retractable landing gear gave the Orion one of the lowest drag coefficients of this era, a value of $C_{D,0} = 0.021$. The Orion, however, lacked a variable-pitch propeller and did not have flaps. Also, its wooden construction was a throwback to earlier times. This is why the DC-3 was so outstanding; it contained all of the modern features of the mature propeller-driven airplane. The parade of configurations in Figure 6.9 continues with two more throwbacks—the Boeing P-26 fighter that still used external wire bracing for its wings and had an open cockpit and fixed landing gear and the Grumman F3F, the U.S. Navy's last biplane fighter, albeit designed as late as 1935. The P-26 and F3F reflected the ultraconservative design philosophy of the military in the early 1930s, a situation existing in Europe as well as the United States. The sleek Seversky SEV-32 racing airplane, a derivative of the Seversky P-35 fighter, an all-metal monoplane with retractable landing gear, is proof that the military was beginning to take advantage of the technology of the golden age and that the fighter was taking on a modern form. The British Spitfire in 1938 was the epitome of this modern form, adopted by all successful World War II fighters such as the North American P-51. The P-51 Mustang, by the way, with its ultrastreamlined, beautiful airframe had the lowest drag coefficient of all World War II piston engine airplanes, $C_{D,0} = 0.0163$. Large, multiengined aircraft such as the Boeing B-29 bomber, and transports such as the Lockheed Constellation and the Douglas DC-4, all containing the technical features of the era of the mature propeller-driven airplane, populated the sky. The last, and perhaps best of these, was the Douglas DC-7, which dated from 1953. Lurking on the horizon, however, was a new type of airplane, the jet-propelled airplane, a harbinger of which is included in Figure 6.9. This is the Messerschmitt

Me-262 twinjet fighter, developed in Germany in the early 1940s and deployed by the German Luftwaffe at the end of the war. The Me-262 was an early first of yet another era, the era of the jet-propelled airplane, which overlapped the era of the mature propeller-driven airplane in the late 1940s and early 1950s. (The era of the jet-propelled airplane is the subject of the next chapter.)

ADVANCES IN AERODYNAMICS

The design revolution in the 1930s was paralleled by an explosive growth of knowledge in aerodynamics, and the applications of this knowledge. Although advances in aerodynamics were many and varied during this period, four success stories stand out as the most pivotal. Let us look at each of these in turn.

Streamlining

To understand the role of streamlining in the advancement of the technology of the airplane, we first need to examine the three types of drag experienced by an airplane flying at subsonic speeds (speeds below the speed of sound): skin-friction drag, form drag, and induced drag. Fundamentally, an airflow over a body creates 1) a pressure distribution that is exerted over the surface of the body and 2) a shear-stress distribution, due to friction, that is exerted over the surface of the body. The pressure acts locally perpendicular at each point on the surface, and the shear stress acts tangentially at each point on the surface. The pressure and shear-stress distributions are the two hands by which nature grabs hold of the body and exerts an aerodynamic force on it. The component of that force that acts in the direction of the freestream is, by definition, the drag. Hence drag is produced both by friction and by pressure.

For a purely subsonic airflow over an airplane, the total drag is made up of contributions from three sources:

1) *Skin-friction drag.* Shear stress, which is the tugging action of friction between the air and the surface of the airplane, creates a force in the drag direction (Figure 6.10a). The force is called *skin-friction* drag (or sometimes simply friction drag).

2) *Form drag.* There are situations in which the airflow separates from the surface of an aerodynamic body (Figure 6.10b). The pressure in the low-energy, recirculating, separated region is relatively low, and thus, the surface pressure exerted on the body in that region is less than it would be if the flow were still attached. In turn, that creates a pressure imbalance between the front and back surfaces of the body; the lower pressure acting on the back of the body trying to push the body forward is overwhelmed by the higher pressure acting on the front of the body trying to push the body backward. That pressure imbalance creates a force in the drag direction, known as "pressure drag due to flow separation," also called *form drag.* If on an airplane there were absolutely no regions of separated flow, then the form drag would be zero. Unfortunately, aeronautical engineers have not yet been able to design that ideal airplane.

3) *Induced drag.* An airplane wing produces lift because the pressure on the bottom of the wing is higher than the pressure on the top of the wing. A by-product of that pressure difference between the top and bottom surfaces of the wing is that,

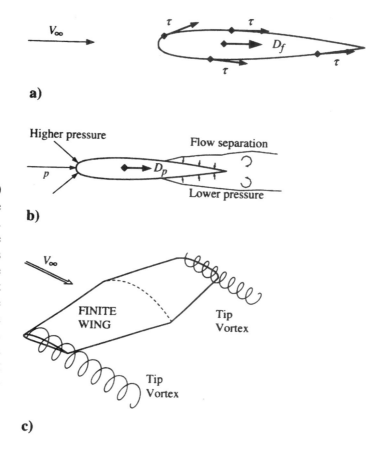

FIGURE 6.10
Sketches showing the physical sources of drag. a) Skin-friction drag, due to frictional shear stress acting tangentially to the surface; D_f is the resultant friction drag. b) Pressure drag due to flow separation from the surface, D_p; sometimes labeled form drag. c) Induced drag associated with vortices generated on a finite wing, sometimes called vortex drag.

at the tips of the wing, the flow is pushed from the high-pressure region on the bottom surface to the low-pressure region on the top surface. That is, the flow tends to curl around the wingtip from bottom to top. The curling action, superimposed on the main flow over the wing, produces a vortex at each wingtip that flows downstream (Figure 6.10c). Those wing-tip vortices are like minitornadoes. Imagine a small tornado swirling around next to you. You would certainly feel a change in air pressure due to the presence of the tornado. The wing also experiences a change in pressure, for the same reason. That change in pressure acting on the surface of the wing always creates an extra pressure imbalance in the drag direction, thus increasing the drag on the wing. That increase in drag is called *induced drag*. It is strictly a pressure drag, and it is caused by the presence of the wingtip vortices. Clearly, the high pressure on the bottom of the wing and the low pressure on the top of the wing combine to cause both the lift and the wingtip vortices. Hence, induced drag is directly related to lift. Indeed, Prandtl's lifting-line theory (to be discussed later) shows that $C_{D,i} \propto C_L^2/AR$, where $C_{D,i}$ is the induced-drag coefficient, C_L is the lift coefficient, and AR is the wing aspect ratio. Designing to achieve lift on an airplane is not without its price; induced drag is the cost paid for the production of lift. The induced drag can be decreased by increasing the aspect ratio.

It will be helpful to keep these three sources of drag in mind in our subsequent discussions; in the age of the mature propeller-driven airplane, they become the fundamental drivers of aerodynamic research and development.

Streamlining was not a new idea in the 1930s. Nature, while evolving the shapes of fish and birds, has been using streamlining for eons. Being observers of nature, such men as Leonardo daVinci and George Cayley intuitively felt that the resistance experienced by a body moving through a fluid (liquid or gas) would be reduced if the body were streamlined. But the design of streamlined shapes in the early days of flight (such as the Duperdussin in Figure 5.3 and the Albatros D-Va in Figure 5.37) was more intuitive than based on hard data or intellectual understanding. In the era of the mature propeller-driven airplane, however, streamlining was an idea whose time had come. Moreover, aeronautical engineers began to understand the physics behind the advantages of streamlining and, therefore, became more comfortable with the idea.

In regard to the importance of streamlining, aeronautical engineers received a wake-up call on the evening of April 6, 1922, when Louis-Charles Breguet read a paper before the Royal Aeronautical Society in London, "Aerodynamical Efficiency and the Reduction of Air Transport Costs." Breguet was already famous as a successful pilot and airplane designer. Born in Paris in 1880, he had been educated in electrical engineering at French technical universities and had joined the family electrical-engineering firm, Maison Breguet. However, motivated by the spectacular flying demonstrations by Wilbur Wright in 1908 in France, Breguet built and flew his first airplane. After that, he plunged headlong into aviation. He immediately opened an airplane assembly factory in Douai, France, and by 1912, he had an assembly line turning out a biplane powered by a Renault 80-horsepower engine. During World War I he manufactured the Breguet 14 bomber in large numbers for the French forces. In 1919, he founded a commercial airline company that later grew into Air France. Thus, on that evening in London as Louis Breguet addressed the Royal Aeronautical Society, the audience listened attentively to the famous French aviation pioneer.

What the audience heard was one of the first important calls for major improvements in the aerodynamic efficiency of airplanes. Breguet's measure of aerodynamic efficiency was the drag-to-lift ratio. (In the United States, it is conventional to work with the reciprocal of that number, namely, the lift-to-drag ratio. However, in Europe, even today, the drag-to-lift ratio is frequently quoted.) Breguet called the drag-to-lift ratio the "fineness" of the airplane; the smaller the fineness, the more aerodynamically efficient the aircraft. Moreover, he referred to the equation for the range of an airplane, which shows that the range is directly proportional to the lift-to-drag ratio, or inversely proportional to the fineness. That equation was first used by Breguet during World War I and today is known worldwide as the Breguet range equation. About that equation, Breguet stated that "one at once realizes the very great importance of the fineness which in that formula is the only term depending upon the aerodynamic qualities of the aeroplane." Later in his talk he elaborated as follows:

> The conclusion is that one must bring to the minimum the value of the fineness. It can be obtained by choosing the best possible profile for the wings, the best designs for the body, empennage, etc. Moreover, the undercarriage should be made to disappear inside the body or the wings when the airplane is in flight, etc.

Breguet was emphasizing that the aerodynamics of the airplane should be as to minimize the fineness, that is, maximize the L/D ratio, and his suggestions to achieve minimum fineness all centered on the reduction of drag. His recommendation for "choosing the best possible profile for the wings, the best designs for the body, empennage, etc.," implied streamlining those geometric shapes to reduce the pressure drag due to flow separation (form drag). That was especially true of his idea for retractable landing gear. The fixed landing gear used on airplanes during that period were simply blunt bodies exposed to the flow, with consequent massive flow separation on their back surfaces and, thus, high form drag. He knew that a substantial reduction in drag could be achieved by retracting the landing gear out of the flow. (The first ideas for retractable landing gear can be traced to some of da Vinci's sketches for flying machines and to Alphonse Penaud in France in 1876, who patented a design for his "airplane of the future," which included a retractable undercarriage with compressed-air shock absorbers. It was not until 1920 that the first practical retractable landing gear was used—on the Dayton–Wright RB high-wing monoplane built for the Gordon–Bennett air races in France. As we have already discussed, as a regular feature of airplane designs, retractable landing gear did not become common until the 1930s.)

Breguet went on to note: "an airplane of high standard quality now has a fineness [D/L] equal to 0.12." That was an L/D of 8.3, in keeping with the values shown in Chapter 5 for typical strut-and-wire biplanes. He gave an example of a typical transport airplane with that fineness and calculated a payload cost of 35 francs per ton per kilometer. If the aerodynamics could be improved to give that airplane a fineness of 0.065 ($L/D = 15.4$), then Breguet calculated a cost of 7.4 francs per ton per kilometer—a cost reduction by almost a factor of 5. Clearly, streamlining, with its consequent reduction in form drag and, hence, increase in L/D, would pay off financially for civil air transport, which was a major focus of Breguet's remarks to the Royal Aeronautical Society that night. His "improved" fineness value of 0.065, pulled out of thin air in 1922 during the age of the strut-and-wire biplane, would not be achieved until the mid-1930s and the development of the Douglas DC-3, which had an L/D of 14.7, or a fineness of 0.068. It was the insistence of Breguet and others like him who campaigned for improvements in aerodynamic efficiency that finally led to significant efforts to achieve drag reductions through streamlining; Breguet's 1922 paper was an important precursor to the aerodynamics of the era of the mature propeller-driven airplane.

Breguet went on to practice what he preached. He designed a number of airplanes during the 1920s and 1930s that set long-range records, including the first nonstop crossing of the South Atlantic in 1927. Breguet was active in running his airplane company until his death in 1955, and his influence permeates a substantial part of French aviation history.

The progress in drag reduction during the age of mature propeller-driven airplanes was facilitated by the spread of Prandtl's boundary-layer theory in the 1920s and the widespread applications of various aspects of that theory in the 1930s. Boundary-layer theory made it possible to calculate the skin-friction drag on an aerodynamic surface. We will discuss the concept of the boundary layer, and the development of its theoretical analysis by Ludwig Prandtl in Germany, when we address advances in aerodynamic theory in a later section. Whereas boundary-layer theory led to reasonably accurate estimations of skin-friction drag, the same cannot be said in regard to flow separation and the resulting form drag. The best that the theory could do was to allow one to estimate the *location* on the surface where separation would occur, and that estimation was frequently in great error. The only means for obtaining aerodynamic information on form drag was empirical—principally wind-tunnel testing and, to a lesser extent, actual flight tests.

Against that background, in 1929 there came a second resounding call for streamlining—in this case from the famous British aeronautical engineer Sir B. Melvill Jones. Addressing the Royal Aeronautical Society, as had Breguet seven years earlier, Jones entitled his lecture "The Streamline Airplane." Like Breguet, Jones was highly respected, but whereas Breguet was an aeronautical industrialist, Jones was a professor of aeronautical engineering at Cambridge University, England. Jones's analysis of the advantages of streamlining was so compelling that it was said that designers were shocked into greater awareness of the value of streamlining. Jones's paper marked a turning point in the practice of aerodynamics during the age of the advanced propeller-driven airplane.

Jones led off his discussion with the following thought:

> Ever since I first began to study aerodynamics, I have been annoyed by the vast gap which has existed between the power actually expended on mechanical flight and the power ultimately necessary for flight in a correct shaped aeroplane. Every year, during my summer holiday, this annoyance is aggravated by contemplating the effortless flight of the sea birds and the correlated phenomena of the beauty and grace of their forms.

Jones went on to underscore the importance of drag reduction, pointing out that such reduction for an airplane with a given power output from the engine would result in a higher cruising velocity, or a lower fuel consumption. Taking a page from Breguet's analysis, this would result in increased range and/or payload, which in Jones's words are "both factors of the first importance in aeronautical development."

Jones clearly identified the kind of drag that was most in need of reduction: *form drag*. He correctly pointed out that induced drag was important at low speeds (because the airplane flies at high C_L at low speeds, hence, high $C_{D,i}$), but that its importance diminished as the speed increased. Also, he noted that significant reductions in induced drag could not be achieved without using much larger wingspans, that is, higher aspect ratios. Thus, Jones suggested that the major area in which drag reduction could be achieved was "head resistance," a term deriving from as far back as Chanute's *Progress in Flying Machines*—simply the sum of skin-friction drag and form drag for the airplane. Jones quoted a characteristic typical of airplanes in the 1920s, namely, that the power required by an airplane to overcome head resistance was 75–95 percent of the total power used. Because little could be done to reduce skin-friction drag, except to reduce the exposed surface area of the airplane, the primary target reduction had to be form drag, the pressure drag due to flow separation: "We all realize the way to reduce this item in the power account is to attend very carefully to *streamlining*."

With that in mind, Jones defined what he called the "perfectly streamlined airplane" as one that 1) generates a flow identical (except in a very thin boundary layer) with the flow of an inviscid fluid (a fluid with no friction); 2) experiences a pressure distribution identical with that due theoretically to the inviscid fluid, that is, no flow separation; and, therefore, 3) experiences a drag that is the sum of the induced drag and the tangential skin-friction forces resolved in the downwind direction.

Thus Jones's ideal airplane was simply one with no form drag. He went on to describe what would be necessary to achieve that lofty goal:

Unless bodies are "carefully shaped," they do not necessarily generate streamline flow, but shed streams of eddies from various parts of their surface.... The power absorbed by these eddies may be, and often is, many times greater than the sum of the powers absorbed by skin friction and induced drag. The drag of a real aeroplane therefore exceeds the sum of the induced power and skin friction drag by an amount which is a measure of *defective streamlining.*

Jones went on at length about the importance of designing the perfectly streamlined airplane, but he did not specify how it should be shaped. To underscore that importance, he estimated the power required to overcome skin-friction drag on several generic airplanes and then compared that with the power required for various real airplanes. His skin-friction calculations assumed that the friction drag on an airplane was the same as that exerted by a turbulent boundary layer on a flat plate of equal exposed area; he called that assumption "convenient and safe." In fact, he suggested that flat-plate turbulent skin friction would be a good estimate for the drag coefficient for any "good streamlined body."

The aspect of Jones's paper that most shocked airplane designers into greater awareness was his plot of horsepower required versus velocity, which compared Jones's ideal, "perfectly streamlined" airplane with various real airplanes of that time (Figure 6.11). The solid curves at the bottom of Figure 6.11 show the power required for the ideal airplane. (They take into account only skin-fiction drag and induced drag.) Four different curves are shown for four different combinations of span loading (W/b^2) and wing loading (W/S), where W is the weight of the airplane and b and S are the span and area of the wing, respectively. The solid

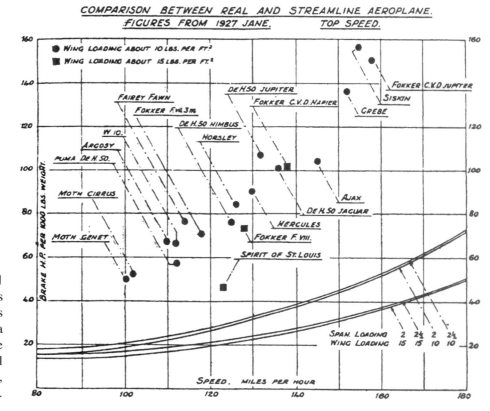

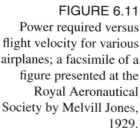

FIGURE 6.11
Power required versus flight velocity for various airplanes; a facsimile of a figure presented at the Royal Aeronautical Society by Melvill Jones, 1929.

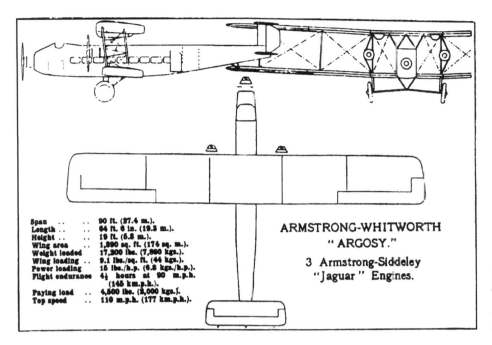

Span ..	..	90 ft. (27.4 m.).
Length ..	..	64 ft. 6 in. (19.3 m.).
Height ..	..	19 ft. (5.8 m.).
Wing area	..	1,890 sq. ft. (174 sq. m.).
Weight loaded	..	17,500 lbs. (7,860 kgs.).
Wing loading ..		9.1 lbs./sq. ft. (44 kgs.).
Power loading	..	15 lbs./h.p. (6.8 kgs./h.p.).
Flight endurance		4½ hours at 90 m.p.h. (145 km.p.h.).
Paying load	..	4,500 lbs. (2,000 kgs.f.
Top speed	..	110 m.p.h. (177 km.p.h.).

ARMSTRONG-WHITWORTH
" ARGOSY."

3 Armstrong-Siddeley
"Jaguar" Engines.

FIGURE 6.12
Three-view of the
Armstrong-Whitworth
Argosy.

symbols are data points for real airplanes. Jones obtained those data from the 1927 edition of *Jane's*, the annual compendium of aircraft performance and design characteristics. Jones pointed out that the vertical distance between any of these data points and the solid "ideal" curve was the power expended by the real airplane in "the generation of unnecessary eddies." That is, the power expended in overcoming form drag, and that "unnecessary" power consumption was considerable for all of the airplanes listed. That is no surprise. Consider the data point for the Argosy. (The Armstrong–Whitworth Argosy was one of the first multiengine airplanes to be designed for a specific buyer, Imperial Airways in the United Kingdom. Introduced in 1926, it was widely used on the routes from London to Paris; Basel; Salonika, Greece; Brussels; and Cologne, Germany. Only seven were built, but they were popular airliners for that day. The last Argosy was retired from service in 1935.) A three-view of the Argosy is shown in Figure 6.12, which shows a rather boxy configuration, with fixed, protruding landing gear and the wires and struts typical of the early 1920s designs. Clearly the Argosy was a long way from Jones's ideal of the perfectly streamlined airplane. The vertical distance between the Argosy data point and the ideal curve in Figure 6.11 is intuitively explainable simply from the three-view. The Argosy was a perfect example of the conservative design approach common in the late 1920s and the early 1930s, especially in Europe. Miller and Sawers in their book *The Technical Development of Modern Aviation* (1970) described it this way: "Designers had acquired the attitude of the practical man, who knew how airplanes should be designed, because that was how they had designed them for the previous 20 years." No wonder the designers were shocked by what Jones had to say.

Another way of interpreting Jones's graph (Figure 6.11) is to examine the horizontal distance between a given data point for a real airplane and the ideal curve. That represents the *increase in velocity* that could be achieved at the given power available to the airplane if there were no form drag. For example, with no form drag, the top speed of the Argosy would have been a blistering 175 miles per hour rather than the actual value of 110 miles per hour. Any way they looked at it, Jones's graph made a strong case for streamlining. It is interesting that of all of the late-1920s aircraft listed in Figure 6.11, the Spirit of St. Louis came closest to Jones's ideal airplane.

After Jones finished his presentation, one very impressed member of the audience, identified only as Mr. Bramson, declared Jones's findings to be as important as the statement of the Carnot cycle in thermodynamics. Jones was more modest than that in response, noting that his findings could not be considered on the same plane as the Carnot theory of heat engines, though their practical outcomes were similar—the provision of an ideal toward which to work. Jones noted that whereas "the Carnot cycle is a precise theorem, my paper is more in the nature of an exercise in approximations." Jones was referring primarily to the approximate formula he used for flat-plate, turbulent skin-friction drag, for lack of a more precise equation for the turbulent case. In any event, by the late 1920s, streamlining was an idea whose time had come. It meant drag reduction, which would be the primary concern in applied aerodynamics during the age of the mature propeller-driven airplane.

That aeronautical engineers in the 1930s and 1940s took up the cause of streamlining goes without saying. Just take another look at Figure 6.9 and especially single out the Douglas DC-3, the Supermarine Spitfire, and the North American P-51—wonderful examples of beautifully streamlined airplanes. Melvill Jones lived until 1975; he must have been satisfied with what he saw.

In 1930, "Streamline!" was the call to action in applied aerodynamics. The objective was to design aerodynamic bodies with the lowest possible form drag—to approach Melvill Jones's ideal airplane. Although there had been considerable progress in aerodynamic theory by that time, it offered only an *understanding* of the mechanisms of flow separation and the resulting form drag; it could not yet provide accurate methods for calculating such phenomena, especially in turbulent flow. Thus, to meet that call to action, aerodynamicists had to turn to the wind tunnel.

The technical development of the wind tunnel paralleled the technical development of the airplane in the 20th century. The rapid growth in aviation after 1903 was paced by the rapid growth of wind tunnels, both in numbers and in technology. The Wright brothers were not by any means the first to use a wind tunnel. After the British engineer Francis Wenham invented the wind tunnel in 1871 (see Chapter 3), nearly a dozen such devices had been built and used before the Wrights constructed their wind tunnel. Indeed, the year 1903 started a boom in new wind-tunnel construction. Over the following nine years, tunnels were built at the National Physical Laboratory in London in 1903; in Rome in 1903; in Moscow in 1905; in Göttingen, Germany in 1908; in Paris in 1909 (including two built by Gustave Eiffel, of tower fame); and again at the National Physical Laboratory in 1910 and 1912. A major advance in the number and technology of wind tunnels was made by NACA after 1915. The first NACA wind tunnel became operational at the Langley Memorial Aeronautical Laboratory at Hampton, Virginia, in 1920. It had a 5-foot-diameter test section that accommodated models up to 3.5 feet wide. Then in 1923, to simulate the higher Reynolds numbers associated with flight, NACA built the first variable-density wind tunnel, a facility that could be pressurized to 20 atmospheres in the flow and, therefore, obtain a 20-fold increase in density, hence, Reynolds number, in the test section. During the 1930s and 1940s, low-speed subsonic wind tunnels grew larger and larger. In 1931, a NACA wind tunnel with a 30 × 60-foot oval test section went into operation at Langley with a 129-mile per hour maximum wind speed in the test section. This was the first million-dollar tunnel in history. (Built during the Great Depression, NACA paid bargain-basement prices.) Called the Full-Scale Tunnel, whole airplanes could be mounted in the test section. It was in this wind tunnel where efforts to streamline airplanes and to obtain drag reduction hit their zenith. Let us get back to that story.

The aerodynamicists put the final touches on their evocations of Melvill Jones's ideal airplane in the late 1930s and early 1940s, when the concept of streamlining was pushed to the maximum and every effort was made to reduce or eliminate even the slightest sources of local flow separation on an airplane. In the laboratory, there could be no better way to locate small regions of drag production than to dispense with small wind-tunnel models and instead to put a real airplane in a wind tunnel. During the 1930s, the only wind-tunnel facility in which that could be done was the 30 × 60-foot Full-Scale Tunnel at NACA Langley. So NACA began a series of detailed, laborious wind-tunnel tests whose purpose was to reduce the drag coefficients for conventional airplanes as much as possible without interfering with their practical operation. Within NACA those early wind-tunnel tests were collectively referred to as the drag-cleanup program, which started in 1938 and lasted essentially through the end of World War II.

The typical drag-cleanup process was one of parameter variation: The airplane was first put in its most faired and sealed condition (protuberances removed, gaps sealed, etc.) and mounted in the wind tunnel, and the drag was measured. Then, one by one, each element was restored to its service condition, and the drag was measured each time. In that fashion, the increment in drag due to each element was measured. Although the drag increment for each element usually was small, the total accumulation due to all of the drag-producing elements usually was large. For example, the drag-cleanup series began in 1938 with the testing of a Brewster XF2A Buffalo single-seat U.S. Navy pursuit airplane; the Navy had become concerned when the experimental prototype had been unable to fly faster than about 250 miles per hour. The airplane was flown to Langley and mounted in the Full-Scale Tunnel (FST) (Figure 6.13). After a detailed series of tests, a number of drag-producing protuberances were identified (landing gear, exhaust stacks, machine-gun installation, gunsight, etc.). That led to some modifications of the airplane, after which the maximum speed was found to be 281 miles per hour, a 31-mile per hour increase over the original prototype. Referring to Jones's Figure 6.11, that drag cleanup was a push toward the right-hand side of the graph.

The drag cleanup for the Brewster Buffalo was such a success that within 18 months 18 different military prototypes were tested in the FST. A quantitative example of the drag-cleanup technique, that for the XP-41, is shown in Figure 6.14. Starting with the most streamlined configuration (condition 1), for which the drag coefficient was 0.0166, the airplane was restored to its original configuration through 17 different steps. The drag coefficient for the fully restored configuration was 0.0275, a 66 percent increase over the most streamlined condition. Many of the sources of drag appear rather pedestrian, for example, sanded walkway added and oiler cooler installed, but collectively they accounted for considerable drag.

The drag-cleanup procedures begun toward the end of the 1930s represented an important step in the evolution of mature propeller-driven airplanes. Although

FIGURE 6.13
Brewster XF2A Buffalo
mounted in the Full-Scale
Tunnel at NACA Langley
Aeronautical Laboratory,
1938.

the tests were mainly for military aircraft because of wartime priorities, they
provided an educational experience and a massive aerodynamic database that
would later be used to design aircraft of all types.

Completing something of an international full circle, on December 17, 1937,
eight years after his famous paper on streamlining to the Royal Aeronautical
Society, Melvill Jones arrived at Columbia University in New York to deliver the
first Wright Brothers Lecture to the Institute of Aeronautical Sciences and
addressed 300 members and guests of the institute, including Orville Wright. Jones
took that opportunity to discuss some new data on boundary-layer behavior,
obtained during flight experiments at Cambridge University using a Hawker Hart
military biplane. Boundary-layer measurements, including velocity profiles, the
location of the transition from laminar flow to turbulent flow, and boundary-layer
thickness, had been obtained on the lower wing of the airplane at airspeeds from
60 to 120 miles per hour in level flight and 240 miles per hour in long, steep dives.
Jones's lecture was a fitting closure to one phase in the development of applied
aerodynamics in the era of the mature propeller-driven airplane. Much had been
accomplished in the decade since his original call for streamlining, and he was

Airplane Condition

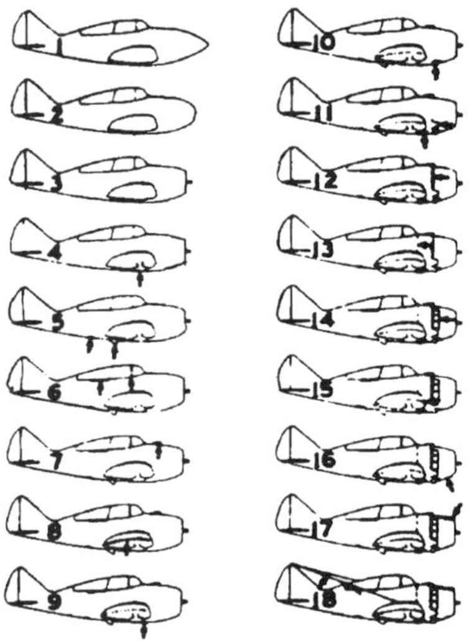

Condition number	Description	C_D ($C_L = 0.15$)	ΔC_D	ΔC_D, percent[a]
1	Completely faired condition, long nose fairing	0.0166		
2	Completely faired condition, blunt nose fairing	.0169		
3	Original cowling added, no airflow through cowling	.0186	0.0020	12.0
4	Landing-gear seals and fairing removed	.0188	.0002	1.2
5	Oil cooler installed	.0205	.0017	10.2
6	Canopy fairing removed	.0203	−.0002	−1.2
7	Carburetor air scoop added	.0209	.0006	3.6
8	Sanded walkway added	.0216	.0007	4.2
9	Ejector chute added	.0219	.0003	1.8
10	Exhaust stacks added	.0225	.0006	3.6
11	Intercooler added	.0236	.0011	6.6
12	Cowling exit opened	.0247	.0011	6.6
13	Accessory exit opened	.0252	.0005	3.0
14	Cowling fairing and seals removed	.0261	.0009	5.4
15	Cockpit ventilator opened	.0262	.0001	.6
16	Cowling venturi installed	.0264	.0002	1.2
17	Blast tubes added	.0267	.0003	1.8
18	Antenna installed	.0275	.0008	4.8
Total			0.0109	

[a]Percentages based on completely faired condition with long nose fairing.

FIGURE 6.14
Progression of the drag cleanup for the Republic XP-41 carried out in the NACA Full-Scale Tunnel, 1939.

directing his attention to one of the remaining major sources of drag, namely, friction drag. Jones repeated his Wright Brothers Lecture at the California Institute of Technology on December 21, described in the January 1938 issue of the *Journal of the Aeronautical Sciences* as "the most outstanding meeting of the Institute of the Aeronautical Sciences ever held on the Pacific Coast." One member of the audience, Francis Clauser, at that time with the Douglas Aircraft Company, recognized the historical full-circle significance of Jones's talk:

> It was a pleasure to hear from the man who provided the stimulation some years ago which has led to the practical elimination of unnecessary form drag in modern airplanes and it is reassuring that this same man is now engaged in research which may conceivably reduce the remaining skin friction to some fraction of its present value.

Today, at the beginning of the 21st century, aerodynamicists are still striving to "reduce the remaining skin friction to some fraction of its present value."

Six years later, the achievements in drag reduction due to streamlining were nicely summarized by another English aeronautical engineer, William S. Farren, who delivered the seventh Wright Brothers Lecture to the Institute of Aeronautical Sciences in New York. Farren, who at that time was director of the Royal Aircraft Establishment, had been a member of Melvill Jones's research group at Cambridge during the 1920s and 1930s. Farren was an experimentalist, who specialized in instrumentation. He built the first wind tunnel at Cambridge and later designed the

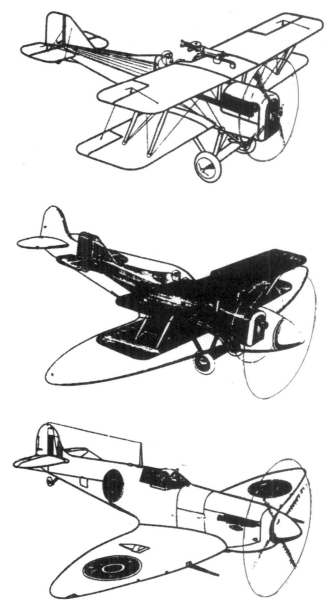

FIGURE 6.15
Examples of streamlining:
a) evolution for the S.E.5
of World War I to the
Spitfire of World War II;
b) evolution from the
Handley Page 0/400
bomber of World War I to
the Avro Lancaster of
World War II. (From a
presentation to the
Institute of Aeronautical
Sciences by William S.
Farren, 1944.)
(*Continued*)   **a)**

instrumentation for the in-flight boundary-layer measurements described earlier.
Although his remarks to the Institute of Aeronautical Sciences centered on the role
of research in aeronautics, he singled out drag reduction as a major example of the
progress in aerodynamic research. His presentation involved some excellent
illustrations of the metamorphosis of the airplane over the period from 1918 to
1944: At the top in Figure 6.15a is the British S.E.5 single-seat fighter from 1917.
The middle figure shows how aerodynamic research during the 1920s and early
1930s transformed the 1917 biplane shape into the streamlined monoplane
configuration typical of the Supermarine racers that finally won the Schneider
Trophy for the United Kingdom. At the bottom is the famous Spitfire from World

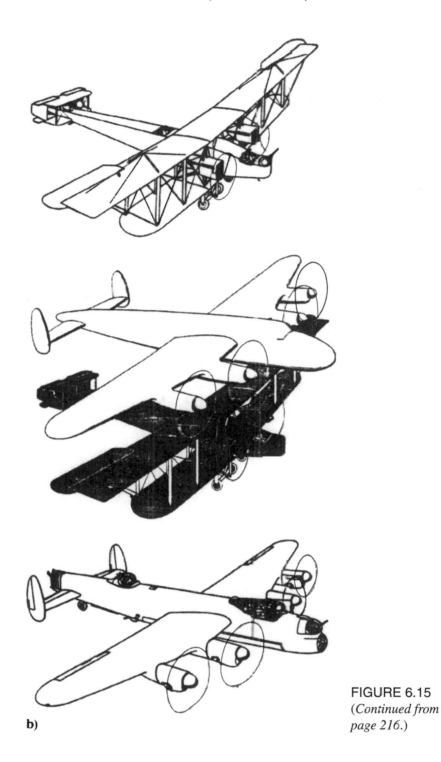

b)

FIGURE 6.15
(*Continued from
page 216.*)

War II, which incorporated the latest advances in aerodynamic streamlining. A similar progression for multiengine bombers is shown in Figure 6.15b. At the top is the Handley Page 0/400 twin-engine bomber from 1917. The middle figure shows the transformation of the old biplane configuration into the streamlined airliner shape of the late 1930s. At the bottom is the Lancaster bomber from World War II, a product of the advances in streamlining. Figures 6.15 provide graphic testimony to the advances in applied aerodynamics during the era of the mature propeller-driven airplane.

NACA Cowling

In 1926, airplanes could be divided into two general categories on the basis of the type of piston engine used—the liquid-cooled in-line engine or the air-cooled radial engine. The former was generally enclosed within the fuselage and did not present much of a problem in regard to streamlining. The latter relied on the airflow over the cylinders to cool the engine, and thus, the cylinders, arrayed like the spokes on a wheel, were directly exposed to the airstream. As a consequence, air-cooled radial engines created a lot of drag—just how much was yet to be realized. However, radial engines had several advantages that led to their use in many airplane designs: lower weight per horsepower, fewer moving parts, and lower maintenance costs. The U.S. Navy was partial to air-cooled radial engines because they continued to perform well despite the jarring impacts of carrier landings. In June 1926, the chief of the U.S. Navy's Bureau of Aeronautics requested that NACA study how a cowling could be wrapped around the cylinders of radial engines so as to reduce drag without interfering with cooling capacity. This set into motion one of the important aerodynamic developments in the era of the mature propeller-driven airplane—the NACA cowling.

The idea of cowlings was not new. For example, the French Deperdussin racing airplane in 1913 had a rounded and streamlined shroud wrapped around a Gnome 14-cylinder two-row rotary engine (Figure 5.3). Also, many of the rotary engines used on World War I airplanes were housed inside curved metal cowlings. Those cowling designs were based more on art than on science or any sound knowledge of aerodynamics. Fortunately, cooling was not a problem for those cowled rotary engines because the cylinders were always rotating through the air behind the cowling. The problem arose with the stationary radial engines that became prevalent in the 1920s.

On May 24, 1927, representatives of the major U.S. aircraft manufacturers met at NACA Langley to become more familiar with NACA's work and facilities and to make suggestions regarding future NACA research that would benefit the industry. That second meeting in what was to become an annual series at NACA played an important role in guiding the development of aerodynamic research at Langley, and the cowling program in particular, as recounted in the 1927 NACA annual report:

> At a preliminary meeting held in the morning the functions and work of the committee were briefly outlined, following which the representatives of the industry were conducted on a tour of inspection of the laboratory and the investigations under way were explained. This occasion marked the formal opening of the committee's new propeller research equipment. In the afternoon the conference proper convened and after a brief statement by the chairman as to the purpose of the meeting, there was general discussion of the problems of commercial aviation in which the representatives of the industry participated. Among the problems which were mentioned as of importance to commercial aviation were the various factors relating to the comfort and convenience of passengers in airplanes and particularly the elimination of noise; the question of controllability at low speeds; and the effect of protuberances on an otherwise faired stream-line body. One of the problems suggested, the study of the

effect of cowling and fuselage shape on the resistance and cooling characteristics of air-cooled engines, was promptly incorporated in the committee's research program.

Although the U.S. Navy had asked NACA to begin research on cowlings a year earlier, it took the political clout of the collective aircraft industry to have such work "promptly incorporated in the committee's research program."

NACA cowling research was the first major test program to be carried out in the newly operational Propeller Research Tunnel (PRT) at NACA Langley. This large tunnel had a test section 20 feet in diameter and a maximum airspeed of 110 miles per hour. The test section could accommodate full size airplane fuselages with installed engines and propellers. Fred Weick, a relatively young aeronautical engineer from the University of Illinois, had just become director of PRT. At the end of the May 24 conference, Weick was given responsibility for the NACA cowling program because PRT was the logical place to carry out the research.

For the next 10 years NACA carried out research on cowlings, most of it experimental. It was not until 1935 that any emphasis was placed on an analytical understanding of the aerodynamic processes associated with cowlings. Within a year after beginning the program, Weick and his associates had demonstrated that a properly designed cowling could dramatically reduce the form drag associated with radial engines without adversely affecting engine cooling—findings that were immediately snapped up by industry and incorporated into new airplane designs. The research method used by Weick was an experimental variation of parameters, and that approach in experimental aerodynamics was to take root at Langley and elsewhere during the 1930s.

The method of experimental parameter variation was the procedure of repeatedly determining the performance of some material, process, or device while systematically varying the parameters that define the object or its conditions of operation. Weick described his approach in the first NACA publication on the cowling research:

> The program as finally arranged included ten main forms of cowling to be tested on a J-5 engine in connection with two fuselages, three on an open cockpit fuselage and seven on a closed cabin type. The seven forms of cowling on the cabin fuselage range from the one extreme of an engine entirely exposed except for the rear crank case, to the other extreme of a totally enclosed engine. One of the cowlings with the open cockpit fuselage includes individual fairings behind each cylinder. Three forms of cowling, two of which are on the cabin fuselage, afford direct comparisons with and without a propeller spinner. The program involves the measurement of the engine cylinder temperatures, each cowling being modified, if necessary, until the cooling is satisfactory. The cowling is then tested for its effect on drag and propulsive efficiency.

The key to the success of the NACA cowling program was that while they experimented with configurations that would reduce form drag through external streamlining, they were careful to maintain effective cooling of the engine by internal ducting of the flow. The cowling found most successful by Weick was cowling number 10 in the NACA series, which was really a cowling within a cowling. Cowling number 10 was devised by taking cowling number 5 (Figure 6.16) (consisting of a smooth, rounded fairing enclosing only part of the cylinders) and wrapping around it an exterior rounded and streamlined shroud that totally enclosed the cylinders (Figure 6.17). The aerodynamically tailored

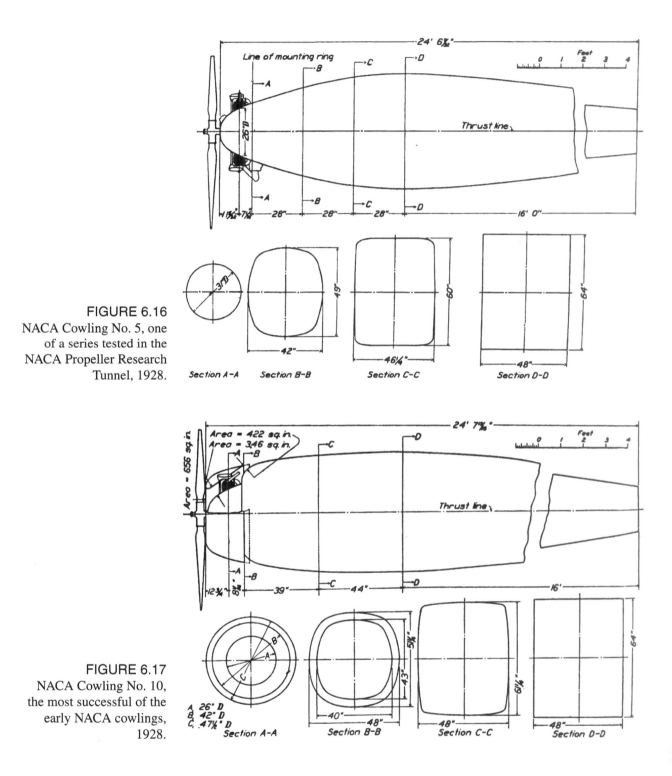

FIGURE 6.16
NACA Cowling No. 5, one
of a series tested in the
NACA Propeller Research
Tunnel, 1928.

FIGURE 6.17
NACA Cowling No. 10,
the most successful of the
early NACA cowlings,
1928.

internal flow in the passage formed by those two walls allowed effective cooling of
the engine.

The results of the initial NACA testing were published in a graph, reproduced
here in its original form in Figure 6.18. These results were stunning! In Figure 6.18,
we see a plot of the measured drag versus the dynamic pressure (or the velocity)
for various cowling designs, which clearly showed the outstanding performance

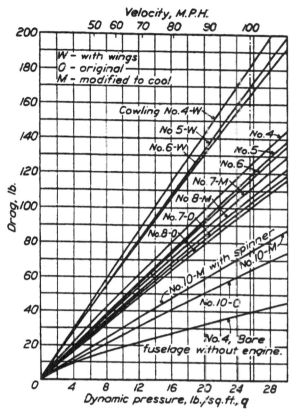

FIGURE 6.18
Experimental results for drag versus velocity for various NACA cowlings, showing that Cowling No. 10 had the lowest drag.

achieved with the NACA cowling, that is, cowling number 10. The bottom line was for the bare fuselage with no engine, and the top line was for the fuselage with the engine installed, but with the cylinders totally exposed. In comparing those two extremes, it was seen that addition of the uncowled engine increased the drag by an absolutely stunning factor of 4.76. Until that measurement, no one had ever understood the devastating extent to which the exposed cylinders were increasing the drag on such airplanes. The lines labeled "No. 10" in Figure 6.18 were for the number 10 cowling ("No. 10-0" was the cowling shown in Figure 6.17, and "No. 10-M" had a slight modification of the cowling inlet to improve the engine cooling.) Compared with the case of totally exposed cylinders, cowling number 10-M reduced the drag by a factor of 0.41 (almost 60 percent). Indeed, with the cowling, the drag was reduced almost back to the value measured without the engine installed.

That was a dramatic finding, and the normally staid NACA was in a state of euphoria. It lost no time in getting the word out. The U.S. aircraft industry was given advance notice of the findings well before the public announcement. (That policy is still followed today, giving the U.S. aerospace industry first access to critical NASA-generated data to enhance its position relative to foreign competitors.) In 1928 Weick wrote an article for the weekly periodical *Aviation* (forerunner of *Aviation Week and Space Technology*) on the dramatic performance of the NACA cowling: "In conclusion, it would seem from the tests made to date that a very substantial increase in high speed and all-around performance can be obtained on practically all radial engined aircraft by the use of the new NACA complete cowling," the article said. In view of the normal policy of NACA at that time to be very conservative and guarded in any communications to the public (data and analyses had to be authenticated beyond question before publication), Weick's statement in *Aviation* must have been quite revealing of the excitement at NACA.

Actually, NACA had remained conservative in one respect. Before releasing the cowling data, NACA engineers had flight tested the cowling, as reported by Thomas Carroll, who had been responsible for flight tests:

> In order that the practical value of the information in the foregoing report might be demonstrated, simple flight tests have been made of the Number 10 cowling.
>
> Through the courtesy of the Army Air Corps at Langley Field, VA, a Curtiss AT-5A airplane was obtained on which an adaptation of the Number 10 cowling was installed. . . . A series of flights were made by the three pilots of the laboratory.
>
> The maximum speed of this type airplane as in use at Langley Field had been reported at 118 miles per hour. This was checked by making a series of level runs with a Curtiss AT-5A airplane at low altitude over the water at full power. The maximum speed was found to be 118 miles per hour at 1,900 R.P.M., both air speed and R.P.M. being measured on calibrated instruments. Similar high speed runs made with the modified AT-5A showed a performance of 137 miles per hour at 1,900 R.P.M, increase of 19 miles per hour. The original speed of 118 miles per hour was attained at 1,720 R.P.M. on the modified airplane.
>
> While the type of cowling as normally installed on an AT-5 is not particularly adaptable to speed, the increase is considered remarkable. Furthermore, the improvement of flying qualities in smoothness of operation was also very favorably commented upon by all pilots who have flown it. The air flow over the fuselage and over the tail surfaces is very obviously improved.
>
> The cooling of the engine was found to be normal in these tests. The oil temperature reached 58° and was fairly constant, and there was no other indication of overheating. Likewise, there was no interference to the pilot's vision in any useful field.

Given the data, the aircraft industry was quick to adopt the NACA cowling, and the expense of the conversion was almost trivial; NACA estimated that it would cost about $25 to build and install a cowling on an existing aircraft. The Lockheed Vega was the first production-line airplane to use the NACA cowling. The Vega first flew in 1927, with its cylinders exposed to the airflow, as was conventional at that time. In 1929, with the NACA cowling added, the maximum speed of the Vega was increased from 165 miles per hour to 190 miles per hour. The cowling-equipped Vega (Figure 6.19) became one of the most famous airplanes of the early 1930s, used by pilots such as Wiley Post and Amelia Earhart. With its cowling and aerodynamically streamlined wheel pants, its zero-lift drag coefficient was 0.0278, quite low for that day.

In 1929 the NACA cowling won the Collier Trophy, an annual award commemorating the most important achievement in American aviation. It would be the first of many Colliers to be won by NACA and NASA in years to come.

After the initial euphoria of 1928 and 1929, the NACA cowling research program settled down to a series of tests intended to further improve the design and, perhaps, to provide an understanding of why the cowling worked the way it did. That latter concern was particularly important because the cowling program had been and continued to be totally empirical. It may have been a bit of an embarrassment that there was no fundamental understanding of the detailed aerodynamic processes involved, particularly in regard to the internal flow used to cool the engine.

FIGURE 6.19
Lockheed Vega with the
NACA Cowling.

In April 1929, Weick left Langley to take a job with the Hamilton Aero
Manufacturing Company (part of the United Aircraft companies) in Milwaukee,
Wisconsin, to design propellers. Donald H. Wood, his colleague and assistant from
the start of the PRT program, took charge of the wind tunnel and the NACA
cowling research program. For the next few years, Wood faced a posteuphoria
period of cowling tests, during which questions were raised about the propriety of
the NACA claims. Worse yet, additional testing led more to confusion than
understanding of the fundamental aerodynamics of the cowling.

The propriety question stemmed
from work carried out at the National Physical Laboratory in England by
Hubert C. Townend, beginning in 1927.
Townend developed a ring with an airfoil cross section that wrapped around
the outside of the exposed cylinders of a
radial engine for the purpose of reducing
drag. His work was published in 1929 by
the British Aeronautical Research Council, a few months before publication of
Weick's report. Neither man was aware
of the work by the other. Because the "Townend ring" left the cylinders more or
less exposed, it did not interfere with cooling, which was reassuring to airplane
designers at the time. As a result, a number of airplanes designed in the early 1930s
used Townend rings rather than the NACA cowling. Boeing particularly favored
the ring, using it on several fighter and bomber designs of the period; the
three-view of the 1932 Boeing P-26A single-seat fighter in Figure 6.20 clearly
shows the Townend ring. To assess the competition, Wood compared the
aerodynamic performances of the Townend ring and the NACA cowling in the

The Lockheed 5-C Vega,
1929. One of the first
commercially built
airplanes to use the NACA
cowling, the Vega's
internal structure and outer
skin were made from
wood. (Harold Andrews
Collection.)

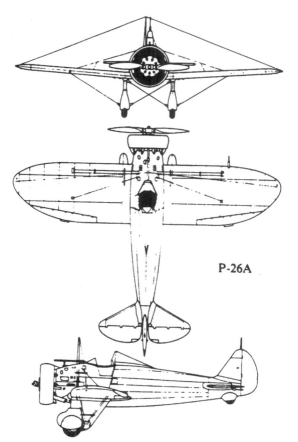

FIGURE 6.20
Boeing P-26 with the
Townend ring.

The Boeing P-26C, 1935.
The P-26 was based on a
design started in 1931.
Although it was the U.S.
Army's first all-metal
monoplane fighter, it
carried over the old open
cockpit and fixed landing
gear features. It continued
Boeing's use of the
Townend ring, although by
1935 the NACA cowling
made the Townend ring
obsolete. (American
Aviation Historical
Society, AAHS, from
John Stewart.)

PRT. The ring produced a considerably larger drag and was clearly inferior to the
NACA cowling. On the strength of those data, George Lewis at NACA
Headquarters in Washington, D.C., convinced Glenn Martin to replace the
Townend ring on the Martin B-10 bomber with the NACA cowling. Equipped with
the NACA cowling, the B-10's maximum speed increased from 195 miles per hour
to 225 miles per hour; also, its landing speed was significantly reduced. As a result,
in 1933 and 1934 the U.S. Army bought more than 100 B-10s, which kept the
Martin Company solvent during the worst of the depression. Martin's use of the

NACA cowling may have been why Martin won the U.S. Army contact over the Boeing B-9, which used Townend rings.

A less well known byproduct of the NACA cowling research program, but of almost as much importance for aircraft with wing-mounted engines, was its study of the proper placements for engine nacelles on a wing. Shortly after Weick's initial tests of the NACA cowling, and as a complement to those tests, Wood performed a series of parametric studies of nacelle placement. Using the PRT, Wood examined 21 possible positions for a nacelle on a thick wing (Figure 6.21). As in the tests of the Townend ring, a 4/9-scale model of the Wright J-5 radial engine was installed in a nacelle with the NACA cowling. The crosses in Figure 6.21 indicate the different positions of the propeller hub during the tests. From his experimental data, Wood reached the following conclusions:

Martin B-10B bomber, 1935. By far the most technically advanced U.S. Army bomber at the time, the Martin B-10B reflected all the features of the design revolution in the 1930s. When it was first introduced, it was faster than the Army's fighters of that day. (American Aviation Historical Society, AAHS, from Richard Koethoff.)

> Taking into account the lift, interference, and propulsive efficiency, the best location of the nacelle, with tractor propeller on a monoplane wing, for high speed and cruising, is with the thrust axis in line with the center of the wing and with the propeller about 25 percent of the chord ahead of the leading edge. This same location also appears to be the best in climb and landing, therefore excels in all conditions of flight.

In Figure 6.21, the best location was found to be point B. The engine locations for airplanes such as the Douglas DC-3, Boeing B-17, and Consolidated B-24 were derived from Wood's data obtained in 1932.

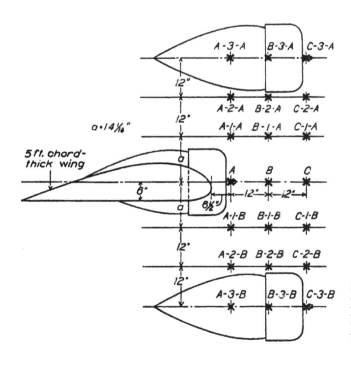

FIGURE 6.21
Different engine nacelle locations on a wing, as tested by NACA in 1932.

In the posteuphoria period, the NACA cowling program continued its experimental testing using the parameter-variation method that had been initiated Weick in 1928, but the euphoria occasioned by the early experiments faded over the next seven years of testing. Weick had been lucky in choosing his test conditions and parameters, which were very favorable for highlighting the advantages of the NACA cowling. Essentially, Weick had skimmed the cream off the top. As time went on, new data gathered over a wider range of parameters yielded mixed findings. For example, when the NACA cowling was tested on a Fokker trimotor with its wing engines mounted below the wings, virtually no improvement in performance was achieved. It was quickly recognized that the configuration of the airplane downstream of the cowling had some effect on the drag. It had been fortuitous that NACA had chosen a Curtiss AT-5A for the first series of flight tests with the cowling, for which the findings were spectacular, as discussed earlier. All of the experimental data on the cowling generated by NACA during the period 1928–1935, however, were obtained without a fundamental understanding of the aerodynamics of the cowling. Of course, such a situation was common in aerodynamics, even at that time. We have seen that the early researchers such as Lilienthal, Langley, the Wright brothers, and Eiffel amassed large bodies of useful aerodynamic data and effectively applied them, without ever understanding the fundamental aerodynamic principles involved. However, a hallmark of the empirical advances in aerodynamics during the era of the mature propeller-driven airplane was that they were accompanied by an increasing degree of understanding of the basic principles involved. The NACA cowling program was not meeting that standard. The noted aeronautical historian James Hansen described that period of cowling research as a time of "paralyzing confusion" leading to an "experimental impasse."

That situation was soon to change. For its first eight years, the cowling program had been run by engineers who were pure experimentalists. That worked well in the beginning, because the initial state of streamlining was so abysmal that even approximate solutions from applied aerodynamics led to great improvements, and the wind tunnel and actual flight testing were the most readily available tools with which to attack the problem. But in the summer of 1935, Henry Reid, Langley's "Engineer in Charge" (the title formerly held by the director of Langley), transferred most of the responsibility for cowling research to Theodore Theodorsen, the most respected theoretician in NACA at that time. Theodorsen had been born in Norway in 1897. He earned an engineering degree from the Norwegian Institute of Technology at Trondheim in 1922 and received his Ph.D. in physics from Johns Hopkins University in 1929, joining NACA Langley Memorial Laboratory as an associate physicist that same year. Theodorsen soon became head of the Physical Research Division, the smallest of the three research divisions at Langley at that time, the others being Engine Research and Aerodynamics. He quickly made his mark in a variety of research areas—airfoil theory, propeller theory, icing problems, wind-tunnel theory, aircraft flutter, and aircraft noise, to name only a few. Theodorsen believed in a balance between theoretical and experimental research. In 1931 he wrote,

> A science can develop a purely empirical basis for only a certain time. Theory is a process of systematic arrangement and simplification of known facts. As long as the facts are few and obvious no theory is necessary, but when they become many and less

simple theory is needed. Although the experimentation itself may require little effort, it is, however, often exceedingly difficult to analyze the results of even simple experiments. There exists, therefore, always a tendency to produce more test results than can be digested by theory or applied by industry.

By 1935 NACA leadership at Langley had decided that Theodorsen's approach was just what was needed to correct the problems in cowling research, and he was given responsibility for the cowling research program and free rein to use the PRT to delve further into the aerodynamic fundamentals underlying the empirically successful cowlings.

Theodorsen was liked and respected by most of the people who worked for him. Much later, in 1992, I. Edward Garick, a talented mathematician who worked closely with Theodorsen in the 1930s and 1940s, commented on Theodorsen's style:

> When a problem captured his attention, he would work on it during relatively short periods of intense concentrated activity, almost incommunicado, followed by periods of apparent desultory inactivity. Often, some of us would walk with him among the trees and orchards then still existing at Langley, and he would discuss foibles of mankind. As head of a division, he had the major virtue, now rare, of protecting his staff from routine and time-draining demands of government, allowing a person to develop his own talents and resources. When one had a finished or semifinished product, Theodorsen would then be a helpful though severe critic.

When Theodorsen took charge of the cowling research program in 1935, it entered its third and final phase, with the aim of achieving fundamental understanding of the aerodynamics of cowlings. Whereas Fred Weick's reports on the NACA cowlings in 1928–1929 had been devoid of analysis and contained no equations, by 1937 Theodorsen had studied the aerodynamic details of the internal and external flows through and over the cowling and had developed an approximate engineering analysis for the aerodynamic processes. On January 26, 1938, he presented a paper at the sixth annual meeting of the Institute of Aeronautical Sciences (IAS) in New York, in which he discussed the latest NACA findings—the first rational analysis of the aerodynamics of cowlings. That analysis focused on the balance between the internal airflow that would effectively cool the engine and yet would keep drag (called "cooling drag") to a minimum, and it examined the nature of the external flow and how it could be directed to achieve minimum form drag. His presentation was an excellent example of engineering analysis—making appropriate assumptions that would be adequate for engineering design.

The Lockheed Vega flown by Amelia Earhart, on display at the National Air and Space Museum, Smithsonian Institution.

NACA was quick to package the new analysis and data into a form useful to airplane designers. George Stickle, author of the resulting NACA Technical Report, wrote the following in 1939:

Inasmuch as the designer of an airplane has neither the time nor the opportunity to acquire a detailed knowledge of every part of the airplane, he wants a simple method of obtaining the optimum cowling dimensions and, perhaps, some of the more important reasons for selecting these dimensions. It is the purpose of this report to present such a method and to illustrate the method with a discussion of practical examples.

That report went on to present design-oriented calculations based on Theodorsen's analysis, treating the geometric design of proper cowlings for given flight conditions and emphasizing how cooling drag and external form drag could be minimized. With that report, the NACA cowling research program reached its high point. Eleven years after Fred Weick's initial breakthrough in empirical design, a better theoretical understanding of the aerodynamics of cowlings had finally become an integral part of the state of the art in aeronautics and was having a major impact on the design of airplanes.

Systematic Progress—Airfoil Aerodynamics

Picking up the thread of airfoil design from Chapter 5, we recall that the airfoil shape of choice during the era of the strut-and-wire biplanes was usually a thin profile, although Junkers and Fokker in Germany were using thick airfoils on practical airplanes by the end of World War I. Aeronautical engineers in England and the United States, originally slow to pick up on the aerodynamic and structural advantages of thick airfoils, by the mid-1920s were beginning to make the conversion. A historical sequence of airfoil shapes is shown in Figure 6.22, which first appeared in a 1941 aerodynamics text book *Aerodynamics of the Airplane* by the noted Cal Tech professor Clark B. Millikan. In Figure 6.22, you can see the chronological progression of various airfoil shapes, each well known in its day. Clearly, starting with the Clark Y and M-6 airfoils in the United States and the RAF 34 airfoil in England, the pioneering German work on thick airfoils was finally gaining some appreciation outside of Germany.

Of particular note was the Clark Y airfoil, shown in Figure 6.22. This airfoil was the most popular of a series of airfoils designed in the 1920s by Virginius Clark, a flamboyant, leading figure in the formative years of aviation in the United States. A distinguished graduate of the Naval Academy in 1907, Clark learned to fly at San Diego, California, while still in the U.S. Navy. Before World War I, he transferred to the U.S. Army's Aviation Section and was sent to the Massachusetts Institute of Technology for courses in aeronautical engineering. During World War I, Clark served in Washington, D.C., and later became the commander of the Army's McCook Field in Dayton, Ohio, the Army's

A close-up of the Lockheed Vega at the National Air and Space Museum, Smithsonian Institution, highlighting the NACA cowling.

major aeronautical research center, rising to the rank of colonel. He designed the Clark Y airfoil in 1922, initially for use as an airfoil section for propellers. It gradually gained acceptance, however, for use as a wing section because wind-tunnel tests showed it to have a relatively high maximum lift coefficient and low drag. The prestigious magazine *Aviation* wrote on October 17, 1927, "Most of the successful airplanes in the United States use airfoils designed by Colonel Clark." This included Charles Lindbergh's Spirit of St. Louis designed by Ryan.

Seversky P-35, 1935. This airplane was the first U.S. Army fighter to reflect all the aspects of the design revolution of the 1930s. It had an enclosed cockpit, NACA cowling, constant-speed propeller, retractable landing gear, wing flaps, and streamlining. (American Aviation Historical Society, AAHS, from Roger F. Besecker.)

The Clark Y airfoil, however, was a perfect example of the ad hoc way in which airfoils were being designed, even by the late 1920s. In a published interview with *Aviation* magazine in October 1927, Colonel Clark was asked, "How do you go about designing these airfoils of yours? What is the secret?" Virginius Clark laughed and replied, "I would gladly tell you the secret if I knew of any. The airfoil sections just seem to lay themselves out and, when good luck attends, fair results are obtained." He went on to elaborate:

> My airfoils have been selected for various airplanes because comparative tests made in wind tunnels at a low value of the Reynolds numbers have indicated that they are fairly good. But, you know, the tests made by our National Advisory Committee for Aeronautics in their variable pressure tunnel at Langley Field prove, if we are to accept them, that even for the purpose of comparison, tests made at a low value of Reynolds number are useless and misleading in many ways. Airfoil A may appear far superior to Airfoil B for a particular purpose when tested with a pressure of one atmosphere, whereas when tested at twenty atmospheres, Airfoil B appears to be much better than Airfoil A for the same purpose.

Here, Clark is referring to the Variable Density Tunnel at Langley, where the test section was pressurized to 20 atmospheres, allowing airfoil testing at a Reynolds

Designation	Date	Diagram	Designation	Date	Diagram
Wright	1908		Göttingen 387	1919	
Bleriot	1909		Clark Y	1922	
R.A.F. 6	1912		M-6	1926	
R.A.F. 15	1915		R.A.F. 34	1926	
U.S.A. 27	1919		N.A.C.A. 2412	1933	
Joukowsky (Göttingen 430)	1912		N.A.C.A. 23012	1935	
Göttingen 398	1919		N.A.C.A. 23021	1935	

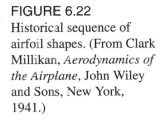

FIGURE 6.22
Historical sequence of airfoil shapes. (From Clark Millikan, *Aerodynamics of the Airplane*, John Wiley and Sons, New York, 1941.)

Beech 17 Staggerwing, 1932. Called the "Staggerwing" because its top wing was located *behind* the bottom wing, a rarely used design feature, the airplane contained some features of the design revolution, such as an enclosed cockpit and a NACA cowling. (American Aviation Historical Society, AAHS, from John Stewart.)

number 20 times larger than the same model tested in a conventional wind tunnel with a test section pressure of one atmosphere. The Reynolds numbers obtained in the NACA Variable Density Tunnel were close to those encountered by a full-size airplane in actual flight through the air; hence, the data from the Variable Density Tunnel were considered to be much more applicable to actual flight conditions than the lower Reynolds number testing carried out in other, conventional wind tunnels. Clark, whose airfoils had been tested in conventional wind tunnels, went on to modestly say, "Therefore, it is fair to assume that there are many airfoils which would be more popular than mine if they had been tested with twenty atmospheres pressure." Clark noted that the NACA did not have the time or resources to test most of the multitude of new airfoils, including some of his own, in the Variable Density Tunnel. This led Clark to summarize the state of airfoil design in 1927 as follows:

> Hence if low scale tests (low Reynolds number) are not indicative of comparative merit, and since high scale tests (high Reynolds number) are unattainable, and as the mathematics have not yet been developed for the precise prediction of practical airfoil performance without supporting experimentation, it may be that we must, for a while forget about wind tunnels, for this particular purpose, and, as each new design problem arises, design an airfoil as we think it should be to best meet the requirements of the particular case—build our wings accordingly, and hope for the best in full flight results.

Hope for the best! That was the situation with airfoil design in 1927. It was a situation not very becoming to aeronautical engineers of that day. But the situation was about to change dramatically in the early 1930s, primarily because of the work of Eastman Jacobs on the experimental side, Theodore Theodorsen on the theoretical side, and the Langley Variable Density Tunnel.

Eastman N. Jacobs joined NACA Langley Memorial Aeronautical Laboratory in 1925, one year after graduating with honors from the University of California at Berkeley. He was soon recognized as an outstanding addition to the Langley staff, often taking innovative approaches to challenging problems. Assigned to the Variable Density Tunnel, Jacobs played an important role in the early aerodynamic research at high Reynolds numbers. By the time of the NACA experimental airfoil program in the early 1930s, Jacobs had become head of the Variable Density Tunnel section, a position he held for the next decade.

From April 1931 to February 1932 Jacobs and his colleagues carried out a series of airfoil measurements that provided a standard for the era of the mature propeller-driven airplane. Jacobs used a systematic approach to obtain what was to become the family of NACA "four-digit" airfoils. The scheme was simplicity itself. Construct a single curved line, called the mean camber line, and wrap a mathematically defined thickness distribution around the camber line. Writing in NACA Technical Report 450 in 1933, Jacobs noted,

The major shape variables then become two, the thickness form and the mean-line form. The thickness form is of particular importance from a structural standpoint. On the other hand, the form of the [mean line] determines almost independently some of the most important aerodynamic properties of the airfoil section, e.g., the angle of zero lift and the pitching-moment characteristics.

The thickness distribution chosen by the NACA was patterned after that of "well-known airfoils of a certain class including the Göttingen 398 and the Clark Y." This thickness distribution is shown in Figure 6.23. Airfoils of different thickness-to-chord ratios were obtained simply by multiplying the thickness distribution by a constant factor. When the prescribed thickness distribution was wrapped around the prescribed mean camber line, the resulting airfoil shape was as shown in Figure 6.24. The family of airfoils designed by NACA in 1931 using that simple technique was the famous NACA four-digit series of airfoils, shown in Figure 6.25. Here, the first digit gave the maximum camber in hundredths of the chord length, the second digit gave the location of the in tenths of the chord length maximum camber measured from the leading edge, and the last two digits gave the maximum thickness of the airfoil in hundredths of the chord length. For example, the NACA 2412 had a maximum camber of 0.02 of the chord length, located at 0.4 of the chord length from the leading edge, with a maximum thickness of 0.12 of the chord length. The lift, drag, and moment coefficients for that entire family of airfoils were carefully measured in the Variable Density Tunnel at Langley. The models used in the wind tunnel were finite rectangular wings with the aspect ratio of 6, and the data were modified and plotted for an infinite aspect ratio using the

appropriate formulas from Prandtl's lifting-line theory, to be discussed shortly. Because the measurements were made in the Variable Density Tunnel, the Reynolds numbers were on the order of 3 million, well within the range encountered in practical flight at that time.

The airfoil data from those studies were used by aircraft manufacturers in the United States, Europe, and Japan during the 1930s. The combination of Jacobs's engineering talent, the rational simplicity of the NACA design process, and the high Reynolds number conditions of the Variable Density Tunnel had finally produced a useful database on the aerodynamic properties of airfoils—a classic, a designer's bible. That contribution to applied aerodynamics in the early 1930s was a major step toward the development of mature propeller-driven airplanes.

Concurrent with Jacobs's experimental work on airfoils, a major theoretical advance in the calculation of airfoil properties was reported by Theodore Theodorsen. As discussed earlier, Theodorsen, educated in the European tradition, an engineer with a strong background in advanced mathematics, brought a large dose of theory to counterbalance the massive experimental emphasis at NACA during the 1930s. Considered the best theoretical aerodynamicist in the United States at the time, Theodorsen was responsible for a major advance in airfoil

Grumman F3F-1, 1935. The Grumman F3F was the U.S. Navy's last biplane fighter. The F3F-1 reflected all of the design features of the design revolution, except it was a biplane rather than a monoplane. (American Aviation Historical Society, AAHS, from P. W. Black.)

design. In 1931, Theodorsen published the first general analysis for airfoils of any arbitrary shape and thickness, and he took that opportunity to criticize the fact that the major emphasis in airfoil design at that time was on empirical experimentation. He wrote,

> Investigations are carried on with little regard for the theory and much testing of airfoils is done with insufficient knowledge of the ultimate possibilities. This state of affairs is due largely to the very common belief that the theory of the actual airfoil necessarily would be approximate, clumsy, and awkward, and therefore useless for nearly all purposes.

Theodorsen's efforts went a long way toward correcting the imbalance between the experimental and theoretical approaches to airfoil design. His work was based on the mathematical theory of complex variables, which had been used by others before him to tackle the problem of airfoil analysis. These earlier analyses, however, were limited in some respect or another to special shapes, or to airfoils that were thin at small angles of attack. Theodorsen's new method eliminated those restrictions; it was the first theoretical analysis for airfoils of any arbitrary shape and thickness at any angle of attack, and it proved to be the most important advance in airfoil theory during the age of the mature propeller-driven airplane.

Despite the importance of Theodorsen's new method, the problem of theoretical calculation of airfoil properties was far from being solved. A case in point involves the comparisons between experimental and theoretical pressure distributions over the surface of an airfoil presented by Theodorsen in 1932. Figure 6.26 shows the variation of the pressure coefficient over the top and bottom surfaces of a Clark Y airfoil at an angle of attack of 5.3 degrees. On this graph, *decreasing* pressures are plotted in the *upward* direction, and negative values of the pressure coefficient mean that the pressure is below the freestream pressure; as the pressure coefficient becomes more negative, the pressure itself is dropping more and more below the freestream value. Also, the top curves pertain

Boeing 307 Stratoliner, 1939. The Stratoliner was the first pressurized passenger aircraft. With the advent of World War II, the development of the Stratoliner was put on hold, and the airplane was overtaken by later advanced transport designs. Only 10 were built before the war broke out. (American Aviation Historical Society, AAHS, from J. Richard Dubois.)

to the upper surface of the airfoil and the bottom curves to the lower surface. The solid curve shows Theodorsen's calculations, and the dashed curve plots experimental data from the Variable Density Tunnel. Note that the theoretical results do not fall on top of the experimental results—there is still a lack of agreement between theory and experiment. Nevertheless, Theodorsen's method allowed the calculation of pressure distributions and lift and moment coefficients for airfoils of arbitrary shape and thickness, and those calculations usually were within 10 percent of the measured values—a tremendous accomplishment in the early 1930s.

Theodorsen's reaction to such comparisons between his theory and the experimental data was to suggest, almost heretically, that the accuracy of the *experimental* data should be reexamined. His only comment about one such comparison with experimental data was a single sentence: "The experimental values are from original data sheets for the N.A.C.A. Technical Report No. 353,

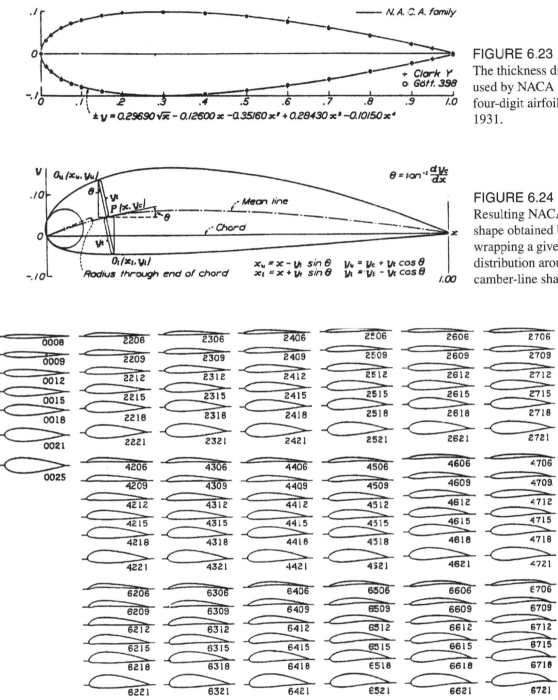

FIGURE 6.23
The thickness distribution used by NACA for the four-digit airfoil series, 1931.

FIGURE 6.24
Resulting NACA airfoil shape obtained by wrapping a given thickness distribution around a given camber-line shape, 1931.

FIGURE 6.25
Family of NACA four-digit airfoils, 1931.

and are not entirely consistent due to difficulties experienced in these experiments." Given the importance of Theodorsen's work and his background in mathematics, the fact that virtually no effort was made to explain the discrepancies between theory and experiment, no matter how slight, is very curious. On the basis of the author's experience with theoreticians and experimentalists over the past 44 years, the guess is that a lot more was being said behind the scenes, but that the normal NACA conservatism, especially during the editorial process for NACA

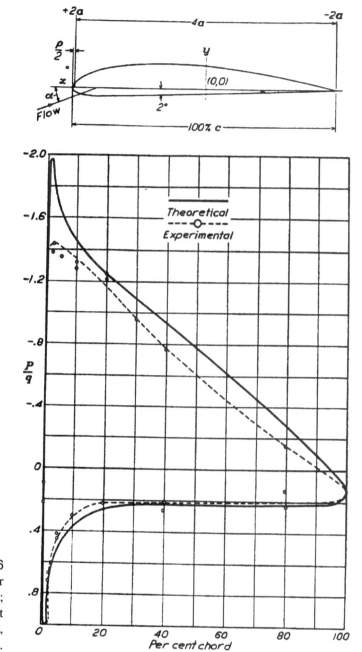

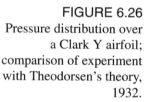

FIGURE 6.26
Pressure distribution over
a Clark Y airfoil;
comparison of experiment
with Theodorsen's theory,
1932.

technical reports, was a very strong filter. Keep in mind that the experimental data
were being produced by Eastman Jacobs and his colleagues in the Variable Density
Tunnel. By that time, Jacobs was the leading experimentalist in NACA, and
Theodorsen was the leading theoretician in NACA, and there was no love lost
between them. In 1987, the aeronautical historian James Hansen wrote,

> Beneath the basic difference in their approaches to gaining aeronautical knowledge,
> there existed a strong personal rivalry and mutual dislike that moved most of their
> confrontations beyond more objective disagreement. At Langley both men controlled

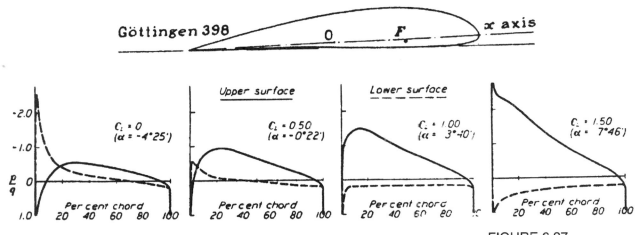

FIGURE 6.27
Theoretical pressure distributions over a Göttingen 398 airfoil; calculations by Garrick using Theodorsen's theory, 1933.

fiefdoms, and because both men were so valuable to the NACA, George Lewis (director of research at NACA Headquarters in Washington) had permitted the feudal arrangement to flourish.

Jacobs joined NACA in 1925, and Theodorsen arrived in 1929. Within two years after his arrival, Theodorsen had published his airfoil theory and had made known his views that too many experiments were being conducted with too little regard for theory. Clearly, the Jacobs–Theodorsen enmity had early roots, and the fact that there was virtually no discussion of the discrepancy between experiment and theory in cases such as that shown in Figure 6.26 suggests that their hostility, filtered by the NACA editorial process, was the reason why.

Theodorsen's airfoil theory was accorded almost instant respect. Within a year, the U.S. Navy's Bureau of Aeronautics asked NACA to carry out a series of calculations of the pressure distributions on airfoils for use in determining the structural loads on wings. Edward Garrick applied Theodorsen's theory to calculate the pressure distributions and lift coefficients for 20 different airfoils, ranging from the earlier U.S.A. 27 and Göttingen 398 airfoils to the most recent NACA four-digit series. The production-line nature of Garrick's calculations is typified in Figure 6.27, which shows his pressure distribution findings for the Göttingen 398 airfoil at four different angles of attack. Garrick's prolific calculations were reminiscent of the earlier NACA compilations of empirical airfoil data in the 1920s and the contemporary experiments on the NACA four-digit series of airfoils by Jacobs. Finally the overwhelming tendency for airfoil data to be determined experimentally was being redressed.

Jacobs continued to design and develop improved airfoil shapes through the 1930s. The second popular NACA series was the five-digit series of airfoils, developed by Jacobs in 1935—a family of related airfoils having the position of maximum camber unusually far forward, within 5–15 percent of the chord length from the leading edge. Exhaustive tests were carried out in the Variable Density Tunnel, with the amount and location of the camber and the thickness ratio being systematically varied. With the forward location of the maximum camber, those new airfoils had higher maximum lift coefficients and lower pitching moments than the NACA four-digit series—attributes that were appealing to aircraft designers. Jacobs found that the best airfoil in that series was the NACA 23012

FIGURE 6.28
The NACA 23012 airfoil,
1935.

airfoil (Figure 6.28); note the mean camber line, with maximum camber near the leading edge. Although the 5-digit airfoils had larger maximum lift coefficients than the previous airfoils, the decrease in lift at the point of stall was abrupt and dramatic. That was a distinct disadvantage compared with the earlier four-digit series, which had smoother and more gradual decreases in lift at the point of stall. Nevertheless, NACA five-digit airfoils were widely used by the aircraft industry. For example, the Douglas DC-4, a four-engine transport that saw service in World War II as the C-54 and was a mainstay of airlines in the United States immediately after the war, used a NACA 23012 airfoil section.

The final chapter in airfoil research and design in the era of propeller-driven airplanes was also written by Jacobs—the development of the *laminar-flow airfoil*. The impetus for that work can be traced back to Melvill Jones's paper on the ideal airplane, one in which perfect streamlining would eliminate pressure drag due to flow separation, leaving only induced drag and skin-friction drag to be dealt with by the designers. During the 1930s the progress in streamlining was such that airplanes began to approach Jones's ideal, and aerodynamicists then began to turn their attention to reduction of skin-friction drag. That was what motivated Jacobs to begin thinking in terms of the laminar-flow airfoil. It was well known that the skin-friction drag in a laminar flow was less (often considerably less) than that in a turbulent flow. Unfortunately, nature prefers turbulent flows, and therefore, it is extremely difficult (sometimes impossible) to maintain a laminar flow over a surface.

In late 1935, Jacobs visited the major European aeronautical laboratories and spent some time at Cambridge University, where he had conversations with Geoffrey I. Taylor and Melvill Jones, England's leading fluid dynamicist and aerodynamicist, respectively. Their attention was focused on the boundary layer, that thin region of flow adjacent to a solid surface where friction was dominant. Taylor and Jones shared with Jacobs some of their preliminary findings that a laminar boundary layer would remain laminar if the surface pressure continued to decrease in the flow direction (a favorable pressure gradient) and that a transition to turbulent flow would occur at about the location where the pressure began to increase in the flow direction (an adverse pressure gradient). Jones showed Jacobs his findings from actual flight experiments in which large regions of laminar flow over a wing were observed in areas where there were favorable pressure gradients. Jacobs returned to the United States convinced that airfoils could be designed to maintain laminar flow simply by shaping them to have large running lengths of decreasing pressure along the surface. It was a nice idea, but it would be difficult to implement. At that time, the recent advances in airfoil theory had been oriented toward calculating the pressure distribution for a given airfoil shape. Jacobs needed to turn that theory inside out and design an airfoil for a given pressure distribution. By background and nature, Jacobs, an experimentalist, would not appear the ideal person to take on that theoretical challenge. One of his colleagues and close friends at Langley, Robert T. Jones, who later would be recognized as NACA's leading theoretician in the postwar period, said that Jacobs, "one of the most skillful and innovative American aerodynamicists, had a wide appreciation of science but did not devote much time to theoretical studies. Rather, he used his theoretical understanding to devise intelligent experiments." Nevertheless, Jacobs ultimately took on that theoretical challenge. He turned to Theodorsen's 1931 airfoil theory and began to examine how it could be reversed to design an airfoil shape from a given pressure distribution. He received no help from Theodorsen, who was quite negative about the whole idea. Later, one of Jacobs's engineers in the Variable Density Tunnel, Ira Abbott, stated, "we were told that even the statement of the problem was mathematical nonsense with the implication that it was only our ignorance that encourages us." Much later, James Hansen wrote, "encouraged now by hearing this negative peer response, Jacobs stubbornly persisted in directing an all-out effort to devise a satisfactory inversion of the Theodorsen method." The Jacobs–Theodorsen enmity was surfacing again.

Jacobs, becoming the theoretician by necessity, in the peace and quiet of his home, studied Theodorsen's theory carefully for a few days. Finally, he managed to modify the theory to allow the design of airfoil shapes with large regions of favorable pressure gradients. From that he designed a completely new family of NACA airfoils, the laminar-flow airfoils. Figure 6.29a shows the shape of the standard NACA 0012 airfoil and its surface pressure distribution at a zero angle of attack. Note that the favorable pressure gradient (decreasing pressure) would exist only over the most forward portion of the airfoil; over the remaining 90 percent of the airfoil, there would be an adverse pressure gradient (increasing pressure). For that airfoil, the transition to turbulent flow would occur near the leading edge, and virtually the entire remaining airfoil surface would experience a turbulent boundary layer, with its attendant high skin-friction drag. In contrast, Figure 6.29b shows the shape of a NACA laminar-flow airfoil, the NACA 66-012, and its surface pressure distribution at a zero angle of attack. Note that the favorable pressure gradient would exist over more than 60 percent of the airfoil surface. That would encourage laminar flow over at least the first 60 percent of the airfoil surface—a dramatic change compared with the NACA 0012 airfoil. Both of these airfoils were symmetric airfoils with 12 percent thickness, but their shapes were completely different, the laminar-flow airfoil having its maximum thickness much farther back from the leading edge than the conventional airfoil.

From one perspective, Jacobs's persistence with the concept of the laminar-flow airfoil yielded a great success. Wind-tunnel tests showed a considerable decrease in drag for the new airfoils, and the excitement within NACA was much like that generated by the NACA cowling in 1928. But in 1938, with war clouds on the horizon, security restrictions prevented NACA from going totally public with Jacobs's important new findings. Nevertheless, some of that excitement was evident in the 1939 annual report of NACA, in the following cryptic statement having to do with experiments in the new low-turbulence wind tunnel at Langley: "These preliminary investigations were started by the development of new airfoil forms that, when tested in the new equipment, immediately gave drag coefficients of one-third to one-half the values obtained for conventional sections." The actual data on the laminar-flow airfoils were not publicly released until after the war, but it was clear from the wind-tunnel data that

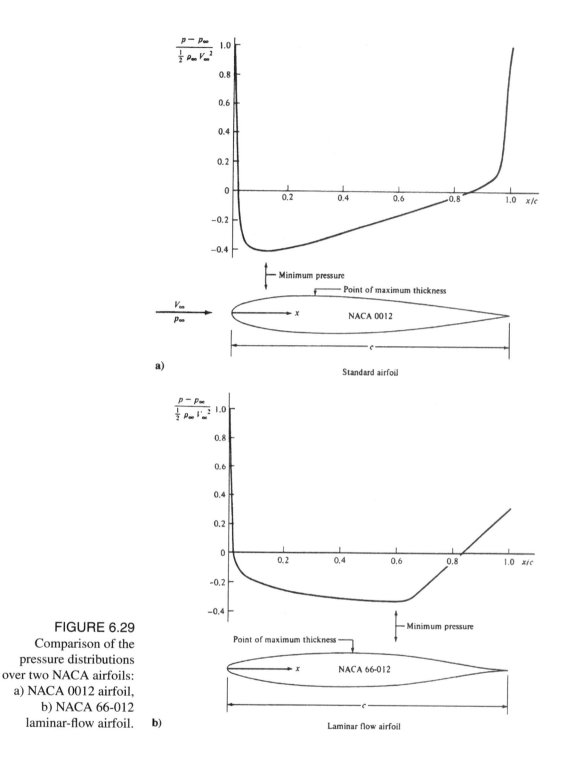

FIGURE 6.29
Comparison of the
pressure distributions
over two NACA airfoils:
a) NACA 0012 airfoil,
b) NACA 66-012
laminar-flow airfoil.

the laminar-flow airfoils worked, at least in the laboratory, and those findings were
quickly put to use by North American Aircraft in the design of the P-51 Mustang
wing, the first airplane to use NACA's laminar-flow airfoil.

But from another perspective, that of the real world of airplane manufacture
and operation, the laminar-flow airfoils did not work. The NACA wind-tunnel
models were like finely polished jewels with very smooth surfaces. Real airplanes

were not. The realities of manufacturing introduced surface roughness and nonuniformities. When used in the field, bug splatters and other foreign-object impacts added to the surface roughness. The net result was that such surface roughness, which led to turbulent flow, won out over the effect of the favorable pressure gradients. In the field, the NACA laminar-flow airfoils experienced almost totally turbulent flow, like any other standard airfoil.

But from a final perspective, the NACA laminar-flow airfoils would enjoy success. Those airfoil shapes with the maximum thickness far back from the leading edge, and with the resulting large regions of favorable pressure gradients, were found to have excellent *high-speed* characteristics; they had higher critical Mach numbers than conventional airfoils. (High-speed effects will be discussed in Chapter 7.) That was almost a fluke—one of those rare instances in the history of technology in which a system becomes a success because it unexpectedly excels at something for which it was not originally designed. The most successful of the NACA laminar-flow airfoils was the "six series," of which the airfoil in Figure 6.29b is an example. Because of their desirable high-speed characteristics, the NACA six-series laminar-flow airfoils were used on almost all high-speed airplanes in the 1940s and 1950s and are still in use today. (However, most aircraft manufacturers now have sophisticated computer programs to design their airfoil shapes for their own purposes, which in a sense is a return to the custom-made product and the ad hoc approach of the early 20th century, but certainly no longer in ignorance.)

In the end, the development of the laminar-flow airfoil series was the crowning achievement from a decade of important airfoil research by NACA led by Eastman Jacobs. The decade of the 1930s brought an increased understanding of airfoil aerodynamics, the derivation of an airfoil theory for arbitrary shapes, and the compilation of a massive collection of substantive wind-tunnel data on airfoils—all substantial factors in the development of mature propeller-driven airplanes.

Aerodynamic Theory

The advances in airfoil theory that fed directly into improving airfoil design were but a small part of the overall advancement in aerodynamic theory that took place in the first three decades of the 20th century. This advancement did not pace advances in airplane design: Wings and whole airplanes were being designed, and airplanes were flying successfully, without benefit of precise scientific understanding. Indeed, the design revolution that brought about the era of the mature propeller-driven airplane was based primarily on empirical data, innovative thinking, and hard experience. On the other hand, the fact that airplanes *were* flying was a tremendous stimulus to academicians and researchers to figure out what was really going on—what physical laws governed the performance of these airplanes, and how could mathematics be used to calculate this performance from first principles? As a result, concurrent with the design revolution, aerodynamic theory experienced substantial advancements. Let us take a quick look.

The groundwork for the growth of aerodynamic theory was laid even before the era of the strut-and-wire biplane, starting with Russia's famous aerodynamicist, Nikolay Joukowski (Zhukovsky). Joukowski, head of the Department of Mechanics at Moscow University, visited Otto Lilienthal in Berlin in 1895. Very impressed with what he saw, Joukowski bought a glider from Lilienthal, one of only eight that

Lilienthal ever managed to sell to the public. Joukowski took this glider back to his colleagues and students in Moscow, put it on display, and vigorously examined it. *This is the first time that a university-educated mathematician and scientist, and especially one of some repute, had become closely connected with a real flying machine, literally getting his hands on such a machine.* Joukowski did not stop there. He was now motivated about flight—he had actually seen Lilienthal flying. The idea of getting up in the air was no longer so fanciful—it was real. With that, Joukowski turned his scholarly attention to the examination of the dynamics and aerodynamics of flight on a theoretical, mathematical basis. In particular, he directed his efforts toward the calculation of lift. He envisioned bound vortices fixed to the surface of the airfoil along with the resulting circulation that somehow must be related to the lifting action of the airfoil. A similar concept was advanced independently by the English engineer Frederick Lanchester, who published his thinking in 1907 in his book *Aerodynamics*. One year earlier, however, Joukowski published two notes, one in Russian and the other in French, in two rather obscure Russian journals. In these notes he derived and used the following relation for the calculation of lift for an airfoil:

$$L = \rho V \Gamma$$

where L is the lift, ρ is the air density, V is the velocity of the air relative to the airfoil, and Γ is the *circulation*, a technically defined quantity equal to the line integral of the flow velocity taken around any closed curve encompassing the airfoil. (Circulation has physical significance as well. The streamline flow over an airfoil can be visualized as the *superposition* of a uniform freestream flow and a circulatory flow; this circulatory flow component is the *circulation*. Figure 6.30 is a schematic illustrating the concept of circulation.) *With this equation, Joukowski revolutionized theoretical aerodynamics.* For the first time, it allowed the calculation of lift on an airfoil with mathematical exactness, as long as one could find the value of the circulation, which depends on the body shape, size, and angle of attack. This was, and still is, not an easy job. This equation has come down through the 20th century labeled as the *Kutta–Joukowski* Theorem. It is still taught today in university-level aerodynamics courses and is still used to calculate lift for airfoils in low-speed flows.

The label of this theorem is shared with the name of Wilhelm Kutta, who wrote a doctoral dissertation on the subject of aerodynamic lift in 1902 at the

FIGURE 6.30
A schematic of the idea of representing the flow over an airfoil as the superposition of a uniform flow and a circulatory flow, fundamental to the circulation theory of lift.

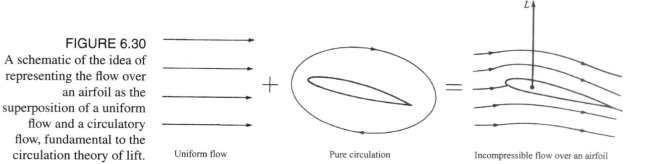

Uniform flow   Pure circulation   Incompressible flow over an airfoil

University of Munich, Germany. Like Joukowski, Kutta was motivated by the flying success of Lilienthal. In particular, Kutta knew that Lilienthal had used a cambered airfoil for his gliders and that when cambered airfoils were put at a zero angle of attack to the freestream, positive lift was still produced. This lift generation at zero angle of attack was counterintuitive to many mathematicians and scientists at that time, but experimental data unmistakenly showed it to be a fact. Such a mystery made the theoretical calculation of lift on a cambered airfoil an excellent research topic at the time—one that Kutta readily took on. By the time he finished his dissertation in 1902, Kutta made the first mathematical calculations of lift on cambered airfoils. Kutta's results were derived without recourse to the concept of circulation. Only after Joukowski published his equation in 1906 did Kutta show in hindsight that the essence of the equation was buried in his 1902 dissertation. For this reason, the equation bears the names of both men.

The Kutta–Joukowski Theorem became the quantitative basis for the *circulation theory of lift*. For the first time, some semblance of a mathematical and scientific *understanding* of the generation of lift was obtained. The development of the circulation theory of lift was the first major element of the evolution of aerodynamics in the 20th century, and it was in the realm of *science*. The objective of Kutta and Joukowski, both part of the academic community, was *understanding* the nature of lift and obtaining some quantitative ability to predict lift. Their work was not motivated, at least at first, by the desire to design a wing or airfoil. Indeed, by 1906 wings and airfoils had already been designed and were actually flying on piloted machines, and these designs were accomplished without benefit of science. The circulation theory of lift was created *after the fact*.

Twenty years later the circulation theory of lift was being used as a practical engineering tool for calculating lift and moments on airfoils. Max Munk, a German aerodynamicist and colleague of Ludwig Prandtl at Göttingen University, developed in the early 1920s a simplified airfoil theory applicable to thin airfoils at small angle of attack—a theory from which the lift is easily obtained. Munk immigrated to America shortly after World War I; NACA welcomed him with open arms. During the 1920s, working for NACA, Munk designed a series of airfoils, designated by the letter M. For example, the M-006 and M-012 airfoils were used on 39 different airplane designs during that period. (By comparison, the ubiquitous Clark Y airfoil, designed without the help of any theory, appeared on 176 different airplane designs during the same period. These numbers come from extensive research by Dr. Howard Wolko at the National Air and Space Museum.) In any event, Munk's thin airfoil theory laid the groundwork for Theodorsen to come along in 1931 and develop a generalized theory to calculate the lift and moments for airfoils of any shape at any angle of attack, as we have already discussed. With this, at the beginning of the era of the mature propeller-driven airplane, the circulation theory of lift finally become a direct engineering tool for use in the design of new airfoils.

The most important engineering result to come from the circulation theory of lift, however, was Prandtl's lifting-line theory for whole wings (not just airfoils). Developed during World War I, and polished in the years immediately after the war, the lifting-line theory allowed the direct calculation of lift and induced drag for finite wings. Dramatically, this theory explained physically why the *aspect ratio* of the wing had such a strong effect on both lift and induced drag, and moreover, it provided engineering formulas that allowed the direct calculation of the aspect ratio effects. For example, the induced drag coefficient $C_{D,i}$ is defined as

$$C_{D,i} = \frac{D_i}{\frac{1}{2}\rho_\infty V_\infty^2 S}$$

where D_i is the induced drag, ρ_∞ and V_∞ are the freestream density and velocity, respectively, and S is the planform (top view) area of the wing. In the same vein, the lift coefficient C_L is defined as

$$C_L = \frac{L}{\frac{1}{2}\rho_\infty V_\infty^2 S}$$

where L is the lift. Prandtl's lifting-line theory gives the following formula for $C_{D,i}$:

$$C_{D,i} = \frac{C_L^2}{\pi e AR}$$

where e is called the span efficiency factor (a number equal to, or usually less than, one), and AR is the aspect ratio of the wing, defined as $AR = b^2/S$, where b is the wing span. (When applied to a whole airplane, e in the preceding formula is the Oswald efficiency, named after Bailey Oswald, the Douglas aerodynamicist who worked on the DC-3.) The preceding formula shows the powerful effect of aspect ratio; for example, doubling the aspect ratio cuts the induced drag coefficient in half. With these formulas, the importance of high aspect ratio clearly comes into focus, and the effect of aspect ratio can actually be calculated. Similar formulas exist for the effect on lift coefficient, showing that an increase in aspect ratio results in a higher lift coefficient.

These results were a theoretical gold mine after World War I. The empiricism and confusion surrounding the effect of aspect ratio that prevailed in the earlier days of flight, as we have discussed in earlier chapters, were swept away by the fruits of Prandtl's lifting-line theory. Although several years were to pass before these results were known and appreciated by aeronautical engineers in England and the United States, by 1930 they were well accepted and were part of the theoretical tool box of all airplane designers. In terms of the maturity of theoretical aerodynamics, they were an integral part of the era of the mature propeller-driven airplane.

Contemporary with the advent of the circulation theory of lift was an equally if not more important intellectual breakthrough in the understanding and prediction of aerodynamic drag. The main concern about the prediction of lift on a body inclined at some angle to a flow surfaced in the 19th-century, beginning with George Cayley's concept of generating a sustained force on a fixed wing. In contrast, concern over drag goes all of the way back to ancient Greek science. The retarding force on a projectile hurtling through the air has been a major concern for millennia. Therefore, it is somewhat ironic that the breakthroughs in the theoretical prediction of both drag and lift came at almost precisely the same time, independent of how long the two problems had been investigated.

What allowed the breakthrough in drag was the origin of the concept of the boundary layer. In 1904, a young German engineer who had just accepted the

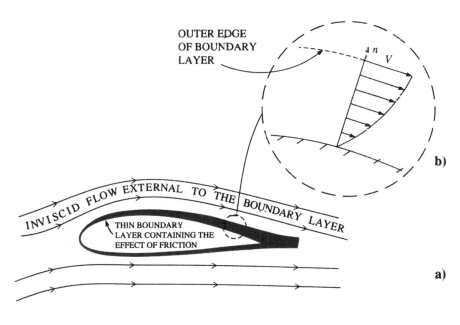

FIGURE 6.31
Sketch showing the boundary layer concept. a) The flow over a body is divided into two parts; the thin boundary layer adjacent to the surface, where the effects of friction are dominant, and a frictionless (inviscid) external flow outside of the boundary layer. b) Enlarged sketch of the boundary layer showing the variation in flow velocity across the boundary layer as a function of the normal distance, perpendicular to the surface.

position as professor of applied mechanics at Göttingen University, gave a paper at the Third International Mathematical Congress at Heidelberg, Germany, that was to revolutionize aerodynamics. Only eight pages long, it was to prove to be one of the most important fluid dynamics papers in history. In it, Prandtl described the following concept. He theorized that the effect of friction was to cause the fluid immediately adjacent to the surface to stick to the surface and that the effect of friction was felt only in the near vicinity of the surface, that is, within a thin region that he called the boundary layer. Outside the boundary layer, the flow was essentially uninfluenced by friction. It was the inviscid, potential flow that had been studied for the past two centuries. This conceptual division of the flow around a body into two regions, the thin viscous boundary layer adjacent to the body's surface and the inviscid, potential flow external to the boundary layer (as shown in Figure 6.31), suddenly made the theoretical analysis of the flow much more tractable. Prandtl explained how skin friction at the surface could be fundamentally understood and calculated from the properties of the flow inside the boundary layer. In turn, the flow inside the boundary layer could be calculated from a set of special equations called the boundary layer equations. He also showed how the boundary layer concept explained the occurrence of flow separation from the body surface—a vital concept in the overall understanding of drag. Flow separation is illustrated in Figure 6.32 for an airfoil at large angle of attack, beyond the stall. Here, the flow literally separates from the top surface near the leading edge, creating a dead-air region over the rest of the surface and causing a severe loss in lift and a large increase in drag. This is the nature of airfoil stall. Boundary layer theory gives some help in predicting the location where separation occurs, but it can not predict the properties of the separated flow itself.

Since 1904, many aerodynamicists have spent their lives studying boundary layer phenomena—it is still a viable area of research today. Boundary layer theory, however, was slow to be picked up by aeronautical engineers. From 1904 to the end of World War I, Prandtl and his colleagues at Göttingen University developed and extended the theory in virtual isolation. After the war, however, Prandtl's work

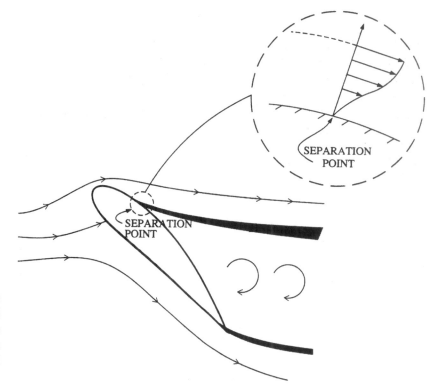

FIGURE 6.32
Schematic of separated
flow over the top surface
of an airfoil at a very high
angle of attack—beyond
the stall.

in aerodynamics, including that with boundary layer, began to seep into the English language. The value of boundary layer theory, which allowed the ready calculation of skin-friction drag, was soon appreciated in the 1920s. Indeed, when Melvill Jones discussed the virtues of streamlining and defined his "ideal airplane" in 1928 as one where the form drag was zero, he used boundary layer theory to calculate the skin-friction drag. Referring back to Jones's graph in Figure 6.11, the solid curves at the bottom include skin-friction drag as calculated from boundary layer theory. By the time of the design revolution and the era of the mature propeller-driven airplane, boundary layer theory was an established and respected tool in the hands of aeronautical engineers.

In summary, the author suggests that Prandtl's boundary layer concept was a contribution to science of Nobel-prize stature. Perhaps one of the best accolades for Prandtl's boundary layer paper delivered in 1904 was given by the noted fluid dynamicist Sydney Goldstein, who was moved to state the following in 1969: "The paper will certainly prove to be one of the most extraordinary papers of this century, and probably of many centuries."

Impact on Flying Machines

During the era of the mature propeller-driven airplanes, the state of the art in aerodynamics was directly reflected in the flying machines to a much greater extent than in previous eras in the history of aerodynamics. During the 1920s and 1930s, airplane designers became acutely aware of the need for aerodynamic improvements. Airplanes were continually flying faster and farther, and new technology had to be developed to keep pace with the steadily increasing challenges. Effective channels for communication between the two worlds of aerodynamics research and airplane design had to be developed during the period between the two world wars. Prandtl's research findings spread to countries outside of Germany through translations of his publications, as well as the export of some of his students, such as the immigration of Max Munk and Theodore von Kárman to the United States. During the 1920s and 1930s the research findings of government agencies (particularly the Royal Aeronautical Establishment in the United Kingdom and NACA in the United States) were published in technical reports that were widely disseminated across the aeronautics community. Indeed, NACA technical reports from that period became classics—data from careful research presented in terms readily understood by both researchers and airplane designers. The annual industry conferences hosted by NACA served to expedite the flow of government research findings to industry. Certainly airplane designers were still conservative by nature, and it took time for them to assimilate and develop trust in the state-of-the-art applications flowing from research in aerodynamics. By the end of the 1930s, the propeller-driven airplane had become a sophisticated flying machine that clearly reflected such assimilation and trust.

ADVANCES IN PROPULSION

Liquid cooling, or air cooling? That was the question facing the airplane engine designer after World War I. The answer was both. The era of the mature propeller-driven airplane saw the development of powerful liquid-cooled engines, most of which were used in military airplanes—especially fighter airplanes where streamlining was all-important. The same era saw the development of highly successful air-cooled radial engines, which by the end of World War II were, by far, the dominant powerplants for most airplanes. These engines, in combination with the development of the variable-pitch propeller, constitute a vital part of the technology of the airplane during the era of the mature propeller-driven airplane. Let us take a closer look.

Liquid-Cooled Engines

The Hispano–Suiza liquid-cooled engine, discussed in Chapter 5, was the state of the art at the end of World War I; its success led to a long line of liquid-cooled engines of ever-increasing horsepower and efficiency over the next 25 years. The major driver for the use of liquid-cooled engines was that they could be made long and slim, with relatively small frontal area, which was very attractive to aeronautical engineers designing highly streamlined airplanes. A beautiful example is shown in Figure 6.33; here three airplanes designed in progressive years for the Schneider Trophy races are shown with their liquid-cooled engines, each airplane becoming more streamlined as allowed by longer, slimmer engines. In the United States, immediately after World War I, the Wright Aeronautical Corporation continued to produce liquid-cooled engines for a few years, but Curtiss, with its applications to high-speed racing airplanes, took the lead with its D-12 liquid-cooled engine. In England, Rolls–Royce embarked on a long development program that eventually led to the Merlin, perhaps the most famous of all liquid-cooled engines with its fame derived in part because it powered the

TABLE 6.2   Liberty/Merlin engine comparison

Engine	Liberty (1918)	Packard Merlin (1948)
Number of cylinders	12	12
Maximum horsepower	420	2250
Weight per horsepower, lb	2.04	0.78

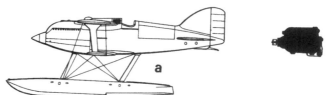

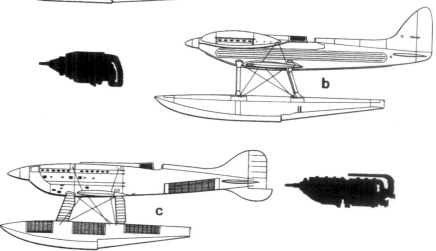

FIGURE 6.33
Racing airplanes and their engine shapes (from David Mondey, Editor, *The International Encyclopedia of Aviation*, Crown Publishers, 1977). a) Curtiss R3C racer powered by a Curtiss V-1500 engine; b) Supermarine S-6B powered by a Rolls-Royce R engine; c) Macchi 72 powered by a Fiat AS.6 engine.

popular and beautiful Supermarine Spitfire during World War II (Figure 6.34). The tremendous engineering advances made in liquid-cooled engines during the era of the modern propeller-driven airplane are dramatically seen in Table 6.2, which compares the Liberty engine of 1918 (discussed in Chapter 5) with the Merlin engine produced in the United States by Packard in 1948. A photograph of the Rolls-Royce Merlin engine is shown in Figure 6.35—a picture of power.

Speed and Power. We interject a note here about speed and the power required for speed. Near the beginning of Chapter 5, we demonstrated that the power required to propel airplanes to certain speeds varies as the cube of the speed. So if we wish to double the speed of a given airplane, we have to increase the engine power by at least two cubed, or a factor of eight. During the era of the mature propeller-driven airplane, top speeds increased from about 200 to above 400 miles per hour. The desire for speeds in the 400-mile per hour range required engines of substantially more power. (Note that in Table 6.2 the Packard Merlin produced about six times more power than the Liberty.) It is this simple reality from

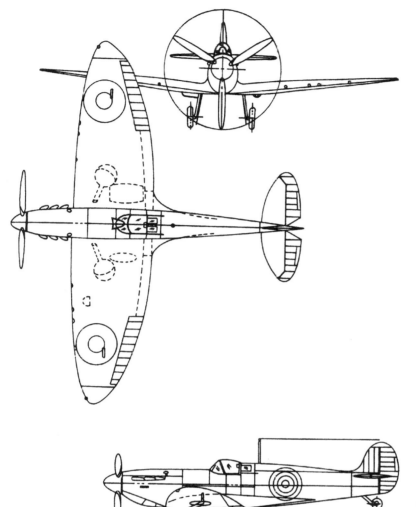

FIGURE 6.34
Three-view of the British
Supermarine Spitfire.

physics that resulted in the development of aircraft engines of tremendous power
packed in relatively small, lightweight packages, such as shown in Figure 6.35. In
terms of such lightweight packages of tremendous power, however, the
liquid-cooled engine was not the last word; the air-cooled radial engine surpassed
it. This is our next story.

Air-Cooled Radial Engines

The development of air-cooled radial engines, unlike that of the liquid-cooled
engine, was not a seamless, continuous series of developments from World War I
radials. Indeed, we have already seen that the major type of air-cooled engine from
that period was the rotary engine. The many disadvantages of having the whole
engine rotate about a fixed crankshaft made the rotary unpopular by the end of the
war. In 1918, the liquid-cooled engine reigned supreme, and the air-cooled engine
appeared to become an artifact of history.

FIGURE 6.35
The Rolls-Royce liquid-cooled Merlin engine, which powered the Spitfire. This engine is on display in the World War II Gallery of the National Air and Space Museum, Smithsonian Institution.

Not for long, however. On the scene came two men, Samuel D. Heron, originally in England, and Charles L. Lawrance in the United States. Heron, an apprenticed mechanic, had worked for Rolls–Royce, Napier, and Siddeley aircraft engine companies before being hired by the Royal Aircraft Factory at Farnborough, England, during World War I. There he was involved in the design of the first successful aluminum air-cooled cylinders. This work eventually led to the development of the Bristol Jupiter air-cooled radial engine in 1922, which produced about 400 horsepower. Large numbers of the Jupiter were manufactured in England and Europe and were employed mainly on military airplanes. The Jupiter had a problem, however. Because of poor exhaust valve cooling, the engine required frequent maintenance. As noted by C. F. Taylor in his monograph on *Aircraft Propulsion* in the *Smithsonian Annals of Flight*, Sam Heron once said about the Jupiter that its consumption should be given in terms of pounds of exhaust valves, rather than in pounds of fuel, per horsepower–hour! In 1921, Heron came to the United States, where he worked for the U.S. Army Aeronautical Research and Development Laboratory at the McCook Field in Dayton during the early 1920s. It was at McCook Field that Heron pioneered the liquid-filled valve concept for cooling; he had some success using a mixture of sodium and potassium nitrate. By 1928, Heron's sodium-filled valve had been adapted on high-performance engines. It was a major contribution to engine technology and was one of the primary reasons for the improvement of engine reliability and endurance during the era of the mature propeller-driven airplane.

At the same time that Heron was working on air-cooled cylinders in England, Charles L. Lawrance was working to develop a practical air-cooled engine in the United States. Lawrance was a New Englander, with a B.A. degree from Yale in 1905 and a Diplome Ecole des Beaux Arts, Paris, in architecture in 1908. While he was in Paris, he became interested in aircraft engines. On returning to the

United States at the start of World War I, Lawrance formed a small company, the Shinnecock Airplane Company, for the purpose of producing a light private airplane powered by a small air-cooled engine that he designed. In 1917 he founded the Lawrance Aero-Engine Corporation and began to design air-cooled engines for the U.S. Army and the U.S. Navy. In 1921 Lawrance created the popular and successful 9-cylinder, 200-horsepower, J-1 air-cooled radial engine. The Navy ordered 200 of the engines, starting a long-duration love affair between the Navy and air-cooled radial engines. These engines had fewer moving parts and were less susceptible to impact damage during carrier landings than liquid-cooled engines. The Navy became the champion of air-cooled radials. Unfortunately, Lawrance's company was small and did not have the mass production facilities desired by both the Army and the Navy. With the Navy's explicit encouragement, Lawrence's company was bought by the Wright Aeronautical Corporation. Gradually, and initially reluctantly, Wright began to shift away from its earlier line of liquid-cooled engines to focus on air-cooled radials. The Wright Aeronautical Corporation built improved versions of Lawrance's engine, known in the 1920s as the Wright J-3 and J-4.

The Ryan NYP "Spirit of St. Louis," 1927, hanging in the Milestones of Flight Gallery at the National Air and Space Museum, Smithsonian Institution.

Sam Heron left McCook Field in 1926 to join the Wright Aeronautical Corporation, of which Lawrance was now president, hence bringing together the two pioneer developers of the air-cooled radial engine. The immediate joint product of these two men was the Wright J-5 Whirlwind, one of the most successful engines in the 200-horsepower class. Shown in Figure 6.36, the Whirlwind was used by Charles Lindbergh in his Spirit of St. Louis, and it won the coveted Collier Trophy in 1927 for aviation's most important development of the year. With experience from the Whirlwind, Lawrance designed a completely new engine, the Wright Cyclone, which in its various forms grew from 500 horsepower in the early 1930s to 1900 horsepower by the beginning of World War II. Wright Cyclone engines powered most versions of the Douglas DC-3.

Pleased with the success of air-cooled radial engines in the 1920s, the Navy felt it needed a second source of supply. With the promise of engine orders from the Navy if they produced a suitable engine, a small group of Wright Aeronautical employees, led by the then-president of the company, F. B. Rentschler, left to form the Pratt and Whitney Aircraft Company in Hartford, Connecticut. It was easy for Rentschler to leave Wright because he became more and more at odds with the company's directors; he resigned in 1924. Within a year he had attracted away from Wright its Chief Engineer, George J. Mead, and its Assistant Engineer in Charge of Design, A. V. D. Willgoos. By 1926, the fledgling Pratt and Whitney group produced the first of a highly successful line of Wasp air-cooled radial engines. For the remainder of the era of the mature propeller-driven airplane, Wright and Pratt and Whitney would be the two primary suppliers of powerful air-cooled radial engines.

TABLE 6.3   Lawrence J-1/Wright Turbo-Compound power comparison

Engine	Lawrence J-1 (1922)	Wright Turbo-Compound (1955)
Number of cylinders	9	18
Maximum horsepower	200	3700
Weight (pounds) per horsepower	2.38	0.96

FIGURE 6.36
Wright Whirlwind J-5
aircooled engine, 1927.
An engine of this type
powered Charles
Lindbergh's "Spirit of St.
Louis."

The competition between these two companies drove the power output from these engines to new heights. With the addition of superchargers and improved fuels, the reciprocating aircraft engine achieved horsepower levels only dreamed of in the early days of aviation. For example, let us compare the original Lawrance J-1 from 1922 with the ultimate Wright Turbo-Compound from 1955 (Table 6.3). By the end of the era of the mature propeller-driven airplane, engine design had become one of its most mature aspects.

Supercharging

The power output of a reciprocating engine varies directly as the density of the ambient air surrounding it. For example, an aircraft engine that produces 1000 horsepower at sea level will produce only about 500 horsepower at an altitude of

22,000 feet, where the air density is only half that at sea level. The lower the ambient density, then the lower the density of the air–fuel mixture in the manifold of the engine, the lower the pressure created by combustion in the cylinder, the lower the force acting on the piston during the power stroke, and hence, the lower the horsepower output. This basic fact has been recognized since the time of the Wright brothers, and for the first 20 years of powered flight, the progressive power loss with increasing altitude was simply accepted. Fortunately, it is not as devastating to airplane performance as one might think because the aerodynamic drag also depends on the

The Pratt & Whitney R-2800 18-cylinder radial engine, 1944, at the National Air and Space Museum, Smithsonian Institution. This engine is typical of the powerful reciprocating engines near the end of the era of the mature propeller-driven airplane.

ambient density: the lower the density, the lower the drag. The net result in those days was that the maximum velocity of a propeller-driven airplane decreased with an increase in altitude, but not as much as one might think just based on the decreased engine power.

On the other hand, if something would be done to maintain the engine power output with increasing altitude, then the airplane's performance at altitude would be greatly enhanced; the drag would go down with increasing altitude, but the power available from the engine would remain the same. This is something particularly important to military airplanes, as well as high-performance civil transports. Indeed, something can be done to maintain engine power with increasing altitude—supercharging. A supercharger is a mechanical device that compresses the air before entering the engine manifold; it is usually in the form of a centrifugal blower that is driven from the main engine via a gear connection to the main crankshaft (a gear-driven supercharger), or by a turbine inserted in the exhaust gas stream from the engine (a turbo-supercharger). The power to drive a gear-driven supercharger is drained from the engine itself, which overall makes the supercharging slightly less efficient. The power to drive a turbo-supercharger comes from the otherwise wasted energy of the exhaust gas, which makes the supercharging more efficient. In either case, the supercharger increases the pressure, hence the density, of the air flowing into the reciprocating engine. As the airplane climbs to higher altitudes, the amount of supercharging increases to maintain the inflow density at a constant level. There is, however, a cutoff altitude above which a given supercharger is unable to maintain the same engine power; above this altitude, the engine power starts to decrease. Typical cutoff altitudes are around 20,000 feet.

The practical implementation of superchargers is a hallmark of the era of the mature propeller-driven airplane. The origin of the supercharger, however, took place during the previous era, that of the strut-and-wire biplane. In 1914, the Swiss engineer A. J. Buchi advanced the idea of a turbosupercharger for aircraft engines. Rateau in France developed some experimental models that were tested during World War I. Concurrently, the Royal Aircraft Factory in Britain experimented with gear-driven superchargers. Neither type of supercharger, however, saw service during the war. Nevertheless, supercharger development gained momentum in 1917 when the fledgling NACA was confronted with the challenge of maintaining the power output of the Liberty engine at altitude. Sanford Moss, an engineer with a doctorate degree in mechanical engineering from Cornell University, was working in the gas turbine division of the General Electric Company at the time. Moss was a natural for this work, and he was directed to begin a study of the turbosupercharger. In 1918, the Engineering Division of the U.S. Army Air Service at McCook Field in Dayton issued a contract with Moss and General Electric to develop a working machine. (It is appropriate to note that in the early years following World War I, NACA and the Army via McCook Field worked closely together on several major problem areas of flight; we will see another example in the next chapter.) In September 1918, Moss and his colleagues hauled a Liberty engine equipped with a Moss-designed turbosupercharger to the top of Pike's Peak just outside Colorado Springs, Colorado. At an altitude of 14,109 feet, the engine with supercharger produced a satisfactory level of horsepower. Moss's invention was a success, but it was too late to be used in World War I.

Engineers at McCook Field continued the work on turbosuperchargers after the war, albeit at a reduced level of activity. Early in 1920, they equipped a Le Pere biplane with a Liberty engine and Moss's turbosupercharger. Then began one of the many examples of man–machine interactions that peppers the history of technology. The only way to find out whether Moss's supercharger would really work at high altitudes on an airplane was to fly the airplane and see what happened. On February 27, 1920, McCook Field test pilot Rudolph W. Schroder took off in the supercharged Le Pere; after a long climb, the airplane and pilot reached 30,000 feet and was still climbing. At that moment, Schroeder's oxygen system failed. At altitudes above about 18,000 feet, the air is so thin that there is not enough oxygen to keep a human being functioning. At slightly above 30,000 feet, suddenly with no auxiliary supply of oxygen, Schroeder knew he was about to black out. He cut off the engine, and just before he lost consciousness, he nosed the airplane over, diving for lower altitude. The airplane plunged five miles before Schroeder came to and regained enough consciousness to land the airplane. Army personnel rushing to his aid found everything, pilot and airplane, encrusted in ice. Schroeder sat helpless in his cockpit, his eyes frozen open. Schroeder recovered and was credited with setting a new world altitude record of 33,143 feet on that day. With the fortitude of an excellent test pilot, and the engineering genius of Sanford Moss, the turbosupercharger had been proven.

C. Fayette Taylor, a leading expert on aircraft engines and at that time Director of the Engine Laboratory at McCook Field, hints that the robustness of the Liberty engine itself contributed to the success of these flight tests, which continued for the next two years, setting yet new altitude records. Taylor, in his monograph *Aircraft Propulsion* published in the *Smithsonian Annals of Flight* in 1971, writes the following of one incident:

> Supercharging was hard on an engine not originally designed for it, and I remember when Major Schroeder, who made the 1920 record, returned from a flight with the Liberty engine and its nacelle cut in two by a failed connecting rod at the third crank from the front end. The only elements holding the four forward cylinders and the propeller in place were the crankshaft and the two camshaft housings. In spite of this condition, and the loss of all its cooling water, the Liberty engine was still running!

In spite of the McCook field tests, and continued U.S. Army and NACA work on the concept, practical turbosuperchargers were not used on production airplanes until the late 1930s. The primary stumbling block was finding suitable materials for the turbine wheels that had to endure the high-temperature exhaust gases. In March 1939, however, turbosuperchargers were successfully tested on a Boeing B-17 bomber and were finally accepted by airplane designers. They were used on the B-17 and B-24 bombers and the P-38 Lightning and P-47 Thunderbolt fighters in World War II.

Geared superchargers had a much easier run. Curtiss and the Wright Aeronautical Corporation were experimenting with such superchargers in 1925, but Pratt and Whitney was the first company in America to use one on a production line engine, the Wasp, in 1927. A year before, Siddeley in England started manufacturing its Jaguar 14-cylinder, two-row radial engine with a geared supercharger. Almost all military and civil transport airplanes after 1930 were powered with engines equipped with geared superchargers. Perhaps the epitome of this type of application was the Merlin engine produced by Rolls–Royce in World War II, the engine that powered the famous Spitfire, among others. The Merlin, equipped with a two-stage, two-speed geared supercharger seen attached to the front of the engine, is shown in Figure 6.37, with all its gears and two centrifugal blowers shown in full glory.

Variable-Pitch Propellers

A propeller is the device that converts the power from a reciprocating engine to forward thrust, the actual force that propels the airplane forward. The propeller, therefore, is a purely aerodynamic device. It is essentially a twisted wing. Why the twist? Consider a rotating propeller mounted on an airplane in forward flight. Each local airfoil section of the propeller sees a local airstream direction that is a *combination* of the forward motion of the propeller and its circular motion. Imagine that you are an airfoil section located near the hub of the propeller. Your speed due to the rotation of the propeller is small because you are close to the center of rotation. Hence, the relative airflow you feel is mainly coming from the forward motion of the airplane, and thus, your chord line should be oriented almost in the forward direction of the airplane. Now imagine that you are located near the tip of the propeller. Your speed due to the rotation of the propeller is now quite large because you are at a large distance from the center of rotation. (A speck of dust at the outer edge of a record on a rotating turntable moves much faster than another speck of dust near the center of the record.) Your speed due to this rotation may be much larger than the forward motion of the airplane. Hence, the relative airflow you feel is mainly coming from the direction of rotation, and thus, your chord line should be oriented almost in the direction of rotation. As a result, the propeller blade must be twisted. Indeed, each airfoil section located along the span of the propeller should see essentially the same angle of attack relative to the local airflow direction, namely, that angle of attack corresponding to the maximum lift-to-drag ratio for the airfoil section. The twist of a propeller and the relative orientation of the airfoil sections along the blade is shown in Figure 6.38, obtained from an early airplane design book from 1920. An old diagram is chosen here because it illustrates the typical shape of a propeller from the early 1920s—the type of fixed-pitch propeller that was soon to be replaced by dramatic new

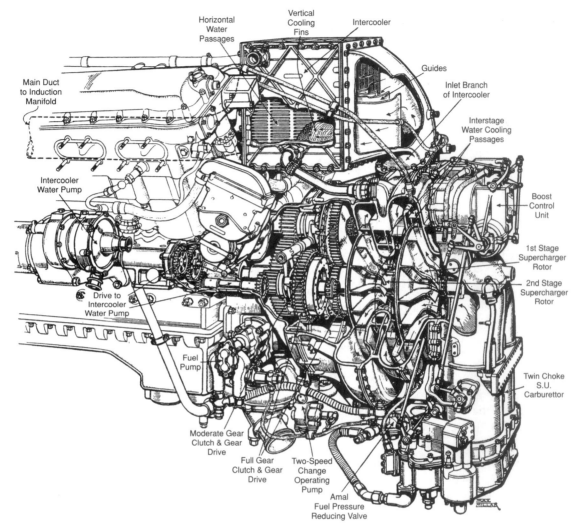

Horizontal
Water
Passages

Vertical
Cooling
Fins

Intercooler

Main Duct
to Induction
Manifold

Guides

Inlet Branch
of Intercooler

Interstage
Water Cooling
Passages

Intercooler
Water Pump

Boost
Control
Unit

1st Stage
Supercharger
Rotor

2nd Stage
Supercharger
Rotor

Drive to
Intercooler
Water Pump

Twin Choke
S.U.
Carburettor

Fuel
Pump

Moderate Gear
Clutch & Gear
Drive

Full Gear
Clutch & Gear
Drive

Two-Speed
Change
Operating
Pump

Amal
Fuel Pressure
Reducing Valve

FIGURE 6.37
Perspective of the
supercharged Rolls-Royce
Merlin 61 engine.

developments during the design revolution. In Figure 6.38, the straight lines emanating from the left top corner are the directions of the relative local wind seen by each airfoil section. Note that *each* airfoil is at a 3-degree angle of attack to the local relative wind.

The pitch of a propeller is the angle of the blade referenced to the plane of rotation; the pitch angle obviously varies along the span of the blade due to the twist of the propeller. In Figure 6.38, the pitch angle of the first airfoil section on the left is 55 degrees and 36 minutes, that of the second airfoil is 46 degrees and 7 minutes, and so forth. A *fixed-pitch* propeller is one where all of the local pitch angles are fixed, such as a propeller blade that is simply locked into its hub, with no provision of rotating the blade about its own axis. The one-piece propeller of the Wright flyer was a fixed-pitch propeller. Indeed, the propeller for all of the standard airplanes during the era of the strut-and-wire biplane were fixed-pitch propellers. Such propellers have a major disadvantage. Because the angle of attack of each airfoil section of the blade is designed to be a specific value corresponding to that for maximum lift-to-drag, and the local angle of attack is dependent on the

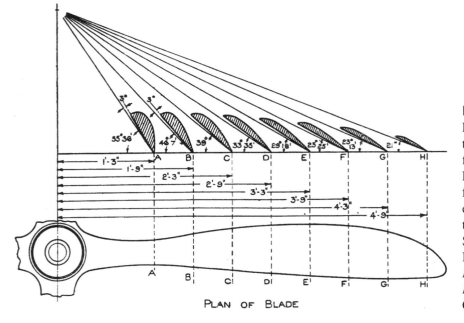

PLAN OF BLADE

FIGURE 6.38
Propeller layout showing twist and pitch. (This figure is the same as Figure 5.25, repeated here for convenience to emphasize the concepts of twist and pitch.) (From S. T. G. Andrews and S. F. Benson, *The Theory and Practice of Aeroplane Design*, E. P. Dutton and Co., New York, 1920.)

local direction of the relative wind, then the propeller will operate at maximum efficiency at only one speed of the airplane. For all other flight speeds, the propeller will be operating off-design, and propeller efficiency (hence, thrust) will decrease. For the low speeds of airplanes before and during World War I, this was not much of a problem. For many of these airplanes, the difference between takeoff speed and maximum speed was about 30 or 40 miles per hour, and the propellers were never far off their design conditions. But in the early 1930s, with the advent of higher performance and faster airplanes, such as the Boeing 247, the difference between takeoff speed and maximum speed was substantial. If a fixed-pitch propeller is designed for optimum performance at takeoff, then its high-speed performance is compromised and the maximum velocity of the airplane is reduced. Conversely, if the propeller is designed for optimum performance at high speed, then the takeoff performance of the airplane is greatly compromised. The first versions of the Boeing 247 transport were equipped with fixed-pitch propellers. During the acceptance trials for United Air Lines in 1932, the airplane performed so poorly in flights over the Rocky Mountains that the success of the new transport was in doubt. The fixed-pitch propeller was the major problem.

The solution to this problem was known well before World War I, namely, design the propeller so that its pitch angle could be changed in flight—the *variable-pitch propeller*. Indeed, the first suggestion for a variable-pitch propeller was made by the Frenchman J. Croce-Spinelli, in 1871, and was suggested again in 1876 by Alphonse Penaud (see Chapter 3), in both cases long before the Wright Flyer came on the scene. Because of the mechanical complexities of rotating the propeller, nothing came of these early suggestions. World War I provided a mild stimulation for work on variable-pitch propellers, with developments in Germany, England, Canada, and the United States, but again, due to the mechanical complexities, no practical solutions came from these efforts. One problem was the design of a mechanical mechanism that could take the wear and tear of propeller operation. Another problem was the wooden propeller itself; attached to a variable-pitch mechanism, such propellers frequently disintegrated during testing.

The successful solution to the problem of variable pitch did not happen until the metal propeller was developed, and both hydraulic and electric mechanisms were successfully designed for changing the pitch. These developments finally came together in the early 1930s, just in time for the higher performance airplanes that were the products of the design revolution. One person stands out as the principal developer of the first successful variable-pitch propeller, Frank W. Caldwell. The story of his persistence, technical knowledge, and innovative ideas is an inherent part of the history of the technology of the airplane. The story of Caldwell's life and his contributions to aeronautical technology is nicely told in the recent paper by J. R. Kinney, Curator for Propulsion at the National Air and Space Museum, entitled "Frank W. Caldwell and Variable-Pitch Propeller Development, 1918–1938," found in the *Journal of Aircraft*, Vol. 38, September–October 2001, pp. 967–976. In the following paragraphs, we summarize some of the salient aspects of Caldwell—his life and contributions to propeller design.

Caldwell was born in 1889 at Lookout Mountain near Chattanooga, Tennessee. He attended the University of Virginia and the Massachusetts Institute of Technology, where he obtained a bachelors degree in mechanical engineering in 1912. His bachelor's thesis entitled "Investigation of Air Propellers" contained pioneering ideas on propeller testing and launched him on a lifetime career dealing with propellers. Caldwell then joined the Curtiss Aeroplane and Motor Company in Buffalo as foreman and process engineer in the propeller department. In 1917, he became the civilian chief engineer of the propeller department of the new aeronautical research and development facility at McCook Field, established by the Airplane Engineering Division of the U.S. Army Air Service. It was at McCook Field that Caldwell began his work on both the metal and variable-pitch propellers. (McCook Field was a crossroads for a number of productive aeronautical engineers beginning in 1918 through the 1920s. We have already mentioned Virginius Clark, who designed airfoil shapes and entire airplanes while at McCook Field, and Sam Heron who made major contributions to air-cooled radial engines during his five-year employment at McCook Field.)

As Caldwell was starting his work at McCook Field, the aeronautical community was well aware of the need for a variable-pitch propeller and a better material than wood for its construction. For example, in the NACA Annual Report for 1918 NACA Chairman William F. Durand, himself an important contributor and expert on the fundamental aerodynamics of propellers while a professor at Stanford University, wrote that the invention of a variable-pitch propeller was "of the highest order of importance" and "outstanding as one of the appliances for which the art of air navigation is definitely in wanting." In regard to the construction of a metal propeller, NACA identified it as one of the "very important problems now confronting the air services of the nation." In England, after the Royal Aircraft Factory at Farnborough built and flight tested a variable-pitch propeller, the resulting report on the tests stated that "there can be little doubt about the aerodynamical advantages of the variable-pitch propeller." The mechanism used for varying the pitch, however, was not satisfactory, and the same report threw cold water on the tests by stating that "the chief objections to the propeller are mechanical."

Caldwell squarely and methodically faced the challenge. He first developed a new multipiece propeller, the detachable blades of which were fixed to a central hub; the mechanism of changing the pitch would be located in the hub. Then Caldwell searched for new materials that would be better than wood. After briefly experimenting with Bakelite micarta (so-called plastic propellers), he found that metal was a better solution. As early as 1918, the propeller department began work on a drop-forged steel propeller and in 1920 contracted with the Standard Steel Propeller Company in Pittsburgh, Pennsylvania, to construct several different designs of steel propellers. Because of flutter problems and structural weakness where the steel blades were threaded to the propeller hub, this work was put on the shelf in 1923. Caldwell turned to Duralumin, the same metal used by Junkers for his all-metal airplanes (see Chapter 5). Using Duralumin blades, the engineer at Standard Steel designed a new steel hub split in two pieces into which the individual Duralumin propeller blades were clamped. This design allowed the pitch angle to be adjusted on the ground before a flight, picking a particular pitch angle that would be appropriate for the anticipated conditions of the flight. As stated by Jeremy Kinney in his recent paper, "A major milestone in propeller design and construction was achieved by 1925: the introduction of a standardized metal ground-adjustable pitch propeller." The U.S. Navy quickly wrote a contract with Standard Steel for a hundred of these propellers; the Navy was interested because one of their new Martin T3M torpedo bombers, powered by the 575-horsepower Wright T-3B Typhoon radial engine, lost a wooden propeller on takeoff.

Problems with the development of new propellers at that time were illustrated by a story told by C. Fayette Taylor, director of the engine laboratory at McCook Field in the 1920s. He relates the following:

> In 1921 Caldwell tested a steel-bladed propeller on his electric whirling machine to twice its rated power. He then, very innocently, presented it to me for a "routine" test on a Hispano–Suiza 300 horsepower engine. After a few minutes at rated power, a blade broke off, came through the control board between the heads of two operators, climbed a wooden staircase, and went through the roof. The engine was reduced to junk.

Leaving McCook Field, Caldwell became the chief engineer at Standard Steel in 1929. In that same year, he patented a hydraulically actuated (in contrast to mechanically actuated) variable-pitch propeller. Also in 1929, Standard Steel was merged with Hamilton Aero Manufacturing to create the Hamilton Standard Corporation, which was part of the large United Aircraft and Transport Corporation (United Technologies, today). Hamilton Standard was soon to become the largest and most important manufacturer of propellers in the world mainly because they took up the development of Caldwell's hydraulic variable-pitch propeller. Although Caldwell meant his design to allow continuous adjustment of the propeller pitch during flight, to save time the work at Hamilton Standard was concentrated on a two-position controllable pitch propeller—one setting for takeoff and another, actuated by the pilot, for cruising flight. Although only a halfway measure, this design proved a major success. It was ready for production in 1932, just in time to save the life of the new Boeing 247 transport (Figure 6.39). As mentioned earlier, the performance of the first versions of the 247, with their fixed-pitch propellers, fell far below expectation, badly enough to jeopardize the

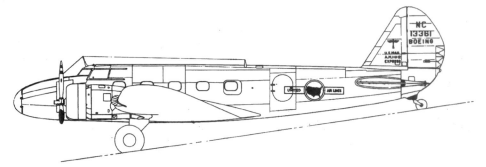

FIGURE 6.39
The Boeing 247D.

whole project. Hamilton Standard sent Caldwell to Boeing to examine the problem. He was able to demonstrate in tests that the new variable-pitch propeller reduced the takeoff run of the 247 by 20 percent, increased the rate of climb by 22 percent, and increased the cruising speed by 5.5 percent. Boeing replaced the old propellers on all its 247s with Hamilton Standard two-position controllable-pitch propellers, and the program was saved.

And so was Hamilton Standard, which at the time was suffering economically in the Great Depression. After Boeing adopted the variable-pitch propeller for the 247, other airplane companies and designers were quick to see the advantages. Douglas installed the two-position variable-pitch propellers on the DC-1, as well as the production versions of the DC-2. By the spring of 1934, Hamilton Standard had sold 1000 of the new propellers. Moreover, by 1935 it had sold foreign rights for their manufacture to deHavilland in Britain, Hispano–Suiza in France, and Junkers in Germany.

Not only was Hamilton Standard's economic status looking up, but so was its professional status. Caldwell and Hamilton Standard shared the 1933 Collier Trophy for the two-position, hydraulically actuated, variable-pitch propeller. In presenting the award, President Franklin D. Roosevelt stated that the new propeller enabled "modern planes and engines to realize to the full the improvements in design." He went on to say, "The success of (Caldwell's) propeller has revealed a new horizon of aeronautics and taken the limits off speed. Henceforth, our pace through the air will be as fast as the daring and imagination of the engineers." Because of his invention, Caldwell would go on to receive from the IAS its prestigious Sylvanus A. Reed Award in 1935. Later, he would serve as president of the IAS in 1941. (The IAS merged with the American Rocket Society in 1962 to form the present-day AIAA.)

Caldwell enjoyed one final major development, the crowning glory of all his propeller work. He had always felt that the ultimate propeller would be one where the pitch is continuously variable during flight, not just two positions. In fact, what made most sense was to have the pitch continuously and automatically changing so that the reciprocating engine would operate at constant speed (constant revolutions per minute) no matter what changes take place in the flight environment. The power output of a reciprocating engine is directly proportional to its revolutions per minute. By continuously changing the propeller pitch in the face of changing conditions, the load on the engine would be maintained to keep the revolutions per minute constant, close to the value corresponding to the engine's maximum power

FIGURE 6.40
Mechanical mechanism
for Hamilton Standard's
constant speed propeller,
designed by Frank
Caldwell.

output. In this way, both the engine and the propeller are working synergistically to obtain maximum available power for flight. To help design a control that could handle frequent changes in engine speed, Caldwell employed the services of the Woodward Governor Company in Rockford, Illinois. The work of this team, in the space of two years, led to a working, *constant-speed propeller* by 1934. Hamilton Standard placed the constant-speed propeller in production in late 1935, just in time for it to be used on the new DC-3 by Douglas. Within four years, Hamilton Standard sold more than 25,000 constant-speed propellers. A diagram of Caldwell's constant-speed mechanism is shown in Figure 6.40.

In the same period that Caldwell was developing his hydraulic actuator for variable-pitch propellers, the Canadian W. R. Turnbull was working on an electrically operated mechanism for the same purpose. Beginning in 1923 with a grant from the Canadian National Research Council, Turnbull developed a reliable propeller where the pitch was changed by an electric motor in the propeller hub and was totally controlled by the pilot. Like Caldwell, Turnbull eventually went to industry for the final development. In 1928, impressed with Turnbull's success, Curtiss–Wright took an exclusive license to further develop and build Turnbull's electric propellers. Curtiss–Wright was already in the propeller business through its subsidiary, the Reed Propeller Company, making steel fixed-pitch propellers. Curtiss–Wright, however, was more conservative than Hamilton Standard and took more time to develop its variable-pitch propeller. When Hamilton Standard marketed its constant-speed propeller, Curtiss–Wright realized that their Turnbull, electrically actuated propeller with continuously variable pitch was a natural for this application. By late 1935, the first Curtiss–Wright constant-speed propellers were fitted to a U.S. Army airplane, the PB2A, and in 1937, they found their first commercial application on the twin-engine Lockheed 14 (Figure 6.9). Curtiss–Wright quickly became a major competitor to Hamilton Standard for the constant-speed propeller, and both types were used extensively during World War II.

Jeremy Kinney labels the constant-speed propeller as the "automatic gearshift in the air." Without it, the tremendously powerful engines that evolved during World War II would never have realized their full potential. The variable-pitch propeller was one of the most important technical developments in the era of the mature propeller-driven airplane.

High-Octane Fuels

One of the lesser known but nevertheless important developments in aeronautics during the 1930s was the advent of high-octane fuels. These fuels allowed engines of a given size to produce more power and were one of the major contributions to the rapid increase of engine power during the era of the mature propeller-driven airplane.

The power output of a reciprocating engine is dependent on the pressure ratio achieved during the compression stroke because the higher the pressure, the more efficient the combustion of the air-fuel mixture. If the pressure is too high, however, the combustion process, instead of being a well-behaved controlled burning mechanism, will instead be a detonation that is less efficient and that can damage the pistons and cylinders—an audible phenomenon called "pinging" or "knocking." The problem of knocking limits the allowable design compression ratio of the engine, hence limiting the design power output of the engine.

In the 1920s, two developments occurred that improved this situation. In 1921, T. Midgley of General Motors discovered that tetra–ethyl–lead used as an additive to gasoline improved the antiknock properties of the fuel. It was adopted as an additive in 1926 by the U.S. Army and in 1927 by the U.S. Navy. Of more importance, however, was the discovery of the effect of isooctane on knocking by Graham Edgar of the Ethyl Corporation in 1926. Isooctane, a paraffin with the chemical formula C_8H_{18}, is a normal product of the distillation of petroleum. The octane rating of gasoline is the amount of isooctane present by volume. In the 1920s, the octane ratings of aviation fuel was essentially that for automobiles at the time—about 50 octane, or 50 percent isooctane by volume. Edgar discovered that with more isooctane present in the fuel, the compression ratio could be made higher before knocking occurred. The Army quickly adopted 87-octane gasoline in 1930, and by 1937 it was the standard for civil aviation as well. Engineers at the Army's Wright Field in Dayton, however, pushed for more. As a result, the Army adopted 100-octane fuel as the military standard in 1936. This fuel became the norm for the military during World War II; it was one of the factors that gave Allied airplanes during World War II a technical advantage.

ADVANCES IN STRUCTURES

The all-metal airplane came into its own at the beginning of the era of the mature propeller-driven airplane. Hugo Junkers's conviction in 1915 that the all-metal airplane was the airplane of the future finally came to fruition. Although other all-metal airplanes were designed in the decade following Junkers' pioneering J.1

in 1915 (see Chapter 5), this type was not generally accepted by the airplane design community at the time. Three advances, one in materials and two in aircraft structures, however, changed this situation, all occurring during the 1920s. Let us take a look.

The advance in materials involved the protection of aluminum alloys from corrosion. The concern over corrosion was a major impediment to the adoption of Duralumin in both Britain and the United States, in spite of the fact that Junkers forged ahead with his successful all-metal airplanes after World War I. This objection to aluminum was gradually removed when G. D. Bengough and H. Sutton, working for the National Physical Laboratory in the United Kingdom in the mid-1920s, developed a technique of anodizing aluminum alloys with a protective oxide coating, and when E. H. Dix in the United States in 1927 discovered a method of bonding pure, corrosion-resistant aluminum to the external surface of Duralumin. The latter, in manufactured form, is called Alclad. NACA, after carrying out corrosion tests on Alclad, gave its approval, and Alclad was accepted by the U.S. Army and U.S. Navy for new all-metal aircraft. The first major civil airplane to use corrosion-resistant aluminum was the Boeing 247, which was fabricated from Alclad 17-ST.

The two major advances in structural design took place in Germany. The first was the practical introduction of the stressed-skin concept. Junkers had designed his all-metal airplanes with the idea that the metal skin would carry loads. In his 1923 paper to the Royal Aeronautical Society, Junkers stated, "The theoretically best design appeared to be the system of the so-called supporting cover, that is, all tensile, compressive and shear forces are taken up by the wing cover." Except for a few exceptions, however, Junkers used corrugated metal to obtain stiffness of the skin. The corrugations added extra surface area, thus increasing the skin-friction drag on the airplane; moreover, the corrugations interfered with the smooth aerodynamic flow over the surface. The practical use of a smooth stressed-skin structure is largely due to Adolf Rohrback, who is also responsible for coining the term "stressed skin" in 1924 during a paper delivered to the Royal Aeronautical Society. Born in 1889 in Gotha, Germany, Rohrback received his engineering diploma from the Technische Hochschule Darmstadt and went on to earn his doctorate in engineering from the Technische Hochschule Berlin–Charlottenburg in 1921. Afterward, he established the Rohrbach Metal Airplane Company in Copenhagen, Denmark, the location chosen to circumvent the strict restrictions imposed on the German aircraft industry by the Treaty of Versailles. He concentrated on the design and construction of all-metal flying boats. In contrast to Junkers' airplanes of corrugated aluminum, Rohrback's airplanes had smooth metal skins, hence lower overall friction drag. Moreover, the internal structure of Rohrback's wings involved a strong, metal box beam with a rounded nose in front and a tapered section in back, all made from aluminum. This design is shown schematically in Figure 6.41, which contrasts the early evolution of metal wing structures. (As Howard Wolko has pointed out to this author, box beams were not new in 1922. They had been built for years in large sizes, namely as ships, and clearly antedate the airplane.) Rohrback's wing design was considered revolutionary at the time; later, it served as a model for the stressed-skin wing structures that have dominated airplane design from 1930 to the present.

Rohrback's rectangular skin panels were fastened to a frame, which supported the panels on all four sides. Prevailing practice at the time dictated that

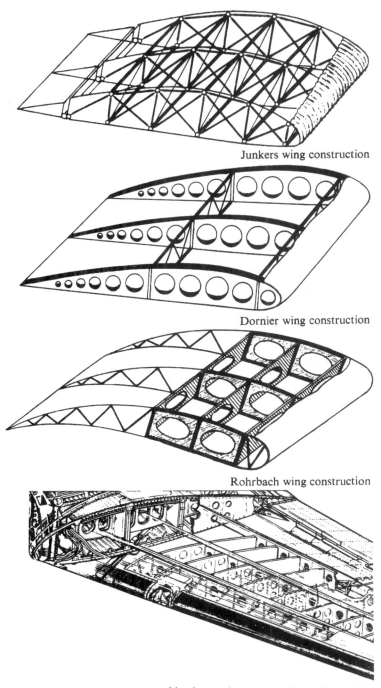

Junkers wing construction

Dornier wing construction

Rohrbach wing construction

FIGURE 6.41
Four different structural
designs for wings. (From
R. Miller and D. Sawers,
*The Technical
Development of Modern
Aviation*, Praeger
Publishers, New York,
1970.)

Northrop wing construction—the DC-3

the frame plus panel combination should be strong enough to prevent the panel
from buckling because buckling was viewed as structural failure. This laid the
groundwork for the second major advance in metal aircraft structures, namely the
discovery that a structure of mutually perpendicular members covered with a thin
skin did not fail if the skin buckled. Herbert Wagner, an engineer working for
Rohrback, made this discovery in 1925, although he did not publish his findings

until 1929. When the skin is allowed to carry the maximum possible load, the spacing between frames could be increased, resulting in lighter-weight structures.

Without knowledge of Rohrback's or Wagner's work, Jack Northrop in the United States pioneered a multicellular wing structure of spars, ribs, and stringers covered with smooth, stressed-skin sheets. He independently discovered that the sheets did not fail even after they began to buckle. The Northrop wing was adopted for several aircraft, including the DC-1–2–3 series. The DC-3 wing structure is shown in Figure 6.41. This wing structure proved to be exceptionally long lasting. Each of the many load-carrying elements of the wing carried lower stress, which greatly increased the fatigue life of the DC-3. (Some people have criticized the DC-3 structure as being "over-designed" and, therefore, not an optimum structure in terms of weight. That may be true intellectually, but the structural toughness of the DC-3 was a boon to its user.)

In short, the all-metal, mostly aluminum, semimonocoque, stressed-skin aircraft structure became the norm during the era of the mature propeller-driven airplane. The all-vegetable airplane became a thing of the past.

ADVANCES IN THE PROCESS OF AIRPLANE DESIGN

The state of the art of airplane design in 1927 was nicely summarized by Edward P. Warner in his design textbook *Airplane Design: Aerodynamics*. Warner, at that time the new appointed Assistant Secretary of the Navy for Aeronautics, and past professor of aeronautical engineering at the Massachusetts Institute of Technology, reflected on the past:

> The pioneers of aircraft design traveled in a wilderness, dependent upon their own resources at every step. No path was marked for them, and the illumination along the way was only such as they themselves might provide. Of research, in its application to aeronautical engineering, there had been hardly even a beginning, and its place had often to be supplied by inspiration, intuition, or empiricism, or go unsupplied.

Warner then contrasted the past with the situation that existed in 1927:

> The student who embarks upon aeronautical studies in 1927 is subject, in some degree, to a contrary embarrassment. Experimental data inundate him. Their ever-growing bulk overwhelms him. The underbrush of obscurity has been cleared away, the field ever more brightly illuminated by the fruits of governmental, institutional, and private research, yet the uniformity with which enlightenment is being cast over the subject in its several parts may prove confusing, leaving the exact course to be followed still in doubt.

He went on to say what was still needed for the process of airplane design:

> The veteran of airplane design may be able to keep pace with the output of the laboratories, assimilating new information as it arrives and fitting it into its appropriate place with those concepts which he has already formed. The shelves upon shelves of books and pamphlets that house the primary expression of the studies that have, during the past two decades, extended over the whole world, have piled upon him gradually. To the novice, confronted with the whole mass of material all at once, it brings bewilderment. The need is for systematization, correlation, coordination, that the prior art and the existing state of knowledge may be presented as a whole in some harmonious scheme.

In the 1930s, the intellectual process of airplane design became marinated in a sauce spiced with new technology in aerodynamics, propulsion, structures, and flight control. This was a distinct improvement over the intuitive, seat-of-the-pants airplane design of the era of the strut-and-wire biplane. One of the major sources of the new technology was NACA in the United States. NACA was created on March 3, 1915, when the Congress passed Public Law 271, which in part read as follows:

> It shall be the duty of the Advisory Committee for Aeronautics to supervise and direct the scientific study of the problems of flight, with a view to their practical solution, and to determine the problems which should be experimentally attacked, and to discuss their solution and their application to practical questions.

Right from the start, NACA was oriented toward research to be applied to practical problems of flight. During the era of the modern propeller-driven airplane, NACA Langley Memorial Aeronautical Laboratory in Hampton, Virginia, put out a continuous flow of practical research results, primarily in the form of NACA technical reports and technical notes, which became an essential part of the library of the airplane designer, both in the United States and throughout the world. (Indeed, NACA technical reports were printed on high-quality glossy paper and were official archive publications as formally recognized by the Library of Congress.)

Also, in the 1930s airplane design became an essential part of the curriculum in university programs in aeronautical engineering that were cropping up at various colleges and universities around the country. For example, between 1926 and 1930, the Daniel Guggenheim Fund for the Promotion of Aeronautics endowed six schools of aeronautical engineering in American universities: Cal Tech, Stanford University, University of Michigan, MIT, University of Washington, and the Georgia School of Technology (later to become Georgia Institute of Technology). In 1926, Michigan and MIT already had major aeronautical engineering programs, and the Guggenheim grants simply reinforced them. At the other schools, the Guggenheim grants jump-started new departments of aeronautical engineering. Also, New York University had been a recipient of earlier Guggenheim funding and already had a viable program in aeronautical engineering. The oldest aeronautics department was at the University of Michigan, formally established in 1916 as part of a newly reorganized Department of Naval Architecture, Marine Engineering, and Aeronautics. In 1923, Michigan established the Department of Aeronautical Engineering, the oldest separate, autonomous department giving bachelor's degrees in aeronautical engineering. (We note that Kelly Johnson, the famous airplane designer for Lockheed, who designed such airplanes as the Lockheed P-80, America's first mainline jet fighter, the U-2, and the Mach 3+ SR-71, was a 1932 Michigan aeronautical engineering graduate.) Graduates of these formal programs came out with a much stronger intellectual background in airplane design than existed in the past, and these graduates went on to contribute to the first golden age of aeronautical engineering that took place in the 1930s.

The design of the Douglas DC-3, as related at the beginning of this chapter, is an excellent example of airplane design during the era of the mature propeller-driven airplane. The Douglas designers themselves did not create any pioneering new technology breakthroughs; rather, the DC-3 embodied for the first time *all* of the new technical developments of the day in a synergistic design. The designers at Douglas were familiar with the new technology, and they were bold enough to use it.

Design of the P-51 Mustang

Let us look at another example, the design of the famous P-51 Mustang, to help understand the transformation that came over the airplane design process in the 1930s. Designed by North American in early 1940, the P-51 became the best and most famous U.S. fighter airplane of World War II. And for good reasons, as discussed in the following.

New airplanes are not designed just of thin air—they are prompted by very specific requirements. This is a characteristic of the era of the mature propeller-driven airplane. In the previous era, especially in World War I and before, new airplanes were frequently conceived in the mind of one or more individuals who were simply responding to the challenge of building a flying machine that could get off the ground; designing such a machine based on a set of narrowly defined specifications for well-defined performance characteristics was something to come in the late 1920s and afterward. (Ryan's Spirit of St. Louis designed in 1927 for Charles Lindbergh is a perfect example of a point-designed airplane—everything was focused on maximizing range and reliability to help Lindbergh get safely across the Atlantic Ocean.) The specific requirements that led to the P-51 came from a need by the U.K. Royal Air Force (RAF) for more fighter airplanes in 1940. The RAF wanted U.S. P-40s made by Curtiss, or some other airplane of similar performance. North American was approached about applying their successful mass-production skills to the manufacture of Curtiss P-40s for the British. North American's top design engineers were not happy about stamping out somebody else's airplane, especially the P-40, which was already obsolete at the time. Edgar Schmued, a German immigrant in 1930, was North America's chief designer. Schmued in his 1990 biography entitled *Mustang Designer* by Ray Wagner (Orion Books, recently reprinted by the Smithsonian Press) tells the following story:

> We desperately wanted to build a fighter. It started very peculiarly. First there were rumors of North American Aviation building the Curtiss P-40 to ensure quick delivery to the British. . . . One afternoon in March (1940), Dutch Kindelberger came to my office (Kindelberger had been the chief engineer for Douglas at the inception of the DC-1 and, in 1934, moved on to become president and general manager of General Aviation Manufacturing Corporation, which later became North American Aviation) and said "Ed, do we want to build P-40's here?" From the tone of his voice, I knew what kind of answer he expected. I said, "Well, Dutch, don't let us build an obsolete airplane, let's build a new one. We can design a better one and build a better one." And that's exactly what he wanted to hear. So he said "Ed, I'm going to England in about two weeks, and I need an inboard profile, three-view drawing, performance estimate, weight estimate, specifications, and some detail drawings on the gun installation to take along. Then I would like to sell that new model airplane that you develop."

Kindelberger laid down the rules for the design in a simple fashion: "Make it the fastest airplane you can and build it around a man that is 5 feet 10 inches tall and weighs 140 pounds. It should have two 20-mm cannons in each wing and should meet all design requirements of the United States Army Air Corp." And that was the full extent of the original design specifications for the P-51.

Schmued was not starting from scratch. In the previous year, he had "a burning ambition to build the best fighter." Working alone, he prepared sketches of a low-wing monoplane, which were sitting in his desk when Kindelberger laid down the specifications. With these sketches, Kindelberger went to England and returned later with a British contract for 400 P-51s. This is how the best U.S. fighter of World War II was born.

The revolution that took place in the process of airplane design in the 1930s is reflected is part by the growing acceptance of new technology by many airplane designers. The design of the P-51 is an excellent example. Driven by Kindelberger's instruction to "make it the fastest airplane you can," Schmued and his designers were awake to any new technology that would either decrease drag, or increase engine power, or both. To their credit, both happened. Let us take a closer look.

Originally, the North American design team planned to use a standard five-digit NACA 23 series airfoil for the wing. During the early design stage, however, two NACA engineers, Russ Robinson and Ed Hartman, paid a visit to North American and informed the company's aerodynamicist Ed Horkey (the company had only one aerodynamicist at the time) about the NACA research on laminar-flow airfoils. As noted earlier, this research was considered by NACA to be so important and so sensitive that the results were classified; as a result, information about the existence of the laminar-flow airfoils was not common knowledge. Horkey was impressed with the NACA wind tunnel measurements that showed more than a 30 percent reduction in drag for the laminar flow airfoil shapes. Rather than adopting one of the NACA airfoil shapes directly, Horkey instead adopted the NACA *theoretical technique* used for designing the shapes and designed a thinner laminar-flow airfoil tailored specifically for the P-51 wing. The resulting wing design incorporated a 16-percent thick airfoil at the root and 11-percent thick at the tip. Hedging their bets, however, North American also designed a wing using a more conventional NACA 23-series five-digit airfoil shape. They made wind-tunnel models of both wings and tested them in the 10-foot GALCIT wind tunnel at Cal Tech. These tests were considered unsatisfactory because of high-turbulence levels in the boundary layer on the tunnel walls, although the laminar-flow wing did exhibit lower drag. The University of Washington had a larger, 8 × 12 foot wind tunnel, where the walls would be farther away from the wing models. So, in Horkey's words, "I got on a DC-3 and went up to Seattle with the model tucked away in the back of the airplane. We tested for both maximum lift, drag, and stall characteristics, and they came out great, so that was our shape from then on." That was how the P-51 became the first airplane designed with a laminar-flow wing. (Ironically, the P-51 and all other later airplane designs that used the laminar-flow airfoil did not enjoy laminar flow over the wing. The wind-tunnel models used by NACA for their measurements of the laminar-flow airfoil properties were like finely polished jewels with very smooth surfaces. In contrast, the rough realities of actual fabrication of the wings in the factory resulted in comparably rough surfaces, which became even more rough during use of the airplane in the field. Surface roughness encourages turbulent flow, and as a result the laminar-flow wings of the P-51 were instead bathed in higher drag turbulent boundary layers. But once again serendipity stepped in. The laminar-flow airfoils turned out to have higher critical Mach numbers—something that was not the intent of the original airfoil design. As a result, the P-51 and other airplanes with laminar-flow wings had superior performance at high speeds where compressibility effects are important. So the P-51 wing was a winner, but for a different reason than its original intent.)

North American P-51D, arguably the best fighter airplane of World War II. (Harold Andrews Collection.)

This episode illustrates not only the acceptance of new technology in the airplane design process in the late 1930s, but also the growing use of wind-tunnel data during the preliminary design process. Until the 1930s, new airplanes were designed by industry with little or no use of wind-tunnel data. This is reflected by the fact that aircraft companies at that time had no large wind tunnels of their own, let alone the staff to operate them. Clark Millikan, a Cal Tech professor, recognized this vacuum in the U.S. aircraft industry, and in 1926 began the design of a large wind tunnel at Cal Tech that would geographically be at the center of California's growing aircraft industry and would be available for testing the future generations of new airplane designs. This wind tunnel became operational in the early 1930s, and many of the important designs from the era of the mature propeller-driven airplane were tested in this facility. (One of the first was the Douglas DC-1, followed by the DC-2 and DC-3 as discussed in the first part of this chapter.) Likewise, the large wind tunnel at the University of Washington became a major servant to Boeing. The process of airplane design during the 1930s took a large technological leap forward when it began to include the intelligent use of wind-tunnel data in specific airplane designs.

Another example of advanced technology incorporated in the design of the P-51 was the radiator for cooling the engine. A side view of the prototype P-51, the North American NA-73X, is shown in Figure 6.42. As seen in Figure 6.42, the radiator is located underneath the fuselage and wing, about halfway along the fuselage. Although this was an unconventional location for an engine cooling radiator, its position was considered optimum by the North American designers. Under varied flight conditions, all of the air that enters the opening of the radiator can not go through the core of the radiator itself; the excess spills out around the edges, causing local adverse aerodynamic interactions with either the wing or fuselage, resulting in an increase in drag. With the radiator of the P-51 in the position shown in Figure 6.42, this interaction and drag increase was minimized. But its location is only part of the story. As a matter of serendipity, the heated

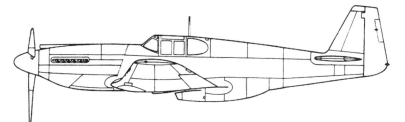

FIGURE 6.42
Side view of the North American NA-73X, prototype of the P-51 Mustang.

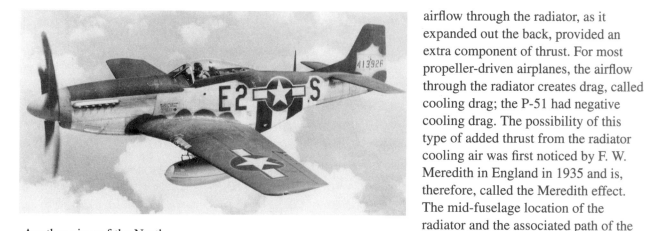

Another view of the North American P-51D, with Normandy D-Day markings. The P-51D had a drag coefficient of 0.0163, to this author's knowledge the lowest drag coefficient of any propeller-driven fighter. (Harold Andrews Collection.)

airflow through the radiator, as it expanded out the back, provided an extra component of thrust. For most propeller-driven airplanes, the airflow through the radiator creates drag, called cooling drag; the P-51 had negative cooling drag. The possibility of this type of added thrust from the radiator cooling air was first noticed by F. W. Meredith in England in 1935 and is, therefore, called the Meredith effect. The mid-fuselage location of the radiator and the associated path of the airflow was just right to give the P-51 the benefit of the Meredith effect. And yet another novel aspect of the radiator design was the boundary-layer bleed feature of the upper lip of the radiator. Note in Figure 6.42 the small gap between the upper part of the radiator inlet and the bottom of the fuselage. This gap allowed the turbulent boundary layer on the surface of the fuselage to flow over the radiator inlet rather than through the inlet, thus, preserving a better quality airflow into the radiator. Such boundary-layer bleed geometry is common today on inlets of modern jet fighter airplanes; in the day of the P-51, it was a novel feature.

The P-51 was the epitome of the low-drag streamlined airplane; its zero-lift drag coefficient of 0.0163 was the lowest of all of the World War II propeller-driven airplanes. This was no accident. The North American designers used all of their ploys to achieve such low drag. In addition to the aerodynamic features already discussed, the P-51 nose was wrapped around a liquid-cooled engine of low frontal area; the early versions were powered by Allison engines, and later versions were equipped with more powerful supercharged Rolls–Royce Merlin engines. North American's design philosophy for the low-drag fuselage, as explained by Edgar Schmued, was to create a shape such that "the air can flow evenly around the body." Schmued used mathematically precise curves generated by conic sections to shape the fuselage. The P-51 was the first airplane to be shaped by such second-degree curves. Schmued relates, "I laid out the lines myself and it was a first."

The prototype NA-73X was rolled out exactly 100 days after the design began—a miraculous feat. The first flight was delayed because the Allison engine was not ready. Finally, on Saturday, October 26, 1940, the prototype P-51 took to the air for the first time, just six and a half months after the British had signed the letter of intent to purchase 400 airplanes from North American.

The P-51 Mustang went on to become the greatest American fighter airplane of World War II. One of its later and most widely used versions, the P-51D, is shown in Figure 6.43. Look carefully at Figure 6.43; what you see is one of the best products of the design process that evolved during the era of the mature propeller-driven airplane.

Air Racing—Did it Enhance Technology?

On September 13, 1931, a highly streamlined airplane, the Supermarine S.6B, flashed through the clear afternoon sky near Portsmouth, along the southern English coast. Piloted by Flight Lieutenant John N. Boothman, that racing airplane averaged a speed of 340.1 miles per hour around a long, seven-lap course, winning

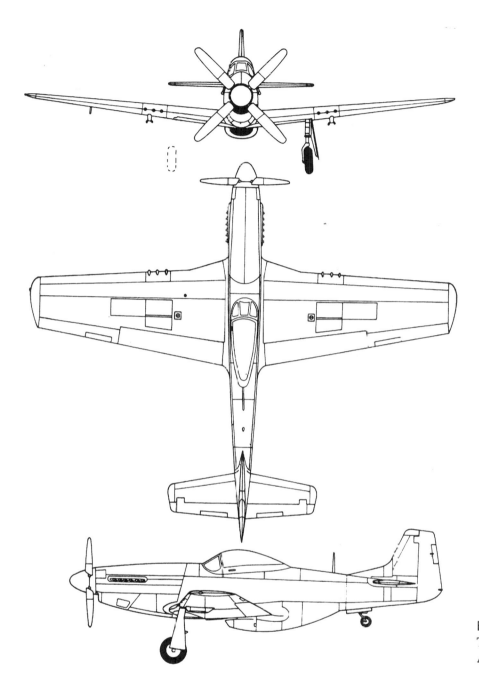

FIGURE 6.43
Three-view of the North
American P-51D Mustang.

the coveted Schneider Trophy permanently for the United Kingdom. Later that
month, Flight Lieutenant George H. Stainforth set the world's speed record of
401.5 miles per hour in the same S.6B. This airplane, shown in Figure 6.44,
embodied aerodynamic streamlining with a powerful Rolls–Royce "R" racing
engine, producing 2300 horsepower for limited durations.

      The S.6B was a product of the fascination with air racing during the period
between the two world wars. Serious competitions were held in Europe and the
United States. Among the most popular were the international Schneider trophy
races limited to seaplanes and the Pulitzer, Thompson Trophy, and National Air
Races in the United States. Very specific, point-designed racing airplanes were

FIGURE 6.44
The Supermarine S-6B.
Winner of the Schneider
Trophy, 1931. (From E.
Angelucci, *Airplanes
From the Dawn of Flight
to the Present Day*,
McGraw-Hill, New York,
1973.)

built for these races, where brute force engine power was the dominant characteristic and more than the usual attention was paid to drag reduction. As a result, it is natural to expect that air racing played some role in advancing the technology of the airplane. On closer examination, however, the reality is quite the opposite; for the most part, racing airplanes incorporated as much of the cutting-edge, but *existing*, technology as the designers were willing to use. To the author's knowledge, no pioneering new technical development came out of the design and operation of racing airplanes that subsequently was transferred to conventional airplanes. What gives racing airplanes the appearance of introducing new technology is their usually "spiffy" looks, sleek, streamlined, and power personified, at a time when conventional airplanes sometimes were rather "clunky" and pedestrian looking. But these spiffy looks were a result of the point-design feature of racing airplanes. The designer usually had one and only one specification in mind, speed. So racing airplanes had souped-up engines tweeked for operation at maximum power; these engines only had to run for short periods of time—enough time to complete the race. If they had been used on conventional airplanes for long-duration flights, many of the engines would have self-destructed. Racing airplanes were also lightweight. They did not have to carry a lot of fuel, more than one human (the pilot), or baggage or other commercial or military payload. So the design specifications of racing airplanes were completely different than conventional airplanes. The designer of racing airplanes was unfettered by other considerations; racing airplanes were point designed for only one characteristic—speed.

On the other hand, driven by the quest for speed some new technology was developed, but this remained parochial to the family of racing airplanes and did not transfer to conventional designs. A classic example was radiator design. The cooling of high-powered engines was critical. Conventional technology yielded large, bulky radiators for liquid-cooled engines. Cooling air would pass through these radiators, with the attendant high-cooling drag. As early as 1920, engineers at the Curtiss Company conceived an innovative radiator design for the single purpose of reducing the cooling drag. Glenn Curtiss was personally enamored with speed, and he led his company in the design of a series of highly successful and spectacular air racers in the early 1920s. In an effort to reduce the drag of these racers to a minimum, the Curtiss designers spread the passages for the liquid coolant over thin regions of very large surface area installed in the surfaces of the wing and fuselage. Figure 6.45 shows the Curtiss R2C-1 racer that won the 1923 Pulitzer Air Race, setting an unofficial world speed record of 243.7 miles per hour.

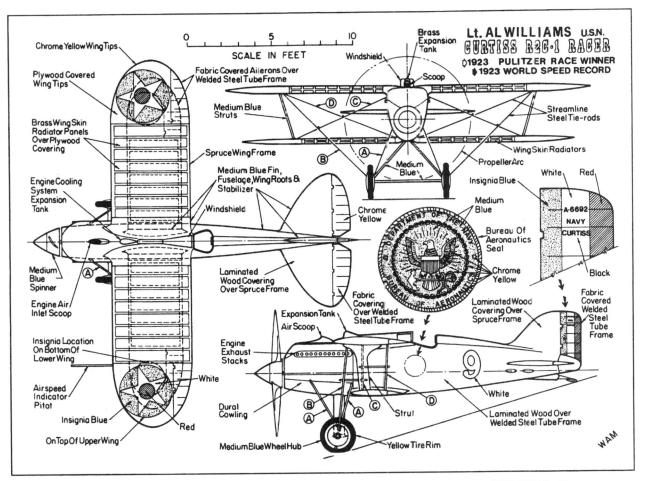

FIGURE 6.45
Curtiss R2C-1 racer,
winner of the 1923 Pulitzer
Race. (American Aviation
Historical Society, AAHS,
Walter Musciano.)

The radiator panels on the wings are clearly seen in the top and front views in Figure 6.45. The airflow over the wings and fuselages would cool the hot liquid, which was then pumped back to the engine. Hence, engine cooling was provided by the natural aerodynamic flow over the airplane with (hopefully) little adverse effect on the aerodynamics, providing a virtual elimination of cooling drag. Much later, in 1929, NACA ran some wind-tunnel tests on a wing panel with skin-mounted radiator panels. They found that the Curtiss-designed cooling passages, which protruded about a quarter of an inch above the natural wing surface and were oriented in the flow direction, caused a higher than expected increase in drag compared with that for a perfectly smooth wing surface. Nevertheless, the tradeoff was still beneficial when compared with the increase in drag that would have been caused by the standard large, bulky radiator design. Finally, the British refined the surface radiator concept by replacing the corrugated protrusions of the Curtiss racers with rectangular flow passages buried flush inside the skin surface, with a smooth outer skin. When this configuration was used on the Supermarine Schneider racers, there was virtually no increase in drag due to the radiator panels.

Skin-mounted radiator surfaces were appropriate for point-designed air racers, but they were impractical for conventional airplanes. The radiator surfaces were easily damaged on the ground during routine handling and maintenance of the airplane. The deflection of the wing structure by large aerodynamic loads

The Curtiss R3C-2 racer in which Jimmy Doolittle won the 1925 Schneider Cup race. Doolittle's racer now hangs in the Pioneers of Flight Gallery at the National Air and Space Museum, Smithsonian Institution.

during maneuvering would strain and break soldered joints, causing coolant leakage. Also, for military airplanes designed for combat use, the large surface areas of the radiator panels were very vulnerable to battle damage. As a result, this technology did not transfer to conventional airplanes. This was no real loss, however, because, as we have already discussed in regard to the design of the P-51, other, more practical solutions to reduce cooling drag were subsequently found.

The question as to how air racing advanced the technology of the airplane is a primary focus of a recent book by the late Birch Matthews (*Race with the Wind: How Air Racing Advanced Aviation*, Motor Books International, 2001). It appears to this reader that Matthews started the book with the conviction that air racers did advance the technology of the airplane, but by the time he finished his detailed and thorough analysis of the question, he had come to the opposite conclusion. Matthews points out that in the early 1920s, when air racers were designed by established airplane manufacturers such as Curtiss and funded by the government, there was an overall small but positive influence on military fighter airplanes. You might see this by comparing the Curtiss R2C-1 racer of 1923 shown in Figure 6.45 with the Navy Curtiss F6C-4 Hawk of 1926 shown in Figure 6.46. Designed by the same company, the Curtiss Hawk has a few genes from the earlier, more streamlined R2C-1 racer. But the practical design requirements for a U.S. Navy fighter did not allow the luxury of a "spiffy" airplane design like the R2C-1. We note also that the airplanes in Figures 6.45 and 6.46 are still examples of the era of the strut-and-wire biplane; for this era, any experience with high-performance racing airplanes was a contribution, no matter how minor. On the other hand, in a detailed and lengthy analysis of air races from the 1930s, Matthews shows that advanced technology flowed from conventional airplanes to the racing airplanes rather than vice versa. Shown in Figures 6.47–6.49 are detailed drawings of three famous racing airplanes from the 1930s. The Laird "Solution" that won the 1930 Thompson Trophy race with an average speed of 202 miles per hour is shown in Figure 6.47. The Solution had adopted the existing new technology of a ground adjustable propeller and the NACA cowling, but also contained the anachronistic biplane configuration with fixed landing gear. The Howard DGA-6 "Mister Mulligan," shown in Figure 6.48, won the 1935 Thompson Trophy with an average velocity of 220 miles per hour. This monoplane had a controllable pitch propeller and a NACA cowling, but had fixed landing gear. Perhaps the most impressive racing airplane of the period was the Hughes 1B racer shown in Figure 6.49. This airplane set a U.S. transcontinental speed record, covering the distance from Burbank, California, to Newark, New Jersey, in 7 hours and 28 minutes on January 19, 1937. In Figure 6.49, we see an aesthetically beautiful, ultrastreamlined racing airplane with the latest Hamilton–Standard hydromatic controllable pitch propeller, NACA cowling, and retractable landing gear. But these same features were to be found on a number of conventional airplanes at the time, including the Douglas DC-3. In the final analysis, Matthews ends his book with the following:

The notion that 1930's air racing was an aerial proving ground influencing World War II fighter design is a romantic myth. It just did not happen. Racing was then, as it is now, a tremendously exciting sport enjoyed by tens of thousands. It was a diversion during a time of national economic depression. It was a fascinating spectacle during a time of exceptional public aviation interest. It was a forum in which women could participate, during a time of male domination in virtually all matters outside the home. That was all it was. That was enough. . . .

A final comment is worth making before we leave this question. Although the author knows of no specific pioneering contribution made by racing airplanes to the technology of the airplane, there was an unquantifiable contribution to the maturation of airplane designers as professionals. One specific case is that of the designer of the famous British Supermarine Spitfire of World War II, Reginald Mitchell. Working for Supermarine in the earlier days, Mitchell designed the S6.B that won the Schneider Trophy for the United Kingdom in 1931 (Figure 6.44). Comparing the S6.B in Figure 6.44 with the Spitfire shown in Figure 6.9, we see two basically different airplanes. This point is further brought home by comparing the three-view of the S6.B in Figure 6.50 with the three-view of the Spitfire in Figure 6.34. But the Spitfire was designed by the same man who designed the S6.B five years earlier. When Mitchell began the design of the Spitfire in 1935, he was professionally more mature than when he designed the S6.B. Part of this professional maturity came from Mitchell's experience in the design of air racers. The author is convinced that this type of maturation process in the minds of airplane designers was fed in some unquantifiable and maybe even subconscious manner by air racing.

A detail of the Curtiss R3C-2 racer at the National Air and Space Museum, Smithsonian Institution, highlighting the radiator panels buried in the surface of the wings, a design feature unique to some racing airplanes.

BLIND-SIDED BY THE FUTURE

Faster and higher—those were the goals of most new airplanes designed during the 1930s. This period was a golden age of aeronautical engineering. But some advanced thinkers were getting worried; some of the gold gilt was beginning to wear thin. The propeller-driven airplane was achieving a pinnacle of success and advancement hardly dreamed possible just 20 years prior. Some World War II

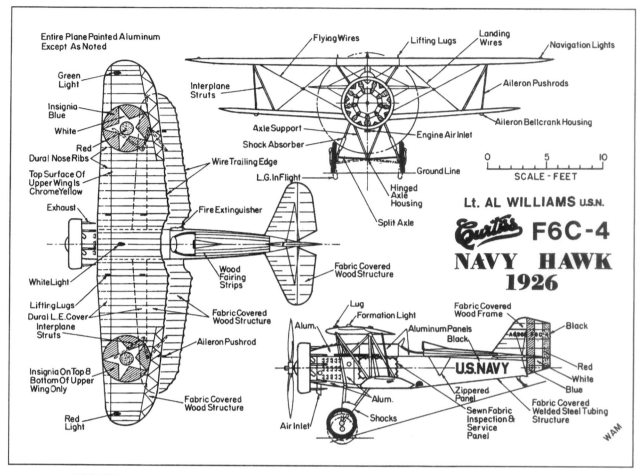

FIGURE 6.46
Curtiss F6C-4 Hawk,
Navy fighter airplane,
1926. (American Aviation
Historical Society, Walter
Musciano.)

fighter airplanes were nudging the speed of sound in high-speed dives; for example, the British Spitfire could reach Mach 0.92. By that time, it was well known that the aerodynamic drag of an airplane increases dramatically as it approaches Mach 1, so much so that no existing engine–propeller combination could produce enough thrust to overcome this drag increase. As a result, the speed of sound loomed as a barrier to faster speeds—this was popularly labeled the "sound barrier." Indeed, there was virtually no hope that propeller-driven airplanes would ever penetrate the sound barrier. In addition to shock waves that occur locally on the wings and fuselages of airplanes as the flight speed approaches Mach 1, there will be strong shock waves on the propeller that dramatically reduce the propeller's efficiency and its thrust. To this day, no propeller-driven airplane has ever flown faster than the speed of sound.

Put yourself in the shoes of an aeronautical engineer in 1936 and reflect on the future of aeronautics from that perspective. You would be in the same situation as Theodore P. Wright, Vice President for engineering at Curtiss, who on December 29, 1936 stepped forward and delivered a paper to the Aeronautic Meeting of the American Association for the Advancement of Science at Atlantic City on the subject of "Speed—And Airplane Possibilities." In his paper, Wright presented a graph showing speed versus chronological year for airplanes, reproduced here as Figure 6.51. The solid curves are reality for the period before

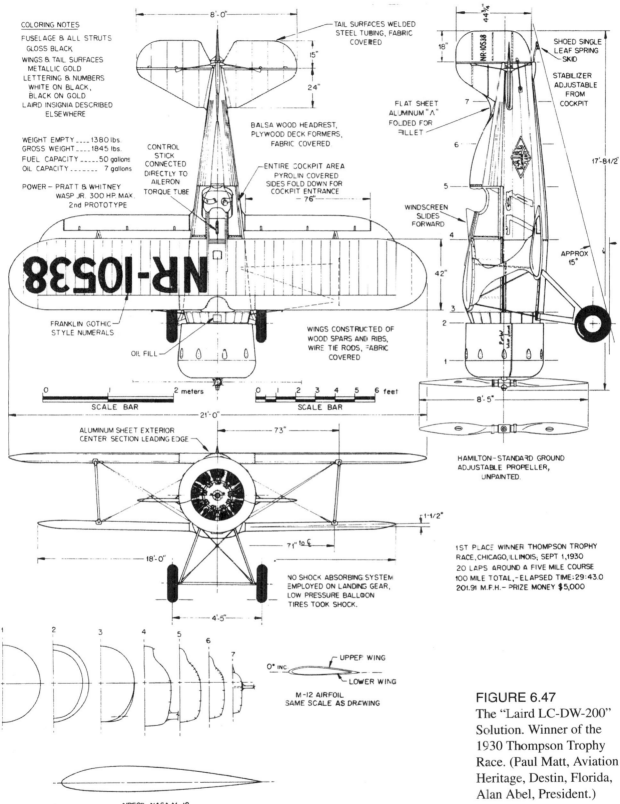

COLORING NOTES

FUSELAGE & ALL STRUTS
   GLOSS BLACK
WINGS & TAIL SURFACES
   METALLIC GOLD
LETTERING & NUMBERS
   WHITE ON BLACK,
   BLACK ON GOLD
LAIRD INSIGNIA DESCRIBED
   ELSEWHERE

WEIGHT EMPTY ____ 1380 lbs.
GROSS WEIGHT ____ 1845 lbs.
FUEL CAPACITY _____ 50 gallons
OIL CAPACITY _____ 7 gallons

POWER – PRATT & WHITNEY
   WASP JR. 300 H.P. MAX.
   2nd PROTOTYPE

TAIL SURFACES WELDED
STEEL TUBING, FABRIC
COVERED

BALSA WOOD HEADREST,
PLYWOOD DECK FORMERS,
FABRIC COVERED.

CONTROL
STICK
CONNECTED
DIRECTLY TO
AILERON
TORQUE TUBE

ENTIRE COCKPIT AREA
PYROLIN COVERED
SIDES FOLD DOWN FOR
COCKPIT ENTRANCE
— 76" —

FRANKLIN GOTHIC
STYLE NUMERALS

OIL FILL

WINGS CONSTRUCTED OF
WOOD SPARS AND RIBS,
WIRE TIE RODS, FABRIC
COVERED

SCALE BAR   2 meters

SCALE BAR   6 feet

ALUMINUM SHEET EXTERIOR
CENTER SECTION LEADING EDGE

FLAT SHEET
ALUMINUM "A"
FOLDED FOR
FILLET

WINDSCREEN
SLIDES
FORWARD

SHOED SINGLE
LEAF SPRING
SKID

STABILIZER
ADJUSTABLE
FROM
COCKPIT

APPROX
15°

NO SHOCK ABSORBING SYSTEM
EMPLOYED ON LANDING GEAR,
LOW PRESSURE BALLOON
TIRES TOOK SHOCK.

HAMILTON-STANDARD GROUND
ADJUSTABLE PROPELLER,
UNPAINTED.

1ST PLACE WINNER THOMPSON TROPHY
RACE, CHICAGO, ILLINOIS; SEPT 1, 1930
20 LAPS AROUND A FIVE MILE COURSE
100 MILE TOTAL, - ELAPSED TIME: 29:43.0
201.91 M.P.H. – PRIZE MONEY $5,000

UPPER WING

0° INC.

LOWER WING

M-12 AIRFOIL
SAME SCALE AS DRAWING

AIRFOIL NACA M-12
(DEVELOPED INTO NACA 2212)

FIGURE 6.47
The "Laird LC-DW-200"
Solution. Winner of the
1930 Thompson Trophy
Race. (Paul Matt, Aviation
Heritage, Destin, Florida,
Alan Abel, President.)

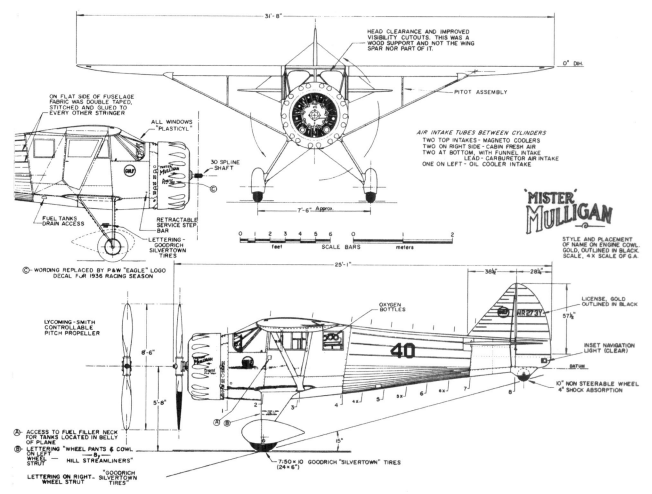

FIGURE 6.48
Howard DGA-6 "Mister Mulligan," 1934–36. (Paul Matt, Aviation Heritage, Destin, Florida)

1936. The dashed curves are Wright's guess for the ensuing 10 years, and all of the dashed curves bend over and approach limits that are at 500 miles per hour or slower. This was the future as far as knowledgeable people could see. Wright discussed how incremental improvements in drag reduction, propeller efficiency, reduced weight, wing loading, and higher altitude flight would increase airplane speeds, but only incrementally and only up to a certain limit. He stated, "At a figure of slightly over 500 miles per hour the factor of compressibility, neglected throughout in the development of aerodynamic theory, will commence to play an important part which will eventually at slightly higher speeds represent a probable ultimate limit." To dedicated and enthusiastic aeronautical engineers, this "ultimate limit" had to have been depressing.

World War II served to focus aeronautical engineering on the incremental improvements discussed by Wright in his 1936 paper. In the United States, the design of new airplanes was frozen, and the emphasis during the war was the mass production of existing designs. Virtually every U.S. airplane that saw service during the war was designed before December 7, 1941. The experimental facilities of NACA were dedicated to the improvement of existing airplane types, and the type of advanced, leading-edge research characteristic of NACA was put on hold

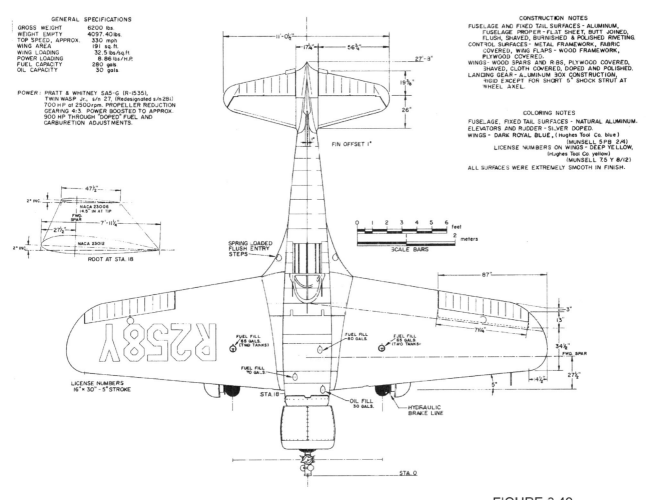

GENERAL SPECIFICATIONS
GROSS WEIGHT   6200 lbs.
WEIGHT EMPTY   4097.40 lbs.
TOP SPEED, APPROX.   330 mph
WING AREA   191 sq.ft.
WING LOADING   32.5 lbs/sq.ft.
POWER LOADING   8.86 lbs/H.P.
FUEL CAPACITY   280 gals.
OIL CAPACITY   30 gals.

POWER: PRATT & WHITNEY SA5-G (R-1535),
       TWIN WASP Jr., s/n 27, (Redesignated s/n 28)
       700 H.P. at 2500rpm. PROPELLER REDUCTION
       GEARING 4:3. POWER BOOSTED TO APPROX.
       900 HP THROUGH "DOPED" FUEL AND
       CARBURETION ADJUSTMENTS.

CONSTRUCTION NOTES
FUSELAGE AND FIXED TAIL SURFACES - ALUMINUM,
    FUSELAGE PROPER - FLAT SHEET, BUTT JOINED,
    FLUSH, SHAVED, BURNISHED & POLISHED RIVETING.
CONTROL SURFACES - METAL FRAMEWORK, FABRIC
    COVERED, WING FLAPS - WOOD FRAMEWORK,
    PLYWOOD COVERED.
WINGS - WOOD SPARS AND RIBS, PLYWOOD COVERED,
    SHAVED, CLOTH COVERED, DOPED AND POLISHED.
LANDING GEAR - ALUMINUM 30X CONSTRUCTION,
    RIGID EXCEPT FOR SHORT 5" SHOCK STRUT AT
    WHEEL AXEL.

COLORING NOTES
FUSELAGE, FIXED TAIL SURFACES - NATURAL ALUMINUM.
ELEVATORS AND RUDDER - SILVER DOPED.
WINGS - DARK ROYAL BLUE, (Hughes Tool Co. blue)
                              (MUNSELL 5PB 2/4)
    LICENSE NUMBERS ON WINGS - DEEP YELLOW,
    (Hughes Tool Co. yellow)
                              (MUNSELL 7.5 Y 8/12)
ALL SURFACES WERE EXTREMELY SMOOTH IN FINISH.

FIGURE 6.49

Hughes 1B Racer. Set the U.S. transcontinental speed record, Burbank, California, to Newark, New Jersey, 7 hours, 28 minutes, 25 seconds, January 19, 1937. (Paul Matt, Aviation Heritage, Destin, Florida). (*Continued*)

for most of the duration of the war. The golden age of aeronautical engineering that began with the design revolution in the early 1930s had run its course.

But a new golden age was about to burst on the scene, a second golden age of aeronautical engineering of which nobody had dreamed. Known by only a few people, the jet engine was being invented independently in Germany and England during the late 1930s. The advent of the jet engine would bring to an end the development of the airplane as known by Wilbur and Orville Wright and would open a new era—the era of the jet-propelled airplane. The inventors of the jet engine created a revolution in aeronautics fully equivalent to the revolution started by the Wright brothers on December 17, 1903. The era of the jet-propelled airplane is the subject of the next chapter; because we are still living in that era, it is also the last chapter of this book.

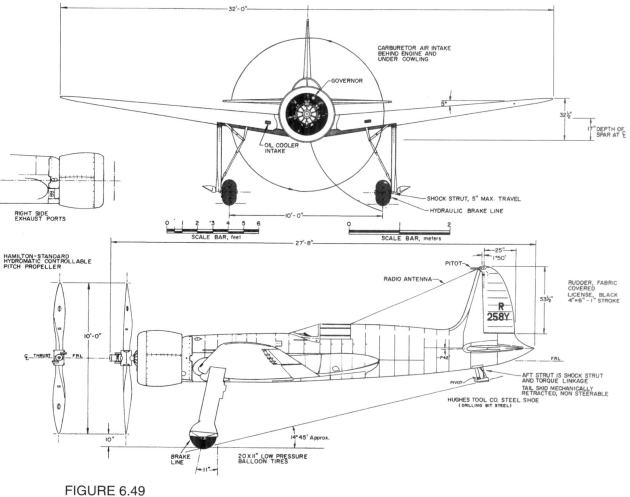

FIGURE 6.49
(*Continued from page 277.*)

The Hughes 1B racer, 1935, in the Golden Age of Flight Gallery at the National Air and Space Museum, Smithsonian Institution.

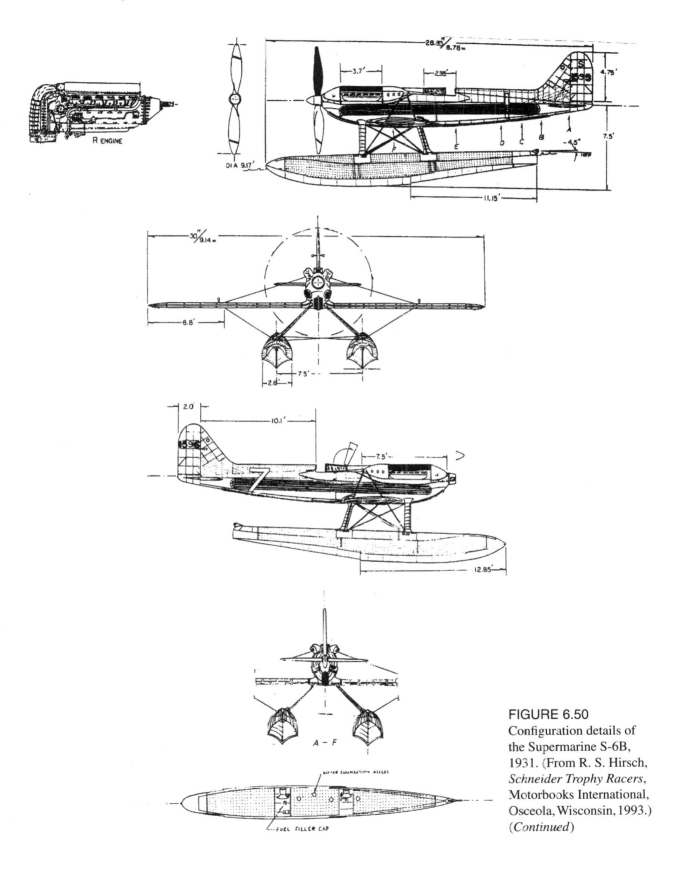

FIGURE 6.50
Configuration details of
the Supermarine S-6B,
1931. (From R. S. Hirsch,
Schneider Trophy Racers,
Motorbooks International,
Osceola, Wisconsin, 1993.)
(*Continued*)

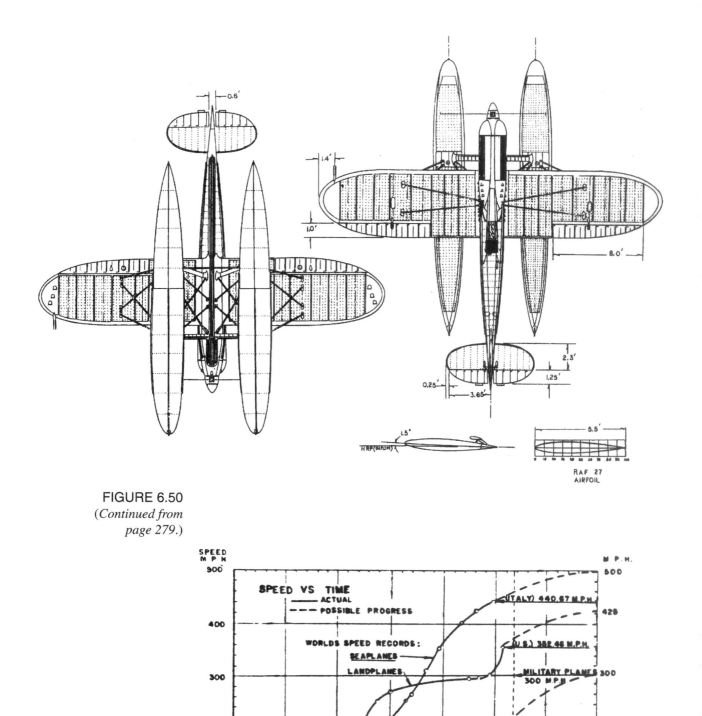

FIGURE 6.50
(*Continued from page 279.*)

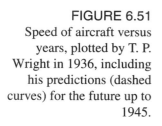

FIGURE 6.51
Speed of aircraft versus years, plotted by T. P. Wright in 1936, including his predictions (dashed curves) for the future up to 1945.

Bob Love's P-51D racing airplane; this photo was taken in 1965 at Las Vegas. The P-51 has remained a favorite of air racing pilots to the present day, a testimonial to its superb design. (American Aviation Historical Society, AAHS, from Bob Lawson.)

Lockheed P-38 Lightning, 1944. Based on the original P-38 design of 1939, the P-38L was the last version of this famous airplane to be produced. The P-38 was the first airplane to encounter severe compressibility effects at high speeds, resulting in the destruction of several early P-38s. (American Aviation Historical Society, AAHS, from Ray Wagner.)

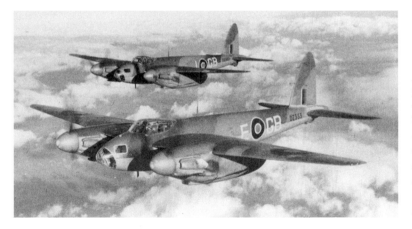

DeHavilland D.H. 98 Mosquito IV, 1942. Made from wood for lightness and reduced radar detection, the Mosquito could fly higher than existing fighter airplanes. (Harold Andrews Collection.)

Avro Lancaster B.II, 1943.
(Harold Andrews
Collection.)

Republic P-47D-25, 1941.
The Thunderbolt is a
classic example of the
fighter airplane during the
era of the mature
propeller-driven airplane.
(American Aviation
Historical Society, AAHS,
from Republic Aviation.)

CHAPTER

The Second Design Revolution: The Era of the Jet-Propelled Airplane

We have the aerodynamic knowledge, the structural materials, the power plants, and the manufacturing capacities to perform any conceivable miracle in aviation. But miracles must be planned, nurtured, and executed with intelligence and hard work.

Glenn L. Martin
Aviation pioneer and manufacturer
1954

The morning of Tuesday, October 14, 1947, dawned bright and beautiful over Muroc Dry Lake, a large expanse of flat, hard surface in the Mojave Desert in California. At 6:00 a.m., teams of engineers and technicians at the Muroc Army Air Field began to prepare a small rocket-powered airplane for flight. Painted orange and resembling a 50-caliber machine-gun bullet mated to a pair of straight, stubby wings, the Bell X-1 research vehicle was carefully installed in the bomb bay of a four-engine B-29 bomber of World War II vintage. At 10:00 a.m., the B-29 took off and climbed to an altitude of 20,000 feet. As it rose past 5000 feet, Captain Charles ("Chuck") Yeager, a veteran P-51 pilot from the European theater during World War II, struggled into the cockpit of the X-1. Yeager was in pain from two broken ribs incurred during a horseback accident the previous weekend, but not wishing to disrupt the events of the day, he informed no one except his close friend Captain Jack Ridley, who was helping him to squeeze into the X-1 cockpit. At 10:26 a.m., at a speed of 250 miles per hour, the brightly painted X-1 dropped free from the B-29. Yeager fired his Reaction Motors XLR-11 rocket engine, and, powered by 6000 pounds of thrust, the sleek airplane accelerated and climbed rapidly. Trailing an exhaust jet of shock diamonds from the four convergent–divergent rocket nozzles of the engine, the X-1 was soon flying faster than Mach 0.85, the speed beyond which there were no wind-tunnel data in 1947—and beyond which no one knew what problems might be encountered in

FIGURE 7.1
The Bell X-1, the first
piloted airplane to fly
faster than sound, October
14, 1947.

transonic flight. Entering that unknown realm, Yeager momentarily shut down two of the four rocket chambers and carefully tested the controls of the X-1 as the Mach meter in the cockpit registered 0.95 and still increasing. Small invisible shock waves were dancing back and forth over the top surface of the wings. At an altitude of 40,000 feet, the X-1 began to level off, and Yeager fired one of the two shutdown rocket chambers. The Mach meter moved smoothly through 0.98 and 0.99 to reach 1.02. There the meter hesitated and then jumped to 1.06. A stronger bow shock wave was formed in the air ahead of the needle nose of the X-1 as Yeager reached a velocity of 700 miles per hour, Mach 1.06, at 43,000 feet. The flight was smooth; there was no violent buffeting of the airplane and no loss of control, as had been feared by some engineers. At that moment, Yeager became the first pilot to fly faster than the speed of sound, and the small, streamlined Bell X-1 (Figure 7.1) became the first supersonic airplane in the history of flight.

As the sonic boom from the X-1 propagated across the California desert, that flight became the most significant milestone in the history of the technology of the airplane since the Wright brothers' first flight at Kill Devil Hills 44 years earlier. The sound barrier had been broken—indeed, it was not a barrier at all. A new future had been opened for flight—high-speed flight at and beyond the speed of sound. Along with that, a second golden age of aeronautical engineering dawned. The present chapter deals with this new golden age of aeronautical engineering, which fits squarely in the era of jet-propelled airplane. The gestation of this era took place in the 1930s, but the birth of the new breed of high-speed airplanes powered by jet engines started about 1945 and continues to the present.

A REVOLUTION IN AERONAUTICS—THE JET ENGINE

Anybody who has inflated a balloon and then let go of the neck and watched the balloon skitter through the air has witnessed jet propulsion in action. The concept of jet propulsion is not new; obtaining thrust in one direction by exhausting a jet of liquid or gas in the opposite direction out of some type of device has been known (but not necessarily understood) for centuries. The application of this principle for propelling an airplane through the air was seriously examined in the United States as early as 1923 by the National Bureau of Standards under contract to NACA. In a report entitled "Jet Propulsion for Aeronautics" by Edgar Buckingham, and published by NACA as Technical Report 159, the practical application of jet propulsion to airplanes was carefully studied. The results were pessimistic. Buckingham concluded that the fuel consumption of a jet engine would be four times as high as that of conventional reciprocating engines with propellers and would be heavier and more complicated. These conclusions were correct for the 250 miles per hour or less flight speeds considered in the report; however, they were not applicable to high-speed flight near or above the speed of sound. Nevertheless, this was enough for NACA to put jet propulsion for aircraft on a back burner. Another negative assessment of gas turbine engines for aircraft came from a committee of scientists appointed by the National Academy of Sciences in 1938. It is not in the least surprising that not only NACA, but also the rest of the aeronautical community in the United States, was lulled into complacency about jet propulsion before World War II.

The opposite of complacency was the mind of a young Royal Air Force (RAF) officer attending the flight instructors course at the Central Flying School at Whittering, England, in 1929. Pilot Officer Frank Whittle had graduated from the RAF technical college at Cranwell the previous year, where he had written a senior thesis entitled "Future Developments in Aircraft Design." In that paper he examined two new concepts for propulsion devices for airplanes—rocket engines and gas turbines driving propellers. Whittle later wrote,

> At that time it did not occur to me to combine the two ideas. The very low efficiency of rockets ruled them out for long range aircraft, and the gas turbine propeller combination did not look promising for the order of speed I was thinking about, namely 500 miles per hour. So my thesis did not provide the answer I was looking for. Nevertheless, it marked the beginning of my quest for an alternative to the piston engine propeller combination.

During his course at the Central Flying School, Whittle had an epiphany: Increase the compressor compression ratio and substitute a turbine for the piston engine. Whittle later labeled this instant as "the birth of the turbojet."

Drawing some sketches of his engine concept, Whittle discussed his idea with his commandant, who was impressed, and who directed Whittle to officials in the Air Ministry. The resulting discussions led nowhere; the Ministry considered any form of gas turbine totally impractical. Whittle went on to file for a patent on January 16, 1930, and it was granted about 19 months later. Because the government was totally uninterested, the concept was not considered to be secret material, and the patent was published and made available worldwide. For the next six years Whittle was busy with his RAF duties, which included two years at

Cambridge University, where he graduated with First Class Honors in mechanical sciences in June 1936. During the interim, Whittle's jet engine concept essentially was put out to pasture. To make things worse, his original patent expired because he failed to pay the renewal fee.

At the time Whittle was filing his patent, 500 miles to the east, a fated, young German college student was studying physics at Göttingen University, Germany. Hans von Ohain was beginning five years of study that would lead to a Ph.D in physics with minors in aerodynamics, aeromechanics, and mathematics; he received his Ph.D degree in November of 1935. While at Göttingen, he attended lectures of the famous aerodynamicist Ludwig Prandtl and became active in the gliding club. His first experience with powered flight was in 1931 on a flight from Cologne to Berlin on a Junkers Trimotor; he was not impressed. Later he recalled,

> The propellers made a horrendous noise. The airplane rattled because it had piston engines. The elegance of flying was totally taken away by the reciprocating ch-ch-ch and vibratory thing, by the shaking, vibrating, noisy, stinking, reciprocating engine. You couldn't even talk to your neighbor. It was difficult to believe you were flying at all unless you looked out of the window. It was not as romantic as I thought it would be. So I got interested and said, 'Well, gee, that isn't good.' As an uninhibited thinking physicist you come up with another process.

This experience piqued von Ohain's interest in aircraft propulsion, and almost as a hobby he began to give the subject some thought at Göttingen. For the next three years, he formulated the idea of an engine that would produce thrust associated with an exhaust jet rather than turning a propeller. Confident of the merits of his design, he patented it in November of 1935; the patent was considered sensitive enough that it was classified "secret," in contrast to the open patent given to Whittle. On the basis of his calculations, von Ohain, with the help of a friend who was an automobile mechanic, built a small device, 3 feet in diameter and about 1 foot in length, to test a compressor and turbine, with combustion in between. Von Ohain called it "a working model born of optimism." Testing began in the back room of his friend's garage. When the device was turned on, yellow flames streaked out the back end. "It looked more like a flame thrower than a gas turbine," von Ohain recalled, but "at least the flames came out of the right place." And they did so at high velocity. Unlike the noisy conventional reciprocating engine, the device provided a smooth source of power, producing a new sound—the whine of rotating machinery and the screeching of a high-speed jet of gas. The device, however, did not produce any meaningful thrust. Moreover, von Ohain had been paying for this work out of his own pocket, and his personal funds were running out. At the encouragement of his mentor, Professor Robert Pohl, von Ohain sought help from industry. With a letter from Professor Pohl opening the door for him, von Ohain walked into the office of Ernst Heinkel on March 18, 1936. Later, von Ohain recounted his visit:

> I did not take the model with me; it was too heavy. This was only the first visit at the Heinkel company, and I did have photographs of the model. Heinkel let his engineers look at the photographs and gave me a chance to explain my ideas. This was my first serious contact with engineers. You know, I was a physicist; in a sense, a self-appointed *applied* physicist. The engineers had many thoughts. They told me that the idea of a turbojet was already known, but no one had produced a practical one. On the other hand, they felt that perhaps the time had come to have another try at it.

Heinkel quickly employed von Ohain, and the company, which had built only airplanes before, embarked on the design of a practical jet engine.

Meanwhile, virtually at the moment that von Ohain was walking into Ernst Heinkel's office, Frank Whittle's effort to design a jet engine, which had been moribund for five years, was getting a shot in the arm. With some encouragement from professors at Cambridge University, Whittle found private support, and, along with a small group of investors, he founded a small company, Power Jets, Ltd., in March 1936, for the sole purpose of building and testing a jet engine. A year later, the engine was completed, and on April 12, 1937, it was started up on a test stand—the first jet engine in the world to successfully operate in a practical fashion.

The Whittle W1X turbojet engine, 1941, in the Jet Flight Gallery of the National Air and Space Museum, Smithsonian Institution.

However, it was not the first to fly. Completely without knowledge of Whittle's work, von Ohain and the engineers at Heinkel moved ahead to design and build a jet engine. The initial design used hydrogen as a fuel and, therefore, was not a practical device. This test engine, however, operated successfully for the first time on a test stand one month before Whittle started up his engine at Power Jets. The closeness of the timing of these two independent efforts is remarkable, an example of an idea whose time had come. Being a designer of airplanes, the Heinkel Company was in a position to custom-design an airframe for the jet engine. Von Ohain shifted to gasoline as a fuel for his subsequent jet engine, making it practical for flight. Three years after their work began, the team mated von Ohain's engine to a specially designed Heinkel airplane, the He 178, shown in Figure 7.2. On August 27, 1939, the He 178, powered by von Ohain's engine,

FIGURE 7.2
The German He 178, the first jet-propelled airplane to fly successfully, August 27, 1939.

FIGURE 7.3
The Gloster E28, the first British airplane to fly with jet propulsion, May 15, 1941.

successfully flew—it was the first gas turbine-powered, jet-propelled airplane in history to fly. It was strictly an experimental airplane, but von Ohain's engine produced 838 pounds of thrust and pushed the He 178 to a maximum speed of 360 miles per hour, in spite of the fact that the test pilot Erich Worsitz was unable to retract the landing gear, which had locked in the down position. With that flight, the era of the jet-propelled airplane had begun.

Meanwhile, in England, Whittle's success in operating a jet engine on a test stand finally overcame the Air Ministry's reluctance, and in 1938 a contract was let to Power Jets, Ltd., to develop a revised power plant for installation in an airplane. Simultaneously, Gloster Aircraft received a contract to build a specially designed jet-propelled aircraft. Success was obtained when the Gloster E.28/39 airplane (Figure 7.3) took off from Cranwell on May 15, 1941, the first airplane to fly with

Bell P-59B Airacomet, 1942. This was America's first jet airplane. Only 50 production Airacomets were made. (American Aviation Historical Society, AAHS, from K. Kistler.)

a Whittle jet engine. The engine produced 860 pounds of thrust and powered the Gloster airplane to a maximum speed of 338 miles per hour. The Gloster E.28/39 now occupies a distinguished berth in the Science Museum in London, hanging prominently from the top-floor ceiling of the massive brick building in South Kensington, London. The technology gained with the Whittle engine was quickly exported to the United States and eventually fostered the birth of the highly successful Lockheed P-80 Shooting Star, the first significant U.S. production-line jet airplane.

In 1948, Frank Whittle retired from the RAF as an air commodore and was knighted for his contributions to British aviation. In 1976 he moved to the United States, where he worked and taught at the U.S. Naval Academy in Annapolis, Maryland. On August 8, 1996, he died at his home in Columbia, Maryland, where he was cremated.

Hans von Ohain was among the large group of German scientists and engineers who were brought to the United States at the end of World War II. He pursued a distinguished career at the Air Force's Aeronautical Research Laboratory at Wright–Patterson Air Force Base, Ohio, where he led a propulsion group doing research on advanced concepts. Indeed, the present author had the privilege of working for three years in the same laboratory with von Ohain and shared numerous invigorating conversations with this remarkable man. Later, von Ohain became affiliated with the U.S. Air Force Aeropropulsion Laboratory at Wright Field, from which he retired in 1980. He remained active after retirement as a tireless spokesman for aeronautics. In 1984, he served a year at the National Air and Space Museum of the Smithsonian Institution in the prestigious Charles Lindbergh Chair (a chair that the present author was honored to occupy two years after von Ohain). Hans von Ohain died at his home in Melbourne, Florida, on March 13, 1998. He is buried in Dayton, Ohio. Within a span of two years, the world lost the two coinventors of the jet engine. History has already shown that these two gentlemen created a revolution in aeronautics, the jet revolution, perhaps on a par with the invention of the practical airplane by the Wright brothers.

Lockheed P-80A Shooting Star, 1945. This airplane was America's first mass-produced jet fighter. Later designated the F-80, the Shooting Star was the first combat jet airplane to see service in the Korean War. (American Aviation Historical Society, AAHS, from Arthur L. Schoeni.)

A NOTE TO THE READER

The exponential increase in speed during the era of the jet-propelled airplane, as noted in Figure 7.4, is accompanied by an exponential development of the technology of the airplane during the same era. To treat the history of this technology in the same detail as in our preceding chapters would make this last chapter a book in itself. Consequently, out of necessity, the discussions in the present chapter are analogous to a logarithmic scale—truncated at the higher numbers. Here, we will discuss a series of historic advancements in the technology of the airplane since 1950, where the choice of the particular material is strictly the author's and which (unabashedly) reflect this author's biases. This is not so bad, however, because we are still living in the era of the jet-propelled airplane, and the history of this era is still being written. In some sense, this is not unlike a discussion of modern art; it is still not clear what will have lasting value. In the remainder of this chapter, we will discuss technical developments that are felt indeed will have lasting value and that are reflective of the age. At the same time, many important aspects of our modern technology of the airplane will go unmentioned. You are encouraged to fill in the blanks by additional reading in the literature.

SETTING THE MOLD FOR JET TRANSPORTATION—
THE BOEING 707

McDonnell FD-1 Phantom, 1946. This airplane was the U.S. Navy's first carrier jet aircraft. Underpowered, only 60 of these aircraft were built. (Harold Andrews Collection.)

Figure 7.5 shows the Boeing 707-320 intercontinental jet airliner, one of the first airplanes to make convenient and fast transoceanic flight a modern reality. We highlight the 707 here because it is representative of an extremely successful design configuration in the era of the jet-propelled airplane. In Figure 7.5, we see a highly streamlined airplane with swept-back wings and pod-mounted jet engines slung under the wings—the type of configuration that set the mold for most jet transports for about the last 50 years and is still considered the norm today. Flip back to Figure 6.7, which shows the Douglas DC-3, the epitome of the mature propeller-driven airplane, and compare these two configurations. Between the DC-3 and the 707, there clearly has been a second design revolution, one that opened the second golden age of aeronautical engineering—the age of high-speed jet flight. The first flight of the DC-3 was on December 17, 1935. The first flight of the Boeing model number 367-80, the prototype of the 707, was on July 15, 1954. Fewer than 19 years separated these

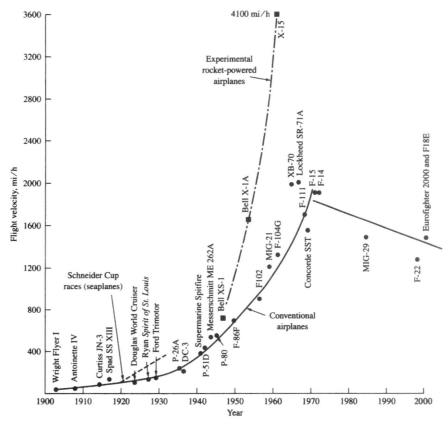

FIGURE 7.4
Trends in flight velocity over the years.

two airplanes. The 707-320 shown in Figure 7.5 cruised at 605 miles per hour with a range of 4300 miles. The DC-3 cruised at 188 miles per hour with a range of 1260 miles. What a difference in just a short time span. How did this come about? Let us take a look.

The swept-wing configuration of the 707 had its beginning on May 7, 1945 when an intelligence team of U.S. scientists and engineers swept into a research laboratory at Braunschweig, Germany and discovered a mass of German aerodynamic data on swept wings. A member of this team was George Schairer, at that time a young aeronautical engineer working for Boeing on a preliminary design for a new generation of jet-powered bombers. After studying the German data, Schairer quickly wrote a letter to his colleague, Ben Cohn, at Boeing, alerting the design team to the interesting features of such wings. Overcoming some internal administrative resistance, the design team, which initially was designing a straight-wing bomber, dropped this early design and pressed ahead with the swept-wing concept. The result was the Boeing B-47, the first U.S. swept-wing bomber. The design evolution of the B-47 is shown in Figure 7.6, taken from William Cook's excellent book, *The Road to the 707* (TYC Publishing, 1991). Notice the evolution from a straight to a swept wing and the various engine arrangements resulting in the final choice of pod-mounted engines slung under the wing. The prototype B-47 first flew on December 17, 1947, and later became the U.S. Air Force Strategic Air Command's first viable and successful jet bomber. The striking similarity between the design of the B-47 and the 707 transport is shown in Figure 7.7. Both aircraft have a 35-degree swept wing, and the jet engines are mounted in pods slung under the wing on struts. The major design changes reflected in the 707 were the low-wing configuration to allow a long body deck for carrying passengers or freight and the use of a tricycle landing gear.

Grumman F9F-2B Panther, 1948. The Panther, in various versions, was the U.S. Navy's primary carrier jet fighter at the start of the Korean War. (Harold Andrews Collection.)

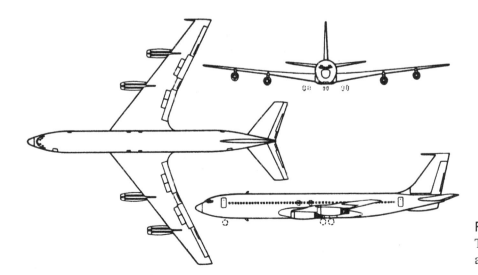

FIGURE 7.5
The Boeing 707-320 jet airliner.

The Boeing 707-320. (American Aviation Historical Society, AAHS, from K. Kistler.)

We will save the rest for the design section later in this chapter, where we will go into a more detailed case study of the design of the 707 as an example of the art of airplane design in the era of the jet-propelled airplane. Our purpose in the present section simply is to offer the Boeing 707 as a good example of the new breed of airplanes that helped to usher in the era of the jet-propelled airplane. All you have to do is to look at and compare the SPAD XIII in Figure 5.5, the Douglas DC-3 in Figure 6.7, and the Boeing 707 in Figure 7.5 to appreciate how far the technology of the airplane came in such a relatively short period of time and that the 707 is an example of the second "design revolution" in the history of the technology of the airplane, helping to foster a second golden age of aeronautical engineering in the jet age.

PARADE OF CONFIGURATIONS—1950 TO THE PRESENT

The advancement in the technology of airplanes since 1950 is reflected in the parade of configurations shown in Figure 7.8. This parade is dominated by sleek, swept-wing aircraft, which are examples of form following function—the function being flight near or beyond the speed of sound. The North American F-86 Sabre is a classic example of the first generation of swept-wing jet-fighter aircraft. The first U.S. swept-wing jet fighter, the F-86, entered squadron service in February 1949, in time to play a strong role during the Korean War. By the time production ended at the end of the 1950s, this airplane had been used by more than 30 countries as

The Boeing 707-121. This photograph shows one of the first 707s, in Pan American markings. Pan American was the first airline to use the 707 on transatlantic flights. (Harold Andrews Collection.)

their primary fighter. During the 1960s and 1970s, the McDonnell (later McDonnell–Douglas) F-4 Phantom became extremely successful as a multipurpose fighter, used in great quantities by the U.S. Navy, U.S. Air Force, and a number of other countries. Whereas the earlier F-86 was a high-speed *subsonic* airplane, the F-4 was capable of speeds in excess of Mach 2. The next generation of jet fighter is represented by the McDonnell–Douglas F-15 Eagle, which first flew in 1972. The F-15 is perhaps the epitome of jet fighters designed for maximum speed; it is capable of almost Mach 3 flight. Just the outside appearance of the F-15 exudes power and speed, and the technical specifications back this up. Comparing thrust-to-weight ratios and wing loadings, we have the values given in Table 7.1.

The progressive increase in thrust-to-weight ratio is the primary reason for the progressive increase in speed. Also, everything else being equal, an increase in wing loading increases the maximum speed; the wing loading of the F-4E is twice that of the F-86E. The wing loading of the F-15C was intentionally designed to be

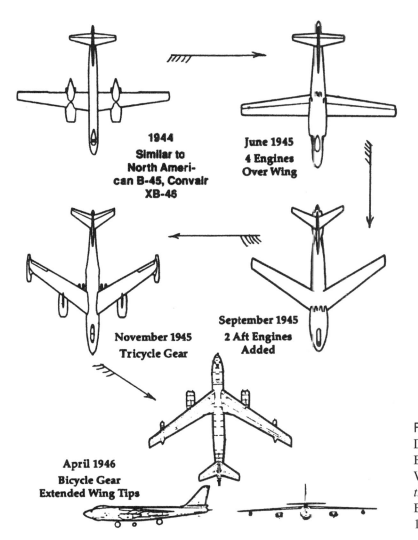

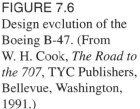

FIGURE 7.6
Design evolution of the Boeing B-47. (From W. H. Cook, *The Road to the 707*, TYC Publishers, Bellevue, Washington, 1991.)

a lower value to enhance maneuverability at some sacrifice in speed, but the high thrust-to-weight ratio of the F-15 more than compensated.

The Boeing 707 (Figures 7.5 and 7.8) was not the only Boeing design spawned by the revolutionary B-47 (Figure 7.6). Perhaps the best and most successful heavy bomber ever designed, the Boeing B-52 Stratofortress reflects the now-classic features of the earlier B-47: swept wings with underslung pod-mounted engines. Powered by eight Pratt and Whitney turbofan engines, the B-52H has a maximum Mach number of 0.91 and a maximum range of over 10,000 miles. The first B-52 flew in 1952. Considered obsolete by technical standards today, the B-52H still remains the main strategic bomber of the U.S. Air Force, most recently seeing combat in 2001 in Afghanistan. The B-52H is planned to remain in active service until 2040, which would give this airplane the distinction of being in main-line service for almost *90 years*, the longest by far of any airplane ever designed! (We remark that longevity of a given airplane design is a hallmark of the era of the jet-propelled airplane. More on this later.)

Civil jet transports are dominated by the design configuration pioneered by Boeing, starting with the 707 and evolving to the large 747 jumbojet seen in

TABLE 7.1   Comparison of the F-86E, F-4E, and F-15C

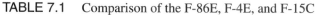

Parameter	F-86E	F-4E	F-15C
Thrust-to-weight ratio	0.35	0.66	1.07
Wing loading, pounds/ft^2	51.6	101.6	73.2
Maximum Mach number	0.91	2.25	2.54

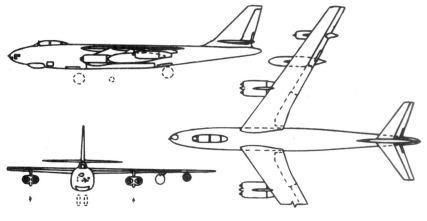

Boeing B-47

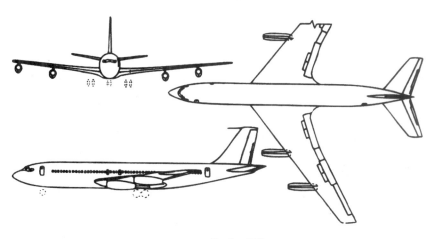

FIGURE 7.7
Comparison of the
configurations of the
Boeing B-47 and the 707.

Boeing 707

Figure 7.8. These are high-speed subsonic jets, and we will have more to say about them later in this chapter.

The era of the jet-propelled airplane is also the era of supersonic flight, introduced by the historic first supersonic flight of the Bell X-1 on October 14, 1947; we have already told this story in the introduction to this chapter. The configurations of supersonic airplanes evolved along the lines of "good supersonic aerodynamics," that is, configurations that minimized wave drag due to the presence of shock waves at supersonic speeds. To minimize the strength of a shock wave, and hence, minimize wave drag, you want airplanes with sharp, pointed

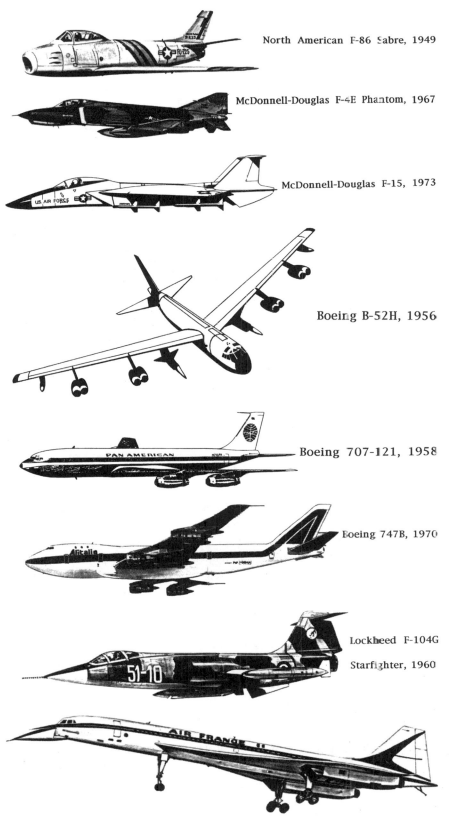

North American F-86 Sabre, 1949

McDonnell-Douglas F-4E Phantom, 1967

McDonnell-Douglas F-15, 1973

Boeing B-52H, 1956

Boeing 707-121, 1958

Boeing 747B, 1970

Lockheed F-104G Starfighter, 1960

Anglo-French Concorde supersonic transport, 1969

FIGURE 7.8
Parade of Configurations:
The Era of the
Jet-Propelled Airplane.
(From Angelucci,
*Airplanes from the Dawn
of Flight to the Present
Day*, McGraw-Hill, 1973.)

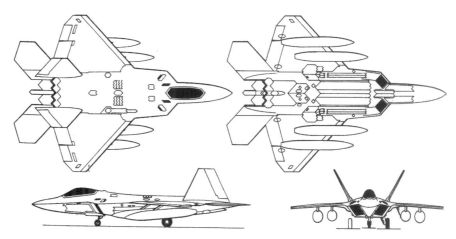

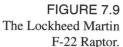

FIGURE 7.9
The Lockheed Martin
F-22 Raptor.

noses, slender fuselages, and thin wings with super-sharp leading edges. The Lockheed F-104 Starfighter is an excellent case in point. Shown in Figure 7.8, the F-104 has all of these design features. Indeed, the wing leading edge is so sharp that a protective glove must be placed on the leading edge to protect it and maintenance personnel from damage and injury while on the ground. The F-104 embodies late 1950s technology; it was the first fighter airplane designed for sustained flight at Mach 2. The F-104 has short, stubby wings with a very low aspect ratio of 2.45. Very low aspect ratio straight wings are one of the two classic wing design choices for supersonic aircraft; the other is to use highly swept wings, with enough wing sweep so that the wing leading edge lies inside the shock wave cones produced at the fuselage nose and at the juncture of the wing root with the fuselage. An example of the latter design approach is the Anglo–French Concorde supersonic transport designed to cruise at Mach 2.2. Note the highly swept leading edge of the wing on the Concorde in Figure 7.8. Returning to the McDonnell-Douglas F-15 in Figure 7.8, note that its wing combines both high wing sweep and a low aspect ratio of 3.02. Modern supersonic jet fighter design takes advantage of both features.

The latest generation of air dominance fighter is exemplified by the Lockheed Martin F-22 Raptor, shown in a four-view perspective in Figure 7.9. The F-22 is earmarked to replace the F-15 Eagle during the first decade of the 21st century. The first flight of the YF-22 prototype was in 1990, and the first flight of the final engineered version destined for production was in 1997, reflecting the long development period for modern piloted combat aircraft. (In comparison to first flights of aircraft in the era of the strut-and-wire biplane, where success meant getting off the ground and into the air without crashing, the first flight of the production model F-22 in 1997 lasted for 58 minutes with speeds up to 300 miles per hour.) Characteristic of today's combat aircraft design, the F-22 is a tradeoff between a low-observable configuration and combat maneuverability (agility). No longer is high speed the major design driver; indeed, the F-22 is designed for a maximum Mach number of only 1.58 without afterburner (called "supercruise") and 1.7 with afterburner. Combat agility in the high-subsonic regime (where the combat arena of most jet fighters is found) is most important. To aid the combat maneuverability, the two engine exhaust nozzles have rectangular cross sections (rather than the usual round cross section) and can be rotated 20 degrees up or down for thrust vectoring in the longitudinal plane of the aircraft. The wing aspect ratio is small, only 2.4, with the leading edge swept through 42 degrees, both of which are important for low wave drag at supersonic cruise. The thrust-to-weight ratio is 1.17, and the wing loading is 71.4 pounds per square foot, both very respectable for a high-performance supersonic fighter. The airfoil section is a custom-designed biconvex shape (circular arc sections for both the upper and lower airfoil surfaces) with thickness-to-chord ratios of 0.0592 at the root and 0.0429 at the wing tip. One reason for the long time between the prototype YF-22 flight in 1990 and the first flight of the final production version in 1997 is the use of high-technology materials; the F-22 structure is 40 percent titanium, 24 percent thermoset composites (both epoxy resin and bismaleimide), only 16 percent aluminum, 6 percent steel, and 14 percent miscellaneous materials. The relatively large percentage of composites is just a harbinger of things to come in future aircraft structures.

When the airplanes shown in Figures 7.8 and 7.9 are examined, there is no doubt that the era of the jet-propelled airplane contains the second golden age of aeronautical engineering.

ADVANCES IN AERODYNAMICS

The era of the jet-propelled airplane is the era of high-speed flight. Airplanes today routinely fly faster than the speed of sound, and almost every commercial jet transport cruises at a speed just slightly below the speed of sound. During the first 45 years of airplane flight, however, the speed of sound was popularly viewed as a barrier to higher speeds. Some people felt that an aircraft could not fly faster than sound, creating the myth of the sound barrier that was rife during the 1930s and 1940s. As a result, aerodynamicists were challenged to understand the physical and mathematical characteristics of flight near and beyond the speed of sound, with a view toward designing aircraft that could possibly "break the sound barrier." This section highlights some of the excitement of this learning process.

Most golfers know the following rule of thumb: When you see a flash of lightening in the distance, start counting at a rate of one count per second. For every count of five before you hear the thunder, the lightning bolt will have struck a mile away. Clearly, sound travels through air at a definite speed, much slower than the speed of light. Indeed, the standard sea-level speed of sound is 1117 feet per second, and in 5 seconds a sound wave will travel 5585 feet, slightly more than a mile. That is the basis for the golfer's count-of-five rule of thumb.

The speed of sound is one of the most important parameters in aerodynamics; it is the dividing line between subsonic flight (speeds less than that of sound) and supersonic flight (speeds greater than that of sound). The Mach number is the ratio of the speed of a fluid flow to the speed of sound in that flow. If the Mach number is 0.5, the velocity of the fluid flow is one-half the speed of sound a Mach number of 2.0 means that the flow velocity is twice that of sound. The physics of a subsonic flow are totally different from those of a supersonic flow—a contrast as striking as that between day and night. That was why there was such drama and anxiety at the first supersonic flight of the X-1, and that is why the precise value of the speed of sound is so important in aerodynamics.

By the 17th century it was understood that sound propagates through the air at some finite velocity. By the time Issac Newton published his *Principia* in 1687, artillery tests had already shown that the speed of sound was approximately 1140 feet per second. The 17th-century gunner had prefigured the modern golfer's experience: The tests were performed by standing a known large distance away from a cannon and noting the elapsed time between the flash from the cannon and the sound of its firing. In Proposition 50, Book II, of the *Principia*, Newton correctly theorized that the speed of sound was related to the "elasticity" of the air. However, he made the erroneous assumption that a sound wave was an isothermal process (i.e., he assumed that the air temperature inside the sound wave was constant) and consequently proposed an incorrect expression for the speed of sound. Much to his dismay, he calculated a value of 979 feet per second—15 percent lower than the value indicated by gunshot data. Undaunted, he resorted to a familiar ploy of theoreticians: He proceeded to try to explain away the difference on the basis of the presence of solid dust particles and water vapor in the atmosphere. That misconception was corrected a century later by the French mathematician Laplace, who properly assumed that a sound wave was adiabatic, not isothermal. Therefore, by the 1820s, the process and relationship for the propagation of sound in a gas was fully understood.

Compressibility Problems—The First Hints (1918–1923)

From the time of the Wright Flyer to the beginning of World War II, it was assumed that changes in air density were negligible as air flowed over an airplane. That assumption of *incompressible flow* was reasonable for the relatively slow (less than 350 miles per hour) airplanes of that era. In dealing with the theory, it was a considerable advantage to assume constant density, and physically the low-speed aerodynamic flows usually exhibited smooth variations, with no sudden changes or surprises. All of that changed when flight speeds began to edge up close to the speed of sound. At that point, aerodynamic theory had to begin to account for changes in air density in the flowfield around the airplane, and physically the flowfield sometimes acted erratically, frequently springing surprises that greatly challenged aerodynamicists. In the 1930s, all of those phenomena were tossed into one basket and called "compressibility problems."

The first hints of compressibility problems came during the era of the strut-and-wire biplane, and they came from only one part of the airplane: the propeller. Although typical flight speeds for World War I airplanes were less than 125 miles per hour, the tip speeds of their propellers, because of their combined rotational and translational motions through the air, were quite large, sometimes exceeding the speed of sound. That was understood by aeronautical engineers at the time, and it prompted the British Advisory Committee for Aeronautics to take an interest in the theory of compressible flows. (The Advisory Committee for Aeronautics was created in 1909 by the British government to define the important problems in aeronautics and "to seek their solution by the application of both theoretical and experimental methods of research." Lord Rayleigh was appointed the first president. When NACA was created in the United States in 1915, the British Advisory Committee for Aeronautics was used as a model.) In 1918 and 1919, G. H. Bryan, working for the committee at the Royal Aircraft Establishment, carried out theoretical analyses of subsonic and supersonic flows over a circular cylinder, a simple geometric shape chosen for convenience. His analysis was cumbersome, but it was one of the earliest attempts to calculate the effects of compressibility on a flowfield.

At the same time, Frank Caldwell and Elisha Fales, at the U.S. Army Air Service Engineering Division, McCook Field, Dayton, Ohio, were taking a purely experimental approach to the problem. (Yes, this is the same Frank Caldwell who pioneered the variable-pitch propeller in the 1920s and 1930s, as discussed in Chapter 6.) Their work was the beginning of a divide between the British and American approaches to research on compressibility effects; over the next two decades, the major experimental contributions to an understanding of compressibility effects would be made in the United States, principally by NACA, and the major theoretical contributions would come from England. In 1918 Caldwell and Fales designed and built the first high-speed wind tunnel in the United States, solely to investigate the problems associated with propellers. Its velocity range was from 25 miles per hour to a stunning 465 miles per hour. It had a length of almost 19 feet, and the test section was 14 inches in diameter—a big, powerful machine for its day. They tested six different airfoils with thickness ratios (ratio of the maximum thickness to the chord length) from 0.08 to 0.2. At the higher speeds, the data showed "a decreased lift coefficient and an increased drag coefficient, so that the lift–drag ratio is enormously decreased." They denoted the airspeed at which those dramatic departures took place as the "critical speed" (that would appear to have been the origin for the term "critical Mach number" that was to come into wide use in aerodynamics beginning in the late 1930s). The critical Mach number is defined as the freestream Mach number at which sonic flow is first encountered on the surface of a body. The large drag rise due to compressibility effects normally occurs at a freestream Mach number slightly above the critical Mach number; that is called the drag-divergence Mach number. Caldwell and Fales had reached and exceeded the drag-divergence Mach number in their experiments.

These first hints of compressibility effects on airfoils at high speeds should not have been any surprise, because a suggestion that aerodynamic forces could do strange things near Mach 1 had first been advanced by Benjamin Robins in 1742 (as discussed in Chapter 2). On the basis of his ballistic-pendulum measurements, Robins observed that projectiles experienced a large increase in drag when the speeds approached the speed of sound. Specifically, he reported that the aerodynamic force began to vary as the velocity cubed (not squared as in the lower speed case). At the beginning of the 20th century, ballistics measurements on projectiles carried out by Bensberg and Cranz in Germany yielded the variations of the drag coefficient with velocity shown in Figure 7.10 for the transonic and supersonic regimes. That curve shows the large rise in the drag coefficient near Mach 1 and the gradual decrease in drag coefficient in the supersonic region. Although those data were obtained by ballistics engineers for use with artillery, they should have alerted aerodynamicists to the problems that they should have expected to encounter with high-speed airplanes later in the century. But there was no reference to that work in the literature on high-speed aerodynamics early in the 20th century; the aerodynamicists who carried out the pioneering work on compressibility effects acted as if they were unaware of such data.

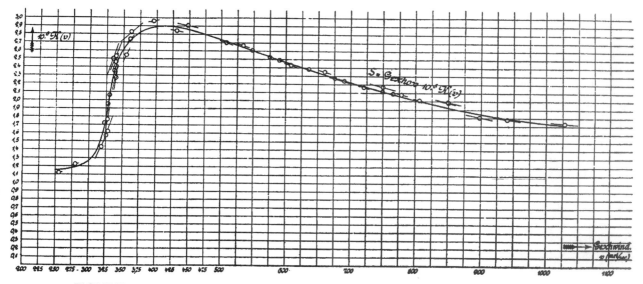

FIGURE 7.10
Projectile drag coefficient versus velocity (in meters per second) in the transonic and supersonic regimes, as measured by Bensberg and Cranz in Germany, 1910.

The Compressibility Burble—NACA's Seminal Research (1924–1929)

During the 1920s, NACA sponsored a series of fundamental experiments in high-speed aerodynamics at the Bureau of Standards, conducted by Lyman J. Briggs and Hugh L. Dryden. In 1919, at age 20, Dryden had a doctorate in physics from Johns Hopkins University. (He would later become director of research for NACA, 1947–1958). That work progressed in three stages that covered the period from 1924 to 1929, the primary motivation being to understand the compressibility effects at the tips of propellers.

The first stage simply confirmed the trends already observed by Caldwell and Fales four years earlier. Briggs and Dryden, with the help of G. F. Hull of the U.S. Army Ordnance Department, jury-rigged a high-speed wind tunnel by connecting a vertical standpipe 30 inches in diameter and 30 feet high to a large centrifugal compressor at the Lynn works of the General Electric Company in Massachusetts. At the other end of the pipe was a cylindrical orifice 12.24 inches in diameter that served as a nozzle. With that device, Briggs and Dryden noted that "air speeds approaching the speed of sound were obtained." Rectangular planform models, with a span of 17.2 inches and a chord length of 3 inches, were placed in the high-speed airstream, and the lift, drag, and center of pressure were measured. The findings supported the earlier trends observed by Caldwell and Fales. In particular, Briggs and Dryden found the following:

1) The lift coefficient for a fixed angle of attack decreased very rapidly as the speed increased.
2) The drag coefficient increased rapidly.
3) The center of pressure moved back toward the trailing edge.
4) The critical speed at which those changes occurred decreased as the angle of attack was increased and the airfoil thickness was increased.

In 1924, the effect of that work, as well as the research that had gone before, was to raise a red flag. Compressibility effects were a nasty lot, and they markedly degraded airfoil performance. But nobody had a fundamental understanding of the physical features of the flowfield that were causing those adverse effects—nor would anyone for another decade.

An important step toward such a fundamental understanding came with the second stage of the work by Briggs and Dryden in 1926. Because the compressor at the Lynn works was no longer available to them, they moved their experimental activity to the U.S. Army's Edgewood Arsenal, where they constructed another high-speed wind tunnel, much smaller, with an airstream only 2 inches in diameter. By careful design of the small airfoil models, two pressure taps could be placed in each model. Seven identical models were used, all with different locations of the pressure taps. They employed 13 pressure-tap locations, 7 on the upper surface and 6 on the lower surface. (For the reader who is counting, the seventh model had only one tap.) With that technique, Briggs and Dryden measured the pressure distributions over the airfoil at Mach numbers from 0.5 to 1.08. The findings were dramatic. Beyond the critical speed, the pressure distributions over the top of the airfoil exhibited a sudden pressure jump at about one-third to one-half the distance from the leading edge, followed by a rather long plateau toward the trailing edge. Such a pressure plateau was familiar (it was similar to that over the top surface of an airfoil in a low-speed flow when the airfoil stalls at a high angle of attack), and it was well known at that time that airfoil stall was caused by separation of the flow off the top surface of the airfoil. Briggs and Dryden concluded that the adverse effects of compressibility were caused by flow separation over the top surface, even though the airfoil was at low (even zero) angles of attack. To substantiate that, they conducted oil-flow tests: An oil, with pigment added to make it visible, was painted on the model surface, and when the model was placed in the high-speed airstream, the telltale line of flow separation was revealed by the oil pattern. Clearly, beyond the critical speed, flow separation was occurring on the top surface of the airfoil. But what was causing the flow to separate? The answer to that question was eight years in the future.

The third stage of the work by Briggs and Dryden was utilitarian, in keeping with the stated duty of NACA to work toward practical solutions. At the end of the 1920s, they carried out a large number of detailed measurements of the aerodynamic properties of 24 different airfoils at Mach numbers from 0.5 to 1.08. The airfoils tested were those conventionally used by the U.S. Army and U.S. Navy for propellers—the standard family of British-designed RAF airfoils and the U.S.-designed Clark Y family. Their data were the first definitive measurements to show compressibility effects on the standard series of airfoils.

By the time of World War I, aerodynamicists were well aware that an airfoil would stall at a high angle of attack because the flow would separate from the top surface. The resulting drastic loss of lift was termed the "lift burble." When Briggs and Dryden found that the drastic loss of lift at high speeds, beyond the critical speed, was also due to flow separation, it was natural to call that effect the "compressibility burble," and that NACA terminology was used in the literature on high-speed aerodynamics through the 1930s.

In contrast to these experimental advances, progress toward theoretical solutions for the compressibility effects in a high-speed subsonic flow was virtually nonexistent during the 1920s. The only major contribution was made by the British aerodynamicist Hermann Glauert, who rigorously derived a correction to be applied to the lift coefficient for low-speed, incompressible flows to correct it for compressibility effects. Because Ludwig Prandtl in Germany had independently obtained the same theoretical result, but never published it, the compressibility correction became known as the "Prandtl–Glauert Rule." It was simple to apply, but the theory was only approximate, and the Prandtl–Glauert rule only could be used with some confidence for thin airfoils at small angles of attack for Mach numbers less than 0.7. For all practical purposes, the flight regime near and beyond Mach 1 remained a theoretical as well as an experimental mystery.

The Mystery Explained

By 1928, two of the three elements essential for a fundamental understanding of the high-speed compressible flow over an airfoil were in hand:

1) From the work of Caldwell and Fales in 1920, and the investigations that followed, it was clear that something dramatic happened to the aerodynamics of an airfoil when the freestream velocity approached the speed of sound. Beyond some "critical speed," the lift would drop precipitously, and the drag would suddenly and rapidly increase.

2) The work of Briggs and Dryden in 1926 showed that those precipitous changes corresponded to a sudden separation of the flow over the airfoil surface, even at low angles of attack.

But what caused the flow to separate? The answer to that question would provide the third element, but the breakthrough to that understanding would take another six years.

In July 1928, John Stack, born and raised in Lowell, Massachusetts, began his career with the NACA Langley Memorial Aeronautical Laboratory. Having just graduated from MIT with a B.S. degree in aeronautical engineering, he was assigned to the Variable Density Tunnel (VDT), the world's premier wind tunnel at that time. Stack had long been dedicated to aeronautical interests. While in high school, he worked to earn enough money for a few hours of flight instruction in a Canuck biplane, and he helped out with the maintenance of a Boeing biplane owed by one of his part-time employers. He had made up his mind to study aeronautical engineering, but his father, a carpenter who was also very successful in real estate, wanted him to study architecture at MIT. When Stack entered MIT, he enrolled in aeronautical engineering, keeping it a secret from his father for the first year, but with the approval of his mother. Much later, Stack commented that "when Dad heard about it, it was too late to protest."

When John Stack arrived at NACA Langley Memorial Aeronautical Laboratory in 1928, a year's worth of design work had already been done on Langley's first high-speed wind tunnel, and the facility was already operational, with an open-throat test section. Stack was given the responsibility for upgrading the High-Speed Tunnel by designing a closed throat, and that improved facility became operational in 1932. It was his participation in the design and development of the 11-inch High-Speed Tunnel that launched Stack's career in high-speed aerodynamics.

While Stack was working on the High-Speed Tunnel, he was impressed by an event in England that would lead to a rapid refocusing of the NACA high-speed research program. In wining the Schneider Trophy for England in 1931, the Supermarine S.6B (see Chapter 6) averaged a speed of 340 miles per hour over a long seven-lap course. A few weeks later, the same airplane set a world's speed record of 401.5 miles per hour. It does not take an aerodynamic expert to appreciate that by 1931 the concept of streamlining to reduce drag had taken root: The Supermarine S.6B simply looked fast, and at 400 miles per hour (Mach 0.53, over half the speed of sound), it was. Suddenly, in the face of that kind of speed, the prior concern over propeller compressibility effects, which for propeller tips posed an important but tolerable problem, became transformed into an absolutely vital concern about the compressibility effects on the entire airplane, and the complexities of those effects raised a problem of showstopping proportions.

Stack was acutely aware of the new compressibility challenge. In 1933, he published the first data to come from the newly modified, closed-throat High-Speed Tunnel. Although the airfoils tested were propeller sections, Stack obviously had the Schneider Trophy racer in mind. He wrote,

> A knowledge of the compressibility phenomenon is essential, however, because the tip speeds of propellers now in use are commonly in the neighborhood of the velocity of sound. Further, the speeds that have been attained by racing airplanes are as high as half the velocity of sound. Even at ordinary airplane speeds the effects of compressibility should not be disregarded if accurate measurements are desired.

For the most part, Stack's data in 1933 confirmed the trends observed earlier. His measurements of the variations of the lift, drag, and moment coefficients with Mach number for a Clark Y 10-percent thick airfoil are shown in Figure 7.11; the precipitous drop in lift and the large decrease in drag at high speeds are clearly evident. He also confirmed that when there were increases in airfoil thickness, or angle of attack, or both, the adverse compressibility effects began to appear at lower Mach numbers. One of his conclusions reflected the theory of the Prandtl–Glauert compressibility correction discussed earlier. His measurements indicated that "the limited theory available may be applied with sufficient accuracy for most practical purposes only for speeds below the compressibility burble," presaging almost 40 years of a theoretical void. The term "compressibility burble" was coined by Stack. He wrote the following in NACA Technical Report 463, published in 1933:

> The lift coefficients increase as the speed is increased, slowly as the speed is increased over the lower portion of the range, then more rapidly as speeds over half the velocity of sound are exceeded, and finally at higher speeds, depending on the airfoil section and the angle of attack, the flow breaks down as shown by a drop in the lift coefficient. This breakdown of the flow, hereinafter called the *compressibility burble*, occurs at lower speeds as the lift is increased by changing the angle of attack of the model.

Driven by the conviction and foresight of John Stack, NACA continued to alert the worldwide aeronautics community to the problems of compressibility effects. In January 1934, the first significant professional aeronautical society in the United States, the Institute of Aeronautical Sciences (precursor to AIAA), began publishing its *Journal of the Aeronautical Sciences*, which contained an article by Stack emphasizing what would be an important NACA theme for the next several decades:

FIGURE 7.11
Compressibility effects on the lift, drag, and moment coefficients for a Clark Y airfoil of 10% thickness, measured by John Stack at the NACA Langley Laboratory, 1933. From left to right are plots of the lift, drag, and moment coefficients versus the speed ratio V/V_o, where V is the freestream velocity and V_o is the speed of sound of the freestream. Although the term "Mach number" had been coined in Europe in 1929, NACA did not identify the speed ratio V/V_o as Mach number until the late 1930s.

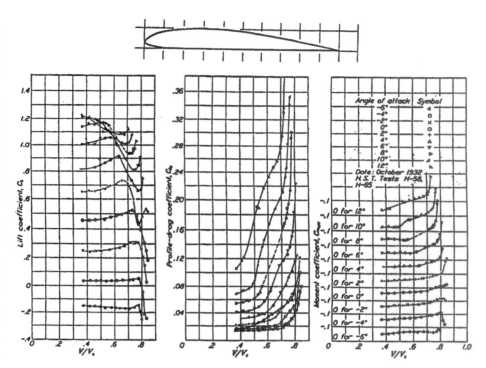

The effects of compressibility have commonly been neglected because until the relatively recent development of the last Schneider trophy aircraft the speeds have been low as compared with the velocity of sound, and the consequent local pressures over the surfaces of high speed airplanes have differed but slightly from atmospheric pressure. At the present time, however, the speeds associated with the fastest airplanes approach 60 percent of the velocity of sound, and the induced velocities over their exposed surfaces lead to local pressures that differ appreciably from the pressure of the atmosphere. When this condition exists, air can no longer be regarded as an incompressible medium. The effects of compressibility on the aerodynamic characteristics of airfoils have been under investigation by the N.A.C.A. in the high speed wind tunnel, and it is the purpose of this paper to examine the possibility of further increases in speeds in the light of this relatively recent research.

By that time, NACA was clearly the world's leading research institution in the area of compressibility effects. Through its influence and sponsorship of the experiments in the 1920s by Caldwell and Fales at McCook Field and by Briggs and Dryden at the Bureau of Standards, and more recently its own carefully conducted experiments at Langley, NACA had been able to identify the first two elements essential for an understanding of the basic nature of compressibility effects: 1) the finding that, above a certain "critical speed," the lift decreased dramatically, and the drag skyrocketed almost beyond comprehension and 2) the finding that such behavior was caused by a sudden, precipitous flow separation over the top surface of the wing or airfoil. The missing third element was an explanation for such behavior.

In 1934, Stack and NACA were able to provide that explanation. By that time, Stack had a new instrument to work with—a schlieren photographic system, an optical arrangement that made the density gradients in the flow visible. One of nature's mechanisms for producing very strong density gradients is a shock wave,

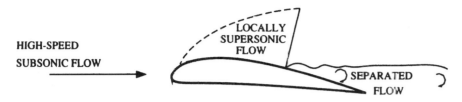

HIGH-SPEED

SUBSONIC FLOW

LOCALLY SUPERSONIC FLOW

SEPARATED FLOW

FIGURE 7.12
Sketch of the physical nature of transonic flow over an airfoil.

and hence, such waves would be visible with the schlieren system. Stack's boss, Eastman Jacobs, was familiar with such optical systems through his hobby of astronomy, and he suggested to Stack that the use of a schlieren system might make some of the unknown features of the compressible flow over an airfoil visible and might shed some light on the nature of the compressibility burble. It did just that, and more. With the 11-inch High-Speed Tunnel running above the critical speed for the NACA 0012 symmetric airfoil mounted in the test section, and with the aid of the schlieren system, Stack and Jacobs recorded the first observation of a shock wave in the flow over the top surface of the airfoil. It was immediately clear that the separated flow over the top surface of the airfoil and the resulting compressibility burble, with all its adverse consequences, were caused by the presence of a shock wave. The nature of that flow is shown in Figure 7.12. When the freestream velocity is high enough, the rapid expansion of the flow over the airfoil creates a local pocket of supersonic flow over the top surface of the airfoil. That pocket is terminated by a shock wave. In turn, the shock wave interacts with the thin, friction-dominated boundary layer adjacent to the surface of the airfoil and causes the boundary layer to separate in the region where the shock impinges on the surface. A massive region of separated flow trails downstream, greatly increasing the drag and decreasing the lift. One of the pioneering schlieren pictures of the flow over the NACA 0012 airfoil taken by Stack in 1934 is shown in Figure 7.13; the quality is poor by modern standards, but it is certainly sufficient for identifying the phenomena. For that case, which was flow over a symmetric airfoil at a zero angle of attack, shocks appeared on both the upper and lower surfaces of the airfoil. That photograph reflected an important discovery in the history of high-speed aerodynamics, one that led to a complete understanding of the physics of the compressibility burble. It was a breakthrough of enormous theoretical and practical importance. It was due to the work of two innovative aerodynamicists at the Langley Memorial Aeronautical Laboratory, John Stack and Eastman Jacobs, operating in a creative atmosphere promoted throughout NACA.

Almost any new scientific discovery will encounter some initial skepticism, and Theodore Theodorsen was skeptical about Stack's findings. As discussed in Chapter 6, Theodorsen was the leading theoretical aerodynamicist in NACA, with a worldwide reputation for his pioneering papers on airfoil theory. John Becker, who joined NACA in 1936 and went on to become one of the most respected high-speed aerodynamicists at Langley Memorial Aeronautical Laboratory reported Theodorsen's reaction to the schlieren photographs taken by Stack, illustrating that the new findings constituted a radical departure from the expected norm:

The first tests were made on a circular cylinder about 1/2 inch in diameter, and the results were spectacular in spite of the poor quality of the optics. Shock waves and

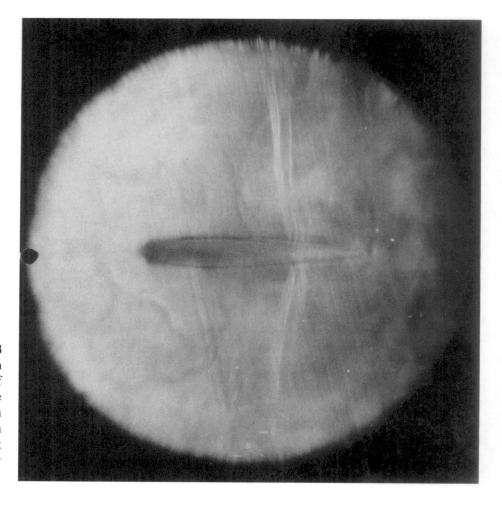

FIGURE 7.13
The first photograph showing the existence of shock waves in the transonic flow over an airfoil. The photograph was taken by John Stack at the NACA Langley Laboratory, 1934.

attendant flow separations were seen for the first time starting at subsonic stream speeds of about 0.6 times the speed of sound. Visitors from all over the Laboratory, from Engineer-in-Charge H. J. E. Reid on down, came to view the phenomena. Langley's ranking theorist, Theodore Theodorsen, viewed the results skeptically, proclaiming that since the stream flow was subsonic, what appeared to be shock waves was an "optical illusion," an error in judgment which he was never allowed to forget.

NACA was soon provided with a timely opportunity to inform the international research community of the breakthrough to a fundamental understanding of compressibility effects and the compressibility burble, namely, the fifth Volta conference held in Italy in 1935. That conference was the most important assemblage of aerodynamicists in the early years of high-speed aerodynamics. Let us take a closer look.

Threshold to Modern High-Speed Aerodynamics and the Concept of the Swept Wing—The 1935 Volta Conference

Because of the rapidly growing interest in high-speed flight, by 1935 it was time for an international meeting of those few researchers of fluid mechanics dealing with compressible flows. The time was right, and in Italy the circumstances were right. Since 1931 the Royal Academy of Science in Rome had been conducting a series of important scientific conferences sponsored by the Alessandro Volta Foundation. (Alessandro Volta was the Italian physicist who invented the electric battery in 1800, and the unit of electromotive force, the volt, was named in his honor.) The first conference dealt with nuclear physics, and subsequent conferences dealt with the sciences and the humanities in alternate years. The second Volta conference carried the title "Europe," and in 1933 the third conference dealt with immunology, followed by "The Dramatic Theater" in 1934. During that period, Italian aeronautics was gaining momentum, led by General Arturo Crocco, an aeronautical engineer who became interested in ramjet engines in 1931 and, therefore, was well aware of the importance of compressible-flow theory and experiments in the future of aviation. The topic chosen for the fifth Volta conference was "High Velocities in Aviation." Participation was by invitation only.

The technical content of the fifth Volta conference ranged from subsonic to supersonic flows and from experimental testing to theoretical considerations. Because of his work in the design and testing of the NACA four-digit airfoil series, and the fact that he was the section head for the NACA VDT, which had put NACA on the international aerodynamics map in the 1920s, Eastman Jacobs also received an invitation to the Volta conference. He took the opportunity to present a paper on the new NACA compressibility research carried out under his supervision by John Stack. Jacobs described the NACA High-Speed Tunnel, the schlieren, and the airfoil experiments carried out in the tunnel. Then he showed, for the first time in a technical meeting, some of the schlieren pictures that he and Stack had taken, for example, Figure 7.13. In keeping with NACA's penchant for perfection, especially in its publications, Jacobs apologized for the quality of the photographs, a fault that detracted little from their technical and historical importance: "Unfortunately the photographs were injured by the presence of bent celluloid windows forming the tunnel walls through which the light passed. The pictures nevertheless give fundamental information in regard to the nature of the flow associated with the compressibility burble." With that, the NACA high-speed research program was not simply on the map, it was leading the pack.

One of the most farsighted and important papers at the fifth Volta conference was presented by Adolf Busemann. The paper was entitled "Aerodynamic Forces at Supersonic Speeds," and it introduced the concept of the swept wing as a means to reduce the large drag increase encountered beyond Mach one. (The swept-wing concept, and its development in both Germany and the United States, will be discussed in a subsequent section.)

The fifth Volta conference was accorded special treatment by the Italian government. Its prestige was reflected in its location; It was held in an impressive Renaissance building that had served as the city hall during the Holy Roman Empire. Moreover, the Italian dictator Benito Mussolini chose the conference as a place to make his announcement that Italy had invaded Ethiopia—a curious setting for such a political announcement.

The conference fueled the excitement about the future of high-speed flight and provided the first major international exchange of information on compressible flows, but in many areas its impact was delayed. For example, Busemann's ideas on swept wings were withdrawn from public view. (The German Luftwaffe recognized their military significance and classified such work in 1936.) The Germans went on to produce a large body of swept-wing research during World War II and the first operational jet airplane, the Me-262, which had a moderate degree of sweep (although the principal design reason was for center-of-gravity location). After the war, technical teams from England, Russia, and the United States descended on the German research laboratories at Peenemunde and Braunschweig and gathered all of the data they could find. The United States also gathered Aldolf Busemann, who was moved to the NACA Langley Memorial Aeronautical Laboratory. Later, Busemann became a professor at the University of Colorado. Virtually all modern high-speed airplanes can trace their lineage back to the original data obtained in Germany and ultimately Busemann's paper at the fifth Volta conference.

On a more positive note, the Volta conference led to some increase in high-speed flight research in the United States. There were renewed efforts at NACA to obtain data on the compressibility effects on high-speed subsonic airfoils. But, in general, the United States reacted slowly to the stimulus provided by the Volta conference. On his return from Italy in late 1935, Theodore von Kármán urged both the U.S. Army and NACA to develop high-speed supersonic facilities, to no avail. Finally, when the war came to the United States in 1941, such urging got a more receptive hearing. In 1942, at the California Institute of Technology (Cal Tech), von Kármán established the first major university curriculum in compressible flow, a course of study that was heavily attended by military officers. Finally, in 1944, the first practical operational supersonic wind tunnel in the United States was built at the U.S. Army's Ballistics Research Laboratory in Aberdeen, Maryland, designed by von Kármán and his colleagues at Cal Tech. Twelve years after Busemann began to collect data in his supersonic tunnel in Germany, and nine years after the fifth Volta conference and the construction of supersonic tunnels at Guidonia in Italy, the United States finally was seriously into the business of supersonic research.

Filling in the Aerodynamic Gaps—The High-Speed Research Airplane

Jacobs's paper at the fifth Volta conference was very much a celebration of the second phase of the NACA research program on high-speed flight. The first phase had been the embryonic wind-tunnel compressibility work of the 1920s, clearly oriented toward applications to propellers. The second phase was a refocusing of that high-speed wind-tunnel research on the airplane itself, and that second phase would soon be augmented by a new initiative—the design and development of an actual research airplane.

The idea of a research airplane, an airplane designed and built strictly for the purposes of probing unknown flight regimes, can be traced to the thinking of John Stack in 1933. On his own initiative, Stack went through a very preliminary design analysis "for a hypothetical airplane which," as he stated, "however, is not beyond the limits of possibility." The purpose of the airplane, as presented in a 1933 article in the *Journal of the Aeronautical Science*, was to fly very fast, well into the compressibility regime. The airplane he designed (Figure 7.14) was highly streamlined for its time, with a straight, tapered wing having a NACA 0018 symmetric airfoil section at the center, thinning to a NACA 0009 airfoil 9 percent

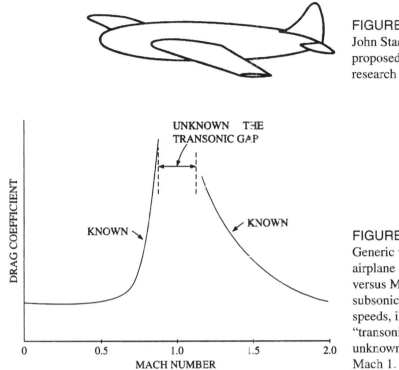

FIGURE 7.14
John Stack's sketch for a proposed high-speed research aircraft, 1933.

FIGURE 7.15
Generic variation of airplane drag coefficient versus Mach number for subsonic and supersonic speeds, illustrating the "transonic gap," the unknown regime near Mach 1.

thick at the tip. Stack even went so far as to test a model of that design (without tail surfaces) in the Langley VDT. He estimated the drag coefficient for the airplane using the data he had measured in the 11-inch High-Speed Tunnel. Assuming a fuselage large enough to hold a 2300-horsepower Rolls–Royce engine, Stack calculated that the propeller-driven airplane would have a maximum speed of 566 miles per hour—far beyond that of any airplane flying at the time and well into the regime of compressibility. NACA did not help Stack find a developer for the airplane, but in the words of the aeronautical historian, James Hansen, "The optimistic results of his paper study convinced many people at Langley that the potential for flying at speeds far in excess of 500 miles per hour was there."

The state of high-speed aerodynamics in 1939 can be illustrated by the trends shown in Figure 7.15, where the generic variation of the drag coefficient for an airplane is shown as a function of the freestream Mach number. On the subsonic side, below Mach 1, wind-tunnel data had indicated the rapid increase in the drag coefficient as Mach 1 was approached. On the supersonic side, ballisticians had known for years how the drag coefficient would behave above Mach 1. Of course, all airplanes at that time were on the subsonic side of the curve shown in Figure 7.15. Stack summarized the situation in 1938 as follows:

> The development of the knowledge of compressible-flow phenomena, particularly as related to aeronautical applications, has been attended by considerable difficulty. The complicated nature of the phenomena has resulted in little theoretical progress, and, in general, recourse to experiment has been necessary. Until recently the most important experimental results have been obtained in connection with the science of ballistics, but this information has been of little value in aeronautical problems because the range

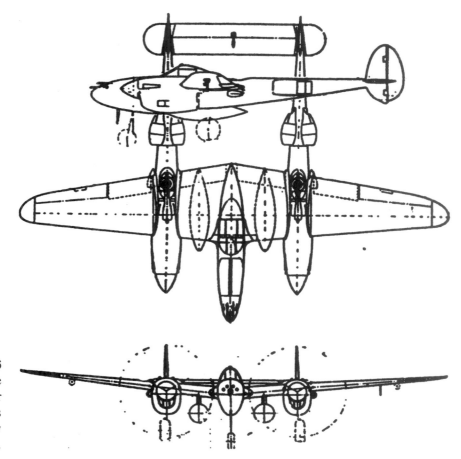

FIGURE 7.16
The Lockheed P-38, the first airplane to encounter serious, and sometimes fatal, compressibility effects.

of speeds for which most ballistic experiments have been made extends from the speed of sound upward; whereas the important region in aeronautics at the present time extends from the speed of sound downward.

In essence, the flight regime just below and just above the speed of sound was unknown—a transonic gap, as shown schematically in Figure 7.15.

The aeronautics community was suddenly awakened to the dangers of that unknown flight regime in November 1941, when Lockheed test pilot Ralph Virden, putting the new, high-performance P-38 through a high-speed dive, could not pull out in time and crashed. That was the first fatality due to adverse compressibility effects, and the P-38 (Figure 7.16) was the first airplane to suffer from those effects. Virden's P-38 had exceeded its critical Mach number in an operational dive and had penetrated well into the regime of the compressibility burble at its terminal dive speed. The problem encountered by Virden and many other P-38 pilots at that time was that, beyond a certain speed in a dive, the elevator controls suddenly felt as if they were locked, and to make things worse, the tail suddenly produced more lift, pulling the P-38 into an even steeper dive. That was called the tuck-under problem at the time. Lockheed consulted various aerodynamicists, including von Kármán at Cal Tech, but it turned out that John Stack at NACA Langley Memorial Aeronautical Laboratory, with his accumulated experience in compressibility effects, was the only one to diagnose the problem properly. The wing of the P-38 lost lift when it encountered the compressibility burble, and as a result, the downwash angle of the flow behind the wing was reduced. That, in turn, increased the effective angle of attack at which the flow encountered the horizontal tail, increasing the lift on the tail and pitching the P-38 to a progressively steeper dive, totally beyond the control of the pilot. Stack's solution was to place a special flap under the wing, to be employed only when those compressibility effects were encountered. The flap was not a conventional dive flap intended to reduce the airplane's speed; rather, it was used to maintain lift in the face of the compressibility burble, thus, eliminating the change in the downwash angle and, therefore, allowing the horizontal tail to function properly. That was a graphic example, from the early days of high-speed flight, of the vital importance of NACA compressibility research as real airplanes began to sneak up on Mach 1.

By the late 1930s, it was time for real airplanes to be used to probe the mysteries of the unknown transonic gap illustrated in Figure 7.15, time for the high-speed research airplane to become a reality. The earliest concrete proposal along those lines came from Ezra Kotcher, a senior instructor at the U.S. Army Air Corps Engineering School at Wright Field (a forerunner of today's Air Force Institute of Technology). Kotcher was a 1928 graduate of the University of California, Berkeley, with a B.S. degree in mechanical engineering. The same year that John Stack began work at Langley as a junior aeronautical engineer, Kotcher began work at Wright Field in a similar position; both interested in high-speed aerodynamics, they would later work together on the development of the Bell X-1. Kotcher's proposal, drafted in August 1939, was in response to Major General Henry "Hap" Arnold's request for an investigation into the future of advanced military aircraft. The proposal contained a plan for a research program of actual high-speed flight. Kotcher pointed out the unknown aspects of the transonic gap and the problems associated with the compressibility burble, as elucidated by NACA, and he concluded that the next important step should be a full-scale flight research program. The U.S. Army Air Corps did not immediately respond to his proposal.

At Langley Memorial Aeronautical Laboratory, the idea of a high-speed research airplane was gaining momentum. By the time the United States entered World War II in December 1941, Stack had studied the behavior of the flow in a wind tunnel when the flow in the test section was near or at Mach 1. He repeatedly found that when a model was mounted in the flow, the flowfield in the test section essentially broke down, making any aerodynamic measurements worthless. He concluded that the development of a truly transonic wind tunnel would be an extremely difficult problem, probably far into the future. It appeared that the best way to learn about the aerodynamics of transonic flight would be to build a real airplane that would fly in that regime, and during several visits by George Lewis, NACA's director of aeronautical research, Stack continued to push that idea. Lewis, who appreciated the work that Stack had done at NACA, was not immediately receptive to the idea of a research airplane, but in early 1942 he left the door open just a crack: "He left Stack with the idea, however, that some low-priority, back-of-the-envelope estimates to identify the most desirable design features of a transonic airplane could not hurt anyone, providing they did not distract from more pressing business," as noted by historian James Hansen.

Given Stack's commitment to the idea, that was all that was needed. With the blessing of the local management at Langley Memorial Aeronautical Laboratory, Stack immediately gathered a small group of engineers and began to work on the preliminary design aspects for a transonic research airplane, and by the summer of 1943 the group had produced such a design. The design established a mind-set that would guide NACA's thinking on the transonic research airplane for the next five years, though it would be in conflict with some later ideas coming from Kotcher and the U.S. Army. The principal features of the preliminary NACA design were as follows:

1) It would be a small turbojet-powered airplane.
2) It would take off under its own power from the ground.
3) It would have a maximum speed of Mach 1, but the main concern would be its ability to fly safely at high subsonic speeds.
4) It would carry a large payload of scientific instruments to measure the aerodynamic parameters and its dynamic behavior in flight near Mach 1.
5) It would start its test program at the low end of the compressibility regime and progressively sneak up to Mach 1 in later flights. The important goal would be to gather aerodynamic data at high subsonic speeds, not necessarily to fly into the supersonic regime.

Those features came to be considered as almost inviolable in the mind-set of the Langley engineers and of Stack in particular.

The exigencies of wartime mandated accelerated research into high-speed aerodynamics, and compressibility problems finally had the attention not only of NACA but also of the U.S. Army and Navy. Stack, who had become Eastman Jacobs's assistant section chief for the VDT in 1935, and head of the high-speed wind tunnels in 1937, was made chief of the newly formed Compressibility Research Division in 1943, giving him his most advantageous position thus far to push for the high-speed research airplane.

Note: On a chronological basis, the first aerodynamic advances in the basic understanding of high-speed compressibility effects took place during the era of the mature propeller-driven airplane. We chose, however, not to discuss these aerodynamic advances in Chapter 6 because their impact was not felt until the era of the jet-propelled airplane. This is an example of the state of the art in aerodynamics beginning to catch up with, and even pacing, the design of airplanes. The high-speed research airplane is a case in point. Although the first X-airplane, the X-1, was designed to probe the unknown aerodynamic regime through Mach 1, it could not have been successfully designed without the knowledge about compressibility effects already at hand at that time.

Point and Counterpoint—The Bell X-1

Although NACA had the theoretical knowledge, the experience, and the data to deal with compressibility problems, the U.S. Army and Navy had the money that would be necessary to design and build a research airplane. The Bell X-1 was conceived on November 30, 1944, when Robert J. Woods of Bell Aircraft visited the office of Ezra Kotcher. Woods, who had NACA ties because of having worked at Langley Memorial Aeronautical Laboratory during 1928–1929 on the VDT, had joined with Lawrence D. Bell in 1935 to form the Bell Aircraft Corporation in Buffalo, New York. Woods had dropped by Kotcher's office simply to chat. During the conversation, Kotcher mentioned that the Army, with the help of NACA, wanted to build a special, nonmilitary, high-speed research airplane. After detailing the Army's specifications for the aircraft, Kotcher asked if Bell Aircraft would be interested in designing and building the airplane. Woods said yes, and the die was cast.

When Kotcher was talking with Woods, he was not operating out of a vacuum. During 1944, U.S. Army and NACA engineers were meeting to outline the nature of a joint-research airplane program, and by mid-1944 Kotcher had received the Army's approval for the design and construction of such an airplane. However, the Army's reasons for wanting the high-speed research airplane were somewhat in conflict with those of NACA. To understand that conflict, we need to consider two factors operative at that time.

The first factor was that there was a common public belief in a sound barrier, a myth that had originated in 1935 when the British aerodynamicist W. F. Hilton had described to a journalist some of the high-speed experiments he was conducting at the National Physical Laboratory. Pointing to a plot of airfoil drag (similar to that shown at the left in Figure 7.15), Hilton described "how the resistance of a wing shoots up like a barrier against higher speed as we approach the speed of sound." The next morning, the leading British newspapers were misrepresenting Hilton's comment by referring to the sound barrier. The idea of a physical barrier to flight, that airplanes could never fly faster than the speed of sound, became widespread among the public. Furthermore, even though most engineers knew that that was not the case, they still had no idea how much the drag would increase in the transonic regime, and given the low levels of thrust produced by airplane powerplants at that time, dealing with the speed of sound certainly loomed as a tremendous challenge.

The second factor in the conflict between the U.S. Army and the NACA was that Kotcher was convinced that the research airplane had to be powered by a rocket engine, rather than a turbojet. That stemmed from his experience in 1943 as a project officer on the proposed Northrop XP-79 rocket-propelled flying-wing interceptor, as well as the Army's knowledge of Germany's new rocket-propelled interceptor, the Me-163.

Therefore, the U.S. Army viewed the high-speed research airplane as follows:

1) It should be rocket powered.
2) Early in its flight schedule, it should attempt to fly supersonically, to show everybody that the sound barrier could be broken.
3) Later in the design process it was determined that it should be air launched, rather than take off from the ground.

All of those requirements were in conflict with NACA's more careful, more scientific approach, but the Army was paying for the X-1, and the Army's views prevailed.

Although John Stack and NACA did not agree with the U.S. Army's specifications, they nevertheless provided as much technical data as possible throughout the design of the X-1. Lacking appropriate wind-tunnel data and theoretical solutions for transonic aerodynamics, NACA developed three stopgap methods for acquisition of transonic aerodynamic data. In 1944, tests using the drop-body concept were carried out at Langley Memorial Aeronautical Laboratory. Wings were mounted on bomblike missiles, which were dropped from a B-29 at an altitude of 30,000 feet. The terminal velocities of those models sometimes reached supersonic speeds. The data were limited, mainly consisting of estimates of the drag, but NACA engineers considered them reliable enough to estimate the power required for a transonic airplane. Also in 1944, Robert R. Gilruth, chief of the Flight Research Section, developed the wing-flow method, wherein a model wing would be mounted perpendicularly at just the right location on the wing of a P-51D. During a dive, the P-51 would pick up enough speed (to about Mach 0.81) so that locally supersonic flow would occur over its wing (as shown in Figure 7.12). The small model wing mounted perpendicularly on the P-51 wing would be totally immersed in that supersonic-flow region, providing a unique high-speed-flow environment for the model. Ultimately, those wing-flow tests gave NACA the most systematic and extensive plots of transonic data yet assembled. The third stopgap method was rocket-model testing, wherein wing models were mounted on rockets, which were fired from NACA's facility at Wallops Island on the coast of Virginia's Eastern Shore. The data from all of those methods, along with the existing body of compressibility data obtained by NACA over the preceding 20 years, provided the scientific and engineering base from which Bell Aircraft designed the X-1.

Breaking the Sound Barrier

This chapter began by describing how Chuck Yeager flew the Bell X-1 through the sound barrier in 1947. The first supersonic flight of the Bell X-1 was the culmination of 260 years of research into the mysteries of high-speed aerodynamics, especially the 23 years of research by NACA—one of the most important stories in the history of applied aerodynamics. A three-view of the X-1 is shown in Figure 7.17.

On December 17, 1948, President Harry S. Truman presented the Collier Trophy for 1947 jointly to three men for "the greatest aeronautical achievement since the original flight of the Wright Brothers' airplane." That trophy was the highest possible official recognition for the accomplishments embodied in the X-1. John Stack was one of the three, recognized as the scientist, along with Lawrence D. Bell, the manufacturer, and Captain Charles E. Yeager, the pilot. The citation to Stack read "for pioneering research to determine the physical laws affecting supersonic flight and for his conception of transonic research airplanes," but an entire team of NACA researchers had worked to earn the 1947 Collier Trophy for the NACA high-speed research program.

At the time of that award, Stack was assistant chief of research at NACA Langley Memorial Aeronautical Laboratory, and in 1952 he was made assistant director of Langley. By that time, he had been awarded the 1951 Collier Trophy for development of the slotted-throat wind tunnel. In 1961, three years after NACA had been absorbed into NASA, Stack became director of aeronautical research at NASA Headquarters in Washington. Despairing at the deemphasis of aeronautics relative to space funding within NASA, Stack, after 34 years of government service with NACA/NASA, retired in 1962 and became vice president for engineering at Republic Aircraft Corporation. When Republic was absorbed by Fairchild–Hiiller in 1965, he became a vice president of that company, retiring in 1971. On June 18, 1972, Stack fell from a horse on his farm in Yorktown, Virginia, and was fatally injured. He was buried in the churchyard cemetery of Grace Episcopal Church in

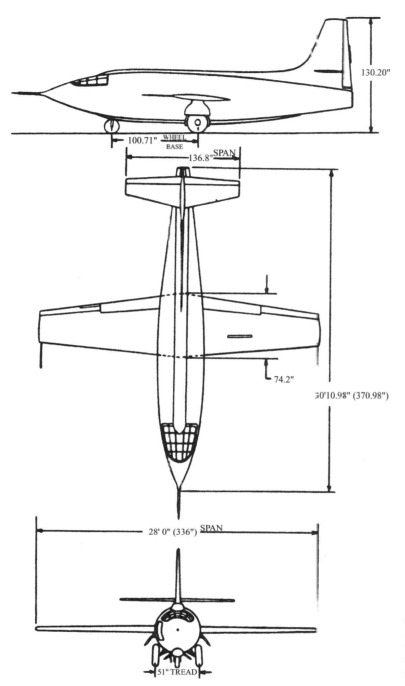

FIGURE 7.17
Three-view of the Bell X-1, the first piloted airplane to fly faster than sound.

Yorktown, only a few miles from NASA Langley Research Center. Today, F-15s from nearby Langley Air Force Base fly over the churchyard—airplanes that can routinely fly at almost three times the speed of sound, thanks to the legacy of John Stack and the NACA high-speed research program.

Probing the Mysteries—Transonic Aerodynamics

The flights of the Bell X-1 proved beyond any doubt that airplanes could fly safely in the mysterious aerodynamic region around Mach 1, in spite of the lack of theory

FIGURE 7.18
Wind-tunnel model of the
Bell X-1 in the Langley
8-foot wind tunnel, 1947.

and experimental data concerning the aerodynamic characteristics in that
"transonic gap." In 1947, a great deal was known about the subsonic and
supersonic regions that bracketed that gap, but very little was known about the
transonic region of the gap itself.

In regard to wind-tunnel testing in the late 1940s, measurements of transonic
flows below $M_\infty = 0.95$ and above $M_\infty = 1.1$ could be carried out with reasonable
accuracy in the NACA high-speed wind tunnels, but the data obtained between
0.95 and 1.1 were of questionable accuracy. For Mach numbers very near 1, the
flow was quite sensitive, and if a model of any reasonable cross-sectional area was
placed in the tunnel, the flow would become choked. ("Choking" is the breakdown
of flow in the test section when the proper mass flow cannot pass through.) That
choking phenomenon was one of the most difficult aspects of high-speed tunnel
research; small models had to be used. Figure 7.18 shows a small model of the Bell
X-1, with a wingspan slightly over 1 foot whereas the test-section diameter was
8 feet. In spite of that small model size, valid data could not be obtained at
freestream Mach numbers above 0.92 because of choking in the tunnel at higher
Mach numbers. Even when the flow did not choke, the shock waves from the
model, which were nearly perpendicular to the flow at Mach numbers near 1,
reflected off the tunnel walls and impinged back on the model itself. In either case,
the aerodynamic data from the model were essentially worthless.

The Mach number gap between 0.95 and 1.1, in which valid data could not
be obtained using the existing high-speed wind tunnels in the late 1940s,
contributed greatly to the aerodynamic uncertainties that dominated the Bell X-1
program up to its first supersonic flight (which was why the Bell engineers made
the X-1 fuselage precisely the shape of a 50-caliber machine-gun bullet, a shape
whose attributes were well known to ballisticians by that time). Moreover, the
advancement of basic aerodynamics in the transonic range was greatly hindered by
that situation. Throughout the late 1930s and 1940s, NACA engineers attempted to
alleviate the choking problem in their high-speed tunnels by using various
test-section designs (closed test sections, totally open test sections, a bump on the

test-section wall to tailor the flow constrictions), as well as various methods for supporting a model in the test section to minimize blockage. None of those ideas solved the problem. But the stage was being set for a technical breakthrough, which came in the late 1940s—the slotted-throat transonic tunnel.

In 1946, Ray H. Wright, a theoretician at NACA Langley Memorial Aeronautical Laboratory, carried out an analysis that indicated that if the test section were given a series of long, thin, rectangular slots parallel to the flow direction that would leave about 12 percent of the test-section periphery open, then the blockage problem might be greatly alleviated. That idea met with some skepticism, but it was almost immediately accepted by John Stack, who by that time was a highly placed administrator at Langley. A decision was made to slot the test section of the small, 12-inch high-speed tunnel, which resulted in greatly improved performance in early 1947. However, that was simply an experiment, and much skepticism remained. On the surface, NACA made no plans to further implement that idea. On the other hand, Stack confided privately to his colleagues that he favored slotting the large 16-foot high-speed tunnel. Without fanfare, that work began in the spring of 1948, buried in a larger project to increase the horsepower of the tunnel. By December of 1950, the modified 16-foot tunnel became operational. Subsequent operation of this facility proved that the slotted-throat concept allowed smooth transition of the tunnel flow through Mach 1 simply because of the increase in tunnel power. With that, the problem of blockage was basically solved. Those tunnels became the first truly transonic wind tunnels, and for that accomplishment John Stack and his colleagues at NACA Langley were awarded the Collier Trophy in 1951. The problem of measuring transonic flows in the laboratory was well in hand.

The same could not be said for the problem of computing transonic flows. The analysis of such flows was exceptionally difficult in the period before the development of the high-speed digital computer. In 1951, there was virtually no useful aerodynamic method for the calculation of transonic flows. Clearly, in 1951, computational analysis of transonic flowfields was lagging greatly behind the experimental progress. That situation prevailed until the advent of modern computational fluid dynamics. By the 1980s, with a few exceptions, the problem of calculating transonic flows was reasonably well in hand, because of the power of computational fluid dynamics.

The Area Rule and the Supercritical Airfoil

There were two major developments having to do with configuration that made transonic flight practical—the area rule and the supercritical airfoil, both products of the transonic wind-tunnel research at Langley Memorial Aeronautical Laboratory directed by Richard Whitcomb. On a technical basis, the area rule and the supercritical airfoil had the same objective, which was to reduce drag in the transonic regime. However, their drag reductions were accomplished in different ways. Consider the qualitative sketch of the drag coefficient versus Mach number in Figure 7.19 for a transonic body. The variation for a standard body shape without the area rule and without a supercritical airfoil is given by the solid curve.

Now let us consider the area rule by itself. The area rule is a simple statement that the cross-sectional area of the body should have a smooth variation with longitudinal distance along the body; there should be no rapid or discontinuous

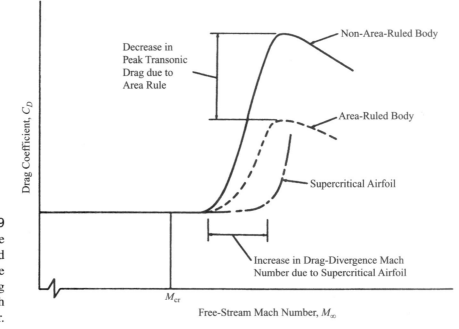

FIGURE 7.19

Illustration of the separate effects of the area rule and supercritical airfoil on the variation of drag coefficient with Mach number.

changes in the distribution of cross-sectional areas. For example, a conventional wing–body combination will have a sudden increase in cross-sectional area in the region where the wing cross section is added to the body cross section. The area rule says that, to compensate, the body cross section should be decreased in the vicinity of the wing, producing a wasplike or soda-bottle shape on the body. The aerodynamic advantage of the area rule is shown in Figure 7.19, where the drag variation for the area-ruled body is given by the dashed curve. Simply stated, application of the area rule reduces the peak transonic drag by a considerable amount.

The supercritical airfoil, on the other hand, acts in a different fashion. A supercritical airfoil is shaped somewhat flat on the top surface, to reduce the local Mach number inside the supersonic region below what it would be for a conventional airfoil under the same flight conditions. As a result, the strength of the shock wave is lower, and the boundary-layer separation is less severe, and thus, a higher freestream Mach number can be reached before the drag-divergence phenomenon sets in. The drag variation for a supercritical airfoil is shown in Figure 7.19 by the broken curve. The role of a supercritical airfoil is clearly evident. Although the supercritical airfoil and an equivalent standard airfoil may have the same critical Mach number, the drag-divergence Mach number for the supercritical airfoil will be much larger. That is, the supercritical airfoil can tolerate a much larger increase in the freestream Mach number above the critical value before drag divergence is encountered. Such airfoils are designed to operate far above the critical Mach number—hence the term "supercritical" airfoils.

The area rule was introduced in a spectacular fashion in the early 1950s. Although there had been some analysis that had produced oblique hints in the direction of the area rule, and although workers in the field of ballistics had known for years that projectiles with sudden changes in their distributions of

a)

b)

FIGURE 7.20
a) The Convair YF-102, without application of the area rule. b) The Convair YF-102A, with area-ruled fuselage. Note the wasp-like shape of the fuselage of the YF-102A in comparison with the YF-102.

cross-sectional areas exhibited high drag at high speeds, the importance of the area rule was not fully appreciated until Richard Whitcomb conducted a series of wind-tunnel tests on various transonic bodies in the slotted-throat wind tunnel. Those data, and an appreciation of the area rule, came just in time to save a new airplane program at Convair. In 1951, Convair was designing one of the "century series" fighters intended to fly at supersonic speeds. Designated the YF-102 (Figure 7.20), that aircraft had a delta-wing configuration and was powered by the Pratt and Whitney J-57 turbojet, the most powerful engine in the United States at that time. Aeronautical engineers at Convair expected the YF-102 to fly supersonically. On October 24, 1953, flight tests of the YF-102 began at Muroc Air Force Base (now Edwards Air Force Base), and a production line was being set up at Convair's San Diego, California, plant. However, as the flight tests progressed, it became painfully clear that the YF-102 could not fly faster than sound—the transonic drag rise was simply too great for even the powerful J-57 engine to overcome. After consultation with NACA aerodynamicists and inspection of the area-rule findings that had been obtained in the Langley Memorial Aeronautical Laboratory tunnel, the Convair engineers modified the airplane to become the YF-102A, with an area-ruled fuselage. Wind-tunnel data on the YF-102A looked promising. Figure 7.21, produced from those data, shows the variation of the drag coefficient with freestream Mach number for the YF-102 and YF-102A. At the top is the cross-sectional-area distribution for the YF-102, showing how it built up

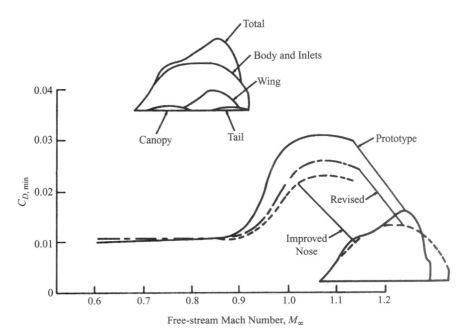

FIGURE 7.21
Variation of the drag
coefficient with Mach
number for the YF-102
(labeled "prototype") and
the YF-102A (labeled
"revised").

from the different body components. Note the irregular, bumpy nature of the total cross-sectional-area distribution. At the bottom right, shown by the dashed line, is the cross-sectional-area distribution for the YF-102A, a much smoother variation than that for the YF-102. The comparison between the drag coefficients for the conventional YF-102 (solid curve) and the area-ruled YF-102A (dashed curve) dramatically illustrates the tremendous transonic drag reduction to be obtained with the use of the area rule. (Recall from Figure 7.19 that the function of the area rule is to decrease the peak transonic drag; Figure 7.21 quantifies that function.) Encouraged by those wind-tunnel findings, the Convair engineers began a flight-test program for the YF-102A. On December 20, 1954, the prototype YF-102A left the ground at Lindbergh Field, San Diego, California, and exceeded the speed of sound while still climbing. The use of the area rule had increased the top speed of the airplane by 25 percent. The production line rolled, and 870 F-102As were built for the U.S. Air Force. The area rule made its debut in dramatic style.

The supercritical airfoil, also pioneered by Richard Whitcomb, based on data obtained in the 8-foot wind tunnel, was a development of the 1960s. Recall from Figure 7.19 that the function of the supercritical airfoil was to increase the increment between the critical Mach number and the drag-divergence Mach number. The data in the Langley tunnel indicated a possible 10-percent increase in cruise Mach number due to the use of a supercritical-airfoil wing. NASA introduced the technical community to the supercritical-airfoil data in a special conference in 1972. Since that time, the supercritical-airfoil concept has been employed on virtually all new commercial aircraft and some military airplanes. Physical data for a supercritical airfoil and for the standard NACA 64-A215 airfoil are compared in Figures 7.22 and 7.23, along with their shapes. At the top of Figure 7.22, the regions of supersonic flow over the airfoils are shown, and the corresponding variations of the pressure coefficients over the airfoil surfaces are shown at the bottom of Figure 7.22. Notice that, for the supercritical airfoil, the region of supersonic flow is terminated by a weaker shock wave and that the

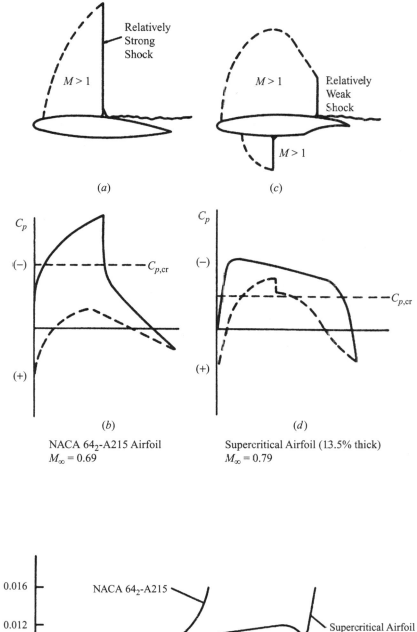

FIGURE 7.22
Flowfield and pressure distribution comparison between a standard NACA 6-series airfoil and a supercritical airfoil, based on Whitcomb's work at the NACA Langley Research Center, 1965.

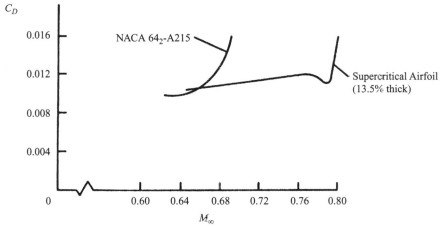

FIGURE 7.23
Drag coefficient versus Mach number for a standard NACA 6-series airfoil and a supercritical airfoil. The transonic drag rise is delayed to a higher Mach number for the supercritical airfoil.

pressure change is less severe. That delays the onset of the transonic drag rise to a higher freestream Mach number, as shown in Figure 7.23. The performance advantage of the supercritical airfoil is clearly evident. Whitcomb's original publication on the supercritical airfoil was at first classified, but was released to the public in the early 1970s.

This section has provided a brief glimpse into what was one of the most exciting chapters in the history of aerodynamics and aeronautical engineering. We have seen how the secrets of transonic flow were slowly and painstakingly uncovered; how a concerted, intelligent attack on the problem eventually led to useful wind-tunnel data, as well as to modern methods of computation for transonic flows; and, finally, how those transonic data ultimately led to two of the major aerodynamic breakthroughs in the latter half of the 20th century—the area rule and the supercritical airfoil.

An Aerodynamic Breakthrough in High-Speed Flight—The Swept Wing

The concept of the swept wing for high-speed flight was introduced by Adolf Busemann at the 1935 Volta conference in the presence of the world's leading high-speed aerodynamicists, as discussed earlier. It should have startled the conference delegates like an electric shock. Instead, it was virtually ignored by the audience. Even von Kármán and Eastman Jacobs did not mention the idea on their return to the United States. Indeed, 10 years later, when World War II was reaching its conclusion and jet airplanes were beginning to revolutionize aviation, the idea of swept wings was suggested independently by Robert T. Jones, an ingenious aerodynamicist at NACA Langley Memorial Aeronautical Laboratory. When Jones presented his proposal to Jacobs and von Kármán in 1945, neither man seemed to remember Busemann's idea from the Volta conference. Von Kármán mentioned that oversight in his autobiography, "I must admit that I did not give this suggestion much attention until years later." Being human, von Kármán offered an excuse, "My direction of effort at this time was not in design, but in developing supersonic theory." However, Busemann's idea was not wasted on the German Luftwaffe, which recognized its military significance and classified the concept in 1936, one year after the conference. That set into motion a research program on swept wings in Germany that had produced a mass of technical data by the end of the war, to the great surprise and concern of the Allied technical teams that swooped into the Germany research laboratories at Pennemunde and Braunschweig in early 1945.

At the time of the Volta conference, Adolf Busemann was a relatively young (age 34) but accomplished aerodynamicist. Born in Lubeck, Germany, in 1901, he completed high school in his home town and received his engineering diploma and Ph.D. in engineering in 1924 and 1925, respectively, from the Technische Hochschule at Braunschweig. Busemann was one of the few important German aerodynamicists of that era who did not begin as one of Prandtl's students, but in 1925 Busemann began his professional career at the Kaiser Wilhelm Institute in Göttingen and soon entered Prandtl's sphere. From 1931 to 1935, Busemann broke away from that sphere to teach in the Engine Laboratory of the Technische Hochschule in Dresden, Germany. In 1935, he went to Braunschweig as chief of the Gas Dynamics Division of the Aeronautical Research Laboratory. When the Allied technical teams moved into German laboratories at the end of the war, they not only scooped up masses of technical aerodynamic data, but also effectively

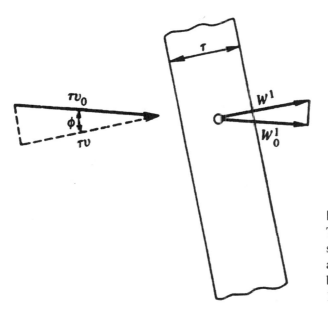

FIGURE 7.24
The first concept of a swept wing to reduce drag at high speeds; presented by Adolf Busemann in 1935.

scooped up Busemann, who accepted an invitation to join NACA Langley Memorial Aeronautical Laboratory under Operation Paperclip (an American operation that brought a large number of German Scientists and engineers to the U.S.) in 1947. Busemann continued his research on high-speed aerodynamics for NACA after joining Langley. He subsequently became chairman of the advanced-study committee at Langley and, among other responsibilities, supervised the preparation of science lectures used for training the early groups of astronauts in the manned space program. Later, Busemann became a professor in the Department of Aerospace Engineering Sciences at the University of Colorado in Boulder. After retirement, he remained in Boulder, leading an active life until his death in 1986.

Busemann's paper at the 1935 Volta conference was based on the simple idea that the aerodynamic characteristics of a wing are governed mainly by the component of the flow velocity perpendicular to the leading edge. Figure 7.24 shows the sketch used by Busemann to illustrate that normal component of the velocity. The angle of sweep is the angle ϕ. As the wing sweep is increased (as ϕ is increased) for a fixed freestream velocity, the component of velocity normal to the leading edge will decrease. Because the wing essentially "sees" the normal component rather than the full-stream velocity, the onset of high-speed compressibility effects on the wing will be delayed to a higher free-stream Mach number. The meaning of that for transonic flight is that as the wing is swept, the critical Mach number for the wing will be increased, and hence, the freestream Mach number at which the large rise in drag is encountered will be increased. Its meaning for supersonic flight is that the onset of wave drag will be delayed, and its magnitude will be reduced.

The swept-wing concept in Busemann's 1935 Volta conference paper was, for everybody outside of Germany, an idea before its time. It is difficult to understand how von Kármán and other attendees failed to appreciate the significance of Busemann's idea, even forgetting it entirely. That very evening, Busemann went out to dinner with von Kármán, Hugh Dryden from the National Bureau of Standards, and General Arturo Crocco, the organizer of the conference.

During dinner, Crocco sketched on the back of a menu card an airplane with swept wings, swept tail, and swept propeller, calling it, facetiously, "Busemann's airplane of the future."

There was no such facetiousness in Germany. Under the Nazi government, the Luftwaffe was expanding rapidly. With Busemann in charge of aerodynamics research at Braunschweig, high-speed wind-tunnel testing of swept wings began. By 1939, the data confirmed the aerodynamic advantage of swept wings. In 1942, the senior airplane designer at Mersserschmitt, Woldemar Voigt, used Busemann's idea during the paper design for an advanced experimental jet fighter. Designated Projekt 1101, the airplane had sharply swept wings, in contrast to the mild sweep of the Me-262 twin-jet fighter that Voight was also designing. Because of the high priority placed on the Me-262, Voigt was not able to spend enough time on Projekt 1101. By the end of the war, there had been only wind-tunnel tests on models of the highly swept jet. The data, however, were most promising.

In May 1945, von Kármán led one of the teams of U.S. scientists and engineers that swept into a crumbling Germany to search for information on German research and development. Because of his education in Germany and familiarity with the leading German scientists, von Kármán was a particularly effective member of the team. On May 7, the day before the surrender was signed, the team arrived at Braunschweig and was amazed to find numerous swept-wing wind-tunnel models and a mass of swept-wing data.

One member of that team was George Schairer, now a retired vice president of The Boeing Company, but at that time a young Boeing aeronautical engineer working on a preliminary design for a new generation of jet-powered bombers. As we noted earlier, after studying the German data on swept wings, Schairer quickly wrote a letter to his colleague, Ben Cohn, at Boeing, alerting the design team to the interesting features of such wings. Moreover, Schairer asked Cohn to distribute copies of his letter to all of the major aircraft manufacturers so that the entire aeronautical community would know about the benefits of swept wings for high-speed airplanes. In the short run, only two companies would take advantage of that information—Boeing and North American.

It is unlikely that the swept wing would have revolutionized airplane design so soon after the war if it had not been for the independent discovery of its advantages by Robert T. Jones, an aerodynamicist at the NACA Langley Memorial Aeronautical Laboratory. Jones was a self-made person in much the same mold as 19th-century aerodynamicists like Cayley, Wenham, and Phillips. Born in Macon, Missouri, in 1910, Jones was totally captivated by aeronautics at an early age. He later wrote the following:

> All during the late twenties the weekly magazine *Aviation* appeared on the local newsstand in my hometown. *Aviation* carried technical articles by eminent aeronautical engineers such as B. V. Korvin-Krovkovsky, Alexander Klemin, and others. Included in both *Aero Digest* and *Aviation* were notices of forthcoming *NACA Technical Reports and Notes*. These could be procured from the Government Printing Office usually for ten cents and sometimes even free by simply writing NACA Headquarters in Washington. The contents of these reports seemed much more interesting to me than the regular high school and college curricula, and I suspect that my English teachers may have been quite perplexed by the essays I wrote for them on aeronautical subjects.

Jones attended the University of Missouri for one year, but left to take a series of aeronautics-related jobs, first as a crew member with the Marie Meyer Flying

Circus and then with the Nicholas–Beazley Airplane Company in Marshall, Missouri, which was just starting to produce a single-engine, low-wing monoplane designed by the noted British aeronautical engineer Walter H. Barling. At one time, Nicholas–Beazley was producing and selling one of those aircraft each day. However, the company became a victim of the Depression, and in 1933 Jones found himself working as an elevator operator in Washington, D.C., and taking night classes in aeronautics at Catholic University. In 1934, the Public Works Administration created a number of temporary scientific positions in the federal government. On the recommendation of Congressman David J. Lewis, from Jones's hometown, Jones received a nine-month appointment at the NACA Langley Memorial Aeronautical Laboratory. That was the beginning of a lifetime career for Jones at NACA/NASA. Through a passionate interest and self-study in aeronautics, Jones had become exceptionally knowledgeable in aerodynamics theory. His talents were recognized at Langley, and he was kept on at the laboratory through a series of temporary and emergency reappointments for the next two years. Unable to promote him into the lowest professional engineering grade because of civil-service regulations that required a college degree, in 1936 the laboratory management was finally able to hire Jones permanently via a loophole. It hired Jones at the next grade above the lowest, for which the requirement of a college degree was not specifically stated (although presumed).

By 1944, Jones was one of the most respected aerodynamicists in NACA. At that time he was working on the design of an experimental air-to-air missile for the U.S. Army Air Force and was also studying the aerodynamics of a proposed glide bomb having a low aspect ratio delta wing. The Ludington-Griswold Company of Saybrook, Connecticut, had carried out wind-tunnel tests on a dart-shaped missile of their design, and Roger Griswold, president of the company, showed the data to Jones in 1944. Griswold had compared the lift data for the missile's low aspect ratio delta wing with calculations made from Prandtl's tried-and-proved lifting-line theory. Jones realized that Prandtl's lifting-line theory was not valid for low aspect ratio wings, and he began to construct a more appropriate theory for the delta-wing

planform. Jones obtained rather simple analytical equations for the low-speed, incompressible flow over delta wings, but considered the theory to be "so crude" that "nobody would be interested in it." He placed his analysis in his desk and went on with other matters.

In early 1945, Jones began to look at the mathematical theory of supersonic flows. When applied to delta wings, Jones found that he was obtaining equations similar to those he had found for incompressible flow using the crude theory that was now buried in his desk.

The Lockheed F-104 at the National Air and Space Museum, Smithsonian Institution, last used as an experimental aircraft by NASA.

Searching for an explanation, he recalled that the aerodynamic characteristics of a wing were governed mainly by the component of the freestream velocity perpendicular to the leading edge. The answer suddenly was quite simple. For the delta wing, the reason his supersonic finding were the same as his earlier low-speed findings was that the leading edge of the delta wing was swept far enough that the component of the supersonic freestream Mach number

A close-up of the wing of the Lockheed F-104 at the National Air and Space Museum, Smithsonian Institution, highlighting the wing with a very thin (3.5 percent thick) airfoil with a razor-sharp leading edge. The straight, low aspect ratio, thin wing of the F-104 is one of the two classic design solutions to supersonic flight.

perpendicular to the leading edge was subsonic, and, hence, the supersonic swept wing acted as if it were in a subsonic flow. With that revelation, Jones had independently discovered the high-speed aerodynamic advantage of swept wings, albeit 10 years after Busemann's paper at the Volta conference.

Jones began to discuss his swept-wing theory with colleagues at NACA Langley Memorial Aeronautical Laboratory. In mid-February 1945, he outlined his thoughts to Jean Roche and Ezra Kotcher of the U.S. Army Air Force at Wright Field. On March 5, 1945, he sent a memo to Gus Crowley, chief of research at Langley, stating the following:

> [I have] recently made a theoretical analysis which indicates that a V-shaped wing traveling point foremost would be less affected by compressibility than other planforms. In fact, if the angle of the V is kept small relative to the Mach angle, the lift and center of pressure remain the same at speeds both above and below the speed of sound.

In the same memo, Jones asked Crowley to approve experimental work on swept wings. Such work was quickly initiated by the Flight Research Section of Langley, under the direction of Robert Gilruth, beginning with a series of free-flight tests using bodies with swept wings dropped from high altitude.

Jones finished a formal report on his low aspect ratio wing theory in late April 1945, including the effects of compressibility and the concept of a swept

The Douglas D-558-2 Skyrocket, the first airplane to fly at Mach 2, with Scott Crossfield at the controls, November 20, 1953, now hangs at the National Air and Space Museum, Smithsonian Institution. This airplane shows the second classic design solution to supersonic flight—a highly swept wing.

wing. However, during the in-house editorial review of that report, Theodore Theodorsen raised some serious objections. Theodorsen did not like the heavily intuitive nature of Jones's theory, and he asked Jones to clarify the "hocus-pocus" with some "real mathematics." Furthermore, because supersonic flow was so different physically and mathematically from subsonic flow, Theodorsen could not accept the "subsonic" behavior of Jones's highly swept wings at supersonic speeds. Criticizing Jones's entire swept-wing concept, calling it "a snare and a delusion," Theodorsen insisted that Jones take out the part about swept wings.

Theodorsen's insistence prevailed, and publication of Jones's report was delayed. However, at the end of May 1945, Gilruth's free-flight tests dramatically verified Jones's predictions, showing a factor-of-4 reduction in drag due to sweeping the wings. Quickly following those data, wind-tunnel tests carried out in a small supersonic wind tunnel at Langley Memorial Aeronautical Laboratory showed a large reduction in drag on a section of wire in the test section when the wire was placed at a substantial angle of sweep relative to the flow in the test section. With that experimental proof of the validity of the swept-wing concept,

Langley forwarded Jones's report to NACA Headquarters in Washington, D.C., for publication. However, Theodorsen would not give up. The transmittal letter of NACA Headquarters contained the statement that "Dr. Theodore Theodorsen [still] does not agree with the arguments presented and the conclusions reached and accordingly declined to participate in editing the paper." Such recalcitrance on the part of Theodorsen is reminiscent of his refusal to believe that the shock waves seen in John Stack's schlieren photographs of the transonic flow over an airfoil 11 years earlier were real. Theodorsen certainly made important contributions to airfoil theory in the 1930s, but he was also capable of errors in judgment. That is, he was human.

The XP-86, the prototype of America's first swept-wing fighter, 1947. Later designated the F-86 Sabre, this airplane went on to fame in the Korean War. The F-86, with its swept wing, was one of the most technically significant airplanes early in the era of the jet propelled airplane. (Harold Andrews Collection.)

On June 21, 1945, NACA issued Jones's report as a confidential memorandum chiefly for the U.S. Army and Navy. Three weeks later, the report was reissued as an advance confidential report, sent by registered mail to those people in industry with a "need to know." Entitled "Wing Plan Forms for High-Speed Flight," Jones's report quickly spread the idea of the swept wing to selected members of the aeronautical community in the United States, but, by that time, information about the German swept-wing research was beginning to reach the same aeronautical community. Jones's work appeared in the open literature about a year later, as NACA TR 863, a technical report only five pages long, but a classic explanation of how a swept wing works aerodynamically.

Credit for the idea of a swept wing for high-speed flight is shared between Busemann and Jones. Separated by a time interval of 10 years, and the closed shops of military security in both Germany and the United States, each independently developed the concept, not knowing of each other's work. The full impact of the swept-wing concept on the aeronautical industry came directly after the end of World War II, with almost simultaneous release of similar information from both sides of the ocean, thus, promoting confidence in the validity of the concept.

This is the aerodynamic legacy behind all of the swept-wing aircraft that are flying today. The development of the swept-wing concept for a high-speed airframe, in concert with the development of the jet engine, created a revolution in the technology of the airplane, and they represent two of the most important hallmarks of the era of the jet-propelled airplane.

Aerodynamics of Hypersonic Flight—The Blunt-Body Revolution

We reiterate that throughout most of the 20th century the technical advancement of the airplane was been driven by the quest to fly faster and higher. This is clearly seen in Figures 7.4 and 7.25. In Figure 7.4, the exponential increase in speed with time throughout most of the century is blatantly obvious. Starting at 30 miles per hour with the Wright Flyer in 1903, the blistering speed of over 2000 miles per

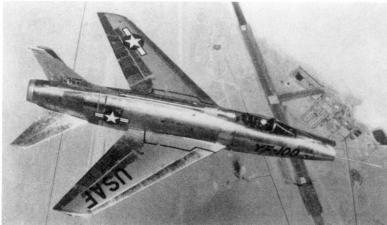

The YF-100 (North American Model 180), 1953. This airplane was the prototype of the North American F-100 Super Sabre, the first fighter airplane capable of supersonic speed in level flight. (Harold Andrews Collection.)

hour was achieved by 1970 with the Lockheed SR-71. The corresponding progressive increase in flight altitudes versus time is shown in Figure 7.25. The successes achieved in this quest for speed and altitude were due in no small part to the aeronautical research programs of NACA and later NASA. (Note that the phenomenal increase in speed and altitude from 1903 to 1970 has not continued in recent years. This is a reflection that performance parameters other than speed and altitude are dictating the design of many modern airplanes, such as energy efficiency and increased flight agility.)

Returning to Figure 7.4, note the dashed curve labeled "experimental rocket-powered airplanes." In the 1960s, with the increased thrust available from a rocket engine, the first hypersonic airplane, the North American X-15, achieved speeds in excess of 3600 miles per hour and altitudes up to 314,000 feet. (Rule of thumb: Flight speeds in excess of five times the speed of sound, Mach 5, are conventionally labeled *hypersonic*.) Since the early 1950s, research on hypersonic flight has been an integral part of the aeronautical scene, and NACA and NASA have led the way.

Examine Figure 7.26; this is a three-view of the Lockheed F-104 fighter airplane—the first aircraft to be designed for sustained flight at Mach 2. This airplane is the epitome of good supersonic design. Note the sleek, slender fuselage, the pointed nose, and the wing with a very thin airfoil and extremely sharp leading edge—so sharp that a protective cover must be placed over it when the airplane is on the ground to protect the ground crew from injury. All of these design features have one purpose—to reduce the strength of shock waves on the airplane in

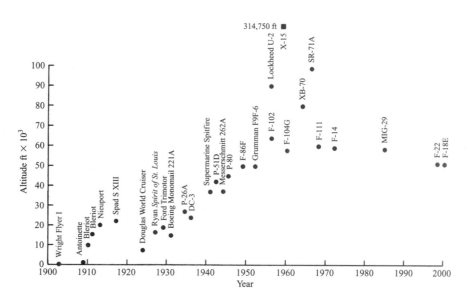

FIGURE 7.25
Typical flight altitudes over the years.

supersonic flight and, hence, to reduce the supersonic wave drag. Extrapolating these design features to higher-speed aircraft, your intuition might say that hypersonic airplanes should be more of the same, even more slender and sharper. But take a look at Figure 7.27, which shows the North American X-15 hypersonic research vehicle, the first aircraft to fly at nearly Mach 7. If anything, this aircraft is a little *less* sleek, with a slightly rounded nose and a more blunt wing leading edge. Finally, examine Figure 7.28, which shows the Space Shuttle, also designed by North American. The Space Shuttle is a hypersonic vehicle designed to enter the Earth's atmosphere at Mach 25 on return from orbit—an extremely fast hypersonic

General Dynamics F-111B, 1965. The first "swing-wing" jet airplane, so-called because the sweep angle of the wings can be changed in flight. A high sweep angle is optimum for high-speed flight, and a low sweep angle is optimum for low-speed flight, such as take-off and landing. (Harold Andrews Collection.)

speed. What we see in Figure 7.28 is a blunt-nosed body with thick wings, embodying a rounded leading edge. This is in direct contrast to the design trend set by the supersonic F-104 shown in Figure 7.26. So, we have to conclude that hypersonic aerodynamics, and its associated effect on the design of hypersonic vehicles, is physically *different* than at supersonic speeds.

What makes the difference is a new phenomenon that is relatively unimportant at supersonic speeds—*aerodynamic heating*. Believe it or not, and totally counter to intuition, aerodynamic heating to the nose and leading edges of hypersonic vehicles is *reduced* by making the nose and leading edges *blunt* rather than sharp. The blunt-body concept for reducing aerodynamic heating of hypersonic vehicles was *revolutionary* in its conception. And it was strictly the brain-child of one of the most innovative NACA/NASA researchers—Harvey Allen. Let us take a closer look.

Imagine a space vehicle, such as the Space Shuttle, in orbit around the Earth. Its altitude is more than 200 miles; hence, due to this tremendous height, the vehicle has a lot of potential energy, which is proportional to its height above the Earth. Moreover, it is moving with a velocity of about 26,000 feet per second. Because of this extreme speed, the vehicle has a lot of kinetic energy, which is proportional to the square of the velocity. Now imagine this vehicle entering the Earth's atmosphere and returning to the Earth's surface, where the vehicle comes to rest. At the surface, both the potential and kinetic energies of the vehicle are zero. Question: Where has all of the energy gone? Answer: The energy has gone into the only two media possible—into the air and into the vehicle. If one is concerned with preventing the vehicle from burning up during its hypersonic entry through the atmosphere, clearly we want *more* of the energy to go into the air and *less* into the body. How do we ensure that this happens? For the answer to this question, consider the two generic body shapes shown in Figure 7.29. At the left is a slender body with a pointed nose, and at the right is a blunt-nosed body. At hypersonic speeds, the shock wave generated by the slender body is attached to the nose and, relatively speaking, is a weaker shock. The air temperature behind this weaker

The Chance-Vought F8U-1 Crusader, 1955. This Navy jet is technically unusual because the wing can be inclined at different angles relative to the fuselage. In this photo, the variable-incidence shoulder-mounted wing is in its most inclined position, which keeps the fuselage horizontal on takeoff and landing for improved pilot visibility, while giving the wing the necessary higher angle of attack for low speed. (Harold Andrews Collection.)

shock typically is on the order of 5000 °F at velocities such as 26,000 feet per second. In contrast, the shock wave generated by the blunt body is much stronger, and it stands off of the body surface by a certain small distance called the shock detachment distance. The air temperature behind this stronger shock typically is on the order of 14,000 °F when the vehicle is moving at 26,000 feet per second. Clearly, this much higher air temperature means that a great deal of the initial vehicle energy is going into the air rather than the body. In contrast, for the slender body, less energy is going into the air, and, hence, more goes into the body. The moral of this story is that, to reduce aerodynamic heating to a hypersonic vehicle, the body should have a *blunt* nose and blunt wing leading edges; the body should *not* be a sharp, slender shape.

The hypersonic blunt-body concept was revolutionary and counterintuitive at the time. Its conception was the brainchild of a NACA research engineer who embodies the best of the qualities that NACA offered in its intellectual manpower. This person was Harry (Harvey) Julian Allen. Harvey Allen received his B.S. and M.S. degrees from Stanford University in 1932 and 1935, respectively. In 1936, he joined NACA Langley Memorial Aeronautical Laboratory as a researcher on the staff of the VDT, working for Eastman Jacobs. In 1940, as part of a contingent of other Langley researchers, he was transferred to the new NACA Ames Research Laboratory just being created in California. Harvey Allen was a perfect example of the innovative, intelligent, and hard-driving aeronautical engineer that formed the lifeblood of NACA's research program. While at Langley, he had participated in the design of the new and secret family of NACA laminar-flow airfoils, earning the respect of Eastman Jacobs for his aptitude in aerodynamic theory, as well as for experimental work. NACA transferred some of its best and brightest from Langley to form the embryonic new staff at NACA Ames—Harvey Allen was one of them.

It was not long until Allen became the head of the Theoretical Aerodynamics Section of the Research Division at Ames in mid-1941. Although he was in charge of theoretical research, Allen had a major impact on a number of new experimental

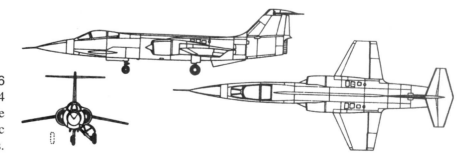

FIGURE 7.26
The Lockheed F-104 Starfighter—an example of good supersonic aerodynamics.

facilities. Along with his boss Don Wood, Allen did much of the design work on the huge 40 × 80 foot subsonic wind tunnel—what was to become the largest wind tunnel in the world at that time. Moreover, Harvey Allen strongly argued to pressurize the new 1 × 3-foot supersonic wind tunnel at NACA Ames Research Laboratory to allow experiments to be made over a wide range of Reynolds numbers. Allen felt that the Reynolds number effect on aerodynamic drag and flow separation would be

The F8U Crusader with the variable-incidence wing in its zero inclination position for high-speed flight. (Harold Andrews Collection.)

equally as important at supersonic speeds as it was at subsonic speeds, thus, directly contradicting and overriding the opposite opinion voiced by Cal Tech professor Theodore von Kármán, arguably the leading aerodynamicist in the United States at that time. Allen had the faith of his convictions. Later, tests in the 1 × 3-foot supersonic tunnel showed Reynolds number effects to be important, vindicating Allen's strong stance.

Right from its inception, the NACA Ames Research Laboratory emphasized high-speed flight. Harvey Allen was an integral part of this activity. In 1945 he was made chief of the new High Speed Research Division at Ames. However, Allen was not satisfied with just administering a research activity; he had to get personally involved with it and exercise his innovative, original thinking on the research aspects. In 1945, he conceived the idea of changing the Mach number in a supersonic wind tunnel simply by sliding one side of the nozzle block back and forth, thus changing the ratio of the exit-to-throat area. It is this ratio that determines the Mach number at the nozzle exit. In 1946, he conceived the

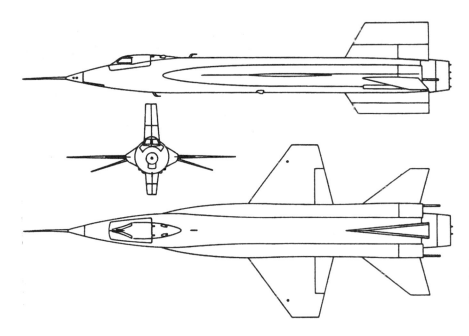

FIGURE 7.27
The North American X-15, a hypersonic airplane designed for Mach 7.

The Lockheed F-104C-5 Starfighter, 1958. The F-104 was the first jet fighter designed for sustained flight at Mach 2. (American Aviation Historical Society Collection.)

supersonic free-flight tunnel, a combination of a supersonic wind tunnel blowing air in one direction and a gun that fired a test model in the opposite direction into this airstream. In this fashion, the relative air velocity over the model is the sum of the tunnel airflow velocity and the projectile velocity from the gun. A relative airflow of Mach 10–12 could be achieved over the model using a supersonic wind tunnel of moderate Mach number. The tunnel was in operation at NACA Ames by 1949. Allen also developed the vapor screen technique for visualizing the flow over supersonic and hypersonic bodies. In this approach, a small amount of water vapor is introduced into the tunnel airstream; this water vapor condenses at the cooler air temperatures created by the nozzle expansion, producing a fine fog in the test section. A narrow sheet of bright light is made to shine through the test section perpendicular to the flow. When there is no model in the test section, the sheet of light appears as a uniformly lighted screen of fog particles. With a model in the tunnel, the flow disturbances change the fog

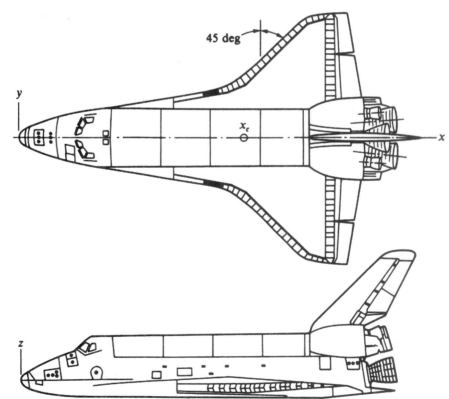

FIGURE 7.28
The Space Shuttle, a hypersonic vehicle designed for Mach 25.

pattern, which allows a visualization of various features of the flow, such as shock waves and vortices. In 1949, when this technique was introduced, it was a dramatic and unique contribution to supersonic and hypersonic wind-tunnel testing.

In short, Harvey Allen was a gifted idea person. It was this gifted nature that led him to the hypersonic blunt-body concept—the concept that made hypersonic flight possible beginning in the 1950s.

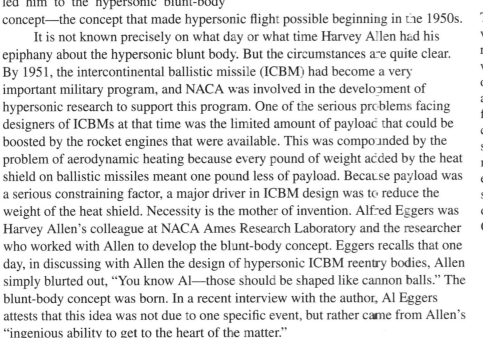

The Lockheed F-104. This view shows the low aspect ratio, very thin, straight wing design of the F-104, one of the two basic design approaches for supersonic flight. This, in combination with the slender pointed fuselage, makes the F-104 an excellent example of good supersonic aerodynamic design. (Harold Andrews Collection.)

It is not known precisely on what day or what time Harvey Allen had his epiphany about the hypersonic blunt body. But the circumstances are quite clear. By 1951, the intercontinental ballistic missile (ICBM) had become a very important military program, and NACA was involved in the development of hypersonic research to support this program. One of the serious problems facing designers of ICBMs at that time was the limited amount of payload that could be boosted by the rocket engines that were available. This was compounded by the problem of aerodynamic heating because every pound of weight added by the heat shield on ballistic missiles meant one pound less of payload. Because payload was a serious constraining factor, a major driver in ICBM design was to reduce the weight of the heat shield. Necessity is the mother of invention. Alfred Eggers was Harvey Allen's colleague at NACA Ames Research Laboratory and the researcher who worked with Allen to develop the blunt-body concept. Eggers recalls that one day, in discussing with Allen the design of hypersonic ICBM reentry bodies, Allen simply blurted out, "You know Al—those should be shaped like cannon balls." The blunt-body concept was born. In a recent interview with the author, Al Eggers attests that this idea was not due to one specific event, but rather came from Allen's "ingenious ability to get to the heart of the matter."

Allen and Eggers together published a classified report, Research Memorandum A53028, in August 1953, containing an analysis proving that the heat transfer to a blunt hypersonic body was considerably less than that to a slender body. This work was later unclassified in NACA Technical Note 4047 published in 1957 and finally placed in the unclassified archive literature as NACA TR 1381 titled "A Study of the Motion and Aerodynamic Heating of Ballistic Missiles

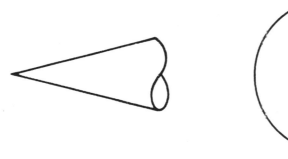

Slender Body   Blunt Body

FIGURE 7.29
Comparison of slender and blunt body shapes.

Entering the Earth's Atmosphere at High Supersonic Speeds." This report still stands today as the definitive classic work on the subject.

In spite of all this, the blunt-body concept was not immediately accepted. Conventional wisdom at the time held that ICBMs should impact the Earth's surface at very high velocity, near Mach 7. Early U.S. Air Force specifications drove the industry to think of long, slender cones with low drag coefficients so that the Mach 7 requirement could be satisfied. The whole thought process was the faster you go, the sleeker the missile. So, in Egger's words, there was an "emotional block dealing with the blunt body." But aerodynamic heating was *the* important consideration in heat shield weight, which, in turn, was a determining factor in the allowable payload weight. And evidence kept accumulating to support Harvey Allen's idea that a blunt-body shape greatly reduced the aerodynamic heating. The concept was tested and verified by Allen and Eggers in the Supersonic Free-Flight Tunnel. Other data obtained in high-performance shock tubes and hypersonic wind tunnels showed the same thing. By 1955, the value of Allen's blunt-body concept was accepted, at least enough to earn him the prestigious Sylvanus Albert Reed Award of the IAS and, in 1957, the NACA Distinguished Service Medal. Harvey Allen was further honored by the IAS when he was chosen as their 21st Wright Brothers Lecturer in 1957. He delivered his Wright Brothers paper to the institute on December 17, 1957, in Washington, D.C., the 54th anniversary of the first flight of the Wright Flyer. Entitled "Hypersonic Flight and the Re-Entry Problem," Allen's paper not only detailed the work on the aerodynamic heating and motion of hypersonic blunt bodies, but it was also a clarion call for research in the new, unknown frontier of hypersonic flight. He ended his paper with the following thoughts:

> This discussion of new problems has only touched upon a few of the known phenomena which become of interest in consideration of high-speed rockets. Certainly numerous others will appear as the conquest of space progresses. Faced with such a nebulous state of affairs it is not surprising that our approach to these new problems is a cautious one. It is well to note, however, that in this regard the present situation is certainly analogous to that which the Wright brothers faced at the turn of the century. If we give the same painstaking and intelligent treatment to our problems as they gave to theirs a half century ago, our success seems assured.

Research on hypersonic aerodynamics continues to the present day. It represents the very frontier of today's quest for speed and altitude.

ADVANCES IN PROPULSION

In terms of aircraft propulsion, the invention of the jet engine in the 1930s, with its subsequent use for the first jet-propelled airplanes in the 1940s, was a revolution on par with the invention of the first practical airplane by the Wright brothers. Both Frank Whittle's and Hans von Ohain's early designs, however, were centrifugal flow jet engines—engines where the airflow coming into the engine is funneled into the center of large compressor blades, which then slings the air outward, increasing the airflow velocity by centrifugal force. The outward flowing air is then turned and slowed, achieving the desired pressure increase across the compressor before entering the combustor. Some of the early production jet engines, such as the Allison J33 (a direct descent of the Whittle design), which powered the

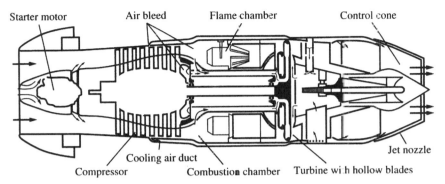

Starter motor   Air bleed   Flame chamber   Control cone

Cooling air duct   Jet nozzle

Compressor   Combustion chamber   Turbine with hollow blades

FIGURE 7.30
The Junkers Jumo 004B
turbojet engine, the first
practical axial-flow jet
engine, 1942.

FIGURE 7.31
The Messerschmitt
Me-262, the first practical
jet airplane, 1942.

Lockheed P-80 jet fighter, were centrifugal-flow jet engines. These engines,
however, presented a large frontal area, making them less desirable for installation
in the sleek, streamlined airframes demanded by high-speed airplanes. As the jet
revolution progressed, centrifugal-flow jet engines receded to the background,
replaced by the more slender axial-flow engines.

The origin of the practical axial-flow jet engine was in Germany during
World War II. Finally mobilized by the success that von Ohain and Heinkel
achieved with the first jet-propelled airplane, the He 178 (Figure 7.2), enlightened
officials at the Air Ministry in Berlin encouraged the further development of jet
propulsion by German industry. Responding, Junkers Motoren began work on an
axial-flow turbojet engine, under the direction of Dr. Anselm Franz. The airflow
through such an engine is compressed by passing through an alternating series of
rotating blades (the rotor) and stationary blades (the stator), where the overall flow
path is essentially along the axis of the engine—hence, the label "axial flow." At
the time that he was given this new responsibility, Dr. Franz was in charge of the
supercharger group. The engine that Franz and his engineers developed at Junkers
was the Jumo 004, shown in Figure 7.30. The eight-stage axial-flow compressor
is clearly seen. The Junkers Jumo 004 was the designated powerplant for the
Me 262, the first practical jet fighter (see Figures 6.9 and 7.31). The first flight
of the Me 262 was on July 18, 1942; it was powered by the two Jumo 004A
turbojets.

TABLE 7.2 Jumo 004 development and production schedule

Development	Date
Start of development	Fall 1939
First test run	October 11, 1940
First flight in Me-262	July 18, 1942
Preproduction	1943
Beginning of production	Early 1944
Introduction of hollow blades	Late 1944
About 6000 engines delivered	May 1945

Much later, Hans von Ohain wrote,

> The Jumo 004, developed under the leadership of Anselm Franz, was perhaps one of the truly unique achievements in the history of early jet propulsion development leading to mass production, for the following reasons:
>
> 1. It emphasized axial-flow turbomachinery and straight throughflow combustors.
> 2. It overcame the nonavailability of nickel by air-cooled hollow turbine blades made out of sheet metal.
> 3. The manufacturing cost of the engine amounted to about one-fifth that of a propeller/piston engine having the equivalent power output.
> 4. The total time from the start of development to the beginning of large scale production was a little over 4 years.
> 5. It incorporated a variable-area nozzle governed by the control system of the engine, and model 004E incorporated afterburning.

The Jumo 004 development and production schedule is given in Table 7.2.

Virtually every jet engine in operation today is an axial-flow engine; the forerunner of them all is the Junkers Jumo 004. In terms of the basic components and the overall thrust-producing mechanism of an axial-flow jet engine, the Jumo 004 had all of the necessary features. The three main types of gas turbine aircraft engine in use today, the turbojet, the turboprop, and the turbofan, are shown in Figure 7.32. The heart of these engines is the compressor–burner–turbine core, labeled the "gas generator" in Figure 7.32. The Jumo 004 in Figure 7.30 has the same type of gas generator. Although Frank Whittle and Hans von Ohain share the credit as being the coinventors of the jet engine, the design and engineering marvel created by Anselm Franz and his team at Junkers during World War II basically ushered in the era of the practical jet-propelled airplane.

A Revolution within a Revolution—The Turbofan

The high pressure created within the gas generator is the fundamental source of thrust that pushes the engine (and airplane) forward. As a consequence, this high pressure also results in a high-speed jet of gas that blasts out the back end of the engine. (This is a kind of "cause-and-effect" process. The high pressure created inside the engine by the gas generator presses on the internal surfaces of the engine components, pushing the engine forward—this is the *cause* of the generation of

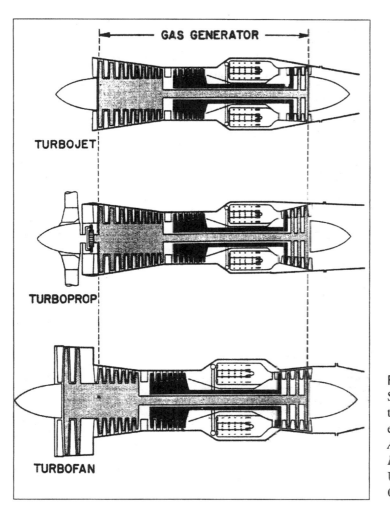

FIGURE 7.32
Schematic of the turbojet, turboprop, and turbofan engines. (From *The Aircraft Gas Turbine Engine and Its Operation*, United Technologies Corporation, 1974.)

thrust. As an equal-and-opposite reaction to the thrust, the gas exiting the gas generator is pushed out through the exit nozzle at high speed—this is the *effect* of the generation of thrust.) The gas velocity at the exit of a turbojet is quite high—typically near or slightly above the speed of sound. Imagine that a jet-propelled airplane zooms right past you. After the airplane has gone past you, you feel the jet exhaust moving at high speed in the opposite direction. Before the airplane came, the air around you was relatively still with little or no kinetic energy. After the airplane has gone past, the air around you is moving at high speed with a lot of kinetic energy. This high-energy jet of air is doing nothing for you. It is simply wasted energy and, therefore, is a source of inefficiency associated with the jet engine. The higher the jet exhaust velocity, the more inefficient is the engine, everything else being equal. This is why turbojet engines are less efficient than propellers. The slip stream from a propeller has a much lower velocity than the jet exhaust from a gas turbine engine, and, therefore, much less energy is wasted. On the other hand, the turbojet can produce much more thrust than a propeller. So we have a classic compromise. When we need high thrust from an aircraft powerplant (say, for speed), we use a jet engine and put up with the lower overall propulsive efficiency.

As seen in Figure 7.32, the turbofan engine has a turbojet as its core, but some of the power from the gas generator is used to turn a large ducted fan. The fan acts much like a propeller, producing thrust and a consequent lower velocity exhaust stream that flows outside the engine core, mixing with the jet exhaust downstream. Because of the lower overall velocity of the jet exhaust (from the fan plus turbojet core), the turbofan is more efficient than a turbojet while at the same time producing a lot of thrust. Measuring efficiency in terms of thrust specific fuel consumption (pounds of fuel consumed per hour per pound of thrust produced), a typical turbojet has a specific fuel consumption of around 1 (pound of fuel)/(pound of thrust)(hour), whereas turbofans have values around 0.5 (pound of fuel)/(pound of thrust)(hour)—a considerable savings of fuel consumed for producing the same thrust.

Today, almost all civil jet airplanes and many military jets are powered by turbofan engines. For example, the twin-engine Boeing 777 is powered by two huge turbofans producing 90,000 pounds of thrust each, with a specific fuel consumption of 0.4 (pound of fuel)/(pound of thrust)(hour). The development of the turbofan was a revolution within the jet engine revolution—it represented a quantum leap in efficiency and is a primary facilitator for low-cost air transportation today. How did this happen? The story of the development of the turbofan engine is an important part of the history of the technology of the jet-propelled airplane. Let us take a closer look.

The idea of shunting some of the air processed by the compressor around the rest of the engine and mixing it as a cold jet downstream of the main flow was patented by Frank Whittle in 1936. Over the next 10 years, this "bypass" concept was examined sporadically by various engine companies in the United Kingdom, but with no successful designs. The problem was that the core engines themselves did not produce enough power per unit of airflow (specific power) to produce the high-pressure ratios required for effective bypass fan operation. The idea languished into the background, in spite of the recognition of the efficiency improvements inherent in the bypass concept. The only exception to this was the development of the Rolls–Royce Conway in the early 1950s. The Conway was a bypass engine with only a small amount of bypass air relative to the amount of air flowing through the core; the bypass ratio was only 0.3, and, hence, the Conway did not achieve anything close to the true potential of a turbofan. Nevertheless, the Conway was the first bypass engine of any kind to be produced in numbers. Unfortunately, the path of heredity stopped there; the Conway did not evolve into the modern turbofan engine. That engine evolved along a completely different path, as we will see.

In the meantime, the development of the turbojet progressed at full speed during the 1950s. A major advancement was the two-spool engine by Pratt and Whitney, where the compressor was divided into two sections—the low-pressure and high-pressure compressors, driven respectively by the low-pressure and high-pressure turbines. A two-spool turbojet is shown in Figure 7.32, where the low-pressure compressor connected to the low-pressure turbine is shown in light shading, and the high-pressure compressor connected to the high-pressure turbine is shown in dark shading. Using this concept, Pratt and Whitney designed the J-57 turbojet that powered the B-52 bomber beginning in the early 1950s. Later in the decade, the commercial version of the J-57, labeled the JT3, powered the first U.S. jet transports, the Boeing 707 and the Douglas DC-8. General Electric and

Rolls–Royce pursued other, equally effective design concepts for producing higher pressure ratios across the compressor. The specific power of turbojets designed during this period gradually increased.

In April 1955, Dr. G. F. Wislicenus of Pennsylvania State University gave a paper to the Society of Automotive Engineers at their Golden Anniversary Aeronautical Meeting, entitled "Principles and Applications of Bypass Engines." Dr. Wislicenus was a leading academic expert on turbomachinery, and his paper reawakened the engine industry to the advantages of such engines. The specific power of engines at that time, such as the J-57, was reaching the threshold where they might effectively serve as core engines for bypass designs. Still, not much was done. Another problem reared its head; the tip speeds of the bypass fan blades could exceed the speed of sound, creating local shock waves and causing dramatic losses in efficiency. Mounting an intensive compressor research program, NACA researchers, mainly at the Lewis Laboratory in Cleveland, Ohio, and the Langley Memorial Aeronautical Laboratory in Hampton, Virginia, studied these transonic and supersonic blade-tip problems during the period 1946–1956, when the program was stopped to concentrate on nuclear and rocket propulsion. As Drs. George Smith and David Mindell have written in their recent history of the turbofan ("The Emergence of the Turbofan Engine," in *Atmospheric Flight in the Twentieth Century*, edited by Peter Galison and Alex Roland, Kluwer Academic, 2000, pp. 107–155),

> NACA engineers designed and tested an impressively large number of experimental supersonic stages between 1946 and 1956. Virtually all of these research compressors performed poorly when judged by the standards that would have to be met for flight. In the last years of the effort, however, some designs began showing promise.... An approach to designing much higher Mach number stages was beginning to emerge.

When NACA curtailed compressor research in 1956, the experience gained was propagated by a small group of engineers who left NACA and went to work for General Electric (GE). The company had an advocate of the turbofan engine, Peter Kappus, who immediately put the ex-NACA group to work on the design of a turbofan, where the fan was placed *behind* the gas generator. Kappus pushed the aft-fan design, where the fan was not mechanically connected to the core engine. Rather, the exhaust from the core engine drove turbine blades mounted on the fan rotor, where the fan blades extended from the tips of these turbine blades. The motivating advantage of this arrangement was that the core engine would not be affected by the need to operate the fan mechanically, and, therefore, GE could use one of their standard turbojet engines for the core without having to design a new core engine. GE chose to use their J-79 for the core, which had enough specific power to do the job. The commercial version of the J-79 was GE's CJ805 turbojet.

The company committed funds in 1956 for the development of the aft-fan engine; because of the use of the standard CJ805 for the core, most of the effort went into the design of the fan, where the prior experience of the transplanted NACA engineers was particularly useful. The CJ805 turbojet produced 11,000 pounds of thrust, with a specific fuel consumption of around 0.7 (pounds of fuel)/(pounds of thrust)(hour). The GE engineers calculated that the aft-fan version would increase the thrust to 15,000 pounds with a specific fuel consumption of 0.55 (pounds of fuel)/(pounds of thrust)(hour)—a stunning improvement in

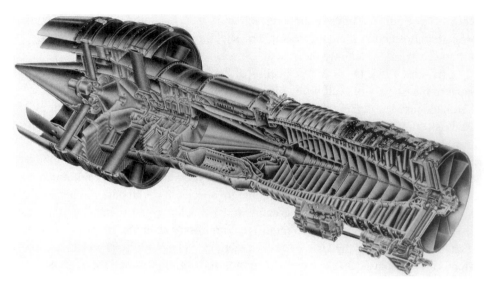

FIGURE 7.33
The General Electric
CJ805-23 turbofan.

performance. The tip of the fan moved at Mach 1.25, higher than any blades in the company's previous experience, but based on their earlier work at NACA, the GE engineers felt that it would not be a showstopper. In addition, GE developed an advanced computer program called the "streamline curvature program," which gave the engineers the ability to calculate aspects of the flow past the blades; this type of computer program greatly enhanced the design of axial compressors. The product of this high technology effort was GE's CJ805-23 turbofan engine, shown in Figure 7.33. Note the large fan at the aft end of the engine. First tested on December 26, 1957, the engine produced the expected 15,000 pounds of thrust, and the specific fuel consumption was actually less than the predicted value of 0.55. In the words of Smith and Mindell, "GE had its turbofan engine at remarkably little development cost." GE moved swiftly toward qualifying the CJ805-23 for commercial transports. The turbofan revolution for the airlines was at hand. GE had developed the first practical turbofan engine.

This is not the end of the story, however. Early in 1958, Pratt and Whitney found out about the rapid progress GE was making toward flight qualifying the CJ805-23. Pratt and Whitney was publicly conservative about the idea of turbofan engines, stating that properly designed turbojet engines were as good as bypass engines. Privately, they dived into a crash program to develop a turbofan. In contrast to GE's revolutionary high-technology development of a new concept, the aft fan, Pratt and Whitney took a more conservative evolutionary approach. Using their experience with large fan design for a potential nuclear-powered engine, Pratt and Whitney chose to mate this fan to the low-pressure compressor of the J-57, commercially known as the JT3C-6. Within weeks, Pratt and Whitney had a front-fan engine operating on a test stand. Without the benefit of a sophisticated streamline curvature computer program or the experience base of transplanted NACA researchers, the Pratt and Whitney engineers designed, on a strictly empirical basis, the JT3D turbofan, with the JT3C-6 turbojet as the core. A photograph of the JT3D is shown in Figure 7.34. Remarkably, the JT3D had almost exactly the same specific fuel consumption and thrust-to-weight ratio as GE's CJ805-23 and actually produced about 1000 pounds more thrust. This was a

FIGURE 7.34
The Pratt and Whitney
JT3D turbofan.

revolutionary leap in performance compared with the JT3C-6 turbojet, but it was achieved through the evolutionary development of existing Pratt and Whitney hardware.

The JT3D turbofan engine first flew on an airplane in July 1959; this was seven months before the first flight of GE's CJ805-23. The JT3D fit both the Boeing 707 and the Douglas DC-8, and the airlines quickly adopted the engine for these aircraft. The CJ805-23 also fit these airplanes, but Pratt and Whitney had beaten GE to the punch. Pratt and Whitney later delivered 8550 JT3Ds, whereas the GE CJ805-23 had to wait for a new airplane, the Convair 990, of which only 37 were ultimately sold. The irony of it all. GE was the first engine company to risk the development of the first turbofan engine, using high technology and a revolutionary design to accomplish the job, whereas Pratt and Whitney, spurred into action by leaked news of GE's program, clapped together an evolutionary design of a turbofan using existing hardware and was the company with the "firstest with the mostest" in terms of a flight-rated turbofan for the airlines using the Boeing 707 and Douglas DC-8. Much later, in 1990, Jack Parker, the head of GE Aerospace and Defense, remarked about this historical event, "We converted the heathen but the competitor sold the bibles."

Today, the three major aircraft engine companies, Pratt and Whitney, GE, and Rolls–Royce, manufacture an extensive line of turbofan engines. Some of these are large engines with thrust levels close to 100,000 pounds. The bypass ratio, defined as the amount of air passing through the fan divided by the amount of air passing through the core, which was 1.56 for the GE CJ805-23, has increased to 5.9 for the GE CF6 (Figure 7.35). Although turbojet engines are still manufactured, mainly for applications to supersonic airplanes, the term "jet engine" today conjures up the turbofan.

ADVANCES IN STRUCTURES

The basic structural elements of modern airplanes are essentially the same as those developed during the era of the mature propeller-driven airplane—the use of metal ribs, stringers, spars, stressed-skin construction, etc. The design and manufacturing of these elements, however, have been revolutionized by the use of the modern

FIGURE 7.35
The General Electric CF6
turbofan.

high-speed digital computer. Structural designers use a modern computational method called finite element analyses to design complex structures. In this analysis, the entire structure is divided into a large number of interconnected tiny elements, and the stress and strain on these elements are computed; such elaborate computations sometimes take days on mainframe computers. A common finite element program in wide use for structural analysis is NASTRAN, developed in the 1960s by NASA. In addition, manufacturing processes are now heavily based on computers, with machine tools, large and small, being controlled by computers—numerical controlled machine tools. A modern example is the automated span assembly tool (ASAT), the gigantic tool used for the manufacture of the wing spar for the Boeing 777. ASAT is designed to fasten up to 30 metal parts ranging from 2 to 100 feet in length. When the ASAT was laid out on the floor of Boeing's hangerlike assembly building, its C-shaped metal frames stood 30 feet high, and the whole machine simply stretched off into the distance. The parts of ASAT were transported to Boeing from its manufacturers in Wisconsin by 90 trucks. The building up and fastening of the elements of the 777 wing *spar* by ASAT is all carefully measured and controlled by computers.

Another revolution involved the materials used for aircraft. All-metal airplanes from the era of the mature propeller-driven airplane, and from the early part of the current era of the jet-propelled airplane were made from aluminum. As the speeds of the jet-propelled airplanes increased from one generation to the next, the aerodynamic heating of the skin of the airplane became more of a problem; the heating is caused by intense frictional dissipation in the boundary layer adjacent to the surface. For example, at sustained cruise at Mach 2, the skin temperature can reach 300 °F. Aluminum begins to lose its strength at this temperature. Steel has better high-temperature properties, and beginning in the 1950s, those parts of Mach 2 aircraft exposed to such temperatures were made from stainless steel honeycomb sandwich material, such as illustrated in Figure 7.36. The skin of

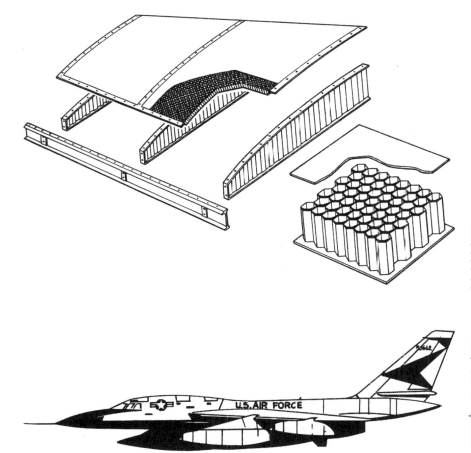

FIGURE 7.36
Brazed stainless-steel honeycomb sandwich panel.

FIGURE 7.37
The Convair B-58A Hustler, 1959. (From E. Angelucci, *Airplanes from the Dawn of Flight to the Present Day*, McGraw-Hill, New York, 1973.)

America's first supersonic bomber, the Convair B-58 (Figure 7.37), was mainly stainless steel honeycomb. Aerodynamic heating increases almost as the cube of the flight velocity, and so the materials problem for yet higher speed aircraft becomes even more severe. Not only is the high-temperature strength of the material a problem, but thermal stresses induced within the metal due to thermal expansion of the material become important. Higher speed aircraft have to use more exotic materials to withstand aerodynamic heating. The Lockheed SR-71 Blackbird, which can fly above Mach 3, is mainly made from titanium, which is much lighter than steel, with good high-temperature properties. The Mach 7 North American X-15, thus far the only powered, piloted hypersonic aircraft, is made from Inconel-X, a nickel-alloy steel capable of withstanding temperatures of up to 1200 °F. How far we have come from the primitive all-metal Junkers J-1 of 1915.

ADVANCES IN THE PROCESS OF AIRPLANE DESIGN

The advent of the jet airplane brought about a second design revolution, beginning in the late 1940s and continuing with increasing fervor to the present day. This is to be compared with the first design revolution, which took place in the early 1930s, resulting in the mature propeller-driven airplane that dominated military and commercial aviation through the end of World War II. The current design revolution has produced the modern jet transports commonplace as part of modern society today, as well as a stable of extremely high-performance jet fighters and bombers. The advances in technology that fostered the first design revolution were part of the first golden age of aeronautical engineering in the 1930s. Similarly, the spectacular increases in technical and scientific knowledge, as well as the awesome challenges associated with flying at and beyond the speed of sound, created a second golden age of aeronautical engineering beginning about 1950 and continuing in ever-changing forms today.

The intellectual process by which airplanes are designed changed dramatically with the second design revolution. We can identify three major shifts in the process of design:

1) There is willingness on the part of the designers sometimes to incorporate new, promising technology that has not been totally proven, to achieve a necessary leap in performance of the new design. This is in contrast to the very conservative design philosophy during the era of the strut-and-wire biplane, where each new airplane was usually a small incremental change from a previous one. In that era, just getting a new design to lift into the air and fly was an accomplishment, and there was always some hope of success when the new design was simply an incremental improvement over a previously successful aircraft. Even during the era of the mature propeller-driven airplane, new designs were still evolutionary products of previous airplanes, and when new technology was incorporated in the new design, only that technology that had been well proven in the laboratory and in flight tests was used.

2) Very extensive wind-tunnel testing is used directly right from the very beginning of the preliminary design process through the final design phase. This is in contrast to the designers from the era of the strut-and-wire biplane, who used virtually no wind-tunnel data at any time during the design process mainly because they had no confidence in the accuracy of such wind-tunnel data. Airplane design at that time was mainly intuitive, and the viability of any new design was established only on its first test flights, after which design modifications were made based on the flight performance. During the era of the mature propeller-driven airplane, improvements in wind-tunnel design and instrumentation gave airplane designers more confidence in wind-tunnel data and resulted in more extensive use of the wind tunnel to fine tune an already existing preliminary design.

3) The use of the high-speed digital computer allows designers to quickly home in on optimum design configurations right at the beginning of the preliminary design process and to enhance the design process all of the way to the production line. In the last two decades, the computer has brought about a revolution within the overall design revolution. The Boeing 777 is said to be the first "paperless" airplane—its design and production tooling were all done on computers. Designers from the previous eras had nothing comparable.

Design of the Boeing 707

Look again at the Boeing 707 in Figure 7.5. The process used for the design of this airplane is a good example of the second design revolution. For all practical purposes, the design of the 707 began with the design of the Boeing B-47 strategic bomber in the late 1940s. When Boeing aeronautical engineer George Schairer

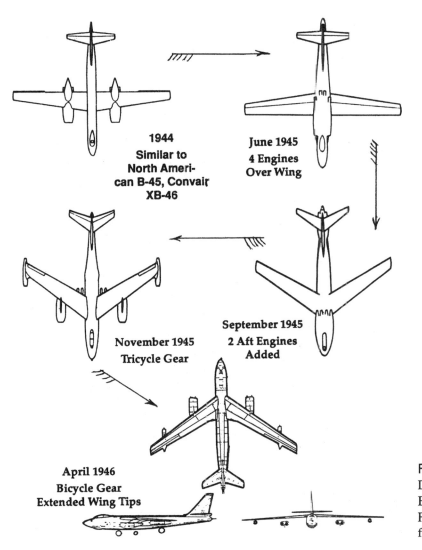

1944
Similar to North American B-45, Convair XB-46

June 1945
4 Engines Over Wing

November 1945
Tricycle Gear

September 1945
2 Aft Engines Added

April 1946
Bicycle Gear Extended Wing Tips

FIGURE 7.38
Design evolution of the Boeing B-47. (Same as Figure 7.6, repeated here for convenience.)

sent his letter from Germany in May 1945 to his colleagues about the German work on swept wings, he set into motion a radical design change that we see all around us today. Let us take a closer look at how this happened.

The Boeing designers had been working on a straight-wing jet bomber in response to U.S. Army Air Force specifications issued in April 1944 for a four-engine jet bomber. North American, Convair, and Martin also responded to this specification—all with straight-winged airplanes. Boeing already had a competitive advantage over the other companies. It had a large high-speed wind tunnel, which it built in 1941. At the insistence of their consultant, Theodore von Kármán at Cal Tech, the tunnel was designed for speeds close to the speed of sound, much higher than envisioned for Boeing airplanes at that time. The Boeing tunnel with a model in the test section could reach Mach 0.87, which for the U.S. aircraft industry put it in a league of its own. The new Boeing jet bomber design, designated the XB-47, benefited right from the beginning from tests in this tunnel. Two early straight-winged versions of the XB-47 are illustrated at the top of Figure 7.38. The design at the top left had the engine nacelles mounted directly into the wing, similar to the preferred arrangement seen on most multiengine propeller-driven airplanes at that time. Wind-tunnel tests showed an undesirable decrease in the critical Mach number for this design—the engines in the wings compromised the high-speed characteristics of the otherwise thin wings. The engines were then moved to the fuselage; the design at the top right of Figure 7.38 shows the four engines mounted on top of the fuselage. Although this arrangement was an aerodynamic improvement over the wing-mounted engines, it had serious practical disadvantages, not the least of which was serious damage to the top of the fuselage from the jet exhausts and the increased danger of cabin fires. The XB-47 design was at this stage when Schairer's letter, dated May 10, 1945, arrived at Boeing.

The essence of this letter directed the Boeing designers to investigate swept wings for the new jet bomber. This represented a radical departure from previous designs; the idea of swept wings was brand new to most people, and aeronautical engineers in the United States had no experience whatsoever with such a configuration. However, the Boeing design team was not happy with their straight-wing designs, and they were ready to try something new that might allow a substantial leap in performance. Against skepticism and opposition from other parts of the company, the design team initiated a series of tests of a swept-wing version of the jet bomber shown at the middle-right of Figure 7.38; the engines were still located on the fuselage. When the Boeing design team leaders Ed Wells and Bob Jewett took this configuration to Wright Field in Dayton in October 1945, the U.S. Army Air Forces Project Office resoundingly rejected it, and properly so. The project office wanted the engines to be mounted on the wing, as was typical on past bombers. On the trip back to Seattle, Washington, Wells and Jewett conceived the idea of mounting the engines in pods suspended below the wing on struts. It was yet another radical idea for its time, but Boeing felt it had no choice because Wright Field had so firmly rejected the previous design. Once again, the Boeing high-speed wind tunnel was vital. The pod-on-strut configuration was tested and refined. The results showed that if the pods were located low enough under the wing that the jet exhaust did not impinge on the trailing-edge flaps when fully deployed, and if the location were forward enough such that the exit of the engine tailpipe was forward of, or just in line with, the wing leading edge, then there was virtually no unfavorable aerodynamic interference between the pods and the wing. In the words of Bill Cook, one of the design engineers on the XB-47, "The wing was performing like the pods were absent." (Wilham H. Cook tells a good story about the history of Boeing's airplane design process going back to the early 1930s and carrying through to the 707 in his book, *The Road to the 707*, TYC Publishing, Bellevue, Washington, 1991.)

George Schairer's letter from Germany also included a short calculation indicating that the minimum amount of sweep back should be 29 degrees, but that even more sweep might be practical. The German data on swept wings was useful, but Boeing started from scratch, testing models with a wide variation of the sweep angle. On the basis of these wind-tunnel tests, a wing sweep of 35 degrees was selected and locked in during the subsequent XB-47 development. Later on, Boeing stuck with this sweep angle for the 707. (We note that Boeing's choice for the sweep angle for its subsequent jet transport designs ranged from a low of 32 degrees for the 727 to a high of 37.5 degrees for the 747, all essentially centered around the original wing sweep for the XB-47.)

The final configuration of the XB-47 is shown at the bottom of Figure 7.38. In addition to the 35-degree sweep, the XB-47 had a very high aspect ratio of 9.43; no other swept-wing airplane since has had such a high aspect ratio. The wing was thin, with an airfoil thickness of 12 percent—so thin that the Boeing designers did not want to retract the landing gear into the wings, but rather choose a bicycle gear that retracted into the fuselage.

The first flight of the XB-47 took place on December 17, 1947 (44 years to the day after the flight of the Wright Flyer). The U.S. Air Force agreed to purchase two prototypes, but amazingly enough did not show great enthusiasm for the new bomber of revolutionary design. This was mainly due to the poor performance of the earlier straight-wing jet bombers, such as the North American B-45, which had soured Wright Field on the idea of jet bombers in general. Even top Boeing management was cautious about the XB-47, and the flight tests, which took place at Moses Lake airfield, about 120 miles from Seattle, were initially carried out without fanfare. The exception was the small flight test crew at Moses Lake, who immediately witnessed the tremendous performance characteristics of the airplane. Indeed, the early tests quickly proved that the drag of the XB-47 was 15 percent less than the predicted value, a cause for great celebration because this meant the range of the airplane was greater than expected, something of real importance for a bomber. The low-drag results finally got the attention of Boeing management in Seattle, and after that, interest in the airplane suddenly picked up within the company. This was followed by an event that was essentially a happenstance. Although the U.S. Air Force test pilots flying the XB-47 were almost finished with their test program, the Air Force was still not showing great interest; the project office at Wright Field had turned its attention to turboprop bombers, in the belief that turboprops were the only engines that would give the necessary long range for bombers. General K. B. Wolfe, head of bomber production at Wright Field made a brief visit to Moses Lake on his way back to Dayton from a meeting with Boeing in Seattle on the design of a new piston engine bomber labeled the B-54. General Wolfe took a 20-minute flight in the XB-47. He was so impressed with the airplane's performance that immediately after landing he declared that the Air Force would buy it "as is." In the end, the Air Force bought 2000 B-47s.

The design of the XB-47 was an early example of the second design revolution that jump-started the era of the jet-propelled airplane. First, the design was revolutionary—no previous airplane was anything like it. The swept wings and the podded engines slung underneath the wings were radical new technical features, which the Boeing engineers embraced to achieve a leap in performance. This overall configuration became the norm for future jetliners, carrying through to the present day. Second, the extensive use of the wind tunnel from the very beginning of the design process was pivotal to the success of the design; this established a trend in airplane design unique to the era of the jet-propelled airplane. In Boeing's case, their large high-speed wind tunnel went into operation in 1944 after a three-year period of development and was able to achieve Mach 0.975 with an empty test section. It was the right facility at the right time. The original decision in 1941 to build the wind tunnel was somewhat of a gamble on the part of Boeing executives. The gamble paid off royally after the war.

The pioneering design technology that accrued during the B-47 project evolved into the first successful jet transport, the Boeing 707. These two airplanes are compared in three-view in Figure 7.7. The design of the B-47 had been

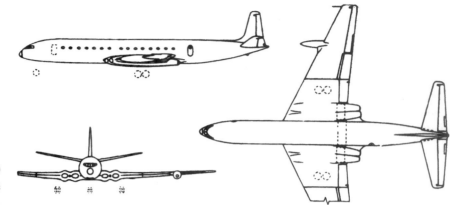

FIGURE 7.39
Three-view of the
deHavilland Comet 4.

revolutionary; the design of the 707 was evolutionary from the B-47. This is obvious from the comparison shown in Figure 7.7. The dominant features of the 707, the 35-degree swept wing and the jet engines mounted in pods slung under the wing on struts, were pioneered with the B-47. The major design changes reflected in the 707 were the low-wing configuration to allow a long body deck for carrying passengers or freight and the use of a tricycle landing gear. The reason for the tricycle gear was purely and simply because airline pilots were familiar with this type of landing gear; it allowed them to lift the nose at takeoff and depress the nose at landing.

At the time the Boeing 707 was designed, the only extant jet airliner was the British de Havilland Comet; the Comet 4 is shown in three-view in Figure 7.39. The Comet was a bold move on the part of the British; the first version, the Comet 1, entered service with the British Overseas Airways Company (BOAC) on May 2, 1952. It was the first jet passenger service in the world. Passengers flocked to fly the Comet; the flights were smooth because it flew at high altitudes generally above the worst of the weather, and flight times between such distant cities as London and Johannesburg and London and Singapore, were cut almost in half. In 1954, however, the Comets experienced two catastrophic accidents. On January 10 and April 8 of that year, two Comets virtually disintegrated at cruising altitude. The problem was structural failure near the corners of the nearly square windows on the fuselage, caused by repeated stress cycles during pressurization of the fuselage for each flight. Once a hole appeared in the fuselage, the pressurized vessel would explosively decompress, causing catastrophic failure of the airplane. The Comets were taken out of service. De Havilland redesigned the Comet, and in 1958 the Comet 4 went into service. By then, however, the British initiative in commercial jet transports had been lost. Only 74 Comet 4s were built.

The designs for the Comet and the 707 were quite different, as can be seen by comparing Figures 7.7 and 7.39. The Comet had a moderately swept wing of 20 degrees but no sweep of the horizontal and vertical tails. The engines were buried in the root of the wing, which took up valuable internal wing volume that could have been used to store fuel. Instead, some of the fuel was stored in bulbous tanks further out on the wings, as seen in Figure 7.39. Also, with the engines buried in the wing, the wings had to be thick enough to accommodate the engines, hence reducing the critical Mach number of the wing. In no way was the 707 a derivative of the Comet—the design philosophies were quite different. So was the performance. The Comet cruised at Mach 0.74 at 35,000 feet, whereas the 707 cruised at Mach 0.87 at 30,000 feet. The Comet was a much smaller airplane; the gross weight of the Comet 1A was 225,000 pounds with a wingspan of 115 feet, whereas the gross weight of the Boeing 707-320B was 336,000 pounds with a wingspan of 146 feet. The Comet had a relatively short range of 1750 miles, which required it to make intermediate stops for refueling. By comparison, the range of the Boeing 707-320B is 6240 miles. The configuration of the Boeing 707 set a model for many subsequent jet transport designs; in contrast, the configuration of the Comet had virtually no impact on future design.

With the success of the B-47, and then later with the large B-52 (Figure 7.8), Boeing management knew they were in an advantageous position to produce the first jet airliner in the United States. The decision to go ahead with such a project did not come easily. The airlines were cautious, waiting to see how successful the Comet might be. Boeing felt that any initial orders for a new commercial jet transport would not be large enough to cover the development and tooling costs. This led to the idea for a military version to be used as a jet tanker for in-flight refueling, almost identical to the civil transport design. In this fashion, business from the U.S. Air Force would make up the startup losses for the development of the civil transport. But the Air Force dragged its heels on such an idea. Nevertheless, on April 22, 1952, the same year that the British Comet first went into airline service, Boeing management authorized the building of a prototype jet airliner. With that decision, the fortune and future destiny of The Boeing Company were forever changed. A company that had produced mainly military airplanes for most of its existence was to become the world's leading manufacturer of civil jet transports in the last half of the 20th century.

However, in 1952, nobody knew this. Boeing's decision in 1952 was a bold one; the prototype jet transport was to be privately financed. The estimated cost of the prototype was $16 million. Boeing, however, decided to use some of its independent research and development (IRD) funds, which came from prorated allotments taken from military contracts. These IRD funds were the government's way of providing some discretionary funding to companies to help them carry out their own research and advanced development. So the government would indirectly end up paying most of the cost of the prototype anyway; the direct cost to Boeing was estimated to be only $3 million. Boeing labeled the prototype with a company internal designation of 367-80; the airplane quickly became known as the "Dash-80."

The Boeing 367-80, more commonly known as the "Dash-80." This airplane was the historic forerunner of the Boeing 707; it first flew in 1954. (Harold Andrews Collection.)

The Dash-80 was powered by four Pratt and Whitney J-57 turbojet engines, which had proven to be very reliable on the B-52 bomber. The civil version of the J-57 (as described in the propulsion section earlier) was designated the JT3C; each engine produced 10,000 pounds of thrust. Although the Dash-80 was an evolutionary derivative of the B-47, there were still some major design challenges.

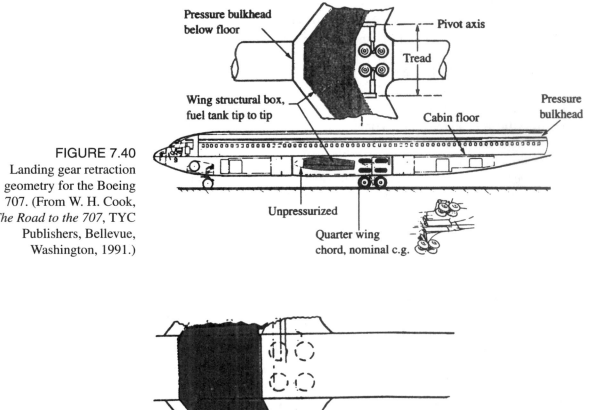

FIGURE 7.40
Landing gear retraction
geometry for the Boeing
707. (From W. H. Cook,
The Road to the 707, TYC
Publishers, Bellevue,
Washington, 1991.)

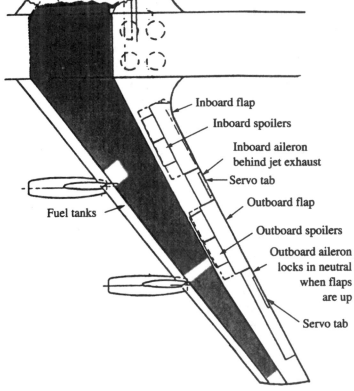

FIGURE 7.41
Trailing-edge flap, aileron,
and spoiler locations for
the Boeing 707. (From
W. H. Cook, *The Road to
the 707*, TYC Publishers,
Bellevue, WA, 1991.)

For one, the use of a tricycle landing gear in conjunction with a swept wing posed a
problem: How would the main gear retract and be stowed in the swept wing? The
structural design of the swept wing involved internal spars that were also swept,
hence, making it geometrically difficult for the main landing gear, which retracted
in a line at right angles to the plane of symmetry, to be stowed in a convenient
vacant space in the wing. The Boeing designers solved this problem by placing the

main gear closer to the plane of symmetry and having the main gear retract into the bottom of the fuselage, as shown in Figure 7.40.

Another challenge was flight control. A well-known aerodynamic characteristic of swept-back wings is that the backward sweep induces a spanwise component of flow over the wing toward the wingtip. Hence, the flow in the tip region tends to separate before that over other parts of the wing, with a consequent loss of control from ailerons placed near the tip. This problem had been noticed in both the B-47 and the B-52, but was not dealt with in a way totally acceptable for a civil transport. To provide proper and reliable lateral control, the Boeing aerodynamicists concentrated on that half of the wing closest to the root, where the spanwise induced flow was minimal, and, hence, flow separation was not a problem. The control surfaces for the Dash-80 wing are shown is Figure 7.41; shown here is Boeing's innovative solution for lateral control. Sandwiched between the inboard and outboard flaps is an inboard aileron positioned behind the jet exhaust from the inboard engine. Furthermore, two sets of spoilers, inboard and outboard, are positioned in front of the inboard and outboard flaps. Spoilers are essentially flat plates that deflect upward into the flow over the top surface of the wing, "spoiling" that flow and, hence, decreasing lift and increasing drag. The combination of the wing upper surface spoilers and the small aileron behind the inboard engine provided the necessary degree of lateral control at high speeds; the outboard aileron near the tip was locked in the neutral position except at low speeds with the flaps down, when the outboard aileron was reasonably effective. This lateral control arrangement proved to be quite successful on the Boeing 707.

The first flight of the Dash-80 took place on July 15, 1954. Success followed success. The first production 707s were delivered to Pan American Airlines in September 1958. On October 26, the first jet service by a U.S. flag carrier was initiated when Pan American flight 114 departed Idlewild Airport, New York, at 7:20 p.m. and landed at Paris's LeBourget about 9 hours later, with an intermediate stop at Gander, Newfoundland, for refueling. (The early model 707 did not have quite the sufficient range, fully loaded, to make the trip from New York to Paris nonstop.) However, this was not the first transatlantic flight by a jet airliner. The British carrier BOAC beat Pan American by a few weeks. On October 4 two redesigned de Havilland Comets, the Comet 4 (Figure 7.39), made simultaneous departures, one from Heathrow Airport in London, and the other from Idlewild in New York, with full loads of passengers. Although those Comets crossed the Atlantic Ocean in both directions that day, the ultimate success belonged to the Boeing 707. Carrying 100 more passengers at 100 miles per hour faster, the 707 outperformed the Comet 4 and soon became the jet airliner of choice for airlines around the world.

The Presidential 707, more commonly known as "Air Force One." In 1962, the 707 became the first presidential jet airplane. (Harold Andrews Collection.)

The turbofan revolution (discussed earlier) and the jet transport revolution met each other in 1958, just as the first versions of the 707 were entering airline service. GE had been working on their aft-fan CJ 805-23 in secrecy, and the airframe companies, including Boeing, were virtually in the dark. This proved to be a fatal flaw by GE. Today, the airframe and propulsion companies work closely together on new designs and new technology to ensure compatibility of the engines with the airplanes. Bill Cook, Boeing's chief of technical staff in the Transport Division, tells of the first time they found out about the General Electric Turbofan engine:

> The first time that we in the 707 engineering organization heard about the new GE engine was when a young GE engineer showed up at the Boeing plant in Renton with some drawings and performance data. It seemed that GE had finally decided they better tell the rest of the airplane manufacturers about their new product. The early GE sales approach was naïve in not aiming at a broader market from the start, and in not obtaining Boeing's reactions as to the suitability of the installation. GE did not seem to realize that Boeing had originated the pod engine concept and had accumulated a lot of data and experience pertaining to its design. Boeing wind tunnel tests had shown that a restriction of the air flowing over the engine pod and under the wing could reduce the top speed of the airplane unless the designers had considered this possibility.

The aft location of the fan in the GE engine was the worst possible location from the point of view of adverse aerodynamic interference between the pod and the wing. Nevertheless, Boeing carried out wind-tunnel tests using the 707 model with a model of the GE aft-fan engine. As the Boeing engineers expected, the wind-tunnel tests showed an intolerable increase in drag. "So we put the GE design concept aside," Cook said, "that is, until American Airlines became interested in the Convair 990 with the GE aft-fan."

Secretly, GE had been working closely with Convair to produce a revolutionary new jet transport, the Convair 990, designed right from the start to be powered by the GE aft-fan engine. Convair kept this project close to the vest, and announcements about its existence were not made until development was well along. When Boeing found out about it, their concern was understandable. Boeing was already moving on to the design of the 720, a shortened-body version of the 707, and was ready to close a deal with American Airlines for a purchase of the 720. Things came to a head in New York during the January 1958 annual technical meeting of the IAS (now AIAA), at which engineers and executives from Boeing and American Airlines were present. Capital Airlines had just announced a buy of Convair 990s the Sunday before the meeting. Capital and American were competitors on the lucrative New York–Chicago route, among others, and with Convair claiming lower fuel consumption, longer range, and higher speeds for the aft-fan powered 990, American Airlines was not about to commit to the Boeing 720 without some changes. During a Monday meeting at the hotel, Bill Littlewood and Frank Kolk of American Airlines made it clear that they wanted a turbofan powered 720. At the hotel ballroom for the afternoon cocktail hour, the chief engineer for Boeing, Maynard Pennell, collared Art Smith, vice president of engineering at Pratt and Whitney, and pressed him about Pratt and Whitney developing a turbofan for the 720. The timing was perfect, because Pratt and Whitney had already started to work on the JT3D with a forward-mounted fan, which would pose no aerodynamic interference between the pod and the wing. The Boeing engineers stayed over in New York to make new performance calculations for a turbofan-powered 720. With the help of additional engineers quickly called in from Seattle, enough estimates had been made to allow Boeing's Ed Wells to meet a week later with American Airlines president C. R. Smith. The deal was clinched, and American Airlines got their Boeing 720s powered by Pratt and Whitney's brand new JT3D turbofan. The turbofan revolution had begun. After that, virtually all new jet transports were powered by turbofans, and indeed many of the earlier 707s and B-52s were reengined to accommodate the JT3D.

This incident underscores another aspect of the process of airplane design during the era of the jet-propelled airplane—the need for close integration of all of the parts of an airplane, as well as all of the different manufacturers that build these parts. Much later, Boeing engineers working on the 777, the latest in Boeing's long series of jet transports, described the 777 as "four million parts all moving in close formation."

The Paperless Airplane

The same degree of intensive wind-tunnel testing that characterized the design of the B-47 and B-52 continued unabated during the design of the 707 and other subsequent Boeing aircraft. Wind-tunnel testing became a seamless part of the process of airplane design during the era of the jet-propelled airplane. But wind tunnel testing has now acquired a new partner in the process of airplane design—the high-speed digital computer. Today, using the sophisticated discipline of computational fluid dynamics (CFD), complete flowfields around airplanes can be calculated on the computer. This tool has taken on some of the responsibility previously delegated to wind tunnels in examining the aerodynamic characteristics of a myriad of different configurations during the conceptual and preliminary design process. Using CFD, the number of expensive wind-tunnel tests can be reduced, and they can be organized in a more efficient manner. However, contrary to some earlier euphoric opinion, CFD will never replace wind tunnels. Mother Nature is simply too complex to allow herself to be accurately modeled by computations. Indeed, the use of CFD as a design tool is going through a confidence-building stage analogous to that suffered through by wind-tunnel data in the 1920s and early 1930s. Although most airplane designers now accept some CFD results as valid to some extent, the wind tunnel is still the gold standard.

On the other hand, in the process of preliminary and detailed design, where the final dimensions of the four million parts are being determined, where the different parts are all supposed to fit together, and where production tooling is being designed and prepared for the manufacture of the airplane, the computer has created a revolution. When Boeing committed itself to the design of the 777, the decision was to make all "drawings" on the computer rather than on paper. With modern three-dimensional graphics programs, computers can be used to help design complex three-dimensional shapes, check for interferences with other parts, and instantly send this information to Boeing's subcontractors located all over the world. Previously, several stages of full-scale mock-ups of the airplane had to be built to check on systems and parts that interfered with each other and to find serious manufacturing problems. Some problems were not discovered until the new airplane started in production. With Boeing's computer system for the design of the 777, engineers could check parts continuously and make instant corrections without having to wait for a mock-up. Even the machine tools and the manufacturing processes were designed this way. Because all of the designers shared all of the information through their computers, there was no need for paper drawings and the countless blueprints of old. The Boeing 777 is the first paperless airplane to be designed in this manner—it has created a revolution within the process of modern airplane design.

THE ERA OF THE JET-PROPELLED AIRPLANE— IT GOES ON AND ON

As mentioned at the beginning of this chapter, the era of the jet-propelled airplane could occupy a book by itself. The technology continues to develop and progress exponentially. But the present book must come to an end, and we will end our discussion of the history of the technology of the airplane with a few additional, very brief comments.

In regard to civil jet transports, Boeing made another bold move on April 15, 1966, when the decision was made to "go for the big one." Boeing had lost the U.S. Air Force's C-5 competition to Lockheed; the C-5 at the time was the largest transport airplane in the world. Taking their losing design a few steps further, Boeing engineers conceived of the 747, the first wide-body commercial jet transport. Bill Allen, president of Boeing at that time, and Juan Trippe, president of Pan American Airlines, shared the belief that the large, wide-body airplane offered economic advantages for the future airline passenger market, and they both jointly made the decision to pursue the project. This was an even bolder decision than that concerning the 707. The words of the authoritative aeronautical historian James Hansen follow:

> In the opinion of many experts, the 747 was the greatest gamble in the history of the aircraft business. At risk were the lives of both companies, as well as the solvency of several private lending institutions.
> Financed with private money, if the 747 had failed, half the banks west of the Mississippi would have been badly shaken. Another important meaning of big aircraft is thus clear; big dollars go along with them.

The gamble paid off. The Boeing 747 (Figure 7.8) first flew in February 1969, and it entered service for the first time in January 1970 on Pan American's New York–London route. At the time of this writing, some 34 years later, 747s are still being produced by Boeing.

The 747 set the design standard for all subsequent wide-body transports. It has done much more. It opened the opportunity for huge numbers of people to fly quickly and relatively cheaply across oceans and to travel to all parts of the globe. The 747 has had a tremendous sociological impact. It has brought people of various nations closer to one another. It has fostered the image of the "global village." It has had a direct impact on society, business, and diplomacy in the last third of the 20th century. It is a wonderful example of the extent to which airplane design can favorably mold and influence society in general.

We have discussed examples of subsonic commercial airplane designs that are a major part of the era of the jet-propelled aircraft. But what about commercial transportation at supersonic speeds? In the 1960s this question was addressed in Russia, the United States, England, and France. The Tupolev Design Bureau in Russia rushed a supersonic transport design into production and service. The Tu-144 supersonic transport first flew on December 31, 1968. More than a dozen of these aircraft were built, but none entered extended service, presumably due to unspecified problems. The Tu-144 was destroyed in a dramatic accident at the

1973 Paris Air Show. In the United States, the government orchestrated a design competition for a supersonic transport; the Boeing 2707 was the winner in December 1966. The design turned into a nightmare for Boeing. For two years, a variable-sweep wing supersonic transport (SST) configuration was pursued, and then the design was junked. Starting at the beginning again in 1969, the design was caught up in an upward spiral of increased weight and development costs. When the predictions for final development costs hit about $5 billion, Congress stepped in and refused to appropriate any more funds. In May 1971, the SST development program in the United States was terminated. Only in England and France was the SST concept carried to fruition.

The first, and so far only, supersonic commercial transport to see long-term, regular service is the Anglo–French Concorde (Figure 7.8). In 1960, both the British and French independently initiated design studies for an SST. It quickly became apparent that the technical complexities and financial costs were beyond the abilities of either country to shoulder alone. Hence, on November 29, 1962, England and France signed a formal treaty aimed at the design and construction of an SST. (By the way, this reality is becoming more and more a part of modern airplane design; when certain projects exceed the capability of a given company or even a given country, the practical solution is sometimes found in national or international consortia. It might be worthwhile for future airplane designers in the United States to learn to speak French, German, or Japanese.) The product of this treaty was the Aerospatiale–British Aerospace Corporation's Concorde. Designed to cruise at Mach 2.2 carrying 125 passengers, the Concorde first flew on March 2, 1969. It first exceeded Mach 1 on October 1, 1969, and Mach 2 on November 4, 1970. Originally, orders for 74 Concordes were anticipated. However, when the airlines were expected to place orders in 1973, the world was deep in the energy crises. The skyrocketing costs of aviation jet fuel wiped out any hope of an economic return from flying the Concorde, and no orders were placed. Only the national airlines of France and Britain, Air France and British Airways, went ahead, each signing up for seven aircraft after considerable pressure from their respective governments. After a long development program, the Concorde went into service on January 21, 1976. In the final analysis, the Concorde was a technical, if not financial, success. It has been in regular service since 1976. It represents an almost revolutionary (rather than evolutionary) airplane design in that no such aircraft existed before it. However, the Concorde designers were not operating in a vacuum. Examining the Concorde in Figure 7.8, we see a supersonic configuration that incorporates good supersonic aerodynamics—a sharp-nosed slender fuselage and a cranked delta wing with a thin airfoil. The Concorde designers had at least 15 years of military airplane design experience with such features to draw on. Today, we know that any future second-generation SST will have to be economical in service and environmentally acceptable. The design of such a vehicle is one of the great challenges in aeronautics. Perhaps some of the readers of this book will someday play a part in meeting this challenge.

We end this chapter with a mention, albeit brief, of the design of certain aircraft that do not "fit the mold" of previous, conventional airplanes, that is, unconventional airplane designs. We have focused on airplanes that set the standard for airplane design, airplanes that came to be accepted as representative of the *conventional airplane*. However, this is not to downgrade the importance of unconventional thinking for the design of new aircraft that look different and/or fly

FIGURE 7.42
The Hawker Siddeley Harrier, the first production vertical-takeoff-and-landing airplane, 1969. (From Angelucci, *Airplanes from the Dawn of Flight to the Present Day*, McGraw-Hill, New York, 1973.)

differently. A case can be made that George Cayley's concept of what today we call the modern configuration airplane was, in its time, quite "unconventional" when viewed against the panorama of flapping-wing ornithopter concepts that preceded it.

Airplanes that takeoff and land vertically are unconventional airplanes. Any such airplane is classified as a *vertical-takeoff-and-landing* (VTOL) airplane. (We are considering fixed-wing VTOL airplanes here, not helicopters, which are a completely different consideration.) One of the best examples of a successful VTOL airplane, one that has been in continuous service since the 1970s, is the Harrier jet-propelled fighter aircraft, shown in Figure 7.42. The Harrier is a British design; first conceived by Hawker Aircraft, a prototype called the P-1227 Kestrel first flew in 1960. Later, the production version, called the Harrier, was built in numbers for the Royal Air Force and the Royal Navy. A version of the Harrier, the AV-8, was adapted and manufactured by McDonnell–Douglas in the United States in the early 1980s, and it is in service with the U.S. Marine Corps. There are many approaches to providing the vertical thrust for a VTOL craft. In the case of the Harrier, the jet exhaust from the single Rolls–Royce Pegasus jet engine passes through four nozzles, two located on each side of the engine. Vanes in these nozzles deflect the exhaust in the downward, vertical direction for vertical takeoff and landing and in the horizontal, backward direction for conventional, forward flight.

Another unconventional airplane concept is the flying wing. From a purely aerodynamic viewpoint, a fuselage is mainly a drag-producing element of the airplane; its lift-to-drag ratio is much smaller than that of a wing. Hence, if the whole airplane were simply one big wing, the maximum aerodynamic efficiency could be achieved. The idea for such flying wings is not new. For example, the famous airplane designer Jack Northrop began working with flying-wing designs in the early 1930s. During and just after World War II, Northrop built several flying-wing bombers. However, the longitudinal stability and control normally provided by the horizontal tail and elevator at the end of a fuselage of a conventional airplane must instead be provided by flaps and unusual curvature of the camber line near the trailing edge of the flying wing. This caused stability and control problems for flying-wing aircraft—problems severe enough that no practical flying wings were produced until recently. In the modern aeronautical engineering of today, airplanes can be designed to be unstable, and the airplane is flown with the aid of a computer that is constantly deflecting the control surfaces to keep the airplane on its intended flight path—the fly-by-wire concept. Such new flight management systems now make practical the design and operation of flying wings. One spectacular modern example, the B-2, is discussed next.

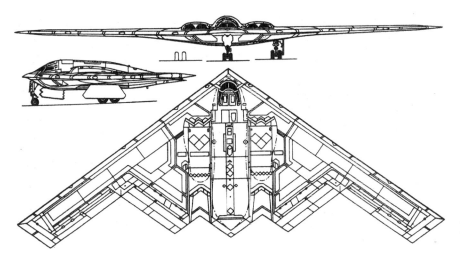

FIGURE 7.43
Northrop Grumman B-2A
stealth bomber.

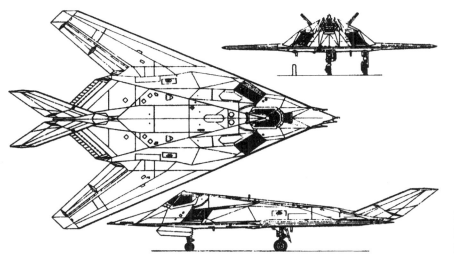

FIGURE 7.44
Lockheed F-117 stealth
fighter.

A class of highly unconventional aircraft has come on the scene in recent years, namely, *stealth aircraft*. Here, the primary design objective is to have the smallest radar cross section possible, to make the airplane virtually invisible on any enemy's radar screen. Two modern stealth airplanes are shown in Figures 7.43 and 7.44, the Northrop B-2 and the Lockheed F-117, respectively. Look at these aircraft. You see configurations with sharp edges and flat angled surfaces, all designed to reflect radar waves away from the source rather than back toward it. Moreover, these airplanes are made of special radar-absorbing material. The design features you see in Figures 7.43 and 7.44 are dictated mainly by radar reflection considerations and not by aerodynamic considerations. Good subsonic aerodynamic design is embodied by rounded leading edges, smoothly curving surfaces, and slender, streamlined shapes. You do not see these features in the B-2 and F-117. Here is an extreme example of the compromises that always face airplane designers. The overriding design concern for these stealth aircraft is very low radar cross section; good aerodynamics had to take a back seat. Sometimes these airplanes are jokingly referred to as "airplanes designed by electrical engineers." This is not far from the truth. However, the fact that both the B-2 and F-117 have acceptable aerodynamic performance implies that the aeronautical engineer faced up to and partially solved a very difficult problem—that of integrating the electrical engineering features with the aeronautical engineering features to produce an effective flying machine. Finally, in reference to the preceding paragraph, note that the B-2 is indeed a flying wing, made possible by the advanced fly-by-wire technology of today.

There are many other unconventional concepts for airplanes, too numerous for us to treat in any detail. For example, since the 1930s, the concept of a combined automobile and airplane, the autoplane, has come and gone several times, without any real success. Another idea, one that has been relatively successful, is the ultralight airplane—essentially an overgrown kite or parafoil, with a chair for the pilot and an engine equivalent to that of a lawn mower for power. These ultralights are currently one of the latest rages at the time of this writing. Another concept, not quite as unconventional, is the *uninhabited air vehicle* (UAV), an updated label for what used to be called a remotely piloted vehicle (RPV). For the most part, these UAVs are essentially overgrown model airplanes, although some recent UAV designs for high-altitude surveillance are large aircraft with very high aspect ratio wings and wingspans on the order of 80 feet. At the time of writing, the design of UAVs for combat purposes, uninhabited combat air vehicles (UCAVs) is of major interest.

The Future?

What about the future of the airplane and its technology? At one time there was a temptation to finish this book with a final chapter dealing with thoughts about the future. But if history tells us anything, predictions about the future become more tenuous with every hour that passes by after the predictions are made. None of the major revolutions in the technology of the airplane discussed in this book were predicted far in advance. So instead of a long discourse on predictions about the future, the book will end with the following thoughts.

Return to Figure 1.1 showing the Wright Flyer on its way toward historic destiny. That flight took place approximately 100 years ago—a scant speck on the whole timeline of recorded history. The exponential growth of aeronautical technology that has taken place since 1903 is evident just by leafing through the subsequent pages of this book. In retrospect, the only adjective that can properly describe this progress is mind-boggling. Indeed, there are those who describe aeronautics as a mature technology today. This may be so, but just as a mature person is in the best position to decided his or her own future destiny, the mature aeronautical technology of today is in its best position ever to determine its destiny in the 21st century. Readers of this book who will influence and guide this destiny are to be envied.

A case in point is hypersonic flight. During the 1980s and early 1990s, work on hypersonic airplanes was vigorously carried out in several countries, including the United States. The U.S. effort was focused on the concept of an aerospace plane, an aircraft that would take off from a normal runway as a normal airplane would and then accelerate to near-orbital speeds within the atmosphere, using airbreathing propulsion (in this case, supersonic combustion ramjet engines). In the United States, this work was intended to produce an experimental hypersonic flight vehicle, the X-30. Although much technical progress was made during this design effort, the program foundered because of the projected enormous cost to bring it to the actual flight vehicle stage. However, in this author's opinion, this hiatus is just temporary. If the history of flight has told us anything, it has shown us that aeronautics has always been paced by the concept of faster and higher. Although this has to be somewhat mitigated today by the need for economically viable and environmentally safe airplanes, the overall march of progress in aeronautics will continue to be faster and higher. In some sense, practical, everyday hypersonic flight may be viewed as the final frontier for aeronautics. This author feels that most young readers of this book will see, in their lifetime in the 21st century, much pioneering progress toward this final frontier.

Hypersonic flight is not the only challenge for the future. As long as civilization as we know it today continues to exist in the world, we will always design and build new and improved airplanes for all the regimes of flight—low speed, subsonic, transonic, supersonic, and hypersonic. From our viewpoint at the beginning of the 21st century, we see unlimited progress and opportunities in the enhancement of airplane performance and design in the 21st century.

Bibliography

This is a partial list of recommended reading material related to the subject of this book. It is just the tip of the iceberg. The author apologizes if your favorite book is not listed, but the literature is vast, and time and space do not allow a more complete list.

Anderson, J. D., Jr., *A History of Aerodynamics*, Cambridge University Press, New York, 1997 (hardback), 1998 (paperback).

Anderson, J. D., Jr., *Introduction to Flight*, 4th ed., McGraw-Hill, Boston, 2000.

Angelucci, E., *Airplanes from the Dawn of Flight to the Present Day*, McGraw-Hill, New York, 1973.

Chanute, O., *Progress in Flying Machines*, Lorenz and Herwey, Long Beach, 1976 (originally published in 1894).

Combs, H., *Kill Devil Hill*, Houghton Mifflin, Boston, 1979.

Cook, W. H., *The Road to the 707*, TYC Publishers, Bellevue, WA, 1991

Crouch, T., *A Dream of Wings*, Norton, New York, 1981.

Crouch, T., *The Bishop's Boys*, Norton, New York, 1989.

Gibbs-Smith, C. H., *Aviation, An Historical Survey*, Her Majesty's Stationery Office, London, 1970.

Gibbs-Smith, C. H., *Sir George Cayley's Aeronautics, 1796–1855*, Her Majesty's Stationery Office, London, 1970.

Greenwood, J. T., (ed.), *Milestones of Aviation*, Hugh Lauter Levin Associates, New York (Distributed by Macmillan Publishing Co., New York, 1989).

Hallion, R. P., *Supersonic Flight*, Macmillan, New York, 1972.

Hallion, R. P., *Designers and Test Pilots*, Time-Life Books, Alexandria, VA, 1983.

Hansen, J. R., *Engineer in Charge*, NASA SP-4305, National Aeronautics and Space Administration, Washington, D.C., 1987.

Jakab, P. L., *Visions of a Flying Machine*, Smithsonian Institution Press, Washington, D.C., 1990.

Langley, S. P., *Experiments in Aerodynamics*, Smithsonian Contributions to Knowledge, Vol. 27, No. 3, Smithsonian Institution, Washington, D.C., 1891.

Langley, S. P., and Manly, C. M., *Langley Memoir on Mechanical Flight*, Smithsonian Contributions to Knowledge, Vol. 27, No. 3, Smithsonian Institution, Washington, D.C., 1911.

Lilienthal, O., *Der Vogelflug als Grundlage der Fliegekunst*, R. Gaertners Verlagsbuchhandlung, 1889. (Translated into English by I. W. Isenthal and published as *Birdflight as the Basis of Aviation*, Longmans Green, London, 1911.)

Loftin, L. K., *Quest for Performance: The Evolution of Modern Aircraft*, NASA SP-468, National Aeronautics and Space Administration, Washington, D.C., 1985.

McFarland, M. W. (ed.), *The Papers of Wilbur and Orville Wright*, McGraw-Hill, New York, 1953.

Mondey, D. (ed.), *The International Encyclopedia of Aviation,* Crown Publishers, New York, 1977.

van der Linden, F. R., *The Boeing 247, The First Modern Airliner,* University of Washington Press, Seattle, 1991.

Vincenti, W. G., *What Engineers Know and How They Know It,* Johns Hopkins University Press, Baltimore, 1990.

Index